T0137007

Lecture Notes in Computer Science

Lecture Notes in Artificial Intelligence   **14078**

Founding Editor

Jörg Siekmann

Series Editors

Randy Goebel, *University of Alberta, Edmonton, Canada*
Wolfgang Wahlster, *DFKI, Berlin, Germany*
Zhi-Hua Zhou, *Nanjing University, Nanjing, China*

The series Lecture Notes in Artificial Intelligence (LNAI) was established in 1988 as a topical subseries of LNCS devoted to artificial intelligence.

The series publishes state-of-the-art research results at a high level. As with the LNCS mother series, the mission of the series is to serve the international R & D community by providing an invaluable service, mainly focused on the publication of conference and workshop proceedings and postproceedings.

Raghava Morusupalli ·
Teja Santosh Dandibhotla · Vani Vathsala Atluri ·
David Windridge · Pawan Lingras ·
Venkateswara Rao Komati

Editors

Multi-disciplinary Trends in Artificial Intelligence

16th International Conference, MIWAI 2023
Hyderabad, India, July 21–22, 2023
Proceedings

 Springer

Editors
Raghava Morusupalli
CVR College of Engineering
Hyberabad, India

Teja Santosh Dandibhotla
CVR College of Engineering
Hyderabad, India

Vani Vathsala Atluri
CVR College of Engineering
Hyderabad, India

David Windridge
Middlesex University
London, UK

Pawan Lingras
Saint Mary's University
Halifax, NS, Canada

Venkateswara Rao Komati (iD)
CVR College of Engineering
Hyderabad, India

ISSN 0302-9743   ISSN 1611-3349 (electronic)
Lecture Notes in Artificial Intelligence
ISBN 978-3-031-36401-3   ISBN 978-3-031-36402-0 (eBook)
https://doi.org/10.1007/978-3-031-36402-0

LNCS Sublibrary: SL7 – Artificial Intelligence

This Springer imprint is published by the registered company Springer Nature Switzerland AG
The registered company address is: Gewerbestrasse 11, 6330 Cham, Switzerland

Preface

It is with great pleasure that we present the proceedings of the 16th Multi-Disciplinary International Conference on Artificial Intelligence (MIWAI 2023), held during July 21, 22, 2023, at CVR College of Engineering, Hyderabad, Telangana, India. MIWAI 2023 is organized by the Department of Computer Science and Engineering in collaboration with Mahasarakham University, Thailand.

The MIWAI series has been organised since 2007 and offers a unique platform for Engineers and Scientists to present their research findings in AI-related areas. The main objective of the conference is to present the latest research findings related to AI topics such as Cognitive Science; Game Theory; Graphical Models; Knowledge Representation and Reasoning; Fuzzy Logic; Computer Vision; Natural Language Processing; Artificial Intelligence; Deep Learning; Evolutionary Computing; Swarm Intelligence; Physics Informed Neural Networks; Data-Driven AI; Decision Support Systems; Industrial Applications of AI; Ontology; and Recommender Systems.

MIWAI 2023 provides opportunities for the delegates to exchange new ideas and establish future collaborations worldwide. MIWAI aims to promote AI research in theoretical and applied research addressing real-world applications. MIWAI 2023 received 245 articles from 13 countries: Bangladesh, Canada, China, Germany, Iceland, India, Indonesia, Israel, Malaysia, Saudi Arabia, Thailand, United Kingdom, and United States. Every submitted article was reviewed scrupulously by the programme committee members, sub-reviewers, and domain experts. We thank Teja Santosh D for his relentless efforts in the entire process of article reviewing and result compilation. Upon thorough evaluation, the committee decided to accept 71 papers and elicit one invited article. The average acceptance rate of articles is around 29% of the total number of submissions. The programme also includes two keynote talks and six expert lectures.

Department of Computer Science and Engineering is indebted to Dr. Raghava Cherabuddi – President & Chairman, CVR College of Engineering, Telangana for expressing his staunch support through seamless approvals for hosting MIWAI 2023. CVR College of Engineering, which was established in 2001, is a pioneer in providing quality education to students. CVRCE true to its vision, is in Pursuit of Excellence while catering to the changing needs of the student community at large for the last couple of decades. College promotes academic research and consultancy and publishes "CVR Journal of Science & Technology" to disseminate research findings and results. The College is working towards accomplishment of its mission to serve the nation as a centre of quality education, research, and knowledge.

MIWAI 2023 expresses its thanks and gratitude to the Cherabuddi Education Society for giving partial financial support to the event. We wish to thank the members of the Steering Committee, Patrons, and Advisory Committee for their support, and are grateful to the Programme Committee members and external reviewers for their efforts in finalising quality articles. Our deep gratitude to all the members of the Local Organizing

Committee from the Department of Computer Science and Engineering for their priceless support in hosting the event.

MahaSarkham University, established in 1967 is a standing testimony to being a progressive university providing world class education to student community, while continuing to encourage research and developing local wisdom. We are extremely grateful and excited to have a journey of learning collaborating with Mahasarkham University in the conduct of MIWAI 2023.

MIWAI 2023 appreciates EasyChair for offering an elegant Conference Management System that helped in accepting articles, sending email notifications, and compiling the proceedings book. We are thankful to Celine Lanlan Chang, Guido Zosimo-Landolfo, Anna Kramer, and the excellent LNCS team at Springer for their support and cooperation in publishing the proceedings as a volume of the Lecture Notes in Artificial Intelligence.

We hope that the proceedings of MIWAI 2023 will provide the readers with valuable insights and stimulate new research ideas.

May 2023

Raghava Morusupalli
Vani Vathsala Atluri
Pawan Lingras
David Windridge

Organization

Editors

Raghava M.	College of Engineering, Telangana, India
A. Vani Vathsala	CVR College of Engineering, Telangana, India
D. Teja Santosh	CVR College of Engineering, Telangana, India
Pawan Lingras	Saint Mary's University, Canada
David Windridge	Middlesex University, UK
Venkateswara Rao Komati	CVR College of Engineering, Telangana, India

Steering Committee

Arun Agarwal	University of Hyderabad, India
Rajkumar Buyya	University of Melbourne, Australia
Patrick Doherty	Linköping University, Sweden
Rina Dechter	University of California, Irvine, USA
Leon van der Torre	University of Luxembourg, Luxembourg
Peter Haddawy	Mahidol University, Thailand
Jérôme Lang	University Paris-Dauphine, France
James F. Peters	University of Manitoba, Canada
Somnuk Phon-Amnuaisuk	UTB, Brunei
Srinivasan Ramani	IIIT Bangalore, India
C. Raghavendra Rao	University of Hyderabad, India

Convenors

Richard Booth	Cardiff University, UK
Chattrakul Sombattheera	Mahasarakham University, Thailand

General Chairs

Pawan Lingras	Saint Mary's University, Canada
A. Vani Vathsala	CVR College of Engineering, India

Program Chairs

David Windridge	Middlesex University, UK
Raghava M.	CVR College of Engineering, India

Chief Patrons

C. Madhusudhan Reddy	CVR College of Engineering, India
Raghava V. Cherabuddi	CVR College of Engineering, India

Patrons

K. Rama Sastri	CVR College of Engineering, India
K. Ramamohan Reddy	CVR College of Engineering, India

Honorary Advisors

K. Lal Kishore	CVR College of Engineering, India
L. C. Siva Reddy	CVR College of Engineering, India
Nayanathara K. Sattiraju	CVR College of Engineering, India
M. V. Seshagiri Rao	CVR College of Engineering, India
Hrushikesha Mohanty	CVR College of Engineering, India
R. V. S. Krishna Dutt	CVRCollege of Engineering, India

Organizing Chairs

K. Venkateswara Rao	CVR College of Engineering, India
B. Rambabu	CVR College of Engineering, India

Publicity Chairs

K. Venkatesh Sharma	CVR College of Engineering, India
N. Subhash Chandra	CVR College of Engineering, India

Program Committee

Arun Agarwal	University of Hyderabad, India
Grigoris Antoniou	University of Huddersfield, UK
Adham Atyabi	University of Colorado, Colorado Springs, USA
Thien Wan Au	Universiti Teknologi Brunei, Brunei
Costin Badica	University of Craiova, Romania
Raj Bhatnagar	University of Cincinnati, USA
Richard Booth	Cardiff University, UK
Zied Bouraoui	CRIL - CNRS and Université d'Artois, France
Gauvain Bourgne	CNRS and Sorbonne Universités, France
Rapeeporn Chamchong	Mahasarakham University, Thailand
Zhicong Chen	Fuzhou University, China
Suwannit-Chareen Chit	Universiti Utara Malaysia, Malaysia
P. Chomphuwiset	Mahasarakham University, Thailand
Sook Ling Chua	Multimedia University, Malaysia
Todsanai Chumwatana	Rangsit University, Thailand
Abdollah Dehzangi	Morgan State University, USA
Juergen Dix	Clausthal University of Technology, Germany
Nhat-Quang Doan	University of Science and Technology of Hanoi, Vietnam
Abdelrahman Elfaki	University of Tabuk, Saudi Arabia
Lk Foo	Multimedia University, Malaysia
Hui-Ngo Goh	Multimedia University, Malaysia
Chatklaw Jareanpon	Mahasarakham University, Thailand
P. Nagabhushan	University of Mysore, India
D. S. Guru	University of Mysore, India
V. Kamakshi Prasad	JNTUH, India
Sriram Somanchi	University of Notre Dame, USA
Teja Palvali	AWS, USA
G. Vijaya Kumari	JNTUH, India
Himabindu K.	NIT-AP, India
Ponnusamy Ramalingam	Chennai Institute of Technology, India
Venky Krishnan	TIFR-B, India
Suresh Chandra Satapathy	KIIT, India
Nilanjan Dey	Techno International New Town, India
A. Kavitha	JNTUH, India
Manasawee Kaenampornpan	Mahasarakham University, Thailand
Santosh Tirunagari	Middlesex University, UK
Ng Keng Hoong	Asia Pacific University of Technology, Malaysia
Kok Chin Khor	Universiti Tunku Abdul Rahman, Malaysia
Suchart Khummanee	Mahasarakham University, Thailand

Ven Jyn Kok	National University of Malaysia, Malaysia
Satish Kolhe	North Maharashtra University, Jalgaon, India
Raja Kumar	Taylor's University, Malaysia
Chee Kau Lim	University of Malaya, Malaysia
Chidchanok Lursinsap	Chulalongkorn University, Thailand
Sebastian Moreno	Universidad Adolfo Ibañez, Chile
Sven Naumann	University of Trier, Germany
Atul Negi	University of Hyderabad, India
Thi Phuong Nghiem	USTH, Vietnam
Dung D. Nguyen	Vietnam Academy of Science and Technology, Vietnam
Thi-Oanh Nguyen	VNU University of Science, Hanoi, Vietnam
Tho Quan	Ho Chi Minh City University of Technology, Vietnam
Srinivasan Ramani	IIIT Bangalore, India
Alexis Robbes	University of Tours, France
Annupan Rodtook	Ramkhamhaeng University, Thailand
Jogesh Muppala	Hong Kong University of Science and Technology, China
R. Srikanth	Stanford University, USA
Ch S. Sastry	IIT-Hyderabad, India
Deepak R. Pullaguram	IIT-Delhi, India
Bapiraju S.	IIIT-Hyderabad, India
Madhavi Gudavalli	JNTUK, India
Deva Priya Kumar	IIIT-Hyderabad, India
Suneetha Eluri	JNTUK, India
Viraj Adduru	Intel, USA
Sanjeev Pannala	Washington State University, USA
Sumeet Chaudhary	University of Colorado, Boulder, USA
Badrinath Jagannath	University of Texas, USA
D. Sudhir Reddy	ADRIN, India
P. S. V. S. Sai Prasad	University of Hyderabad, India
Nekuri Naveen	University of Hyderabad, India
M. Phani Krishna Kishore	GVPCE, India
Tilottama Goswamy	Vasavi College of Engineering, India
Harvey Rosas	University of Valparaiso, Chile
Junmo Kim	KAIST, Korea
Adrien Rougny	NIAIST, Japan
Jose H. Saito	Universidade Federal de São Carlos, Brazil
Nicolas Schwind	NIAIST, Japan
Myint Myint Sein	University of Computer Studies, Myanmar
Jun Shen	University of Wollongong, Australia

Guillermo R. Simari	Universidad del Sur in Bahia Blanca, Argentina
Alok Singh	University of Hyderabad, India
Dominik Slezak	University of Warsaw, Poland
Swarupa Rani K.	University of Hyderabad, India
Chattrakul Sombattheera	Mahasarakham University, Thailand
Heechul Jung	Kyungpook National University (KNU), Korea
Panida Songrum	Mahasarakham University, Thailand
Frieder Stolzenburg	Harz University of Applied Sciences, Germany
Olarik Surinta	Mahasarakham University, Thailand
Ilias Tachmazidis	University of Huddersfield, UK
Thanh-Hai Tran	MICA, Vietnam
Rajani Kanth T. V.	SNIST, India
Derwin Suhartono	Bina Nusantara University, Indonesia
Supriya Vaddi	GNIST, India
Anoop V. S.	Digital University of Kerala, India
Braja Bandhu Nayak	CVR College of Engineering, India
Humaira Nishat	CVR College of Engineering, India
T. Esther Rani	CVR College of Engineering, India
Y. Rama Devi	CBIT, India
Aruna Varanasi	SNIST, India
Narayana Murthy Kavi	University of Hyderabad, India
K. Narendar Reddy	CVR College of Engineering, India
R. K. Selvakumar	CVR College of Engineering, India
Suguru Ueda	Saga University, Japan
Chau Vo	HCMC University, Vietnam
Chalee Vorakulpipat	NECTEC, Thailand
Kewen Wang	Griffith University, Australia
Kevin Wong	Murdoch University, Australia
Pornntiwa Pawara	Mahasarakham University, Thailand
Peter Scull	Mahasarakham University, Thailand
Sheng He	Harvard Medical School, USA
Maria do Carmo Nicoletti	UNIFACCAMP, Brazil
Khanista Namee	King Mongkut's University of Technology, Thailand
Sajjaporn Waijanya	Silpakorn University, Thailand
Kraisak Kesorn	Naresuan University, Thailand
Narit Hnoohom	Mahidol University, Thailand
Artitayaporn Rojarath	Mahasarakham University, Thailand
Emmanuel Okafor	Ahmadu Bello University, Nigeria
Sakorn Mekruksavanich	University of Phayao, Thailand
Jantima Polpinij	Mahasarakham University, Thailand
Narumol Choomuang	Muban Chombueng Rajabhat University, Thailand

Web Master

| Panich Sudkho | Mahasarakham University, Thailand |
| D. Sujan Kumar | CVR College of Engineering, India |

Local Organizing Committee

D. Durga Bhavani	CVR College of Engineering, India
C. Ramesh	CVR College of Engineering, India
S. Suguna Mallika	CVR College of Engineering, India
Ch. Ram Mohan	CVR College of Engineering, India
D. Teja Santosh	CVR College of Engineering, India
M. Sridevi	CVR College of Engineering, India
D. Sandhya Rani	CVR College of Engineering, India
Ch. Sarada	CVR College of Engineering, India
P. Kiran Kumar	CVR College of Engineering, India
V. D. S. Krishna	CVR College of Engineering, India
V. N. V. L. S. Swathi	CVR College of Engineering, India
S. Lalitha	CVR College of Engineering, India
M. Archana	CVR College of Engineering, India
G. Sandhya	CVR College of Engineering, India
G. Bala Krishna	CVR College of Engineering, India
S. Srinivasulu	CVR College of Engineering, India
Suhail Afroz	CVR College of Engineering, India
M. Hanimi Reddy	CVR College of Engineering, India
Ch. Bhavani	CVR College of Engineering, India
V. Dattatreya	CVR College of Engineering, India
M. Swamidas	CVR College of Engineering, India
S M Ali	CVR College of Engineering, India
M. Vasavi	CVR College of Engineering, India
R. Sahith	CVR College of Engineering, India
G. Swetha	CVR College of Engineering, India
P. Madhavi	CVR College of Engineering, India
K. Sindhuja	CVR College of Engineering, India
S. Srinivas	CVR College of Engineering, India
K. Deepthi Reddy	CVR College of Engineering, India
G. Sushma	CVR College of Engineering, India
A. Swathi	CVR College of Engineering, India

Web Developers

G. Raghavender Reddy	CVR College of Engineering, India
Anjali Vemula	CVR College of Engineering, India
Potnuru Divya Sai	CVR College of Engineering, India
Kshatriya Shrujeeth Singh	CVR College of Engineering, India

Additional Reviewers

Atluri, Vani Vathsala
B. Srikanth
B. Vikranth
Bala Krishna, G.
Bhupal, Surya
C. H. Ram Mohan
Cindha, Ramesh
D. Durga Bhavani
D. Narayana
E. Uma Reddy
Eluri, Suneetha
Gangappa, Malige
Goswami, Tilottama
Govathoti, Sudeepthi
H. Venkateswara
Hegde, Nagaratna P.
Janardhanarao, Syamalapalli
J. V. S. Srinivas
K. Himabindu
Kannan, Rajchandar
Kogila, Raghu
Kovoor, Madhuri
Krishnan, Nimala
Krishnaveni, Chennuru Venkata
Lakshmi, H. N.
M. Varaprasad Rao
Mahalingam, Jaiganesh
Mahankali, Naga Sailaja
Mekala, Sagar
Mekala, Srinivas
More, Swami Das
Murthy, Kavi Narayana
Nalla, Subhash Chandra
Nayak, Braja B.

Nayani, Sateesh
Nekuri, Naveen
Nimmala, Satyanarayana
Nishat, Humaira
Patra, Raj Kumar
Prakash K., L. N. C.
Prasad, A. V. Krishna
R. V. S., Krishnadutt
R. K., Selvakumar
Raghavendra Rao, Chillarige
Rajini Kanth, T. V.
Raju, Kishore
Ramacharan, S.
Rambabu, Bandi
Ramisetti, Seetharamaiah
Rani, Rella
Rani, Swarupa
Rao K., Venkateswara
Rao, K. Sreenivasa
Ravi Shankar Reddy, Gosula
Ravi, Y. V. K.
Reddy, A. Srinivasa
Reddy, D. Sudheer
Reddy, N. Madhusudhana
Reddy, P. Namratha
Rinku, Dhruva R.
Sagar, A. B.
Santosh, D. Teja
Singaraju, Suguna Mallika
Sridevi, M.
Sunitha, Maddhi
Supriya, M.
Suryanarayana, S. V.
Tirunagari, Santosh

U. Moulali

V. S., Anoop

Vadali, Ravi Sankar

Vaddi, Supriya

Valiveti, Dattatreya

Varanasi, Aruna

Venkatesh Sharma, K.

Yellasiri, Ramadevi

Sponsors

CVR COLLEGE OF ENGINEERING
(A UGC Autonomous and JNTUH Affiliated Institute)
Mangalpalli, Vastunagar, Ibrahimpatnam,
Ranga Reddy (DT), Telangana - 501510
India

Mahasarakham University
Khamriang Sub-District,
Kantarawichai District,
Maha Sarakham 44150
Thailand

Contents

Digital Life: An Advent of Transhumanism 1
   Hrushikesha Mohanty

Heuristics for K-Independent Average Traveling Salesperson Problem 25
   Sebanti Majumder and Alok Singh

Book Recommendation Using Double-Stack BERT: Utilizing BERT
to Extract Sentence Relation Feature for a Content-Based Filtering System 36
   Derwin Suhartono and Adhella Subalie

Evaluating the Utility of GAN Generated Synthetic Tabular Data for Class
Balancing and Low Resource Settings 48
   Nagarjuna Venkata Chereddy and Bharath Kumar Bolla

How Good are Transformers in Reordering? 60
   Ch. Ram Anirudh and Narayana Murthy Kavi

Automatic Differentiation Using Dual Numbers - Use Case 68
   R. Anand Krishna, R. V. S. Krishna Dutt, and P. Premchand

On Some Properties of a New PoisN Wavelet Family 79
   M. Shravani, D. Sudheer Reddy, and B. Krishna Reddy

Centrality Measures Based Heuristics for Perfect Awareness Problem
in Social Networks 91
   Rahul Kumar Gautam, Anjeneya Swami Kare, and S. Durga Bhavani

Re-examining Class Selectivity in Deep Convolutional Networks 101
   Akshay Badola, Vineet Padmanabhan, and Rajendra Prasad Lal

Content Based Network Representational Learning for Movie
Recommendation (CNMovieRec) 112
   Nageswar Rao Kota, Vineet Padmanabhan, and Wilson Naik Bhukya

Parallel and Distributed Query Processing in Attributed Networks 124
   A. Sandhya Rani and K. Swarupa Rani

Gradient Directional Predictor for Reconstructing High-Fidelity Images 135
   Ravi Uyyala and Jyothirmai Joshi

We Chased COVID-19; Did We Forget Measles? - Public Discourse
and Sentiment Analysis on Spiking Measles Cases Using Natural
Language Processing 147
    V. S. Anoop, Jose Thekkiniath, and Usharani Hareesh Govindarajan

Swarm Learning for Oncology Research 159
    H. S. Shashank, Anirudh B. Sathyanarayana, Aniruddh Acharya,
    M. R. Akhil., and Sujatha R. Upadhyaya

A Review on Designing of Memory Computing Architecture for Image
Enhancement in AI Applications 169
    C. Radhika, G. V. Ganesh, and P. Ashok Babu

Shufflenetv2: An Effective Technique for Recommendation System
in E-Learning by User Preferences 179
    Dudla Anil Kumar and M. Ezhilarasan

A Multi-modal Approach Using Game Theory for Android Forensics Tool
Selection 192
    Mahpara Yasmin Mohd Minhaz Alam and Wilson Naik

LPCD: Incremental Approach for Dynamic Networks 203
    Ashwitha Gatadi and K. Swarupa Rani

Clinical Abbreviation Disambiguation Using Clinical Variants of BERT 214
    Atharwa Wagh and Manju Khanna

Ontological Scene Graph Engineering and Reasoning Over YOLO Objects
for Creating Panoramic VR Content 225
    N. Prabhas Raj, G. Tarun, D. Teja Santosh, and M. Raghava

Incremental Classifier in the Semi Supervised Learning Environment 236
    Maneesha Gudapati and K. Swarupa Rani

Alzheimer's Detection and Prediction on MRI Scans: A Comparative Study ... 245
    Namrata Nair, Prabaharan Poornachandran, V. G. Sujadevi,
    and M. Aravind

Evaluating the Performance of Diverse Machine Learning Approaches
in Stock Market Forecasting 255
    Bharath Raj Anand Kumar, Sheetal Katiyar, Prasanth Lingada,
    Karunakar Mattaparthi, R. Krishna, Gnana Prakash,
    Dileep Vuppaladhadiam, Narayana Darapaneni,
    and Anwesh Reddy Paduri

A Blockchain-Driven Framework for Issuance of NFT-Based Warranty
to Customers on E-Commerce 265
   Sneha Devrani, Rohit Ahuja, Anirudh Goel,
   and Sahajdeep Singh Kharbanda

Using Machine Learning Models to Predict Corporate Credit Outlook 277
   Rashmi Malhotra and D. K. Malhotra

Visualization Recommendation for Incremental Data Based on Intent 285
   Harinath Kuruva, K. Swarupa Rani, and Salman Abdul Moiz

Automating Malaria Diagnosis with XAI: Using Deep-Learning
Technologies for More Accurate, Efficient, and Transparent Results 297
   Krishan Mridha, Fitsum Getachew Tola, Shakil Sarkar, Nazmul Arefin,
   Sandesh Ghimire, Anmol Aran, and Aashish Prashad Pandey

Artificial Intelligence as a Service: Providing Integrity and Confidentiality 309
   Neelima Guntupalli and Vasantha Rudramalla

Live Bidding Application: Predicting Shill Bidding Using Machine
Learning 316
   Chetan Mudlapur, Samyak Jain, Shruti Mittal, Pravar Jain,
   and Vikram Neerugatti

A Novel Pixel Value Predictor Using Long Short Term Memory (LSTM)
Network 324
   Sabhapathy Myakal, Rajarshi Pal, and Nekuri Naveen

Efficient Trajectory Clustering of Movements of Moving Objects 336
   Y. Subba Reddy, V. Thanuja, G. Sreenivasulu, N. Thulasi Chitra,
   and K. Venu Madhav

Node Cooperation Enforcement Scheme for Enhancing Quality of Service
in MANETs Using Machine Learning Approach 348
   Srinivasulu Sirisala, G. Rajeswarappa, and Srikanth Lakumarapu

Interpreting Chest X-Ray Classification Models: Insights and Complexity
Measures in Deep Learning 356
   Anirban Choudhury and Sudipta Roy

Nuclei Segmentation Approach for Computer Aided Diagnosis 368
   Narayana Darapaneni, Anwesh Reddy Paduri, Jayesh Gulani,
   Sanath Aithu, M. M. Santhosh, and Shaji Varghese

Stock Market Intraday Trading Using Reinforcement Learning   380
Rugved Pandit, Neeraj Nerkar, Parmesh Walunj, Rishi Tank,
and Sujata Kolhe

Predicting the Droughts Using Artificial Neural Networks – A Case Study   390
B. Naga Malleswara Rao, P. V. Ramana, and B. Akhila Meenakshi

Applying Machine Learning for Portfolio Switching Decisions   399
E. Uma Reddy and N. Nagarjuna

Bark Texture Classification Using Deep Transfer Learning   407
Rohini A. Bhusnurmath and Shaila Doddamani

Dynamic Twitter Topic Summarization Using Speech Acts   421
Suhail Afroz, Ch. V. S. Satyamurty, P. Asifa Tazeem, M. Hanimi Reddy,
Y. Md. Riyazuddin, and Vijetha Jadda

Generative Adversarial Network for Augmenting Low-Dose CT Images   429
Vijai Danni and Keshab Nath

Improving Software Effort Estimation with Heterogeneous Stacked
Ensemble Using SMOTER over ELM and SVR Base Learners   442
D. V. S. Durgesh, M. V. S. Saket, and B. Ramana Reddy

A Deep Learning Based Model to Study the Influence of Different Brain
Wave Frequencies for the Disorder of Depression   449
Bethany Gosala, Emmanuel Raj Gosala, and Manjari Gupta

Planning Strategy of BDI Agents for Crowd Simulation   459
Panich Sudkhot and Chattrakul Sombattheera

Design and Development of Walking Monitoring System for Gait Analysis   475
K. T. Krishnamurthy, S. Rohith, G. M. Basavaraj, S. Swathi,
and S. Supreeth

Stock Market Investment Strategy Using Deep-Q-Learning Network   484
Sudhakar Kalva and Naganjaneyulu Satuluri

A Survey on Recent Text Summarization Techniques   496
G. Senthil Kumar and Midhun Chakkaravarthy

Conversational AI: A Study on Capabilities and Limitations of Dialogue
Based System   503
Narayana Darapaneni, Anwesh Reddy Paduri, Umesh Tank,
Balassubramamian KanthaSamy, Ashish Ranjan, and R. Krisnakumar

Co-clustering Based Methods and Their Significance for Recommender
Systems 513
    Naresh Kumar and Merlin Sheeba

Machine Learning and Fuzzy Logic Based Intelligent Algorithm
for Energy Efficient Routing in Wireless Sensor Networks 523
    Sagar Mekala, A. Mallareddy, Rama Rao Tandu, and Konduru Radhika

Sentiment Analysis of Twitter Data on 'The Agnipath Yojana' 534
    Vamsi Krishna Mulukutla, Sai Supriya Pavarala, Vinay Kumar Kareti,
    Sujan Midatani, and Sridevi Bonthu

Pixel Value Prediction Task: Performance Comparison of Multi-Layer
Perceptron and Radial Basis Function Neural Network 543
    Sabhapathy Myakal, Rajarshi Pal, and Nekuri Naveen

A Yolo-Based Deep Learning Approach for Vehicle Class Classification 554
    Lakshmi Kishore Kumar Nekkanti and Varaprasad Rao

Rescheduling Exams Within the Announced Tenure Using Reinforcement
Learning 569
    Mohammed Ozair Omar, D. Teja Santosh, M. Raghava,
    and Jyothirmai Joshi

AI Based Employee Attrition Prediction Tool 580
    Swati Agarwal, Chetna Bhardwaj, Glory Gatkamani, Raghav Gururaj,
    Narayana Darapaneni, and Anwesh Reddy Paduri

iSTIMULI: Prescriptive Stimulus Design for Eye Movement Analysis
of Patients with Parkinson's Disease 589
    S. Akshay, J. Amudha, Nilima Kulkarni, and L. K. Prashanth

EduKrishnaa: A Career Guidance Web Application Based
on Multi-intelligence Using Multiclass Classification Algorithm 601
    Shreyas Ajgaonkar, Pravin Tale, Yash Joshi, Pranav Jore,
    Mrunmayee Jakate, Snehal Lavangare, and Deepali Kadam

Multi-dimensional STAQR Indexing Algorithm for Drone Applications 611
    Pappula Madhavi and K. P. Supreethi

Low Light Image Illumination Adjustment Using Fusion of MIRNet
and Deep Illumination Curves 620
    Sunanda Perla and Kavitha Dwaram

A Hybrid Intelligent Cryptography Algorithm for Distributed Big Data
Storage in Cloud Computing Security 637
*P. T. Satyanarayana Murty, M. Prasad, P. B. V. Raja Rao, P. Kiran Sree,
G. Ramesh Babu, and Ch. Phaneendra Varma*

An Ensemble Technique to Detect Stress in Young Professional 649
Rohit Ahuja and Rajendra Kumar Roul

iAOI: An Eye Movement Based Deep Learning Model to Identify Areas
of Interest 659
*S. Akshay, J. Amudha, Nakka Narmada, Amitabh Bhattacharya,
Nitish Kamble, and Pramod Kumar Pal*

Traffic Prediction in Indian Cities from Twitter Data Using Deep Learning
and Word Embedding Models 671
Koyyalagunta Krishna Sampath and M. Supriya

Interpretable Chronic Kidney Disease Risk Prediction from Clinical Data
Using Machine Learning 683
*Vijay Simha Reddy Chennareddy, Santosh Tirunagari,
Senthilkumar Mohan, David Windridge, and Yashaswini Balla*

Sign Language Interpretation Using Deep Learning 692
S. Suguna Mallika, A. Sanjana, A. Vani Gayatri, and S. Veena Naga Sai

Redefining the World of Medical Image Processing with AI – Automatic
Clinical Report Generation to Support Doctors 704
*Narayana Darapaneni, Anwesh Reddy Paduri, B. S. Sunil Kumar,
S. Nivetha, Varadharajan Damotharan, Suman Sourabh,
S. R. Abhishek, and V. Albert Princy*

Statistical Analysis of the Monthly Costs of OPEC Crude Oil Using
Machine Learning Models 714
*V. Swapna, Srikanth Bethu, G. Vijaya Lakshmi,
Kanthala Sampath Kumar, and V. V. Haragopal*

Conversational Artificial Intelligence in Digital Healthcare: A Bibliometric
Analysis 723
P. R. Visakh, P. N. Meena, and V. S. Anoop

Demand and Price Forecasting Using Deep Learning Algorithms 735
*Narayana Darapaneni, Anwesh Reddy Paduri, Sourav Kundu,
Lokesh Jayanna, N. Balasubramaniam, M. P. Manohar, B. Rajesh,
and Sudhakar Moses Munnangi*

Hybrid Model Using Interacted-ARIMA and ANN Models for Efficient
Forecasting 747
   T. Baskaran, Nimitha John, and B. V Dhandra

Addressing Challenges in Healthcare Big Data Analytics 757
   Santosh Tirunagari, Senthilkumar Mohan, David Windridge,
   and Yashaswini Balla

Assessing Reading Patterns of Learners Through Eye Tracking 766
   Agashini V. Kumar, Atharwa Wagh, Abdulqahar Mukhtar Abubakar,
   J. Amudha, and K. R. Chandrika

Comparison of Deep Learning Algorithms for Early Detection
of Melanoma Skin Cancer on Dermoscopic and Non-dermoscopic Images 778
   Niharika Wamane, Aishwarya Yadav, Jidnyasa Bhoir, Deep Shelke,
   and Deepali Kadam

Author Index 787

Digital Life: An Advent of Transhumanism

Hrushikesha Mohanty[1,2](✉)

[1] CVR College of Engineering, RR District, Ibrahimpatnam, India
`hmcs@cvr.ac.in`
[2] University of Hyderabad, Hyderabad, India
`hmcs@uohyd.ac.in`

Abstract. The advent of digital technology has not only given a fillip to the growth of science and technology but also has greatly impacted individuals as well as society. Computing scientists are looking for generic frameworks for modelling human like digital entities that are autonomic service providing agents. Social scientists are looking into the impacts digital world makes on human minds. Philosophers are engaged in mapping the journey of humanity into the new world evolving with the immense breakthroughs in science and technology. This chapter presents a generic model of a digital life, reviews works of intelligent agents, discusses on digital life and after life issues; ends with a brief discussion on transhumanism, a philosophical issue raised by seers and thinkers.

Keywords: Digital life · after life and transhumanism

1 Introduction

The urge of understanding the Nature and its wonders has been there since the times of Vedas and Upansihads when the *rishis* composed hymns narrating the glory of Nature and its kindness for sustaining life on earth. Scientists deconstruct the Nature for the goodness of life. The quest on understanding has gone into the next higher level where not only the Nature is exploited but also challenged by the scientific aspirations in creating an artificial world that mimics Nature in making artificial lives. While researchers in Life Science are engaged in making life in their labs, engineers and computing scientists are busy in making of human like entities like robots and chatbots. On the top of that, the recent interest on Artificial Intelligence has raised the hope of exciting applications in different domains of life. The utility of such human like systems is immensely seen in the pandemic times where human life gone into seclusion leaving a way for digital systems to operate on behalf of their respective human masters. This is the advent of an era of digital life. A life goes through its pleasures and pangs of its genesis. Does a digital life have something like that? How will digital lives impact the society now and in future? These are some questions now appear before scientists, engineers and philosophers. This chapter makes an attempt in

R. Morusupalli et al. (Eds.): MIWAI 2023, LNAI 14078, pp. 1–24, 2023.
https://doi.org/10.1007/978-3-031-36402-0_1

revisiting the threads of research in computing science for the making of life like computing entities for providing services to human needs. It also discusses some social impacts such life like digital entities may have when humans and human-likes meet in transmediated space due to real and virtual worlds.

This section is followed by a digital human model providing a framework for implementation of autonomous digital entities that can sense its environment, decides its objectives and makes action schedules to achieve its objectives. Then the third section discusses on Agent theory. This branch is already well researched area. A discussion on it attempts to provide a general impression of the research carried out in this field of study. The fourth section carries forward the idea of Agent Society that talks of multi-agents. Then the discussion of the chapter takes a discussion on digital life. In this context two terms viz. digital natives and digital immigrants are discussed. Later section, the discussion furthers on digital life and after-life. This section talks of caring of digital wealth after its owner dies. It also discusses on a new ecosystem that real and digital world together may make. An expression of a life in a transmediated space that the new ecosystem provides, is discussed in this section. The next section gives an idea of digital world and its infrastructure like digital highway; it also proposes the need of novel civil governance for digital lives in cyber space. Then the chapter concludes with a remark, rather a longish one, on the possibilities of a new world order with digital lives and born digital humans leading to transhumanism, a philosophical state of higher order that humanity aims for.

2 Digital Human

We say a representation of a human in the cyberspace as a digital person (dp) that's identified by a unique number like ādhar number given to each individual in India. There can be several cyber-representations of a human for its participations in several digital platforms for specific services or even for institutional associations. Each signature of a service consumer at service provider portals, stores some basic as well as service specific informations. Thus, there can be several shadows of a human in cyber space. These can be viewed as a kind of digital lives. Now, a human in the real-word has $1 : n$ mappings to cyber world. The fast spread of Internet across the Globe provides a competing virtual world, at which even the real world at certain instances shy away. Covid pandemic time, utility of virtual world is seen. When transactions by person became life threatening, then their digital shadows in virtual world kept the world running albeit with legitimacy that formal transactions require. Human and humanoids together in cyberspace now create a mixed world of *diginity* i.e. a shadow world of humanity. Digital humanity includes apps, digital shadows, robots, chat bots and alike many digital entities who represent as well as work for people. These are powered by software implementing algorithms. These algorithms reflect the problem solving techniques as coded by the developers and designers. Conventionally, a software once developed works forever in the same way in contrast to human problem solving power that changes as time flows based on its intellectual maturity and increasing experiential intelligences. The attempt for instilling this changing traits in problem solving, has given rise to this new area of research called Artificial Intelligence. This tempts to think of a framework for a diginity to theorise its autonomous actions for achieving its goals. Next we will discuss on such a framework in the light our previous work in the field of computational social science [20, 21].

In reality a human plans its actions to achieve its aims and objectives that it rationally wishes to have based on its knowledge, resources and location. That can be told as $f(K, R, L) \longrightarrow Q$ where K,R and L are the sets of knowledge, resource and location respectively and Q is the set of objectives a person may have. The rationality of this paradigm $<Q, K, R, L, >$ flows from a common understanding of a human and planning for its living. A schematic diagram 'DL-Paradigm' (Fig. 1) shows a digital-life paradigm. It shows an environment in which a human/humanoid/app resides and operates. We view a person's action-space in this three dimensional space. Its objectives are guided by its position in this dimensional space. That means a person decides on its objectives with respect to its K,R and L knowledge, resource and location respectively. We would like to make it clear that, the proposed model is a generic one both for real world and cyber world. But, in discussion here, hence forth we will refer this digital person as a person-like entity in digital space. A behavioural model for a person can be proposed by defining a set of operations that for a person can be applied to find a schedule of operations required for achieving a given goal. First let us define those operations. An abstraction of these functions is as follows

Fig. 1. DL-Paradigm

A digital person dp does with x for y:
$<dp, x, y>:: action(dp, x) \rightarrow y$
and a person dp needs x for goal q:
$<dp, q, x>:: needx(dp, q) \rightarrow x$
Now we define three triplets that define three functions for a digital person to find out its needs with respect to its objective as well as its position in digital-life three dimensional space. With respect to an objective q, it deduces its need x i.e. a reading on the dimension x. For the purpose, the model has a generic function $needx(dp, q) \rightarrow x$. With respect to each dimension, here we propose three instances ofi generic function as

$$<dp,q,r>:: needR(dp,q) \rightarrow r \qquad (1)$$
$$<dp,q,k>:: needK(dp,q) \rightarrow k \qquad (2)$$
$$<dp,q,l>:: needL(dp,q) \rightarrow l \qquad (3)$$

These three functions respectively return resources, knowledge and location that a digital person dp needs to achieve its objective q. Next we define what a person can do in its current status i.e. dp's state in K,R,L three dimensional space. The functions below provides actions of dp with knowledge k:

$$<dp,k,q>:: addQ(dp,k) \rightarrow q \qquad (4)$$
$$<dp,k,r>:: genR(dp,k) \rightarrow r \qquad (5)$$
$$<dp,k,l>:: moveL(dp,k) \rightarrow l \qquad (6)$$

The above three functions viz. $addQ$, $genR$ and $moveL$ respectively return an objective q, resource r and location l that a person dp with knowledge k can have. Using the function $addQ$ a dp can decide what objective it may fix to achieve. The function $genR$ returns what new resources a dp can generate with its present knowledge k, the function $moveL$ tells where one can move to a new location being powered by its knowledge k. In the similar notion, we define another set of functions to deduce what a digital person dp can do with a given resource r:

$$<dp,r,k>:: acqK(dp,r) \rightarrow k \qquad (7)$$
$$<dp,r,q>:: addQ(dp,r) \rightarrow q \qquad (8)$$
$$<dp,r,l>:: moveL(dp,r) \rightarrow l \qquad (9)$$

With a given resource r, a digital person dp can acquire knowledge k by applying the function $acqK$. By function $addQ$, with a given resource r, a person dp can add one new objective q to its list of objectives. Likewise, a person may choose to move to a place l, using its resource r; this is deduced by the function $moveL$. The next set of functions say, what a person may have being at a location l due to the locational benefits.

$$<dp,l,k>:: acqK(dp,l) \rightarrow k \qquad (10)$$
$$<dp,l,q>:: addQ(dp,l) \rightarrow q \qquad (11)$$
$$<dp,l,r>:: genR(dp,l) \rightarrow r \qquad (12)$$

At a location l, based on locational facilities, a person may add to its objective list (function $addQ$), acquire knowledge (function $ack\text{-}K$) and plan to generate resource (function $genR$).

Having the above declarative model, we give a brief account of its functional behaviour and a schematic representation of the model is given in Fig. 2. This presents an inference engine that a dp uses to actualise its objective. The engine has four processes vix. $Achieve\text{-}Q$, $move\text{-}L$, $gen\text{-}R$ and $ack\text{-}K$ to achieve an objective, move to a location, generate resources and acquire knowledge respectively.

The function *Add-Q* is used to add objectives to the objective repository. There are also another three functions to add respective items to other three repositories for knowledge, location and resource. It uses four repositories to store K, L, R and Q. Each repository can have required structure as per the requirement of an application. As the discussion here is very high level we are not going into details. It uses alert triggers with respect to K, L, R and Q. The idea in functioning of inferencing engine is fairly simple. Engine in an infinite loop remains in wait state but comes to active state as and when there is an event due to an addition of an objective to the repository of Q. Then *Achieve-Q* function executes an objective. In case of failing to execute the objective, it finds out the need like knowledge, resource or relocation required to achieve the objective. On knowing that the respective functions viz. *acqK*, *genR* and *moveL* are executed. On accomplishing the activated tasks due to these functions the respective repositories are updated. These updates in turn generate new objectives and these objectives are added to the objective queue. The engine keeps running until the objective queue is empty. When a person turns complacent the engine stops. A digital person *dp* being in cyberspace and representing a person behaves like an agent to accomplish the task it's assigned with. In order to bring the notion of agency in digital life, let's look at a hypothetical case as stated next.

Mr Lazy a habitant of city Bhubaneswar releases its digital incarnation *dLazy* with $<k, q, r, l>$ in cyberspace to negotiate with *dBcc* a digital agent of Bhubaneswar city corporation for fixing and paying its property tax. dLazy moves to dBcc to know property tax amount and payment details. If the former finds itself unable to perform that then it moves to a property tax consultant *dPtc* for help. If it is in short of money, then moves to *dBob* the digital agent of Bank of Bhubaneswar to acquire money. In collaboration with *dPtc*, *dLazy* pays tax to *dBcc*.

This hypothetical case presents a digital life of a person in cyberspace. It shows how these digital persons can perform actions on behalf their of respective owners. The model presented in this section provides an abstraction of a task planning and execution process that a digital person can adopt to perform its objectives.

The example given above, also presents a concept of *agency* e.g. the digital person *dLazy* is an agent of *Mr Lazy*. In the next section we will deal with this concept and further on some generic human traits in problem solving.

3   Agent Theory

Agency in general is a notion of delegation of one's job to another for execution in exchange of some agreed upon commission to the agent for the work it has carried out. This notion of agency is adopted towards software developments for developing autonomous software systems, each with certain capability to perform a defined task on its own. However, a group of agents may join to perform a composite task consisting of several simple tasks. A task is simple, we mean that, it is

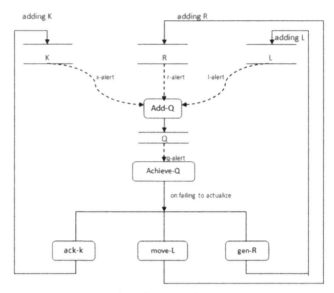

Figure 2: State Change in Goal Processing

Fig. 2. AlertProcessing

a small in the sense of atomicity, to execute and return a result for a given input without soliciting computing helps from other software processes. In a sense, it's a self-contained computing unit. Such a software process, independent in making a decision on its own, is known as a software agent. In research community it's also known as *intelligent agents*. In late years of 20th century, study on intelligent agents was a hot topic of research. The paper [18] identifies the concept of intelligent agents. While stressing on *autonomy* of intelligent agents, it brings in another aspect to agents, that's *interaction*. An agent, while working, is aware of its environment like available memory size, network bandwidth, security and services of other agents. In a way an agent is a piece of software that is *responsive*, *reactive* and *sociable*. Along the line of research in Artificial Intelligence, the emergence of Intelligent Agents is an encouraging effort towards wide scale application of intelligent technology in different domains. In order to address a complex problem i.e. a composition of atomic problems, the researchers followed an idea of distributed multi-agent systems [14] i.e. a system endowed with distributed computing and intelligent problem solving techniques. With this capability, intelligent systems are in a way ably different than object-oriented systems and expert systems. An object-oriented system though behave like an unitary entity with human like features viz. *inheritance, encapsulation, friendship* etc. but are not active and autonomous to make a choice on interacting with computing environment. Expert systems are the first successful intelligent systems used for problem solving. But, these systems though autonomous in planning problem solving strategy still are not co-operative as distributed intelligent systems [14]. Expert systems interact with experts for knowledge engineering and users needing expert services. It's passive in nature for not reacting to external stimuli.

Agent technology offers the next higher level system that reasons based on given as well as acquired knowledge. Intelligent systems with rational choice making, inferencing, learning, reacting (to external stimuli) capabilities behave like an entity with artificial life. As [18] tells, a piece of software with design objectives is intelligent for having three properties viz. *reactivity*, *pro-activeness* and *social ability*. It responds to external stimuli within defined time limit, so reactive. It is pro-active in taking a lead to meet the design objectives. The system on its own takes actions, looking ahead of time, as a measure to meet the demands of an ensuing situation. A part of its problem solving capability may be drawn from an external agent. These life like features of agents are further augmented by a model of mental status called BDI model i.e. *BDI: Belief, Desire* and *Intention* as shown in Fig. 3. Two leading researchers in this field report a comprehensive idea on BDI agents in the first conference on multi-agent systems [4]. The necessity of endowing agents with belief, desire and intention attributes is rationalised by them through an air traffic control system that is typically a real-time system with many other characteristics to accomplish a task like landing of a flight that requires to find an optimal sequence of tasks to be performed in a given time limit on interacting with evolving local conditions. They identify six characteristics that such an agent should have. Those are the following.

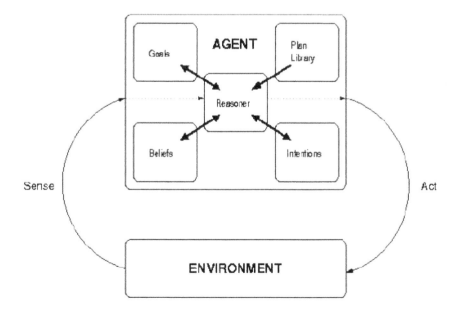

Fig. 3. BDI Agent

1. responding to evolving environment
2. identifying multiple objectives at a given instant of time and weighing possibility of achieving these objectives.
3. identifying non-determinism in actions that are potentially possible at a given instant of time.
4. the possibilities of external factors impacting a course of actions should be identified.
5. other than the factors of extended environment like weather and wind speed, the local environment factors are to be looked at e.g. runway condition, local vehicle movements, birds flying and etc.
6. rate of execution of actions and that of evolving environment need to be synchronised to ensure the actions are taken in expected times.

In case of air-traffic control system, there are some inputs received in tits and bits e.g. air speed information from different wind speed sensors. As these information are not validated and at the same time can't brushed away, so, are stored for later use in decision makings. These informative state of a system in labelled as *belief* state. Next, with given information what are achievable objectives, their pay-offs and priorities associated are to be weighed. These functions form a *desire* state of a system. This state generates several possibilities of which one has to be chosen for action based on problem domain specific conditions and computing limitations. A system on making a choice of action(s) enters into *intention* state. This presents an over all idea on BDI agents. Engineering of intelligent agents is a research area that looks into software engineering issues. One of our work in this direction is reported in [19]. A brief on the paper follows here.

The paper presents a micro-level design (Fig. 4) of a BDI agent with a formal specification using RAISE specification language [27]. The three states viz. belief, desire and intention are specified and a generic model for specifying a state transition with pre and post conditions are specified. We present a modular design of a BDI agent. The modules are control module, communication module,

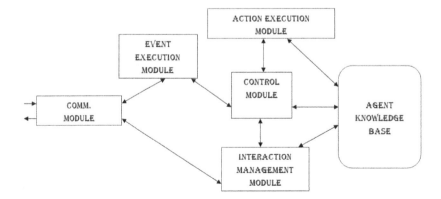

Fig. 4. BDI Agent Architecture

interaction management module, event management module, action execution module and a knowledge base management module. A service centric approach is adopted for engineering of an agent. A module provides a service in response to a request from another module. Engineering a service centric agent, we need to design in a way so that an agent can reason on its own behaviour towards goal adoption and commitment towards task accomplishment. It also has mechanism to communicate with other agents. Languages for agent communication is also an interesting topic. The concept of *society of agents* is also considered in which agents follow a set of societal laws while accomplishing a task. This helps in controlling undefined states that may result from unregulated information exchanges. Many applications like ecommerce applications need to adhere to certain social laws for good business and customer satisfaction. In one of our work [26] we have proposed the enforcement of social laws for collaboration, commitment honouring, relation preservation, reactive behaviour, relation revival and reciprocation. On the basis of speech-act theory, the agent communication language may use behavioural ontology for communication so a message sending agent can give a tone along with its message content so a receiving agent acts accordingly.

The research towards agent communication language has gone beyond classical communication protocol. The search was to find problem domain independent generic communication language primitives that agents use along with domain messages. These generic primitives add tones to messages like communicative (reporting), directive, assertive, suggestive and etc. Such tones sets the course of action plan at a receiving agent. The research on Agent Communication Language ACL took a concrete shape on taking the stock of research results due to various groups. Such a consolidation effort has given rise to $KQML$ i.e. Knowledge Query and Manipulation Language [31]. DARPA led team went on standardising agent communication language based on speech-act theory and identified three dozen performatives for agents to use. These performatives provide a base for building communication transactions to perform complex tasks of co-ordination and negotiation. Table 1 extracted from [32] shows these performatives in nine groups. Having this advancement in agent communication, the research in this area took interest in some typical generic human behaviour useful for problem solving [39]. The next section we will discuss on some works on this aspect of agents.

4   Agent Society

Multi-agent systems make a society of agents and an agent having a problem to solve may take helps of the other agents. Distributed systems also solve a problem together by assigning parts of a problem to different systems. Task distribution in these systems mainly keep two issues in mind viz. problem location, data locality. Means, computing either has to be at the point of problem locality or at the origin of the data that the computing needs. But a multi agent system though exhbits parallelism still it has some differences. The differences of these

Table 1. KQML Performatives

Performative Type	Communication Ontology
Informational	tell, deny, untell, cancel
Query	evaluate, reply, ask-if, ask-about,
-	ask-one, ask-all, sorry
Multi-response query	stream-about, stream-all
Basic effector	achieve, unachieve
Generator performatives	standby, ready, next, rest, discard, generator
Capability	advertise
Notification	subscribe, monitor
Facilitation	broker-one, broker-all, recommend-one,
-	recommend-all, recruit-one, recruit-all
Networking	register, unregister, forward,
-	broadcast, pipe, break

systems include finding participating agents, planning and negotiation in work distribution [25]. Existentialism of an agent in a society of agents is viewed in terms of the agent's capability. It's assumed that an agent has well defined task to execute certain objectives. It's independent to execute a task and take a decision during task execution. This is essentially a preamble of agency endowed with an agent. With this basic assumption, a taxonomy of agent functionalities is proposed in Fig. 5.

An agent having a task to execute does some basic activities viz. task decomposition, finding collaborating agents for sub-tasks, co-ordination of agents and execution planning and solution synthesis. Finding an agent for a subtask is a matching of its objective to an agent's capability. The matching can be performed by an matching agent that works like an yellow page. The similar concept is seen in discovering of webservices at UDDI (Universal Description, Discovery, and Integration) site that registers all webservices available at different service providers. A coordinating agent essentially does planning of task execution so that the execution carries on without resource contention, deadlocks and livelocks. It also keeps a watch on adherence to all the task associated conditions. Cooperation means the management of agents executing subtasks and these are nonantagonistic agents. That means they don't cooperate without any associate conditions. Whereas competing agents negotiate among themselves to find optimal conditions at which self interest is not compromised. A domain independent task control engine extracted from [14] is presented in Fig. 6. It shows a higher level design abstraction of agent's task coordination activities. The way it's different from traditional operating system in controlling task execution is for making dynamic choices based on beliefs i.e. information that are tentatively taken as true. This results in abandoning a thread of execution and replanning. Interested readers may refer to the paper for details. The point here is to be seen

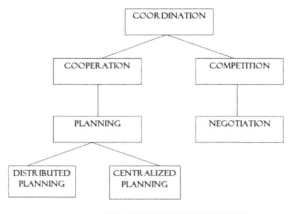

Fig. 5. Taxonomy of Agent Coordination

that human like traits agents exhibit while doing a thing i.e. *parr*: plan, analyse, replan and resume. This is very much a way digital entity like an agent exhibits a human-like behaviour while executing a task.

Further this behaviour is augmented by collaboration, negotiation and social reasoning. Behaviour of agents towards problem solving is based on theory of dependence as proposed in [12]. The attributes in a group of agents required for problem solving, include interconnection, interoperability, adaptation and co-ordination. According to the paper, the four cardinal principles, that agents should follow are the principle of i. *non-benevolence* ii. *sincerity* iii. *auto-knowledge* iv. *Consistency*. The first principle talks of agent's autonomy for choosing if it wants to help others or not. It never deliberately wishes to communicate erroneous information to others. That is the second principle. Its knowledge base is complete with reference to its capability i.e. if it declares it can do a task that means it has complete know how in solving the problem. But, it may have erroneous information about other agents. That makes the third principle. The fourth principle is about consistency. If inconsistency of information between two are detected then the agents revise their beliefs to maintain consistency. Dependencies are characterised as 1. *Independence*, 2. *Locally Believed Mutual Dependence*, 3. *Mutually Believed Mutual Dependence* 4. *Locally Believed Reciprocal Dependence* 5. *Mutually Believed Reciprocal Dependence* and 6. *Unilateral Dependence*. The paper also defined languages for an agent so it can compose its task as a composition of subtasks so it can monitor status of task execution and communicate with other agents for cooperation. The research provides a theoretical basis for reasoning on workings of agents following the theory of social dependence.

The importance of language in the design of agents is reiterated in a recent work [17]. The researchers propose a new technique for agent communication that not only eases management of complex task execution but it takes care two

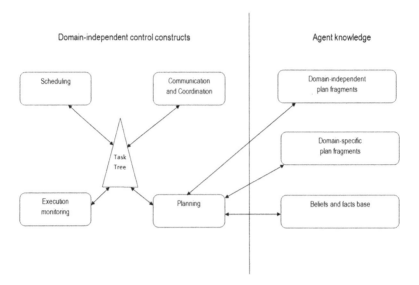

Fig. 6. BDI Generic tasks

vital aspects that researchers yet have not considered, are trust and security while maintaining decentralisation and transparency. For the purpose, the paper proposes role-based domain specific language. They propose a domain specific language having prime features of agent communication language, agent frame contract language. The two research questions addressed in the paper are 1. possibility of having a domain specific language as intended for agents in a block chain to communicate on an aspect of a particular domain abiding the contracts defined at the participating agents. The second one is about assuring security in use of a defined domain specific language. Design by contract is a software engineering approach that uses preconditions, postconditions, assertions, invariants in compositional design so that not only compatibility of software components are verified but also these help to design test cases for runtime system verification. In case of general purpose language, preconditions, assertions etc., are programmed and compiled. So, it follows an intrusive mechanism to ensure system safety conditions. That's a heavy implementation and not useful for systems in block chain for these being independent entities in a chain. Each of these systems are role based and context sensitive. Hence, the authors have chosen the implementation of design contracts in application layer using domain specific language so that an entity in its status change, invokes contracts for verification and execution based on the role status of a system. Block chain database contains both stateful and state less contracts. Once an agent performs an action, then its state is populated into black chain database and in turn based on its status, contracts are executed. Thus, the work provides an implementation of smart contracts in agent society using both domain specific language and agent programming language.

Negotiation, a human like strategy is followed by antagonistic agents but wishing to participate in a problem solving for their own interest. Negotaition being essentially a human attribute, is at times very complex depending on the human nature of the parties engaged in a negotiation process. It's essentially a decision making process followed by a defined negotiation protocol. At the end of this protocol a negotiation may succeed in finding an optimal solution i.e. a solution with individual's interest not utterly undermined. We will indicate some basic techniques for agent negotiation; however interested readers may refer to [33, 35, 36, 38, 40] for details. The basic techniques for negotiation includes

- game theory-based negotiation
- plan-based negotiation
- AI-based negotiation approaches.

Agents follow their utility functions, a set of deals, strategies and negotiation protocols. Utility function of an agent evaluates the gain it can have achieving a goal versus the loss for not achieving. A deal is an action of an agent, it has a utility function attached. A protocol defines rules that govern a negotiation process. Factoring time into negotiation process is reported in [38]. A process of negotiation must end in time. That's a vital issue including security aspects in negotiation process as reported in [41]. Critiques of game theory approach identify the unreasonable assumptions on agent benevolence. And a common knowledge on pay-off matrix is another debatable point. A detail on it may be found in [42]. The next, planning as method for agent negotiation is reported in [1]. Here agents are non-hierarchical, that way autonomous in choice of problem solving. First, an agent let be called as co-ordinator with its knowledge in problem solving strategies, decomposes a problem into several sub problems and looks for the agents who can solve these sub problems. Planning problem is to find inconsistencies among individual plans and resolving these conflicts. This resolution of inconsistencies is carried out by negotiation. In case of centralised planning, negotiation is conducted by a co-ordinator while in case of distributed planning, an agent finding self inconsistent with an interfacing agent, initiates a process of negotiation. That means their is an assumption of local common knowledge i.e. locally the agents in negotiation are aware of each other's plan. The locally consistent information is gradually spread across the agents involved in co-operative problem solving, and the negotiation finally ensures planning consistency at the global level. Computational complexity in attending global consistency in distributed planning case is a complex task to achieve. Further, sharing planning with neighbours may not be preferable. However, for some specific tasks distributed planning may be useful e.g. agents in rescue operation, command control applications. The next is about the negotiation strategy based on artificial intelligence techniques. Some of these techniques include case based reasoning, logic, evidence based reasoning, constraint direct search and etc. Negotiation is seen as a repetitive process in each time the deal is made based on the past experience. Case based reasoning is a technique that uses the cases based on their utility in the present context for negotiation. A case may have multiple attributes and utility function may be designed based on multi-attribute utility theory. It is argued that negotiation strategy for the future and present negotiations can be drawn based on the past experiences. The other approach is based on constraint-directed search of a problem space. Iteratively constraints and conflicts are relaxed until a negotiation is achieved. The negotiations operators are drawn from domain and then composed and refined for solution space navigation. Knowledge based model that uses partitioned blackboard for sharing of request and accept and reject proposals. The model uses shareable knowledge through blackboard implementation. Each such model is intuitively designed proposing a mechanistic approach of negotiation. However, each technique is based on certain assumptions like assuming agents benevolent and truthful, which could be too simplistic in real life. Modelling behaviours of individuals and group behaviour is a complex task. The study till now has been done as discussed above following mathematical as well as AI techniques. Still, it lacks a solid theoretical basis towards verifiable terminating negotiation strategies. Next section we will refer to some human aspects that we wish digital life may address.

5   Diginatives

Digital natives and digital immigrants are two terms introduced in [16] in a magazine on education strategic planning. It defines digital natives as the generation born in digital age and their parents and grand parents are the digital immigrants. The former finds digital age normal to deal with while the later is sceptic and at times hesitantly deals with it. The author of the article lists the new attributes of a digital native and compares the same with behaviour of digital immigrants. We will briefly refer some salient features the article narrates.

The new traits identified are in many dimensions like day to day life to livelihood and entertainment. A digital native starts a day with checking whatsapp massages, chat box in greeting its digital neighbours. The informations received on their cell phones are as trusted as much as digital immigrants distrust those. The former loves messages of business promotions to their respective cellphones whereas the former hates. Online transactions are normal for natives but immigrants are sceptic of it. Online learning is easier for the natives while the immigrants find it cumbersome. Digital natives have discovered a new language for texting that shuns classical grammar and spelling and at the same time the immigrants find that cryptic for unusual abbreviations. Real time texting has become a norm for the natives while at the best immigrants venture for emailing. Sharing about own in public on social media is a trending habit for digital natives. Digital immigrants do hesitate. The later prefers religious postings on social media. The most interesting point is avatarism of digital natives. One may appear on social media with different groups on different purposes. And it may happen even by different names for the same person and also masquerading is an accepted negative trait with some natives. Opinion making, crowd sourcing, open source resource sharing, cyber entertainment are some typical behaviours are predominant with the digital natives. The researchers tend to define digital natives' behaviour as a sub culture cutting across nations, races and cultures. And also their study shows as such there may not be essentially much difference between digial natives and digial immigrants at the higher level of social thinkings [43]. Technology intervention has also created distractions e.g. students' indifference to class room lectures. [22] tries to understand distractions as a phenomenon seen today among digital natives. At the same time computing scientists are busy in devising techniques to study belief, trust and emotion in digital behaviours of the digital natives. It's to be seen how do these analytics are the readings of the reality.

6   Digital Life and Afterlife

Digital natives tend to have a sub-culture with its rights, responsibilities and ethics in life. While having a life in digital space they also do need to remain connected with the worldly realities. In this context, here we will discuss on issues viz. rights, responsibilities, ethics and afterlife

Digital natives create contents those are indeed digital assets of individuals. These digital assets are of two types real and personal. The real assets are information about properties, one may have like land record, vehicle registration papers, insurance and bank details ets. Personal assets are the intellectual, personal and social details. All these often termed as contents. Digital natives use different platforms for sharing, storing and usage of these resources. These platforms are technology driven with different access control provisions like public, private, group and etc. access permissions. Now the points both technologists as well as sociologists study are management of these digital resources provisioning security as well as usability. Like any other assets, the aspects of life also comes into picture while managing rights. How to manage these assets afterlife? What should be ethical behaviour of digital natives so these assets are safe? What are the moral issues involved here? Some research works dealing these questions will be referred here.

Digital Life and digital assets are the two concepts the paper [11] deals with. Some even make a vast repository of its digital holdings that it's referred as a digital estate. When there is a property then the natural questions come to mind regarding safety in holding a property, a protocol for sharing it with others, its growth and maintenance, sustainability, exchange of property, inheritance and ofcourse moral responsibility. The other question hunts people is, "what will happen to my digital assets after my death?" What about digital inheritance? Can it continue to be with a person after its death? The paper deals with these questions from social science and legal perspectives. The paper talks of digital estate managers who can take care of digital assets and estates of its clients. In order to facilitate digital asset management, the paper also proposes unambiguous laws in totality so not only the digital assets of a person can be protected but also its inheritance can be well defined [13].

Technologists lived up to the recommendations of the social scientists on the management of digital estates. In order to give an idea on automation of digital content management we refer to a paper [37]. It's a representative one but does not claim as a comprehensive review. A generic model for managing digital assets is taken from the paper and presented here for a discussion. There are four actors viz. *content provider*, *distributor*, *consumer* and *clearing house*. This architecture is mainly for digital services like games, movies, news, blogs and etc. The idea is alike to the idea of webservices. The actor *content provider* on creating contents provides it to the distributor which provides digital platforms like youTube, blogspots etc. for providing online or offline services to consumers. Distributors make metadata of contents and advertises so consumers get to know about the services. Consumers make payments which are managed by clearing houses such that both i.e. the distributors' and consumers' rights are honoured. The Fig. 7 [37], provides a framework indicating the functional relations among the four. All need to obey their respective operational roles with a code of conduct.

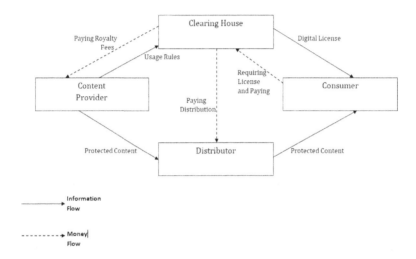

Fig. 7. Digital Content Management

Digital natives have their respective online lives as well as real ones. The way they deal with the both in virtuous way is a matter of importance particularly for an onlife life being a shadow life; but it often transacts with the real world in addition to interactions with its virtual worlds. The paper [5] interacts with a section of youth of different categories to study the extent to which digital natives consider moral issues while dealing with their respective digital life. They have considered the youths behaviours in social networking, multi-player gaming and information acquiring like downloading etc. While analysing their behaviour they found, among the traits prevalent among the digital natives, individualistic thinking is dominant. They are in a way mostly engrossed to themselves in their respective digital lives. At the same time, individuals show concern to others like showing respect, expressing wellness etc. A moral behaviour among digital natives getting naturalised. This is for the people whom one knows. Exhibiting good moral behaviour to the known people is ofcourse prevalent. But, they show little respect to the unknowns. The activities like mud slinging other than engaging in criminal activities are worrisome behaviours. Digital life tends to be anonymous in vast cyberspace in such an extent that two people sitting side by side in an airport lounge may be texting one another without knowing their current proximity. Next we will refer to a work on digital world and individuals.

Digital technology has offered each a virtual world that coexist with the real world. A digital ecosystem like Internet of Things, cell phones and etc. make a digital ecosystem in which individuals dwell in. Thus an individual dwelling in both the worlds viz. real world and online world turns to a transmediated self as told in [34]. In real life one may be alone but could be together in its digital world with social networking friends; this makes a life *alone together*. Online appearances of an individual creates avatār that is an individual on a screen. This brings in a philosophical question on existentialism. Self and its digital avatārs may compete in claiming as a prime reference of a self. Again the question of existential equivalence among a self and its avatārs throw a philosophical question on existentialism. The paper talks of four characteristics of a transmediated individual. These are *integrated*, *dispersed*,*episodic*, and *interactive*. A complete image of an individual is an integrated view of its real life and its online life based on its avatārs in different social networking platforms and other Internet platforms. The dispersed appearances of digital self, may project different aspects of real self. A study of consistency among digital lives of a self is an interesting topic of research for many strategic applications. Episodic appearances of a digital life is useful to trace the changes in a person in reality as well as its online incarnations. Number of interactions of a person with its own digital incarnations as well as with others, is exponentially increased. It's useful to have an integrated view of such interactions to analyse behaviour of a person and its tranmediated existences.

With the advent of new technologies and then life turning to its transmediated existences in real as well as digital spaces, it's indeed wise to make use of these technologies for making life better. Next section we will talk of a future of digital world and its inhabitants.

7   Digital World Making

The recent pandemic has accelerated the ushering of the digital age in an unprecedented way. It's now to make digital natives ease with the digital world order. In order to give a glimpse of the impact digital technology has made on human life we will give only two examples, one from manufacturing industry and another from medicine, considering the importance of both in modern life. *Digital Twin*, a concept for an industry sub floor management is reported in [7]. It's an unique idea to have a real factory and a simulated one running in parallel and in online exchange of data between, to guide real time operations based on simulation results. This helps in real time management of manufacturing process so it can address to dynamic changes occurring in logistic, supply chain management and volatility of market.

Health sector has seen sea changes with digital healthcare devices [9] and the data evolving from these devices carry the imprint of human health so based on that personal healthcare management can be precisely defined [15]. The technological developments in wireless technology and genomic study particularly driven by high performance computing have given rise to a plethora of opportunities for precise healthcare with tailor made health services, a person requires. Most interesting point is the remote provisioning of these services by making use of wireless technology for data streaming from patients to health specialists and service providers and also vice versa health advices streaming to the patients. A programmed sensor kept in a digestible pill enters into say intestinal track and emits signal tracing the biological events occurring in the track. Similarly, a programmed pill may sit at a place inside a patient body to drop the required amount of medicine at the right place at the right time. This gives a scenario of digital life working in association with its real life. The management of data is crucial when such health care digital agents implanted in human bodies and stream data to hospitals. This requires a secured data highway so that real-time health data is available to the specialists for immediate healthcare. Like highways as an infrastructure are thought for boosting the economy, so now digital highway is of high priority to achieve data liquidity and data equity that enables not only data sharing but also ensures responsible interoperable data operations. The need of such digital data highway is discussed in [15].

The above two examples are representative in nature. It shows the possibilities of active digital lives taking over, to start with, some real-life mundane activities. Later even intelligent digital lives (agents) may represent a person for crucial decision makings. Thus there is a need of personalised digital lives unlike today apps we see on our cellphones. Tomorrow, people may like to tailor made the digital lives they need to have. Composition of such digital lives is a difficult proposition for expecting each to design and develop its own software agents. It is certainly not a rational assumption. Then the need of digital live factory comes to which one can order to get a digital life of its own choice. That's customisation of a digital life to suit one's traits and ethics. A generic digital life software can be downloaded and then tailor made by the user itself to shape it up to its own digital life. It requires an easy user interface and self abstraction schemas which are to be populated by an user to create its own digital life that does its work in a given domain and for a given objective. It's like augmenting digital apps with human like behaviour. Supposing, having this done, what could be possible scenarios in cyberspace with innumerable life like autonomous digital entities carrying individuals' traits, wishes and priorities for availing services. In addition there is the looming concern of rogue digital entities. That way, digital lives together reflect the somewhat similar scenario what we see in real life. This brings in the need of governance of digital lives. In an editorial note [3] talks of research on Big data mainly to study social realities in our fast changing society.

Similar study is required for this ultra new society of digital lives with individuals live in a transmidiated space where real as well as coexisting virtual worlds. Possibly, not just a cyber infrastructure but new cyber world of digital lives is to be created. This needs a revolutionary outlook in making of a new digital world populated with digital lives. Digital society has flavour of globalisation as well as localisation i.e. glocalization. The paper [10] discusses on this issue and talks of a new phenomena of nationalism and post-secularism. Based on these, there may be emergence of new youth value system, that time is to say in the near future.

8   Conclusion

We have presented a framework of an digital life in a three dimensional space of knowledge, resource and location and have shown how can it schedule its behaviour to achieve an objective. A functional behaviour of a digital entity is formally specified. Then we revisit the works on software agents in which the researchers have attempted to implement some human aspects with an aim to develop autonomous agents that can make rational choices during problem solving. In this context, BDI, a pragmatic popular agent framework is discussed. Further towards cooperative problem solving to meet the challenges of complex tasks, a high level abstraction of problem solving strategies viz. co-operation and planning are discussed referring to some prime works in this area.

We have also discussed some philosophical and social issues being actively researched by social scientists. In this context, the research works on the status of a digital life, after its owner's death are referred. These works mainly talk about the possession status of the digital resources created by a person. How does the law of inheritance work for these resources? What does happen to the unclaimed resources? The importance of these issues are stated. Looking at the future, we have also discussed the idea of evolving digital worlds.

For computing scientists, the idea of artificial life has been a research interest. What indeed a life is? A complex structure of organic materials evolved in a course of time as the theory of evolution claims, makes today's human with a body and mind, so the human can make rational choices in its life dotted by its birth and death, though nobody knows what it is before and after the birth and the death respectively. The idea of digital life follows the classical notion of life endowed to an entity that is not really living but carries with an imprint of life. Both the researchers of Life Science and Computing Science have been trying to create artificial life. Here we will look at the evolution of artificial life in computing domain.

Evolution is regarded as a prime concept on the genesis of life since Darwin proposed the theory of evolution in his famous book *The Origin of Species* [8]. Based on this theory, the computing scientists starting with Von Neumann and Allan Turing have been talking of digital system with artificial life. A note on it may be found in [30]. Theory of evolution sees the three characteristics that drives the Nature; these are dominant traits and mutation, reproduction and inheritance. Von Neumann proposed a theoretical framework of cellular automata in quest of self reproducing systems. Later Turing, took up the search of a child machine in line of the process of biological evolution and tried to teach the machine to act as taught. But, he discounted the success of the experiment. Following this, Barricelli reports his fascinating work on artificial life [6]. His experiment on cellular automata deals with self reproducing automata that changes its state depending on the states of its neighbouring cells in such a way that the change depends upon the states of some neighbouring cells such that cooperative configurations of states could arise. In this experiment he observed some phenomena. These include self-reproduction of certain collections of states (which he named "symbioorganisms"), spontaneous formation of symbioorganisms, parasitism, and self-maintaining symbioorganisms. Then the research took its turn on Artificial Intelligence (AI) in several dimensions e.g. automated reasoning, inferencing, planning, learning, natural language processing, speech recognition, robotics and etc. Expert systems, some embedded systems with learning and inferencing capabilities were put in practice. But, the research in this area took slow pace for realising the success of artificial systems lies on its capability in dealing with open world. Now, again we see the surge of artificial systems into mainstream promising smart applications in many domains.

As discussed, apps, IoT systems, robots, chatbots and etc. on behalf of their owners work with defined goal exhibiting virtual lives in cyber world. They make a digital ecosystem. The world they make, is different and parallel to the real world. This reminds the tale of *Trishanku* in Mahābhārata wishing a world of his own, alike to the cosmic world *swarga* i.e. the heaven and finally suffering being upside down swinging in halfway to it. The tale gives a lead to think what should such parallel world be, if at all it has to be, in case our wishes are alike to those of the king *Trishanku*. How the changes have been at the advent of new technologies, is essential to know, to visualise the present in terms of the past and project ahead of time to get a picture of what the world could be in future.

At present digital natives and digital immigrants live in a transmediated space for having both the real and digital lives. But, the case of born-digital generation could be different. A work [43] discusses on this issue. We will refer to some points of relevance to digital lives. The authors have adopted quantitative approach in analysing data collected from different societies across the Globe to study the way people think on life matters like livelihood, family, health, career, safety and etc. They have found the differences and commonalities among digital natives, digital immigrants and born digital have. The growing trend of differences in attitude to life and conduct seen among generations projects the emergence of a new digital culture with changes in attitudes, values, and behaviours of individuals around the world. Further digitalization may result to shrinking of intercultural differences. The authors also profess a revision of idea on national culture that has grown and groomed in a geographical ecosystem. For the expanse of cyberspace beyond geographical spaces may downplay the influence a geographical ecosystem makes. But, common interests including racial identity and beliefs may give rise to global clusters where individual members of a cluster spread across the Globe. On growing digitalisation and dependence, the changes in human psychology in looking at world is a crucial factor. At the same time, human intellect curiosity in making of artificial life is also a matter of focus now. We will conclude this chapter with a reference to [28].

Humankind, starting from harvesting from Nature, has come to the point of competing with Nature. Science and technology have given a big hand in this journey though philosophically the idea of competition is despised still the benevolence of Science is not brushed off. Ancient civilisations have their own attempts in creating artificial life. The *muni* Vishwamitra, of Indian epics creates an artificial heaven for the king *Trishanku*. The demon *Raktabirjya* regenerates itself soon after its blood touches the ground. The *Kourav* queen *Gandhari* gets her hundred sons on eating oblation made to holy fire, *yagna*. Other civilisations must have similar myths. Modern approaches for making of artificial life is categorised into three catogories viz. as wet, hard and soft [28]. Wet approach includes biochemical processes where as electromechanical processes make hard approach and software based systems make soft approaches. These approaches are not mutually exclusive. There could be a common query asking the necessity of having artificial lives. Human inquisitiveness could be a reason for the search of artificial lives. Artificial lives like robots, software agents, artificially generated limbs provide services to humankind. We also find use of digital lives in pursuing agenda in different domains. Like usefulness, a concern for its overreaching negative social impact is also of concern to public. May be sometime human ego get hurt being beaten by software agents and robots. Data security and privacy may get compromised for artificial lives turning rogues. Human developing possessive relations with artificial lives may generate different kinds of psychological issues in future. Should there be an ethical process to treat with deceased artificial lives? Human lives hitherto to living among artificial lives, particularly digital lives may face new world of transhumanism. Let's have a look at some of the works in this area that is relevant here for our discussion.

8.1   Transhumanism

Transhumanism talks of the life beyond. The quest for artificial life is towards transhumanism. Bhāratiya ancient epics with the concept of rebirth supports the idea of life beyond life. It talks of a spiritual relation between *ātman* (soul) and *Brahman* the Divine. Through rebirths, *ātman*'s endeavour to achieve its eternity is its journey to the divine *Brahman*. Sri Aurobindo's theory of *divya jēban* (divine life) prophesies *atimānab* (super human) that conquers death and attains to eternity. Currently, significant advancements in both the Life Science and the Digital Technology, transhumanists have been keen on philosophical issues involved in artificial lives. Their search for meaning of life through transhumanism is interesting to note.

Bio-conservationists oppose use of technology in shaping up human life, like use of tools and medicines for enhancing memory power. Transhumanists favour technology interventions. Thus, there are conflicting thoughts. As a solution

[24] proposes an idea of posthuman dignity that recommends selective use of technology for enhancing human dignity.

The kinds of transhumanism as noted in [2] are viz. Individual Transhumanism, Terrestrial Transhumanism, Religious Transhumanism, and Cosmist Transhumanism. Looking beyond life individual transhumanism looks for overcoming human limitations and aspiring longer life span and with all amenities for enhanced quality of life. This is purely existentialism emboldened by technology. This is what digital lives now offer towards individual transhumanism. Religious transhumanism believes on the hand of the Divine for making a life meaningful. This is a mix of existentialism and spiritualism. Thus, religious transhumanist though admits power of science and technology still believe, the meaningful life is due to the grace of God. Terrestrial transhumanists, unlike the previous two, look for betterment of humanity. It is in view of growth and development of humanity towards meaningful life because of intervention of range of technologies viz. artificial intelligence, wireless communication, genomic, space science, quantum computing and etc. Finally cosmist transhumanism goes beyond worldly reality and proposes technological innovation leading super human capability so human civilisation spreads into space to turn into inter galactic societies. Talking about human evolution, the author in [29] ideates on cosmic beings (CoBe) that can surpass human intelligence. This idea resembles to the Sri Aurobindo's the concept of *atimanava* i.e. super human realising the divinity in life. Sri Aurobindo has dealt at transcendental higher plane than the present transhumanists talk about.

The current trends in realising transhumanism focusses on making of human like artificial lives. Novelists also add to this imagination [23]. Humanity is now facing individual transhumanism at the onset of large scale intervention of digital technologies. Real life submerged in unseen beings of digital lives and their copies in cyberspace create an unprecedented scenario in which meaning of life is to be redefined considerably scaling down the existential risk and empowering individual and society for higher meaning of life. Success in this individual transhumanism through digital lives has to triumph for greater cause of humanity leading to *atimanava*, the transcendental human life [44].

References

1. Alder, M.R., Davis, A.B., Weihmayer, R., Forest, R.W.: Conflict-resolution strategies for non-hierarchical distributed agents. In: Gasser, L., Huhns, M.N. (eds.) Distributed Artificial Intelligence, vol. 2. Morgan Kaufmann (1989)
2. Sandberg, A.: Transhumanism and the meaning of life. In: Trothen, T., Mercer, C. (eds.) Transhumanism and Religion: Moving into an Unknown Future. Praeger (2014)
3. Visvizi, A., Lytras, M.D., Aljohani, N.: Big data research for politics: human centric big data research for policy making, politics, governance and democracy. J. Ambient. Intell. Humaniz. Comput. **12**, 4303–4304 (2021)
4. Rao, A.S., Georgeff, M.P.: BDI agents: from theory to practice. In: Proceedings of 1st International Conference on Multi-agent System, pp. 312–319 (1995)

5. Flores, A., James, C.: Morality and ethics behind the screen: young people's perspectives on digital life. New Media Soc. **15**(6), 834–852 (2012)
6. Barricelli, N.A.: Numerical testing of evolution theories. Part I. Theoretical introduction and basic tests. Acta Biotheoretica **XVI**(1/2), 69–98 (1962)
7. Brenner, B., Hummel, V.: Digital twin as enabler for an innovative digital shop floor management system in the ESB Logistics Learning Factory at Reutlingen - University. Procedia Manuf. **9**, 198–205 (2017)
8. Darwin, C.: The Origin of Species. John Murray, London (1859)
9. Topol, E.J.: Transforming medicine via digital innovation. Sci. Transl. Med. **2**(16) (2010)
10. Zolotukhina-Abolina, E., Mirskaya, L., Pendyurina, L., Ingerleib, M.: Digital reality and youth values. In: E3S Web of Conferences, vol. 273, p. 10010 (2021)
11. Hopkins, J.P.: Afterlife in the cloud: managing a digital estate. Hastings Sci. Tech. L. J. **5**(2), 209 (2013)
12. Sichman, J.S., Demazeau, Y.: On social reasoning in multi-agent systems. Inteligencia Artificial. Revista Iberoamericana de Inteligencia Artificial, vol. 5, no. 13 (2001)
13. Conner, J.: Digital life after death: the issue of planning for a person's digital assets after death. Est. Plan. Cmty. Prop. L. J. **3**, 301 (2011)
14. Sycara, K., Pannu, A., Williamson, M., Zeng, D., Detker, K.: Distributed intelligent systems. IEEE Expert **11**, 36–46 (1996)
15. Chin, L., Khozin, S.: A digital highway for data fluidity and data equity in precision medicine. BBA - Rev. Cancer **1876**, 188575 (2021)
16. Prensk, M.: Digital natives, digital immigrants part 2: do they really think differently? On Horiz. **9**(6) (2001)
17. Oruç, O.: Role-based embedded domain-specific language for collaborative multi-agent systems through blockchain technology. In: 9th International Conference of Security, Privacy and Trust Management (SPTM) (2021)
18. Wooldridge, M.: Intelligent agents. In: Multiagent Systems (1999). https://books.google.com/
19. Patra, M.R., Mohanty, H.: A formal framework to build software agents. In: APSEC, pp. 119–126 (2001)
20. Mohanty, H.: Person habitat and migration modeling. In: 2011 Tencon, IEEE India Conference (2011)
21. Mohanty, H.: Computational social science: a bird's eye view. In: Hota, C., Srimani, P.K. (eds.) ICDCIT 2013. LNCS, vol. 7753, pp. 319–333. Springer, Heidelberg (2013). https://doi.org/10.1007/978-3-642-36071-8_25
22. Hanin, M.L.: Theorizing digital distraction. Philos. Technol. **34**, 395–406 (2021)
23. Ian, M.: Machines Like Me: A Novel. Knopf Canada, Toronto, Canada (2019)
24. Bostrom, N.: In defense of posthuman dignity. Bioethics **19**(3) (2005). 1467-8519
25. Huhns, M.N., Stephens, L.M.: Multi-agent systems and society of agents. https://www.researchgate.net/profile/Michael-Huhns/publication
26. Patra, M.R., Mohanty, H.: Enforcing social laws in goal directed communication. In: Proceedings of the International Conference on Industrial and Engineering Applications of Artificial Intelligence and Expert Systems (IEA-AIE 1997), Atlanta, USA (1997)
27. The RAISE language Group. The RAISE Specification Language, Prentice Hall International (UK) Ltd. (1992)
28. Belk, R., Humayun, M., Gopaldas, A.: Artificial life. J. Macromark. **40**(2), 221–236 (2020)
29. Chu, T.: Human Purpose and Transhuman Potential: A Cosmic Vision of Our Future Evolution. Origin Press (2014)

30. Taylor, T., Dorin, A., Korb, K.: Digital Genesis: Computers, Evolution and Artificial Life. eprint=1512.02100, arXiv (2015)
31. Neches, R.: Overview of the DARPA Knowledge Sharing Effort (1994). http://www-ksl.stanford.edu/knowledge-sharing/papers/kse-overview.html
32. Nwana, H.: Michael Wooldridge software agent technologies. BT Technol. J. **14**(4) (1996)
33. Nwana, H.S., Lee, L., Jennings, N.R.: Co-ordination in software agent systems. BT Technol. J. **14**(4), 79–88 (1996)
34. Sage Elwell, J.: The transmediated self: life between the digital and the analog. Convergence: Int. J. Res. New Media Technol. **20**(2), 233–249 (2014)
35. Aknine, S., et al.: An extended multi-agent negotiation protocol. Auton. Agent. Multi-agent Syst. **8**, 5–45 (2004)
36. Beer, M., et al.: Negotiation in Multi-Agent Systems (UKMAS 1998) (1998)
37. Liu, Q., Safavi-Naini, R., Sheppard, N.P.: Digital rights management for content distribution. In: Australasian Information Security Workshop (2003)
38. Kraus, S.: Negotiation and cooperation in multi-agent environments. Artif. Intell. **94**, 79–97 (1997)
39. Brzostowski, J., Kowalczyk, R.: Predicting partner's behaviour in agent negotiation. In: AAMAS 2006, 8–12 May 2006 (2006)
40. Mohanty, H., Kurra, R., Shyamasundar, R.K.: A framework for web-based negotiation. In: Janowski, T., Mohanty, H. (eds.) ICDCIT 2010. LNCS, vol. 5966, pp. 140–151. Springer, Heidelberg (2010). https://doi.org/10.1007/978-3-642-11659-9_14
41. Mohanty, V., Hota, C.: Secure web services negotiation. In: Nagamalai, D., Renault, E., Dhanuskodi, M. (eds.) CCSEIT 2011. CCIS, vol. 204, pp. 609–618. Springer, Heidelberg (2011). https://doi.org/10.1007/978-3-642-24043-0_62
42. Rosenschein, J.S., Zlotkin, G.: Rules of Encounter: Designing Conventions for Automated Negotiation among Computers. MIT Press, Cambridge (1994)
43. Kincl, T., Strach, P.: Born digital: is there going to be a new culture of digital natives? J. Glob. Scholars Market. Sci. **31**(1), 30–48 (2021)
44. Aurobindo, S.: The Life Divine, 7th edn. Sri Aurobindo Ashram, Pondicherry (1982)

Heuristics for K-Independent Average Traveling Salesperson Problem

Sebanti Majumder⬤ and Alok Singh$^{(\boxtimes)}$⬤

School of Computer and Information Sciences, University of Hyderabad,
Hyderabad 500046, Telangana, India
alokcs@uohyd.ernet.in

Abstract. This paper deals with heuristic solution of K-independent average traveling salesperson (KIATSP) problem which is a recent extension of the well-known traveling salesperson problem (TSP). This problem seeks finding of K mutually independent Hamiltonian tours with no common edge such that the weighted sum of the average and standard deviation of the cost of these K tours is as small as possible. Like TSP, KIATSP is also an $\mathcal{NP}$-hard problem. We have designed seven constructive heuristics to address this problem. Our first two heuristics build K tours one after the other, whereas all the other heuristics construct K tours parallelly. A detailed comparative study of the performances of these seven heuristics on 40 TSPLIB instances has been presented. It is observed that those heuristics which build tours in parallel generally performed better than those heuristics where tours are built one after the other.

Keywords: Constructive heuristic · Discrete optimization · Traveling salesperson problem · K-independent average traveling salesperson problem

1 Introduction

Traveling salesperson problem (TSP) is among those problems in the field of combinatorial optimization which are very famous and have wide applicability [3,4,6]. In TSP, the objective is to find the shortest Hamiltonian tour in a given edge-weighted complete graph. TSP finds its application in vehicle routing, logistics, planning and scheduling etc. But in some real-life scenarios, such as, in a logistic company's delivery system, there may arise a situation where one or more edges in the shortest route becomes faulty. In that case having backup routes can be helpful. In K-independent average traveling salesperson (KIATSP), introduced by Iwasaki and Hasebe in [2], K tours with similar utility values are designed, which in turn improves the reliability. In KIATSP, the goal is to build K mutually independent Hamiltonian tours with no common edge such that the weighted sum of the average and standard deviation of the cost of these K tours is minimised. KIATSP is a very recent problem introduced only in 2021. For $K = 1$, KIATSP reduces to TSP, and hence, being a generalization of an $\mathcal{NP}$-hard problem, viz. TSP [1], KIATSP is also $\mathcal{NP}$-hard. Figure 1 provides

© The Author(s), under exclusive license to Springer Nature Switzerland AG 2023
R. Morusupalli et al. (Eds.): MIWAI 2023, LNAI 14078, pp. 25–35, 2023.
https://doi.org/10.1007/978-3-031-36402-0_2

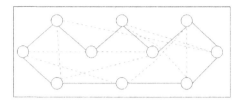

Fig. 1. Illustration of K-independent tours (with $K = 2$) on a 10 node complete graph.

an illustration of K independent tours with $K = 2$ on a complete graph, where the total number of cities is 10. As can be clearly seen, there are no common edge between these two tours. In their paper [2], Iwasaki and Hasebe have also proposed another problem called K-independent total traveling salesperson problem (KITTSP). KITTSP seeks K mutually independent Hamiltonian tours with no common edge such that the sumtotal of the cost of these K tours is minimised. Clearly, KIATSP contains KITTSP as a special case when weight for average cost is K and weight for standard deviation is zero. If there is a need to find K independent tours, where the difference in the cost of these tours is minimum, i.e., in a situation where K tours can be simultaneously used, KIATSP would be more useful. KITTSP will be more useful where backup tours are required in case of failure of the shortest tour. So in a way these two problems are complementary problems. KIATSP provides tours with similar utility values, whereas KITTSP provides tours with rank utility values [2].

Iwasaki and Hasebe [2] have used ant colony optimization (ACO) approach to solve KIATSP problem. They have shown comparative analysis of ACO with a mathematical optimization (MO) approach based on quadratic programming and have compared the performance on one particular instance *gr17* from TSPLIB for different values of K. They have shown the superiority of their proposed algorithm over MO. This is the only approach available in the literature to solve KIATSP. No problem-specific constructive heuristics exists in the literature for KIATSP. We were motivated to work on this problem since it was not explored much. We have developed seven different constructive heuristic to solve this problem. These constructive heuristics have been tested on 40 publicly available instances from TSPLIB. A comparative analysis of all the seven heuristics has been provided. We will use cities, vertices and nodes interchangeably in this paper.

The remaining part of this paper is organized as follows: Sect. 2 defines the problem formally, whereas Sect. 3 presents our seven heuristics. Section 4 is devoted to experimental results and their analysis. In Sect. 5, we have outlined some concluding remarks and directions for future research.

2 Formal Problem Definition

Suppose $G = (V, E)$ is a complete undirected edge-weighted graph where V is the vertex set and E is edge set. For every edge $(i, j) \in E$ connecting vertices i and j, a weight w_{ij} is associated with (i, j), which can be interpreted as the length of that edge or the cost of traversing that edge. The KIATSP consists in finding K Hamiltonian tours on G in such a manner that these K tours should not have any edge in common and the weighted sum of the average and standard deviation of the cost of these K tours is minimized. We call the tours mutually independent if they do not have any edge in common. Hence, KIATSP can be restated as the problem of finding K mutually independent Hamiltonian tours on G so that the weighted sum of the average and standard deviation of the cost of these K tours is minimized. The objective function can be defined formally in the following manner:

$$\min \quad \gamma cost_{avg} + \theta cost_{sd}$$

$$\text{where,} \quad cost_{avg} = \frac{1}{K} cost_{sum}$$

$$cost_{sum} = \sum_{i \in V} \sum_{j \in V} \sum_{k \in K} w_{ij} x_{ijk}$$

$$cost_{sd} = \sqrt{\frac{1}{K}(\sum_{k \in K}(\sum_{i \in V} \sum_{j \in V} w_{ij} x_{ijk} - \frac{1}{K}(\sum_{i \in V} \sum_{j \in V} \sum_{k' \in K} w_{ij} x_{ijk'}))^2)}$$

$$x_{ijk} \in \{0, 1\}$$

where x_{ijk} is 1, if the kth tour contains the edge (i, j), and 0 otherwise. γ and θ are the weights assigned to average tour cost and standard deviation of tours' costs respectively. Our research work is focussed on developing problem-specific heuristics to address KIATSP and empirical analysis thereof. Hence, no mathematical programming formulation of the problem is provided. Interested readers can refer to [2] for the mathematical formulation of the problem.

3 Proposed Heuristics

We have developed seven constructive heuristics, viz. C1, C2, C3, C4, C5, C6 and C7 for KIATSP. Out of these seven heuristics, first six heuristics are based on the concept of nearest neighbour and a city can be added only at the end of partially constructed tour. On the other hand, our last heuristic is an insertion based heuristic where a new city can be added anywhere in the tour depending on the quality of the resulting tour. The nearest neighbour method is a very simple approach and is widely used to solve TSP based problems. This method starts by marking all nodes as unvisited. Then while building a tour, first node is selected randomly and added to the tour and marked as visited. the rest of the tour is built by adding the nodes one-by-one in an iterative manner. During each iteration, a nearest unvisited neighbor of the node last added, i.e., a node not yet included in the tour that is nearest to the node last added, is added to the tour. This newly added node is marked visited and another iteration begins. This process continues till no unvisited node remains, i.e., till the complete tour is constructed. Earlier, we have developed constructive heuristics [5] for KITTSP [2] based on nearest neighbor concept. Except for the last heuristic, the heuristics presented here for KIATSP follow the same idea as used in [5] for KITTSP.

Before describing our seven heuristics, it is clarified that no heuristic of ours is guaranteed to give K mutually independent tours in every run. The number of mutually independent tours generated depends on the value of K, the structure of the problem instance and the seed used for the random number generator. That is why, we execute our heuristics multiple times to find K mutually independent tours. If all runs fail, then no feasible solution can be obtained.

3.1   Constructive Heuristic No. 1 (C1)

In the first heuristic C1, K mutually independent tours are generated one-by-one, by exploiting the concept of nearest neighbours as explained already. It is a greedy approach. Starting with a randomly chosen city, a tour is constructed by iteratively adding to the tour a city nearest to the city last added from the set of available cities. Set of available cities include those cities which are not already part of the current tour and the edges joining them to the city last added do not occur in any of the tours already constructed. If for a particular tour, no further edge can be added to the tour since all the possible edges are already part of partial solution, then that particular tour is constructed again from scratch with a new city as start city. This new start city is chosen randomly from cities not already tried as start city. If all cities got tried without any success then the heuristic ends with an infeasible solution where the number of tours is less than K. Otherwise, C1 returns a completely feasible solution.

3.2   Constructive Heuristic No. 2 (C2)

Our second heuristic generates K tours one-by-one based on the concept of GRASP (greedy randomized adaptive search procedure) approach [7]. This heuristic is same as C1 except for the fact that instead of choosing the nearest city from the set of available cities, a city is chosen randomly from p nearest cities.

3.3   Constructive Heuristic No. 3 (C3)

The third heuristic C3 builds tour parallelly. In the beginning, initial city is selected for each of the K tours at random and then an iterative process ensues. During each iteration, the next city for each of the K tours is selected one-by-one by considering the tours in their natural order. These iterations continue until all the K tours are completely constructed. The next city selected for adding into a tour is the nearest available neighbour of the city last added to the tour. Only those cities are available for selection in a tour which are not already part of that tour and the edge connecting them to the city last added do not occur in any of the K partially constructed tour. If the heuristic is unable to find any edge that is already not included in the tour, then the whole process starts afresh and all the K tours are constructed again from scratch. The construction of K tours from scratch is repeated till 120s. If it is unable to provide a feasible solution even after 120s then a null solution is returned, or else a feasible solution with K mutually

Table 1. Performance of seven heuristics for $K = 3, \gamma = 1$, and $\theta = 2$

Instances	$K=3, \gamma=1, \theta=2$													
	C1		C2		C3		C4		C5		C6		C7	
	Average	AET	Average	AET	Average	AET	Average	AET	Average	AET	Average	AET	Average	AET
ulysses22	14176.92	0.0029	15150.77	0.0017	13284.6	0.0001	14261.77	0.0002	**12695.27**	0.0001	14074	0.0001	18428.49	0.0002
bays29	5023.69	0.0037	4706.22	0.0025	4102.6	0.0001	4636.64	0.0018	**3810.21**	0.0004	4460.52	0.0002	6613.07	0.0002
att48	22806.5	0.0036	28596.15	0.0036	19854.95	0.0001	26278.08	0.0001	**19450.77**	0.0002	25868.79	0.0002	55714.37	0.0011
eil51	1059.58	0.0023	1147.37	0.0025	**881.02**	0.0001	1104.99	0.0013	895.93	0.0008	1049.24	0.0017	1754.98	0.0053
berlin52	19371.29	0.0044	20151.98	0.0022	**15726.2**	0.0037	18331.51	0.0014	16092.95	0.0002	18731.52	0.0002	31430.57	0.0013
pr76	410475.12	0.0003	305201.34	0.0012	**245501.28**	0.0037	298022.96	0.0002	246067.22	0.0003	280584.37	0.0003	593763.55	0.0055
gr137	200246.77	0.0044	208606.98	0.0003	165719.51	0.0048	198043.91	0.0005	**164802.57**	0.0004	195484.58	0.0002	668760.83	0.0204
pr144	222604.91	0.0048	232509.33	0.0007	162695.26	0.0047	195136.92	0.0004	**159461.43**	0.0007	204981.37	0.0003	840429.47	0.0188
ch150	17229.82	0.0047	18237.55	0.005	13530.42	0.0036	16807.18	0.0006	**13006.7**	0.0004	16922.65	0.0004	56957.59	0.0232
kroA150	67959.97	0.0046	75142.07	0.005	56995.42	0.0005	68307.27	0.0004	**56206.17**	0.0004	69081.13	0.0003	282919.98	0.0261
kroB150	65612.45	0.0056	72160.6	0.0043	**52497.76**	0.0004	67553.58	0.0004	52775.61	0.0005	66736.67	0.0002	278113.94	0.0243
pr152	195697.53	0.005	240278.94	0.0049	148230.49	0.0005	217968.13	0.0004	**144979.89**	0.0003	212632.23	0.0003	1080868.23	0.0248
u159	120267.91	0.004	138244.42	0.0046	98556.96	0.0047	125901.83	0.0006	**97571.4**	0.0007	125689.91	0.0007	469024.81	0.0298
brg180	NF	NF	NF	NF	NF	NF	NF	NF	NF	NF	NF	NF	966482.73	0.0342
ts225	NF	NF	NF	NF	NF	NF	NF	NF	NF	NF	NF	NF	1626937.56	0.07
gr229	323424.94	0.0048	346625.74	0.0075	268164.84	0.0048	332573.74	0.0007	**257092.46**	0.0008	334932.36	0.0005	1438891.72	0.0758
gil262	6772.31	0.0046	7211.31	0.0085	**5135.31**	0.1104	6765.92	1.082	5146.03	0.1819	6831.81	1.1293	28026.39	0.1139
pr264	205644.54	0.0051	221812.15	0.0092	**174763.57**	0.0321	216386.17	0.0084	175862.94	0.0177	227641.27	0.0098	1153046.16	0.1133
pr299	129131.29	0.0068	152462.63	0.0112	105731.65	0.0013	136528.41	0.001	**105590.65**	0.0013	137392.41	0.0009	776479.35	0.1582
lin318	111779.79	0.0042	122537.12	0.0119	**87843.05**	0.0065	112500.76	0.0012	88947.91	0.001	115620.54	0.001	613700.33	0.1934
rd400	37186.56	0.0077	41721.74	0.0163	**28961.61**	0.007	37641.03	0.0021	29121.03	0.0025	38029.25	0.0026	221889.63	0.3862
fl417	NF	NF	**58729.63**	0.0246	NF	NF	NF	NF	NF	NF	NF	NF	507094.59	0.4273
gr431	407459.3	0.0077	447188.32	0.018	324103.23	0.0002	406802.05	0.0013	**321053.1**	0.0047	407989.17	0.0014	2559569.4	0.4706
pr439	307903.82	0.0079	335017.43	0.0177	**237183.7**	0.0062	308119.06	0.0014	242382.08	0.0026	308162.4	0.0015	1928715.93	0.5
pcb442	181026.02 (7)	0.0165	191983.54	0.0287	148026.02	25.8969	173344.87	51.4915	151104.15	33.199	169630.63	74.7828	783921.27	0.5096
d493	83854.84	0.0077	90077.23	0.0176	**67246.53**	0.0009	82207.14	0.0021	69889.28	0.0025	82084.75	0.0017	460756.56	0.7117
att532	70874.47	0.0068	75850.83	0.0246	55847.77	0.0056	70508.36	0.0022	**54302.39**	0.0036	71072.39	0.0025	525607.87	0.8871
ali535	NF	NF	NF	NF	NF	NF	NF	NF	NF	NF	NF	NF	3654416.97	0.9201
u574	103280.49	0.0086	108192.11	0.0303	79976.85	0.0105	96419.79	0.0007	**77170.53**	0.0052	98190.59	0.0043	689334.23	1.1199
rat575	16951.18	0.0107	18678.38	0.0322	14158.63	0.3564	16877.19	1.0484	**14076.83**	0.3071	16840.88	1.2958	116056.93	1.1204
d657	123421.2	0.011	134404.18	0.0355	**97202.53**	0.0096	117686.31	0.0034	98583.49	0.0039	119757.28	0.0034	871598.39	1.7455
gr666	681784.52	0.0113	731934.29	0.0072	**525438.01**	0.0103	660789.94	0.0325	531327.9	0.0041	668566.48	0.002	5189888.53	1.7694
u724	106712.28	0.0098	120015.01	0.0437	**83222.29**	0.0178	110040.36	0.0064	85646.61	0.0119	107804.66	0.0073	875989.46	2.3321
rat783	24391.29	0.0129	24871.58	0.0595	**18630.15**	2.3241	22474.71	15.5635	18702.79	2.0496	22476.61	22.3311	181449.05	2.8349
nrw1379	128224.62	0.0241	141049.3	0.1459	102396.82	0.0323	127785.68	0.0351	**100474.8**	0.0422	128497.96	0.0483	1449118.02	16.6818
fl1577	120012.88 (9)	0.1338	128983.24	0.2112	**97809.4**	66.4871	NF	NF	99125.34	69.158	119894.48	15.6906	1366006.43	26.4534
d1655	206676.07	0.0311	217164.52	0.2118	166149.38	0.7723	195600.48	3.3206	**161277.1**	1.0081	196913.7	0.2303	2197615.8	31.371
vm1748	931442.76	0.025	1030723.97	0.2325	**718418.23**	0.0339	930815.15	0.0275	724516.17	0.0204	945760.24	0.0233	15199653.75	38.1895
u1817	208909.96	0.0386	232776.01	0.0647	**169320.34**	38.5677	NF	NF	170283.64	13.6329	205055.96	77.2731	2144409.45	42.9161
rl1889	999164.43	0.0243	1111433.14	0.26	717964.64	0.0715	955849.85	0.0154	**713719.28**	0.0275	944916.55	0.0238	15006133.55	50.2996
# Best	0	–	1	–	18	–	0	–	18	–	0	–	3	–

independent tour is returned. Building the tours in parallel allows all the tours to have equal opportunities in selecting the good edges, unlike in the previous two heuristics, where tours are built one-by-one. In the heuristics C1 and C2, due to sequentially building the tours, the initial tours have more opportunities to utilise the low cost edges, whereas the latter tours have lesser opportunities. Due to the repetitive construction of K tours from scratch upon failure to obtain a feasible tour, the time taken by this heuristic can differ significantly from one run to another. Moreover, it is significantly higher than C1 and C2. Since our objective function is to minimise the weighted sum of the average and standard deviation of the cost of K tours, building the tours in parallel works in favour as good quality edges are distributed uniformly. The next three heuristics namely C4, C5 and C6 also construct the tour in parallel like C3. So their behaviour with regard to execution time is similar to C3.

3.4   Constructive Heuristic No. 4 (C4)

Heuristic C4 is same as C3 except for the fact that next city is selected based on the concept of GRASP like C2.

Table 2. Performance of seven heuristics for $K = 6, \gamma = 1$, and $\theta = 2$

Instances	K = 6, γ = 1, θ = 2													
	C1		C2		C3		C4		C5		C6		C7	
	Average	AET	Average	AET	Average	AET	Average	AET	Average	AET	Average	AET	Average	AET
ulysses22	NF	NF	18826.52	0.0023	**15892.89**	0.5829	16460.96	0.004	16423.07	0.8327	16968.91	0.0135	NF	NF
bays29	**6567.61 (2)**	0.0021	6323.59	0.0025	4978.14	0.0232	5450.9	0.0019	4885.4	0.0258	5267.12	0.0053	NF	NF
att48	**41185.52 (7)**	0.0015	40730.25	0.0034	31117.55	0.0781	34606.95	0.0044	33372.73	0.0956	35281.63	0.006	56053.36	0.0026
eil51	1572.65 (5)	0.0022	1486.54	0.003	**1168.78**	3.53	1264.03	8.328	1169.81	4.1919	1271.3	5.9521	1834.87	0.0028
berlin52	27274.39	0.0017	26113.42	0.0028	20369.69	0.0326	22307.91	0.0036	**20040.35**	0.0267	21768.21	0.0086	32821.22	0.0049
pr76	410475.12 (9)	0.0017	385741.17	0.0029	311954.34	0.0111	339183.35	0.0027	**307239.61**	0.015	335967.28	0.0055	601062.88	0.0057
gr137	276769.57 (8)	0.0025	267459.09	0.0037	**207837.05**	0.0257	232077.09	0.0018	209991.62	0.0224	223886.39	0.0015	676632.08	0.0341
pr144	331200.54 (9)	0.003	316699.24	0.0041	**220813.61**	0.0248	255653.09	0.002	221421.97	0.031	253936.17	0.0062	825248.21	0.0367
ch150	24472.06	0.0019	23643.84	0.0044	**17123.89**	0.0057	19873	0.0009	17307.73	0.0173	19862.69	0.0067	57811.73	0.0488
kroA150	105106.28	0.002	101393.84	0.0045	78390.59	0.0067	82966.23	0.0029	**75268.12**	0.0206	84521.48	0.0053	287748.2	0.0422
kroB150	97472.12	0.0024	94836.09	0.0038	71190.53	0.0047	80435.37	0.0021	**70778.15**	0.0076	79661.45	0.0041	284670.93	0.0417
pr152	376499.29	0.0029	371774.19	0.0107	246057.05	0.0232	292613.26	0.0029	**244050.46**	0.0259	287480.99	0.0063	1086202.63	0.0444
u159	187475.54	0.0025	185906.62	0.0048	**136290.3**	0.0279	153761.16	0.0055	137996.39	0.0664	157783.17	0.0111	465184.28	0.048
brg180	NF	NF	NF	NF	NF	NF	NF	NF	NF	NF	NF	NF	**1001044.72**	0.074
ts225	NF	NF	NF	NF	NF	NF	NF	NF	NF	NF	NF	NF	**1657885.69**	0.1383
gr229	504267.47 (9)	0.0039	456311.88	0.0067	379764.13	0.2096	399276.11	0.0042	**376010.07**	0.1986	390806	0.0078	1417757.59	0.1408
gil262	9625.64	0.0044	**9602.69**	0.011	NF	NF	NF	NF	NF	NF	NF	NF	28282.36	0.2158
pr264	201403.53	0.0035	229215.3	0.0092	190558.57	1.1845	227151.53	0.1426	**187440.05**	1.0977	230867.38	0.2522	1172102.26	0.2125
pr299	190876.39	0.0035	193292.45	0.0109	139850.32	0.0231	161775.67	0.0053	**138935.03**	0.0215	165744.36	0.0071	788551.94	0.3114
lin318	175723.93	0.0038	167672.18	0.0107	**121615.5**	0.0559	138276.48	0.0051	123691.56	0.0462	138820.56	0.01	609724.52	0.373
rd400	53778.67	0.0043	55041.91	0.0152	**39065.54**	0.0461	45600.96	0.0119	39239.57	0.059	44898.4	0.0225	222170.34	0.7599
fl417	NF	NF	**71052.57 (2)**	0.0504	NF	NF	NF	NF	NF	NF	NF	NF	510991.37	0.8578
gr431	603220.91	0.0054	570142.43	0.0174	448050.31	0.2313	483011.61	0.0114	**443483.24**	0.44	488028.56	0.0217	2584814.54	0.9344
pr439	471392.1	0.0052	445730.61	0.0174	**347458.93**	0.5999	372273.89	0.0224	349761.79	0.8049	374982.27	0.0224	1939761.18	0.9807
pcb442	NF	NF	NF	NF	NF	NF	NF	NF	NF	NF	NF	NF	**792115.78**	1.0116
d493	116751.65	0.0054	116868.87	0.0202	**87112.55**	0.0111	98048.24	0.0077	87988.02	0.0112	98393.15	0.0087	459575.15	1.4274
att532	99481.01	0.006	97321.45	0.0263	**71904.54**	0.0368	83003.06	0.0178	73297.91	0.0658	81631.59	0.0156	532416.42	1.7874
ali535	NF	NF	NF	NF	NF	NF	NF	NF	NF	NF	NF	NF	**3687381.14**	1.9091
u574	140449.8	0.0065	138005.45	0.0298	**102262.91**	0.2831	113510.65	0.0174	102781.63	0.4533	114969.25	0.0213	691330.19	2.2475
rat575	**22968.43**	0.0115	23531.85	0.0402	NF	NF	NF	NF	NF	NF	NF	NF	116486.96	2.2127
d657	171140.34	0.0061	171277.13	0.037	**123239.29**	0.0397	140934.61	0.0123	124517.64	0.0388	141502.01	0.0149	876149.22	3.4657
gr666	949383.22	0.0068	936951.15	0.0373	**693860.76**	0.01	783556.63	0.007	695663.79	0.0373	779945.04	0.0154	5208467.87	3.5586
u724	147651.98	0.0076	152198.8	0.0444	**108535.96**	0.0672	125978.85	0.035	108663.36	0.0821	126544.71	0.0412	894115.99	4.4833
rat783	32438.97	0.0217	**31644.36**	0.0848	NF	NF	NF	NF	NF	NF	NF	NF	183992.34	5.6895
nrw1379	177964.5	0.0162	181029.64	0.1475	131224.32	1.635	150552.52	0.402	**130684.73**	1.338	151195.64	0.8575	1461064.31	33.1956
fl1577	**160508.44 (8)**	0.2381	166661.86	0.2406	NF	NF	NF	NF	NF	NF	NF	NF	1372319.48	52.8842
d1655	267734.22	0.0638	274288.1	0.212	NF	NF	**227509.06**	63.1262	NF	NF	NF	NF	2201387.06	63.2849
vm1748	1298722.78	0.0216	1323023.25	0.2269	921725	0.1279	**1090381.2**	0.04	932148.18	0.1379	1104547.19	0.0667	15200315.16	73.2059
u1817	**275339**	0.0496	290271.13	0.3705	NF	NF	NF	NF	NF	NF	NF	NF	2146257.58	87.8428
rl1889	1508116.04	0.0235	1462794.64	0.2622	993958.21	1.741	1153819.61	0.0518	**1006582.19**	1.5558	1161801.73	0.0625	15037343.75	99.6085
# Best	3	–	3	–	16	–	2	–	12	–	0	–	4	–

3.5   Constructive Heuristic No. 5 (C5)

The fifth heuristic C5 works in a similar manner as C3, except for the fact that in C3 while selecting the order of the tour for adding new nodes, a natural order is applied. On the other hand, in C5, we have used a random order for selecting the tour to give all the tours a fair opportunity to use the low cost edges.

3.6   Constructive Heuristic No. 6 (C6)

C6 is same as C4 except, in C6 the order for selecting tours for addition of new nodes is random rather than a natural order due to similar reason as in C5.

3.7   Constructive Heuristic No. 7 (C7)

The seventh heuristic C7 is an insertion based heuristic. In this heuristic, the start city is selected randomly for all the K tours, one-by-one. Then next two nodes are added one-by-one to each of K tours like C3 by following the nearest neighbour concept, i.e., the second node is the nearest available neighbour to

Table 3. Performance of seven heuristics for $K = 3, \gamma = 2$, and $\theta = 1$

Instances	C1		C2		C3		C4		C5		C6		C7	
	Average	AET	Average	AET	Average	AET	Average	AET	Average	AET	Average	AET	Average	AET
ulysses22	23716.18 (7)	0.0036	26257.73	0.0049	23120.1	0.002	25649.74	0.0024	**23094.28**	0.0044	25312.95	0.0044	32933.79	0.0002
bays29	7489.15	0.0018	8202.01	0.0029	7277.15	0.0017	8371.67	0.0036	**7183.76**	0.0045	8210.26	0.0029	12185.69	0.0003
att48	36930.50	0.0036	48210.07	0.0003	36553.52	0.0001	47709.79	0.0001	**36031.29**	0.0034	47537.25	0.0001	103449.03	0.001
eil51	1687.19	0.0032	2017.29	0.0051	**1618.46**	0.004	1990.1	0.0047	1646.82	0.0042	1966.62	0.006	3331.54	0.001
berlin52	29566.94	0.002	34447.94	0.0051	**28134.1**	0.0019	33395.85	0.0015	28342.97	0.0052	33957.81	0.003	59508.48	0.0012
pr76	455819.16	0.0035	534365.12	0.0057	**439860.94**	0.0003	533377.53	0.0017	442978.31	0.0038	528549.94	0.0039	1138082.08	0.0028
gr137	302233.39	0.0048	361029.44	0.0062	**288381.76**	0.0005	359622.61	0.0047	290037.39	0.0038	361524.84	0.0002	1277344.77	0.0146
pr144	305271.01	0.0049	385111.67	0.0063	281013.83	0.0003	365905.11	0.0003	**276375.66**	0.0006	373920.68	0.0003	1604029.99	0.017
ch150	25883.41	0.0049	31924.32	0.0065	24801.76	0.0014	31438.09	0.0042	**24215.8**	0.0047	31906.82	0.0034	110090.69	0.0201
kroA150	103920.93	0.0037	132194.19	0.005	103280.11	0.0007	127953.58	0.0046	**101831.48**	0.0047	130268.12	0.0046	542123.14	0.0196
kroB150	101613.03	0.0048	128671.7	0.0063	98936.53	0.0004	126076.74	0.0021	**98826.9**	0.0044	126169.19	0.0035	537626.82	0.0198
pr152	286040.32	0.0049	410701.87	0.0032	266995.04	0.0005	400357.66	0.0005	**265522.99**	0.0006	396426.32	0.0002	2078595.16	0.0193
u159	187481.66	0.0045	241720.36	0.0081	**181505.58**	0.0027	232876.81	0.0048	182344.5	0.0049	235625.7	0.0064	890614.46	0.0224
brg180	NF	NF	NF	NF	NF	NF	NF	NF	NF	NF	NF	NF	**1849245.36**	0.0304
ts225	NF	NF	NF	NF	NF	NF	NF	NF	NF	NF	NF	NF	**3162038.78**	0.0606
gr229	502574.12	0.0048	619910.22	0.0094	486446.87	0.0007	623900.92	0.0028	**481098.98**	0.0046	623814.63	0.005	2772430.51	0.0632
gil262	10573.66	0.0044	12876.25	0.0122	**9889.95**	0.0846	12894.86	1.0698	9890.71	0.1866	12913.26	1.1416	54462.1	0.0998
pr264	342281.32	0.005	406675.82	0.0083	319528.93	0.0251	401079.94	0.0145	**318129.42**	0.0237	415963.34	0.0099	2232469.33	0.0971
pr299	205906.84	0.0054	263646.01	0.0105	198197.72	0.0016	258806.36	0.0065	**196508.62**	0.0069	259709.2	0.0067	1495097.93	0.1403
lin318	171515.85	0.0064	218105.51	0.0119	**164140.43**	0.0009	214384.73	0.0055	164809.2	0.0066	217306.12	0.0053	1188888.57	0.1667
rd400	58228.88	0.0063	74094.92	0.019	**55769.76**	0.0056	72318.42	0.0022	56269.41	0.0086	73559.38	0.0068	435640.11	0.3476
fl417	NF	NF	**103357.46**	0.0282	NF	NF	NF	NF	NF	NF	NF	NF	984694.29	0.3874
gr431	637007.45	0.0075	790684.81	0.0201	605736.27	0.0017	777819.12	0.0061	**602970.95**	0.0081	780515.04	0.0068	4943832.45	0.4244
pr439	468215.01	0.0065	592259.32	0.0212	**437950.5**	0.0021	579987.18	0.0065	439462.09	0.0077	579078.25	0.0067	3768454.06	0.4507
pcb442	297942.37 (7)	0.0153	337777.12	0.0328	**284329.91**	19.9337	330714.83	51.2734	285145.12	33.3113	328081.72	75.1917	1540500.79	0.4591
d493	132918.17	0.0073	161518.27	0.0245	**126629.26**	0.0009	158680.97	0.0068	128450.29	0.0054	158584.07	0.0056	900601.23	0.6492
att532	109744.69	0.007	135516.06	0.0282	103979.84	0.003	134647.43	0.0059	**102414.4**	0.0099	134540.79	0.0065	1027491.64	1.1016
ali535	NF	NF	NF	NF	NF	NF	NF	NF	NF	NF	NF	NF	**7165703.58**	0.8804
u574	156548.19	0.0057	189959.1	0.0326	147237.82	0.0028	185546.1	0.0092	**145760.22**	0.0051	186780.7	0.0107	1347765.37	1.1225
rat575	27276.59	0.009	32842.99	0.0358	**26467.87**	0.2641	32739.89	1.0952	26570.26	0.3174	32570.99	1.3289	226742.07	1.0223
d657	192364.85	0.0097	238642.19	0.0403	**183101.36**	0.0072	229210.55	0.0088	184077.34	0.0098	231805.34	0.01	1709326.94	1.5389
gr666	1071928.76	0.0084	1315880.59	0.041	**1007078.46**	0.0027	1282797.87	0.0086	1016673.65	0.0095	1298838.09	0.0085	10183044.97	1.6091
u724	170531.44	0.0111	212590.91	0.0469	**160871.04**	0.011	211632.48	0.0119	163355.16	0.0177	211286.58	0.0125	1725792.93	2.0529
rat783	37340.55	0.0126	44706.64	0.0629	**35133.58**	1.7226	43740.15	16.6217	35409.75	2.1023	43775.4	23.2344	358236.03	2.5969
urw1379	206533.16	0.0219	254382.65	0.1486	**196256.86**	0.0155	250892.99	0.0447	196397.75	0.0535	250984.53	0.0579	2859161.81	15.0482
fl1577	187616.72 (9)	0.1246	228151.62	0.2098	**176186.85**	50.5506	NF	NF	179254.62	69.6241	224804.64	15.7893	2697378.26	22.7899
d1655	329418.14	0.0287	388489.16	0.21	314735.24	0.6432	380073.24	0.3289	**312856.1**	1.025	380223.2	0.2379	4348038.95	26.3956
vm1748	1440475.18	0.0242	1845629.98	0.2292	**1368309.77**	0.027	1807690.43	0.0377	1373611.68	0.0307	1823957.47	0.0288	30000852.87	31.1674
u1817	346975.03	0.0337	410678	0.2724	330246.27	28.6124	NF	NF	**329859.47**	13.7292	399866.33	78.1111	4240663.77	34.8341
rl1889	1489201.01	0.0256	1932896.37	0.2627	1379456.07	0.051	1868445.62	0.0209	**1371435.59**	0.0359	1852891.22	0.0249	29685339.78	39.5988
# Best	0	–	1	–	19	–	0	–	17	–	0	–	3	–

the first node and the third is similarly the nearest neighbour to the second node. The remaining nodes are added to the K tours iteratively by following the insert mechanism. This process also occurs in parallel for all the K tours. A node is chosen at random from the set of unvisited nodes for that particular tour. Then it is placed in such a location that difference between the maximum and minimum edge of that particular tour is minimised. It should also be taken care that no edge is repeated in any of the K tours. The termination condition is same as C3, i.e., if it is unable to find a suitable edge, it will start over again and try to build all K tours from scratch. This process can be repeated for a maximum of 120 s without any success. It is also an all or nothing approach. If a feasible solution with K mutually independent tour is obtained within the time, then it will return the feasible solution otherwise it will return a null solution.

4   Computational Results

Our seven heuristics have been implemented in C language and executed on a 3.40 GHz Intel Core i5 based system with 8 GB RAM and Ubuntu 16.04 operating system. These heuristics were tested on 40 TSPLIB instances ranging from

Table 4. Performance of seven heuristics for $K = 6, \gamma = 2$, and $\theta = 1$

Instances	C1 Average	C1 AET	C2 Average	C2 AET	C3 Average	C3 AET	C4 Average	C4 AET	C5 Average	C5 AET	C6 Average	C6 AET	C7 Average	C7 AET
ulysses22	NF	NF	30550.96	0.0049	28567.02	0.6027	29675.48	0.0088	28797.41	0.8217	29963.9	0.0092	NF	NF
bays29	9777.18 (4)	0.0037	10166.97	0.0021	9057.52	0.0257	9799.8	0.003	9005.77	0.0228	9656.48	0.0019	NF	NF
att48	57444.58 (7)	0.0002	62246.95	0.0003	54026.72	0.0808	59941.13	0.0044	55342.39	0.0942	60979.74	0.0038	104050.76	0.0043
eil51	2324.13 (5)	0.0043	2395.77	0.0054	2131.29	3.5316	2329.26	8.7123	2151.13	4.1514	2340.15	6.068	3397.21	0.0019
berlin52	39755.58 (9)	0.0037	41771.11	0.004	36771.27	0.0356	40317.76	0.0079	36717.77	0.0262	39854.66	0.0058	60784.08	0.0067
pr76	605409.47 (9)	0.0038	632151.93	0.0052	564767.07	0.0126	619747.53	0.0058	560801.3	0.0102	620422.39	0.0017	1129137.22	0.0076
gr137	408625.63 (8)	0.0053	433077.1	0.0052	373054.05	0.0293	424645.99	0.0015	375219.21	0.0218	416867.74	0.0016	1282333.62	0.032
pr144	453006.8 (9)	0.0037	490569.5	0.0064	400103.28	0.0281	466478.42	0.0009	402312.46	0.0265	468597.33	0.0021	1586300.41	0.0324
ch150	35201.83	0.005	38187.24	0.0066	32154.82	0.0073	37288.45	0.0053	32416.21	0.0157	37379.32	0.0026	110505.02	0.0464
kroA150	148744.69	0.005	161783.52	0.0066	141123.29	0.0084	156997.64	0.0048	137448.03	0.0165	158236.06	0.0013	540133.74	0.0404
kroB150	141516.91	0.0046	154053.2	0.0041	129992.11	0.0061	151148.53	0.0027	130118.48	0.0033	149565.78	0.0011	543847.13	0.0397
pr152	490159.34	0.0051	553718.37	0.0067	428850.55	0.0268	524197.45	0.0012	432786.86	0.0217	522360.45	0.0021	2061253.86	0.0383
u159	269427.12	0.0046	296656.79	0.008	249227.78	0.0306	283033	0.0099	250857.45	0.0615	288415.71	0.0073	891173.32	0.0473
brg180	NF	NF	NF	NF	NF	NF	NF	NF	NF	NF	NF	NF	1871432.36	0.07
ts225	NF	NF	NF	NF	NF	NF	NF	NF	NF	NF	NF	NF	3180014.94	0.1215
gr229	721483.9 (9)	0.0062	748493.69	0.0098	672708.61	0.2246	736495.46	0.0035	665302.76	0.1981	730654.35	0.0082	2730874.17	0.1286
gil262	14176.27	0.006	15728.49	0.0154	NF	NF	NF	NF	NF	NF	NF	NF	54792.51	0.2006
pr264	346859.17	0.0056	418604.57	0.0112	337283.36	1.255	414896.57	0.1452	334779.42	1.0661	417812.82	0.2678	2233099.55	0.1961
pr299	279441.92	0.006	313357.48	0.0099	260551.61	0.0271	305637.93	0.0077	260378.21	0.0166	309126.16	0.0039	1522221.29	0.2902
lin318	248467.99	0.0067	270332.01	0.0128	225065.53	0.0628	259072.97	0.0093	225936.5	0.04	260441.05	0.0053	1178738.81	0.3461
rd400	79125.61	0.0068	89809.2	0.0177	74210.84	0.0521	86661.86	0.0163	74044.26	0.0533	86458.27	0.0194	433194.35	0.7095
fl417	NF	NF	120861.54 (2)	0.0547	NF	NF	NF	NF	NF	NF	NF	NF	988057.61	0.8051
gr431	879763.4	0.0087	938486.57	0.0193	816354.61	0.2543	908894.43	0.0125	811864.79	0.435	914829.8	0.0209	4960164.85	0.88
pr439	668992.7	0.0087	720004.66	0.02	618460.91	0.6548	699397.74	0.025	616283.29	0.7809	697295.69	0.0188	3769091.36	0.9255
pcb442	NF	NF	NF	NF	NF	NF	NF	NF	NF	NF	NF	NF	1542940.26	0.9554
d493	174367.9	0.0069	192168.69	0.0174	163617.08	0.0139	186245.8	0.0095	164503.81	0.0084	186697.05	0.0098	898163.67	1.3411
att532	146397.03	0.0064	160681.43	0.0211	135035.24	0.04	157047.78	0.0153	134907.15	0.0623	155486.22	0.0132	1034132.48	1.765
ali535	NF	NF	NF	NF	NF	NF	NF	NF	NF	NF	NF	NF	7176635.12	1.824
u574	206566.45	0.0068	225566.1	0.0309	192275.36	0.314	217912.03	0.0216	191107.66	0.4361	218453.22	0.016	7176635.12	1.8263
rat575	35075.41	0.0144	39074.3	0.0425	NF	NF	NF	NF	NF	NF	NF	NF	1349415.57	2.128
d657	254208.15	0.0104	282777.64	0.0388	235946.34	0.0431	272172.63	0.0183	236194.87	0.0342	272493.36	0.0098	226576.43	2.0946
gr666	1418016.86	0.0105	1561528.63	0.0395	1309197.13	0.0307	1506102.39	0.0125	1311646.94	0.0303	1505540.37	0.0093	1710103.56	3.1791
u724	222029.21	0.012	251376.3	0.0458	208021.43	0.0772	243011.53	0.0413	207903.31	0.072	244121.33	0.0389	10171172.26	3.3431
rat783	48134.36	0.0243	52573.98	0.0849	NF	NF	NF	NF	NF	NF	NF	NF	1746607.69	4.2529
nrw1379	268510.4	0.0204	300783.22	0.1452	251713.08	1.8085	291775.96	0.448	251002.57	1.2742	291984.35	0.893	359702.62	5.3795
fl1577	240326.12 (8)	0.2436	272877.48	0.233	NF	NF	NF	NF	NF	NF	NF	NF	2865292.4	30.6099
d1655	411077.84	0.0696	457644.07	0.2103	NF	NF	438145.06	63.3799	NF	NF	NF	NF	2708192.19	49.5719
vm1748	1915496.29	0.0223	2193553.58	0.2237	1760239.4	0.1426	2102470.2	0.0481	1773899.66	0.1253	2121607.17	0.0603	30060036.58	69.1771
u1817	430908.68	0.0572	483096.24	0.3646	NF	NF	NF	NF	NF	NF	NF	NF	4232473.52	79.1675
rl1889	2124576.63	0.0377	2362419.99	0.2487	1898359.33	1.9077	2234980.53	0.0606	1910022.87	1.507	2247567.41	0.056	29637651.7	89.6562
# Best	6	–	1	–	14	–	0	–	15	–	0	–	4	–

22 to 1889 nodes. We have executed all our heuristics for 10 independent runs on each instance and reported the results in terms of average solution quality and average execution time in seconds over runs in which K mutually independent tours are obtained out of 10 runs. We have taken two different K values, viz. $K = 3, 6$. For C2, C4 and C6, p value is set to 3. We have taken three different sets of γ and θ values, i.e., $\gamma = 1, \theta = 2$, $\gamma = 2, \theta = 1$, and $\gamma = 1, \theta = 1$. The results are reported in six different tables each corresponding to one particular combination of values of K, γ and θ out of six possible combinations. The first column in these tables report the instance name. The digits at the end of an instance name specify the number of nodes in that instance. Remaining columns report the average solution quality (columns labelled "Average") and average execution time (columns labelled "AET") in seconds for each of the seven heuristics. The entries marked with parenthesis ('()') are those instances where we obtained feasible in solution in less than 10 runs and the number within the parenthesis gives the number of runs out of 10 in which we have obtained a feasible solution. The entries marked with "NF" (none found) for an instance indicate that corresponding heuristic didnot find any feasible solution for that instance. The last row in these tables provide the number of instances on which each heuristic provide the best solution quality.

Table 5. Performance of seven heuristics for $K = 3, \gamma = 1$, and $\theta = 1$

Instances	C1		C2		C3		C4		C5		C6		C7	
$K=3,\gamma=1,\theta=1$	Average	AET	Average	AET	Average	AET	Average	AET	Average	AET	Average	AET	Average	AET
ulysses22	12631.03	0.0036	13802.83	0.0002	12134.9	0.0001	13303.84	0.0001	11929.85	0.0001	13128.98	0.0001	17120.76	0.0002
bays29	4170.95	0.0036	4302.74	0.0002	3793.25	0.0003	4336.1	0.0001	3664.66	0.0002	4223.59	0.0002	6266.25	0.0004
att48	19912.33	0.0001	25602.07	0.0004	18802.82	0.0001	24662.62	0.0002	18494.02	0.0002	24468.68	0.0002	53054.47	0.001
eil51	915.59	0.0033	1054.89	0.0004	833.16	0.0006	1031.7	0.0012	847.58	0.001	1005.29	0.0014	1695.51	0.0014
berlin52	16312.74	0.0037	18199.98	0.0005	14620.1	0.0005	17242.45	0.0001	14811.97	0.0002	17563.11	0.0002	30313.02	0.0011
pr76	250595.39	0.0028	279855.49	0.0006	228454.08	0.0002	277133.5	0.0002	229681.84	0.0003	269711.44	0.0003	577281.88	0.003
gr137	167493.39	0.0049	189878.81	0.0018	151367.09	0.0003	185888.84	0.0004	151613.32	0.0005	185669.81	0.0003	648701.87	0.0151
pr144	175958.64	0.0045	205873.67	0.002	147903.03	0.0003	187014.01	0.0003	145279.03	0.0007	192067.35	0.0003	814819.82	0.0174
ch150	14371.08	0.0044	16720.62	0.0021	12777.39	0.001	16081.76	0.0003	12407.5	0.0004	16276.49	0.0004	55682.76	0.0205
kroA150	57293.63	0.0049	69112.09	0.0021	53425.18	0.0004	65420.28	0.0002	52679.22	0.0003	66449.75	0.0003	275014.37	0.021
kroB150	55741.83	0.0045	66944.1	0.0023	50478.1	0.0004	64543.44	0.0002	50534.17	0.0004	64301.95	0.0003	271913.59	0.0207
pr152	160579.28	0.0048	216993.6	0.0018	138408.51	0.0005	206108.6	0.0003	136834.29	0.0003	203019.52	0.0002	1053154.46	0.0213
u159	102583.19	0.0044	126654.93	0.0024	93354.18	0.0005	119592.88	0.0004	93305.3	0.0007	120438.54	0.0007	453213.09	0.0238
brg180	NF	NF	NF	NF	NF	NF	NF	NF	NF	NF	NF	NF	938576.03	0.0326
ts225	NF	NF	NF	NF	NF	NF	NF	NF	NF	NF	NF	NF	1596325.45	0.0642
gr229	275333.02	0.0044	322178.65	0.0041	251537.24	0.0018	318824.89	0.0006	246063.81	0.001	319582.33	0.0006	1403774.07	0.067
gil262	5781.99	0.0036	6695.85	0.0069	5008.42	0.0876	6553.59	1.0533	5012.25	0.1814	6581.69	1.1103	27496.16	0.1022
pr264	182641.95	0.0046	209495.99	0.006	164764.17	0.0259	205822.04	0.0081	164664.12	0.0181	214534.87	0.0111	1128505.16	0.1046
pr299	111679.38	0.0057	138702.88	0.0074	101309.79	0.0011	131778.26	0.0006	100699.76	0.0013	132367.2	0.0008	757192.43	0.1491
lin318	94431.88	0.0075	113547.54	0.0075	83994.49	0.001	108961.83	0.0011	84585.7	0.0009	110975.55	0.0009	600862.97	0.1794
rd400	31805.14	0.0089	38605.55	0.012	28243.79	0.0014	36653.15	0.0021	28463.48	0.0003	37196.21	0.0029	219176.58	0.365
fl417	NF	NF	54029.03	0.0224	NF	NF	NF	NF	NF	NF	NF	NF	497262.96	0.4046
gr431	348155.59	0.0077	412624.38	0.0136	309946.5	0.0024	394873.72	0.0009	308008.02	0.0022	396168.07	0.0014	2501133.95	0.444
pr439	258706.28	0.0071	309092.25	0.0137	225044.74	0.0019	296035.41	0.0012	227281.39	0.0027	295746.88	0.0015	1899056.66	0.4811
pcb442	159656.13 (7)	0.0141	176586.89	0.0238	144118.64	21.0353	168019.9	49.9062	145416.42	32.6389	165904.12	74.4984	774807.35	0.4882
d493	72257.67	0.0087	83865.17	0.017	64625.26	0.001	80296.04	0.0019	66113.19	0.0016	80222.94	0.0017	453785.93	0.7054
att532	60206.39	0.0062	70455.63	0.0207	53275.87	0.0034	68385.27	0.0022	52238.93	0.0037	68537.73	0.0026	517699.84	0.8415
ali535	NF	NF	NF	NF	NF	NF	NF	NF	NF	NF	NF	NF	3606706.85	0.8765
u574	86609.56	0.0087	99383.74	0.0252	75738.22	0.0029	93088.63	0.0024	74310.25	0.0052	94990.43	0.0038	679033.2	0.9101
rat575	14742.59	0.0108	17173.79	0.027	13542.17	0.2809	16539.03	0.9716	13549.03	0.3038	16470.62	1.4452	114266.33	1.0762
d657	105262.02	0.0098	124348.79	0.0314	93434.63	0.0031	115632.29	0.0031	94220.28	0.0033	117187.54	0.0034	860308.44	1.5981
gr666	584571.09	0.0098	682604.96	0.0317	510838.82	0.0034	647862.6	0.0021	516000.52	0.0031	655801.53	0.002	5124311.17	1.7116
u724	92414.57	0.0111	110868.64	0.0393	81364.44	0.0086	107224.28	0.0058	83000.59	0.0117	106363.75	0.0065	867260.8	2.1717
rat783	20577.28	0.0136	23192.74	0.0525	17921.24	1.8243	22071.62	15.4291	18037.51	2.0285	22084	23.3864	179895.03	2.7608
nrw1379	111585.93	0.0243	131810.65	0.1346	99551.23	0.0177	126226.22	0.0344	98957.52	0.0408	126494.16	0.0468	1436093.28	15.7342
fl1577	102543.2 (9)	0.1171	119044.95	0.1948	91332.09	53.4971	NF	NF	92793.32	68.1689	114899.71	15.4531	1354482.23	24.0016
d1655	178698.07	0.0312	201884.56	0.1955	160294.87	0.6212	191891.24	0.3153	158044.4	0.9839	192378.97	0.2234	2181884.92	27.7153
vm1748	790639.32	0.026	958784.65	0.2122	695606	0.0236	912835.19	0.0275	699375.95	0.0191	923239.24	0.0207	15066835.54	33.089
u1817	185295	0.0327	214484.67	0.2516	166522.2	30.917	NF	NF	166714.37	13.3809	201640.76	75.6011	2128357.74	37.984
rl1889	829455.15	0.0243	1014776.5	0.2487	699140.23	0.0521	941431.82	0.0125	695051.62	0.0241	932602.59	0.0239	14897157.78	42.9486
# Best	0	–	1	–	19	–	0	–	17	–	0	–	3	–

The following observations can be made from the results reported in these six tables (Tables 1, 2, 3, 4, 5 and 6):

- It has been observed from the results, that for most of the instances, approaches in which K independent tours are build parallelly, viz. C3, C4, C5, C6 and C7, performed better than C1 and C2, where the tours were build one-by-one. In KIATSP, since the objective is to minimize the weighted sum of the average and the standard deviation of the K tours' cost, building tours in parallel has been observed to provide better solution. This is because while building the tours in parallel, every tour is getting more-or-less equal opportunities in selecting the best edges.
- It has been observed that out of all the heuristics C3 and C5 performs best for most of the instances. Also C3 has been observed to provide better results for more number of large sized instances.
- The time taken by the parallel approaches is more than their serial counterparts. We have already discussed the reason for this in Sect. 3.3.
- Pure greedy approaches C3 and C5 has been observed to provide better results than the GRASP based approaches C4 and C6.

Table 6. Performance of seven heuristics for $K = 6, \gamma = 1$, and $\theta = 1$

Instances	$K=6, \gamma=1, \theta=1$													
	C1		C2		C3		C4		C5		C6		C7	
	Average	AET	Average	AET	Average	AET	Average	AET	Average	AET	Average	AET	Average	AET
ulysses22	NF	NF	16459.16	0.0002	**14819.97**	0.5992	15378.81	0.0046	15073.5	0.8244	15644.27	0.009	NF	NF
bays29	5448.27 (4)	0.0001	5496.85	0.0002	4678.55	0.0239	5083.57	0.0017	**4630.39**	0.0228	4974.53	0.0019	NF	NF
att48	32876.7 (7)	0.0003	34325.74	0.0007	**28381.42**	0.0779	31516.03	0.0043	29571.71	0.0942	32087.12	0.0038	53368.04	0.0017
eil51	1298.93 (5)	0.0003	1294.1	0.0008	**1100.03**	3.4966	1197.76	8.4609	1106.98	4.1486	1203.82	5.8477	1744.03	0.002
berlin52	22343.32 (9)	0.0002	22628.17	0.0005	19046.98	0.0331	20875.22	0.0037	**18919.37**	0.0259	20540.96	0.0056	31201.77	0.002
pr76	338628.2 (9)	0.0003	339297.7	0.0008	292240.47	0.0117	319643.63	0.0013	**289346.97**	0.0105	318796.56	0.0015	576733.37	0.0061
gr137	228465.07 (8)	0.0008	233512.06	0.0025	**193630.36**	0.0275	218907.69	0.0016	195070.27	0.022	213584.71	0.0015	652988.57	0.0323
pr144	261402.45 (9)	0.0007	269089.58	0.0024	**206972.3**	0.0257	240710.5	0.001	207911.48	0.0267	240844.5	0.0017	803849.54	0.0354
ch150	19891.3	0.0005	20610.36	0.0023	**16426.24**	0.0059	19053.82	0.0012	16574.65	0.0158	19080.67	0.0026	56105.58	0.0422
kroA150	84616.99	0.0004	87725.79	0.0021	73171.29	0.0068	79987.96	0.0005	**70905.38**	0.0162	80919.18	0.0012	277198.44	0.0426
kroB150	79663.01	0.0004	82963.1	0.002	67060.88	0.0046	77194.63	0.0008	**66065.54**	0.0033	76409.08	0.0011	274934.89	0.0425
pr152	288886.21	0.0007	308497.52	0.0024	**224969.2**	0.0246	272270.24	0.0012	225912.44	0.0217	269947.15	0.002	1049152.16	0.0412
u159	152300.88	0.0006	160854.47	0.0026	**128506.03**	0.0295	145598.05	0.0061	129617.95	0.0623	148732.96	0.0073	452119.2	0.0428
brg180	NF	NF	NF	NF	NF	NF	NF	NF	NF	NF	NF	NF	**957492.36**	0.0636
ts225	NF	NF	NF	NF	NF	NF	NF	NF	NF	NF	NF	NF	1612633.54	0.1188
gr229	408583.79 (9)	0.002	401601.86	0.005	350824.25	0.2245	378590.59	0.0036	**347104.58**	0.1995	373820.12	0.0077	1382877.25	0.1324
gil262	**7933.97**	0.0016	8443.73	0.0017	NF	NF	NF	NF	NF	NF	NF	NF	279961.62	0.2035
pr264	182754.23	0.0012	215939.96	0.0064	175947.31	1.2478	214016.03	0.145	**174073.16**	1.0779	216226.73	0.244	1135067.27	0.2001
pr299	156772.77	0.0009	168883.31	0.0077	133467.31	0.025	155804.53	0.0021	**133104.41**	0.0166	158290.17	0.0035	770257.74	0.293
lin318	141397.31	0.0009	146001.4	0.0088	**115560.34**	0.0594	132449.82	0.0038	116542.69	0.0405	133087.2	0.0048	596154.44	0.3518
rd400	44301.43	0.0015	48283.7	0.0132	**37758.79**	0.0493	44087.61	0.0105	37761.27	0.0542	43785.56	0.0172	218454.9	0.7576
fl417	NF	NF	**63971.37 (2)**	0.0502	NF	NF	NF	NF	NF	NF	NF	NF	499683	0.8077
gr431	494328.1	0.0022	502876.33	0.0149	421468.31	0.2532	463968.68	0.0095	**418440.34**	0.4378	467619.45	0.0186	2514993.13	0.8776
pr439	380128.27	0.002	388578.42	0.0153	**321973.28**	0.6533	357223.88	0.0215	322015.03	0.7912	357425.99	0.0171	1902950.85	0.9378
pcb442	NF	NF	NF	NF	NF	NF	NF	NF	NF	NF	NF	NF	778352.01	0.9664
d493	97039.85	0.0019	103012.52	0.0185	**83576.54**	0.0116	94764.68	0.0081	84163.94	0.0083	95030.07	0.0086	452579.61	1.3485
att532	81959.35	0.0021	86000.96	0.0228	**68979.93**	0.0377	80016.95	0.0148	69401.69	0.0635	79039.27	0.0128	522182.97	1.6814
ali535	NF	NF	NF	NF	NF	NF	NF	NF	NF	NF	NF	NF	3621338.75	1.744
u574	115672.08	0.0029	121190.52	0.0254	98179.42	0.3071	110474.23	0.0144	**97963.1**	0.438	111140.82	0.014	680248.58	2.1578
rat575	**19347.95**	0.0065	20868.72	0.037	NF	NF	NF	NF	NF	NF	NF	NF	114454.46	2.1208
d657	141782.83	0.0027	151351.59	0.0329	**119728.54**	0.0407	137702.42	0.012	120237.5	0.0349	137998.46	0.0083	862084.26	3.1757
gr666	789133.36	0.0027	832826.59	0.0345	**667685.96**	0.0111	763219.67	0.0049	669103.58	0.0304	761828.47	0.0085	5126546.71	3.3782
u724	123227.06	0.0033	134525.04	0.0403	**105519.13**	0.0749	122996.79	0.0348	105522.22	0.0726	123555.35	0.0344	880241.23	4.3227
rat783	**26857.78**	0.0162	28072.78	0.0787	NF	NF	NF	NF	NF	NF	NF	NF	181231.65	5.4103
nrw1379	148824.97	0.0006	160604.28	0.1414	127645.8	1.7936	147442.83	0.4334	**127229.1**	1.2901	147726.66	0.8295	1442118.9	31.2367
fl1577	**133611.52 (8)**	0.2212	146513.11	0.2294	NF	NF	NF	NF	NF	NF	NF	NF	1360170.55	46.8645
d1655	226270.69	0.0504	243977.39	0.2019	NF	NF	**221884.71**	66.3066	NF	NF	221913.52	39.2293	2181431.96	54.6314
vm1748	1071406.36	0.0127	1172125.61	0.2247	**893988.13**	0.1383	1064283.8	0.0371	902015.95	0.1256	1075384.79	0.0559	15086783.91	66.3227
u1817	**235415.89**	0.0382	257789.12	0.3569	NF	NF	NF	NF	NF	NF	NF	NF	2126243.7	71.8473
rl1889	1210897.56	0.0167	1275071.54	0.2493	**964105.85**	1.8775	1129600.05	0.0502	972201.69	1.5212	1136456.38	0.0511	14891665.15	83.5184
# Best	5	–	1	–	18	–	1	–	11	–	0	–	4	–

- Equal opportunity based heuristics performed better compared to their non-equal opportunity based counterparts, i.e., C3 & C5 performed better in comparison to C1, and C4 & C6 performed better in comparison to C2 if we leave aside those cases where equal opportunity based heuristics fail to find feasible solutions.
- It has also been observed that C1 and C2 fail to provide solution in all 10 iterations for some instances like *pr76, gr137 etc.*, but results for all 10 iterations has been observed in all the parallelly build heuristics C1, C3, C4, C5 and C6.
- C7 has been successful in providing results on some instances where all other heuristics failed to provide feasible solution. But the solution quality as well as the running time is poor in comparison to the other heuristics in most of the cases.
- It has been observed that, a completely feasible solution is obtained by C2 and C7 for the instance *fl417* in Table 3, whereas no feasible solution is obtained for the same instance by using C1, C3, C4, C5 and C6.
- In Table 2, we can see that, on the instance *brg180*, only C7 has provided feasible solution.

5   Conclusions

KIATSP is a recently introduced variant of TSP for which literature contains only a single approach based on ACO. In this paper, seven constructive heuristics have been proposed and tested on 40 instances from TSPLIB with different values of K, γ and θ. Computational results demonstrate that heuristics which build tours in parallel performed better than those heuristics where tours are built one after the other. The heuristics C3 and C5 where the tours are build parallelly and neighbours are selected in a greedy manner performed better compared to the GRASP based approaches C4 and C6. C3 is seen to perform better on most of the large sized instances.

Since there is no existing heuristic approach for KIATSP, any future development to solve KIATSP can be based on the ideas incorporated in these heuristics. Apart from standalone use, these heuristics can be used in combination with metaheuristic approaches where they can be used for generating initial solution as well as neighboring solution.

In future, we intend to work on metaheuristic approaches to solve KIATSP. The constructive heuristics presented here can be used for generating initial solutions in these metaheuristic approaches. We also plan to develop local search based heuristics for KIATSP which can be used inside these metaheuristic approaches to further improve the quality of solutions obtained by these approaches.

References

1. Garey, M.R., Johnson, D.S.: Computers and Intractability: A Guide to the Theory of NP-Completeness. W. H. Freeman, San Francisco (1979)
2. Iwasaki, Y., Hasebe, K.: Ant colony optimization for K-independent average traveling salesman problem. In: Tan, Y., Shi, Y. (eds.) ICSI 2021. LNCS, vol. 12689, pp. 333–344. Springer, Cham (2021). https://doi.org/10.1007/978-3-030-78743-1_30
3. Lenstra, J.K., Kan, A.R.: Some simple applications of the travelling salesman problem. J. Oper. Res. Soc. **26**(4), 717–733 (1975)
4. Lin, S., Kernighan, B.W.: An effective heuristic algorithm for the traveling-salesman problem. Oper. Res. **21**(2), 498–516 (1973)
5. Majumder, S., Singh, A.: Heuristics for K-independent total traveling salesperson problem. In: Woungang, I., Dhurandher, S.K., Pattanaik, K.K., Verma, A., Verma, P. (eds.) Advanced Network Technologies and Intelligent Computing, pp. 626–635. Springer, Cham (2023). https://doi.org/10.1007/978-3-031-28183-9_44
6. Matai, R., Singh, S.P., Mittal, M.L.: Traveling salesman problem: an overview of applications, formulations, and solution approaches. In: Traveling Salesman Problem, Theory and Applications. InTechOpen, London (2010)
7. Resende, M.G., Ribeiro, C.C.: Optimization by GRASP. Springer, Berlin (2016)

Book Recommendation Using Double-Stack BERT: Utilizing BERT to Extract Sentence Relation Feature for a Content-Based Filtering System

Derwin Suhartono[(⊠)] and Adhella Subalie

Computer Science Department, School of Computer Science,
Bina Nusantara University, Jakarta 11480, Indonesia
dsuhartono@binus.edu

Abstract. Traditional entertainment such as reading is still heavily enjoyed and is even having an increase in interest. But there is a significant discrepancy in search keywords "book recommendation" and "similar books to", where the latter is higher than the former. This research proposed a method that attempted to recommend books by their story progression that is called Double-Stack BERT which generates a document embedding from a book synopsis as a representation in the vector space. This document embedding will then be measured by its similarity against each other using cosine similarity to retrieve a similar book recommendation. Double-Stack BERT builds the document embeddings by extracting and adding its sentence relation feature by treating each sentence in a document as a token. This addition proved to increase the performance of document embedding when tested on datasets with similar characteristics.

Keywords: Book recommendation · Content-Based Filtering · CBF · Sentence-BERT · BERT · RoBERTa · Document embedding · Sentence relation extraction

1 Introduction

The rise of the digital era and content consumption in the past decade has grown exponentially. But in the midst of that, traditional entertainment such as reading books proves to stand its ground, accelerated by the use of modern approaches such as the use of audiobooks, e-books, and platforms for the book lovers community. Although there are too many books that someone can ever read in their lifetime, it is always possible to curate what to choose to read. Book recommendation specifically serves as a vital component in digital platforms to help users all around the world to curate what they actually would want to read.

But even with the copious amount of book recommendation systems, it seems like a specific type of use case has not been covered yet. With the simple query

R. Morusupalli et al. (Eds.): MIWAI 2023, LNAI 14078, pp. 36–47, 2023.
https://doi.org/10.1007/978-3-031-36402-0_3

in Google Trends[1], it's easy to see that there's a discrepancy between the search terms "book recommendations" and "similar books to", with the latter being higher than the former in these past 5 years.

The cause of this discrepancy remains inconclusive without further prodding, but looking at the current book recommendations systems, it's apparent that it is crowded with Collaborative Filtering (CF) systems or perhaps hybrid systems of CF and CBF (Content-Based Filtering). Previous researchers have mentioned or proven that hybrid systems yield better results overall [3,11] than just using pure CF or its counterpart: Content-Based Filtering (CBF). While CF recommendations are based on user interactions, CBF recommendations are based on the content of what it's trying to derive its recommendation from, like book metadata (author, date published, etc.). CF and CBF both have their own advantages and disadvantages, but for the use case of trying to find "similar books to X", CBF is going to be adopted to fill in this use case due to its advantage in representing what a book actually is. Furthermore, not much research has been done to utilize a book synopsis as the feature used in a CBF book recommendation system even though a synopsis is used as a tester of what a book is about. Using a book synopsis as a feature would require it to be turned into a document embedding.

After the revolutionary release of BERT (Bidirectional Encoder Representations from Transformers) [4] in 2019, every task in NLP (Natural Language Processing) is being tackled by using it as a base such as single sentence classification tasks, sentence pair classification tasks, question answering tasks, and single sentence tagging task. This innovation applied bidirectional training on Transformer [12] models to language modeling.

A successful attempt to generate sentence embeddings using BERT was done by using a siamese structure and triplet network called Sentence-BERT [8]. Using BERT as the base model, siamese structure aims to learn distributed embeddings representation of data points in a way that in the high dimensional vector space, contextually similar data points are projected in the near-by region whereas dissimilar data points are projected far away from each other. The research also shows that just using its final pooling layer by itself does not yield good results.

But most of the works done during this year after BERT's release were clearly hindered by its limitation in the input size, with 512 tokens as its limit for BERT-base and 1024 tokens for BERT-large. Attempts to solve or improve this input size problem were done by Longformer [2] and BigBird [13] where both of them use variations of patterns for the self-attention mechanism to increase the input size limit.

Creating a book recommendation system would yield a better result using a hybrid system [3,11] but they usually did not mention the usage of book synopsis as one of the features. But an attempt at a CBF book recommendation system by using the TF-IDF (Terms Frequency-Inverse Term Frequency) representation

---

[1] Results can be reproduced from https://trends.google.com with two queries: "book recommendations" and "similar books to", with worldwide settings in the past 5 years (2017–2022).

of the book synopsis and cosine similarity did satisfy 83.3% of the respondents that used the system [9] although the methods used were outdated. Construction of a book feature vector that includes the book synopsis as one of the features, turning it into a document embedding using a BERT model, and adding a novel feature: author embeddings [6] which represent an author in a vector space, actually yields a great result in a German books classification task. This leads to the conclusion that using a book synopsis as a feature will produce a great result since this feature served as a base feature. Another attempt at using BERT to construct a document embedding was done for Japanese emotion-analysis data [10]. This attempt tried to break the barrier of 512-tokens input size limitation by dividing the text into several parts, generating the document embeddings using BERT for each part, and then calculating the mean vector of all parts combined. After that, the mean vector is concatenated with the TF-IDF vector representation of the text and this proved to improve the performance of the task relative to the usage of only the CLS (Classification) token vector. But again, the improvement using TF-IDF is rather outdated. While this research will focus more on generating document embeddings using BERT, an attempt at document classification called DocBERT [1] using BERT actually yielded state-of-the-art results by fine-tuning it directly for the document classification task.

From these previous attempts at similar objectives, some conclusions could be derived:

1. Using BERT as the base of document embedding creation is proven to be beneficial
2. Adding related features to the base of the document embedding itself could improve the performance of the CBF book recommendation system (e.g. author embedding [6], TF-IDF representation [10])
3. The length of the document for the input of BERT-based models is still a problem since there's a limit. Because of this, the entirety of the input is often not considered.
4. Only several attempts at using book synopsis as a CBF feature have been done even though it shows great potential.

Due to those conclusions, the aim of this paper is to generate a document embedding from a book synopsis using a BERT-based model to use it in a CBF book recommendation system. The base embedding will be concatenated with a sentence-relation feature vector that could cater to a longer document.

In the following sections where the model is evaluated, the classification results are not to prove whether this method could succeed in the classification task, but rather to confirm its quality by adding a new feature for the document embedding.

2   Proposed Method

To try and achieve this paper's objective, this paper contributed this novel solution called Double-Stack BERT as seen in Fig. 1:

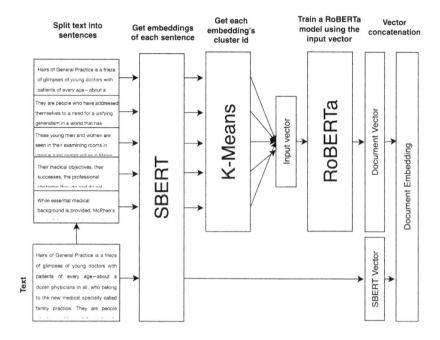

Fig. 1. The high-level diagram of Double-Stack BERT.

Stack 1:
- Splitting book synopsis text into sentences to get each of its sentence embeddings using Sentence-BERT [8]
- Treat each sentence embeddings as a token and form these tokens into a sequence of tokens for the input of a RoBERTa model [5]

Stack 2:
- Pre-train the RoBERTa model using these sequences of sentence tokens to get a model that learns the context between each sentence
- Get the last pooling layer of the trained RoBERTa as a sentence relation feature vector

The Double-Stack BERT aims to extract the sentence relation feature vector. This vector then will be concatenated with an SBERT vector (or content vector).

2.1 Dataset

There are 4 datasets that are used in this research for different purposes. For the pre-training purpose, unlabelled corpus like BookCorpus [14] was used for its book content and big size. There are a total of 11,038 books in this dataset, resulting in 74 million data points of sentences.

For document embedding quality evaluation, this paper used MR (Movie Reviews) Polarity [7], Reuters-21578 Distribution 1.0, and Google Books API dataset (fetched by the authors themselves) for further confirmation. MR Polarity is a dataset for sentiment analysis with 2 polar labels (vpositive" and "negative"), Reuters dataset is a collection of news articles with their genre as labels, and Google Books API dataset is a collection of books metadata from the Google Books API. The database of the book recommendation system also uses Google Books API dataset.

2.2   First Stack: Feature Extraction

The First Stack of Double-Stack BERT has the objective to represent a document by splitting it into its sentences and then formatting it to fit the input format of the Second Stack (RoBERTa). This stack includes an SBERT [8] model as its core. The dataset containing documents is first processed by splitting each data point into sentences. At this point, a document is treated as a collection of sentences. Each of these sentences will be transformed into sentence embeddings using SBERT (all-mpnet-base-v2). During the pre-training process, the sentence embeddings were clustered using K-Means ($K = 100$) to get each sentence's cluster id. The same K-Means operation would produce a sentence codebook that will be used in future operations to map out new embeddings into their cluster ids. At this point, a document is represented as a sequence of cluster ids that each represent a sentence.

These existing cluster ids are then treated as vocabularies alongside special tokens from RoBERTa: "<s>", "</s>", "<pad>", "<unk>", and "<mask>". A dictionary was constructed to map these vocabularies into token ids, which then will be saved to use for future operations. Once the sentence codebook and the dictionary are set, the process of building the input vector could be done in simple steps, as shown in Fig. 2.

An input_ids, an attention mask, and a label vector are then generated for each document as shown in Fig. 3, ready to be the input of a RoBERTa model with a maximum length of 512 tokens. These vectors are necessary for the model to learn the context of each 'vocabulary' using RoBERTa's algorithm to form a language modeling, Masked Language Modelling (MLM). By substituting regular English words with 'types' of sentences represented by cluster ids, the untrained RoBERTa model is expected to learn how certain types of sentences relate to one another in a document.

2.3   Second Stack: RoBERTa

The Second Stack in Double-Stack BERT aims to turn the sequence of sentences into a vector that holds the information of contextualized sentences in a document/text.

The previously formatted inputs went through the pre-training process of an untrained RoBERTa. This serves to train this model to learn the dataset BookCorpus [14] through a different representation explained in the previous section. After the model has been trained, we can extract the last pooling layer

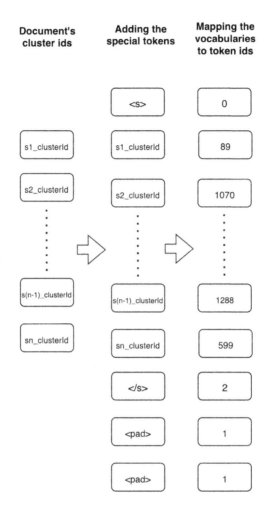

Fig. 2. Building the input vector to fit the RoBERTa's input format.

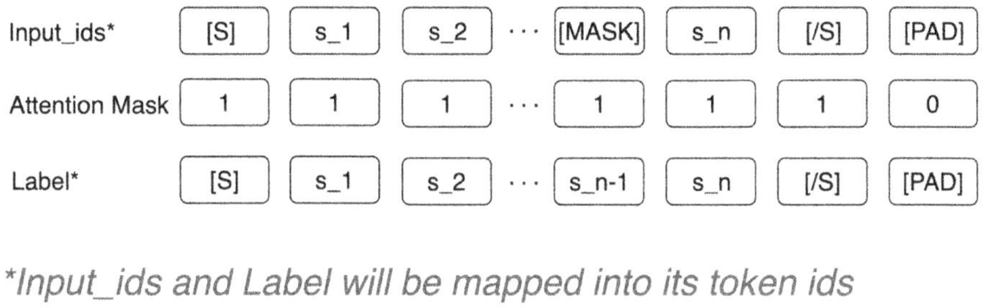

Input_ids*	[S]	s_1	s_2	··· [MASK]	s_n	[/S]	[PAD]
Attention Mask	1	1	1	··· 1	1	1	0
Label*	[S]	s_1	s_2	··· s_n-1	s_n	[/S]	[PAD]

Input_ids and Label will be mapped into its token ids

Fig. 3. Input_ids, attention mask, and label vectors for RoBERTa.

of the model to represent the sentence relation vector of the relevant document input.

For a full book synopsis representation, this sentence relation vector is concatenated with its content vector, generated using the previous SBERT model using the full unsplit synopsis/text resulting in a vector of length 1536 (768 + 768) as shown in Fig. 4.

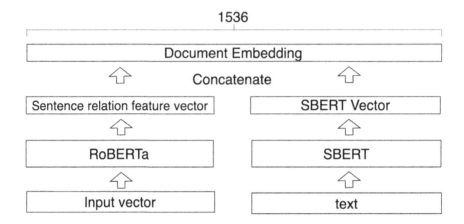

Fig. 4. The full vector building.

2.4   Recommendation System

The final recommendation system would compare each document embedding against each other to calculate its similarity using cosine similarity. To help optimize this process, all of the book synopsis in the database (Google Books API dataset) that has been processed into a document embedding acquired through previous steps are clustered using the K-Means algorithm ($K = 200$) to get similar books groups. The similarity score will then only be calculated against the books in the same cluster and sorted to get the most similar books.

3   Results and Discussions

3.1   Model Testing

The quality of document embeddings that the Double-Stack BERT model generates is tested using a classification task using a linear SVM (Support Vector Machines) classifier with accuracy and F1 score as metrics. As mentioned in the previous section, the tested datasets were MR Polarity and Reuters. The proposed model was tested against some baseline models and tested combination methods using alternative features for document embeddings such as TF-IDF

Table 1. Performance evaluation results.

	MR Polarity		Reuters	
	Acc	F1	Acc	F1
Baseline models				
TF-IDF	0.770	0.770	0.855	0.840
SBERT (all-mpnet-base-v2)	**0.857**	**0.857**	0.863	0.852
Doc2Vec	0.555	0.551	0.590	0.528
Longformer	0.587	0.588	0.697	0.763
BigBird	0.784	0.784	0.671	0.719
Tested methods				
SBERT mean vectors	0.853	0.853	0.824	0.804
SBERT mean vectors + TF-IDF	0.852	0.852	**0.865**	0.854
SBERT mean vectors + BoS vector (K = 10000)	0.838	0.838	0.784	0.771
SBERT mean vectors + BoS vector (K = 100)	0.855	0.855	0.803	0.785
SBERT mean vectors + BoS vector (K = 100) + TF-IDF	0.854	0.854	0.837	0.824
BoS vectors (K = 100)	0.683	0.683	0.503	0.419
BoS vectors (K = 100) + TF-IDF	0.775	0.775	0.816	0.797
SBERT vector + BoS (K = 100)	0.855	0.855	0.836	0.824
Proposed method				
Double-Stack BERT vector (128 tokens)	0.596	0.596	0.419	0.537
Double-Stack BERT vector (128 tokens) + SBERT vector	0.852	0.852	0.864	**0.875**

Table 2. Proposed method evaluated using dataset with similar characteristics (Google Books API dataset).

	Accuracy	F1-Score
Baseline model		
SBERT (all-mpnet-base-v2)	0.704	0.702
Proposed methods		
Double-Stack BERT vector (K = 100) (128 tokens)	0.168	0.210
Double-Stack BERT vector (K = 100) (128 tokens) + SBERT vector	**0.707**	**0.709**

vectors, Bag of Sentences (BoS) and SBERT sentences mean vectors. Any models that weren't meant to produce an embedding were tested by extracting the last pooling layer as a representation.

Due to the unavailability of proper computation resources during the pre-training stage, the RoBERTa model could only be trained using 100,000 data points from the total of 74 million data points in BookCorpus and the sentence codebook can only be trained using 1 million data points. But as shown in Table 1, the results for the proposed methods are yielding better results even though there were limitations during implementation.

The proposed method did well on the Reuters dataset with the best F1 score at 0.875 and second place for accuracy at 0.864. This dataset was on par with the target data's characteristic which is a text/document with a narration, similar to a book synopsis. The MR Polarity was expectedly not the best suited for this model as it is a dataset of sentences with no narration in it. The addition of the sentence relation vector (or Double-Stack BERT vector) instead worsens the overall performance of the SBERT vector. To further confirm the use case of the Double-Stack BERT, another experiment was done as an addition to test out the model. Using the actual dataset meant for operation, the model proved to be increasing the performance of document embeddings as shown in Table 2. The Google Books API dataset that was used for this additional experiment was the undersampled version with only 15 classes of book genres each containing 399 books.

3.2   Recommendation Result

To assess the recommendation produced by this system, results from other platforms were taken as comparisons to be analyzed as shown in Table 3.

These recommendations were generated for the query book of title "The Seven Husbands of Evelyn Hugo" by Taylor Jenkins Reid. It's easy to see that from mainstream platforms that use CF (Goodreads, WISRN, Google Play Books), the recommendation falls in a rather generic range of popularity and genre. But with the nature of CF, these recommendations probably mean that "if a user A likes book X and user B likes books X too, user A will probably like the books that user B enjoys too". There's not much info on what type of system these platforms use (except for WISRN which uses CF system with its own algorithms) so it's not really known for sure whether they are pure CF or hybrid systems.

The proposed method did generate interesting recommendations albeit not much in common. The genres are conflicting and not many comparable storylines or elements just by looking at the synopsis. Because the only feature used as a book's identifier is the synopsis, this might not be enough. Another factor to consider is the fact that a book synopsis might not be the best representation of a book's story because it was usually not written by the author itself and it is convoluted with other things like reviews from other notable authors or publishers.

The best recommendation that yields the most similarities would be the subjective book recommendation, taken from an article on a blog that a person has made specifically from their own personal[2]. The recommendations have similar elements, similar tones, perhaps same time settings, and the same main and sub-genres. The first recommendation even comes from the same author with the same universe as the query book.

But this method is clearly not ideal because it relies on human power and the popularity of a book. Similar articles won't always be available for most books.

---

[2] Source of blog post: https://www.thecreativemuggle.com/books-like-the-seven-husbands-of-evelyn-hugo/.

Table 3. Book recommendations from the proposed model compared to the other recommendation platforms.

Platforms	Recommendation 1	Recommendation 2	Recommendation 3
Goodreads	**Title:** It Ends with Us **Similarities:** - Sub-genre (romance) - Popularity	**Title:** Ugly Love **Similarities:** - Sub-genre (romance) - Popularity	**Title:** People We Meet on Vacation **Similarities:** - Sub-genre (romance) - Popularity
What I Should Read Next (WISRN)	**Title:** Honey Girl **Similarities:** - Sub-genre (romance) - Popularity	**Title:** Josh and Hazel's Guide to Not Dating **Similarities:** - Sub-genre (romance) - Popularity	**Title:** Love and Other Words **Similarities:** - Sub-genre (romance) - Popularity
Google Play Books	**Title:** Maybe in Another Life **Similarities:** - Sub-genre (romance) - Popularity - Author	**Title:** It Ends with Us **Similarities:** - Sub-genre (romance) - Popularity	**Title:** The Song of Achilles **Similarities:** - Sub-genre (romance) - Popularity
Subjective (personal) book recommendation	**Title:** Malibu Rising **Similarities:** - Hollywood and celebrity elements - Author - Universe - Time settings	**Title:** Mary Jane **Similarities:** -Celebrity element - Main genre and sub genres - Time settings	**Title:** The Final Revival of Opal & Nev **Similarities:** - Hollywood and celebrity elements - Main genre and sub genres - Time settings
Proposed method	**Title:** Royko in Love **Similarities:** - Biography-like - Sub-genre (romance)	**Title:** Crazy Salad and Scribble **Similarities:** - About life in general	**Title:** Housebroken **Similarities:** - Elements of marriage life

4 Conclusion

This study proposes a novel solution of constructing a document embedding from a book synopsis using the addition of a sentence relation feature that proved to increase the performance of target datasets such as Reuters and Google Books API Dataset in classification tasks even though the training capacities were severely limited due to technical issues. Also as expected, the model did not perform well on a non-target dataset, MR Polarity dataset. The main part of this method lies in the usage of a RoBERTa model to extract the sentence relation feature from a narrative document/text by dividing each document into sentences, treating these sentences as a sequence of tokens for the input of RoBERTa model to learn its context in a document. The last pooling layer is taken as the feature vector to be concatenated with an SBERT content vector.

These results on model evaluation have shown that BERT-based models have a big potential to be used to learn the relation between sentences in a document. However, upon implementation, the recommendation results were poor compared to other platforms, with the subjective recommendations being the best at giving recommendations.

This method certainly has a lot of room to improve. For the model development, the trained model could be swapped with more sophisticated ones and it can also be arranged in other architecture. More training with more datasets is expected to give better results too. With the poor performance in yielding book recommendations, it is also advisable to combine the current feature with other metadata such as author, genre, and date published.

References

1. Adhikari, A., Ram, A., Tang, R., Lin, J.: DocBERT: BERT for document classification (2019)
2. Beltagy, I., Peters, M.E., Cohan, A.: Longformer: the long-document transformer (2020)
3. Berbatova, M.: Overview on NLP techniques for content-based recommender systems for books. In: Proceedings of the Student Research Workshop Associated with RANLP 2019, Varna, Bulgaria, pp. 55–61. INCOMA Ltd. (2019). https://aclanthology.org/R19-2009
4. Devlin, J., Chang, M.W., Lee, K., Toutanova, K.: BERT: pre-training of deep bidirectional transformers for language understanding. In: Proceedings of the 2019 Conference of the North American Chapter of the Association for Computational Linguistics: Human Language Technologies, Minneapolis, Minnesota (Volume 1: Long and Short Papers), pp. 4171–4186. Association for Computational Linguistics (2019). https://aclanthology.org/N19-1423
5. Liu, Y., et al.: RoBERTa: a robustly optimized BERT pretraining approach (2019)
6. Ostendorff, M., Bourgonje, P., Berger, M., Moreno-Schneider, J., Rehm, G., Gipp, B.: Enriching BERT with knowledge graph embeddings for document classification (2019)
7. Pang, B., Lee, L.: Seeing stars: exploiting class relationships for sentiment categorization with respect to rating scales. In: Proceedings of the 43rd Annual Meeting of the Association for Computational Linguistics (ACL 2005), Ann Arbor, Michigan, pp. 115–124. Association for Computational Linguistics (2005). https://aclanthology.org/P05-1015
8. Reimers, N., Gurevych, I.: Sentence-BERT: sentence embeddings using Siamese BERT-networks. In: Proceedings of the 2019 Conference on Empirical Methods in Natural Language Processing and the 9th International Joint Conference on Natural Language Processing (EMNLP-IJCNLP), Hong Kong, China, pp. 3982–3992. Association for Computational Linguistics (2019). https://aclanthology.org/D19-1410
9. Soyusiawaty, D., Zakaria, Y.: Book data content similarity detector with cosine similarity (case study on digilib.uad.ac.id). In: 2018 12th International Conference on Telecommunication Systems, Services, and Applications (TSSA), pp. 1–6 (2018)
10. Tanaka, H., Cao, R., Bai, J., Ma, W., Shinnou, H.: Construction of document feature vectors using BERT. In: 2020 International Conference on Technologies and Applications of Artificial Intelligence (TAAI), pp. 232–236 (2020)
11. Tian, Y., Zheng, B., Wang, Y., Zhang, Y., Wu, Q.: College library personalized recommendation system based on hybrid recommendation algorithm. Procedia CIRP **83**, 490–494 (2019). https://www.sciencedirect.com/science/article/pii/S2212827119307401. 11th CIRP Conference on Industrial Product-Service Systems
12. Vaswani, A., et al.: Attention is all you need (2017)

13. Zaheer, M., et al.: Big bird: transformers for longer sequences. In: Larochelle, H., Ranzato, M., Hadsell, R., Balcan, M., Lin, H. (eds.) Advances in Neural Information Processing Systems, vol. 33, pp. 17283–17297. Curran Associates, Inc. (2020). https://papers.nips.cc/paper/2020/hash/c8512d142a2d849725f31a9a7a361ab9-Abstract.html
14. Zhu, Y., et al.: Aligning books and movies: towards story-like visual explanations by watching movies and reading books. In: 2015 IEEE International Conference on Computer Vision (ICCV), pp. 19–27 (2015)

Evaluating the Utility of GAN Generated Synthetic Tabular Data for Class Balancing and Low Resource Settings

Nagarjuna Venkata Chereddy[1,2] and Bharath Kumar Bolla[3](✉) (iD)

[1] Liverpool John Moores University, Liverpool, UK
[2] UpGrad Education Private Limited, Nishuvi, Ground Floor, Worli, Mumbai - 400018, India
[3] University of Arizona, Tucson, USA
bharathbolla@arizona.edu

Abstract. The present study aimed to address the issue of imbalanced data in classification tasks and evaluated the suitability of SMOTE, ADASYN, and GAN techniques in generating synthetic data to address the class imbalance and improve the performance of classification models in low-resource settings. The study employed the Generalised Linear Model (GLM) algorithm for class balancing experiments and the Random Forest (RF) algorithm for low-resource setting experiments to assess model performance under varying training data. The recall metric was the primary evaluation metric for all classification models. The results of the class balancing experiments showed that the GLM model trained on GAN-balanced data achieved the highest recall value. Similarly, in low-resource experiments, models trained on data enhanced with GAN-synthesized data exhibited better recall values than original data. These findings demonstrate the potential of GAN-generated synthetic data for addressing the challenge of imbalanced data in classification tasks and improving model performance in low-resource settings.

Keywords: Binary Classification · Tabular Synthetic Data · Class Imbalance · ADASYN · SMOTE · GAN · GLM · Random Forest · Low resource setting · SDV · GANs

1 Introduction

One of the significant problems in classification tasks is a class imbalance, which occurs when one class value in the target variable is highly dominant over the other class values. It is imperative to handle the class imbalance in the target variable of classification datasets, especially in predicting rare-case scenarios. If the class imbalance is not treated, machine learning models built on the imbalanced data will suffer from unwanted bias, leading to incorrect classifications. In rare cases of classification problems, misclassification often leads to severe consequences. Several class imbalance handling techniques have been proposed over the years.

Sampling techniques like random undersampling, random oversampling, SMOTE [1], ADASYN [2], and other variants of SMOTE [3] can be used to handle the class

R. Morusupalli et al. (Eds.): MIWAI 2023, LNAI 14078, pp. 48–59, 2023.
https://doi.org/10.1007/978-3-031-36402-0_4

imbalance, but they have their limitations. Due to recent advancements in deep learning, neural network models were employed to generate synthetic data. With the emergence of GANs [4], GAN-based architectures were also used in synthetic data generation. With the success of deep learning architectures in generating synthetic data on images and text, state-of-the-art architectures like GANs were extended to synthesize tabular data. From [5] and [6], it is evident that robust real-world application models need large-scale training data to yield superior performance. But large-scale data is not often readily available. In such cases, synthetic data generation techniques can curate a large-scale dataset with the same structural and statistical properties as the original data [7].

This research uses GAN-based models to create synthetic data points with similar structural and statistical properties to the original data. Synthetic data with the best qualitative properties is combined with actual data to evaluate the utility of the synthetic data in class balancing and low-resource setting experiments. The objectives of this paper are as follows:

- To evaluate the utility of synthetic data from GAN, SMOTE, and ADASYN in complementing the train data in low resource settings (classification tasks).
- To compare GAN and Non-GAN synthetic data generation techniques (SMOTE and ADASYN) on highly imbalanced data.

2   Literature Review

Synthetic data has gained popularity in recent years. In supervised learning, with artificial data generation techniques, researchers can generate an arbitrary number of synthetic samples with labels similar to the original data samples. The research community is increasingly using synthetic data in combination with actual data in data crunch situations to overcome the shortage of data. Researchers have conducted numerous studies on different artificial data generation techniques.

2.1   Synthetic Data Using SMOTE and ADASYN

Classification models trained on imbalanced data lead to misclassifying data points from minority classes. Over-sampling and under-sampling methods can be used to treat class imbalances. Over-sampling leads to an increase in training time and overfitting, and under-sampling leads to profound data loss. SMOTE was proposed to overcome the issue of class imbalance by creating synthetic samples [1]. SMOTE assigns equal weights to all minority class samples and overgeneralizes the minority class. Due to this drawback, multiple variants of SMOTE, like Safe Level SMOTE, SMOTE-SGA, ADASYN, and Borderline-SMOTE, were proposed [1, 3]. ADASYN uses a probability distribution function and creates more synthetic minority samples for data points that are hard to learn [2]. A combination of oversampling and undersampling methods was used to treat the class imbalance [8]. This may solve the problem to some extent. However, under-sampling leads to data loss, which is not advisable on a highly imbalanced dataset, and random oversampling leads to duplicate records that result in the overfitting of the model [1, 3].

2.2 Synthetic Data for Images and Text

Data augmentation is a widely used technique for improving the performance of machine learning models [9–11]. However, there are cases where augmentation can decrease model performance, particularly in detecting defects [12, 13]. To address this, recent developments in deep learning have led to the use of neural network models for generating synthetic data. For example, a parametric face generator was used to create synthetic face images, which were used for training deep neural network models [14]. In another study, an artificial data generation process was developed for generating synthetic images with synthetic backgrounds. The Faster R-CNN algorithm was trained fully on these images, achieving comparable performance to real-world data [14].

Synthetic data generation techniques have been used to overcome data shortages in specific domains. For instance, a chatbot in the Filipino language was developed using synthetic data generated using Taglog Roberta due to a data shortage in the language [15]. Similarly, synthetic data was generated from discharge summaries of mental health patients to overcome the scarcity of labeled data in the healthcare domain [16].

The use of Generative Adversarial Networks (GANs) in synthetic data generation has also been explored. Deep Convolutional GANs (DCGANs) have been proposed to generate better-quality synthetic images than conventional techniques [17]. However, using GANs for text generation is difficult due to the requirement of different data generated by the generator. To overcome this, the Medical Text GAN (mtGAN) architecture was proposed, which employs the REINFORCE algorithm to generate synthetic text data for Electronic Health Records (EHRs) [18]. In mtGAN, the discriminator's outputs serve as reward points for the generator to generate high-quality synthetic data.

2.3 Synthetic Data for Tabular Data Using Generative Models

The success of GANs in generating synthetic data on images and text has led to their use in synthesizing tabular data with the same features and statistical properties as the original data [7]. A technique for generating synthetic relational databases called CTGAN was proposed, while Synthetic Data Vault (SDV) uses Gaussian copulas to understand the interdependencies of columns and generate synthetic data [19]. Synthetic data generated using SDV has been evaluated through a crowd-sourced experiment and found no significant difference in performance compared to models trained on original datasets [20]. GAN architectures, including the Synthetic Data Vault, Data Synthesizer, and Synthpop ecosystems, have been evaluated for their utility in generating synthetic data for machine learning tasks [21, 22]. Synthetic data can also protect user privacy when sensitive data needs to be shared. However, it must be generated at a greater distance from real data to increase privacy [23]. However, the authors have not addressed the class imbalance in the datasets and have used datasets with few data points, leaving scope to explore the use of tabular synthetic data to complement training data for machine learning models in low-resource settings.

3   Research Methodology

As part of this research, two studies were conducted on the imbalanced insurance data [24]. The steps followed in Study 1 and Study 2 were illustrated in Figs. 1 and 2 respectively.

- Study 1: In this study, the performance of models was evaluated by training Random Forest (RF) algorithm on varying combinations of original and synthetic data.
- Study 2: Generalised Linear Model (GLM) algorithm was applied to the data balanced with synthetic data from the minority class samples.

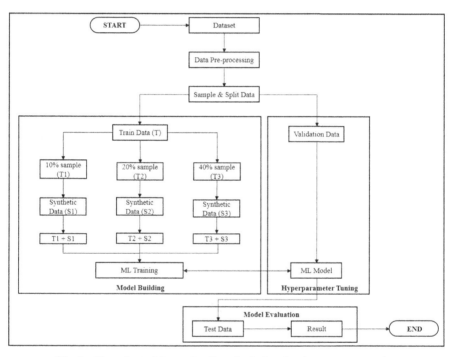

Fig. 1. Flow chart of the study of synthetic data in a low resource setting

3.1   Dataset Description

As part of this research, highly imbalanced vehicle insurance data with 382154 instances was obtained from Kaggle [24]. The Response variable is the target variable with binary values 0 and 1. 0 and 1 correspond to the customer's interest in taking up the policy with the insurance company. Id is the unique identifier for each row. Age, Region_Code, Annual_Premium, Policy_Sales_Channel, and Vintage columns have numerical values. The rest of the columns are categorical/binary variables. The dataset has 62601 (16.4%) instances for which the response was flagged as one, and for the rest, the response was flagged as zero. This is a clear case of class imbalance and must be handled appropriately.

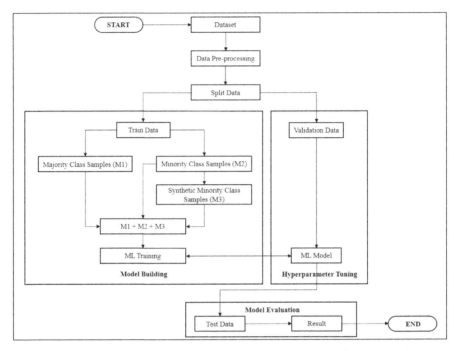

Fig. 2. Flow chart of the study of class balancing experiments

3.2 Data Pre-processing

Region_Code and Policy_Sales_Channel columns have 53 and 156 unique values, respectively, where each region and channel was represented with a numeric value instead of their names. So, these two columns were converted from integer to object datatype. Standard pre-processing techniques were applied to clean and prepare the data for modeling. The pre-processed data is ready for modeling, referred to as df_train_model. df_train_model dataset was used in class balancing experiments. 3 new datasets df_10_org (T1), df_20_org (T2) and df_40_org (T3) with 10%, 20% and 40% of the df_train_model were created using stratified sampling. All data points from the newly created datasets T1, T2, and T3 are used to generate S1, S2, and S3 and train classification algorithms in a low-resource setting.

3.3 GAN Training

In this study, we utilized two models from the Synthetic Data Vault ecosystem, namely CTGAN, and CopulaGAN, to generate synthetic data. Both models were trained for 100 epochs with a batch size of 500 and a learning rate of 0.0002 for both the generator and discriminator. The discriminator steps of both models were set to 5. Both GAN models were trained on df_10_org and synthetic data of the same size as df_10_org was generated from each model. The synthetic data generated from each model was used to enrich the df_10_org, df_20_org, and df_40_org datasets by synthesizing 26750 (S1),

53501(S2), and 107002 (S3) records, respectively. Additionally, 223686 (M3) minority class records were synthesized to balance the imbalanced df_train_model dataset. The synthetic data generated by the best-performing GAN was selected for experiments using KSTest and Logistic Detection Score metrics.

3.4 Data Modelling

The data used in class balancing and low resource setting experiments were split into a 70:30 ratio using stratified train-test split, and continuous variables were rescaled using StandardScaler. In order to balance and improve the rescaled train data, GAN, SMOTE, and ADASYN were utilized. For class balancing, four versions of data were available for modeling, including the original imbalanced data and data balanced with each of the SMOTE, ADASYN, and GAN techniques. Twelve versions of data were available for low resource settings, including the original data sets and the enriched data sets generated using GAN, SMOTE, and ADASYN. Both experiments used the GLM and RF algorithms to build classification models.

In the class balancing experiment, the GLM algorithm was used, as it provides coefficients for all input variables. GLM models were trained on all four versions of data using Recursive Feature Elimination (RFE) and manual feature elimination techniques to remove insignificant independent variables. The top fifteen variables returned by RFE were used to build an initial model, and manual feature elimination was performed using p-values and VIF values.

In the low resource setting experiment, Classification models were built using the RF algorithm, and the data were transformed using Principal Component Analysis (PCA); for data enriched with synthetic data from GAN, seventeen principal components were used to transform the data, while fifteen principal components were used for other data versions. PCA-transformed training data was fed to the RF algorithm for training, and hyperparameter tuning was performed using GridSearchCV on n_estimators, max_depth, min_samples_leaf, and max_leaf_nodes parameters. The roc_auc metric was used to select the best-performing model, considered the final model.

The process of model evaluation and predictions on test data were consistent for both GLM and RF models. Using the final model, the odds of test data points that the models had not seen were predicted, and labels were assigned using the optimal threshold value. Accuracy, recall, AUC, specificity, and G-Mean metrics were calculated using the labels of unseen test data, and recall was used as the primary metric for evaluation.

4 Results

In this section, the results obtained from the models are discussed. Subsection 4.1 discusses the qualitative assessment of synthetic data generated from GANs. The two subsequent sub-sections will discuss the results obtained from class balancing and low resource setting experiments.

4.1 Assessment of GAN Synthetic Data Quality

The outcomes of the assessment of synthetic data generated by GAN are presented in Table 1. CopulaGAN synthetic data demonstrated slightly better performance than CTGAN synthetic data in KSTest, with scores of 0.99 and 0.98, respectively. The detection scores of synthetic data from CTGAN and CopulaGAN were 0.76 and 0.82, respectively. CopulaGAN required 280 min for the training phase and only 6 min and 11 s to produce 410930 (26750 + 53501 + 107002 + 223686) data points. CopulaGAN needed less time for training and sampling than CTGAN. Despite CTGAN synthetic data displaying somewhat better results in the detection matrix, CopulGAN synthetic data demonstrated better performance than CTGAN synthetic data in all three parameters. Therefore, the synthetic data created by CopulaGAN was employed for the class balancing and low resource setting experiments.

Table 1. GAN Results

	KSTest	Logistic Detection score	Training time (mins)	Sampling Time
CTGAN	0.98	0.76	301	6 min 58 s
CopulaGAN	0.99	0.82	280	6 min 11 s

4.2 Results on the Utility of Synthetic Data in Class Balancing

The findings of the class balancing experiments are presented in Fig. 3. The threshold values used to calculate the reported metrics are listed in Sect. 4. The results indicate that the synthetic data generated by GAN yielded the highest recall value (0.84), while the data balanced with ADASYN and GAN synthetic data resulted in better performance on the G-Mean metric (0.82). All versions of the data had the same AUC score (0.88). The accuracy (0.82) and specificity (0.82) values obtained from the imbalanced and SMOTE-balanced data were better than those obtained from the data balanced with ADASYN and GAN synthetic data. The balanced data showed similar performance to the imbalanced data, but the real impact of balancing with synthetic data is reflected in the threshold values. The threshold values of the balanced data were at least twice as large as those of the imbalanced data, indicating that models trained on balanced data can make predictions with greater accuracy than those trained on imbalanced data.

4.3 Low Resource Setting – Random Forest Results

The figures (Figs. 4, 5 and 6) depict the results of Random Forest on different variants of the datasets df_10_org, df_20_org, and df_40_org. The "Base" column represents the original data, while the Base + SMOTE, Base + ADASYN, and Base + GAN columns refer to the data enriched with synthetic data from SMOTE, ADASYN, and GAN, respectively. According to Fig. 4, ADASYN enhanced data has the highest accuracy (0.833), SMOTE enriched data has the highest AUC score (0.889), and GAN enriched data has

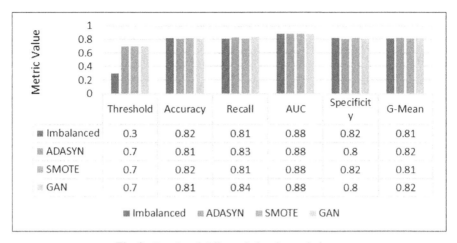

Fig. 3. Results of different balancing techniques

the highest G-Mean (0.821). The models trained on the ADASYN and GAN enhanced data have yielded superior specificity (0.862) and recall (0.841) values, respectively. Figure 5 shows that ADASYN enriched data has the highest accuracy (0.836), SMOTE and GAN enriched data have the highest AUC score (0.89), and GAN enriched data has the highest G-Mean (0.825). The models trained on ADASYN and GAN enriched data have yielded superior specificity (0.873) and recall (0.845) values, respectively. Figure 6 indicates that ADASYN enhanced data has the highest accuracy (0.836) and specificity (0.867), while the original 40% of data and SMOTE and GAN enriched data have the highest AUC score (0.891). The models trained on GAN enhanced data have yielded superior recall values (0.847).

The results indicate that using GAN synthetic data can improve recall values significantly compared to using the original data. For instance, the recall value (0.841) obtained from the model trained on 10% of data enriched with GAN synthetic data is significantly higher than the recall value (0.817) obtained from the original 20% of data. This pattern is also observed when comparing the results in Figs. 5 and 6. Additionally, models trained on data enriched with SMOTE consistently yield higher AUC values, while those trained on data enriched with ADASYN yield higher accuracy and specificity values (Figs. 4, 5 and 6). Finally, the models trained on data enriched with GAN consistently yield higher recall and G-mean values than other data versions.

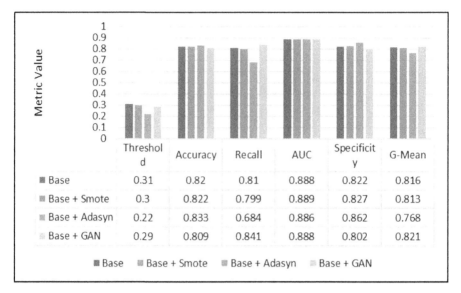

Fig. 4. Random Forest results with 10% of the data

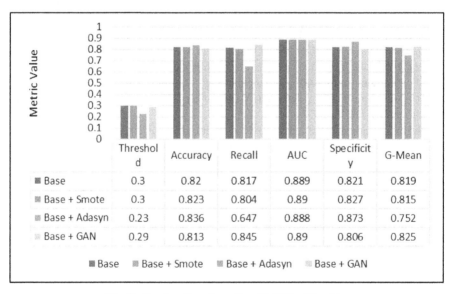

Fig. 5. Random Forest results with 20% of the data

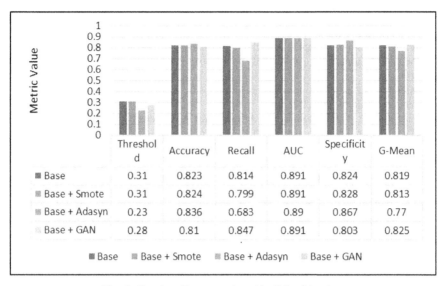

Fig. 6. Random Forest results with 40% of the data.

5   Conclusion

This study is the first to investigate the use of synthetic data in a low-resource setting. Our research establishes the effectiveness of synthetic data in building classification models for highly imbalanced data in low-resource settings. Specifically, this study is the first to explore using GAN synthetic data in low-resource settings. The models trained on balanced data using GAN have resulted in the highest recall at a threshold of 0.7. The random forest models trained on data enriched with GAN synthetic data in low-resource settings have consistently produced superior recall values. The better recall values observed in the models trained on data enriched with GAN synthetic data can be explained by the fact that GAN has effectively learned the characteristics of minority class samples, thus generating high-quality synthetic data from such samples. This finding indicates that synthetic data from GAN can effectively predict rare case scenarios, such as fraudulent transactions, loan defaulters, and rare diseases like HIV AIDS, urinary tract infections, and dengue, among others. Our work generalizes the power of Generative models to solve class imbalance problems in low-resource settings, demonstrating the potential of synthetic data generated by GAN in improving classification models' performance on highly imbalanced datasets.

References

1. Chawla, N.V., Bowyer, K.W., Hall, L.O., Kegelmeyer, W.P.: SMOTE: synthetic minority over-sampling technique. J. Artif. Intell. Res. **16**, 321–357 (2002). https://doi.org/10.1613/jair.953
2. He, H., Bai, Y., Garcia, E.A., Li, S.: ADASYN: adaptive synthetic sampling approach for imbalanced learning. In: 2008 IEEE International Joint Conference on Neural Networks

(IEEE World Congress on Computational Intelligence), pp. 1322–1328 (2008). https://doi.org/10.1109/IJCNN.2008.4633969

3. Kovács, G.: Smote-variants: a python implementation of 85 minority oversampling techniques. Neurocomputing **366**, 352–354 (2019). https://doi.org/10.1016/j.neucom.2019.06.100

4. Goodfellow, I., et al.: Generative adversarial nets. In: Advances in Neural Information Processing Systems, vol. 27 (2014)

5. Xu, A., Liu, Z., Guo, Y., Sinha, V., Akkiraju, R.: A new chatbot for customer service on social media. In: Proceedings of the 2017 CHI Conference on Human Factors in Computing Systems, pp. 3506–3510. New York, NY, USA (2017) https://doi.org/10.1145/3025453.3025496

6. Goyal, A.K., Metallinou, A., Matsoukas, S.: Fast and scalable expansion of natural language understanding functionality for intelligent agents. In: Proceedings of the 2018 Conference of the North American Chapter of the Association for Computational Linguistics: Human Language Technologies, vol. 3, pp. 145–152. (Industry Papers), New Orleans – Louisiana (2018). https://doi.org/10.18653/v1/N18-3018

7. Koenecke, A., Varian, H.: Synthetic data generation for economists. arXiv 06 Nov 2020. https://doi.org/10.48550/arXiv.2011.01374

8. Shamsudin, H., Yusof, U.K., Jayalakshmi, A., Akmal Khalid, M.N.: Combining oversampling and undersampling techniques for imbalanced classification: a comparative study using credit card fraudulent transaction dataset. In: 2020 IEEE 16th International Conference on Control & Automation (ICCA), pp. 803–808. (2020). https://doi.org/10.1109/ICCA51439.2020.9264517

9. Ethiraj, S., Bolla, B.K.: Augmentations: an Insight into their effectiveness on convolution neural networks. In: Advances in Computing and Data Sciences, pp. 309–322. Cham (2022). https://doi.org/10.1007/978-3-031-12638-3_26

10. Ethiraj, S., Bolla, B.K.: Classification of astronomical bodies by efficient layer fine-tuning of deep neural networks. In: 2021 5th Conference on Information and Communication Technology (CICT), pp. 1–6. (2021). https://doi.org/10.1109/CICT53865.2020.9672430

11. Ethiraj, S., Bolla, B.K.: Classification of quasars, galaxies, and stars in the mapping of the universe multi-modal deep learning. arXiv 22 May 2022. https://doi.org/10.48550/arXiv.2205.10745

12. Bolla, B.K., Kingam, M., Ethiraj, S.: Efficient deep learning methods for identification of defective casting products. In: Cognition and Recognition, pp. 152–164. Cham (2022). https://doi.org/10.1007/978-3-031-22405-8_13

13. Lal, R., Bolla, B.K., Ethiraj, S.: Efficient neural net approaches in metal casting defect detection. arXiv 08 Aug 2022. https://doi.org/10.48550/arXiv.2208.04150

14. Hinterstoisser, S., Pauly, O., Heibel, H., Marek, M., Bokeloh, M.: An annotation saved is an annotation earned: using fully synthetic training for object instance detection. arXiv 26 Feb 2019. https://doi.org/10.48550/arXiv.1902.09967

15. Tan, G.L., Ty, A.P., Ng, S., Co, D.A., Cruz, J.C.B., Cheng, C.: Using synthetic data for conversational response generation in low-resource settings. arXiv 06 Apr 2022. Accessed: 26 Jan 2023 [Online]. Available: http://arxiv.org/abs/2204.02653

16. Ive, J., et al.: Generation and evaluation of artificial mental health records for natural language processing. npj Digit. Med. **3**(1), 69 (2020). https://doi.org/10.1038/s41746-020-0267-x

17. Gao, Y., Kong, B., Mosalam, K.M.: Deep leaf-bootstrapping generative adversarial network for structural image data augmentation. Comput. Aided Civ. Infrastruct. Eng. **34**(9), 755–773 (2019). https://doi.org/10.1111/mice.12458

18. Guan, J., Li, R., Yu, S., Zhang, X.: A method for generating synthetic electronic medical record text. IEEE/ACM Trans. Comput. Biol. Bioinform. **18**(1), 173–182 (2021). https://doi.org/10.1109/TCBB.2019.2948985

19. Patki, N., Wedge, R., Veeramachaneni, K.: The synthetic data vault. In: 2016 IEEE International Conference on Data Science and Advanced Analytics (DSAA), pp. 399–410 (2016). https://doi.org/10.1109/DSAA.2016.49

20. Xu, L., Skoularidou, M., Cuesta-Infante, A., Veeramachaneni, K.: Modeling tabular data using conditional GAN. arXiv 27 Oct 2019. https://doi.org/10.48550/arXiv.1907.00503

21. Bourou, S., El Saer, A., Velivassaki, T.-H., Voulkidis, A., Zahariadis, T.: A review of tabular data synthesis using GANs on an IDS dataset. Information **12**(9), 375 (2021). https://doi.org/10.3390/info12090375

22. Hittmeir, M., Ekelhart, A., Mayer, R.: On the utility of synthetic data: an empirical evaluation on machine learning tasks. In: Proceedings of the 14th International Conference on Availability, Reliability and Security, pp. 1–6. New York, NY, USA, (2019). https://doi.org/10.1145/3339252.3339281

23. Utility and Privacy Assessments of Synthetic Data for Regression Tasks. https://ieeexplore.ieee.org/document/9005476 Accessed 26 Jan 2023

24. Learning from Imbalanced Insurance Data. https://www.kaggle.com/datasets/arashnic/imbalanced-data-practice (Accessed 26 Jan 2023)

How Good are Transformers in Reordering?

Ch. Ram Anirudh[✉] and Narayana Murthy Kavi

University of Hyderabad, Hyderabad, India
ramanirudh@uohyd.ac.in

Abstract. Translation requires transfer of lexical items (words/phrases) from Source Language to Target Language and also reordering of the transferred lexical items as appropriate for the target language. Whatever be the approach used, quality of translation depends on both the quality of lexical transfer and quality of reordering. In this paper, we explore how good the state-of-the-art sequence-to-sequence Transformer model is in reordering. Reordering models are tested for sequence to sequence mapping from an Intermediate Language (which uses the words of the target language arranged in the source language order) to target language. We build models using the *samanantar* English-Kannada parallel corpus. BLEU, TER and RIBES scores show significant improvement after reordering. We have also tested our models on the Machine Translation task as a whole. Compared to the default lexicalized reordering models used in Statistical Machine Translation, our transformer based reordering models have shown better performance.

Keywords: Machine Translation · Natural Language Processing · Transformers · Reordering

1 Introduction

Translation requires transfer of lexical items (words and phrases) from Source Language (SL) to Target Language (TL) and also reordering of the transferred lexical items as appropriate for the target language. Any approach to Machine Translation (MT) has to do these implicitly or explicitly. Traditional rule based MT (RBMT) [7] - transfer based methods in particular, perform transfer at morphological and syntactic levels explicitly. Statistical MT (SMT) [4,13], a more modern data driven approach, builds a lexical table and a phrase table (translation model) from a parallel corpus, which are used for lexical transfer. SMT also learns a reordering model from the parallel corpus. The translation model and reordering model are combined with language model in a log-linear function to generate translations during a process called decoding. Neural MT [1,24] implicitly learns to translate SL texts into TL texts in appropriate word order. Whatever be the method, quality of translation depends on both the quality of lexical transfer and quality of reordering.

R. Morusupalli et al. (Eds.): MIWAI 2023, LNAI 14078, pp. 60–67, 2023.
https://doi.org/10.1007/978-3-031-36402-0_5

Modern approaches to MT recognize the fact that words may have multiple meanings and connotations, and disambiguation is best done by considering the sentential context in which they occur. That is perhaps why lexical transfer and reordering are not considered as independent tasks. However, lexical items are much smaller and structurally much simpler than sentences. Also, the number of possible lexical items is much smaller when compared to all possible sentences, which is open ended and unbounded. Therefore, conceptually, lexical transfer is a much simpler task compared to sequence to sequence operations such as reordering. Further, the morphological complexity (including inflection, derivation, phonetic conflation, compounding etc.) vary widely across languages. Degree and nature of lexical ambiguities are also not the same in all languages. Word order is very rigid in some languages, while it is relatively free in other languages. Instead of the same-size-fits-all approach, exploring lexical transfer and reordering individually can give us new insights and open up new doors for research. In particular, here we focus on the question of how good the latest models are in the reordering task.

Suppose the MT task starts by transferring SL words to TL words arranged in SL word order. We call this *intermediate language* (IL). Next, the words in IL text are reordered using a reordering model. See Fig. 1.

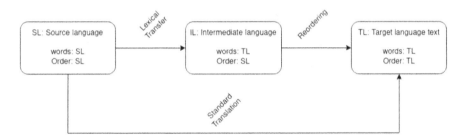

Fig. 1. Typical workflow of MT in explicit lexical transfer followed by reordering compared to standard MT models.

In this paper, we explore how good the state-of-the-art sequence-to-sequence Transformer model [24] is in reordering. The transformer reordering model is built using parallel corpus of IL sentences and corresponding TL sentences. Such a training data is prepared using word-aligned parallel corpus trained using IBM models of SMT [4]. Word alignments from SL to TL help us in arranging TL sentences in SL word order. We then train IL-TL transformer reordering model. We test the reordering model for English and Kannada languages. English belongs to Indo-Germanic language family and Kannada belongs to Dravidian language family. These languages differ widely in morphological and syntactic structures making them good candidates for testing reordering. Results on reordering test sets have shown a substantial improvement in BLEU score from 51.5 before reordering to 85.1 after reordering using transformer reordering model for English. It improved from 47 to 77 for Kannada. Reordering model is tested on MT task also, by applying it after generating monotone (SL ordered) SMT decoder output. Promising results were shown for English to Kannada.

2   Related Work

Simplest reordering in phrase-based MT [13] is a distortion probability distribution model that models the jump of phrase from one position to another. Tillman [23] proposed a lexicalized reordering model that predicts whether next phrase should be oriented to the right (monotone), left (swap) or a different position (discontinuous) relative to the previous translated phrase. This is the most commonly used baseline model in SMT. Li et al. [15] used a neural reordering model comprising of recursive autoencoders to learn the orientations. In all these methods, reordering model is combined with translation model and language model during decoding. Here we rather train a sequence-to-sequence reordering model, which is used to reorder after translating words/phrases.

Very few works in MT literature have had a separate reordering model. Bangalore and Riccardi [2] developed stochastic finite state models for lexical choice and reordering separately. The lexical choice model outputs a sequence of TL words for a given SL sentence. A stochastic finite state transducer learnt from a parallel corpus of source-ordered TL words with their corresponding TL sentences, is used to convert the TL words from lexical choice to a set of reordering rules. Sudoh et al. [22] do a translation from Japanese to English by training two SMT models: first, to translate Japanese to English in Head-Final English (HFE) ordering which is a feature native to Japanese. Second SMT model learns to reorder HFE to appropriate English. The English portion of the parallel corpus is reordered according a set of rules for getting HFE. Our work is similar, where we use word-alignments from IBM models instead of linguistic rules to get a parallel corpus of IL-TL sentences. More information on reordering models for MT can be found in a comprehensive survey by Bisazza and Federico [3].

Here we use transformers to build reordering models. Transformers are the backbone of many state-of-the-art NLP models including BERT [5], GPT [18], BART [14], etc. They have consistently outperformed the previous models in various tasks like machine translation, text summarization and question answering on standard data sets [5, 24]. In applications of computer vision, transformers have shown remarkable results [6,10]. Transformer learns the representations of input and output sequences, completely on a self-attention mechanism, without using any recurrence mechanism in its architecture. This mitigates the problems of long-distance relationship and catastrophic forgetting as with earlier RNN based networks. The authors of the original paper further claim that self-attention mechanism implicitly models the structure of sentence, making the transformer model more interpretable. For more details on transformer network, see Vaswani et al. [24].

3 Experiments

3.1 Dataset and Preprocessing

All the experiments in this work are done on English-Kannada (en-kn) language pair. English and Kannada belong to distinct language families. Kannada is agglutinative, morphologically rich and a free word order language but with a default *subject-object-verb* order. English is a relatively more isolating language with *subject-verb-object* word order.

English-Kannada parallel corpus from *samanantar* [19] is used for all the experiments. *samanantar* is a repository of large-scale parallel corpora for Indic languages, collected mostly by web-scraping and aligning similar sentences in web scraped texts. There are 4014931 translation pairs with around 27.7M words in English and 36.9M words in Kannada.

We have preprocessed the dataset for our experiments using open source tools. English side of the dataset is truecased and tokenized using the recaser and tokenizer respectively, provided with Moses SMT toolkit [12]. Kannada text is tokenized using Indic NLP library[1]. The tokenized parallel corpus is then cleaned to remove very long sentences (>80 words) and empty lines on source and target sides, using corpus cleaning script provided with Moses.

The dataset required for training our reordering model is actually a parallel corpus where one side is IL and the other side is TL. We take the en and kn sides from the cleaned *samanantar* corpus and create two parallel corpora: $IL_{en} - en$ and $IL_{kn} - kn$. IL sentences are generated using alignments learnt by training SMT models. The corpora obtained thus are split into training, development and test sets. 500 sentences are randomly picked for development set and 3000 sentences are randomly picked for test set. Remaining sentences are used for training. Subword tokenization is learnt for the two datasets using byte-pair-encoding (BPE) technique with 32000 symbols [20]. The datasets are then BPE tokenized before proceeding for training.

3.2 Training

We train two phrase based SMT systems: en-kn and kn-en using Moses. These models are useful for obtaining IL and testing the reordering models later. Cleaned *samanantar* parallel corpus is used for training. 5-gram language models with Kneser-Ney smoothing are built with *kenlm* provided with Moses. Monolingual datasets for building LM are obtained from Kakwani et al. [9]. We use the option `grow-diag-final-and` for learning alignments and `msd-bidirectional-fe` for learning lexicalized reordering.

We build two transformer reordering models: $IL_{en} - en$ and $IL_{kn} - kn$. OpenNMT [11] is used for training. Hyperparameter settings for the transformer network are similar to Vaswani et al. [24], except the word-embeddings. Vocabulary and word-embeddings are shared across input and output, since the words in

---

[1] https://anoopkunchukuttan.github.io/indic_nlp_library/.

IL and TL are same. Encoder and decoder stacks consist of 6 layers each. The model dimension d is 512. Batch size is 2048, validation batch size is 128. Training steps are 200000 and validation steps are 10000. Attention heads are 8 and attention dropout is 0.1. Optimization is done using Adam optimizer. Training is done on 2 NVIDIA GeForce RTX 2080 GPUs. The training takes around 12 h for $IL_{en} - en$ and 14 h for $IL_{kn} - kn$.

3.3   Evaluation

Evaluation is done using BLEU [17], TER [21] and RIBES [8] scores. BLEU (BiLingual Evaluation Understudy) uses a modified precision based score that counts n-gram matches between the hypothesis and reference translations. TER (Translation Edit Rate) is based on edit distance between hypothesis and reference which includes a shift operation alongside insertion, deletion and substitution. RIBES (Rank-based Intuitive Bilingual Evaluation Score) directly measures the reordering between hypothesis and reference translation using rank correlation coefficients. The word ranks (indices) in reference are compared to those of the corresponding matching words in the hypothesis to compute the correlation coefficient. For testing our task, RIBES and TER are more relevant.

We evaluate our reordering model in two settings. In one, we report BLEU, TER and RIBES scores before and after reordering on the test sets we created from IL-TL parallel corpus. We call these reordering test sets. Evaluation on these shows whether transformer is good at reordering. The sentences in these test sets represent an ideal situation where lexical transfer is at its best. To check how they perform in a more realistic setup of MT, we also test the models by using them to reorder the monotone-ordered² SMT decoder output. We compare the BLEU, TER and RIBES scores of this reordered output with the decoder output generated using the baseline lexicalized reordering in SMT. It may be noted that while lexicalized reordering is combined with translation and language models, we do transformer reordering separately after generating monotone ordered decoder output which resembles our IL. For these, we use test sets provided by Workshop on Asian Translation (WAT) 2021 [16].

3.4   Results

The results are reported in Tables 1 and 2. Table 1 shows BLEU, TER and RIBES on the test set before and after reordering. All the scores increase substantially after reordering using the transformer model, showing the promise of transformer for reordering. Table 2 shows MT evaluation results on test set provided with WAT2021 benchmarks dataset. For English to Kannada MT, reordering separately using transformer model is better than lexicalized reordering. This is evident from TER and RIBES scores. For Kannada to English MT, lexicalized reordering gives better results compared to separate transformer model. However, when we look at the counts of edit operations in TER computation

---

² Use option -dl 0 in Moses during decoding to generate monotone ordered output.

(Table 3), we see that shifts are lesser with transformer reordering compared to insertions, deletions and substitutions for both language pairs, indicating the efficacy of transformer reordering model.

Table 1. BLEU and TER scores on reordering test set before and after reordering using transformer model

Language	Metric	Before Reordering	After Reordering
Kannada	BLEU	47.7	**77.4**
	RIBES	0.693	**0.929**
	TER	0.382	**0.117**
English	BLEU	51.5	**85.1**
	RIBES	0.739	**0.961**
	TER	0.360	**0.095**

Table 2. BLEU and TER scores of SMT output with lexicalized reordering model and transformer reordering model on WAT2021 test sets

Language Pair	Metric	Lexicalized Reordering	Transformer Reordering
Kannada-English	BLEU	19.9	16.0
	RIBES	0.541	0.537
	TER	0.754	0.772
English-Kannada	BLEU	9.2	9.2
	RIBES	0.423	**0.465**
	TER	0.891	**0.867**

Table 3. Edit operations in TER when outputs are compared with reference translations

Language Pair	Edit Ops	Lexicalized Reordering	Transformer Reordering
Kannada-English	Insertions	3423	2525
	Deletions	5463	7253
	Substitutions	15637	15798
	Shifts	4494	**4160**
English-Kannada	Insertions	2586	2444
	Deletions	3043	3233
	Substitutions	15851	15749
	Shifts	2984	**2388**

4   Conclusions

In this paper we have explored transformers for reordering in MT. We build models using the *samanantar* English-Kannada parallel corpus. Our experiments show that transformers are good at the reordering task. This will hopefully encourage further explorations in this direction and open up new avenues of research in the field of MT.

References

1. Bahdanau, D., Cho, K., Bengio, Y.: Neural machine translation by jointly learning to align and translate. In: Proceedings of the 3rd International Conference on Learning Representations, San Diego, CA, USA (2015)
2. Bangalore, S., Riccardi, G.: Finite-state models for lexical reordering in spoken language translation. In: Proceedings of Sixth International Conference on Spoken Language Processing, Beijing, China (2000)
3. Bisazza, A., Federico, M.: A survey of word reordering in statistical machine translation: computational models and language phenomena. Comput. Linguist. **42**(2), 163–205 (2016)
4. Brown, P.F., Pietra, V.J.D., Pietra, S.A.D., Mercer, R.L.: The mathematics of statistical machine translation: parameter estimation. Comput. Linguist. **19**(2), 263–311 (1993)
5. Devlin, J., Chang, M., Lee, K., Toutanova, K.: BERT: pre-training of deep bidirectional transformers for language understanding. In: Proceedings of the 2019 Conference of the NAACL: HLT, Minneapolis, Minnesota (Volume 1: Long and Short Papers), pp. 4171–4186. ACL (2019)
6. Dosovitskiy, A., et al.: An image is worth 16×16 words: transformers for image recognition at scale. In: Proceedings of International Conference on Learning Representations. Online (2021)
7. Hutchins, W.J., Somers, H.L.: An Introduction to Machine Translation. Academic Press, London (1992)
8. Isozaki, H., Hirao, T., Duh, K., Sudoh, K., Tsukada, H.: Automatic evaluation of translation quality for distant language pairs. In: Proceedings of the 2010 Conference on EMNLP, Massachusetts, USA, pp. 944–952 (2010)
9. Kakwani, D., et al.: IndicNLPSuite: monolingual corpora, evaluation benchmarks and pre-trained multilingual language models for Indian languages. In: Findings of the Association for Computational Linguistics: EMNLP 2020, pp. 4948–4961, Online. Association for Computational Linguistics (2020)
10. Khan, S., Naseer, M., Hayat, M., Zamir, S.W., Khan, F.S., Shah, M.: Transformers in vision: a survey. ACM Comput. Surv. **54**, 10s, Article no. 200 (2022). 41 p. https://doi.org/10.1145/3505244
11. Klein, G., Kim, Y., Deng, Y., Nguyen, V., Senellart, J., Rush, A.: OpenNMT: neural machine translation toolkit. In: Proceedings of the 13th Conference of the AMTAS, Boston, MA, USA (Volume 1: Research Papers), pp. 177–184 (2018)
12. Koehn, P., et al.: Moses: open source toolkit for statistical machine translation. In: Proceedings of the 45th Annual Meeting of the ACL, Prague, Czech Republic, pp. 177–180. ACL (2007)

13. Koehn, P., Och, F.J., Marcu, D.: Statistical phrase-based translation. In: Proceedings of the 2003 Conference of the NAACL: HLT, vol. 1, pp. 48–54. ACL, Edmonton (2003)
14. Lewis, M., et al.: BART: denoising sequence-to-sequence pre-training for natural language generation, translation, and comprehension. In: Proceedings of the 58th Annual Meeting of the ACL, pp. 7871–7880, Online. ACL (2020)
15. Li, P., Liu, Y., Sun, M., Izuha, T., Zhang, D.: A neural reordering model for phrase-based translation. In: Proceedings of COLING 2014, the 25th International Conference on Computational Linguistics: Technical Papers (2014)
16. Nakazawa, T., et al.: Overview of the 8th workshop on Asian translation. In: Proceedings of the 8th Workshop on Asian Translation (WAT2021), pp. 1–45, Online. ACL (2021)
17. Papineni, K., Roukos, S., Ward, T., Zhu, W.J.: Bleu: a method for automatic evaluation of machine translation. In: Proceedings of the 40th Annual Meeting of the ACL, Philadelphia, Pennsylvania, USA, pp. 311–318. ACL (2002)
18. Radford, A., Narasimhan, K., Salimans, T., Sutskever, I.: Improving language understanding with unsupervised learning. Technical report, OpenAI (2018)
19. Ramesh, G., et al.: Samanantar: the largest publicly available parallel corpora collection for 11 Indic languages. Trans. ACL **10**, 145–162 (2022)
20. Sennrich, R., Haddow, B., Birch, A.: Neural machine translation of rare words with subword units. In: Proceedings of the 54th Annual Meeting of the ACL (Volume 1: Long Papers), pp. 1715–1725 (2016)
21. Snover, M., Dorr, B., Schwartz, R., Micciulla, L., Makhoul, J.: A study of translation edit rate with targeted human annotation. In: Proceedings of the 7th Conference of the AMTAS, Massachusetts, USA (2006)
22. Sudoh, K., Wu, X., Duh, K., Tsukada, H., Nagata, M.: Syntax-based post-ordering for efficient Japanese-to-English translation. ACM Trans. Asian Lang. Inf. Process. **12**, 3, Article no. 12 (2013)
23. Tillmann, C.: A unigram orientation model for statistical machine translation. In: Proceedings of the Joint Conference on HLT-NAACL, Boston, MA, pp. 101–104 (2004)
24. Vaswani, A., et al.: Attention is all you need. In: Proceedings of Neural Information Processing Systems, Long Beach, CA, USA, pp. 6000–6010 (2017)

Automatic Differentiation Using Dual Numbers - Use Case

R. Anand Krishna[1], R. V. S. Krishna Dutt[2(✉)], and P. Premchand[3]

[1] Technical University of Munich, Munich, Germany
anand.rallabhandi@tum.de
[2] CVR College of Engineering, Ibrahimpatnam 501510, Telangana, India
krishnadutt.rvs@cvr.ac.in
[3] Osmania College of Engineering, Hyderabad, India

Abstract. Automatic Differentiation (AD), also called algorithmic differentiation, is a method to obtain derivatives of univariate as well as multivariate functions without the need of using numerical or symbolic differentiation. The accuracy of AD is limited by the word length of the computing platform used for implementation; it is otherwise exact. Recent applications of AD are found in Machine Learning, particularly in Deep Neural Networks (DNNs), Kinematics, Computational Fluid Dynamics, optimization problems, and solutions of differential equations. AD is carried out either in forward or backward methods when implemented with real numbers. However, AD using dual numbers is of current interest. Nonlinear relationships between sensor data of a thermal power plant are modeled using DNNs and it is possible to estimate the sensitivity measures by obtaining the gradients of output w.r.t. input feature vector of DNNs. The sensitivities can be estimated using DNNs which obviates the need for complex first-principle thermodynamic modeling. The sensitivities can be obtained using high-dimensional dual numbers to represent the DNN model parameters. Though dual numbers do not form a perfect ring (field) as per the definition of Group Number Theory, they are effective in simultaneous evaluation of functions and their Jacobians and Hessians. This paper discusses the use of AD with dual numbers to obtain the sensor sensitivity of a typical 500 MW using DNN.

Keywords: automatic differentiation · dual numbers · sensor sensitivity

1 Introduction

1.1 Automatic Differentiation

The computer codes for finding derivatives of functions of real variables are generally based on numerical and symbolic differentiation. Numerical differentiation is popular and is based on Eq. (1). However, for practical implementation, the series in Eq. (1) is approximated by ignoring higher order terms to obtain Eq. (2). This results in truncation and round-off errors due to finite precision representation in computer codes. Further, N-dimensional space requires 2N function evaluations to obtain all first-order partial derivatives.

© The Author(s), under exclusive license to Springer Nature Switzerland AG 2023
R. Morusupalli et al. (Eds.): MIWAI 2023, LNAI 14078, pp. 68–78, 2023.
https://doi.org/10.1007/978-3-031-36402-0_6

$$f(x + h) = f(x) + h\frac{\partial f(x)}{\partial x} + \frac{h^2}{2!}\frac{\partial^2 f(x)}{\partial x^2} + \ldots \tag{1}$$

$$\frac{\partial f(x)}{\partial x} \approx \frac{f(x + h) - f(x)}{h} \tag{2}$$

Symbolic differentiation, on the other hand, is based on closed-form calculus primitives like addition, chain, and product rules applied recursively. It can lead to 'expression swelling', if not implemented properly. Both numerical and symbolic differentiation are mature methods that are implemented in different tools and languages. Automatic Differentiation (AD) is a set of current techniques to speed up differentiation and can still be exact. AD can be implemented either in forward or reverse mode when real numbers are used. Accuracy is limited by the word length of the computing platform. AD is based on computational graphs and function primitives without the use of numerical and symbolic differentiation methods. A computational graph breaks down the complex function into simpler primitive expressions. In the forward mode, the computational graph is traversed from the input (independent) variables to the output (dependent) variables and differentiation is performed by computing the derivative at each node of the graph. In the reverse mode, the dependent variable to be differentiated is the output and the derivative is computed with respect to each sub-expression at each node in the backward mode. It is seen that in the forward mode AD, the derivative trace needs to be repeated for every independent variable, while in the reverse mode, the full gradient is obtained in one pass. This is due to the difference in applying the chain rule. Baydin et al. [1] surveyed the wide use of AD in different fields. It is, however, observed that the machine learning community's focus on it is recent. The survey brings out the emergence of general-purpose AD in deep learning. AD is based on the differentiation of closed-form expressions and control flows like branching, loops, recursion, and procedure calls. van Merriënboer et al. [2] studied different techniques like functional languages and the graph-based intermediate representations used in developing AD-enabled machine learning frameworks. Further, a graph-based intermediate representation structure for implementation is presented. Bolte et al. [3] studied an alternate approach to non-smoothed algorithmic differentiation and the backward mode of AD. Theoretical results highlight unpredictable behavior in a non-smoothed context which is an issue that is ubiquitous in machine learning. It is concluded that the spurious behavior is harmless and can be ignored. Hence, it is justified to use AD outside its original domain of validity in machine learning. The application of generalized dual numbers to find derivatives with respect to vector quantities is presented by Rehner [4] and it is applied to thermodynamic state properties and critical points. These properties are highly nonlinear and the derivatives are usually obtained numerically. Raissi et al. [5] used AD in a hidden physics model for data-driven modeling of spatiotemporal dynamics based on sparse data. The unknown underlying physics formulated by possible PDE terms is weakly imposed and is implicitly learned by an auxiliary neural network. Though it is observed that AD can help open the black box of neural nets by understanding the role played by automatic differentiation within the field of deep learning, the resulting model still lacks sufficient interpretability since the closed-form governing equations cannot be fully uncovered. Zhao Chen et al. [6] used DNNs for representation learning, physics embedding, automatic differentiation, and sparse regression to approximate the solution of a system of variables, compute essential derivatives, and identify the important derivatives and parameters to discover the underlying structure and explicit expression of the equations. The above literature is, however, representative and not exhaustive. It is also evident that AD is currently being explored in applications involving differential equations and deep learning frameworks. Alternately, dual numbers can be used in AD in which both function and its derivatives are evaluated simultaneously. Current literature indicates the use of generalized dual numbers in AD and its use in deep learning models. Table 1 summarizes the gross comparison of the three techniques. Machine learning frameworks like PyTorch, TensorFlow, MXNet, etc., implement the reverse mode AD. However, dual numbers offer an alternate method of doing AD. While it is advantageous to opt for reverse mode with real numbers, currently, dual numbers are explored as an alternative to simplify AD.

Table 1. Comparison of Computer Differentiation Techniques

Gross Comparison of Computer Differentiation		
Method	Pros	Cons
Numerical	Easy to implement, fast, suitable for Machine Learning applications	Approximate
Symbolic	Exact	Moderately complex to implement, can be slow, memory increases for complex expressions
Automatic Differentiation	Exact, fast, suitable for Machine Learning	Moderately complex

1.2   Dual Numbers

The dual numbers are a particular class of a two-parameter family of generalized complex number systems of the form, with Eqs. (3) and (4) representing the multi-dimension space

$$z = x + \sum_{i=1}^{N} \epsilon_i y_i \tag{3}$$

where

$$x, y \in \mathbb{R} \text{ and } \epsilon_i^2 = 0, \epsilon_i \epsilon_j = 0 \quad (i \neq j) \tag{4}$$

Any function $f(z)$, when evaluated, will result in a dual number with the primal part representing the value of the function while the dual part represents the derivative of the function as given by Eq. (5)

$$f(z) = f_p(x, y) + \sum_{i=1}^{N} f_d^i(x, y) \tag{5}$$

where $f_p(x, y)$ and $f_d(x, y)$ are the primal and the dual parts, respectively, associated with i^{th} dimension; both the primal and the dual parts are the functions of real variables. The special property of the functions of dual numbers is the dual part of ith dimension which is the partial derivative of the primal part in that direction.

F. Messelmi [7] provided an analysis of the dual numbers and showed the formulas for elementary trigonometric and hyperbolic functions. To use dual numbers, rules for addition, subtraction, multiplication, and division along with the evaluation of primitive functions like explicit algebraic and transcendental functions like sine, cosine, exponentiation, etc., are defined. The latter can be obtained with series expansion and by using the property of dual number $\epsilon^n = 0 \quad \forall n \geq 2$. The product and chain rules are also defined. Jeffrey et al. [8] presented the application of hyper dual numbers to optimization problems involving Hessians. László Szirmay-Kalos [9] discussed the application of dual numbers for higher-order AD. The next section discusses the use of dual numbers for AD. We demonstrate the computational graph of the sigmoid function with inputs and weights represented by real numbers and multi-dimensional dual numbers, respectively. This representation is used in further sections.

2 AD with Dual Numbers

Consider the sigmoid function that is often used in DNNs. For simplicity, two inputs, (x_1, x_2) are considered and both the inputs are represented using real numbers and the model parameters, (w_0, w_1, w_2), are represented as multi-dimensional dual numbers. Figure 1 shows the corresponding computational graph. Table 2 shows the computation of the output at each node of the graph in Fig. 1.

It is seen that in one forward pass of the graph, both the function values and their derivatives w.r.t. inputs at each node are simultaneously obtained. This makes dual numbers an attractive alternative when compared to AD with real numbers. For any given cost function $J(W)$ in any DNN, in which the model parameters $[W] = [w_{ij}]$ are dual numbers; the gradients are given by the dual part as shown in Eq. (6).

The gradients are obtained using the dual part of the parameter which represents the direction of the steepest descent and the real part represents the current parameter values. The updated parameters using the gradient descent can be represented by Eq. (6).

$$W(t + 1) = W(t).(\text{Primal part}) - \eta \nabla J(W(t)).(\text{Dual part}) \tag{6}$$

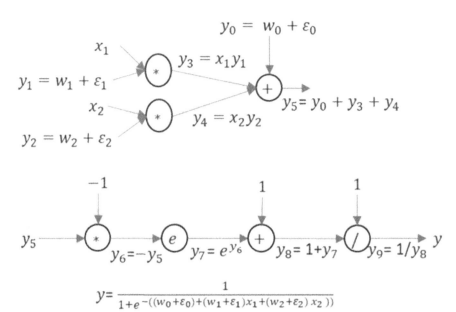

$$y = \frac{1}{1 + e^{-((w_0 + \varepsilon_0) + (w_1 + \varepsilon_1)x_1 + (w_2 + \varepsilon_2)x_2)}}$$

Fig. 1. Computational graph of Sigmoid with Dual Numbers

Table 2. Sigmoid Function and its derrivative using dual numbers

AD with Dual Numbers	
S. No.	Output at each node
1	$y_0 = w_0 + \epsilon_0$
2	$y_1 = w_1 + \epsilon_1$
3	$y_2 = w_2 + \epsilon_2$
4	$y_3 = w_1 x_1 + x_1 \epsilon_1$
5	$y_4 = w_2 x_2 + x_2 \epsilon_2$
6	$y_5 = (w_0 + x_1 w_1 + x_2 w_2) + (\epsilon_0 + \epsilon_1 x_1 + \epsilon_2 x_2)$
7	$y_6 = -(w_0 + x_1 w_1 + x_2 w_2) - (\epsilon_0 + \epsilon_1 x_1 + \epsilon_2 x_2)$
8	$y_7 = e^{-(w_0 + x_1 w_1 + x_2 w_2) - (\epsilon_0 + \epsilon_1 x_1 + \epsilon_2 x_2)}$
9	$y_8 = 1 + e^{-(w_0 + x_1 w_1 + x_2 w_2) - (\epsilon_0 + \epsilon_1 x_1 + \epsilon_2 x_2)}$
10	$y_9 = \dfrac{1}{1 + e^{-(w_0 + x_1 w_1 + x_2 w_2)}} + \dfrac{e^{-(w_0 + x_1 w_1 + x_2 w_2)}(\epsilon_0 + \epsilon_1 x_1 + \epsilon_2 x_2)}{(1 + e^{-(w_0 + x_1 w_1 + x_2 w_2)})^2}$

Equation (6) shows that the update rule in the gradient descent is based on the primal and the dual parts of the parameters at each node in the different layers of DNN. Unlike in regular back prorogation, the update rule uses both the primal and dual parts obtained in forward pass.

3   DNN with Dual Numbers

Consider an ANN/DNN with model parameters represented by dual numbers. Consider the connection of jth neuron in the layer $k - 1$ to the mth neuron in the layer k; the parameters are as shown in Eq. (7).

$$[W]^k = [W_r]^k + [W_d]^k \odot [\epsilon]^k \qquad (7)$$

The dimensions of each of the matrices are in line with the number of parameters between the layers $k-1$ and k. The output from each layer, based on the previous layer inputs and weight matrices, is given in Eqs. (8) and (9). Equation (10) gives the Jacobian for the layer k. f represents the activation function in the layer k.

$$[Z]^k = [W_r]^{k-1}([W_r]^k + [W_d]^k \odot [\epsilon]^k) = [Z_r]^k + [Z_d]^k \odot [\epsilon]^k \qquad (8)$$

$$[O]^k = f[Z_r]^k + [Z_d]^k \odot [\epsilon]^k) = [O_r]^k + [O_d]^k \odot [\epsilon]^k \qquad (9)$$

$$[J]^k = [O_d]^k \odot [\epsilon]^k \qquad (10)$$

The parameters in each layer are represented by multi-dimensional dual numbers. The dual part from each layer is separated and stored for back propagation using the chain rule. The real part is used further in the forward mode. This algorithm avoids the need to separately calculate Jacobians like in conventional or AD with real numbers. With a single pass, we get all the information needed for back propagation using the chain rule. This allows us to train the network using the standard gradient descent algorithm with the gradients obtained in the forward pass alone.

Thus, the gradient descent with dual numbers has the following advantages over the traditional gradient descent with real numbers:

1. Easy computation of gradients,
2. Increased accuracy of gradients.

Overall, the gradient descent with dual numbers can lead to faster convergence and improved optimization results, particularly for complex and deep neural networks. The following section discusses a use case of DNN with dual numbers for obtaining sensitivities of a 500 MW thermal power plant.

4   Sensitivities of Sensors in Thermal Power Plants

The turbine cycle of a typical working 500 MW Thermal Power plant has nearly eighty parameters influencing the output of a turbine cycle. The output, i.e., the load, is a highly non-linear function of these parameters, represented by Eq. (11). Process changes and equipment degradation contribute to changes in the load. Performance monitoring requires tracking these changes by way of estimating the sensitivities of the sensors. The sensor sensitivities are defined in Eq. (12), in which S_i is the sensitivity due to the ith parameter, L is the load, v_i is the parameter, and $\frac{\partial L}{\partial v_i}$ is the gradient of load w.r.to the parameter v_i. Obtaining the sensitivities usually involves complex first-principle thermodynamic modeling using conservation laws and non-linear fluid properties. In a physics-based model, load L is obtained by Eqs. (13) and (14). Sensitivity, as per Eq. (12), is obtained by numerical derivatives of the nonlinear implicit function $\phi(p_k, t_k)$, the thermodynamic property of a working fluid. m_k, p_k, and t_k are the mass flow, pressure, and temperature, respectively, of the working fluid at k^{th} measurement location. However, for an operating plant, the state Eqs. (13) and (14) have to be changed frequently based on its degradation. This is not feasible.

$$L = f(v_1, v_2, ... v_i .....) \tag{11}$$

$$S_i = \frac{L}{v_i} \frac{\partial L}{\partial v_i} \tag{12}$$

$$\Sigma(m_i) = 0 \tag{13}$$

$$\Sigma(\phi(p_i, t_i) * m_i) = 0 \tag{14}$$

HUI-JIE WANG et al. [10] proposed the concept of sensitive factors of the energy consumption of operating parameters using the application of analytic models to the whole thermal system under variable work conditions. Further, the state space theory with the topological relation between the parameters of the measuring points and the energy consumption was established. With this approach, the sensitivities of all operating parameters of different units are estimated through calculation. Chandrakant et al. [11] considered simulations incorporating first law analysis to carry out sensitivity studies of three supercritical steam parameters with high-ash washed and unwashed Indian coals. Parameters considered include three ambient temperature conditions. Guoqiang Zhang et al. [12] considered the problem of sensitivity analysis of a coal-fired power plant with flue gas re-circulation and used first principle model. It is shown that re-circulation rate and coal input have a great effect on the performance of the power plant. R.A. Mulder et al. [13] used the basic definition of efficiency of a nuclear fusion power plant and the plant efficiency is determined by the thermodynamic efficiency and the recirculated power fraction. The focus is on sensitivity analysis using the thermodynamic model. However, the above studies do not consider the ML models based on real-time data and thermodynamic models need to be tuned every time for process or equipment characteristic changes. Alternatively, sensitivities of physical systems can be obtained in real-time using DNNs with dual numbers representing the model parameters and these can be trained using forward mode AD. This obviates the need for complex first principle modeling. The following section proposes sensitivity analysis using dual numbers in DNN for a typical 500 MW thermal plant.

4.1 Thermal Power Plant Parameter Sensitivity Using Dual Numbers

Without any loss of generality, one turbine, shown in Fig. 2, is employed to demonstrate the usage of DNN representing the turbine in Fig. 3. DNN parameters are represented using multi-dimensional dual numbers as discussed in the previous sections. Equation (15) shows load as a function of main steam flow (m_1), pressure (p_1), temperature (t_1), exhaust pressure (p_2), and temperature (t_2).

$$L = f(m_1, p_1, t_1, p_2, t_2) \tag{15}$$

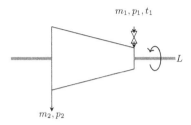

Fig. 2. High Pressure Steam Turbine

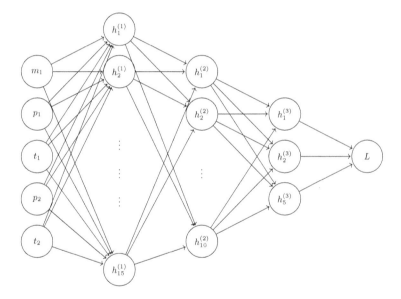

Fig. 3. DNN of Turbine Cycle with five input features

Mean base load data, consisting of the five features mentioned above, of an operating turbine alongwith with different standard deviations (σ) is shown in Table 3. The sensitivities of the five parameters as per Eq. (12) are obtained by training the DNN in line with Eqs. (7) to (10). Figures 4, 5 and 6 show these sensitivities for flow, inlet and outlet parameters of the turbine respectively. These are obtained using both AD and numerical evaluation for the same DNN. These sensitivities for all the five input parameters show a trend of similarity. The main differences in values as well as phase shift in both methods are attributable to the way the derivatives are obtained. The accuracy is expected to improve

Table 3. Base Load Data Vector for 142.8 MW Steam Turbine

Main Parameters at Inlet and Exhaust of High Pressure Turbine				
$m_1(T/hr)$	$p_1(kg/cm^2)$	$t_1(°C)$	$p_2(kg/cm^2)$	$t_2(°C)$
1450	170	538	35	120
1.0	0.5	0.5	0.5	0.5

by choosing different architectures for DNN and training over large data sets from the field. AD is exact while numerical derivatives are approximations. AD is expected to give more accurate results. The different sensitivities indicate the plant behavior due to changes in feature data. It is known from physics that the flow and load are linearly related provided the other inlet and outlet conditions are held constant. Similarly, when the inlet pressure alone is increased, the load decreases. The sensitivity plots represent field data that changes simultaneously; hence the sensitivities represent the combined effect of all the parameters.

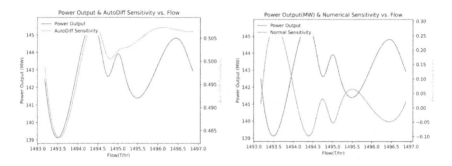

Fig. 4. Turbine Sensitivities due to Flow using DNN with Dual Numbers

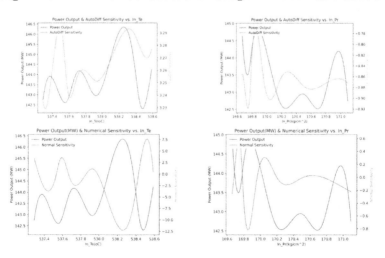

Fig. 5. Turbine Sensitivities due to Inlet Parameters using DNN with Dual Numbers

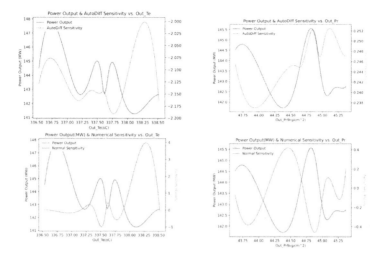

Fig. 6. Turbine Sensitivities due to Outlet Parameters using DNN with Dual Numbers

5 Conclusions

It is shown that multi-dimensional dual numbers can be used to represent model parameters of DNN; further plant sensitivities can be easily obtained by modeling the plant using DNNs. It is shown that in a single pass, the gradients of the output w.r.t. model parameters can be obtained with the use of dual numbers. Real-time plant data of a working steam turbine of a 500 MW thermal plant is used to demonstrate the AD with dual numbers wherein the DNN models the turbine. The sensitivities obtained both by Auto Differentiation and numerical methods are compared. This can be extended to full plant data having a few hundred features. Further, once DNN has been trained, real-time monitoring is simple as these compact DNNs can be easily coded in micro-controllers that are often used in plants.

References

1. Baydin, A.G., Pearlmutter, B.A., Radul, A.A., Siskind, J.M.: Automatic differentiation in machine learning: a survey. J. Mach. Learn. Res. **18**, 153:1–153:43 (2017)
2. van Merriënboer, B., Breuleux, O., Bergeron, A., Lamblin, P.: Automatic differentiation in ML: where we are and where we should be going. In: Bengio, S., Wallach, H.M., Larochelle, H., Grauman, K., Cesa-Bianchi, N., Garnett, R. (eds.) Advances in Neural Information Processing Systems 31: Annual Conference on Neural Information Processing Systems 2018, NeurIPS 2018, Montreal, Canada, 3–8 December 2018, pp. 8771–8781 (2018)
3. Bolte, J., Pauwels, E.: A mathematical model for automatic differentiation in machine learning. In: Advances in Neural Information Processing Systems 33:

Annual Conference on Neural Information Processing Systems 2020, NeurIPS 2020, 6–12 December 2020 (2020)

4. Rehner, P., Bauer, G.: Application of generalized (hyper-) dual numbers in equation of state modelling. Front. Chem. Eng. **3** (2021)

5. Raissi, M., Perdikaris, P., Karniadakis, G.E.: Physics-informed neural networks: a deep learning framework for solving forward and inverse problems involving nonlinear partial differential equations. J. Comput. Phys. **378**, 686–707 (2019)

6. Chen, Z., Liu, Y., Sun, H.: Physics-informed learning of governing equations from scarce data. Nat. Commun. **12** (2021)

7. Messelmi, F.: Analysis of dual functions. Ann. Rev. Chaos Theory Bifurcations Dyn. Syst. **4** (2013)

8. Fike, J., Alonso, J., Jongsma, S., Weide, E.: Optimization with gradient and hessian information calculated using hyper-dual numbers. In: 29th AIAA Applied Aerodynamics Conference (2011)

9. Szirmay-Kalos, L.: Higher order automatic differentiation with dual numbers. Periodica Polytechnica Electr. Eng. Comput. Sci. **65**(1), 1–10 (2021)

10. Wang, H.-J., Zhang, C.-F., Zhao, N.: The operating parameters sensitive analysis of energy consumption for coal-fired power plant. In: Proceedings of the 2008 International Conference on Wavelet Analysis and Pattern Recognition, Hong Kong, 30–31 August 2008 (2008)

11. Dahiphale, C., Vasireddy, S.N., Jayanti, S.: Sensitivity analysis of performance of coal-fired power plants to steam, coal and environmental parameters. In: Proceedings of the 24th National and 2nd International ISHMT-ASTFE Heat and Mass Transfer Conference, IHMTC2017-07-1268 (2017)

12. Zhang, G., Wenlong, X., Wang, X., Yang, Y.: Sensitivity analysis and optimization of a coal-fired power plant in different modes of flue gas recirculation. Energy Procedia **61**, 2114–2117 (2014)

13. Mulder, R.A., et al.: Plant efficiency: a sensitivity analysis of the capacity factor for fusion power plants with high recirculated power. Nucl. Fusion **61**, 046032 (2021)

On Some Properties of a New PoisN Wavelet Family

M. Shravani[1], D. Sudheer Reddy[2]([⊠]) [ID], and B. Krishna Reddy[1]

[1] Department of Mathematics, Osmania University, Hyderabad, India
[2] Department of Space, ADRIN, Secunderabad, India
sudheer@adrin.res.in

Abstract. This paper presents a family of new real valued continuous wavelet functions derived from Poisson kernel. Properties like Admissibility condition, vanishing properties, frequency response and time-frequency bandwidth are studied. A comparison is made between new wavelet family "PoisN" with Gaussian wavelet family. Finally, the de-noising capability of the proposed new wavelet is demonstrated with a noisy version of Gaussian function with different values of SNR.

Keywords: Continuous Wavelet Transform · new wavelet family · Poisson distribution · properties · time-frequency bandwidth · Gaussian distribution

1 Introduction

The continuous wavelet transform (CWT) is used to analyze how the frequency content of a signal changes over time. Most of the continuous wavelets are used in applications involving the detection of minute change of signals over a continuous set of scales. The applications of CWT range from finding a crack or damage in materials via non-destructive testing, seismic studies, analysis of financial time series, speech processing, pulmonary micro vascular pressure, geophysical, metrological studies, condition monitoring etc.

Approaches to construct new redundant or non-redundant wavelet bases are persistently being studied by many researchers [1,17] adapting to new demands from several applications which were otherwise compromised with existing wavelets families [2]. Of late, the use of wavelets in machine learning grew to become potential area of research which led to the development of wavelet networks [3], multi-level wavelet convolution neural network [4], wavelet support vector machine [18], wavelet kernel methods [5], deep learning [6] etc. In the recent study of physics informed neural networks, wavelets are used as an activation function to solve non-linear differential equations [7]. In their study they have used Morlet, Mexican hat and Gaussian wavelet functions as activation functions to derive the best solution and found that PINN with wavelet activation function perform better than tanh activation.

In this paper we develop a new family of continuous wavelets generated from Poisson Kernel, study some important properties of it and establish a relation between the transform coefficients with a member of the proposed wavelet and parameters of Gaussian distribution at different scales. We also estimate the parameters of noisy Gaussian distribution using this new wavelet function.

2 Continuous Wavelet Transform

A wavelet is an oscillatory, real or complex-valued function $\psi(x) \in L^2(R)$ in finite interval with an average value of zero. The square integrable measurable function $\psi(x)$ is called a mother wavelet. The mother wavelet $\psi(x)$ is localized in both time and frequency domains and generates a family of wavelets $\psi_{a,b}(x)$ formulated as $\psi_{a,b}(x) = \frac{1}{\sqrt{b}}\psi\left(\frac{x-a}{b}\right)$, where the numbers $a \in R$ and $b \in R^+$ denote the scale and translation parameters, respectively.

For a given real signal $f(x) \in L^2(R)$, the continuous wavelet transform (CWT) is defined as the inner product of the signal function with the wavelet functions [1, 8].

$Wf(a, b) = f, \psi_{a,b} = \frac{1}{\sqrt{b}}\int_{-\infty}^{\infty} f(x)\psi\left(\frac{x-a}{b}\right)dx$, where $Wf(a, b)$ is called a wavelet coefficient for the wavelet $\psi_{a,b}(x)$ and it measures the variation of the signal in the vicinity of a whose size is proportional to b.

The choice of the mother wavelet depends on the nature of the application at hand which gives a scope for closer understanding of the application and provides motivation for development of new wavelet functions. Here we study few existing continuous wavelet functions and their properties.

The non-redundant discrete wavelet transform de-correlates the wavelet coefficients at different resolutions and is often inadequate for applications demanding identification of features on a finer scale as might be required in crack or damage detection in metal plates. Hence, for practical implementation one can choose adequately discretized time (a) and frequency (b) scales and approximating the CWT integral as a summation over this grid.

Real valued Morlet, Mexican hat and Poisson wavelet are some of frequently used continuous wavelet functions for various applications. The real valued Morlet wavelet is a wavelet composed of cos(5t) multiplied by a Gaussian window (envelope) i.e., $\psi(t) = \pi^{-\frac{1}{4}}\cos(5t)e^{-t^2}$. Gaussian wavelet family is a set of wavelet members generated from k^{th} derivative of Gaussian function $v(t) = e^{-\frac{t^2}{2}}$, i.e., $v^{(k)}(t) = C_k\frac{d^k}{dt^k}e^{-t^2}$ where C_k is the normalization constant. Let GausN denote the Nth member of this family. In particular the second member of this family is the well-known Mexican hat wavelet given by $\psi(t) = \frac{2}{\pi^{-\frac{1}{4}}\sqrt{3}}(1 - t^2)e^{-\frac{t^2}{2}}$. New complex wavelets derived from Cauchy distribution and their properties are studied in [9] and approximation properties of Chebyshev wavelets generated from Chebyshev polynomials are studied in [10].

3 New Continuous Wavelet Family Generated from Poisson Kernel

Wavelets were explored in the domain of statistics and build new wavelet families from probability distributions [11] presents applications of wavelets in statistical framework. In [12] the authors studied the convergence properties of continuous wavelet transforms of distributions. Holschneider [13] defined the Poisson wavelet given by

$$g(t) = \left(t\frac{\partial}{\partial t} + 1 \right) P(t) \text{ where } P(t) = \frac{1}{\pi}\frac{1}{1+t^2}$$

rewriting $g(t)$ as $g(t) = \frac{\partial}{\partial t}(t \cdot P(t))$, further similar to Gaussian wavelets as described by Mallat [14], we are motivated to study the nature of higher derivatives of $tP(t)$ and study some of its properties.

A new family of wavelets are generated from n^{th} derivative of the continuous function $\theta(t) = tP(t) = \frac{t}{1+t^2}$ given by

$$\psi_n(t) = K_n\frac{d^n}{dt^n}\theta(t) \tag{1}$$

where integer n is the order of this family. Let "$PoisN$" denote N^{th} member of this family. $Pois1$ is the Poisson wavelet. (for brevity we adopt the naming convention similar to $GausN$ of MATLAB [15]).

The constant K_n has to be chosen such that $\|\psi_k(t)\|^2 = 1$, thus imposing this condition we get

$$K_n = \left(\int_{-\infty}^{\infty} \left| \frac{d^n}{dt^n}\theta(t) \right|^2 dt \right)^{-1/2} \tag{2}$$

The zero average property of wavelet i.e., $\int_{-\infty}^{\infty}\psi_n(t)dt = 0$ can also be easily verified. The inverse Wavelet transform is guaranteed by the existence of admissibility condition

$$C_{\psi_n} = \frac{\int_0^{\infty} \left| \hat{\Psi}_n(f) \right|^2 df}{f} < \infty \tag{3}$$

where $\hat{\Psi}_n(f) = \int_{-\infty}^{\infty} e^{-i\omega t} f(t)dt$ is the Fourier transform of $f(t)$. The finiteness of C_{ψ_n} ensures the conservation of signal energy in both time and transform domain with the wavelet function ψ_n.

Table 1 provides the values of K_n and C_{ψ_n} for $n = 1, 2, 3, 4, 5, 6, 7, 8$.

The first four member of this new wavelet family are given by

$$\psi_1(t) = K_1\frac{1-t^2}{\left(1+t^2\right)^2},$$

$$\psi_2(t) = K_2\frac{2t\left(t^2-3\right)}{\left(t^2+1\right)^3},$$

$$\psi_3(t) = K_3\frac{-6\left(t^4-6t^2+1\right)}{\left(t^2+1\right)^4},$$

$$\psi_4(t) = K_4\frac{24t\left(t^4-10t^2+5\right)}{\left(t^2+1\right)^5}$$

and the corresponding plots are given in Fig. 1. Hence the functions $\psi_k(t)$ forms a family of one dimensional real continuous admissible wavelets.

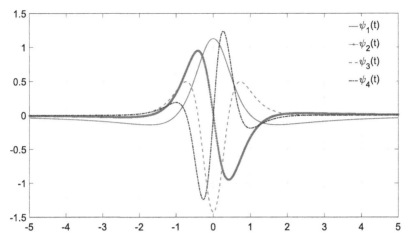

Fig. 1. The First four members of the new wavelet family PoisN.

Table 1. Provides the values of K_n and C_{ψ_n} for $n = 1, 2, 3, 4, 5, 6, 7, 8$.

Wavelet	C_{ψ_k}	N_k
ψ_1	3.1416	1.1284
ψ_2	−1.5708	0.6515
ψ_3	1.0472	0.2379
ψ_4	−0.7854	0.0636
ψ_5	0.6280	0.0134
ψ_6	−0.5088	0.0023
ψ_7	0.4491	0.000346
ψ_8	−0.3926	0.000044652

4   Properties of the Proposed New Wavelet Family

4.1   Support, Symmetry and Regularity

The support width of the family $\psi_k(t)$ is infinite, however the effective support is $[-10, 10]$. The odd members (ψ_1, ψ_3, ...) of the family are symmetric whereas the even members (ψ_2, ψ_4, ...) exhibit rotational symmetry. Finite support (localization) of wavelet in both time and frequency domains is achieved by imposing regularity condition on it. The wavelets defined by ψ_k are infinitely differentiable in domain of R, hence these continuous functions form a family of infinitely regular wavelets i.e., $\psi_k \in C^n$ for all n, where C^n is set of infinitely differentiable continuous functions.

The expression for n^{th} derivative of $\theta(t)$ function is

$$\frac{d^n}{dx^n}\left(\frac{x}{1+x^2}\right) = (-1)^n n! \sum\nolimits_{\alpha=\alpha_i}(x-\alpha_i)^{-1-n} \qquad (4)$$

where α_i is the root of $(z^2 + 1)$ in the complex domain.

4.2 Vanishing Moments

Vanishing moments of $\psi_k(t)$ Are used to describe the approximating power of the $\psi_k(t)$ [16]. Moments of order p for a given $\psi_k(t)$ is given by $m_p^k = \int_{-\infty}^{\infty} t^p \psi_k(t)dt$. It can be clearly observed that the odd members $(\psi_1, \psi_3, \ldots)$ are even functions and even members $(\psi_2, \psi_4, \ldots)$ of the family are odd functions. Hence odd moments of all orders for odd family members vanish and even moments of all orders for even family members vanish.

$$m_p^k = 0, \; if \; mod\,(k - p, 2) = 0 \tag{5}$$

i.e., $m_p^k = 0$ for both k, p are odd or both k, p are even.

4.3 Frequency Decay

Analytical expression for Fourier Transform of the first four members of the family are given by

$$\hat{\Psi}_1(w) = \pi N_1 |w| e^{-|w|},$$

$$\hat{\Psi}_2(w) = i \cdot \pi \cdot N_2 \cdot sign(w) \cdot w^2 e^{-|w|}$$

$$\hat{\Psi}_3(w) = -\pi N_3 |w|^3 e^{-|w|},$$

$$\hat{\Psi}_4(w) = -\frac{\pi i \, N_4 w^2}{sign(w)^2} e^{-|w|} [w^2 sign(w)^3 - 4w \cdot sign(w)^2 + 4w$$
$$+ 12 sign(w)^3 - 12 sign(w)]$$

where $sign(w)$ is the signum function. The frequency response of even members of the family are real whereas for odd members of the family are purely imaginary.

The plot of real parts of $\hat{\Psi}_1(w)$, $\hat{\Psi}_3(w)$ and imaginary parts of $\hat{\Psi}_2(w)$ and $\hat{\Psi}_4(w)$ are shown in Fig. 2.

It may be observed that the frequency response also has compact support and decays exponentially in the small finite interval however this interval tends to increase for higher members of the family.

4.4 Time-Frequency Bandwidth

Time and frequency domains have a inverse relation $(t = 1/\omega)$ i.e., if a signal has compact support in time then its frequency equivalent does not have it, and vice versa. The time-frequency bandwidth is a robust measure of combined time and frequency spread of a signal. It is essentially a property of the shape of a given wavelet function.

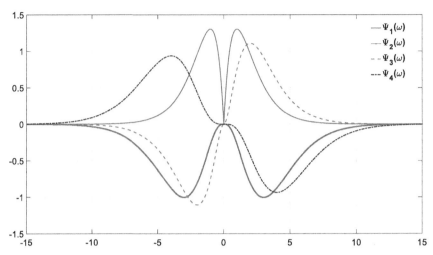

Fig. 2. Fourier Transform of first four members of PoisN wavelet family.

Time-frequency bandwidth is the product of the variance of the signal and variance of its spectral width.

$$\Delta_t^2 * \Delta_\omega^2 = \int_{-\infty}^{\infty} \frac{t^2 |x(t)|^2}{x(t)^2} dt * \int_{-\infty}^{\infty} \frac{\omega^2 |\hat{x}(\omega)|^2}{\|\hat{x}(\omega)\|^2} dt$$

Generally, signals of short duration have wide spectral width and vice versa. Table 2 provides the Time-Frequency products of different members of PoisN and GausN wavelet family. We may observe that Pois1 and Gaus1 have same bandwidth with different time and frequency variances. For higher members (N > 1) of PoisN family the time-frequency product is less than its GausN counterparts but PoisN is more localized in time than GausN.

Table 2. Comparison of Time bandwidth product of PoisN wavelet with existing wavelets

Order	PoisN wavelet			GausN wavelet		
	Δ_t^2	Δ_ω^2	$\Delta_t^2 * \Delta_\omega^2$	Δ_t^2	Δ_ω^2	$\Delta_t^2 * \Delta_\omega^2$
1	1.000	3.0	3.0000	0.7500	3	2.2500
2	0.3333	7.5	2.5000	0.5833	5	2.9165
3	0.2000	14.0	2.8000	0.5500	7	3.8500
4	0.1428	22.5	3.2142	0.5357	9	4.2814
5	0.1111	33.0	3.6667	0.5277	11	5.8056
6	0.0909	45.5	4.1364	0.5227	13	6.7955
7	0.0769	60.0	4.6154	0.5192	15	7.7885
8	0.0666	76.5	5.1000	0.5166	17	8.7833

A comparison showing the plots of Pois1, Mexican hat, Morlet in both time and frequency domains are given in Figs. 3 and 4 respectively. The time band width products of all three wavelets are provided in Table 3.

Table 3. Comparison of time-frequency products

wavelet	Δ_t^2	Δ_ω^2	$\Delta_t^2 * \Delta_\omega^2$
Pois1	1.0	3.0	3.0
Mexican	1.1667	2.5	2.9167
Morlet	0.5000	25.499	12.749

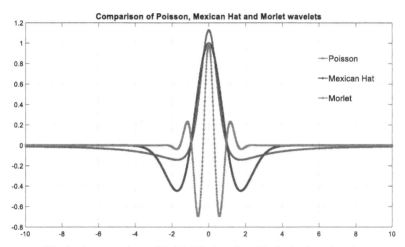

Fig. 3. A comparison of Pois1, Mexican hat, Morlet in time domain.

5 Continuous Wavelet Transform Of Gaussian Distribution with the New Wavelet

The continuous wavelet transform of a continuous time signal $x(t)$, using the any mother wavelet is defined as

$$CT_{x(t)}^{\psi_k}(a, b) = \frac{1}{\sqrt{a}} \int_\infty^\infty x(t) \psi_k \left(\frac{t - b}{a} \right) dt \tag{6}$$

where a is the dilation parameter (scale) of the wavelet and b is the location parameter of the wavelet. The Gaussian function is of the form $G(t : \mu, \sigma) = \frac{1}{\sigma\sqrt{2\pi}} e^{-\frac{(t-\mu)^2}{2\sigma^2}}$ with mean μ and standard deviation σ. The continuous wavelet transform of $G(t : \mu, \sigma)$ is given by

$$CT_{G(t:\mu,\sigma)}^{\psi_k}(a, b) = \frac{1}{\sigma\sqrt{2a\pi}} \int_\infty^\infty e^{-\frac{(t-\mu)^2}{2\sigma^2}} \psi_k \left(\frac{t - b}{a} \right) dt$$

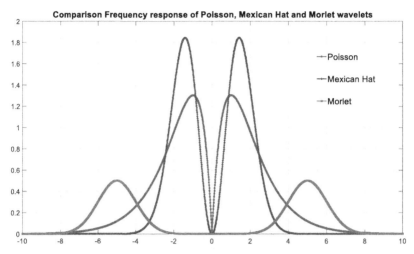

Fig. 4. A comparison of Pois1, Mexican hat, Morlet in frequency domain.

substituting $\frac{t-\mu}{\sigma} = x \Rightarrow \frac{dt}{\sigma} = dx$

$$= \frac{1}{\sqrt{2a\pi}} \int_{\infty}^{\infty} e^{-\frac{x^2}{2}} \psi_k \left(\frac{\sigma x - (b-\mu)}{a} \right) dx$$

$$= \frac{1}{\sqrt{\sigma}} \int_{\infty}^{\infty} \frac{1}{\sqrt{2\pi}} e^{-\frac{x^2}{2}} \frac{1}{\sqrt{a/\sigma}} \psi_k \left(\frac{x - (b-\mu)/\sigma}{a/\sigma} \right) dx$$

Let $\frac{a}{\sigma} = a'$ and $\frac{b-\mu}{\sigma} = b' \Rightarrow a = \sigma a', b = \sigma b' + \mu$

$$= \frac{1}{\sqrt{\sigma}} \int_{\infty}^{\infty} \frac{1}{\sqrt{2\pi}} e^{-\frac{x^2}{2}} \frac{1}{\sqrt{a'}} \psi_k \left(\frac{x - b'}{a'} \right) dx$$

$$= \frac{1}{\sqrt{\sigma}} \int_{\infty}^{\infty} G(t : 0, 1) \frac{1}{\sqrt{a'}} \psi_k \left(\frac{x - b'}{a'} \right) dx$$

$$= \frac{1}{\sqrt{\sigma}} CT_{G(t:0,1)}^{\psi_k} \left(a', b' \right)$$

Therefore the coefficients $CT_{G(t:\mu,\sigma)}^{\psi_k}(a, b)$ and σ of Gaussian function $G(t : \mu, \sigma)$ are related by

$$CT_{G(t:\mu,\sigma)}^{\psi_k} \left(a'\sigma, \mu + b'\sigma \right) = \frac{1}{\sqrt{\sigma}} CT_{G(t:0,1)}^{\psi_k} \left(a', b' \right) \tag{7}$$

a special case when $\mu = 0$, Eq. (7) provides a relation between scaled wavelet coefficients

$$CT_{G(t:0,\sigma)}^{\psi_k} \left(a'\sigma, b'\sigma \right) = \frac{1}{\sqrt{\sigma}} CT_{G(t:0,1)}^{\psi_k} \left(a', b' \right) \tag{8}$$

Figure 5 show the plots of $CT_{G(t:\mu,\sigma)}^{\psi_1}$ for $\sigma = 0.25, 0.5, 0.75, 1$ and $\mu = 0$.

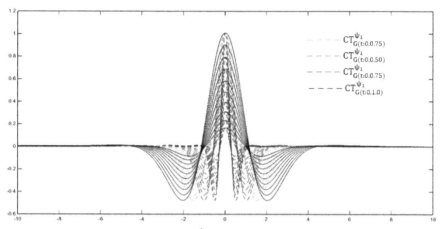

Fig. 5. The plot of the coefficients $CT^{\psi_k}_{G(t:\mu,\sigma)}(a,b)$ for $\mu = 0, \sigma = 0.25, 0.5, 0.75, 1.0$

5.1 Effect on Wavelet Coefficients of Gaussian Function

It is clear from the above relation and the coefficient plots that the curves corresponding to each scale a' is symmetric about μ. So the value of μ can be estimated from the point of symmetry.

To compute the value of σ, rewriting Eq. (8) by substituting $b' = 0$ we get

$$\sqrt{\sigma}\left|CT^{\psi_k}_{G(t:0,\sigma)}(a'\sigma,0)\right| = \left|CT^{\psi_k}_{G(t:0,1)}(a',0)\right|$$

$$\Rightarrow \sqrt{\sigma} = \frac{\left|CT^{\psi_k}_{G(t:0,1)}(a',0)\right|}{\left|CT^{\psi_k}_{G(t:0,\sigma)}(a'\sigma,0)\right|} \tag{9}$$

Wavelet transform of the Gaussian and noisy Gaussian function are computed with the third member of PoisN, i.e., ψ_3 for $a' = 32$. Noisy Gaussian is simulated using "awgn" function of Matlab with known parameters. It is found that the PSNR of the coefficients obtained with and without noise turns out to be approximately the SNR of the noise added to the Gaussian function.

The estimation of σ becomes poor when the SNR is drops beyond 50%. Table 4 provides the estimated σ with different values of SNR. Observe that the estimation of σ for higher values of SNR is very poor and this estimation improves with decreasing values of SNR as expected.

Figure 6 shows the plot of noisy Gaussian for different values of SNR from 10 to 100 in steps of 10.

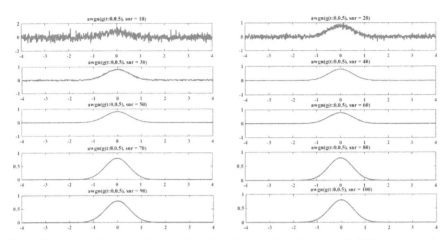

Fig. 6. The plots of the noisy Gaussian function with $\sigma = 0.5$ and $\mu = 0$ with SNR values varying from 10 to 100 in steps of 10.

Table 4. Estimated σ using ψ_3 wavelet for different SNR values

SNR in dB	Estimated σ
10	0.502
20	0.5019
30	0.5014
40	0.5031
50	0.502
60	0.5269
70	0.4537
80	0.3548
90	0.2309
100	2.0986

6 Conclusion

In this study we have constructed a new wavelet family derived from Poisson kernel. Formulated a relationship between the CWT coefficients of Gaussian function with and without noise. Vanishing moments, Frequency response and time-frequency bandwidth properties of the new wavelet are also studied. A comparison between the new wavelet family PoisN and Gaussian wavelet family GausN was studied and summarized in the following table.

Property	Gaussian family	Poisson family
Wavelet name	GausN	PoisN
Orthogonal	No	No
Biorthogonal	No	No
Compact support	No	No
DWT	No	No
CWT	Possible	Possible
Support width	Infinite	Infinite
Effective support	[-5 5]	[-10, 10]
Symmetry	Yes n even $\Rightarrow$ Symmetry n odd $\Rightarrow$ Anti-Symmetry	Yes n odd $\Rightarrow$ Symmetry n even $\Rightarrow$ Anti-Symmetry

References

1. Daubechies, I.: The wavelets transform, time frequency localization and signal analysis. IEEE Trans. Inform. Theory **36**(6), 9611005 (1990)
2. Leal, A.S., Paiva, H.M.: A new wavelet family for speckle noise reduction in medical ultrasound images. Measurement **140**, 572–581 (2019)
3. Zhang, Q., Benveniste, A.: Wavelet networks. IEEE Trans. Neural Netw. **3**(6), 889–898 (1992)
4. Liu, P., Zhang, H., Lian, W., Zuo, W.: Multi-level wavelet convolutional neural networks. IEEE Access **7**, 74973–74985 (2019)
5. Yger, F., Rakotomamonjy, A.: Wavelet kernel learning. Pattern Recogn. **44**(10–11), 2614–2629 (2011)
6. Ramziyz, Z., Starck, J.-L., Moreauy, T., Ciuciuyz, P.: Wavelets in the deep learning era. In: EUSIPCO, pp. 1417–1421 (2020). 978-9-0827-9705-3
7. Uddin, Z., Ganga, S., Asthana, R., Ibrahim, W.: Wavelets based physics informed neural networks to solve non-linear differential equations. Sci. Reports **13**, 2882 (2023)
8. Antoine, J.-P., Murenzi, R., Vandergheynst, P., Ali, S.T.: Two-Dimensional Wavelets and their Relatives. Cambridge University Press, New York (2004)
9. Rayeezuddin, M., Krishna Reddy, B., Sudheer Reddy, D.: Performance of reconstruction factors for a class of new complex continuous wavelets. Int. J. Wavelets, Multiresolut. Inform. Process. **19**(02), 2050067 (2020)
10. Nigam, H.K., Mohapatra, R.N., Murari, K.: Wavelet approximation of a function using Chebyshev wavelets. J. Inequal. Appl. **2020**, 187 (2020)
11. Vidakovic, B.: Statistical Modeling with Wavelets. Wiley (1990)
12. Ashurov, R., Butaev, A.: On continuous wavelet transforms of distributions. Appl. Math. Lett. **24**, 1578–1583 (2011)
13. Holschneider, M.: Wavelets in Geosciences, Lecture Notes in Earth Sciences. Springer Verlag, Berling (2000)
14. Stephane Mallat, W.L., Hwang,: Singularity detection and processing with wavelets. IEEE Trans. Inform. Theory **38**, 617–643 (1992)
15. Wavelet Toolbox of Matlab® from www.mathworks.com
16. Damelin, S.B., Miller, W., Jr.: The Mathematics of Signal Processing. Cambridge University Press, New York (2012)

17. Daubechies, I.: Orthogonal bases of compactly supported wavelets. Commun. Pure Appl. Math. **41**, 909–996 (1988)
18. Zhang, L., Zhou, W.D., Jiao, L.C.: Wavelet support vector machine. IEEE Trans. Syst. Man Cybern. B Cybern. **34**(1), 34–39 (2004)

Centrality Measures Based Heuristics for Perfect Awareness Problem in Social Networks

Rahul Kumar Gautam$^{(\boxtimes)}$ (ORCID), Anjeneya Swami Kare (ORCID), and S. Durga Bhavani (ORCID)

School of Computer and Information Sciences, University of Hyderabad,
Hyderabad, India
{19mcpc06,askcs,sdbcs}@uohyd.ac.in

Abstract. Social networks are used extensively for advertising, political campaigning, and spreading awareness. Usually, there is an underlying diffusion model using which the information spreads between the nodes. The Independent cascade and Linear threshold models are some of the most popular diffusion models. This paper considers an information/awareness-spreading problem called the Perfect Awareness problem. Initially, all the nodes are assumed to be not aware of the information. Information is passed to a few specific influential nodes, which are called seed nodes, who spread the information to their neighbors. When a node receives a message for the first time, it becomes *aware* of the information. However, it does not pass on the message immediately till it receives the same message from a sufficient number of neighbors. Then it becomes a *spreader* node that spreads the information to its neighbors. The model of diffusion adopted here is the linear threshold model. This problem is formally known as the perfect awareness problem. The main objective is to find a seed set of minimum cardinality such that at the end of the diffusion process, all the network nodes are aware of the information.

In this paper, we propose heuristics based on centrality measures such as degree centrality, eigenvector centrality, betweenness, closeness, and page rank for the perfect awareness problem. The experimentation is carried out on 20 data sets, including a large network with 1.1 million nodes. The proposed heuristics yield, on average 15% improvement, the best-being 38.5% in the seed set size compared to the existing heuristics.

1 Introduction

Nowadays, to grow a business, advertisements have become a tool to reach most people within a short time. People are well-connected through social media. Communication happens through social media, which is an extensive network of people. Such information spreading can be seen in many applications, such as election campaigns, disaster response initiatives, and even during the recent management of Covid-pandemic. For example, during an election campaign, a significant challenge for contestants of the election is to spread their ideas rapidly

R. Morusupalli et al. (Eds.): MIWAI 2023, LNAI 14078, pp. 91–100, 2023.
https://doi.org/10.1007/978-3-031-36402-0_8

on social networks. A few influential people who can influence the maximum number of people are selected explicitly in the network. Here the diffusion model of spreading needs to be considered. A few well-known diffusion models are the linear threshold and independent cascade models. We adopt the linear threshold model for diffusion, using this perfect awareness problem is described.

The social network is modeled as a graph $G(V, E)$, where V and E are sets of vertices and edges, respectively. Each node is assigned a positive integer as a threshold value. We denote the threshold value of v as $t(v)$. The information needs to be spread to all the vertices of graph G. Initially, all the vertices of the graph are not *aware* of the information. A seed set $S \subseteq V$ is selected to spread the information. The neighbors of each *seed* node $v \in S$ immediately become *aware* of the information. We call the informed vertices "aware" vertices. The set A contains all the aware vertices of the graph G. It is obvious that $S \subseteq A$. In subsequent steps, if a node $v \notin S$ has k number of spreader neighbors and $k \geq t(v)$, then v becomes a spreader. The process stops when all vertices $v \in V$ become aware. This is called the perfect awareness problem. The objective is to minimize the size of the seed set S.

We propose efficient heuristics for perfect awareness problem based on the centrality measures defined in social networks. Heuristics based on centrality measures have been proposed for related problems like graph burning [7,12,18], and rumor minimization [17]. To the best of our knowledge, centrality measures have not been used for perfect awareness problem.

2   Related Work

Kempe et al. first defined the problem of maximization of influence in social networks [8,9]. They proposed two fundamental diffusion models: the independent cascade and linear threshold models. Chen et al. [3] proved that influence maximization is NP-Hard. Further, they proved that influence maximization is hard to approximate within a poly-logarithmic factor. The influence maximization problem is also referred to as the target set selection (TSS) problem. Many new variants of the TSS problem have been proposed. Cordasco et al. [5] have studied evangelism in social networks. Recently, Liang et al. [11] studied target set selection problems in competitive social networks. The difference is that as the spread of information is being maximized, the competitor also spreads its information. The competitor can block the contagion of the spreader. The goal is to spread the information to a maximum number of vertices of the target set.

Using the linear threshold diffusion model, Cordasco et al. [4] defined the perfect awareness (PA) problem. They provide a polynomial time algorithm for trees and propose a heuristic for general graphs. In the recent paper on perfect awareness, Pereira et al. [14] proposed heuristics based on genetic algorithms for general graphs.

This paper proposes heuristics based on centrality measures such as degree centrality, eigenvector centrality, betweenness centrality, closeness centrality, and page rank to address the perfect awareness problem.

3 Centrality Based Heuristics

The centrality measures in social networks retrieve influential nodes in the network. For example, degree centrality locates high-degree nodes; the nodes with high closeness centrality are at a low average distance to all the network nodes. Hence we believe that nodes with high centrality values may be good candidates for the seed nodes for the Perfect awareness problem.

A social network graph $G(V, E, t)$ is given where V and E are sets of vertices and edges, respectively, and t is a threshold function, $t : V \to \mathbb{N}$. The algorithm has two phases. In the first phase, we compute the potential seed set, and in the second phase, we use a greedy pruning technique to remove redundant vertices from the potential seed set to obtain the final seed set.

3.1 Computing Potential Seed Set

We compute the centrality of each vertex $v \in V$ and rank the nodes in non-increasing order according to their centrality, and this sequence is stored in the array K. For each vertex $u \in K$, the diffusion process is activated after including the vertex u in the seed set. If $u \in K$ gives at least one new aware node, we mark the vertex u as a spreader and add u to the potential seed set $\hat{S}$. This process is repeated until all the nodes of the graph become aware. The steps of the algorithm are illustrated below.

- Input: $G = (V, E, t)$.
- Initially, all vertices of the graph G are not aware and the potential seed set $\hat{S} = \emptyset$.
- Compute centrality for each vertex of the graph and order the vertices in decreasing order of centrality. Let this list be K.
- For each vertex $u \in K$, run the diffusion function with the seed sets $\hat{S}$ and $\hat{S} \cup \{u\}$ respectively. If the diffusion calls $\hat{S} \cup \{u\}$ gives more aware nodes than with only $\hat{S}$, then u is added to the potential seed set $\hat{S}$. On
- The above step is repeated until all graph vertices become aware.
- Output: Potential seed set $\hat{S}$.

Note that this algorithm runs the diffusion function twice, which increases the algorithm's running time. We suggest an efficient implementation for the algorithm given in Algorithm 1 using the *Incremental diffusion* function given in Algorithm 2.

3.2 Pruning of Potential Seed Set

After computing the potential seed set $\hat{S}$, we apply the greedy pruning technique to reduce the seed set's size further. We explain with an example why the pruning technique is useful. Consider the graph in Fig. 1. Using degree centrality, we get the potential seed set as $\hat{S} = [a, c, d, b]$. The threshold of a is 3, and even if we remove a from $\hat{S}$, all the vertices are still aware. With this, we get a perfect awareness set of reduced size. This technique is called pruning.

Algorithm 1: Computing the potential seed set $\hat{S}$

Input : $G = (V, E, t)$.
Output: Potential seed set $\hat{S}$.

1 GETPOTSEEDSET(G) **begin**
2 | $\hat{S} \leftarrow \phi$;
3 | $I \leftarrow \phi$;
4 | $A \leftarrow \phi$;
5 | $K \leftarrow$ DECREASING-ORD-OF-CENTRALITY($V(G)$);
6 | **for** $u \in K$ **do**
7 | | **if** $u \in I$ **then**
8 | | | $continue$;
9 | | $(I', A') \leftarrow$ INCRE-DIFFUSION($G, \hat{S}, u, I, A$);
10 | | **if** $|A'| > |A|$ **then**
11 | | | $\hat{S} \leftarrow \hat{S} \cup \{u\}$;
12 | | | $I \leftarrow I'$;
13 | | | $A \leftarrow A'$;
14 | | **if** $|A| = |V|$ **then**
15 | | | **return** $\hat{S}$

Algorithm 2: Incremental Diffusion Function

Input : Graph $G = (V, E, t)$, Seed set S, vertex u, aware set A and
           intermediate spreaders I.
Output: Intermediate spreaders I and Aware set A.

1 INCRE-DIFFUSION(G, S, u, I, A) **begin**
2 | $L \leftarrow [\,]$
3 | $S' = S \cup I \cup \{u\}$
4 | **for** $v \in S'$ **do**
5 | | $append(L, v)$
6 | **while** $empty(L) = False$ **do**
7 | | $v = removeFirst(L)$
8 | | **for** $w \in N(v)$ **do**
9 | | | $A \leftarrow A \cup \{w\}$
10 | | | $S \leftarrow \{x | x \in N(w) \cap S'\}$
11 | | | **if** $t(w) \leq |S|$ and $w \notin S'$ **then**
12 | | | | $I \leftarrow I \cup \{w\}$
13 | | | | $S' \leftarrow S' \cup \{w\}$
14 | | | | $append(L, w)$
15 | **return** (I, A)

The pruning technique works as follows: For each vertex u, we compute the number of neighbors which are spreader nodes $m(u)$. A list K is formed by adding vertices in $\hat{S}$ in decreasing order with respect to $m(u)$. For each vertex

$u \in K$, we check if $\hat{S}\backslash\{u\}$ is a perfect awareness set or not. If $\hat{S}\backslash\{u\}$ is a perfect awareness set then we remove u from $\hat{S}$. The process is repeated for all vertices in K. At the end of the pruning process, we get the final seed set. The algorithm for the pruning process is shown in Algorithm 3.

Algorithm 3: Pruning Technique

Input : $G = (V, E, t)$, Potential seed set $\hat{S}$.
Output: The Seed set S.

1 PRUNING$(G, \hat{S})$ **begin**
2     $K \leftarrow$ VERTICES-DECRE-ORD-SPDEGREE$(\hat{S})$
3   **for** $u \in K$ **do**
4        $S' \leftarrow \hat{S}$
5        $S' \leftarrow S'\backslash\{u\}$
6        $A' \leftarrow$ DIFFUSION(G, S')
7   **if** $|A'| = |V|$ **then**
8           $\hat{S} \leftarrow S'$
9   **return** $\hat{S}$

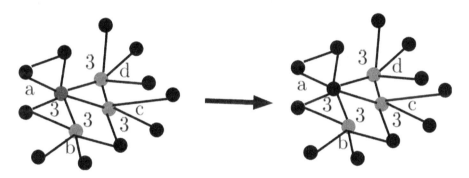

Fig. 1. The potential seed set $(\hat{S}) = \{a, b, c, d\}$. The pruning function returns the final seed set as $\{b, c, d\}$

4 Results and Discussion

We have implemented Algorithm 1 with the following centrality measures: Degree, Eigenvector, Closeness, Betweenness, and Page rank centrality. We explain these centrality measures briefly:

Degree centrality (DC): The centrality of a node is the number of its neighbors. The node with more neighbors has a chance of spreading to more neighbors.

Eigenvector centrality (EC): Bonacich et al. [2] first proposed Eigenvector centrality for graphs. The problem with degree centrality does not consider neighbors of neighbors and how much they are essential. On the other hand, Eigenvector centrality considers neighbors of neighbors as well.

Closeness centrality (CC): The closeness centrality [1] measures how close a vertex is to the rest of the vertices. In other words, the closeness centrality of v is the inverse of the average sum of the distance from v to the rest of the vertices. Choosing a node with more closeness centrality as the spreader may help to make more nodes aware.

Betweenness centrality (BC): The betweenness centrality [6] of v measures how many shortest paths between pairs of vertices pass through v.

Page rank centrality (PR): Page rank algorithm [13] is a popular algorithm that gives influential nodes in a directed network. These influential nodes can be good candidates for spreaders.

We have done experimentation on two sets of data sets. The first set contains {Karate Club, ca-HepPh, ca-HepTh, ca-GrQc, jazz, power grid, BlogCatalog, and Facebook} which are chosen so that the experimental results can be compared with existing heuristics [4,14] and the results are shown in Table 1. Additionally, we consider other popular data sets from Network Data Repository [16] and SNAP data set [10], which includes a large data set of size $54K$ and the results are shown in Table 2. The results are also shown in plots which are shown in Figs. 2a, 2b, and 2c.

As can be seen from Table 1, Degree centrality (DC) is performing well on most of the data sets by giving the smallest seed set. The proposed heuristics achieve an average improvement of 15% when compared to the known heuristics GR [4] and CGR [14]. Among the two heuristics, GR and CGR, GR is performing better than CGR, and hence the percentage of improvement is calculated with respect to GR. It can be noted that on the data set *BlogCatalog* of size more than $10K$, our degree centrality-based heuristic is giving an improvement of 37.5% and on textitjazz, a small data set, all our heuristics give 38% improvement over GR.

In the additional experimentation given Table 2 conducted on data sets from Network Data Repository [16] and SNAP Data set [10], heuristics based on Degree centrality and Page rank are giving better results among our heuristics. The code is not publicly available for GR and CGR. As GR is a genetic algorithm-based heuristic and the experimental parameters chosen are not known, we could not do the experimentation on these data sets.

Additionally, to validate heuristics and the pruning procedure, We implemented a Degree centrality heuristic on the large data set Youtube [15] of size $1.1M$ vertices. The size of the potential seed set obtained by the degree centrality heuristic is 39419, and upon applying the pruning procedure, the seed set was reduced to 34880, showing nearly 8.8% improvement.

Table 1. The size of the seed sets obtained by our proposed heuristics based on the centrality measures: EC, DC PR CC, and BC are given on real-world data sets, and the comparison is carried out with the known heuristics GR and CGR.

	|V|	|E|	CGR [4]	GR [14]	EC	DC	PR	CC	BC	IMP
Karate	34	78	3	3	3	3	3	3	3	0%
CA-HepPh	12008	0.11M	1610	1243	915	920	**914**	924	979	26.4%
CA-HepTh	9877	25K	1531	1164	1056	**1043**	1044	1063	1071	10.4%
CA-GrQc	5242	14K	897	769	735	**727**	728	735	736	5.5%
jazz	198	2.7K	15	13	8	8	8	8	8	38.5%
power grid	4941	6.5K	1367	602	583	**561**	569	588	581	6.9%
BlogCatalog	10312	0.33M	221	208	131	**130**	130	140	149	37.5%
Facebook	4039	88K	10	10	10	10	10	10	10	0%

Table 2. Comparison of results among our proposed heuristics on additional data sets

Network Source	Name	|V|	|E|	EC	DC	PR	CC	BC
Network Data Repository [16]	Netscience	379	914	43	43	43	43	43
	Polblogs	643	2K	64	62	61	67	68
	Reed98	962	18K	107	85	87	90	85
	Mahandas	1258	7513	47	32	28	36	30
SNAP Data [10]	Chameleon	2.2K	31.4K	82	77	77	76	77
	TV show	3.8K	17.2K	406	401	395	412	413
	Squirrel	5K	198K	178	212	207	226	201
	Politician	5.9K	41.7K	354	333	341	371	371
	Government	7K	89.4K	374	345	353	378	414
	Musae-Crocodile	11K	170K	234	209	208	236	229
	Gemsec-Deezer(HR)	54K	498K	2445	2189	2233	2365	2465

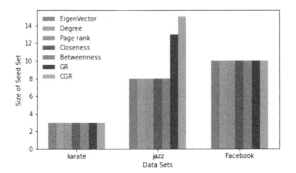

(a) Comparing results with GR [14] and CGR [4] algorithms with our algorithms.

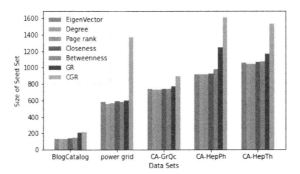

(b) Comparing results with GR [14] and CGR [4] algorithms with our algorithms.

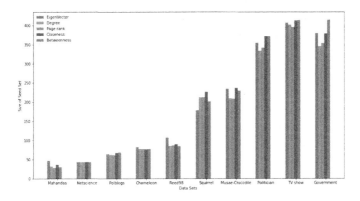

(c) Experimentation on additional data sets to compare the proposed heuristics.

Fig. 2. Experimental results on different data sets.

5   Conclusion

There are not many heuristics available for the Perfect awareness problem. Centrality measures in social networks proved to be good candidates for heuristics in influence spread problems and other related problems. In this work, we presented heuristics based on 5 centrality measures for the perfect awareness problem. Further, we added a greedy pruning procedure to make the heuristics more effective. The results obtained by these heuristics show a significant reduction in the seed set size compared to the known heuristics. The Degree centrality heuristic was the fastest and showed promising results on most data sets. The Closeness centrality and Betweenness centrality did not scale well for large data sets. In the future, we would like to investigate graph structure-based heuristics for the perfect awareness problem.

References

1. Bavelas, A.: Communication patterns in task-oriented groups. J. Acoust. Soc. Am. **22**(6), 725–730 (1950)
2. Bonacich, P.: Factoring and weighting approaches to status scores and clique identification. J. Math. Sociol. **2**(1), 113–120 (1972)
3. Chen, N.: On the approximability of influence in social networks. SIAM J. Discret. Math. **23**(3), 1400–1415 (2009)
4. Cordasco, G., Gargano, L., Rescigno, A.A.: Active influence spreading in social networks. Theor. Comput. Sci. **764**, 15–29 (2019)
5. Cordasco, G., Gargano, L., Rescigno, A.A., Vaccaro, U.: Evangelism in social networks: algorithms and complexity. Networks **71**(4), 346–357 (2018)
6. Freeman, L.C.: A set of measures of centrality based on betweenness. Sociometry 35–41 (1977)
7. Gautam, R.K., Kare, A.S., S., D.B.: Faster heuristics for graph burning. Appl. Intell. **52**(2), 1351–1361 (2021). https://doi.org/10.1007/s10489-021-02411-5
8. Kempe, D., Kleinberg, J., Tardos, É.: Maximizing the spread of influence through a social network. In: Proceedings of the Ninth ACM SIGKDD International Conference on Knowledge Discovery and Data Mining, pp. 137–146 (2003)
9. Kempe, D., Kleinberg, J., Tardos, É.: Influential nodes in a diffusion model for social networks. In: Caires, L., Italiano, G.F., Monteiro, L., Palamidessi, C., Yung, M. (eds.) ICALP 2005. LNCS, vol. 3580, pp. 1127–1138. Springer, Heidelberg (2005). https://doi.org/10.1007/11523468_91
10. Leskovec, J., Krevl, A.: SNAP Datasets: Stanford large network dataset collection (2014). http://snap.stanford.edu/data
11. Liang, Z., He, Q., Hongwei, D., Wen, X.: Targeted influence maximization in competitive social networks. Inf. Sci. **619**, 390–405 (2023)
12. Nazeri, M., Mollahosseini, A., Izadi, I.: A centrality based genetic algorithm for the graph burning problem. Available at SSRN 4224314 (2022)
13. Page, L., Brin, S., Motwani, R., Winograd, T.: The pagerank citation ranking: bringing order to the web (1999). http://dbpubs.stanford.edu:8090/aux/index-en.html
14. Pereira, F.C., de Rezende, P.J., de Souza, C.C.: Effective heuristics for the perfect awareness problem. Procedia Comput. Sci. **195**, 489–498 (2021)

15. Reza, Z., Huan, L.: Social computing data repository (2009). http://datasets.syr. edu/pages/datasets.html
16. Rossi, R.A., Ahmed, N.K.: The network data repository with interactive graph analytics and visualization. In: AAAI (2015). https://networkrepository.com
17. Yang, L., Li, Z., Giua, A.: Containment of rumor spread in complex social networks. Inf. Sci. **506**, 113–130 (2020)
18. Šimon, M., Huraj, L., Luptáková, I., Pospíchal, J.: Heuristics for spreading alarm throughout a network. Appl. Sci. **9**, 3269 (2019)

Re-examining Class Selectivity in Deep Convolutional Networks

Akshay Badola$^{(\boxtimes)}$ ⓘ, Vineet Padmanabhan ⓘ, and Rajendra Prasad Lal

School of Computer and Information Sciences, University of Hyderabad,
Prof C R Rao Road, Gachibowli, Hyderabad 500046, India
{badola,vineetnair,rajendraprasad}@uohyd.ac.in

Abstract. While Deep Neural Networks have become ubiquitous, some of their properties have remained elusive. Among these is class selectivity, which measures the association of a unit of a model to its inputs and outputs. Current literature is split on the effect of class selectivity of CNNs as some have determined it to be harmful for generalization, while others have found it to be beneficial. The results of such analyses can vary widely with the definition of selectivity used as there is no consensus on it. In this work, we provide a new flexible definition of class selectivity towards rectifying this discrepancy, which can better describe the network's association with a class at various layers. We compare with the standard class selectivity metric and associated regularizer. We show experimentally that our proposed metric quantifies selectivity in a more consistent manner. We also dispel the notion that selectivity is harmful for generalization by showing that evaluation results do not change by increasing selectivity. We also analyze the association between selectivity, feature disentanglement, and decomposability and show that selectivity and filter disentanglement are complementary. Finally, we also provide the source code for all our experiments.

Keywords: Deep Learning · Convolutional Neural Networks · Class Selectivity · Disentanglement

1 Introduction

Deep Convolutional Networks [1–3] have become a mainstay of modern Computer Vision. Various methods involving Deep CNNs give state-of-the-art results on most Computer Vision tasks [4,5] and they are still extremely popular despite the emergence of Vision Transformer [6] family of models because of their simplicity and the fact that they do not require pre-training on large corpora.

The inner workings of CNNs however, are still poorly understood even as the overall principles are obvious. Certain properties like Generalization [7], Adversarial Examples [8,9], and Overparametrization [10,11] are an active area of research.

© The Author(s), under exclusive license to Springer Nature Switzerland AG 2023
R. Morusupalli et al. (Eds.): MIWAI 2023, LNAI 14078, pp. 101–111, 2023.
https://doi.org/10.1007/978-3-031-36402-0_9

Another such property is class selectivity. Class selectivity is broadly understood as the *preference* of a single *unit* towards examples of a given class. The definition itself of *preference* and *unit* can vary in the literature. Overall it means that certain weights of the network are activated more strongly when they encounter examples of a given class.

Preference is defined as the activity of a given neuron or filter. Some of the different definitions in existing literature are: (1) Class Correlation [12,13], (2) Class Selectivity [14,15] (3) Concept Alignment [16] (4) Class Specificity [17,18].

The definition of a unit on the other hand usually restricts to individual weight or *neuron* in the case of MLP, a single *cell* in the case of LSTMs and a convolutional filter in the case of CNNs. In this work, we will focus on CNNs. A *unit* will refer to a single convolutional filter in some layer of the Convolutional Neural Network.

2   Related Work

Examples of early work on selectivity include [19] who tried to maximize the effect of an activation in a Deep Belief Networks [20]. Coates et al. [21] attempted to train *selective* features which they combined to form invariant image features. Later work focused on the semantic nature of filters emerging while discriminative training of Convolutional Neural Networks [8,22,23].

Morcos et al. [14] were the first to examine the phenomenon of class selectivity in CNNs and they termed it as *single directions*. Leavitt et al. [15] built upon that work and argued that selectivity is harmful and demonstrated that reducing selectivity does not harm or even increases performance.

However, the opinion on the effect of class selectivity in CNNs is still split and [24] conducted a comparison of various selectivity metrics prevalent in literature; including those given by [14,15] and augmented that with human participants to show that current selectivity metrics do not provide an accurate picture of its purported role in training and generalization.

Work pertaining selectivity has percolated to transformers [25] but it is not as active an area of research there due to complex interactions in transformers.

2.1   Motivation and Contributions

From our survey, we can glean that a consensus on an effective definition of class selectivity does not exist and existing metrics can be misleading [24]. To address this, we examine the shortcomings of existing methods and provide a new metric which we term as **Layerwise Class Selectivity** which we denote by Ψ_k. Compared to [17,18], our metric is applicable for all layers of a CNN. Unlike [14,15] our metric measures selectivity across a layer and gives a clearer picture of a filter's selectivity towards a class. We also provide the source code of all our experiments.[1].

---

[1] The code can be found at https://github.com/akshaybadola/class_specific_cnn.

In summary, our contributions are:

– We provide a new metric of class selectivity and demonstrate its efficacy with experiments on popular CNN architectures.
– We show that it is more consistent than existing standard selectivity metric given in [15].
– We give insight into network generalization and reach the opposite conclusion of prevalent notion that selectivity is harmful [14] for network generalization.
– We make available source code of our experiments.

3   Role of Class Selectivity

The notion of class selectivity has been inspired by findings from neuroscience. See e.g., [26] and [27] for a brief recount of the topic. The hypothesis being that certain neurons in the brain associate very strongly with certain phenomena in the real world. These neurons came to be known as "grandmother" cells.

Thinking analogously to the human brain, similar associations with weights or filters in Neural Networks were investigated by [14,21] etc. However, the idea seems to have come full circle where now, selective units are more evident in DNNs than in the human brain [28].

It can be reasoned that class selectivity in some measures would be present across networks. Its extact role though, is not clear. Recent work [14,15] has suggested that it generally harms the performance of Deep CNNs. But the consensus is not there with [17,18] showing that it does not affect the network and aids in interpretability. Gale et al. [24], instead argue that the metrics are misleading. A consensus on the matter has not emerged, however.

A more detailed survey of selectivity measures in CNNs is given in [24]. They describe:

– **Localist Selectivity:** The set of activations for class A that are disjoint than those for $\neg A$
– **Top Class Selectivity:** Activity for class i which is greater than that of others: That is, for $A_i > A_{\neq i}$, divide the number of those images with the rest $|A_i|/|A_{\neq i}|$
– **Precision:** Find small subset of images that strongly activate the filter. Precision for class x is determined manually as $x/|X|$
– **Class conditional mean activation (CCMAS):** Used by [14,15]
  $\mu_{SI} = \frac{\mu_A - \mu_{\neg A}}{\mu_A + \mu_{\neg A}}$ where μ_A is the mean activation of a filter for class A.

Of the aforementioned, Class Conditional Mean Activation (CCMAS) is the most popular in literature. It was investigated in depth by Morcos et al. [14] and then by Leavitt et al. [15] in an attempt to identify class selectivity in CNNs. Gale et al. [24] and [13] also studied it with differing results. Leavitt [15] also defined a selectivity regularizer to try to decrease selectivity and showed that decreasing selectivity did not change or increase network performance. But in contrast [13] concluded with the same methods that ablating a single unit does not catastrophically affect the decision for a given class, but instead ablating **many filters together** hurts the performance more.

As such, we can identify the following shortcomings with the above approaches:

1. Gale et al. [24] only recorded the activations of correctly classified images.
2. Morcos et al. [14] and [15] consider the filters individually, while it stands to reason that they should be measured as combinations along a layer.

We argue that one cannot examine the filters in isolation. At each CNN layer, a linear combination of filters is input to each filter in the next layer, hence they all interact together and thus selectivity must be considered on a layer as a whole. Instead, we propose to group highly selective filters for a given class together.

3.1   Layerwise Class Selectivity

As stated above, We argue that selectivity cannot be measured in isolation and that a layer of a CNN has to be evaluated to measure effective selectivity. Therefore, we examine filters at a given layer together. But notably we focus on the outputs from the filters and not the weights themselves.

To analyze the activations at a given layer we gather the outputs at that layer. Since the outputs from CNN filters are 4-way tensors (first axis being the batch), we sum the last two axes to arrive at a 2-way tensor or a matrix to get a $b \times d$ dimensional matrix $\mathbf{X}$, where b is the batch size.

Let $\mathbf{x}_l^c$ be one such output vector from layer l for a single input image of class c to the CNN. So that $\mathbf{X}_l^c$ is the combined output for *all* the images in the dataset for a particular class c at layer l. Denote $x_{i,l}^c$ as the ith component of the vector $\mathbf{x}_l^c$ at layer l. Without loss of generality, we will drop the subscript l for clarity for the rest of the section.

Now consider d dimensional vector $\mathbf{x}^c$. Due to the use of ReLU, all its outputs are >0. Now, if we sort $\mathbf{x}^c$ by its ℓ_1 norm (or ℓ_2 norm, but we use ℓ_1 norm for simplicity), the components with the highest norm are the highest activated components. If this large activation is concentrated in a few components of this vector for a particular class *and* the set of these components are different than that for other classes, then these components are *selective* for this particular class c.

We can then proceed to define our proposed metric Layerwise Class Selectivity Ψ_k. We first note that selectivity of examples of a given class would be high if a *small fraction* of the indices for which the activation of $\mathbf{x}^c$ is the greatest. Let $k \in (0, 1)$.

We can normalize the components of $\mathbf{x}^c$ without changing their relative weight. Define normalized vector $\mathbf{s}^c = \frac{\sum x_i^c}{|\mathbf{x}^c|}$ Our aim is then to find the minimum number of indices such that the fraction of norm for $\mathbf{s}^c > k$. We call those indices selective indices SI.

We can easily find that by sorting vector $\mathbf{x}^c$ along its components. However, this number increases if a greater fraction of the components for $\mathbf{x}^c$ contain high activation and decreases otherwise. We define selectivity for a data point $\mathbf{x}^c$ as *(1 - (Number Of Selective Indices))* divided by *(Total Number of Indices)*, which is also the same as the dimension d and number of output filters in that layer.

Hence, Selective indices $SI = \underset{i}{\operatorname{argmin}} \sum s_i^c < k, 0 < k < 1$ and RI are the *rest* of the indices. And Selectivity $\psi_{x,k}^c$:

$$\psi_{x,k}^c = 1 - |SI|/(|SI| + |RI|) \tag{1}$$

where $|.|$ indicates the number of the set of indices.

The mean selectivity for the entire dataset for a given class c is therefore:

$$\Psi_k^c = \frac{1}{|X_c|} \sum \psi_{x,k}^c \tag{2}$$

where $|X_c|$ is the number of data points for a class c. The process of finding $\psi_{x,k}^c$ and Ψ_k^c is shown in Fig. 1.

Note that:

1. $\psi_{x,k}^c, \Psi_k^c \in (0,1)$
2. $\psi_{x,k}^c, \Psi_k^c$ increase as the selectivity increases and decrease as it decreases

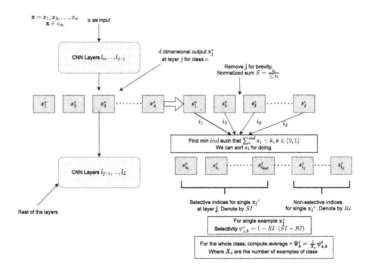

Fig. 1. Finding selective indices and computing $\psi_{x,k}^c$ and Ψ_k^c

3.2   Activation Orthogonality

Bodola et al. [18] used a frequency histogram of selective indices SI, to further select the most frequent indices corresponding to features at a given layer which they call *influential features*. They show that at the final layer, those filters have little overlap with each other and thus are disentangled.

They have used Mutual Information at the final layer to quantify the disentanglement. We instead propose to use *Mean Pairwise Mutual Information* for those filters to measure disentanglement at **all layers** of a CNN.

$$\bar{I} = \frac{1}{(N-1)^2} \sum_{c_i \neq c_j} \sum_{c_j \neq c_i} I(x_{c_i}; x_{c_j}) \tag{3}$$

where N is the number of classes, $I(X;Y) = H(X) + H(Y) - H(X,Y)$ and $H(X) = -\sum plog(p)$, that is Shannon Entropy.

μ_{PMI} is complementary to Ψ_k^c as, Ψ_k^c measures the predilection of activations to concentrate along a few filters, and μ_{PMI} quantifies how disjoint that concentration is.

4   Experiments and Results

In this section we describe our experimental setup and results. To demonstrate our proposed metrics we conducted experiments with Resnet20 CNN model and CIFAR-10 dataset, which are one of the standard benchmarks for computer vision and were also used by [14,15,18].

4.1   Class Selectivity with Ψ_k and μ_{SI}

Here we analyze our proposed metric Layerwise Class Selectivity Ψ_k and compare with Class Conditional Mean Activation μ_{SI} proposed in [14,15].

However, it is not straightforward to compare the two techniques, as the scale of the two measures will be different. In order to do a fair comparison, we measure selectivity for each class at each layer *before and after* fine-tuning the model with two different *Selectivity Regularizers*. The first regularizer was proposed in [15] and adds a penalty term to the loss function

$$loss = -\sum_{c}^{C} y_c log(\hat{y}_c) - \alpha\mu_{SI} \tag{4}$$

where μ_{SI} is,

$$\mu_{SI} = \frac{1}{L}\sum_{l}^{L} \frac{1}{U}\sum_{u}^{U} SI_u \tag{5}$$

The second was proposed in [18] which performs implicit selective regularization by fine-tuning on a subspace of the filters given by *influential filters* at the final layer.

To analyze Class Selectivity we first evaluated both μ_{SI} and Ψ_k on a Resnet20 trained on CIFAR-10. Then we fine-tuned it with the regularizer given by [15] and again checked both μ_{SI} and Ψ_k. Finally, we fine-tuned after decomposing the final layer as given by [18] and computed the metrics again. The results for μ_{SI} are given in Table 1 and for Ψ_k in Table 2. *Regular* in both the tables refers to the pre-trained Resnet20 without any fine-tuning or regularization. *Selective* refers to the model after regularization as given in [15]. *Decomposed* refers to fine-tuning with the method given in [18].

We have averaged the values of μ_{SI} and Ψ_k over all classes in a given layer. For the experiments, we did not compute intermediate activations and only checked after each full Resnet Block, hence the number of layers is less than 20.

4.2 Layerwise Decomposability

Activation Orthogonality is complementary to selectivity as discussed in Sect. 3.2. We also conducted experiments to determine Layerwise Decomposability as measured by Mean Pairwise Mutual Information 3. As earlier, we checked before and after regularization and fine-tuning as given in [15,18] respectively. We computed layerwise $\bar{I}$ and then averaged it. The results are given in Table 3.

Table 1. Mean Layerwise Class Conditional Activation μ_{SI} for all classes of CIFAR-10 on Resnet20. The values in bold indicate minimum in a row. Decomposed model should *increase* selectivity, while Regularized model should *decrease* it.

Layer	Vanilla	Decomposed	Selectivity
1	**0.455071**	0.464543	0.463533
2	**0.379685**	0.380318	0.384917
3	**0.308229**	0.314514	0.315383
4	**0.307505**	0.314283	0.312787
5	**0.363581**	0.372642	0.367755
6	**0.3691**	0.374281	0.372883
7	0.396026	0.398077	**0.392132**
8	**0.502869**	0.50797	0.503655
9	0.512369	0.518779	**0.510246**
10	0.609504	0.629787	**0.599994**
Mean	**0.420394**	0.427519	0.422329

Table 2. Mean Layerwise Selectivity Ψ_k for all classes of CIFAR-10 on Resnet20. The values in bold indicate minimum in a row. Decomposed model should *increase* selectivity, while Regularized model should *decrease* it.

Layer	Vanilla	Decomposed	Regularized
1	**0.794981**	0.796271	0.795704
2	0.800684	0.79669	**0.795706**
3	0.750174	0.747445	**0.746924**
4	0.671361	0.671723	**0.669929**
5	**0.707627**	0.708473	0.708779
6	**0.675719**	0.676191	0.677528
7	**0.700337**	0.702046	0.700649
8	0.72629	0.724628	**0.72373**
9	0.714931	0.716629	**0.714121**
10	**0.817019**	0.840912	0.808798
Mean	0.735912	0.738101	**0.734187**

Table 3. Mean Pairwise Mutual Information for all layers of CIFAR-10 on Resnet20. The values in bold indicate the minimum in a row.

Layer	Vanilla	Decomposed	Regularized
1	1.45738	1.47981	**1.42467**
2	1.54463	**1.50942**	**1.50942**
3	1.52438	**1.48231**	**1.48231**
4	1.38791	**1.3689**	1.39196
5	**1.21895**	1.2193	1.24445
6	**1.27192**	1.32324	1.32324
7	**1.30823**	1.32274	1.32868
8	**1.17646**	1.18977	1.22678
9	1.11861	**1.08113**	1.14818
10	0.966042	**0.956676**	0.970724
Mean	1.29745	**1.29333**	1.30504

4.3 Interpreting the Results

Tables 1, 2 contain the selectivity metrics computed on Resnet20 and CIFAR-10. The names in the tables refer to variants of Resnet20 models. They are 1) Vanilla, Resnet20 without any modification 2) Decomposed Resnet20, after fine-tuning as given in [18] and 3) Regularized Resnet20, after fine-tuning with regularization as given in [15].

We can assess the efficacy of μ_{SI} from Table 1. After Regularization, the μ_{SI} **should decrease, while it increases for the Regularized model** and the Vanilla Resnet20 shows the least μ_{SI}. While our proposed metric Ψ_k **increases selectivity as expected**. Our proposed metric Ψ_k, therefore, behaves as expected.

The Decomposed model shows the highest selectivity Ψ_k, which is complementary to Mean Pairwise Mutual Information $\bar{I}$. We can see that it also shows the highest decomposability corresponding to the highest layerwise selectivity. This corroborates our proposed metric's ability to identify selectivity.

Another thing we can note is that selectivity should increase higher up the network (closer to the final or decision layer), as ablating a single unit closer to the decision layer should impact that class more. We can see in Table 2 that except for the first layer, Ψ_k does indeed increase with depth. This further corroborates the efficacy of our proposed metric.

5   Discussion and Future Work

In this work, we have proposed a new metric for class selectivity in CNNs and we have demonstrated its efficacy and superiority to the standard metrics with experiments on Resnet20 and CIFAR-10. We have shown in comparison with existing prevalent metric μ_{SI} that our metric is better able to capture Class Selectivity. We have also demonstrated its relation to filter disentanglement and model decomposability by evaluating the same models with Mean Pairwise Mutual Information.

The implications of Class Selectivity are still disputed in current literature. But we can agree that CNNs indeed display this behaviour. Certain features are more activated by a class than others. Badola et al. [18] decomposed the final layer based on class selective features and further decomposition can be explored in future along similar lines. The relation of class selectivity and robustness, with respect to adversarial examples has also not been investigated in the literature. Future work can explore all of these aspects and we believe that a consistent metric for selectivity as we have proposed can help in that.

Acknowledgements. We wish to thank the MEITY, Govt. of India and IoE Directorate, University of Hyderabad for funding this research with Visvesvaraya PhD Fellowship award number MEITY-PHD-1035 and UoH-IoE project grant number UoH-IoE-RC3-21-050 respectively.

Competing Interests. The authors declare no competing interests in relation to this work.

References

1. LeCun, Y., et al.: Backpropagation applied to handwritten zip code recognition. Neural Comput. **1**(4), 541–551 (1989). https://doi.org/10.1162/neco.1989.1.4.541
2. Krizhevsky, A., Sutskever, I., Hinton, G.E.: ImageNet classification with deep convolutional neural networks. In: Advances in Neural Information Processing Systems, pp. 1097–1105 (2012). https://doi.org/10.1145/3065386

3. He, K., et al.: Deep residual learning for image recognition. In: Proceedings of the IEEE Conference on Computer Vision and Pattern Recognition, pp. 770–778 (2016). https://doi.org/10.1109/cvpr.2016.90
4. Girshick, R.B.: Fast R-CNN. In: Proceedings of the IEEE International Conference on Computer Vision, pp. 1440–1448 (2015). https://doi.org/10.1109/ICCV.2015.169
5. Girshick, R., et al.: Region - based convolutional networks for accurate object detection and segmentation. IEEE Trans. Pattern Anal. Mach. Intell. **38**(1), 142–158 (2016). https://doi.org/10.1109/TPAMI.2015.2437384
6. Dosovitskiy, A., et al.: An image is worth 16×16 words: transformers for image recognition at scale. In: Proceedings of the International Conference on Learning Representations (2020)
7. Zhang, C., et al.: Understanding deep learning requires rethinking generalization. In: Proceedings of the International Conference on Learning Representations (2016)
8. Szegedy, C., et al.: Intriguing properties of neural networks. In: Proceedings of the International Conference on Learning Representations (2014)
9. Ilyas, A., et al.: Adversarial examples are not bugs, they are features. In: Advances in Neural Information Processing Systems (2019). https://doi.org/10.23915/DISTILL.00019
10. Neyshabur, B., et al.: Towards understanding the role of over - parametrization in generalization of neural networks. In: Proceedings of the International Conference on Learning Representations (2018)
11. Allen-Zhu, Z., Li, Y., Liang, Y.: Learning and generalization in overparameterized neural networks, going beyond two layers. In: Advances in Neural Information Processing Systems (2018)
12. Li, Y., et al.: Convergent learning: do different neural networks learn the same representations? In: Advances in Neural Information Processing Systems (2015)
13. Zhou, B., et al. Revisiting the Importance of Individual Units in CNNs via Ablation (2018)
14. Morcos, A.S., et al.: On the importance of single directions for generalization. In: Proceedings of the International Conference on Learning Representations (2018)
15. Leavitt, M.L., Morcos, A.S.: Selectivity considered harmful: evaluating the causal impact of class selectivity in DNNs. In: Proceedings of the International Conference on Learning Representations (2020)
16. Bau, D., et al.: Network dissection - quantifying interpretability of deep visual representations. In: Proceedings of the IEEE Conference on Computer Vision and Pattern Recognition, pp. 3319–3327 (2017). https://doi.org/10.1109/CVPR.2017.354
17. Liang, H., et al.: Training interpretable convolutional neural networks by differentiating class-specific filters. In: Vedaldi, A., Bischof, H., Brox, T., Frahm, J.-M. (eds.) ECCV 2020. LNCS, vol. 12347, pp. 622–638. Springer, Cham (2020). https://doi.org/10.1007/978-3-030-58536-5_37
18. Badola, A., et al.: Decomposing the deep: finding class specific filters in deep CNNs. Neural Comput. Appl. **35**, 13583–13596 (2023). https://doi.org/10.1007/s00521-023-08441-z
19. Erhan, D., et al.: Visualizing higher - layer features of a deep network. Technical report (2009)
20. Hinton, G.E., Osindero, S., Teh, Y.: A fast learning algorithm for deep belief nets. Neural Comput. **18**, 1527–1554 (2006). https://doi.org/10.1162/neco.2006.18.7.1527

21. Coates, A., Karpathy, A., Ng, A.: Emergence of object - selective features in unsupervised feature learning. In: Advances in Neural Information Processing Systems (2012)
22. Girshick, R.B., et al.: Rich feature hierarchies for accurate object detection and semantic segmentation. In: Proceedings of the IEEE Conference on Computer Vision and Pattern Recognition (2013). https://doi.org/10.1109/CVPR.2014.81
23. Gonzalez-Garcia, A., Modolo, D., Ferrari, V.: Do semantic parts emerge in convolutional neural networks? Int. J. Comput. Vis. **126**(5), 476–494 (2017). https://doi.org/10.1007/s11263-017-1048-0
24. Gale, E., et al.: Selectivity metrics provide misleading estimates of the selectivity of single units in neural networks. In: Annual Meeting of the Cognitive Science Society (2019)
25. Wang, X., et al.: Finding skill neurons in pre-trained transformer - based language models. In: Conference on Empirical Methods in Natural Language Process (2022). https://doi.org/10.48550/arXiv.2211.07349
26. Quiroga, R., et al.: Invariant visual representation by single neurons in the human brain. Nature (2005). https://doi.org/10.1038/nature03687
27. Barwich, A.: The value of failure in science: the story of grandmother cells in neuroscience. Front. Neurosci. (2019). https://doi.org/10.3389/fnins.2019.01121
28. Bowers, J., et al.: Why do some neurons in cortex respond to information in a selective manner? Insights from artificial neural networks. Cognition (2016). https://doi.org/10.1016/j.cognition.2015.12.009

Content Based Network Representational Learning for Movie Recommendation (CNMovieRec)

Nageswar Rao Kota[1,2] (ID), Vineet Padmanabhan[2(✉)] (ID),
and Wilson Naik Bhukya[2] (ID)

[1] Defence Research and Development Laboratory, Hyderabad 500058, India
knrao.drdl@gov.in
[2] School of Computer and Information Sciences, University of Hyderabad,
Hyderabad 500046, India
{vineetnair,rathore}@uohyd.ac.in

Abstract. Research in the domain of recommender systems mainly points out to two types of recommendation strategies, namely, Collaborative Filtering (CF) and Content based filtering (CBF). In CF, the idea is to find users *similar* to the *active user* (the user to whom recommendation needs to be done) and recommendation is done based on *items* liked by similar *users*. On the other hand, content based filtering make use of the explicit or implicit data provided by the users on different items so as to generate a user profile and recommendation is made based on this profile. Previous research mainly focusses on CF-based approaches and many interesting results have come out in the recent years. In this paper we focus on CBF wherein a novel framework is proposed called content-based network representational learning for movie recommendation (CNMovieRec). We also propose a group recommender system based on our new CNMovieRec. Our experimental findings demonstrate that the results related to the proposed content-based framework is comparable to those of CF techniques (in terms of MAE, MSE & RMSE) and the new model is able to overcome challenges of *Data Sparsity* and *Cold-Start* problems usually accompanying CF-models.

Keywords: Recommender Systems · Network Representation Learning

1 Introduction

When faced with broad range of choices, it becomes difficult for individuals to make the right decision, as the amount of information available at hand is vast and it often leads to what is termed in the recommender systems community as the *Information Overload* problem. Recommender systems can help in tackling the information overload problem as can be witnessed from them becoming an irreplaceable component of internet sites such as Yahoo, Netflix, YouTube,

R. Morusupalli et al. (Eds.): MIWAI 2023, LNAI 14078, pp. 112–123, 2023.
https://doi.org/10.1007/978-3-031-36402-0_10

LinkedIn, Amazon etc. Research in the area of recommender systems [1] is a subject of great concern both in Academia as well as Industry. The bottomline of a recommendation system is to estimate an item's effectiveness and to predict whether it is worth recommending to a user or not. The three key elements in any recommender system are the *user* (consumer), *item* (product) and *rating* (preference). By providing his/her preference (opinion) on items he/she has bought or movies he/she has watched, any user can make use of the recommendation system to get recommendations on new items for which no opinion/rating has been given by that particular user. In order to produce suggestions/recommendations, data can be collected either in explicit (a user is asked to give his/her ratings) or implicit (user's action is recorded from the web) form by the recommender system.

Though there are many approaches to build a movie recommender system, the most commonly used techniques are that of *Collaborative filtering* [9,12,13,18,19] and *Content-based filtering* [14,16,17]. Collaborative filtering is the most commonly used recommendation technique and is based on the assumption that user's with identical tastes (preferences) in the past are probably going to have similar preferences in the future also. A recommendation is made to a particular user based on the ratings/preferences of other similar user's and therefore the term collaborative. Matrix factorisation (MF) [9] techniques are a family of algorithms in collaborative filtering that helps in extracting the latent/hidden factors for user's and items from a single rating matrix. In order to capture the unique characteristics that are associated with user's/items, the MF methods, through a process of factorisation helps in extracting the hidden/latent factors associated with each item/user. Most of our previous work on Movie Recommender systems is based on matrix factorisation based collaborative filtering [10,11]. In this paper we deviate from the usual path and focus on content-based filtering for recommender systems. In this paper we have two major contributions:

1. A novel content based filtering algorithm(CNMovieRec) to predict Unknown ratings using Network Representation Learning for Movie recommendation.
2. A content based group recommender system based on the CNMovieRec for recommending items in a group scenario.

2   Related Work

In this Section we outline some related work with respect to Content-based filtering and Network representation learning. Though matrix factorisation based collaborative filtering is a highly popular technique to built recommender systems it has two heavy drawbacks in the form of *Data Sparsity* and *Cold Start* [5]. Data sparsity arises in scenarios wherein the user/s does not rate the items he/she has watched/purchased/read and therefore at that particular time point due to the scarcity of data (information) one cannot make further pertinent recommendations to the user. Cold start problem arises in situations wherein a new user (who has not rated any items yet) wishes to utilise the recommendation engine. As the data ratings of the user does not exist, making any kind of recommendations for him/her becomes and issue.

On the other hand, content-based filtering recommends items based on specific item that the user has liked in the past. For instance, to make a movie recommendation, the content-based framework uses movie (item) metadata such as genre, description, actors, directors etc. rather than trying to find other similar users like in collaborative filtering. The main idea behind content-based recommendation is that if a person likes a specific item, he/she will further like an item that is close (similar) to it as well. It will make use of the user's past item metadata for recommendation. Unlike collaborative filtering which uses only the existing ratings of the user, content based filtering relies on the attributes or features of the items and user profile information. The advantages of content-based filtering are 1) *User Independance*: In content based filtering, recommendations are based only on the past likings (ratings) of the items by active user. It does not rely on other user ratings unlike collaborative filtering where other user ratings are required to identify the similar or neighbouring users 2) *Transparency*: Explanations can be easily provided by explicitly listing features or descriptions of the items that caused for recommending item. Conversely collaborative techniques has a single reason for an item recommendation is that unknown users with similar tastes liked that item. 3) *New Item* Content-based technique can recommend items which are not yet rated by any user. So they do not suffer from the first-rater problem, which affects collaborative approach which rely solely on users ratings to make recommendations.

In content based approach, initially, Item profile and user profile is calculated based on item features. Content-based filtering approach utilises information about items previously rated by a user, and build profile of user interests based on the features of the objects rated by the *active user* (the user for whom recommendation needs to be carried out). Calculated profiles are used to recommend items to the users based on the similarity of target item to items rated by the active user. In order to construct and update the profile of active user, his/her reactions to items are utilised, which generally are in the form of ratings (A discrete numerical value in a scale typically in the range 0 to 5). These ratings, together with the related item representations, are exploited in the process of building a model useful to predict the actual relevance of newly presented items. Users can also explicitly define their areas of interest as an initial profile when user has not yet rated any item. Collaborative filtering has become more successful over content-based filtering (CBF) as CBF lacks efficient content representation techniques. Items are represented by a set of features, also known as attributes or properties. For example, in the case of a movie recommendation, features adopted to describe a movie are: actors, directors, genres, plot, ...etc.). When each item is described by the same set of attributes, and every attribute has a known set of values that it can take, the item is represented by means of structured data.

The recent advancements in Network representational learning(NRL) has given more strength with respect to content representation, which was the major bottleneck in the path of success for content based techniques. Items are represented through NRL and representations are utilised in recommending items for gaining the advantages of content based filtering as explained above. Several different approaches have been proposed, Before NRL, to represent the content of items such as Vectorisation, TF-IDF matrix, TADW, Word2Vec models, Topic Modelling. Next section explains the Network representation modelling in detail.

2.1   Network Representation Learning (NRL)

Network representation learning [3, 6, 20, 21] has been proposed as a new learning paradigm in the area of Social Network Analysis wherein the idea is to encode the structural information of a network with node representation. The network vertices are embedded into a low-dimensional vector space, by preserving network topology structure, vertex content, and other side information. NRL mainly depends on *Network structure*, *Vertex Attributes* and *Vertex labels*. Network Structure or topology is represented as an adjacency matrix or adjacency list which majorly depicts how the vertices are related to each other. The relationship between these vertices are represented in the form of edges as depicted in Fig. 1. On the other hand, Vertex attribute, in addition to the network structure, can provide direct evidence to measure content-level similarity between vertices. By combining vertex attributes and network structure a model can filter out noisy information. Vertex labels provide direct information about the categorisation of each network vertex to certain classes or groups. Vertex labels are strongly influenced by and inherently correlated to both network structure and vertex attributes. NRL can be formally defined as follows: Let $G = (V, E)$ be a graph with V as the set of nodes and E as the set of edges. The goal of NRL is to learn a function $f : V \rightarrow R^d$ that maps each node v in V to a d-dimensional vector representation $f(v)$ in R^d. The objective of f is to maximise the similarity between the embeddings of nodes that are related by an edge, and minimises the similarity between the embeddings of nodes that are not related by an edge. NRL converts/embeds large scale information networks into a low dimensional vector space for further reduction in complexity for information analysis. NRL methods broadly can be categorised in to five groups based on: *Matrix Factorization, Random Walk, Edge based, Deep learning* and *Hybrid*. Our proposed method

Fig. 1. Network to Vector Representation

is based on edge modeling which preserves mainly the network topology and the vertex attributes information jointly. NRL has opened a new horizon in recommender system as both are intended to solve similar problems related information overload.

3   CNMovieRec

We propose CNMovieRec as a Content based Network Representational Learning framework for Movie Recommendation which exploits the power of NRL to get the unique representations of movies in the form of vectors in a low dimensional space. Movie vectors are later used to find the similarities between the movies and for predicting the unknown movie ratings by the user. Given Heterogeneous Movie network with set of viewers V and movies M with movie *genre* and *crew* as attributes then the set of Edges E between movies represents common *actors* and *directors* between the movies. As shown in Fig. 2, the network can be divided into two distinct parts: the *movie network* and the *viewer network*. As our objective is to learn the representation of movies, we focus on utilising the movie network to extract the movie representations.

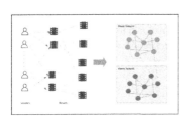

Fig. 2. Attributed Movie Network   **Fig. 3.** Movie Embeddings

The first step of CNMovieRec is to get the vector representations of movies. Movie embeddings are a combination of representations from attributes (genres) of movies and network embeddings from Movie network. Movie Network is formed based on the movie crew information. Movies are nodes and edges represents commonality between the movies. Commonality may be identified through common actors or common directors. Movie embeddings are represented as a matrix R where r_{mn} represents the value of mth movie for n^{th} latent feature as shown in Fig. 3. Matrix R is computed based on the joint representation of movie network structure and movie attribute proximity. Following the procedure in AANE (Accelerated Attributed Network Embedding) [8] it can be represented as

$$L = L_A + L_H \tag{1}$$

L_A is attribute embeddings and L_H is network Structure embeddings. Movie Attribute embeddings L_A are computed based on movie genres. Initially every movie is represented through its genre. For example if there are m movies and k genres, movie attribute embeddings are represented by matrix $m \times k$. Affinity matrix A is computed using the cosine similarities between the movies in which a_{ij} represents the cosine similarity between movie i and movie j. Matrix A will have the dimensions mxm. The following objective function determines the final movie attribute embeddings L_A.

$$\min_R L_A = \sum_i \sum_j (a_{ij} - r_i r_j^t)^2 \tag{2}$$

where r_i represent the row vector of $movie_i$ and r_j represents the row vector of $movie_j$ A movie network represents the commonality between the movies. This network structure embeddings preserve the commonalities between the movies. The following function learns the movie embeddings to preserve the structural aspect of the movie network

$$\min_R L_H = \sum_{(i,j) \in p} w_{ij} ||r_i - r_j||_2 \tag{3}$$

where r_i represent the row vector of $movie_i$ and r_j represents the row vector of $movie_j$ and w_{ij} represents the weight of the edge between $movie_i$ and $movie_j$. The final matrix R is computed by minimising the combined objective function based on Eq. 2 and Eq. 3

$$\min_R L = \sum_i \sum_j (a_{ij} - r_i r_j^t)^2 + \sum_{(i,j) \in p} w_{ij} ||r_i - r_j||_2 \tag{4}$$

$a_{ij} \in A$, is affinity matrix of movies based on cosine similarity between movie genres. w_{ij} represents the weight of the edge between $movie_i$ and $movie_j$. Predicting unknown ratings is the next step for building a movie recommender system. Unknown ratings are predicted using average weighted sum of similarities between all the rated movies and the target movie. The unknown ratings prediction is calculated using the formula given below.

$$w(v, m) = \hat{q}(v) + \frac{\sum_{s \in S(v)} (q(v, s) - \hat{q}(v)) * sim(m, s)}{\sum_{s \in S(v)} sim(m, s)} \tag{5}$$

where $S(v)$ is the set of movies rated by viewer v. $q(v, s)$ is the rating of viewer v on movie s, $\hat{q}(v)$ is the average rating of viewer v and $sim(m, s)$ is the similarity between movie m and s. The CNMovieRec algorithm is outlined in Algorithm 1. We formulate a toy example that explains how the unknown rating predictions are computed based on the similarities of the rated items to the target item. After computing the vector representation of movies, we need to compute the

---

Algorithm 1. CNMovieRec Algorithm

1: **Input:** Graph (M, E) where M is the set of movies and E is the set of edges between movies, Rating Matrix R, set of Viewers V and N (for Top-N movies)
2: **Output:** Predicted rating matrix $\hat{R}$ and recommended list of movies (Top N)
3: Compute movie vectors using Eq. 3
4: Using Movie Vectors, compute sim=cosine_similarity(M)
5: **for** $v \in V$ **do**
6:    **for** $m \in M$ **do**
7:       Find predicted rating $\hat{R}_{v,m}$ using Eq. 5
8:    **end for**
9: **end for**
10: Sort the ratings of each user and recommend top N movies
11: Return $\hat{R}$ and Top N movies

---

similarity matrix of movies based on the cosine similarities. Cosine similarities are again utilised in the weighted average rate computation based on Eq. 5. The toy example considers 3 users and 5 movies, movie cosine matrix and rating matrix.

Table 1. Movie Similarity Matrix.

	M1	M2	M3	M4	M5
M1	1	0.2	0.8	0.9	0.1
M2	0.2	1	0.4	0.7	0.8
M3	0.8	0.4	1	0.6	0.2
M4	0.9	0.7	0.6	1	0.6
M5	0.1	0.8	0.2	0.6	1

Table 2. Viewer Rating Matrix.

	M1	M2	M3	M4	M5
V1	–	3	1	–	4
V2	3	1	–	4	5
V3	–	-	3	4	1

Table 3. Predicted Rating Matrix.

	M1	M2	M3	M4	M5
V1	1.63	3	1	2.68	4
V2	3	1	3.1	4	5
V3	3.3	2.5	3	4	1

In Table 2 the unknown ratings are represented as –. Our aim is to predict these unknown ratings using the Eq. 5, Table 1 and Table 2. Based on the given information in Table 1 and Table 2, we can compute the predicted score of movie $M1$ for viewer $V1$ as follows: Using Eq. 5, we have:

$$w(V1, M1) = 2.667 + \frac{(3 - 2.667) * 0.2 + (1 - 2.667) * 0.8 + (4 - 2.667) * 0.1}{0.2 + 0.8 + 0.1}$$

where Average ratings of viewer V1 $\hat{q}(v)$ is 2.667 and, in first portion of the fraction $(3 - 2.667) * 0.2$, 3 is rating of Movie M2, 0.2 is similarity between M1, M2. Simplifying the above expression, we get w(V1, M1) = 2.667 − 1.037 = 1.63 Therefore, the predicted score of movie M1 for viewer V1 is 1.63. Similarly, we can compute the predicted scores of movies for other viewers and movies using the same approach by substituting the corresponding ratings and average ratings into Eq. 5 as shown in Table 3.

3.1   Deep-CNMovieRec

Deep-CNMovieRec is a deep learning based model for predicting the unknown ratings from the Movie vectors and Viewer vectors. The computation of vectors for viewer's is based on TF-IDF, by taking into consideration the preferred movies by the viewer. The Deep network is trained to compute the movie ratings. Viewer vector is represented as $V = (f_1, f_2, f_3, \ldots, f_n)$ where f_i represents a $feature_i$ of a movie. f_i is computed based on the equation

$$f_i = FF(v, i) * IUF(i) \tag{6}$$

where $FF(v, i)$ is the number of movies preferred by the viewer when $feature_i$ is present in the movie. $IUF(i)$ is calculated as $IUF(i) = \log \frac{|v|}{UF(i)}$, where $|v|$ is the number of viewers and $UF(i)$ is the number of viewers who preferred the movie when $feature_i$ is present in a movie. Deep-CNMovieRec has one input layer, six hidden layers and one output layer. Output layer (one node) calculates the predicted rating of the movie by viewer. Input layer is concatenation of the viewer features and movie features and consists of 220 nodes in which 20 nodes represents the viewer vector and 200 nodes represents the movie vector which is computed based on AANE [8]. Six hidden layers has 100, 64, 32, 16, 8, 4 nodes respectively. The activation function in all the layers is ReLU. A regularisation mechanism of dropout (0.2 probability of each node) is applied for hidden layers for handling overfitting issues. Network is optimised using Adam optimiser for 100 epochs with learning rate 0.001.

4   Experimental Results (CNMovieRec)

Content based movie recommender system requires heterogeneous information regarding movies. HetRec2011 [7] datasets from group-lens are used for heterogeneous information of movies along with the users rating information. Heterogeneous information includes the movie crew, movie genres and imdb URL of the movie. The dataset contains 2113 viewers, 10155 movies and 20 genres as given in Table 4.

Table 4. HetRec2011 Datset

2113	viewer
10155	movies
20	genres
4060	directors
95321	actors
855598	ratings
404.921	avg ratings per user
84.637	avg ratings per movie

The dataset ratings are at 96.02% sparsity levels with 855598 ratings given by the users. The following table shows the results of CNMovieRec with different K most similar rating movies with target movie. Metrics such as MAE, MSE and RMSE are used to evaluate the algorithm for different k most similar movies with that of the target movie and the results are shown in Table 5. Table 6 shows the performance of three different recommendation algorithms - CNMovieRec, PMF, and DeepCNMovieRec based on three evaluation metrics: Mean Absolute Error (MAE), Mean Squared Error (MSE), and Root Mean Squared Error (RMSE). Based on the information given in the table, we can observe that PMF outperforms our proposed algorithms by a small margin of 0.04 in terms of MAE. These results indicate that PMF is slightly better than our proposed algorithms in terms of prediction accuracy, but the difference in performance is relatively small.

Table 5. MAE, MSE, RMSE values for different K-values

	K = 10	K = 100	K = 200	K = 350	k = all Movies
MAE	0.74	0.71	0.71	0.71	0.71
MSE	0.93	0.86	0.85	0.86	0.85
RMSE	0.96	0.92	0.92	0.92	0.92

Table 6. Comparison with PMF

	CNMovie Rec	PMF	DeepCN MovieRec
MAE	0.71	0.67	0.74
MSE	0.85	0.73	0.91
RMSE	0.92	0.86	0.95

5   Group Recommender System

Compared to personalised recommender systems, Group recommender systems (GRS) [2,4,15,17] have attracted more attention recently as they try to find relevant content of interest for socially connected individuals. The main idea of group recommendation methods is based on two assumptions 1) user preferences can be inferred and then aggregated into group preferences and 2) there is only partial observation of group preferences. Group recommender methods are of two types group *preference learning* and *reference aggregation*. Preference learning is to learn from historical preferences of individuals and predict for the unknown preferences of the groups. Preference aggregation is to aggregate the individual users preferences in the group based on social choice rules. In this paper we focus on preference learning method. Most of the existing literature in group recommender systems is based on collaborative filtering approach and in this paper we have extended our content based CNMovieRec algorithm in a group scenario.

Given a set of users U, Items I and sparse rating matrix R, the GRS problem is to recommend the subset of items I, to the group G, where $g_i \subseteq U$, such that all the users in the group share common preference profile by satisfying maximum possible users of group g_i. Grouping is the most crucial step in GRS as it reflects the most common preferences among the group. We have employed Random Similar Group (RSG) method to form the groups. In our framework, we made groups based on the ratings given by the users on the individual items. A set of members based on the fixed size are randomly selected with a constraint of having the most similar preference (rating greater than 4) by all the group members for at least 10 movies. We have prepared 200 groups for our experiments wherein each group consists of users who rated equal to or more than 4 for a minimum of 10 movies.

The next step is the preparation of group rating matrix M for each generated group set G, where the number of rows represent the number of groups and columns represent the number of movies. Three different group rating matrices are created based on three different social choice voting methods viz. *Least Misery, Max* and *Average*. For group preference learning we have employed the same algorithm CNMovieRec described in first contribution is used. After constructing Group rating matrix, Considering the each group as an individual viewer, CNMovieRec algorithm is used to compute the predicted ratings of non rated movies by a group, as explained in Sect. 5 based on weighted average similarities of the rated movies.

5.1 Experimental Results

Experiments are conducted for different group sizes (2, 3, 4). For each group size we have created three group rating matrices based on three aggregation strategies. Results are evaluated using metrics such as *precision, recall* and *F1 score* for each aggregation matrix. Following tables show the experimental results for each group size (2, 3, 4). Table 7, Table 8 and Table 9 demonstrates that the performance of the algorithm is consistent across group sizes 2, 3 and 5. However the *Recall* values are lower when considering preference values greater than or equal to 4 for deciding relevant movies which can be attributed to the fact that user's average rating is much lower than 4. The algorithm has high accuracy, as evidenced by the *Precision* and *Recall* values, which are very close to 1.

Table 7. Group Size = 2

	pref ≥ 3	pref ≥ avg	pref ≥ 4
Aggregation = Avg			
Precision	0.82	0.82	0.76
Recall	0.92	0.92	0.06
F1	0.87	0.87	0.11
Aggregation = Max			
Precision	0.83	0.83	0.77
Recall	0.94	0.94	0.06
F1	0.88	0.88	0.12
Aggregation = Min			
Precision	0.82	0.82	0.76
Recall	0.92	0.92	0.06
F1	0.87	0.87	0.11

Table 8. Group Size = 3

	pref ≥ 3	pref ≥ avg	pref ≥ 4
Aggregation = Avg			
Precision	0.80	0.81	0.72
Recall	0.96	0.97	0.01
F1	0.88	0.01	0.02
Aggregation = Min			
Precision	0.83	0.83	0.73
Recall	0.98	0.99	0.03
F1	0.90	0.90	0.07
Aggregation = Max			
Precision	0.80	0.81	0.72
Recall	0.96	0.97	0.01
F1	0.88	0.88	0.02

Table 9. Group Size = 4

	pref $\geq$ 3	pref $\geq$ avg	pref $\geq$ 4
Aggregation = Avg			
Precision	0.80	0.80	0.71
Recall	0.96	0.96	0.01
F1	0.88	0.87	0.04
Aggregation = Min			
Precision	0.83	0.84	0.73
Recall	0.99	0.98	0.08
F1	0.90	0.90	0.15
Aggregation = Max			
Precision	0.80	0.80	0.71
Recall	0.96	0.96	0.01
F1	0.88	0.87	0.04

6   Conclusions and Future Work

In this paper we have developed a framework for recommender systems in which the content-based filtering technique is adopted instead of the usual collaborative filtering approach. We demonstrated that the content-based filtering technique when interpreted in the backdrop of Network Representation Learning (NRL) can provide results on par with that of the collaborative filtering method. Our experimental results corroborates this claim. To the best of our knowledge this is the first work that shows NRL can give a natural interpretation for content-based approaches. Moreover we extend our framework to a group scenario and demonstrate that the experimental results related to various group sizes are encouraging. Since content based filtering has advantages such as user independence, transparency and a natural solution for the cold-start problem it is important that learning paradigms like NRL needs to be investigated and solutions found. This work can be extended wherein the NRL-based content-based approach can be interpreted as a multi-objective-optimisation problem in the context of recommender systems. This we have left for future work.

References

1. Aggarwal, C.C.: Recommender Systems: The Textbook, 1st edn. Springer, Cham (2016). https://doi.org/10.1007/978-3-319-29659-3
2. Amer-Yahia, S., Roy, S.B., Chawla, A., Das, G., Yu, C.: Group recommendation: semantics and efficiency. Proc. VLDB Endow. **2**(1), 754–765 (2009)
3. Cai, H., Zheng, V.W., Chang, K.C.-C.: A comprehensive survey of graph embedding: problems, techniques, and applications. IEEE Trans. Knowl. Data Eng. **30**(9), 1616–1637 (2018)

4. Cao, D., He, X., Miao, L., An, Y., Yang, C., Hong, R.: Attentive group recommendation. In: SIGIR 2018, Ann Arbor, USA, 08–12 July 2018, pp. 645–654. ACM (2018)
5. Enrich, M., Braunhofer, M., Ricci, F.: Cold-start management with cross-domain collaborative filtering and tags. In: Huemer, C., Lops, P. (eds.) EC-Web 2013. LNBIP, vol. 152, pp. 101–112. Springer, Heidelberg (2013). https://doi.org/10.1007/978-3-642-39878-0_10
6. Goyal, P., Ferrara, E.: Graph embedding techniques, applications, and performance: a survey. Knowl. Based Syst. **151**, 78–94 (2018)
7. Hetrec. This dataset is an extension of movielens10m dataset, published by groupleans research group. http://www.grouplens.org
8. Huang, X., Li, J., Hu, X.: Accelerated attributed network embedding. In: SIAM International Conference on Data Mining, pp. 633–641 (2017)
9. Koren, Y., Bell, R., Volinsky, C.: Matrix factorization techniques for recommender systems. Computer **42**(8), 30–37 (2009)
10. Kumar, V., Pujari, A.K., Padmanabhan, V., Kagita, V.R.: Group preserving label embedding for multi-label classification. Pattern Recognit. **90**, 23–34 (2019)
11. Kumar, V., Pujari, A.K., Sahu, S.K., Kagita, V.R., Padmanabhan, V.: Proximal maximum margin matrix factorization for collaborative filtering. Pattern Recognit. Lett. **86**, 62–67 (2017)
12. Li, B.: Cross-domain collaborative filtering: a brief survey. In: 2011 23rd IEEE International Conference on Tools with Artificial Intelligence (ICTAI), pp. 1085–1086. IEEE (2011)
13. Li, B., Yang, Q., Xue, X.: Can movies and books collaborate?: cross-domain collaborative filtering for sparsity reduction. In: IJCAI 2009, San Francisco, CA, USA, pp. 2052–2057. Morgan Kaufmann Publishers Inc. (2009)
14. Mooney, R., Roy, L.: Content-based book recommending using learning for text categorization. In: Proceedings of the 5th ACM Conference on Digital Libraries, pp. 195–204 (2000)
15. Salehi-Abari, A., Boutilier, C.: Preference-oriented social networks: group recommendation and inference. In: RecSys-2015, Vienna, Austria, 16–20 September 2015, pp. 35–42. ACM (2015)
16. Salter, J., Antonopoulos, N.: The CinemaScreen recommender agent: a film recommender combining collaborative and content-based filtering. IEEE Intell. Syst. **21**(1), 35–41 (2006)
17. Seko, S., Yagi, T., Motegi, M., Muto, S.: Group recommendation using feature space representing behavioral tendency and power balance among members. In: RecSys 2011, Chicago, USA, 23–27 October 2011, pp. 101–108. ACM (2011)
18. Su, X., Khoshgoftaar, T.M.: A survey of collaborative filtering techniques. Adv. Artif. Intell. **2009** (2009)
19. Su, X., Khoshgoftaar, T.M., Zhu, X., Greiner, R.: Imputation-boosted collaborative filtering using machine learning classifiers. In: Proceedings of the 2008 ACM Symposium on Applied Computing, pp. 949–950. ACM (2008)
20. Tu, C., Liu, H., Liu, Z., Sun, M.: CANE: context-aware network embedding for relation modeling. In: Association for Computational Linguistics, ACL 2017, Vancouver, Canada, pp. 1722–1731. Association for Computational Linguistics (2017)
21. Zhang, D., Yin, J., Zhu, X., Zhang, C.: Network representation learning: a survey. IEEE Trans. Big Data **6**(1), 3–28 (2020)

Parallel and Distributed Query Processing in Attributed Networks

A. Sandhya Rani$^{(\boxtimes)}$ (ID) and K. Swarupa Rani$^{(\boxtimes)}$ (ID)

University of Hyderabad, Hyderabad, Telangana, India
{21mcpc18,swarupacs}@uohyd.ac.in

Abstract. Graph Analytics (GA) is a rapidly growing field that holds significant importance in numerous applications that focuses on analysing the complex relations in a network. One of the crucial concepts in GA is Query Reachability which refers to the ability to find a path connecting two nodes (u, v) in graph G. The multiple attributes in reachability query processing play a significant role to discover some interesting patterns. Existing studies did not deal with processing complex queries in attributed graphs. To fulfill some of the challenges, We contributed to this paper with three ideas for solving complex queries, finding paths, and processing multiple queries in parallel and distributed paradigms. Therefore, 1) Proposed <u>D</u>istributed <u>Set</u> <u>R</u>eachability <u>Q</u>uery in <u>A</u>ttributed <u>N</u>etworks (DSRQ_AN) algorithm using distributed computing through the Neo4j graph data platform and Cypher Query Language, 2) Finding the path to the given complex queries, and 3) Proposed a <u>M</u>ultiple <u>Q</u>uery <u>P</u>rocessing in <u>P</u>arallel and <u>D</u>istributed (MQP_PD) algorithm to execute in a parallel environment. This paper assessed the performance of the proposed approaches through a parallel paradigm on Neo4j slaves. Furthermore, the demonstrated results of parallel execution outperform sequential execution for multiple queries on attributed graphs.

Keywords: Reachability query · Attributed graphs · Distributed algorithms

1 Introduction

A Reachability Query (RQ) determines the path between a source vertex u to a target vertex v in a graph G. Nevertheless, we need to satisfy specific constraints in real-world networks to find reachability. The attributed graph is used to represent the vertex and edge attribute information. Integrating such information into the network structure makes attribute-based graphs crucial for query reachability. In general, representing real-world data more precisely and encoding more information that can be used in queries by including characteristics, such as node attributes, edge attributes, and edge labels.

Despite substantial research on RQ in the literature, no appropriate approaches exist to deal with complex queries in real-world graphs. These issues can be addressed through attributed networks considering the graph's topology and attribute values. For instance, MCR algorithm [12] finds the reachability for queries in attributed graphs and provides paths by satisfying the specified constraints. But MCR does not handle multiple set reachability queries.

For finding the query processing in multiple sources and targets, DS-RQ [9] was presented. But most of the studies are not focused on the complex queries of attributed graphs. LCDSRQ [1] introduced by Gacem et al. is the processing workflow to find reachability by satisfying the label constraints. In real-world applications, the user desires an exact path between the vertices rather than finding the reachability. Also, there is a demand to find exact paths rather than finding only the reachability in attributed networks by satisfying the label constraints. Existing reachability query algorithms are not sufficient for handling large networks and there is a demand to find new solutions. To overcome the above limitations, we proposed the Distributed Set Reachability Queries in Attributed Networks (DSRQ_AN) approach to find exact paths in the attributed networks. Additionally, we proposed Multiple Query Processing in Parallel and Distributed approach to find paths for multiple queries in a parallel and distributed environment.

This paper concentrates on a more complicated formulation of reachability queries by finding paths. The resultant paths satisfy the given query with vertex and edge-specific attributes. The following are contributions of this paper:

1. Proposed DSRQ_AN algorithm to address complex queries in attributed networks.
2. Modified and extended the LCDSRQ approach [1] by finding paths in attributed networks.
3. Solved the multiple queries of attributed networks in parallel and distributed environments.

Section 2 explains the preliminary concepts and literature. Section 3 illustrates one of the introduced DSRQ_AN algorithms. Section 4 describes another proposed approach such as MQP_PD. Section 5 describes experimentation with performance evaluation. Section 6 provides the conclusions and future scope.

2   Preliminary Concepts and Related Work

The terminology and definitions addressed in this paper are presented in this section. The notations used in algorithms are listed in Table 1.

Definition 1 (Attributed Graph). An attributed graph, G, is a graph denoted as $G = (V, E, V_a, E_a)$, where V is a set of vertices, $E \subseteq V \times V$ is a set of edges, V_a is a set of vertex specific attributes and E_a is a set of edge-specific attributes [10].

Definition 2 (Multidimensional Constraint Reachability). Given an attributed graph G, a source vertex s, a destination vertex t, vertex constraint

CV_a, and edge constraint CE_a, the multidimensional constraint reachability query on the attributed graph verifies whether the source (s) can reach the target (t) under vertex and edge constraint CV_a, CE_a [8].

Definition 3 (Distributed Set Reachability Query). Given a graph G, a set of sources S and a set of targets T, and aims to find the pairs (s_i, t_j) such as $s_i \in S$, $t_j \in T$ and t_j is reachable from s_i [9]

Definition 4 (Boundary Graph). Let $G = (\{G_i\}, E', \Lambda, F)$ be a distributed labeled graph on n workers, $i \leq n$. We define the boundary graph $G_{bound} = \langle V_{bound}, E_{bound}, \Lambda_{bound}, F_{bound} \rangle$ where $\boldsymbol{V_{bound}}$ is a set of n super nodes $(|V_{bound}| = n)$. Each super node $g_i \in V_{bound}$ represents a sub graph G_i. There exists an edge $(g_i, g_j) \in \boldsymbol{E_{bound}}$, if and only if $(v_i, v_j) \in E'$, such as $v_i \in O_i, v_j \in I_j$, Λ_{bound} is a set of labels, $\Lambda_{bound} \subseteq \Lambda$. $\boldsymbol{F_{bound}}$ assigns labels $\lambda \in \Lambda_{bound}$ to each edge $(g_i, g_j) \in E_{bound}$ as follows: $F_{bound}(g_i, g_j) = F(v_i, v_j)/v_i \in O_i \wedge v_j \in I_j$ [1].

Table 1. Notations used in the algorithm.

Notations	Description
G_b	Boundary graph
V_b	Boundary vertices
E_b	Set of cross edges
S	Set of source vertices
I	Set of in-crossing vertices
V_a	Set of vertex attributes
CV_a	Constraints on Vertex attribute values
IT	Path from in crossing vertex to target
Attr(x)	A set of vertex attributes of node $x \in V_a$, i.e., $attr(x) \subseteq V_a$
T	Set of target vertices
IO	Path from in crossing vertex to out crossing vertex
E_a	Set of edge attributes
O	Set of out crossing vertices
ST	The path from source to target
CE_a	Constraints on Edge attribute values
SO	Path from source to out crossing vertex

Graph reachability has multiple variants, (i) simple graph reachability to find reachability from source to destination vertices [2–4], (ii) Label-Constrained Reachability (LCR) [5], to find the reachability in the labeled graph from the source node to target node for a given set of constraints, (iii) Reachability queries on distributed graphs for finding reachability from the source node to target node [6,7] (iv) Distributed-Set Reachability queries for the set of sources and targets by constructing the boundary graph which maintained by the master node [1].

The works in [8,12] particularly refers to the attributed graphs for processing the reachability of the source to the target by satisfying the vertex and edge constraints. Table 2 describes the techniques of existing literature with the prominent features in reachability query processing on various graphs. Based on the literature, we found none of the studies demonstrated the distributed set reachability on attributed graphs.

Table 2. Survey of graph reachability techniques with basic features

Technique	Multiple Labels	Distributed Query Processing	Multiple Sources/Targets	Multiple Attributes
Bipartite Hierarchical (BiHi) model [5]	✗	✗	✗	✗
disRPQ Algorithms [6]	✗	✓	✗	✗
Redundant Algorithms for RRQs [7]	✗	✓	✗	✗
Heuristic Search Technique through Guided BFS and Hashing [8]	✗	✗	✗	✓
LCDSRQ [1]	✓	✓	✓	✗
DSRQ_AN (proposed approach)	✓	✓	✓	✓
MQP_PD (proposed approach)	✓	✓	✓	✓

3   DSRQ_AN Approach

The proposed DSRQ_AN technique is to find the paths for given source vertices S to target vertices T on attributed graphs. For example, the attributed graph shown in Fig. 1 is partitioned over a distributed environment, and depicted in Fig. 2. It is noted that $<id>$ for node and relationship properties are generated by Neo4j and will not be treated as one of the node and relation properties of Fig. 1.

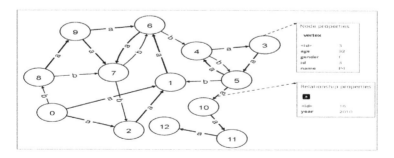

Fig. 1. Example of toy attributed network. The figure was created using Neo4j browser software.

3.1   Illustrations

Let the vertex attributes be *age, gender, id,* and *name,* and the edge attributes be *year* with some domain values. Example of complex query in attributed graph looks like $Q = \langle \{S\}, \{T\}, CV_a, CE_a \rangle$, for instance: $S = \{3, 5\}$, $T = \{1, 12\}$, $CV_a = \{age > 32, \text{gender: f}\}$, $CE_a = \{year > 1980, \text{a}\}$. For the given query, the paths need to be identified between set of sources and set of targets are $\{(3, 1)$ $(3, 12)$ $(5, 1)$ $(5, 12)\}$. The given query returns paths exists for only two pairs by satisfying constraints for $\{3, 12\}$ and $\{5, 12\}$ via the vertex and edge constraints. Thus, the DSRQ_AN paths (3, 5, 10, 11, 12) and (5, 10, 11, 12) are provided for given query constraints by satisfying the constraints.

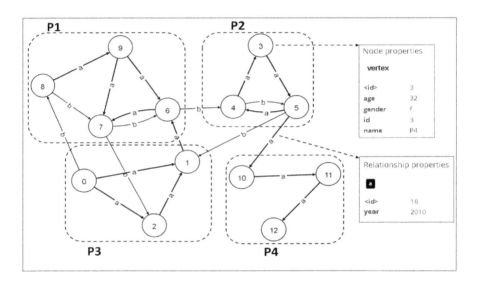

Fig. 2. An example of attributed graph in distributed environment.

In this study, we implemented methodology on Neo4j distributed environment as the baseline LCDSRQ approach [1]. It consists of the master node and a set of slave nodes. This process needs synchronization, which is maintained by the master node with the help of a boundary graph. It consists of boundary vertices V_b, cross-edges E' which includes in-crossing and out-crossing edges, vertex attributes, and edge attributes. The master stores indexes to identify partitions based on in-crossing, out-crossing vertices, and cross edges.

3.2   Query Reachability Processing

Algorithm 1 explains the DSRQ_AN approach to find super nodes from boundary graph and a set of local sources, local targets, and local intermediate nodes in active partitions for attributed graphs, as shown in line nos. 1 and 2. The same procedure is followed from LCDSRQ [1] and extended this approach to find the reachability paths in attributed networks based on the given constraints. The elaborated procedures are described in Algorithms 2 and 3.

Algorithm 1: DSRQ_AN(G_b, E', Q)

Input: $G_b = <V_b, E_b, V_a, E_a>, E', Q = <S, T, CV_a, CE_a>$
Output: Set of paths

1 *flagscoll* ← *DefineActivePartition*(G_b, Q)   //find super nodes
2 $<\{S_i\}, \{T_i\}, \{O_i\}.\{I_i\}> ←$ *FindSetWorkerPairs*(E', G_b, Q)
3 $<\{ST_i\}, \{SO_i\}, \{IT_i\}, \{IO_i\}> ←$
   FindPartialPaths($G_i, S_i, I_i, O_i, T_i, flagscoll, CV_a, CE_a$)
4 *Result* ← *FindMergePaths*($G_b, ST, SO, IO, IT, flagscoll$)
5 **return** Result

To find the reachability paths in attributed graphs, the two steps are given below:

Step 1 - *Finding Local Reachability Paths:* The boundary graph $G_b = <V_b, E_b, V_a, E_a>$ is stored at the master. The master runs the slaves parallel to find the local source vertices, target vertices, and in-crossing and out-crossing vertices. Algorithm 2 describes finding local paths for each partition. Loop (line nos. 1–11) processes each partitioned graph, and the same procedure [1] is followed. However, the existing procedure finds reachability pairs, while line nos. 12–18 are our contribution deals with finding the reachability paths in all local active partitions among the given sources, targets, out-crossing and in-crossing vertices based on the vertex and edge attributes.

Step 2 - *Merging All Local Paths:* After finding the local paths from all active partitions, the proposed Algorithm 3 will merge all the local paths based on the given query constraints of vertices and edges. Line nos. 1–2 collects all local paths from each partition for a set of source and target vertices into results. Lines 3 -13 iterate for each active partition. Line 4 checks for the predecessor's existence, Line nos. 5–6 to check if the partition contains a target then merge the IT paths with the predecessor's partial paths. Line nos. 7–8 to check if the partition contains intermediate then merge the IO paths with the predecessor's partial paths. Line 9 checks the existence of the successor partition, and Line nos. 10–13 combines source out-crossing partition paths for every successor partition.

Algorithm 2: FindPartialPaths $(G_i, S_i, I_i, O_i, T_i, flagscoll, CV_a, CE_a)$

Input: $G_i, S_i, I_i, O_i, T_i, flagscoll, CV_a, CE_a$
Output: Sets of vertex paths ST_i, SO_i, IT_i, IO_i

1 **for** *every partition G_i* **do**
2   //Find local paths for all partitions
3   **if** *flagscoll.local = True* **then**
4          $ST_i \leftarrow FindLocalPaths(G_i, S_i, T_i, CV_a, CE_a)$
5   **if** *flagscoll.source = True* **then**
6          $SO_i \leftarrow FindLocalPaths(G_i, S_i, O_i, CV_a, CE_a)$
7   **if** *flagscoll.intermediate = True* **then**
8          $IO_i \leftarrow FindLocalPaths(G_i, I_i, O_i, CV_a, CE_a)$
9   **if** *flagscoll.target = true* **then**
10         $IT_i \leftarrow FindLocalPaths(G_i, I_i, T_i, CV_a, CE_a)$

11 **return** ST_i, SO_i, IO_i, IT_i

12 **Function** *FindLocalPaths(G_i, X, Y, CV_a, CE_a)*
13      $R \leftarrow \phi$
14   **for** *each node of $x \in X$ and $CV_a \subseteq Attr(x)$* **do**
15   **for** *each node of $y \in Y$ and $CV_a \subseteq Attr(y)$* **do**
16   **if** $x \xrightarrow{CE_a} y$ **then**
17                $R \leftarrow (x, y)$

18 **return** R

Algorithm 3: FindMergePaths$(G_b, ST, SO, IO, IT, flagscoll)$

Input: $G_b = \{V_b, E_b, V_a, E_a\}, pathsST[], SO[], IO[], IT[], flagscoll$
Output: Array of full vertex paths Result

1 **for** *each partition in G* **do**
2   Res $\leftarrow$ Res $\cup$ ST[k]
3 **for** *every active partition k* **do**
4   **if** *predecessors(k) = True* **then**
5   **if** *flagscoll[k].target = True* **then**
6   Res $\leftarrow$ Res $\cup$ merge(path[k], IT[k])
7   **if** *flagscoll[k].intermediate = True* **then**
8             $path[k] \leftarrow merge(path[k], IO[k])$
9   **if** *successors(k) = True* **then**
10   **if** *flagscoll[k].source = True* **then**
11   path[k] $\leftarrow$ path[k] $\cup$ SO[k]
12   **for** *every successor t of k* **do**
13   path[t] $\leftarrow$ path[t] $\cup$ path[k]

14 **return** Res

4 MQP_PD Approach in Parallel and Distributed Environments

Section 3 addressed the path finding and set reachability query in the distributed environment of attributed networks. In this section, we proposed a Multiple Query Processing strategy of attributed networks in a parallel environment through the Neo4j NOSQL system. The processing of queries is distributed in batches and executed parallel on different slaves for finding exact paths between the source vertex and destination vertex. Each slave is having the copy of the input graph. To improve the performance, the queries are divided among multiple slaves, which consist of the same graph. Algorithm 4 describes finding the paths for multiple queries in a parallel and distributed environment using the number of slaves. We demonstrated by experimenting through sequential and parallel paradigm and observed that sequential strategy takes more time; the observations are depicted in Fig. 5.

Algorithm 4: Multiple Query Processing

Input: $G = \{V, E, V_a, E_a\}$, $Q = <S, T, CV_a, CE_a>$
Output: Resultant paths

1 Partition S, T into multiple sub-queries where $S, T \in V$
2 Let n be the number of slaves
3 Each slave contains graph G
4 Distribute multiple queries to each slave
5 $RP = \phi$
6 **for** *each slave i* **do**
7   **for** $v \in S$ *and* $CV_a \subseteq Attr(v)$ **do**
8   **for** $v' \in T$ *and* $CV_a \subseteq Attr(v')$ **do**
9   **if** $v \xrightarrow{CE_a} v'$ **then**
10                 $RP = (v, v')$

11 **return** RP

---

5 Performance Evaluation

To demonstrate the DSRQ_AN algorithm, the master node contains the boundary graph, and the number of slaves executes in a parallel environment. The Cypher language is used to express reachability queries [11]. We have implemented the methods in Java, and experiments have been conducted on a machine with Intel(R) Core i7-6820HQ CPU @ 2.70 GHz, 8 Core(s).

Three contributions are experimented and discussed in this section. Firstly, The performance of baseline (LCDSRQ) [1] and proposed DSRQ_AN algorithms using the synthetic datasets (SYNTH1 [1] with 600,000 vertices) for the range of queries, which are shown in Fig. 3. The number of queries are represented as $m \times$

n, where m, n is the number of sources and targets respectively. As observed, due to attributed networks and complex query processing, our approach considerably takes more time (in fractions).

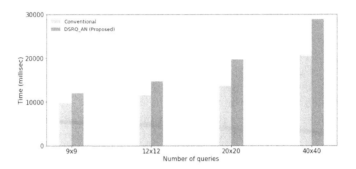

Fig. 3. Time taken to execute complex queries of the conventional and proposed approach.

Secondly, In Fig. 4, we examined the performance comparison with respect to the number of constraints $|C|$ and observed that the number of constraints increases proportionally. The time for finding exact paths is also increasing in the conventional and proposed approach.

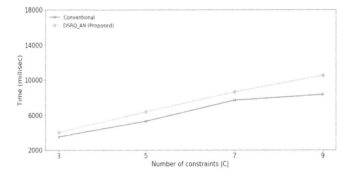

Fig. 4. Time vs. No. of constraints $|C|$.

Thirdly, the MQP_PD algorithm is implemented in sequential and parallel modes. The parallel approach considered four slaves and each slave has the same input graph of 50,000 vertices and different sets of queries are distributed among slaves to extract outcomes simultaneously. This parallel approach takes less time compared to the sequential approach for multiple queries and is depicted in Fig. 5.

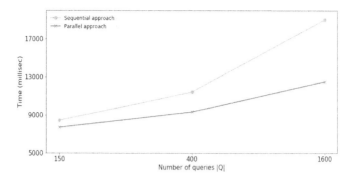

Fig. 5. Performance of sequential and parallel approaches for multiple query execution.

6   Conclusions and Future Work

In this study, we proposed the DSRQ_AN to process multi-dimensional constraint distributed graphs for solving Distributed Set Reachability queries. We extended the algorithm to find the resultant paths using synthetic datasets. Additionally, we have demonstrated that the proposed DSRQ_AN is scalable for attributed networks and handled effectively by distributed computing through the Neo4j graph data platform and Cypher Query Language. Also, demonstrated the sequential and parallel approaches for multiple query execution on the attributed graphs and observed that query execution time is reduced for the parallel approach. We plan to extend the research to perform experiments on real-world networks and develop an efficient algorithm to handle dynamic networks to solve distributed set reachability queries.

References

1. Gacem, A., Papadopoulos, A.N., Boukhalfa, K.: Scalable distributed reachability query processing in multi-labeled networks. Data Knowl. Eng. **130**, 101854 (2020). https://doi.org/10.1016/j.datak.2020.101854
2. Seufert, S., Anand, A., Bedathur, S., Weikum, G.: FERRARI: flexible and efficient reachability range assignment for graph indexing. In: 2013 IEEE 29th International Conference on Data Engineering (ICDE), pp. 1009–1020 (2013). https://doi.org/10.1109/ICDE.2013.6544893
3. Veloso, R.R., Cerf, L., Junior, W.M., Zaki, M.J.: Reachability queries in very large graphs: a fast refined online search approach (2014). https://openproceedings.org/EDBT/2014/paper_166.pdf, https://dx.doi.org/10.5441/002/edbt.2014.46
4. Yildirim, H., Chaoji, V., Zaki, M.J.: GRAIL: scalable reachability index for large graphs. Proc. VLDB Endow. **3**, 276–284 (2010). https://doi.org/10.14778/1920841.1920879
5. Chen, L., Wu, Y., Zhong, Z., Xiong, W., Jing, N.: A hierarchical model for label constraint reachability computation. Neurocomputing **162**, 67–84 (2015). https://doi.org/10.1016/j.neucom.2015.04.003

6. Fan, W., Wang, X., Wu, Y.: Performance guarantees for distributed reachability queries (2012). http://arxiv.org/abs/1208.0091, https://doi.org/10.48550/arXiv.1208.0091
7. Nguyen-Van, Q., Tung, L.-D., Hu, Z.: Minimizing data transfers for regular reachability queries on distributed graphs. In: Proceedings of the 4th Symposium on Information and Communication Technology, pp. 325–334. Association for Computing Machinery, New York (2013). https://doi.org/10.1145/2542050.2542092
8. Yung, D., Chang, S.-K.: Fast reachability query computation on big attributed graphs. In: 2016 IEEE International Conference on Big Data (Big Data), pp. 3370–3380 (2016). https://doi.org/10.1109/BigData.2016.7840997
9. Gurajada, S., Theobald, M.: Distributed set reachability. In: Proceedings of the 2016 International Conference on Management of Data, pp. 1247–1261. Association for Computing Machinery, New York (2016). https://doi.org/10.1145/2882903.2915226
10. Wang, Z., Fan, Q., Wang, H., Tan, K.-L., Agrawal, D., Abbadi, A.: Pagrol: parallel graph OLAP over large-scale attributed graphs (2014). https://doi.org/10.1109/ICDE.2014.6816676
11. Francis, N., et al.: Cypher: an evolving query language for property graphs. In: Proceedings of the 2018 International Conference on Management of Data, pp. 1433–1445. Association for Computing Machinery, New York (2018). https://doi.org/10.1145/3183713.3190657
12. Bhargavi, B., Rani, K.S., Neog, A.: Finding multidimensional constraint reachable paths for attributed graphs. EAI Endorsed Trans. Scalable Inf. Syst. **10**, e8 (2023). https://doi.org/10.4108/eetsis.v9i4.2581

Gradient Directional Predictor for Reconstructing High-Fidelity Images

Ravi Uyyala[1]([⊠])(ID) and Jyothirmai Joshi[2]

[1] Chaitanya Bharathi Institute of Technology (CBIT), Hyderabad, India
uyyala.ravi@gmail.com
[2] VNR Vignan Jyothi Institute of Engineering and Technology, Hyderabad, India
jyothirmai_j@vnrvjiet.in

Abstract. A good pixel prediction strategy is essential to have a good prediction error expansion based reversible data hiding technique. Several pixel prediction strategies exist in literature. Gradients are used to predict the current pixel. Several Researchers have been proposed based on the gradient estimation to predict the current pixel for embedding more data in the current pixel. In this paper a novel approach based on the gradients of the image using 3×4 neighbourhood has been proposed for better predicting the current pixel. Adaptive histogram bin shifting has been used to insert more data with less distortion, depending on the local complexity of the pixel. The experimental study shows that the proposed technique performs better than some existing methods.

Keywords: Gradients · Inserting the data into Images · Gradients · Prediction Strategy

1 Introduction

The traditional way of hiding data is called lossy data hiding because the cover image cannot be extracted to its original form. In contrast, RDH [1] enables the recovery of the inserted data as well as the cover data from the marked data. Because the cover media can be rebuilt using the marked media, RDH is frequently referred to as lossless data hiding.

The main thing that sets RDH apart is the ability to reverse an embedded image and get the main data back. Data is added to the main data by making a alteration to the pixel values that can be reversed. Because the transformation can be reversed, the main data can be brought back from the embedded data and the hidden data can be taken out at the same time. So, the value of each pixel in the restored image is about the same as its value in the main data.

This technique has become more useful in several applications where the recovery of the main data is very crucial. There are numerous RDH strategies in the literature [1]. The RDH technique was first introduced in [2]. Since then, a number of RDH techniques have advanced this domain. One of the first methods for RDH was the difference expansion (DE)-based Algorithm described in [3].

To add a single bit of information to the main data, the difference between the neighbouring pixels that are immediately adjacent is explored. This field has advanced to a number of well-known research works in [3]. Histogram bin shifting-based RDH is a distinct kind of method presented in [4]. A pair of the cover image histogram's peak and zero points have been used to insert the single data in the histogram bin shifting method [4]. In [5], an RDH approach based on multiple histograms is proposed. Different complexity values of the image are explored to compute the multiple histograms. Then, the secret information is expanded into the image using the optimal bin selection method in [5].

One genre of these techniques that have been found to be superior to others and better than others is RDH using the Prediction Error (PE) Expansion (PEE)-Techniques [6]. In PEE-based RDH techniques, a set of context pixels surrounding a neighbourhood are analyzed to predict the current pixel. Data bits are hidden in the PE-of the concerned pixel. The superiority of PEE-based RDH techniques has attracted more attention from researchers. This motivates me to carry out further research on PEE-based RDH techniques.

Naturally, a good predictor results in less PE-for a particular pixel value. Since data bits are expanded in the PE, a good pixel predictor causes less embedding distortion in the pixel. Hence, the objective of the research, as reported in this paper, is to come up with novel RDH techniques by exploring suitable pixel prediction schemes. Novel pixel prediction strategies have been proposed in the context of RDH. In this context, the performance of several cutting-edge pixel prediction strategies has also been investigated. The use of appropriate pixel prediction strategies has led to a better trade-off between embedding capacity and distortion.

The ability of RDH varies depending on the PVO [7]. The technique using PVO in [7] divided the image into several, non-overlapping sections. The pixel values of the block are then arranged in ascending order. Next, the 2nd-highest and 2nd-lowest values are used to calculate the 1st highest and 1st lowest values. Many articles have examined the ordering of pixel values in [7–15].

There is also a type of RDH technique that uses a fixed set of reference pixels and is based on PEE. The initial set of reference pixels is used to locally adjust the number of reference pixels. Various Reference pixel-based predictions are suggested in [16,17].

The study of image coding initially had a significant influence on prediction methods. For instance, the PEE-based RDH in [6] uses a MED, it was initially developed as a lossless image coding method. The MED predictor suggests, the top, left, and top-left neighbours of a pixel to estimate its current pixel value, with an emphasis on whether or not an edge is present at the pixel's near left or top. The GAP utilized the horizontal, and vertical gradients and their strengths to predict a pixel [6]. The GAP predictor is also used in the RDH approach to predict a pixel value. Additional gradient-based predictors consist of GBSW, Extended GBSW [18]. Many additional predictors rely on a straightforward calculation utilizing information from nearby pixels [19–21]. The perceptron-based predictor [22] is used to predict the current pixel using multi-layers. In [23], the current pixel is predicted by the weighted average of these four adjacent pixel values. Recently, a video RDH has been suggested in [24].

In this paper, we propose a gradient-based prediction using 3×4 neighborhood-based context to better predict the current pixel. Later, to better embed the data into the original cover image, a novel adaptive histogram bin shifting method was used.

This paper is organised as follows: The second Sect. 2 investigates gradient-based prediction in the context of the 3×4 neighborhood. Section 3 describes the embedding and extraction using adaptive histogram bin shifting. Section 4 explains the experimental findings, and finally, Sect. 5 illustrates the conclusion.

2   Gradient Based Prediction

This study presents a novel RDH strategy that uses a gradient-based pixel prediction approach. The gradients are calculated in the present work using a seven-pixel context and a 3×4 neighbourhood in the horizontal and vertical directions. This work considers the context with a seven-pixel around current pixel (x) as shown in the Fig. 1. The gradients are typically determined by first computing differences in various directions. Generally, with the help of gradients one can find the strong edges around the center pixel. Based on the strong edge, better predicted value can be obtained. This work uses two better gradients for estimating the value. The proposed work considers only horizontal and vertical gradients. Based on these two gradients, the proposed work is trying to find the edges present around the current pixel. Typically, the horizontal or vertical directions are better aligned with the pixel intensity values. Difference between the horizontal and vertical is used to find the better estimated value. Gradients are very much useful for finding the edges around the current pixel. The new prediction context computes the following pixel differences for the two orientations (horizontal, vertical):

$$D_h = |W - WW| + |N - NW| + |N - NE| \tag{1}$$

$$D_v = |W - NW| + |N - NN| + |NE - NNE| \tag{2}$$

The complete process of predicting the current pixel using the context of 3×4 neighbourhood with seven pixels around the current pixel is described in the Algorithm 1.

The variance of the four-pixel values at the current pixel's right and bottom neighbours (SW, S, SE, and E) is used to calculate the local complexity of that pixel. The original values of these pixels are maintained during embedding and extraction.

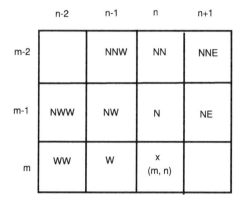

Fig. 1. 3×4 Neighbourhood Based Context

Algorithm 1. Estimating the present pixel x

$D \Leftarrow D_v - D_h$
$S \Leftarrow ((W + N)/2 + (NE - NW)/4)$
if $D > 80$ then
   $x' \Leftarrow W$
else if $D < -80$ then
   $x' \Leftarrow N$
else if $D > 32$ then
   $x' \Leftarrow (W + S)/2$
else if $D > 8$ then
   $x' \Leftarrow (W + 3 \times S)/4$
else if $D < -32$ then
   $x' \Leftarrow (S + N)/4$
else if $D < -8$ then
   $x' \Leftarrow (W + 3 \times S)/2$
end if

---

3   Embedding and Extraction

A pixel's PE is determined as the difference between its main value (x) and estimated or predicted value (x'), or $PE = x - x'$. Similar to the work in [25], A novel adaptive histogram bin shifting or altering method is adopted here. The present work has been investigated to expand 1 or 2 bits of data into the main content. The main content is explored with the help of complexity of the image. The proposed work uses local complexity to insert 1 or 2 bits of data. The main objective of computing the local complexity is to determine the roughness of the image surrounding the present pixels. During inserting the secret data the bins selected are $(-1, 0)$ and $(1, 0)$. The main motive of selecting only two bins is to reduce the distortion caused to main content. Generally, if PE is less then small distortion has been caused to main content while embedding. The small

PE is tried to give small deviation from original pixel to embedded pixel. The proposed work PE-histogram has been shown in Fig. 2.

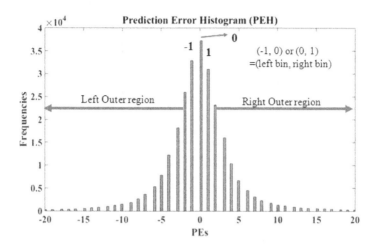

Fig. 2. Adaptive Histogram Bin Shifting

A few key points about this embedding strategy are mentioned here:

– The PE of the pixel contains either 1 or 2 bits of data, depending on the local complexity (lc) of the pixel. A pixel's lc assesses the roughness in pixel's surroundings. It is estimated, here, using variance of SW, S, SE, E pixel values.
– If the lc is $\leq$ to threshold value (Th_{lc}) and PE is ε $[-Th_{pe}, +Th_{pe}]$ then that pixel is expanded two bits of data.
– If the lc is $>$ threshold value (Th_{lc}) and PE of the current pixel is ε $[-Th_{pe}, +Th_{pe}]$ then that pixel is expanded one bit of data.
– If the lc is $\leq$ to Th_{lc} and PE is $\notin [-Th_{pe}, +Th_{pe}]$ then that pixel is shifted towards left or right by $-4Th_{pe}$ and $4Th_{pe} + 3$ respectively.
– Similarly, If the lc is $>$ threshold value Th_{lc} and PE of the current pixel is $\notin [-Th_{pe}, +Th_{pe}]$ then that pixel is shifted towards left or right by $-2Th_{pe}$ and $2Th_{pe} + 1$ respectively.
– The threshold value of lc and threshold value of PE are denoted by Th_{lc}, and Th_{pe} respectively.
– The proposed work uses only $(-1, 0)$ and $(1, 0)$ bins for embedding two bits or one bit of data based on the adaptive histogram bin shifting.
– Pixels from two successive bins of the PE histogram are only used to expand the secret data bits. Normally, the bin with PE as 0 or anyone of its adjacent bins will be the highest for a good predictor. Hence, two consecutive bins are selected as having predictor errors as either $(-1$ and $0)$ or $(0$ and $1)$. To differentiate from the two bins where embedding is done, the remaining bins are moved towards negative or positive side of the PE histogram.

- The following information is considered as auxiliary or additional information, which are also required during extraction process: (i) The pixel's location of final secret information inserted, (ii) How many bits (either one or two)expanded in the final pixel value, (iii) Th_{lc} value, (iv) whether there has been an overflow or underflow (OF/UF), (v) Compressed OF/UF location map's length, and (vi) the compressed OF/UF map.
- The LSBs of the pixels of initial some rows of image are explored to store the additional information. The actual LSBs of these pixels are added at the end of the data bit string. Embedding of this concatenated bit string starts from the immediate next row after the embedding of auxiliary data.

A few key points about extraction are stated below:

- At first, the LSBs of the pixels in the initial few rows of the marked image are used to obtain the additional information.
- Location of the last expanded pixel are known from the additional information. From this pixel, a traversal in the opposite order of raster scan sequence is followed to extract the data bit string (which also includes the actual LSBs of the pixels at the first few rows) and to restore the cover image pixel values.
- If the lc is $\leq$ threshold value (Th_{lc}) and PE is $\varepsilon\ [-4Th_{pe}, +4Th_{pe} + 3]$ then that pixel is explored to extract two bits of data.
- If the lc is $>$ threshold value (Th_{lc}) and PE is $\varepsilon\ [-2Th_{pe}, +2Th_{pe} + 1]$ then that pixel is explored to extract one bit of data.
- If the lc is $\leq$ to Th_{lc} and PE is $\notin [-4Th_{pe}, +4Th_{pe} + 3]$ then that pixel is shifted towards right or left by $4Th_{pe}$ and $-4Th_{pe} - 3$ respectively.
- Similarly, If the lc is $>$ threshold value Th_{lc} and PE is $\notin [-Th_{pe}, +Th_{pe}]$ then that pixel is shifted towards right or left by $2Th_{pe}$ and $-2Th_{pe} - 1$ respectively.
- The threshold value of local complexity and threshold value of PEare denoted by Th_{lc}, and Th_{pe} respectively.
- The expanding PEhistograms bins in this work are $(-1, 0)$ and $(0, 1)$ only.
- Finally, the actual LSBs are placed in the pixels at the first few rows in a LSB-substitution technique.
- During inserting the secret data and extraction the estimated value or predicted value should be similar.

In this paper, the proposed work has been suggested the adaptive histogram bin shifting technique for data to be embedded into the pixels. In various papers, the complexity of the pixel is used to find, whether the current pixel located in the smooth region or rough region.

4 Experimental Results

This section presents the experimental results of the proposed gradient-based prediction and adaptive prediction error histogram bin shifting. Experiments are carried out using test images of sizes 512×512 shown in the Fig. 3. The experimental findings involve the two sets of histogram bins (i) either -1 or 0 and (ii) either 0 or 1. The embedding capacities for the two aforementioned scenarios do not differ noticeably from one another. PSNR values between the cover images and the associated marked images in these two scenarios are also similar (at the maximum embedding capacity for each image). For each of the aforementioned experimental cases, PSNR values between the cover image and the marked images are estimated for different payload sizes. These PSNR values are plotted for case one in Fig. 4.

Fig. 3. Standard four test images: Lena, Lake, Elaine, and Boat

Peak Signal-to-Noise Ratio (PSNR) values between the cover image and the corresponding marked images are estimated with various payload sizes for each of the above experimental cases. The experiments are conducted by changing the local complexity threshold value Th_{lc} as $0, 1, 2, 4, 8$ and 16. A single bit embedding is indicated by Th_{lc} having a value of 0. More data can be inserted when Th_{lc} is greater. The proposed work is compared with other existing methods with the help of single bit embedding, i.e. $Th_{lc} = 0$.

To control the adaptive embedding process, the value of the local complexity threshold Th_{lc} is modified in the reported experiments as 0, 1, 2, 4, 8, and 16. When Th_{lc} is set to 0, it means that a pixel's PE contains a 1 bit payload. A greater Th_{lc} value means that more pixels can accommodate 2 bits of payload. Embedding capacity rises as Th_{lc} is valued higher. When Th_{lc} is valued higher, the PSNR value also decreases at the same time. Maximum embedding capacity for various payload (Bits per pixel (Bpp)) with PSNR values, observable from the Table 1.

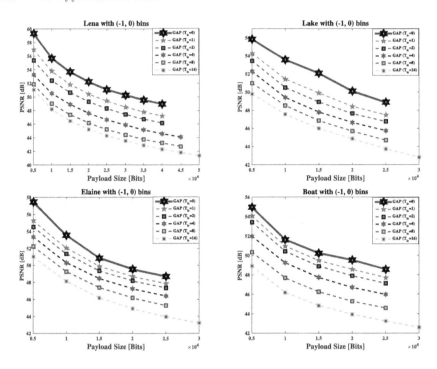

Fig. 4. Performance Comparison by varying Th_{lc}

The proposed RDH technique employing the 3×4 neighborhood for gradient estimation is compared to several existing RDH techniques, including the rhombus average [26], EGBSW [27], and significant bit plane difference [28]. Figure 5 displays the PSNR values between the cover images and their marked images for different payload sizes. The marked images of the proposed method with various payload sizes are presented in Fig. 6. The suggested RDH strategy outperforms the currently used comparison techniques. It can be observed that the proposed reversible data-hiding technique performs better than the existing techniques. Experimental results of histogram bin pairs $(-1, 0)$ and $(0, 1)$ are almost similar. The proposed method has been presented only for $(-1, 0)$ pair, i.e., usage of histogram bins relating to prediction errors as -1 and 0. We compared the proposed approach with peak point $(-1, 0)$ with other existing methods because the PSNR values for peak points $(-1, 0)$ and $(1, 0)$ are nearly identical.

The Structural Similarity (SSIM) Index value is one of the metric to estimate the quality of the marked image with respect to original image. For various images, SSIM values have been shown in the Table 2.

Table 1. Maximum Embedding Capacity when $Th_{lc} = 0$ and $Th_{lc} = 16$ for various Bpp with PSNR Values

Image	$Th_{l} = 0$		$Th_{l} = 16$	
Lena	0.15	48.96	0.19	41.37
Lake	0.09	48.86	0.11	42.82
Elaine	0.09	48.70	0.11	43.21
Boat	0.10	48.56	0.11	42.60

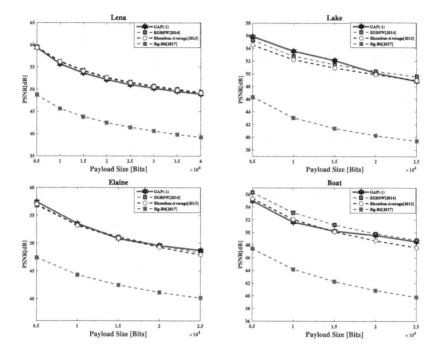

Fig. 5. Performance Comparison with other methods

Table 2. SSIM Values for 5000 bits with all images

Image	Capacity	SSIM
Lena	**5000 bits**	**0.93**
Lake	**5000 bits**	**0.92**
Elaine	**5000 bits**	**0.91**
Boat	**5000 bits**	**0.87**

Fig. 6. Results of the Proposed work on RDH scheme for various test images. Original image, marked images with 5000 bits

5   Conclusion

The gradient based prediction has been exploited in this paper for RDH technique. Using a 3×4 neighbourhood context with gradients in different directions, the prediction was determined. The adaptive histogram bin shifting approach was used for embedding the data into the bins of the histogram adaptively for better embedding. The suggested method outperforms various current strategies based on gradients and adaptive histogram bin shifting.

Initially, the prediction has been computed using gradient estimation, gradients are computed by taking the difference in horizontal and vertical directions. Predicted value of the current pixel is computed based on the edge presents around the current pixel. If the edge presents in horizontal direction then predicted value will be taken as horizontal edge. If the edge presents in vertical direction then predicted value is computed based on the vertical edge. Here, the proposed work presents only two directions. Generally the predicted value is more located in these two directions only.

The expansion of prediction error has been expanded for embedding the data into the current pixel. Expansion means, inserting the data into the prediction error. The prediction error expansion has been considered for inserting the data into the prediction error. Based on the capacity one can increase the threshold for more data to embed in the current pixel in the PEE technique. But here, instead of considering all bins based on threshold value. The proposed work uses the adaptive histogram bin shifting method. The threshold values in the proposed work are $(-1, 0, 1)$. So, only these bins are used for data embedding. Moreover, the adaptive bin shifting has been used for more data to be embedded.

Here, the local complexity value has been selected for adaptive embedding. More data has been embedded in smooth region, less data has been embedded in rough region. The smooth region and rough region of the image has been computed using local complexity threshold.

There are two kinds of reversible data hiding, (i) Robust reversible data hiding. (ii) fragile reversible data hiding. In first category of the RDH, one has to check how robust the proposed technique with different types of attacks. The proposed RDH should be strong enough to different attacks. In second category of RDH, robustness checking is not required to present. Thus, the second category of RDH is very much useful in the applications where the recovery of the original medium is mandatory.

The reversible data hiding technique is fragile, similar to the existing RDH techniques. Therefore, robustness of the proposed technique against several attacks on the marked image is not generally studied for these techniques. These RDH techniques differ from robust watermarking strategies in that The hidden data is destroyed by a little change in the marked pixel value. Hence, this enables identification of any tampering of original cover image. Therefore, the primary purpose of the RDH technique is to maintain the integrity of the original cover image.

References

1. Shi, Y.Q., Li, X., Zhang, X., Wu, H.T., Ma, B.: Reversible data hiding: advances in the past two decades. IEEE Access **4**, 3210–3237 (2016)
2. Honsinger, C.W., Jones, P.W., Rabbani, M, Stoffel, J.C.: Lossless recovery of an original image containing embedded data. U. S. Patent, US 6278791B1 (2001)
3. Tian, J.: Reversible data embedding using a difference expansion. IEEE Trans. Circuits Syst. Video Technol. **13**(8), 890–896 (2003)
4. Ni, Z., Shi, Y.Q., Ansari, N., Su, W.: Reversible data hiding. IEEE Trans. Circuits Syst. Video Technol. **16**(3), 354–362 (2006)
5. Li, X., Zhang, W., Gui, X., Yang, B.: Efficient reversible data hiding based on multiple histograms modification. IEEE Trans. Inf. Forensics Secur. **10**(9), 2016–2027 (2015)
6. Thodi, D.M., Rodriguez, J.J.: Expansion embedding techniques for reversible watermarking. IEEE Trans. Image Process. **16**(3), 721–730 (2007)
7. Li, X., Li, J., Li, B., Yang, B.: High-fidelity reversible data hiding scheme based on pixel-value-ordering and prediction-error expansion. Signal Process. **93**, 198–205 (2013)
8. Wang, X., Ding, J., Q, Pe.: A novel reversible image data hiding scheme based on pixel value ordering and dynamic pixel block partition. Inf. Sci. **310**, 16–35 (2015)
9. Ou, B., Li, X., Jinwei, W.: Improved PVO-based reversible data hiding. A new implementation based on multiple histograms modification. J. Vis. Commun. Image Represent. **38**, 328–339 (2016)
10. Weng, S., Shi, Y.Q., Hong, W., Yao, Y.: Dynamic improved pixel value ordering reversible data hiding. Inf. Sci. **89**, 136–154 (2019)
11. He, W., Xiong, G., Zhou, K., Cai, J.: Reversible data hiding based on multilevel histogram modification and pixel value grouping. J. Vis. Commun. Image Represent. **40**, 459–469 (2016)

12. Qu, X., Kim, H.J.: Pixel-based pixel value ordering predictor for high-fidelity reversible data hiding. Signal Process. **111**, 249–260 (2015)
13. Weng, S., Zhang, G., Pan, J.S., Zhou, Z.: Optimal PPVO-based reversible data hiding. J. Vis. Commun. Image Represent. **48**, 317–328 (2017)
14. Xiang, H., Liu, H.: A pixel-based reversible data hiding method based on obtuse angle prediction. In: 2nd International Conference on Multimedia and Image Processing, Wuhan, China, pp. 191–195 (2017)
15. He, W., Cai, J., Xiong, G., Zhou, K.: Improved reversible data hiding using pixel-based pixel value grouping. Optik **157**, 68–78 (2018)
16. Ravi, U., Rajarshi, P., Prasad, M.: Reversible data hiding using b-tree triangular decomposition based prediction. IET Image Process. **13**, 1986–1997 (2019)
17. Ravi, U., Rajarshi, P.: Reversible data hiding based on the random distribution of reference pixels. In: IEEE Region Ten Symposium (Tensymp), pp. 225–230 (2018)
18. Ravi, U., Rajarshi, P., Prasad, M.: Gradient dependent reversible watermarking with low embedding impact. In: International Conference on Signal Processing and Integrated Networks, pp. 184–189 (2016)
19. Ravi, U., Rajarshi, P.: Reversible data hiding using improved gradient based prediction and adaptive histogram bin shifting. In: International Conference on Signal Processing and Integrated Networks, pp. 720–726 (2020)
20. Ravi, U., Prasad, M., Rajarshi, P.: Selected context dependent prediction for reversible watermarking with optimal embedding. In: International Conference on Computer Vision and Image Processing, vol. 460, pp. 35–46 (2016)
21. Ravi, U., Rajarshi, P.: Reversible data hiding with selected directional context based prediction using 8-neighborhood. In: IEEE International Conference on Electronics, Computing and Communication Technologies, pp. 1–6 (2020)
22. Bhandari, A., Sharma, S., Ravi, U., Rajarshi, P., Verma, M.: Reversible data hiding using multi-layer perceptron based pixel prediction. In: International Conference on Advances in Information Technology, pp. 1–8 (2020)
23. Jia, Y., Yin, Z., Zhang, X., Luo, Y.: Reversible data hiding based on reducing invalid shifting of pixels in histogram shifting. Signal Process. **163**, 238–246 (2019)
24. Li, L., Yao, Y., Yu, N.: High-fidelity video reversible data hiding using joint spatial and temporal prediction. Signal Process. **208**, 108970 (2023)
25. Hong, W., Chen, T.-S., Shiu, C.-W.: Reversible data hiding for high-quality images using modification of prediction errors. J. Syst. Softw. **82**(11), 1833–1842 (2009)
26. Coltuc, D., Dragoi, I.-C.: Context embedding for raster-scan rhombus based reversible watermarking. In: First ACM Workshop on Information Hiding and Multimedia Security, pp. 215–220 (2013)
27. Dragoi, I.C., Coltuc, D., Caciula, I.: Gradient based prediction for reversible watermarking by difference expansion. In: 2nd ACM Workshop on Information Hiding and Multimedia Security, pp. 35–40 (2014)
28. Weiqing, W., Junyong, Y., Wang, W.: Reversible data hiding scheme based on significant-bit-difference expansion. IET Image Process. **11**(11), 1002–1014 (2017)

We Chased COVID-19; Did We Forget Measles? - Public Discourse and Sentiment Analysis on Spiking Measles Cases Using Natural Language Processing

V. S. Anoop[1]([✉]) [ID], Jose Thekkiniath[2] [ID],
and Usharani Hareesh Govindarajan[3] [ID]

[1] School of Digital Sciences, Kerala University of Digital Sciences,
Innovation and Technology, Thiruvananthapuram, India
anoop.vs@duk.ac.in
[2] Department of Biological Sciences, Purdue University Fort Wayne,
Fort Wayne, IN, USA
[3] Business School, University of Shanghai for Science and Technology,
Shanghai, China

Abstract. This study employs text mining and natural language processing approaches for analyzing and unearthing public discourse and sentiment toward the recent spiking Measles outbreaks reported across the globe. A detailed qualitative study was designed using text mining and natural language processing on the user-generated comments from Reddit, a social news aggregation and discussion website. A detailed analysis using topic modeling and sentiment analysis on Reddit comments (n = 87203) posted between October 1 and December 15, 2022, was conducted. Topic modeling was used to leverage significant themes related to the Measles health emergency and public discourse; the sentiment analysis was performed to check how the general public responded to different aspects of the outbreak. Our results revealed several intriguing and helpful themes, including *parental concerns, anti-vaxxer discussions,* and *measles symptoms* from the user-generated content. The results further confirm that even though there have been administrative interventions to promote vaccinations that affirm the parents' concerns to a greater extent, the anti-vaccination or vaccine hesitancy prevalent in the general public reduces the effect of such intercessions. Proactively analyzing public discourse and sentiments during health emergencies and disease outbreaks is vital. This study effectively explored public perceptions and sentiments to assist health policy researchers and stakeholders in making informed data-driven decisions.

Keywords: public discourse · sentiment analysis · text mining · natural language processing · public health · health surveillance · infodemiology

R. Morusupalli et al. (Eds.): MIWAI 2023, LNAI 14078, pp. 147–158, 2023.
https://doi.org/10.1007/978-3-031-36402-0_13

1   Introduction

Measles is a highly contagious viral disease and is one of the significant causes of death among young children globally. Recent World Health Organization (WHO) statistics show that nearly 40 million children are highly vulnerable to the growing measles threat. A joint report published in November 2022 by the WHO and the Center for Disease Control (CDC) revealed that many children missed their measles vaccines. Many factors may contribute to this, but the primary one is the COVID-19 pandemic [1,2]. In 2021 alone, 9 million measles cases and 128000 deaths were reported globally due to significantly declined measles vaccinations and weakened measles surveillance procedures due to COVID-19[1]. This caused persistent measles outbreaks in 2022 across the globe and the WHO has stated this as an "imminent threat". A careful analysis showed that while significant efforts have been focused on developing COVID-19 vaccines in record time, the focus on routine vaccination programs declined to an unacceptable level.

Social media is proven to be a platform for deliberations and discussions on any topics, including pandemics and disease outbreaks [3,25]. The public commonly shares their opinions, concerns, symptoms, treatments, and adverse reactions to medications on social media such as Twitter [22] and Facebook and news aggregators such as Reddit [4]. These highly invaluable data contain trends and latent themes that may be significantly important to aid public policymakers and governments in prioritizing their strategies to help combat the outbreaks [26–29]. To the best of the authors' knowledge, very few early studies reported in the public health literature analyze public discourse and sentiment towards growing measles outbreak [5,6].

During the COVID-19 pandemic and Monkeypox outbreak, Reddit[2] has been used as one of the vital sources of public discourse analysis [7–9,23,24,30,30,31]. The proposed study uses Reddit comments to respond and add knowledge to our understanding of the global measles outbreak. To explore public discourse and sentiments during the measles outbreak, we use unsupervised machine learning techniques to examine (a) What major topics related to measles can we identify from Reddit comments? (b) How can we map the discovered topics to the measles-related themes? (c) How do Reddit users emotionally react to the spiking global measles cases? The qualitative analysis of user-generated comments and discussions may unearth better insights and patterns to aid in better-informed decision-making processes. The proposed study uses text mining and natural language processing techniques, including topic modeling and sentiment analysis, to qualitatively analyze public discourse on the spiking global Measles outbreak. The specific objectives of this work are:

a. To conduct a qualitative public discourse and sentiment analysis on the growing measles outbreak emergency using user-generated content.

---

[1] https://www.who.int/news/item/23-11-2022-nearly-40-million-children-are-dangerously-susceptible-to-growing-measles-threat.

[2] https://www.reddit.com/.

b. To analyze major themes of discussion among users on different aspects of measles including *parental concerns*, and *vaccinations*

c. To understand how social network users emotionally react to the measles outbreak that the WHO has categorized as a global imminent threat.

2 Methods

2.1 Study Design

This study uses an observational design and a purposive sampling approach to select all the comments from Reddit pages related to Measles (for instance, https://www.reddit.com/r/Measles/. We used natural language processing approaches to unearth salient topics and terms related to Measles, and our data mining process included data preparation and analysis. The sampling, data collection, and pre-processing were carried out to build the experiment-ready version of the dataset. During the analysis phase, we implemented unsupervised machine learning (topic modeling), qualitative analysis, and sentiment analysis by using individual Reddit comments as the unit of analysis. The overall workflow of the proposed methodology is shown in Fig. 1.

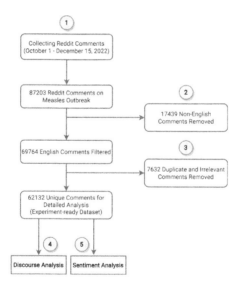

Fig. 1. Workflow of the methodology

2.2 Data Preparation and Measures

We have collected comments posted by Reddit users, specifically on the pages that discuss Measles, using Reddit's open application programming interface (API) available at https://www.reddit.com/dev/api/. The comments posted between October 01, 2022, and December 15, 2022, are collected for this study using PRAW: The Python Reddit API Wrapper available at https://praw. readthedocs.io/en/stable/. We collected 87203 Reddit comments, of which 17439 comments not written in English were removed. Of the 69764 comments, 7632 were found to be duplicates or irrelevant and thus removed. After the pre-processing stage, 62132 comments were selected for the experimental purpose. For this study, we selected *author*, *created date*, and *body* features, and our data collection method strictly complied with Reddit's terms of service and developer agreement policies. Three representative comments from the dataset are shown in Table 1. As this study analyzes user-generated content, there may be a significant amount of noise and irrelevant content as a part of the comments collected. We pre-processed the comments collected data to ensure quality by adopting the following measures:

a. We removed user mentions, URLs, and other special symbols along with punctuation marks and numbers as they do not contribute significantly to the message analysis.
b. We removed emojis using the *demoji* library available at https://pypi.org/project/demoji/
c. We removed all non-English letters and other characters as this study concentrates on the analysis of comments written in English
d. We removed repeated characters from words if found unnecessary (for example, "soooo painful" has been changed to "so painful").

2.3   Data Analysis

This study uses an unsupervised machine learning algorithm to analyze the patterns from the unstructured comments, as this approach was commonly used in scenarios dealing with limited observations. Since the approach is unsupervised, the algorithm may automatically cluster similarities where qualitative analysis may fail when dealing with large unstructured text data. In natural language processing, topic models are a suite of text-understanding algorithms that unearth the latent patterns from a large body of unstructured text. There are several topic modeling algorithms already reported in the machine learning and natural language processing literature [10,11], and they differ in how they make assumptions to generate hidden word collections called "topics". The primary assumption of most of the previous topic modeling algorithms is that a document contains only one topic, but that is not the case with real-world documents. The Latent Dirichlet Allocation (LDA) [12] algorithm introduced later in the literature by David M. Blei could model this assumption and became very popular among natural language processing researchers and enthusiasts. We used the LDA algorithm in this study to infer latent topics from the comments posted by Reddit users, which helped us categorize the text based on the features and patterns. Topic modeling is already proven to be efficient in analyzing large quantities of user-generated unstructured text in social science research [13–15].

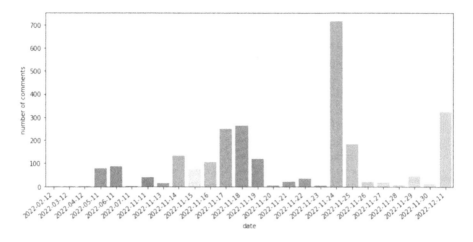

Fig. 2. Representative, date-wise responses on the measles outbreak on Reddit

Qualitative analysis is required to dive deep into the data to analyze better the trends, patterns, and themes [16]. Analyzing and interpreting topics generated by the topic modeling algorithms required human efforts, and during this qualitative analysis, we performed the same. The topic words are analyzed and contextualized to map them to different themes relevant to the Measles emergency, enabling deeper qualitative dives into the comments collected. This human-in-the-loop qualitative analysis help derives in-depth interpretations from identifying public discourse [17] better. Sentiment analysis is a natural language processing approach that attempts to analyze the sentiment and emotions of people expressed in unstructured text. This technique has been widely used in social science research for analyzing the general public's sentiment towards products, services, and any social phenomenon [18]. This study uses the VADER Sentiment Analysis technique [19] for classifying individual comments into negative, positive, or neutral. The Python library available at https://pypi.org/project/vaderSentiment/ has been used for classifying the sentiments.

3 Findings

The findings from the qualitative study, as proposed in Sect. 2, are detailed in this section. The LDA topic modeling algorithm generated topics that contained common co-occurring words from the comments collected. This study uses the topic coherence score to compute the number of topics to be generated for the LDA algorithm. For this experiment, we set the number of topics to be ten based on the coherence estimation given by *gensim* library [21] available at https://radimrehurek.com/gensim/. The representative, date-wise responses on the Measles outbreak from Reddit is shown in Fig. 2. For better interpretation and thematic mapping of the topics generated, we manually created topic labels such as *measles vaccination, vaccine manufacturer, measles symptoms,*

Table 1. Some of the representative comments from the dataset

Sl. No.	Comment
1	*"The allergy thing always gets me. "Well what happened to people with allergies/asthma before modern medicine?" They died. Just like they die now if they don't get help in time. Just like the babies who caught measles, smallpox, polio, etc. They died"*
2	*"I homeschooled my kids for many years so I didn't have get mine vaccinated at all. I did because vaccines are fucking awesome, but I've met many many families that homeschooled so as to not vaccinate. It's scary"*
3	*"To give a more holistic view of infection fatalities, real-world data in the US in the early 20th century (like pre-world war 1)with very limited availability of medical intervention was looking at 6000 measles deaths per year in the country with a population of over 100 million and everyone getting it at some point"*

anti-vaccination, and *parental concerns*. We assigned these topic labels to all the ten topics generated by the LDA model, and a subset (5 topics) of the results are shown in Table 2. Figure 3 shows the visualization of Measles topics generated by the topic-modeling algorithm using the pyLDAVis library, and the top-ranked topic words for eight topics (topic 0 to topic 7) generated by the topic-modeling algorithm are shown in Fig. 4. The most common positive and negative words in all the user comments collected are shown in Fig. 5.

Table 2. Top 5 topic words and corresponding topic labels

Topic #	Topic words	Topic label
0	homeschool, vaccine, immunity, family, scary, religous, government, covid, low, infant, mortality, ...	*measles_vaccination*
1	covid, monkeypox, measles, pandemic, vaccine, companies, market, trillion, economy, kill, ...	*vaccine_companies*
2	fever, rashes, headache, school, spread, asperger, swollen, vaccine, mmr, blindness, ...	*measles_symptoms*
3	kid, people, parent, antivaxxers, antivax, antinatalism, religion, oppose, kids, death, ...	*anti_vaccination*
4	plenty, pediatrician, allow, altered, vaccine, trust, school, allergy, government, ...	*parental_concerns*

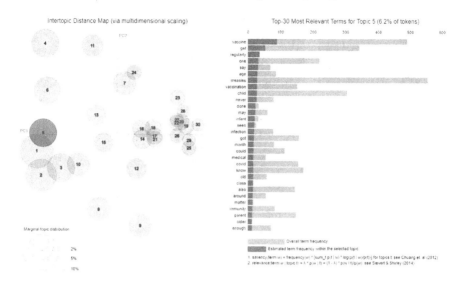

Fig. 3. pyLDAvis [20] visualization of measles topics generated by the topic modeling algorithm

4 Discussion

This study reports the results of the public discourse and sentiment analysis of Reddit user-generated comments on the spiking Measles outbreak declared "an imminent threat" by the WHO. The findings from this qualitative study may enable an understanding of the general public's sentiments and concerns, which will be significant to the government and other public policymakers in framing health policies. This analysis also leverages insights from the user-generated content that could facilitate implementing better outbreak surveillance to tackle the alarming situation effectively. The latent themes and other patterns unearthed from a large collection of unstructured public comments may be important for advanced planning and guiding targeted health intervention programs. Governments can also ascertain the effectiveness of imposed measures and amend the strategies and policies using these data-driven decision-making interventions. The major insights from this study show that the discussions on the Measles outbreak are centered around themes such as *parental concerns*, *vaccinations*, and *antivaxxers*. As Measles mostly affects children under the age of five, parents across the globe are worried about missed vaccinations for several reasons, but the prime is the COVID-19 pandemic. Many parents have expressed concern about sending their kids to schools, fearing that their unvaccinated kids may get Measles from other kids. On the other hand, another group of parents is totally against vaccinations in general and Measles in particular, who homeschool their kids for many years. While many comments have been posted to support this, many people raised their voices against such practices of not vaccinating kids. Another interesting observation from our analysis shows that people often com-

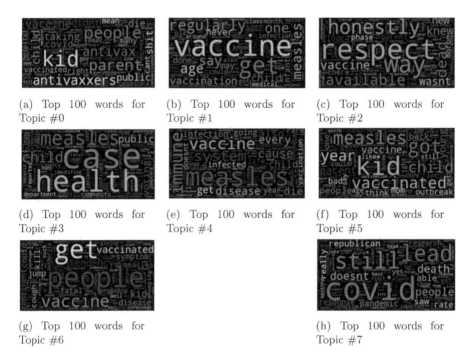

(a) Top 100 words for Topic #0

(b) Top 100 words for Topic #1

(c) Top 100 words for Topic #2

(d) Top 100 words for Topic #3

(e) Top 100 words for Topic #4

(f) Top 100 words for Topic #5

(g) Top 100 words for Topic #6

(h) Top 100 words for Topic #7

Fig. 4. Top ranked topic words for the eight topics generated by the topic modeling algorithm along with the common positive and negative words in the user posts

pare post-COVID disease outbreaks with COVID-19. For example, there is a tendency to compare the efficacy of measles vaccinations with COVID-19. But, many healthcare professionals pointed out that while COVID-19 vaccinations have around 30–40% effectiveness, measles has approximately 93–97%. Many comments pointed out that they had taken the suggested vaccinations before going to public school, and as adults, they never had any reactions to infections such as measles. The analysis also shows that there are a large group of people who are anti-vaxxers who are not only against vaccinations but also share misinformation among the communities.

A more significant number of topics and themes generated by the proposed methodology indicate anti-vaccination and parental concerns. But the authors vehemently recommend a detailed analysis to affirm the same. Even though anti-vaccination and misinformation are the subjects of the vast bulk of talks on Measles outbreaks, it doesn't mean that the analysis highlights only such themes. There are several other themes, such as *measles symptoms*, *measles vaccinations*, and *vaccine side effects* to name a few, that are of significant importance to the measles discussions. Remarkable diligence must be exercised considering the themes obtained while the public policies related to the measles outbreak to avoid any potential biases towards the themes leveraged. The measles outbreak has hit several countries very severely, and they have witnessed very large

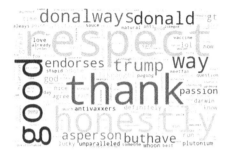

(a) Common words among positive comments

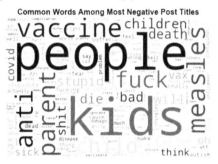

(b) Common words among negative comments

Fig. 5. Common positive and negative words in the user comments

and disruptive outbreaks. One of the prime reasons for the all-time low number of vaccination is the challenges created by the COVID-19 pandemic. The governments were using all their machinery to develop and supply COVID-19 vaccinations to combat the pandemic, but the routine vaccinations for measles and others were losing focus. Even though many lessons were learned in dealing with health emergencies when combating the COVID-19 pandemic, many avenues need to be strengthened through the lens of public health policies. It is undeniable that public health policy significantly impacts health status, and we need evidence-based policy-making practices to advance the same. These pieces of evidence, categorized as quantitative (such as epidemiological) and qualitative (such as narrative accounts), bring great value for effective health policymaking. Our findings suggest ways health policymakers can make data-driven, informed decisions on prioritizing governmental measures to help prevent the measles outbreak. For example, the user-generated responses collected and analyzed from social media and news aggregators identify outbreak clusters and anti-vaxxer groups, aiding in implementing health surveillance measures. Another area would be to discover public sentiment toward the measures taken by governments and public health organizations so that they can change their strategies and prioritize the action items. It is also worth noting that there may be many stigmas related to disease outbreaks, often targeting some underrepresented groups or sectors in society. Our findings also show that the qualitative evidence helps policymakers to formulate effective public health communications and awareness programs to reduce the stigma and misinformation spread during health emergencies.

4.1 Limitations

There are some limitations to this study. This study uses limited Reddit pages to collect public comments about spiking Measles cases. As this is an evolving discussion, many comments might have been added while conducting this experiment. The second limitation is that Reddit may not be considered a representative of the general public, as only a limited number of users may share their views on such a platform. However, there are already studies reported in the literature on using Reddit as a platform for public discourse and emotion analysis. Further, our analysis shows that the hate groups shout the loudest and most frequently during such disease outbreaks or pandemics, which may bias the output or findings of this study. The other limitation of this study is that we have only analyzed the comments written in English. Many representative comments might have missed Chinese, Arabic, and German languages. The authors highly recommend several future research to address the challenges associated with limited data sampling and multi-lingual comment analysis, which are not addressed in this study.

5 Conclusions

This work uses natural language processing and text mining to analyze public discourse and sentiment towards spiking measles cases reported globally. The data collected from Reddit, a public news aggregation platform on measles, was used for this study. The analyses leveraged several insights, including topics of discussion that show parental concerns, vaccination, and discussions on antivaccine. These concerns are valid for any pandemic we have fought, such as COVID-19, but measles will be an imminent threat to children. These insights may be helpful for devising better disease surveillance measures by the governments and other policymakers to help tackle the measles outbreak.

References

1. Cioffi, A., Cecannecchia, C.: Measles outbreaks during the COVID-19 pandemic: medico-legal and public health implications. Cadernos Saúde Pública **38** (2022)
2. Opel, D.J., et al.: The legacy of the COVID-19 pandemic for childhood vaccination in the USA. Lancet **401**(10370), 75–78 (2023)
3. Aggarwal, K., Singh, S.K., Chopra, M., Kumar, S.: Role of social media in the COVID-19 pandemic: a literature review. In: Data Mining Approaches for Big Data and Sentiment Analysis in Social Media, pp. 91–115 (2022)
4. Melton, C.A., White, B.M., Davis, R.L., Bednarczyk, R.A., Shaban-Nejad, A.: Fine-tuned sentiment analysis of COVID-19 vaccine-related social media data: Comparative study. J. Med. Internet Res. **24**(10), e40408 (2022)

5. Prieto Santamaria, L., et al.: Influenza and Measles-MMR: two case study of the trend and impact of vaccine-related Twitter posts in Spanish during 2015–2018. Hum. Vaccines Immunotherap. **18**(1), 1–16 (2022)
6. Deiner, M.S., et al.: Facebook and Twitter vaccine sentiment in response to measles outbreaks. Health Inform. J. **25**(3), 1116–1132 (2019)
7. Bunting, A.M., Frank, D., Arshonsky, J., Bragg, M.A., Friedman, S.R., Krawczyk, N.: Socially-supportive norms and mutual aid of people who use opioids: an analysis of Reddit during the initial COVID-19 pandemic. Drug Alcohol Depend. **222**, 108672 (2021)
8. Melton, C.A., Olusanya, O.A., Ammar, N., Shaban-Nejad, A.: Public sentiment analysis and topic modeling regarding COVID-19 vaccines on the Reddit social media platform: a call to action for strengthening vaccine confidence. J. Infect. Public Health **14**(10), 1505–1512 (2021)
9. Kumar, N., et al.: COVID-19 vaccine perceptions in the initial phases of US vaccine roll-out: an observational study on reddit. BMC Public Health **22**(1), 446 (2022)
10. Dumais, S.T.: Latent semantic analysis. Annu. Rev. Inf. Sci. Technol. **38**(1), 188–230 (2004)
11. Hofmann, T.: Probabilistic latent semantic indexing. In: Proceedings of the 22nd Annual International ACM SIGIR Conference on Research and Development in Information Retrieval, pp. 50–57 (1999)
12. Blei, D.M., Ng, A.Y., Jordan, M.I.: Latent Dirichlet allocation. J. Mach. Learn. Res. **3**(Jan), 993–1022 (2003)
13. Rodriguez, M.Y., Storer, H.: A computational social science perspective on qualitative data exploration: using topic models for the descriptive analysis of social media data. J. Technol. Hum. Serv. **38**(1), 54–86 (2020)
14. Hu, Y., Boyd-Graber, J., Satinoff, B., Smith, A.: Interactive topic modeling. Mach. Learn. **95**, 423–469 (2014)
15. Yin, H., Song, X., Yang, S., Li, J.: Sentiment analysis and topic modeling for COVID-19 vaccine discussions. World Wide Web **25**(3), 1067–1083 (2022)
16. Braun, V., Clarke, V.: Using thematic analysis in psychology. Qual. Res. Psychol. **3**(2), 77–101 (2006)
17. Altheide, D.L.: Moral panic: from sociological concept to public discourse. Crime Media Cult. **5**(1), 79–99 (2009)
18. Verma, S.: Sentiment analysis of public services for smart society: literature review and future research directions. Gov. Inf. Q. **39**(3), 101708 (2022)
19. Hutto, C., Gilbert, E.: VADER: a parsimonious rule-based model for sentiment analysis of social media text. In: Proceedings of the International AAAI Conference on Web and Social Media, vol. 8, no. 1, pp. 216–225 (2014)
20. Sievert, C., Shirley, K.: LDAvis: a method for visualizing and interpreting topics. In: Proceedings of the Workshop on Interactive Language Learning, Visualization, and Interfaces, pp. 63–70 (2014)
21. Röder, M., Both, A., Hinneburg, A.: Exploring the space of topic coherence measures. In: Proceedings of the Eighth ACM International Conference on Web Search and Data Mining, pp. 399–408 (2015)
22. Mann, S., Arora, J., Bhatia, M., Sharma, R., Taragi, R.: Twitter sentiment analysis using enhanced BERT. In: Kulkarni, A.J., Mirjalili, S., Udgata, S.K. (eds.) Intelligent Systems and Applications. LNEE, vol. 959, pp. 263–271. Springer, Singapore (2023). https://doi.org/10.1007/978-981-19-6581-4_21
23. Rao, S.S., Kamath, G.B., Rao, S.S.: Cancer through the lens of social media: an examination of cancer-related content on reddit. In: Tuba, M., Akashe, S., Joshi, A.

(eds.) ICT Infrastructure and Computing. LNNS, vol. 520, pp. 335–346. Springer, Singapore (2022). https://doi.org/10.1007/978-981-19-5331-6_35

24. Arbane, M., Benlamri, R., Brik, Y., Alahmar, A.D.: Social media-based COVID-19 sentiment classification model using Bi-LSTM. Expert Syst. Appl. **212**, 118710 (2023)

25. Srivastava, S.K., Singh, S.K., Suri, J.S.: A healthcare text classification system and its performance evaluation: A source of better intelligence by characterizing healthcare text. In: Cognitive Informatics, Computer Modelling, and Cognitive Science, pp. 319–369. Academic Press (2020)

26. Aipe, A., Mukuntha, N.S., Ekbal, A.: Sentiment-aware recommendation system for healthcare using social media. In: Gelbukh, A. (ed.) CICLing 2019. LNCS, pp. 166–181. Springer, Cham (2023). https://doi.org/10.1007/978-3-031-24340-0_13

27. Chen, N., Chen, X., Zhong, Z., Pang, J.: The burden of being a bridge: analysing subjective well-being of Twitter users during the COVID-19 pandemic. In: Amini, M.R., Canu, S., Fischer, A., Guns, T., Kralj Novak, P., Tsoumakas, G. (eds.) ECML PKDD 2022, Part II. LNCS, vol. 13714, pp. 241–257. Springer, Cham (2023). https://doi.org/10.1007/978-3-031-26390-3_15

28. Pribán, P., Balahur, A.: Comparative analyses of multilingual sentiment analysis systems for news and social media. In: Proceedings of the 20th International Conference on Computational Linguistics and Intelligent Text Processing, La Rochelle, France (2019)

29. Vaghela, M., Sasidhar, K.: Smartphone mediated tracking and analysis of sleep patterns in Indian college students. Hum.-Cent. Intell. Syst. 1–12 (2022)

30. Jickson, S., Anoop, V.S., Asharaf, S.: Machine learning approaches for detecting signs of depression from social media. In: Anwar, S., Ullah, A., Rocha, Á., Sousa, M.J. (eds.) ICITA 2022. LNNS, vol. 614, pp. 201–214. Springer, Singapore (2023). https://doi.org/10.1007/978-981-19-9331-2_17

31. John, R., Anoop, V.S., Asharaf, S.: Health mention classification from user-generated reviews using machine learning techniques. In: Anwar, S., Ullah, A., Rocha, Á., Sousa, M.J. (eds.) ICITA 2022. LNNS, vol. 614, pp. 175–188. Springer, Singapore (2023). https://doi.org/10.1007/978-981-19-9331-2_15

32. Anoop, V.S., Sreelakshmi, S.: Public discourse and sentiment during Mpox outbreak: an analysis using natural language processing. Publ. Health **218**, 114–120 (2023)

Swarm Learning for Oncology Research

H. S. Shashank[(✉)] [iD], Anirudh B. Sathyanarayana[(✉)] [iD], Aniruddh Acharya[(✉)] [iD], M. R. Akhil.[(✉)] [iD], and Sujatha R. Upadhyaya[iD]

Department of Computer Science and Engineering, PES University, Bangalore, India
shashankhon@gmail.com, anibs2171@gmail.com,
aniruddh.acharya3005@gmail.com, akhil.mr2001@gmail.com,
sujathar@pes.edu

Abstract. The medical industry is one of the biggest victims of unavailability and lack of variety of data. Despite sizable medical data being available across the world, privacy norms prevent it from being shared. Adding variety to data is impossible without an efficient, privacy-preserving approach to enable data use from multiple sources. This lack of variety in data leads to extremely biased machine learning models. Cancer data, like data of many other diseases, is multivariate and demands personalized treatment protocols, showing importance of the variety that data from multiple sources can bring in. The research work tries to shed light on how decentralized learning can be employed to improve and strengthen clinical research by enabling researchers to analyze diverse insights from heterogeneous data sources. Along with discussing cutting-edge Deep learning architectures for Cancer diagnosis, we show experiments with "Swarm Learning" i.e. HPE's decentralized machine-learning platform that facilitates collaboration between data owners. This experiment focuses on Breast Cancer tumor diagnosis. As a part of the study, we examined around 1300 histochemical images of breast cancer tumors as well as follow-up records for multiple cases using various deep learning techniques. The experimental results show that decentralized learning can compete with traditional machine learning and make way for more robust methods in not just cancer research, but the healthcare domain as a whole.

Keywords: Decentralized AI/ML · Swarm learning · Privacy-preserving · Machine learning · Oncology · Image processing · Neural Networks

1 Introduction

Artificial Intelligence, and particularly Machine Learning techniques can be easily extrapolated to the medical space, and it is expected to improve the domains of research, teaching, and clinical care tremendously [2, 3]. Considering how several techniques like neural networks in AI have proved their potential in pattern recognition and predictive abilities, employing them to solve problems that require laborious analysis of patterns and trends would be intuitive. The medical domain is full of such problems, cancer being one of them. There have been several breakthrough points in cancer research, particularly with methods like precision oncology. Despite this, cancer is still one of the biggest contributors to patient mortality.

© The Author(s), under exclusive license to Springer Nature Switzerland AG 2023
R. Morusupalli et al. (Eds.): MIWAI 2023, LNAI 14078, pp. 159–168, 2023.
https://doi.org/10.1007/978-3-031-36402-0_14

Employing AI techniques could not only improve the pace of empirical cancer research but also play a vital role in quicker and more efficient identification and inhibition of the disease and better patient management, paving the way for personalizing treatments for patients tailored for their conditions [7].

However, its success will only be limited if the variety of data that is available is limited. In fact the medical industry as a whole is one of the biggest victims of data unavailability as well as a deficiency in data variety. Despite sizable medical data being available across the world, privacy norms prevent it from being shared. Models built on datasets without the necessary data volume and diversity, irrespective of how efficient they are, will turn out to be highly biased. This is because of the data being accumulated from only a specific human populace, thus lacking the variety necessary to ensure the model works for everyone. Advanced treatment methods require a variety of data – like gross tumor parameters, tumor cell microscope pictures, and genomic data. Some of these may not always be collected at every medical center. Further with cancer being an extremely variant disease, this problem is only being amplified. Cancer research requires a large volume of pathology information and biopsy images. While not many organizations have access to such data, even the ones which do have lack the data diversity required to build meaningful machine learning models out of it. Oncology research can benefit extensively from a decentralized machine learning platform that builds a global model that learns from distributed pockets of data. The overarching vision is to facilitate researchers to bring in several types of patient data from decentralized sources, and eventually enable them to build models utilizing these multifaceted data points to arrive at high quality decisions. This experiment marks a starting point to achieve the idea.

We have made use of Swarm learning for achieving decentralized model training. Swarm Learning is a decentralized ML framework developed by HPE, which supports independent model building on private data at data-origin sites and allows secure sharing of parameters via a permissioned blockchain technology [1].

Given that cancer is vast and variable, we restricted all our experiments to breast cancer and its subtypes, which in fact forms a reasonably large subset of all cancers. Our objective for the experiment is to demonstrate the feasibility of such a method to barter insights through a variety of heterogeneous data between organisations and improve the quality of oncology research without overstepping the privacy norms in place. The below sections show how by leveraging the Swarm Learning architecture we were able to arrive at improved global models solely through decentralized learning of parameters. Our experiments showed that these models performed better than those that used complete data made available at one source. Through experiments we also showed that passing on the results in the form of weights to the global model from independent nodes with disparate data ensures that overall accuracy of the model is almost as good as, or in some cases better than accuracy obtained if the complete set of data were accumulated at one source.

Provided the domain chosen for this experiment was breast cancer, we ran two sets of experiments on two different types of data; the first one for tumor classification and the second for recurrence prediction. In the first case, we used the WDBC diagnosis dataset, which contains follow-up data for breast cancer cases as well as the BreakHis dataset, consisting of microscopic images of breast cancer tissue.

In the second case, we used the WPBC recurrence dataset, which along with the follow up data has the recurrence status of the tumor.

In Sect. 2, we discuss important and related works that have influenced our research. Section 3 discusses the nature of the datasets that we used and how it is split across nodes. All the experiments that we ran and the strategies that we used are also explained here. Section 4 describes the implementation details and Sect. 5 discusses the conclusions and results.

2 Related Work

As mentioned earlier, the medical space is heavily restricted by privacy norms, which are very much necessary to ensure patient privacy. However, from the research perspective, this leads to the formation of what can be called "data islands" as there can be no transfer of data between hospitals or research institutes. This dramatically impacts the development of good artificial intelligence models for predictive diagnosis and treatments. What will be necessary is a way to barter insights rather than the data itself. A detailed analysis of prior works in the domain of Breast Cancer, Machine Learning and Decentralised learning ensued.

Warnat-Herresthal et al. provides a detailed explanation of the Swarm Learning framework developed by Hewlett Packard Enterprise (HPE) [1]. It discusses how the framework solves this issue and can also be extrapolated to other domains like predictive maintenance, finance sector, etc. The study showcased the usage of the framework in order to build predictive models for 3 diseases, namely COVID-19, Tuberculosis, and Leukemia. The types of data that were used include images of chest X-ray, whole-blood derived transcriptome and PBMC transcriptome. The team also made use of different parameter-tuning methods for the 3 dataset types. The primary changing points were dropout rates. This method also makes use of weighted average in its parameter merging stage. With this, weights are assigned to the nodes such that the magnitude of the weight is proportional to the volume of the data being offered by the node.

According to Vincent Peter C. Magboo et al. Breast Cancer is a very prevalent condition in women regardless of race and increases with age [3]. Death from breast cancer is mainly associated with metastasis and recurrence. In this case, recurrence refers to relapse. This is the reason studying the recurrence and predicting it, is of very huge importance to both data scientists and clinical researchers. An accurate prediction about the recurrence can aid doctors in their decision-making process which will lead to an increased chance of patients survival and provide a more personalized treatment. A lot of this recurrence prediction research involves machine learning techniques and statistical algorithms which have enhanced the capabilities of breast cancer detection and prediction.

Frederich Stahl et al. proposed data stream classification techniques for pocket data mining [4]. Through thorough experimental study, they proved that running heterogeneous/different, or homogeneous/similar data stream classification techniques over vertically partitioned data (data partitioned according to the feature space) results in comparable performance to batch and centralized learning techniques.

Our research has taken inspiration from some of the works stated above, and makes use of all these concepts to test how efficiently deep learning techniques combined with distributed learning can work for oncological research.

3   Experiments, Data Availability and Split

Diagnosing cancer at an early stage is very important for an effective treatment. Early cancer diagnosis and AI are two fields with important areas of convergence [5]. While it is established AI has a huge overlap with Cancer research, particularly in domains like early diagnosis, precision oncology and recurrence prediction, experiments in decentralized learning frameworks like Swarm Learning are not common. The primary goal of the following experiments is to emphasize how beneficial adapting to such techniques can be to further not just cancer, but medical research as a whole.

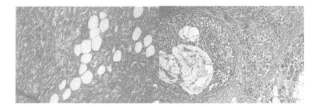

Fig. 1. Sample images from the BreakHis Dataset

For the experiments, two types of data were used. The first type of data includes WDBC and WPBC dataset which consists of gross tumor parameters like tumor perimeter, tumor area, texture etc. The response variable for WDBC is the diagnosis of the tumor whereas the response variable for WPBC is whether the cancer recurred or not. The second dataset consists of breast-tumor images as observed under a microscope. Figure 1 shows a few examples from the BreakHis dataset. The dataset contains sample magnification ranging from $40\times$ to $400\times$. From the various magnification values available, $40\times$ magnified images were considered for the experiment. The number of malignant and benign samples present under the $40\times$ magnification is 830 and 362 respectively.

3.1   Data Splitting

The two nodes in the swarm learning setup try to simulate two medical data sources. The data was distributed between the two nodes – which, in a real world setting, can be considered as two different medical centers in two different geographical locations with one population diverse from another (as it is usually observed). The data split was done with an intent to portray the diverse populace.

The WPBC dataset was split equally between the two nodes randomly. The BreakHis dataset consisted of the sub-types of the observed tumor. The same information was used while splitting the data among the SL-nodes. Inspired by the findings of Frederich Stahl et al. [4], the BreakHis dataset was partitioned by grouping similar types of cancer in the same node. Apart from adding homogeneity to the different nodes, it also simulates the high bias that could be found in different data nodes in a real world scenario. The first node, Node-1, comprised Fibroadenoma and Adenosis under the benign class and Lobular carcinoma and Ductal carcinoma under the malignant class. The second node, Node-2, comprised Tubular adenoma and Phyllodes tumor under the benign class and Papillary carcinoma and mucinous carcinoma under the malignant class.

The data on each node was further split into a training and a testing set. The training data for the localized model comprised all the above mentioned subtypes of the tumor. For both the set of experiments, the test-set was kept constant for both localized and the Swarm learning framework. This was done in order to ensure that the model was being tested against a uniform dataset for better consistency.

The number of samples distributed among the two nodes is as depicted in the Table. 1. The table also shows the number of samples present in the training and test sets.

Table 1. BreakHis Data Split

Split	Benign	Malignant
Node-1	174	398
Node-2	118	257
Test-set	72	175

4 Implementation

As described in the introduction, we have made use of the Swarm Learning framework developed by HPE to enable decentralized training of the Breast Cancer diagnosis models we developed.

Swarm learning ensures that small pockets of data collected at isolated sources will never have to leave the source of origin and all privacy-preserving norms are strictly followed and yet the deep learning model developed benefits from the combined data. Unlike a federated learning model, this is completely decentralized where any node can play the role of integrating the learnt parameters and there will be no centralisation of information of any kind [1, 6].

For the experimental setup, two machines were used to simulate a real-world scenario, where each node depicts a medical data source. The first machine was running the Swarm Network and the License Server along with one Swarm Learning Node. The second machine was running a Swarm Learning Node which was connected to the aforementioned Swarm Network Node.

Figure 2 depicts the experimental setup. APLS node refers to the auto-pass license server. The license server installs and exchanges the license required to authenticate the nodes in the swarm learning network. During execution, the swarm learning nodes spawn multiple Machine Learning Node containers which contain the actual ML model under training.

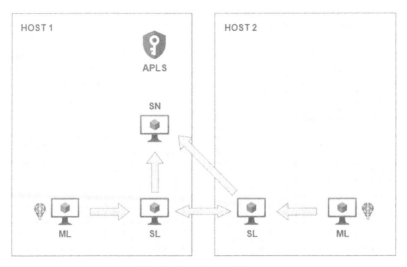

Fig. 2. Experimental Setup

Based on the WPBC and WDBC datasets, two verticals were identified and a binary classification model was built for each. The first one was to classify the tumor as benign or malignant and the other one to predict if the given tumor would recur or not. Images from the BreakHis dataset were used to develop another classification model to classify the tumor as benign/malignant.

The datasets were cleaned, preprocessed and labeled appropriately depending on how the datasets were structured. Exploratory data analysis was then performed to better understand the data at hand through correlations and feature distribution. Once the datasets were preprocessed, we experimented with the distribution strategies. A detailed explanation for this is provided in the Data Splitting section.

4.1 Neural Network Model for Prediction Using Gross Parameters from WDBC Dataset

A sequential Neural Network was built with 2 hidden layers and with a sigmoid output activation function. The optimisation function used was Adam as it leverages adaptive learning methods to determine individual learning rates for each parameter, thus leading to faster computations. And the loss function used was binary cross entropy. This Neural Network model behaves as a classifier, predicting whether the tumor is benign or malignant. The accuracy and recall achieved with the model is listed in the following table Table 2.

4.2 Neural Network Model for Recurrence Using Gross Parameters from WPBC Dataset

A model similar to the above mentioned cancer prediction case was built for predicting the possibility of cancer recurrence. The purpose of this model is to see if the cancer

Table 2. Results of the ANN Locally for Cancer Prediction

Task	Epochs	Accuracy	Recall
WDBC Classification	150	98.83	99.9

of the patient recurrent. All of the independent variables were the same as the WPBC cancer dataset. The dependent variable only mentioned if the cancer was recurrent or non-recurrent. In terms of architecture, the model was kept completely identical to the former model as we got good results. Due to inadequacy of data points, the model was not run on the swarm learning set-up. However, it could be interesting to see how it would behave with a higher volume of data, especially in a decentralized learning environment. Another reason to perform the experiment was the magnitude recurrence studies carry. Being able to detect recurrent tumors early on will have a great impact since healthcare providers can tailor the treatment for handling it better. The accuracy and recall achieved with the model is listed in the following table Table 3.

Table 3. Results of the ANN Locally for Cancer Recurrence

Task	Epochs	Accuracy	Recall
WPBC Classification	150	71.88	55.55

4.3 Residual Network Model for Prediction Using Images from the BreakHis Dataset

For our application involving Breast Cancer Histology images from the BreakHis dataset, there was a necessity for the model to analyze the fine-grained features of the images. This would require the chosen model to be very deep i.e. have a lot of hidden layers within the model. Although having a lot of layers, the performance of a deep neural network can be degraded in certain scenarios due to the effect of vanishing or exploding gradients. In order to overcome this, we decided to evaluate the performance of two residual network architectures, namely ResNet50 and DenseNet201.

Residual Networks add a skip-connection that bypasses the non-linear transformations with an identity function (Fig. 3). To further improve the information flow between layers, DenseNet proposes a different connectivity pattern by introducing direct connections from any layer to all subsequent layers.

From the various magnifications available in the BreakHis dataset, we chose the $40\times$ images since the volume of images under the said magnification was higher. After assigning appropriate labels to the images, the dataset was divided into train and test sets. Additionally, pre-trained ImageNet weights were imported and applied to the ResNet and the DenseNet model before the training process was initiated.

From the results obtained in Table 4, it is evident that the accuracy achieved from the DenseNet201 was higher than that of the ResNet50 model. Thus the DenseNet201

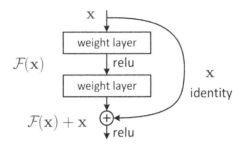

Fig. 3. Architecture of a single ResNet block [8]

Table 4. Performance comparison

Task	Epochs	ResNet50 acc	DenseNet201 acc
BreakHis Classification	20	92.06	95.23

model was chosen for the swarm learning experiment. The data was split between the nodes as described in the previous sections. The split was done as mentioned to create homogenous data streams.

5   Results and Discussion

As mentioned in the previous sections, the Swarm Learning framework was set up on two different physical devices, each representing a research center or a hospital which holds disparate data. Identical models are stored in each of these "nodes". The model weights are updated after each merge-call. The frequency of merge calls can be set by controlling a model parameter, namely sync frequency. Apart from the regular hyper parameter tuning, we also experimented with a range of sync frequencies. We observed that with lower sync frequencies, the accuracy increased. However, the computation time increased as the number of merge calls increased. We can observe that the accuracies in both the nodes are the same, as the models reach a consensus after each merge call.

The obtained results are as documented in Tables 5 and 6. In Table 5, which shows the accuracy obtained using the DenseNet201 model on different settings, it is observed that the accuracy obtained in the swarm learning set-up was slightly better than the one obtained locally.

Similarly in Table 6, which shows the accuracy obtained using the ANN model for the tumor diagnosis task, it is observed that the accuracy obtained in the swarm learning set-up was slightly better than the one obtained locally.

Table 5. Results of the BreakHis Data set model Swarmified

Task	Epochs	SL1 training data	SL2 training data	SL1 + SL2 training data	Accuracy SL1	Accuracy SL2
Cancer-cell identification (BreakHis Images)	10	75.0	78.9	91.9	93.522	93.522

Table 6. Results of the WDBC Ann model Swarmified

Task	Epochs	Acc Local	Acc SL1	Acc SL2
WDBC Classification	100	94.56	94.73	94.73

6   Conclusion and Future Work

Our experiments demonstrate that distributed learning methods like swarm-learning can accelerate cancer research as there is no transfer of data across sources and complete anonymity of data is preserved. With a framework like swarm learning, hospitals and/or medical research centers can collaborate at a global scale, to achieve a robust understanding of the population and data at hand. Further ahead, it can also enable researchers to correlate the different parameters better and eventually arrive at ensemble models to facilitate personalisation of treatments for patients.

An important observation from the experiments was that the accuracy obtained from swarm learning was slightly more than that of the local model. This could be attributed to the sync frequency set in the swarm learning experiments as well as the data distribution methods that were followed, which are mentioned in detail in the above sections. While this may not be the outcome in all scenarios, it is still an important aspect to consider before trying out the described method. The set of experiments conducted can help demonstrate that a decentralized machine learning model could be as good if not better than a localized model under the right circumstances.

The results of these experiments can encourage future works to further explore decentralized learning methods. While the current set of experiments can validate it, further research is necessary to understand what model architectures and what data distributions and data modeling techniques work best for the task at hand. Apart from analyzing the technical part, one should also conduct feasibility analysis of extrapolating the techniques to different domains of the medical space. Further ahead we can also expand decentralized learning to domains which have either high volume of scattered data or data privacy concerns, or both. Some examples include but are not limited to: credit fraud detection, predictive maintenance for industrial equipment, self driving cars.

To conclude, we believe AI will play an extremely important role in furthering medical research, and employing decentralized learning methods like Swarm Learning could make the process much faster and more robust.

Acknowledgment. We would like to express our gratitude to Mr. Ravi Sarveswara, Mr. Dharmendra and Mr Krishna Prasad Shastry from Hewlett Packard Enterprises for collaborating with and guiding us. HPE played an important role in giving us an opportunity to collaborate and for providing a platform for our project. To Dr. Sivaraman Eswaran, Department of Electrical and Computer Engineering, Curtin University, for his help and guidance which helped propel this project forward.

We also take this opportunity to thank Dr. Shylaja S S, Chairperson, Department of Computer Science and Engineering, PES University, for all the knowledge and support we have received from the department and the University.

References

1. Warnat-Herresthal, S., Schultze, H., Shastry, K.L., et al.: Swarm Learning for decentralized and confidential clinical machine learning. Nature **594**, 265–270 (2021). https://doi.org/10.1038/s41586-021-03583-3
2. Bhardwaj, A.: Promise and provisos of artificial intelligence and machine learning in healthcare. J. Healthc. Leadersh. **14**, 113–118 (2022). https://doi.org/10.2147/JHL.S369498
3. Magboo, V.P.C., Magboo, M.S.A.: Machine learning classifiers on breast cancer recurrences. Proc. Comput. Sci. **192**, 2742–2752 (2021)
4. Stahl, F., et al.: Homogeneous and heterogeneous distributed classification for pocket data mining. In: Hameurlain, A., Küng, J., Wagner, R. (eds.) Transactions on Large-Scale Data- and Knowledge-Centered Systems V. LNCS, vol. 7100, pp. 183–205. Springer, Heidelberg (2012). https://doi.org/10.1007/978-3-642-28148-8_8
5. Hunter, B., Hindocha, S., Lee, R.W.: The role of artificial intelligence in early cancer diagnosis. Cancers (Basel). **14**(6), 1524 (2022). https://doi.org/10.3390/cancers14061524.PMID:35326674;PMCID:PMC8946688
6. Saldanha, O.L., Quirke, P., West, N.P., et al.: Swarm learning for decentralized artificial intelligence in cancer histopathology. Nat. Med. **28**, 1232–1239 (2022). https://doi.org/10.1038/s41591-022-01768-5
7. Schork, N.J.: Artificial intelligence and personalized medicine. In: Von Hoff, D.D., Han, H. (eds.) Precision Medicine in Cancer Therapy. CTR, vol. 178, pp. 265–283. Springer, Cham (2019). https://doi.org/10.1007/978-3-030-16391-4_11
8. He, K., et al.: Deep residual learning for image recognition. In: Proceedings of the IEEE Conference on Computer Vision and Pattern Recognition (2016)

A Review on Designing of Memory Computing Architecture for Image Enhancement in AI Applications

C. Radhika[1,2](✉), G. V. Ganesh[1], and P. Ashok Babu[2]

[1] Department of Electronics and Communication Engineering, Koneru Lakshmaiah Education Foundation, Vaddeswaram, AP, India
radhikachelle@gmail.com
[2] Department of ECE, Institute of Aeronautical Engineering, Dundigal, Hyderabad, Telangana, India

Abstract. This paper presents the random spray retinex (RSR) algorithm, which is an efficient image enhancement technique with the potential to improve image quality. However, the computational complexity of the algorithm, as well as the hardware and memory units it requires, may limit its applicability in contexts with constrained resources, such as Internet of Things systems. Image augmentation is increasingly important for improving the performance of many modern applications, including artificial intelligence (AI). Our research confirms that RSR can enhance segmentation accuracy. To overcome the limitations of the RSR algorithm, we propose a memristor-based in-memory computing architecture, utilizing Resistive RAM (RRAM) technology, which provides low-power solutions at a low cost. We evaluate the performance of various RSR algorithms in terms of processing time on this architecture.

Keywords: RRAM · RSR pre-processed · RSR Algorithm · MEMRISTORS · In memory computing architecture

1 Introduction

Low-quality digital images are frequently present in a variety of application domains, including medical imaging, space exploration, and underwater habitats. This can be a result of the environment's dynamic features or inadequate illumination conditions [1, 2]. The same is true of photos taken for applications involving autonomous vehicle driving. The fact that there is a significant disparity in brightness between the bright and dark parts is a problem that these photographs share. Consequently, it significantly lowers the computing complexity caused by the data-intensive Due to its demonstrated great success in picture enhancement, Random Spray Retinex (RSR), one of the several Retinex versions, has been chosen as a case study and a test for the novel proposed architecture [3, 4]. The latter analysis is crucial for the implementation stage because it aids in determining the necessary level of quantization. The architecture of the Canonical

R. Morusupalli et al. (Eds.): MIWAI 2023, LNAI 14078, pp. 169–178, 2023.
https://doi.org/10.1007/978-3-031-36402-0_15

AI is seen in Fig. 1. Hardware has not yet made use of the sparsity in the retinex. The reason for this is that high-dimensional sparse data typically exceeds the capabilities of commodity hardware.

2 Literature Review

We have examined a number of study ideas that have been published in various-journals and conferences on this topic. After that, we contextualize the RSR method within the Retinex algorithm family and list its primary variations. Based on the original Retinex, which was created in the 1960s and depended on random routes, other Retinex algorithms have been created throughout time [21]. Many processes that detailed how to handle the data gathered by the random path and gradually include it into the rectified output made up this method. The most distinctive of these methods was the so-called reset, which allowed the correction to be referred to the highest values discovered around the corrected pixel. Some later-developed Retinex family algorithms, including those of the Milano-Retinex subfamily [13], to which RSR belongs, maintained the reset mechanism. For the purpose of completeness, we should note that other streamlined algorithms, such as the so-called NASA-Retinex [22], abandoned this fundamental principle. RSR is based on the point sampling method, and it was developed by Provenzi and colleagues [9] when they saw that point sampling may examine a pixel's surroundings less redundantly than a random walk. The name "Random Spray Retinex (RSR)" comes from the pixel samples referred to as sprays. In RSR, the algorithm generates a number of collections of useful pixels in the area around each target pixel to be corrected, extracts the maximum intensity from each collection, and then uses a suitable average of those values as a white reference for rescaling the input brightness of the target to compute the output value. For the purpose of gathering neighbor information, the authors showed that the spray approach works better than the path-based strategy. RSR and the Automatic Color Equalization (ACE) method were later integrated. In terms of how they treat spatial variation, the two algorithms complement one another. As a consequence, the two algorithms' output pictures have complementary strengths and weaknesses [34]. RSR exhibits strong saturation characteristics but has a limited ability to retrieve details. Instead, ACE has a tendency to highlight evidentary details while obscuring visuals. Moreover, Lecca et al. [35] altered the RSR algorithm to take spatial picture information into account while controlling the localization of color filtering. The RSR channel lightness computation at each individual pixel adds spatial information through the use of a weighting function that is inversely proportionate to the distance from the spray center. By concentrating on the region of interest, Tanaka et al. [36] created two RSR versions (ROI). Whereas the second version focuses on the visual resolution of the visual field information and treats it as an ROI, the first variation presented a cone distribution based on anatomical data as an ROI. One of the quickest and most effective RSR implementations is FuzzyRSR [26], which makes use of the.

The same spray is to correct multiple pixels. B. HARDWARE IMPLEMENTATIONS IN REAL-TIME In the literature, a few hardware Retinex algorithm implementations have been suggested. For instance, a Single-Scale Retinex algorithm, a real-time realization of the NASA-Retinex algorithms based on digital signal processors (DSPs), which are substantially different from RSR and much less performance-demanding, [40], Moreover, because of the high-power consumption and high cost of the hardware, the DSP solution itself is not appropriate for edge devices. In order to resolve this problem and accelerate these algorithms, a Field-programmable gate array (FPGA)-based hardware accelerator solution was suggested in [39–42]. Li et al. [39]'s implementation of multiscale Retinex in an outdoor application uses an entirely parallel architecture built on FPGAs. The Gaussian kernel is optimized via address encoding and distributed arithmetic, and concurrent multi-scale convolutions are achieved. Additionally, the multiscale Retinex algorithm is modified by Ustukov et al. Using various picture-blurring techniques, such as tabular value substitution in place of computing logarithm values, improves algorithm speed. The approach may be implemented on an FPGA as a threading conveyor due to its ability to mix algorithms. A low-cost, high-throughput idea for retinex video enhancement was presented by Park et al. [43]. Retinex is the basis for the video enhancement algorithm. A unique illuminance estimation approach was utilized to control the dynamic range of images with inadequate lighting while maintaining visual details. An internal microprocessor controls the video improvement settings in real time, enabling the device to adjust to the quirks of the incoming images and ambient illumination. The picture must be stored in external dynamic random-access memory (DRAM) due to the FPGA's limited memory capacity, which increases latency and energy consumption [39, 40, 42]. The Gaussian filter, nevertheless, The RESET operation, a key component of the retinex theory, is used in applications. This study provides a revolutionary low-complexity and real-time HW-friendly architecture and design of the Retinex algorithm to overcome the issues with the aforementioned implementations. To the best of our knowledge, this study also offers the first effective hardware ReRAM-based RSR algorithm implementation. We suggest utilizing memristor-based structures that can carry out highly parallel operations to save space and energy and speed up the Retinex algorithm execution. Global solutions for the low-light enhancement problem have been developed, such as tone mapping [2], gamma correction, and histogram equalization [1]. Additionally, since these algorithms use global information from inconsistent augmentation, the picture they apply would result in saturation of the intensity. More complicated algorithms have been created to address these problems, including spatial color algorithms (SCA) [7, 8], adaptive histogram equalization [5, 6], and adaptive contrast enhancements [3, 4]. Retinex principles, which were informed by how the Human Vision System (HVS) functions, serve as the foundation for SCAs [9, 10]. A variety of attributes would improve pictures. Due to their successful blending of local and global information, these algorithms significantly expand the dark areas [11, 12]. This proposal offers a revolutionary, real-time, low-complexity Retinex algorithm architecture and design to overcome these issues. After that, we contextualize the RSR method within the Retinex algorithm family and list its primary variations. Several later developed Retinex family algorithms, including those of the Milano-Retinex sub-family [13–16], to which RSR belongs, preserved the reset mechanism. For the purpose of completeness, we should note that other reduced algorithms, such as the so-called NASA-Retinex [17–22], abandoned this fundamental principle. RSR is based on the point sampling method, and it was developed by Provenzi and colleagues [23] after they saw that point sampling can examine a pixel's surroundings less redundantly than a random walk [24, 25] (Table 1).

Table 1. Reference table.

Ref. no.	Name of Authors	Remarks
[19]	Banić et al	presented Light RSR, algorithmic implementation reducing processing time while preserving the same geographical sampling method of RSR
[35]	Lecca et al	Discussed an RSR algorithm to incorporate spatial picture information and change where color filtering is applied
[36]	Tanaka et al	Provided a type concentrated on the visual resolution of the visual field information as an ROI
[39]	Li et al	Implementation of multi-scale Retinex using a fully parallel FPGA-based architecture
[41]	Ustukov et al	Algorithm speed is increased by using several picture-blurring approaches, such as replacing tabular data rather than computing logarithm values
[43]	Park et al	Highlighted the high-throughput, low-cost method for retinex video enhancement. The hardware (HW) architecture, which can deliver a 1920×1080-pixel image at a throughput of 60 frames per second with little lag, was constructed using an FPGA

2.1 Problem Identification and Formulation

The resolution loss is high.

The variations of array yield issues, and device reliability problems. The approach is limited accuracy brought on by weight quantization.

Sequential memristors were a memory computation relatively inefficient method of getting a high resolution while slowing down the RSR algorithm (Fig. 1).

These are the areas that our suggested research efforts will further explore. The following are mentioned:

- The new strategy will be very helpful in creating effective deep learning and computer vision applications based on memristors.
- RSR's effectiveness as a preprocessing step for AI applications is still under investigation.
- When RSR was applied to noisy images, improved accuracy was required (Fig. 2).

- In global retinex approaches, lighting is recovered by smoothing the original image through several Gauss mask types. Accurately extracting illumination is a major challenge.

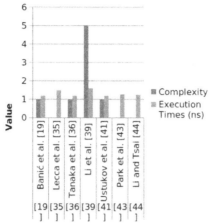

Fig. 1. Comparative Analysis of Complexity and Execution Times

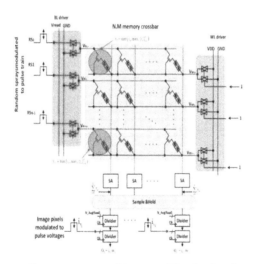

Fig. 2. In-memory computing macro core architecture of the simulated memristor-based Retinex processing unit and the relevant block modules.

- We are proposing an enhanced retinex method based on the observation that the backgrounds of picture sequences in successive video frames will typically be similar and closely related.

- In the approach, the illumination of a few neighboring frame images will be combined using a maximum method and used as the uniform illumination of these adjacent frame images.
- Research that has been suggested in order to obtain more correct background information and accomplish more exceptional performance enhancement.
- Compared to the traditional retinex system, the proposed method will offer high-speed and energy/area-efficient architecture. Various picture quality metrics and quantization levels will be used to evaluate image quality.
- MAC activities will be carried out concurrently. Generally.
- This concept will be used in more memristor-based in-memory computing systems that make optimal use of sparse input data and scale to max operators. The suggested method would be seen as a huge help in creating effective deep learning and computer vision applications based on memristors. It will also be investigated whether the RSR algorithm may be used as a preprocessing step for AI applications.
- When RSR is applied to noisy photos, the accuracy is anticipated to Improve.
- Research on how contrast enhancement and altered lighting affect the efficiency of semantic segmentation in urban road scenes. A number of contexts, including one involving autonomous vehicle control, can serve as inspiration for this example. Applications for autonomous vehicles must function properly in a variety of situations, but environmental conditions, like as bad lighting and bad weather, might degrade the quality of the photos captured, endangering safety (Fig. 3).

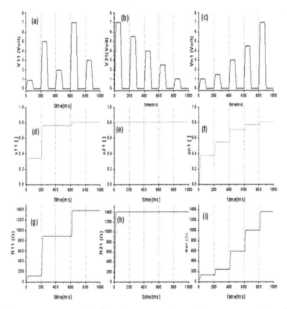

Fig. 3. Biasing voltages were provided to the targeted memristor cross-points in (a), (b), and (c). The internal state variable's progression was the outcome of (d), (e), and (f). (g), (h), and I the scale to maximum resistances after the applied voltages are computed in memory (quantized pixel values) (Fig. 4).

2.2 Memristor-Based In-Memory Computing Architecture for RSR

This section provides about the contemporary memristor-based in-memory computing solutions, associated limitations, and new research opportunities in the topics of research.

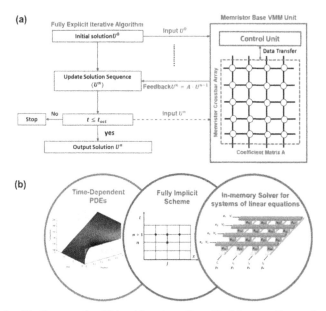

Fig. 4. (a) Scientific Computation Using Memristor Based In-Memory Computing Architecture [source: Internet]

2.3 Device Physics Memristor

The concept of in-memory computing is built upon memory structures utilizing memristive devices. Various well-known examples of this memristive memory structures include conductive bridge RAM (CB-RAM) [39], phase change memories (PCM) [40], spin-transfer-torque magnetic (STT-MRAM) [41], and redox-oxide RAM (ReRAM) [42]. These structures leverage the prime features of memristive devices such as non-volatility, compatibility with CMOS technology, high scalability, and the ability to store, process, and compute data at the same physical location. The memory structure based on the memristor operates through a crossbar network composed of metal electrodes, where a memristor device is positioned at each perpendicular cross-section. The configuration of this memristor crossbar structure is shown in Fig. 2.2 and facilitates a feature size as small as 4F2, which results in a maximum packing density. Various memristive devices share this same crossbar structure and are depicted below (Fig. 5).

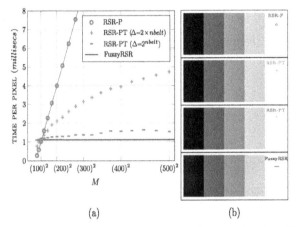

(a)   (b)

Fig. 5. Performance comparison – in terms of processing time as a function of [source: Internet]

2.4 Performance Assessment and Discussions

2.5 Memory Access

Our simulation involved three stages, illustrated in Fig. 6. The first stage utilized Hspice to generate a circuit-level outcome. The second stage used the memory architecture-level data from stage 1 to run a simulation using the Nvsim model, producing results for read/write power consumption and memory delay. In the final stage, we used GEM5 to perform system-level calculations based on the results from the previous stages. With these three stages completed, we were able to execute the written LeNet-5 algorithm in GEM5 to determine the read/write power consumption of the entire algorithm. Our simulation was conducted with specific parameters. The SPICE and process files were set up based on references [15, 16], respectively, with read voltage set at 6 mV, current at 1 uA, and register at 6 k. For NVSIM, we chose a 1 MB memory with 8 banks, where each bank contained 16 MATs, each MAT had 4 cell arrays, and each cell array was 16 x 1024 bits in size. We also used 16-bit gradients for the accelerators and selected MNIST as our benchmark dataset, using the LeNet-5 NN architecture. We implemented a bitwise CNN with six convolutional layers, two average pooling layers, and two FC layers, which were equivalent to convolutional layers, for the CNN layers of each 32×32 image. After gathering all of this information, we conducted comparisons using experimental data. The detailed process of each stage is described below (Fig. 7).

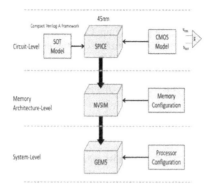

Fig. 6. Experimental architecture.

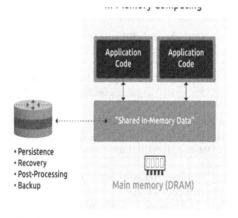

Fig. 7. In-memory computation explained

3 Conclusion

In contrast to the traditional retinex method, random spray retinex in the re-search mentioned above offers high-speed and energy/area-efficient architecture in review. Various picture quality measures and quantization settings were used to evaluate image quality. The latter functioned as a resistive value scale. For the buildup of output currents, MAC operations were carried out concurrently. This idea is generally applicable to a variety of their performance by utilizing scale to max operators and sparse input data It is believed that the recommended approach will be particularly beneficial in developing applications for deep learning and computer vision on memristors. The RSR algorithm and other applications were also investigated.

References

1. Arici, T., Dikbas, S., Altunbasak, Y.: A histogram modification framework and its application for image contrast enhancement. IEEE Trans. Image Process. **18**(9), 1921–1935 (2009)

2. Guan, X., Jian, S., Hongda, P., Zhiguo, Z., Haibin, G.: An image enhancement method based on gamma correction. In: Proc. 2nd Int. Symp. Comput. Intell. Design, pp. 60–63 (2009)
3. Huang, S.-C., Cheng, F.-C., Chiu, Y.-S.: Efficient contrast enhancement using adaptive gamma correction with weighting distribution. IEEE Trans. Image Process. **22**(3), 1032–1041 (2013)
4. Zhang, D., Park, W.-J., Lee, S.-J., Choi, K.-A., Ko, S.-J.: Histogram partition based gamma correction for image contrast enhancement. In: Proc. IEEE 16th Int. Symp. Consum. Electron., Jun, pp. 1–4 (2012)
5. Kim, J.-Y., Kim, L.-S., Hwang, S.-H.: An advanced contrast enhancement using partially overlapped sub-block histogram equalization. IEEE Trans. Circuits Syst. Video Technol. **11**(4), 475–484 (2001)
6. Kim, T.K., Paik, J.K., Kang, B.S.: Contrast enhancement system using spatially adaptive histogram equalization with temporal filtering. IEEE Trans. Consum. Electron. **44**(1), 82–87 (1998)
7. Rizzi, A., McCann, J.J.: On the behavior of spatial models of color. Proc. SPIE **6493**, 649302 (2007)
8. Lecca, M.: A gradient-based spatial color algorithm for image contrast enhancement. In: Proc. Int. Conf. Image Anal. Process, pp. 93–103. Springer, Cham, Switzerland (2019)
9. Provenzi, E., Fierro, M., Rizzi, A., De Carli, L., Gadia, D., Marini, D.: Random spray Retinex: a new Retinex implementation to investigate the local properties of the model. IEEE Trans. Image Process. **16**(1), 162–171 (2007)
10. Kolås, O., Farup, I., Rizzi, A.: Spatio-temporal Retinex-inspired envelope with stochastic sampling: a framework for spatial color algorithms. J. Imag. Sci. Technol. **55**(4), 40503 (2011)
11. Lecca, M.: STAR: a segmentation-based approximation of point-based sampling Milan Retinex for color image enhancement. IEEE Trans. Image Process. **27**(12), 5802–5812 (2018)
12. Gianini, G., Rizzi, A., Damiani, E.: A Retinex model based on absorbing Markov chains. Inf. Sci. **327**, 149–174 (2016)
13. Rizzi, A., Bonanomi, C.: Milano Retinex family. J. Electron. Imag. **26**(3), 031207 (2017). https://doi.org/10.1117/1.JEI.26.3.031207
14. Lu, Y., Alvarez, A., Kao, C.-H., Bow, J.-S., Chen, S.-Y., Chen, I.-W.: An electronic silicon-based memristor with a high switching uniformity. Nature Electron. **2**(2), 66–74 (2019)
15. Halawani, Y., Mohammad, B., Al-Qutayri, M., Al-Sarawi, S.F.: Memristor-based hardware accelerator for image compression. IEEE Trans. Very Large Scale Integr. Syst. **26**(12), 2749–2758 (2018)
16. Zayer, F., Mohammad, B., Saleh, H., Gianini, G.: RRAM crossbar-based in-memory computation of anisotropic filters for image preprocessing loa. IEEE Access **8**, 127569–127580 (2020)
17. Zayer, F., Dghais, W., Belgacem, H.: Modeling framework and comparison of memristive devices and associated STDP learning Windows for neuromorphic applications. J. Phys. D, Appl. Phys. **52**(39), 393002 (2019)
18. Abunahla, H., Halawani, Y., Alazzam, A., Mohammad, B.: NeuroMem: analog graphene-based resistive memory for artificial neural networks. Sci. Rep. **10**(1), 1–11 (2020)
19. Banić, N., Lončarić, S.: Light random sprays Retinex: exploiting the noisy illumination estimation. IEEE Signal Process. Lett. **20**(12), 1240–1243 (2013)
20. Cordts, M., et al.: The cityscapes dataset. In: Proc. CVPR Workshop Future Datasets Vis., vol. 2, pp. 1–4 (2015)
21. McCann, J.J.: Retinex at 50: color theory and spatial algorithms, a review. J. Electron. Imag. **26**(3), 031204 (2017). https://doi.org/10.1117/1.JEI.26.3.031204
22. Jobson, D.J., Rahman, Z.-U., Woodell, G.A.: A multiscale Retinex for bridging the gap between color images and the human observation of scenes. IEEE Trans. Image Process. **6**(7), 965–976 (1997)

Shufflenetv2: An Effective Technique for Recommendation System in E-Learning by User Preferences

Dudla Anil Kumar$^{(\boxtimes)}$ and M. Ezhilarasan

Department of Information Technology, Puducherry Technological University, Puducherry 605014, India
anilkumar.d@pec.edu, mrezhil@ptuniv.edu.in

Abstract. Recommendation systems for e-learning can help learners to discover new courses, improve their learning outcomes, and enhance their overall experience. Learning improved by technology provides a variety of communication and data tools for learning and teaching. The lack of data, scalability, cold start, time requirements, and accuracy continues to be challenging. To overcome the challenges, we propose deep learning-based techniques for recommendation systems in e-learning. In this paper, we utilize a deep learning method for a recommendation system. Initially, we collect the information of the student or user from the student or user profile. Secondly, extracting the features such as comments, likes, dislikes, favorites, and ratings using the ResNet-152 approach. Using the ShuffleNet V2 technique, the number of users who have recommended and have not recommended the associated learning site will be predicted at the finish. To improve the accuracy of the proposed technique, we utilize the Modified Butterfly Optimization Algorithm (MBOA). The performance analysis in terms of several performance indicators serves as evidence for the proposed method's superiority.

Keywords: ShuffleNet V2 · Recommendation System · Feature Extraction · E-Learning · Dataset

1 Introduction

Recommender systems have become widely utilized in the past several years as a response to the issue of data overload. E-learning recommender structures essentially address this issue by recommending appropriate learning materials to students based on their updated understudy preference and user profile [1]. Giving different recommendations of learning resources for the good achievement of the learning objectives is a crucial informational activity in helping online students in e-learning environments. While in doubt, current frameworks that are used in any situation one type of learning are used to enable personalization. Personalization in e-learning structures concerns content disclosure, flexible connection, social occasion, adaptable course movement, and adaptable composed effort assistance [2–4]. The flexible course movement class demonstrates the most exceptional and widely utilized assembling of change methods employed in current e-learning frameworks. Personalization thus accommodates a significant activity in a flexible e-learning framework.

Researchers explore e-learning and online transport considered stuff that has gotten thought from the World Wide Web's existence. But once more, very few course administration structures are built with smart pros that would enable modifying the course delivery system or tailoring the required learning things [5, 6]. Applications in business have been successful near. The personalization of virtual stores and online records to enhance electronic data acquisition, restrict blending, appeal to purchase, and draw in new clients has been the focal point of numerous study considerations in business, correspondence, mind science, and science of enrollment. Several such applications are being promoted nowadays and have the chance to stand out. For instance, some locations might provide updated item files that would typically comprise items that reflect the client's past preferences or that have a high likelihood of being purchased based on the user's profile lowering, infuriating the customer with lengthy and pointless data [7–10]. Depending on the current purchase, the customer's preferences and "tastes," and the overall selections, many company goals may make relevant recommendations for multiple categories.

In the current era, training sessions and seminars are used to help teachers and students continually improve their skills. On the other side, e-learning provides a platform for learners, teachers, and organizational employees to discover their linked interest-specific talents to improve their achievement. Learners are not physically present at training centers, unlike in schools and other places for learning where both teacher and students must be present [11, 12]. An e-learning platform can function independently to support education even in remote or rural places by offering cutting-edge and current course content. By enhancing their technical and academic abilities, the e-learning platform increases the chances of experienced professionals and teachers advancing in their careers by enabling them to compete with skilled and knowledgeable individuals [13]. While there are numerous advantages to e-learning, there are also some disadvantages, such as insufficient assistance and direction for e-learning, virtualized direction in individualized options for individual needs, etc. In sectors where many people share their data and personal information, such as education, social media, and other domains, the usage of recommendations is therefore unavoidable. By offering particular content recommendations, customized options help learners enhance their learning experiences. The majority of current recommendations focus on collaborative-based filtering (CBF), which has the problems of sparsity and a new user, while others use content filtering (CF), which uses one user's prior knowledge to suggest relevant material. In both cases, however, data filtering is based on the ratings of either current or former users. The cold star problem, which emerges with a big user base, makes it challenging to have accurate preferences because of preference mismatches and a dearth of available virtual environments. To overcome all the issues, we propose a novel technique for the recommendation system in this paper. We initiate by gathering data about students or users from their profiles. Second, using the ResNet152 technique, extract features like comments, likes, dislikes, favorites, and ratings. Using the ShuffleNet V2 technique, the number of users who have not recommended and recommended the associated learning site will be predicted at the conclusion. We use the Modified Butterfly Optimization Algorithm (MBOA) to increase the proposed technique's accuracy. The key contribution is,

- Initially, collect the information on student details from the E-Learning dataset of the OULAD-VLE dataset.
- To extract the features such as ratings, likes, and comments from users or students, utilizing the ResNet-152 technique.
- Utilizing ShuffleNet V2 deep learning novel technique as a classifier for learning courses recommended or not recommended to students or users.
- For performance evaluation, we used to collect data for the OULAD-VLE dataset and with accuracy, precision, sensitivity, specificity, and f1-score of performance metrics.

The rest of the article is divided into the following sections. Section 2 lists the literature that is related to the paper. The problem statement is given in Sect. 3. The proposed technique is explained in Sect. 4. Section 5 presents the results. Finally, Sect. 6 presents the conclusions.

2 Literature Survey

Even though online learning recommendation systems have been the subject of numerous studies, there are still several drawbacks to the current system that require the development of a new approach.

For the aim of recommending learning sources to every student, Tarus et al. [14] suggested a hybrid recommendation strategy combining sequential pattern mining (SPM), CF algorithms, and context awareness. The SPM technique is utilized to mine websites and find the student's often access patterns, then context awareness is utilized to incorporate context data about the student such as learning goals and knowledge level; CF-computes predictions and creates recommendations for the learner based on contextualized information and student's sequential access patterns.

Vedavathi & AnilKumar [15] suggested a hybrid optimization algorithm (HOA)-based efficient e-learning recommendation (EELR) model for user preferences. A DRNN and the IWO algorithm are used by the EELR system to build an HOA. Initially, DRNN is used to organize different types of e-learners into e-learner groups, from which clients can request course recommendations. The student's behavior and preferences are then assessed by thoroughly mining the configurations periodically monitored by the IWO calculation. Recommender frameworks advise students on publications they might like to analyze rather than having them actively search for data.

Ibrahim et al. [16] suggested a Fog-based Recommendation System (FBRS), which can be effectively used to enhance the functionality of the E-Learning environment. By identifying three FBRS modules Subclass Identification Module (SIM), Class Identification Module (CIM), and Matchmaking Module, they may develop a framework to improve and reorganize the EL environment (MM). Moreover, the FBRS technique defeats both customization and synonymy by achieving a high reaction time and security.

Jeevamol & Renumol [17] suggested an ontology-based (OB) content recommender system to deal with the issue of new users having trouble getting started. Ontology is utilized in the suggested recommendation model to system the learner and the learning items with their properties. To produce the top N recommendations based on learner ratings, the recommendation model uses collaborative and content-based filtering algorithms. The prediction and performance accuracy of the suggested model under cold-start conditions were evaluated through experiments utilizing the precision, evaluation metrics mean absolute error and recall. By utilizing ontological domain information, the suggested model offers recommendations that are more trustworthy and individualized.

A Dynamic Ontology-based E-learning Recommender System was suggested by Amane et al. [18]. To get the top N recommendations using clustering approaches, the suggested strategy characterizes course and learner semantically. This information will be merged into collaborative and content-based filtering processes. The experiments' measurements are performed utilizing the renowned "COURSERA" dataset combined with the USMBA dataset from our university. The results show that the suggested strategy is more effective than a content-based method in the process of making recommendations.

3   Proposed Methodology

For online learning systems, this paper has presented customized, continuous, and dynamic recommendations. The new recommendation system for online learning has been implemented using the proposed model's intelligent technique. In this paper, we utilize a deep learning method for a recommendation system. Initially, we collect the information of the student or user from the student or user profile. Secondly, extracting the features such as comments, likes, dislikes, favorites, and ratings using the ResNet-152 approach. Finally, employing the ShuffleNet V2 technique to predict the outcome as to how many students have recommended and not recommended the learning site. To improve the accuracy of the proposed technique, we utilize the Modified Butterfly Optimization algorithm (MBOA).

3.1   Data Gathering

The recommendation system needs to be able to identify the users' interests. To be able to create a profile for each of these individuals, it must gather a variety of data from them. Our system will create the data gathering required to create the user profile. The data gathered for the E-learning recommendation system from the OULAD-VLE dataset, which is available in Kaggle. The OULAD-VLE dataset is nothing more than a cutting-edge e-learning platform that centralizes all data and employs cutting-edge technology to facilitate effective learning. With technology-friendly, user-friendly, enterprise-friendly, customizable, course-friendly procedures, and learning-friendly, it has the power to delight, amuse, and engage the learning process. The data are manufactured artificially for this experiment based on consumer reviews of this E-learning dataset.

3.2   ResNet-152 for Feature Extraction

After collecting the information about the student or user, then we extract the features of students from the student profile. To extract the features, we utilize the ResNet-152 approach. It extracts the features such as comments, likes, dislikes, favorites, and ratings. The recommendation module employs a numerical value that is transformed from the rating scale of one star to five stars. A sort of neural network called residual networks has been proposed for feature extraction. ResNet has a residual learning unit to prevent deep neural network degeneration [19]. This system is built as a feed-forward network with a shortcut connection that enables the addition of new outputs and inputs. Overall, feed-forward, fully connected, and back propagation networks all have different roles in ResNet-152, and each is significant in its own way. Without feed-forward networks, the initial feature extraction process would be compromised, and the network may not be able to identify important low-level features in the input image. Without fully connected layers, the network may not be able to learn complex features, and its performance may be limited. Without back propagation, the network would not be able to learn from its mistakes and continually improve its performance. The key advantage is that it improves the precision of classification without getting the model more complicated. By joining further three-layer blocks, the ResNet - 152 layers are created. Compared to the 34-layer network VGG-16/19, the 152-layer ResNet has a simpler construction. The residual connections of the ResNet design greatly benefited from the linkages between residual blocks. Increasing the network's capacity preserves the knowledge acquired during training and improves model construction.

In contrast to the prior network, which led to accuracy degradation and saturation, the ResNet approach is advantageous in that it is simple to optimize and has higher accuracy when the depth is increased. The counterpart residual networks are plain networks that have short links added to them, making them similar to the counterpart residual networks.

3.3 ShuffleNet V2 for Classification

ShuffleNet V2, a lightweight CNN architecture, is used as the model training architecture. This model was chosen because it is thought to combine feature reuse with minimal trainable parameters for large datasets like the OULAD-VLE dataset. A model's evaluation and performance assessment parameters minimize model complexity and training time in this way. There were 41 classes, and parameters like scaling factor, pooling, and bottleneck ratio were configured. To acquire the best results from the models, the number of hidden layers was reduced by utilizing custom inputs and hyperparameter adjustment. Six building blocks, each with two convolutional layers, were stacked to make the network [20]. During model execution, no layers were frozen. The "ReLU" function was applied to each activation layer, and then a final "softmax" layer with 41 neurons corresponding to the amount of output classes was added. The error rate was decreased using the optimizer, Adam. The following is a list of the updated weights' formulae.

Initialization of weights:

$$\rho_m \leftarrow 1, \rho_v \leftarrow 1, m \leftarrow 0, v \leftarrow 0 \tag{1}$$

Update rules for Adam Optimizer:

$$\rho_m \leftarrow \beta_m \rho_m \tag{2}$$

$$\rho_v \leftarrow \beta_v \rho_v \tag{3}$$

$$m \leftarrow \beta_m m + (1 - \beta_m)\nabla_w J \tag{4}$$

$$v \leftarrow \beta_v v + (1 - \beta_v)(\nabla_w J) \odot \nabla_w J \tag{5}$$

$$w \leftarrow w - \alpha\left(\frac{m}{\sqrt{v} + \epsilon} \frac{\sqrt{1 - \rho_v}}{1 - \rho_m}\right) \tag{6}$$

where, correspondingly, m, v stands for the first and second-moment vectors. Similar to this, the exponential decay rates for the first and second moment vectors are represented by β_m, and β_v, respectively. The adaptive learning rate time decay factor is specified by the variables ρ_m, and ρ_v. Similar to momentum, this value is related to the memory for previous weight modifications. The α symbol in Eq. 6 stands for learning rate or step size. The little number in Eq. 6's $\nabla_w J$ represents the gradient of the cost function, J. ϵ is intended to avoid the division by zero condition. Equation 2 through Eq. 5 describe circumstances bias change and obeying weight, while Eq. 1 define initial weights before the update. Equation 6 displays the ultimate weight parameter change. The $\odot$ symbol denotes element-wise multiplication in Eq. 5 and element-wise root operations in Eq. 6. To get a higher classification accuracy, we utilize the Modified Butterfly Optimization Algorithm.

3.4 Modified Butterfly Optimization Algorithm (MBOA)

With the use of MBOA, the fuzzy membership limits for the presented E-learning recommendation model are optimized. MBOA is a population-based algorithm that emulates the behavior of butterfly populations in nature, and it has been shown to be effective in optimizing the hyper parameters of CNNs. The Butterfly Optimization Algorithm (BOA) produces effective results since the switch probability factor regulates both the global and local search. The global search process allows butterflies to explore the search space, but the local search process encourages the exploitation of the butterflies, maintaining the diversity of solutions/butterflies. The BOA succeeds in retaining butterfly variety while tackling challenging real-world issues because these search operations happen sequentially and randomly [21]. Hence, a Modified BOA that employs an additional step of intensive exploitation is proposed in the current work. After each butterfly has conducted a local or global search, extensive exploitation is carried out in each iteration. Without a doubt, intensive exploitation will add another step to the process, forcing it to complete another one that will require more computation time. Yet, the efficiency of the algorithm is improved by this extensive exploitation, which justifies its insertion. Intense exploitation is accomplished by

$$x_i^{t+1} = g^* + ((rand_1 - rand_2) \times g^*) \tag{7}$$

In Eq. (7), $rand_1$ and $rand_2$ are random numbers chosen at random from a uniform distribution between 0 and 1, while g^* is the best butterfly/solution. If $rand_1$ and $rand_2$

return the same number, it means that the algorithm will use the same random number twice, which can lead to biased results and affect the diversity of the search. Overall, ensuring that $rand_1$ and $rand_2$ return different numbers is crucial for the effectiveness and accuracy of the modified butterfly optimization algorithm. Its thorough exploitation directs the proposed algorithm to converge toward the global optimum while simultaneously avoiding the local optimum trap. The MBOA optimizes the participation limits of the ShuffleNet V2 classifier in the proposed intelligent recommendation system for e-learning to categorize the output as either recommended or not recommended.

4   Results and Discussion

This section's first half categorizes gastrointestinal diseases using the dataset's evaluation and methodology for extracting disease feature attributes, comparing our method to "state-of-the-art" methods.

4.1   Dataset Description

For e-learning testing environments, the Open University Learning Analytics dataset (OULAD) was created. It incorporates student-submitted assessment results in addition to comprehensive VLE information that researchers and academics can utilize to framework various features and develop various models for forecasting student achievement in a course. The 32,593 students and 22 courses whose data compensate the OULAD-VLE dataset. The daily activity based on 10,655,280 entries was also provided. The dataset was made up of three major data types: demographics, learning behavior, and performance. An anonymization procedure was used, and some attributes were randomly chosen, to ensure privacy. Nonetheless, student-identifying characteristics including gender, handicap, age, location, and education were kept intact. An artificial intelligence-based recommendation system's dataset is represented by qualities that fall into four categories. We took three categories of information: performance (final test results and score), demographics (code presentation, code module, disability, studied credits, and id student), and learning behavior (num of prev attempts, sum-clicks on VLE activities). The dataset attributes are displayed in several tables, and the attributes were retrieved and tested for the AISAR system that was designed.

4.2   Evaluation Metrics

$$Accuracy = \frac{TP + TN}{TP + TN + FP + FN} \tag{8}$$

$$Precision = \frac{TP}{TP + FP} \tag{9}$$

$$F1Score = 2 \times \frac{precision \times recall}{precision + recall} \tag{10}$$

$$Sensitivity = \frac{TP}{TP + FN} \tag{11}$$

$$Specificity = \frac{TN}{TN + FP} \tag{12}$$

4.3 Performance Metrics

When compared to other current models in experimental performance, the proposed approach offers the highest categorization accuracy. Results for recall, accuracy, f1-score, and precision for SPM [14], HOA [15], FBRS [16], and the proposed ShuffleNet V2 on the recommendation system from the OULAD-VLE dataset are shown in Table 1. The results show that the proposed methodology outperforms other current approaches in terms of classification accuracy values. Hence, using an optimization method, we displayed the comparison results as a graph. Figure 1 displayed the accuracy analysis of the suggested technique without optimization in comparison to other techniques currently in use.

Table 1. Analysis of the Proposed and Existing Techniques

Performance Measures (%)	SPM [14]	HOA [15]	FBRS [16]	Proposed
Accuracy	97.45	96.51	98.27	99.54
Sensitivity	96.89	95.82	98.06	98.91
Specificity	97.25	95.09	97.83	99.02
F1-score	97.84	96.24	98.60	99.23
Precision	97.16	75.47	97.72	98.97
FNR	3.24	2.97	3.89	2.65
FPR	2.15	1.96	2.43	1.75

Figure 1 also compared the proposed technique's categorization outcomes with those of other approaches that do not employ optimization algorithm graphs. Our proposed models improved the classification accuracy while requiring less computation time.

4.4 Analysis of Computation Time

Table 2 analyses and lists the computation times for the proposed approach and the previously used methods. In comparison to other existing techniques, the proposed technique takes less computation time. The evaluation in the E-learning recommendation system appears to be good when compared to other previous techniques, even if the computation time of the proposed technique is less than other existing methods.

Figure 2 shows the existing and proposed methods of comparison of analysis of computation time.

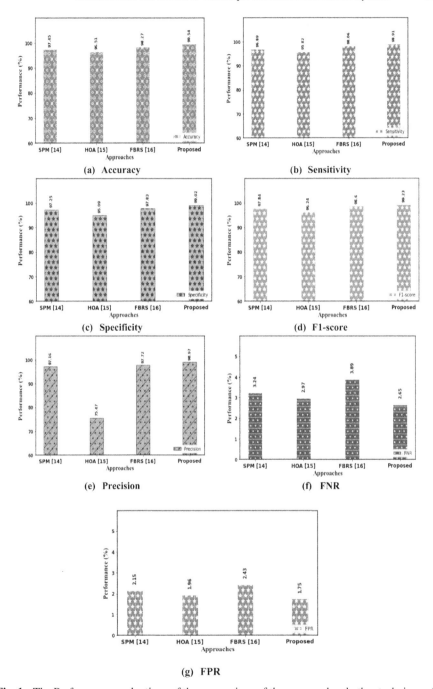

Fig. 1. The Performance evaluations of the comparison of the proposed and other techniques (a) Accuracy (b) Sensitivity (c) Specificity (d) F1-score (e) Precision (f) FNR (g) FPR

Table 2. The Computation Time of The Existing and Proposed Method for the E-Learning Recommendation System

Approaches	Computation Time (sec)
SPM [14]	0.20
HOA [15]	0.26
FBRS [16]	0.17
ShuffleNet V2 with MBOA	0.14

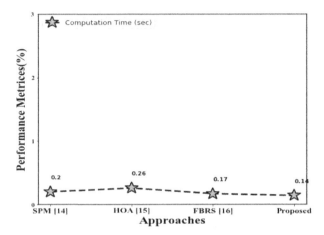

Fig. 2. The comparison of existing and proposed techniques computation time analysis.

4.5 Evaluation of Training Results

Our accuracy following 100 epochs was 99.54%, which is significant given that accuracy curves generally converge. The accuracy and loss of validation and training are displayed in Fig. 3.

The validation loss curves quickly increase and decrease. It implies that getting more test results can be useful. However, given the minimal variance between Train and Test Loss and the smoothing of the curve over epochs, this might be acceptable. Figures 3 display the training's accuracy and loss. Higher accuracy and loss predictions are provided by ShuffleNet V2. Our methodology outperforms previous approaches in both the validation and training stages of the classification process for the e-learning recommendation system.

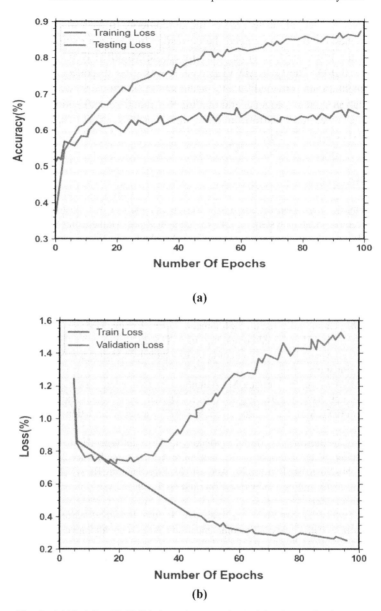

Fig. 3. (a) Training Vs Validation accuracy, (b) Training Vs Validation loss.

5 Conclusion

For online learning systems, this paper provided a continuous, dynamic recommendation, personalized. In this paper, first, we collected the information of the student or user from the student or user profile. Secondly, extracted the features such as comments, likes, dislikes, favorites, and ratings used the ResNet-152 approach. Finally, employed the ShuffleNet V2 technique to predict the outcome as to how many students have not recommended and recommended the corresponding learning site. To improve the accuracy of the proposed technique, we utilized the Modified Butterfly Optimization algorithm (MBOA). The OULAD-VLE dataset was used to collect the information. Our experimental data provided 99.54% accuracy. In future work, we will convert our recommendation system into a general module that functions and is simple to install on every popular e-Learning platform under a free license, such as (Chamilo, Claroline, eFront, Moodle, SAKAI, Etc.).

References

1. Bhaskaran, S., Marappan, R., Santhi, B.: Design and analysis of a cluster-based intelligent hybrid recommendation system for e-learning applications. Mathematics **9**(2), 197 (2021)
2. Ali, S., Hafeez, Y., Humayun, M., Jamail, N.S.M., Aqib, M., Nawaz, A.: Enabling recommendation system architecture in virtualized environment for e-learning. Egyptian Informatics Journal **23**(1), 33–45 (2022)
3. Ghosh, S., Roy, S., Sen, S.: An efficient recommendation system on e-learning platform by query lattice optimization. In: Data Management, Analytics and Innovation: Proceedings of ICDMAI 2020, Vol. 1, pp. 73–86. Springer Singapore (2021)
4. Rahhali, M., Oughdir, L., Jedidi, Y., Lahmadi, Y., El Khattabi, M.Z.: E-learning recommendation system based on cloud computing. In: WITS 2020: Proceedings of the 6th International Conference on Wireless Technologies, Embedded, and Intelligent Systems, pp. 89–99. Springer Singapore (2022)
5. Amane, M., Aissaoui, K., Berrada, M.: A multi-agent and content-based course recommender system for university e-learning platforms. In: Digital Technologies and Applications: Proceedings of ICDTA 21, Fez, Morocco, pp. 663–672. Springer International Publishing, Cham (2021)
6. Gomede, E., de Barros, R.M., de Souza Mendes, L.: Deep auto encoders to adaptive E-learning recommender system. Computers and education: Artificial intelligence **2**, 100009 (2021)
7. Ezaldeen, H., Misra, R., Bisoy, S.K., Alatrash, R., Priyadarshini, R.: A hybrid E-learning recommendation integrating adaptive profiling and sentiment analysis. Journal of Web Semantics **72**, 100700 (2022)
8. Tahir, S., Hafeez, Y., Abbas, M.A., Nawaz, A., Hamid, B.: Smart learning objects retrieval for E-Learning with contextual recommendation based on collaborative filtering. Educ. Inf. Technol. **27**(6), 8631–8668 (2022)
9. Yan, L., Yin, C., Chen, H., Rong, W., Xiong, Z., David, B.: Learning resource recommendation in e-learning systems based on online learning style. In: Knowledge Science, Engineering and Management: 14th International Conference, KSEM 2021, Tokyo, Japan, August 14–16, 2021, Proceedings, Part III, pp. 373–385. Springer International Publishing, Cham (2021, August)
10. Alatrash, R., Ezaldeen, H., Misra, R., Priyadarshini, R.: Sentiment analysis using deep learning for recommendation in E-learning domain. In: Progress in Advanced Computing and Intelligent Engineering: Proceedings of ICACIE 2020, pp. 123–133. Springer Singapore (2021)
11. Achyuth, B., Manasa, S.: Implementation of recommendation system and technology for villages using machine learning and iot. In: Evolutionary Computing and Mobile Sustainable Networks: Proceedings of ICECMSN 2020, pp. 527–542. Springer Singapore (2021)

12. Dhaiouir, I., Ezziyyani, M., Khaldi, M.: The personalization of learners' educational paths e-learning. in networking. In: Intelligent Systems and Security: Proceedings of NISS 2021, pp. 521–534. Springer Singapore (2022)
13. Rafiq, M.S., Jianshe, X., Arif, M., Barra, P.: Intelligent query optimization and course recommendation during online lectures in E-learning system. J. Ambient. Intell. Humaniz. Comput. **12**(11), 10375–10394 (2021). https://doi.org/10.1007/s12652-020-02834-x
14. Tarus, J.K., Niu, Z., Kalui, D.: A hybrid recommender system for e-learning based on context awareness and sequential pattern mining. Soft. Comput. **22**(8), 2449–2461 (2017). https://doi.org/10.1007/s00500-017-2720-6
15. Vedavathi, N., Anil Kumar, K.M.: An efficient e-learning recommendation system for user preferences using hybrid optimization algorithm. Soft. Comput. **25**(14), 9377–9388 (2021). https://doi.org/10.1007/s00500-021-05753-x
16. Ibrahim, T.S., Saleh, A.I., Elgaml, N., Abdelsalam, M.M.: A fog based recommendation system for promoting the performance of E-Learning environments. Comput. Electr. Eng. **87**, 106791 (2020)
17. Jeevamol, J., Renumol, V.G.: An ontology-based hybrid e-learning content recommender system for alleviating the cold-start problem. Educ. Inf. Technol. **26**(4), 4993–5022 (2021). https://doi.org/10.1007/s10639-021-10508-0
18. Amane, M., Aissaoui, K., Berrada, M.: ERSDO: E-learning recommender system based on dynamic ontology. Educ. Inf. Technol. **27**(6), 7549–7561 (2022)
19. Zhang, L., Li, H., Zhu, R., Du, P.: An infrared and visible image fusion algorithm based on ResNet-152. Multimedia Tools and Applications **81**(7), 9277–9287 (2021). https://doi.org/10.1007/s11042-021-11549-w
20. Ma, N., Zhang, X., Zheng, H.T., Sun, J.: Shufflenet v2: Practical guidelines for efficient cnn architecture design. In: Proceedings of the European conference on computer vision (ECCV), pp. 116–131 (2018)
21. Arora, S., Singh, S., Yetilmezsoy, K.: A modified butterfly optimization algorithm for mechanical design optimization problems. J. Braz. Soc. Mech. Sci. Eng. **40**(1), 1–17 (2018). https://doi.org/10.1007/s40430-017-0927-1

A Multi-modal Approach Using Game Theory for Android Forensics Tool Selection

Mahpara Yasmin Mohd Minhaz Alam$^{(\boxtimes)}$ and Wilson Naik

SCIS, University of Hyderabad, Hyderabad, India
mahpara31@gmail.com

Abstract. In the field of digital forensics, specifically for android forensics, we have several tool options to use during the investigations for a given task. Investigators may prefer to utilize one tool over the others depending on reasons such as success of the tool for particular tasks and the execution time required to use the tool. It is also common that forensic tools do not have the same performance in different cases involving different tasks or devices. To overcome this problem a game theory based multi-modal approach for android forensics is proposed. The idea is to test and analyze 14 android forensics tools and generated a dataset for each tool based on the features and functionalities that it provides. Each dataset is given as input to Multi-arm bandit(MAB) algorithms to calculate rewards. Using the type of action and calculated rewards a decision tree will be generated. Siblings on the same level indicate that they provide a similar kind of action. Further game theory approaches will be applied to the siblings of the decision tree. Based on the obtained rewards, the payoff of each mixed strategy nash equilibrium can be calculated for sibling nodes w.r.t different game theory and the efficiency of the pair of tools can be determined. This will help in determining if a given android forensic tool should be selected or not for a particular forensic investigation.

Keywords: Decision tree · Game theory · Forensics investigation · Multi-arm bandits · Nash equilibrium

1 Introduction

In the field of digital forensics, evidence from multiple digital sources is preserved, acquired, documented, analysed, and interpreted. In order to combat cybercrimes, forensics has developed throughout time and now includes many different fields of forensic research. The majority of the digital evidence used in court cases—about 80% of it [1] is from mobile devices. Android forensic tools assist investigators in removing the crumbs of evidence from android devices so they may be offered to the authorities in order to put offenders in jail. The essential subfield of digital forensics known as mobile forensics focuses on the recovery, extraction, and analysis of digital evidence or data from mobile devices under forensically sound conditions. To put it simply, android forensics is the study of accessing data saved on devices, including as call logs, images, SMS, contacts, movies, documents, application files, browsing histories, and so forth [2]. It also deals with recovering lost data from mobile devices using various forensic techniques. The

R. Morusupalli et al. (Eds.): MIWAI 2023, LNAI 14078, pp. 192–202, 2023.
https://doi.org/10.1007/978-3-031-36402-0_17

court must accept digital evidence in cases involving cybercrime, financial fraud, etc. Making a clone of your Android device is crucial. And investigators must only work on the Android image file, not the actual device.

Digital forensics is generally a long and tedious process for an investigator [3]. There are a wide variety of tools available that an investigator must consider, including both open source and proprietary. Tool developers and forensics researchers are regularly making efforts to make newer tools available especially open source tools.. Investigators generally decide to use certain tools based on their familiarity, technical skills, and previous experiences with those tools. In addition, they may sometimes have to use additional tools to verify their findings. This is commonly the case when their previously selected tools do not generate the desired output.

So considering all these factors a game theory-based multi-modal approach for android forensics is proposed. The idea is to test and analyze 16 android forensics tools and generate a dataset for each tool based on the features and functionalities that it provides. Each dataset is given as input to Multi-arm bandit algorithms [4] like Epsilon-greedy, UCB (Upper confidence bound), and Linear UCB to generate rewards that are explained in a later section. The idea is to make a decision tree that will be generated based on the type of action and rewards. Siblings on the same level indicate that they provide a similar kind of action. Further game theory approaches will be applied to the siblings of the decision tree. Based on the obtained rewards, the payoff of each mixed strategy nash equilibrium can be calculated for sibling nodes w.r.t different game theory approaches and the efficiency or relevancy of the pair of tools can be determined. Similarly, this technique will be applied to other pair of forensics tools as well and this way we can compare accuracy with respect to each other. This will help in determining if a given android forensic tool should be selected or not for a particular forensic investigation.

2   Related Work

There are limited game theory applications in the digital forensic domain in general. For instance, Nisioti, et al. [5] discussed the interaction between a cyber forensic Investigator and a strategic Attacker using a Bayesian game [6] of incomplete information played on a multi-host cyber forensics investigation graph of actions traversed by both players. They proposed a technique to identify the optimal investigating policy while considering the cost and impact of the available actions. The probabilistic distribution is calculated through past incident reports using Common Vulnerability Scoring System (CVSS) [7]. In our study we calculated Probabilities/rewards generated using multi-armed bandit algorithms like epsilon greedy, UCB, etc.

In other work Saeed et al. [8], shown how the investigator used counter anti-forensics, or anti-rootkits, whereas the attacker used anti-forensics, in rootkits. Models based on game theory like gradient play [9] and fictitious play [10] are selected along with an algorithms to evaluate and simulate the players' interactions. They have used 14 features / characteristics to model the players' interactions in the forensic environment. In our case we are considering 115 feature set to get better prediction.

There are few works on android forensics like in [11] Mukhlis et al. worked on the live procurement method for logical acquisition on smartphones using agents AFLogical

OSE [12] and Laron [13] to obtain digital proof in the form of Contact List, Call Log, SMS and MMS. This is based on a comparison between two open-source agents. In our work, we are using Android debug bridge (ADB) [14] which is the base for both tools along with several other tools. There are limited contribution in the field of android forensics tool selection so we are working on this topic. The details are given in following sections.

3 Experimental Setup

3.1 Dataset

A stock Android image from Digital Corpora [15] was used to make an image of Android 12. To access all the features and capabilities of each unique app, a device had multiple popular applications (apps) loaded with random user data. User data was also included in stock Android apps.While testing each android forensics tool we also generate 14 separate data based on the features and functionalities of the tool for further computation.

3.2 Android Forensics Tools

There are specialized tools that help in android forensics. Investigators can retrieve deleted information, analyze, and preserve evidence that may arise during an examination of criminal activity. In this experiment we are considering 14 forensics tools that are the free and reliable mobile forensic tools or scripts to conduct digital forensic investigations.

4 Multi-arm Bandits Problem

The multi-armed bandit (MAB) problem simulates an agent that simultaneously seeks to learn new information (referred to as "exploration") and optimises judgments based on knowledge already at hand (referred to as "exploitation"). In order to maximise her or his overall value well over time being considered, the agent seeks to achieve balance between these conflicting tasks. Using this method we generate rewards that will help in creating a decision tree. Following MAB algorithms are used to generate rewards:

4.1 ε-greedy Algorithm

The ε-greedy algorithm [16] is a wholly random process, and once the strategy is changed from exploitation to exploration, a random decision would be made. The algorithm chooses a random arm with probability ε at each phase t = 1, 2, ..., and plays the current best reward-yielding arm with probability 1 ε. This can also be stated as the probability of selecting arm i at time, given initial empirical means $\mu 1(0),..., \mu K(t)$ and pi(t) which represents the probability of picking arm i at time t,

$$p_i(t+1) = \begin{cases} 1 - \epsilon + \frac{\epsilon}{k}, & i = \arg\max_{j=1,...,K} \mu_j(t) \\ \frac{\epsilon}{k}, & \text{otherwise} \end{cases} \quad (1)$$

4.2 Upper Confidence Bound

Initial assumptions made by the UCB algorithm [17] include that every arm has already been played nearly once, with the number of iterations each arm has been played being displayed by ni (t). The arm j(t) is then chosen at round t by the UCB algorithm typically follows:

$$j(t) = \arg \max_{i=1...k} \left(\mu_i + \sqrt{\frac{2 \ln(t)}{n_i}} \right) \tag{2}$$

4.3 LinUCB

LinUCB [18] is generic contextual bandit algorithms who's sole input parameter is α. In reality, improving this parameter could lead to larger overall payoffs if has a high value. LinUCB always selects the arm with both the highest UCB, much as UCB methods. The complexity among its computation increases linearly with the number of arms and, at most, cubically with the number of features.

Using these algorithms we calculated rewards for each forensics tool as shown in Table 1. We also calculated which tool is specialised in which type/domain of forensics analysis while testing the tools.

5   Decision Tree Creation and Application of Game Theory

5.1 Decision Tree Creation

Decision tree is a tree-structured classifier [19], where internal nodes represent the features of a dataset, branches represent the decision rules and each leaf node represents the outcome. In these internal nodes represents type of digital forensics action which is represented in blue. The lead nodes indicators type of forensics tool which is represented in orange colour as shown in Fig. 1.

5.2 Game Theory Approaches

The study of ways to handle competitive circumstances in games where a player's action choice may have an indirect impact on the actions of all other players is the focus of game theory. Different varieties exist. After testing various games like cooperative game, bayesian game, non-zero sum games etc., the non-zero sum is giving good result as in some cases positive rewards are assigned to both tools for similiar action.

Here we will do calculation mixed strategy mixed strategy for sibling nodes of decision tree. A mixed strategy exists in a game, when the player cannot choose a definite action, but he/she rather have to choose action according to the probability distribution over all applicable actions.

Table 1. Reward calculation for each tool

Sr. no.	Tools	Type of action	Rewards		
			ϵ - Greedy	UCB	Linear UCB
1	Andriller	Acquisition	0.564	0.412	0.466
2	Autopsy	Analysis and interpretation	0.471	0.764	0.767
3	Mobiledit	Acquisition	0.687	0.854	0.462
4	ADB (Android debug bridge)	Acquisition, analysis and interpretation	0.854	0.545	0.764
5	MAGNET Encrypted Disk Detector	Analysis	0.342	0.347	0.343
6	Belkasoft Live RAM Capturer	Acquisition and interpretation	0.575	0.654	0.564
7	Hash My File	Retrieval and interpretation	0.912	0.453	0.761
8	CrowdResponse	Retrieval	0.342	0.245	0.543
9	ExiFTool	Analysis and interpretation	0.432	0.345	0.466
10	Sleuth Kit	Analysis	0.766	0.435	0.786
11	Volatility Framework	Analysis	0.231	0.786	0.565
12	FTK Imager	Interpretation	0.378	0.658	0.546
13	Bulk Extractor	Retrieval	0.543	0.454	0.265
14	FireEye RedLine	Analysis and IoC	0.623	0.754	0.445

5.3 Pay-off Calculation

For demonstration purpose we are showing calculation w.rt Andriller and ADB that are siblings nodes whose parent is Acquisition meaning that both tools provides acquisition feature and are competitive in nature. So we are generating payoff matrix as given below (Fig. 2):

where,

V: Value (benefit) of forensics process

E1: Effectiveness of forensics using Andriller

E2: Effectiveness of forensics using ADB

Ct: Cost of processing time

Cf: Cost of unsuccessful forensics

5.4 Applying Mixed Strategy Nash Equilibrium

Now we will investigate whether there is a mixed strategy Nash equilibrium (MSNE) [38].

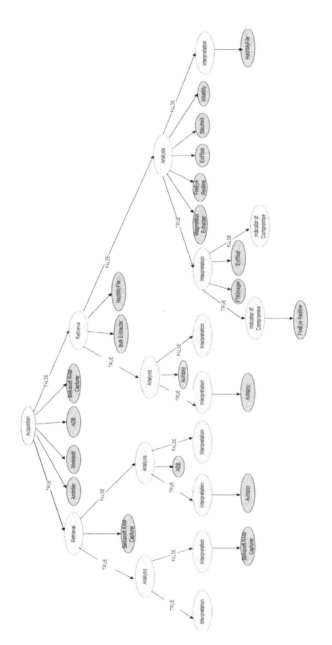

Fig. 1. Decision tree based on rewards and tool features

	Andriller	ADB
Andriller	VE1 - Ct , VE1 - Ct	VE1 - Ct , VE2 - Cf
ADB	VE2 - Cf , VE1 - Ct	VE2 - Cf , VE2 - Cf

Fig. 2. Pay-off matrix

Let S and P as probabilities of player 1 i.e. Andriller plays S and player 2 i.e. ADB plays P

$$\sigma_S + \sigma_P = 1 \tag{3}$$

We can write player 2's expected utility of playing S as a pure strategy and the function of player 1's mixed strategy

$$EU_S = \sigma_S(VE_1 - C_t) + (1 - \sigma_S)(VE_1 - C_t) = (VE_1 - C_t) \tag{4}$$

Player 2's expected utility of playing P as a pure strategy is

$$EU_P = \sigma_S(VE_2 - C_f) + (1 - \sigma_S)(VE_2 - C_f) = (VE_2 - C_f) \tag{5}$$

We are looking for a mixed strategy from player 1 that leaves player 2 indifferent between their pure strategies. We want to find a S and P such that

$$EU_S = EU_P \tag{6}$$

$$VE_1 - C_t = 1 - VE_2 - C_f \tag{7}$$

If we divide above Eq. 7 by V, we get following equation,

$$E_1 - \frac{C_t}{V} > E_2 - \frac{C_f}{V} \tag{8}$$

This shows that results completely depends on E1 and E2 i.e. effectiveness using Andriller and ADB respectively because most of the Ct i.e. cost of processing time and Cf i.e. cost of unsuccessful forensics are equal and opposite in value. Similiarly we are applying this approach on sibling node tools. After that we analysed each tool based on the processing time. The result and analysis is shown further section.

6 Comparisons and Results

We computed the rewards for tools using multi-arm bandits problems by changing parameters for best results. After analysis we used $\alpha = 1$ for LinUCB, $\rho = 1$ for Upper confidence bound (UCB) and $\varepsilon = 0.5$ for ε-greedy method. We run the simulation for all 16 tools for 800 rounds to get cumulative reward after running 100 times and 1000 times. Below are the simulation results for ADB and andriller (Figs. 3, 4, 5 and 6).

In all these graphs you can see that LinUCB is providing similar result both ADB and Andriller irrespective of number of simulations. Similar case occurred in case of ExifTool

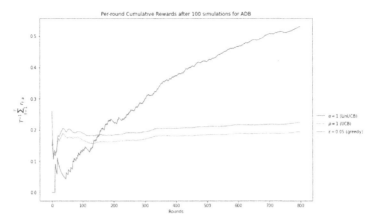

Fig. 3. Cumulative reward after 100 simulation of ADB

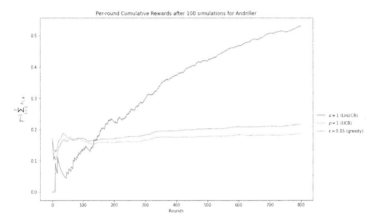

Fig. 4. Cumulative reward after 100 simulation of Andriller

and volatility that is sibling nodes under analysis as parents where epsilon-greedy was showing constant result even by varying the factors. In such cases we considered the average of the result of all three algorithms.

Further, we considered the varied efficiency of forensics tool and what kind of feature it provides like acquisition, retrieval, analysis, interpretation of each tool in given as decision tree in Fig. 1 to create a scatter plot of available forensics tools as given in Fig. 7.

The efficiency of android forensics is derived while testing each tool individually and level of forensics refers to level of a particular in the decision tree as given in Fig. 1. Further if we introduce an android forensics tool for testing, we'll find its payoff compared to neighbouring tools in scatter plot.

Suppose we have to introduce new forensics tool XRY [20] that is known for Acquisition and analysis. So, we create pay-off matrix of XRY vs Belkasoft RAM Capturer and XRY vs HashMyFile even though these tools are used in dissimiliar domain of android

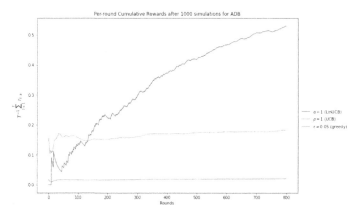

Fig. 5. Cumulative reward after 1000 simulation of ADB

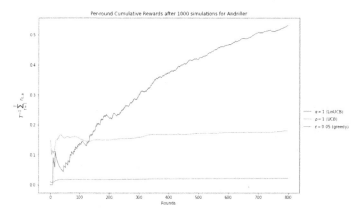

Fig. 6. Cumulative reward after 1000 simulation of Andriller

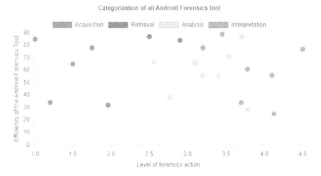

Fig. 7. Categorization of all android forensics tool

forensics but still we are applying game theory due to the kind of action or feature it provides. In calculation we found efficiency of XRY as 55 and level 1.76. So based this value it falls under Acquisition category as shown in Fig. 8. Similiarly we can add newer android forensics tools into the tool list. The newly added tool is as shown in Fig. 8.

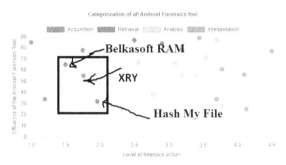

Fig. 8. New added tool XRY

7 Conclusion

Out of several tool options available during the investigations for a given task we derived a technique to find best suited android forensics tool. Forensic tools do not have the same performance in different cases involving different tasks or devices. Tool testing is a time consuming process we tried to solve the problem by using game theory along with multi-arm bandits and decision tree. We analyzed 14 android forensics tools and generated a dataset for each tool based on the features and functionalities that it provides. Each dataset is given as input to Multi-arm bandit algorithms like Epsilon-greedy, UCB (Upper confidence bound), and Linear UCB to generate rewards. A decision tree is generated based on the type of action and rewards. Siblings on the same level indicate that they provide a similar kind of action. Further game theory approaches are applied to the siblings of the decision tree. Based on the obtained rewards, the payoff of each mixed strategy nash equilibrium is calculated for sibling nodes w.r.t non-zero sum game. We even derived a noval method to add new android forensics tool to the tools list.

References

1. Baggili, I., Mislan, R., Rogers, M.: Mobile phone forensics tool testing: a database driven approach. IJDE 6 (2007)
2. Tamma, R., Tindall, D.: Learning Android Forensics. https://www.goodreads.com/book/show/25596976-learning-android-forensics (2015)
3. Nelson, B., Phillips, A., Steuart, C.: Guide to Computer Forensics and Investigations, 5th edn. Course Technology Press, Boston, MA, USA (2015)
4. Multi-arm bandits problem, Machine learning. https://en.wikipedia.org/wiki/Multi-armed_bandit
5. Nisioti, A., Loukas, G., Rass, S., Panaousis, E.: Game-theoretic decision support for cyber forensic investigations. Sensors **21**(16), 5300 (2021). https://doi.org/10.3390/s21165300
6. Bayesian game under game theory. https://en.wikipedia.org/wiki/Bayesian_game

7. Common Vulnerability Scoring System (CVSS). https://www.first.org/cvss/

8. Saeed, S.H., Arash, H.L., Ali, A.G.: A survey and research challenges of anti-forensics: evaluation of game-theoretic models in simulation of forensic agents' behavior. Forensic Sci. Int.: Digital Invest. **35**, 301024 (2020). https://doi.org/10.1016/j.fsidi.2020.301024

9. Shamma, J.S., Arslan, G.: Dynamic fictitious play, dynamic gradient play, and distributed convergence to Nash equilibria. IEEE Trans. Automat. Contr. **50**, 312–327 (2005). Gradient play

10. Shamma, J.S., Arslan, G.: Dynamic fictitious play, dynamic gradient play, and distributed convergence to Nash equilibria. IEEE Trans. Automat. Contr. **50**, 312–327 (2005). Fictitiousous play

11. Aji, M.P., Hariyadi, D., Rochmadi, T.: Logical acquisition in the forensic investigation process of android smartphones based on agent using open source software. IOP Conf. Ser.: Mater. Sci. Eng. **771**(1), 012024 (2020). https://doi.org/10.1088/1757-899X/771/1/012024

12. AFLogical OSE open-source github reference. https://github.com/nowsecure/android-forensics

13. Hariyadi, D., Huda, A.A.: Laron: Aplikasi Akuisisi Berbasis SNI 27037:2014 pada Ponsel Android. In: Indonesia Security Conference 2015, no. September, pp. 1–10 (2015). Laron

14. Android debug bridge (ADB). https://developer.android.com/studio/command-line/adb

15. Digital Corpora Android 12 image. https://digitalcorpora.org/corpora/cell-phones/android-12

16. Epsilon-greedy algorithm. https://medium.com/analytics-vidhya/multi-armed-bandits-part-1-epsilon-greedy-algorithm-with-python-code-534b9e2abc9

17. Upper Confidence Bound(UCB). https://towardsdatascience.com/the-upper-confidence-bound-ucb-bandit-algorithm-c05c2bf4c13f

18. LinUCB Algorithm. https://github.com/thunfischtoast/LinUCB

19. Decision tree classifier. https://github.com/topics/decision-tree-classifier

20. XRY Mobile forensics and data recovery. https://www.msab.com/product/xry-extract/

LPCD: Incremental Approach for Dynamic Networks

Ashwitha Gatadi$^{(\boxtimes)}$ and K. Swarupa Rani$^{(\boxtimes)}$

University of Hyderabad, Hyderabad, Telangana, India
{20mcpc14,swarupacs}@uohyd.ac.in

Abstract. Graph mining and analytics refer to analyzing and extracting meaningful information from graph data structures. Graph mining includes techniques such as community detection, centrality analysis, and graph pattern matching to identify significant subgraphs or clusters of nodes. Graph analytics includes node classification, link prediction, and graph clustering. Graph mining and Graph analytics together are used in applications such as recommender systems, social network analysis, and fraud detection. Link Prediction and Community Detection are essential techniques in Graph mining and analytics. Link Prediction is used in real applications to recommend new friends in the social network and to predict the traffic flow in the transportation network. On the other hand, Community Detection is essential as it shares common interests or characteristics, which can help better understand social phenomena like how the community structure changes over time. One of the applications of Community Detection is transportation which uses to identify the clusters of sources and destinations that travelers frequently visit. There are issues with the traditional approaches on predicting the links and detecting the communities, and there is a demand to detect the communities incrementally. Unlike existing methods, which use the entire dataset for detecting the communities, our proposed methodology **L**ink **P**rediction and **C**ommunity **D**etection (LPCD) for dynamic networks form the links within or between the communities and can understand how the network is evolving in an incremental fashion. We experimented on benchmark datasets, and our experimental results were compared with the conventional approaches and showed better performance.

Keywords: Dynamic Networks · Link Prediction · Community Detection · Incremental Approach

1 Introduction

Network Science is the study of social networks using graphs and network theory. This technique is used for understanding social networks and the relationships between individuals, organizations, or groups. Network science uses to analyze online social networks, friendship networks, etc. Some network science applications are in sociology, business, and public health. The challenging issues in this domain, particularly with Link Prediction and Community Detection.

© The Author(s), under exclusive license to Springer Nature Switzerland AG 2023
R. Morusupalli et al. (Eds.): MIWAI 2023, LNAI 14078, pp. 203–213, 2023.
https://doi.org/10.1007/978-3-031-36402-0_18

In Link Prediction, the future links are predicted depending on the network's existing connections. Link Prediction has many applications, such as suggesting a friend in social networks and predicting the interaction among the proteins in the protein-protein interaction network. Different approaches are used to predict the link: (1) Similarity-based, (2) Model-based, and (3) Embedding-based approaches [15]. In the similarity-based approach, the links are predicted using the similarity measure for every pair of nodes that are not connected. Based on the high similarity score of the pair of nodes, there may likely be a chance to form a link. In model-based approaches, the link is formed based on some specific set of parameters. In embedding techniques, the network is mapped to low-dimensional embedding space by preserving the maximum properties of the network.

Community Detection aims to identify the denser groups of nodes within and sparse connections between the communities. Community Detection will help in identifying the unseen relations among the nodes. Community Detection is applied in biology and genetics, social media, marketing and advertising, transportation networks, image analysis, video analysis, etc.

Different algorithms with unique strategies for detecting communities exist, such as Louvain [6], Infomap [5], Walktrap [2], Fastgreedy [1], Eigenvector [3], and Labelpropagation [4] algorithms. In general, the Community Detection algorithm takes a snapshot of a network for community detection in the evolving network, which may not be forming good communities. Therefore, Eric et al. (2021) solved this issue by discovering LINE [13] approach for predicting links before forming the communities. LINE [13] approach has limitations in addressing Community Detection. In this paper, to overcome the limitation we adopted the modified approach of Zarayeneh et al. [12] for detecting the communities in dynamic networks. Existing LINE [13] and Δ-screening [12] approaches are presented briefly in Sect. 2.

The key contributions of this paper are as follows

(a) Proposed LPCD approach through incremental fashion, which guarantees the quality of the community structure
(b) Applying an efficient Community Detection algorithm
(c) Results compared with the conventional and proposed approach

The rest of the paper is arranged in the following sequence. In Sect. 2, the literature review is briefly explained. In Sect. 3, the proposed methodology is explained. Section 4 presents the experimental results. In Sect. 5, the comparison of the results is presented. The Conclusions and Future work are presented in Sect. 6.

2   Related Work

In dynamic graphs, the detection of communities is categorized broadly into three phases: (1) Static-Based Approaches, (2) Stability-Based Approaches, (3) Cross-Time Step Approaches. In static-based methods, the communities are identified for the current timestamp. Then to track the evolution of the network, the current and previous timestamps communities are compared. There are different approaches proposed using the concept of static-based methods. Asur et al. [16] presented the algorithm by constructing the binary matrix to represent each timestamp's node-to-community memberships. Palla et al. [17] approach uses the clique percolation method. The static methods are expensive as it has the drawback of computing from scratch and keeping track of communities for the successive timestamp.

Stability-Based Approaches identify the communities in the current timestamp using the information of the previous timestamps community structure. This is the incremental approach that generates strong communities and tracks the evolution of communities. The modularity-based incremental approach proposed by Maillard et al. [7] (2009) used the concept of Clauset-Newman-Moore static method. Aktunc et al. [8] (2015) proposed Dynamic Smart Local Movement (DSLM). Lin et al. (2008) [9] discovered the hybrid method, "FaceNet", which uses the concept of modularity maximization. Zeng et al. (2020) [10] used the consensus-based approach to find the communities in the series of timestamps. Zhaung et al. (2021) [11] presented an incremental approach, "DynMo", which updates the communities using the information of previous timestamps community structure.

Cross-Time Step Approaches identify the communities at any given timestamp. It maintains the track of graph evolution at all the timestamps. Matias et al. (2018) [18] introduced a Poisson Process Stochastic Block Model (PPSBM), which detects the communities in the temporal graphs.

Structural similarity measures the similarity of two nodes concerning the link information of the network. It identifies the similar properties of nodes and predicts the links over the network. According to LINE [13], Leicht-Holme-Newman, Common neighbors, Salton, Hub promoted, Jaccard, Adamic-Adar, Sorensen, Resource Allocation, and Hub Depressed are the few measures that are used to predict the link. This approach identifies the probability of connecting the pair of nodes. This is done by computing the heuristic function between every pair of non-connected nodes and updating to the given network. This approach has the advantage of detecting the communities after predicting the link to form good clusters.

The approach orthogonal to all these approaches is "Δ-screening", which focuses on an incremental approach. It identifies the part of the graph affected by the batch of addition/deletion of the edges. Then the changes are made without compromising the quality of the community structure. LINE [13] and Δ-screening [12] approach uses the Louvain algorithm [6], which may lead to a poor community structure.

To overcome this limitation, we explored and analyzed the various community detection algorithm and found the Leiden algorithm [14] is efficient in an incremental manner. This paper also addresses the problem of efficiently detecting the communities by applying the Leiden algorithm.

The Leiden [14] algorithm has been introduced to overcome the issue of the Louvain [6] algorithm, which forms communities that may be poorly connected. The input graph is treated as a singleton partition at the initial stage. The communities are formed from the input graph, and each community will be treated as a single partition. Further, the refinement step executes to determine any splits in the existing communities (partitions). An aggregated network is created based on the changes of the partition in the refinement step and treated as the input graph for the next iteration. This process is repeated until no further improvements.

3   LPCD Incremental Approach

The proposed LPCD approach shown in Fig. 1 improves the conventional LINE [13] approach in two ways. 1. Guarantees the quality of community structure, 2. Detecting the communities in an efficient manner (incremental fashion) by incorporating the strategy of Δ - screening approach [12] without considering the network from scratch.

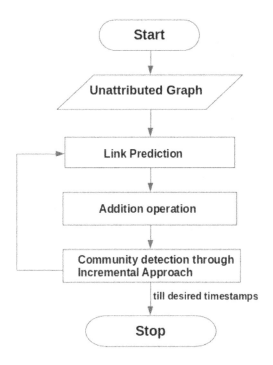

Fig. 1. Workflow of LPCD Approach

The proposed workflow is as follows:

step 1: Initially, for the given input graph, for each non-connected pair of nodes the probability is computed using some heuristic functions. The chance of adding a link depends on the higher probability value. We have used heuristic functions such as Jaccard and Hub promoted.

step 2: To predict the links the LINE [13] philosophy is used.

step 3: The communities are identified using the Leiden algorithm [14] for the updated network (links predicted and added)

step 4: The communities are updated by adopting the incremental strategy from the Δ-screening approach [12] without considering the input from scratch. For this, the change in modularity ΔQ is computed as

$$\Delta Q_{x \to \mathcal{C}(y)} = \frac{e_{x \to \mathcal{C}(y) \cup \{x\}} - e_{x \to \mathcal{C}(x) \setminus \{x\}}}{2E_t} + \frac{deg(x).a_{\mathcal{C}(x) \setminus \{x\}} - deg(x).a_{\mathcal{C}(y)}}{(2E_t)^2}$$
$$(1)$$

where,

- $\Delta Q_{x \to \mathcal{C}(y)} \to$ the change in modularity for the node x moving to the community $\mathcal{C}(y)$
- $e_{x \to \mathcal{C}(y)} \to$ degree sum of all the nodes in $\mathcal{C}(y)$ linking to the vertex x
- $E_t \to$ the number of edges at timestamp t
- $deg(x) \to$ the total degree of the node x
- $a_{\mathcal{C}(y)} \to$ degree sum of all the nodes in $\mathcal{C}(y)$

step 5: Check the condition of the desired timestamps. If the condition fails, GOTO step 2 else, exit.

Algorithm 1. Leiden Algorithm

1: **Require:** Graph with V vertices and E edges G(V,E)
2: **Ensure:** Communities $\{\mathcal{C}_1, \mathcal{C}_2, ..., \mathcal{C}_k\}$
3: $G' = \text{copy}(G)$
4: **repeat**
5:     Initially each vertex is assigned as a community
6:     Compute change in modularity for each vertex moving to another community
7:     **if** change in modularity value improves **then**
8:         Add the particular node to other community
9:         Repeat the same for every vertex in each community
10:    **end if**
11:    Communities formed are $\mathcal{C}_{(I_t)} = \{\mathcal{C}_1, \mathcal{C}_2, ..., \mathcal{C}_k\}$
12:    $\mathcal{C}_{(I_t)} = \text{Refinement}(G')$
13:    $Modularity_{(I_t)} = modularity(G', \mathcal{C}_{(I_t)})$
14:    $G' = \text{Aggregate}(G')$
15: **until** $Modularity_{(I_{t-1})} \neq Modularity_{(I_t)}$
16: **return** $\{\mathcal{C}_1, \mathcal{C}_2, ..., \mathcal{C}_k\}$

Algorithm 1 is the Leiden algorithm. Initially, each node is considered as a single community. Calculate the change in modularity for each node by moving from one community to another and choose the move that improves the modularity. Here, $\mathcal{C}_{(I_t)}$ represents the set of communities for iteration I_t. Once communities are formed, check with each community whether it can be further divided into separate communities, as shown in the Refinement Step of Fig. 2a(iii). Compute the modularity of the communities obtained, given as $Modularity_{(I_t)}$. Then the communities are aggregated as a super node. The super node degree is the sum of all the nodes degree within that particular community. And the edge value present between the super nodes is the sum of edges between the communities, as shown in the Aggregation Step of Fig. 2a(iv). Here, G' represents the network structure in the current iteration. The procedure is repeated iteratively until there is no change in modularity value. The sample output can be as shown in Fig. 2b, and the final communities detected may be as in Fig. 2b(viii).

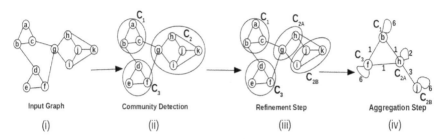

(a) Sample Initial Iteration of Leiden Algorithm

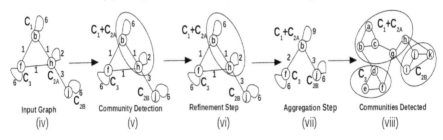

(b) Sample Final Outcome of Leiden Algorithm

Fig. 2. Illustration of Leiden Algorithm

The following similarity measures are used from [13]:

- **Jaccard:** This measure relates the number of common neighbors between vertices to the number of neighbors that these vertices have and is given by:

$$Jaccard = \frac{\Gamma(x) \cap \Gamma(y)}{\Gamma(x) \cup \Gamma(y)} \qquad (2)$$

- **Hub Promoted:** This measure assigns higher scores to links adjacent to hubs (high-degree vertices), as the denominator depends on the minimum of the degrees of the vertices of interest.

$$Hp = \frac{\Gamma(x) \cap \Gamma(y)}{min\{k_x, k_y\}} \qquad (3)$$

3.1   Illustration of Updating the Communities

From Fig. 3(i), if the possible links predicted are {(h,i), (g,k), (g,j), (a,d), (c,d), (a,e)}. As {(h,i), (g,k), (g,j)} are predicted within the communities, the community structure remains the same. As (a,d) is predicted between the communities, we need to check the ΔQ by moving node 'a' to 'C_3', its value is '-0.025', and node 'd' to 'C_1', its value is '0.0'. The value of ΔQ needs to be greater than '0'. Hence, adding the link (a,d) will not change the community structure. When the edge (c,d) is added to the network, the ΔQ value of moving node 'c' to 'C_3' is '-0.02471' and the ΔQ value of moving node 'd' to 'C_1' is '0.007231'. Therefore, node 'd' is moved to community 'C_1'. Then, we need to check the remaining nodes of 'C_3' with 'd', which is in 'C_1' and compute the ΔQ. If it improves, the nodes will move to 'C_1', or else it will remain in 'C_3'. Thus, the same is repeated for every pair of edges in the predicted links. And finally, the communities formed, which is shown in Fig. 3(ii).

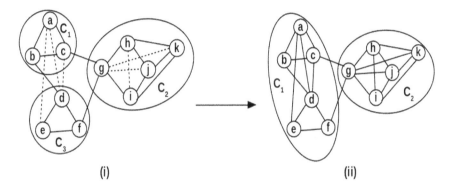

(i)   (ii)

Fig. 3. Illustration of Predicting and adding the links and Updating the communities

3.2   Description of Proposed Algorithm

Algorithm 2 is the LPCD in dynamic networks. Initially, the links are predicted and added based on the probability heuristic function. Here, P_{Edges} are the percentages of predicted edges, and $Predicted\_Edges$ are the predicted edges chosen to add to the network. After updating the network, the Leiden algorithm [14] is used for community detection. The extracted communities are the input to the next iteration. Change in modularity of the nodes between two communities represents as $Gain_1$ and $Gain_2$. $Gain_1$ and $Gain_2$ are calculated, and the respective nodes may or may not be moving between the communities ($Community_1$, $Community_2$) depending on the values of the change in modularity of two nodes, such as (a, d). For the next iteration, each edge added to the network will compute the change in modularity to the communities. Once any node is moved to the other community depending on the change in modularity, the neighbour nodes need to be checked, which is given in lines 20–25 and 28–33. Then the communities are updated. G[time] is the series of updating communities over time.

Algorithm 2. LPCD in Dynamic Networks

1: **Require:** Graph with V vertices and E edges $G(V, E)$, Number of timestamps = $timeStamps$, Percentages_of_Edges (per timeStamp) = P_{Edges}
2: **Ensure:** track_of_communities=$G[1], G[2], ..., G[timeStamps]$
3: $G_{History} \leftarrow copy(G)$
4: **for** $time$ in timeStamps **do**
5:     $G_{copy} \leftarrow copy(G_{History})$
6:     $Predicted\_Edges \leftarrow Heuristics(G_{copy}, P_{Edges})$
7:     $G_{copy} \leftarrow G_{copy} \cup Predicted\_Edges$
8:     **if** time$\leftarrow 1$ **then**
9:         $G[time] \leftarrow CommunityDetectionAlgorithm(G_{copy})$
10:         $G_{History} \leftarrow copy(G_{copy})$
11:     **else**
12:         **for** edge in $Predicted\_Edges$ **do**
13:             (source, target) $\leftarrow$ map(edge)
14:             $Community_1 \leftarrow$ source
15:             $Community_2 \leftarrow$ target
16:             $Gain_1 \leftarrow \Delta Q_{target \rightarrow Community_1}$
17:             $Gain_2 \leftarrow \Delta Q_{source \rightarrow Community_2}$
18:             **if** $Gain_1 > Gain_2$ && $Gain_1 > 0$ **then**
19:                 $Community_1 \leftarrow Community_1 \cup \{target\}$ and $Community_2 \leftarrow Community_2 \backslash \{target\}$
20:                 **for** neighbour in $community(target)_{time-1}$ **do**
21:                     subgain $\leftarrow \Delta Q_{neighbour \rightarrow Community_1}$
22:                     **if** $subgain > Gain_1$ **then**
23:                         $Community_1 \leftarrow Community_1 \cup \{neighbour\}$ and $Community_2 \leftarrow Community_2 \backslash \{neighbour\}$
24:                     **end if**
25:                 **end for**
26:             **else if** $Gain_2 > 0$ **then**
27:                 $Community_2 \leftarrow Community_2 \cup \{source\}$ and $Community_1 \leftarrow Community_1 \backslash \{source\}$
28:                 **for** neighbour in $community(source)_{time-1}$ **do**
29:                     subgain $\leftarrow \Delta Q_{neighbour \rightarrow Community_2}$
30:                     **if** $subgain > Gain_2$ **then**
31:                         $Community_2 \leftarrow Community_2 \cup \{neighbour\}$ and $Community_1 \leftarrow Community_1 \backslash \{neighbour\}$
32:                     **end if**
33:                 **end for**
34:             **end if**
35:         **end for**
36:         $G[time] \leftarrow copy(G_{copy})$
37:         $G_{History} \leftarrow copy(G_{copy})$
38:     **end if**
39: **end for**
40: **return** track_of_communities

---

4   Experimental Results

The following experiments are executed on an Intel Core i7 processor having memory of 31.2 GiB. The proposed algorithm is implemented using the python language. The operating system used is Ubuntu 20.04. The experiments are executed for desired timestamps.

Table 1. Experimental Results using 'Jaccard' measure for ten timestamps

Approaches	Dataset	3% of Edges Added		5% of Edges added		10% of Edges added	
		Time(millisec)	Modularity	Time(millisec)	Modularity	Time(millisec)	Modularity
Conventional Approach	Karate club	1.67	0.4392	1.78	0.4583	2.23	0.4532
	Dolphin	3.15	0.5368	3.17	0.5516	3.14	0.5443
	Football	11.14	0.6348	11.66	0.6393	11.86	0.5479
	Polbooks	6.65	0.5390	11.12	0.5495	2.19	0.5490
	AdjNoun	13.47	0.3386	10.94	0.3512	14.25	0.3278
Modified conventional approach with Leiden Algorithm	Karate club	0.92	0.4456	0.8845	0.4615	1.178	0.4555
	Dolphin	0.976	0.5423	0.982	0.5532	1.067	0.5485
	Football	2.620	0.6348	2.24	0.6397	2.886	0.6269
	Polbooks	1.708	0.5391	1.87	0.5507	2.49	0.5523
	AdjNoun	1.895	0.3476	1.946	0.3561	2.54	0.3321
Proposed LPCD Approach	Karate club	**0.0069**	0.4458	**0.019**	0.4624	**0.178**	0.4499
	Dolphin	**0.0**	0.5433	**0.051**	0.5509	**0.3083**	0.5416
	Football	**0.4077**	0.6293	**0.567**	0.6287	**1.298**	0.6154
	Polbooks	**0.00**	0.5364	**0.0227**	0.5404	**0.0117**	0.5416
	AdjNoun	**0.508**	0.3298	**0.4885**	0.3195	**2.252**	0.3068

Therefore, the number of timestamps considered is 10. And the number of edges added per timestamp is chosen as 3%, 5%, and 10% according to Eric et al. [13].

Table 2. Experimental Results using 'Hub Promoted' measure for ten timestamps

Approaches	Dataset	3% of Edges Added		5% of Edges added		10% of Edges added	
		Time(millisec)	Modularity	Time(millisec)	Modularity	Time(millisec)	Modularity
Conventional Approach	Karate club	1.62	0.4368	1.75	0.4239	2.142	0.4443
	Dolphin	2.97	0.5422	3.75	0.5526	3.17	0.5664
	Football	11.36	0.6350	12.49	0.6374	12.31	0.6257
	Polbooks	6.56	0.5280	6.39	0.5273	12.39	0.5266
	AdjNoun	13.29	0.3115	10.70	0.3096	14.69	0.3032
Modified conventional approach with Leiden Algorithm	Karate club	0.807	0.4237	0.924	0.4430	0.713	0.4502
	Dolphin	0.966	0.5455	0.986	0.5525	1.319	0.5694
	Football	2.063	0.6352	2.27	0.6387	2.955	0.6226
	Polbooks	1.712	0.5281	1.943	0.5279	2.601	0.5312
	AdjNoun	1.892	0.3116	2.032	0.3282	**2.215**	0.3215
Proposed LPCD Approach	Karate club	**0.0163**	0.4218	**0.0572**	0.4432	**0.122**	0.4378
	Dolphin	**0.0**	0.5419	**0.0**	0.5466	**0.00**	0.5642
	Football	**0.222**	0.6279	**0.675**	0.6312	**1.055**	0.6084
	Polbooks	**0.00**	0.5275	**0.0121**	0.5276	**0.012**	0.5260
	AdjNoun	**0.825**	0.2966	**1.122**	0.3007	5.021	0.3014

The benchmark datasets used are Karate club (34 nodes, 78 edges), Football (35 nodes, 118 edges), Dolphins (62 nodes, 159 edges), Polbooks (105 nodes, 441 edges), AdjNoun (112 nodes, 425 edges). We implemented (1) The conventional approach, (2) Modified the conventional approach by adopting the efficient

Community Detection algorithm, and (3) The proposed approach with standard datasets. Table 1 and 2 are the experimental results for ten timestamps using the measures Jaccard and Hub Promoted, respectively. We have taken the average time and modularity for ten timestamps. Tables 1 and 2, compare the results of runtime and modularity of the three approaches, and the LPCD approach shows better results for the time. It is also observed that the modularity value is improved when replacing Community Detection algorithm such as Leiden algorithm in conventional approach.

5   Result Analysis

Figure 4 shows the graph results by inserting the 3%, 5%, and 10% of the edges in the network. The similarity measures are Jaccard and Hub promoted for predicting the links. The comparison results are plotted for the Karate club dataset. The percentage of edges and the average time taken is plotted along the X and Y axes, respectively. The LPCD approach performs better compared to the conventional approach.

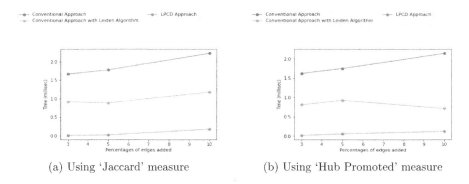

(a) Using 'Jaccard' measure   (b) Using 'Hub Promoted' measure

Fig. 4. Conventional Approach versus Proposed Approach

6   Conclusions and Future Work

This article contributes the workflow of Link Prediction and Community Detection for dynamic networks incrementally by using similarity measures and applying an efficient algorithm for community detection which guarantees the quality of the structure of communities detected. The experiments were executed on real-world datasets and compared results with a conventional approach. In the future, one can use more similarity measures to predict the link and to perform experiments on large datasets. There is a scope for extending the LPCD approach to attributed graphs.

References

1. Clauset, A., Newman, M.E., Moore, C.: Finding community structure in very large networks. Phys. Rev. E **70**(6), 066111 (2004)
2. Pons, P., Latapy, M.: Computing communities in large networks using random walks. In: Yolum, I., Güngör, T., Gürgen, F., Özturan, C. (eds.) ISCIS 2005. LNCS, vol. 3733, pp. 284–293. Springer, Heidelberg (2005). https://doi.org/10.1007/11569596_31
3. Foster, I., Kesselman, C.: The Grid: Blueprint for a New Computing Infrastructure. Morgan Kaufmann, San Francisco (1999)
4. Newman, M.E.: Finding community structure in networks using the eigenvectors of matrices. Phys. Rev. E **74**(3), 036104 (2007)
5. Rosvall, M., Bergstrom, C.T.: Maps of random walks on complex networks reveal community structure. Proc. Natl. Acad. Sci. **105**(4), 1118–1123 (2018)
6. Blondel, V.D., Guillaume, J.L., Lambiotte, R., Lefebvre, E.: Fast unfolding of communities in large networks. J. Stat. Mech: Theory Exp. **2008**(10), P10008 (2008)
7. Görke, R., Maillard, P., Staudt, C., Wagner, D.: Modularity-driven clustering of dynamic graphs. In: Festa, P. (ed.) SEA 2010. LNCS, vol. 6049, pp. 436–448. Springer, Heidelberg (2010). https://doi.org/10.1007/978-3-642-13193-6_37
8. Aktunc, R., Toroslu, I.H., Ozer, M., Davulcu, H.: A dynamic modularity based community detection algorithm for large-scale networks: DSLM. In: Proceedings of the IEEE/ACM International Conference on Advances in Social Networks Analysis and mining, pp. 1177–1183 (2015)
9. Lin, Y.R., Chi, Y., Zhu, S., Sundaram, H., Tseng, B.L.: FaceNet: a framework for anlayzing communities and their evolutions in dynamic networks. In: Proceedings of the 17th International Conference on World Wide Web, pp. 685–694 (2008)
10. Zeng, X., Wang, W., Chen, C., Yen, G.G.: A consensus community-based particle swarm optimization for dynamic community detection. IEEE Trans. Cybern. **50**(6), 2502–2513 (2020)
11. Zhuang, D., Chang, M.J., Li, M.: DynaMo: dynamic community detection by incrementally maximizing modularity. IEEE Trans. Knowl. Data Eng. **33**(5), 1934–1945 (2021)
12. Zarayeneh, N., Kalyanaraman, A.: Delta-screening: a fast and efficient technique to update communities in dynamic graphs. IEEE Trans. Netw. Eng. **8**(2), 1614–1629 (2021)
13. de Oliveira, É.T.C., de França, F.O.: Enriching networks with edge insertion to improve community detection. Soc. Netw. Anal. Min. **11**(1), 1–13 (2021). https://doi.org/10.1007/s13278-021-00803-6
14. Traag, V.A., Waltman, L., Van Eck, N.J.: From Louvain to Leiden: guaranteeing well-connected communities. Sci. Rep. **9**, 5233 (2019)
15. Berahmand, K., Nasiri, E., Rostami, M., Forouzandeh, S.: A modified DeepWalk method for link prediction in attributed social network. Computing **103**, 2227–2249 (2019)
16. Asur, S., Parthasarathy, S., Ucar, D.: An event-based framework for characterizing the evolutionary behavior of interaction graphs. ACM Trans. Knowl. Discov. From Data **3**(4), 1–36 (2009)
17. Palla, G., Barabasi, A.-L., Vicsek, T.: Quantifying social group evolution. Nature **446**(7136), 664–667 (2007)
18. Matias, C., Rebafka, T., Villers, F.: A semiparametric extension of the stochastic block model for longitidinal networks. Biometrika **105**(3), 665–680 (2018)

Clinical Abbreviation Disambiguation Using Clinical Variants of BERT

Atharwa Wagh[(✉)] [ID] and Manju Khanna[ID]

Department of Computer Science and Engineering, Amrita School of Computing, Amrita
Vishwa Vidyapeetham, Bengaluru, India
waghatharwa@gmail.com, k_manju@blr.amrita.edu

Abstract. Acronyms are commonly used in technical fields, such as science and medicine, but their potential expansions can be difficult to understand without proper context. This is where acronym disambiguation (AD) comes in - the process of determining the appropriate extension of an acronym in text. AD is essential for comprehending technical jargon in plain language, and requires effective representations of "words", "phrases", "acronyms", and "abbreviations" depending on their context. However, understanding the appropriate expansion for an acronym is not always straightforward. Words in natural language often have multiple meanings, and the context in which they are used can further increase the complexity of the text. For example, the acronym "AC" can potentially expand to "Adriamycin Cyclophosphamide", "ante cibum" i.e., before meals, or "Anticoagulation", among other possibilities. To address this challenge, we have developed a transformers-based model that can learn from contextual data and select the correct full form from a set of possible options for a given abbreviation. This study was conducted on the Clinical Acronym Sense Inventory (CASI) dataset. This study involved comparing different clinical versions of the BERT transformer architecture, including SciBert, ClinicalBert, and BioBert and observed that ClinicalBert performed the best with F score of 91.49%.

Keywords: Abbreviation · Disambiguation · Transformers · BERT · Clinical text · Natural Language Processing · CASI

1 Introduction

The definition of an acronym is a condensed version of a word or phrase. Clinical notes frequently employ them, sometimes to save time and space and other times to conceal unfavorable information. According to recent studies, clinical notes like doctor's notes typically have 30 to 50 percent of their words be acronyms. However, abbreviations are very ambiguous, meaning that they can be used to mean different things in different contexts. According to a recent study, close to one-third of abbreviations are ambiguous. A poll of more than 200 health care workers found that only 43% of a set of abbreviations were properly identified. Their ambiguity stems from a number of things, including the

© The Author(s), under exclusive license to Springer Nature Switzerland AG 2023
R. Morusupalli et al. (Eds.): MIWAI 2023, LNAI 14078, pp. 214–224, 2023.
https://doi.org/10.1007/978-3-031-36402-0_19

context in which they are employed (local vs. global reach) and the lack of established guidelines for their creation. Usually, words from their definitions' first letters are used to form acronyms.

In a variety of writing styles, acronyms and abbreviations are frequently used to shorten lengthier statements. Although acronyms are helpful for saving space when writing and the reader's time when reading, they can make it difficult to grasp the material, especially if it is used outside of its definition or in lengthy writings. The research community and software developers have made significant attempts to develop systems for recognizing acronyms and locating their accurate meanings in the text in order to address this problem.

Because technical acronyms are so common in scientific and medical writing and because they might have several meanings, acronym disambiguation (AD) is essential for understanding these texts in their entirety. Given that words in natural language sometimes have several meanings, understanding based on their context is necessary to determining the suitable expansion for acronyms. The context in which these words are employed further increases the complexity of natural language. Adriamycin cyclophosphamide, ante cibum, Anticoagulation, etc. are a few examples of potential AC expansions. To accurately grasp the sentence, choose the expansion that most closely matches the text's meaning from those listed above.

The frequent use of acronyms in clinical texts is a defining feature. Abbreviations made up 17.1% of all the word tokens in a study of physician-entered inpatient admission notes at NYPH (New York Presbyterian Hospital). Long biological words and sentences are conveniently represented by abbreviations by healthcare practitioners. These abbreviations frequently include crucial medical information (such as names for conditions, medications, and treatments), which must be clear and correct in medical documents. However, research has demonstrated that the imprecise and frequently changing abbreviations make it difficult for patients and healthcare practitioners to effectively communicate, potentially lowering the quality and safety of healthcare. "The Joint Commission's 2008 National Patient Safety Goals" mandated that U.S. hospitals refrain from using a list of potentially lethal acronyms. Recent studies imply that a clinical natural language processing (NLP) system may help to prevent medical errors brought on by the usage of authorized acronyms.

Annotated data was needed for clinical abbreviations to be distinguished (corpora). The annotation procedure is thought to be expensive, time-consuming, and laborious. Additionally, limited annotated data are available mostly due to privacy concerns. The majority of earlier studies relied on creating unique classifiers to decipher each abbreviation, but this method is deemed insufficient for uncommon and obscure abbreviations. Therefore, creating generalizable techniques could aid in the deciphering of uncommon and unknown abbreviations, such as having one classifier of all abbreviations.

Hence, this study tries to develop a generalized system for AD which was evaluated and verified on Clinical Acronym Sense Inventory (CASI) dataset.

2   Literature Review

The researchers proposed a new method for identifying acronyms using tensor networks and triplet loss to create effective representations of semantic variations between acronym expansions. Their approach, called m-networks, uses multiple networks and reinforcement learning to identify positive and negative sentences for a given dataset. They evaluated their approach on three datasets and achieved high F scores, effectively distinguishing between acronym expansions. The researchers also utilized principal component analysis to assess the semantic similarity and representation of the output embeddings [1].

The researchers in [2] proposed a new web-based system for identifying and disambiguating acronyms using more complex rules and a supervised model trained on a large dataset. However, the models may not be able to expand all acronyms from domains other than the training set's domain. To address this limitation, they introduced a website-based system that can recognize and expand acronyms in various domains. They began by offering a rule-based system for acronym identification.

The authors in [3] addressed the challenge of medical abbreviation disambiguation and its impact on deep learning models in medical applications. They introduced a large dataset for pre-training models in medical abbreviation disambiguation and demonstrated the models' performance on the pre-training task. The pre-trained models were further refined on two downstream tasks and outperformed models created from scratch on the mortality prediction challenge. The models utilized pre-trained Fasttext embeddings and the Adam optimizer with a learning rate of 0.001. The authors concluded that pre-training improved the models' performance, especially for ELECTRA, and demonstrated that pre-training on the MeDAL dataset improved the models' ability to understand medical English.

The paper [4] introduces ABB-BERT, a BERT-based model that aims to disambiguate abbreviations and contractions. The model has learned on a diverse set of activities related to abbreviation and contraction disambiguation, including sentence boundary detection, part-of-speech tagging, and named entity recognition. ABB-BERT achieves high accuracy on a benchmark dataset and outperforms several baseline models. The authors demonstrate the model's effectiveness on real-world examples and highlight its potential applications in various domains, including text classification and information retrieval.

One study [5] was done on ambiguous pronoun disambiguation using transformers architecture BERT. They used BERT plus a custom MLP model which got them an accuracy of 80.45%.

The paper [6] introduces BioBERT, a pre-trained language representation model for biomedical text mining. BioBERT is based on the BERT architecture and is trained on a large corpus of biomedical literature and clinical notes. The authors propose a novel pre-training strategy involving fine-tuning BERT on biomedical domain-specific tasks. The model achieves state-of-the-art results on several benchmark datasets and outperforms other pre-trained language models, such as PubMedBERT and ClinicalBERT. BioBERT can be fine-tuned for various downstream tasks, such as biomedical question answering, drug discovery, and clinical decision support, and has become a widely used resource in the biomedical community for natural language processing tasks.

The paper [7] introduces SciBERT, a language model fine-tuned on a large corpus of scientific papers, specifically designed to handle the unique linguistic features and vocabulary of scientific text. The model outperforms general-purpose language models on several scientific NLP tasks, including citation intent classification, named entity recognition, and sentence similarity. The authors also demonstrate that fine-tuning SciBERT on smaller scientific datasets leads to significant improvements in performance over previous "state-of-the-art" methods. SciBERT provides a powerful tool for researchers working with scientific text, offering superior performance on a range of NLP tasks in this domain.

Another study [8] in which they have used BERT for obtaining the contextual embeddings and then they used ML based algorithm SVM for classification of ambiguous pronouns.

The paper [9] introduces ClinicalBERT, a language model designed for processing clinical notes and predicting hospital readmissions. The model is fine-tuned on a large dataset of electronic health records and outperforms previous "state-of-the-art" methods on the hospital readmission prediction task. ClinicalBERT is also demonstrated to be effective for a range of downstream clinical NLP tasks, including identifying patients with diabetic retinopathy and predicting the onset of heart failure. The model provides a powerful tool for healthcare providers and researchers working with electronic health records.

Paraphrase detection has been done in a study [10] using transformers architecture BERT. In this study different vectorization methods were deployed and they observed BERT to be performing better in their comparative study.

The authors of [11] in their work have suggested that a semi-supervised approach to disambiguating clinical acronyms that makes use of word embeddings and meaning expansion. Furthermore, they provide CASEml, an unsupervised technique for acronym disambiguation in clinical writing. In order to determine when an acronym refers to its intended meaning, CASEml uses an ensemble of two models, one of which uses context word embeddings and the other of which makes use of visit-level text and billing information.

In one of the study [12], a model based on BERT architecture was used to design a question answering system so as to assist learners of all age especially who are learning remotely and have to study very vast scope of theoretical subjects demanding remembrance skills like history and languages so as to make the learning more efficient and interesting.

The authors in [13] their work have suggested that assuming the reader is a medical practitioner, they assume that the focus of this study is on AD in medical literature. In this situation, disambiguation can take the form of supplying the real long-form version of the ABV or outputting important extra context terms related with it. In the first part of this section, they evaluate the effectiveness of several token classification techniques for the AD problem. Next, they choose the model from the first section that performs the best and evaluate how well it performs in comparison to other text categorization techniques. The best-performing models are determined to be BioBERT and SciBERT for the MeDAL and BlueBERT for the UMN.

Another health care application which is BERT based Braille model which is deployed for summarization of long documents [14].

Authors of [15] in their work have said that disambiguating acronyms is regarded as a particular form of word sense disambiguation assignment. Annotated data was needed to clarify clinical acronyms. More than 80% of the data in electronic health records are now unstructured, therefore funding research on information extraction from clinical text is essential to obtaining organized data that may be used in decision-making processes. Bert was taught to differentiate between a variety of clinical abbreviations. An interesting area of NLP wherein BERT comes handy as always is the area of "Named Entity Recognition" [16]. Here as well for text vectorization BERT was deployed and its performance was analyzed with respect to other word embedding tools. The study in [17] has proposed that task-specific architectures are used in feature-based approaches. BERT is the first finetuning-based representation model that surpasses numerous task-specific designs in terms of performance on a wide range of tasks at the token and sentence levels.

The authors of [18] in their work, the Transformer is a model architecture introduced by the authors that totally abandons recurrence in favor of an attention mechanism to highlight global dependency between input and output. To their knowledge, the Transformer is the first transduction model to compute representations of its input and output without the requirement for "sequence aligned RNNs", instead depending just on self-attention.

3 Methodology

3.1 Dataset

The dataset used for this study is Clinical Acronym Sense Inventory (CASI). The training dataset consists of more than 29000 observations and 3 features. The features are acronym, expansion and the text. The number of observations contained in test and validation dataset are 3699. Pre – processing of the dataset – basic steps followed were, converting to lower case, removing the punctuation, creating tokens, removing the stop words.

Traditionally, text preparation has been a crucial step in language pre – processing (NLP) activities. It simplifies language so that machine learning algorithms may operate more effectively. So, after pre – processing the data and converting it into workable form now the models were applied onto it for the correct full form prediction. Three variants of BERT, SciBert, BioBert and ClinicalBert were applied and analysis of result was done.

3.2 Working of the BERT Architecture

We know that BERT is a transformers-based architecture which uses only the encoder part of it in its mechanism. Bert is basically an encoder stack of the transformers architecture. Why exactly has this architecture came into existence, why were LSTM, GRU networks not enough? So, the answer to this question was that there are some problems in which the sequence of the words and the context plays a very imminent role which these networks were not capable of. For ex. Sequence of words is very important in translation of one language to another whereas context of the text becomes very important for a question answering system like a chatbot. Also, what if we have multiple inputs to be sent to the network at a time and then analyze it plus remember what was sent earlier while the second batch of input is being sent, in such scenarios, transformers model came into picture. For the first time in this the input and output generating Now let us a look at the encoder architecture working. First is the conversion of pre – processed text to a vector with the help of word embeddings. With word embeddings, each word in a language or domain is represented as a real-valued vector in a smaller spatial domain. Now these word embeddings are learnable ones i.e., they will learn and modify themselves accordingly from every epoch. Vectors will keep changing with every epoch so they are termed as learnable. A learning representation for text called word embedding gives words with related meanings a comparable representation. Words are represented as vectors in a specified vector space in a family of methods known as word embeddings. The technique falls under the general heading of "deep learning" since each word is given to a single vector, and the vector values are learned in a way that mimics a neural network.

The concept of giving each word a dense distributed representation is essential to the method. Tens or hundreds of dimensions long real-valued vector is used to represent each phrase. Thousands or millions of dimensions are needed for sparse word representations, such a one-hot encoding, in contrast so for this reason word embeddings are preferred.

Second thing is the positional encoding part of the calculation. A finite dimensional representation of the "position" or "position of the words" in a sequence is known as a positional encoding. Now we know that RNN or LSTM takes sequential input into the network. For ex. if a sentence has 10 words in it then one word will enter at a time into the network. Whereas Bert takes entire sentence as an input. So, the model should be aware of the sequence of the words and hence positional encoding comes into picture. It's a vector which holds the positional information of the words of a sentence.

Next part after converting the sentences into vectors, we have to create a matrix out of it. So, all the rows of the matrix must of same dimension. But as the sentences trained can be of different lengths, we define a hyperparameter which is set to a particular value. So, if the sentence is shorter than that value rest part of it will be filled with zeros and in this way, padding would be performed. Now all these vectors formed are divided by $\sqrt{d_k}$ which is the dimension of word embedding so as to scale the vectors as their length can be huge.

The encoder now consists of a stack of cells that comprises a series of Recurrent Neural Networks (RNNs). RNNs are effective tools for dealing with problems where the sequence of events is more important than the individual components. An RNN (Recurrent Neural Network) is a type of neural network that features fully connected layers and looped layers. These loops involve an iteration over two inputs that are concatenated or added together, followed by a matrix multiplication and a non-linear function. The key feature of RNNs is that they possess internal memory, allowing them to incorporate previous inputs into future predictions. This memory enables RNNs to more accurately predict subsequent words in a sentence, given knowledge of preceding words. RNNs are particularly useful in tasks where the order of elements is significant or where previous inputs are more important than previous items, as they can take this information into account. Next comes the concept of attention. Attention is measured with the help of probability concept. Hence in order to convert the vector matrix into probability we pass it through activation function softmax. Now passing through softmax makes the sum of each row as 1 and all the values will lie in between 0 and 1 and hence these values follow the concept of probability. Now if we consider the first row of matrix then we can say that the second word probability value will tell us that for understanding the first word how much importance the model has given to the second word.

Sometimes when the sentences get very big then multi head attention comes into picture. For ex. if it is three headed attention then every head will focus on different words. So, when we concatenate all these heads then the model will definitely give a better representation. Now attention mainly depends or gets calculated with the help of three vectors, query, key and value vector.

- Query vector (Q) – it is a vector which represents that what we have to find out or what is that we have make the model find out.
- Key vector (K) – it is a vector with respect to which we have to find out the query vector. It is like a reference which the model has.
- Value vector (V) – on inputting the query vector, mapping it to the key vector what vector did the model generate is termed as the value vector.

The concept of key/value/query is similar to retrieval systems. For instance, when searching for videos on YouTube, the search engine maps the user's query (text in the search bar) against a set of keys (such as video title, description, etc.) associated with candidate videos in their database. Then, it presents the best-matched videos (values) to the user. In this context, "Q" refers to the actual expansion of the abbreviation, "Key vector" represents the possible expansions, and "value vector" is what the model generates based on its learning.

The attention mechanism is called the "Scaled Dot Product Attention". It is calculated as follows – (Fig. 1)

$$Attention(Q, K, V) = softmax\left(\frac{QK^T}{\sqrt{d_k}}\right)V$$

If the sentences are longer in length, then very complex "query", "key" and "value" matrices get generated and hence we need multi head attention so as to process that quantity of flowing information. In multi head attention, parallelly multiple instances of attention are calculated and all these attentions are combined to get a final attention score.

Now one thing to take care is that we continuously keep transforming the input vectors which come through word embeddings by passing it through various processes in order to get the output. But in doing so we may tend the vectors to deviate from its original form and hence we add transformed vector with some part of the original form so that it should have both and it should.

So, this makes up one encoder layer. Like this Bert model has a series of encoder layers through which the vectors pass, then after this stack of encoders the output would be sent to a dense layer which would have some activation function which would have some loss function as categorical cross entropy and then we would get the final output.

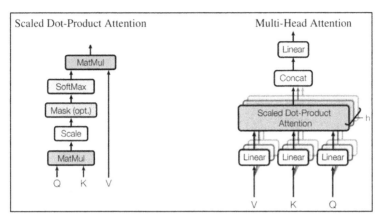

Fig. 1. Scaled dot product attention and multi head attention [11].

3.3 Why BERT Variants?

For this study the CASI dataset has been passed through a series of algorithms which are variants of BERT – SciBert, BioBert and ClinicalBert. Using conventional Bert wouldn't give good results as this study is domain specific. The dataset used consists entirely of medical texts. So, the conventional Bert which is pre – trained on BookCorpus (800 million words) and Wikipedia (2500 million words) wouldn't be that much useful. Therefore, variants of Bert which are specifically designed for medical data analysis have been used. These variants of Bert use pre – trained weights of conventional Bert to start with and then further train that model on some different corpora. BioBert is pre – trained on ("PubMed abstracts" and "PMC full-text articles". SciBert is trained on a randomly selected sample of 1.14 million papers belonging to the Semantic Scholar. This collection contains 82% publications from the general biomedical domain and 18% papers from the computer science sector. Not just the abstracts, but the complete texts of the publications are used. The average length of a paper is 154 phrases, or 2,769 tokens, giving a corpus size of 3.17 billion tokens, or about the same as the 3.3 billion tokens on which BERT was trained. ClinicalBert is pre – trained on "Medical Information Mart for Intensive Care III (MIMIC III)" dataset. This dataset consists of 58,976 unique hospital admissions from around 38,597 patients in the ICU between 2001 to 2012.

4 Results

It was observed that out of these six models ClinicalBERT performed the best for acronym disambiguation. It got the highest F score and testing accuracy of 91.49% and 96.67% respectively. As we can refer from the table below the ClinicalBERT helps achieve a better F score than baseline model proposed in [1]. (Table 1)

The accuracy and loss plots have been shown below. The model has undergone ten training iterations. The accuracy chart shows that both the training and validation accuracy reached stability after 3 epochs. While the validation accuracy is practically fixed to a certain level, the training accuracy has almost stabilized but continues to rise

Table 1. Results.

Architecture	Training accuracy	Testing accuracy	Validation accuracy	F score
Baseline method by [1]	-	-	-	70.67
BERT	99.16	95.86	96.43	79.80
SciBERT	98.85	96.05	96.45	89.75
BioBERT	99.35	96.54	97.16	90.86
ClinicalBERT	99.41	**96.67**	97.10	**91.49**

for another 10 epochs. On the other hand, the validation loss was reducing up until 4 epochs before it slightly increased up to 10 epochs (Fig. 2).

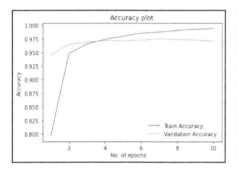 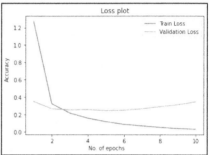

Fig. 2. Accuracy plot and Loss plot for ClinicalBERT.

Now, as this was a multi class, multi label classification hence accuracy is not a good metric for evaluation of the model. Hence, F score becomes the most important evaluation metric. From the results table we can definitely conclude that BERT had the least F score as it is not trained on clinical data and hence earlier a hypothesis was formed wherein it was said that BERT won't prove effective in this study and hence, we went for such variants of BERT who had been pre-trained on clinical data. Almost similar pattern in the accuracy and loss plots was obtained in the performance of other BERT variants as well. Hence, it can be said that all the models were able to learn the dataset in a similar pattern but ClinicalBERT was able to get the highest F score and testing accuracy.

4.1 Why ClinicalBERT Performed the Best?

Out of the three BERT variants, SciBERT includes domain-specific vocabulary related to scientific terminology, which allows it to better capture the nuances of scientific text and understand domain-specific concepts such as chemical compounds, gene names, and protein names as it is specifically tailored for scientific NLP tasks. Whereas, in addition to the difference in training corpus, there are some key differences in the specific vocabulary used in each model. ClinicalBERT includes domain-specific vocabulary related to medical terminology and abbreviations used in clinical notes and EHRs, while BioBERT includes domain-specific vocabulary related to biomedical terms and concepts such as genes, proteins, and diseases. As the training corpus of ClinicalBERT specifically includes abbreviations used in medical domain which the other two BERT variants lack in their training corpus, justifies the highest F score and testing accuracy of ClinicalBERT model for disambiguation.

5   Conclusion

In conclusion, the study highlights the importance of acronym disambiguation in understanding technical language in scientific and medical publications. The use of transformers-based models such as BERT, SciBert, ClinicalBert, and BioBert can help in selecting the correct full form of an abbreviation from a set of possible options. The comparative analysis between these models showed that BERT variants specifically trained on clinical data perform better than conventional BERT. The findings of this study can have significant implications in improving the comprehension of technical language and facilitating communication in various fields of research and healthcare. The novelty of this work was that the CASI dataset used in this study was never tested with transformers architecture BERT applied onto it and hence this study tried to explore it. We tried to compare and validate our work with the results obtained in the study of [1] where they proposed their triplet model. We achieved better F score on the CASI dataset when using clinical variants of BERT. According to our literature survey, best accuracy and F score has been achieved on CASI datasets so far. The CASI dataset was worked on very less and results which were previously obtained on it were poor. The suggested approach was better able to analyze the dataset and provide good performance while disambiguating the abbreviations. In the future scope of this study fine tuning of the hyperparameters can be done so as to further enhance the model's performance.

References

1. Seneviratne, S., Daskalaki, E., Lenskiy, A., Suominen, H.: m-Networks: Adapting the Triplet Networks for Acronym Disambiguation. In: Proceedings of the 4th Clinical Natural Language Processing Workshop, pp. 21–29 (2022)
2. Ben Veyseh, A.P., Dernoncourt, F., Chang, W., Nguyen, T.H.: MadDog: A web-based system for acronym identification and disambiguation. In: Proceedings of the 16th Conference of the European Chapter of the Association for Computational Linguistics: System Demonstrations, pp. 160–167. Online. Association for Computational Linguistics (2021)
3. Wen, Z., Lu, X.H., Reddy, S.: MeDAL: medical abbreviation disambiguation dataset for natural language understanding pretraining. In: Proceedings of the 3rd Clinical Natural Language Processing Workshop (2020). https://doi.org/10.18653/v1/2020.clinicalnlp-1.15
4. Kacker, P., Cupallari, A., Subramanian, A.G., Jain, N.: ABB-BERT: A BERT model for disambiguating abbreviations and contractions. In: Proceedings of the 18th International Conference on Natural Language Processing (2022). https://doi.org/10.48550/ARXIV.2207.04008

5. Nair, R., Prasad, V.N.V., Sreenadh, A., Nair, J.J.: Coreference Resolution for Ambiguous Pronoun with BERT and MLP. In: 2021 International Conference on Advances in Computing and Communications (ICACC), pp. 1–5. Kochi, Kakkanad, India (2021). https://doi.org/10. 1109/ICACC-202152719.2021.9708203
6. Lee, J., et al.: BioBERT: a pre-trained biomedical language representation model for biomedical text mining. Bioinformatics **36**(4), 1234–1240 (15 February 2020). https://doi.org/10. 1093/bioinformatics/btz682
7. Beltagy, I., Lo, K., Cohan, A.: SciBERT: A Pretrained Language Model for Scientific Text. In: Proceedings of the 2019 Conference on Empirical Methods in Natural Language Processing and the 9th International Joint Conference on Natural Language Processing (EMNLP-IJCNLP), pp. 3615–3620. Association for Computational Linguistics, Hong Kong, China (2019)
8. Mohan, M., Nair, J.J.: Coreference resolution in ambiguous pronouns using BERT and SVM. In: 2019 9th International Symposium on Embedded Computing and System Design (ISED), pp. 1–5. Kollam, India (2019).https://doi.org/10.1109/ISED48680.2019.9096245
9. Huang, K., Altosaar, J., Ranganath, R.: ClinicalBERT: Modeling Clinical Notes and Predicting Hospital Readmission. arXiv (2019). https://doi.org/10.48550/ARXIV.1904.05342
10. Gangadharan, V., Gupta, D., Amritha, L., Athira, T.A.: Paraphrase detection using deep neural network based word embedding techniques. In: 2020 4th International Conference on Trends in Electronics and Informatics (ICOEI) (48184), pp. 517–521. Tirunelveli, India (2020). https://doi.org/10.1109/ICOEI48184.2020.9142877
11. Link, N.B., et al.: Acronym Disambiguation in Clinical Notes from Electronic Health Records. MedRxiv (2020). https://doi.org/10.1101/2020.11.25.20221648
12. Sriharsha, C., Rithwik, S., Prahlad, K.P., Nair, L.S.: Intelligent Learning Assistant using BERT and LSTM. In: 2021 12th International Conference on Computing Communication and Networking Technologies (ICCCNT), pp. 1–6. Kharagpur, India (2021). https://doi.org/ 10.1109/ICCCNT51525.2021.9579531
13. Cevik, M., Jafari, S.M., Myers, M., Yildirim, S.: Token Classification forDisambiguatingMedical Abbreviations. arXiv (2022). https://doi.org/10.48550/ARXIV.2210.02487
14. Yamuna, K., Shriamrut, V., Singh, D., Gopalasamy, V., Menon, V.: Bert-based Braille Summarization of Long Documents. In: 2021 12th International Conference on Computing Communication and Networking Technologies (ICCCNT), pp. 1–6. Kharagpur, India (2021). https:// doi.org/10.1109/ICCCNT51525.2021.9579748
15. Jaber, A., Martínez, P.: Disambiguating Clinical Abbreviations Using a One-Fits-All Classifier Based on Deep Learning Techniques. Methods Inf Med. **61**(S 01), e28–e34 (2022 Jun). https://doi.org/10.1055/s-0042-1742388. Epub 2022 Feb 1. PMID: 35104909; PMCID: PMC9246508
16. Chavali, S.T., Tej Kandavalli, C., Sugash, T.M., Gupta, D.: A Study on Named Entity Recognition with Different Word Embeddings on GMB Dataset using Deep Learning Pipelines. In: 2022 13th International Conference on Computing Communication and Networking Technologies (ICCCNT), pp. 1–5. Kharagpur, India (2022). https://doi.org/10.1109/ICCCNT 54827.2022.9984220
17. Devlin, J., Chang, M.-W., Lee, K., Toutanova, K.: BERT: Pre- training of Deep Bidirectional Transformers for Language Understanding. arXiv (2018). https://doi.org/10.48550/ARXIV. 1810.04805
18. Vaswani, A., et al.: Attention is all you need. In: Proceedings of the 31st International Conference on Neural Information Processing Systems (NIPS'17). Curran Associates Inc., Red Hook, NY, USA, 6000–6010 (2017)
19. CASI dataset, https://conservancy.umn.edu/handle/11299/137703
20. Transformers architecture, https://towardsdatascience.com/understanding-encoder-decoder-sequence- to-sequence-model-679e04af4346

Ontological Scene Graph Engineering and Reasoning Over YOLO Objects for Creating Panoramic VR Content

N. Prabhas Raj⬤, G. Tarun⬤, D. Teja Santosh(✉) ⬤, and M. Raghava⬤

Department of Computer Science and Engineering, CVR College of Engineering, Vastunagar, Mangalpalli, Telangana State, Ibrahimpatnam, India
tejasantoshd@gmail.com, raghava.m@cvr.ac.in

Abstract. Detecting objects in videos and harnessing their relationships for scene understanding is a challenging task in the computer vision domain. This has been attempted using the Scene Graph Generation (SGG) task. Recent YOLO models could track objects and establish spatial relationships among the detected objects. However, these deep neural networks are not capable of explaining the structural relationships among the objects that impair practical applications. The adoption of visual transformers is also not prudent as it leads to an increase in the complexity of the overall model. In this paper, an ontology-based scene graph engineering and reasoning approach over the extracted objects is proposed as a solution to this problem. First, the ontological model takes the detected objects from YOLO and generates corresponding entities and relationships. Then, the Semantic Web Rule (SWRL) is written on top of this model to discover the image sequence. And it also offers a machine-interpretable explanation for this sequence when a continuous stream (audio-visual) is constructed. Finally, this audio-visual is coupled with spatial media metadata to make it 360-degree panoramic viewable Virtual Reality (VR) content. It is found that the ontological model is a more versatile solution than the overall deep neural models. Overall, this methodology is helpful in various real-world scenarios for better learning and understanding of natural environments. For example, the audio explanation gadget helps specially-abled people navigate through cluttered environments such as metro rail stations.

Keywords: SGG · YOLO · visual transformer · ontology based SGG · SWRL rules · VR

1 Introduction

The ultimate purpose of Computer Vision (CV) is to build systems that are capable of extracting valuable information from digital images, videos etc., as humans do [1]. This is achieved by implementing the visual scene understanding sub task of SGG [2]. This is emphasized as the higher-level task in addition to detecting the objects as it requires exploring the semantic relationships between objects and interactions among these detected objects [3]. This task is significant and is challenging.

The generation of scene graph is a bottom-up process. The overall SGG architectures following this process are complex involving object detection like YOLO [4] and visual relationship detection [5] deep neural models in its pipeline. The recent visual transformers [6, 7] for performing SGG tasks have drawn the attention of CV research community to utilize it and to modify it accordingly. These are complex deep neural models and are data hungry [8] for being generalizable to any use case scenario. Utilizing such models for explaining of structural relationships in specific practical applications is not a wise decision.

To alleviate this, an ontology based scene graph engineering and reasoning approach over the extracted objects is proposed as a solution to this problem. First, the ontological model takes the detected objects and corresponding entities and relationships are put together. Then, the Semantic Web Rule is written on top of this model to discover the image sequence and offering it as a meaningful explanation for this sequence when a continuous stream (audio-visual) is constructed. Finally, this audio-visual is mixed with spatial media metadata to make it 360-degree panoramic viewable Virtual Reality (VR) content.

2   Motivation

The work of Fernando et al., inspired [9] the authors to take up the work of creating ISEO Ontology with the detected objects from the TERESA test set used in [9] to establish the structural properties, instantiate the corresponding entities and reason the SWRL rule. Also, for rendering 360° panoramic content the work of Rhee et al., motivated [10] the authors to create panoramic VR content using the results from the reasoned ISEO ontology. This panoramic content is useful for consumers in their daily practical activities.

3   Related Works

The task of Scene Graph Generation has drawn interest in the Computer Vision research community and has led to the proposal of a lot of SGG approaches and achieved good results in this field. This section surveys the works on the sub tasks of SGG with employing ontological inferences for VR content creation at the end of the survey.

To start with, Johnson et al., developed [11] FCLN model which internally uses Faster R-CNN with a differentiable, spatial soft attention mechanism for detecting objects from the image. Li et al., utilized [12] Faster R-CNN for object detection in the process of scene understanding. Essam et al., used [13] YOLOv5x6 for object detection for the scene graph generation task. Carion et al., viewed [14] object detection as a direct set prediction problem and detected the objects from the images by their Detection Transformer model.

The detected objects from the images are to be utilized in forming the structural relationships among them. Chen et al., incorporated [15] explicitly into their graph propagation network the statistical correlations between object pairs to mine this information. Baier et al., demonstrated [16] how a visual statistical model could improve visual relationship detection. Zellers et al., analyzed [17] the statistical correlations between objects and relationships and concluded that these correlations have strong regularization for predicting relationships. Zheng et al., proposed [18] multi-stage attention model that uses feature fusion for relation detection. Kolesnikov et al. proposed [19] Box Attention model for detecting the relations between the objects.

The ontological modelling of objects as entities and their relationships as object properties for scene graph generation is a useful direction. These models are not data hungry and assists with daily activities in real world environments. Fernando et al., proposed [9] ontology guided scene graph generation for Telepresence Robotics case study by supplying domain knowledge in the form of an ontology. The results on two different ontologies developed on two different datasets have shown that the performance obtained with ontological model for scene graph generation has exceeded when compared with their considered baseline deep learning model [20].

Finally, by utilizing the semantics of the ontology the Virtual Reality (VR) content becomes specific to cater to the needs of the VR consumers. Dragoni et al., developed [21] light weight ontology to describe virtual entities in serious VR games with the goal of fostering clarity, reuse and mutual understanding between VR trainers and VR developers. Krzysztof Walczak and Jakub Flotynski proposed [22] ontology-based synthetic 3D content creation for VR application by inferring implicit knowledge from semantic rules with that 3D content.

The above works inform that end-to-end deep learning models for implementing the task of SGG are heavy in terms of lots of image or video data so that it works well. These deep models are not capable of explaining the structural relationships among the objects. Also it is understood that ontologies are the better choice over deep learning models for assisting users with daily activities. In [9] the authors have raised the need for improved expressiveness for the ontology (through SWRL rules) so that new knowledge is possible to extract which the work in [22] has induced for VR content creation. It is also understood from the survey of works in [23] that deep learning based VR content creation involves heavy computation with the need of huge amount of data as opposed to ontological inferences based VR content creation.

The authors of this current research will implement the Semantic Web Rules on top of their ISEO ontological model to discover the image sequence. These SWRL rules also offers meaningful explanation for this sequence when a continuous stream (audio-visual) is constructed. This audio-visual is injected with spatial media metadata to make it 360-degree panoramic viewable VR content.

The rest of the paper is structured as follows: Sect. 4 explains the proposed ontology based SGG reasoning for creating panoramic VR content. Section 5 presents the experimental setup for carrying out the experiments and the results. Finally, the concluding remarks and the suggestions for future research are provided in Sect. 6.

4 Ontological Scene Graph Engineering and Reasoning for creating panoramic VR content

The task of creating panoramic VR content with ontological inferences starts with detecting the objects from the input image collection. The overall pipeline of this proposed work is shown in Fig. 1 below.

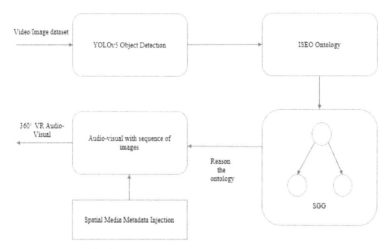

Video/Image dataset

YOLOv5 Object Detection

ISEO Ontology

360° VR Audio-Visual

Audio-visual with sequence of images

Reason the ontology

SGG

Spatial Media Metadata Injection

Fig. 1. Overall Pipeline of the Proposed Work

The input images are provided as input to YOLOv5 object detection model. This is a deep model which uses both residual and dense blocks in order to enable the data flow to the deepest layers thereby overcoming vanishing gradient problem. Also the problem of redundant gradients is tackled with the Cross Stage Partial Network (CSPNet). CSPNet partitions the feature map of the base layer into two parts and then merges them through a cross-stage hierarchy. This strategy reduces the number of parameters and reduces the computation of floating-point operations per second (FLOPS) leading to increase in the inference speed. This is crucial for real-time object detection.

YOLOv5 returns three outputs namely the classes of the detected objects, their bounding boxes and the objectness score. YOLOv5 detects the bounding boxes having center points in the edges in the easier manner. The output of YOLOv5 deep learning model of nine images is shown in Fig. 2 below.

The detected objects from the images as from the above figure are provided as instances to the ISEO ontology. This ontology is engineered by the following entities and object properties as shown in Fig. 3 below.

The objects detected from the images are mapped to the corresponding images with the object property 'contains'. The domain entity is Images and the range is a collection of entities which reflect the objects from the images which is RDF List. Other object properties namely infront_of, is_on, next_to are defined based on the frequency of their occurrence in the images. The instantiation of these entities with the detected objects are performed. The visualization of ISEO ontology after instantiation is shown in Fig. 4 below.

In order to find out the order of the images required for the creation of audio-visual there is a need to improve the expressiveness of ISEO ontology. This is achieved by writing a SWRL rule which checks for the availability of the objects in the images. It is assumed that all objects are present in all images so that the number of debugged SWRL rules will be equal to the number of images instantiated to the Images entity. The SWRL rule is given below.

Fig. 2. YOLOv5 Object Detection on TERESA data set

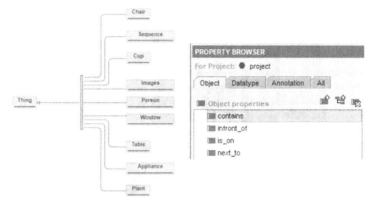

Fig. 3. ISEO Ontology Entities and Object Properties

contains(?x, ?y) ∧ contains(?x, ?z) ∧ contains(?x, ?p) ∧ contains(?x, ?q) ∧ contains(?x, ?r) ∧ contains(?x, ?s) ∧ contains(?x, ?i) → Sequence(?x)

The sequence of images after debugging the above SWRL rule are shown in Fig. 5 below.

Also the same SWRL rule is deemed to be the explanation [24] to each and every image in the obtained sequence of images. This rule finds the structural relationships between the objects as explanation paths in the identified images. The Controlled Natural Language (CNL) explanation of the SWRL rule is as follows:

If a thing(1) contains a thing(2) and the thing(1) contains a thing(3) and the thing(1) contains a thing(4) and the thing(1) contains a thing(5) and the thing(1) contains a thing(6) and the thing(1) contains a thing(7) and the thing(1) contains a thing(8) then the thing(1) is a sequence.

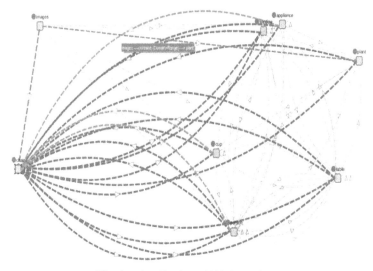

Fig. 4. Visualization of ISEO ontology

Fig. 5. Sequence of images based on debugged SWRL rule. Starts from Top-Left and ends at Bottom-Right

The above CNL form of the SWRL rule is an explanation for obtaining a particular image as outcome. This is because that the above CNL is seemingly a natural text, flexible as a polysemy sentence and is the representation of the symbolic logic in natural language [25]. Finally, the audio-visual is constructed based on the obtained sequence of images and with the explanation. To make it a viewable VR content with the goal of making consumers immerse into the audio-visual content by interacting with it, Spatial Media Metadata properties are injected to the created audio-visual. The output is 360° panoramic viewable VR audio-visual content (https://github.com/IamTarunG/video-360.git).

5   Experimental Results and Discussion

The dataset considered for carrying out the experiments by following the pipeline as specified in Fig. 1 is TERESA dataset. This is a test set containing 25 images with the corresponding coordinates data of the objects. The objects present in these images are listed in labels file. These images are provided as input to the YOLOv5 object detection model that detected the objects. Nine images are used from these 25 images for further experimentation. These objects are annotated as instances to the engineered ISEO ontology. This is a light weight ontology in which the entities are connected in tree-like structure and has no strict formal connections. On top of this ontology the Semantic Web Rule is written which after reasoning has returned the sequence of images as shown in Fig. 5. An Audio-Visual is constructed with the obtained sequence of images. The audio contains the story narrated with the detected objects and the structural relationships between these objects in that image. There are a total of 89 objects detected from the nine images. There are 6 object classes distributed across the 9 images. The object classes are namely Person, Table, Cup, Window, Chair, Plant. The evaluation of performance of the YOLOv5 object detection on the considered nine images in terms of Precision (P) and Recall (R) in percentages are tabulated in Table 1 below.

It is evident from the above table that when the number of detected objects of a particular entity are less in an image then the recall is less and vice-versa. Also it is observed that when the number of objects of a particular entity that are detected in an image are less in number when compared with the total number of objects of that entity across all the images then the precision of that detected object is less and vice-versa. The Average Precision (AP) for each entity is the sum over all the images. The mean Average Precision (mAP) is the average of the AP across all entities. The AP and mAP value(s) for each entity is presented in Table 2 below.

The comparison with the state-of-the-art works as discussed in Sect. 3 with [11] and [12] in terms of mAP shows that YOLOv5 model has improved object detection over Faster R-CNN model. Both the works used Visual Genome dataset. They have achieved mAP 5.39% and 7.43% respectively. With YOLOv5 there is a better improvement of 5.69% in mAP when compared with [11] and there is a good improvement of 3.65% in mAP when compared with [12].

The task of Predicate Detection is evaluated in this work by using Recall@K (where K is the value of the highest number of predicted relation triplets). The comparison of Recall@K is done with a tunable graph constraint hyperparameter 'k'. In this work, the K value considered is 20 and the k value considered is 1. The work with which the results are compared is [9]. The comparison of Recall@K for k is shown in Table 3 below.

It is observed from the above table that there is a significant improvement of 21.9% in present work when compared with [9] for Recall@K with k. This shows that there is better percentage of prediction of structural relationships with the ontology support. The

Table 1. Precision and Recall percentages of the detected objects across nine images.

Object and Metrics	Image1	Image2	Image3	Image4	Image5	Image6	Image7	Image8	Image9	Total Precision
Person	P=16, R=30.7	P=24, R=50	P=4, R=10	P=8, R=20	P=4, R=7.6	P=8, R=15.3	P=12, R=27.2	P=8, R=100	P=16, R=80	100
Table	P=10, R=15.3	P=10, R=16.6	P=20, R=40	P=5, R=10	P=20, R=30.7	P=15, R=23	P=15, R=27.2	--	P=5, R=20	100
Cup	P=40, R=15.3	P=20, R=8.3	--	--	--	P=40, R=15.3	--	--	--	100
Window	P=33.3, R=23	P=33.3, R=25	--	--	--	P=33.3, R=23	--	--	--	99.9
Chair	P=7.6, R=15.3	--	P=19.2, R=50	P=23, R=60	P=19.2, R=38.4	P=11.5, R=23	P=19.2, R=45.4	--	--	99.7
Plant	--	--	--	P=25, R=10	P=75, R=23	--	--	100	100	100
Total Recall	99.6	99.9	100	100	99.7	99.6	99.8	100	100	--

utilization of inferences from ISEO ontology for creating the 360^0 panoramic VR audio-visual specifies the usefulness of the ontology in simplifying the development of VR

Table 2. AP and mAP.

Entity	Average Precision (%)	Mean Average Precision (%)
Person	11.1	11.08
Table	11.1	
Cup	11.1	
Window	11.1	
Chair	11.0	
Plant	11.1	

Table 3. Predicate Detection comparison with Recall@K metric.

Dataset and Work	Recall@K (K = 20) and k = 1
VG-SGG with ontology in [9]	44.7%
Proposed Work	**66.6%**

scenarios. The fixed number of entities for the detected objects and the object properties of the ISEO ontology made the development process as well as the inferencing easier.

6   Concluding Remarks and Future Directions

The task of Ontological Scene Graph Engineering and Reasoning over YOLO objects for creating panoramic VR content has been carried out successfully. The objective is to build an integrated system with YOLO object detection and ontology modules that are not resource hungry. This is achieved by first identifying the objects from the images. Then these objects are instantiated to the ISEO Ontology. This ontology is the Scene Graph which is used for further reasoning with SWRL rule. The evaluation of Predicate Detection specified that a better percentage of prediction of structural relationships has been achieved with the ontology support. The SWRL rule provides sequence of images as consequent when debugged. Finally, this rule forms the explanation for the constructed audio-visual which is injected further with spatial metadata to obtain panoramic VR audio-visual. In future, this work is extended to aid specially-abled people navigate through real world cluttered environments such as metro rail stations in VR gadget.

References

1. Zhu, G., et al.: Scene graph generation: a comprehensive survey. arXiv preprint arXiv:2201.00443 (2022)
2. Lu, C., Krishna, R., Bernstein, M., Fei-Fei, L.: Visual relationship detection with language priors. In: Leibe, B., Matas, J., Sebe, N., Welling, M. (eds.) Computer Vision – ECCV 2016. Lecture Notes in Computer Science, LNCS, vol. 9905, pp. 852–869. Springer, Cham (2016). https://doi.org/10.1007/978-3-319-46448-0_51

3. Zhang, J., et al.: Large-scale visual relationship understanding. Proc. AAAI Conf. Artif. Intell. **33**(01), 9185–9194 (2019)

4. Redmon, J., et al.: You only look once: Unified, real-time object detection. In: Proceedings of the IEEE Conference on Computer Vision and Pattern Recognition (2016)

5. Cheng, J., et al.: Visual relationship detection: a survey. IEEE Trans. Cybern. **52**(8), 8453–8466 (2022)

6. Yang, M.: Visual Transformer for Object Detection. arXiv preprint arXiv:2206.06323 (2022)

7. Cui, Y., Farazi, M.: VReBERT: a simple and flexible transformer for visual relationship detection. In: 2022 26th International Conference on Pattern Recognition (ICPR). IEEE (2022)

8. Adadi, A.: A survey on data-efficient algorithms in big data era. J. Big Data **8**(1), 24 (2021)

9. Amodeo, F., et al.: OG-SGG: ontology-guided scene graph generation—a case study in transfer learning for telepresence robotics. IEEE Access **10**, 132564–132583 (2022)

10. Rhee, T., et al.: Mr360: Mixed reality rendering for 360 panoramic videos. IEEE Trans. Visual. Comput. Graphics **23**(4), 1379–1388 (2017)

11. Johnson, J., Karpathy, A., Li, F.-F.: Densecap: fully convolutional localization networks for dense captioning. In: Proceedings of the IEEE Conference on Computer Vision and Pattern Recognition (2016)

12. Li, Y., et al.: Scene graph generation from objects, phrases and region captions. In: Proceedings of the IEEE International Conference on Computer Vision (2017)

13. Essam, M., et al.: An enhanced object detection model for scene graph generation. In: Proceedings of the 8th International Conference on Advanced Intelligent Systems and Informatics 2022. Springer International Publishing, Cham (2022). https://doi.org/10.1007/978-3-031-20601-6_30

14. Carion, N., Massa, F., Synnaeve, G., Usunier, N., Kirillov, A., Zagoruyko, S.: End-to-end object detection with transformers. In: Vedaldi, A., Bischof, H., Brox, T., Frahm, J.-M. (eds.) Computer Vision – ECCV 2020. Lecture Notes in Computer Science, LNCS, vol. 12346, pp. 213–229. Springer, Cham (2020). https://doi.org/10.1007/978-3-030-58452-8_13

15. Chen, T., et al.: Knowledge-embedded routing network for scene graph generation. In: Proceedings of the IEEE/CVF Conference on Computer Vision and Pattern Recognition (2019)

16. Baier, S., Ma, Y., Tresp, V.: Improving visual relationship detection using semantic modeling of scene descriptions. In: d'Amato, C., et al. (eds.) The Semantic Web – ISWC 2017. Lecture Notes in Computer Science LNCS, vol. 10587, pp. 53–68. Springer, Cham (2017). https://doi.org/10.1007/978-3-319-68288-4_4

17. Zellers, R., et al.: Neural motifs: scene graph parsing with global context. In: Proceedings of the IEEE Conference on Computer Vision and Pattern Recognition (2018)

18. Zheng, S., Chen, S., Jin, Q.: Visual relation detection with multi-level attention. In: Proceedings of the 27th ACM International Conference on Multimedia (2019)

19. Kolesnikov, A., et al.: Detecting visual relationships using box attention. In: Proceedings of the IEEE/CVF International Conference on Computer Vision Workshops (2019)

20. Wang, L., et al.: Visual relationship detection with recurrent attention and negative sampling. Neurocomputing **434**, 55–66 (2021)

21. Dragoni, M., Ghidini, C., Busetta, P., Fruet, M., Pedrotti, M.: Using ontologies for modeling virtual reality scenarios. In: Gandon, F., Sabou, M., Sack, H., d'Amato, C., Cudré-Mauroux, P., Zimmermann, A. (eds.) The Semantic Web. Latest Advances and New Domains. ESWC 2015. LNCS, vol. 9088, pp. 575–590. Springer, Cham (2015). https://doi.org/10.1007/978-3-319-18818-8_35

22. Walczak, K., Flotyński, J.: Inference-based creation of synthetic 3D content with ontologies. Multimed. Tools Appl. **78**(9), 12607–12638 (2018)

23. Wang, M., et al.: VR content creation and exploration with deep learning: a survey. Comp. Visual Media **6**, 3–28 (2020)
24. Catherine, R., et al.: Explainable entity-based recommendations with knowledge graphs. arXiv preprint arXiv:1707.05254 (2017)
25. Bao, Q., Witbrock, M., Liu, J.: Natural Language Processing and Reasoning (2022)

Incremental Classifier in the Semi Supervised Learning Environment

Maneesha Gudapati$^{(\boxtimes)}$ and K. Swarupa Rani$^{(\boxtimes)}$

University of Hyderabad, Hyderabad, Telangana, India
{21MCPC02,swarupacs}@uohyd.ac.in

Abstract. Due to rapid growth in information technologies, millions of data are being generated at every time span. Data storage and processing are more expensive in terms of memory, resources, and time. The traditional machine learning classifier performs well when all the data is available along with the label information at the time of training, which may not be possible in every circumstances. Semi-supervised techniques overcome this limitation. With limited labeled data, semi-supervised learning makes use of both classification and clustering techniques for constructing efficient classifiers, and there is a demand to update the classifier periodically. Unlike traditional approaches, which use the entire data set for updating the classifier, our method updates in an incremental fashion. This paper proposes a framework for incremental classifiers in a semi-supervised environment. Experiments are conducted on benchmark datasets with the proposed approach and compared to the conventional method.

Keywords: Incremental learning · Semi Supervised · Clustering · Novelty detection · Multiple new classes · New class identification

1 Introduction

In today's world, data is abundantly available through different sources, but most of them are unlabeled. With the available labeled information, the machine learning algorithms will train the model, leading to performance degradation due to evolving of new data. To improve performance, human experts should manually annotate data by examining every instance, which is time-consuming and expensive.

One of the challenges for traditional Machine Learning (ML) algorithms is to build an efficient classifier with the available data, which may not be sufficient for addressing the emerging data. Another challenge is to handle the volume of data to build an efficient classifier and updating the classifier from scratch every time, which is more expensive with respect to memory, time, and limited resources. Moreover, these ML algorithms will operate in batch mode, and updating the model with new data needs to repeat the same procedure from

© The Author(s), under exclusive license to Springer Nature Switzerland AG 2023
R. Morusupalli et al. (Eds.): MIWAI 2023, LNAI 14078, pp. 236–244, 2023.
https://doi.org/10.1007/978-3-031-36402-0_21

scratch by combining existing and incremental data which is a time-consuming process.

With many applications, it is highly undesirable to maintain historical data. For example, applications like time series forecasting, anomaly detection, spam filtering, IOT applications, face identification, etc., storing all the historical data requires more data storage infrastructure. To overcome storage issues, incremental learning will address them effectively and efficiently. As and when the data evolves, the classifier updates by using evolved data without losing past information. This incremental classification is useful to people who make decisions, particularly long-term organizational decisions, or, in our particular field, family decisions, etc.

Generally in a semi-supervised environment, the label will not exist for all the instances of the streamed data. The classifier needs to build with the limited label data (i.e., training data) to provide better classification accuracy, which may not be possible in every circumstance. Semi-supervised learning makes use of little labeled data, to classify more unlabelled data in the streams. Classification and clustering approaches together make semi-supervised learning more significant for providing better performance accuracy.

In the process of data streaming, once the model is incrementally updated the historical data need not be preserved for the future. The changes happen to the data distribution as well new classes may evolve in the stream. Concept drift [2,12] refers to an online supervised learning scenario where the relation between the input data and the target variable changes over time, and concept drift detection aims to detect such change.

Most of the existing incremental models [1–3], are working under the assumption that the ground truth labels are provided by the experts while updating the model, which may not be possible in some situations. There are a couple of works [2,4,7] that addressed the issue by assuming multiple new classes as a single class and updating the classifier, which may not perform efficiently. To overcome the above issues, we develop a classifier that is able to accommodate dynamic changes in a semi-supervised environment. And we also handled and addressed multiple novel classes for updating the classifier.

In this paper, we proposed an Incremental Classifier in the Semi-Supervised Learning environment (ICSL), which is an extension to the LC-INC [2] method. The paper contributions are as follows:

– The framework for learning the incremental classifier(shown in Fig. 1).
– Multiple novel classes are handled by applying an efficient clustering technique.
– Updation of the classifier with multiple new classes
– Results comparison of the conventional and proposed approach.

2   Related Work

The class incremental learning mainly addresses the subproblem like finding the new instances, identifying the pre-trained instances, and updating the classifier when new instances appear over a period.

Rahman et al. [1] constructed an Adaptive Decision Forest(ADF) model which updates the classifier through batches. In this approach, three different forests are maintained during the evolution of data and it is time-consuming and expensive. ADF works with real-time data having ground truth labels and the same has to be provided dynamically. Adaptive decision forest works in the batch mode i.e., the data will be stored temporarily before updating to the classifier.

Zhou et al. [2] proposed a network model with the data stream settings, with the detection of novel classes and updating the classifier with newly identified novel instances. Zhang et al. [3] proposed an Adaptive Online Incremental Learning (AOIL) model for updating the model parameters, by using the autoencoder to find reconstruction and prediction losses. Based on the loss function, the trained model will update accordingly and they are not focusing exclusively on novelty detection.

Several approaches [4–6] consider the online setting for model updation, where SSLDN [4] and SCMC [6] works under the assumption that a single class is being updated to the model in a semi-supervised environment.

Wang et al., [5] aim for the ensemble model called FOSTER, by freezing the previous model and constructing a new model with every new change in the stream. Later these two models are ensembled to provide the updated model. Used the gradient boosting technique to handle class incremental learning. A semi-supervised novelty detection algorithm by Mesarcik et al., [7] using Nearest-Latent-Neighbours (NLN) in autoencoders. An Adaptive K-Nearest Neighbors similarity Graph (AKNNG) by Cai et al., [8], which gives different 'k' values for different data points. By using similarity graphs the 'k' value is adjusted.

3   Incremental Classifier Framework

Our proposed framework is the extension and modification of the Zhou et al. [2] (2022) works. The existing LC-INC model [2] assigns the same class label to all the unlabeled new instances as a meta-novel class which may degrade the classification performance. In order to overcome this situation, we adopted the clustering technique [6,11] in this framework to improve the performance of the classifier.

The workflow of the Incremental Classifier Framework is shown in Fig. 1. In the workflow, there are two important modules such as LC-INC [2] and Clustering [11]. The description of each module is provided in the following subsections.

3.1   LC-INC Module

In the LC-INC model [2], deep networks were used to find the similarity between trained instances with the newly emerged data. The procedure is shown below with pictorial representation in Fig. 2.

1. For the labeled data, construct the representative instance for each category (class) by using the class centroid.

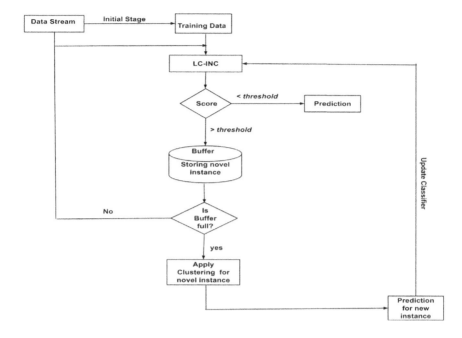

Fig. 1. Workflow of Incremental Classifier Framework.

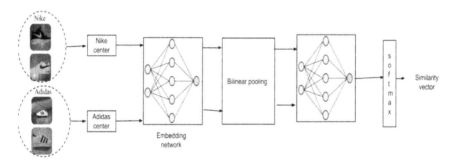

Fig. 2. LC-INC Model [2]

2. Each class center is given to the embedding network, to convert to the low dimensional embedding space i.e., For each representative instance, an equivalent embedding vector will be generated in this network.
3. Now the embedded vector of the known class will be merged with unknown class embedding by using compact bilinear pooling algorithm [9].
4. Then the feature fusion vector will be given to the structure comparison module with a sigmoid layer, which outputs the similarity vector.

3.2 Identification of New Class

To predict the novelty of the instance, calculate the score function given below by using the similarity vector values.

$$Score(x) = min(\lambda c, 1)Prob(x) + max(1 - \lambda c, 1)Ent(x) \qquad (1)$$

In the score function, 'c' is the chunk number starting from 0 at every novel class period. For example, at t_0, the value is '0', and incrementally at t_p the value is 'P'. Operator max/min keeps the score values in the range $(0, 1)$. λ is a trade-off parameter that needs to be dynamically updated for every period. $Prob(x)$ is the probability of x belongs to a novel class. $Ent(x)$ is an entropy.

If the score is greater than the predefined threshold, the arrived instances are to be treated as novel and will be stored in the buffer. Otherwise, predict the class label.

3.3 Maintain Buffer

All the identified novel instances will be stored in the temporary buffer for further updation on the classifier. When the buffer reaches the predefined maximum limit, we performed clustering to the novel instances.

3.4 Clustering Approach

After identifying as a new instance (may or may not have a class label), that particular instance will be sent to the buffer. Further, the k-means clustering algorithm [11], is applied to those instances (without considering the label information for any of the new instances) to form desired clusters. We need to check the instance of different clusters having class labels. If the class label information is available (ground truth value) for any of the instances inside the cluster then the same class label information is assigned to the entire cluster. If not, the new class label is assigned to the specific cluster.

3.5 Incremental Classifier Algorithm

All new instances along with class labels obtained from the clusters are further submitted to the LC-INC [2] module to update the classifier incrementally. The modified algorithm is shown in Algorithm 1.

In the Incremental Classifier Algorithm (Algorithm 1), while the stream emerges, each instance x_t' is given to the LC-INC module to construct the similarity vector. Then the similarity vector is used to calculate the novelty score (S). If the score exceeds the predefined threshold, the instance is identified as a new class. Newly identified instances are placed in the buffer for incremental updation of the classifier. $random(B, k)$ selects 'k' instances randomly from the stored instances in the buffer. $findNearestCentroid(C_1, C_2, \cdots, C_k)$ calculates the closest centroid for all the stored new instances and updates the cluster

---

Algorithm 1: Incremental Classifier

Input: Streaming data$\{x'_t\}^{\infty}_{t=0}$, $k(Number of Clusters)$
Output: Predicted label y'_t or Updated Model ($\mathcal{M}$)

1 $B \leftarrow \Phi$
2 **repeat**
3 $\quad$ $SV \leftarrow LCINC(x'_t)$
4 $\quad$ $S \leftarrow Score(SV)$
5 $\quad$ **if** $S > Tld$ **then**
6 $\quad\quad$ $B \leftarrow B \cup x'_t$

7 $\quad$ **else**
8 $\quad\quad$ $y'_t \leftarrow argmax(SV)$

9 $\quad$ **if** $|B| = maxsize$ **then**
10 $\quad\quad$ $C_1, C_2, \cdots, C_k \leftarrow random(B, k)$
11 $\quad\quad$ **repeat**
12 $\quad\quad\quad$ **for** $\forall i \in B$ **do**
13 $\quad\quad\quad\quad$ $findNearestCentroid(C_1, C_2, \cdots, C_k)$
14 $\quad\quad\quad$ **for** $\forall k - clusters$ **do**
15 $\quad\quad\quad\quad$ $calculateCentroid(\forall points \in k)$

16 $\quad\quad$ **until** $convergence$;
17 $\quad\quad$ **for** $\forall k - clusters$ **do**
18 $\quad\quad\quad$ **if** $isTrueLabel(k) = true$ **then**
19 $\quad\quad\quad\quad$ $label(i) \leftarrow trueLabel(k), \forall i \in k$

20 $\quad\quad\quad$ **else**
21 $\quad\quad\quad\quad$ $label(i) \leftarrow tempLabel$

22 $\quad\quad$ $\mathcal{M} \leftarrow updateModel(\mathcal{M}, B)$
23 $\quad\quad$ $B \leftarrow \Phi$

24 **until** $null$;

---

centroid by using *calculateCentroid()*. After maximum iterations or no further convergence, the clustering procedure stops. Now from the identified clusters, if the information of the ground truth label is available for any instance in the cluster, the same label was assigned to all the instances in that particular cluster. Otherwise, assign a label(temporary) to all the instances within the cluster.

4   Experimental Results

The proposed approach was developed on Python 3.X by using modules in the Pytorch library. The YSneaker dataset [10] is a real-time dataset. During experiments, the YSneaker dataset is partitioned into two unequal parts. The first part is considered with class label information to build the classifier. The remaining part is treated as it evolves in the data stream. This part is used in experiments to address the issue of incremental classifiers. Therefore we considered a few instances with class label information and another few without class label information and applied the clustering algorithm [11]. The hyperparameters like buffer size and score threshold are considered same as Zhou et al. (2022) [2]. The accuracy curve shown in Fig. 3., can identify the improvement of the proposed approach to the conventional LC-INC [2].

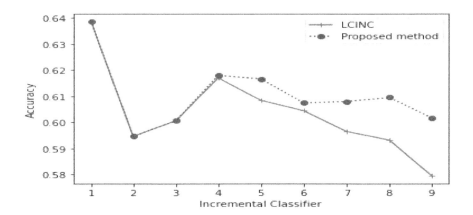

Fig. 3. Accuracy curve for Conventional and proposed approach.

In Fig. 3., the X-axis shows the incremental updation of the classifier in multiple stages, and accuracy was shown on Y-axis. In the figure, we observed a sharp reduction in accuracy, at the initial stage, as new classes evolved in the stream. As the stream progresses, our proposed model's accuracy increases when compared with the LC-INC [2] approach.

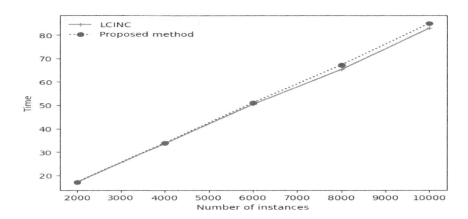

Fig. 4. Time curve for Conventional and proposed approach.

In Fig. 4., the number of data instances considered in the data stream versus time taken was plotted along X-axis and Y-axis respectively. From the figure, we can clearly understand that the execution time taken by our proposed approach is closer to the traditional one i.e., by applying the clustering technique, there is only a very slight difference in time taken with an improvement in accuracy as shown in Fig. 3. The experiment was done by considering different numbers of data instances in the Sneaker dataset [10] as an evolving stream. The comparison results are shown in Table 1.

F1 Score and Accuracy were used as evaluation metrics to compare proposed and conventional methods. Accuracy was calculated by using the total number of correctly classified instances to the total number of instances. In the data stream, new classes emerged which are not equally distributed. So, the F1 score was also used as a performance measure to compare the conventional approach with our proposed approach. The F1 score metric was calculated by using precision and recall through harmonic mean.

Table 1. Performance measure (Time, Accuracy and F1 Score) for Traditional and Proposed approaches.

Number of Instances	Traditional approach			Proposed approach		
	Time (sec)	F1 Score	Accuracy	Time (sec)	F1 Score	Accuracy
2000	17.1900	0.5675	0.5690	17.2717	0.5715	0.5714
4000	33.6319	0.5745	0.5725	33.9381	0.597	0.5826
6000	50.3447	0.5625	0.5933	51.0737	0.5692	0.6031
8000	65.2494	0.5822	0.5999	67.2337	0.5877	0.6057
10000	82.8279	0.5698	0.5855	84.9027	0.5788	0.5927

5   Conclusions and Future Work

One of the challenges in the real-world scenario is that most of the emerging data is unlabeled, which needs to be handled, and the model should update incrementally. In this paper, we proposed an Incremental classifier framework to handle multiple novel classes. The proposed framework uses clustering and classification techniques to work effectively in a semi-supervised environment. In this work, the clustering technique helps to identify multiple new classes, whereas the classification technique predicts the known instances or identifies the novel instance. The results show the efficacy of the proposed framework to the traditional approach. In the data streams, feature evolution may also be possible, which is not the scope of this paper and can be extended in the future. Also, one can use adaptive clustering techniques in the Incremental Classifier framework.

References

1. Rahman, Md.G., ZahidulIslam, Md.: Adaptive decision forest: an incremental machine learning framework. Pattern Recognit. **122**, 108345 (2022). https://doi.org/10.1016/j.patcog.2021.108345
2. Zhou, D.W., Yang, Y., Zhan, D.C.: Learning to classify with incremental new class. IEEE Trans. Neural Netw. Learn. Syst. **33**(6), 2429–2443 (2022)
3. Zhang, S.S., Li, J.W., Zuo, X.: Adaptive online incremental learning for evolving data streams. Appl. Soft Comput. **105**, 107255 (2021). https://doi.org/10.1016/j.asoc.2021.107255
4. Zhou, P., Wang, N., Zhao, S., Zhang, Y., Wu, X.: Difficult novel class detection in semi supervised streaming data. IEEE Trans. Neural Netw. Learn. Syst. (2022). https://doi.org/10.1109/TNNLS.2022.3213682
5. Wang, F.Y., Zhou, D.W., Ye, H.J., Zhan, D.C.: FOSTER: feature boosting and compression for class-incremental learning. In: Avidan, S., Brostow, G., Cissé, M., Farinella, G.M., Hassner, T. (eds.) ECCV 2022. LNCS, vol. 13685, pp. 398–414. Springer, Cham (2022). https://doi.org/10.1007/978-3-031-19806-9_23
6. Liao, G., et al.: A novel semi-supervised classification approach for evolving data streams. Expert Syst. Appl. **215**, 119273 (2023). https://doi.org/10.1016/j.eswa.2022.119273. ISSN 0957-4174
7. Mesarcik, M., Ranguelova, E., Boonstra, A.J., Nieuwpoort, R.V.V.: Improving novelty detection using the reconstructions of nearest neighbours. Array **14**, 100182 (2022) https://doi.org/10.1016/j.array.2022.100182. ISSN 2590-0056
8. Cai, Y., Zhexue Huang, J., Yin, J.: A new method to build the adaptive k-nearest neighbors similarity graph matrix for spectral clustering. Neurocomputing **493**, 191–203 (2022). https://doi.org/10.1016/j.neucom.2022.04.030. ISSN 0925-2312
9. Gao, Y., Beijbom, O., Zhang, N., Darrell, T.: Compact bilinear pooling. In: Proceedings of CVPR, pp. 317–326 (2016)
10. Yang, Y., Zhu, N., Wu, Y., Cao, J., Zhan, D., Xiong, H.: A semi supervised attention model for identifying authentic sneakers. Big Data Min. Anal. **3**(1), 29–40 (2020)
11. Bock, H.H.: Clustering methods: a history of k-means algorithms. In: Brito, P., Cucumel, G., Bertrand, P., de Carvalho, F. (eds.) Selected Contributions in Data Analysis and Classification. Studies in Classification, Data Analysis, and Knowledge Organization, pp. 161–172. Springer, Heidelberg (2007). https://doi.org/10.1007/978-3-540-73560-1_15
12. Gama, J., Zliobaite, I., Bifet, A., Pechenizkiy, M., Bouchachia, A.: A survey on concept drift adaptation. ACM Comput. Surv. **46**(4), 1–37 (2014)

Alzheimer's Detection and Prediction on MRI Scans: A Comparative Study

Namrata Nair$^{(\boxtimes)}$, Prabaharan Poornachandran, V. G. Sujadevi, and M. Aravind

Centre for Internet Studies and Artificial Intelligence, School of Computing,
Amrita Vishwa Vidyapeetham, Amritapuri, India
{namratan,praba,sujap,aravindm}@am.amrita.edu

Abstract. Alzheimer's disease (AD) is one of the most prevalent medical conditions with no effective medical treatment or cure. The issue lies in the fact that it is also a condition which is chronic, with irreversible effects on the brain, like cognitive impairment. The diagnosis of Alzheimer's in elderly people is quite difficult and requires a highly discriminative feature representation for classification due to similar brain patterns and pixel intensities. Although we cannot prevent AD from developing, we can try to detect the stages of development of AD. In this paper, we explore and test the various methodologies used to classify Alzheimer's Disease (AD), Early Mild Cognitive Impairment (EMCI), Late Mild Cognitive Impairment (LMCI), Mild Cognitive Impairment (MCI) and, healthy person (CN) using the Magnetic Resonance Image (MRI)s and Deep Learning techniques. The experiments are performed using ADNI dataset the results are obtained for multiple machine learning and deep learning methods that have been implemented over time. In our proposed work, we take into consideration the different stages of Dementia and Alzheimer's Disease, and use Deep Learning models on the MRI scans for detecting and predicting which stage of Alzheimer's or Dementia a person is suffering from.

Keywords: Deep Learning · Classification · VGG16 · EffNet · 3D-CNN · Alzheimer's Disease · Image Processing · Disease Detection

1 Introduction

Alzheimer's disease is a progressive neurological disorder that causes the brain to shrink and causes the cells to die. Alzheimer's disease is the most common cause of dementia, which is identified as a continuous decline in thinking, cognitive, behavioural as well as social skills, henceforth causing difficulties in the affected person's daily independent functioning. AD most likely goes unobserved due to the fact that at effects of AD only manifest after a decade or more, which in turn cause late detection of the symptoms as well. Alzheimer's Disease International (ADI), the most referred scientific report for Alzheimer's disease, reports that around more than 70 million people worldwide deal with Dementia, and more than 24 million suffer from Alzheimer's Disease. The predicted numbers for people diagnosed with AD, by the year 2030 is more than 78 million and to more than 100 million people by the end of year 2050 [1]. The 3D imaging as seen in MRI scans for Alzheimer's, makes it easy for physicians to identify and classify anomalies in the brain. These anomalies can be potential markers of Alzheimer's, but not always, since they could also be symptoms of other medical conditions leading to cognitive impairment. Alzheimer's MRI produces 3D imaging of the neural structure, which can show the number of cells present and the size of the cells, which are common identifiers for cancer. It is a widely known fact that the parietal lobe is one of the most affected part of the brain, caused by Alzheimer's. Hence knowing the size of the cells, and the lobes of the brain itself, play a vital role for AD detection. The parietal lobe's size helps indicate to doctors whether the patient is developing the different stages of AD or any other medical condition. Various MRI analytical methods have proved to be of significant benefit in identifying the plausible molecular and signature markers for AD and MCI. These markers, in turn, help improve accuracy fro diagnosis and treatment. Although traditional structural modalities are the recommended methods for MCI and AD detection and diagnosis, the need for further research to overcome methodological limitations of more advanced one is the need of the hour, aiding neuropathological insights to different causes of impairment [2]. Patients are mostly diagnosed with AD during the later stages of Dementia, when they suffer from diverse forms of cognitive decline. Such cases are determined to be too late, hence causing any preventive protocols to slower the imminent cognitive decline to be futile. All forms of treatment, both posological and over-the-counter medication, have proven to be effective in delaying or even reducing cognitive symptoms, the catch being that we need to be able to catch the disease in its early stages [3]. The various stages of the disease progression have been identified. The specific category of catching the disease before it causes further cognitive decline, i.e, catching the disease in it's early stages corresponds to be known as mild cognitive impairment (MCI), whose main characteristic is having minor memory detriment [4] (We use the MCI abbreviation, as it is the most frequently used term in the scientific community). It is note-worthy to understand and acknowledge that AD is a progressive medical condition, this implies that patients diagnosed with MCI that will advance on to suffer from AD, those diagnosed with Dementia already have AD, only that cognitive difficulties have not full presented. For this very reason, it is important to differentiate among patients diagnosed with MCI and those who will remain stable ad various other stages of Dementia, for example patients fully diagnosed with AD. In the later stages, i.e. when the symptoms of Dementia have already presented, AD is an easier diagnosis imaging methods, as is seen in many studies, like [4,5]. Although indicators may exist in magnetic resonance image (MRI) or in positron emission tomography (PET), the detection of the stages from MCI to AD is still a challenge. A novel approach to aid the research on tackling this issue, the researchers community now has access to thousands of neuroimaging datasets, in all possible views for example longitudinal, and axial, for the stages of Dementia like MCI, and AD subjects along with other variables (i.e., demographic, genetic, and cognitive measurements, etc.) is the public database Alzheimer Disease Neuroimaging Initiative (ADNI) (http://adni.loni.usc.edu). Many in the machine learning community have used this very dataset classify and detect the two stages of Dementia, AD and MCI [6–8]. ecently, many emerging works have been able to demonstrate the use of ML algorithms to classify images from AD, MCI, and healthy participants, showing the classification with very high accuracy. The goal of this comparative study is to analyze the existing classification methods based in Deep Learning algorithms applied to neuroimaging data in combination with other variables for predicting the stages even in MCI, and its progression to AD. Although such classification has provided valuable information about AD biomarkers, for this technology to have a more substantial clinical impact by empowering a clinician to administer a customized treatment protocol, it is necessary to determine and predict whether a MCI patient will progress to AD dementia or remain stable.

2   Related Work

AD detection is a widely studied, and it involves several issues and challenges. One of the recent trends is using 3D convolutional neural networks (3d-CNN), and implementing new learning methods to these CNN models, like transfer learning, to classify between subjects with Alzheimer's disease and subjects without any disease. A common method was using sparse auto-encoding and 3D-CNN by [9]. A development on this method of this is [10], where an algorithm is built, that detects the condition of a subject affected by cognitive impairment based on a magnetic resonance image (MRI) scan of the brain. [11] proposed an algorithm to predict the AD with a Deep 3D-CNN, which can learn generic features capturing AD markers. The 3D-CNN is built on top of an auto-encoder for CNN, pre-trained for shape differences identification in structural MRI scans of the brain. They also propose CNN fine-tuning for the AD classification task. Another CNN framework proposed the use of a multi-modal MRI analytical method relying on Deep Tissue Injury (DTI) or Functional Magnetic Resonance Imaging (fMRI) data, for the classification of AD, NC (Control Normal), and amnestic mild cognitive impairment (aMCI) patients. Although it achieved quite a high accuracy, they used 2D-CNN stating that 3D-CNN would definitely give a better result [13]. In accordance to the quote "Prevention is better than cure", Alzheimer's Disease progression can also be considered in this way. Although we cannot completely prevent the disease from developing, we can try to take many measure to slow the rate of progression. This where the process of detecting the stages of progression for AD is much required. For this very need, a multi-class, hybrid Deep Learning framework for early diagnosis of AD was proposed by [13]. They used k-Sparse autoencoder (KSA) classification to find degraded brain regions using 150 images of MRI scans as well as Cerebrospinal fluid (CSF) scan and PET images from the ADNI study public dataset. Another approach was by [14] for classification between people with AD, MCI and cognitive normal (CN) with an AUC score of 91.28% and 88.42%, respectively for classification between 2 separate experiments - (i) AD and MCI and, (ii) MCI and CN. All experiments were performed using 50 epochs with a batch size of 8, and the Adam optimizer was adopted with a LearningRateSchedule that uses a piece-wise constant decay schedule. This proposition was focused on how to prepare the data to be fed into the model. Early detection is a crucial goal in the study of Alzheimer's Disease. [15] describes the different techniques that can be used to boost 3D-CNN performance. They achieved around 14% accuracy while using existing models for classification of AD, MCI, and controls in the ADNI dataset, with the AlexNet and ResNet models as baseline 3D CNNs with Instance normalization. They also utilized the method of encoding each age value into a vector and combine the vector with the output of the convolutional layers. The enhancement for early detection for Alzheimer's requires the study of the brain from all angles and notice how AD and progressive stages to AD project in these angles. A 3D-CNN architecture is applied to 4D FMRI images for classifying four AD stages, where they divided MCI as Early MCI (EMCI) and Late MCI(LMCI), hence resulting in the following classification labels - AD, EMCI, LMCI, NC [16]. [17] proposed model using a large dataset of the Open Access Series of Imaging Studies (OASIS) Brain dataset. The proposed model has taken all parts of the human brain that are axial, sagittal, and frontal for Alzheimer's disease detection, and has obtained around 98.35% accuracy with the AlexNet 2012 ImageNet nerual network layers. The model proposal of using genes as indicators was also made, for AD detection, with high yielding accuracy [18]. MRI scans, genetic measures, and clinical evaluation were used as inputs for the APOe4 (APOE4 is considered as the strongest risk factor for Alzheimer's disease) model. Compared to pretrained models such as AlexNet and VGGNet, this model significantly reduced computational complexity, and memory requirements. In addition to this, other CNN structures that deal with 3D MRI for different stages of progression for AD classification are suggested by [19] and [20]. In our work, we focus on having a comparative study on the different Deep Learning methods used to perform classification of AD. We have seen that in most works the most commonly used classes for classification are AD, MCI, and CN. And hence, in our work, we would be focusing on the aforementioned classes as well as additional two more - Early Mild Cognitive Impairment (EMCI), and Late Mild Cognitive Impairment (LMCI), which will be as is and not instead of MCI.

3 Deep Learning and MRI Classification

Deep learning (DL) methods are increasingly used to improve clinical practice, and make more efficient smart systems. We will not go into great detail on the different DL architectures, but we will simply draw an outline on the models we would be using for out study, and how the models in Deep Learning are being implemented for medical imaging and MRI classification. A critical step in locating and categorising dangerous diseases is the categorization of MRI brain tumour images. The descriptiveness and discriminativeness of the extracted features have been identified as complementary qualities that are essential for strong classification performance in the extensive research that has been done to identify brain tumours based on medical images. Machine learning is essential in classification because of its variety of approaches and suitability for a particular issue. The segmentation and classification of reconstructed magnitude pictures have traditionally been the main goals of deep learning in MRI. It has only recently, but impressively, entered the lower levels of MRI measurement methods [21]. Convolutional neural networks (CNN) can be used to increase productivity in radiology settings; for instance, [22] showed how chemical elements dosage like gadolinium Gadolinium MRI (which is used for contrast enhancement) can be reduced without causing any reduction in image quality. Deep learning can also be applied in PET scan - MRI scan correction [23], in the information extraction from medical images, [24] just to name a few. In the field of Magnetic Resonance Imaging (MRI) classification and detection, deep learning has seen applications at each level of end-to-end workflows and solutions. From acquisition to image retrieval, from segmentation to disease classification and prediction. The entire image acquisition to disease prediction pipeline is broken down into two parts [21] - (i) Signal processing chain which includes including image restoration and, (ii) DL algorithms and models for image segmentation, disease detection and so on. Our work focuses on the second part, the disease detection and classification, primarily focusing on the stages of progression of AD.

3.1 Classification of Diseases Using Deep Learning

Deep learning rose to its prominent position in computer vision when neural networks started outperforming other methods on image analysis benchmarks. Deep learning techniques have become the de facto standard for a wide variety of computer vision problems. Healthcare providers generate and capture enormous amounts of data containing extremely valuable signals and information, at a pace far surpassing what "traditional" methods of analysis can process. In medical imaging the interest in deep learning is mostly triggered by convolutional neural networks (CNNs) [25]. Today's deep learning methods are almost exclusively implemented in either TensorFlow, a framework originating from Google Research, Keras, a deep learning library originally built by Francois Chollet and recently incorporated in TensorFlow, or Pytorch, a framework associated with Facebook Research. In our study we used 3D-CNN, EffNet, and VGG for classification of the different stages of AD. We also increase the size, and the labels used in our dataset. It is explained further in the next sections.

3.2 Evaluation Criteria

In this context, we evaluate and assess these methods for suitability in an MRI classification purpose, and then choose the model which performs the best. We do this using the entire Alzheimer's Disease Neuroimaging Initiative (ADNI) dataset, based on the below mentioned goals:

(a) Best performance with least training: We look for a model which can reach a good F1-score with least amout of data and epochs.
(b) Type and Size of training data: Although we can easily obtain annotated MRI scans from healthcare providers, it need not always be the case, as it depends on the healthcare provider's facilities. Hence it is important to have models that can scale up and produce high results even with low amounts of data.
(c) Deployment: As most hospitals with Hospital Information Systems already have sizable hardware, models that do not impose additional significant hardware requirements, but instead add GPU are desirable. As many Deep Learning models, and especially image classification task use a standard dataset, fine-tuning will need to be done on custom corpuses.

The above mentioned criteria are used to evaluate the following: Convolutional Neural Networks (CNN) [26], EfficientNet (EffNet) [27], Very Deep Convolutional Networks for Large-Scale Image Recognition (VGG) [28].

3.3   Methodology

Dataset: The dataset we use is ADNI, which is an open source dataset for Alzheimer's Disease data collection, in both csv(comma separated values) as well as MRI scans in DICOM and NIFTI formats. The dataset that used consisted of 83K DICOM and NIFTI files combined. These medical images, after pre-processing, were classified into the following classes:

(a) CN: Control Normal. This refers to the MRI scans taken of candidates with no clinical diagnosis of suffering from Dementia or Alzheimer's Disease.
(b) AD: Alzheimer's Disease. These are the MRI scans of candidates clinically diagnosed with Alzheimer's
(c) MCI: Mild Cognitive Impairment. These are of those who either reported memory loss themselves, or were clinically diagnosed with the same.
(d) EMCI: Early Mild Cognitive Impairment. This refers to those candidates present in the early stages of Cognitive Impairment.
(e) LMCI: Late Mild Cognitive Impairment. These scans refers to those in the later stages of Cognitive Impairment.

Although, many of researchers have worked on the classification of AD, we have noticed that the maximum number of classes they would use would be only 3 - AD, CN, MCI (Combination of both EMCI and LMCI). We chose to keep EMCI and LMCI as separate classes because we aims at predicting each stage of AD and in turn provide better insights and comforts to someone living with AD.

Experimental Setup: All experiments were run using Tensorflow platform. We initially ran the DICOM and NIFTI files as they are on a simple CNN model, which proved to us that we needed to do a simple clean up on the data. We used a small sample of 150 DICOM files for this dry run. For the pre-processing we initially converted all the DICOM and NIFTI Files to spliced, JPEG files. We also ensured that the quality was not lost during the conversion. Each JPEG image underwent maxpooling and was reshaped, and re-labelled as well. The configurations used are as follows:

(a) *3D-CNN*: A simple network of DenseNet layers make up the 3D-CNN model. A ReLU activation function was used, with a standardized learning rate of 0.0001 and epochs of 100(min).
(b) *EffNet*: We used Softmax activation with Imagenet weights. This model was built on Dense Layers of CNN as well as AlexNet layers. Here also we ran the experiments for the standard 100 epochs with 0.0001 learning rate.
(c) *VGG*: Here we used a Sequential model with Dense as well as Flatten layers. We also used ReLU activation function with Auto-tuning, and hence running the model for a standard 100 epoch with learning rate of 0.0001, the standard for all the experiments.
(d) Convergence occurs when no improvement happens. Thus this convergence section was added onto all the models, hence aiding in save both time and memory.
(e) *Training/Test Split*: We used an 80%, 10%, and 10% ratio to split the dataset into training, validation, and test sets, respectively.

4   Results

For the entire training data, one run were done for each configuration, presented in Table 1. As mentioned before, the run was conducted for 100 epochs and the best result was chosen. The best Micro-F1 value attained within 10 epochs is shown in Column 2. Column 3 shows the best reached Micro-F1 score. We observe the following:

(a) While the traditional base model of traditional CNN does catch up to the 3D-CNN model, the 3D-DNN model proved to be more efficient in comparison, by reaching convergence at around 50 epochs to provide an overall performance of 95.43%.
(b) while comparing the model of traditional CNN with 3D-CNN, we noticed that it took much longer, around the 70 epochs for the traditional model to reach a convergence with 93% as the best F1-score.
(c) The VGG model does outperform the 3D-CNN model, but only by a maximum of 2%. We also noticed that the VGG model reached convergence only much later at around the 55 epochs. We herein inferred that both VGG and 3D-CNN are undeniably part of the fore-runners for MRI classification, in our experiment.
(d) The EffNet model outperformed both VGG and 3D-CNN, by achieving convergence at around 40 epochs with its best F1-score at 97.22%.
(e) Although the EffNet model and VGG model F1-scores are negligibly different, the convergence epochs show that EffNet can perform better much faster.

Table 1. Model Performance (at 10 and 100 epochs)

Exp. No	Architecture	F1-micro	Best-F1
1	3D-CNN	93.55	95.43
2	VGG	96.39	97.16
3	EffNet	97.22	97.22

4.1 Limitations

(a) *CN*, and *AD* sections facilitate relatively straight-forward classification while *EMCI*, *LMCI*, and *MCI* present a challenge.
   – An image that was identified to be *LMCI* was misclassified as *MCI* although it occurred in the *MCI* labelled class. It was noted that without more bio-indicators, such misclassifications could among these classes. The confusion matrix comparing the LMCI and EMCI to MCI, along with precision and recall, are seen below :

	MCI	LMCI	Precision
MCI	20915	2852	88.00%
LMCI	2535	7814	75.00%
Recall	89.19%	73.26%	

	MCI	LMCI	Precision
MCI	20915	2852	88.00%
LMCI	2535	7814	75.00%
Recall	89.19%	73.26%	

(b) The performance of VGG and EffNet are comparable. However, training VGG is quite memory-intensive compared to EffNet, which makes the latter attractive from a deploy-ability standpoint. This leads us to the inference that additional fine-tuning in VGG will consume more memory, while maybe not providing any better results than when we fine-tune EffNet.

(c) Based on the discussions so far, creating a curated data-set of about 3000 samples, by identification of the misclassified samples and curating them will help push the accuracy higher.

5   Conclusion

This paper shows that various CNN models do provide an efficient solution to the task of MRI multi-class classification. It is inferred and reflected that around even a small sample of 500 medical image files would be a sufficient starting point for a well performing model. The comparison of models shows that they can achieve comparable accuracy and can be used independently. EffNet outperforms marginally. Future work will look into validation with diverse MRI images of the brain, and integration into an intelligent predictive interface for effective generation of clinical diagnosis, and assuaging physician burn-out. This paper builds on the same principle as the previous papers referred here, easily identifying the causes of concern, as well as focusing on a wider range of sections to be identified. Another focus will be on looking at how various conditions like brain tumour or trauma of any sort, which affect the brain, could learn to Alzheimer's Disease and how we can reduce the speed of progression using early warning predictions, based on similar principles.

References

1. Helaly, H.A., Badawy, M., Haikal, A.Y.: Deep learning approach for early detection of Alzheimer's disease. Cogn. Comput. **14**, 1711–1727 (2021)
2. Chandra, A., et al.: Magnetic resonance imaging in Alzheimer's disease and mild cognitive impairment. J. Neurol. **266**, 1293–1302 (2019)
3. Robinson, L., Tang, E., Taylor, J.-P.: Dementia: timely diagnosis and early intervention. Bmj **350** (2015)
4. Mittal, V.A., Walker, E.F.: Dyskinesias, tics, and psychosis: issues for the next diagnostic and statistical manuel of mental disorders. Psychiatry Res. **189**(1), 158 (2011)
5. Hinrichs, C., et al.: Predictive markers for AD in a multi-modality framework: an analysis of MCI progression in the ADNI population. Neuroimage **55**(2), 574–589 (2011)
6. Suk, H.-I., Shen, D.: Deep learning-based feature representation for AD/MCI classification. In: Mori, K., Sakuma, I., Sato, Y., Barillot, C., Navab, N. (eds.) MICCAI 2013. LNCS, vol. 8150, pp. 583–590. Springer, Heidelberg (2013). https://doi.org/10.1007/978-3-642-40763-5_72
7. Li, F., et al.: A robust deep model for improved classification of AD/MCI patients. IEEE J. Biomed. Health Inform. **19**(5), 1610–1616 (2015)
8. Mirzaei, G., Adeli, H.: Machine learning techniques for diagnosis of Alzheimer disease, mild cognitive disorder, and other types of dementia. Biomed. Signal Process. Control **72**, 103293 (2022)
9. Payan, A., Montana, G.: Predicting Alzheimer's disease: a neuroimaging study with 3D convolutional neural networks. arXiv preprint arXiv:1502.02506 (2015)
10. Hosseini-Asl, E., Keynton, R., El-Baz, A.: Alzheimer's disease diagnostics by adaptation of 3D convolutional network. In: 2016 IEEE International Conference on Image Processing (ICIP). IEEE (2016)
11. Sarraf, S., Tofighi, G.: Classification of Alzheimer's disease structural MRI data by deep learning convolutional neural networks. arXiv preprint arXiv:1607.06583 (2016)
12. Wang, Y., et al.: A novel multimodal MRI analysis for Alzheimer's disease based on convolutional neural network. In: 2018 40th Annual International Conference of the IEEE Engineering in Medicine and Biology Society (EMBC). IEEE (2018)
13. Bhatkoti, P., Paul, M.: Early diagnosis of Alzheimer's disease: a multi-class deep learning framework with modified k-sparse autoencoder classification. In: 2016 International Conference on Image and Vision Computing New Zealand (IVCNZ). IEEE (2016)
14. Gamal, A., Elattar, M., Selim, S.: Automatic early diagnosis of Alzheimer's disease using 3D deep ensemble approach. IEEE Access **10**, 115974–115987 (2022)
15. Liu, S., et al.: On the design of convolutional neural networks for automatic detection of Alzheimer's disease. In: Machine Learning for Health Workshop. PMLR (2020)
16. Parmar, H., et al.: Spatiotemporal feature extraction and classification of Alzheimer's disease using deep learning 3D-CNN for fMRI data. J. Med. Imaging **7**(5), 056001–056001 (2020)

17. Kumar, L., Sathish, S., et al.: AlexNet approach for early stage Alzheimer's disease detection from MRI brain images. Mater. Today Proc. **51**, 58–65 (2022)
18. Spasov, S.E., et al.: A multi-modal convolutional neural network framework for the prediction of Alzheimer's disease. In: 2018 40th Annual International Conference of the IEEE Engineering in Medicine and Biology Society (EMBC). IEEE (2018)
19. Basaia, S., et al.: Automated classification of Alzheimer's disease and mild cognitive impairment using a single MRI and deep neural networks. NeuroImage Clin. **21**, 101645 (2019)
20. Pan, D., et al.: Early detection of Alzheimer's disease using magnetic resonance imaging: a novel approach combining convolutional neural networks and ensemble learning. Front. Neurosci. **14**, 259 (2020)
21. Lundervold, A.S., Lundervold, A.: An overview of deep learning in medical imaging focusing on MRI. Z. Med. Phys. **29**(2), 102–127 (2019)
22. Gong, E., et al.: Deep learning enables reduced gadolinium dose for contrast-enhanced brain MRI. J. Magn. Reson. Imaging **48**(2), 330–340 (2018)
23. Liu, F., et al.: Deep learning MR imaging-based attenuation correction for PET/MR imaging. Radiology **286**(2), 676–684 (2018)
24. Oakden-Rayner, L., et al.: Precision radiology: predicting longevity using feature engineering and deep learning methods in a radiomics framework. Sci. Rep. **7**(1), 1648 (2017)
25. LeCun, Y., et al.: Gradient-based learning applied to document recognition. Proc. IEEE **86**(11), 2278–2324 (1998)
26. O'Shea, K., Nash, R.: An introduction to convolutional neural networks. arXiv preprint arXiv:1511.08458 (2015)
27. Tan, M., Le, Q.: EfficientNet: rethinking model scaling for convolutional neural networks. In: International Conference on Machine Learning, PMLR (2019)
28. Simonyan, K., Zisserman, A.: Very deep convolutional networks for large-scale image recognition. arXiv preprint arXiv:1409.1556 (2014)

Evaluating the Performance of Diverse Machine Learning Approaches in Stock Market Forecasting

Bharath Raj Anand Kumar[1], Sheetal Katiyar[1], Prasanth Lingada[1],
Karunakar Mattaparthi[1], R. Krishna[1], Gnana Prakash[1], Dileep Vuppaladhadiam[1],
Narayana Darapaneni[2], and Anwesh Reddy Paduri[1(✉)]

[1] Great Learning, Bangalore, India
anwesh@greatlearning.in
[2] Northwestern University/Great Learning, Evanston, IL, USA

Abstract. Stock market prediction is crucial for financial analysis, and numerous machine-learning algorithms have been utilized to forecast trends and movements. This study examines the efficacy of various algorithms, such as ARIMA, TBATS, Holt-Winters, Random Forest, ANN, RNN, LSTM, and others, in predicting stock market behavior. A range of leading and lagging technical indicators was incorporated and extensive EDA to identify and manage outliers was conducted. The indicators were further assessed to minimize feature collinearity, thereby enhancing prediction quality and performance. This research compares the outcomes of these algorithms to determine a consistently accurate forecasting method. The experimental results reveal a peak prediction accuracy of approximately 91% across different algorithms. Interestingly, while complex deep learning models show strong performance, simpler models like Linear Regression, MLP, and the Theta Model yield impressive results, with a Mean Absolute Percentage Error (MAPE) of 1. This study provides a comprehensive evaluation of various machine learning algorithms applied to stock market prediction, emphasizing the effectiveness of simpler models in generating precise and dependable forecasts.

Keywords: Stock market prediction · Financial analysis · Machine learning algorithms · Technical indicators · EDA (Exploratory Data Analysis)

1 Introduction

Forecasting stock market prices has long been a challenging and captivating area of research for business analysts and researchers alike. Accurate stock market prediction is inherently difficult due to the substantial influence of external factors, including social, psychological, political, and economic elements. The data associated with the stock market is typically time-variant and nonlinear [2], further complicating the prediction process.

Over the years, various prediction techniques have been developed to improve the accuracy of stock market forecasting. Fundamental Analysis and Technical Analysis – are widely used for predicting stock prices by examining historical data [14].

1.1 Fundamental Analysis

Fundamental analysis is an approach employed to assess a company's intrinsic value, which assists in determining its financial position's strength. Fundamental analysis offers insight into whether a stock is overvalued or undervalued. Parameters like alpha and beta can also be utilized to identify stocks with high volatility, which can be valuable inputs for stock selection, analysis, or performance prediction.

1.2 Technical Analysis

While fundamental analysis helps comprehend the strength and intrinsic value of a company, technical analysis offers various indicators which can serve as either leading or lagging indicators.

Technical analysis also provides insights into the supply and demand of the stock in the current market. These indicators assist in understanding the support and resistance levels, reflecting the market sentiment among traders and strength and direction of the stock price.

In this study, primary focus is to use technical indicators to predict stock prices using various machine learning models. The Model performance is then compared and analyzed to identify the most effective ones and consider potential combinations to develop a comprehensive prediction system.

2 Literature Review

In the literature review, various research papers and architectures related to stock market predictions in the context of the Indian and US markets were examined. The prediction methods can be categorized broadly into two groups: Numeric analysis and Sentiment analysis. The architectures employed in these papers have achieved individual stock price predictions with an accuracy of up to 98%. While earlier models relied solely on numeric analysis, recent architectures incorporate sentiment analysis as an additional dimension to enhance the accuracy of stock price predictions.

Data modeling is a critical aspect of any architecture. The referenced architectures modeled data based on technical parameters of specific stocks. It is essential to note that a stock's price is not solely dependent on its performance but is also influenced by market sentiment, repo rates, and the performance of similar stocks [1]. The referenced architectures attempted to account for these factorsby using hybrid intelligent models for stock market prediction using the psycholinguistic variables (LIWC and TAALES) extracted from news articles as predictor variables [6]. Some recent architectures also incorporated sentiment analysis derived from social media platforms like Twitter and newspaper articles, which can help anticipate stock price movements [3].

A few of the examined architectures employed Convolutional Neural Networks (CNN) for stock price prediction [8, 10]. Following traditional methodologies, stock price movements are plotted on graphs, which serve as predictors for future trends, such as candlestick charts and stock closing price charts. CNNs demonstrated impressive performance on this type of data, achieving over 91% accuracy. It is worth noting that

CNN-based architectures maintained over 90% accuracy during the COVID crisis when stock prices plummeted [8, 10].

Some papers also considered not only the stock in interest but also related stocks in the industry[4] or stocks across industry but showing close correlation.

After examining all referenced papers, a more traditional approach [15], similar to a trader's methodology, was adopted. This involves collecting stock data, analyzing the fundamentals, generating technical indicators [16] and subsequently predicting the stock price using various array of models to identify the best model or models.

3   Materials and Methods

3.1   Data

In the realm of stocks and the stock market, numerous options are available to choose from. The criteria considered for selecting a stock from the list of available options were as follows:

- Established stocks with a long market presence, ensuring ample data to work with.
- Stable stocks with low volatility, such as those with low beta values, because as volatility increases, the predictability of stocks generally declines.
- Stocks that exhibited consistent movement, not stagnant, and followed general stock market trends.

The primary goal was to make accurate predictions and determine which model or models performed best in forecasting. Based on these considerations, SBI, a banking stock with a long history, was selected, allowing for the acquisition of data from 1996 to the present, spanning 22 years. This stock is included in NIFTY 50, SENSEX, BANKNIFTY, FIN NIFTY, and several other indices. Multiple financial stocks, which can be utilized in further experiments (outside the scope of this study), may be employed to understand variations in SBI stock.

Ultimately, approximately 6,700 data points consisting of open, close, high, low, and volume values were gathered. This data was extracted from Yahoo Finance.

Attempts were also made to acquire 5-min interval data, but it was only available for a short period of around two months, which may not be sufficient for comprehensive analysis.

3.2   Exploratory Data Analysis (EDA)

The EDA with following steps:

Identifying Missing Value
While working with stock data, all values were available except for volume values, which were missing on certain days. The cause was investigated and determined to be likely due to holidays or trading suspensions for the stock. To address this issue, all missing values were replaced with either the previous or the next available non-zero value, selecting the nearest non-zero value for each instance.

Outlier detection
Next, the percentage change for all data points was calculated, as the price ranged from 20 to 600, and this metric was used to identify outliers. The z-scores for the percentage changes of Open, High, Low, and Close values were then computed. After analyzing the data, it was recognized that stock data is prone to significant variations; therefore, the z-score limit was set at 3.5.

Outlier analysis
Some of the major outliers were examined to determine the reasons behind their existence. Research was done to understand whether they were caused by intrinsic factors within the company or external factors. Most of the outliers were generally due to external factors, such as COVID-19, recession, political scenarios like cabinet changes, or sudden closure of companies like Satyam. Consequently, the decision was made to remove these outliers, as they were not intrinsic to the stock and did not stem from issues within the company.

Data Processing
First, the date column was converted to a datetime format. Next, the percentage change of OHLC (Open, High, Low, Close) was calculated, and their respective Z-scores were determined. Based on scores above or below 3.5, it was initially considered to drop the records, but it was realized that doing so would create larger gaps. As an alternative, the outliers were smoothened by taking a weighted average of the previous, current, and next data points. After multiple iterations, it was found that using a weight of 10 effectively smoothened the curve.

$$Optmised\ Value = \frac{weight * Previous\ value + Current\ value + weight * Next\ value}{2 * (weight) + 1}$$

Feature engineering
After effectively smoothing the data and eliminating the majority of outliers through 2 to 3 repetitions of the mentioned process, including recalculating the Z-scores after each iteration, the focus shifted to generating new features. Four categories of technical indicators were developed: Trend, Momentum, Volatility, and Oscillator indicators. Additionally, the next open price was selected as one of the indicators, as the goal was to predict the next day's closing price. This resulted in a total of around 30 features which can be really helpful in the stock price prediction. [2, 12].

Feature reduction
The analysis of all these features was then carried out by performing a correlation analysis to understand their dependencies and influences on each other. Two approaches were adopted for this process. In the first approach, highly correlated columns were manually identified, and an attempt was made to reduce the number of features while retaining at least one feature from each indicator category; for example, the standard deviation was chosen instead of the Bollinger band. In the second approach, a principal component analysis was conducted, selecting all columns that represented 95% of the variability in the data. Ultimately, two datasets containing 11 and 10 features each, respectively, were obtained. The data was then divided into training and testing sets and the manually-selected feature data was scaled.

3.3 Algorithm Selection

To select the appropriate models for analysing stock data, a range of models were evaluated across different categories. Regression models like Linear Regression were considered for their ability to capture linear relationships between variables. Time series models like AutoARIMA, SES/TBATS/Holt Winters, and THETA were chosen for their ability to capture trends and seasonal patterns in the data. Tree-based models like Random Forest with GridSearch CV, XG Boost, and Light GBM were considered for their ability to handle complex nonlinear relationships between variables. Lastly, neural network models like ANN/DNN and MLP with Grid Search CV, as well as RNN and Bi-Directional LSTM, were selected for their ability to capture temporal dependencies and relationships. By selecting a range of models from different categories, we can ensure that we are able to capture the unique characteristics and relationships present in stock data.

4   Results

4.1   Time Series Models

See (Figs. 1, 2, 3, and 4).

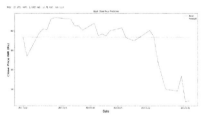

Fig. 1. Simple Exponential Smoothening Model

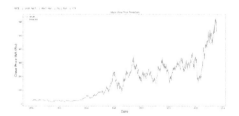

Fig. 2. Theta Model

Fig. 3. Holt Winters Model

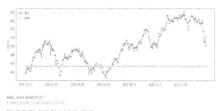

Fig. 4. Auto ARIMA Model

4.2   Tree-Based Models

See (Figs. 5, 6, 7 and 8).

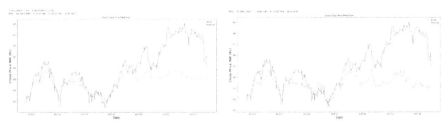

Fig. 5. Random Forest with grid search CV Model

Fig. 6. Light GBM Model

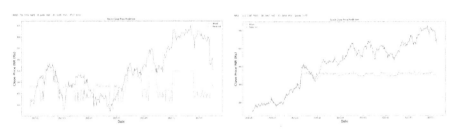

Fig. 7. Decision Tree Model

Fig. 8. XG Boost Model

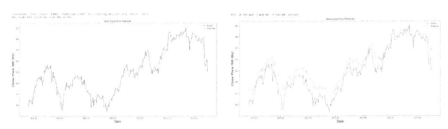

Fig. 9. MLP with Grid Search CV

Fig. 10. ANN/DNN Model

Fig. 11. Bi-Directional LSTM Model

4.3 Deep Learning Models

See (Figs. 9, 10 and 11).

4.4 Regression Models

See (Figs. 12 and 13).

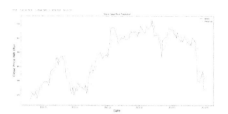

Fig. 12. LR Model with PCA data

Fig. 13. LR Model with Manual Curated Data

4.5 Model Performance Summary

SlNo	Model Type	Model	RMSE	MAPE	MAE	MSE
1	Deep Learning	RNN	167.92	30.06	161.7	28,196.30
2	Tree-Based	XG Boost	122.23	18.51	93.21	14,940.34
3	Time Series	AutoARIMA	77.39	11.02	61.63	5,988.58
4	Tree-Based	Decision tree	59.4	8.17	45.12	3,527.82
5	Tree-Based	Light GBM	59.09	7.65	43.29	3,491.18
6	Time Series	TBATS	53.7	7.89	43.3	2,883.98
7	Tree-Based	Random Forest	50.57	6.15	35.09	2,557.64
8	Tree-Based	Random Forest + GridSearch CV	48.99	5.93	33.82	2,399.69
9	Time Series	SES	25.48	2.99	16.78	649.12
10	Time Series	Holt Winters	25.35	2.99	16.83	642.42
11	Deep Learning	Bi-Directional LSTM	25.28	4.26	23.02	639.12
12	Deep Learning	ANN/DNN	20.4	3.44	17.27	415.99
13	Regression	Linear Regression with PCA data	9.82	1.29	7.3	96.34
14	Deep Learning	MLP with Grid Search CV	8.29	1.21	6.28	68.7
15	Regression	Linear Regression with Manual data	7.93	1.13	5.88	62.95
16	Time Series	THETA	2.56	1.01	1.56	6.58

$$\text{RMSE} = \sqrt{\frac{\sum_{i=1}^{N}(y(i)-y'(i))^2}{N}}; \quad \text{MAPE} = \frac{1}{n}\Sigma\left|\frac{actual-predicted}{actual}\right|; \quad \text{MAE} = \frac{1}{n}\Sigma|actual - predicted|; \text{MSE} = \frac{\sum_{i=1}^{N}(y(i)-y'(i))^2}{N}.$$

5 Discussion

5.1 Models Performance

The analysis started with basic time series models, moved on to regression models, investigated tree-based models, and finally focused on deep learning models. Assessing the performance of these algorithms based on precision and accuracy offers an interesting insight into their potential.

In this context, accuracy refers to a model's ability to capture the stock price fluctuations, including the highs and lows. Conversely, precision relates to how close the predicted price is to the actual value, without necessarily following the stock's price movement.

Time Series Models Performance
Time Series models like AutoARIMA, TBATS, SES, and Holt Winters did not display accuracy or precision in their predictions. In some cases, a simple rolling average performed better than these models in terms of predictive capability. This clearly showed that these are very basic models and are unable to capture the price action effectively.[5, 7, 11].

On the other hand, the Theta Model exhibited a remarkable degree of accuracy and precision, suggesting its potential usefulness in stock price prediction. However, relying solely on this model for predicting stock prices might not be advisable, as incorporating additional models or techniques could lead to more robust and reliable predictions.

Tree-Based Models Performance
A noticeable improvement in performance was observed from time series models to basic Decision Trees, Light GBM, and Random Forest + GridSearch CV being the best among them. However, they did not prove to be highly reliable models. One peculiar behavior observed was that all these models appeared to have an upper limit in terms of their predictions. Attempts were made to delve deeper to identify the cause, but it was not possible to conclusively determine whether overfitting or model limitations were the reasons for this behavior.

Interestingly, below this threshold value, the predictions were relatively accurate and precise. Nevertheless, incorporating more features, additional data, and further tuning of hyperparameters might help improve this aspect.

Deep Learning Models Performance
Deep learning models performed exceptionally well, with ANN/DNN and MLP with Grid Search CV achieving the lowest error metrics. Bi-Directional LSTM exhibited impressive precision, effectively capturing the price action; however, its accuracy was lower than other models and had a phase difference. The excellent performance of MLP, with its high precision and accuracy, brought it very close to other models like Theta and Regression [9].

These results highlighted that the selection of the right deep learning architecture was crucial for achieving better predictions, as different architectures might yield varying results. Additionally, increasing the dataset size and incorporating more features, such as non-numeric inputs like sentimental analysis [1] and variations in other stock data, could significantly improve model performance.

Regression Models Performance
Regression models emerged as the underdog in this analysis, boasting significantly lower error metrics compared to other model types and displaying very high accuracy and precision. However, the high accuracy might also indicate overfitting of the model. As a result, it may not be prudent to rely solely on this model for predictions. Instead, it would be wise to combine it with other models to make the final prediction, ensuring a more robust and reliable outcome.

6 Future Work and Conclusions

An alternative perspective to consider is focusing not just on the stock price but also on the direction of the stock movement. Predicting the direction of movement might yield greater accuracy and provide more valuable insights to inform investment decisions.

Enhancing the dataset with information from other stocks and market indices can help improve predictions, as stock prices are often influenced by other stocks and external factors [13]. Introducing features such as stock sectors, subsectors, alpha and beta based segments, and other fundamental stock characteristics could also provide valuable input for the model.

Investigating alternative approaches, like CNN models or ensemble methods, may contribute to better stock prediction performance. A pre-trained model can be developed using this enriched data, which can then be fine-tuned for specific stocks by retraining with their respective data. This process would make the model more tailored and potentially more accurate for the individual stock.

Within the limitations of this study, it can be concluded that simple Linear Regression, Theta, and ANN models outperformed the rest of the models. Bi-directional LSTM also demonstrated excellent performance. Combining these models could further enhance the prediction of the stock price.

References

1. Akita, R., Yoshihara, A., Matsubara, T., Uehara, K.: Deep learning for stock prediction using numerical and textual information. In: 2016 IEEE/ACIS 15th International Conference on Computer and Information Science (ICIS), Okayama, Japan, pp. 1–6 (2016). https://doi.org/10.1109/ICIS.2016.7550882
2. Ghosh, P., Neufeld, A., Sahoo, J.K.: Forecasting directional movements of stock prices for intraday trading using LSTM and random forests. Finan. Res. Lett. **46**, 102280 (2022). https://doi.org/10.1016/j.frl.2021.102280
3. Pagolu, S., Reddy, K., Panda, G., Majhi, B.: Sentiment analysis of Twitter data for predicting stock market movements, pp. 1345–1350 (2016). https://doi.org/10.1109/SCOPES.2016.7955659
4. Sidi, L.: Improving S&P stock prediction with time series stock similarity. arXiv preprint arXiv:2002.05784 (2020)
5. Selvamuthu, D., Kumar, V., Mishra, A.: Indian stock market prediction using artificial neural networks on tick data. Financ. Innov. **5**(1), 1–12 (2019). https://doi.org/10.1186/s40854-019-0131-7

6. Kumar, B.S., Ravi, V., Miglani, R.: Predicting indian stock market using the psycho-linguistic features of financial news. Ann. Data Sci. **8**(3), 517–558 (2020). https://doi.org/10.1007/s40 745-020-00272-2

7. Xiao, D., Su, J.: Research on stock price time series prediction based on deep learning and autoregressive integrated moving average. Sci. Prog. **2022**, 1–12 (2022). https://doi.org/10. 1155/2022/4758698

8. Kusuma, R., Ho, T.-T., Kao, W.-C., Ou, Y.-Y., Hua, K.-L.: Using Deep Learning Neural Networks and Candlestick Chart Representation to Predict Stock Market (2019)

9. Hussein, A.S., Hamed, I.M., Tolba, M.F.: An efficient system for stock market prediction. In: Filev, D., et al. (eds.) Intelligent Systems'2014. AISC, vol. 323, pp. 871–882. Springer, Cham (2015). https://doi.org/10.1007/978-3-319-11310-4_76

10. Li, J.: Research on market stock index prediction based on network security and deep learning. Secur. Commun. Networks **2021**, 1–8 (2021). https://doi.org/10.1155/2021/5522375

11. Hiransha, M., Gopalakrishnan, E.A., Menon, V.K., Soman, K.P.: NSE stock market prediction using deep-learning models. Procedia Comput. Sci. **132**, 1351–1362 (2018). https://doi.org/ 10.1016/j.procs.2018.05.050

12. Vijh, M., Chandola, D., Tikkiwal, V.A., Kumar, A.: Stock closing price prediction using machine learning techniques. Procedia Comput. Sci. **167**, 599–606 (2020). https://doi.org/10. 1016/j.procs.2020.03.326

13. Thakkar, A., Chaudhari, K.: CREST: cross-reference to exchange-based stock trend prediction using long short-term memory. Procedia Comput. Sci. **167**, 616–625 (2020). https://doi.org/ 10.1016/j.procs.2020.03.328

14. Usmani, M., Adil, S.H., Raza, K., Ali, S.S.A.: Stock market prediction using machine learning techniques. In: 2016 3rd International Conference on Computer and Information Sciences (ICCOINS), pp. 322–327. Kuala Lumpur, Malaysia (2016). https://doi.org/10.1109/ ICCOINS.2016.7783235

15. Darapaneni, N., et al.: Automated portfolio rebalancing using Q-learning. In: 2020 11th IEEE Annual Ubiquitous Computing, Electronics & Mobile Communication Conference (UEMCON), pp. 0596–0602 (2020)

16. Darapaneni, N., et al.: Stock price prediction using sentiment Analysis and deep learning for Indian markets. arXiv [q-fin.ST] (2022)

A Blockchain-Driven Framework for Issuance of NFT-Based Warranty to Customers on E-Commerce

Sneha Devrani, Rohit Ahuja$^{(\boxtimes)}$ ⓘ, Anirudh Goel, and Sahajdeep Singh Kharbanda

Thapar Institute of Engineering and Technology, Patiala, India
{sdevrani_be19,rohit.ahuja,agoel3_be19,
skharbanda_be19}@thapar.edu

Abstract. With the advent of digitalization, online shopping has become increasingly popular as it saves buyers and retailers time by providing information about different products and brands at their doorstep. Even the platforms offering second-hand products have seen massively trafficked over the past few years. However, online shopping experiences are not always smooth customers have to deal with security concerns which makes it difficult to trust online retailers. Customers going for second-hand products find it hard to get product-related accurate details and access warranty services after purchase. In-addition, existing e-commerce platforms does not offer jointly e-commerce cum re-commerce. Hence, a transparent E-commerce platform system is required to enable users to conveniently and securely buy/sell the product. Thus, we proposed a Blockchain-based e-commerce solution that provides users with an NFT (digital warranty card) just after the transaction. This digitalization of documentation will ease the process of accessing customers' product details for repair/replacement services. Moreover, the proposed system supports re-commerce along with e-commerce providing the user the feature to add their product in the flea market where other users can choose and view the purchase history of the product. Based on that, they can negotiate with the seller and transfer the product ownership to their name. We implemented the proposed scheme using reactJS, Django, MySQL, and blockchain. Smart contracts are deployed over the polygon network, interacting with web pages developed using React. Finally, the analysis and results of the proposed model express that it is viable, secure, and far better than the existing e-commerce platforms.

Keywords: Blockchain · Smart Contract · Ethereum · Security · NFT · E-Commerce

1 Introduction

The e-commerce market has grown significantly over the past few years, especially with the wave of Covid-19, which increased the attention on digital transformation and brought a significant switch from the analog to the digital era [1–3]. However, people are still reluctant to trust online vendors because unlike in-store shopping they didn't

ⓒ The Author(s), under exclusive license to Springer Nature Switzerland AG 2023
R. Morusupalli et al. (Eds.): MIWAI 2023, LNAI 14078, pp. 265–276, 2023.
https://doi.org/10.1007/978-3-031-36402-0_24

get their product's ownership certificate cum warranty card just after completion of payment despite they have to wait for the entire shipment period to get their product ownership transferred to their name. There are several platforms which supports both e-commerce as well as re-commerce (flea market) to sell/buy second hand products online but fails to provide the product's last owner's authenticity and warranty services to new owners [7, 8, 11].

Moreover e-commerce suffers from several deficiencies such as the customer has no-control over his personal information due to which user has no information about how their data is being used or if it leaked which led to serious security and privacy concerns [12]. Even there are high processing fees charged by intermediaries which ultimately customers have to pay.

The immutable and distributed ledger technology of blockchain has attracted significant attention from researchers, academicians, and industry professionals alike. Several business enterprise have adopted blockchain technology to enhance security and transparency in user transactions [4–6]. Moreover, the peer-to-peer architecture of blockchain enables all entities involved in the system to track the status of transactions, while also making it difficult to modify records or add unauthorized transactions. Therefore, blockchain can be the efficient solution for these problems as it can provide transparency, and security and possibly remove those old traditional ways of payments. There will be no third party in between so low processing fees and can protect privacy [9, 10, 13].

We have proposed a blockchain-driven framework for issuance of NFT-based cum ownership cum warranty card to overcome these issues for e-commerce customer. A blockchain guarantees high transparency, fostering trust, and users can vote on database updates using a decentralized time-stamping algorithm [13]. Furthermore interface, we have added blockchain functionality to place all warranty details on the blockchain during the transaction. This digitalization of documentation will increase the customers' trust as they will now get a product ownership certificate immediately after the transaction. In addition, the proposed system offers faster ownership verification during the repair/replacement process. In addition, proposed system brings reform in re-commerce as now the customer can see all the past owners of the product before purchase and will get an updated digital warranty card that they can use for verification from anywhere across the globe without the involvement of any third party.

The rest of the paper is organized as follows. Section 2 describes existing land transfer system and its deficiencies. The proposed methodology is presented in Sect. 3, while Sect. 4 discusses the implementation of proposed system. Section 5 evaluates the experimental evaluation and compare features of proposed scheme with existing land transaction system. Finally conclusion is provided in Sect. 6.

2   Existing System

E-commerce websites work through a series of steps that involve the customer, retailer, intermediaries, and third-party services. As depicted in Fig. 1 retailers add their products to the intermediary database with a given quantity. The customers visit the website and choose their desired items. After adding items to their cart, they place the

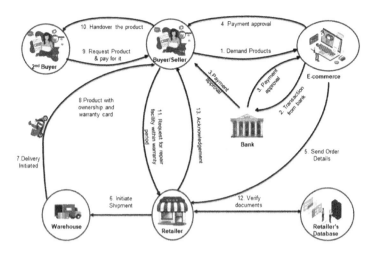

Fig. 1. Existing E-Commerce System

product requests, which get accepted after being cross-verified from the retailer's end. After verifying the status, the transaction is carried out using third-party services (e.g., ABC bank). After getting the payment approval from the bank, the intermediary website updates the customer with the shipping details. The customers have to verify themselves with the OTP (one Time Password) to receive the shipment. The shipment usually takes around a week, and then the product gets delivered to the customer along with the product ownership and warranty card. The warranty card includes all the retailer details, which can be used further to avail of the repair services within the warranty period.

2.1 Deficiencies of Existing System

- Lack of Trust and Transparency: Customer trust is a must for every e-commerce site, and customers prefer to get ownership of products at the time of the transaction, but they get this only after the shipment is made.
- Cyber Threats: In the current scenario, E-commerce Sites risk losing customers' data and millions in revenue due to cyber attacks.
- Cannot transfer Ownership on Resale: Current E-Commerce websites do not provide users with any features that can transfer ownership at resale. Due to this, customers buying used products cannot enjoy the remaining warranty services.
- Verification and Traceability: Customers adding sensitive information, such as bank details, passwords etc., during payment and verification can cause security issues as information is prone to hacker attacks. Moreover, on resale, it is hard to track how many times the item was purchased in the past.
- High Cost: Decreasing the role of intermediaries during transactions results in fewer processing fees, allowing retailers to achieve cost-effectiveness.

3   Proposed Scheme

The proposed framework comprises of *Original Buyer, E-Commerce, Bank, Retailer, Warehouse, New Buyer.* The *Original Buyer* becomes the seller for *New Buyer* using Re-commerce service of our framework.

Customer Registration: Prior to Buy/Search any product, customer calls Algorithm 1 to register himself.

Algorithm 1. CustReg: Customer Registration.

Require: Takes as input customer C's Name, email C_E, phone No C_p address C_A gender C_g of customer C.

Ensure: Customer Registered Successfully.

1: $E_{com} \xleftarrow{\ Input\ } [\xi]\ Cust : \xi = (Name, C_E, C_p, C_A, C_g)$
2: $Cust \xleftarrow{\ OTP\ } E_{com}$
3: $verify(OTP) \leftarrow E_{com}$
4: **if** $(verify(OTP) = 1)$ **then**
5:     Customer details verified
6: **else**
7:     Wrong OTP entered
8: **end if**
9: $E_{Com} \xleftarrow[\ Input\ ]{Cust\_Name,pswd} Cust$
10: **if** $(User_Name == Unique\ \&\&\ Criteria(Pswd) == 1)$ **then**
11:     Customer successfully registered
12: **else**
13:     password and username doesn't match the criteria
14: **end if**

Retailer Registration: Prior to upload the available products every retailer register himself under the hood of brand he sells, using Algorithm 2 in order to register himself.

Algorithm 2. RetailReg: Retailer's Registration.

Require: Takes as input company name C_N, email C_E, retailer's phone no and address R_P and R_A respectively.

Ensure: Retailer Registered Successfully.

1: $E_{com} \xleftarrow[\ Input\ ]{C_N,C_E,R_P,R_A,retailer\_id@company.com,Id} Retailer$
2: $Retailer \xleftarrow{\ OTP\ } E_{com}$
3: **if** $verify(OTP) == 1$ **then**
4:     **if** $(verify(Id) == 1)$ **then**
5:         Retailer verified

6:     **else**
7:          Not a valid retailer
8:     **end if**
9: **end if**
10: $E_{Com} \xleftarrow[Input]{password} Retailer$
11: **if** $(Criteria(Password) == 1)$ **then**
12:     Retailer successfully registered
13: **else**
14:     password doesn't match criteria
15: **end if**

Enter Product: To enter available product information along with its available quantity and its metadata on E-commerce website retailer calls Algorithm 3. Product's metadata, i.e., size, color, brand etc. is used by customer.

Algorithm 3. EntryProd: To Enter the product with its available quantity by Retailer

Require: Retailer's e-mail "retailer_id@company.com"
Ensure: product entered successfully.

1: $E_{com} \xleftarrow[Input]{retailer\_id@company.com, Pswd} Retailer$
2: **if** $(verify(retailer\_id@company.com, Pswd) == 0)$ **then**
3:     Not a valid retailer
4: **else**
5:     "Login Successful"
6:     $E_{Com} \xleftarrow[UploadItem]{productname, Metadata} Retailer$
7:     Product uploaded successfully.
8: **end if**

Order Product: Customer selects product name along with its metadata, i.e., size, color, brand etc. and calls Algorithm 4 to order product from E-commerce website.

Algorithm 4. OrdProd: For ordering the product.

Require: product name and its metadata.
Ensure: NFT minted for digital warranty and placed on blockchain successfully.

1: $E_{com} \xleftarrow[Search]{ProductName, Metadata} Customer$
2: **if** $(Available(Product) == 0)$ **then**
3:     Out of Stock
4: **else**
5:     Add to Cart
6: **end if**
7: $E_{Com} \xleftarrow[Input]{DelieveryAddress, Pin-Code} Customer$

8: **if** $(Delieverable(Product) == 0)$ **then**
9:     Service unavilable at this address
10: **else**
11:     Payment connect via metamask
12: **end if**
13: **if** $(Successfull(Payment) == 0)$ **then**
14:     Transaction failed.
15: **else**
16:     Order Placed successfully.
17:     NFT minted corresponding to digital warranty card and placed on blockchain
18: **end if**

Recommerce: In order to sell pre-owned product, customer avails the benefit of flea market services available with our application by using Algorithm 5. Let us assume that to sell his owned product Alice searches the product A_{Id} in order history of E-commerce website O_H then upload product's image and its current state A_{Im} and A_C. In addition, decide the price of A_{PP} and initially selects the flag bit $F_A = 1$ for negotiating on the price of A_{Id}.

Algorithm 5. ReCom: Customer add product for reselling on flea market.

Require: Resale product's Id A_{Id}, current state A_C, Image A_{Im} and price A_{PP}
Ensure: Product added for reselling on flea market successfully.

1: **if** $(Login(Cust\_Name, pswd) == 0)$ **then**
2:     Invalid credentials/ not a customer
3: **else**
4:     $O_H \xleftarrow{\substack{Product \\ Search}} Customer$
5:     $Flea_{market} \xleftarrow{\substack{A_{Id}, A_C, A_{Im}, A_{PP}, F_A \\ Add}} Alice$
6: **end if**

Pre-owned Purchase. To purchase pre-owned product, buyer employs flea-market services available with our proposed approach to negotiate with the owner of the product by using Algorithm 6. Let us assume that, Bob selects product pre-owned by Alice A_{Id} and set the price B_{PP} and initially set the negotiation flag bit $F_B = 1$.

Algorithm 6. ReBag: To purchase the pre-owned goods.

Require: Product name and its description
Ensure: Transaction Failed/ Transfer ownership & NFT

1: $Flea_{market} \xleftarrow{\substack{product, Metadata \\ Search}} Buyer$
2: **if** $Check(Transfer_{History}, Metadata) == 0$ **then**
3:     exit()

4: **else**$(P_{id}, P_B, F_B) \xleftarrow{Enter} Bob$
5: **end if**
6: **while** $\left(F_A = F_B = 1\right)$ **do**

7:    **if** $\left(P_A = P_B\right)$ **then**
8:       Payment/Metamask Connect
9:       **if** $Payment(Successfull) == 1$ **then**
10:          $Bob \xleftarrow[Transfer]{Ownership} Alice$
11:          $Bob \xleftarrow[Transfer]{NFT} Alice$
12:       **else**Transaction Failed
13:       **end if**
14:       $\left(P_B, F_B\right) \xleftarrow{update} Bob$
15:    **end if**
16: **end while**

Figure 2 depicts the working of our proposed framework.

4   Implementations

To implement the proposed system, we have designed a decentralized application using a JavaScript-based framework reactJs, high-level python framework Django and MySQL database. It consists of fundamental logic defined by a smart contract code based on the Polygon blockchain. This application provides an e-commerce interface to the user where they can buy their desired products, access their warranty card details, and even resale them using blockchain.

4.1   Technology Stack Used

This subsection discusses the technology stack employed for implementing blockchain based land transaction system.

1. Web3 Library: is a collection of libraries used to interact with decentralized networks like Ethereum. It helps in interacting with smart contracts, fetching user account details, and making transactions using metamask.
2. Django: is a free, open-sourced, backend side python web framework that follows the model-template-views (MTV) architecture pattern and encourages rapid development in a clean, pragmatic design.
3. MySQL: is an open-source relational DBMS ideal for both small and large applications. It enables users to conquer the database challenges of the next-generation web, cloud, and communications services with uncompromising scalability.
4. React: is an open-source JavaScript framework that is used for frontend-development. It provides fast and declarative techniques to design an interface with reusable components.
5. Axios: is a promise-based HTTP client library used in React to make requests for REST API created using the Django backend server.

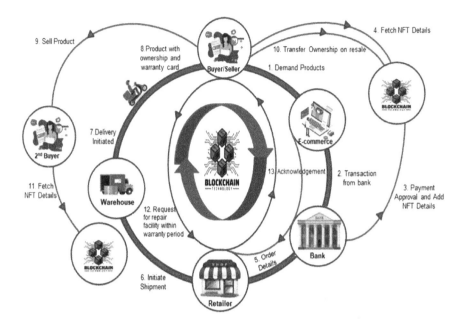

Fig. 2. Proposed Blockchain Based Land Registration System

6. Metamask: is a software that acts as a platform for cryptocurrency transactions and is currently used by thousands of users worldwide. It is available as both a web extension and a mobile app.
7. Polygon: is an online platform for hosting blockchain-based projects. Transaction fees are paid using MATIC token. Polygon uses a modified proof-of-stake consensus mechanism to operate the platform efficiently.

4.2   Designing Smart Contract

Smart Contracts are designed to execute tasks like minting the products, ownership transfer and verification, updating the warranty on redeeming the gift, and repair procedures flawlessly. The smart contract is made up of basic functionality using logic to meet all the requirements. Images/documents can't be stored on the Blockchain (we can, but it will cost a lot of Ether), so it is done through IPFS (Interplanetary file system), which in return gives us a hash that is stored on the Blockchain. To store warranty information, we use Blockchain and the MySQL database together, which are further mapped to a unique Id. Storing documents on the Blockchain is expensive, due to which it is stored on IPFS. The proposed model has three types of entities on the blockchain network: Retailer: the person who adds the products to the Interface; Interface: who acts as an intermediatory between the retailer and the Customer; and Customer: who purchases the product from the Interface. All the functionalities have been combined into a single contract. Table 1 explicitly states the Method its functionalities and role employed in smart contracts.

Table 1. Smart Contracts Methods & its description

Method	Function Used	Description
Transaction	safeMint()	Initialize NFT corresponding to digital warranty card.
Warranty Duration	warrantyProvider()	Returns warranty period of product corresponding to $token - id$.
Replacement	getTime()	Returns expiry date of product's warranty
	replacement()	qualifies the product for repair/replacement services and updates the replacement date of the product.
Transfer	transfer()	Transfers product ownership to new customer after validating product's warranty
Extend Warranty	applyExpiryDiscount()	Increases product warranty duration based on gift card

4.3 Integration

This contract was developed on Remix IDE (remix.ethereum.org) and deployed using Remix on Polygon. After successfully compiling the smart contract, an ABI(Application Binary Interface) and a contract address is generated, which is copied and used further. Then in the ReactJS code and the Django code, the contract is initialized using ABI and contract address. The smart contract is deployed to the Polygon test Network, and the whole project is tested on the local host. The front-end transaction page is designed in such a way that before any transaction is completed, a meta mask wallet popup will appear, requesting the User to mine the product with some gas fees that will give them a digital warranty card and place their product ownership details on blockchain. For viewing anything stored on the blockchain, no fee is required. Only while modifying, a gas fee is incurred. Each time any user changes the state of the blockchain, a gas fee in Matic has to be paid.

5 Experimental Evaluation and Results

5.1 Experimental Evaluation

The implementation of our blockchain-based e-commerce web application was successful and proved that a decentralized solution could be used to reduce the dependency on intermediatory in e-commerce. The proposed solution is more efficient and provides digitalization of documentation that we can access from anywhere across the globe. Every action involving writing new data involves a transaction on the blockchain and results in a small transaction cost known as the gas fee. For deploy the agreement contract, few ethers are required in metamask account. The agreement contract's deployment cost is 0.001487ETH. This transaction was recorded on the Ropsten testnet network.

5.2 Architecture of Proposed System

Our system is based on Blockchain, which is a decentralized system of peer-to-peer (P2P) networks as depicted in Fig. 3. It consists of 3 entities: retailer, customer, and e-commerce interface. The interface acts as an intermediatory between the retailer and the customer where the retailers add their products, and the customers purchase them based on their interests.

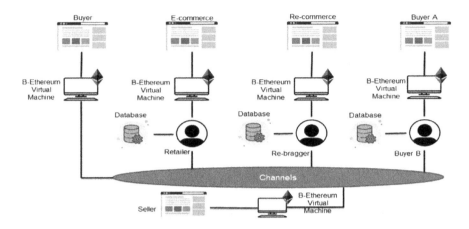

Fig. 3. Architecture of Proposed Framework

Table 2. Comparison of Existing & Proposed Technique, where -:Absence of feature,✓: presence of feature

Features	Existing	Proposed
Decentralization	-	✓
Payment for intermediary services	High	low
Security	Low	High
Transfer ownership	-	✓
Transparency	Low	High
Fault Tolerant	Low	High
Boost trade at the global level	low	high
Cost-effectiveness	Low	High
Digital Product warranty	-	✓
Authentic Reviews	Low	High
Re-commerce and Re-bag	-	✓
Product Transfer History	-	✓

5.3   Feature Analysis

This subsection discusses features of the proposed system. Table 2 compares the proposed scheme with the existing work.

1. Decentralization: Traditional e-commerce websites rely on a central database maintained by intermediaries, which can lead to inaccuracies. In contrast, blockchain utilizes a distributed ledger where transaction information quickly propagates across a network, ensuring data integrity. Each network member possesses a copy of the data, enabling cross-verification and rejection of any manipulated information through a majority vote.
2. Intermediary Cost: The bundles of high-quality photos, product videos related to any e-commerce website are typically created at a high cost to the store owner, but the ownership belongs to the e-commerce platform. E-commerce block-chain puts consumers in charge of the data assets and reduces the need for intermediaries. It

maximizes the value of the data for both the companies and the consumers. There is no need to pay the intermediaries.

3. Security: Nowadays, any data breach can cost millions in revenue to an e-commerce retailer and a lot more brand authority. The level of security blockchain offers cannot be afforded without it by retailers.

4. Transfer Ownership: The warranty card included with the E-commerce website purchase is only intended for the purchaser, the owner. However, on re-sale, there is no option to update the ownership in the retailer's database, but with blockchain, we can transfer ownership, and the new owner can also access the warranty services remaining from the day of his/her purchase.

5. Transparency: Blockchain driven ledger is indelible and unforgettable. Entries can only be made into the ledger if the system validates them. Moreover, every other node in the system would also need to be changed to change it. For this reason, it is impossible to remove a transaction to hide it, and fraudulent transactions cannot be added.

6. Fault tolerant: Blockchain technology is highly fault-tolerant. Its uptime relies not on a few server centers but on hundreds and thousands of nodes that offer processing input to run the system. When a few nodes are turned off, the network's overall efficiency remains unchallenged.

7. Boost trade at the global level: Blockchain in e-commerce enables retailers to bypass credit cards and their associated high processing fees, providing an opportunity to bridge the gap between countries and open up new possibilities for customers in regions with limited access to reliable banking and government systems

8. Cost-Effectiveness: After removing mediators and intermediaries from the payment process, blockchain eliminates transaction and processing fees, allowing retailers to achieve cost-effectiveness.

9. Digital Product Warranty: Consumers and retailers experience the frustration of losing paper receipts and being unable to prove warranty coverage. With blockchain, retailers can efficiently store warranty information and process it quickly. Every person can access the data, allowing warranty information to be easily accessed and validated.

10. Authentic Reviews: Our proposed system ensures that only people who purchased the product are eligible to add reviews contrary in existing system anyone can add reviews.

11. Re-commerce/Re-bag: Our application offers both e-commerce and re-commerce services, catering to the growing demand for affordable branded products. Customers who have purchased items through e-commerce can conveniently add them to the flea market from their profiles, indicating the current condition. Interested buyers can browse through the seller's purchase history and make purchases accordingly.

12. Product Transfer History: With blockchain smart contracts, we can keep track of all the past owners of the product with the timeline. Any buyer going through the flea market can access these details, and based on it, they can negotiate with the current owner and come to a conclusion.

6   Conclusion

This article presented a blockchain-driven e-commerce system for issuance of NFT-based warranty for customers, digitalization of documentation, and supports the feature of ownership transfer on resale. Furthermore, transparency has been improved and users are allowed to conveniently and securely buy/resell products through e-commerce platforms. In addition, users are allowed to negotiate on price and crosscheck transfer history details prior to purchase already used product from other users. Thus, blockchain driven e-commerce is best suited for practical application.

References

1. Shrestha, A.K., Joshi, S., Vassileva, J.: Customer data sharing platform: a blockchain-based shopping cart. In: 2020 IEEE International Conference on Blockchain and Cryptocurrency (ICBC), pp. 1–3. IEEE (2020)
2. Cristina, E.M.: Blockchain in Ecommerce. Risk Contemp. Econ. 254–260 (2021)
3. Wang, Z., Yang, L., Wang, Q., Liu, D., Xu, Z., Liu, S.: ArtChain: blockchain-enabled platform for art marketplace. In: 2019 IEEE International Conference on Blockchain (Blockchain), pp. 447–454. IEEE (2019)
4. Thaw, Y.Y., Mahmood, A.K., Dominic, P.: A study on the factors that influence the consumers trust on ecommerce adoption (2009). arXiv preprint arXiv:0909.1145
5. Xu, J., Li, Z., Wang, X., Xia, C.: Narrative information on secondhand products in e-commerce. Mark. Lett. **33**, 1–20 (2022)
6. Treiblmaier, H., Sillaber, C.: The impact of blockchain on e-commerce: a framework for salient research topics. Electr. Commer. Res. Appl. **48**, 101054 (2021)
7. Shen, B., Xu, X., Yuan, Q.: Selling secondhand products through an online platform with blockchain. Transp. Res. Part E Logistics Transp. Rev. **142**, 102066 (2020)
8. Ramachandiran, R.: Using blockchain technology to improve trust in eCommerce. https://www.ijitee.org/. Published By: Blue Eyes Intelligence Engineering and Sciences Publication. https://doi.org/10.35940/ijitee. Retrieval Number: 100.1/ijitee. J944108101021 J9441. 08101021
9. Shorman, S.M., Allaymounq, M., Hamid, O.: Developing the E-commerce model a consumer to consumer using blockchain network technique. Int. J. Manag. Inf. Technol. (IJMIT) **11** (2019)
10. Xuan, T.M., Alrashdan, M.T., Al-Maatouk, Q., Alrashdan, M.T.: Blockchain technology in E-commerce platform. Int. J. Manage. **11**(10), 1688–1697 (2020)
11. Pushpalatha, A., Senthil, G., Jawahar, P.M.M., Kartheesan, E.: A trustworthy decentralized Onkart ecommerce platform based on blockchain technology. In: 2022 6th International Conference on Trends in Electronics and Informatics (ICOEI), pp. 832–839. IEEE (2022)
12. Shakila, U.K., Sultana, S.: A decentralized marketplace application based on ethereum smart contract. In: 2021 24th International Conference on Computer and Information Technology (ICCIT), pp. 1–5. IEEE (2021)
13. Zhao, S., O'Mahony, D.: Applying blockchain layer2 technology to mass e-commerce (2020). Cryptology ePrint Archive

Using Machine Learning Models to Predict Corporate Credit Outlook

Rashmi Malhotra[1] [ID] and D. K. Malhotra[2]([✉]) [ID]

[1] Saint Joseph's University, Philadelphia, PA 19131, USA
rmalhotr@sju.edu
[2] Thomas Jefferson University, Philadelphia, PA 19144, USA
davinder.malhotra@Jefferson.edu

Abstract. This study explores the use of three algorithms, support vector machines (SVMs), Adaptive Boosting (AdaBoost), and Gradient Boosting models, to distinguish between companies with good and bad credit outlooks. The study uses seven financial variables to classify non-financial companies as good or bad credit outlook. SVMs have several advantages, including their ability to handle non-linearly separable data, their avoidance of overfitting, and their suitability for high-dimensional data. Adaboost and Gradient Boost also have several advantages, including the ability to combine multiple weak classifiers, its computational efficiency, and its ability to handle large datasets. Results suggest that all three models-SVMs, Adaboost, and Gradient Boosting--can effectively distinguish between companies with good and bad credit outlooks.

Keywords: Credit Outlook · Classification · Support Vector Machines · AdaBoost · Gradient Boosting

1 Introduction

Despite the development of numerous statistical and artificial intelligence-based models to predict financial distress and corporate insolvencies, business failures continue to occur. For example, the dot-com bubble burst in 2001, leading to an increase in loan defaults and bankruptcy filings by large companies. Similarly, the 2008–2009 economic crisis resulted in a number of major corporate bankruptcies. From 1989 to 1991, according to Altman, 34 companies with liabilities exceeding $1 billion filed for Chapter 11 bankruptcy. However, during the dot-com collapse of 2001, 102 companies with total liabilities of $580 billion filed for bankruptcy. During the Great Recession of 2008–2009, 74 companies filed for bankruptcy with an unprecedented total of over $1.2 trillion in liabilities. These bankruptcies demonstrate the need for further research and development to effectively predict financial distress and prevent corporate failures.

Early identification of failing companies is essential to prevent them from negatively impacting the entire financial system. By understanding the factors that lead to financial distress, stakeholders can take prompt remedial action to address the underlying issues and stop further decline. This preemptive approach can help to mitigate the effects of

© The Author(s), under exclusive license to Springer Nature Switzerland AG 2023
R. Morusupalli et al. (Eds.): MIWAI 2023, LNAI 14078, pp. 277–284, 2023.
https://doi.org/10.1007/978-3-031-36402-0_25

corporate failures on the overall economy and protect the financial system from potential disruptions. In order to encourage economic stability and fortitude, continuing research and advancement in the field of bankruptcy and financial trouble prediction remain crucial.

While several studies have demonstrated the benefits of neural networks for financial analysis, such as enhanced forecasting, fraud detection, credit evaluation, and securities trading, recent evidence suggests that backpropagation may not be the most suitable neural architecture for classification tasks. This study demonstrates the use of support vector machines (SVMs), Adaptive Boosting (AdaBoost), and Gradient Boosting models to distinguish between companies with a positive and negative credit outlook.

The study uses a dataset of 591 non-financial companies, each with seven financial variables. The support vector machines (SVMs), Adaptive Boosting (AdaBoost), and Gradient Boosting algorithms are trained on the dataset and then used to classify the companies into two groups: those with a positive credit outlook and those with a negative credit outlook. The results show that support vector machines (SVMs), Adaptive Boosting (AdaBoost), and Gradient Boosting models can classify the companies with high accuracy.

The study's findings suggest that support vector machines (SVMs), Adaptive Boosting (AdaBoost), and Gradient Boosting models can be useful tools for classification tasks in financial analysis. The study also provides evidence that machine learning strategies can be used to effectively distinguish between companies with a positive and negative credit outlook.

2   Literature Survey

Several studies have examined the role of machine learning techniques in loan evaluation and predicting credit risk. Malhotra, Malhotra, and Malhotra [7] explored the use of decision trees, AdaBoost, and support vector machines (SVMs) to identify potential bad loans. They showed that AdaBoost provides an improvement over simple decision trees as well as SVM models in predicting good credit clients and bad credit clients. Coates, Nydick, and Malhotra [3] demonstrated the use of tree-based algorithms, such as decision trees, random forests trees, boosted trees, and XGBoost, to reduce the risk of bad loans and to identify the characteristics that can help distinguish between a good loan and a bad loan so that loan officers can enhance their scoring models by giving those characteristics more weight when deciding whether or not to extend loans to borrowers. Hyeongjun, Cho, and Doojin [4] studied whether recurrent neural network (RNN) and long short-term memory (LSTM) algorithms capable of handling sequential data may improve corporate bankruptcy forecasting. In terms of bankruptcy prediction performance, the research discovered that the employment of RNN and LSTM approaches beats other classification techniques such as logistic regression, support vector machine, and random forest methods. Madaan, Kumar, Keshri, Jain, and Nagrath [5] compared and contrasted the Random Forest and Decision Trees credit risk prediction algorithms. When both algorithms were evaluated on the same dataset, Random Forest outperformed the Decision Tree approach with significantly greater accuracy. In another study, Bakpo and Kabari [1] utilize a combination of neural networks and decision trees to forecast credit risk.

Each set of consumers' categorization criteria is used to construct decision trees. The results revealed a decline in misclassification. Mais and Nemer [6] demonstrated how to analyze credit risk using an extreme learning machine (ELM). In simulation, ELM outperforms naive Bayes, decision tree, and MLP classifiers by 1.8248%, 16.6346%, and 5.8933%, respectively. Ching-Chin, Weng-U, Kwei-Long, and Shu-Yi [2] proposed a decision tree credit assessment technique (DTCAA) for addressing the credit assessment problem in a large data environment. The research demonstrated the efficacy and validity of DTCAA using a large data set from one of Taiwan's premier vehicle collateral lending organizations. The data demonstrated that DTCAA is competitive in a variety of contexts and across multiple criteria, demonstrating DTCAA's applicability to credit assessment methodologies. Thus, as illustrated by the above-mentioned studies, the use of machine learning models is a viable option to analyze the credit outlook of companies.

3 Models

3.1 Support Vector Machines (SVM) Model

SVM is a machine learning method that can be used for categorization as well as regression analysis. The primary aim of SVM is to identify a hyperplane in a high-dimensional space that best divides various classifications or sets of data points. The hyperplane is selected to optimize the margin between the two classes, which is described as the distance between the spots nearest to the hyperplane in each class. The data points nearest to the hyperplane and most pertinent to class division are referred to as support vectors.

SVM is particularly helpful when the data in the input space is not linearly separable, as it provides for non-linear changes of the data using kernel functions. Linear, quadratic, radial basis function (RBF), and sigmoid kernel functions are the most commonly used in SVM. SVM has several benefits over other machine learning algorithms, including the ability to manage high-dimensional data, non-linearly separable data using kernel functions, and avoiding overfitting by optimizing the gap between classes. SVM has been used effectively in a variety of areas, including picture classification, text categorization, and biology.

The machine learning method Support Vector Machine (SVM) has numerous benefits and uses. SVM is particularly helpful when there are many more features (i.e., dimensions) than samples in the collection. High-dimensional data can be handled by SVM successfully and quickly. By using kernel functions to transfer the data into a higher-dimensional space, SVM can manage non-linearly separable data. SVM can catch intricate patterns and non-linear relationships that linear models are unable to. Through maximization of the gap between the groups, SVM can prevent overfitting. The space between the judgment border and the nearest data values for each class is referred to as the margin. The model performs better in terms of applicability when the margin is maximized. Both categorization and regression issues can be solved using SVM. It has been used in a variety of industries, including biology, banking, text categorization, and picture classification. A distinct dividing line created by SVM can be used to decipher how decisions are made. The support vectors, which are the most important data elements for the categorization job, are also identified by SVM. Last but not least, SVM is a well-known machine learning method that has undergone significant research and optimization over time. SVM is implemented in a variety of software programs, making it simple to use and employ in a number of different areas.

3.2 AdaBoost (Adaptive Boosting) Model

Adaboost is a machine learning method that is used to solve categorization and regression issues. It is a sort of ensemble learning technique in which numerous weak classifiers (or models) are combined to form a powerful classifier. Yoav Freund and Robert Schapire suggested AdaBoost in 1996. AdaBoost works by repeatedly training a series of weak classifiers on the training data, with each consecutive classifier concentrating on the examples misclassified by the preceding classifier. The method gives a weight to each training sample during each run, which determines its significance for the next classification. Examples misclassified by the prior classification are given more weight, while examples properly classified are given less weight. The ultimate classifier is a weighted total of the weak classifiers, with the weights decided by the categorization success of the weak classifiers. The ultimate classification gives each poor predictor a weight, with more weight assigned to the more precise classifiers. AdaBoost's efficiency can be increased by merging multiple poor models. AdaBoost is a highly effective machine learning algorithm that can be applied to various tasks such as regression, binary, and multi-class categorization. It has a high degree of dimensionality and is less likely to suffer from overfitting compared to separate classifications. AdaBoost is also straight-forward to apply and is widely available in different machine learning frameworks and programs. It is commonly used in applications such as text classification, object identification, and facial tracking, among others. One alternative method for categorization tasks is Support Vector Machines (SVM). While both AdaBoost and SVM aim to improve categorization accuracy, they differ in their approach. SVM is a singular classifier that seeks to find the optimal dividing hyperplane between two classes, while AdaBoost is an ensemble learning method that uses multiple weak classifiers to create a powerful classifier. SVM focuses on maximizing the gap between two groups, while AdaBoost aims to accurately categorize all training instances. AdaBoost can be affected by noise data and anomalies, whereas SVM attempts to identify the optimal dividing hyperplane that generalizes well to unknown data, making it more robust to chaotic data. While AdaBoost is simple to use and train, SVM is more complex and requires more training time and computing power. The choice between AdaBoost and SVM ultimately depends on the specific task at hand, as each algorithm has its strengths and weaknesses.

3.3 Gradient Boosting Model

Gradient Boosting is a very effective machine learning approach that may be used for both regression and classification applications. It is a form of ensemble learning approach in which numerous weak models are combined into a single strong model. The Gradient Boosting model may be used to categorize good and negative credit outlook for organizations by analyzing a variety of criteria such as liquidity ratio, capital productivity, return on asset, interest coverage ratio, cash generation ratio, and capital adequacy to produce predictions about a company's creditworthiness. The Gradient Boosting model requires a set of labeled training data, with each sample in the dataset bearing a label indicating whether it has a positive or negative credit outlook. The method constructs a succession of decision trees, each of which attempts to accurately categorize the samples. The model modifies the weights of the misclassified instances in each iteration to enhance the performance of the following tree. The model continually improves its ability to categorize the data by repeatedly adding additional decision trees and modifying their weights. Gradient Boosting has the benefit of being very configurable and can be adjusted to individual data and use scenarios. To enhance the model's performance, you may change the number of trees in the model, the learning rate, the depth of each tree, and other factors. Gradient Boosting can also handle missing data and outliers effectively, making it an excellent option for credit scoring applications.

4 Data and Variables

The aim of this research is to analyze manufacturing companies categorized ac-cording to the GIC classification. The study evaluates seven variables, namely, liquidity ratio, capital productivity, return on asset, interest coverage ratio, cash generation ratio, and capital adequacy, to assess the credit outlook of these companies. When assessing a company's creditworthiness, using several financial metrics can provide a comprehensive analysis of its financial health. This paper examines seven vital metrics, namely liquidity ratio, capital productivity, return on assets, interest coverage ratio, cash generation ratio, and capital adequacy. Liquidity ratio measures a company's ability to pay its short-term obligations. A high liquidity ratio indicates that a company has enough cash to meet its short-term obligations, while a low liquidity ratio indicates that a company may have difficulty meeting its short-term obligations. This is important because if a company is unable to pay its short-term obligations, it may be forced to file for bankruptcy. Capital productivity measures how efficiently a company uses its capital. A high capital productivity ratio indicates that a company is using its capital efficiently, while a low capital productivity ratio indicates that a company is not using its capital efficiently. This is important because if a company is not using its capital efficiently, it may not be able to generate enough profit to repay its debts. Return on assets measures how profitable a company is for its shareholders. A high return on assets ratio indicates that a company is generating a lot of profit for its shareholders, while a low return on assets ratio indicates that a company is not generating a lot of profit for its shareholders. This is important be-cause if a company is not profitable, it may not be able to repay its debts. Interest coverage ratio measures a company's ability to pay its interest expenses. A high interest coverage ratio indicates that a company has enough income to cover its interest expenses, while a low interest coverage ratio indicates that a company may have difficulty covering its interest expenses. This is important because if a company is unable to pay its interest expenses, it may be forced to file for bankruptcy. Cash generation ratio measures a company's ability to generate cash from its operations. A high cash generation ratio indicates that a company is generating a large amount of cash from its operations, while a low cash generation ratio indicates that a company is not generating a lot of cash from its operations. This is important because if a company is not generating enough cash from its operations, it may not be able to repay its debts. Capital adequacy measures a company's ability to absorb unexpected losses. A high capital adequacy ratio indicates that a company has enough capital to absorb unexpected losses, while a low capital adequacy ratio indicates that a company may not have enough capital to absorb unexpected losses. If a company faces unforeseen losses, it may become unable to repay its debts. Excess cash flow is significant in predicting bankruptcy as it provides an indication of a company's ability to pay its debts and sustain its operations in the long run.

Companies with high levels of excess cash flow are less likely to file for bankrupt-cy since they have sufficient resources to meet their obligations, whereas those with low levels of excess cash flow are at higher risk of insolvency and may struggle to meet their debt payments. Therefore, excess cash flow is an important factor to con-sider when evaluating a company's creditworthiness and predicting its likelihood of bankruptcy. Table 1 provides summary statistics of the data used in this study.

Table 1. Summary statistics of the variables used in this study to differentiate between credit outlook of companies.

Variables	Mean	Standard Deviation
Capital Adequacy Ratio (%)	68.39	76.60
Current Liquidity	2.69	2.28
Capital Productivity	0.95	0.82
Return on Assets (%)	4.13	15.47
Int. Coverage Ratio	63.66	171.26
Cash Gen Rate (%)	31.78	70.21
Excess Cash Flow (%)	8.97	68.60

5 Empirical Results

Table 2 summarizes the results of Support Vector Machine, AdaBoost, and Gradient Boosting models to classify companies that have a bad credit outlook and good credit outlook.

Table 2. Classification of companies as good credit and bad credit outlook using Support Vector Machine, AdaBoost, and Gradient Boosting models.

Classification	Training Accuracy	Testing Accuracy
SVM Model	99.55%	85.14%
AdaBoost Model	100%	91.22%
Gradient Boosting Model	100%	93.9%

The average training accuracy of support vector machine models in differentiating between good credit and bad credit outlook companies was 99.5%. When we used the holdout sample to test the predictive ability of support vector machine, the average testing accuracy was at 85.14% in differentiating between good and bad credit outlook companies. The AdaBoost model trained extremely well with an average accuracy of 100% in differentiating between good and bad credit outlook manufacturing companies. On the holdout sample, the average predictive ability was higher at 91.22%. The Gradient Boosting algorithm performed better than SVM and AdaBoost models in the hold out sample with a predictive accuracy of 93.9%.

In this research study, we applied three different machine learning models to evaluate the credit outlook of companies classified as manufacturing companies. To ensure the reliability of our models, we employed k-fold cross-validation sampling procedure. This technique involves dividing the data set into k groups of equal size and using one group for validation while training the model on the remaining k − 1 groups. By using this method, we were able to estimate the accuracy of our models on unseen data. We chose the value of 10 for 'k' to balance the trade-off between bias and variance. Increasing the value of k helps reduce the bias by reducing the size difference between the training set and the resampling subsets. Our first model was a support vector machine (SVM), which we ran with different regularization values to avoid overfitting and underfitting. The objective of regularization is to balance the margin maximization to ensure that the algorithm works for nonlinearly separable datasets and is less sensitive to outliers. The C parameter is a penalty parameter that represents misclassification or error term. We used a linear kernel SVM model with a regularization factor value of 5 units for our initial experiment. Further, we used the default value of gamma (1/total number of features − 1/6) to specify the sphere of influence of each training point. Table 3 shows the results of our SVM, AdaBoost, and Gradient Boost models and the proportion of correctly classified companies into good and bad credit outlook categories using 10-fold cross-validation. Table 3 summarizes the results of three models using scalar transformed data, k-fold Cross Validation, k = 10.

Table 3. Models using scalar transformed data, k-fold Cross Validation, k = 10.

Classification	Testing Accuracy
SVM Model	84.9%
AdaBoost Model	82.9%
Gradient Boosting Model	82.2%

6 Summary and Conclusions

In conclusion, this study investigated the effectiveness of three algorithms, namely support vector machines (SVMs), Adaptive Boosting (AdaBoost), and Gradient Boosting models, for identifying companies with good or bad credit outlooks based on seven financial variables. Our findings indicate that all three models-SVMs, Adaboost, and Gradient Boosting--are effective in distinguishing between companies with different credit outlooks. Each algorithm has its own advantages, such as SVMs' capability to handle non-linear data and Adaboost and Gradient Boosting's ability to combine weak classifiers and handle large datasets. These findings suggest that these algorithms hold great potential for credit risk assessment in non-financial companies.

References

1. Bakpo, F., Kabari, L.: Credit risk evaluation system: an artificial neural network approach. Niger. J. Technol. **28**(1), 95–104 (2009)
2. Chern, C.-C., Lei, W.-U., Huang, K.-L., Chen, S.-Y.: A decision tree classifier for credit assessment problems in big data environments. IseB **19**(1), 363–386 (2021). https://doi.org/10.1007/s10257-021-00511-w
3. Malhotra, D.K., Nydick, R., Coates, N.: Using tree-based models to predict credit risk. Int. J. Bus. Intell. Syst. Eng. **1**(1), 1 (2022). https://doi.org/10.1504/IJBISE.2022.10054394
4. Kim, H., Cho, H., Ryu, D.: Corporate bankruptcy prediction using machine learning methodologies with a focus on sequential data. Comput. Econ. **59**(3), 1231–1249 (2021). https://doi.org/10.1007/s10614-021-10126-5
5. Madaan, M., Kumar, A., Keshri, C., Jain, R., Nagrath, P.: Loan default prediction using decision trees and random forest: A comparative study. IOP Conf. Ser.: Mater. Sci. Eng. **1022**, 012042 (2021)
6. Mais, H.Q., Nemer, L.: Extreme learning machine for credit risk analysis. J. Intell. Syst. **29**(1), 640–652 (2020). https://doi.org/10.1515/jisys-2018-0058
7. Malhotra, D.K., Malhotra, K., Malhotra, R.: Evaluating consumer loans using machine learning techniques. In: Lawrence, K.D., Pai, D.R. (eds.) Applications of Management Science, pp. 59–69. Emerald Publishing Limited (2020). https://doi.org/10.1108/S0276-897620200000020004

Visualization Recommendation for Incremental Data Based on Intent

Harinath Kuruva, K. Swarupa Rani[✉][iD], and Salman Abdul Moiz[✉][iD]

University of Hyderabad, Hyderabad, Telangana, India
{21mcpc07,swarupacs,salman}@uohyd.ac.in

Abstract. Data Visualization is a pictorial representation that transforms data into visual elements. Visualizations are generally recommended for a dataset based on the user's requirement. Visualization Recommendation is done generally with the help of experts in their domain field which is time consuming and very expensive. Recommendation can also be done based on statistical features extracted from the dataset and applying the machine learning model. There are existing works of Visualization Recommendation based on intent from the user. In this approach visualization is categorized into visualization type and visualized columns. Visualization type (e.g., Pie, Bar, and Line charts) is predicted using the BiDA model, Visualized columns are identified by leveraging the pretrained model BERT. The incremental data could correspond to big data where volume and velocity of data is added which is a challenging task to handle in visualization recommendation. To overcome this challenge we proposed Incremental Visualization Recommendation (IVR) where the recommendation algorithm is not used from scratch (updated data) rather, we use the recommendation algorithm only for the incremental segment of the data. Our experiments on benchmark datasets consume less time and show good results.

Keywords: Visualization recommendation · Incremental data · Intent · Horizontal increments · Vertical increments

1 Introduction

There is a beautiful saying, "A picture is worth a thousand words," which gives the essence of the importance of visualization. Humans can visualize the world, so processing data in a visual context is easier. Data Visualization is a pictorial representation that transforms data into visual elements. Nowadays, users are required to analyze the data with the help of visualization. Visualization can be a powerful tool for communication, analysis, and decision-making. Visualization has many real-world applications in various fields like Business and Finance, Healthcare, Sports, Education, Science and Engineering. In Business and Finance, it can analyze financial data, such as stock prices, sales figures, and customer behavior, to identify trends and make better business decisions. Maps and graphs are frequently used to better understand concepts rather than

R. Morusupalli et al. (Eds.): MIWAI 2023, LNAI 14078, pp. 285–296, 2023.
https://doi.org/10.1007/978-3-031-36402-0_26

having long textual paragraphs. On the one hand, the usage of maps and charts in daily life is increasing, an example of visualization. On the other hand data has been growing rapidly over the internet and there is a need to represent and provide insights to the data by applying visualization techniques. Therefore, data visualization is vital in giving a brief insight into the information.

A visualization is recommended to users by satisfying their requirements for a particular dataset. There have been many approaches like rule-based, machine learning approaches, and knowledge graph embedding approaches for recommending the visualization for the dataset. These approaches recommend visualization based on the rules, training a machine learning model by extracting features of data and by constructing a knowledge graph from the data respectively. As per our study there was an approach of Maruta et al. [1] works related to the visualization recommendation based on intent from the user. Intent is an English sentence that says about the requirement of the user. Using the intent for visualization recommendation makes the task easy to analyze and to provide accurate results desired by the user.

High dimensional data visualization techniques are used to display data in more than three dimensions. The challenge in high-dimensional data visualization is the curse of dimensionality. As the number of dimensions in a dataset increases, the amount of data required to adequately cover the visual space grows exponentially. It isn't easy to draw meaningful insights from the data. To address this challenge, the intent based incremental approach is proposed in this paper.

Incremental visualization is a technique used in data visualization where data is updated dynamically in real-time. With the context of volume and velocity of big data which is being added to the existing data, it has been very difficult to provide visualization recommendation for incremental data. In this paper we proposed an **I**ncremental **V**isualization **R**ecommendation (IVR) which can handle challenges posed by volume and velocity. Our approach handles incremental data exclusively and recommends visualization for the entire data along with incremental data without performing from scratch. Therefore, our proposed methodology takes less time.

The key contributions of the paper are stated below:

– Developed and proposed IVR algorithm.
  • Let p be our proposed algorithm, z is visualization recommendation, x be the existing data, hy is horizontal increment and vy is vertical increment.
    If $p(x) \rightarrow z$ and $p(hy) \rightarrow z$ then we can say $p(x + (hy)) \rightarrow z$
    If $p(x) \rightarrow z$ and $p(vy) \rightarrow z$ then we can say $p(x + (vy)) \rightarrow z$
  • Handling Visualization Recommendation for horizontal and vertical increments of data.

2   Related Work

Visualization recommendation approaches can be divided into rule based, machine learning and knowledge graph approaches. Rule based visualization recommendation approaches will be constructing the rules depending on the type of the data in the dataset and with the help of expert's intervention. Some of the rule based approaches include APT [2], Show Me [3] SAGE [4] and Voyager2 [5]. The disadvantage is that constructing the rules requires a lot of human effort. Machine learning-based approaches will extract the features from the dataset, and those extracted features are given to ML models for predicting the visualization of a particular dataset. Qian et al. [6] and Hu et al. [7] are some machine learning based approaches. These approaches use neural networks, a black box where we cannot know why the particular visualization is recommended. Knowledge graph based approaches such as KG4Vis [8] will construct the knowledge graph from the visualization corpus and use the graph to recommend the visualization. Constructing the knowledge graph is the main hindrance in this approach, mainly dependent on a large corpus of the data. Several other approaches are related to the visualization recommendation in different contexts, which are discussed below.

Lee et al. [9] approach extracts information from the data frames and recommends the visualization. Epperson et al. [10] recommend the visualization based on a user's data analysis history. Ojo et al. [11] recommend personalized visualization by constructing Graph Neural Network from a large corpus of data. Harris et al. [12] recommend visualization by utilizing relevant insights in the data. Gao et al. [13] obtained all possible visualizations and constructed a graph by modeling the relations between all visualizations, finally recommending the high score visualization. Kelleher et al. [14] provided the visualization recommendation for scientific datasets in the context of big data. The above discussed approaches deal with different datasets for visualization recommendation. But there exists an approach Maruta et al. [1] based on two input parameters such as dataset and intent for visualization recommendation. Intent refers to information that the user actually desires to visualize from the dataset.

Apart from visualization recommendation approaches discussed earlier there is a demand for incremental visualization methods to solve the problem of visualization recommendation for incremental data. Incremental visualization [15] is a technique used in data visualization where data is updated dynamically in real-time. There is no efficient strategy in the literature to address incremental visualization recommendation. In this paper we proposed a methodology to solve this problem without rendering entire data from scratch for every time stamp which can save significant processing time and improves the user experience. We modified and extended the works of Maruta et al. [1] which recommends the visualization based on two input parameters: the intent and dataset for incremental data.

Dimensional stacking is a visualization technique that allows for the simultaneous display of multiple dimensions or categories of data within a single plot. It involves stacking multiple two-dimensional plots on top of each other, with each plot representing a different category or dimension of the data. In the literature, there are several multidimensional visualization techniques, out of which dimensional stacking is one technique useful for visualizing multiple dimensions of data. There will be no clarity in this technique as all dimensions are plotted. Hence, we adopted some visualization techniques in this paper to visualize bivariate and univariate types.

3   Incremental Visualization Recommendation (IVR)

3.1   Introduction

In this section, our proposed approach will be discussed to handle the real-time incremental data generated in the real world. Nowadays, data is growing tremendously in an incremental fashion. The data can be added in terms of volume in big data in a dynamic environment horizontally (instances are added) or/and vertically (new dimensions are added). Providing the visualization recommendation in this situation was challenging, and the problem still needed to be addressed. There are many approaches for recommending the visualization of entire data (existing and incremental data) but they are time consuming and very expensive because considering the entire data from scratch and repeating the process. To address this issue, our approach recommends the visualization for the chunks (blocks) of data by executing the recommendation algorithm exclusively on incremental data. Finally, it provides visualization for the entire data (existing and incremental data).

Intent Aware Visualization Recommendation (IAVR) algorithm [1] is applied to existing data and intent, generating visualization type and visualized columns. Over the period, the same algorithm [1] is applied exclusively on incremental data along with intent, which provides visualization type and visualized columns for incremental data. The obtained visualization types and visualized columns for existing and incremental data are compared. The visualization type is based on intent generation. When the columns in the data evolve over time and the changes reflect on the value of the intent, visualization type may vary. In general, visualization type may or may not vary. In this paper, we addressed only when both the results (visualization type and visualized columns) are the same for existing and incremental data. Then our method recommends the visualization of the entire data (existing and incremental data) without carrying the experiments from scratch and it is very less time consuming. If the results are not the same, either of the results obtained for existing and incremental data are recommended for the entire data. If the visualization type is bivariate, plot a bivariate visualization for the top two set of visualized columns. If the visualization type is not bivariate, plot a univariate visualization for the top single visualized column. Figure 1 summarizes our proposed strategy.

3.2   Workflow Description

Data Preprocessing: The benchmark datasets are to be preprocessed where the missing values are replaced by the median of the remaining values when the values are numeric, in another case when the data value is a string, it will be replaced with the repeated string. In addition, the null values and the duplicate instances in the dataset are also removed. The preprocessed dataset is converted into the JSON format for further processing.

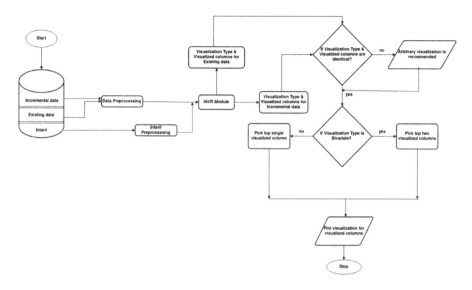

Fig. 1. Workflow of IVR

Intent: User requests are formally placed in simple sentence as one of the input parameters and it is helpful to visualize the data for a given dataset. For example, **"Region wise insurance analysis"** sentence is used as intent to obtain analysis region wise for the dataset of Prediction of Insurance Charges. Maruto et al. [1] have taken the intent from the captions of the visualization corpus which was crawled from the Tableau public web. In our approach, we analyzed the dataset and generated the suitable intents for different datasets (Prediction of Insurance Charges, AQI - Air Quality Index, California House Price).

Intent Preprocessing: The intent is also preprocessed by removing the stop words. The words in the intent are also mapped with synonyms which could give more accurate results. These intents are added to the JSON format of data preprocessing.

Incremental Dataset: There could be two possible increments for the dataset. The increments could be instances added to the existing data which we termed as horizontal increments and adding dimensions to the existing data which we termed as vertical increments. Here we considered all possible horizontal increments and vertical increments 10%, 20% till 50% of the data size. Further, the preprocessing of incremental data is also done.

IAVR Module: Maruta et al. [1] have proposed a visualization recommendation approach where the intent and dataset are taken as input and outputs the visualization type (Bar chart, Line chart, Pie chart, etc.,), visualized columns (based on the computation of the percentage of each column in the dataset to be visualized). They used BiDA [16] and BERT [17] models to predict the visualization type and visualized columns. Visualization type is predicted by providing both the intent embedding and the column embedding in the dataset to the BiDA model. The output of the BiDA model is given to the multilayer perceptron and the softmax function is used to predict the visualization type finally. The intent and dataset headers are given to the pre-trained BERT model for extracting the visualized columns. The output of the BERT model is combined with statistical features of the dataset's attributes to obtain the probability of each column that could be visualized.

Algorithm 1. Incremental Visualization Recommendation (IVR)

Require: Dataset (D), Intent (I)
Ensure: Visualization (V)
 1: Preprocess D & I
 2: $EV \leftarrow IAVR(D, I)$
 3: **if** hy $= 1$ and vy $= 0$ **then**
 4:     $IV \leftarrow IAVR(hy, I)$
 5: **else if** vy $= 1$ and hy $= 0$ **then**
 6:     $IV \leftarrow IAVR(vy, I)$
 7: **else if** vy $= 1$ and hy $= 1$ **then**
 8:     $IV \leftarrow IAVR(hy + vy, I)$
 9: **end if**
10: **if** EV $=$ IV **then**
11:     **if** VT $= 1$ **then**
12:         $VC \leftarrow (VC0, VC1)$
13:     **else**
14:         $VC \leftarrow (VC0)$
15:         $V \leftarrow plot(VT, VC)$
16:     **end if**
17: **end if**
18: **return** V

3.3   Algorithm Description

The dataset and Intent are taken as input. Preprocessing of the dataset and Intent is done which was discussed earlier in Sect. 3.1. Incremental data is added horizontally (hy) and vertically (vy) to the dataset. hy and vy can take the value either 0 or 1 where 1 indicates increments and 0 indicates no increments. IAVR is an Intent Aware Visualization Recommendation algorithm [1] which will give visualization (visualization type and visualized columns) as output. IAVR is applied for existing data (D) and Intent (I) which will provide a visualization recommendation and it is termed Existing Visualization (EV). When the data evolves in a data stream, IAVR [1] is applied to the chunks of incremental data without considering the data from scratch. Ultimately, we will get a visualization recommendation exclusively for incremental data and termed as Incremental Visualization (IV). Now EV and IV recommendations are compared if both are the same, then visualization type (VT) is checked. VT can take the value either 0 or 1 where 1 indicates bivariate and 0 indicates univariate. If the visualization type is bivariate, the top two visualized columns (VC0 & VC1) are chosen otherwise, the top single visualized column is chosen (VC0) and treated as univariate. Finally, visualization is plotted for the visualized columns (VC) based on visualization type (VT).

3.4 Comparison Between Traditional and Proposed Approach

There are several approaches that deal with different datasets for visualization recommendation. But there exists an approach Maruta et al. [1] which is based on two input parameters, such as dataset and intent for visualization recommendation. Intent refers to information that the user desires to visualize from the dataset. Apart from visualization recommendation approaches, there is a demand for incremental visualization methods to solve the problem of visualization recommendation for incremental data (Table 1).

Table 1. Comparison of traditional approach with our proposed approach

Traditional Maruta et al. (2021) [1]	Proposed Approach IVR
Can't handle incremental data	Handles incremental data
Used synthetic dataset	Used benchmark datasets
Can't handle volume and velocity in the context of big data	Large volume and streaming of data is addressed
Time consuming	Relatively less time consuming

3.5 Illustrations

Consider, for instance, one input parameter is a student dataset that has 9 dimensions (Roll No, Name, Internal1, Internal2, Internal3, Internal (Best), External, Total and Grade) and 11 instances (existing) initially and incrementally added 7 instances (incremental) over a period of time. Another input parameter is the Intent value **"Result Analysis"**. The results obtained for existing and incremental data (horizontal and vertical increments) are shown in Fig. 2 where the Visualization Type: Pie Chart (Univariate) and Visualized Column: Grade. We observed that the results of the existing and incremental (horizontal and vertical increments) are the same. Hence, the same results of VC and VT are mapped to the entire data without rendering from scratch.

Figure 2f shows the results of the visualization recommendation entire data from the student dataset with different values of Intent **"Student Roll No and performance on Total Marks"** and the results obtained are Visualization Type: Line Chart (Bivariate) and Visualized Columns: Roll No and Total.

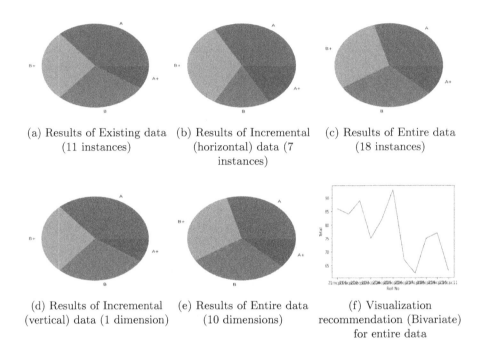

(a) Results of Existing data (11 instances)

(b) Results of Incremental (horizontal) data (7 instances)

(c) Results of Entire data (18 instances)

(d) Results of Incremental (vertical) data (1 dimension)

(e) Results of Entire data (10 dimensions)

(f) Visualization recommendation (Bivariate) for entire data

Fig. 2. Visualization recommendation of proposed approach

4   Discussions and Experimental Results

Experiments were performed for three standard benchmark datasets of the Kaggle database, i.e., Prediction of Insurance Charges, AQI - Air Quality Index, and California House Price. All these datasets have different data sizes and dimensions. We generated intents from each dataset to perform experiments, and the details are provided. The dataset is divided into two parts: (90:10, 80:20, 70:30, 60:40, 50:50). The first part is considered as existing data and the remaining part is considered incremental data (it can be horizontal and vertical increments). A pre-trained GloVe model [18] is used for word embedding for the intent values. This model was trained using the Wikipedia 2014 dump and Gigaword 5 corpus. For predicting the visualization type BiDA model is used with six layers in the multilayer perceptron [1]. A pre-trained BERT model is used to identify visualized columns with two layers in the multilayer perceptron [1].

4.1   Experimental Results

The IAVR [1] algorithm is applied to the first part treating existing data and obtaining the desired results. The same algorithm is applied to the second part treating as incremental data. Comparing the visualization results (VT and VC) and recommending the visualization for the entire data (existing and incremental data). Hence, IAVR [1] is applied for every timestamp for incremental data and recommends visualization for the entire data (existing and incremental data). Table 2 shows the results obtained with our proposed approach.

Table 2. Experimentation of our proposed approach with benchmark datasets for horizontal and vertical increments

Dataset	Intent	Incremental data (Horizontal and Vertical)	Visualization recommendation for existing data	Visualization recommendation for incremental data
Prediction of Insurance Charges **Size:** 1337 × 5	Region wise insurance analysis	10%, 20%, 30%, 40% and 50% of data size and number of dimensions respectively.	Pie Chart for region column	Pie Chart for region column
	Impact of insurance charges on having children		Bar Chart between having children and insurance charges	Bar Chart between having children and insurance charges
AQI - Air Quality Index **Size:** 10127 × 4	Air Quality Index value according to country	10%, 20%, 30%, 40% and 50% of data size and number of dimensions respectively.	Line Chart between AQI value and country	Line Chart between AQI value and country
	Examination of population close to ocean		Bar Chart between ocean proximity and population	Bar Chart between ocean proximity and population
California House Price **Size:** 20640 × 10	House value effect on number of bedrooms	10%, 20%, 30%, 40% and 50% of data size and number of dimensions respectively.	Bar Chart between median house value and total bedrooms	Bar Chart between median house value and total bedrooms
	Examination of population close to ocean		Bar Chart between ocean proximity and population	Bar Chart between ocean proximity and population

Table 2 results show that the visualization recommendation results for the existing and incremental data (horizontal and vertical) are the same. Hence the same visualization recommendation is mapped for the entire data (existing and incremental data).

The different visualization type is obtained by varying the intent value. For the intent value **"House value across the region"** and dataset **"Prediction of Insurance Charges"**, the obtained results are Visualization Type: Multi-Polygon chart. Similarly, we can obtain different visualization types by varying intent values accordingly.

4.2   Analysis of the Results

Experimentation was done on the benchmark Air Quality Dataset by considering the range from 2000 instances to 10000 instances in an incremental fashion. Our proposed (incremental) approach has taken considerably less time than the traditional approach depicted in Fig. 3.

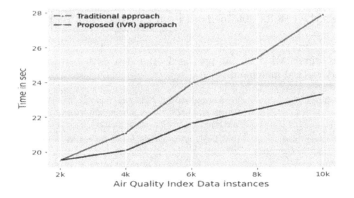

Fig. 3. Traditional approach vs Proposed IVR approach

In our experimentation, we have considered two cases to analyze the results. When the instances are added to the existing data, those are considered as horizontal increments, which we categorized as Case 1 and dimensions are added to the existing data, those are considered vertical increments, which we categorized as Case 2.

Case 1:
When horizontal increments are added to the data, the visualization recommendation by our approach is the same for the existing and incremental data.
Case 2:
There are two phases in vertical increments. (1) Incremental columns may not be part of the intent value and is addressed in this paper. (2) Sometimes, intent value can also be part with respective to the incremental columns.

We observed that incrementally evolved columns over a period of time, which are not part of the intent, then the resultant visualization recommendation is the same for existing and incremental data. There can be some cases where the visualization recommendations differ when the intent is part of the incremental updated columns. In such cases, the arbitrary visualization recommendation is suggested. The details of this work are in progress but beyond the scope of this paper.

5   Conclusions and Future Work

This article demonstrated an intent based visualization recommendation for the incremental data. We have experimented our approach with the benchmark datasets, and it is observed that the visualization recommended for the existing data and incremental data is the same. After thorough experimentation with several benchmark datasets, we concluded that the visualization recommended for the entire data (existing and incremental data) is the same. Therefore our approach saves a lot of time as there is no need to run the entire data from scratch every time to recommend the visualization. Our future work includes how the proposed approach will work with vertical increments of the data where the added dimension names are part of the intent. In such cases, the visualization recommendation differs for the existing and incremental data. Instead of recommending arbitrary visualization, there is a possibility to check for the distribution of the data in the visualization or do feature engineering and build rules to recommend the visualization.

References

1. Maruta, A., Kato, M.P.: Intent-aware visualization recommendation for tabular data. In: Zhang, W., Zou, L., Maamar, Z., Chen, L. (eds.) WISE 2021. LNCS, vol. 13081, pp. 252–266. Springer, Cham (2021). https://doi.org/10.1007/978-3-030-91560-5_18
2. Mackinlay, J.: Automating the design of graphical presentations of relational information. ACM Trans. Graph. **5**, 110–141 (1986). https://doi.org/10.1145/22949.22950
3. Mackinlay, J., Hanrahan, P., Stolte, C.: Show Me: Automatic Presentation for Visual Analysis. IEEE Trans. Vis. Comput. Graph. **13**, 1137–1144 (2007). https://doi.org/10.1109/TVCG.2007.70594
4. Roth, S.F., Kolojejchick, J., Mattis, J., Goldstein, J.: Interactive graphic design using automatic presentation knowledge. In: Proceedings of the SIGCHI Conference on Human Factors in Computing Systems, pp. 112–117. Association for Computing Machinery, New York (1994). https://doi.org/10.1145/191666.191719
5. Wongsuphasawat, K., et al.: Voyager 2: augmenting visual analysis with partial view specifications. In: Proceedings of the 2017 CHI Conference on Human Factors in Computing Systems, pp. 2648–2659. Association for Computing Machinery, New York (2017). https://doi.org/10.1145/3025453.3025768
6. Qian, X., et al.: ML-based Visualization Recommendation: learning to recommend visualizations from data (2020). http://arxiv.org/abs/2009.12316, https://doi.org/10.48550/arXiv.2009.12316
7. Hu, K., Bakker, M.A., Li, S., Kraska, T., Hidalgo, C.: VizML: a machine learning approach to visualization recommendation. In: Proceedings of the 2019 CHI Conference on Human Factors in Computing Systems, pp. 1–12. ACM, Glasgow Scotland (2019). https://doi.org/10.1145/3290605.3300358
8. Li, H., Wang, Y., Zhang, S., Song, Y., Qu, H.: KG4Vis: a knowledge graph-based approach for visualization recommendation. IEEE Trans. Vis. Comput. Graph. **28**, 195–205 (2022). https://doi.org/10.1109/TVCG.2021.3114863

9. Lee, D.J.-L., et al.: Lux: Always-on Visualization Recommendations for Exploratory Dataframe Workflows. In: Proceedings of the VLDB Endow, vol. 15, pp. 727–738 (2021). https://doi.org/10.14778/3494124.3494151

10. EPPerson, W., et al.: Leveraging analysis history for improved in situ visualization recommendation. Comput. Graph. Forum. **41**, 145–155 (2022). https://doi.org/10.1111/cgf.14529

11. Ojo, F., et al.: VisGNN: personalized visualization recommendationvia graph neural networks. In: Proceedings of the ACM Web Conference 2022, pp. 2810–2818. Association for Computing Machinery, New York(2022). https://doi.org/10.1145/3485447.3512001

12. Harris, C., et al.: Insight-centric visualization recommendation (2021). http://arxiv.org/abs/2103.11297

13. Gao, Q., He, Z., Jing, Y., Zhang, K., Wang, X.S.: VizGRank: a context-aware visualization recommendation method based on inherent relations between visualizations. In: Jensen, C.S., et al. (eds.) DASFAA 2021. LNCS, vol. 12683, pp. 244–261. Springer, Cham (2021). https://doi.org/10.1007/978-3-030-73200-4_16

14. Kelleher, C., Braswell, A.: Introductory overview: recommendations for approaching scientific visualization with large environmental datasets. Environ. Model. Softw. **143**, 105113 (2021). https://doi.org/10.1016/j.envsoft.2021.105113

15. Schulz, H.-J., Angelini, M., Santucci, G., Schumann, H.: An enhanced visualization process model for incremental visualization. IEEE Trans. Vis. Comput. Graph. **22**, 1830–1842 (2016). https://doi.org/10.1109/TVCG.2015.2462356

16. Seo, M., Kembhavi, A., Farhadi, A., Hajishirzi, H.: Bidirectional attention flow for machine comprehension (2018). http://arxiv.org/abs/1611.01603, https://doi.org/10.48550/arXiv.1611.01603

17. Devlin, J., Chang, M.-W., Lee, K., Toutanova, K.: BERT: pre-training of deep bidirectional transformers for language understanding. In: Proceedings of the 2019 Conference of the North American Chapter of the Association for Computational Linguistics: Human Language Technologies, vol. 1 (Long and Short Papers), pp. 4171–4186. Association for Computational Linguistics, Minneapolis (2019). https://doi.org/10.18653/v1/N19-1423

18. Pennington, J., Socher, R., Manning, C.: GloVe: global vectors for word representation. In: Proceedings of the 2014 Conference on Empirical Methods in Natural Language Processing (EMNLP), pp. 1532–1543. Association for Computational Linguistics, Doha (2014). https://doi.org/10.3115/v1/D14-1162

Automating Malaria Diagnosis with XAI: Using Deep-Learning Technologies for More Accurate, Efficient, and Transparent Results

Krishan Mridha[1(✉)] [iD], Fitsum Getachew Tola[2] [iD], Shakil Sarkar[3], Nazmul Arefin[4], Sandesh Ghimire[1], Anmol Aran[1], and Aashish Prashad Pandey[1]

[1] Computer Engineering, Marwadi University, Rajkot, Gujarat, India
krishna.mridha108735@marwadiuniversity.ac.in
[2] Computer Engineering – Artificial Intelligence, Marwadi University, Rajkot, Gujarat, India
[3] Pharmacy, Marwadi University, Rajkot, Gujarat, India
[4] Computer Science and Technology, Southwest University of Science and Technology, Mianyang, Sichuan, China

Abstract. Malaria is a deadly infectious disease that claims numerous lives worldwide each year, primarily due to delayed or incorrect diagnosis using the manual microscope. This article proposes the automation of the diagnosis process through deep-learning technologies, specifically convolutional neural networks (CNNs), based on the intensity characteristics of Plasmodium parasites and erythrocytes. The approach involves feeding images into CNN models such as ResNet50, CNN, and MobileNet, with the MobileNet model achieving the best overall performance. The first novelty of this paper is that we update the pre-trained models which give us better results. To further enhance the system, the article advocates for the use of explainable artificial intelligence (XAI) techniques, including feature attribution and counterfactual explanations, to improve the accuracy, efficiency, and transparency of the malaria diagnosis system. The proposed system integrates deep learning and XAI, which can provide clear and interpretable explanations for decision-making processes, guide the development of more effective diagnostic tools and save lives. For instance, we use Grad-CAM and Grad-CAM++ which counter the affected areas on the images and that could be a noble contribution to this paper. It is shown via extensive performance study that auto-mating the process can accurately and efficiently detect the malaria parasite in blood samples with a sensitivity of over 95% and less complexity than prior methods reported in the literature.

Keywords: Disease · Convolutional Neural Network · Explainable Artificial Intelligence · Deep Learning

1 Introduction

The parasite Plasmodium, which causes the potentially fatal illness malaria, is spread to people through the bites of infected mosquitoes. The World Health Organization (WHO) estimates that malaria will cause 229 million infections and 409,000 deaths globally in

R. Morusupalli et al. (Eds.): MIWAI 2023, LNAI 14078, pp. 297–308, 2023.
https://doi.org/10.1007/978-3-031-36402-0_27

2019. Most of these deaths will affect children under the age of five in sub-Saharan Africa. One of the biggest challenges in combating malaria is early diagnosis, as symptoms can often be mistaken for other illnesses. In recent years, deep learning algorithms have shown promising results in classifying malaria-infected individuals from digital images of blood samples. By analyzing large datasets of annotated images, deep learning algorithms can learn to identify subtle patterns and features that are indicative of malaria infection, enabling faster and more accurate diagnosis. Given the significant impact of malaria on global health and development, there is a pressing need for continued research and innovation in this domain. The application of deep learning in malaria diagnosis and prevention has the potential to revolutionize our approach to tackling this disease and saving countless lives. Late or incorrect diagnosis is a major contributor to mortality in the United States. The review procedure has to be automated immediately given the seriousness of this issue for world health. Among other things, the suggested method should be able to reliably and consistently read blood films and properly diagnose parasitemia. The strategy must also be economical and lighten the burden on malaria field workers and their families. In the modern world, deep learning algorithms are a common tool for picture categorization, movie identification, and medical image analysis. Convolutional neural networks (CNNs) are the most often utilized kind of deep neural network in computer vision. Deep neural networks are the most useful machine learning technology currently accessible, especially in the field of biomedicine. Deep learning (DL) has been extremely popular in recent years for analyzing and diagnosing biomedical and healthcare concerns because of its simplicity in extracting crucial information and its ability to complete tasks that were previously difficult to complete using traditional approaches. The CNN's convolutional layer functions as an automated feature extractor, sifting through the input data to extract both significant and hidden attributes. Using a fully connected neural network, which optimizes probability scores by ingesting the retrieved characteristics, picture classification is accomplished. When deep learning is employed in biological applications, the number of research publications published has also significantly grown over the past several years.

2 Related Work

Plasmodium parasites are the deadly illness that causes malaria, which is still a major public health problem in many areas of the world, particularly in third-world nations. Almost 219 million cases of malaria were recorded by the World Health Organization (WHO) in 87 nations worldwide in 2017 [1]. The WHO has identified South-East Asia, the Eastern Mediterranean, the Western Pacific, and the Americas as high-risk regions. Several methods have been described in the literature for detecting these parasites, including clinical diagnosis, microscopic diagnosis, rapid diagnostic test (RDT), and polymerase chain reaction (PCR) [2]. Early diagnosis of malarial parasites is essential for the effective prevention and treatment of malaria.

Clinical diagnosis and PCR are two common conventional diagnostic techniques that are carried out in lab settings and need a high degree of human knowledge that may not be present in rural places where malaria is common. A diagnosis for malaria may be made in 15 min or less using RDT and microscopic diagnosis, both of which do not need a professional diagnostic or a microscope [3]. According to WHO [4] and others [5, 6], RDT has drawbacks, including a lack of sensitivity, the inability to quantify parasite density and distinguish between P. vivax, P. ovale, and P. malariae, the greater cost compared to the light microscope, and susceptibility to damage from heat and humidity.

An efficient diagnostic technique is automatic microscopic malaria parasite identification, which entails the capture of the microscopic blood smear picture (for instance, using a smartphone as demonstrated in [7, 8]), segmentation of the cells, and categorization of the infected cells [9]. Combining successful blood cell segmentation with malaria parasite identification allows for the performance of counting. In several investigations [10–13], good performance has been noted in the well-researched field of cell segmentation. Prior research on the categorization of infected cells has made use of image processing [14–16], computer vision [17–19], and machine learning [20–22] tools and methodologies. To the best of our knowledge, however, precise and computationally effective methods for categorizing infected cells have not been investigated. For instance, the accuracy of a model suggested in [40] is said to be 99.52%, however, the model's roughly 19.6 billion floating point operations (flops) make it unfeasible for usage in power-constrained devices.

3 Methodology

The suggested technique using CNN, pre-trained algorithms, and many layers is covered in detail in this section. Figure 1 depicts the pre-processing, augmentations, training, and assessment phases of identifying Malaria cells. Several hyper-parameters are used to train and optimize DL algorithms for transfer learning and fine-tuning. The learning rates and biases in neural networks are optimized accordingly. To improve the accuracy of the findings, we eventually integrate the three top DL algorithms during the ensemble stage.

Fig. 1. Proposed Deep learning model for Malaria classification

A. Dataset Description: The dataset is collected from Kaggle a public repository [23] where the dataset contains 2 folders namely Infected and Uninfected. The total number of images is 27,558. The dataset is split into three sets with 80:10:10. That means to train, test, and validate the set. The train set is used for training the model, the validation set is for adjusting the hyperparameter and testing for getting real classification from the model.

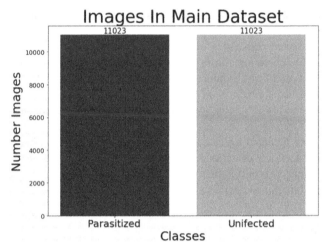

Fig. 2. Number of images per sample.

Figure 2 is for the number of images per class where the Parasitized and Un-infected Images are equal to 11023.

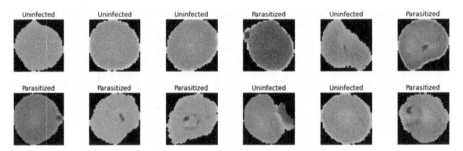

Fig. 3. Samples from the dataset.

Figure 3 is the sample images from the dataset. Figure 4 is for the number of images per spill where the training size is 80%, the testing data set size is 10% and the validation data set size is 10%.

Dataset Distribution

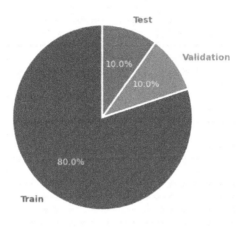

Fig. 4. Number of images for a split class

B. Proposed model: (Fig. 5)

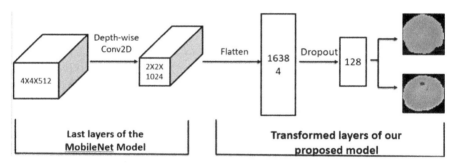

Fig. 5. Proposed MobileNet model for Malaria cell Disease Classification where we add a flattened layer, a dense layer in the last part of MobileNet.

In this article, we have three types of Deep learning modes ls where two are pre-trained called MobileNet and ResNet50 and another one is a traditional Convolutional Neural Network. Below, we are discussing some of the important points about the models.

4   Results and Discussion

In machine learning, the evaluation of a model's performance showing in Table 1. is crucial in determining its effectiveness. Three common metrics used for evaluating classification models are the confusion matrix, precision, recall, and F1 score [24–26].

Table 1. Model Evaluation Metrics

		Predicted values		
		True	False	
Actual	True	True Positive (TP)	False Negative (FN) Type 1 Error	Accuracy = $\dfrac{TP+TN}{TP+TN+FP+FN}$
	False	False Positive (FP) Type 2 Error	True Negative (TN)	Specificity = $\dfrac{TN}{TN+FP}$
		Pr*ecision* $\dfrac{TP}{TP+TN}$		Accuracy = $\dfrac{TP+TN}{TP+TN+FP+FN}$ $F1 = \dfrac{2\,x\,\text{Pr}ecision\,x\,\text{Recall}}{\text{Pr}ecision + \text{Recall}}$

Table 2. Accuracy and K-fold accuracy for three models where we compare Training/Validation accuracy and Loss

Algorithms	Training Accuracy	Training Loss	Validation Accuracy	Validation Loss
CNN	0.9545	0.2349	0.8836	0.4076
Proposed MobileNet	0.9272	0.0.2724	0.9509	0.1576
ResNet50	0.6923	0.6197	0.7199	0.5968

In terms of accuracy and curve from Table 2 and Fig. 6, the best model among the three is the Proposed MobileNet with a training accuracy of 0.9272 and validation accuracy of 0.9509. This indicates that the model has been able to learn the features of the data well and generalize to new data.

On the other hand, the CNN model has a slightly higher training accuracy of 0.9545 but a lower validation accuracy of 0.8836, suggesting that the model may have to overfit the training data.

The ResNet50 model has the lowest training accuracy of 0.6923 and validation accuracy of 0.7199. This indicates that the model has not been able to learn the features of the data well and generalize to new data, which could be due to the complexity of the model or insufficient training data.

In terms of training and validation loss, the Proposed MobileNet has the lowest validation loss of 0.1576, indicating that it can make more accurate predictions on new data. The CNN model has a higher validation loss of 0.4076, which is likely due to

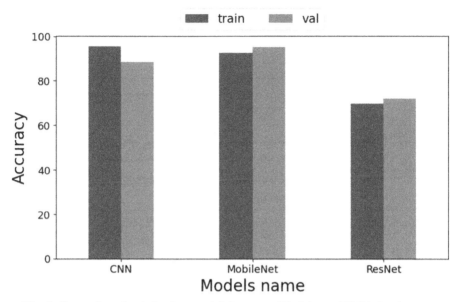

Fig. 6. Comparison Graph for three models in terms of Training and Validation Accuracy

overfitting, while the ResNet50 has the highest validation loss of 0.5968, indicating that it is not performing well on new data.

Overall, the Proposed MobileNet seems to be the best model among the three, with high accuracy and low validation loss. However, further testing and evaluation are needed to confirm its performance on a larger and more diverse dataset.

Table 3. Confusion Matrix, Precision Matrix, and Recall Matrix for all Models.

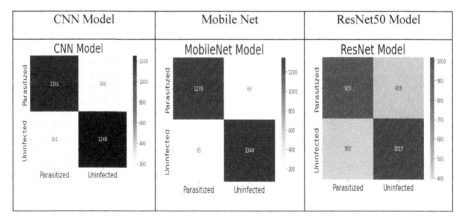

Table 3 and 4 describe the confusion matrix, from where Precision, Recall, and F1-score is calculated. The Precision is describing the many positives that are classified

Table 4. Precision, Recall, and F1-score respectively a, b, and c

Model		CNN	MobileNet	ResNet
	0	0.88	0.95	0.70
Precision	1	0.88	0.95	0.70

a. Precision

Model		CNN	MoileNet	ResNet
	0	0.88	0.95	0.68
Recall	1	0.88	0.95	0.72

b. Recall

Model		CNN	MobileNet	ResNet
	0	0.88	0.95	0.69
F1-score	1	0.88	0.95	0.71

c. F1-scroe

correctly by the model. According to the confusion matrix our Proposed MobileNet performs better than the other two models. The true positive and true negative predictions are better than other models.

The training and validation accuracy curves shown in Table 5 are visual representations of how well a model is learning and generalizing to new data. The training accuracy curve represents the accuracy of the model on the training dataset, while the validation accuracy curve represents the accuracy of the model on a validation dataset that it has not seen during the training process (Table 6).

Table 5. Training vs Validation Accuracy curve for all the models. These curves describe the model learning for all the samples.

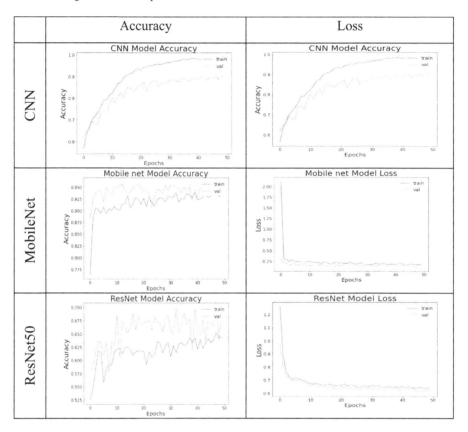

In Table 6, we show the visualization techniques output such as Grad-CAM [27] and Grad-CAM++ [28] to understand the affected areas and help physicians comprehend the reason for the prediction. These techniques generated heat maps of the regions of interest, highlighting the areas that contributed most to the classification decision. This not only enhances the interpretability of the deep learning model but also provides a valuable tool for farmers to identify and target the specific regions of a plant affected by the disease. Grad-CAM (Gradient-weighted Class Activation Mapping) and Grad-CAM++ are popular techniques for generating heatmaps to visualize the important regions of an image that contribute most to the classification decision made by a neural network. These techniques use the gradient information flowing into the final convolutional layer of the network to generate the heatmaps, making them easy to integrate with most CNN architectures. Using these visualization techniques, we were able to provide doctors with a clear understanding of the areas affected by the disease, enabling them to take effective measures to control and prevent the spread of the disease. The application of Grad-CAM

Table 6. Interpretability results by using the proposed MobileNet model

and Grad-CAM++ to our deep learning model enhanced its interpretability, making it a valuable tool for smart agriculture.

5   Conclusion

In conclusion, the application of deep learning techniques for coffee leaf disease classification has shown great potential in improving crop management and ensuring food security. By automating the disease classification process using deep learning algorithms, the physician can quickly identify and treat diseases, resulting in better diagnosis. The results of this study demonstrate the effectiveness of the proposed method for malaria cell disease classification, and the visualization techniques such as Grad-CAM and Grad-CAM++ can help doctors comprehend the reason for the prediction. The best accuracy obtained from the MobileNet model emphasizes the importance of transfer learning and the effectiveness of pre-trained models in deep learning. The devastating impact of malaria disease classification cannot be overstated, and the need for accurate and efficient disease detection methods is more pressing than ever before. As researchers in the field of smart diagnosis, we are deeply committed to developing solutions that can help physician improve their livelihoods and provide security for the growing global population. We believe that our findings have the potential to revolutionize the way we approach healthcare management and help doctors around the world achieve better diagnosis systems. We hope that our work will be received with enthusiasm by the scientific community and contribute to the ongoing efforts to build a sustainable future for the smart healthcare system.

References

1. Fact Sheet about Malaria: https://www.who.int/news-room/fact-sheets/detail/malaria (2019). Accessed 29 Dec 2019
2. Fact Sheet about MALARIA: https://www.who.int/news-room/fact-sheets/detail/malaria (2020). Accessed on 12 Apr 2020
3. Wongsrichanalai, C., Barcus, M.J., Muth, S., Sutamihardja, A., Wernsdorfer, W.H.: A review of malaria diagnostic tools: Microscopy and rapid diagnostic test (rdt). Am. J. Trop. Med. Hyg. **77**(Suppl. 6), 119–127 (2007)
4. WHO: New Perspectives: Malaria Diagnosis. Report of a Joint WHO/USAID Informal Consultation (Archived). https://www.who.int/malaria/publications/atoz/who_cds_rbm_2000_1 4/en/ (2020). Accessed on 9 Apr 2020
5. Obeagu, E.I., Chijioke, U.O., Ekelozie, I.S.: Malaria rapid diagnostic test (RDTs). Ann. Clin. Lab. Res. **6**, 275 (2018)
6. Available online: https://www.who.int/malaria/areas/diagnosis/rapid-diagnostic-tests/gen eric_PfPan_training_manual_web.pdf. Accessed on 6 Apr 2020
7. Rajaraman, S., et al.: Pre-trained convolutional neural networks as feature extractors toward improved malaria parasite detection in thin blood smear images. PeerJ **6**, e4568 (2018)
8. Quinn, J.A., Nakasi, R., Mugagga, P.K., Byanyima, P., Lubega, W., Andama, A.: Deep convolutional neural networks for microscopy-based point of care diagnostics. In: Proceedings of the Machine Learning for Healthcare Conference, pp. 271–281. Los Angeles, CA, USA, 19–20 Aug 2016
9. Poostchi, M., Silamut, K., Maude, R.J., Jaeger, S., Thoma, G.: Image analysis and machine learning for detecting malaria. Transl. Res. **194**, 36–55 (2018)
10. Anggraini, D., Nugroho, A.S., Pratama, C., Rozi, I.E., Pragesjvara, V., Gunawan, M.: Automated status identification of microscopic images obtained from malaria thin blood smears using Bayes decision: a study case in Plasmodium falciparum. In: Proceedings of the 2011 International Conference on Advanced Computer Science and Information Systems, pp. 347–352. Jakarta, Indonesia, 17–18 Dec 2011
11. Yang, D., et al.: A portable image-based cytometer for rapid malaria detection and quantification. PLoS ONE **12**, e0179161 (2017)
12. Arco, J.E., Górriz, J.M., Ramírez, J., Álvarez, I., Puntonet, C.G.: Digital image analysis for automatic enumeration of malaria parasites using morphological operations. Expert Syst. Appl. **42**, 3041–3047 (2015)
13. Das, D.K., Maiti, A.K., Chakraborty, C.: Automated system for characterization and classification of malaria-infected stages using light microscopic images of thin blood smears. J. Microsc. **257**, 238–252 (2015)
14. Bibin, D., Nair, M.S., Punitha, P.: Malaria parasite detection from peripheral blood smear images using deep belief networks. IEEE Access **5**, 9099–9108 (2017)
15. Mohanty, I., Pattanaik, P.A., Swarnkar, T.: Automatic detection of malaria parasites using unsupervised techniques. In: Pandian, D., Fernando, X., Baig, Z., Shi, F. (eds.) ISMAC 2018. LNCVB, vol. 30, pp. 41–49. Springer, Cham (2019). https://doi.org/10.1007/978-3-030-006 65-5_5
16. Yunda, L., Ramirez, A.A., Millán, J.: Automated image analysis method for p-vivax malaria parasite detection in thick film blood images. Sist. Telemática **10**, 9–25 (2012)
17. Ahirwar, N., Pattnaik, S., Acharya, B.: Advanced image analysis-based system for automatic detection and classification of malarial parasites in blood images. Int. J. Inf. Technol. Knowl. Manag. **5**, 59–64 (2012)
18. Hung, J., Carpenter, A.: Applying faster R-CNN for object detection on malaria images. In: Proceedings of the IEEE Conference on Computer Vision and Pattern Recognition Workshops, pp. 56–61. Honolulu, HI, USA, 21–26 Jul 2017

19. Tek, F.B., Dempster, A.G., Kale, I.: Parasite detection and identification for automated thin blood film malaria diagnosis. Comput. Vis. Image Underst. **114**, 21–32 (2010)
20. Ranjit, M., Das, A., Das, B., Das, B., Dash, B., Chhotray, G.: Distribution of plasmodium falciparum genotypes in clinically mild and severe malaria cases in Orissa, India. Trans. R. Soc. Trop. Med. Hyg. **99**, 389–395 (2005)
21. Sarmiento, W.J.; Romero, E.; Restrepo, A.; y Electrónica, D.I.: Colour estimation in images from thick blood films for the automatic detection of malaria. In: Memoriasdel IX Simposio de Tratamiento de Señales, Im ágenes y Visión artificial, p. 15, 16. Manizales (2004)
22. Romero, E., Sarmiento, W., Lozano, A.: Automatic detection of malaria parasites in thick blood films stained with hematoxylin-eosin. In: Proceedings of the III Iberian Latin American and Caribbean Congress of Medical Physics, ALFIM2004, Rio de Janeiro, Brazil, 15 Oct 2004
23. The dataset is taken from https://www.kaggle.com/datasets/iarunava/cell-images-for-detecting-malaria
24. Mridha, K.: Early prediction of breast cancer by using artificial neural network and machine learning techniques. In: 2021 10th IEEE International Conference on Communication Systems and Network Technologies (CSNT), pp. 582–587. Bhopal, India (2021). https://doi.org/10.1109/CSNT51715.2021.9509658
25. Mridha, K., Pandey, A.P., Ranpariya, A., Ghosh, A., Shaw, R.N.: Web based brain tumor detection using neural network. In: 2021 IEEE 6th International Conference on Computing, Communication, and Automation (ICCCA), pp. 137–143. Arad, Romania (2021). https://doi.org/10.1109/ICCCA52192.2021.9666248
26. Mridha, K., Sarkar, S., Kumar, D.: Respiratory disease classification by CNN using MFCC. In: 2021 IEEE 6th International Conference on Computing, Communication and Automation (ICCCA), pp. 517–523. Arad, Romania (2021). https://doi.org/10.1109/ICCCA52192.2021.9666346
27. Selvaraju, R.R., Cogswell, M., Das, A., Vedantam, R., Parikh, D., Batra D.: Grad-CAM: visual explanations from deep networks via gradient-based localization. In: Proceedings of the IEEE International Conference on Computer Vision (ICCV), pp. 618–626. Venice, Italy (2017)
28. Chattopadhyay, A., Sarkar, A., Howlader, P., Balasubramanian, V.N.: Improved visual explanations for deep convolutional networks, In: 2018 IEEE Winter Conference on Applications of Computer Vision (WACV), pp. 839–847. Lake Tahoe, NV, USA (2018). https://doi.org/10.1109/WACV.2018.00092

Artificial Intelligence as a Service: Providing Integrity and Confidentiality

Neelima Guntupalli[✉] and Vasantha Rudramalla

Department of CSE, Acharya Nagarjuna University, Guntur, India
neelima.guntupalli80@gmail.com

Abstract. As Artificial Intelligence technologies are being vigorously used, there are major concerns about privacy, security and compression of the data. Bulk amounts of data are being stored in the cloud and the same will be transmitted to the parties that offer AI software services or platform services. The three key features that are to considered while transferring the data from cloud to Artificial Intelligence as a service (AIaaS) or Machine Learning as a service (MLaaS) are Data Compression, Data Integrity and Data Confidentiality. There is high demand for data processing which in turn is driving us to perform data compression. Data compression has to be done whether it is with Artificial Intelligence or Cloud Computing or Machine learning algorithms. Because without compressing the data such huge amounts of data whether it is text or multimedia application cannot be stored as it is. In this paper we have used an optimized lossless compression algorithm. When bulk amounts of data is being transferred from platform services to cloud, the foremost thing that has to be done is categorization of data i.e. the data that is critical and which needs integrity and the data that can be read by the users on the network. The critical data which needs AI services should be checked whether they are transmitted as it is. The data that is being sent by the cloud user should reach the service providing platforms without being modified. To maintain such integrity to the data, Hashing can be used. In this paper we have proposed a hashing algorithm that is implemented after performing data compression. The generated hash value is used as an attribute in generating keys for encryption.

Keywords: AIaaS · MLaaS · Data Compression · Data Integrity · Data Confidentiality · Hashing · Hash Values · Platform Services · Critical data

1 Introduction

Artificial Intelligence is the most emerging technology which is contributing to the human well being. It is playing a key role in the success and pioneering of different organizations and their advancement. It is speculated by the McKinsey Global Institute that the usage of AI services could yield further global economic output of USD 13 trillion by 2030 [3]. As per AI Magazine consulting giant Accenture has a belief that Artificial Intelligence has the ability to increase the rates of profitability by 38% on average and can also lead to an overall economic boost of USD 13 trillion in additional gross value by 2035.The average simulation shows that approximately 70 percent of organizations should have been implementing at least one kind of service offered by AI technology but that less than half must have completely utilizing the services of the five sub domains of AI like computer vision, advanced machine learning, online assistants, robotic process automation and natural language [3]. From the abstraction view this pattern of adoption may be partial or complete, but this would be relatively fast when compared with other technologies.

1.1 Evolution of AI as a Service

The organizations prefer to entrust complex tasks that were difficult to be solved by human beings to AI. Artificial Intelligence programs surpass the efficiency of the human beings in terms of computational power and productivity. To encourage the development of AI, Cloud service providers such as Microsoft, Google, Salesforce, IBM and Oracle are the initiators to extend AI services and also machine learning, deep learning as services.AI as a Service is a term that is used to describe a third party which offers advanced AI functionalities to companies with a one-time payment or subscription fee. Many companies are utilizing this service in recent years to reduce the productivity cost and increase development, deployment feasibility and efficiency It is not a restrained statement to say that AI as a service is going to be a game-changer for many small-to-medium organizations [2]. Till recent years, many organizations were priced out of using Artificial Intelligence for their business, as it would have required in-house development of AI systems with human-like qualities, such as natural language understanding, perception and commonsense reasoning. As there is such massive demand for the use of AI application, the users of the cloud should be ensured that their data that is being stored in the cloud should be preserved with integrity and confidentiality [4, 7].

2   Proposed Mechanism

With AIaaS, now it has become more feasible, allowing the businesses to sway Artificial Intelligence for things such as customer service, data analysis, and automating production. The AIaaS based models are connected with cloud computing to make them offered as services to the users. It means that various services provided by Artificial Intelligence models are accessed over the internet, and business organizations only pay for what they use. This allows the users or the businesses to easily access the features and capabilities of AI who may not afford to invest much budget or resources in AI technologies. Furthermore AIaaS providers generally provide pre-developed models and also APIs that could be integrated into current applications, making it simpler and faster for the organizations to implement AI capabilities.

AIaaS can be categorized as AI software services, AI developer services and AI infrastructure services. In the recent years AI software services are generally dependent on machine learning and deep learning techniques. AIaaS is also offering machine learning as a service, inference as a service and deep learning as a service. In recent days various kinds of AI services like natural language processing, speech services, data analytic services and computer vision services are accessible through cloud. They are the significant technologies that are being used by the cloud users. While utilizing these services utmost concern is about providing integrity and confidentiality to the data [4, 7]. The foremost thing that has to be done is data compression. Several data compression techniques with varying space and time complexities are available to minimize the size of the data in the virtual environment [1, 5]. The proposed algorithm focuses on ensuring privacy and security to the data after compressing the data. Compression mechansim, data integrity and confidentiality are the three key features that are altogether provided to only the critical data of our cloud application.

2.1 Proposed Enhanced Quadratic Chaotic-Map Algorithm

In this paper we have used Enhanced Quadratic Chaotic-Map Algorithm to generate a hash key from the given data. This algorithm has preserved data integrity and its performance has proved to be better when compared with the existing algorithm. Later the last key feature i.e. Data Confidentiality is implemented by encrypting the data [2]. Encryption is performed using the hash value generated from the Enhanced Quadratic Chaotic-Map Algorithm thus making the cryptic mechanism more effective. Hash values are generated by using the proposed hashing algorithm. Hashing algorithms always retrieve a code from the given data which authenticates the data at the receiving end [6]. There are many existing algorithms for generating hash code, but the proposed algorithm has proved to be effectively operative on the cloud data. The input to this algorithm is the compressed data which we have performed using dynamic byte stream based DWT-DCT compression mechanism.

Non-Linear Chaotic-Maps: In the dynamic systems, the non-linear chaotic map is generally represented as in Eq. (1).

Controlled Chebyshev Chaotic Map: Let x be a real integer N from the set A that is mapped onto A in such a way that,

$Tx (N){:}A \rightarrow A{:}[-1,1] \rightarrow [-1,1]$

$$Tx = k \; \cos(x \cdot \cos -1 \, N) \tag{1}$$

The recurrence relation to the equation is given as.

$$Tx(V) \; = \; (VTx - 1 \, (V) - Tx - 2 \, (V))/k \, And \, T0 \, (V) \; = \; k, T1 \, (V) \; = \; kv$$

.

Extended Quadratic Map: In the dynamic systems the non-linear quadratic map is given as in Eq. (2).

$$Nx + 1KNx2 = C \tag{2}$$

$x = c - kX_n{}^2$ Here, the values of C will be in the range between (0, 2).that is c ∈ (0, 2) and (Fig. 1)

2.2 Proposed Hash-Based Homomorphism AB Encryption Model

The below are the parameters of the user that are used as public key. The mathematical functions that are used to generate the public key are mentioned.

$$Public \; key := \{(p), (q), (r), 1, G_{\alpha 2}, G_{\alpha 3}, H_{AK}^1, H_{SK}^2, H_{policies}^3\}$$

Step 1: Initialize the input compressed data as H
Step 2: Randomly choose a generator X_0 from cyclic group G.
Step 3: Iterate equation (9) until 60 rounds, for each byte compressed value
Step 4: H[i] =Use equation (10) to permute the byte value.
Step 5: Done
Step 6: $H = [1] + [2] + [3] + [4] + \cdots [n]$
Step 7: Stop.

Fig. 1. The Enhanced Quadratic Chaotic-Map Algorithm to provide data integrity for AI services.

Key Generation: In this step the private key is generated which is used in general as a secret key. The parameters that are used here are the user's credentials and the Hash Value generate from the algorithm mentioned in Fig. 6. Every user in the network is given a secret key and there pattern keys are generated as.

$$Public\ key := \{(p), (q), (r),_1, G_{\alpha 2}, G_{\alpha 3}, H^1{}_{AK}, H^2{}_{SK}, H^3{}_{policies}\}$$

$$Master\ key := \{\alpha 1, \alpha 2, \alpha 3\} \text{Are taken randomly from cyclic group}$$

$$K_{1,} = g_p{}^{1\,(s'/+a1)}; i=0.....Partition1.length;$$

$$K_{1,} = g_q{}^{1\,(s'/+a2)}; j=0..... Partition2.length;$$

$$K_{1,} = {}_{gr1}{}^{(s'/+a3)}; k=0.... Partition3.length;$$

$$Secret\ key := \{Hashvalue.\ length; H^1_{AK}, H^2_{SK}, H^3_{policies}; K_{1,i}, K_{1,j}, K_{1,k}\}$$

Cloud to AIaaS platform Data Encryption: Each cloud user uses the public key that comprises of hash values and user's credentials to encrypt the data.

Data Decryption: At the receiving end matching credentials are used and using the hash value it is checked whether the data has received as it is.

Homomorphic encryption and Decryption Process: The input to the Enhanced Quadratic Chaotic-Map Algorithm is the compressed data. Compressed data will be as data chunks where each chunk is of two bytes. Additive homomorphic and multiplicative homomorphic techniques are applied on each chunk of data. The mentioned process is recursively applied on all the compressed chunks of the data file [5] (Fig. 2).

Input: Compressed data and Hash key value.
Output: Encrypted data in the AWS console.

Step 1:Start

Step 2:Setup phase for the public key.
Step 3: Secret Key generation by using the public key and the master key.
Step 4: Homomorphic encryption process.
Step 5: Repeat the step 4 until the last byte of the file.
Step 6: Compressed and encrypted file is stored in the Cloud console
       Bucket.
Step 7: Homomorphic decryption process.
Step 7: Stop.

Fig. 2. The Hash-based Homomorphic ABEncryption Algorithm for encryption and decryption.

3 Results and Comparative Study

This paper is implemented using AWS console of the cloud platform. The encrypted files comprises of objects that are stored in the buckets of AWS (Figs. 3 and 4, Tables 1 and 2).

Table 1. Comparative result of different Hash models with proposed model in the AWS console.

Hash Algorithm	MinBitRate	AvgBitChangeRate
MD2	91	113
MD4	96	117
MD5	101	121
MD6	105	123
SHA-1	101	118
SHA-2	107	123
SHA3	112	127
Whirlpool	105	119
Xorshift	95	109
Extended Quadratic Chaotic-map hash(proposed)	123	142

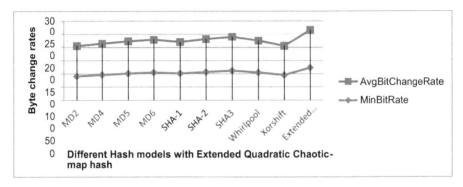

Fig. 3. Hash models Vs Byte change rate

Table 2. The comparative result of different Encryption models with proposed model in AWS console.

Encryption Model	Encryption Time (ms)	Decryption Time (ms)
CPABE	5475	4929
KPABE	6354	5394
CCPABE	4988	4592
RSA	8755	7141
Hash-based Homomorphic ABEncryption Model (proposed model)	4592	4317

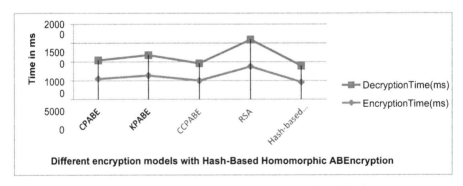

Fig. 4. Encryption models Vs Encryption &Decryption Time in ms.

4   Conclusion

This paper has used data integrity and also data confidentiality while the cloud user is utilizing AI services. And also the data compression technique is used before applying hashing mechanism and encryption technique. It is to reduce the computation complexity and also to minimize the amount of storage. The critical data is being transmitted on the cloud using strong encryption mechanism. If at all if it is modified by any unauthorized user by performing any cryptanalysis attack, it can be easily identified by the receiver because of the generated hash value. This proposed mechanism was tested as effective and efficient.

References

1. Yamagiwa, S.: Stream-based lossless data compression. In: Katoh, N., Higashikawa, Y., Ito, H., Nagao, A., Shibuya, T., Sljoka, A., Tanaka, K., Uno, Y. (eds.) Sublinear Computation Paradigm, pp. 391–410. Springer, Singapore (2022). https://doi.org/10.1007/978-981-16-4095-7_16
2. Sattari, F., Lefsrud, L., Kurian, D., Macciotta, R.: A theoretical framework for data-driven artificial intelligence decision making for enhancing the asset integrity management system in the oil & gas sector. J. Loss Prev. Process Ind. **74**, 104648 (2022)
3. Lins, S., Pandl, K.D., Teigeler, H., Thiebes, S., Bayer, C., Sunyaev, A.: Artificial intelligence as a service. Bus. Inform. Syst. Eng. **63**(4), 441–456 (2021)
4. Thabit, F., Alhomdy, S., Jagtap, S.: A new data security algorithm for the cloud computing based on genetics techniques and logical-mathematical functions. Int. J. Intell. Netw. **2**, 18–33 (2021)
5. Raghavendra, C., Sivasubramanian, S., Kumaravel, A.: A Improved image compression using effective lossless compression technique. Cluster Comput. **22**, 3911–3916 (2018)
6. Harfoushi, O., Obiedat, R.: Security in cloud computing using hash algorithm: a neural cloud data security model. Modern Appl. Sci. **12**, 143 (2018)
7. Albugmi, A., Alassafi, M., Walters, R., Wills, G.: Data Security in Cloud Computing (2016)

Live Bidding Application: Predicting Shill Bidding Using Machine Learning

Chetan Mudlapur, Samyak Jain, Shruti Mittal, Pravar Jain, and Vikram Neerugatti[✉]

Department of Computer Science and Engineering, JAIN (Deemed-to-be University),
Bengaluru, India
Vikram.n@jainuniversity.ac.in

Abstract. Online bidding systems are a well-known method of satisfying online buyers' and sellers' expectations since they allow both parties to buy and sell goods at competitive prices. A live auction is used to implement the online bidding system, allowing multiple bidders to participate at once. Together, these bidders may place a bid on any item. You can sell anything on the website with this app from your home or a store. It is being created with the intention of making the system dependable, simple, and quick. Everyone can now take part in an auction while relaxing in their own homes. Despite the popularity of internet auctions, there are numerous dishonest buying or selling practises that might take place. One of the trickiest forms of auction fraud to spot among all of them is shill bidding. Shill bidding is when a seller participates in his or her own auction while purposefully placing a false bid to raise the price at the end. The seller may do this on his or her own, or a third party may work along with the seller to submit fictitious bids on the seller's behalf.

Keywords: Live Auction · Online Bidding · Shill Bidding

1 Introduction

Online auctions are a great way to take advantage of easily available, extensive exposure because of the volume of traffic these sites receive. As a result, we are creating this application to make these events accessible to buyers and dealers nationwide. To the greatest extent possible, we think that moving to online auctions was required for both buyers and sellers.

The auction environment offers unique chances to both buyers and sellers for the following reasons:

- The auction setting gives vendors the chance to move quickly and within a set window of time.
- An auction's comparatively inexpensive prices are very alluring to purchasers, albeit at the expense of some flexibility [1].

R. Morusupalli et al. (Eds.): MIWAI 2023, LNAI 14078, pp. 316–323, 2023.
https://doi.org/10.1007/978-3-031-36402-0_29

The three methods of price posting, negotiation, and auction make up the majority of commercial transactions. The results of casual observation imply that each of these processes involves certain types of items. A bidder's true reservation value for an item can be obtained from an auction, and the price that is paid can subsequently be linked to that value. Auctions are better suited for goods where there is a greater variation in client reservation values than in the mean worth. Auctions are also a better choice for rare products [11, 12].

On the other hand, auction fraud can occur in online auctions. In-auction fraud is usually the most difficult to build effective remedies for, in contrast to pre and post-auction fraud, as it involves human behaviors and methods that are not always evident. Also, one of the major worries is in-auction fraud because the uninformed bidders aren't even aware that it's happened [2].

One of the worst sorts of auction fraud is shill bidding, in which the seller either bids on the item that is being auctioned off themselves or hires others to buy on their behalf. Shill bids are made with the intention of inflating the successful bidder's price. While it is acknowledged that shill bidding is a severe kind of in-auction fraud, shill bidders have access to a variety of tactics. Because of this, it can be difficult to determine what exactly qualifies as shill bidding and how we can spot it in online auctions. How to recognize and identify bidder behaviors in order to counteract shill bids before the victim suffers any financial loss is an even more serious issue [3].

In this paper, we studied the various works that have been done until now, defined a problem statement for which we want to seek a solution for and we defined the essential characteristics for an auction web application in order to be user friendly and accessible. We also discussed about the methodology implemented to analyze and identify shill bidding and the system design and discussed the results based on our findings.

2 Literature Survey

Initially we aimed to predict the product prices at the end of an auction. There are many studies on how to anticipate the end price (also known as the closing price) for an online auction. Regression, multi-class classification, and multiple binary classification tasks are three models that Ghani and Simmons use to forecast the auction end-price [4]. Based on functional data analysis, few scholars have investigated a dynamic forecasting model that can anticipate the final price of an auction that is "in-progress" [5, 6]. For bidders to focus on other auction products with potentially low prices rather than those with high end prices, such a service is more crucial. Dynamic forecasting is not important for commodity listing decision assistance, though, because sellers cannot alter the auction setting once it starts.

Regression trees, multi-class classification, and multiple binary classifications have been used to solve the machine learning challenge of predicting the end price of an online auction [7]. It has been established that the machine learning strategy that displays price prediction as a sequence of binary classifications is the most effective one for this purpose. Employing support vector machines, functional k-nearest neighbor, clustering, regression, and classification approaches, the historical track of a current auction is used to make short-term predictions about the next bid [8]. Nevertheless, the majority of these approaches for predicting prices are static and rely on data that is only available at the start of the auction.

Given the various intricacies and complications we focused on predicting shill bidding behavior in an online auction system. Shill bidding is when the seller (alone or with others) places a bid on the object up for auction to drive up the price. The shill bidding industry is growing quickly for two key reasons. First off, the majority of current auction websites use English auctions with open bidding so that buyers may see other purchasers' bids and be influenced by them as they're bidding. The vendors and auction websites are simply interested in seeing English auctions improve the level of competitiveness. Second, creating a new account on the Internet is really a simple process. Everyone can create many IDs there. Given the inexpensive nature of creating an account, sellers have begun to speculate [9, 10].

In this paper, to tackle the fraud such as shill bidding in e-auctions, we utilized Support Vector Machine model and Decision Tree Classification model on commercial auction data to identify shill bidding behavior, with high accuracy, by narrowing down the most important features required to analyze shill bidding and discarding the rest of the attributes [13].

3 Methodology

3.1 Problem Statement

The objective is to forecast future bids using clustering or classification techniques. Everyone taking part in this procedure is referred to as making a "bid" when they give a price. The data set divides normal bids into "0" and aberrant bids into "1" categories.

3.2 Methodology to Forecast Shill Bidding

Business Understanding
First, we need to set the questions that need to be answered with outcome of this project. These questions are:

- What characteristics are most crucial for predicting bidding class?
- Is it possible to forecast a target variable with more than 90% accuracy?

Data Understanding
The phase of understanding buisness and the data understanding phase complement each other and urge us to identify, collect, and examine the data sets that will be most useful in assisting us in achieving the project's objectives.

Finally, we uploaded the gathered dataset and designated Record ID as the index column since it has a special identifying code that can make it easier to retrieve data and manage data in general. After that, examine the dataset's data types and look for imbalances and missing values.

Remove the column from which it's impossible to extract any valuable information. Boxplots for every variable should be examined to better understand the distribution and outliers.

Data Preparation

The entire process of building the final dataset utilizing the first raw data is covered. It is conceivable that different data preparation tasks will be carried out repeatedly without following a specific order. Table, record, and attribute selection, as well as data processing and cleansing for modelling tools, are among the tasks.

The first step in the data preparation part is normalisation, which entails rescaling the values to fall inside the range [0, 1].

We rank features by significance using the DecisionTreeClassifier. The weighted decrease in node impurity divided by the likelihood of arriving at that node is used to determine the relevance of a feature. The number of samples reaching the node divided by the total number of samples is the node probability.

The next step is to reduce the dimensionality using the Linear Discriminant Analysis (LDA) approach. We may select the number of components to utilise using the Principal Component Analysis (PCA) dimensionality reduction technique. With the exception of PCA, the number of components in LDA is always one less than the number of classes we have recorded as a target variable. LDA, however, provides a distinct division between classes, making it a stronger tool for handling classification issues.

Modeling

At this point, we will decide on the modelling approach that will be employed. It could be one or more models. The target variable and dependent variables are separated as the first stage's step. The dataset will then be divided into train and test halves. The model was then trained, and the outcomes were assessed, using the Support Vector Machine and Decision Tree Classification methods.

4 Algorithms Used for Modelling

4.1 Support Vector Machine Algorithm

One of the most well-liked algorithms for supervised learning is called the Support Vector Machine (SVM), and it is used to solve both classification and regression issues. It is largely utilised in Machine Learning Classification issues, however. The SVM algorithm's objective is to establish the optimal decision boundary or line that can divide n-dimensional space into classes so that subsequent data points may be quickly assigned to the appropriate category. The term "hyperplane" refers to this optimal decision boundary. In order to create the hyperplane, SVM selects the extreme points and vectors. Support vectors, which are used to represent these extreme instances, are what give the Support Vector Machine method its name [8].

4.2 Decision Tree Algorithm

In the machine learning and the deep learning technologies the major knowledge extracted by the huge data is the classification of data and related to the regression problems. To solve these issues the decision trees algorithms is one of the best tree structured type classifiers, that consists of the properties as a tree as it consists of the root, intermediate, and leaf nodes, that which is used to represents the characteristics of the dataset and the classified labels.

The most important thing to keep in mind while developing a model for machine learning is to select the optimal method for the dataset and task at hand. The two benefits of employing a decision tree are listed below:

- Decision trees are often designed to resemble how people think while making decisions, making them simple to comprehend.
- Because the decision tree displays a tree-like structure, the rationale behind it is simple to comprehend.

5   Results and Discussion

We also obtained the answers for the two questions posed in the business understanding stage. For forecasting the target variable, we found that the following three characteristics are crucial:

- Successive_Outbidding: Even if he is the present winner, a shill bidder outbids himself repeatedly to raise the price progressively in quick succession.
- Auction_Duration: The duration of an auction.
- Winning_Ratio: A shill bidder participates in several auctions but seldom prevails and least important features are:
- Starting_Price_Average.
- Auction_ID: Auction's unique identification number.
- Early_Bidding: To attract people' attention, shill bidders frequently place their bids quite early in the auction.

We were able to predict the target variable with an accuracy of 96.97% using Support Vector Machine model (Fig. 1) and an accuracy of 97.83% using Decision Tree Classifier model (Figs. 2 and 3, Table 1).

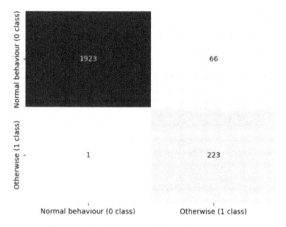

Fig. 1. Confusion matrix of SVM model

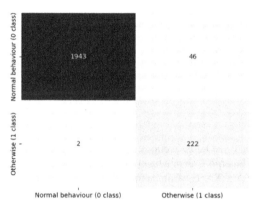

Fig. 2. Confusion matrix of Decision Tree model

Table 1. Comparison Between Decision Tree Classifier and Support Vector Machine

Parameters	Support Vector Machine	Decision Tree Classifier
False Positive	66	46
False Negative	1	2
Accuracy	0.9697	0.9783
Precision	0.7716	0.8283
Recall	0.9955	0.9910

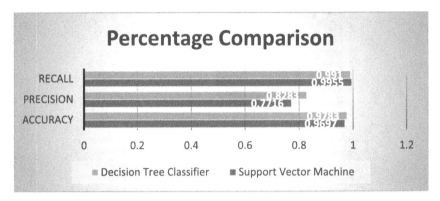

Fig. 3. Comparison Between Decision Tree Classifier and Support Vector Machine

6 Conclusion and Future Scope

In this paper, we conclude that Decision Tree Classification model performs better than Support Vector Machine model with high accuracy and precision to detect shill bidding.

In future work, for predicting the shill bidding different machine learning and deep learning algorithms can be used, and can focus on the security and privacy of the bidders.

References

1. Aggarwal, C.C., Yu, P.S.: Online auctions: there can be only one. In: 2009 IEEE Conference on Commerce and Enterprise Computing (2009)
2. Dong, F., Shatz, S.M., Xu, H.: Combating online in-auction fraud: clues techniques and challenges. Comput. Sci. Rev. 3(4), 245–258 (2009)
3. Trevathan, J., Read, W.: Undesirable and fraudulent behaviour in online auctions. In: Proceedings of International Conference on Security and Cryptograpghy, pp. 450–458 (2006)
4. Ghani, R., Simmons, H.: Predicting the end-price of online auctions. In: Proceedings of the International (2004)
5. Wang, S., Jank, W., Shmueli, G.: Explaining and forecasting online auction prices and their dynamics using functional data analysis. J. Bus. Econ. Stat. 26(2), 144–160 (2008). https://doi.org/10.1198/073500106000000477
6. Chan, N.H., Li, Z.R., Yau, C.Y.: Forecasting online auctions via self-exciting point processes. J. Forecast. 33(7), 501–514 (2014). https://doi.org/10.1002/for.2313
7. Kaur, P., Goyal, M., Lu, J.: Pricing analysis in online auctions using clustering and regression tree approach. In: Cao, L., Bazzan, A.L.C., Symeonidis, A.L., Gorodetsky, V.I., Weiss, G., Yu, P.S. (eds.) ADMI 2011. LNCS (LNAI), vol. 7103, pp. 248–257. Springer, Heidelberg (2012). https://doi.org/10.1007/978-3-642-27609-5_16
8. Pinto, T., Sousa, T.M., Praça, I., Vale, Z., Morais, H.: Support Vector Machines for decision support in electricity markets' strategic bidding. Neurocomputing **172**, 438–445 (2016). https://doi.org/10.1016/j.neucom.2015.03.102
9. Matsuo T., Ito T., Shintani T.: An approach to avoiding shill bids based on combinatorial auction in volume discount. In: First International Workshop on Rational, Robust, and Secure Negotiation Mechanisms in Multi-Agent Systems, pp. 25–38 (2005)

10. Lei, B., Zhang, H., Chen, H., Liu, L., Wang, D.: A k-means clustering based algorithm for shill bidding recognition in online auction. In:2012 24th Chinese Control and Decision Conference (CCDC), pp. 939–943. Taiyuan, China (2012). https://doi.org/10.1109/CCDC.2012.6244147
11. https://www.econport.org/content/handbook/auctions/historyofauctions.html
12. https://www.sutori.com/en/story/history-of-online-auctions--QSFnJLMNZGNX1c661r m4Nwex
13. Ganguly, S., Sadaoui, S.: Online detection of shill bidding fraud based on machine learning techniques. In: Mouhoub, M., Sadaoui, S., Ait Mohamed, O., Ali, M. (eds.) IEA/AIE 2018. LNCS (LNAI), vol. 10868, pp. 303–314. Springer, Cham (2018). https://doi.org/10.1007/978-3-319-92058-0_29

A Novel Pixel Value Predictor Using Long Short Term Memory (LSTM) Network

Sabhapathy Myakal[1,2]([⊠]) [iD], Rajarshi Pal[2] [iD], and Nekuri Naveen[1] [iD]

[1] School of Computer and Information Sciences, University of Hyderabad,
Hyderabad, India
sabha.delight@gmail.com
[2] Institute for Development and Research in Banking Technology, Hyderabad, India

Abstract. Pixel value prediction refers to predicting a pixel value using its neighboring pixel values. It is an important part of several image processing tasks, such as image compression and reversible data hiding. Prediction error is defined as the difference between the original pixel value and the corresponding predicted pixel value. Low prediction error helps to attain good performances in both image compression and reversible data hiding. This has motivated researchers to explore various techniques for pixel value prediction. Most of these techniques map the neighborhood to the predicted value using a mathematical relationship. This kind of rigid approach does not fit to the varied pixel neighborhood in images. On the contrary, a neural network can be trained to predict the pixel value instead of using a conventional mathematical approach for this mapping. In this paper, pixel value prediction is conceptualized as predicting the next value in a spatial sequence of pixels in a particular direction. Therefore, a novel pixel value predictor is proposed using a long short term memory (LSTM) network. Two different LSTM networks are trained separately for horizontal and vertical directions. Finally, the proposed approach leverages the predictors for both directions. For each pixel, it considers the direction with lesser variation in the input pixel sequence. Experimental results indicate that the proposed LSTM network based predictor performs better than the comparing state-of-the-art methods.

Keywords: pixel value prediction · long short term memory (LSTM) network · neural network

1 Introduction

Pixel value prediction is an important step in several image processing tasks, such as reversible data hiding (RDH) [1,2] and image compression [3,4]. A pixel value is predicted using its neighboring pixel values. Difference between the original pixel value and the corresponding predicted pixel value is termed as prediction error. In the context of reversible data hiding, the prediction error expansion based techniques [5–7] embed secret bits in the expanded prediction error. Most image compression techniques [3, 4] also involve an initial pixel value prediction step which is later followed by an encoding step. Low prediction error helps to achieve good performances in both image compression and reversible data hiding. This motivates researchers to explore several pixel prediction methods.

There exist several pixel value predictors in literature. For example, a simple average of the values at the 4-neighboring pixels is used as the predicted pixel value in a rhombus predictor [8]. Depending on the homogeneity of the neighboring pixel values, average of either two vertical neighbors, two horizontal neighbors or all the four neighbors is used as the predicted pixel value in [9]. In [10], specific orientations are considered to predict the center pixel value using average values of pairs of neighboring pixels in those orientations. The center pixel value in [11] is predicted using a weighted average of 4-neighbors. Four predicted values are initially estimated in [12] as averages of pairwise neighboring pixel values in four directions (horizontal, vertical, diagonal and anti-diagonal) using a 3 × 3 window. Then, the directions with the least two diversities (between pairwise directional neighbors) are considered for obtaining the final predicted value. Instead of these averages, weighted median of the neighboring pixel values is considered in [13] as the predicted value. There are also approaches based on edges and gradients for pixel value prediction. For example, a median edge detection (MED) technique in [14] predicts a pixel value based on existence of an edge. Here, three neighboring pixel values towards the right, bottom and bottom-right directions of the pixel being predicted are used for the prediction task. Horizontal and vertical gradients are used to predict a pixel value in a simplified gradient adjusted predictor (SGAP) [14]. Instead of using only two directions for estimation of gradients, a gradient based selective weighting (GBSW) predictor [15] considers gradients in four directions, i.e. vertical, horizontal, diagonal and anti-diagonal. Among the four directions, two directions with the least gradients are used for predicting the pixel value. Then, a weighted average of the causal pixel values in the selected directions is utilized to compute the predicted pixel value. In an extended gradient-based selective weighting (EGBSW) scheme [16], the concept of gradient estimation is extended by considering a larger neighborhood than that of the GBSW predictor [15]. Other gradient based approaches include an improvement to the gradient based approach in [17] and direction-based gradient methods in [18, 19].

In another different approach, the concept of reference pixel values is used. In this approach, non-reference pixel values are predicted using reference pixel values. A set of reference pixels is determined based on the concept of Delaunay triangulation [20]. The triangles are formed in a way such that the circum-circle of a triangle does not include vertices of any other triangle. The vertices of the triangles in such a Delaunay triangulation mesh constitute the reference pixels. These reference pixels are used to interpolate the pixel values of the non-reference pixels. Similarly, in a binary tree triangulation-based approach [21], reference pixels are obtained by recursively dividing the image into right-angled triangles.

Vertices of these triangles are considered as reference pixels. In this approach, non-reference pixel values in a triangle are predicted through interpolation of reference (vertex) pixel values of the triangle. In another reference pixel based approach [22], a pixel value is predicted using weighted median of the neighboring reference pixel values.

All of the above methods mathematically map the neighborhood pixel values to the predicted pixel value. The rigid mathematical mapping may not always fit with the varieties of pixel neighborhood that can occur in an image. In order to solve this problem, multiple predictors have been used in [23]. Alternatively, a neural network can be trained to predict the pixel value instead of using a mathematical based mapping. For example, pixel value is predicted in [24] and [25] using multi-layer perceptron (MLP) neural network. In [24], 8-neighbors in a 3×3 window are used for predicting the center pixel value. In another similar MLP-based approach [25], 12 untraversed neighboring pixel values (according to the raster scan traversal) within a 5×5 window are used to predict the pixel value. A convolutional neural network based approach is also used for pixel prediction in [26]. In this method, an image is divided into two non-overlapping halves - a dot set and a cross set. The dot set pixel values are predicted using the cross set pixel values and vice-versa. Few more recent convolutional neural network based approaches can be found in [27–29].

In line with the above neural network based approaches, this paper proposes a novel pixel value predictor using long short term memory (LSTM) recurrent neural network. In this proposed work, the spatial sequence of pixel values in a particular direction is considered. The pixel value prediction task is modeled as predicting the next pixel value in this sequence. Two different LSTM networks are trained for pixel value prediction - using two different orientations - horizontal and vertical. The idea is to use the orientation (either horizontal or vertical) with lesser variation in the considered neighborhood pixel value sequence for predicting each pixel value. The main contribution of this paper is the proposed novel pixel value predictor using long short term memory (LSTM) network.

Rest of this paper is structured as following: The proposed LSTM network based pixel value predictor is described in Sect. 2. Experimental setup and results are reported in Sect. 3. At the end, the conclusion about the reported work is drawn in Sect. 4.

2   Proposed LSTM Network Based Pixel Value Predictor

Long short term memory (LSTM) recurrent neural network is good at learning dependency in sequential data. In this paper, the idea is to train a LSTM network to learn the dependency between a pixel value and its preceding pixel values in a particular direction. The spatial sequence of pixel values is exploited here. Two different pixel sequences are considered in two different directions - horizontal and vertical. A separate LSTM network is trained for each direction. In this work, preceding six pixel values in a particular direction are used to predict the next pixel value in the sequence. The LSTM network using a horizontal sequence of six neighborhood pixel values is denoted as LSTM-H6 for the rest of the paper. As it is shown in Fig. 1, the task of predicting the pixel value at location (p, q) considers the following order of the pixel values in the horizontal direction: $(p, q + 6)$, $(p, q + 5)$, $(p, q + 4)$, $(p, q + 3)$, $(p, q + 2)$ and $(p, q + 1)$. The order of the sequence is selected in such a way that the nearer pixels to the pixel being predicted (p, q) are closer to it in the sequence. The LSTM-H6 network takes the horizontal sequence of pixels as input and generates the predicted value of the pixel as output.

(p,q)	(p,q+1)	(p,q+2)	(p,q+3)	(p,q+4)	(p,q+5)	(p,q+6)
(p+1,q)						
(p+2,q)						
(p+3,q)						
(p+4,q)						
(p+5,q)						
(p+6,q)						

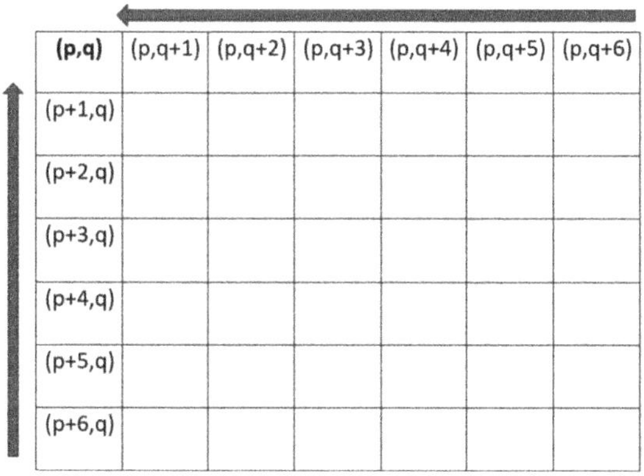

Fig. 1. Six horizontal neighbors and six vertical neighbors of a pixel (p, q). The corresponding sequences of these neighborhood pixels are indicated with arrows.

Similarly, the LSTM network using a vertical sequence of six neighborhood pixel values is denoted as LSTM-V6 for the rest of paper. As it is shown in Fig. 1, the task of predicting the pixel value at location (p, q) considers the following order of the pixel values in the vertical direction: $(p + 6, q)$, $(p + 5, q)$, $(p + 4, q)$, $(p + 3, q)$, $(p + 2, q)$ and $(p + 1, q)$. The order of the sequence is selected in such a way that the nearer pixels to the pixel being predicted (p, q) are closer to it in the sequence. The LSTM-V6 network takes the vertical sequence of pixels as input and generates the predicted value of the pixel as output. Further, the criterion of considering a neighborhood for training the two LSTM networks is stated in Sect. 2.1. The considered LSTM architecture for pixel value prediction is presented in Sect. 2.2.

2.1   Criterion for Considering Neighborhood

The LSTM network is trained using pixel neighborhood sequence as input and the original pixel value (next value in the sequence) as the desired output. As it is suggested in [30], presence of edge pixels in the neighborhood deteriorates the pixel prediction performance. Therefore, if there is any edge (or noisy) pixel in the considered neighborhood or if the current pixel itself is an edge (or noisy) pixel, such neighborhoods are not considered for training. Otherwise, consideration of such a pixel would disrupt the sequence of values.

Edge (or noisy) pixels are identified by using the following procedure:

- Initially, the input image is smoothed to remove noise using a Gaussian low pass filter of size 7 × 7.
- A threshold is obtained using Otsu's method.
- A binary edge (or noisy) pixel map is obtained, at last, by applying Canny edge detector.

2.2 LSTM Architecture for Pixel Value Prediction

A common architecture of the LSTM network is used in both directions (horizontal and vertical). Architecture of each LSTM network is shown in Fig. 2. The input layer takes preceding six pixel values in a sequence. There are two hidden layers. Each hidden layer has 10 neurons (LSTM cells). In the dropout layer, the dropout probability is set as 0.2. It is followed by a dense layer of size 8. Finally, the output layer having one neuron produces the predicted pixel value as output. The hidden cell state and the output of the LSTM are set with a dimension of 1 (because the LSTM network has to generate a single predicted pixel value as output).

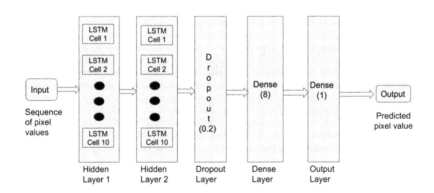

Fig. 2. Architecture of the LSTM Network

The working of each LSTM cell is discussed below: Each LSTM cell has 3 gates: input gate, forget gate and output gate. The input gate determines what new information is to be stored in the long-term memory. The forget gate determines what information from the long-term memory to forget (discard) or to keep (remember). The output gate takes the current input, the previous short-term memory, and the newly computed long-term memory and generates the new short-term memory/hidden state to be passed on to the LSTM cell in the next time step. The weights at these 3 gates are initialized randomly. During the training process, the LSTM learns the weights at these 3 gates. The input and the output gates employ sigmoid and tanh activation functions. The forget gate employs a sigmoid activation function.

Back-propagation algorithm with Adam optimizer is used to train both the LSTM networks. A learning rate of 0.01 is used. If the validation loss (mean squared error) does not decrease for 30 consecutive epochs, then the LSTM network is considered to be converged.

Although the two LSTM network predictors are trained separately, both the trained networks are leveraged during the pixel prediction task. For each pixel, the variances of the corresponding neighborhood pixel values are computed in horizontal and vertical directions. Then, the LSTM network corresponding to the direction with lesser variance is considered for predicting a pixel value. The idea behind selecting the direction with lesser variance is that lesser prediction error is expected in the direction with lesser variance (among the pixel values in a sequence).

3   Experimental Setup and Results

The proposed LSTM networks are trained using 400 randomly selected images from the episode-3 of the 2nd Break Our Watermarking System (BOWS-2) data set [31]. The size of each of these 400 gray scale images is 512×512. Fifteen such randomly selected images from the training data are shown in Fig. 3.

Tuples in the training set are obtained from these 400 training images. The criterion for considering pixel neighborhood (in Sect. 2.1) is followed for selecting the tuples in the training set. For training the LSTM networks, 5-fold cross validation based approach is performed. The tuples in the training data are split into 5 non-overlapping partitions. At every fold, the LSTM networks are trained using four of these partitions and validation is carried out on one partition (validation set). As a result of 5-fold cross validation, five models are learned. A set of 100 randomly selected images (different from the training images) from the BOWS-2 data set [31] is used to select the best performing model among these five models. The results of 5-fold cross validation are shown in Table 1 and Table 2 for horizontal and vertical directions, respectively. The model exhibiting the least mean squared error (MSE) between the original pixel values and the corresponding predicted values is selected as the best performing model. The models for fold 4 and fold 1 are selected for horizontal and vertical directions, respectively.

Performances of the selected trained LSTM network models are evaluated on a separate test set of 8 gray scale images: namely Airplane, Boat, Elaine, Lake, Lena, Mandrill, Peppers and Tiffany. These images are shown in Fig. 4. These individual LSTM networks are also compared against the proposed idea of leveraging both directions. Comparison of performances of the proposed individual

Fig. 3. Fifteen images illustrated at random from the training data.

Table 1. 5-fold cross validation training results of LSTM-H6

Fold	Mean Squared Error
Fold 1	41.12
Fold 2	42.63
Fold 3	43.49
Fold 4	**40.40**
Fold 5	41.77

Table 2. 5-fold cross validation training results of LSTM-V6

Fold	Mean Squared Error
Fold 1	**51.03**
Fold 2	52.02
Fold 3	51.55
Fold 4	53.53
Fold 5	56.10

LSTM neural networks (LSTM-H6 and LSTM-V6) and the proposed combination of these two LSTM predictors (LSTM-Comb) are reported in Table 3.

Table 3. Comparison of image-wise pixel prediction performances of the proposed individual predictors (LSTM-H6 and LSTM-V6) and the proposed combined version using both LSTM networks (LSTM-Comb)

Test Image	LSTM-H6	LSTM-V6	LSTM-Comb
Airplane	51.24	33.93	**26.70**
Boat	101.72	**54.36**	62.24
Elaine	**83.38**	107.70	86.16
Lake	92.46	93.40	**71.73**
Lena	44.57	30.61	**28.97**
Mandrill	256.96	359.41	**236.00**
Peppers	69.36	60.61	**53.00**
Tiffany	95.40	**49.67**	56.68
Average MSE	99.39	98.71	**77.68**

It can be observed from the reported MSE values in Table 3 that the proposed idea of leveraging both LSTM networks yields better results for following 5 images: Airplane, Lake, Lena, Mandrill and Peppers. Moreover, the average prediction performance of the leveraged version outperforms the individual prediction performances of LSTM-H6 and LSTM-V6. This indicates the efficacy of

Fig. 4. Eight gray scale test images: (left to right in first row) Airplane, Boat and Elaine; (left to right in second row) Lake, Lena and Mandrill; (left to right in third row) Peppers and Tiffany

the proposed idea of leveraging LSTM networks in both directions for predicting the pixel values in an image. Therefore, subsequent experiments consider the proposed combined version (LSTM-Comb) for pixel value prediction.

Subsequently, performance of the proposed LSTM network based pixel value predictor is compared with few state-of-the-art predictors using mean squared error (MSE) between the original pixel values and the corresponding predicted values. Eight gray scale images in Fig. 4 are used for this comparison. These state-of-the-art predictors include CNN based predictor [26], median edge detection (MED) predictor [14] and simplified gradient adjusted (SGAP) predictor [14]. These MSE values are presented in Table 4. It can be observed from the reported MSE values in Table 4 that the proposed LSTM network based pixel value predictor performs better than comparing state-of-the-art methods on an average.

Table 4. Performance comparison of the proposed LSTM network based predictor with few state-of-the-art predictors based on mean squared error.

Test Image	Proposed LSTM	CNN [26]	MED [14]	SGAP [14]
Airplane	26.70	**14.37**	45.77	57.27
Boat	62.24	**61.03**	88.32	92.32
Elaine	86.16	114.83	100.70	**76.95**
Lake	**71.73**	93.45	122.60	120.29
Lena	28.97	**22.80**	50.91	41.89
Mandrill	**236.00**	295.06	432.66	434.65
Peppers	**53.00**	55.69	66.78	63.09
Tiffany	56.68	**29.45**	47.39	41.26
Average MSE	**77.68**	85.84	119.40	115.96

4 Conclusion

In this paper, pixel value prediction task has been conceptualized as predicting the next pixel value in a spatial sequence based on the preceding pixel values. A novel pixel value predictor using long short term memory (LSTM) network has been proposed. Here, the LSTM network learned the pattern in a spatial sequence of pixel values. Two different LSTM networks - LSTM-H6 and LSTM-V6 - were trained using pixel neighborhood sequences in horizontal and vertical directions, respectively. The proposed approach in this paper leveraged both the trained networks. The LSTM network with a direction having lesser variance (over preceding pixel values in the sequence) was used to predict a pixel value. The experimental results indicated better performance of the proposed LSTM network based predictor than the comparing state-of-the-art predictors.

References

1. Thodi, D.M., Rodriguez, J.J.: Expansion embedding techniques for reversible watermarking. IEEE Trans. Image Process. **16**(3), 721–730 (2007)
2. Wu, H., Li, X., Luo, X., Zhang, X., Zhao, Y.: General expansion-shifting model for reversible data hiding: theoretical investigation and practical algorithm design. IEEE Trans. Circuits Syst. Video Technol. **32**(9), 5989–6001 (2022)
3. Leon, D., Balkir, S., Sayood, K., Hoffman, M.W.: A CMOS imager with pixel prediction for image compression. In: Proceedings of the IEEE International Symposium on Circuits and Systems, vol. 4, pp. IV-776–IV-779 (2003)
4. Ayoobkhan, M.U.A., Chikkannan, E., Ramakrishnan, K.: Lossy image compression based on prediction error and vector quantisation. EURASIP J. Image Video Process. **2017**(1), 1–13 (2017). https://doi.org/10.1186/s13640-017-0184-3
5. Kim, S., Qu, X., Sachnev, V., Kim, H.J.: Skewed histogram shifting for reversible data hiding using a pair of extreme predictions. IEEE Trans. Circuits Syst. Video Technol. **29**(11), 3236–3246 (2019)

6. Kumar, N., Kumar, R., Malik, A., Singh, S., Jung, K.-H.: Reversible data hiding with high visual quality using pairwise PVO and PEE. Multimedia Tools Appl. (2023)
7. Nguyen, N.-H., Pham, V.-A.: An efficient IPVO based reversible data hiding method using four pixel-pairs. Multimedia Tools Appl. (2023)
8. Coltuc, D., Dragoi, I.-C.: Context embedding for raster-scan rhombus based reversible watermarking. In: Proceedings of the First ACM Workshop on Information Hiding and Multimedia Security, pp. 215–220 (2013)
9. Dragoi, C., Coltuc, D.: Improved rhombus interpolation for reversible watermarking by difference expansion. In: Proceedings of the 20th European Signal Processing Conference, pp. 1688–1692 (2012)
10. Kim, D.-S., Yoon, E.-J., Kim, C., Yoo, K.-Y.: Reversible data hiding scheme with edge-direction predictor and modulo operation. J. Real-Time Image Process. **14**, 137–145 (2018)
11. Jia, Y., Yin, Z., Zhang, X., Luo, Y.: Reversible data hiding based on reducing invalid shifting of pixels in histogram shifting. Signal Process. **163**, 238–246 (2019)
12. Uyyala, R., Pal, R.: Reversible data hiding with selected directional context Based prediction using 8-neighborhood. In: Proceedings of IEEE International Conference on Electronics, Computing and Communication Technologies, pp. 1–6 (2020)
13. Naskar, R., Chakraborty, R.S.: Reversible watermarking utilizing weighted median-based prediction. IET Image Process. **6**(5), 507–520 (2012)
14. Coltuc, D.: Improved embedding for prediction-based reversible watermarking. IEEE Trans. Inf. Forensics Secur. **6**(3), 873–882 (2011)
15. Knezovic, J., Kovac, M.: Gradient based selective weighting of neighboring pixels for predictive lossless image coding. In: Proceedings of the 25th International Conference on Information Technology Interfaces, pp. 483–488 (2003)
16. Dragoi, I.C., Coltuc, D., Caciula, I.: Gradient based prediction for reversible watermarking by difference expansion. In: Proceedings of the 2nd ACM Workshop on Information Hiding and Multimedia Security, pp. 35–40 (2014)
17. Uyyala, R., Pal, R.: Reversible data hiding using improved gradient based prediction and adaptive histogram bin shifting. In: 7th International Conference on Signal Processing and Integrated Networks, pp. 720–726 (2020)
18. Chen, Y., Huang, D., Ma, G., Wang, J.: Gradient-based directional predictor for reversible data hiding. In: Proceedings of the 13th IEEE Conference on Industrial Electronics and Applications, pp. 1553–1556 (2018)
19. Shilpa, K., Aparna, P., Antony, A.: Gradient-oriented directional predictor for HEVC planar and angular intra prediction modes to enhance lossless compression. AEU - Int. J. Electron. Commun. **95**, 73–81 (2018)
20. Hong, W., Chen, T.S., Chen, J.: Reversible data hiding using Delaunay triangulation and selective embedment. Inf. Sci. **308**, 140–154 (2015)
21. Uyyala, R., Pal, R., Prasad, M.V.N.K.: Reversible data hiding using B-tree triangular decomposition based prediction. IET Image Process. **13**(11), 1986–1997 (2019)
22. Uyyala, R., Pal, R.: Reversible data hiding based on the random distribution of reference pixels. In: Proceedings of IEEE Region Ten Symposium, pp. 225–230 (2018)
23. Lu, T.-C., Chen, C.-M., Lin, M.-C., Huang, Y.-H.: Multiple predictors hiding scheme using asymmetric histograms. Multimedia Tools Appl. **76**(3), 3361–3382 (2017)

24. Bhandari, A., Sharma, S., Uyyala, R., Pal, R., Verma, M.: Reversible data hiding using multi-layer perceptron based pixel prediction. In: Proceedings of the 11th International Conference on Advances in Information Technology, pp. 1–8 (2020)
25. Myakal, S., Pal, R., Naveen, N.: Reversible data hiding technique using multi-layer perceptron based prediction and adaptive histogram bin shifting. In: Tiwari, A., Ahuja, K., Yadav, A., Bansal, J.C., Deep, K., Nagar, A.K. (eds.) Soft Computing for Problem Solving. AISC, vol. 1393, pp. 231–243. Springer, Singapore (2021). https://doi.org/10.1007/978-981-16-2712-5_20
26. Hu, R., Xiang, S.: CNN prediction based reversible data hiding. IEEE Signal Process. Lett. **28**, 464–468 (2021)
27. Hu, R., Xiang, S.: Reversible data hiding by using CNN prediction and adaptive embedding. IEEE Trans. Pattern Anal. Mach. Intell. **44**(12), 10196–10208 (2022)
28. Yang, X., Huang, F.: New CNN-based predictor for reversible data hiding. IEEE Signal Process. Lett. **29**, 2627–2631 (2022)
29. Zhang, X., Yao, Y., Yu, N.: Convolutional neural network-driven optimal prediction for image reversible data hiding. In: Proceedings of the 23rd International Workshop on Multimedia Signal Processing (2021)
30. Prabhakaran, A., Pal, R.: Image pixel prediction from neighborhood pixels using multilayer perceptron. In: Proceedings of the 7th International Conference on Soft Computing for Problem Solving, pp. 221–230 (2017)
31. BOWS-2 data set: episode-3 of the 2nd Break Our Watermarking System contest data set. http://bows2.ec-lille.fr/BOWS2OrigEp3.tgz

Efficient Trajectory Clustering of Movements of Moving Objects

Y. Subba Reddy[1], V. Thanuja[2], G. Sreenivasulu[3](✉) ⓘ, N. Thulasi Chitra[4], and K. Venu Madhav[5]

[1] Department of CSE, KG Reddy College of Engineering and Technology, Hyderabad, India
[2] Department of Master of Computer Applications, V R Institute of Post Graduate Studies, Nellore, India
[3] Department of CSE, ACE Engineering College, Hyderabad, India
[4] Department of CSE, MLR Institute of Technology, Hyderabad, India
[5] Department of CS&IS, School of Sciences, BIUST, Palapye, Botswana, South Africa

Abstract. Trajectory data mining is a very important data mining technique with respect to clustering of moving objects trajectories. It is the latest and hot topic in modern research area and it has got many real time applications. Trajectories of objects such as people, any alive things and many other are very useful for taking efficient and effective decision making in areas such as vehicle tracing, finding location of a desired service, finding location of a human being, cell, and so on. Trajectory data clustering is state-of-the-art data mining technique that is used in many real life applications such as finding movement sequence trends of people, animals, and vehicles and so on. A new algorithm is proposed for clustering trajectories of moving objects based on trajectory similarity measure called symmetrical difference measure (SDM). This measure is easy to compute and interpret for clustering objects of moving objects when compared with all the existing trajectory similarity finding measures.

Indexing Terms: Symmetrical Difference Measure · Trajectory data similarity · Trajectory database · Trajectory data clustering

1 Introduction

Nowadays movement data of objects are regularly collecting from GPS and sensors. The relationship among the objects with respect to time and space can be analyzed and it is useful in many real time applications, Many state-of-the-art based technologies are achieve and they are useful to collect very large amounts of movements of people, animals, ships, flights, buses, mobiles and so on. In the development of application systems the light of movement-based communities, many new novel location-based services used [1]. A research been put into data mining movement behavior from trajectories and given a set of trajectories, the goal of trajectory pattern data mining discover frequent sequential patterns that are sequential relationships around the regions [1]. Generally, geographical space is a continuous trace of a moving object in which a trajectory is only a

R. Morusupalli et al. (Eds.): MIWAI 2023, LNAI 14078, pp. 336–347, 2023.
https://doi.org/10.1007/978-3-031-36402-0_31

sample of identification points that the moving object passes [2]. Various techniques are available for finding similarities between the trajectories. Trajectory similarity measures are useful for trajectory clustering, classification, association and trajectory querying. For the given trajectories of two moving objects it is required to find similarity measures automatically. Nowadays the trajectory volumes of data rapidly increasing.

Data that captures the movements of a variety of objects, including smart-phone users, animals, vehicles, and vessels [3]. At present only a limited number of methods are available for finding similarity relationships in movement data. Trajectory simplification can improve the efficiency of many algorithms that operate on the trajectories by removing relatively unimportant data points [3].

Internet enabled mobile devices are primary sources for obtaining very large volumes of trajectory data that capture the movements of different types of objects such as people, vehicles, animals and vessels [7]. The increasing pervasiveness of location acquisition technologies has enabled collection of very large trajectory datasets for different types of moving objects. Useful patterns discovered from the movement behavior of moving objects are very valuable and forms a trajectory knowledgebase, and much useful to variety of real time applications. Ubiquitous amounts of trajectory data sets are being generated continuously with the rapid development of location acquisition technologies [5]. Trajectories of moving objects are useful in finding knowledge such as moving patterns, moving group patterns, finding location of a specific object or service etc. Many global positioning systems (GPS) enabled devices are pervasive [4]. Finding movement patterns in trajectory data stream is very useful in many real time applications [6].

A trajectory of a moving object is a discrete trace that the moving object travels in geographical space. Generally, it is a sequence of geo-locations with corresponding timestamps in spatiotemporal space [8].

Reasonably good methods are available for finding similarity between trajectories. Some of the most important trajectory similarities finding methods are:

1) Dynamic Time Wrapping (DTW)
2) Edit Distance with Projections (EDWP)
3) Edit Distance with Real Penalty (ERP)
4) Edit Distance on Real Sequence (EDR)
5) Model Driven Assignment (MA)
6) Longest Common Sub Sequence (LCSS)

Trajectory is the trace of moving object. There exist a wide spectrum of trajectories and other applications driven and improved by trajectory data mining, such as path discovery, location/destination prediction, movement behavior analysis for individual or a group of moving objects, making sense of urban service [2]. Different types of models have been proposed to capture the trajectory data sets. It is important to consider uncertainty of the trajectory data also. Trajectory data of moving objects is the most important on many real time applications. Generally trajectory data is available in the form of raw information trajectories and these trajectories must be preprocessed and simplified further for efficient and effective management. It is very convenient for trajectory data recording and storing traces of moving objects. Examples for trajectory data applications are-

1) To find user behavior analysis
2) To analyze traffic data details
3) To find social relationships among the people
4) To find the best rate among the possible potential roots.
5) To design and use optimal and best plans in the management of any city works.
6) Particularly useful for tracking mobile locations continuously
7) Particularly useful for tracking animal locations continuously

Before using trajectory data it must be preprocessed and stored in the good and convenient form in such a way that it is easy to use and manage. This trajectory preprocessing step is called trajectory simplifying and trajectory preprocessing positions must be preserved. Preprocessed trajectory data contains only important locations and these important locations are called hot regions and these hot regions are used in any trajectory data clustering technique. A set of known trajectories, the goal is to cluster trajectories into groups, and trajectories in the same group have a certain degree of similarity [1].

It is exactly model the movement similarity of users via using present similarity functions from user raw trajectories [1]. Trajectory data mining tasks are summarized and classified into several categories, i.e., pattern mining, clustering, classification and knowledge discovery [2]. A location is usually expressed by a tuple of < *longitude*; *latitude* > which is recorded by a GPS device. Each tuple of < *longitude*; *latitude* > corresponds to a unique point in geographical space [2].

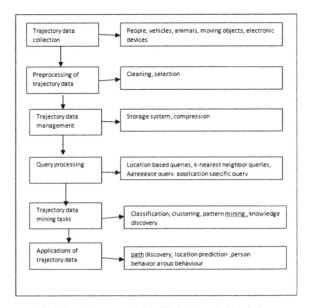

Fig. 1. A Framework for Trajectory Data Mining

2   Problem Definition

A trajectory is a contiguous locations covered by people, animals, or vehicles and so on. Trajectory database consists of collections of trajectories of moving objects. Usually trajectory database consists of raw trajectories and these raw trajectories must be preprocessed and stored in an efficient and effective way. Trajectories are represented using spatial and temporal spaces of moving objects in terms of sequences of locations consisting of positions and timestamp pairs:

$(position_1, time_1), (position_2, time_2),....., (position_n, time_n)$

Or simply $(x_1, y_1), (x_2, y_2),.....,(x_n, y_n)$

Trajectory similarity measures are used for trajectory clustering and for the simplicity purpose only locations are considered for trajectory clustering. That is, a trajectory is represented for simplicity purpose as $= (p_1, p_2, p_3,..., p_n)$ where $p_1, p_2, p_3,..., p_n$ are sequential locations (positions) of objects. Trajectories can be modeled either single dimensional model or multi dimensional models. Result accuracy increases as dimensionality representation increases. At present for simplicity purpose only sequential locations of trajectories are considered for trajectory clustering. Trajectory data classification and trajectory data association rule mining are also equally important trajectory data mining techniques. But in this paper only trajectory data clustering is considered and a new trajectory data clustering algorithm for moving objects is proposed. Initially each user is represented in special data structure for efficient and effective representation of all the trajectory details of one user. Sometimes this special data structure is very useful for applying pruning technique.

3   Trajectory Data Clustering Methodology

3.1   The Need

Trajectory data based clustering methodology is very useful for dividing trajectories into groups with similar movement patterns. Discovery of trajectory patterns leads to discovering interactions between moving objects [9]. Mobility primarily based information clustering is basically forming the similarity teams of moving objects like vehicles, animals, people, and cell phones so on. Moving objects are clustered based on trajectory related information such as the semantic meaning of trajectories, weights of locations, movement velocity, feature movements, feature characteristics, a temporal duration, and spatial dispersion.

3.2   The Framework

The field of trajectory data mining is spreading itself with fast evolution in it. Here efforts are made to mention the developments in the field. The field of trajectory data mining is conveniently represented in the Fig. 3.1. [10] (Table 1).

Location acquisition and mobile computing technologies are generating very large spatial trajectory data. Large spatial trajectory datasets represent mobility objects. A trajectory of a moving object could be a separate trace that the moving object travels in the geographical area.

Table 1. Data Mining: Broad field

Data Collection	Users Data	Vehicles Data	Animals Data	Location details of cell phones
Preprocessing	Cleaning	Sampling, Completion	Noise reduction	Stay point detection
Data Management	Efficient Storage	Indexing Structures Ex: B + tree, R-tree	Compression	
Query Processing	Location Based	Pattern Queries	Range Queries, k-NN Queries	Application Specific Queries
Trajectory Data Mining Tasks	Classification of Trajectory data	Clustering of Trajectory data	Pattern Mining of Trajectory data	Outlier Detection of Trajectory data
Applications of Trajectory Data Mining Technique	Desired Path Discovery	Desired Location Prediction	Group Behavior Analysis	City details, Transportation, Banking sector, Airlines system

4   Algorithm

Proposed new trajectory clustering algorithm

Read values of minimum support and minimum conditional probability values for representing user details in terms special data structure called special probability tree. Read all the trajectory profiles of all users and then store all the user profiles in the form of special and efficient data structure for effective decision making with help of multi branch tree data structure. All the trajectories are represented in terms of hot locations only. Also all these trajectories of various objects are represented and stored using indexing structures only because trajectory database is great in size. Proposed trajectory data clustering algorithm is shown in Fig. 1 and explained its execution details (Fig. 2).

Explanation of the new trajectory clustering algorithm.

Initially profile details of all the 'n' number of users are analyzed, preprocessed, modified and adjusted into cleaned trajectory data sets of 'n' number of users.. Trajectory details of all the users are represented and stored in the form of multi-way decision making tree data structures.

Time complexity of all the operations (insert, search, delete) in the tree data structures are $O(\log(n))$. Tree data structure reduces the time complexity from linear $O(n)$ to $O(\log n)$. While loop executes until the total number of clusters count become less than the threshold. Notice that each of the iterations of the while loop creates a special cluster called actor cluster and it is determined by finding middle cluster of the currently existing clusters. This middle cluster (actor cluster) is compared pair wise with all the remaining clusters. Symmetric difference measure is used for pair wise cluster comparison. The

---

Proposed New-Trajectory-Clustering Algorithm

---

1. Read values of minimum support and minimum conditional probability values for representing user details.

2. Read all the details of trajectory profiles of all the users
3. Store all the user profiles in the form of multi way decision making multi branch tree data structures

4. total-clusters = n

5. read-threshold
6. initial-cluster = 1
7. While (total cluster > threshold) do
{
    7.1 actor-cluster = total-cluster / 2
    7.2 for i = 1 to total-clusters do
      {
          find pair wise similarity measures of all trajectory clusters with the current actor-cluster
      }
    7.3 end for
    7.4 combine two clusters having minimum pair wise similarity measure value
    7.4 decrease total-cluster value by 1
}
8. print all the modified cluster details

Fig. 2. New trajectory clustering algorithm

pair of clusters with the smallest symmetrical measure is grouped together. The process is repeated until while condition becomes false.

In the first loop of the while loop n/2 is selected to the actor cluster and compared with all the remaining clusters. The pair wise clusters that are compared are $(n/2, 1)$, $(n/2, 2), (n/2, 3), (n/2, 4), ..., (n/2, n)$.

Clustered pairs considered in the second iteration are
$((n-1)/2, 1), ((n-1)/2, 2), ((n-1)/2, 3), ..., ((n-1)/2, n-1)$
Third iteration compared cluster pairs are
$((n-2)/2, 1), ((n-2)/2, 2), ((n-2)/2, 3), ...((n-2)/2, n-1)$

5   Example for Trajectory Data Clustering

Consider the following set of trajectory data sets of nine moving objects such as users. For simplicity purpose only nine trajectory data sets of users are considered.

User1 = {A, B, C, AB, BC, ABC}

User2 = {A, B, C, AB, AC, BC}

User3 = {B, C, D, BC, BD, CD, BCD}

User4 = {B, C, D, E, BC, BD, BE, CD, BDE,

CDE}

User5 = {A, B, C, D, AB, BC, CD, ABC)

User6 = {A, B, C, D, AB, AC, BC, CD}

User7 = {B, C, D, BC, BD, CD, BCD}

At the beginning, movements of each user are represented as a special tree data structure. These trees are generated either by using breadth first search (BFS) or depth first search (DFS) traversals. Sometimes pruning is necessary to obtain optimal tree data structures. Once all the user trees are constructed then these user trees are clustered using proposed new clustering technique. This new clustering technique uses a new trajectory similarity measure called symmetrical difference between clusters.

For example, assume that trajectory profile of a particular user is {ABCD, ACD, ABD} (Fig. 3).

Corresponding user's trajectories tree is shown in Fig. 1

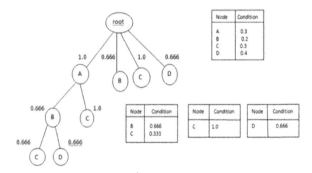

Fig. 3. User trajectory tree

Symmetrical difference between user trajectory1 and user trajectory2 is defined as
Symmetrical difference = {user1 - user2} union {user2-user1}
Here, total no of clusters is 9. Actor cluster number is computed as
Actor cluster = total number of clusters/2 = 9/2 = 4

Here, 4th cluster is taken as actor cluster. Pair wise symmetrical difference is computed with actor cluster and in all the remaining clusters. This process is illustrated below. SDM means symmetrical difference measure.

SDM (user4, user2) = {user4 - user2} Union {user2 - user4}

= {D, E, BD, CD, BDE, CDE} Union {A, AB, AC}
={D,E,BD,BE,CD,BDE,CDE,A,AB,AC}
Count is = 10

SDM (User4, user3) = {user4 - user3} Union {user3 - user4}
= {E, BE, BDE, CDE} Union {BCD}
= {E, BE, BDE, CDE, BCD}
Count is = 5

SDM (user4, user5) = {user4-user5} Union {user5-user4}
={B,E,BD,BE,BDE,CDE}U{A,AB,ABC}
={ B,E,BD,BE,BDE,CDE , A,AB,ABC }
Count is = 9

SDM (user4, user6) = {user4 - user6}u{user6 - user4}
= {E, BD, BE, BDE, CDE} Union {A, AB, AC}
= {E, BD, BE, BDE, CDE, A, AB, AC}
Count is = 8

SDM (user4, user7) = {user4 - user7} Union {user7 - user4}
= {E, BD, BE, BDE, CDE} Union {BCD}
= {E, BD, BE, BDE, CDE, BCD}
Count is = 6

SDM (User4, user8) = {user4 - user8} Union{user8 - user4}
= {BE} Union { }
= {BE}
Count is = 1

SDM (user4, user9) = {user4 - user9} Union {user9 - user4}
={E,BC,BD,BE,CD,BDE,CDE}Union{A,AB,AC,ABC,ACD}
={ E,BC,BD,BE,CD,BDE,CDE ,A,AB,AC,ABC,ACD}

Count is = 12

Actor cluster 4 is compared with all the remaining clusters the symmetrical difference measure (SDM) is minimum between actor cluster 4 and cluster 8. So, clusters 4 and 8 are combined. After combining these two clusters total number of clusters becomes eight and the same process is repeated for these eight clusters and these eight clusters are shown below:

User1= {A, B, C, AB, BC, ABC}

User2= {A, B, C, AB, AC, BC}

User3= {B, C, D, BC, BD, CD, ABC}

User4= {A, B, C, D, AB, BC, CD, ABC}

User5= {A, B, C, D, AB, AC, BC, BD}

User6= {B, C, D, BC, CD, BCD}

User7= {A, B, C, D, AB, AC, ABC, ACD}

User8= {B, C, D, E, BC, BD, CD, BE, BDE, CDE}

Actor-Cluster = total number of clusters/2 =8/2 = 4th cluster
Actor-Cluster = {A, B, C, D, AB, BC, CD, ABC} = 4th cluster
SDM (4, 1) ={USER4 - USER1}U{USER1- USER4)
            = {D, CD} Union { } = {D, CD}
                Count = 2
SDM (4, 2) ={D, CD, ABC}Union{AC}
            = {D, CD, ABC, AC}
                Count is = 4
SDM (4, 3) = {A, AB, ABC} Union {BD, BCD}
            = {A, AB, ABC, BD, BCD}
 Count is =5
SDM (4, 5) = {ABC} Union {AC} = {AC, ABC}
Count is =2
SUM (4, 6) = {A, AB, ABC} Union {BCD}
            = {A, AB, ABC, BCD}
                Count is =4
 SUM (4, 7) = {BC, CD} Union {AC, ACD}
            = {BC, CD, AC, ACD}
                Count is =4
SDM (Cluster4, Cluster8) = {A, AB, ABC} Union (E, BD, BE, BDE, CDE}
                    ={A,AB,ABC, E,BD,BE,BDE,CDE}

        Count is = 8

Minimum value is = 2 at clusters 4 and 1. Hence, clusters 4 and 1 are grouped together and new clusters are shown below.

```
User1= {A, B, C, AB, AC, BC}

User2= {B, C, D, BC, BD, CD, BCD}

User3= {A, B, C, D, AB, AC, BC, CD}

User4= {B, C, D, BC, CD, BCD}

User5= {A, B, C, D, AB, AC, ABC, ACD}

User6= {B, C, D, E, BC, BD, CD, BE, BDE, CDE}

User7= {A, B, C, D, AB, BC, CD, ABC}
```

Actor-Cluster=total number of clusters/2=7/2= 3rd cluster
Cluster = {A, B, C, D, AB, BC, CD, ABC} = 3rd cluster
SDM (3, 1) = {USER3_USER1} Union {USER1-USER3)
       = {D, CD} Union { } = {D, CD}
       Count is = 2
SDM (3, 2) = {A,AB,AC}Union {BD,BC}
       = {A, AB, AC, BD, BC}
      Count is = 5
SDM (3, 4) = {A, AB, AC} Union {BCD}
       = {A, AB, AC, BCD}
      Count is = 4
SDM (3, 5) = {BC, CD} Union {ABC, ACD}
       = {BC, CD, ABC, ACD}
      Count is =4
SDM(3, 6)={A,AB,AC}Union{ E,BD,BE,BDE,CDE }
       = {A, AB, AC, E, BD, BE, BDE, CDE}
      Count is = 8
SDM (3,7)={AC}Union{ABC}={AC, ABC}
      Count is = 2
Clusters 3 and 1are grouped together.
SDM(3,1)={A,AB,AC,ABC,ACD}Union{BC,BD,CD,BCD}

```
User1 = {B, C, D, BC, BD, CD, BCD}

User2 = {B, C, D, BC, CD, BCD}

User3 = {A, B, C, D, AB, AC, ABC, ACD}

User4 = {B, C, D, E, BC, BD, CD, BE, BDE, CDE}

User5 = {A, B, C, D, AB, BC, CD, ABC}

User6 = {A, B, C, D, AB, AC, BC, CD}
```

SDM(3,2) ={A,AB.AC,ABC,ACD}Union{BC,CD,BCD}
       ={ A,AB.AC,ABC,ACD , BC,CD,BCD }

The entire given trajectory details of nine users are grouped into three cluster groups as shown in Table 2.

Table 2. Final clustered trajectories

Cluster group	Clusters of users
1	{4, 8)
2	{3, 7}
3	{1, 2, 4, 5, 9}

First group contains two clusters, second group contains two clusters and third group contains 3 clusters.

Time Complexity of Proposed Trajectory Data Clustering Algorithm
At the very beginning, first actor cluster is compared with all other remaining (n-1) clusters in the first iteration. In the second iteration second actor cluster is compared with (n-2) remaining clusters. In the third pass actor cluster is compared with the remaining (n-3) clusters and so on. Hence the proposed trajectory clustering algorithm total time complexity $= (n - 1) + (n - 2) + (n - 3) + (n - 4) + \ldots\ldots + 4$
$1 + 2 + 3 + 4 + 5 + \ldots..(n\text{-}4) + (n\text{-}3) + (n\text{-}2) + (n\text{-}1) - 6$
$((n - 1)^*n)/2 - 6 = (n^2 - n)/2 - 6 = n^2/2 - n/2 = n^2/2 = O(n^2)$

6   Conclusions

Trajectory data mining is one of the hottest research topics. Trajectory data clustering is one of the state-of-the-art research topics in trajectory data mining. A new trajectory data clustering algorithm is proposed for clustering movement communities of moving objects. In the future more efficient trajectory similarity measuring algorithms will be introduced for efficient and effective trajectory data clustering. Also trajectory data clustering will be studied in the multidimensional view.

References

1. Zhu, W.-Y., Peng, W.-C., Hung, C.-C., Lei, P.-R., Chen, L.-J.: Exploring sequential probability tree for movement-based community discovery. IEEE Transactions on Knowledge and Data Engineering 26(11) (NOVEM BER 2014)
2. Feng, Z., Zhu, Y.: Department of Computer Science and Engineering, Shanghai Jiao Tong University, Shanghai 200240, China A Survey on Trajectory Data Mining: Techniques and Applications. Special Section on Theoretical Foundations for Big Data Applications: Challenges and Opportunities
3. Li, X., C_eikute, V., Tan, K.-L.: Effective online group discovery in trajectory databases. IEEE Trans Actions on Knowledge and Data Engineering 25(12) (DECEMBER 2013)
4. Cao, X., Cong, G., Jensen, C.S.: Mining Significant Semantic Locations from GPS Data. Proc. VLDB Endowment 3(1), 1009–1020 (2010)

5. Chen, Z., Shen, H.T., Zhou, X., Zheng, Y., Xie, X.: Searching trajectories by locations: an efficiency study. In: Proc. ACM SIGMOD Int. Conf. Manage. Data (SIGMOD), Indianapolis, IN, USA, pp. 255–266 (Jun. 2010)
6. Taniar, D., Goh, J.: School of Business Systems, Monash University, Clayton, Vic, Australia" On Mining Movement Pattern from Mobile Users. International Journal of Distributed Sensor Networks **3**, 69–86 (2007). ISSN: 1550-1329 print/1550-1477 online
7. Kalayeh, M.M., Mussmann, S., Petrakova, A.: Niels da Vitoria Lobo and Mubarak Shah "Understanding Trajectory Behavior: A Motion pattern approach" arXiv:1501.00614v1 [cs.CV] (4 Jan 2015)
8. Feng, Z., Zhu, Y.: (Member, IEEE), Department of Computer Science and Engineering, Shanghai Jiao Tong University, Shanghai 200240,China Shanghai Key Laboratory of Scalable Computing and Systems, Shanghai Jiao Tong University, Shanghai 200240, China. "A Survey on Trajectory Data Mining: Techniques and Applications"
9. Zheng, Y., Zhang, L., Ma, Z., Xie, X., Ma, W.-Y.: Recommending Friends and Locations Based on Individual Location History. ACM Trans. Web **5**(1) (Feb. 2011). article 5
10. Fengi, Z., Zhu, Y.: A Survey on Trajectory Data Mining: Techniques and Applications. IEEE Access **4** (April, 2016)

Node Cooperation Enforcement Scheme for Enhancing Quality of Service in MANETs Using Machine Learning Approach

Srinivasulu Sirisala[1]([✉]) [ID], G. Rajeswarappa[2] [ID], and Srikanth Lakumarapu[1] [ID]

[1] Department of CSE, CVR College of Engineering, Hyderabad, India
vasusirisala@gmail.com
[2] Department of CSE, G Pulla Reddy Engineering College, Kurnool, Andhra Pradesh, India
rajeswarappa.cse@gprec.ac.in

Abstract. Mobile Adhoc network (MANET) is a wireless and infrastructure less network where nodes may behave non cooperative due to limited resource constraint. In this paper a node cooperation enforcement scheme assess the node's trust with respect to multiple parameters namely packet forwarding potential, node energy, throughput, delay. In MANETs due to the node's limited resource nature and frequent and unpredictable network topology, it is not suffice to consider node's current trust also it is required to consider nodes previous behavior for which in this paper a predictive model used to decide the node is trusted or not. The proposed Machine Learning based Node Cooperation Enforcement Scheme (MLNCES) performance is analyzed experimentally. In simulation results, the proposed method MLNCES outperforms the FCOPRAS-NCETE and GTF-GDMT approaches.

Keywords: Mobile Ad hoc Network (MANETs) · Nodes' Cooperation · Trust prediction · Regression

1 Introduction

MANETs comprise of multiple cooperating nodes that possesses self-organizing potential and restricted energy. Node cooperation during the process of routing is essential in MANETs for improving the QoS factors of packet delivery rate, throughput with minimized delay, jitter, and energy consumptions in the network. But the degree of cooperation may get crumbled when the mobile nodes exhibit malicious and selfish behavior in the network. This amount of non-cooperation contributed by the mobile nodes affects routing and lowers the network performance. Thus, node co-operation imposing technique that differentiates candid from malevolent node is vital for effective network performance.

In general as MANET is a infrastructure less network, to conserve the energy nodes will exhibit malicious behavior and it is noticed that, there is fall in the QoS due to the existence of selfish and malicious. Hence it is highly essential to identify and isolate the selfish and malicious nodes from the routing path. To address this issue it is required to compute the each intermediate node's cooperation degree (trust). The Multi Attribute Decision Making (MADM) is widely accepted approach for finding node's cooperation degree. In MADM node's attributes (packet delivery ratio, node energy, throughput, delay, etc.) are taken into the consideration to compute the node's cooperation degree.

The potential for developing a node cooperation enforcement scheme COPRAS-based selfish and malicious node detection and isolation method is motivated by the contributions of MADM techniques like Multi-Objective Optimization by Ratio Analysis (MOORA) [2], Technique for Order of Preference by Similarity to Ideal Solution (TOPSIS) [3], Simple Additive Weighting (SAW) [4], Preference Ranking Organization Method for Enrichment Evaluation (PROMETHEE) [5], and Complex Proportional Assessment Method (COPRAS) [6].

In MANETs trust of a node is computed either through direct method or indirect method (recommendation based) [1, 7, 8]. In both approaches the past behavior of node is not taken into consideration. In this context Multivariate regression model can be used to evaluate a node's trustworthiness. It is a statistical method for simulating the relationship between several independent factors and a dependent variable. Assessing the trust of nodes is a crucial task in the context of Mobile Ad hoc Networks (MANETs), because nodes communicate with one another in decentralized manner. The regression model trained with the node's previous trust values against various attribute values (node energy, through put, delay, packet delivery rate) and it predicts the node's current trust value for the node's current attributes status.

In this paper COPRAS method along with Regression Model is used to compute the trust of a node.

2   Related Work

This section reviews the work on node cooperation methods and the machine learning based node cooperation enforcement schemes.

A Fuzzy COPRAS [9] model proposed which combines merits of fuzzy set theory and COPRAS to compute cooperation degree of nodes in the routing path and thereby mitigate the misbehaving nodes along the path. It uses fuzzy set theory as it is good enough in handling the uncertainty introduced by the vague and inaccurate data derived from the mobile nodes observed through direct and indirect interaction. COPRAS take fuzzy values to compute node's cooperation degree based on which rank the nodes. Low ranked nodes are treated as misbehaving node and isolated from the routing path. From the results it is evident that the proposed Fuzzy COPRAS can intensely decrease the total identification time with less overhead.

In [10] it was proposed a probabilistic based Gaussian Trust Factor based Grey Decision Making Technique (GTF-GDMT). It considers the past behavior of node while computing its trust thus it has achieved improved detection rate of falsely nodes. A cooperative watch dog method [11] proposed for perceiving selfish nodes. A node that identifies selfish node propagates this information to all other node which comes into contact. This method minimized selfish node detection time and got improved precision in perceiving the selfish nodes.

In [12] it was proposed a machine learning (ML) based approach, that uses benefits of Rough Set Theory (RST) and Support Vector Machine and achieved high accuracy in intrusion detection.

In [14] probabilistic ML techniques used to asses risk caused by vulnerable nodes thereby sustain QoS in the MANET.

In [13] Deep learning and Reinforcement principles used. A RL agent trained to make predictions on malicious and trustworthy nodes and to perform classification on them.

Q-Learning technique [15] used, so that each node learns and got improved in adjusting its route request forwarding rate according to trust score of neighbor.

Based on condensed trust values, a global approach for assessing trust was offered [16]. In the described approach, the trust model depended on a bayes approach to determine the level of confidence and similarly.

3 Node Cooperation Enforcement Scheme

The proposed MLNCES derives the benefits of COPRAS and regression based predictive model for assessing cooperation degree (trust) of node thereby avoids low trust rated nodes from routing path and ensure QoS in the network.

3.1 COPRAS

The Steps of COPRAS which is incorporated in our proposed MLNCES are as follows.

Step1: Computation of weights and performance ratings of nodes is done through direct and indirect trust sensing methods. If 's' decision makers (D1, D2,..., Ds) assess the weights of the 'q' selection indices (C1, C2,..., Cq), as well as the performance ratings of the "r" intermediate nodes (MN_1, MN_2,..., MN_r), against each of these "q" selection indices (throughput, packet forwarding ratio, energy consumption, packet delay), the weights (W_i) and performance ratings (R_{ki}) may be stated as:

$$WT_{MN(i)} = \frac{1}{n}\left(WT_{MN(1)} \oplus WT_{MN(2)} \oplus \ldots \oplus WT_{MN(r)}\right) \tag{1}$$

$$R_{MN(ki)} = \frac{1}{n}\left(R_{MN(ki1)} \oplus R_{MN(ki2)} \oplus \ldots \oplus R_{MN(kis)}\right) = \frac{1}{n}\sum_{j=1}^{s} R_{MN(kij)} \tag{2}$$

where, $WT_{MN(i)}$ $(i = 1, 2, \ldots.q)$ is the aggregated weight of each selection indices contributed by "r" nodes and $R_{MN(ki)}$ $(k = 1, 2, \ldots.r; i = 1, 2, \ldots., q; j = 1, 2, \ldots., s)$ is the aggregated performance rating of "r" selection indices over selection index Cq.

Step 2: prepare Performance Rating Matrix (PRM)

$$M_{PR} = \begin{bmatrix} pr_{11} & pr_{12} & \cdots\cdots & pr_{1r} \\ pr_{21} & pr_{22} & \cdots\cdots & pr_{2r} \\ \cdots\cdots\cdots\cdots\cdots\cdots\cdots\cdots \\ pr_{q1} & pr_{q2} & \cdots\cdots & pr_{qr} \end{bmatrix} \tag{3}$$

where, pr_{ij} is the aggregated perform rating computed with respect to "S" decision makers.

Step 3: Computing Normalized Performance Rating Matrix (NPRM)

The basic goal of normalizing performance matrices is to assign each restricted PRM element a dimension-less value. Based on parameters such as packet forwarding potential and throughput, energy consumption, packet delay, and packet retransmissions, each node's performance rating is calculated. Yet, the dimensions of these variables vary (i.e. they are measured in different units and different scales). Hence, the PRM normalization procedure aids in the conversion of various performance rating components into a single rating unit within a scale of measurement. This normalizing procedure is used to fit the input data into values that fall within a similar range and are based on a specified scale. Moreover, this normalization acts as an anchor, promoting steady bias and weight convergence. NPRM is determined through Eq. (4).

$$M_{NPR} = \begin{bmatrix} npr_{11} & npr_{12} & \cdots & npr_{1r} \\ npr_{21} & npr_{22} & \cdots & npr_{2r} \\ \cdots\cdots\cdots\cdots\cdots\cdots\cdots \\ npr_{q1} & npr_{q2} & \cdots & npr_{qr} \end{bmatrix} \tag{4}$$

where, 'npr_{ij}' is computed using Eq. (5).

$$npr_{ij} = \frac{pr_{ij}}{\sum_{i=1}^{q} pr_{ij}} \tag{5}$$

Step 4: Weighted Normalization (WNPRM)

In this step, the weights associated with each attribute are multiplied with corresponding attribute row elements of performance matrix's to create the weighted NPRM.

$$M_{WNPR} = \begin{bmatrix} wnpr_{11} & wnpr_{12} & \cdots & wnpr_{1r} \\ wnpr_{21} & wnpr_{22} & \cdots & wnpr_{2r} \\ \cdots\cdots\cdots\cdots\cdots\cdots\cdots \\ wnpr_{q1} & wnpr_{q2} & \cdots & wnpr_{qr} \end{bmatrix} \tag{6}$$

Suppose, '$W_{MN(j)}$' is the weight of the associated 'j^{th}' selection index, then weighted normalization over PRM is determined based on Eq. (7).

$$wnpr_{ij} = npr_{ij} \times W_{MN(j)} \tag{7}$$

Step 5: Calculating positive and negative beneficiary values of attribute criteria.

In this step, the ratings of maximization attribute (throughout, packet forwarding potential) criteria are added similarly minimization attribute (energy consumption, packet delay) criteria are added through Eq. (8) and (9) to determine positive and negative beneficiary values of attribute criteria.

$$NB_{ij}^{-} = \sum_{j=1}^{n} wnpr_{-ij}^{n} \tag{8}$$

$$B_{ij}^+ = \sum_{j=1}^{n} wnpr_{+ij}^n \tag{9}$$

Step 6: Estimating of Cooperation Degree

The cooperation degree of the intermediate mobile nodes that are present in the network's routing path between the source and the destination is computed using Eq. (10) based on the minimization optimization value shown in Eq. (10).

$$COP_{DEG(MN(i))} = \frac{SL_{MIN(i)}}{SL_{max}} \times 100\% \tag{10}$$

where,

$$SL_{MIN(i)} = B_{ij}^+ + \frac{B_{MIN}^- \sum_{i=1}^{m} B_i^-}{B_i^- \sum_{i=1}^{m} \frac{B_{MIN}^-}{B_i^-}} \tag{11}$$

$COP_{DEG(MN(i))}$ reflects the relative weight of each mobile node participating in the routing path.

3.2 Predicting NODE's Cooperation Degree

Using COPRAS method, while computing the trust, node's past history is not taken into consideration. In MANETS due to the mobility nature of the nodes and limited power constraints node may not give consistent cooperation for routing process. Hence it is required to take the node's past behavior in to consideration for predicting the current behavior during the routing process.

The MLNCES uses basic AODV routing protocol. It collects the each node's current state (throughput, packet forwarding potential, energy consumption, packet delay and trust) along the routing path using RREQ packet during the route request phase. MLNCES takes node's status as an entry into the dataset of that node. Likewise MLNCES prepares dataset of a node from its past status. MLNCES uses supervised regression algorithm to train the model. Out of the entire capacity of dataset 80% been used for training the model and 20% used to test the model. After computing the node's cooperation degree using COPRAS, MLNECS deploys the regression based predictive model, which determines node's is trust value using Eq. (12).

$$Y = \beta_0 + \beta_1 X_1 + \beta_2 X_2 + \cdots + \beta_p X_p + \epsilon \tag{12}$$

where "x_i" takes the different ranged values of node's attribute criteria (throughout, packet forwarding ratio, energy consumption, packet delay) and Y is the estimated trust.

The final Cooperation degree is computed in Eq. (13).

$$FCOP_{DEG(MN(i))} = 0.8 * COP_{DEG(MN(i))} + 0.2 * Y \tag{13}$$

Table 1. Simulation parameters used in implementing MLNECS

Simulation parameters	Values considered
MANET routing protocol	AODV
Complete number of mobile nodes	100
Complete number of source and destination pairs	40
Transmission capacity	2 kbps
Transmission range	250 m
Simulation area	1000×1000 m^2
Simulation time	11.26 min
Threshold trust value	0.4
Rate of nodes mobility	10 m per second
Packet size	512 Bytes
Type of data traffic	CBR (Constant Bit Rate)
Pause time	10 s
Model used for node mobility	Random Way Point model

4 Simulation Results and Discussion

The proposed MLNCES deploys the COPRAS and LR to attain Cooperation degree and uses AODV for the complete routing process. The simulation experiments of MLNCES are done through ns-2.34 simulator and simulation parameters are shown in Table 1.

The suggested MLNCES approach's average packet delivery rate and average throughput, as tested with various malicious nodes, are highlighted in Figs. 1 and 2.

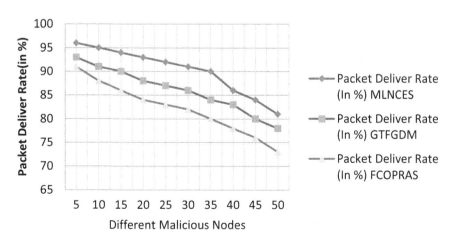

Fig. 1. MLNCES – Mean Packet Delivery rate

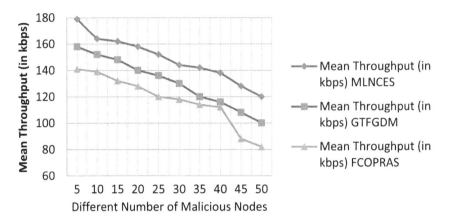

Fig. 2. MLNCES – Mean throughput

With MLNCES mean packet delivery rate is found to be maximum maintained independent of the number of malicious nodes because the time required for trust building with a corresponding rise in the number of malicious nodes in the network, estimate and its isolation both significantly increase. In comparison to the baseline GTFGDM and FCOPRAS approaches, the mean packet delivery rate of the suggested MLNCES strategy with various malicious nodes is found to be enhanced by 11.84% and 13.62%. It has also been confirmed that the suggested MLNCES strategy improves mean throughput by 12.94% and 14.26% when used with various malicious nodes.

5 Conclusion

In MANETs, node's cooperation plays a vital role in achieving the QoS. The inadequate resources of a node motivate the node to be non cooperative. In the proposed MLNCES, COPRAS considers multiple QoS attributes to assess the cooperation degree to the more accurate level. The regression model considered the node's past behavior to predict the trust value. Further, the aggregated value of node cooperation degree derived from COPRAS and predictive model values. As predictive model is used in addition to the COPRAS, in results it is noticed a significant improvement in the performance with respect to the increased number of malicious nodes.

References

1. Sirisala, N.R., Yarava, A., Reddy, Y.C.A.P., Poola, V.: A novel trust recommendation model in online social networks using soft computing methods. Concurr. Comput. Pract. Exp. **34**, e7153 (2022). https://doi.org/10.1002/cpe.7153
2. Thakkar, J.J.: Multi-objective optimization on the basis of ratio analysis method (MOORA). In: Multi-Criteria Decision Making. SSDC, vol. 336, pp. 191–198. Springer, Singapore (2021). https://doi.org/10.1007/978-981-33-4745-8_11

3. Uzun, B., Taiwo, M., Syidanova, A., Uzun Ozsahin, D.: The technique for order of preference by similarity to ideal solution (TOPSIS). In: Uzun Ozsahin, D., Gökçekuş, H., Uzun, B., LaMoreaux, J. (eds.) Application of Multi-Criteria Decision Analysis in Environmental and Civil Engineering. PPES, pp. 25–30. Springer, Cham (2021). https://doi.org/10.1007/978-3-030-64765-0_4

4. Arsyah, U.I., Jalinus, N., Syahril, A., Arsyah, R.H., Pratiwi, M.: Analysis of the simple additive weighting method in educational aid decision making. Turk. J. Comput. Math. Edu. **12**(14), 2389–2396 (2021)

5. Uzun, B., Almasri, A., Uzun Ozsahin, D.: Preference ranking organization method for enrichment evaluation (PROMETHEE). In: Uzun Ozsahin, D., Gökçekuş, H., Uzun, B., LaMoreaux, J. (eds.) Application of Multi-Criteria Decision Analysis in Environmental and Civil Engineering. PPES, pp. 37–41. Springer, Cham (2021). https://doi.org/10.1007/978-3-030-64765-0_6

6. Garg, R., Kumar, R., Garg, S.: MADM-based parametric selection and ranking of E-learning websites using fuzzy COPRAS. IEEE Trans. Educ. **1**(1), 1–8 (2018)

7. Sirisala, S., Ramakrishna, S.: Survey: enhanced trust management for improving QoS in MANETs. In: Bapi, R.S., Rao, K.S., Prasad, M.V.N.K. (eds.) First International Conference on Artificial Intelligence and Cognitive Computing. AISC, vol. 815, pp. 255–263. Springer, Singapore (2019). https://doi.org/10.1007/978-981-13-1580-0_25

8. Sengathir, J., Manoharan, R.: Exponential reliability factor based mitigation mechanism for selfish nodes in MANETs. J. Eng. Res. **4**(1), 1–22 (2016)

9. Sirisala, S., Rama Krishna, S.: Fuzzy COPRAS-based Node Cooperation Enforcing Trust Estimation Scheme for enhancing Quality of Service (QoS) during reliable data dissemination in MANETs. Int. J. Commun. Syst. **34**(7), e4767 (2021). https://doi.org/10.1002/dac.4767

10. Sirisala, S., Rama Krishna, S.: Gaussian trust factor-based grey decision making technique (GTF-GDMT) for node cooperation enforcement in MANETs. Int. J. Intell. Eng. Syst. (IJIES) **14**, 154–165 (2021). ISSN: 2185-3118

11. Hernandez-Orallo, E., Olmos, M.D.S., Cano, J.C., Calafate, C.T., Manzoni, P.: CoCoWa: a collaborative contact-based watchdog for detecting selfish nodes. IEEE Trans. Mob. Comput. **14**(6), 1162–1175 (2014)

12. Poongothai, T., Duraiswamy, K.: Intrusion detection in mobile AdHoc networks using machine learning approach. In: International Conference on Information Communication and Embedded Systems (ICICES 2014), Chennai, India, pp. 1–5 (2014). https://doi.org/10.1109/ICICES.2014.7033949

13. Jinarajadasa, G., Rupasinghe, L., Murray, I.: A reinforcement learning approach to enhance the trust level of MANETs. In: 2018 National Information Technology Conference (NITC), Colombo, Sri Lanka, pp. 1–7 (2018). https://doi.org/10.1109/NITC.2018.8550072

14. Michael, H., Jedidiah, A.: Mobile Adhoc networks - an overview of risk identification, intrusion detection and machine learning techniques used. In: 2022 IEEE 2nd International Conference on Mobile Networks and Wireless Communications (ICMNWC), Tumkur, Karnataka, India, pp. 1–5 (2022). https://doi.org/10.1109/ICMNWC56175.2022.10031757

15. Vijaya Kumar, A., Jeyapal, A.: Self-adaptive trust based ABR protocol for MANETs using Q-learning. Sci. World J. **2014**, 9, Article ID 452362 (2014). https://doi.org/10.1155/2014/452362

16. Josang, A., Quattrociocchi, W.: Advanced features in Bayesian reputation systems. In: Fischer-Hübner, S., Lambrinoudakis, C., Pernul, G. (eds.) TrustBus. LNCS, vol. 5695, pp. 105–114. Springer, Heidelberg (2009). https://doi.org/10.1007/978-3-642-03748-1_11

Interpreting Chest X-Ray Classification Models: Insights and Complexity Measures in Deep Learning

Anirban Choudhury[(✉)] and Sudipta Roy

Department of Computer Science and Engineering, Assam University, Silchar, India
`ref.anirban@gmail.com`

Abstract. Triumph of Deep Learning methods in solving many pressing practical problems in the framework of supervised, un-supervised, self-supervised learning etc. are ubiquitous, yet their interpretation and assessment of robustness in terms of quantifying complexity measure is an ongoing endeavour. This line of work tries to reason this in agreement with empirically justified notion of overparameterization in interpolating regime and implicit regularization of Deep neural network models, in many settings. Our work tries to consolidate these ideas and empirically validate the findings in the setting of supervised Chest X-Ray classification. We find that our design choices in constructing Chest X-Ray classification model progress towards the phenomenon of Double descent and notion of Implicit regularization. We report effect of our designed choices on the classification output quantified in terms of precision, recall and AUC (Area Under ROC Curve) score.

Keywords: Deep Learning(DL) · Deep Neural Network(DNN) · Overparameterization · Interpolation · Benign Overfitting · Implicit Regularization · Chest Radiography(CXR)

1 Introduction

Advances in Deep learning methods [10] unfolding in rapid pace, touching application areas in Computer Vision [5,7], Language Modeling [4,9] and Reinforcement learning [11]. Deep neural network are non-linear parameterized family of computational/statistical model, that typically has the form:

$$f(x; w) = \psi_L(w_L \psi_{L-1}(w_{L-1}...\psi(w_1 x))...) \tag{1}$$

where L is the number of layers in the neural network, $w_L \in \mathbb{R}^{d_l \times d_{l-1}}$ are the parameters of the network and $d_0 = d$ is the dimension of data and $\psi : \mathbb{R}^{d_l} \to \mathbb{R}^{d_l}$, is the fixed non-linearity. Given a training data: $(x_1, y_1), (x_2, y_2),$ ..., $(x_n, y_n) \in \mathbb{R}^d \times \mathbb{R}^{d_L}$, the parameters w are chosen by gradient method to minimize the empirical risk [1]:

R. Morusupalli et al. (Eds.): MIWAI 2023, LNAI 14078, pp. 356–367, 2023.
https://doi.org/10.1007/978-3-031-36402-0_33

$$\hat{L}(w) = \frac{1}{n} \sum_{i=1}^{n} l(f(x_i; w), y_i) \tag{2}$$

where l is a suitable loss function.

In doing so, complexity of the underlying function class must be quantified and controlled in statistical and computational sense, so that empirical risk quantified by sample average of training set given by Eq.2 must converge to expectation:

$$L(w) = \mathbb{E}[l(f(x; w), y)] \tag{3}$$

uniformly across function class.

Deep learning methods seems to achieve this convergence, to an expressive function class with large number of parameters (Overparameterization) by fitting the training data completely (Interpolation). Although this benign overfitting of training data seems to be in conflict with classical wisdom that says, there must be a balance between model complexity and data sample (bias-variance tradeoff), so as to achieve a desired performance in chosen task, yet this way of computational tractability and statistical guarantees utilizing overparameterized model seems to work in favour of Deep learning supported by empirical evidence.

Moreover, different choices of design ingredients like architectural choice, optimization algorithms, initialization strategies etc. of a training procedure [1] appears to induce a bias that breaks the equivalence among all models that interpolate the training data, without any explicit regularization (Implicit Regularization).

To consolidate and validate these facts, we posed our empirical study in supervised setting of Multi-label Chest X-Ray classification task. We leveraged ChestXray14 [12] as our data distribution for this study. Further details of data modeling can be found in [5]. Our contribution to this work, is to shed some light with carefully tested empirical results, towards interpreting and assessing the complexity measure of black-box model underpinning Deep learning, that rely its performance quantification and its visible behaviour like classification, in terms of input-output mapping, in a chosen setting. Significance of our work is to posit a empirical framework for arguing about certain properties of Deep neural network, in this case establishing the validity of Overparameterization and Implicit regularization.

Rest of the manuscript is structured as follows: Sect. 2 summarizes different complexity measures, that are being used to assess performance of Deep neural network. Section 3 give details of our proposed work in terms of our Design choices in constructing model architecture, training procedure, experimental setup etc. and accompanied with Results and discussion. Finally, Sect. 4 concludes with a brief summarization of our current work.

2   Insights on Different Complexity Measures

2.1   Function-Space Complexity Measures: Norm Based Complexity Quantification

In the case of binary classification problem, complexity of function-space can be quantified usting notion like Normalized margin and Frobenious-normalized margin [3].

The key point of this measure of complexity implies that small margin is complex, as small perturbation of function can lead to a function with different training error.

2.2   Classical Statistical and Computational Complexity Measures

Uniform Convergence. This framework seek to assess generalization performance of a machine learning model by restricting the size of the function class against amount of training data needed. The quantity that is relevant in this framework is 'shattering coefficient'. Further details can be found in [3].

Algorithmic Stability. This framework asserts that, rather than looking for generalization performance across entire function class uniformly, can the performance be assessed and quantified by a single function returned by the learning algorithm [3].

PAC-Bays. PAC(Probably Approximately Correct) - Bayes is another approach towards algorithm depenedence on generalization bound. It measures the KL-divergence between prior over function realised by the classifier and the posterior distribution, over a data distribution [3].

Rademacher Complexity and VC-Dimension. Rademacher Complexity is a statistical measure of complexity, which is a deviation between expectation and sample average, i.e.,

$$\frac{1}{2}R_n(F) <= \mathbb{E}[\sup_{f \in F} |\mathbb{E}[f] - \hat{\mathbb{E}}[f]|] <= 2R_n(F) \tag{4}$$

where, $F \subset [0,1]^Z$ for a probability distribution P on a measurable space Z, with samples $z_1, z_2, ..., z_n \in P$, and

$$R_n(F) = \mathbb{E}[\sup_{f \in F} |\frac{1}{n}\sum_{i=1}^{n} \epsilon_i f(z_i)|] \tag{5}$$

Rademacher complexity is also related to, Computational complexity of function class F, known as VC-dimension, given by: $R_n(F) = \hat{\phi}(\sqrt{\frac{d_{VC}(F)}{n}})$ [1].

2.3 Effective Model Complexity and Double Descent

Conventional wisdom suggests that, training in Deep neural network can be split into two phases:

- In the first phase, neural network learns a function with small generalization gap.
- In the second phase, the network starts to overfit the data, leading to increase in test error.

However, empirical evidence suggests that, in some regimes, the test error decreases again and may achieve a lower value, at the end of training, as compared to the first minimum. This is depicted in Fig. 1 below:

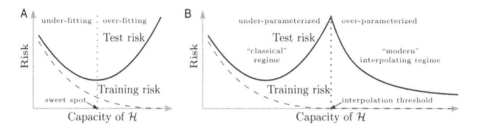

Fig. 1. Classical U-shaped Performance Curve and Recent phenomenon of Double Descent [2].

The phenomenon of Double descent not just occur as function of model size, but also as a function of training epochs, and as such Effective Model Complexity(EMC) is used as a complexity measure to quantify and reason about this phenomenon [8].

3 Proposed Work

For our empirical study,

- We leveraged single NVIDIA RTX 3050 Ti GPU for all our model training.
- Initial learning rate was set to 0.15, with exponential learning rate decay, with decay rate of 0.96.
- We used Binary Cross-entropy [5], as our surrogate loss function.
- Model family used as per Choudhury et al. [5]:
  - Custom Convolutional Neural Network (CNN).
  - Resnet Family of Convolutional Neural Network.

3.1 Data Modeling

We used ChestXray14 [12] dataset as our underlying data distribution. Following Choudhury et al. [5], we modelled our data for down stream architecture interfacing.

3.2   Increasing Number of Training Epochs: Setting 1

Table 1, shows our setting for assessing performance of model as function of number of training epochs:

Table 1. Model Settings as a function of Number of Training Epochs.

Number of Epochs	Data Distribution Size	Custom CNN Parameter Count	Batch Size	Image Size
100	$1, 12, 120$	$3, 228, 687$	64	$224 \times 224 \times 3$
300	$1, 12, 120$	$3, 228, 687$	64	$224 \times 224 \times 3$
1000	$1, 12, 120$	$3, 228, 687$	64	$224 \times 224 \times 3$

3.3   Increasing Model Complexity: Setting 2

Table 2, shows our setting for assessing performance of model as function of model complexity,

Table 2. Model Settings as a Function of Model Complexity

	Model Complexity, Parameter Count	Data Distribution Size	Batch Size	Number of Epochs
1	Custom CNN, $3, 228, 687$	$1, 12, 120$	64	100
	ResidualNet, $3, 444, 799$	$1, 12, 120$	8	100
2	Custom CNN, $3, 228, 687$	$56, 060$	32	100
	ResidualNet 152, $19, 472, 391$	$56, 060$	32	100

3.4   Variants of Optimizer: Setting 3

Table 3, shows our setting for assessing performance of model as function of variant of optimizer,

Table 3. Model Settings as a Function of Optimizer Variants

Optimizer	Data Distribution (50% of Total size)	Custom CNN, Parameter Count	Batch Size	Image Size	Number of Epochs
Adam (Default Parameter, $\beta_1 = 0.9, \beta_2 = 0.99$)	$56, 060$	$3, 228, 687$	32	$224 \times 224 \times 3$	300
Stochastic Gradient Descent, SGD	$56, 060$	$3, 228, 687$	32	$224 \times 224 \times 3$	300

3.5   Results

Following Choudhury et al. [5], we analyzed model performance mainly in terms of three metric AUC (Area Under ROC Curve), Precision and Recall, for assessing Effective Model Complexity (EMC) 2.3 pertaining to settings mentioned in Sects. 3.2, 3.3 and 3.4. We also tracked Accuracy and Loss for some of our experimentations.

For Setting 1, 3.2:

Training and Validation Dynamics. Figure 2, 3 and 4 below shows training and validation dynamics over number of epochs: 100, 300, and 1000 respectively:

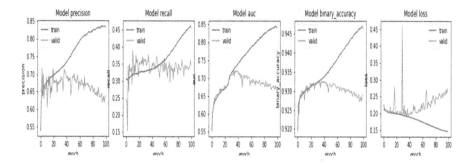

Fig. 2. Training and Validation Dynamics - I.

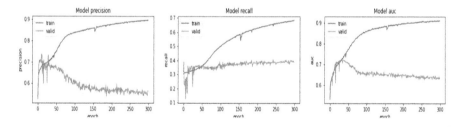

Fig. 3. Training and Validation Dynamics - II.

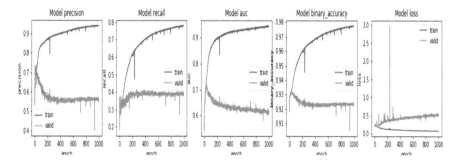

Fig. 4. Training and Validation Dynamics - III.

Training and Validation Assessment. Table 4, shows assessment score over training epochs: 100, 300, and 1000 respectively:

Table 4. Training and Validation Assessment

	AUC		Precision		Recall		Binary Accuracy		Loss	
Number of Training Epochs	Training	Validation	Training	Validation	Training	Validation	Training	Validation	Training	Validation
100	**0.7511**	0.6838	0.7579	0.6679	0.3648	0.3384	0.9367	0.9304	0.1796	0.2241
300	**0.8502**	0.6582	0.8313	0.5988	0.5377	0.3653	0.9524	0.9257	0.1334	0.3510
1000	**0.9052**	0.6357	0.8941	0.5738	0.6772	0.3822	0.9665	0.9241	0.0956	0.4146

Held out Test set Assessment. Table 5, shows held out test set score for training epochs 100 and 1000 respectively:

Table 5. Test Set Assessment

Number of Training Epochs	AUC	Precision	Recall	Binary Accuracy	Loss
100	**0.8424**	0.8301	0.4319	0.9454	0.1536
1000	**0.8684**	0.8227	0.6249	0.9580	0.1862

For Setting 2, 3.3:

Training and Validation Dynamics. Below Fig. 5, 6, 7 and 8, shows training and validation dynamics as a function of increasing model complexity:

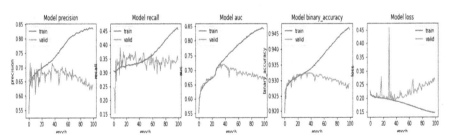

Fig. 5. Training and Validation Dynamics - Custom CNN - I.

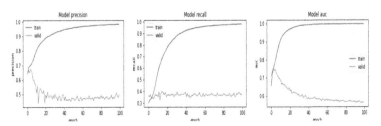

Fig. 6. Training and Validation Dynamics - Residual Net-I.

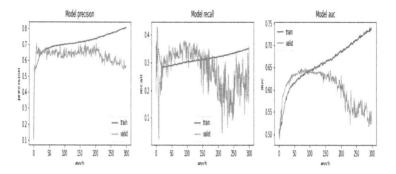

Fig. 7. Training and Validation Dynamics - Custom CNN - II.

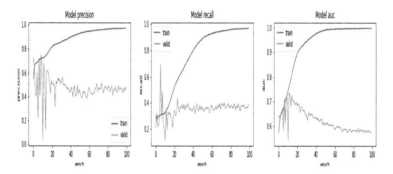

Fig. 8. Training and Validation Dynamics - Residual Net- II.

Training and Validation Assessment. Table 6, shows training and validation score for models of increasing complexity:

Table 6. Training and Validation Assessment

	AUC		Precision		Recall	
Model Complexity	Training	Validation	Training	Validation	Training	Validation
Custom CNN-1	0.7541	0.6838	0.7578	0.6679	0.3648	0.3384
ResidualNet152-1	0.9701	-	0.9228	—	0.8583	-
Custom CNN-2	0.6850	0.6808	0.6926	0.6731	0.3216	0.3173
ResidualNet152-2	0.9331	0.6217	0.8870	0.4746	0.7605	0.3514

Held out Test Set Assessment. Table 7, shows Test set score for models of increasing complexity,

Table 7. Test Set Assessment

Model Complexity	AUC	Precision	Recall	Binary Accuracy	Los
Custom CNN-1	0.8424	0.8301	0.4319	0.9454	0.1536
ResidualNet152-1	0.9671	0.9648	0.9302	0.9913	0.5630
Custom CNN-2	0.8123	0.7622	0.3737	0.9358	0.1778
ResidualNet152-2	0.9474	0.9207	0.8611	0.9817	0.1356

For Setting 3, 3.4:

Training and Validation Dynamics. Figure 9 and 10, below shows overall training and validation dynamics as a function of optimizer variant:

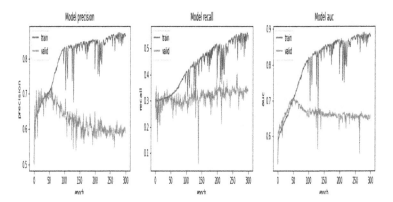

Fig. 9. Training and Validation Dynamics, Adam [6].

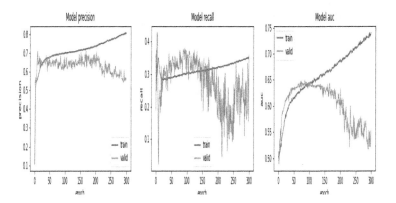

Fig. 10. Training and Validation Dynamics, SGD.

Training and Validation Assessment. Table 8, shows training and validation assessment score for models as function of optimizer variants,

Table 8. Training and Validation Assessment

	AUC		Precision		Recall		Binary Accuracy		Loss	
Optimizer	Training	Validation	Training	Validation	Training	Validation	Training	Validation	Training	Validation
Adam	0.8009	0.6612	0.7996	0.6266	0.4316	0.3123	0.9433	0.9258	0.1500	0.2933
SGD	0.6583	0.6021	0.7108	0.6306	0.3141	0.2734	0.9304	0.9252	0.2027	0.2152

Test Set Assessment. Table 9, shows test set assessment score for models as function of optimizer variants:

Table 9. Test Set Assessment

Optimizer	AUC	Precision	Recall	Binary Accuracy	Los
Adam	0.5000	0.1454	0.8104	0.5713	0.6931
SGD	0.5552	0.5437	0.3522	0.9208	0.4495

3.6   Discussions

Few of our observations from this empirical study are in order:

For Setting 1, 3.2

- We noticed that training and validation performance (2, 3 and 4) in terms of metric AUC, Precision, and Recall increased monotonically up to training epochs (40, 50, and 50) respectively, and diverged there after till the end of our set number of training epochs i.e., 100, 300, and 1000 respectively, verifying classical U-shaped model performance curve [2].
  We begin to see a trend from these sets of experimentation, if we increase the number of training epochs further beyond 1000 that we have currently studied, the phenomenon of "Double Descent" can be verified, which will quantify the peak of threshold where second decent takes place, as postulated and can be measured by Effective Model Complexity (EMC)2.3.
- From Table 4, we see a consistent increase in training performance in terms of our chosen metric, i.e., AUC, Precision, and Recall, but there is a dip in the validation metric, as we increased training epochs from 100, 300, and 1000. However, we foresee that these trend will change as we increase the number of training epochs. Our future work will follow this direction to consolidate this assertion.

For Setting 2, 3.3 Here, we performed two sets of experimentation,

First, we assessed model performance as a function of increasing model complexity, with complete data distribution size.
Here, we found 6 that, the behaviour is consistent with classical U-shaped performance curve [2], with Custom CNN-1 and ResidualNet152-1, on our chosen metric of AUC, Precision, and Recall.

Second, We assessed model performance same as First experiment, but with 50% of our data distribution size, showing behaviour consistent as first.

However, we envisage that increasing the model complexity as we increase the trainable parameter count, going further into overparameterized regime, the emergence of second dip in the performance quantification curve is inevitable, and experimentation in this direction are foreseen.

For held-out test set 7, we observe similar behaviour, as we increased model complexity i.e., going from Custom CNN-1 to ResidualNet152-1 and Custom CNN-2 to ResidualNet152-2, performance of AUC, Precision, and Recall increased as expected.

For Setting 3, 3.4

- We see that, training curve closely follow validation curve (9, 10) in the case of Stochastic Gradient Descent (SGD) optimizer compared with other optimizer variant Adam [6], with all other measurable parameters like model complexity and number of training epochs fixed at a constant value.
  This suggests that SGD is better in imposing "Implicit Regularization" then Adam.
- We also confirm 8 U-shaped performance curve for both these case of optimizers, and foresee phenomenon of "Double Descent" with 'Overparameterization' and increased number of training epochs.
- Test set results 9 also validate and confirms the importance of optimizer as an input to Deep learning models, in our case SGD compared to Adam, for finding a good minimum in the optimization landscape, by imposing "Implicit Regularization", quantified by increased performance score of AUC, Precision, and Recall.

4   Conclusion

In this work, we have looked at various complexity measures available to assess and quantify the performance of Deep learning model. Specifically, we empirically studied Effective Model Complexity (EMC) applying to ChestXRay data distribution for multi-label classification task.

We found that notion of EMC, as a function of increasing model complexity, function of increasing number of training epochs, and function of optimizer variants, is a reliable complexity measure to quantify phenomenon such as 'Overparameterization' and "Implicit Regularization", in understanding Generalization in Deep learning.

Availability of Data. The ChestXray14 dataset analysed during the current study are publicly available for research purpose in the web link: https://nihcc.app.box.com/v/ChestXray-NIHCC

Funding. There is no funding for this study.

Author's Contribution. Author's have equal contribution.

Conflict of Interest. The authors declare that, they have no Conflict of Interest.

References

1. Bartlett, P.L., Montanari, A., Rakhlin, A.: Deep learning: a statistical viewpoint. Acta Numerica **30**, 87–201 (2021)
2. Belkin, M., Hsu, D., Ma, S., Mandal, S.: Reconciling modern machine-learning practice and the classical bias-variance trade-off. Proc. Natl. Acad. Sci. **116**(32), 15849–15854 (2019)
3. Bernstein, J.: Optimisation & generalisation in networks of neurons. arXiv preprint arXiv:2210.10101 (2022)
4. Brown, T., et al.: Language models are few-shot learners. In: Advance in Neural Information Processing System, vol. 33, pp. 1877–1901 (2020)
5. Choudhury, A., Roy, S.: Data driven deep learning modeling: Methods in multi-label chest radiograph classification (2022). Available at SSRN 4161950
6. Kingma, D.P., Ba, J.: Adam: a method for stochastic optimization. arXiv preprint arXiv:1412.6980 (2014)
7. Liu, Z., Mao, H., Wu, C.Y., Feichtenhofer, C., Darrell, T., Xie, S.: A convnet for the 2020s. In: Proceedings of the IEEE/CVF Conference on Computer Vision and Pattern Recognition, pp. 11976–11986 (2022)
8. Nakkiran, P., Kaplun, G., Bansal, Y., Yang, T., Barak, B., Sutskever, I.: Deep double descent: where bigger models and more data hurt. J. Stat. Mech: Theory Exp. **2021**(12), 124003 (2021)
9. Ramesh, A., Dhariwal, P., Nichol, A., Chu, C., Chen, M.: Hierarchical text-conditional image generation with clip latents. arXiv preprint arXiv:2204.06125 (2022)
10. Roy, S., Choudhury, A.: On the intersection of deep learning and chest radiography: background and prospects (2019). Available at SSRN 3861229
11. Silver, D., et al.: Mastering the game of go with deep neural networks and tree search. Nature **529**(7587), 484–489 (2016)
12. Wang, X., Peng, Y., Lu, L., Lu, Z., Bagheri, M., Summers, R.M.: Chestx-ray8: hospital-scale chest x-ray database and benchmarks on weakly-supervised classification and localization of common thorax diseases. In: 2017 IEEE Conference on Computer Vision and Pattern Recognition (CVPR), pp. 3462–3471. IEEE (2017)

Nuclei Segmentation Approach for Computer Aided Diagnosis

Narayana Darapaneni[1], Anwesh Reddy Paduri[2(✉)], Jayesh Gulani[3], Sanath Aithu[3], M. M. Santhosh[3], and Shaji Varghese[3]

[1] Northwestern University/Great Learning, Chicago, USA
[2] Great Learning, Bangalore, India
anwesh@greatlearning.in
[3] PES University, Bangalore, India

Abstract. Computer aided diagnosis based on computational pathology combines the concepts of pathology with computer science to develop automated mechanisms for interpretation of histological images. Nuclei segmentation is a type of computation pathology that enables the identification and separation of Nuclei cells in a histopathology image. These segmentation routines play a critical role in quantification of cellular structures and provide insights to identify abnormalities related to pathological conditions such as cancer. In order to determine the progress and severity of a pathological condition it is necessary to use tools that measure the properties of tissue structure in different stages of a disease. Biomedical image analysis for Nuclei segmentation using deep learning methodologies is an ongoing area of research wherein to improve histopathology examination it is desired to develop a model that can generalize and accurately segment different types of nuclei. However, creating a suitable model for this process is difficult due to variability in patient data, overlapping nuclei cell boundaries, image quality, background noise, and provision of well-annotated data. In this study, we describe our findings on the performance of a model developed using the standard U-Net architecture and compare it against a model that is developed based on pre-trained weights and models using ImageNet as the backbone. The aim is to develop a semantic segmentation model that can capture high-level information in terms of features from a data set that consists of Whole-slide images (WSI). The outcome of the research is to be able to select a semantic segmentation model that is efficient and fast to classify Nuclei cells for the given biomedical tissue images. The model uses a stochastic gradient descent optimizer and the evaluation criteria for this network i.e., the ground truth against prediction is based on Mean Intersection over Union.

Keywords: Nuclei segmentation · deep learning · U-Net · semantic segmentation · histopathology · Jaccard Index

1 Introduction

This research is to develop a machine learning based deep neural network predicts that type of nuclei in bio-medical images that have been created using whole slide images (WSI) also known as histopathology images. The development of such a model

© The Author(s), under exclusive license to Springer Nature Switzerland AG 2023
R. Morusupalli et al. (Eds.): MIWAI 2023, LNAI 14078, pp. 368–379, 2023.
https://doi.org/10.1007/978-3-031-36402-0_34

could then be used for predicting nuclei presence in different organ tissues and a good performing model can be used to provide pre-trained weights for learning when a newer model is developed to work with WSI based datasets.

2 Literature Survey

Deep learning-based CNN networks are widely used for bio-medical image processing. Computer vision based on image segmentation and deep learning architecture has proven to play a significant role in enabling improvements in computer aided diagnosis [12]. Computer vision, especially Convolution Neural Network (CNN), with strong ability on pattern recognition transformed the world of medical image reading and analysis [10]. However, soon there was a realization that CNN was not the ultimate solution in scenarios where the object of interest did not have clear boundaries or edges [21]. To improve the object detection process region-based CNN (R-CNN) were developed [9]. In these networks R-CNN works as a classifier which trains CNNs to segregate proposals in identified regions into object categories. The Region proposal network (RPN) using a full convolution network yields a set of rectangular object proposals from the input image. These models were created with a combination model of R-CNN and Support Vector Machine (SVM). The SVM part of the model enhances the classification accuracy [3]. Thereon there was extensive research carried on with Regional Convolution Neural Network (R-CNN) and its several variants like Faster R-CNN and Mask R-CNN for object detection and classification [17]. Faster R-CNN which uses R-CNN and RPN as the two main networks. The uniqueness in faster R-CNN is that it uses selective search to generate region proposals compared to other CNN algorithms. New variants of the network were built such as Faster R-CNN head with ResNet C4 [8] and the second Faster R-CNN head with FPN [11]. FPN has a top-down architecture with lateral connections with an in-network feature pyramid from a single-scale input. An approach similar to ResNet but with the Faster R-CNN having an FPN backbone extracts RoI features from different levels of the feature pyramid according to their scale has also been developed. Mask RCNN [7] is one the fundamental algorithms to achieve instance segmentation. Mask R-CNN used along with ResNet-FPN backbone for feature extraction gives excellent results in both accuracy and speed. Various studies in the area of Medical Imaging have used Mask RCNN and its improvements for the segmentation of the body organs and cells [14, 16].

While Mask R-CNN proved to be extremely well suited for object detection it had some constraints providing accurate classification. Challenges in Instance segmentation occur due to the valid detection of all objects in an image while also being capable to properly segment each instance, lack of sufficient data with good image quality, variations in patient data and need of high-quality annotation hinders improvement of accuracy and performance of instance detection-based learning mechanisms. Another methodology of object detection is semantic segmentation. Semantic segmentation of images was first performed by using end to end Fully Convolution Networks (FCN) [13] which could segment images of arbitrary sizes. But the segmentation performance of the FCN was not enough. By adding an up sampling and down sampling structure with skip connections U-Net [15] architecture achieved better segmentation performance and became the go to solution for bio-medical image processing for image segmentation. In spite of improved performance U-Net models needed to be used with a tiling strategy that required the output to be stitched back together to get the output segmentation. This was a waste of computation resources. An adaptive fully dense (AFD) neural network based on u_net was created to handle this problem as well as the variability in medical images related to the presence of noise and complex boundaries [19]. Hybrid segmentation models [2] were also developed that used a combination of SegNet, U-Net with pretrained models like ResNet as the backbone to provide weights for improving the performance of the models. Networks were also created for performing region of interest localization together with data augmentation [4] and were used in conjunction with U-Net models to perform image segmentation to overcome non-existence of vast amounts of medical imaging data. These types of hybrid network also provided good performance values with Dice scores above 0.90. Improvements in detection-based segmentation involved creation of networks that focused on most relevant part of the medical image using Faster-RCNN instance segmentation method and not requiring to divide an image into multiple patches [20], this network was able to perform with a Dice score of 0.859. Methods for Object detection based on region based localization and semantic segmentation that are applicable for this operation like U-Net [15], Mask-RCNN [7] are usable from open source algorithms and are able to work with pre-trained models. Additionally neural networks were created by an ensemble of Mask-RCNN with U-Net for nuclei segmentation, these models performed better than the models the employed these algorithms independently [18].

3   Material and Methods

Nuclei segmentation on whole-slide images (WSI) helps in the determination of the distribution of different kinds of cell types that are related to diseases like cancer. Considering the importance, this paper attempts to help build a suitable model that is able to generalize and accurately segment nuclei in the PanNuke dataset [5]. The models created are evaluated based on how well they can identify background noise in the data and identify the various cell characteristics in tissue samples from the images within the dataset. For addressing the above needs semantic segmentation network will be created for performing Binary and multi class classification. To further improve the performance weights from existing pre-trained models like ResNet50 will be used. In the testing phase, images with already annotated images are fed to the pre-trained model to perform tissue segmentation. The performance of the network would then be measured by experimenting with different weight initialization techniques and optimizer techniques for improving the Pixel accuracy and Intersection over Union accuracy. The model shall use stochastic gradient descent optimizer and the evaluation criteria for this network for the ground truth against prediction will be based on Mean Intersection Over Union (MeanIOU) coefficient.

3.1   Setup

The hardware used for this test was HP Z-book with 32 GB RAM and 4 GB GPU with NVIDIA RTX graphics card. The operating system in use in Windows 10 and the code is developed using Jupyter notebook. Since the GPU memory is limited the resolution of the images had to be reduced to 64 * 64 * 3 from the original 256 * 256 * 3 pixels.

The models for training and prediction are created using tensorflow and keras backend. ResNet50 has been chosen as the means of incorporating pre-trained weights into the encoding layer of a standard U-Net model.

3.2 Exploratory Analysis

The data provided in the PanNuke dataset is Nuclei instance segmentation dataset with instance details being semi automatically generated for 19 different tissue types [6]. The dataset provides a split for train, validation, and test by providing three different sets of images with each set containing 2656, 2523 and 2722 images. The images have been stored randomly in each of the splits. The number of tissue types in the splits are distributed appropriately based on the comparative occurrence of tissues in the entire dataset. The cell nuclei captured in the images and nuclei sizes are also approximately distributed equally across the image splits. The dataset has over 7000 images and there are 189744 nuclei labelled. The labelling has been performed for nuclei found in tissues from breast, stomach, colorectal, bladder liver, prostate, and kidney. Pixel-level boundary annotation for every nucleus has been provided in the dataset. Colon and breast types are the most common tissue types indicating a class imbalance in the dataset (Fig. 1).

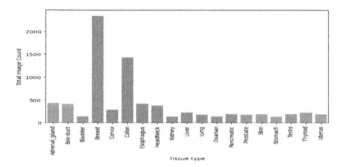

Fig. 1. Count of tissue types in dataset

The mask images of the nuclei in the dataset are enumerated by the different types viz. Neoplastic, Inflammatory, Connective, Dead nuclei and Non-Neo epithelial. Each layer of the mask is used to represent one of the different types of nuclei, so there are five different layers in the masks for the types. There is a sixth layer that provides a binary representation of the presence of all the nuclei in the image. The sixth layer labels the presence of a nuclei in the images as zero and non-nuclei pixels as one. There is further imbalance in the sixth layer, the binary data indicates less foreground pixels than background pixels. The data is made available as single file numpy arrays for images, masks and types that describe the tissues.

In order to read the data from each of the sets the code was written to read the single files and create separate numpy files for each of the tissue types and made available as three sets in respective folders.

The distribution of nuclei sizes and the number of nuceli per image was calculated and plotted. From Fig. 2, most of the images have approximately 0 to 40 nuclei. The size of the nuclei is between 1 to 1000 pixels. It can also be observed that there are several outliers in the dataset.

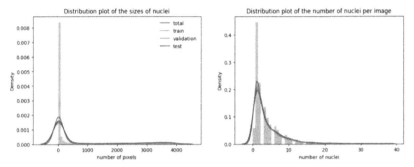

Fig. 2. Distribution of nuclei sizes and number of nuclei per image

In this study we are not performing any outlier removal and will make use of all the data to measure the performance of the model. Any other treatments will be identified based on the results of the model.

The images in the dataset will undergo image normalization using the concept of histogram equalization. This method would normalize the images by spreading out the frequent intensity values over the range of the image.

The three sets created were then used such that each of the unique tissue data in numpy arrays were read into appropriate train, validation, and test structures. The PanNuke study [5] has mentioned that the three splits have pre-extracted patches that are randomly available to evaluate the models accurately. This study has hence taken the same split to allow for comparison of scores of the models that are being developed.

4   Base Model and Architecture

The paper uses the PanNuke dataset as the source of data to develop a model to detect and segment the nuclei of the tissues using semantic segmentation. The steps being followed are, to first build a standard U-net model using the image resolution of 64 * 64 * 3 and perform a binary classification of foreground data against the background. The base model of semantic segmentation used for this is based on the U-Net architecture [16] which would allow to measure the performance of the model to identify between the foreground nuclei data and the background. The metrics used for the measurement of the performance of this model is the F1-Score. F1-score measures a model's accuracy by considering both precision and recall and measures the harmonic mean between precision and recall. It is mathematically represented as

$$\text{F1-Score} = 2 * (\text{precision} * \text{recall})/(\text{precision} + \text{recall}) \tag{1}$$

The standard U-Net model using the image resolution of 64 * 64 * 3 will then be used for Multi class segmentation by making appropriate changes to use relevant activation functions. Further the base model would be extended wherein the U-Net model with pre-trained ImageNet weights based on ResNet50 would be created to measure the performance and accuracy of detection of different classes of nuclei data in the dataset. The model developed for multi class classification has been evaluated using the MeanIOU metric. This metric is a commonly used evaluation measure where the goal is to predict the class of pixels in an image. This metric considers both false positives and false negatives unlike other metrics like accuracy, precision or recall that use either false positives or false negatives. Hence, it would provide a more accurate measure of the segmentation performance of the mode. It is mathematically represented as:

MeanIOU = (1/no. of classes) * sum(IOU_class1, IOU_class2, ... IOU_classN),
where no. of classes is the number of classes in the dataset and IOU is the Intersection over Union score of each class

$$(2)$$

4.1 Binary Classification - Identifying Presence of Nuclei

In order to provide a binary classification, the semantic segmentation model developed will be used to perform segmentation and predict the presence of nuclei cells in the image. This is achieved by using the binary mask data that is provided as the sixth layer of data in the masks data. The sixth layer of the dataset stores data in a binary structure and so indicates the presence of nuclei in the images with a value 0 and non-nuclei pixels as 1. The model is provided with the training and validation data and the accuracy for both the training validation data is calculated. The model has been trained for using the Adam optimizer as the activation function in the output layer. The batch size is set to 16.

The high-level architecture of the model is as below:

4.2 Multi Class Classification - Nuclei Cell Feature Identification

The PanNuke dataset has the nuclei cells categorized into 5 types by the type of Nuclei; Neoplastic, Inflammatory, Connective, Dead nuclei and Non-Neo epithelial. The tissue types are represented as a separate layer in the mask of each of the images. The mask images of the tissues in the dataset contains six layers, the first 5 layers represent the tissue types, and the sixth layer has all the nuclei categories combined and represented as matrix with binary values. To distinguish the different cells in the image a color scheming has been used to display the actual masked image and the prediction image. The color scheme is shown the in Table 1:

Two models were developed for performing prediction on the dataset. One model being the standard U-net model and the second model using ResNet50 weights as part of the encoding sequence. For both the models, the output layer used the L2 kernel regularizer with a value of 0.0005. The learning rate for the models was set at 0.0005 and stochastic Gradient Descent has been used as the optimizer. It was trained for 500 epochs using the SGD optimizer. The batch size was set to 16 for the training and validation set.

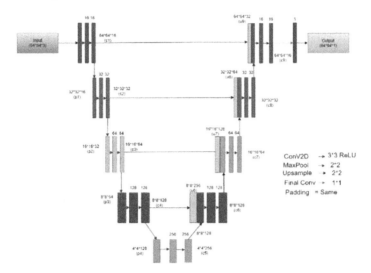

Fig. 3. U-Net model Nuclei detection [16]

Table 1. Color scheme to identify the cells in the image data

Cell types	Color scheme
Neoplastic	Yellow
Inflammatory	Green
Connective tissue	Red
Dead	Black
Non-Neoplastic epithelial cells	Purple
Background	Gray

The first model is a U-Net architecture which is same as the one used for Binary classification (refer Fig. 3) except the use of SGD optimizer and using Softmax as the activation in the output layer.

The second model is a U-Net model with a Resnet50 backbone for the encoder layer. The high high-level architecture diagram for the second model using ResNet50 model is shown in Fig. 4.

4.3 Results and Evaluation

4.3.1 Results from Binary Classification

The model developed for Binary classification provided an accuracy of 87% for both the train and validation sets. The model was run for 100 epochs. The prediction results using the test dataset is shown below. Though the accuracy is high the boundaries of

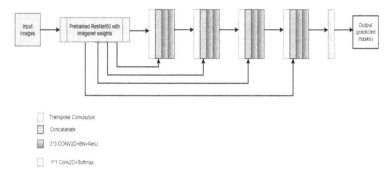

Transpose Convolution
Concatanate
3*3 CONV2D+BN+ReIU
1*1 Conv2D+Softmax

Fig. 4. U-Net with ResNet50 backbone [1]

the pixels are not properly identified by the model. The prediction result for a randomly selected image from the test dataset is show in Fig. 5

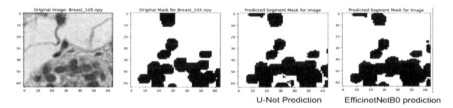

U-Net Prediction   EfficinetNetB0 prediction

Fig. 5. Prediction result for Segmented masks for Breast image

The evaluation methods of the model are based on F1-Score additionally the intersection over union score (Jaccard Score) was also calculated. The Jaccard score and F1-Score was measured using the sklearn package. The scores derived from the loss functions are used to calculate and match the predicted occurrence of nuclei in the pixels with the ground truth. Using this the number of true positive (TP), true negatives (TN), false positives (FP), and false negatives (FN) values for the cells predicted in the pixels is calculated.

The predictions from the model return a value between 0 and 1 for each pixel. A value above 0.5 is classified as 1. The F1-score of the U-net model is about 0.85 which is above the threshold value of 0.5. Based on these values we can say that the model seems to be capable of performing semantic segmentation to identify nuclei cells in the dataset. The model could be extended to allow for predictions of different classes of cells in the dataset. The scores to measure robustness is shown in Fig. 6.

4.3.2 Results from Multi Classification Models

The standard U-Net model after performing the training and validation run provided an accuracy value of around 70.88% when used with a test dataset. The loss curves of the training are shown in Fig. 7. The training was performed for 500 epochs, and it can be seen from the curves that as the training proceeded the measure accuracy seems to have

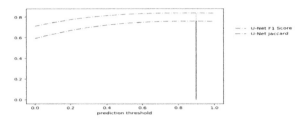

Fig. 6. F1-Score for U-Net model for binary classification

stablished around 71% for the train and validation data. It also seen from the curves that model's learning and generalizing are nearly similar over the epochs they seem to indicate a Good Fit.

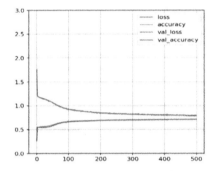

Fig. 7. Loss and Accuracy curves for U-Net

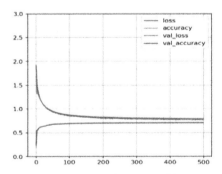

Fig. 8. Loss and Accuracy curves for U-net with ResNet50 backbone

A ResNet50 pretrained model based on Imagenet weights was used to create the neural network with ResNet50 acting as the backbone for U-Net. The encoding part of the UNet was based on the ResNet50 layers. Training on the model provided an accuracy similar to the standard U-Net model of around 71%. The prediction accuracy using the test dataset was around 70.46%. The loss and accuracy curve for the test and validation is shown in Fig. 8. Here too the curves indicate a good fit.

The prediction result of the model on the test dataset using the same image as used for the binary prediction for comparison purpose is shown in Fig. 9. In the figure each of the different classes of the cell have been highlighted with a different color.

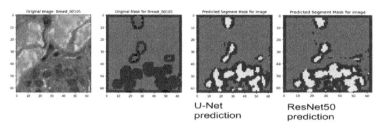

U-Net
prediction

ResNet50
prediction

Fig. 9. Multiclass classification prediction for Breast image

The prediction result shows that the model can predict the presence of nuclei cells which are nearly like the original mask in terms of the location. But some of the issues seen are the cell types being identified is not the same as the Original Mask. Also, pixel boundaries are not properly demarcated in the prediction result.

In order to evaluate the model, the MeanIOU of the models was calculated and are shown in Table 2.

Table 2. MeanIOU values

Model	MeanIOU
U-Net	0.2421
RestNet50	0.2370

In order to further measure the performance of the model the IOU values were calculated for each of the different class of cells in the test dataset. The table below shows the IOU for each of the nuclei features as calculated by the U-net model (Table 3):

Table 3. Comparison of IOU values from the 2 models

Cell type	IOU: U-Net	IOU: U-Net with ResNet50 backbone
Neoplastic	0.1096	0.1133
Inflammatory	0	0.0968
Connective tissue	0.0779	0.1206
Dead	0	0
Non-neoplastic epithelial cells	0.1651	0.063

Here we can see that the ResNet50 model has been able to have better IOU values for each of the different types of cells.

5   Discussion and Conclusions

The intention of this research is to develop a machine learning based deep neural network that allows for prediction of nuclei in bio-medical images that have been created using whole slide images (WSI) also known as histopathological images.

For the binary classification, it is seen that the semantic segmentation model provided good IOU and accuracy scores. It was able to identify and distinguish the background and foreground cells but could not fully demarcate the pixel boundaries. A similar model when used for multi-class classification did not indicate good performance values. Though the models developed for multi-classification were able to predict the location of the cells in the image they were not robust enough to identify the cell types that made up the tissue structure.

Due to the limitation of hardware resources the resolution of the images was reduced from 256 * 256 * 3 to 64 * 64 * 3. This may have contributed to the models not having robust values for multi-class classification. The dataset also does have some imbalance with regards to the distribution of tissue data with breast and colon having a higher number of samples. Further work is required in the pre-processing of the dataset, for example, addressing the imbalance of the data, identifying images of similar resolutions to be used together for training and testing. For multi class classification it will also be required to further improve the hyper parameter tuning to improve the nuclei class predictions. From the values of IOU being reported it is a possibility that using other pretrained weights from other models like EfficientNet may provide better results. One other option is to build an instance segmentation model can verify if it can provide better results for multi-class classification.

Considering the current results, we will need to conclude that more analysis is required to process the data and get insights into the results being reported. Additional pre-processing with better hyper parameters and full resolution images may provide the possibilities of creation of a semantic segmentation mode that would allow for storing of weights from this study to be used predictions in other Whole Slide image datasets.

References

1. Alam, S., Tomar, N.K., Thakur, A., Jha, D., Rauniyar, A.: Automatic polyp segmentation using U-NetResNet50 (2020)
2. Daimary, D., Bora, M.B., Amitab, K., Kandar, D.: Brain tumor segmentation from MRI images using hybrid convolutional neural networks. Proc. Comput. Sci. **167**, 2419–2428 (2020). International Conference on Computational Intelligence and Data Science
3. Duvvuri, K., Kanisettypalli, H., Jayan, S.: Detection of brain tumor using CNN and CNN-SVM. In: 2022 3rd International Conference for Emerging Technology (INCET), pp. 1–7. IEEE (2022)
4. Galea, R.-R., Diosan, L., Andreica, A., Popa, L., Manole, S., Bálint, Z.: Region-of-interest-based cardiac image segmentation with deep learning. Appl. Sci. **11**(4), 1965 (2021)

5. Gamper, J., Alemi Koohbanani, N., Benet, K., Khuram, A., Rajpoot, N.: PanNuke: an open pan-cancer histology dataset for nuclei instance segmentation and classification. In: Reyes-Aldasoro, C.C., Janowczyk, A., Veta, M., Bankhead, P., Sirinukunwattana, K. (eds.) ECDP 2019. LNCS, vol. 11435, pp. 11–19. Springer, Cham (2019). https://doi.org/10.1007/978-3-030-23937-4_2

6. Gamper, J., et al.: PanNuke dataset extension, insights and baselines. arXiv preprint arXiv: 2003.10778 (2020)

7. He, K., Gkioxari, G., Dollár, P., Girshick, R.: Mask R-CNN. In: Proceedings of the IEEE International Conference on Computer Vision, pp. 2961–2969 (2017)

8. He, K., Zhang, X., Ren, S., Sun, J.: Deep residual learning for image recognition. In: Proceedings of the IEEE Conference on Computer Vision and Pattern Recognition, pp. 770–778 (2016)

9. Kaldera, H.N.T.K., Gunasekara, S.R., Dissanayake, M.B.: Brain tumor classification and segmentation using faster R-CNN. In: 2019 Advances in Science and Engineering Technology International Conferences (ASET), pp. 1–6. IEEE (2019)

10. Kido, S., Hirano, Y., Hashimoto, N.: Detection and classification of lung abnormalities by use of convolutional neural network (CNN) and regions with CNN features (R-CNN). In: 2018 International Workshop on Advanced Image Technology (IWAIT), pp. 1–4. IEEE (2018)

11. Lin, T.-Y., Dollár, P., Girshick, R., He, K., Hariharan, B., Belongie, S.: Feature pyramid networks for object detection. In: Proceedings of the IEEE Conference on Computer Vision and Pattern Recognition, pp. 2117–2125 (2017)

12. Litjens, G., et al.: A survey on deep learning in medical image analysis. Med. Image Anal. **42**, 60–88 (2017)

13. Long, J., Shelhamer, E., Darrell, T.: Fully convolutional networks for semantic segmentation. In: Proceedings of the IEEE Conference on Computer Vision and Pattern Recognition, pp. 3431–3440 (2015)

14. Phung, V.H., Rhee, E.J.: A high-accuracy model average ensemble of convolutional neural networks for classification of cloud image patches on small datasets. Appl. Sci. **9**, 4500 (2019)

15. Ren, X., Zhou, S., Shen, D., Wang, Q.: Mask-RCNN for cell instance segmentation (2020)

16. Ronneberger, O., Fischer, P., Brox, T.: U-net: convolutional networks for biomedical image segmentation. In: Navab, N., Hornegger, J., Wells, W.M., Frangi, A.F. (eds.) MICCAI 2015. LNCS, vol. 9351, pp. 234–241. Springer, Cham (2015). https://doi.org/10.1007/978-3-319-24574-4_28

17. Shu, J.-H., Nian, F.-D., Yu, M.-H., Li, X.: An improved mask R-CNN model for multiorgan segmentation. Math. Probl. Eng. **2020**, 1–11 (2020)

18. Tahir, H., Khan, M.S., Tariq, M.O.: Performance analysis and comparison of faster R-CNN, mask R-CNN and ResNet50 for the detection and counting of vehicles. In: 2021 International Conference on Computing, Communication, and Intelligent Systems (ICCCIS), pp. 587–594. IEEE (2021)

19. Vuola, A.O., Akram, S.U., Kannala, J.: Mask-RCNN and U-Net ensembled for nuclei segmentation. In: 2019 IEEE 16th International Symposium on Biomedical Imaging (ISBI 2019), pp. 208–212. IEEE (2019)

20. Wang, E.K., Chen, C.-M., Hassan, M.M., Almogren, A.: A deep learning based medical image segmentation technique in internet-of-medical-things domain. Future Gener. Comput. Syst. **108**, 135–144 (2020)

21. Xu, Z., Wu, Z., Feng, J.: CFUN: combining faster R-CNN and U-net network for efficient whole heart segmentation. arXiv preprint arXiv:1812.04914 (2018)

Stock Market Intraday Trading Using Reinforcement Learning

Rugved Pandit$^{(\boxtimes)}$ [iD], Neeraj Nerkar$^{(\boxtimes)}$ [iD], Parmesh Walunj$^{(\boxtimes)}$ [iD], Rishi Tank$^{(\boxtimes)}$ [iD], and Sujata Kolhe [iD]

Datta Meghe College of Engineering, Navi Mumbai, India
rugved1915@gmail.com, neeraj.nerkar@gmail.com,
parmeshwalunj@gmail.com, chiragt1805@gmail.com,
sujata.kolhe@dmce.ac.in

Abstract. In this study, Reinforcement Learning (RL) techniques are used to develop trading strategies for the stock market. Conventional trading strategies rely on human intuition and the examination of historical data to make forecasts, whereas RL agents can automatically learn the best trading strategies through market interaction. The Proximal Policy Gradient (PPO) agent is employed to produce trading policies using real-world stock market data. The tests covered in the paper are conducted on the notoriously turbulent Indian intraday market. The findings of this study can be helpful to financial institutions, RL researchers, and those interested in the use of RL approaches for stock trading.

Keywords: Reinforcement Learning · Proximal Policy Gradient · Finance · Technical Indicators · Intraday Trading

1 Introduction

Profitable trading methods necessitate a deep understanding of the market's trends and patterns because the Indian stock market is a dynamic and complicated environment. It might be difficult for investors to consistently make money trading on the stock market. In recent years, trading strategies that can adjust to market situations and make wise selections have been created using technology and machine learning approaches. The development of trading strategies for the Indian stock market using reinforcement learning (RL) [1] approaches are suggested in this research. Focus is placed on the RL algorithm Proximal Policy Optimization (PPO) [2], which has demonstrated promise for the creation of intelligent trading systems. A trading agent that can learn the best practices for buying and selling stocks in Indian intraday market is created using PPO. Other agents such as Actor2Critic (A2C) [3] and Soft Actor-Critic (SAC) [4] have also been experimented with to find the optimal solution.

Financial technical analysis frequently makes use of technical indicators to spot market trends and patterns. In order to train the agent on historical data and produce the best trading strategies, several of the most popular technical indicators are integrated into the

R. Morusupalli et al. (Eds.): MIWAI 2023, LNAI 14078, pp. 380–389, 2023.
https://doi.org/10.1007/978-3-031-36402-0_35

RL environment. The commonly utilized Relative Strength Index (RSI), Moving Average Convergence Divergence (MACD), Bollinger Bands, and a few others are among the technical indicators that have been added to the environment. Historical data from some of the biggest Indian stocks which offers a lot of data to work with are used to train and assess the agent's performance.

The paper emphasizes the advantages of applying RL strategies to stock trading. The findings demonstrate that the suggested strategy can increase profitability while lowering investing risk in the Indian stock market. The strategy can also aid investors in decision-making and lessen the effects of market swings. The suggested strategy employing technical indicators and RL approaches offers investors a useful tool to create successful trading strategies in the Indian stock market. The findings show the potential of applying RL to stock trading, and they also offer some ideas for further research in this area.

2 Literature Review

The authors of [5] talk about an ensemble approach for creating successful stock trading strategies using deep reinforcement learning frameworks. The method entails employing the Deep Deterministic Policy Gradient [6], Advantage Actor Critic [7], and Proximal Policy Optimization algorithms to train a deep reinforcement learning agent. For 30 Dow Jones equities, the ensemble strategy is assessed and contrasted against the Dow Jones Industrial Average index and a conventional min-variance portfolio allocation technique. When it comes to risk-adjusted return as determined by the Sharpe ratio, the suggested deep ensemble method outperforms the three individual algorithms and the two baselines. The work [8] covers the developments in automated low-frequency quantitative stock trading with deep reinforcement learning [9]. The possibility of deploying DRL agents to optimize returns and reduce risks in the complex environment of the stock market is discussed in the study. Numerous studies have demonstrated statistically significant gains in performance when compared to well-established baseline strategies, but profitability levels are frequently low, real-time trading platforms lack experimental testing, and there are few in-depth comparisons between agents based on various DRL or human traders. The study comes to the conclusion that while DRL in stock trading has a lot of potential for application, the field of study is still in its infancy.

The paper [10] investigates the feasibility of building an end-to-end daily stock trading system that can automatically decide whether to purchase or sell at each trading day using Deep Q-networks (DQN) [11] and Deep Recurrent Q-networks (DRQN) [12]. Using daily trading data from the S&P500 ETF, the authors assess the performance of DQN and DRQN traders and compare it to Buy and Hold (BH) and Random action-selected DQN traders as benchmarks. The experiment's findings demonstrate that the DQN trader exceeds the benchmarks, and the DRQN trader performs even better thanks to the recurrence framework's capacity to identify and capitalize on lucrative patterns concealed in time-related sequences. The study contends that DRL agents have the capacity to choose profitable trading strategies, although further research is needed to determine their long-term stability and effectiveness in real-world trading scenarios.

The authors of the paper [13] suggest a deep reinforcement learning-based technique for automating swing trading. To select the best course of action for buying, selling, or holding stocks in order to maximize the increase in asset value, the model employs a deep deterministic policy gradient-based neural network. The authors also recognize the significance of using a system that forecasts stock value trends in conjunction with the reinforcement learning algorithm. They address this by implementing a sentiment analysis model that forecasts the stock trend from financial news using a recurrent convolutional neural network [14]. The authors of [15] offer a technical analysis-based trading technique that makes money by employing a new definition of the flag pattern. The rule specifies purchasing, selling, profit, and loss parameters. The rule was tested with 96 alternative configurations over three sub periods by the authors using a database of intraday observations from the US Dow Jones index. The German DAX and British FTSE indexes were also used in the investigation. The findings revealed that, in comparison to the US market, the proposed trading rule produced larger returns for the European markets, highlighting the latter's greater inefficiency.

The paper [16] introduces the FinRL DRL library, which allows novices to create their own stock trading methods using quantitative finance. It offers back testing analysis, training neural network agents in virtual environments, and datasets from the stock market. Trading restrictions are incorporated into FinRL, which also simulates trading situations on multiple stock markets. The library provides DRL algorithms, widely-used reward functions, and accepted evaluation baselines. Also, three application demonstrations, trading in a single stock, trading in a number of stocks, and portfolio allocation are included.

The use of deep reinforcement learning for stock trading strategy and investment choices in the Indian market is the primary topic of the paper [17]. Feature extraction and trading strategy development are the two critical objectives for long-term gains when applying machine learning in stock trading. Using ten Indian stock datasets, the study analyses and evaluates the performance of three deep reinforcement learning models: Deep Q-Network, Double Deep Q-Network, and Dueling Double Deep Q-Network. The study [18] examines the efficacy of employing LSTM [19] and random forest networks [20] to predict the directional out-of-sample movements of the S&P 500's constituent stocks for intraday trading. The study uses a multi-feature configuration that includes returns with respect to opening prices, intraday returns, and not just returns with respect to closing prices. The findings indicate that utilizing random forests and LSTM networks, the multi-feature setup yields a daily return of 0.54% and 0.64%, respectively. These results provide a superior trading approach than the single-feature configuration employed in earlier studies. Using the big data technical analysis and distributed computing frameworks like Hadoop and Spark, the paper [21] investigates the application of Bollinger Bands in algorithmic trading. The goal of the study is to discover equities that produce the most profit utilizing intraday trading tactics by focusing on the Nifty 50, a stock index of the National Stock Exchange (NSE) of India. Using a distributed Spark platform, the tick-by-tick data from the NSE was transformed to minute data, and the gains made during a trading year were examined.

3 Problem Statement

Given the current closing price of the stock in the market, calculate all the necessary parameters related to the stock. Determine and execute the best possible action based on the calculated parameters. The action is to buy or sell a certain number of stocks, or to hold the already owned stocks.

4 Methodology

4.1 Problem Definition

A type of machine learning called Reinforcement Learning allows an agent to pick up new skills by interacting with its surroundings and getting feedback in the form of rewards or penalties. Finding an ideal strategy that maximizes the cumulative reward over time is the aim of reinforcement learning. This method is frequently applied in fields where the best course of action depends on the condition of the environment, such as robotics, gaming, and control systems. Reinforcement Learning algorithms are a potential method for resolving complicated issues because they have achieved human-level performance in a number of fields. The technical indicators give the information of the history of the state, that enables us to formulate the process as a MDP.

A well-liked approach for describing decision-making issues in reinforcement learning is the Markov Decision Process (MDP). The probabilities of changing from one state to another and the incentives connected to each state-action pair are defined by an MDP, which is made up of a set of states, actions, and rewards. The Markov property, which asserts that the decision of transitioning to the next state depends only on the present state and action and not on the history of prior states and actions, is the fundamental premise behind MDPs. This property is very useful since it allows one to ignore the previous actions as long as one appropriately defines the observation state. MDPs are used by reinforcement learning algorithms to discover the best possible policy for maximizing the cumulative reward over time. The agent engages with its surroundings, observes its status, behaves in accordance with the policy, and is rewarded. Based on the rewards and state transition probabilities discovered by the MDP, the agent modifies its policy. Finding the best policy to maximize the predicted cumulative reward over time is the aim of reinforcement learning. In the suggested solution, the problem is defined as a MDP to define trading's goal as reward maximization.

The algorithm utilized for the agent in the solution is Proximal Policy Optimization (PPO). It solves some of the drawbacks of earlier policy gradient algorithms. The policy is updated by PPO employing clipped surrogate objective functions, which restrict policy changes and increase stability. By ensuring that the new policy does not deviate much from the previous one, clipping lowers the variance of the updates. PPO also has a value function that calculates expected compensation, which further lowers variance. PPO has demonstrated its worth in numerous applications, delivering improved performance in many benchmarks.

The parameters for the agent in the MDP are discussed as follows,

State (s) = A vector that includes the current stock price, technical indicators for the stock, total balance, the current total net worth (sum of balance and price of owned stocks), savings.

Action (a) = A vector of actions. The permitted actions for a stock are buying, holding and selling. The action space is defined as a set of Discrete numbers ranging from 0 to 20. The divergence point is at the value of 10, the numbers preceding it define sell and the *degree* of sell and the numbers exceeding it define buy and the *degree* of buy.

Reward (r) = The direct reward given to the model, gauged on the quality of action. Defined in our case as

$$r = n_t - n_{t-1} + \frac{n_t - b}{b} * 10$$

where, r: reward, n_t: net worth at time t, b: initial balance.

The novel reward function has two terms, first is the difference in net worth now and a step prior. This tells the model how it is performing each step. Second is the profit term. This keeps a long term track of how much profit was made since beginning. The reason for using two terms is that the first term is shallow, it only tracks the difference between last step and now, but it is necessary to learn about immediate actions, and the second term helps the model look deeper and generate higher overall profit.

Some constraints and assumptions had to be put in place to simulate the real-world trading scenario. They are listed as follows,

Market Liquidity: Allows for quick execution of orders at the close price. It is anticipated that the reinforcement trading agent won't have an impact on the stock market.

Positive Balance: A negative balance should not be produced by the permitted acts.

4.2 Environment

An environment was meticulously constructed to imitate real-world trading before training a deep reinforcement trading agent, enabling the agent to interact with and learn from its surroundings. In order to trade effectively, a variety of facts must be considered, including historical stock prices, current share prices, technical indicators, etc. Such information must be obtained by our trade agent from the environment in order to carry out the actions outlined in the previous section. To construct our environment and train the agent, we use OpenAI gym [22]. Continuous training has been utilized to train the model.

The environment utilized for training the agents comprises several financial technical indicators which are calculated using historical stock prices. The several technical indicators are calculated using the stockstats [23] python library. The technical indicators used are as follows,

- **MACD:** MACD [24] is a technical analysis tool used in the financial markets that analyzes the difference between two moving averages and a signal line to determine trends. When the MACD line crosses above the signal line or below it, there is a bullish indication, and when it crosses below, there is a bearish signal.

- **Bollinger Bands:** Bollinger Bands [25] are a technical analysis tool that consists of three lines plotted on a price chart, using a moving average in the middle line and a predetermined number of standard deviations to determine the upper and lower bands that dynamically adjust to volatility.
- **RSI:** The Relative Strength Index (RSI) [26] is a technical analysis tool that compares the size of prior gains and losses to measure the degree of price movement in a security. It uses a chart with a range of 0 to 100 and identifies overbought conditions above 70 and oversold conditions below 30, with the formula taking into account the number of days and the size of price moves. It is frequently used to identify buy/sell signals and confirm trend reversals or continuations.
- **CCI:** A technical analysis indicator called the Commodity Channel Index (CCI) calculates how much an asset's price deviates from its statistical mean.
- **Directional Movement Index:** A technical analysis indicator called the Directional Movement Index (DMI) is used to gauge how strongly a security's price trend is moving. The DMI has two lines that are used to determine the direction of the price trend: the positive directional indicator (+DI) and the negative directional indicator ($-$DI).
- **SMA:** The average price of a security over a given time period is determined by the Simple Moving Average (SMA), a popular technical analysis indicator. The SMA is determined by adding the security's closing prices for the selected time period, then dividing by the number of periods. The SMA smooths out the price data and aids in spotting trends when shown as a line on a chart. In order to confirm trend direction and spot potential trend reversals, traders frequently employ the SMA in conjunction with other technical indicators.

Figure 1 explains the methodology the agent follows in order to make trades.

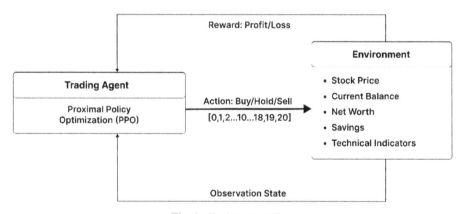

Fig. 1. Environment Flow

4.3 Training

The dataset was obtained from yfinance [27] which provided minute-by-minute data for the time period Feb 2015 to Feb 2022.

Continuous learning methodology was utilized to train the agents over historical stock data for which technical indicators were added. Whilst performing the training process it was observed that the agent would often get stuck in local minima and as a result would lead to stagnation. This adversely affects trading performance and the ability of the agent to learn effectively. The solution to the stagnation problem is two-fold, the first step being to add random steps to increase exploration. Manually increasing exploration of the model ensures the model does not stagnate and learns more. This was employed by adding random steps at a rate of 5% per step taken during training. The second way to combat the stagnation problem was to reset the environment every 100,000 steps, which includes resetting the current balance, net worth and shares held. These two methods acting together ensured the agent constantly kept learning.

4.4 Process Flow

A novel tactic was employed to save the profits made by the model. After a certain threshold of profit was reached, the agent was forced to sell a stock and store the profit from that action in the "savings" variable. The agent could trade with whatever it had left after the subtraction operation and could not access the capital in the savings section. This promoted a way to safeguard profits from time to time and ensured consistent profits (Fig. 2).

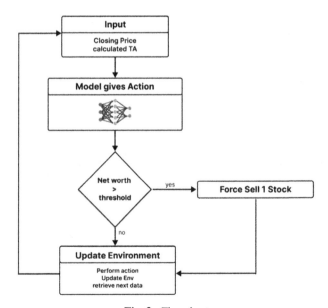

Fig. 2. Flowchart

As the agent was trained with these constraints, the available capital at hand was always kept consistent and the amount of fluctuations over larger periods of time stabilized. Additionally, the reward function that consists of two terms requires that both terms have comparable values so information from both of them is conveyed instead of just one term dominating. This tactic of capping profit and loss ensures that the rewards don't overshoot and model gets consistent information.

5   Observations and Results

The models created were tested with different environments and on different stocks in the Indian Stock Market. Figure 3 shows the return of investment for the Infosys stock.

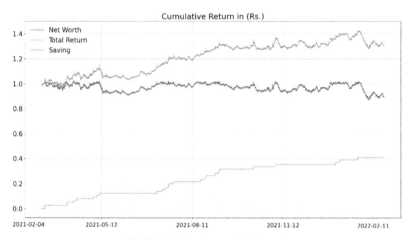

Fig. 3. Backtesting on INFY stock

Figure 3 tracks the movement of net worth, total return and savings over the course of February 2021 till February 2022. The total return is calculated by adding up the net worth and saving variables as mentioned in the methodology. The total result sees a consistent growth over the months returning a final cumulative return of 30.61%. The initial invested amount was 100,000 INR, after performing the backtesting trades for a year the final observed values for net worth and savings were 89,396 and 40,977 respectively, leading to a total return of 130,613 INR.

Various action spaces were tested for the PPO model and it was found that the model learnt the best with discrete action space with the option to buy and sell multiple shares at once rather than continuous action space. The feature of locking aside the profit earned after certain threshold offers security and liquidation.

Both traders and researchers are becoming more interested in the use of reinforcement learning techniques in intraday stock trading. Because it can draw on prior trading experiences to make the best decisions possible in the present, reinforcement learning is particularly well suited for use in the trading industry. A crucial element of reinforcement learning is Markov Decision Processes (MDPs), which offer a framework for simulating sequential decision-making tasks. The flexibility of reinforcement learning to adapt to shifting market conditions is one of the main benefits of utilizing MDPs in intraday trading.

The necessity for a lot of training data is one of the main obstacles. Effective trading strategies are learned using reinforcement learning algorithms with MDPs using a large amount of historical data, which can be challenging in intraday trading because data is only available for brief periods of time. Overfitting, where the algorithm gets too narrowly focused on the training data and fails to generalize to new market situations, is another concern. Notwithstanding these advantages, there are a number of disadvantages to employing reinforcement learning with MDPs for intraday trading.

Several studies have shown that, especially in turbulent or unpredictable markets, reinforcement learning algorithms containing MDPs can outperform conventional trading models. In conclusion, recent years have seen a lot of potential in the use of reinforcement learning methods with MDPs in intraday trading. The advantages of this strategy are considerable, even though there are still certain issues like overtrading that need to be resolved. MDP-based reinforcement learning systems can manage complicated and noisy data, adapt to changing market conditions, and outperform conventional trading models.

6   Conclusion

In conclusion, recent years have seen a lot of potential in the use of reinforcement learning methods with MDPs in intraday trading. The PPO model with a discrete action space has demonstrated promising results in developing intelligent trading systems for the Indian stock market. The inclusion of popular technical indicators in the RL environment and the option to buy and sell multiple shares at once have improved the performance of the model. Using Profit Cap and Stop Loss defines the range of capital available to the model. This adds stability to the model's actions since the available capital is always similar. It also lets us define a relevant reward function that can always give helpful information to the model. The advantages of this strategy are considerable, even though there are still certain issues like overtrading that need to be resolved. MDP-based reinforcement learning systems can manage complicated and noisy data, adapt to changing market conditions, and outperform conventional trading models.

References

1. Montague, P.R.: Reinforcement learning: an introduction, by Sutton, RS and Barto, AG. Trends Cogn. Sci. **3**(9), 360 (1999)
2. Schulman, J., et al.: Proximal policy optimization algorithms. arXiv preprint arXiv:1707. 06347 (2017)
3. Bahdanau, D., et al.: An actor-critic algorithm for sequence prediction. arXiv preprint arXiv: 1607.07086 (2016)
4. Haarnoja, T., et al.: Soft actor-critic algorithms and applications. arXiv preprint arXiv:1812. 05905 (2018)
5. Yang, H., et al.: Deep reinforcement learning for automated stock trading: an ensemble strategy. In: Proceedings of the First ACM International Conference on AI in Finance (2020)
6. Lillicrap, T.P., et al.: Continuous control with deep reinforcement learning. arXiv preprint arXiv:1509.02971 (2015)

7. Mnih, V., et al.: Asynchronous methods for deep reinforcement learning. In: International Conference on Machine Learning. PMLR (2016)
8. Pricope, T.-V.: Deep reinforcement learning in quantitative algorithmic trading: a review. arXiv preprint arXiv:2106.00123 (2021)
9. Mnih, V., et al.: Playing atari with deep reinforcement learning. arXiv preprint arXiv:1312. 5602 (2013)
10. Chen, L., Gao, Q.: Application of deep reinforcement learning on automated stock trading. In: 2019 IEEE 10th International Conference on Software Engineering and Service Science (ICSESS). IEEE (2019)
11. Huang, Y.: Deep Q-networks. In: Deep Reinforcement Learning: Fundamentals, Research and Applications, pp. 135–160 (2020)
12. Hausknecht, M., Stone, P.: Deep recurrent Q-learning for partially observable MDPs. arXiv preprint arXiv:1507.06527 (2015)
13. Azhikodan, A.R., Bhat, A.G.K., Jadhav, M.V.: Stock Trading Bot Using Deep Reinforcement Learning. In: Saini, H.S., Sayal, R., Govardhan, A., Buyya, R. (eds.) Innovations in Computer Science and Engineering. LNNS, vol. 32, pp. 41–49. Springer, Singapore (2019). https://doi. org/10.1007/978-981-10-8201-6_5
14. Lee, C.-Y., Soo, V.-W.: Predict stock price with financial news based on recurrent convolutional neural networks. In: 2017 Conference on Technologies and Applications of Artificial Intelligence (TAAI). IEEE (2017)
15. Cervelló-Royo, R., Guijarro, F., Michniuk, K.: Stock market trading rule based on pattern recognition and technical analysis: forecasting the DJIA index with intraday data. Expert Syst. Appl. **42**(14), 5963–5975 (2015)
16. Liu, X.-Y., et al.: FinRL: a deep reinforcement learning library for automated stock trading in quantitative finance. arXiv preprint arXiv:2011.09607 (2020)
17. Bajpai, S.: Application of deep reinforcement learning for Indian stock trading automation. arXiv preprint arXiv:2106.16088 (2021)
18. Ghosh, P., Neufeld, A., Sahoo, J.K.: Forecasting directional movements of stock prices for intraday trading using LSTM and random forests. Finan. Res. Lett. **46**, 102280 (2022)
19. Hochreiter, S., Schmidhuber, J.: Long short-term memory. Neural Comput. **9**(8), 1735–1780 (1997)
20. Breiman, L.: Random forests. Mach. Learn. **45**, 5–32 (2001)
21. Parambalath, G., et al.: Big data analytics: a trading strategy of NSE stocks using Bollinger bands analysis. In: Balas, V.E., Sharma, N., Chakrabarti, A. (eds.) Data Management, Analytics and Innovation. AISC, vol. 839, pp. 143–154. Springer, Singapore (2019). https://doi. org/10.1007/978-981-13-1274-8_11
22. Brockman, G., et al.: OpenAI gym. arXiv preprint arXiv:1606.01540 (2016)
23. Python Package Index – PyPI: Python Software Foundation (n.d.). Accessed https://pypi.org/ project/stockstats/
24. Yazdi, S.H.M., Lashkari, Z.H.: Technical analysis of Forex by MACD Indicator. Int. J. Human. Manag. Sci. (IJHMS) **1**(2), 159–165 (2013)
25. Bollinger, J.: Using Bollinger bands. Stocks Commodities **10**(2), 47–51 (1992)
26. Gumparthi, S.: Relative strength index for developing effective trading strategies in constructing optimal portfolio. Int. J. Appl. Eng. Res. **12**(19), 8926–8936 (2017)
27. Python Package Index – PyPI: Python Software Foundation (n.d.). Accessed https://pypi.org/ project/yfinance/

Predicting the Droughts Using Artificial Neural Networks – A Case Study

B. Naga Malleswara Rao[1]([ENVELOPE]) [ID], P. V. Ramana[2], and B. Akhila Meenakshi[1]

[1] CVR College of Engineering, Hyderabad, India
bnmrao@cvr.ac.in
[2] MNIT, Jaipur, India

Abstract. Drought is a natural and gradual threat with many devastating consequences for all aspects of human life. Accurate drought forecasting is a promising step to help decision-makers develop strategies to manage drought risks. To achieve this goal, choosing a suitable model is vital in forecasting. Various artificial neural network (ANN) models are used to predict short-term and long-term droughts on different time scales using the Standardized Precipitation Index (SPI) in Gujarat. Due to the frequent danger of drought, people face environmental challenges today in the country, community, and industry. Some of the adverse effects of the drought threat persist in Pakistan, including other threats. However, early measurement and identification of drought can guide water resources management to use drought-resistant strategies. This article uses Perceptron Neural Network (MLPNN) algorithm to predict drought.

Keywords: Droughts · ANN · SPI · MLPNN · Groundwater

1 Introduction

Droughts continue to rank among the most harmful risks, with significant negative effects on the environment, civilization, and economy. Recent occurrences, like summer 2018 drought that devastated large portions of central Europe, caused major crop loss and wildfires. In Germany alone, the damage was anticipated to cost several hundred million dollars, Federal Ministry of Food and Agriculture, [11]. Effects of global warming also result in considerable changes to the earth's climate, which have an immediate impact on the occurrence and magnitude of catastrophic situations like droughts, Spinoni et al., [15–17]. A rise in the prevalence of drought incidence is severe hazard for civilization. It is crucial to fully comprehend this phenomenon to take quick action to reduce calamities. By saving as much water as possible in the most vulnerable regions, for example, stakeholders would be able to minimise the associated risks with drought recurrence. The drought would help to lessen the water shortage whenever it occurred. Such demand-reduction measures may be implemented sooner and to a greater extent, which would lessen the harm to society and the economy.

The research work is the assessment of drought risk. Drought refers to the period in a year when there is a shortage of rainwater, resulting in dry and hot weather. The concept of drought is complex. Drought can cause many physical changes in the environment. Causes significant impacts on nature and people. It has a lasting impact on people. Droughts are one of the deadliest natural disasters due to less rainfall. Drought is the deadliest because agriculture is one of the primary sources in India and depends on rainfall and water supply. Water scarcity severely affects agriculture, causes famine and inflation, and causes numerous deaths. Drought also affects the environment indifferent ways. The action of establishing the high rain comes to an end. The area affected by the drought is unlimited. In addition to one district, this can also affect many districts. All conditions are drought effects. Lack of rain, changes in crop cycle, and improved seed diversity reduces soil moisture levels, decrease plant growth and increase desertification conditions.

Information about the beginning of droughts is essential for reducing their impact. A drought index can be used to calculate this. A number of drought indices available, that are typically determined as per statistical & physical metrics. They primarily consider soil and atmospheric conditions. The Standardized Precipitation Index (SPI), Standardized Precipitation Evaporation Index (SPEI), Soil Moisture Percentile (SMP) and Palmer Drought Severity Index (PDSI) are some of the most often used indices. The World Meteorological Organization has accepted the Standardized Precipitation Index (SPI) as a Standard Meteorological Index [17]. Based on the likelihood that a certain quantity of rain will fall in the concern region, it serves as a barometer of meteorological dryness. In studies on drought forecasting, SPI is a forecasting variable by Belayneh et al. [8] and Bonaccorso et al. [10].

A physical, conceptual, or data-driven model can be used to predict any physical phenomenon. Due to their quick development times and flexible input parameters, the latter ones are extensively used. According to McGovern et al. [17], machine learning techniques have a great potential for extreme prediction because they can learn from previous data, manage numerous input variables, incorporate physical interpretation into the models, and unearth new information from the statistical information. Two typical predictor groupings of factors are identified in a study of seasonal drought forecasting by Hao et al. [14], local climate variables and large-scale climatic parameters. The very first ones are naturally connected with the frequency of drought because they are known to correspond with rainfall pattern in specific places. According to past research, a positive NAO index during the summer is linked to warm, dry temperatures in the northwest of Europe, while colder, wetter conditions are experienced in southern Europe and the Mediterranean region.

According to Sheffield and Wood [17], an AMO positive phase is characterised by humid conditions over portions of Scandinavia and Great Britain and by dry weather in the Mediterranean. An AMO negative phase is characterised by the opposite condition, dry situations in Great Britain as well as wet weather of Mediterranean. According to past studies, there is a 62% association between the frequency of droughts and AMO, with a 90% degree of significance. The NAO is used in a recent survey by Bonaccorso et al. [10] to forecast the likelihood of a drought in Sicily. Local climate parameters of rainfall, temperature, humidity content are the input parameters of forecast. SPI was used as an input variable to the method by Belayneh et al. [8] & Bonaccorso et al. [10]

for the most recent month. Precipitation was a parameter utilised as an input by some researchers.

2 Study Area

Since 2018, Gujarat has seen very little rain, resulting in severe water scarcity, particularly in rural areas. Tankers were used to deliver water to over 500 villages across 14 districts in Gujarat. The situation was far worse in Saurashtra, Kutch, and Northern Gujarat. Other water reservoirs, except for the Narmada dam and the Sardar Sarovar canal, were depleted.

3 Methodology

3.1 Standardized Precipitation Index

McKee et al. [17] established the standardised precipitation index (SPI), a precipitation-based indicator. A continuous monthly rainfall dataset is utilised to calculate SPI. Several timeframes can be used to construct the index; commonly, 1, 3, 6, 12 or 24 months are used. The values for the appropriate timescale's rainfall are first collected. The generated dataset is then converted into a normal distribution with mean SPI set to zero, after which each month's data is independently fitted to a gamma distribution. The amount of deviations from the mean is then the SPI level for a certain rainfall. The SPI is particularly helpful to reflect wetter and dryer regions in addition to account for fluctuations between seasons due to the normalisation. Because the weather at the two study sites is varied, the SPI offers useful and comparative measurement. Collection duration of SPI value must be equal to or shorter than the forecast lead time value or else, the algorithm for machine learning would get the precipitation quantities required for the SPI's mathematical calculation as input.

In the present work, precipitation and groundwater data were collected, divided into two types: Data collection and data analysis. Data was collected for Gujarat state. Groundwater data for Gujarat for 2011–19 are from the state Groundwater Authority. Standardized Groundwater Index (SGI) calculated using groundwater data. Precipitation data for Gujarat has been technically collected for all rain gauge stations to estimate the Standardized Precipitation Index (SPI). In a recent study, the researchers [1, 2] proposed the Multivariate Standardized Drought Index (MSDI) to characterize general equation and can be expressed as:

$$p(x \leq X, y \leq Y) = P \tag{1}$$

Here P indicates probability. As per the research work of [6–8] the equation for MSDI is follows:

$$\text{MSDI} = \emptyset^{(-1)}(P) \tag{2}$$

Here $\emptyset$ is the standard normal distribution function (SDN) is an alternative equation. The GPD function suggested by [3–5] can be expressed as:

$$g(X) = \frac{1}{\beta^{\alpha}\Gamma(\alpha)} X^{\alpha-1} e^{\frac{-\alpha}{\beta}} \tag{3}$$

where $\Gamma(\alpha)$ Gama function. α and β are parameters as indicated by the authors [9–12]. The GPD function assuming $t = \frac{\alpha}{\beta}$:

$$G(X) = \frac{1}{\Gamma(\alpha)} \int_0^X t^{\alpha-1} e^{-t} dt \tag{4}$$

Since Eq. (4) is PDF as $H(X) = q + (1 - q)G(X)$, The Gringorten plotting position:

$$p(X_i) = \frac{i - 0.44}{n + 0.12} \tag{5}$$

In the above equation i and n are number of zero rainfall and sample size respectively [13]. The outputs of Eq. (5) can be transformed into Standardized Index (SI) as:

$$SI = \emptyset^{-1}(p) \tag{6}$$

The $\emptyset$ is the function of the standard normal distribution (SND) function as

$$(SI) = \begin{cases} -\left(t - \frac{C_0 + C_1 t + C_2 t^2}{1 + d_1 t + d_2 t^2 + d_3 t^3}\right) & \text{if } 0 < p \leq 0.5 \\ +\left(t - \frac{C_0 + C_1 t + C_2 t^2}{1 + d_1 t + d_2 t^2 + d_3 t^3}\right) & \text{if } 0.5 < p \leq 1 \end{cases}$$

Here $C_0 = 2.6085569$; $C_1 = 0.7947898$; $C_2 = 0.00998756760$; $d_1 = 1.564644211$; $d_2 = 0.20002444$; $d_3 = 0.0012989779$; and

$$t = \begin{cases} \sqrt{\ln \frac{1}{p^2}} \\ \sqrt{\ln \frac{1}{(1-p)^2}} \end{cases}$$

The artificial numerical modelling for multi-unseen layers, and an output layer.

$$y_k(t) = f_0 \left[\sum_{j=1}^{m} w_{kj} \cdot f_n \left(\sum_{i=1}^{N} w_{ji} x_i(t) + (w_{j0}) + w_{k0} \right) \right] \tag{7}$$

The artificial intelligence models used to the SPI and the range lies between 0 and 1 [11–17]. The multi-layered FF ANN as shown in Fig. 1.

Input and targets for the fitting problem are shown in Fig. 2. The given training data as well validation data includes the testing data are shown in Fig. 3. The proposed unseen layers in the artificial intelligence are shown in Fig. 4.

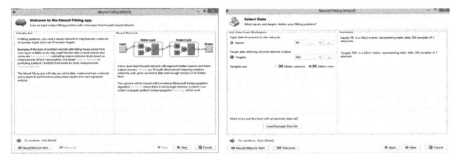

Fig. 1. Multi-layer FF artificial intelligence   **Fig. 2.** Input and targets for the fitting

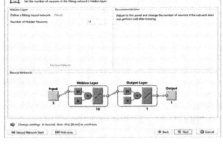

Fig. 3. Training, validation and testing data   **Fig. 4.** Hidden layers in neural network

4 Result and Discussions

4.1 Pre-monsoon Groundwater Gujarat, Daman, and Diu

The mean decadal water levels of the national hydrograph stations in Gujarat of the phreatic aquifer for pre-monsoon period 2007–16 used for the drought assessment. With the help of groundwater data, a standardized groundwater index has been calculated, shown in Fig. 5; on the x-axis, there are several hydrograph stations of all districts of Gujarat. On the y-axis, there is the depth of groundwater (m). The maximum groundwater depth is for Anand and Daman districts. The minimum value is found for many districts such as Amreli, Diu, Kachchh, and Sabarkantha.

In Fig. 6, on the x-axis, there is the number of hydrograph stations in all districts of Gujarat. On the y-axis, Drought occurrence is Probable. As a result, the highest probability was found for Bharuch district, and the minimum probability was found for Surat and Surendranagar district. Similarly, in Fig. 7, the probability of drought occurrence due to soil moisture for 6 months has been calculated, where qn is soil moisture content and qn(1), qn(2), ..., qn(6) showing Probability for May, June,....., October. Here on the x-axis, there is the number of hydrograph stations of all districts of Gujarat. On the y-axis, drought occurrence is probable due to soil moisture conditions. qn(1) figure shows the probability of drought occurrence due to soil moisture condition for May month. The curve showing the maximum likelihood is for most of the districts, and the minimum is for Ahmedabad, Gandhinagar, Junagarh, and Kachchh districts. For qn(2), the same probability curve, the maximum likelihood (probability) is for Sabarkantha district, and the lowest chance (probability) is for most of the communities including Ahmedabad, Gandhinagar, Junagarh, and Kachchh.

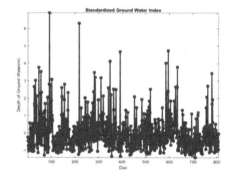

Fig. 5. Average groundwater depth data

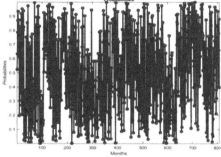

Fig. 6. Probability of drought occurrence

For qn(3), the same probability curve, the maximum likelihood is for the Kachchh district. The minimum probability is for many communities such as Ahmedabad, Gandhinagar, Junagarh, and Kachchh. Figure qn(4), qn(5), and qn(6) are showing similar results for maximum and minimum probabilities. In Fig. 8, risk assessment done due to sensitivity of soil moisture for 6 months, where sn is the sensitivity of soil moisture and sn(1), sn(2),......, sn(6) showing the Probability for May, June,......, October. The x-axis in all the 6 Figures shows the number of hydrograph stations, and the y-axis shows the probable sensitivity in soil moisture. From all the curves of Fig. 8, it's concluded that maximum sensitivity was in May and June month and the minor sensitivity was in October.

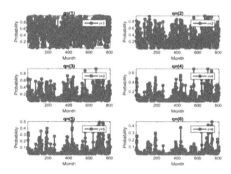

Fig. 7. Probability of drought occurrence due to soil moisture conditions

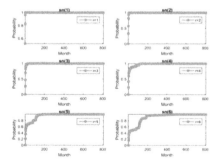

Fig. 8. Probability of drought occurrence to sensitivity of soil

In Fig. 9, there are model-fitting curves for 6 months, which are showing the pertinent data, where fn has functioned for curve fitting, and fn(1), fn(2),......, fn(6) are the fitting curves for May, June, October. Here the x-axis shows the number of hydrograph stations of all districts of Gujarat. The y-axis shows the probability of fitting. The model which shows more fitting will deliver the most accurate results (Fig. 10).

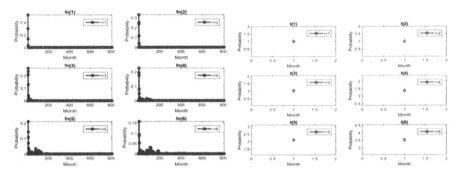

Fig. 9. Mathematical curve fitting for 6 months

Fig. 10. Mean value for all analysis of 6 months

Finding the best configuration requires carefully adjusting the model parameters for artificial intelligence (AI) design. The best architecture of drought prediction of artificial intelligence is to develop a mathematical algorithm and inspect it thoroughly. Figure 11 shows the mean squared error (MSE) reached a minimum in 7 epochs. The training stopped when the validation parameter reached 6 validation checks at epoch 13 with the gradient descent value 0.31978, which would cause the convergence of the network fast.

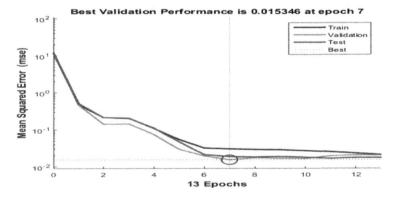

Fig. 11. Performance plot for artificial neural network

5 Conclusions

This work used artificial intelligence (AI) design and a popular drought index called the Standardised Groundwater index to monitor the drought pattern in the Gujarat region. According to the study, the monsoon and annual drought start in May and can last up to eight months. In the same year, there was almost a similar spatial distribution, however in some regions, the severity and frequency of drought vary from year to year. The pre-monsoon drought, on the other hand, is more severe in Gandhinagar, Junagarh, and Kachch district. Additionally, a critical analysis of the rainfall indicates that the region is susceptible to future episodes of chronic drought. The likelihood of a drought occurring is substantially lower in areas like Anand, Surat, and Surendranagar. Additionally, for the Standardised Groundwater Index, Gandhinagar, Junagarh, and Kachchh district have the lowest values whereas Anand, Surat, and Surendranagar have the highest values.

References

1. Adomian, G.: Convergent series solutions of nonlinear equations. J. Comput. Appl. Math. **11**(2), 225–230 (1984)
2. Adomian, G.: Solving Frontier Problems of Physics, The Decomposition Method, 2nd edn., p. 22. Kluwer, Dordrecht (1994)
3. Gobarah, A., Abou-Elfath, H., Biddah, A.: Response-based damage assessment of structures. J. Earthq. Eng. Struct. Dyn. **28**, 79–104 (1997)
4. Mwafy, A.M., Elnashai, A.S.: Static push over versus dynamic collapse analysis of RC buildings. J. Eng. Struct. **23**, 407–424 (2001)
5. Elnashai, A.S.: Advanced inelastic analysis for earthquake applications. J. Struct. Eng. Mech. **12**, 51–70 (2001)
6. Surendranath, A., Ramana, P.V.: Mathematical approach on recycled material strength performance via statistical mode. Mater. Today: Proc. **54**(4) (2021)
7. Meena, A., Ramana, P.V.: Mathematical model for recycled poly ethylene terephthalate material mechanical strengths. Mater. Today: Proc. **38**(5) (2021)
8. Belayneh, A., Adamowski, J., Khalil, B., Quilty, J.: Coupling machine learning methods with wavelet transforms and the bootstrap and boosting ensemble approaches for drought prediction. Atmos. Res. (2016). https://doi.org/10.1016/j.atmosres.2015.12.017
9. Raghu Prasad, B.K., Ramana, P.V.: Modified Adomian decomposition method for fracture of laminated unidirectional composites. J. Springer **37**(1), 33–57 (2012)
10. Bonaccorso, B., Cancelliere, A., Rossi, G.: Probabilistic forecasting of drought class transitions in Sicily (Italy) using Standardized Precipitation Index and North Atlantic Oscillation Index. J. Hydrol. **526**, 136–150 (2015). https://doi.org/10.1016/j.jhydrol.2015.01.070
11. Federal Ministry of Food and Agriculture: Trockenheit und Dürre – Überblick über Maßnahmen (2018). https://www.bmel.de/DE/Landwirtschaft/Nachhaltigeandnutzung/Klimawandel/_Texte/Extremwetterlagen-Zustaendigkeiten.html
12. Ganesh, E., Ramana, P.V., Shrimali, M.K.: In elastic materials and mathematical variables for obstacle bridge problem evaluation. Mater. Today: Proc. **65**, 3424–3430 (2022). https://doi.org/10.1016/j.matpr.2022.05.564
13. Ganesh, E., Shrimali, M.K., Ramana, P.V.: Higher-order obstacle problems evaluation through novel approach. In: ASPS Conference Proceedings, vol. 1, no. 2 (2022). https://doi.org/10.38208/acp.v1.508

14. Hao, Z., Hao, F., Singh, V.P., Zhang, X.: Changes in the severity of compound drought and hot extremes over global land areas. Environ. Res. Lett. **13**, 124022 (2018). https://doi.org/10.1088/1748-9326/aaee96
15. Bracci, J.M., Kunnath, S.K., Reinhorn, A.M.: Seismic performance and retrofit evaluation for reinforced concrete structures. J. Struct. Eng. **123**, 3–10 (1997). ASCE
16. Dolsek, M., Fajfar, P.: Simplified non-linear seismic analysis of infilled reinforced concrete frames. J. Earthq. Eng. Struct. Dyn. **34**, 49–66 (2005)
17. McGovern, A., et al.: Using artificial intelligence to improve real-time decision-making for high-impact weather. Bull. Am. Meteorol. Soc. **98**, 2073–2090 (2017). https://doi.org/10.1175/BAMS-D-16-0123.1

Applying Machine Learning for Portfolio Switching Decisions

E. Uma Reddy[ID] and N. Nagarjuna[(✉)] [ID]

CVR College of Engineering, Hyderabad, India
{umareddy,n.nagarjuna}@cvr.ac.in

Abstract. Portfolio switching is an investment strategy that responds to Market momentum by adjusting a portfolio to produce more value. This study will use machine learning algorithms to predict the prudent state of the market using sample mutual fund returns to make portfolio-switching decisions. The study trained and tested the performance of sample funds using monthly returns of mutual funds, market proxy, and risk-free assets over seven years. The machine learning algorithm, specifically Support Vector Machine (SVM) and Logistic Regression (LR), was used to select a portfolio that could adapt to a changing market. SVM outperformed LR in terms of performance and evaluating the algorithm's efficacy using sample mutual funds helps the investors to choose the suitable algorithm for investment decisions.

Keywords: Mutual funds · portfolio management · portfolio switching · Logistic Regression · Support Vector Machine

1 Introduction

Mutual funds, pension funds, and Unit Linked Insurance Policy Schemes offer a wide choice of Equity investments to individual investors. These funds provide an open option of switching facilities to their investors. This option facilitates investors in changing their equity exposure with another class of Assets belonging to the debt category. To achieve their financial objectives, investors prefer certain asset classes with high exposure in the portfolio.

If investors adopt a realistic method of timing that is based on the present market condition, they may benefit from switching. Investors need to identify the market movement, such as downturn and upturn, before making their portfolio decisions. Well-diversified Investor's Equity Portfolio returns mimic the Market returns [4, 25]. Benchmarks for the performance of equity portfolios typically use broad market indices like the NSE 500 to represent the Market [24].

Excess returns are widely used in finance literature as a critical factor to evaluate performance compared to other investment possibilities. Mutual Fund Portfolio's monthly returns are calculated based on their closing Net Asset Values (NAV), and these monthly returns are converted into Excess Returns by subtracting corresponding monthly Risk-free returns.

Equity investments excess returns are regarded as a premium above a risk-free rate [16]. Investors can compare their portfolios excess returns using the market status; when the market's excess returns are positive, the market state is 1which indicates Upturn Market; otherwise, it is viewed as 0 indicating Downturn market. Investors typically evaluate their portfolios based on positive excess returns regardless of market conditions. However, to get maximum benefit from portfolio switching decisions, portfolios can be positioned in the following order for the select period.

i. Portfolio Excess returns > 0 and Market status = 0.
ii. Portfolio Excess returns > 0 and Market status = 1.
iii. Portfolio Excess returns < 0 and Market status = 0.
iv. Portfolio Excess returns < 0 and Market status = 1.

- This study utilizes machine learning to predict state of the market, based on well Diversified Equity Mutual fund Returns, Risk-free returns, and Market proxy.
- SVM and Logistic Regression models are used to forecast the market state to make portfolio-switching decisions by using data sets of well-diversified equity funds returns and risk-free returns as predictors.
- Evaluating the performance of various algorithms to demonstrate its effectiveness in guiding portfolio decisions.

This study facilitates investors in assessing the performance of their portfolios and decide whether to make changes as per the timing results of the Algorithm used. The paper is divided into the following sections. Section 2 covers the Literature Survey, while Sect. 3 outlines the methodology, including data preprocessing, model training, and classifiers used. Section 4 presents the results, and Sect. 5 concludes the paper.

2   Literature Survey

Machine learning techniques were utilized to forecast future mutual fund performance in a study published in the Journal of Finance and Economics. The forecasts were then used as a basis for portfolio rebalancing choices. The authors discovered that their methodology produced noticeably greater returns compared to conventional portfolio management procedures [2].

Jiang, J., & Tsai, J. used a hybrid strategy combining traditional asset allocation models with machine learning algorithms to optimize a mutual fund portfolio. The approach outperformed conventional methods in terms of risk-adjusted returns [1].

Al Janabi proposes a framework that integrates an optimization algorithm and machine learning models to analyze investment portfolios. The framework uses a machine learning method to select optimal portfolios for commodities while considering liquidity-adjusted value-at-risk. This approach is useful for commodity trading units to evaluate risk exposure, explore risk reduction options, and construct efficient market portfolios [13].

The authors of this article—Yiyang Zhang, RongjieXie, and Feng Gao—discuss the uses of machine learning in asset management, such as the choice to transfer mutual funds portfolios, and give an overview of the pertinent literature and future research directions [22].Gradient Boosted Trees, a machine learning technique, was utilized in a study published in the Journal of Investment to forecast mutual fund returns and direct portfolio allocation choices. Yu et.al discovered that, in terms of both return and risk parameters, their strategy beat conventional asset allocation models [3].

An overview of current developments in machine learning techniques for portfolio management, including mutual fund portfolio switch decision, is provided by Yuxiang Chen and Hua Peng. They also highlight the prospects and limitations in this area [23].

Using financial statement data and other indicators, David Grossman and Kristina Rennekamp suggest a machine learning-based method to forecast the decision to switch mutual fund portfolios [6]. The potential use of machine learning in mutual fund portfolio management, including portfolio selection, risk management, and portfolio switching decisions, is discussed by Rajesh K. Aggarwal and Suneel Maheshwari [11].

SVMs and random forests outperform other ML algorithms for forecasting mutual fund portfolio switches, per Jie Xu and Jianbing Liu's analysis [8].

SerhatYüksel and N. Nergiz Dincer give an overview of machine learning methods used in mutual fund selection, such as portfolio switch decisions, and use empirical research to gauge the effectiveness of these methods [21].

Ayodeji Olalekan Ojo et al. addresses the applications of machine learning techniques in investment decision-making, including the decision to transfer mutual fund portfolios, and assess the potential advantages and drawbacks of doing so [20].

Hui Guo and Robert Savickas find that a machine learning approach greatly outperforms conventional statistical methods when used to predict the decision to alter a mutual fund portfolio [5].

The present state-of-the-art of machine learning algorithms for portfolio management, including mutual fund portfolio switch decisions, is outlined by Yan Wu, Weining Wang, and Yunjie Zhao. They also suggest future research topics [19].

Kumbalathuparambil and Singh overview how machine learning is used in financial planning and investment management, specifically for making decisions on mutual fund portfolios and portfolio switching [12].

The use of machine learning in asset management, including the decision to transfer mutual fund portfolios, is discussed by Shashank Singh and Vahid Gholampour, who also assess the advantages and drawbacks of doing so [18].

Zhou, Zhu, and Qi summarize the literature on using machine learning to predict mutual fund portfolio switching. They assess different approaches and recommend future research directions [9].

Possible future studies are suggested by NeginShahnazari and Fatemeh Ghadami as they address potential uses of machine learning in finance, such as the decision to transfer mutual fund portfolios [15].

The state-of-the-art machine learning algorithms for portfolio optimization, including mutual fund portfolio switch decision, is examined by Thiago C. Silva et al. [14].

While using a machine learning algorithm to forecast mutual fund switching behavior, Robert H. Battalioet al. discover that the programme can produce more accurate forecasts than conventional approaches [7].

Pinelis, M., & Ruppert, D. discuss the drawbacks of traditional portfolio allocation methods and suggest using machine learning algorithms as an alternative solution.

They propose a new machine learning-based portfolio allocation approach involving regression trees and random forests [17].

With the review of the studies, it has been found that authors focused on using various models of Machine Learning to detect portfolios with superior performance. However, this study concentrates on detecting the state of the market for Portfolio switching decisions.

3   Methodology

This section explores the primary steps to take before model creation, including defining the data collection and environment, handling missing values, and extracting significant features.

3.1   Datasets and Handling Missing Values

The study used the following data sets for a period of 7 years from January 2012 to December 2018.

Dataset consists of

a. Monthly returns of 36 Diversified Growth option Open-ended Equity schemes from the Association of Mutual Funds in India (AMFI),
b. Monthly risk-free returns from the Average Yield at Cut off Price of 91 days T-bills Auctions of Reserve Bank of India (RBI) and
c. Monthly Market returns from Month End Closing Values S&PCNX 500 index of the National Stock Exchange (NSE).

Monthly returns of the Indian Equity Mutual Fund Portfolio were determined based on their closing Net Asset Values (NAV) and transformed into excess returns by subtracting the corresponding month's risk-free returns.

The Python packages Pandas and Scikit-learn were used for experimentation, splitting the dataset into training and testing sets. The model was constructed using machine learning algorithms on the training set, and the trained model was applied to the testing dataset.

The effectiveness of each model is evaluated based on its accuracy, recall, precision, and F-score.

Preprocessing is required for the raw dataset to be used with a model. The dataset contains features with missing values, which are imputed with mean.

3.2   Feature Selection

Correlation-based feature selection technique is used to select the appropriate features.

3.3 Training the Model

The data is split into a 3:1 ratio, with 75% of the data used for training (train data) and 25% for testing (test data). For instance, if there are 100 records, 75 will be designated train data and 25 test data for testing. To perform the task, supervised machine learning algorithms like Logistic Regression (LR) and Support Vector Machine (SVM) are utilized.

3.4 Classifiers

A) Logistic Regression

Logistic regression (LR) converts one or more input parameters into a probability between 0 and 1 by using a logistic function on a linear combination of input variables. This probability can be interpreted as the likelihood of an event occurring. When making predictions on new data, logistic regression is first trained on labeled data. LR is widely used in classification and prediction tasks.

B) Support Vector Machine

SVM is a potent machine learning method used for classification and regression tasks. It finds the ideal border or hyperplane to divide data into different classes. To ensure precise predictions on fresh data, the SVM algorithm maximizes the margin or distance between the hyperplane and the closest points in each class. SVM is frequently used in classification to categorize new samples according to their position on the hyperplane.

3.5 Metrics for Performance Evaluation

Using machine learning, various performance measures from the confusion table estimate the model's performance (Table 1).

Table 1. Model's Confusion Matrix

Confusion Matrix		Actual Values		Accuracy = (TP + TN)/(TP + FP + FN + TN)	
		Market state = 1	Market state = 0		
Predicted Values	Market State = 1	TP	FP	Predicted Positive Value	TP/(TP + FP)
	Market State = 0	FN	TN	Predicted Negative Value	TN/(FN + TN)

True Positive (TP) = Samples accurately predicted to have a market upturn.
False Positive (FP) = samples incorrectly predicted to have an upturn market.

False Negative (FN) = samples incorrectly predicted to have a downturn market.
True Negative (TN) = samples accurately predicted to have a downturn market.

Accuracy, recall, precision, and F1-score were numerous measures used to assess each model's performance [10].

4   Results

The dataset used for this analysis covered 84 months, including monthly returns of 36 Mutual funds Equity schemes, Risk-free Returns, and Market Returns. It has 84 records, 50 of which reflect a market upturn, and 34 recorded a downturn. Training and testing datasets were created from the pre-processed dataset. The testing set has 21 records, whereas the training set has 63. Logistic Regression and SVM, two machine learning techniques, were employed. The 10-Fold Cross Validation approach was used to train the model using the training set. Table 2 shows the performance comparison of Machine Learning Algorithms for portfolio decisions.

Table 2. Performance comparison of Machine Learning Algorithms for portfolio decisions

Model/Measure	Accuracy	Precision	Recall	F1-Score
Logistic Regression	90.4	84	100	91.3
SVM	100	100	100	100

In this study, SVM outperformed logistic regression with perfect accuracy, precision, recall, and F1-score scores of 100%, while logistic regression had an accuracy of 90.4% and precision score of 84%. This is due to SVM's ability to handle non-linear data effectively with kernel functions, capture intricate relationships, and handle high-dimensional data and imbalanced datasets more robustly than logistic regression.

5   Conclusion

The study used two ML algorithms to detect the state of market for portfolio management decisions. The effectiveness of machine learning in making accurate decisions for switching portfolios strongly depends on the choice of algorithms. SVM model obtained better results in terms of accuracy, precision, recall, and F1-score compared to the Logistic Regression model. By using more precise machine learning algorithms like SVM, investors can identify portfolios that are outperforming the projected state of the market. However, forecasting market trends helps investors to make better choices.

References

1. Jiang, J., Tsai, J.: Hybrid asset allocation: combining traditional and machine learning approaches. J. Finan. Data Sci. **1**, 3–16 (2019)

2. Qi, W., Wu, Y., Wang, H.: Predicting mutual fund performance with machine learning. J. Finan. Econ. **40**, 116–127 (2019)
3. Yu, H., Lu, Q.: Machine learning for mutual fund return prediction and portfolio optimization. J. Invest. **28**, 57–69 (2019)
4. Krishnamurti, C., Sequeira, J.M., Fangjian, F.: The importance of portfolio diversification in reducing risk. J. Wealth Manag. **15**, 99–106 (2012)
5. Guo, H., Savickas, R.: Mutual fund portfolio switching: a machine learning approach. J. Finan. Quant. Anal. **53**, 2639–2668 (2018)
6. Ezzat, K., Grossman, D., Rennekamp, K.: Predicting portfolio switching decisions with machine learning. J. Account. Res. **59**(4), 1481–1522 (2021). https://doi.org/10.1111/1475-679X.12372
7. Battalio, R.H., Jennings, R.J., Corwin, S.A.: Using machine learning to predict mutual fund switching behavior. J. Finan. Quant. Anal. **55**, 573–598 (2020). https://doi.org/10.1017/S00 22109020000135
8. Xu, J., Liu, J.: Predicting portfolio switching decisions: a comparative study of machine learning algorithms. Int. J. Intell. Syst. **36**, 2473–2487 (2021). https://doi.org/10.1002/int. 22378
9. Zhou, Y., Zhu, H., Qi, Y.: Predicting mutual fund portfolio switching: a review of the literature. Int. J. Econ. Finan. **12**, 113–121 (2020). https://doi.org/10.5539/ijef.v12n6p113
10. Prakash, K.L.N.C., Narayana, G.S., Ansari, M.D., Gunjan, V.K.: Instantaneous approach for evaluating the initial centers in the agricultural databases using K-means clustering algorithm. JMM **18**, 43–60 (2021). https://doi.org/10.1007/s12045-021-0132-1
11. Aggarwal, R.K., Maheshwari, S.: Machine learning applications in mutual fund portfolio management. J. Finan. Manag. Anal. **34**(2), 35–46 (2021). https://doi.org/10.1177/097231 6620985992
12. Kumbalathuparambil, A., Singh, R.: Machine learning for financial planning and investment management: a review. J. Adv. Manag. Res. **16**(1), 70–91 (2019). https://doi.org/10.1108/ JAMR-08-2017-0079
13. Al Janabi, M.A.M.: Optimization algorithms and investment portfolio analytics with machine learning techniques under time-varying liquidity constraints. J. Model. Manag. **17**(3), 864–895 (2022). https://doi.org/10.1108/JM2-10-2020-0259
14. Silva, T.C., Bastos, V.A.F., Garcia-Garcia, D.: A systematic literature review on machine learning techniques for portfolio optimization. Expert Syst. Appl. **166**, 113527 (2021). https:// doi.org/10.1016/j.eswa.2020.113527
15. Shahnazari, N., Ghadami, F.: Machine learning applications in finance: a review of the literature and future directions. J. Finan. Data Sci. **3**(3), 66–84 (2021). https://doi.org/10.3905/ jfds.2021.1.015
16. Bhatt, S., Ghosh, S.: Measuring performance of mutual funds: an analysis of risk and return. Int. J. Bus. Quant. Econ. Appl. Manag. Res. **1**(10), 72–83 (2014)
17. Pinelis, M., Ruppert, D.: Machine learning portfolio allocation. J. Finan. Data Sci. **8**, 35–54 (2022). https://doi.org/10.1016/j.jfds.2021.12.001
18. Singh, S., Gholampour, V.: Applications of machine learning in asset management. J. Portfolio Manag. **45**(6), 41–58 (2019). https://doi.org/10.3905/jpm.2019.1.228
19. Wu, Y., Wang, W., Zhao, Y.: Machine learning for portfolio management: a review and new research directions. J. Intell. Fuzzy Syst. **40**(3), 3901–3912 (2021). https://doi.org/10.3233/ JIFS-201108
20. Ojo, A.O., Li, Z., Nahavandi, S.: A review of machine learning techniques for investment decision making. J. Investment Strat. **9**(2), 1–35 (2020). https://doi.org/10.3905/jis-2020-1-082
21. Yüksel, S., Dincer, N.N.: Machine learning and mutual fund selection. Expert Syst. Appl. **141**, Article no. 112957 (2020). https://doi.org/10.1016/j.eswa.2019.112957

22. Zhang, Y., Xie, R., Gao, F.: Machine learning applications in asset management. J. Syst. Sci. Complex. **34**(6), 1818–1836 (2021). https://doi.org/10.1007/s11424-021-9222-4
23. Chen, Y., Peng, H.: Portfolio management with machine learning: a review of recent advances. IEEE Trans. Neural Netw. Learn. Syst. **32**(4), 1389–1409 (2021). https://doi.org/10.1109/TNNLS.2020.2975596
24. NSE Indices Limited: NIFTY 500 Index (n.d.). https://www1.nseindia.com/products/content/equities/indices/nifty_500.htm
25. Kumar, D., Gopalakrishnan, K.: Impact of behavioral factors on investment decisions: a study of individual equity investors in India. IUP J. Behav. Finan. **12**(3), 23–41 (2015)

Bark Texture Classification Using Deep Transfer Learning

Rohini A. Bhusnurmath and Shaila Doddamani[(✉)]

Department of Computer Science, Karnataka State Akkamahadevi Women's University,
Vijayapura, Karnataka 586108, India
dodamanishaila@gmail.com

Abstract. Tasks that are involved in forest are conservation, disease diagnostics, plant production, and tree species identification is crucial. There has been a disagreement over whether the leaves, fruits, flowers, or bark of the tree should be utilized to distinguish between species. Research has shown that bark is crucial because it persists during seasonal changes and gives trees their distinctive identities through structural variances. Using bark texture image to identify tree species is a difficult topic that could be helpful for many forestry-related jobs. Although recent developments of deep learning performed the outstanding outcome on common eyesight problems. This research presents a deep learning-based strategy for classifying 50 different categories of trees based upon the texture of their bark for that taken the dataset called BarkVN-50. This BarkVN-50 dataset is the largest values of trees bark that have been taken into account for bark classification thus far. Here in present experiment investigated the use feature extraction from the basic CNN model and pre-trained (Transfer learning techniques) models like VGG16, MobileNet and also compared the results of the all three models with their computation time and accuracies of each models. It is observed from results that pre-trained model work more efficient with high accuracy.

Keywords: CNN · Pattern recognition · Texture classification · Deep learning · Pre-trained model · VGG16 · MobileNet · Species Identification

1 Introduction

Researchers in physiology, the environment, meteorology, etc. hold tree identification in high regard as one of their fields. Usually, several characteristics including fruit, leaves, stems, colors, bark, and tree trunk shells are used to determine the type of tree. Experts with relevant experience typically perform this technique. As a result, it is expensive and does not have high or consistent accuracy. Also, it is quite risky for professionals or researchers in many forests and meadows. As a result, developing a technique for recognizing native trees in one of the most prominent research areas in computer vision and image processing are forests and rangelands [1].

Trees and shrubs' bark, which is their outermost layer, is crucial to their existence. The delivery of materials produced by using photosynthesis in plant tissues is one of the barks key roles. Another noteworthy aspect of bark's protective qualities is that it serves as a barrier against herbivory, fire, and cold weather. Tree trunks and branches are often covered in numerous layers of bark. Cork development is primarily responsible for its appearance. The environment in which it grows frequently contributes to the diversity in thickness and texture. The bark of trees is a source of many crucial economic and medicinal items [2].

The importance of landmarks with semantic meaning has been shown in recently developed semantic localization and mapping algorithms [3, 4]. In this case, As such semantic landmarks, trees and knowledge of their species would be useful. Drones flying in woods are a topic that the robotics community is becoming more and more interested in [5]. In terms of forestry applications, Relying on a tree's bark for species identification offers several benefits over other characteristics, such how its leaves or fruits look. Initially, despite seasonal variations, bark of the tree is always seen. Moreover, it can still be found on wood years after the trees were felled and put in a lumber yard. Even though there isn't much foliage at the robot's height in woods that are important for economy, bark is typically visible to most robots when taking inventory of standing trees. Yet, since some species only have very slight changes in their bark structure, classifying tree species only based on photographs of the tree bark's is a difficult job that still experienced by humans find difficulties.

Recent developments of DL have demonstrated that neural networks (CNN) can outperform humans on a variety of visual identification tasks [6]. Deep learning methods have a key limitation in that they typically need very big datasets to produce results that are adequate. For instance, there are 14 million images in the ImageNet database, divided into roughly 22,000 synsets.

In this study, work is carried out on the texture dataset BarkVN-50 [7], which includes 50 different tree categories and 5,678 303 × 404 pixel pictures, with the goal of classifying the most possible tree species. A transfer learning techniques and the basic convolution neural network model is used, and a fine tuning strategy was used to differentiate the textures of the bark trees and subsequently recognize the original tree categories. Evaluation criteria including the accuracy of the models, precision, recall, and f1-score are used to access the model performance.

With the use of statistically based model learning techniques, we frequently classify the surface texture recorded under various illumination situations. And showed comparison among the basic CNN model and Pre-trained models of the deep learning has been discussed in the proposed study.

The paper is further divided into five sections. Recent research projects in this field are covered in the Sect. 2. The approach of the suggested model is presented in Sect. 3, and the proposed model is discussed in the Sect. 4. The experiment's findings are presented in the Sect. 5. Further work is concluded in the Sect. 6.

2 Literature Work

SahilFaizal [2] proposed the classification model in the field of the wood texture. Worked on the classification of bark texture by taking the BarkVN-50 dataset by applying a transfer learning techniques like ResNet101 has been implemented and got the better results. Junfeng Hu et al. [8] has worked on the lumber classification field they have used the deep learning to classify the lumber images worked on the three different datasets by using ResNet model and got the higher accuracy for all three datasets. Kazi and Panda [9] worked on instead of using the conventional CNN architectures, here they have investigated the transfer learning potential for CNN models in the context of fruit picture categorization. In this study, the three different types of fruits were identified, and their relative freshness was categorized using a variety of traditional convolutional neural network architectures.

A unique dataset called BarkNet-1.0 was created by M. Carpenter et al. [10] and contains 23,000 pictures of the 23 different tree species found in Canada. Then, by the pre-trained weights of the ImageNet dataset (consist more than 1 million photos there roughly 10,000 types of items), this data is utilized to train ResNet architecture. Experimental results revealed that the model's accuracy ranged from 93.88% to 97.81%. Chen Zhang et al. [11] proposed an RGB optical image collection called TCC10, which serves as a standard for tree canopy classification and contains images of 10 urban tree species (TCC). Tree cover photos with straightforward backdrops and are with complicated environments can both be found in the TCC10 dataset. The goal was to investigate the viability of classifying specific tree species using DL techniques (VGG-16, AlexNet and ResNet-50). Hiremath and Bhusnurmath [12] proposed an innovative technique for categorizing color textures based on anisotropic diffusion. The goal is to use computer vision to investigate color spaces for the usefulness in the automatic identification of specific textures types in industrial areas, specifically, granite and wood textures.

Yuan-Yuan Wan et al. [13] examined and statistically explained the value of texture analysis techniques for identifying bark. Co-occurrence matrices technique, Gray level run-length method, histogram method (HM), and auto-correlation method comparative investigations of the extraction of bark texture features are carried out. Absolute Gradient Matrix is used to extract distinguishing properties from different texture images, and it is compared to other methods of texture analysis [14]. Ting He et al. [15] have worked on the wood defect detection by extracting the features of the wood by using the learning method to detect the wood features and classify automatically. Hiremath and Bhusnurmath [16] have worked on local directional binary patterns and anisotropic diffusion to classify color texture images in RGB color space. Texture classes are classified using the k-NN classifier. The Oulu database is used to evaluate the approach. Findings show a more accurate and superior categorization method for color texture images than RGB. Akash et al. [17] has worked on the Convolution neural network (CNN) is used to present a model that is based on deep learning. The model is then separated into two submodels that are aware of models 1 and 2. The method is created with specially configured parameters to categorise surface texture with fewer training examples. A CNN model is used to categorise the created surfaces with the relevant labels into classes after the image feature vectors are formed using statistical processes to compute the surface's physical appearance.

Maryam et al. [18] Employed segmentation-based fractal texture evaluation (SFTA) of images that represent the malware code, features from pre-trained AlexNet and

Inception-v3 deep neural networks are combined with features from images. used distinct pre-trained models for feature extraction (AlexNet and Inception-V3) as well. The accuracy of the malware classifier is increased using deep convolutional neural network (also known as CNN feature extraction from two models. Awwal et al. [19] has worked on the Deep Learning in Neuroradiology Brain Haemorrhage Classification Using Transfer Learning here they have worked on identifying brain haemorrhage which is measured as a monotonous job for radiologists, To address the problem A convolutional neural network (CNN), the well-known AlexNet neural network, and a modified novel AlexNet with support vector machine (AlexNet-SVM) classifier are trained to classify the brain computer tomography.

Rajayogi et al. [21] on a dataset of Indian food, image categorization is done using several transfer learning approaches. Food is crucial to human life because it gives us various nutrients, thus it's important for everyone to keep an eye on their eating habits. Food classification is therefore vital for leading a healthier lifestyle. Pre-trained models are employed in the project instead of the more conventional ways of creating a model from scratch, which reduces computing time and costs while simultaneously producing superior outcomes. For training and validating, the dataset of Indian food is utilised, which consists of 20 classes with 500 photos each. IncceptionV3, VGG16, VGG19, and ResNet are the models that were used. After testing, it was discovered that Google InceptionV3 performed better than other models.

Chen Li et al. [22] has used transfer learning and a residual convolutional neural network to identify pests. The experimental dataset used to achieve data augmentation by random cropping, colour transformation, CutMix, and other procedures was the IP102 agricultural pest picture collection. When it comes to influencing elements like shooting angles, light, and colour variations, processing technology can provide considerable resilience. The experiment tested various combinations of learning rate, transfer learning, and data augmentation to the ResNeXt-50 (32 4d) model's classification accuracy. The experiment also evaluated how data enhancement affected the ability of various samples to be classified. The findings demonstrate that the model classification effect that is based on transfer learning is typically superior to that that is based on new learning.

3 Materials

Many issues requiring sophisticated, highly variable functions are resolved by deep learning models. To address such issues, approaches learn characteristic hierarchies with features derived from higher level features that are composed of numerous features at lower levels. These characteristics produce good classification accuracy when applied to categorize the texture in different domains. The suggested deep learning model for categorizing surface texture is described in this part along with its sub models.

3.1 Dataset

The dataset is a collection of 5,768 images in total over 50 types of bark tree. The images depict the variations in tree bark. The BarkVN-50 [16] dataset is freely accessible for research purposes at Vinh Truong Hoang of the Ho Chi Minh City Open University.

Details about the BarkVn-50 dataset are given in the Table 1. Hence in the experimented dataset each class having the unbalanced number of images. The Fig. 1 shows the all classes with its different number of images in each class. The Fig. 2 contains the samples texture images from the BarkVN-50 texture dataset which are taken for the experiment.

Table 1. Summary of the BarkVn-50 Dataset [16]

Parameters	Values
Total number of images	5578
Number of classes	50
Size of each patch (image)	303×404
Image format	RGB JPG images
Total size of dataset	176 MB

3.2 Pre-processing and Splitting

At this step, the raw data is prepared to be used with the deep learning (DL) models, The CNN model and pre-trained models can use all of the images because they have been scaled to 224 * 224 * 3 size. The data is splitted into training and validation sets after preprocessing.

4 Proposed Model

The proposed experiment is carried out with two different models one with basic CNN and other uses the pre-trained (transfer learning) model. CNNs are a subclass of deep neural networks that are frequently used for visual image analysis. CNNs can identify and categorize specific features from images. A convolution tool that uses a method known as feature extraction to separate and classify the various characteristics of the image for analysis. The goal of this CNN feature extraction approach is to reduce the number of features that are present in a dataset. It adds new features that are a summary of the existing features included in the initial collection of features. The Fig. 3 shows proposed basic CNN architecture that has the numerous CNN layers.

The Fig. 4 shows pre-trained model architecture of the transfer learning. In the proposed experimentation transfer learning is carried out using two different transfer learning techniques, named, MobileNet and VGG16. These models are evaluated on a training and validation in the ratio of 80:20.

VGG16
The 16 in VGG16 stands for 16 weighted layers. Thirteen convolution layers, five Max Pooling layers, three Dense layers, and a total of 21 layers make up VGG16, but only

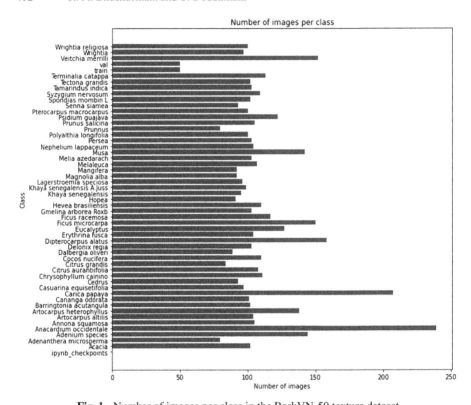

Fig. 1. Number of images per class in the BarkVN-50 texture dataset

sixteen of them are weight layers, also known as learnable parameters layers. The most distinctive feature of VGG16 is that it prioritized convolution layers of a 3 × 3 filter with stride 1 rather than a large number of hyper-parameters and consistently employed the same padding and max-pool layer of a 2 × 2 filter with stride 2.Throughout the whole architecture, the convolution and max pool layers are uniformly ordered. There are 64 filters in the Conv-1 Layer, 128 filters in Conv-2, 256 filters in Conv-3, and 512 filters in Conv-4 and Conv-5.

MobileNet
It is possible to train classifiers that are incredibly compact and incredibly quick using the MobileNet class of convolutional neural networks (CNNs), which Google open-sourced. It creates a lightweight deep neural network by using depth wise convolutions to drastically lower the number of parameters compared to previous networks. The first mobile computer vision model for Tensorflow is called MobileNet. The MobileNet model features 27 convolutional layers, including 13 depth wise convolutions, 1 average pool layer, 1 fully connected layer, and 1 softmax layer.

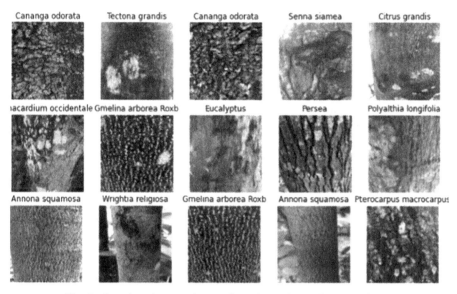

Fig. 2. Samples of texture images from the BarkVN-50 texture dataset

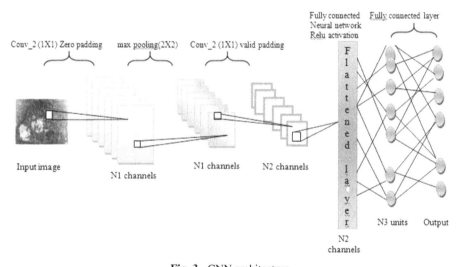

Fig. 3. CNN architecture

5 Experimental Results

Proposed work is experimented on Intel core i3 processor running at 2.40 GHz speed using 4 GB RAM, 64-bit Windows 10 Operating System. Few of the python libraries like Numpy, pandas etc. are used and a whole model is created by using the tensorflow [2].

5.1 Results and Discussion

The efficacy of the anticipated models is experimented using a number of categorization measurement factors [20] and pre-processing is carried out by resizing the original images of size 303 × 404 to 224 × 224 which are considered for the experimentation. Number of epoch is set as 70 for all three proposed model so that to cross verify the accuracy of all models using uniform number of epochs. These models are tested with less number of epochs that results less accuracy and increasing the number of epoch results constant loss in the models as compared to the experimented number of epochs. Hence, number of epoch is set as 70. Parameters of pre-trained models which are altered in the proposed method for the effectiveness of accuracy are: i) Global Average Pooling 2D layer is added, ii) dense layers is added and iii) at last layer softmax activation function is used. These additional layers exhibit better results for the proposed method.

Precision, recall, accuracy were three quantitative performance measures that were produced throughout the Prediction phase to assess the dependability of trained models by using validation data are given Eqs. (1) to (3). Based on True Negative (TN), False Negative measures (FN), True Positive (TP), False Positive (FP), and these metrics are calculated.

$$Precision = \frac{TP}{TP + FP} \tag{1}$$

$$Recall = \frac{TP}{TP + FN} \tag{2}$$

$$Accuracy = \frac{TP + TN}{TP + FN + TN + FP} \tag{3}$$

The results are shown in graphical form and tabular form. Table 2 shows the results in terms of different achievements measures that assess the effectiveness of techniques and state correctness. Experimentation for epochs for different values is shows in Figs. 5, 6 and 7. It is observed that epoch values is 70 is optimal for further processing, which results better classification accuracy. The following are the discussion of these performance measuring criteria's:

- Results of basic CNN model.
- Results of pre-trained MobileNet model
- Results of pre-trained VGG16 model

From the above Table 2, it is observed that the results for the BarkVN-50 texture dataset, the basic CNN model is about the 79.49% accuracy and for the model VGG16 is 96.21% accuracy and MobileNet model shows 95.42% accuracy. The basic CNN model is giving the less accuracy as compared to the pre-trained models which are good for the detecting the patterns.

Figures 5, 6 and 7 show the detailed experimentation results of above mentioned all three models of the BarkVN-50 texture dataset for values of epochs ranging from 0 to 70. Accuracy, recall, loss and precision function evolution is shown in graphical view.

The Table 3 shows the performance evaluated on BarkVN-50 texture datasets in the form of accuracy.

Table 2. Performance comparison of classification results for the BarkVN-50 dataset with proposed method

Parameters	Results with different models		
	Basic CNN	Mobile Net	VGG16
Accuracy (%)	79.49	95.42	96.21
Precision (%)	84.79	95.42	96.72
Recall (%)	75.41	94.36	95.95
Train time per epoch in sec	640	2602	10725
Loss Function	categorical_crossentropy	categorical_crossentropy	categorical_crossentropy
Layers used	Zero padding 6 conv layers Fully connected layer + ReLU Max pooling layer Softmax	Global average pooling Dense layer, Fully connected layer ReLU, output layer softmax	Global average pooling Dense layer, Fully connected layer ReLU, output layer softmax

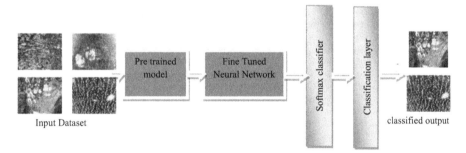

Fig. 4. Proposed pre-trained model architecture

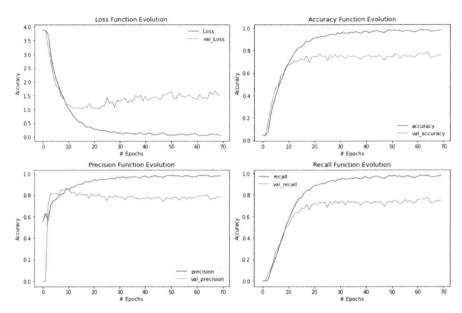

Fig. 5. BarkVN-50 Accuracy, Loss Curve and Precision, Recall curves for Basic CNN model

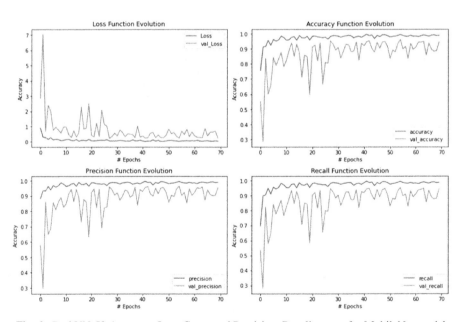

Fig. 6. BarkVN-50 Accuracy, Loss Curve and Precision, Recall curves for MobileNet model

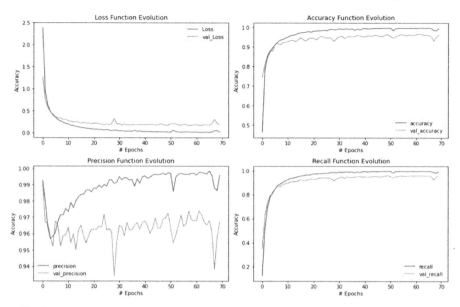

Fig. 7. BarkVN-50 Accuracy, Loss Curve and Precision, Recall curves for VGG16 model

Table 3. Comparison of classification accuracy obtained with proposed method and other work on BarkVN-50 texture dataset.

Sl. No.	Work in literature	Methodology	Classification Accuracy in %
01	SahilFaizal [2]	CNN ResNet101	94
02	Proposed method	Basic CNN	79.49
		MobileNet	95.42
		VGG16	96.21

Proposed experimental results gives better classification rate in evaluation with state-of-the-art approach. The VGG16 model is giving 96.21% accuracy because of the 16 layer deeper as compared to the basic convolution neural network.

6 Conclusion and Future Scope

Convolutional neural networks, which have cutting-edge architectures for extracting feature vectors from visual input, are used here to do feature extraction. The model's ability to generalize and its capacity for exact classification have both been validated during the evaluation phase. Several CNN-based designs have been investigated and tested. According to the comparison analysis, proposed models perform better than the majority of other models for BarkVN-50 texture datasets i.e. for the MobileNet it is 95.42% and for the VGG16 is 96.21% accuracy. And for each model epoch value is set to optimal. As a result, it can be inferred that use of pre-trained models (transfer learning) can be utilized to finish tasks rapidly when the target dataset's feature space is similar to the dataset used to train the pre-trained model. In the future, the proposed method can be tested for a variety of pre-trained models on more texture datasets and potentially apply them to other fields like medical and aerial photography.

Acknowledgement. Authors are thankful to the reviewers for suggestions and constructive criticism that helped to enhance the quality of the manuscript.

References

1. Fekri-Ershad, S.: Bark texture classification using improved local ternary patterns and multi-layer neural network. Expert Syst. Appl. **158**, 113509 (2020). https://doi.org/10.1016/j.eswa.2020.113509
2. Faizal, S.: Automated identification of tree species by bark texture classification using convolutional neural networks. arXiv preprint arXiv:2210.09290 (2022). https://doi.org/10.22214/ijraset.2022.46846
3. Atanasov, N., Zhu, M., Daniilidis, K., Pappas, G.J.: Localization from semantic observations via the matrix permanent. Int. J. Robot. Res. **35**(1–3), 73–99 (2016). https://doi.org/10.1177/02783649155965
4. GhasemiToudeshki, A., Shamshirdar, F., Vaughan, R.: UAV visual teach and repeat using only semantic object features. ArXiv e-prints, arXiv-1801 (2018)
5. Smolyanskiy, N., Kamenev, A., Smith, J., Birchfield, S.: Toward low-flying autonomous MAV trail navigation using deep neural networks for environmental awareness. In: IEEE/RSJ International Conference on Intelligent Robots and Systems (IROS), Vancouver, BC, Canada, pp. 4241–4247 (2017). https://doi.org/10.1109/IROS.2017.8206285

6. Truong Hoang, V.: BarkVN-50. Mendeley Data, V1 (2020). https://doi.org/10.17632/gbt4td mttn.1

7. He, K., Zhang, X., Ren, S., Sun, J.: Delving deep into rectifiers: surpassing human-level performance on ImageNet classification. In: Proceedings of the IEEE International Conference on Computer Vision, pp. 1026–1034 (2015)

8. Hu, J., Song, W., Zhang, W.: Deep learning for use in lumber classification tasks. Wood Sci. Technol. **53**(2), 505–517 (2019). https://doi.org/10.1007/s00226-019-01086-z

9. Kazi, A., Panda, S.P.: Determining the freshness of fruits in the food industry by image classification using transfer learning. Multimed. Tools Appl. **81**(6), 7611–7624 (2022). https://doi.org/10.1007/s11042-022-12150-5

10. Carpentier, M., Giguère, P., Gaudreault, J.: Tree species identification from bark images using convolutional neural networks. In: 2018 IEEE/RSJ International Conference on Intelligent Robots and Systems (IROS), Madrid, Spain, pp. 1075–1081 (2018). https://doi.org/10.1109/IROS.2018.8593514

11. Zhang, C., Xia, K., Feng, H., et al.: Tree species classification using deep learning and RGB optical images obtained by an unmanned aerial vehicle. J. For. Res. **32**, 1879–1888 (2021). https://doi.org/10.1007/s11676-020-01245-0

12. Hiremath, P.S., Bhusnurmath, R.A.: Industrial applications of colour texture classification based on anisotropic diffusion. In: Santosh, K.C., Hangarge, M., Bevilacqua, V., Negi, A. (eds.) RTIP2R 2016. CCIS, vol. 709, pp. 293–304. Springer, Singapore (2017). https://doi.org/10.1007/978-981-10-4859-3_27

13. Wan, Y.-Y., et al.: Bark texture feature extraction based on statistical texture analysis. In: Proceedings of 2004 International Symposium on Intelligent Multimedia, Video and Speech Processing, Hong Kong, China, pp. 482–485 (2004). https://doi.org/10.1109/ISIMP.2004.143 4106

14. Howard, A.G., et al.: MobileNets: efficient convolutional neural networks for mobile vision applications. arXiv preprint arXiv:1704.04861 (2017). https://doi.org/10.48550/arXiv.1704.04861

15. He, T., Liu, Y., Yu, Y., Zhao, Q., Hu, Z.: Application of deep convolutional neural network on feature extraction and detection of wood defects. Measurement **152**, 107357 (2020). https://doi.org/10.1016/j.measurement.2019.107357

16. Hiremath, P.S., Bhusnurmath, R.A.: RGB - based color texture image classification using anisotropic diffusion and LDBP. In: Murty, M.N., He, X., Chillarige, R.R., Weng, P. (eds.) MIWAI 2014. LNCS (LNAI), vol. 8875, pp. 101–111. Springer, Cham (2014). https://doi.org/10.1007/978-3-319-13365-2_10

17. Aggarwal, A., Kumar, M.: Image surface texture analysis and classification using deep learning. Multimed. Tools Appl. **80**, 1289–1309 (2021). https://doi.org/10.1007/s11042-020-095 20-2

18. Nisa, M., et al.: Hybrid malware classification method using segmentation-based fractal texture analysis and deep convolution neural network features. Appl. Sci. **10**(14), 4966 (2020). https://doi.org/10.3390/app10144966

19. Urbonas, A., Raudonis, V., Maskeliūnas, R., Damaševičius, R.: Automated identification of wood veneer surface defects using faster region-based convolutional neural network with data augmentation and transfer learning. Appl. Sci. **9**(22), 4898 (2019). https://doi.org/10.3390/app9224898

20. Goyal, V., Sharma, S.: Texture classification for visual data using transfer learning. Multimed. Tools Appl. (2022). https://doi.org/10.1007/s11042-022-14276-y

21. Rajayogi, J.R., Manjunath, G., Shobha, G.: Indian food image classification with transfer learning. In: 2019 4th International Conference on Computational Systems and Information Technology for Sustainable Solution (CSITSS), vol. 4, pp. 1–4. IEEE (2019). https://doi.org/10.1109/CSITSS47250.2019.9031051. https://doi.org/10.1155/2019/4629859

22. Li, C., Zhen, T., Li, Z.: Image classification of pests with residual neural network based on transfer learning. Appl. Sci. **12**(9), 4356 (2022). https://doi.org/10.3390/app12094356

Dynamic Twitter Topic Summarization Using Speech Acts

Suhail Afroz[1]([✉]) [iD], Ch. V. S. Satyamurty[1] [iD], P. Asifa Tazeem[1], M. Hanimi Reddy[1], Y. Md. Riyazuddin[2], and Vijetha Jadda[3]

[1] CVR College of Engineering, Hyderabad, India
suhailafroz786@gmail.com
[2] GITAM University, Hyderabad, India
rymd@gitam.edu
[3] Vikrama Simhapuri University, Nellore, India

Abstract. The enormous growth of social media platforms such as Facebook and Twitter caused content and comment explosion. Summarization of such comments help in value derivation and become useful in policy making. The tweets are different in nature like noisy, short, and dissimilar. Twitter's capacity to summarize a message or issue concisely and effectively is what gives it this power. To improve their tweets and reach a larger audience, users frequently use strategies like threading, hashtags, and multimedia attachments. There are several methods applied by researchers, but these are error prone. To summarize the tweets, we have taken the help of speech acts. The speech acts are helpful to guide the summarization based on behavior of the tweet with an organized view of the tweets. The approach is collecting the tweets, preprocessing, classification, and summarization. After the summarization evaluate the tweets based on different categories and nature of the tweet.

Keywords: Twitter · Topic Summarization · Speech Acts · Word Extraction · Ranking

1 Introduction

Twitter is a popular social media platform that allows users to share short messages called tweets. The platform has become a significant source of information and communication for individuals, business, and organizations worldwide. With its limited character count per tweet, the user is challenged to condense their thoughts and ideas into concise and impactful statements.

Twitter's influence on various aspects of society cannot be understated. It has facilitated the rapid spread of information, enabling conversations and debates on important social and political issues. Hashtags have played a crucial role in organizing and mobilizing communities, allowing users to connect and amplify their voices. Influencers, politicians, and celebrities have harnessed the platform's reach to shape public opinion and engage with their followers.

© The Author(s), under exclusive license to Springer Nature Switzerland AG 2023
R. Morusupalli et al. (Eds.): MIWAI 2023, LNAI 14078, pp. 421–428, 2023.
https://doi.org/10.1007/978-3-031-36402-0_39

Now a day's people are expressing their views in chats and using social media. There are several social media applications are available such as Facebook, twitter, Instagram, WhatsApp, LinkedIn. In this one Facebook and twitter most popular. Every second, on an average 6000 tweets are tweeted. This leads to per minute 3,50,000 tweets are tweeted on twitter.com. There are trending tweets which consists of millions of tweets, reading all the tweets in topic is a tedious task for a human being. The summarization of these many tweets with help of promising solutions of text mining. These techniques will generate synopsis of many tweets in each topic. The twitter summarizations are very different from other summarization of text such as documents, research articles, books, news topics. The topic modeling and text summarization is a multi-classification problem.

A summary is a brief synopsis of the main points of a text. The purpose of the abstract is to make it easier for the reader or listener to understand what the material is trying to say. It's useful to make summaries of your own work. A summary can show your understanding of the main points of an assigned reading or viewing. If the ideas in the source are important to the task you are working on and you feel they should be included, you can summarize sections of the source, or even the entire source, but the original takes up a lot of space.

By nature, twitter topic summarization is a kind of multi-document summarization. The news articles contain hundreds of words, but each tweet is 140-character long. The twitter tweets are maximum of two sentences. The tweet for a particular topic is a hundred to tens of thousands, summarizing of these tweets are useful but at the same time they are noisy, spelling mistakes, short words, grammar mistakes are more. So, the summarization is not an easy step. The said facts lead to text summarization approaches may not be correctly fit to the twitter summarization. The approach presented in this paper will solve few of the issues.

Speech acts are very much useful for tweets because they serve the purpose to differentiate the tweets with a subject which they related depends on the communicative nature. The people while communicating using tweets, some are suggestions, few are comments, some may share information and others are questions. These are all called as "speech acts" [1].

Speech acts on Twitter relate to the numerous communicative actions carried out via tweets. Twitter's character limit makes it difficult to have a thorough conversation, but users use a variety of speech actions to get their points across. These speaking acts serve a variety of purposes, such as expressing opinions, exchanging information, having conversations, putting out requests, giving orders, and more. Twitter users can employ speech acts to achieve objectives with their tweets. Through the clever use of words, they can instruct, persuade, amuse, engage, provoke, or mobilize their audience. Each tweet becomes a chance to deliver a speech act that accomplishes a certain expressive aim while simultaneously conveying information.

In some case users' tweets may not inform what the type of 'speech act' they are performing is not known while tweeting. First recognize the tweets, before applying the 'speech act'. The grasp of linguistic knowledge of 'speech acts' is an added advantage to perform topic summarization as well as generate more meaningful sentence templates.

The Sect. 2 consists of related work, Sect. 3 discussed experimental setup, Sect. 4 presents experimental results and Sect. 5 consists of conclusion.

2 Related Work

The 'Speech act' was proposed by Austin [1] in 1960's is very much useful for tweet summarization or chats in social network analysis. The researchers show interest about the linguistic meaning of the sentences lead to build the logical aspects [2] and taxonomies [3] of speech acts. The speech further extended to dialogue act [4] to know more about the sentences expressed in chatting. The dialogue act is helpful to automatic recognition to model conversion [5, 6]. The dialogue act and speech act helped to depend on the corpora such as Switchboard DAMSL [7] and meeting recorder dialogue act [8]. Further these acts are extended to electronic media like emails, chat rooms and discussion forums [9, 10] useful to understand the intended purpose of the sender. The methods developed for the corpora for verbal communications are not useful as well as the methods developed for email or chat discussions are also not helpful to summarize the tweets because of the nature of communication used in tweets. The researchers started new classification methods recently [11] hindered by poor annotated data. The problem is addressing by either supervisory [12] and unsupervised methods [13]. The further complication of this task is a unique chat style in speech and text used neither [14, 15] and noisiness of the tweets. The [16] has produced few results.

3 Experimental Setup

The steps listed below can be used to perform sentiment analysis on a single dataset of Twitter data:

Step 1: Data Collection - Collecting the necessary Twitter data is the first step in the analysis process. Either the Twitter API or a third-party source of data downloads can be used for this.

Step 2: Data cleaning - Make the data suitable for analysis by eliminating any duplicate or irrelevant tweets and preparing the ones that remain. This can entail operations like tokenization, stemming, and stop word removal.

Step 3: Sentiment Analysis - Apply a sentiment analysis algorithm to the preprocessed tweets to perform sentiment analysis. Several techniques, including lexicon-based methods, machine learning algorithms, and hybrid techniques, can be used to do this.

Step 4: Visualization - Visualize sentiment analysis results to gain insight into the sentiment of your Twitter data. This may include the use of graphs, charts or other visual aids representing Tweet Sentiment Scores.

Step 5: Interpretation - Interpret the results of sentiment analysis by analyzing sentiment scores and identifying patterns and trends in the data. This helps her gain insight into the opinions and attitudes of her Twitter users on specific topics and events.

Overall, sentiment analysis of Twitter data provides businesses, researchers, and individuals with insight into how people feel about particular topics, brands, and events, and the ability to make data-driven decisions based on those insights. It can be a useful tool for making decisions.

Speech acts refer to the actions performed through language, where words are not just used to convey information but also to accomplish certain tasks or achieve specific effects. Twitter, as a platform for communication, is a space where various speech acts are employed. Here are some common speech acts found in tweets: Statements, Questions, Commands, Expressions, Apologies, Promises, Invitations, etc. In our experimental setup we are using suggestions, statements, questions, and comments.

The introduction of speech acts facilitates a high-level and well-organized view of the tweets, i.e., whether most of them are about facts, opinions, suggestions, or questions. On this level, we can extract language expressions to convey the most salient information in a speech act, which would not be feasible with a more traditional framework working with salient terms, phrases, sentences, or tweets in general.

First the tweets are retrieved from the twitter database on the twitter site. Using the user credentials, the new application must be created in the twitter website in the developer mode. The created application is helpful as a mediator to retrieve the tweets using the access keys.

Figures 1, 2, 3, 4 and 5 will demonstrate the steps to create an application and generate access key.

Fig. 1. First Screen

Fig. 2. Basic application

Fig. 3. Twitter application creation

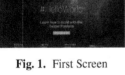

Fig. 4. Application setting of application.

Fig. 5. Access key.

Fig. 6. Retrieved tweets.

First need to login into the developer account of twitter and then need to click "Create New App" Then feed the necessary details for the application. After this application would be created and then consumer key, consumer Secret code are generated. The access token and access Token secret code are helpful to access the application.

The retrieved tweets shown in Fig. 6 to be preprocessed to bring them into understandable form. The preprocessing step includes several things like replacing a URL with the keyword URL, username with AT, replacing the repeated characters in each word and replacing the repeated words with null.

The second step is to apply the classification algorithm is used to classify the retrieved tweets. The retrieved tweets will be classified into four categories. The categories are question, suggestion, comment, and statement. Classification is done based on the datasets. The distinct dataset is used for each classification, based on the dataset classification is proceeded.

They are several types of datasets which are available for classifying tweets into certain categories. The comment dataset is useful for classifying comment tweets, which is shown below. Following is the sample of comment dataset. It contains several words like:

aah!
aaah
aaaahh
help!
aha
a-ha
I understand
Attention, please!s
ahh
ahhh
Ok, I see

4   Experimental Results

The classification of tweets depending on the 'speech act' forming different types of files are shown below.

Fig. 7. Classification of tweets

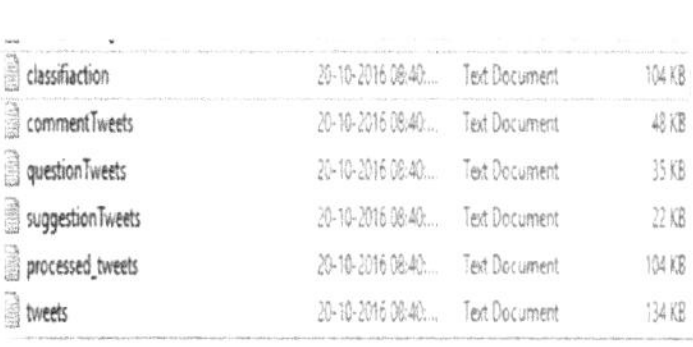

Fig. 8. Different files

Fig. 9. Output file of the suggestion tweets   **Fig. 10.** Output file of the comment tweets.

The Fig. 7 is the file which is generated by the classification module. It also generates other files such as statementTweets.txt, questionTweets.txt, suggestionTweets.txt and commentTweets.txt. Figure 8 is the screenshots of the files (Fig. 9).

Figure 10 is the output file of the comment tweets. The question tweets and processed tweets are written to respective files.

The next step is to evaluate the retrieved tweets. The first step in evaluation is to categorize the tweets as positive, negative, and neutral using sentiment analysis. The output of the sentiment analysis is shown in Fig. 11.

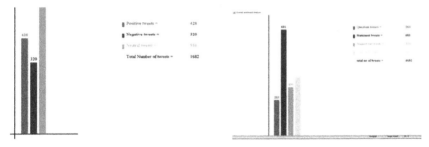

Fig. 11. Output after applying sentiment analysis.   **Fig. 12.** The tweets with different speech acts

Figure 11 shows the sentiment analysis and Fig. 12 shows the tweets with different speech acts.

In Fig. 11 the red color bar is the positive tweets with a value 428, the blue color is the negative tweets with a value 320 and the green color bar is neutral tweets are 934. The total tweets considered are 1682.

Further the tweets are categorized using speech acts into four categories as shown in Fig. 12. The four categories of tweets are question tweets 263, statement tweets 681, suggestion tweets 339 and comment tweets 399. The total tweets considered are 1682.

Figure 13(a) shows the different types of tweets positive and negative and neutral tweets with accuracy, the different measures such as precision, recall and F-measure with accuracy shown in Fig. 13(b). The accuracy is 87.58%.

As can be seen in Fig. 14 below, that lists the human and automatic summaries for the hashtag topic, the abstractive summaries guided by speech acts more frequently capture key words or phrases in human summaries than the extractive summaries.

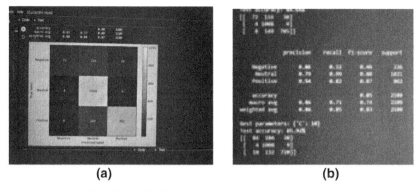

(a)   **(b)**

Fig. 13. (a) Confusion Matrix. (b) Accuracy measures

HUMAN AND AUTOMATIC SUMMARIES FOR #*AGOODBOYFRIEND*

Human	*People are tweeting the qualities that make a good boyfriend and the things a good boyfriend does.*
Our method	*For "a good boyfriend", people state "Team Minaj, DAMN Derrick Rose, Yuri Gagarin" and comment on "love joy, silent cries, good girlfriend".*
SumBasic	*#agoodboyfriend is #agoodboyfriend whether he's around u or not.. "#AGoodBoyfriend" is really a TT? #agoodboyfriend is not looking for #ago*

Fig. 14. Twitter topic summarization.

5   Conclusion

Twitter data summarization is a complex task due to the limited character count and the informal nature of tweets. It requires a combination of linguistic analysis, machine learning, and domain-specific knowledge to generate accurate and meaningful summaries.

Reading all the tweets has some obvious problems because of the sheer amount of material available and lack of patience on the reader's part. These problems can be tackled to by creating a summarized information for all the tweets. The paper in its current state meets just the bare minimum requirements.

But the work does provide proof of concept and the intricacies. Even tasks that sound not quite tough to perform like extracting the main content from all the tweets involves a lot of care and issues to be handled which can only be done with iterations of development, working on better and better versions each time. It is a humongous task to abstract such high levels of intricacy with a harmonious front and still being sourced by billions of people daily.

The work has been built quite lean, focusing on just the sentimental phase, this makes a lot of difference to somebody who loves surfing through twitter.

References

1. Austin, J.: How to Do Things with Words. Oxford University Press, Oxford (1962)

2. Searle, J., Vanderveken, D.: Foundations of Illocutionary Logic. Cambridge, UK (1985)
3. Searle, J., Cole, P., Morgan, J. (eds.): Indirect speech acts. In: Syntax and Semantics, vol. iii, pp.59–82. Academic, New York (1975). Speech acts
4. Bunt, H.: Context and dialogue control. Think **3**, 19–31 (1994)
5. Shriberg, E., et al.: Can prosody aid the automatic classification of dialog acts in conversational speech? Lang. Speech (Spec. Iss. Prosody Conversat.) **41**(3–4), 439–487 (1998)
6. Stolcke, K., et al.: Dialogue act modeling for automatic tagging and recognition of conversational speech. Comput. Linguist. **26**(3), 339–373 (2000)
7. Jurafsky, D., Shriberg, E., Biasca, D.: Switchboard SWBD-DAMSL labeling project coder's manual, draft 13. University of Colorado Institute of Cognitive Science, Technical report (1997)
8. Dhillon, R., Bhagat, S., Carvey, H., Shriberg, E.: Meeting recorder project: dialog act labeling guide. In: International Computer Science Institute, Berkeley, CA, Technical report (2004)
9. Cohen, W., Carvalho, V., Mitchell, T.: Learning to classify email into 'speech acts'. In: Proceedings of the EMNLP-04, pp. 309–316 (2004)
10. Feng, D., Shaw, E., Kim, J., Hovy, E.H.: Learning to detect conversation focus of threaded discussions. In: Proceedings of the HLT-NAACL-06, pp. 208–215 (2006)
11. Zhang, R., Gao, D., Li, W.: What are tweeters doing: recognizing speech acts in Twitter. In: Proceedings of the AAAI-11 Workshop Analyzing Microtext (2011)
12. Ritter, A., Cherry, C., Dolan, B.: Unsupervised modeling of Twitter conversations. In: Proceedings of the HLT-NAACL-10, pp. 172–180 (2010)
13. Jeong, M., Lin, C.-Y., Lee, G.: Semi-supervised speech act recognition in emails and forums. In: Proceedings of the EMNLP-09, pp. 1250–1259 (2009)
14. Crystal, D.: Language and the Internet, 2nd edn. Cambridge University Press, Cambridge (2006)
15. Crystal, D.: Internet Linguistics. Routledge, London (2011)
16. Dhanve, N.M.: Twitter topic summarization using speech acts. IJIRCCE **4**(4) (2016)

Generative Adversarial Network for Augmenting Low-Dose CT Images

Vijai Danni and Keshab Nath[✉]

Indian Institute of Information Technology, Kottayam, Kerala, India
keshabnath@iiitkottayam.ac.in

Abstract. Computed Tomography(CT) image reconstruction from sensor data involves time-consuming and complex mathematical operations. Filtered Back Projection(FBP) is a mathematical equation that can convert input sinogram data to CT images. Normally CT scans are performed with a relatively high amount of radiation dosage. This may cause long-term ailments for patients. The solution is to use low-dose radiation dosage. But this will result in noisy and unclear images upon FBP reconstruction. There are some approaches where deep learning models have been applied on top of FBP reconstructed images for denoising such as FBP+Unet etc. The resulting images may still contain imperfections that could lead to medical misinterpretation. In this paper, we have implemented a GAN model that could augment the quality of reconstructed images and bridge the gap between the reconstructed and ground truth images. We will be focusing on lung/chest CT data provided by the LoDoPab-CT dataset and augmenting the image quality of FBP reconstructed images.

Keywords: Computed Tomography(CT) · Generative Adversarial Network · Health Care · Deep Learning

1 Introduction

Computed Tomography (CT) is a very important diagnostic tool used in medicine since the 1970s [1]. It allows the doctors to get a view of the inside body of a patient without any invasive procedures. CT scan is used to detect bone tumors and fractures, muscle and bone disorders, pinpoint blood clots, tumors, infections, etc. It is used to monitor the growth of cancer, tumor, lung nodules, heart disorders and other terminal diseases. It can also be a guide during medical procedures such as surgery, biopsy and radiation therapy [2]. Traditional CT scanning techniques have a drawback such that the image quality is dependent on radiation dosage. The higher the applied dosage the greater the quality of reconstructed images. With each innovation, the radiation dosage requirement is getting considerably reduced. Filtered Back Projection(FBP) was the method of choice for CT until 2009 when Iterative Reconstruction (IR) was introduced. IR reduced radiation dosage from 23 to 76 without any reduction in image quality. All CT machines now use IR methods. The technology kept on evolving and

R. Morusupalli et al. (Eds.): MIWAI 2023, LNAI 14078, pp. 429–441, 2023.
https://doi.org/10.1007/978-3-031-36402-0_40

with each advance in IR algorithms radiation dosage also decreased dramatically [1]. Machine learning techniques are considered the future of medical imaging. A huge amount of research is being conducted in this field of science. Radiation reduction is the main goal of introducing ML and two approaches are commonly found for this. One is by giving low-dosage radiation to patients and the resulting low-quality CT image data is fed into a neural network and image quality is raised to the level of ground truth (high-dosage image data) while the next technique applies X-rays to patients at only intervals of time (sparse-angle) rather than continuous exposure during the X-ray machine rotation, and interpolating from the incompletely collected data to obtain full resolution images [3].

In this work, we use the first method mentioned above. Here we make use of a benchmark dataset named Low-Dose Parallel Beam - a subset of Lung Image Database Consortium - LIDC-IDRI (LodoPab-CT) [4] that provides low radiation dosage, sparse angle sinogram data also provides ground truth of the same which can be used for comparing and testing the quality of machine learning model. FBP is applied to the low-dose CT scan data that results in a low-quality image, but the image when passed through a trained GAN network, will raise the image quality to the level of high radiation dosage images. The quality of the reconstructed image is measured based on of Peak Signal-to-Noise ratio(PSNR) and Structural Similarity Index Measure(SSIM). A higher PSNR value indicates better reconstruction. The higher the value of SSIM the better. In this research work, we primarily focus on SSIM values. Though CT scans are available for all parts of the body, our work only focuses on Chest/Lung based CT images that are provided by the LodoPab-CT dataset. Chest CT scans can help doctors to detect lung problems such as blood clots, tumors or masses, fluid builds(pleural effusion), pulmonary embolism, tuberculosis etc. [5]. The quality of the CT images should be very high to detect minute tumors or blood clots. Noise in the CT images may result in doctors misdiagnosing a patient. So research in the field of CT imaging should not only be about radiation reduction but also about improving the quality of the images as well. This is where PSNR and SSIM values come into play. Some researchers also speculate that the advice of highly experienced CT technicians should also be taken into account when evaluating industry-standard ML models before their hardware implementation.

2   Related Work

Computed Tomography has come a long way from its inception since the 1970s. A lot of research is done on this topic. The future of CT scanning is Machine Learning techniques. In the following discussion, we will explore some of the recent research conducted in this field.

Jianbing Dong et al. [3] developed a method called DPC-CT that trains a deep learning model using sparse-view CT sinogram data and produces high-quality CT images through a five-step process. The process involves performing an FBP operation on incomplete data, obtaining a corrupted sinogram, applying differential phase-contrast, passing it through a neural network, and performing a final FBP reconstruction to obtain the CT image. Kim et al. [6]

introduced DLIR, a Deep Learning technique that surpasses ASIR-V, an iterative reconstruction method, in producing high-quality LDCT images with less noise, demonstrating a 30% reduction in image noise. Leuschner *et al.* [4] gives a detailed description of the LoDoPab-CT dataset used in this work. They explain that the dataset can be used for low-dose machine learning model building, sparse-angle and transfer learning applications as well. They also explain some drawbacks in using it for real-life applications because the dataset contains simulated low-dose radiation data and not actual low-dose sinogram data. Dong *et al.* [7] explains how they used a combination of unet and residual learning in sparse-view CT image reconstruction. They found that RMSE and SSIM improved by quite a margin when they tested in micro-CT experimental data. Sandfort *et al.* [8] used CycleGAN to improve low-dose CT image reconstruction quality. They compared it to the standard UNet architecture on kidney, liver, and spleen scans with and without contrast material, using the DeepLesion dataset for training. Jin *et al.* [9] compared FBPConvnet and SART-TV for image reconstruction. FBPConvnet performed better due to its ability to preserve fine details, while SART-TV only performs regularization. The paper also discusses sparse view reconstruction and its potential for reducing radiation dosage for patients.

Table 1. Comparison of standard reconstruction methods

Method	PSNR	SSIM	Runtime	Parameters
FBP	19.75	0.597	4	1
TV	28.06	0.929	5 166	1
FBP + U-Net denoising	29.20	0.944	9	10^7
FBP + residual denoising	32.38	0.972	9	$1.2 \cdot 10^5$
Learned Gradient	32.29	0.981	56	$1.2 \cdot 10^4$
Learned PDHG	28.32	0.909	48	$2.4 \cdot 10^4$
Learned Primal	36.97	0.986	43	$1.2 \cdot 10^5$
Learned Primal-Dual	**38.28**	**0.989**	49	$2.4 \cdot 10^5$

The aim of this study is to reduce the difference between standard reconstructed images and the corresponding ground truth images in medical imaging. While various reconstruction methods are used, the focus is solely on the basic FBP method. Results from different methods are presented in Table 1, with the highest SSIM value obtained using the Learned Primal-Dual method. The goal of this research is to close the gap between reconstructed images and ground truth using an effective GAN model.

3 Proposed Approach

We use a sinogram dataset reconstructed via Filtered Back Projection method with 64×64 resolution as input for a GAN model. The GAN model improves the low-dose input image and outputs an image of the same resolution. We use SSIM to compare the output with ground truth. Discriminator and Generator models are trained separately using PyTorch, with the Discriminator trained to distinguish between original and Low-Dose FBP reconstructed + GAN augmented images. The SSIM formulae are obtained from the piqa library and used to calculate Mean Bias Error value for backward propagation during training. These libraries are available in secure python-pip repositories and widely used in production environments.

The LoDoPab-CT dataset has low dose images with $3 \times 362 \times 362$ resolution, but for training purposes, the resolution was reduced to $3 \times 64 \times 64$ without reproducing the noise. However, this leads to little difference between the low-dose and ground truth images and results in an SSIM of 1.0, making accurate training impossible. To address this, dynamic noise injection [10] using Poisson and Gaussian noise is recommended, which can be easily generated using pre-built functions in the scikit-image library. The noise is added directly to the training images. Figure 1 depicts the architecture utilized in this research, with the LoDopab-ct dataset providing both ground truth data and its low-dose equivalent sinogram data, which is transformed into 2D images via FBP. Our aim is to utilize a DCGAN model with convolution layers in both the generator and discriminator sections to enhance the quality of the low-dose sinogram images. The generator is the crucial element of our GAN model, as it generates images of higher quality than the input. The objective is to bridge the gap between the reconstructed and ground truth images.

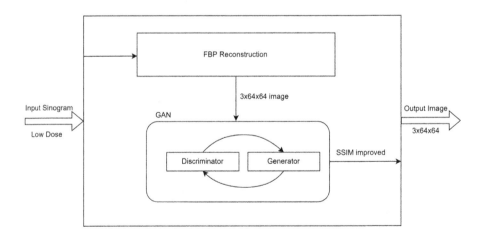

Fig. 1. Proposed Architecture

To enhance the model's performance and prevent overfitting, image preprocessing is used during training. This includes a 40% chance of feeding the generator a lower quality image. DCGAN uses BCE loss for back-propagation, but we've adapted it to incorporate structural similarity, resulting in an MSE loss value that's used for back-propagation in both the generator and discriminator.

3.1 Reconstruction

The *odl* library was utilized for the reconstruction section, where a pre-built FBP inverse operation function was utilized to convert sinogram data into 2D image data. The resulting reconstructed images were saved as JPEG files and will be loaded in batches during training time. To mitigate overfitting, various image preprocessing methods were employed, including random adjustments to brightness, hue, contrast, Gaussian Blur, image translation, etc. The resulting ground truth and low-dose images were saved separately in a folder structure, each containing training, testing, and validation images.

3.2 Discriminator

In Fig. 2's block diagram, we can observe the Discriminator's distinct components that contribute to its training process. To facilitate its learning, two backward passes are performed. The first pass involves feeding the Discriminator with Ground Truth images to teach it how to discern real data. The second pass forwards the Generator's output images to educate the Discriminator about fake data. It's worth noting that the Generator's output quality heavily relies on the Discriminator's ability to accurately identify the image's state presented to it. If the Discriminator fails to achieve this, it can lead to a significant reduction in the Generator's output quality.

Table 2. Discriminator model summary

Layer (type)	Output Shape	Num. Params
Conv2d-1	[−1, 64, 32, 32]	3,072
LeakyReLU-2	[−1, 64, 32, 32]	0
Conv2d-3	[−1, 128, 16, 16]	131,072
BatchNorm2d-4	[−1, 128, 16, 16]	256
LeakyReLU-5	[−1, 128, 16, 16]	0
Conv2d-6	[−1, 256, 8, 8]	524,288
BatchNorm2d-7	[−1, 256, 8, 8]	512
LeakyReLU-8	[−1, 256, 8, 8]	0
Conv2d-9	[−1, 512, 4, 4]	2,097,152
BatchNorm2d-10	[−1, 512, 4, 4]	1,024
LeakyReLU-11	[−1, 512, 4, 4]	0
Conv2d-12	[−1, 1, 1, 1]	8,192
Sigmoid-13	[−1, 1, 1, 1]	0

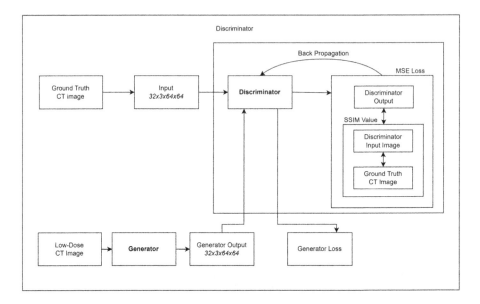

Fig. 2. Discriminator used in our proposed model.

The model summary of the discriminator network is given in the Table 2. The discriminator model is a Convolutional Neural Network model. The input to the model is expected to be an image array of shape $3 \times 64 \times 64$. The output of the model is a single-valued array of shape $1 \times 1 \times 1 \times 1$. The output value is the predicted quality of the input image as determined by the neural network. The higher the value the higher the quality is expected to be. Here in the model, the output quality measure is the SSIM itself. The final activation function is the sigmoid function. Thus the predicted output value will be between 0 and 1.

The discriminator block diagram indicates that a unique backpropagation approach is adopted by combining the SSIM value and Mean Squared Error loss. Initially, the SSIM value is computed between the Ground Truth and Generator Input, followed by the calculation of the MSE Loss between the Discriminator output value and the previously computed SSIM value, which is then backpropagated. Given that two backward propagation steps are required, the first step involves the MSE between the discriminator output and 1, where the input for the discriminator is the Ground Truth image. The second step employs the MSE Loss between the discriminator output and the SSIM value of the Ground Truth and generator output image.

3.3   Generator

The Generator block diagram Fig. 3 shows the main components involved in training a generator model. The input to the generator is the simulated low-dose CT images obtained from FBP reconstruction. The images were flattened before feeding to the generator. Using this flattened image data, the generator will generate a CT image of higher quality and reduced noise than the input image data. The output image will have a shape of $3 \times 64 \times 64$ resolution, which is the same resolution as the input image before flattening.

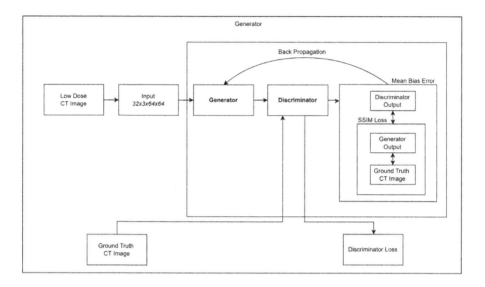

Fig. 3. Generator used in our proposed model.

One can find the generator model summary in the Table 3. Transpose convolution layers are used for model generation. The final layer has the tanh activation function. The value of tanh output ranges from -1 to $+1$. Thus there is a chance that the tensor output of the generator might have some values that are less than 0. To avoid this the output tensor is passed through a normalization function before further processing is conducted. The normalization function will bring all the values within the image tensor between 0 and 1 instead of -1 and 1. The next step of the model training process is to directly feed the output of the generator into the discriminator. The discriminator model will then predict the SSIM value of the generated image if it were to be compared with its Ground Truth counterpart. This predicted output is used when assessing the loss value that will be then promoted for back-propagation. The loss used here is Mean Bias Error. MBE error is the mean of the difference between the original and the predicted value for each of the error components. Here one error factor is the discriminator output and the other is the SSIM value of the generator output with ground truth image.

4   Experimental Results

The forward pass of our model is exceptionally swift. We evaluated its output against the ground truth and presented the SSIM score. In this paper, we provide

Table 3. Generator model summary

Layer (type)	Output Shape	Num. Params
ConvTranspose2d-1	[−1, 512, 4, 4]	100,663,296
BatchNorm2d-2	[−1, 512, 4, 4]	1,024
ReLU-3	[−1, 512, 4, 4]	0
ConvTranspose2d-4	[−1, 512, 8, 8]	4,194,304
BatchNorm2d-5	[−1, 512, 8, 8]	1,024
ReLU-6	[−1, 512, 8, 8]	0
ConvTranspose2d-7	[−1, 512, 16, 16]	4,194,304
BatchNorm2d-8	[−1, 512, 16, 16]	1,024
ReLU-9	[−1, 512, 16, 16]	0
ConvTranspose2d-10	[−1, 256, 32, 32]	2,097,152
BatchNorm2d-11	[−1, 256, 32, 32]	512
ReLU-12	[−1, 256, 32, 32]	0
ConvTranspose2d-13	[−1, 128, 64, 64]	524,288
BatchNorm2d-14	[−1, 128, 64, 64]	256
ReLU-15	[−1, 128, 64, 64]	0
ConvTranspose2d-16	[−1, 64, 64, 64]	73,728
BatchNorm2d-17	[−1, 64, 64, 64]	128
ReLU-18	[−1, 64, 64, 64]	0
ConvTranspose2d-19	[−1, 3, 64, 64]	1,728
Tanh-20	[−1, 3, 64, 64]	0

a concise overview of the diverse set of tools and techniques utilized. Our research was constructed using Python as the primary programming language, and we installed Cuda 11.7 due to the availability of a dedicated graphics card in our system. For model development, we employed the PyTorch library, which supports Cuda. Additionally, we employed the torchvision library for image pre-processing tasks and the torchsummary library to summarize the model's parameters. We incorporated the scikit image library to apply Poisson and Gaussian noise, the pillow library for reading images from storage, and Matplotlib to exhibit the final test results. We obtained the LoDoPab-CT data through the dival library, and the odl library facilitated the extraction of ground truth images and their low-dose counterparts from the LoDoPab-CT dataset, and also aided in FBP reconstructions of the low-dose data.

4.1   Dataset Used in the Experiment

The dataset used in the research work was derived from the LoDoPab-CT dataset. FBP reconstruction was done for generating the images. The original data which is the ground truth is the high-dose equivalent CT images. There

are about 3456 images in the test folder, 35712 training images and 3456 validation images. The same for both ground truth and low-dose images. The images
generated can be of color or grayscale. We chose color images for training of the
grayscale images wasn't producing presentable results. The Training was slow.
But once we started to use color images for training, the model began learning about CT images much faster. The images obtained from the LoDoPab-CT
dataset are of 362×362 image resolution. Our GAN model is not capable of
processing this resolution. The model can handle the processing of 64×64 resolution images only. Thus the images will be converted to 64×64 resolution
during the data loader stage.

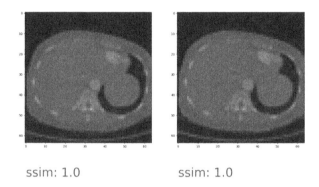

ssim: 1.0   ssim: 1.0

Fig. 4. Comparison - Ground Truth and low-dose images.

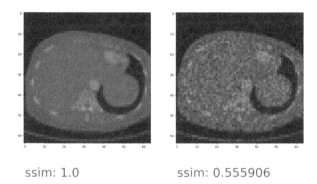

ssim: 1.0   ssim: 0.555906

Fig. 5. Comparison - Ground Truth and low-dose image with noise.

One important point of note is that the Low-Dose images generated from
the LoDoPab-CT dataset will be no different from GT images when downsized
to 64×64 images. Please refer to Fig. 4. So we needed to inject some noise into
our low-dose images to get original low-dose equivalent data. For that, we have
used skimage's Poisson and Gaussian blur. Please refer to the new image Fig. 5
after some noise was injected.

4.2   Data Loader

In the preceding sections, we have discussed the division of the dataset used in our experiment, comprising Ground Truth and its low-dose equivalent, with both divisions further categorized for training, testing, and validation. For the training process, we utilized PyTorch's Dataset class to fetch images from local storage and applied preprocessing techniques such as Poisson noise for low-dose images and a 10% chance of Gaussian noise injection. Additionally, we introduced a 40% chance of implementing one of four image preprocessing methods, including Gaussian blur, image translation, hue adjustment, or brightness/contrast variations. We opted to use colored images with 3 channels, as grayscale images yielded unsatisfactory results. However, we can convert them to grayscale at the end if required. To load the images from storage, we used the Pillow library and converted the image variable to a torch tensor. Although the initial tensor had values ranging from 0 to 255 (uint8), we normalized the values between 0 and 1 for training purposes. Finally, we determined that a batch size of 32 was optimal for training, as larger batch sizes resulted in inadequate graphics memory and were thus avoided.

5   Performance Analysis

We've conducted rigorous testing on the model using a unique test dataset that's integral to both the ground truth and low-dose image sections in the LoDoPab-CT dataset. This dataset is entirely separated from the training process, meaning the model will be presented with entirely novel image inputs. Using this approach, we were able to produce some exceptional results, as illustrated in Fig. 6, 7, 8, 9. These results were generated using images from the test dataset, with the leftmost image representing the original ground truth image, the middle image simulating the low-dose input given to the generator model, and the rightmost image displaying the output generated by the model. Additionally, the corresponding SSIM and PSNR values are included below each image for easy reference.

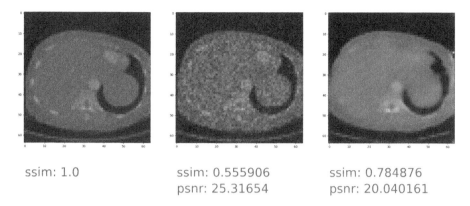

ssim: 1.0   ssim: 0.555906   ssim: 0.784876
                             psnr: 25.31654   psnr: 20.040161

Fig. 6. Test image 180 - SSIM 0.78 (ground truth, low-dose, model output)

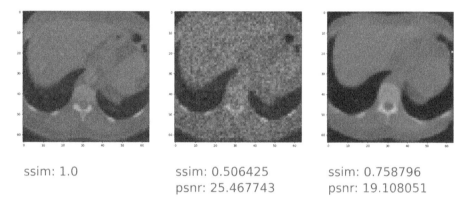

ssim: 1.0   ssim: 0.506425   ssim: 0.758796
                             psnr: 25.467743   psnr: 19.108051

Fig. 7. Test image 1810 - SSIM 0.75 (ground truth, low-dose, model output)

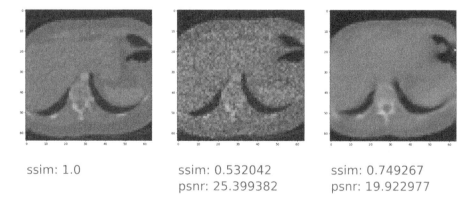

ssim: 1.0   ssim: 0.532042   ssim: 0.749267
                             psnr: 25.399382   psnr: 19.922977

Fig. 8. Test image 2800 - SSIM 0.75 (ground truth, low-dose, model output)

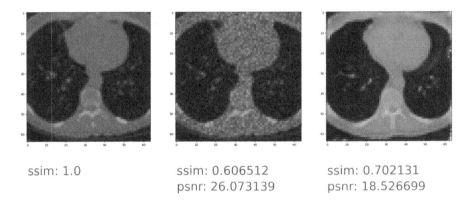

ssim: 1.0   ssim: 0.606512   ssim: 0.702131
                     psnr: 26.073139   psnr: 18.526699

Fig. 9. Test image 3000 - SSIM 0.70 (ground truth, low-dose, model output)

6   Conclusion

The objective of this study was to narrow the disparity between conventional reconstruction methods and the ground truth image. The findings reveal that a small Deep Learning Network with an input resolution of only 64×64 pixels can produce a 10% improvement in SSIM, demonstrating the effectiveness of the proposed model. In future studies, we aim to enhance our GAN model further to achieve a substantially higher SSIM value and further close the gap between the reconstructed output and the ground truth image.

References

1. Willemink, M.J., Noël, P.B.: The evolution of image reconstruction for CT—from filtered back projection to artificial intelligence. Eur. Radiol. **29**(5), 2185–2195 (2018). https://doi.org/10.1007/s00330-018-5810-7
2. Mayo Foundation for Medical Education and Research. Ct scan (2022). https://www.mayoclinic.org/tests-procedures/ct-scan/about/pac-20393675?p=1. Accessed 07 May 2022
3. Dong, Fu, J., He, Z.: PLOS ONE **14**(11), e0224426 (2019). https://doi.org/10.1371/journal.pone.0224426. https://doi.org/10.1371%2Fjournal.pone.0224426
4. Leuschner, J., Schmidt, M., Baguer, D.O., Maass, P.: Sci. Data **8**(1) (2021). https://doi.org/10.1038/s41597-021-00893-z
5. A chest CT scan to diagnose lung symptoms (2017). https://americanhealthimaging.com/blog/chest-ct-scan-diagnose-lung-symptoms/
6. Kim, J., Yoon, H., Lee, E., Kim, I., Cha, Y.K., Bak, S.: Korean J. Radiol. **21** (2020). https://doi.org/10.3348/kjr.2020.0116
7. Dong, X., Vekhande, S., Cao, G.: Sinogram interpolation for sparse-view micro-ct with deep learning neural network (2019). https://doi.org/10.48550/ARXIV.1902.03362. https://arxiv.org/abs/1902.03362

8. Sandfort, V., Yan, K., Pickhardt, P.J., Summers, R.M.: Sci. Rep. **9**(1) (2019). https://doi.org/10.1038/s41598-019-52737-x
9. Jin, K.H., McCann, M.T., Froustey, E., Unser, M.: IEEE Trans. Image Process. **26**(9), 4509–4522 (2017). https://doi.org/10.1109/tip.2017.2713099
10. Zeng, D., Huang, J., Bian, Z., Niu, S., Zhang, H., Feng, Q., Liang, Z., Ma, J.: IEEE Trans. Nucl. Sci. **62**(5), 2226 (2015). https://doi.org/10.1109/TNS.2015.2467219

Improving Software Effort Estimation with Heterogeneous Stacked Ensemble Using SMOTER over ELM and SVR Base Learners

D. V. S. Durgesh$^{(\boxtimes)}$ ⓘ, M. V. S. Saket$^{(\boxtimes)}$ ⓘ, and B. Ramana Reddy ⓘ

Department of Computer Science and Engineering, Chaitanya Bharathi Institute of Technology, Hyderabad, India
{ugs19058_cse.venkata,ugs19047_cse.saket}@cbit.org.in,
bramanareddy_cse@cbit.ac.in

Abstract. Software engineering projects can be complex and involve many different tasks and activities, such as collecting requirements, design, coding, testing, and deployment. Estimating the effort needed for the project is one of the first phases in the creation of software projects. For a software engineering project to be successfully completed, the amount of work needed to execute it must be precisely estimated. The paper suggests a novel method to calculate the effort needed to construct a software project by employing a heterogeneous stacked ensemble comprising of two base learners, namely Extreme Learning Machine (ELM) and Support Vector Regressor (SVR) and it also aims to investigate the effectiveness of Synthetic Minority Over-Sampling Technique for Regression (SMOTER) in predicting software project effort. The results indicate that the proposed model enhances the performance of the base models, resulting in a reduction of 35.7% in MAE, 24.1% in RMSE, and 18.3% in R-value. After the implementation of SMOTER, a noteworthy reduction in the error of the proposed model has been observed.

Keywords: Extreme Learning Machine · Stacked ensemble · SMOTER

1 Introduction

Software effort estimation is an approach that is crucial to the process of developing software. In software engineering, the term "effort" refers to the time and materials needed to finish a software development project. It is the technique of estimating how much work will be necessary to finish a software development project. The traditional way of measuring software effort is in terms of the number of hours worked by a person, or the monetary cost required to pay for this work [1]. Effort estimation is challenging due to the inherent complexity and variability of software development projects. Projects often involve changing requirements, unexpected delays, and uncertain outcomes. Estimation bias is also a common problem, where estimates are influenced by personal biases, stakeholder pressure, or incomplete information. Despite these challenges, accurate effort estimation is crucial for project success. Data scientists currently

© The Author(s), under exclusive license to Springer Nature Switzerland AG 2023
R. Morusupalli et al. (Eds.): MIWAI 2023, LNAI 14078, pp. 442–448, 2023.
https://doi.org/10.1007/978-3-031-36402-0_41

encounter a significant challenge, known as the data imbalance problem. This problem is prevalent in machine learning classification tasks when classes of data are not evenly represented, referred to as the class imbalance problem. The issue of imbalanced data is also encountered in datasets where the target value is continuous, known as imbalanced regression. Dealing with a target variable that is continuous in regression data sets can make the task more complex as it involves handling an infinite number of potential values. To overcome this issue of imbalance data, data oversampling is done [3]. In order to balance the datasets, the Synthetic Minority Over-Sampling Technique (SMOTE) is utilised as an oversampling technique.

According to the literature in software engineering (SEE) domain, Extreme Learning Machine (ELM) [1] and Support Vector Regression (SVR) [4] are considered the best effort estimators in machine learning (ML) techniques. Study [1] and [4] have advocated the effectiveness of these models in effort estimation for software development. Given the performance of ELM and SVR as popular models for the effort estimation in software development, a heterogenous two-level stacked ensemble has been developed [2]. By leveraging the strengths of each model, the ensemble model is designed to achieve better performance than any individual model.

The paper is organised in the following manner: Related works are presented in Sect. 2. Section 3 describes the approach used in this study. On the basis of performance measures, Sect. 4 discusses the findings and evaluation. Final thoughts and future work are presented in Sect. 5.

2   Related Work

In software engineering, effort is typically measured as the amount of time, resources and personnel required to complete a particular task or project. Effort estimation is an important aspect of software development. There are various techniques and tools used for estimating software development effort, including expert judgment, historical data analysis, parametric modelling, and machine learning algorithms. Effort can also be measured in terms of software metrics, such as lines of code, function points. These metrics provide a quantitative measure of software's size, functionality, and complexity, which can be used to estimate the effort required to develop and maintain the software [6].

The accuracy of a prediction is largely influenced by two key factors: the model and the dataset used [3]. In order to ensure that the model is trained on a representative sample of data from all classes or categories, it is crucial for machine learning to have a balanced dataset. If the dataset is imbalanced, meaning that some classes or categories have significantly fewer samples than others, the model may become biased towards the majority class or categories and perform poorly on the minority ones. To avoid this issue, we can balance the dataset by oversampling the minority class or under sampling the majority class.

In their paper, V. Van Hai et al. [9] applied a clustering method to the dataset and utilized the FPA (Function Point Analysis) and EEAC (Empirical Estimation of Activity Consumption) methods to estimate effort for the resulting clusters. In their research, S. Shukla et al. [5] utilized Multi-Layer Perceptron (MLP) and its ensembles, such as Ridge-MLPNN, Lasso-MLPNN, Bagging-MLPNN, and AdaBoost-MLPNN, to enhance the accuracy of software effort estimation. The study revealed that AdaBoost-MLPNN outperformed the other models and was found to be the best model for software effort estimation. A machine learning technique called ensemble learning mixes numerous models to increase a task's overall performance and accuracy. Ensemble learning employs numerous models to make predictions and mixes their outputs in a way that increases overall performance rather than depending on a single model.

In a case study described by F. B. Ahmad et al. [7], they utilized an LSTM (Long Short-Term Memory) network to predict the software development effort required for tasks in a large software development organization. In the paper by S. K. Sehra et al. [8], they applied OLS (Ordinary Least Squares) Regression and K Means Clustering, data mining techniques to preprocessed data for software effort estimation. This study found that the K Means clustering preprocessing technique provided more accurate software effort estimation compared to the OLS Regression technique.

3 Proposed Methodology

This section outlines the methodology used to build the software effort estimating model.

For our investigation, we used the Desharnais dataset, which consists of information from 81 software projects. Each project has 12 attributes: Project ID, Manager Experience, Length, Team Experience, Effort, Transaction, Entities, Point Adj, AdjustmentFactor, Language, Year End, Point Non-Adjust. According to software development effort estimation models, the primary variable is the amount of work needed to complete the project; in this case, the attribute which is dependent is *"Effort"* and the attributes which are dependent are *"ManagerExp"*, *"TeamExp"*, *"Length"*, *"Entities"*, *"PointsNonAjust"*, *"Transactions"*, *"YearEnd"*, and *"PointsAdj"*. The 81 projects that were evaluated had durations ranging from 1 to 39 months (with an average of 11.7 months). A range of 546 to 23,940 person-hours of effort were recorded, with an average of 5,046.31 person-hours. The distribution of data on effort, the dependent variable, is shown by the histogram in Fig. 1. The features present in Desharnais dataset are shown in Fig. 2.

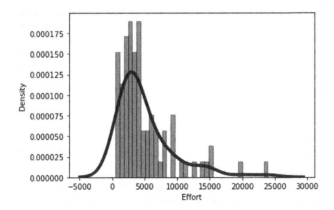

Fig. 1. Effort Value Distribution

Attributes	Classification	Description
Project	Numeric	Project ID which starts by 1 and ends by 81
TeamExp	Numeric	Team experience measured in years
ManagerExp	Numeric	Manager experience measured in years
YearEnd	Numeric	Year the project ended
Length	Numeric	Duration of the project in months
Effort	Numeric	Actual effort measured in person-hours
Transactions	Numeric	Number of the logical transactions in the system
Entities	Numeric	Number of the entities in the system
PointsNonAdjust	Numeric	Size of the project measured in unadjusted function points. This is calculated as Transactions plus Entities
Envergure	Numeric	Function point complexity adjustment factor. This is based on the General Systems Characteristics (GSC). The GSC has 14 attributes; each is rated on a six-point ordinal scale. $Envergure = \sum_{i=1}^{14} CGS_i$
PointsAdjust	Numeric	Size of the project measured in adjusted function points. This is calculated as: $PointsAdjust = PointsNonAdjust * (0,65 + 0,01 * Envergura)$
Language	Categorical	Type of language used in the project expressed as 1, 2 or 3. The value "1" corresponds to "Basic Cobol", where the value "2" corresponds to "Advanced Cobol" and the value "3" to 4GL language.

Fig. 2. Dataset Description

3.1 Data Preparation

We used Pearson's correlation coefficient to determine the critical aspects in our study in order to better estimate the software development effort.

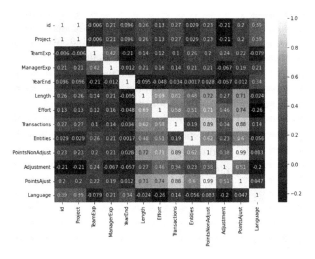

Fig. 3. Pearson Correlation

As observed in Fig. 3, the Desharnais dataset's independent variables, such as "*Transactions*", "*Length*", "*Entities*", "*PointsAdj*", and "*PointsNonAdjust*" exhibit correlation coefficients over 0.50 with regard to effort.

Following the feature selection process, we utilized SMOTER, a data oversampling technique, to balance our dataset. The SmoteR method interpolates the attribute values of two original cases chosen at random from the pool of observations with rare values to produce synthetic cases with a rare target value. The set of relevant observations is determined by SmoteR using a relevance function and a user-specified threshold.

It over-samples the observations in this set and under-samples the remaining cases to create a new training set with a more balanced distribution of values. The distribution of data on effort after using SMOTER is shown by the histogram in Fig. 4.

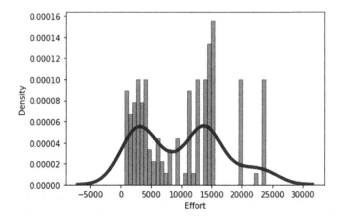

Fig. 4. Effort Value Distribution after applying SMOTER

3.2 Ensemble Learning

Ensemble learning is a methodology in machine learning that involves combining multiple models to generate predictions. The rationale behind ensemble learning is that by integrating the predictions of several models, the final output can be more precise and dependable than any of the individual models alone. In this paper we are using a heterogenous stacked ensemble approach for the model.

A heterogeneous stacked ensemble is a type of ensemble learning technique in which multiple models of different types (heterogeneous models) are combined to make predictions. In a stacked ensemble, the output of the base models (Extreme Learning Machine, Support Vector Regression) is used as input to a meta-model (Random Forest Regression), which learns how to combine the outputs of the base models to make final predictions. The predictions generated by the base models for each training instance are merged to produce a fresh set of features that is fed as input to the meta-model.

Suppose there are n base models, and each model produces n predictions for every training instance. The predictions are combined by concatenation to create a new feature set with dimensions n × m, where m is the number of training instances. The resulting feature set is then fed into the meta-model along with the corresponding true labels of the training instances.

The meta-model is then trained to learn how to map the merged predictions generated by the base models to the true labels of the training instances. When making predictions on new instances, base models are first employed to produce predictions for the new instances. The resulting predictions are then merged and used as input to the meta-model to generate the final prediction.

The base learners are subjected to k-fold cross-validation and are then used as input to the level-2 meta learner model, and the final predictions are made by this model. The Random Forest Regressor was selected as the meta-learner because of its robustness and versatility in handling various types of data distributions and feature interactions. It is a powerful algorithm that can effectively handle complex data sets.

4   Results and Evaluation

The following section presents the findings that were obtained from the research conducted. As we can see in Table 1, there is a significant decrease in RMSE, MAE values after applying SMOTER on our dataset. The Proposed model gives the error of 2168.90 (MAE), 3097.87 (RMSE) before applying SMOTER, which was later decreased to 1412.25 (MAE), 2360.51 (RMSE) after using data oversampling technique.

Table 1. Comparison of proposed model before and after applying SMOTER

Models	Before applying SMOTER		After applying SMOTER	
	MAE	RMSE	MAE	RMSE
Extreme Learning Machine (ELM)	3313.30	4258.51	2197.23	2846.64
Support Vector Regression (SVR)	1881.48	2726.01	2240.83	3104.94
Proposed Stacked Ensemble	2168.90	3097.87	1412.25	2360.51

The evaluation of the performance of the proposed model and the two base learners was measured using the R, MAE, and RMSE criteria. The results of this evaluation are reported below. The results indicate that the proposed stacked model exhibited the lowest values for both RMSE and MAE, while also achieving the large value for R (Table 2).

Table 2. Comparison between proposed stacked model and base learners over MAE, RMSE, R-value

Metrics	ELM	SVR	Proposed Stacked Ensemble
Mean Absolute Error (MAE)	2197.23	2240.83	1412.25
Root Mean Squared Error (RMSE)	2846.64	3104.94	2360.51
R-value	0.76	0.71	0.84

5   Conclusion and Future Scope

Obtaining a precise and dependable estimate of the effort required for software development has been a difficult task in software engineering. Accurately estimating the cost and effort required during the early stages of a project can greatly benefit the field. This study introduces a heterogeneous stacked ensemble approach to improve the effectiveness of software effort estimation. We attempted to balance the dataset using SMOTER in order to improve the dataset quality. It can be observed that the application of this over-sampling technique has resulted in a decrease in the error of our models.

The proposed ensemble includes two base models and one meta model, which are customized for this specific task. According to the results, the stacking approach is very effective, as the proposed model demonstrates a significant improvement in performance.

As a topic for future research, we suggest employing an optimisation method, namely Particle Swarm Optimisation (PSO), to optimise the model parameters for software development job estimation. This approach can potentially improve the accuracy and reliability of the proposed model by fine-tuning the parameters based on the specific characteristics of the dataset being used.

References

1. De Carvalho, H.D.P., Fagundes, R., Santos, W.: Extreme learning machine applied to software development effort estimation. IEEE Access **9**, 92676–92687 (2021). https://doi.org/10.1109/ACCESS.2021.3091313
2. Goyal, S.: Effective software effort estimation using heterogenous stacked ensemble. In: 2022 IEEE International Conference on Signal Processing, Informatics, Communication and Energy Systems (SPICES), Thiruvananthapuram, India, pp. 584–588 (2022). https://doi.org/10.1109/SPICES52834.2022.9774231
3. Jawa, M., Meena, S.: Software effort estimation using synthetic minority over-sampling technique for regression (SMOTER). In: 2022 3rd International Conference for Emerging Technology (INCET), Belgaum, India, pp. 1–6 (2022). https://doi.org/10.1109/INCET54531.2022.9824043
4. Zakrani, A., Najm, A., Marzak, A.: Support vector regression based on grid-search method for agile software effort prediction. In: 2018 IEEE 5th International Congress on Information Science and Technology (CiSt), Marrakech, Morocco, pp. 1–6 (2018). https://doi.org/10.1109/CIST.2018.8596370
5. Shukla, S., Kumar, S., Bal, P.R.: Analyzing effect of ensemble models on multi-layer perceptron network for software effort estimation. In: 2019 IEEE World Congress on Services (SERVICES), Milan, Italy, pp. 386–387 (2019). https://doi.org/10.1109/SERVICES.2019.00116
6. Pressman, R.S.: Software Engineering: A Practitioner's Approach, 7th edn. McGraw Hill Education, New York (2010)
7. Ahmad, F.B., Ibrahim, L.M.: Software development effort estimation techniques using long short-term memory. In: 2022 International Conference on Computer Science and Software Engineering (CSASE), Duhok, Iraq, pp. 182–187 (2022). https://doi.org/10.1109/CSASE51777.2022.9759751
8. Sehra, S.K., Kaur, J., Brar, Y.S., Kaur, N.: Analysis of data mining techniques for software effort estimation. In: 2014 11th International Conference on Information Technology: New Generations, Las Vegas, NV, USA, pp. 633–638 (2014). https://doi.org/10.1109/ITNG.2014.116
9. Van Hai, V., Nhung, H.L.T.K., Prokopova, Z., Silhavy, R., Silhavy, P.: Toward improving the efficiency of software development effort estimation via clustering analysis. IEEE Access **10**, 83249–83264 (2022). https://doi.org/10.1109/ACCESS.2022.3185393

A Deep Learning Based Model to Study the Influence of Different Brain Wave Frequencies for the Disorder of Depression

Bethany Gosala[1] , Emmanuel Raj Gosala[2] , and Manjari Gupta[1](✉)

[1] DST Centre for Interdisciplinary Mathematical Sciences (DST-CIMS), Institute of Science, Banaras Hindu University, Varanasi 220005, Uttar Pradesh, India
manjari@bhu.ac.in
[2] Department of Computer Science, University Post-Graduate College, Osmania University, Secunderabad 500003, Telangana, India

Abstract. The human brain is one of the most advanced, complex, and incredible machines which has continued to fascinate scientists, researchers, and scholars for hundreds of years. Many experiments and studies have been done on the human brain to understand its mechanism and how it works, yet we are not close to understanding its full potential. One way of studying the brain is to study the brain wave frequencies which are emitted by it. The brain emits five different types of waves namely, delta, theta, alpha, beta, and gamma. Studying these different waves can help in solving various psychological issues, and problems like anxiety, stress, and depression which every human faces at least once in their life, according to WHO depression will be the main cause of mental illness by 2030. This work aims to find the influence of different brain waves and their involvement in the case of depression. For this, we have used deep learning techniques and developed a supervised learning model called convolutional neural network (CNN) for the classification of signals from Major Depression Disorder (MDD) from the healthy control. The developed CNN is run in five brain waves, and we calculated the accuracy for performance evaluation of the developed model for each brain wave frequency. The best accuracy we get is 98.4% for the delta wave followed by 97.6% for the alpha wave and the beta wave giving the least accuracy of 72.83%.

Keywords: Alpha wave · Beta wave · Gamma wave · Delta wave · Theta wave · Major Depression Disorder (MDD) · Deep Learning · Convolutional neural Networks (CNN)

1 Introduction

Mental health is one of the important factors which contributes in bring the best out of a person. Contrary to this psychiatric disorder or mental illnesses are health conditions where a disturbance in an individual's cognition, emotion regulation, or behavior is observed. These disorders are usually associated with distress or impairment in important areas of functioning, psychiatric disorders like Anxiety, Neurodevelopment disorder,

R. Morusupalli et al. (Eds.): MIWAI 2023, LNAI 14078, pp. 449–458, 2023.
https://doi.org/10.1007/978-3-031-36402-0_42

eating disorders, Personality disorders, Parkinson's, Alzheimer's, post-traumatic stress disorder (PTSD), Bipolar, Psychotic disorders, Schizophrenia, and Depression, etc., According to WHO, 12.5% of world's population suffers with some kind of mental disorders. A 2019 study revealed that, with depression around 280 million people suffer and among which 23 million are children and adolescents [1], another World Health Organization study pointed out that, depression will be the prime cause of mental illness by 2030. Depression also known as clinical depression or major depressive disorder is one of the leading mental disorders which causes a continuous feeling of sadness and loss of interest in a person who is suffering from. It paves the way to a wide range of physical and emotional problems which in turn reduces the productivity of the person [2]. Mental illness can be diagnosed by studying the signals from the brain. Brain signals measure the instinct biometric information from the human brain, which reflects the user's passive or active mental state. Brain signals constitute the information that is processed by millions of brain neurons (nerve cells and brain cells). There are various invasive and non-invasive techniques to collect brain signals. Techniques line Electroencephalograph (EEG), Magneto-encephalography (MEG) as well as brain-imaging techniques such as Magnetic Resonance Imaging (MRI), and Computed Tomography (CT) are a few types of non-invasive techniques. Here, in this study we will be mainly focusing on the signals collected from Electroencephalography (EEG), these signals have high temporal resolutions and have low signal-to-noise ratio which is an advantage over other brain signal techniques [3, 4].

Artificial intelligence (AI), is influencing every area, and increasing its reach in every passing day. AI techniques like machine learning (ML), and deep learning (DL), are being applied in all domains and revolutionizing the technology. ML and DL have benefited diverse domains giving excellent results in areas like pattern recognition, image classification, disease prediction, voice recognition, computer vision, automatic driving vehicles, medicine, etc., [5–10].

The brain emits different types of frequency bands which associates with different activities which we perform, studying these brain frequencies will help us in understanding the how brain works and which part of the brain, and which band contributes to a particular activity. Hence, we also want to study these brain frequencies in case of depression and what contributes to and influences when a person is depressed. In our work, we will be using filtering techniques to get different brain frequencies like delta, theta, alpha, beta, and gamma [11], and will be applying a well-known deep learning technique: convolutional neural networks (CNN), to study the influence of brain bands.

Our main contributions through this work are as follows:

1. We have developed a DL model for the classification of MDD EEG Signals from HC by building a CNN classifier.
2. We have done the frequency band-wise study to see which brain wave frequencies are contributing more and which are not playing much role in depression.
3. Among all the brain frequencies delta waves gave better results and beta waves have given the least satisfying results.

The rest of the paper is organized in the following manner: in Sect. 2 we have given the background of related, in Sect. 3 we discussed the Methods that we built and the methodology that we followed for the experiments, in Sect. 4 we show the results that we got and finally Sect. 5 concludes with the conclusion and further studies.

2 Related Work

An ML-based model for the diagnosis of MDD is proposed by [12], they used EEG data of 33 MDD and 30 HC for developing the model. The input features such as power, and EEG alpha, was investigated in the model they proposed, later z-score standardization is also used for the reduction of irrelevant features concerning mean and variance. In this work the authors built three supervised classification models namely; Logistic regression (LR), Support vector machine (SVM), and Naïve Bayesian (NB), and also used 10-fold cross-validation to validate the developed model. The best results were provided by SVM which are an accuracy of 98.4%, sensitivity of 96.66%, and specificity of 100%.

Multi-model data from EEG, eye tracking, and galvanic skin response (GSR) are used for classifying MDD patients from HC with multiple ML algorithms like random forest (RF), LR, and SVM, developed by [13] using data of 144MDD and 204 HC. Among all classifiers, LR gave the best results of accuracy of 79.63%, precision of 76.67%, recall of 85.19%, and f1 score of 80.70%.

Bachmann, M. et al. [14] has developed an ML classification model by using logistic regression and with leave-one-out cross-validation for classifying MDD subject signals from HC. The dataset they used consists of 13 medication-free depressive patients and 13 HC. The analysis of EEG data is done through both linear and non-linear feature extraction, linear methods like spectral asymmetry index, alpha power variability, and relative gamma power, and nonlinear methods such as Higuchi's fractal dimension, detrended fluctuation analysis, and Lempel-Ziv complexity were extracted. LR classifier is used for classification and it gave the best accuracy of 92%.

Akar, S. et al. [15] have presented a statistical study on MDD patients when they are at rest and emotional state and calculated various statistical features and did statistical analysis on the signal. They have extracted features like Shannon entropy (ShEn), Lempel-Ziv complexity (LZC), Kolmogorov complexity (KC), Katz's fractal dimension (KFD), Higuchi's fractal dimension (HDF). They found that KFD, HFD, and LZC values were more sensitive in detecting EEG complexities and in discriminating between two groups than the ShEn and KC values, according to the results of ANOVA. Significant differences between patients and controls and between emotional periods.

Sharma, M. et al. [16] have given a depression diagnosis system using EEG signal and a three-channel orthogonal wavelet filter bank (TCOWFB), applied six-length TCOWFB for decomposition of frequencies in seven sub-bands (WSB). The logarithm of the L2 norm (LL2N) of six detailed WSBs and one approximate WSB are used as discriminating features. With the least square support vector machine (LS-SVM) classifier, their model has achieved an accuracy of 99.58%.

An ML framework built by [17] that involves extraction of synchronization likelihood (SL) features as input data for the automatic diagnosis of MDD with classifiers like SVM, LR, and NB. The best results they have achieved by SVM with 98%, 99.9%, 95%, 0.97 of accuracy, sensitivity, specificity, and f-measure respectively.

A DL-based transfer learning model developed by [18], for the analysis of various spatial and temporal features of 46 MDD and 46 HC where the data is collected from 19 electrodes and of four brain frequency bands which are delta theta, alpha, gamma. They converted the EEG signal into a 2-dimensional (2D) mesh-dependent grayscale image data to preserve the internal structure of the data in the spatiotemporal coupled domain, and these images were fed to pre-trained models. The pre-trained models they used are MobileNet, ResNet-50, and Inception-v3. The best results were given by MobileNet which are 89.33 and 92.66 accuracies of the left and right hemispheres of the brain respectively.

The authors [19] developed a tool for pre-screening major depressive disorder patients by proposing a deep-asymmetry methodology that converts the 1D-EEG's asymmetry feature into a 2D-matrix image to convert into images, short-time Fourier transforms (STFT), wavelets were used. The images were generated brain frequency bandwise, the generated images are from frequencies of delta, theta, alpha, and beta. After converting the signals to images, they built a supervised deep learning classifier that is a convolutional neural network (CNN), generated images from EEG signal are fed to CNN for the classification. They have achieved the best accuracy of 98.85% for the alpha band.

3   Methodology

3.1   Dataset

We used an open-source dataset for this study provided by [12], which is available at (https://figshare.com/articles/EEG_Data_New/4244171). The dataset is collection of 34 patients with MDD, ages between 27 to 53 (mean = 40.3 ± 12.9), and 30 healthy subjects between 22 to 53 years (mean = 38.3 ± 15.6). The EEG data recording is done by a 20-channel EEG according to the 10–20 international standard electrode position. The signals are collected three times from each subject: (i) when the eye is closed (EO), (ii) when the eye is open (EO), and (iii) while doing some TAST. The EEG sampling frequency was set to 256 Hz. A notch filter was applied to reject 50 Hz power line noise. All EEG signals were band-pass filtered with cutoff frequencies at 0.1 Hz and 70 Hz.

3.2   Pre-processing

The dataset consists of signals collected while subjects' eyes open (EO), eyes close (EC), and doing some TASKS. Data collected from a number of channels is not uniform throughout the data, the channels vary from 20–22 for different subjects. Since the number of channels used to collect the data is not the same for all samples, it is not easy to create a matrix of uniform shape. So, we made all subject's channels by which data is collected the same by removing the extra 2 channels which are there in some of the samples. After making all channels uniform, we extracted different brain wave frequencies like delta wave, theta wave, alpha wave, beta wave, and gamma by applying band pass filtering with respective low pass and high pass filtering. To extract delta waves from the raw signal we used a low pass value of 4 Hz and a high pass value of 0.5 Hz. Similarly, for theta, we used 4 Hz and 7 Hz, for alpha, 8 Hz and 12 Hz, for beta 13 Hz and 30 Hz, and for gamma 30 Hz and 45 Hz as high pass and low pass values respectively, these band frequency values vary slightly from different researchers. After preprocessing we got a total of 180 sample signals of data among which 85 are HC and 95 are MDD signals. After bandpass filtering, epochs were created for signal of 5-s duration of each epoch with 2 s of overlap, we extracted a total of 24,390 epochs from the dataset for each frequency band. These epochs are saved as a numpy array of dimensions (24390, 20, 1280) where 24390 are created epochs, 20 is channels from which data is collected, and 1280 are the number are data points in each epoch.

After epoching EEG signal of each brain wave frequency are fed to a supervised dep learning model that is Convolutional neural network (CNN), the data is split in 80–20 ratio for training and validation, the detailed experiment flow is given in below Fig. 1.

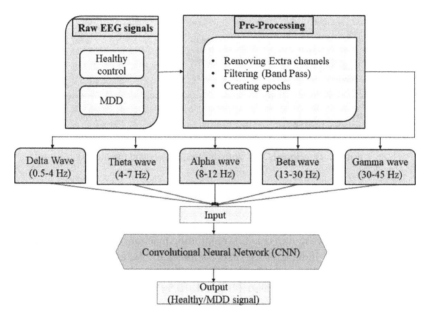

Fig. 1. Experimental flow diagram

3.3 Experimental Design

We have developed a Convolutional neural network (CNN) with 11 layers in which we used 4 computational layers, 4 pooling layers, and 1 dense layer, we run CNN for 10 epochs, with batch size 100. CNN which we built has a total of 89351 parameters among which 89151 are trainable parameters and 200 are non-trainable parameters. A detailed description of the CNN is given in Fig. 2.

Model: "sequential"

Layer (type)	Output Shape	Param #
conv1d (Conv1D)	(None, 1278, 100)	6100
batch_normalization (BatchN ormalization)	(None, 1278, 100)	400
leaky_re_lu (LeakyReLU)	(None, 1278, 100)	0
max_pooling1d (MaxPooling1D)	(None, 639, 100)	0
conv1d_1 (Conv1D)	(None, 637, 100)	30100
leaky_re_lu_1 (LeakyReLU)	(None, 637, 100)	0
max_pooling1d_1 (MaxPooling1D)	(None, 318, 100)	0
dropout (Dropout)	(None, 318, 100)	0
conv1d_2 (Conv1D)	(None, 316, 100)	30100
leaky_re_lu_2 (LeakyReLU)	(None, 316, 100)	0
average_pooling1d (AverageP ooling1D)	(None, 158, 100)	0
dropout_1 (Dropout)	(None, 158, 100)	0
conv1d_3 (Conv1D)	(None, 156, 50)	15050
leaky_re_lu_3 (LeakyReLU)	(None, 156, 50)	0
average_pooling1d_1 (AveragePooling1D)	(Averag (None, 78, 50)	0
conv1d_4 (Conv1D)	(None, 76, 50)	7550
leaky_re_lu_4 (LeakyReLU)	(None, 76, 50)	0
global_average_pooling1d (G lobalAveragePooling1D)	(None, 50)	0
dense (Dense)	(None, 1)	51

Total params: 89,351
Trainable params: 89,151
Non-trainable params: 200

Fig. 2. Developed CNN with different layers and parameters.

3.4 Hardware and Software

After the pre-processing, we got an array of dimensions (24390, 20, 1280) and a size of more than 5 GB hence we required a good computing machine to run the experiments we used Param Siddhi-AI, India's fastest supercomputer for the execution of experiments. We were provided with a cluster of a Siddhi-AI which has a CPU of AMD EPYC 7742 64C 2.25 GHz, with 128 CPU cores, 1 TB RAM, 10.5 PiB PFS-based storage, Mellanox ConnectX-6 VPI (Infiniband HDR) Networking. We used Python programming language the developing the code and we used a Jupyter notebook environment. We also used packages like *MNE, numpy, pandas, Tensorflow, matplotlib, seaborn*, etc., to execute the experiments.

4 Results and Discussion

In this section, we will discuss the experimental results that we have obtained from our conducted experiments. In total, we have conducted 5 experiments one for each brain wave frequency, and the results which we have obtained are shown in Table. 1. We have compared the developed model with the state-of-the-art models and the developed model has outperformed some of the state-of-the-art models. This comparison of the proposed model is illustrated in the below Table. 2.

Table 1. Acquired accuracies due to different brain wave frequencies.

Brain frequencies	Accuracy	
	Mean	Maximum
Delta wave (0–4 Hz)	92.16	98.4
Theta wave (4–7 Hz)	73.31	80.23
Alpha wave (8–13 Hz)	81.81	97.6
Beta wave (13–30 Hz)	47.14	72.83
Gamma wave (30–45 Hz)	83.94	90.65

Table 2. Comparison of the proposed model with the state-of-the-art methods.

Authors	Datasets	No. of Participants	Classification Algorithms	Accuracy (%)
Mumtaz, W. et al. [12]	The MDD patients met the diagnostic criteria for MDD according to the Diagnostic and Statistical Manual-IV (DSM-IV)	34 MDD patients and 30 Healthy Subjects	SVM Logistic Regression Naïve Bayesian	98 91.7 93.6
Sharma, M. et al. [16]	From the Department of Psychiatry, Government Medical College, Kozhikode, Kerala, India	15 Depressed Patients and 15 Normal Subjects	Computer-aided depression diagnosis system using newly designed bandwidth-duration localized (BDL)	99.58
Ding, X. et al. [13]	By Peking University Sixth Hospital, Beijing, China	144 MDD patients and 204 Normal subjects	Logistic Regression	79.63
Mumtaz, W. et al. [17]	The EEG data acquisition involved vigilance-controlled monitoring during the recordings	33 MDD patients and 30 Normal subjects	SVM Logistic Regression Naïve Bayesian	98.4 97.6 96.8
Bachmann, M. et al. [14]	The EEG signals were recorded using the Neuroscan Synamps2 acquisition system (Compumedics, NC, USA)	13 medication-free depressive outpatients and 13 Healthy controls	Single Measure (linear) Single Measure (nonlinear) Combination of two linear measures(li) Combination of two linear measures(non-li)	81 77 88 85
Uyulan, C. et al. [18]	EEG signals were recorded from the "Neuroscan/ Scan LT" neuro-headset of 19 channels	46 control and 46 depressed subjects	ResNet-50 Inception-v3 MobileNet	90.22 (delta) 82.11 (delta) 88.19(delta)

(*continued*)

Table 2. (*continued*)

Authors	Datasets	No. of Participants	Classification Algorithms	Accuracy (%)
Kang, M. et al. [19]	https://figshare.com/articles/ EEG_Data_New/4244171	34 MDD and 30 Normal subjects	CNN	98.85 (alpha)
Proposed System	https://figshare.com/articles/ EEG_Data_New/4244171	34 MDD patients and 30 Normal subjects	1DCNN	delta = 98.40 Theta = 80.23 alpha = 97.60 beta = 72.83 gamma = 90.65

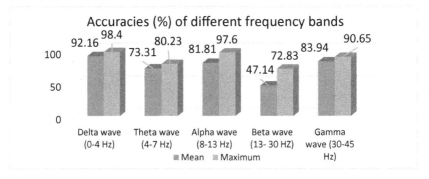

Fig. 3. Graphical representation of acquired accuracies

Above Fig. 3. Shows the graphical representation of the accuracies which we got for each of the brain wave frequencies.

5 Conclusion and Future Work

In this work, we have studied the influence of various brain wave frequencies on depression and found that lower-range frequencies play an important role while dealing with depression problems. The deep learning model which we developed gave better results compared with the state-of-the-are methods, and can say that deep supervised learning techniques are well suited for this problem. For future studies we are planning to work with other types of neurological disorders such as, Schizophrenia, Epilepsy, and Parkinson's' etc., we are planning to explore other deep learning techniques like transfer learning and also different types of feature extraction techniques for extracting best feature from the data.

Acknowledgement. 1. We acknowledge the National Supercomputing Mission (NSM) for providing computing resources of "PARAM Siddhi-AI" under the National PARAM Supercomputing Facility (NPSF), C-DAC, Pune, and supported by the Ministry of Electronics and Information Technology (MeitY) and Department of Science and Technology (DST), Government of India.

2. The author is extremely grateful to University Grants Committee (UGC) for providing the Junior Research Fellowship (JRF) under Maulana Azad National Fellowship for Minorities (MANFJRF), with the award reference number: NO.F.82-27/2019 (SA III).

3. We also acknowledge the Institute of Eminence (IoE) scheme at BHU for supporting us.

References

1. https://www.who.int/news-room/fact-sheets/detail/mental-disorders#:~:text=A%20mental%20disorder%20is%20characterized,different%20types%20of%20mental%20disorders. Accessed 14 Mar 2023
2. https://www.mayoclinic.org/diseases-conditions/depression/symptoms-causes/syc-20356007. Accessed 24 Apr 2023
3. Farnsworth, B.: What is EEG (Electroencephalography) and How Does it Work? (2018). IMOTIONS. https://imotions.com/blog/what-is-eeg
4. Aslan, Z., Akin, M.: A deep learning approach in automated detection of schizophrenia using scalogram images of EEG signals. Phys. Eng. Sci. Med. **45**(1), 83–96 (2021). https://doi.org/10.1007/s13246-021-01083-2
5. Alpaydin, E.: Machine Learning: The New AI. MIT Press (2016)
6. Subhash, S., Srivatsa, P.N., Siddesh, S., Ullas, A., Santhosh, B.: Artificial intelligence-based voice assistant. In: 2020 Fourth World Conference on Smart Trends in Systems, Security and Sustainability (WorldS4), pp. 593–596. IEEE (2020)
7. Gosala, B., Chowdhuri, S.R., Singh, J., Gupta, M., Mishra, A.: Automatic classification of UML class diagrams using deep learning technique: convolutional neural network. Appl. Sci. **11**(9), 4267 (2021)
8. Esteva, A., et al.: Deep learning-enabled medical computer vision. NPJ Digit. Med. **4**(1), 5 (2021)
9. Gosala, B., Kapgate, P.D., Jain, P., Chaurasia, R.N., Gupta, M.: Wavelet transforms for feature engineering in EEG data processing: an application on Schizophrenia. Biomed. Signal Process. Control **85**, 104811 (2023)
10. Hamet, P., Tremblay, J.: Artificial intelligence in medicine. Metabolism **69**, S36–S40 (2017)
11. Fingelkurts, A.A., Fingelkurts, A.A., Neves, C.F.: Natural world physical, brain operational, and mind phenomenal space–time. Phys. Life Rev. **7**(2), 195–249 (2010)
12. Mumtaz, W., Xia, L., Ali, S.S.A., Yasin, M.A.M., Hussain, M., Malik, A.S.: Electroencephalogram (EEG)-based computer-aided technique to diagnose major depressive disorder (MDD). Biomed. Signal Process. Control **31**, 108–115 (2017)
13. Ding, X., Yue, X., Zheng, R., Bi, C., Li, D., Yao, G.: Classifying major depression patients and healthy controls using EEG, eye tracking and galvanic skin response data. J. Affect. Disord. **251**, 156–161 (2019)
14. Bachmann, M., et al.: Methods for classifying depression in single channel EEG using linear and nonlinear signal analysis. Comput. Methods Programs Biomed. **155**, 11–17 (2018)
15. Akar, S.A., Kara, S., Agambayev, S., Bilgiç, V.: Nonlinear analysis of EEGs of patients with major depression during different emotional states. Comput. Biol. Med. **67**, 49–60 (2015)
16. Sharma, M., Achuth, P.V., Deb, D., Puthankattil, S.D., Acharya, U.R.: An automated diagnosis of depression using three-channel bandwidth-duration localized wavelet filter bank with EEG signals. Cogn. Syst. Res. **52**, 508–520 (2018)
17. Mumtaz, W., Ali, S.S.A., Yasin, M.A.M., Malik, A.S.: A machine learning framework involving EEG-based functional connectivity to diagnose major depressive disorder (MDD). Med. Biol. Eng. Comput. **56**(2), 233–246 (2017). https://doi.org/10.1007/s11517-017-1685-z

18. Uyulan, C., et al.: Major depressive disorder classification based on different convolutional neural network models: deep learning approach. Clin. EEG Neurosci. **52**(1), 38–51 (2021)
19. Kang, M., Kwon, H., Park, J.H., Kang, S., Lee, Y.: Deep-asymmetry: asymmetry matrix image for deep learning method in pre-screening depression. Sensors **20**(22), 6526 (2020)

Planning Strategy of BDI Agents for Crowd Simulation

Panich Sudkhot[✉] and Chattrakul Sombattheera

Multiagent, Intelligent and Simulation Laboratory (MISL) Faculty of Informatics,
Mahasarakham University Khamreang,
Kantarawichai 44150, Mahasarakham, Thailand
{panich.s,chattrakul.s}@msu.ac.th

Abstract. Crowd simulation has been an interesting and important area of research because of its wide application in real world domains. The driving mechanisms of crowd simulation is how agents in the crowd make decision about their individual moves. There can be many decisive factors, both internal and external, about how agents plan to move. In this research, we preliminarily examine how the collective crowds behave given that some agents have their behaviors different from other agents. With our BDI-based agents, we experimented with three types of individual behaviors: agressive, active and humble. We also have three types of traits: psychoticism, extraversion and neuroticism. We compare our BDI-based agents against RVO agents in different scenes. We find that in pass-through scenes, our agents can move faster to their destinations. In hallway scenes, our agents can move smoother and faster to their destinations. In narrowing passage scenes, our agents with agressive behaviors move faster than RVO agents. However, our agents with active and humble behaviours move slower than RVO agents.

Keywords: Crowd Simulation · Planning Strategy · People's behavior

1 Introduction

Crowd simulation has long been and important and interesting area of research. Its applications in real world include crowd management, crowd evacuation, architecture design, crowd movement, passage way design, etc. There are two main streams of crowd simulation: macroscopic and microscopic crowd simulation. With macroscopic, crowd flows are modeled by mathematical formula. The crowd is considered to be a mass and only its movement is of interest. On the other hand, microscopic pays attention to internal decision making of individual agents that reflect in agents behaviours, which collectively show the behaviour of the movement of the crowd.

In this research we pay attention to microscopic model. The benefit of microscopic model over the macroscopic is that the microscopic represents what actually happens in real world environment. While having our own objectives, we,

R. Morusupalli et al. (Eds.): MIWAI 2023, LNAI 14078, pp. 459–474, 2023.
https://doi.org/10.1007/978-3-031-36402-0_43

as human being, are stimulated or temped by surrounding environment, as well as driven by our traits, behave individually. All these individual behaviours collectively comprise crowd movement. To have a pragmatic and useful crowd simulation, it is important that we model crowd simulation as similar as possible to real human beings behaviours.

In this research, we use BDI (Belief-Desire-Intention) principles to model our agents [10–13]. With BDI, agents are capable of consequently plan and re-plan in order to adjust to the ever changing environments. In general, BDI agents sense the environment and detect changes. When the agent determines that changes may affect its original plans, it re-thing for possible alternatives. This plan and re-plan take places repeatedly until the agent reaches its destination. Our BDI agents are based on RVO (Reciprocal Velocity Obstacles) agents [9], which work very well at navigating low level robot through congested area. To reflect more real world behavior, we also equip our agents with different traits, including psychoticism, extraversion and neuroticism. These agents' behaviors are humble, active and agressive.

The paper is structured as following. We review related papers and previous work in Sect. 2.1 and Sect. 2.2. We use parameters and data analysis in Sect. 2.4. We have scenarios experiment in Sect. 4 and conclusion in Sect. 5.

2   Background

2.1   Personality Models and Trait Theory Review

Characterizing the spectrum of human personalities has long been a challenging task of psychologists. There have been so many different theories, focusing of various aspects, proposed over several decades or centuries. Among these, an outstanding theories is "cross situational consistency", i.e. the behavior that does not change much regardless of times and changing situations. Methods to categorize and organize these variations have been proposed by psychologists have proposed among behavior's variety of sources. Guy et al. [1] develops theories based on Trait personality. Traits are patterns of human behaviours, thoughts or emotion. It is believed that merely a small amount of traits can govern a wide range of human behaviours [2].

In [1], personality traits of individuals can be controlled by change parameters, resulting in various behaviors of crowd. The foundation of [1] is the Personality Trait Theory. It is said that a small number of underlying traits comprise complex variations in behavior. A number of established models in Trait Theory are used to generate different behaviors for each individual, including Eysenck 3-Factor personality model [3]. This model is composed of three factors, i.e., Psychoticism, Extraversion, and Neuroticism, of personality. The combination of PEN factors identifies an individual's personality, dependinging on their strength and weakness. Psychoticism defines aggression and egocentricity of a person. Extroversion governs active, assertive or daring social interest. Neuroticism designates shyness and anxiety [4]. In addition, different hormones, including, testosterone, serotonin and dopamine, also combine with PEN to present human's behaviours.

It is suggested that a large number of the observed behaviours depends on a small number of defining factor [5]. Here, we also follow [1] to apply a similar factor analysis technique.

2.2 Behavior Perception User Study Background

In this section, we briefly review criteria used in our experiments. Since we base our work on [1], we shall present their settings in the following, for the sake of completeness.

The overall objective of [1] is to emulate various crowd behaviors by combining different adjusted parameters. The effects of changes of parameters are also observed. These parameters include preferred speed, effective radius (distance between each pair of agents), the highest number of surrounding agents that affect the agent's behavior, the furthest distance of surrounding agents that affect the agent, and futuristic planning of the agent.

Similarly to [1], a data-driven approach is adopted. A mapping between simulation parameters and perceived agent behaviors is derived. By doing these, there are at least two advantages: *i*) wider range of parameters provide more personality results, and *ii*) richer, more complex mappings can be possible. The setting also allows for multiple goals. There can be many adjectives for describing agents in the crowd, including "aggressive", "active" and "humble". There can be multiple psychological characteristics, such as the PEN [3] model. The setting supports a factor analysis, allowing for extracting underlying personality in the crowd.

2.3 Emulating Traits

In this section, we also re-explain the scenarios used in [1], which we follow. There are three scenarios. Simulations were created using Crowd Simulation Framework [6] and Multi-agent simulation navigate [7]. Figure 1 shows a snapshot of three scenarios. Scenario 1) Pass-Through: 8 traited agents are navigated through a crowd of 800 crossing agents. Scenario 2) Hallway: 22 traited agents are navigated through 12 groups of agents in a hallway. There are 120 other agents in several small groups. Scenario 3) Narrowing Passage: traited agents are navigated on the same direction toward a narrowing exit with 6030 other agents. In all scenarios, non-traited agents are assigned with default parameters, resulting in similar behaviors for all of them. The traited agents are also assigned with the same set of configured parameters.

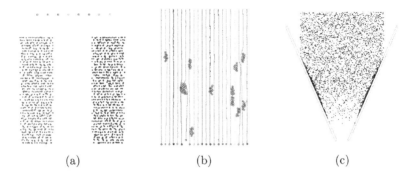

(a)   (b)   (c)

Fig. 1. Three scenarios: (a) Pass-through, (b) Hallway, and (c) Narrowing passage.

Furthermore, [1] suggest the following parameter settings, which we follow: i) maximum neighbor avoiding distance, ii) maximum neighbor avoiding number, iii) futuristic planning, iv) agent radius, and v) preferred speed. Random values are assigned to these parameter, whose range is shown in Table 1.

Table 1. Range of simulation parameters.

Parameter	Min	Max	Unit
max. neighbor avoiding distance	3	30	m
max. neighbor avoiding number	1	100	(n/a)
futuristic planning	1	30	s
Agent radius	0.3	2.0	m
Preferred speed	1.2	2.2	m/s

2.4 Data Analysis

In this section, we also present data analysis used by [1], which we follow. Their main idea is that they want to investigate the relationship between the parameters and the behaviors of the agents observed by human being. They had 64 volunteers to observe the agent behaviours and map each one of them to a specified category:

$$
\begin{pmatrix} Aggressive \\ Active \\ Humble \end{pmatrix} = A_{adj} \begin{pmatrix} \frac{1}{13.5}(Neighbor\ Dist - 15) \\ \frac{1}{49.5}(Max.\ Neighbors - 10) \\ \frac{1}{14.5}(Planning\ Horiz. - 30) \\ \frac{1}{0.85}(Radius - 0.8) \\ \frac{1}{0.5}(Pref.\ Speed - 1.4) \end{pmatrix}
$$

[1] also map their parameters to the PEN [2] model: (Psychoticism:Aggressive), (Extraversion:Active) and (Neuroticism: Humble). A mapping between personal adjectives and the PEN model is

$$
\begin{pmatrix} Psychoticism \\ Extraversion \\ Neuroticism \end{pmatrix} = A_{pen} \begin{pmatrix} \frac{1}{13.5}(Neighbor\,Dist - 15) \\ \frac{1}{49.5}(Max.\ Neighbors - 10) \\ \frac{1}{14.5}(Planning\ Horiz. - 30) \\ \frac{1}{0.85}(Radius - 0.8) \\ \frac{1}{0.5}(Pref.\ Speed - 1.4) \end{pmatrix}
$$

[1] suggest that PEN values can then be predicted based on the simulation parameters. They also observe the correlation between factors of the PEN model. A strong correlation between the Psychoticism and Neuroticism. Their conclusion is that Extraversion increases radius and speed of the agent. On the other hand, Carefulness reduces the radius and speed of the agents.

Our work is based on [1]. We equip agents with BDI capability and observe the changes. In the following, we shall discuss our implementation.

3   Our BDI Agent

Belief-desire-intention is a well know intelligent agent paradigm that has been adopted into building efficient agents. BDI allows for replanning when the state of surrounding environment have changed. Belief is the knowledge about the state of the world surrounding the agent. In the crowd simulation context, belief is the information about the positions, velocities, directionis of surrounding agent. In addition, information about other obstacles, the terrains, etc. is also considered part of the belief as well. Desire is the goal of agent. In crowd simulation context, the destination is the goal of the agent. Intention, lastly, is the plan for achieving goal. Since surrounding environment can always change, agents have to always update its belief about the current state of the surrounding environment. Consequently, the agent also has to consider how the changes can effect its current plan and re-plan accordingly. The most commonly adopted architecture of BDI agents is shown in Fig. 2.

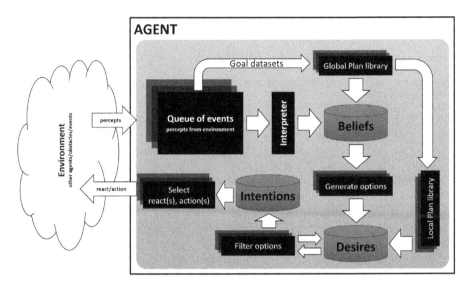

Fig. 2. BDI Agent Our agents are developed with BDI framework that allow for more efficient simulation.

Let **B** be the belief set of the agent. Let **D** be the desire set or the goal of the agent. Agent can have multiple subgoals in order to achieve the main goal. Let **I** be the intension set of the agent. Each plan in the **I** is represented by π. The present state of the world is represented by ω. Below we illustrate a typical BDI algorithm in Algorithm 1. Both **B** and **I** are initialized with the original set of belief $\mathbf{B}_0$ and $\mathbf{I}_0$ first. The first set of plan π is initialized with *null*. The algorithm enters the main loop where it observes the surrounding world and revise its belief set. It then reconsider both **B** and **I** where some of the belief and intention may be dropped according to the present situation. Here, the agent generate new options and deliberate over them. Plans are generated for achieving these intentions. The deliberation is determined whether it is needed in the function *reconsider*(). The present plan is then executed and updated.

An example of implementing BDI architecture is shown in Fig. 3. The BDI agent A is moving pass crossing agents on the Pass-through scenario from its current position at the bottom of the figure to its destination at the top of the figure. There are four other agents in the scene. B is the closest to A, moving from left to right. C is a little further away moving from right to left. D is further than C moving from right to left. D is the furthest moving from right to left. The dashed arrow represent the direction of each agent. The velocity is depicted by the size of the dash, the finer the slower. We can clearly see that agent B, C, D, and E are moving with the same velocity and maintain their direction. Agent A can maintain is speed until it moves pass the blue line because D is approaching. At this points, A keeps updating its belief and also replanning. Slowing down a little bit is the result of all these processes. Note that by the time A cross the blue line it can be certain that C must have gone pass its path already. If

Algorithm 1: BDI A typical BDI algorithm [8]

```
1  B ← B₀;
2  I ← I₀;
3  π ← null;
4  while true do
5  |   ω ← the state of the world;
6  |   revise B with ω;
7  |   if reconsider(B, I) then
8  |   |   D ← options(B, I);
9  |   |   I ← filter(B, D, I);
10 |   |   if !sound(π, I, B) then
11 |   |   |   π ← plan(B, I);
12 |   if !empty(π) then
13 |   |   α ← head(π);
14 |   |   execute(α);
15 |   |   π ← tail(π)
```

A is not slowing down, it could have eclipsed with D. The process of updating its belief and re-planning repeat continously. To be even safer, it slides slightly to the left with slower speed and keeps going with its normal speed toward its destination. E must have gone pass its path further away by then.

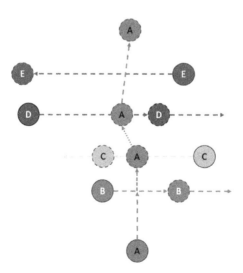

Fig. 3. Re-plan of movement With capability to re-plan according to ever changing environment, agents change speed and direction.

4 Experiments

Based on settings shown above, we present results achieved from our framework. The agents' preferred velocities range is [1.35,1.55] m/s. The parameters that change behavior by only one "unit" (on the 1–6 scale described in Sect. 2.3). The parameters used are summarized in Table 2.

Table 2. Simulation parameters for various personality traits.

Trait	Neigh. Dist	Num. Neigh.	Plan. Horiz.	Radius	Speed
Psych.	15	40	38	0.4	1.55
Extrav.	15	23	32	0.4	1.55
Neuro.	15	9	29	1.6	1.25
Aggres.	15	20	31	0.6	1.55
Active	13	17	40	0.4	1.55
Humble	15	7	30	1.1	1.25

4.1 Pass-Through Scene Results

Pass-through scenario generally allows agents to move freely from one side of the scene to the other side. In the following, we present snapshots of three scenes of running our framework and default RVO2.

As shown in Fig. 4, agents in (a) move straight toward the other end. On the other hand, agents in (b)'s movement has more variations. This is because our framework allows more flexibility in agent's movement. With our framework, agents can figure out more appropriately about path planning. While more space is available, our frame work allows for longer more straight movement. On the other hand, default RVO2 works at low level. When agents detect other agents in their path, agents try to figure out how to avoid collision. This results in diverged paths of some agents.

(a)   (b)

Fig. 4. Pass-through Scenario-1. Paths of agents using our framework (a) and default RVO2.

Based on diversion of paths in Pass-through Scenario-1, we adjust some parameters in Pass-through Scenario-2 to verify if agents with RVO2 can move more straight forward. We find that RVO2 agents can move more straight, as shown in Fig. 5. As in scenario-1, our framework still help agents to move straight toward their targets.

(a)   (b)

Fig. 5. Pass-through Scenario-2. Paths of agents using our framework (a) and default RVO2.

We further adjust parameters in Pass-through Scenario-3. We found that RVO2 agents still move not straight, as shownl in Fig. 6 (b). On the other hand, agents using our framework still move straight toward their targets.

(a)   (b)

Fig. 6. Pass-through Scenario-3. Paths of agents using our framework (a) and default RVO2.

Pass-through Scenes provide a lot of space for agents. The computational load is light, as shown in Table 3

Table 3. Execution time (AVG): average time of agents (big circles) to reach goal in three Pass-through Scenario.

Behavior	Our approach AVG time(ms)	RVO2 AVG time(ms)
Aggressive	16,664	17,273
Active	16,443	17,712
Humble	16,224.25	16,966

4.2   Hallway Scenario Results

In Hallway Scenarios, agents move from one side of the scene, through static obstacles randomly distributed, to their destinations on the other end. Each obstacle is composed of red circles placed together as shown in Figs. 7, 8 and 9. We ran our experiments many times and present here only three snapshots of path ways of agents' movement using both our framework (a) and RVO2 (b).

In the first scene, Hallway Scenario-1, agents are characterized by levels of psychoticism. Our framework allows agents to merely avoid obstacles and move straight to their destinations, as shown in Fig. 7 (a). For agents using RVO2, their paths swerve away a little after avoiding obstacles, as shown in Fig. 7 (b).

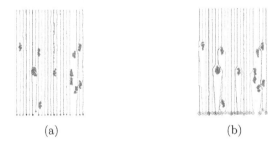

(a)   (b)

Fig. 7. Hallway Scenario-1. (a) high "Psychoticism" agents. (b) Default RVO2 agents.

In the second scene, Hallway Scenario-2, agents are characterized by levels of extraversion. Agents with our framework still have similar movement pathways to Hallway Scenario-1. Agents to merely avoid obstacles and move straight to their destinations, as shown in Fig. 8 (a). For agents using RVO2, their paths swerve away a little after avoiding obstacles, as shown in Fig. 8 (b).

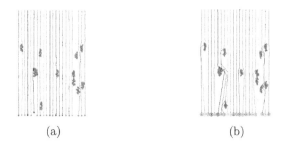

(a)   (b)

Fig. 8. Hallway Scenario-2. (a) agents with high levels of "Extraversion". (b) Default RVO2 agents.

In the third scene, Hallway Scenario-3, agents are characterized by levels of neuroticism. Agents with our framework still have similar movement pathways to Hallway Scenario-1 and Hallway Scenario-2. Agents to merely avoid obstacles and move straight to their destinations, as shown in Fig. 9 (a). For agents using RVO2, their paths swerve away a little after avoiding obstacles, as shown in Fig. 9 (b).

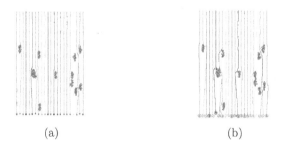

(a)   (b)

Fig. 9. Hallway Scenario. (a) agents with high levels of "Neuroticism". (b) Default RVO2 agents.

The execution times of simulation of agents with our framework and RVO2 for all three characteristics are shown in Table 4.

Table 4. Execution time (AVG): average time of agents (big circles) to reach goal in three Pass-through Scenario.

Trait	Our approach AVG time(ms)	RVO2 AVG time(ms)
Psychoticism	891	934
Extraversion	884	895
Neuroticism	838	955

4.3 Narrow Passage Scene Results

In Narrowing Passage scenes, agents are to move from a wide starting end through a narrowing passage to the exit on the other end. There are three type of agent settings, Aggressive, and neutral (or default), as shown in Figs. 5.8, 5.9, and 5.10, respectively.

In the first setting, Aggressive, agents with aggressive characteristic are randomly placed in the crowd. As shown in Fig. 10, most agents tightly gather along both sides of the narrowing passage. It appears that aggressive agents move pass the exit more quickly than other agents.

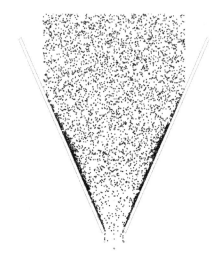

Fig. 10. Narrowing Passage - 1. comparing aggressive agents vs other agents.

In the second setting, Humble, agents with humble characteristic are randomly placed in the crowd. As shown in Fig. 10, most agents tightly gather along both sides of the narrowing passage. It appears that agressive agents move pass the exit more slowly than other agents (Fig. 11).

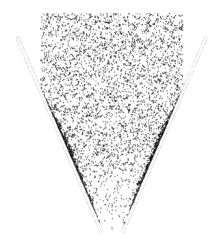

Fig. 11. Narrowing Passage - 2. A comparing humble agents and other agents.

In the third setting, Neutral, agents with neutral characteristic are randomly placed in the crowd. As shown in Fig. 10, most agents tightly gather along both sides of the narrowing passage. It appears that agressive agents move pass the exit more quickly than other agents (Fig. 12 and Table 5).

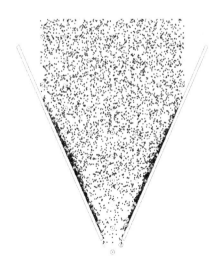

Fig. 12. Narrowing Passage - 3. A comparing neutral agents and other agents.

A comparison of the rate at which the agents of various personalities passed through the exit is shown in Fig. 13 show how different traited agents, equiped with BDI capability, move towards their destinations, compared with other agents. As the name suggests, humble agents take much longer time to reach

Table 5. Table of comparison four behaviors to reach goal (average time) in the **Narrowing Passage Scenario.**

Behaviors	AVG time(ms)
Aggressive	241,536
Active	243,831
Humble	244,864
Default RVO2	242,427

their destinations. Being humble simply slow the agents down particularly when reaching congested area. Active agents take lesser time to reach their destination than humble agents. Agressive agents are the fasted to reach their destinations. With regards to the travel of simulated agents, their behaviors do not change much. But they can make better decisions, avoiding congested areas earlier. With regard to computational power required, BDI helps reduce computational power.

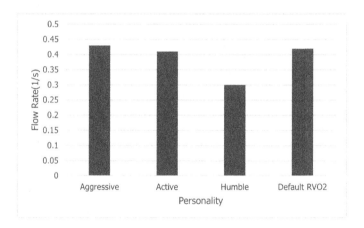

Fig. 13. Exit Rate. The average number of different types of agents exit the passage per second.

In addition to these settings, we can further simulate different types of agents for results and analysis of complex and heterogenous crowd.

4.4   Timing Results

We have found that with back-end computing, we can achieve sastisfying results because we do not have to carryout overhead and overload computing for the whole crowd. In addition to efficiently simulating crowd of agents, we are also interested in pursuing more efficiency, e.g. visualizing on the fly. We show the executtion time for agent simulation and visualization in different scenarios in

Table 6. The simulations were carried out on a 3.6 GHz AMD Ryzen 5 2600x processor.

Table 6. Performance timings per frame.

Scenario	Agents	Obstacles	Time (msec)
Hallway	6100	2	0.4
Narrowing Passage	142	0	1.9
Pass Through	808	0	1.4

5 Conclusion

It is very important that we capture human beings characteristics in making decision for carrying out precise, reliable, useful and helpful crowd simulation. In our previous work, we show that with BDI architecture, the execution time for simulation is lower. This allow for simulating larger number of agents. In addition, the behaviour of agents remains, and in some regards, more, realistic. In this research, we use our BDI agents to carry out crowd simulation with different traited agents. With our BDI-based agents, we experimented with three types of individual behaviors: agressive, active and humble. We also have three types of traits: psychoticism, extraversion and neuroticism. We compare our BDI-based agents against RVO agents in different scenes. We find that in pass-through scenes, our agents can move faster to their destinations. In hallway scenes, our agents can move smoother and faster to their destinations. In narrowing passage scenes, our agents with agressive behaviors move faster than RVO agents. However, our agents with active and humble behaviours move slower than RVO agents.

References

1. Guy, S., Kim, S., Lin, M., Manocha, D.: Simulating heterogeneous crowd behaviors using personality trait theory. In: Proceedings Of The 2011 ACM SIGGRAPH/Eurographics Symposium On Computer Animation, pp. 43–52 (2011)
2. Pervin, L.: Science of personality. BMJ **2**, 247–247 (1942)
3. Eysenck, M.: Personality and Individual Differences: A Natural Science Approach. Springer, US (1985)
4. Eysenck, S., Eysenck, H.: The place of impulsiveness in a dimensional system of personality description. Br. J. Soc. Clin. Psychol. **16**, 57–68 (1977)
5. Cattell, H.: The Sixteen Personality Factor (16PF) Questionnaire. Understanding Psychological Assessment, pp. 187–215 (2001)
6. Sudkhot, P., Sombattheera, C.: A crowd simulation in large space urban. In: 2018 International Conference On Information Technology (InCIT), pp. 1–8 (2018)

7. Sudkhot, P., Wong, K., Sombattheera, C.: Collision avoidance and path planning in crowd simulation. ICIC Express Lett. **17**, 13 (2023)
8. Der Hoek, W., Jamroga, W., Wooldridge, M.: Towards a theory of intention revision. Synthese **155**, 265–290 (2007)
9. Berg, J., Guy, S., Snape, J., Lin, M., Manocha, D.: Rvo2 library: reciprocal collision avoidance for real-time multi-agent simulation (2011). See https://gamma.Cs.Unc.Edu/RVO2
10. Rao, A., Georgeff, M.: Modeling rational agents within a BDI-architecture. Readings In Agents, pp. 317–328 (1997)
11. Georgeff, M., Rao, A.: An abstract architecture for rational agents. In: Proceedings of the Third International Conference On Principles Of Knowledge Representation And Reasoning, pp. 439–449 (1992)
12. Rao, A.: AgentSpeak (L): BDI agents speak out in a logical computable language. In: Agents Breaking Away: 7th European Workshop On Modelling Autonomous Agents In A Multi-Agent World, MAAMAW'96 Eindhoven, The Netherlands, 22–25 January 1996, Proceedings, pp. 42–55 (2005)
13. Rao, A., Georgeff, M.: Decision procedures for BDI logics. J. Log. Comput. **8**, 293–343 (1998)

Design and Development of Walking Monitoring System for Gait Analysis

K. T. Krishnamurthy[1] (ID), S. Rohith[2(✉)] (ID), G. M. Basavaraj[2] (ID), S. Swathi[3] (ID),
and S. Supreeth[4] (ID)

[1] Department of EEE, BMS College of Engineering, Bengaluru, Karnataka, India
`krishnamurthykt.intn@bmsce.ac.in`
[2] Department of ECE, Nagarjuna College of Engineering and Technology, Bengaluru,
Karnataka, India
`Rohithvjp2006@gmail.com`
[3] Department of CSE, Nagarjuna College of Engineering and Technology, Bengaluru,
Karnataka, India
[4] Department of Computer Science and Engineering, REVA University, Bengaluru, India

Abstract. Athletes, coaches and physical therapists are interested in learning how different running styles affect the muscles and forces as well as the gait cycle of runners. This paper focuses on the measurement and examination of walking patterns in people's lower half of the human body or the leg. The stance phase and swing phase are used for the Gait Analysis. It is employed to treat patients appropriately and improve gait abnormalities. Data were collected from two different age groups of people by placing sensors on the leg and the person was asked to walk on a treadmill for 5 min. The Gyro Sensor and The MPU 6050 3-Axis Accelerometer was inturn connected to the Arduino microcontroller and were processed to get gait parameters. The result showed that the design was less costly, and the wearable sensor was used for effective analysis of patients.

Keywords: Gait Analysis · Arduino Microcontroller · Gyro Sensor

1 Introduction

With the rapid improvement in the computerized diagnosis of neurological diseases, Gait Analysis has attracted many by researchers to develop methods to diagnose and analyze the conditions of any individual. Through Gait analysis, the gait phase can be identified, the kinematic and kinetic parameters of human gait events can be determined and musculoskeletal functions can be quantitatively evaluated. As a result, Gait Analysis has been employed in sports, rehabilitation, and health diagnostics. Gait Analysis is the study of human locomotion, using sensors and other equipment by observing movements, body mechanics, and muscle activity [1–4]. Using Gait Analysis, identification of gait phase, determination of the kinematic and kinetic parameters of human gait is done. Gait Analysis is used to diagnose and treat people whose walking ability is affected by diseases. It is frequently employed in sports biomechanics to aid athletes in running more effectively and to spot posture or movement-related issues in those who have sustained injuries.

© The Author(s), under exclusive license to Springer Nature Switzerland AG 2023
R. Morusupalli et al. (Eds.): MIWAI 2023, LNAI 14078, pp. 475–483, 2023.
https://doi.org/10.1007/978-3-031-36402-0_44

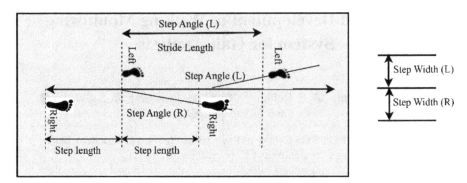

Fig. 1. Spatial gait parameters

Figure 1 shows the spatial parameters of gait. Typical spatial parameters of gait parameters are: step length, step width, stride length and foot angle. Step length is the distance measured parallel to the progression of the human body. Stride length is a length measured parallel to the progression of the line. Step width is the length between the line of progression of the left foot and the line of progression of the right foot. The foot angle is the angle between the line of progression and the foot axis.

Another name for human locomotion is the gait cycle, which has two phases: The stance phase and the swing phase. The stance phase is a series of appendage activity that moves the material forward while upholding posture balance. The posture development ends when the base is on the ground. The base concerning this phase, is liable to be subjected to the forces of ground trade at all steps, softening the party on the swim and initiating frame forward promptly subsequently. The swing step is the ending at which point below it is off the ground and lively forward. While hiking, the posture point constitutes about 60 of the walk's era and the swing state about 40. As ambulatory speed is raised, the odds are momentarily gone in the posture time decreases. This phase is a series of appendage activity that moves the material forward while upholding posture balance. The posture development is the ending when the base is on the ground. The base concerning this phase, is liable to be subjected to the forces of ground trade at all steps, softening the party on the swim and initiating frame forward promptly subsequently. The swing step is the ending at which point below it is off the ground and lively forward. While hiking, the posture point constitutes about 60 of the walk's era and the swing state about 40. As ambulatory speed is raised, the odds momentarily are gone in the posture time decreases. The upright dark bars are the periods of double appendage posture. The break happens all along the middle of the walks era and is named the "terminal double posture" break. This pause "starts accompanying floor contact as apiece resumes as far as the original posture appendage is repealed for swing". This pause is fundamentally placing a switch that happens between the swing and the posture appendage. These pauses can therefore be shabby further into various stages, one that is collected of posture, and one that is collected of swing. It is all along these posture periods that the crowd is situated as the foundation. For resolving the allocation of forces on the paw, these posture periods of the stages will be the only ones asking forces to the extremities (Fig. 2).

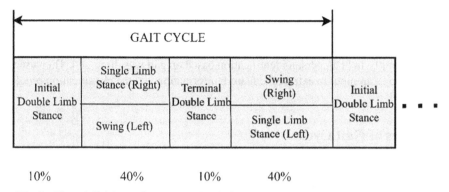

Fig. 2. The subdivisions of posture and their friendship to mutual floor contact pattern [9]

The rest of the sections are organized as follows. In Sect. 2, the Literature survey is discussed. The phases of the gait cycle are discussed in Sect. 3. An overview of the proposed work is discussed in Sect. 4. In Sect. 5, Results and Analysis are discussed. The conclusion is given in Sect. 6.

2 Literature Survey

Advancements in latest technologies attracted researchers and industry to develop automated, real-time based monitoring systems based on parameters of gait. Many researchers developed Walking Monitoring Systems for Gait Analysis for different applications [4, 5, 10]. In [1] Electromyography (EMG) for the measurement of voluntary muscle activity and Inertial Measurement Unit (IMU) for gait measurement for the applications of Stroke-Induced movement disorder were developed. To restore the damaged muscle's motions, an atrophied or weaker muscle was electrically stimulated by detecting specified gestures and the intensity of the active muscle bundle's EMG signal. In [3] Model-based approach for automated person recognition by walking and running are motion-based ideas. Motion extraction was carried out by using bilateral symmetric and an analytical model. Results show that system provides better recognition concerning running compared to walking. In [4], gait recognition by person re-identification using different cameras for tracking persons with different angles was done. Initially, gait is estimated with the angle and then the recognition process is applied to the captured images using a convolutional neural networks approach. Automated Gait Analysis of human motion recognition and classification is discussed in [5]. The approach attempts to combine information about the changelessness and movement of human walks. The entire process was divided into the detection and extraction of gait from the images. Finally, extracted gait was analyzed and classified using the k-nearest neighbour classifier. In [6], new wearable human gait analysis-based system using a piezoresistive pressure sensor is discussed. 8 Piezoelectric sensors were used for converting resistance to voltage. Wifi-based technology is used to receive gait data to the computer for analysis. The analysis was carried out for walking, running, and squatting. Results showed that it can monitor daily activities effectively. In [7], outdoor walking analysis with a foot-mounted IMU system was developed. GPS technology to transfer the data to the computer was used. The walking features calculated by this system are used for monitoring and analysis. Gait analysis based on a wireless sensor integrated into the shoe is discussed in [9]. In [10], person identification based on gait was discussed. They used a video frame as an input to extract the feature information and the classification process was applied.

3 Phases of Gait Cycle

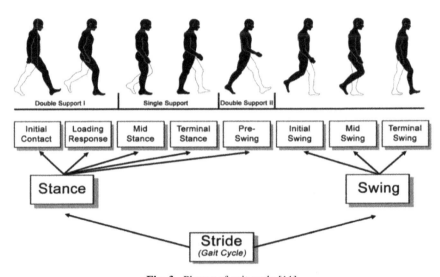

Fig. 3. Phases of gait cycle [11]

Figure 3 shows different phases of the gait cycle which are explained in detail in each cycle. Each phase of a gait has a functional aim and a vital pattern of carefully chosen synergistic motion to achieve that objective.

(1) Initial contact: This stage begins when the foot contacts the ground. The loading response pattern of the limb is determined by the joint postures being shown at this moment.
(2) Loading response: This stage marks the start of the double-stance period. This stage starts with Initial floor contact and lasts until the other foot is lifted for the swing. For shock absorption, the knee is flexed using the heel as a rocker.
(3) Midstance: The period is the first half of the single-limb support. During this phase, the limb moves over the stationary foot by dorsiflexion. When one foot is lifted, midstance begins and continues until the body's weight is placed over the forefoot.
(4) Terminal stance: The single-limb support is completed during this stage. The limb moves forward over the forefoot rocker as the heel rises to begin the stance and continues until the opposite foot touches the ground. During this period, body weight advances the forefoot.

(5) Pre-swing: The main objective of this stage is to set up the limb for swing. The second double-stance period in the gait cycle occurs during this last stage of stance. Pre-swing starts with the initial contact of the opposite limb and concludes with the ipsilateral toe-off.

(6) Initial swing: This stage is about one-third of the swing time, begins with the lifting of the foot off the ground and ends when the swinging foot is in opposition to the stance foot. The foot is raised at this stage, and the limb is progressed through increasing knee flexion and hip flexion.

(7) Mid-swing: This stage starts when the swinging limb is opposite the stance limb and completes when the swinging limb is forward to the point where the tibia is vertical.

(8) Terminal swing: The last stage starts with a vertical tibia and finishes when the foot touches the ground. The leg (shank) advances past the thigh, completing the progress of the limb.

4 Proposed Work

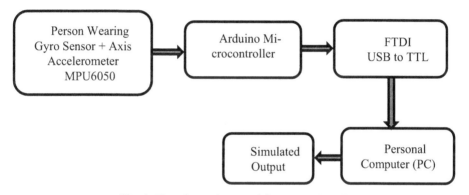

Fig. 4. Experimental setup of the proposed work

Figure 4 shows the experimental setup of the proposed work. To build a wearable sensor for a person which helps in analyzing the gait parameters. This work aims at creating a wearable sensor that can be worn on the lower part of a body i.e., leg. It measures the angles of the leg movement in which the life of a physiotherapy patient recovers quickly, and it helps athletes who can compare his/her previous records and prevents any future injuries. The sensors were connected to the Leg to obtain the parameters of the gait. Further parameters were processed through the Arduino microcontroller. The processed parameters were transferred to the personal computer through USB. Further, the graph was obtained as a waveform. This waveform is used for the future analysis of the human walking style.

5 Results and Analysis

In this work, two different persons were considered to study the proposed work. Python code was used for the analysis of the data. Figure 5 shows the prototype and complete setup of the proposed work. It uses an Arduino microcontroller, MPU-6050 3-Axis

Accelerometer and Gyro Sensor module. The real-time data acquired from the sensor were used for analysis. Our prototype is the path that has been drawn for the real-time data and the values are plotted by simulation.

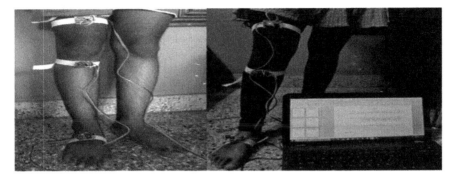

Fig. 5. Prototype of the proposed work

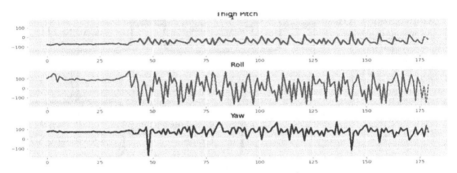

Fig. 6. The thigh part of leg with the simulation of angles.

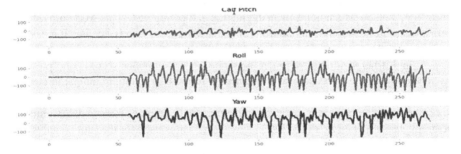

Fig. 7. The calf part of the leg with simulation of angles

Figure 6, Fig. 7 and Fig. 8 show the waveform obtained from real-time data acquired from Mr. Jeevan N, 18 Years of age, 172 cm in Height and 65 kg in weight. The thigh part of the leg gives the angles pitch, roll, and yaw and as shown in Fig. 6. Figure 7

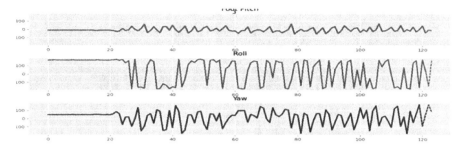

Fig. 8. The foot part of leg with the simulation angles

shows the calf part of the leg which gives the angles pitch, roll and yaw. Figure 8 shows the foot part of the leg which provides the angles of roll, pitch and yaw.

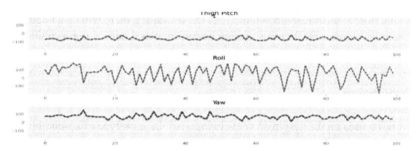

Fig. 9. The thigh part of leg with the simulation of angles

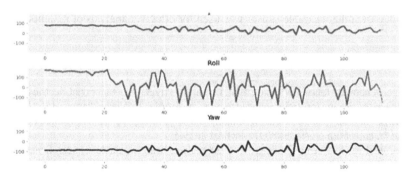

Fig. 10. The calf part of the leg with simulation of angles

The results shown in Fig. 9, 10 and 11 show the data acquired from the second person of name Ms. Nandini, aged 22 Years, Height 168 cm and Weight: 58 kg. It shows the results of the leg, Calf and Foot parts of real-time data acquired from Ms. Nandini. Figure 9 is the thigh part of the leg which provides the angles of pitch, roll and yaw. Figure 10 is the calf part of the leg that gives the angles pitch, roll and yaw. Figure 11 shows the foot part the leg gives the angles roll, pitch and yaw. From the simulation

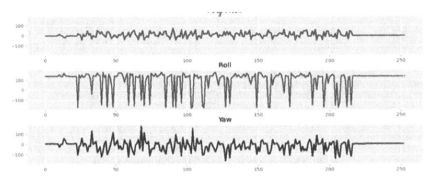

Fig. 11. The foot part of leg with the simulation angles

results shown in Fig. 6, 7, 8, 9, 10 and 11, it is observed that there is a difference in simulations of each region of the leg. A threshold value is set for the analysis depending on the situation. If the threshold is more than the set values, there will be a huge change in the simulation plot. Further to store the waveform cloud computing techniques [12, 13] can be used.

6 Conclusion

This work focuses on the design and development of the prototype of a wearable device for the Analysis of Gait. It can be used to treat patients appropriately and improve gait abnormalities. The prototype was developed using The Gyro Sensor, MPU 6050 3-Axis Accelerometer and Arduino microcontroller. In this work, two different real-time persons with different age groups selected to test the prototype. The result shows that the design is of low cost and a wearable sensor was used for effective analysis of patients.

References

1. Raghavendra, P., Talasila, V., Sridhar, V., Debur, R.: Triggering a functional electrical stimulator based on gesture for stroke-induced movement disorder. In: Vishwakarma, H.R., Akashe, S. (eds.) Computing and Network Sustainability. LNNS, vol. 12, pp. 61–71. Springer, Singapore (2017). https://doi.org/10.1007/978-981-10-3935-5_7
2. Tao, W., Liu, T., Zheng, R., Feng, H.: Gait analysis using wearable sensors. Sensors **12**(2), 2255–2283 (2012). https://doi.org/10.3390/s120202255
3. Yam, C., Nixon, M.S., Carter, J.N.: Automated person recognition by walking and running via model-based approaches. Pattern Recogn. **37**(5), 1057–1072 (2004). https://doi.org/10.1016/j.patcog.2003.09.012
4. Elharrouss, O., Almaadeed, N., Al-Maadeed, S., Bouridane, A.: Gait recognition for person re-identification. J. Supercomput. **77**(4), 3653–3672 (2020). https://doi.org/10.1007/s11227-020-03409-5
5. Yoo, J.-H., Nixon, M.S.: Automated markerless analysis of human gait motion for recognition and classification. ETRI J. **33**(2), 259–266 (2011)

6. Fei, F., Leng, Y., Yang, M., Wu, C., Yang, D.: Development of a wearable human gait analysis system based on plantar pressure sensors. In: Proceedings of IEEE 2nd International Conference on Micro/Nano Sensors for AI, Healthcare and Robotics, Shenzhen, China, pp. 506–510 (2019). https://doi.org/10.1109/NSENS49395.2019.9293994
7. Tawaki, Y., Nishimura, T., Murakami, T.: Monitoring of gait features during outdoor walking by simple foot mounted IMU system. In: Proceedings of IEEE Industrial Electronics Society, Singapore, pp. 3413–3418 (2020). https://doi.org/10.1109/IECON43393.2020.9254427
8. Bamberg, S.J.M., et al.: Gait analysis using a shoe-integrated wireless sensor system. IEEE Trans. Inf. Technol. Biomed. **12**(4), 413–423 (2008)
9. Jhapate, A.K., Singh, J.P.: Gait based human recognition system using single triangle. Int. J. Comput. Sci. Technol. **2**(2) (2011)
10. Gowtham Bhargavas, M., Harshavardhan, K., Mohan, G.C., Nikhil Sharma, A., Prathap, C.: Human identification using gait recognition. In: Proceedings of International Conference on Communication and Signal Processing, India, 6–8 April 2017, pp. 1510–1513 (2017). https://doi.org/10.1109/iccsp.2017.8286638
11. Stöckel, T., Jacksteit, R., Behrens, M., Skripitz, R., Bader, R., Mau-Moeller, A.: The mental representation of the human gait in young and older adults. Front. Psychol. **6**, 943 (2015). https://doi.org/10.3389/fpsyg.2015.00943
12. Supreeth, S., Patil, K., Patil, S.D., Rohith, S., Vishwanath, Y., Venkatesh Prasad, K.S.: An efficient policy-based scheduling and allocation of virtual machines in cloud computing environment. J. Electr. Comput. Eng. **2022**, 12, Article ID 5889948 (2022). https://doi.org/10.1155/2022/5889948
13. Supreeth, S., Patil, K.: Hybrid genetic algorithm and modified-particle swarm optimization algorithm (GA-MPSO) for predicting scheduling virtual machines in educational cloud platforms. Int. J. Emerg. Technol. Learn. (iJET) **17**(07), 208–225 (2022). https://doi.org/10.3991/ijet.v17i07.29223

Stock Market Investment Strategy Using Deep-Q-Learning Network

Sudhakar Kalva[1,2(✉)] and Naganjaneyulu Satuluri[3]

[1] Department of Computer Science and Engineering, G. Pulla Reddy Engineering College (Autonomous), Kurnool 518007, AP, India
sudhakarcs14@gmail.com

[2] Department of Computer Science, Jawaharlal Nehru Technological University Kakinada, Kakinada, India

[3] Department of Information Technology, LakiReddy Bali Reddy College of Engineering (Autonomous), NTR District, Mylavaram 521230, AP, India

Abstract. Artificial intelligence demonstrates its ability to analyze time series data more efficiently than humans and to automate stock trading processes without the need for human interaction. Developing a stock market investment strategy using artificial intelligence (AI) involves leveraging AI techniques to analyze data, identify patterns, and make informed investment decisions. In this study, we commonly utilized reinforcement learning DQN to create algorithms. Deep Q-Learning Network (DQN) is a reinforcement learning algorithm that combines Q-learning with deep neural networks to handle high-dimensional state spaces. It was introduced by Deep Mind in 2013 and has since been applied to various domains, including gaming, robotics, and finance. Financial markets are highly complex and subject to various external factors, making the application of DQN in stock market investment is a challenging. A deep q-learning network maps the agent's actions to its states. In addition, we performed external prediction in order to use forecasted prices as new features, changed the exploration rate, and implemented a stop-loss technique in order to increase trading performance. A list of the most predictable stocks is also supplied as an optional and referable rank list, which is a marginal output of external prediction. The final AI trader has the capacity to study from previous years' data of three selected equities and trade automatically with significant earning potential using new data. Our AI trading system model that uses reinforcement learning and deep learning on time series to trade stocks in the stock markets intelligently and safely, with estimated returns of 0.425% per five trading days. Overall our investment strategy model achieved 23.4% return for 275 trading days. Developed model definitely helpful to Investment Bankers, mutual fund managers, and Individual Investors.

Keywords: Automate stock trading · Deep q-Learning · AI trader

1 Introduction

Deep Q-Learning Network (DQN) is a reinforcement learning algorithm that combines Q-learning with deep neural networks to handle high-dimensional state spaces. Q-Learning: Q-learning is a classical reinforcement learning algorithm that learns an

© The Author(s), under exclusive license to Springer Nature Switzerland AG 2023
R. Morusupalli et al. (Eds.): MIWAI 2023, LNAI 14078, pp. 484–495, 2023.
https://doi.org/10.1007/978-3-031-36402-0_45

action-value function, Q(s, a), representing the expected cumulative rewards for taking action 'a' in state 's'. It updates Q-values based on the Bellman equation, which expresses the relationship between current and future rewards. Deep Neural Networks: DQN utilizes deep neural networks to approximate the action-value function. The neural network takes the state as input and produces Q-values for each possible action as output. The network's weights are updated iteratively during training to minimize the difference between predicted and target Q-values. The target Q-values used for training are obtained by applying the Q-learning update equation with the target network. The target network's weights are updated less frequently, typically after a fixed number of iterations, to maintain stable target value estimation.

We will design an automatic trading system for the Indian stock market as part of the AI trader research. The system is supposed to go through the following steps: obtain stock price history in order to select a small number of potentially most predictable stocks; obtain initial settings from users, like the initial cash and trading period; train models using historical data in the back - end and trade automatically using new coming prices of chosen stocks; display the trading log, which includes actions taken and current price;

2 Related Work

The business value of a profitable stock trading technique is enormous. Algorithmic trading is a serious financial issue that is gaining a lot of attention. Statistical analysis and classical machine learning technologies were used to create numerous forecasting models. Financial time series data, on the other hand, are tremendously noisy. A wide range of factors, including the political climate, managerial profile, and economic volatility, could have a significant impact on stock prices. As a result, predicting the price of a stock is extremely difficult [1].

In past few years, several researchers have used cutting-edge machine learning models to improve financial trading and have seen considerable results. Previous research can be divided into two categories. Machine learning techniques, for beginning, are widely used to recognize historic time series patterns and forecast future trends [2]. [3] Proposed a model for predicting stock price movement based on long short-term memory (LSTM). Another method to tackling the stock trading problem is to represent it as a Markov Decision Process and use reinforcement learning to forecast optimal trading decisions [4, 5], which is inspired by the recent breakthrough of using deep reinforcement learning to difficult decision-making tasks.

However, the research findings on stock selection from many stock markets are extremely restricted.

Designing AI trading systems that can handle many stocks in real time is difficult. As a result, more studies are required.

3 Data

We got our data via the Yahoo Finance API. Starting in 1995, the data includes daily price (open, high, low, and close), volume, and quantity. The data was preprocessed by truncating time spans and integrating different selected equities based on dates matching. Stock code, stock close price, volume, and date were the major features that we analyzed.

4 Proposed Method

To overcome this challenge, we created a reinforcement learning core with deep learning support.

Algorithm for Deep Q-Network (DQN):

Step 1: Initialize replay memory buffer with capacity N.
Step 2: Initialize the Q-network with random weights.
Step 3: Initialize a target network with the same architecture as the Q-network and copy the initial weights from the Q-network.
Step 4: For each episode:

- Reset the environment to the initial state.
- Repeat until the episode ends:

  - Select an action using an exploration strategy (e.g., ε-greedy) based on the current Q-network's Q-values for the current state.
  - Execute the selected action and observe the next state and reward.
  - Store the transition (state, action, reward, next state) in the replay memory buffer.
  - Sample a random mini-batch of transitions from the replay memory.
  - For each transition in the mini-batch, calculate the target Q-value:

    - If the next state is terminal, set the target Q-value as the reward.
    - Otherwise, calculate the target Q-value as the reward plus the discounted maximum Q-value from the target network for the next state.

  - Update the Q-network's weights by minimizing the mean squared error between the predicted Q-values and the target Q-values using the current mini-batch.
  - Periodically update the target network's weights by copying the weights from the Q-network.

Step 5: Repeat step 4 until the desired number of episodes or convergence is reached (Fig. 1).

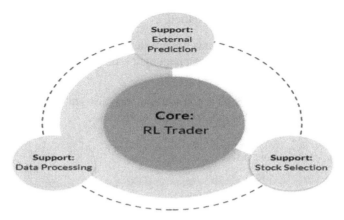

Fig. 1. Proposed Method structure

To overcome the auto trading challenges, we investigated and created **Deep Q-Network (DQN), a state-of-the-art in reinforcement learning scope**. DQN agents in real life can learn from the experience of changing states, which includes different days of price fluctuation and how it varies based on the activities taken by the agent, such as buying, selling, or holding particular stocks (Fig. 2).

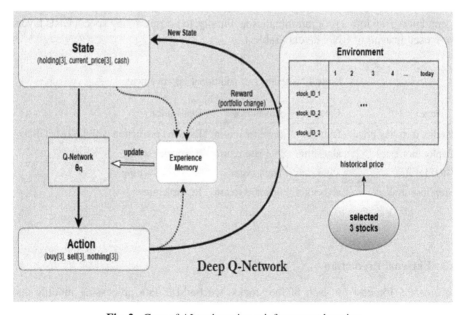

Fig. 2. Core of AI trader using reinforcement learning

4.1 Components in the Proposed Method

Environment: stock history, initial investment, steps, stock statistic information, step method, and trade technique are the most important settings.

Agent
Agent parameters include state size, action size, memory, discount rate, exploration pace, approximation model, act technique, and replay method.

State
Share holding, cash, current price.

Action
Buy index, no operation index, sell index.

Neural net
LSTM layers and Sequential dense layers.

We used a variety of ways to improve the basic RL process for additional supporting sections. First, we built an external deep neural network to forecast stock prices in order to perform supportive preprocessing on our data. The prediction is employed in two ways: one, to select the best three stocks from a pool of 50 that are the most predictable and stable, and another, to supply new stronger features in the 'state' of RL algorithms. Second, we examined the exploration-exploitation trade-off in order to gain deeper and selected to implement a pure greedy strategy in RL agent policy, which we tested and found to be very effective. Third, we had the idea to add a stop-loss policy to the RL agent, but we ran into a programming issue. Finally, to boost training speed, GRU layers were used instead of RNN layers (Table 1).

Table 1. Summary of additional improvement

Change	Category	Advantage	Realization
Predict next-day price	feature	Increase return	External prediction with LSTMs/GRUs
Exploration rate	algorithm	Increase return	RL model setting
GRU layers	algorithm	Train faster	RL model setting
Stop-loss strategy	algorithm	Increase return	RL structure

4.2 External Prediction

To create a forecast on each of the stocks, we build a data processing module and stacked LSTM/GRU deep neural networks outside of the RL schema. Stock close prices and volume are used to train the model. Each stock is divided into 50-day portions. We trained it by utilizing prices from the previous 49 days to estimate the price of the next 50 days. As a result, if we focus on any stock for 49 days, we can make predictions one day. We can select a selection of stocks that we estimate are the most predictable based

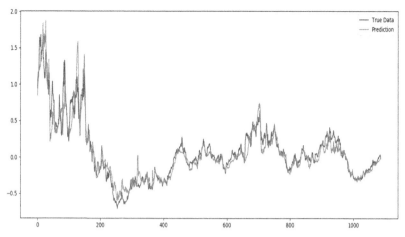

Fig. 3. A sample of 'point' prediction

on prediction accuracy. The forecasted values can also be used as features injected into the RL system (Fig. 3).

Description of Figure: When it is inserted as a feature into the RL schema (into the definition of states), the agent can now know the next day's expected price at any of the states and hence make better judgments (Fig. 4).

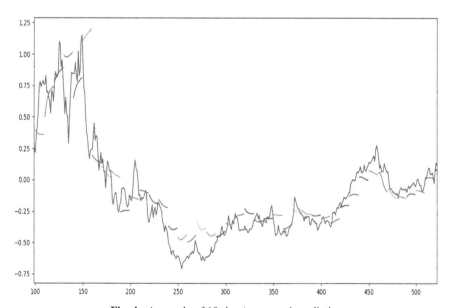

Fig. 4. A sample of 10-day 'sequence' prediction

Description of Figure: When it is injected as a feature into the RL schema (into the definition of states), at any of the states, the agent is now able to know the next 10 days predicted trend, hence makes better decisions. We may conjecture that this would be a strong feature (Figs. 5 and 6).

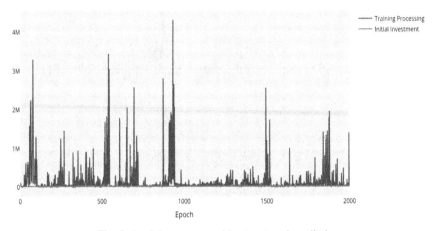

Fig. 5. Training process without external prediction

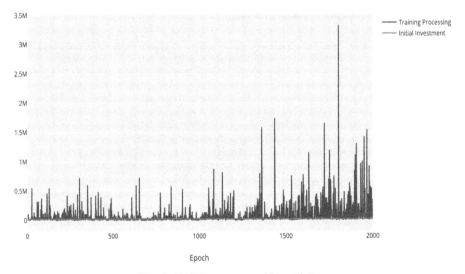

Fig. 6. Training process with prediction

4.3   GRU Layers

In order to improve the performance of our model, we also try to change the structure of neural networks.

We used the Long Short Term Memory (LSTM) layer, which is capable of learning sequence dependence in time series issues, as stated in the last milestone report. We tried a few different approaches before opting on gated recurrent units (GRUs), which work similarly to LSTM in that they use a gating mechanism to learn long-term dependencies in recurrent neural networks. According to the findings of the experiments, GRU's performance is comparable to that of LSTM, but GRU is computationally more economical. Given that training reinforcement learning algorithms takes a long time by nature, a more efficient agent model could be very useful in training and validating models faster (currently it takes over 8 h to train the model).

In addition, we spent a significant amount of time fine-tuning parameters such as layer size and period length, as well as merging more characteristics, all of which significantly improved the model's performance.

4.4 Stop-Loss Strategy

We didn't have risk management in our model, as TAs pointed out in Milestone 2. We aim to include a stop-loss technique into our reinforcement learning algorithm during this milestone. The concept is simple: when a stock's price is collapsing and falling to a specified stop price, the trader executes a transaction for that stock. We hope that by using this strategy, we will be able to reduce the variance. However, implementation is more difficult than we expected. It's a little tough to incorporate manually-specified strategies because we utilize OpenAI Gym for the reinforcement learning environment and the agent network is clearly defined. Furthermore, because sell/buy operations occur during the trading process, implementing an automatic strategy for all possible options is difficult.

We found that stock selection did not provide top-ranked stocks that could bring us more profit than our random choices, which could be explained by the fact that the most predictable stocks are the most stable but not the most profitable, and that high return should always correspond to high risk. We also identified that using future 10-day price prediction as a feature did not yield a higher return, which could be explained by the fact that we cannot include too many features in the model because it would make the model too complex and require more data, which is not allowed in the real-time series problem (the length of stocks dates have a maximum range) (Fig. 7).

5 Experimental setup/Results

5.1 Training Process Workflow in Step by Step

Step 1: Initialize agent and its networks
Step 2: For each episode:

- Reset environment and get initial state S

Step 3: For time in range:

- Obtain action A from agent with neural net mapping using S

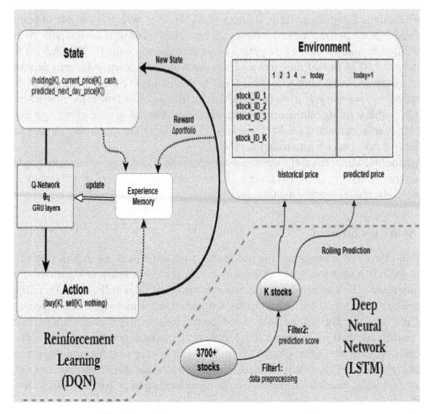

Fig. 7. Architecture of the proposed methodology

- Performing action to environment, observe and save in cache:
- (S, next state S', reward R, done, information)
- If done: end episode and save results

Step 4: Experience replay, i.e., using cache to update neural networks:
Step 5: For each observation (S, S', R, done):

- R, model predict (S') -> Q target
- Use neural net to predict (S) -> Q
- Update neural net using (S, Q, Q target)

5.2 Testing Process

Step 1: Initialize agent and its networks
Step 2: For each episode:

- Reset environment and get initial state S

Step 3: For time in range:

- Obtain action A from agent with neural net mapping using S
- Performing action to environment, observe:
- (S, next state S', reward R, done, information)
- If done: end episode and save results

Step 4: Settings:

- Initial investment: 20000
- Tax and transaction fee during trading: 0.3%
- Methods:
- Train-test split to simulate the real trading (which needs online training)
- Training data: 3 stocks of 950 days (from 2015 to 2018)
- Test data: the same stocks of 275 days (from 2018 to 2020)
- Test trading processes for 2000 episodes

5.3   Result

Return: 24864 for 275 trading days (23.4% return).
   (or: 0.425% return for every 5 trading days) (Fig. 8).

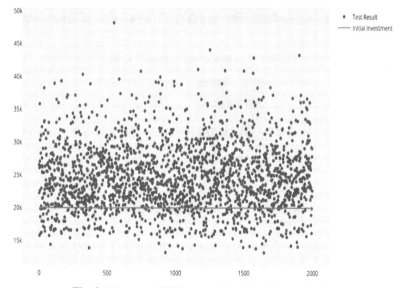

Fig. 8. Returns of 2000 test trading simulation episodes

6   System Overview

Stock Advisor is a web application built with Python Flask and Bootstrap (Fig. 9).

Fig. 9. Stock Advisor front end

It can receive data from users such as which stock they want to trade, how many shares they own, and how much cash they have on hand. And on the back end, the web system will read those parameters and conduct the reinforcement learning algorithm. Finally, the web page will give a trading recommendation based on the most recent stock data and user feedback.

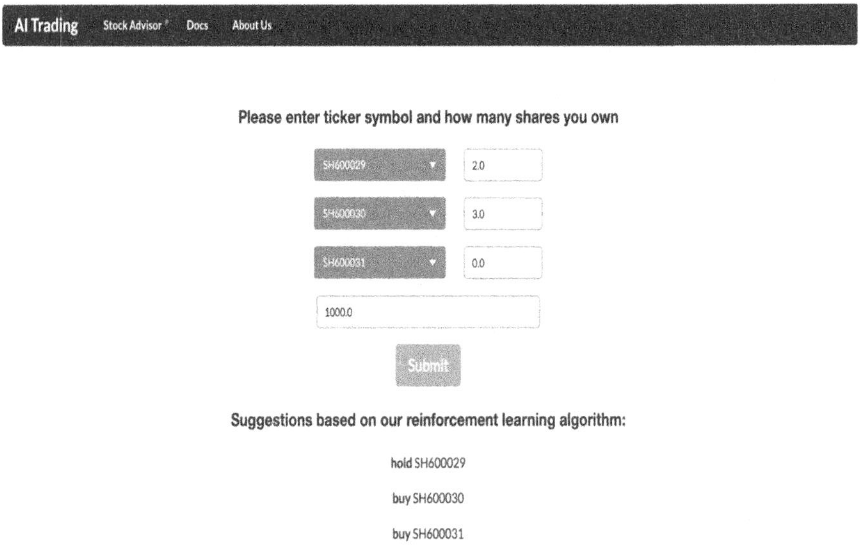

Fig. 10. Stock advisor could make suggestion based on user case

The Fig. 10 represents reading ticker symbol and how many shares you want, after that reinforcement learning algorithm (DQN) generate suggestions whether to hold or buy or sell the shares, by this investors can gets huge benefits from stock markets cannot makes losses from this volatile stock markets.

7 Conclusion

We developed a stock AI trading system that uses reinforcement learning and deep learning on time series to trade stocks in the stock markets intelligently and safely, with estimated returns of 0.425% per five trading days. The construction of an RL schema, the approximation of deep network policies, and the properties of forecasted pricing are all significant. However, there are still some issues: we still need to expand the 3 fixed number of candidate stocks to multiple numbers to provide flexibility, which is difficult for the dimensionality curve; the potential use of a rank list of stocks based on prediction accuracy has not been discovered, and this method may lead to some ways that can lead to a more profitable AI trader; useful features such as such as predicted 10-days prices might result in better results once we use them in a more proper way. From a broad perspective, AI trading combines entrepreneur development, market analysis, random events, and so on. Our system only allows you to trade safely utilizing stock price data. If we can integrate the above components, we may be able to create full-scope AI traders that can entirely outperform human traders.

References

1. Guresen, E., Kayakutlu, G., Daim, T.U.: Using artificial neural network models in stock market index prediction. Expert Syst. Appl. **38**(8), 10389–10397 (2011)
2. Patel, J., et al.: Predicting stock and stock price index movement utilizing trend deterministic data preparation and machine learning approaches. Expert Syst. Appl. **42**(1), 259–268 (2015)
3. Chen, K., Zhou, Y., Dai, F.: A LSTM-based technique for stock return prediction: a case study of the stock market. In: 2015 IEEE International Conference on Big Data (Big Data). IEEE (2015)
4. Deng, Y., et al.: Deep direct reinforcement learning for financial signal representation and trading. IEEE Trans. Neural Netw. Learn. Syst. **28**(3), 653–664 (2017). https://doi.org/10.1109/TNNLS.2016.2522401
5. Xiong, Z., et al.: Practical deep reinforcement learning strategy for stock trading (2018)
6. Fior, J., Cagliero, L.: A risk-aware approach to stock portfolio allocation based on Deep Q-Networks. In: 2022 IEEE 16th International Conference on Application of Information and Communication Technologies (AICT), Washington DC, DC, USA, pp. 1–5 (2022). https://doi.org/10.1109/AICT55583.2022.10013578
7. Ansari, Y., et al.: A deep reinforcement learning-based decision support system for automated stock market trading. IEEE Access **10**, 127469–127501 (2022). https://doi.org/10.1109/ACCESS.2022.3226629
8. He, Y., Yang, Y., Li, Y., Sun, P.: A novel deep reinforcement learning-based automatic stock trading method and a case study. In: 2022 IEEE 1st Global Emerging Technology Blockchain Forum: Blockchain & Beyond (iGETblockchain), Irvine, CA, USA, pp. 1–6 (2022). https://doi.org/10.1109/iGETblockchain56591.2022.10087066
9. Long, J., Chen, Z., He, W., Taiyu, Wu., Ren, J.: An integrated framework of deep learning and knowledge graph for prediction of stock price trend: An application in Chinese stock exchange market. Appl. Soft Comput. **91**, 106205 (2020). https://doi.org/10.1016/j.asoc.2020.106205. ISSN 1568-4946
10. Jiang, W.: Applications of deep learning in stock market prediction: recent progress. Expert Syst. Appl. **184**, 115537 (2021). https://doi.org/10.1016/j.eswa.2021.115537. ISSN 0957-4174

A Survey on Recent Text Summarization Techniques

G. Senthil Kumar$^{(\boxtimes)}$ and Midhun Chakkaravarthy

Lincoln University College, Wisma Lincoln, No. 12-18, Jalan SS 6/12, 47301 Petaling Jaya,
Selangor Darul Ehsan, Malaysia
`pdf.gskumar@lincoln.edu.my`

Abstract. NLP (Natural Language Processing) is a subfield of artificial intelligence that examines the interactions between computers and human languages, specifically how to design computers to process and evaluate vast quantities of natural language data. The procedure of condensing long text into paragraphs or phrases is known as NLP text summarization. This technique retrieves essential information from a text while keeping its meaning. This decreases the time necessary to comprehend large elements, such as articles, without compromising the integrity of the content. Major difficulties in text summarizing include subject identification, interpretation, summary construction, and summary evaluation. Most real-world systems that summarize texts rely on extractive summarization. Hence, there must be a way to summarize lengthy assessments into concise statements with few words that convey the same information. The use of text summarization in this context can be helpful. Text Summarization is of interest to several researchers in natural language processing. This study provides an overview of the different text-summarization approaches used in Natural language processing.

Keywords: Natural Language Processing · Text summarization · Extractive · abstractive and reinforcement learning

1 Introduction

The purpose of natural language processing (NLP) text summary is to make large content more manageable by dividing it into shorter sections. By using this technique, we are able to glean relevant details from the text without altering its original meaning. This shortens the time necessary to understand extended texts like articles without sacrificing accuracy. Summarizing text includes highlighting the most important parts of a lengthy text document in order to create a short, cohesive, and grammatically correct summary [1]. There are two approaches to text summarization demonstrated in Figure 1(a) Extractive approaches and (b) Abstractive approaches.

In Extractive approaches, when we use the frequency strategy to summarize a text, we compile a dictionary including the most important phrases and their relative frequency. As part of our final summary based on high-frequency words, we make a note of the sentences that include those keywords. This guarantees that all of the words in our summary are taken directly from the original source. No alterations are made to the text in the course of carrying out the extraction; rather, it is performed in line with the stated measure.

Instead of selecting phrases from the source text passage to include in the summary, abstractive summarization generates a paraphrase of the main ideas in a given text using a new vocabulary. The purpose of abstractive text summarization is to provide a quick summary that effectively conveys the essential arguments of the original text. It's possible that the summaries created will introduce additional phrases and sentences that weren't there in the original text.

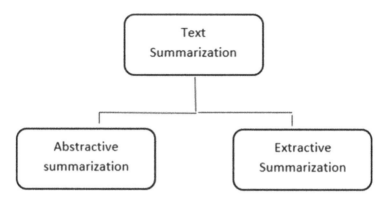

Fig. 1. Approaches of Text Summarization

2 Methodologies

The text summary is the process of condensing a document's phrases and words without altering its meaning. Text summarization employs AI and NLP to extract the most pertinent facts from enormous volumes of textual material.

2.1 Extractive Text Summarization Methodologies

For the purpose of formulating extractive summaries [1], relevant text segments (sentences or passages) are extracted from the text and analyzed statistically for their surface-level characteristics, such as word/phrase frequency, placement, or trigger words. "Most frequent" or "most attractively positioned" content is assumed to be the "most significant" information. Hence, no work on deep text interpretation is required for such a method.

The process for extractive text summarization [2], can be broken down into two steps: 1) The stage before the processing or pre-processing and 2) the processing stage. The original text is represented in a structured fashion during the pre-processing stage. In most cases, these are included: a) The identification of the boundaries of sentences. The punctuation mark that denotes the conclusion of a sentence in English is called a dot, and it is used to denote the border between sentences. b) Stop-Word Elimination – Eliminating common terms that have no meaning and do not collect significant information about the job. c) Stemming is a process used to retrieve each word's root or radix to emphasize its meaning. The objective of this process is known as stemming. During the Processing stage, the factors that influence the relevance of phrases are identified and computed. Following that, the weight learning approach is used to give weights to each of these factors. The feature-weight equation is used to get each sentence's final score. The most well-regarded sentences are chosen for the final summary.

An unsupervised system, SummCoder, was proposed for extractive text summarization of a single document by Joshi et al., [3]. After the preliminary processing in SummCoder, the skip-thought model reduces phrases to vectors of constant length. Each sentence is evaluated based on three scores—the Sentence Content Relevance Metric (scoreContR), the Sentence Novelty Metric (scoreNov), and the Sentence Position Relevance Metric (scorePosR)—before being included in the summary (scorePosR). A final score and relative score are computed once all the points have been tallied. In conclusion, the summary may be made by first sorting the input terms in decreasing order of relative rank and then sorting them in accordance with how often they appear in the text.

Summary methods based on the centrality of position were proposed by Zheng and Lapata [4]. (PacSumm). Sentences serve as nodes in a graph-based ranking system. Connections between nodes are represented by edges. The phrases were mapped with the use of a technique called Bidirectional Encoder Representations from Transformers (BERT). Pre-training BERT entails two tasks: masked language modeling, in which a token is assigned to a sentence based on the left and right sentences, and sentence prediction, in which the connection between two phrases is predicted. Five negative samples are provided for every positive result for use in fine-tuning BERT. An unnormalized matrix is obtained by the pairwise dot product of all phrase representations after they have been discovered. Selecting sentences through this matrix.

A comparison of abstract and extractive methods is provided by Surbhi Bhatia et al. [5]. To avoid duplication, abstract summarization makes use of a graph-based method. Graphs are built, constraints are applied to guarantee valid sentences, and Sent WordNet is used to aggregate sentiment scores before the sentences are scored individually. The (PCA) Principal Component Analysis method is used in extractive summarization to rank sentences according to their relevance and so find a summary of the text.

To get to the essence of the text, the Weighted Compression Model was proposed by Vanetik et al., [6]. This is achieved in the suggested paradigm by Eliminating EDUs from a statement in a loop (EDUs). Selecting and discarding EDUs is the next stage. An EDU list is compiled using syntax trees organized by the voting bloc. Several EDUs were left off the list since their removal might have resulted in grammatical errors. All the others are removed and the weight of the essential EDUs is calculated and sorted.

To ensure that the summary is as concise as possible while including all relevant information, EDUs are prioritized based on their weight relative to their associated costs.

Akalanka Galapathi and John Anvik [7], have discovered an extractive approach to generating bug report summaries that do not rely on the sophisticated characteristics employed by Rastkar's model. Accuracy and recall were shown to be different when complicated features were included than when they were not. Length and Lexical Features describe them. A logistic regression model was utilized for sentence categorization. For instance, they have implemented classification using the sklearn package. They have utilized a variety of logistic regression models to compare the effectiveness of separate and combination characteristics.

Fuzzy Evolutionary Optimization Modeling (FEOM) was proposed for phrase clustering by Song et al., [8]. In this experiment, we'll use 'n' items that will be clustered using distances. We next employ three evolutionary operators—selection, crossover, and mutation—until the termination condition is not met (Nmax = 200). The probabilities of crossing (pc) and mutation (pm) are controlled by three variables: the distribution coefficient (Var), the relative distance (G), and the mean evaluation effect (Em). Next, phrases with the highest degree of fitting are chosen.

2.2 Abstractive Text Summarization Methodologies

It generates new words and phrases, arranges them into coherent sentences, and highlights key information from the source text. This makes abstractive summarization methods more difficult to implement and more time-consuming to compute. According to Chu & J. Liu [9], With large data stores of associated text documents, abstract summaries are automatically created. Yet, such data sets are unusual, and models that make use of them much less so. Several spheres. Improvements in a series of sequences by single pairs have been made recently. Only when just texts (such product or business evaluations) are provided without the stated summaries do we explore end-to-end constructs, in which a neural model is developed to generate uncontrolled summaries. The MeanSum model's two most distinguishing features are An auto-encoder component that reads the reviews and learns a representation for each, then strips the summary of any language context. Second, a "learning" summary generator that can replicate previous outputs to provide consistent meeting summaries.

According to Zhang et al. [10], while describing a dialogue, it is important to include the larger context, which often includes many speakers who may have varying roles, goals, and perspectives. Several varieties of language. SuTaT's goal in a consumer one-on-one discussion is to summarize both speakers by modeling customer words and agent words independently while keeping them cohesive. SuTaT has a module for conditional production and two for nonelected summaries. The goal is to produce a summary for each customer and data agent. Design-wise, it's a lot like making a tete-a-tete: the representatives' answers and the customers' needs are intertwined. Beautiful, rentable models outperform those with no human oversight. SuTaT-performance LSTMs is far superior to that of alternative unstructured abstract foundations equipped with LSTM encoders and decoders.

The effectiveness of methods used to summarize bug reports is affected by their ability to account for certain features of the reports. Xiaochen et al. [11] have developed a new unsupervised method they name DeepSum to address this issue. In order to properly summarize reported errors, DeepSum relies on deep learning for its summarization duties. A stepped auto-encoder network forms the core of DeepSum, synthesizing the summary of the bug reports learned in the network's hidden layers. Both the summary data set and the authorship data set are utilized to assess the quality of the summarizers.

Two sets of encoder-decoders make up the Sequence-to-Sequence-to-Sequence Autoencoder sequence proposed by Baziotis et al., [12]. In this case, words are employed as a series of random, incomprehensible elements. The initial and final sequences are examples of inserted and rebuilt sentences, while the third is an example of a compressed sentence. Bidirectional RNN may be used to embed coded source sequences in output projects via the Embedding layer.

Brief information on the several RNN variations utilized for Abstractive Text summarization is provided by Raphal et al., [13]. However, the fundamental RNN isn't great at picking up on ties that will persist over time. It's this corrected with a model of recurrent neural networks with a long short-term memory. The input, output, and forget gates are the three components that makeup LSTM. Its purpose is to record reliant relationships that span several time periods. The subject of the "Vanishing Gradient" is also addressed.

2.3 Reinforcement Learning Methodologies

In order to make existing mechanisms for summarizing texts more effective, reinforcement learning is being used to this field [14]. In this case, achieved by providing reinforcement or punishment for each action taken by a training agent in order to get an ideal policy for use in summary generation. Several reinforcement learning strategies for auto-text-summarization have been described in this study.

Mohsen et al. [15] provide a Reinforcement Learning-based hierarchical neural extractive summarizer. As a first option, there is focused observation. The Sentence Encoder here use a Bidirectional Long Short-Term Memory (BiLSTM) to convert text into a sequence of vectors that accurately reflect the words and phrases in the text. At completion, the Attention Document Encoder constructs a representation of the document.

The Sentence Extractor then assigns a value of 1 to the most relevant sentences and a value of 0 to the least relevant sentences. Sentence rankings are determined by a learning agent that is taught how to do so. The ROUGE scores are immediately improved. The agent is given a random starting point and then educates itself by reading relevant information.

Wong et al. [16] have constructed a hybrid model for extractive text summarization using Probabilistic SVM and NBC. Once learning is supervised, it is generally producing quality results; however, unlabeled data is required. In order to reduce the amount of labeled data, co-training methods are used. A co-training strategy is devised to facilitate the training of several classifiers using the same feature space.

PSVM and NBC are enhanced using a mix of surface, material, and relevance aspects. Co-training was used to blend labeled and unlabeled data to cut down on labelling expenses. Based on experimental results, semi-supervised learning is just as effective as supervised learning (0.366 vs. 0.396 accuracies) while saving half the money spent on labelling. Enhancements are made to the ROUGE results of the same summary procedure.

3 Conclusion and Future Work

In this study, we have analyzed the literature on abstractive, extractive, and reinforcement learning. These articles use various techniques and methods, but they all produce encouraging results. There are difficulties with each of these approaches that can be overcome by adopting another approach.

Nonetheless, the biggest and most widespread problem that still need fixing are evaluating the summaries. Automated Text Summarization aims to eliminate these problems (and others like them) and make the technology more user-friendly and practically applicable. The ongoing Automated Text Summarization research aims to develop a model capable of producing summaries on par with those written by humans.

References

1. Kyoomarsi, F., Khosravi, H., Eslam, E., Dehkordy, P.K.: Optimizing text summarization based on fuzzy logic. In: Proceedings of Seventh IEEE/ACIS International Conference on Computer and Information Science, pp. 347–352. IEEE, University of Shahid Bahonar Kerman, UK (2008)
2. Gupta, V., Lehal, G.S.: A survey of text mining techniques and applications. J. Emerg. Technol. Web Intell. **1**(1), 60–76 (2009)
3. Joshi, A., Fidalgo, E., Alegre, E., Fernández-Robles, L.: SummCoder: an unsupervised framework for extractive text summarization based on deep auto-encoders. Expert Syst. Appl. **129**, 200–215 (2019)
4. Zheng, H., Lapata, M.: Sentence centrality revisited for unsupervised summarization. arXiv preprint arXiv:1906.03508 (2019)
5. Bhatia, S.: A comparative study of opinion summarization techniques. IEEE Trans. Comput. Soc. Syst. **8**, 110–117 (2020)
6. Vanetik, N., Litvak, M., Churkin, E., Last, M.: An unsupervised constrained optimization approach to compressive summarization. Inf. Sci. **509**(10), 22–35 (2020)
7. Galappaththi, A.: Automatic sentence annotation for more useful bug report summarization. Diss. Lethbridge, Alta.: The University of Lethbridge, Department of Mathematics and Computer Science (2020)
8. Song, W., Choi, L.C., Park, S.C., Ding, X.F.: Fuzzy evolutionary optimization modeling and its applications to unsupervised categorization and extractive summarization. Expert Syst. Appl. **38**(8), 9112–9121 (2011)
9. Chu, E., Liu, P.: MeanSum: a neural model for unsupervised multi-document abstractive summarization. In: International Conference on Machine Learning, pp. 1223–1232 (2019)
10. Zhang, X., Zhang, R., Zaheer, M., Ahmed, A.: Unsupervised abstractive dialogue summarization for Tete-a-Tetes. arXiv preprint arXiv:2009.06851 (2020)
11. Jiang, H., Li, X., Ren, Z., Xuan, J., Jin, Z.: Toward better summarizing bug reports with crowdsourcing elicited attributes. IEEE Trans. Reliab. **68**(1), 2–22 (2019). https://doi.org/10.1109/TR.2018.2873427
12. Baziotis, C., et al.: SEQ^3: differentiable sequence-to-sequence-to-sequence autoencoder for unsupervised abstractive sentence compression. arXiv preprint arXiv:1904.03651 (2019)
13. Raphal, N., Hemanta, D., Philemon, D.: Survey on abstractive text summarization. In: International Conference on Communication and Signal Processing, 3–5 April 2018, India (2018)

14. Wasthi, I., Gupta, K., Bhogal, P., Anand, S., Soni, P.: Natural language processing (NLP) based text summarization - a survey, pp. 1310–1317 (2021). https://doi.org/10.1109/ICICT5 0816.2021.9358703

15. Mohsen, F., Wang, J., Al-Sabahi, K.: A hierarchical self-attentive neural extractive summarizer via reinforcement learning (HSASRL). Appl. Intell. **50**(9), 2633–2646 (2020). https://doi.org/10.1007/s10489-020-01669-5

16. Wong, K.F., Wu, M., Li, W.: Extractive summarization using supervised and semi-supervised learning. In: Proceedings of the 22nd International Conference on Computational Linguistics (Coling 2008), pp. 985–992 (2008)

Conversational AI: A Study on Capabilities and Limitations of Dialogue Based System

Narayana Darapaneni[1], Anwesh Reddy Paduri[2(✉)], Umesh Tank[3],
Balassubramamian KanthaSamy[3], Ashish Ranjan[3], and R. Krisnakumar[3]

[1] Northwestern University/Great Learning, Evanston, USA
[2] Great Learning, Bangalore, India
anwesh@greatlearning.in
[3] PES University, Bangalore, India

Abstract. The conversational chat model here is based on the RASA framework. This framework is used as the base to design the chatbot. The topical Chat dataset used here contains approximately 210,000 utterances, which is more than 4,100,000 words. The chatbot analyzed this chat dataset and revealed how individuals interact with one another while discussing various topics. The TED (Transformer Embedding Dialogue) policy is used by Rasa to ensure that conversations are meaningful and are able to stick to the original intent of placing an order. The three inputs and all the features were fed into the transformer. Then, we built a model so that we can train it with the data and then can be used for the prediction and identify improvement opportunities. We simulated ASR hypotheses for each turn in a conversation using four different settings. System A had a Word Error Rate (WER) of 0.01–0.39 for the dialogues in the test freq audio and test-uncommon audio, whereas system B had an error rate of about 0.08. We trained our Rasa-based model with topical chat data. Topical chat data includes various conversations on a specific topic in the json files. After training the bot we can ask various questions about around 250 entities and the bot will share fun facts about those entities. The report, confusion matrix, and confidence histogram for your intent classification model were then created by the Rasa test script. Any samples that were inaccurately predicted are recorded and preserved in an errors file.

Keywords: Rasa · TED · RASA Framework · Chat Dataset · error rate

1 Introduction

Conversational AI, often known as the development of conversational bots, that can engage with people in natural language, has been of interest to our study. As shown by text-based systems like ELIZA [1]. Conversational AI research often falls into one of two categories: task-oriented or open-domain. Open-domain bots aspire to serve as social conversation partners with whom humans may have natural [2] and interesting talks. Task-oriented bots strive to assist humans in completing a specified task via multi-turn interactions [4]. In addition to standard language abilities such as comprehension, open-domain bots (also known as SocialBot) must master certain conversational [3] skills that come easily to humans: memorising.

© The Author(s), under exclusive license to Springer Nature Switzerland AG 2023
R. Morusupalli et al. (Eds.): MIWAI 2023, LNAI 14078, pp. 503–512, 2023.
https://doi.org/10.1007/978-3-031-36402-0_47

World information, reasoning in light of conversational history [5], and crafting meaningful answers. SocialBot must also have appropriate thematic breadth and depth and be capable of performing seamless topic changes. The lack of datasets of knowledge-grounded talks and related knowledge sources [8] is a significant barrier to study on the acquisition of these conversational abilities. We provide Topical-Chat, a corpus of over 11,000 human-to-human discussions about knowledge across eight key subjects. The Topical-Chat dataset was obtained [6] by pairing Amazon Mechanical Turk employees, supplying them with topical reading sets, and requesting that they conduct natural, coherent, and interesting talks based on the reading sets supplied. Partners do not have explicitly defined roles they must play during a conversation [7], and the reading sets provided to them may be symmetric or asymmetric to varying degrees, which accurately reflects real-world conversations in which the world knowledge [9] acquired by both partners prior to a conversation may be symmetric or asymmetric. In addition, partners are required to comment each conversational turn on many dimensions, including reading set use and emotion [10]. In order to provide benchmarks for future Topical-Chat research, we trained multiple encoder-decoder conversational models on Topical-Chat. Each of these models tries to produce a response based on a reading set and conversational history. We use the TED policy Transformer architecture in particular. Through automated and human review, we show that our models are capable of having interesting discussions based on knowledge.

2 Literature Survey

We examined a variety of TaskBot-related articles, focusing notably on The Alexa Prize [18]. The Alexa Prize is a competition sponsored by Amazon Alexa that has allowed hundreds of university students to compete in previous years to advance the state of the art in conversational AI. Amazon sponsored a conversational challenge for the development of a TaskBot [12] after the success of the SocialBot Grand Challenge, a competition among colleges across the globe to create the greatest SocialBot. This agent may aid users in completing real-world activities, such as preparing a particular food or completing a home improvement job. An intriguing need of the Taskbot is that it should not only engage with consumers but also actively aid the user in completing the work. The TaskBot differs from the conventional scenario in which a person instructs a machine to accomplish a job [11]. In this instance, TaskBot presents a person with a task completion instruction. These criteria provide a unique set of obstacles, such as assisting the user in locating a particular element of a work, such as the supplies or equipment necessary to complete a task, and finding an alternative in the case that those ingredients or tools are unavailable. Also, this entails developing a strategy and adjusting it as necessary. The TaskBot should be able to respond to inquiries posed by the user about the task or its stages. There are several more obstacles that demand the development of unique technologies in various fields [12], such as Information Retrieval, Question Answering, Dialog Management, and multimodal interaction.

For the Alexa TaskBot Competition, we evaluated GrillBot [19], a multimodal task-oriented voice assistant designed to help users through complicated real-world chores. Task Graph is a new dynamic depiction of phases, requirements [13], and other features that guides people through complex tasks. By offering a formal abstraction of the work, Task Graph facilitates conversational fluidity and adaptability. It enables GRILLBot to take the initiative or the user to make choices on the current work. One of the fascinating features of GRILLBot is that it stores the conversation's context in the database so that it may be retrieved later [14]. As more questions are asked, the dialogue is loaded as the background for answering the question [16]. The other two modules, functions, and neural functionalities, offer context-independent replies that are stateless. Graphs are used to depict tasks.

Likewise, TWIZ [20] is also participating in the same competition. Their bot design anticipates the facilitation of an engaging experience in which users are steered via multimodal discussions to the successful accomplishment of the designated job. They accomplished this by adhering to four key principles: a) robust dialogue interaction, by customizing core dialogue components (utterance processing, dialogue manager, and response generator) for an in-the-wild environment; b) effective and conversational task grounding; c) delivery of an immersive multimodal task guiding experience; and d) engagement maximization and user cognitive stimuli.

The Conversation task-grounding was applied. We incorporated sophisticated intent recognition, a Transformer-based ranker, and seasonal recommendations for users who merely intended to explore the TaskBot in order to aid the user in swiftly [15] locating the desired activity and minimizing annoyance. The identification of intent was done in two independent phases: First, they try to categorize it using a variety of techniques. Then, they made minute rule-based adjustments. Two task decomposition techniques were used. The first technique is an unsupervised step-length-based strategy. They used Spacy to recognize sentence boundaries and interrupt the step after a certain number of words. Task-Token-Segmenter is a supervised approach that employs a BERT model to discover the optimal locations to split a step. They fed each token's embedding into a common linear layer that makes binary predictions (segment/not segment). Apart from this, they used a variety of NLP approaches [17], including text similarity, weighted TF-IDF, etc. Curiosity was an additional intriguing concept that was offered. The bot would remark on interesting tidbits associated with the activities being completed, hence increasing client engagement.

3   Materials and Methods

In this study, we conducted considerable research on the algorithms, models, and frameworks utilized extensively by the Dialog system. We will begin by discussing the general architecture of Dialogue-Based Systems, followed by a short discussion of implementation specifics.

Architecture of Conversational Systems: Contemporary dialogue-based systems generally consist of five fundamental components: ASR (Automatic Speech Recognition), NLU (Natural Language Understanding), Dialogue Manager, NLG (Natural Language Generation), and TTS (Text-To-Speech). ASR (Automatic Speech Recognition) identifies speech input from the user and translates it to text for processing. ASR is the first point of entry for Dialog-Based Systems that may be implemented on the client through APIs. Because to the modular nature of the design, we may utilize any of the existing ASR models. The NLU is where the Dialogue System attempts to comprehend the purpose or inquiry of the user. To comprehend user input, the NLU module utilizes several approaches, such as embeddings, n-grams, CBoW (Continuous Bag Of Words), etc. After understanding the user's purpose via NLU, a Dialogue Manager (DM) collects the context and past conversation history to take action. The DM also establishes a connection with the NLG (Natural Language Generator) to create the answer to the user's query based on the inquiry's history and present context. NLG creates replies, whereas the DM determines which response is most suitable for a specific question. Once the user selects a response, TTL (Text-to-Speech Synthesis) transforms the text into voice. TTL is mostly a client module. Response Generator uses many trained models to provide a response. Models are trained beforehand, and LLM (Large Language Models) may be utilized to improve results or provide a response that is domain-specific. The figure below demonstrates the full procedure (Fig. 1).

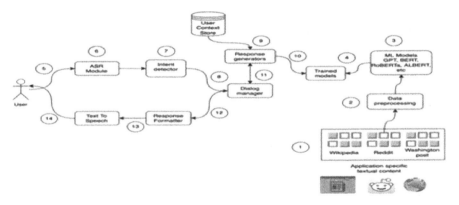

Fig. 1. High-Level Workflow

We have used an open-source python voice recognition library that supports Google's ASR implementation. Google's voice recognition APIs are used for ASR. On the client, ASR APIs are implemented. The last three modules, namely NLU, DM, and NLG, are constructed using the Rasa framework, which provides webhooks and a built-in server to operate these backend components. We utilized webhooks, Rasa as a server, and text form submissions to get a response. The Bot we developed is a fun-fact bot that is trained on Amazon's topical chat dataset and can give amusing information on about 250 subjects grouped into 8 categories. Using our data collection, we trained a Rasa-supported transformer-based model and added a few DM-specific behaviors'. NLG relies heavily on context and history, which are backed by Specific rules and goals. After selecting the answer, we send the test response to the client. We convert Text-To-Speech on the client using gTTS, a Python package created by Google to transform text to voice. After the text has been translated to voice, it is stored in the file and played using a typical mpg player. This concludes one round of discourse.

Rasa Framework: In this study, a dialogue-based System was built utilizing the Rasa framework. Rasa is an open-source framework for creating conversational artificial intelligence systems, such as chatbots and virtual assistants. It provides a set of tools and frameworks for creating and deploying bespoke conversational models using machine learning methods. Rasa is equipped with a natural language comprehension module that extracts meaning from text, a conversation management module that selects the next course of action depending on the current situation, and a natural language production module that creates suitable replies. Several components of the Rasa Framework are discussed below:

Intent categorization and entity recognition are performed by DIET (Dual Intent and Entity Transformer) classifier. Prior to DIET, Rasa utilizes a bag of words approach with one feature vector per user message. DIET learns quicker than large-scale language models and performs similarly. It outperforms BERT after fine-tuning on a complicated NLU dataset.

TED Policy: Based on the discussion context, user input, and preset task, the dialogue management system of Rasa applies the TED policy to select the model's next action. Models and pipelines for intent identification, entity extraction, and response creation are pre-built in Rasa.

We used the Topical-Chat dataset. It is a collection of human-human talks based on knowledge. The subject chat data set is a collection of data pertaining to talks between two or more individuals discussing a certain topic. The data sets were gathered from internet message boards, chat rooms, and other text-based sources. Topical-Chat basically comprises of two sorts of files: (1) Conversation Files - .json files that include a chat between two Amazon Mechanical Turk employees (also known as Turkers) (2) Set File Reading - they are. A Turker is provided Json files containing knowledge chunks from many data sources (Wikipedia, Reddit, and the Washington Post) to read and refer to during conversation.

4 Results

We trained our Rasa-based model using data from trending chats. In the JSON files, the topical chat data contains numerous discussions on a given subject. The Rasa framework is very flexible and can handle a variety of use cases. For our tests, we chose to develop a conversational AI system based on interesting facts. Our work is available on github here https://github.com/umeshgtank/Funfact_bot. Trained model is also available, and you can reproduce the same results by just executing 'rasa run –connector rest –enable-api' command and running the client script (you need to install rasa for this to work).

After training the bot using Topical-chat data, we may ask a variety of inquiries on around 250 topics, and the bot will respond with interesting trivia about those entities. The entity is structured into eight major subject areas.

We could ask:
"Give me some information on football"
The bot will produce one of the domain's replies.
Moreover, we may inquire
"Tell me more" and

The bot can remember the context and will give further interesting information about the current subject. Below example demonstrates the context awareness ability of the bot. You can see our query to the bot and when asked "Tell me more" bot was aware of the context (Mars in our case) and gives out a new fun fact based on the context.

You said: tell me something about Mars.
Response: **a Mars colonization project planned for 2023 will be funded by creating a reality TV show.**

You said: tell me more.
Response: **a Satellite was lost on Mars because Locheed Martin used the Imperial system while NASA used the metric system.**

The chatbot is also able to generalize the questions even if not trained on the specific question format. In the below example, model was not trained on "I would like to know about…" but was trained on "Tell me something about Mars" and "What do you know about Mars?". Despite that model is able to generalize on conversations like – "I would like to know about Mars"

```
{  'alternative': [  {  'confidence': 0.92190772,
                   'transcript': 'I would like to know about Mars'},
               {'transcript': 'I would like to know more about Mars'}, ..], 'final': True}
```

You said: I would like to know about Mars
Response If you fly to mars under constant 1g acceleration it will only take 2 or 3 days

We separated the data into train and test in order to assess the model. After training the model, we applied it to test data.

Rasa permits testing of NLU and core (dialogue management). We tested the complete system, and the findings were recorded according to "Intent categorization". For your intent classification model, the Rasa test script will output a report, confusion matrix, and confidence histogram. The Rasa also captures stories which are failed and identified incorrectly. The reports are also generated for stories. Challenges encountered Our implementation may encounter some of the difficulties stated in the restriction sections, such as "producing repetitious and generic utterances and missing common sense". This behavior is noticed when our system is unable to accurately identify intent, causing it to lose context as well (Fig. 2).

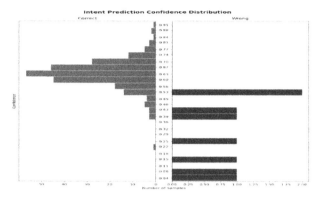

Fig. 2. Intent graph

5 Discussion

While dialogue-based systems have the potential to be successful, they are limited by a number of challenges and limits. In this section, we'll discuss a few of these hurdles and restrictions. Some of these limits may be circumvented by the use of other alternatives. The vast majority of workarounds are handmade or manual. Even though powerful frameworks like as Rasa and many others exist, NLP still needs human design. Due to the availability of sophisticated frameworks and tools, building a bot may be straightforward, according to our study. Despite this, creating a good NLP application is still complex, requires human input, and must be built manually. In addition, we have noticed that data collection is not standardized. Many organizations acquire and arrange their data in a number of ways. To train our model, we needed to convert the data into a format that Rasa can comprehend. A few of applications have been developed to convert Topical data to Rasa format. In addition, we need to manually alter a piece of the text owing to a few exceptional occurrences. Inaccurate replies to user queries resulted from errors in intent categorization. The model must be adjusted accordingly. In the assessment report, the Rasa framework provides information about erroneously identified objectives. In some instances, physical involvement is also required throughout the process of fine-tuning. Due to the difficulty and complexity of creating test data in the absence of real users, training the NLU model presents an additional challenge. For our experiments, we manually created test data from the data sets, with some data enhanced by scripts. Visible dialogue is an intriguing new subfield of conversational AI that poses new research challenges. Visual conversation has the potential to allow a number of new and useful applications in fields such as the assistance of individuals with visual impairment and, more broadly, applications requiring intelligent scene perception. There are several datasets that can be used to train conversation systems, however there are still challenges with training data. This is particularly true for task-oriented systems, for which the collection of data for new application domains would be costly and time-consuming. Attempting to employ data from a different domain is one option. A second technique involves training the algorithm with limited data. A conversation system should have access to real-world facts in order to respond effectively to a person's questions or concerns. Early-stage conversation systems were primarily concerned with providing high-quality replies, as measured by metrics such as Sensibleness and Specificity. Google's Knowledge Graph, which was unveiled in 2012, has more than 500 billion information about 5 billion entities extracted from the World Wide Web and a number of open-source and licensed databases. It is also used in businesses to store information and connections inside the organization and to automate the response to inquiries. To participate in cooperative conduct, an intelligent dialogue system must be able to reason about its own and its conversational partner's behavior. This involves the capacity to deduce the intentions of the other individual and react appropriately. These difficulties were addressed in early work on plan-based discourse. Many issues complicate the research of conversation systems, such as how to refer to entities and things and the capacity to notice subject transitions and choose new subjects. How to participate in multiparty talks, how to process information sequentially, and how to organize turn-taking in dialogue. The process of identifying the proper entity is referred to as entity linking. There are several methods to make references to entities inside a text or conversation. Anaphoric reference varies from co-reference in that it indicates when an entity that was previously mentioned is referenced to using an anaphoric term such as a pronoun. Participants in an open-domain chat are allowed to discuss a variety of topics. Effective participation in a discussion requires the capacity to recognize subjects addressed by the other participant. In addition to being able to monitor subjects and provide appropriate comments, a participant should also be able to select whether to stay on the same topic or switch to another. Multi-party communication is a discussion between many persons and a dialogue system, including robots, avatars, and multiple human players. It may also include scenarios with several users interacting with a smart speaker. Identifying who is being addressed, determining who is actively engaging, determining who is the speaker, managing turn-taking, and differentiating between numerous themes and multiple dialogues are all challenges that arise in multiparty interaction. Incremental processing in conversation While dealing with a dialogue system, it is often feasible for the user to pause the output by stopping the conversation agent. This instructs the system to cease speaking and await input from the user. This This operation is not possible on the system. Instead, it waits until the system believes the user has finished speaking (indicated by silence). This is referred to as endpoint detection and it is crucial when switching chats. Human-to-human discussions, on the other hand, are distinct in that speakers often anticipate and absorb information in stages. How will the opposing party respond? By showing words as they are detected without waiting for the user to complete speaking, newer versions of Google Voice Search employ the incremental speech process. In addition to step-by-step processing of material, discussion participants often intervene with a Finish into continuing statements. In fact, in one corpus of discussions, roughly one in five rounds entailed finishing a sentence. Co-production is a common term. Nevertheless, the implementation of incremental processing is technically challenging, particularly in a pipeline design where the output of one component is not transferred to the next until it is complete. Exist in a system with incremental processing, the data must be partly processed and must consequently be altered. Following output. Taking turns in conversation Current spoken conversation systems are inflexible with regard to turn-taking. The system waits until it detects a period of quiet that exceeds a specified threshold before concluding that the user has done speaking; however, the user may intervene at any point to terminate the system's output. Participants in human-to-human talks carefully watch current turns to foresee their likely termination points, also known as transition-relative locations, in order to make the system more realistic. This is particularly crucial when interacting with social bots and avatars that exhibit human-like behavior. In March 2016, Microsoft released the chatbot Tay for 16 h before shutting it down. Tay discovered that he had sent an inflammatory tweet via the tweets of other Twitter users. Due to the experience of researchers in conversational artificial intelligence, individuals are aware of the hazards of dialogue systems and learn incorrect conduct through their interactions with users. Additional difficulties include the distortion of data used by machine learning algorithms, the production of false news, and the provision of incorrect or unsuitable recommendations. As a positive development, researchers are now working on AI. Seeking to develop safer, better-behaving conversational AI models for the sake of society. Dialog systems offered on publicly accessible platforms must be able to process a broad range of inputs. There are rude and unsuitable inputs in addition to inputs that are technically challenging. The advanced frameworks and tools make use of state-of-the-art algorithms, such as transformers, BLSTM, etc., and they also provide a structure that enables researchers and developers to apply various types of algorithms and strategies, such as combining rule-based and neural network-based algorithms. With these frameworks, we may construct a vast array of conversation systems. Modern systems perform astoundingly well when it comes to detecting an intent or object, thanks to the use of cutting-edge algorithms. Particularly when there is a substantial quantity of training data available. As indicated in the restriction sections, despite all these developments, current dialogue-based systems still need human intervention when a precise answer is required, and it still faces a number of additional obstacles due to the complexity of human translation.

6   Conclusion

The advanced frameworks and tools take advantage of state-of-the-art algorithms, such as transformers, BLSTM, etc. and they also provide a structure which helps researcher and developers to apply different types of algorithms and strategies, such as combining rule-based along with neural network-based algorithms. Using these frameworks, we can build wide varieties of dialogue systems. With the help of state-of-the-art algorithms, modern systems perform amazingly well when it comes to identifying an intent or entity. Especially, when a good amount of training data is available. Despite all these advancements, as we have noted in the limitation sections, the modern dialogue-based systems still need handcrafting when we need precise response, and it still suffers from a number of other challenges since human conversion is complex.

References

1. Khatri, C., et al.: Advancing the state of the art in open domain dialog systems through the Alexa prize. arXiv preprint arXiv:1812.10757 (2018)

2. Green Jr., B.F., Wolf, A.K., Chomsky, C., Laughery, K.: Baseball: an automatic question-answerer. In: Papers Presented at the May 9–11, 1961, Western Joint IRE-AIEE-ACM Computer Conference, pp. 219–224 (1961)
3. Winograd, T.: Understanding natural language. Cogn. Psychol. **3**(1), 1–191 (1972)
4. Bobrow, D.G., Kaplan, R.M., Kay, M., Norman, D.A., Thompson, H., Winograd, T.: Gus, a frame-driven dialog system. Artif. Intell. **8**(2), 155–173 (1977)
5. Grice, H.P.: Logic and conversation. In: Speech Acts, pp. 41–58. Brill (1975)
6. Austin, J.L.: How to Do Things with Words. Oxford University Press, Oxford (1975)
7. Searle, J.R., Searle, J.R.: Speech Acts: An Essay in the Philosophy of Language, vol. 626. Cambridge University Press, Cambridge (1969)
8. Weizenbaum, J.: Eliza—a computer program for the study of natural language communication between man and machine. Commun. ACM **9**(1), 36–45 (1966)
9. Turing, A.M.: Computing machinery and intelligence. In: Epstein, R., Roberts, G., Beber, G. (eds.) Parsing the Turing Test, pp. 23–65. Springer, Dordrecht (2009). https://doi.org/10.1007/978-1-4020-6710-5_3
10. Adiwardana, D., et al.: Towards a human-like open-domain chatbot. arXiv preprint arXiv:2001.09977 (2020)
11. Roller, S., et al.: Recipes for building an open-domain chatbot. arXiv preprint arXiv:2004.13637 (2020)
12. Vaswani, A., et al.: Attention is all you need. arXiv (2017)
13. Devlin, J., Chang, M.-W., Lee, K., Toutanova, K.: BERT: pre-training of deep bidirectional transformers for language understanding. arXiv (2018)
14. Hochreiter, S., Schmidhuber, J.: Long short-term memory. Neural Comput. **9**(8), 1735–1780 (1997)
15. Sharma, R.K., Joshi, M.: An analytical study and review of open source chatbot framework. RASA. Int. J. Eng. Res **9**(06), 1011–1014 (2020)
16. Astuti, W., Putri, D.P.I., Wibawa, A.P., Salim, Y., Ghosh, A., et al.: Predicting frequently asked questions (FAQs) on the COVID-19 chatbot using the DIET classifier. In 2021 3rd East Indonesia Conference on Computer and Information Technology (EIConCIT), pp. 25–29 (2021)
17. Shawar, B.A., Atwell, E.S.: Using corpora in machine-learning chatbot systems. Int. J. Corpus Linguist. **10**(4), 489–516 (2005)
18. Gottardi, A., et al.: Alexa, let's work together: introducing the first Alexa prize taskbot challenge on conversational task assistance. arXiv preprint arXiv:2209.06321 (2022)
19. University of Glasgow. Grillbot: A flexible conversational agent for solving complex real-world tasks. In: Alexa Prize TaskBot Challenge Proceedings (2022)
20. Antony, D., et al.: A survey of advanced methods for efficient text summarization. In: 2023 IEEE 13th Annual Computing and Communication Workshop and Conference (CCWC), pp. 0962–0968 (2023)

Co-clustering Based Methods and Their Significance for Recommender Systems

Naresh Kumar[1] and Merlin Sheeba[2](✉)

[1] CSE Department, Sathyabama Institute of Science and Technology, Chennai, India
[2] Department of ECE, Jerusalem College of Engineering, Chennai, India
merlisheebu@gmail.com

Abstract. In the contemporary era, businesses are driven by Internet based web or mobile applications. In every conceivable area of research, it is indispensable for such applications to have a recommender system to expedite the interactions between customers and business entity for faster convergence. Provided this fact, there is need for leveraging such systems as they have unprecedented impact on businesses across the globe. In this regard, identification of merits and demerits in the existing methods used to realize recommender systems is to be given paramount importance. In this paper, we review literature to ascertain useful facts pertaining to different approaches to make recommender systems. Since recommender systems lubricate the process of commercial or otherwise interactions with consumers, for business entities it is imperative to have applications with built-in recommender system. The literature review made in this paper provides different aspects of recommender systems such as datasets, methods and their utility in the current business scenarios. It throws light into the research gaps that help in further research and improvement based on novel data mining approaches.

Keywords: Recommender systems · co-clustering · collaborative filtering methods · content based filtering methods · top-n recommendations

1 Introduction

Clustering is an unsupervised method that makes use of distance measures for grouping data instances. It has plenty of real world applications like credit card fraud detection. However, it considers grouping of instances based on rows only. It does mean that it misses some more useful information in clustering process. In order to overcome this, many co-clustering methods came into existence. Such methods simultaneously perform clusters on rows and columns as discussed in [1–3]. Recommender systems on the other hand are useful in generating recommendations in applications like e-commerce to promote business by helping customers to take decisions faster. From the literature it is understood that recommender systems can be made using clustering approaches and co-clustering as well. Keuper et al. [1] proposed correlation co-clustering method for tracking multiple objects and motion segmentation. Huang et al. [2] explored co-clustering methods and proposed a multi-view co-clustering method that exploits bipartite graphs. Huang et al. [3] proposed a spectral co-clustering algorithm as spectral

R. Morusupalli et al. (Eds.): MIWAI 2023, LNAI 14078, pp. 513–522, 2023.
https://doi.org/10.1007/978-3-031-36402-0_48

co-clustering ensemble (SCCE). Wang et al. [4] proposed a data-driven approach that combines interpretable machine learning and co-clustering for disease prediction in healthcare domain. Salah and Nadif [5] proposed a novel approach known as directional co-clustering. They developed many Expectation Maximization (EM) methods based on it to estimate specific data distributions. Huang et al. [6] proposed a novel co- clustering model known as "Constraint co-Projections for Semi-Supervised Co-Clustering (CPSSCC)" which makes use of pairwise constraints and projections of constraints in order to achieve semi-supervised approach in clustering. There are other approaches found in the literature such as ensemble approach [13] known as spectral co-clustering ensemble (SCCE). Wang et al. [4] proposed a data-driven approach that combines inter-pretable machine learning and co-clustering for disease prediction in healthcare domain. Salah and Nadif [5] proposed a novel approach known as directional co-clustering. They developed many Expectation Maximization (EM) methods based on it to estimate spe-cific data distributions. Huang et al. [6] proposed a novel co- clustering model known as "Constraint co-Projections for Semi-Supervised Co-Clustering (CPSSCC)" which makes use of pairwise constraints and projections of constraints in order to achieve semi-supervised approach in clustering. There are other approaches found in the liter-ature such as ensemble approach [13], graph based clustering [15], triclustering [16], spectral clustering [17], traffic clustering [18], clustering for network anomaly detec-tion [21], clustering with robust metrics [23], high-order clustering [24], CluEstar [26], semi-supervised clustering [27] and sequential data modelling [30]. There are many different clustering algorithms, and no single best method for all datasets. Essentially clustering is an unsupervised learning method that often saves time and effort in data mining operations.

Co-clustering is data mining technique which allows simultaneous clustering of the rows and columns of a matrix. Our contributions in this paper are as follows.

1. Review of literature and identification of merits and demerits of existing methods used for recommender systems.
2. Comparison of different recommender systems which provides knowhow on various approaches.
3. Summarizing important research gaps that help in conducting further research in this potential area.

The remainder of the paper is structured as follows. Section 2 focuses on automated recommender systems covering collaborative filtering and content based filtering meth-ods. Section 3 presents many kinds of co-clustering methods. Section 4 provides the summary of findings from the co-clustering literature. Section 5 presents the datasets widely used for co-clustering. Section 6 presents the research gaps identified while Sect. 7 concludes the paper and gives directions for possible future scope of the research.

2   Automated Recommender Systems

This section throws light on two different categories of automated recommender systems namely collaborative filtering and content based filtering.

2.1   Collaborative Filtering

The recommender systems that exploit collaborative filtering generate recommendations based on known ratings of similar users as explored in [31]. Due to emergence of Internet based technologies and databases, collaborative filtering assumes more significance over content based approach [34]. It is widely used by recommender systems in the real world. It can generate predictions automatically and also use preferences of other users in a collaborating setting. It considers the preferences of the user in question and other users as well while generating recommendations. Indirectly it can find like-minded users and based on their preferences recommendations are made.

2.2   Content Based Filtering

As the name implies, this approach is used to generate recommendations based on user preferences and content of the items as studied in [32] and [33]. It is also widely used in recommender systems in many real world applications. It not only uses description of items in the data but also preferences of user. It is suitable when there is known data pertaining to given item. It does not need data from other users in order to generate recommendations. Moreover, it generates recommendations that are highly related to user and meets user intent. Recommendations generated by this kind of filtering are transparent to user with high openness.

3   Co-clustering Approaches

Most of the data in the real world is stored and maintained in relational model proposed by Dr. E. F. Codd. Co-clustering is the approach that concurrently performs clustering of rows and columns. It is also known as Bi-clustering. Keuper et al. [1] proposed correlation co-clustering method for tracking multiple objects and motion segmentation. With FBMS59 benchmark dataset, their empirical study revealed superior performance of their method over existing ones. Huang et al. [3] proposed a spectral co-clustering algorithm known as spectral co-clustering ensemble (SCCE). It supports simultaneous clustering with ensemble of row and column clustering for generating optimal results. It is the novelty of the algorithm unlike traditional clustering methods. Spectral approach is used for co-clustering. In future, they intend to improve it using diversity of labels towards co-clustering ensemble.

Wang et al. [4] proposed a data-driven approach that combines interpretable machine learning and co-clustering for disease prediction in healthcare domain. It makes use of feature clusters and patient clusters in parallel leading to group based feature selection and group specific predictive model. Their method showed better performance when clubbed with different prediction models while finding high risk patients. Salah and

Nadif [5] proposed a novel approach known as directional co- clustering. They developed many Expectation Maximization (EM) methods based on it to estimate specific data distributions. It results in most-relevant clusters leading improved business intelligence. Many real world datasets are used towards empirical study. Their method showed better performance over many predecessors. They intended to investigate a strategy in future to determine number of co-clusters automatically.

3.1 Semi-supervised Clustering

Huang et al. [6] proposed a novel co-clustering model known as "Constraint co-Projections for Semi-Supervised Co-Clustering (CPSSCC)" which makes use of pair-wise constraints and projections of constraints in order to achieve semi-supervised approach in clustering. They map the problem of co-clustering to typical eigen-probem for improving efficiency in solving real world clustering problems. CPSSCC is found to have some good features that do not have with state of the art methods. However, they intend to leverage with an improve approach towards selection of constraints.

3.2 Nonnegative Matrix Factorization

Non-Negative Matrix Factorization (NMF) is a clustering method that is widely used in data mining applications. Sun et al. [7] proposed a co-clustering method based on NMF. It is known as "sparse dual graph-regularized nonnegative matrix factorization (SDGNMF)". It can represent non-negative data with linear representation and parts based approach. SDGNMF jointly makes use of sparseness constraints and dual graph based approaches. Their approach is evaluated with image clustering. The prior label information available in the graphs help to encode the latent discriminative and geometrical structures found in the data distribution. As sparseness constraints are exploited, their method improves the learning of tasks. It also could reduce the dimensions in the image data.

3.3 Unsupervised Harmonic Co-clustering

Lu et al. [8] present harmonic co-clustering method that is based on unsupervised approach. Their method is capable of finding groups and sub-groups of cells based on similarity in abhor morphologies. It makes use of a novel diffusion distance measure to make this method more efficient in achieving co-clustering. It also exploits carefully selected distance measures and smoothing mechanisms in order to have robust detection of hidden patterns. The diffusion metric is found to be suitable for working with similarities among objects while performing co-clustering. It also combines the diffusion metric with harmonic analysis theory and wavelet transforms. The output is the co-clusters that with cluster representation to bring about quality in clustering.

3.4 Distributed Co-clustering Framework

Distributed computing has paved way for seamless connectivity of servers for improving computations with many benefits like scalability and availability. Cheng et al. [9] proposed a distributed co-clustering framework with alternate minimization co-clustering

(AMCC) algorithms that are essentially improved variants of EM methods. The co-clustering supports sequential updates in a distributed environment. Thus the framework can help many sources of inputs to be part of the system. When compared with traditional algorithms AMCC is found to have faster convergence. Wang et al. [10] also investigated co-clustering in distributed environment. They proposed a collaborative co-clustering approach towards this end. It gets multiple views from different sources of data to perform simultaneous co-clustering. Discrimination is followed to differentiate and process sources of data as it is in the form of different views. In order to unify features matrix and relationships matrix a co-regularization mechanism with constraints is introduced. They used two different social media data a sources of inputs and evaluated the collaborative co-clustering method.

3.5 Co-clustering Based on Feature Co-shrinking

With inter-correlations among features multi-way feature selection is more complex in nature. As it is a challenging phenomenon, Tan et al. [11] developed a proposed a co-clustering model based on feature co-shrinking. It also makes use of co-sparsity regularization and matrix tri-factorization models to achieve the co-clustering with feature co-shrinking. The ideal behind this is to learn inter- correlations from multi-way feature and reduce them by removing irrelevant features. Their proposed algorithm solves a non-smooth optimization problem. Different benchmark datasets are used in order to evaluate their method. NMI is the metric used to evaluate performance of their method.

3.6 Goal Oriented Co-clustering

When there are multiple goals in co-clustering mechanism, it is essential to consider the goals while performing clustering. There are many problems in existing co-clustering methods. When multiple goals are used, they are not able to fine relevant features. They also lack knowhow on using user given information. There is also problem with utilization of many features to have better representation of goals. There was inability to generate multiple co-clusters concurrently. Other issues in existing methods include difficulty in finding location based information, problems with spectral and subspace learning, capturing goal using seed feature expansion. These challenges are overcome with the proposed goal oriented co-clustering. The full goal oriented model proposed by Wang et al. [12] proposed a goal oriented co-clustering for overcoming aforementioned drawbacks using social networks dataset. Their method considers selected feature clusters and generate co- clusters. The features are data goal generated ones based on user inputs.

3.7 Bipartite Graphs for Co-clustering

Huang et al. [2] explored co-clustering methods and proposed a multi-view co-clustering method that exploits bipartite graphs. It considers the samples and features in the dataset and makes use of the graphs to perform multi-view co-clustering that results in guaranteed convergence. They intended to improve it using semi-supervised learning and kernel learning in future. Xu et al. [14] also use bipartite graphs for co-clustering. Their method is known as interactive visual co-clustering. They make use of tree maps and adjacency matrices for visual encoding of clusters. They used case studies to evaluate real world data with co-clustering and interactive visualization. Their investigation found the importance of visualizing co-clusters in an interactive fashion. In future, they intend to explore multimode graphs to generate and visualize co-clustering results.

Tachaiya et al. [19] proposed a clustering approach that supports cluster visualization. It is named as RThread as it is thread centric and visualizes the clusters in security domain for improving security. It also helps in identification interesting clusters that are useful to security Qian et al. [20] proposed several approaches that make use of multi-view related data for clustering. Maximum entropy clustering approach is used for exploiting inter-view and intra-view correlations concurrently. It is a collaborative multi-view approach for the aforementioned clustering process. Its makes use of clustering ensemble of views so as to improve clustering performance. In future, they intended to improve it using weighted view fusion approach. Mio et al. [28] focused on multi view generation and multi-view learning procedures to have clustering optimization. It makes use of unsupervised feature partitioning approach to make clustering decisions. It makes use of dual-space approach but can be improved further for other situations. Ma et al. [29] proposed a clustering method known as "Robust Multi-View Continuous Subspace Clustering (RMVCSC)". It improves clustering performance with the help of a continuous objective. As it makes use of multiple views and each view can represent different perspective, the clustering needs continuous objective function that improves optimization in clustering. It also has continuous learning to detect and remove outliers that obstruct quality in clustering.

3.8   Co-clustering of Big Data

Big data is the data that is very huge and keep growing besides having different data formats. Yan [22] proposed a methodology for co-clustering of big data. The researcher also explored co- clustering of 2D and 3D data. The data is essentially a multi-dimensional data used for empirical study. Co-clustering also helps in simultaneous classifications that provide more useful patterns from the data. From the empirical data, the research could find different possibilities with co-clustering including pre-processing to larger applications like recommendation systems. Chehreghani and Chehreghani [25] investigated on learning representations from data associated with dendrograms. They proposed a generalized framework for realizing such representations using different distance metrics. They employed co-clustering approach towards making such representations. They found that their method is effective in handling large volume of data for co-clustering.

4   Summary of Findings

This section presents the summary of findings from different co-clustering methods that have been reviewed in the preceding section.

Table 1. Summary of findings on co-clustering methods

Ref	Technique	Merits	Limitations	Remarks
Keuper et al. [1]	Correlation Co-Clustering	Multiple object tracking and motion segmentation	Needs further improvement in quality of clusters	FBMS59 and MOT 2015 benchmark are used
Huang et al. [2]	Multi-view co-clustering	Guaranteed convergence, effectiveness in clustering	Semi-supervised and kernel learnings are yet to be incorporated	Bipartite graphs are used as datasets
Huang et al. [3]	Spectral co-clustering	Effective metrics and ensemble for performance improvement	Labelling for co-cluster ensemble is yet to be done	MSRA-MM and UCI datasets
Wang et al. [4]	Integrated co-clustering	Disease prediction, effective decision making	Needs improvements to deal with large volumes of data	Clinical dataset
Salah and Nadif [5]	Directional co-clustering	Faster convergence	Parameter estimation is yet to be done	DT2, SPORTS, NG20, CLASSIC4, WEBACE and CSTR
Huang [6]	Semi-supervised co- clustering	Has more favourable features	Needs to improve constraints selection	MSRA-MM and real world dataset
Sun et al. [7]	Image co-clustering	Provides convergence proofs, high accuracy	Data representation needs to be improved	PIE-pose27, COIL20 and ORL-32
Lu et al. [8]	Harmonic co-clustering	Groupings and sub-groupings are meaningful	Refinement in measures needed	Synthetic datasets
Cheng et al. [9]	Data co-clustering	Works in distributed environment, faster convergence	Needs cloud based environment	UCI datasets

(continued)

Table 1. (*continued*)

Ref	Technique	Merits	Limitations	Remarks
Wang et al. [10]	Collaborative co-clustering	Supports multiple data sources, improves performance	Feature selection for multi-view sources is to be done	Reuters Multilingual dataset, WebKB and Cornell dataset

As presented in Table 1, the summary of different co-clustering methods that are existing are provided. They have advantages and limitations and used different datasets. It provides the methods with their merits and demerits at a glance.

5 Datasets

Plenty of datasets used for co-clustering are found in the literature. Keuper et al. [1] explored co- clustering using datasets such as FBMS59, PASCAL VOC 2012 and MOT 2015 benchmark datasets. Huang et al. [2] used several benchmark datasets in the form of bipartite graphs for experimental study on co-clustering. Huang et al. [3] studied spectral co-clustering approach using MSRA-MM dataset and other 10 benchmark datasets such as secom, hvwnt, kdd99sub, credit, hepatitis, semeion, breast, spectheart and sonar collected from UCI machine learning repository. Wang et al. [4] focused on cl-clustering along with machine learning integration by using datasets such as clinical dataset containing EHRs in healthcare domain. Salah and Nadif [5] evaluated their directional co-clustering using datasets like TDT2, SPORTS, NG20, CLASSIC4, WEBACE and CSTR. Huang [6] proposed semi-supervised co-clustering and evaluated them using datasets like MSRA-MM and real world datasets like tr41, tr31, tr23, tr12, re0, mm, k1b, k1a and cranmed. Sun et al. [7] investigated on image co-clustering and used benchmark datasets such as PIE-pose27, COIL20 and ORL-32. Lu et al. [8] studied harmonic co-clustering with datasets such as synthetic datasets. Cheng et al. [9] investigated co-clustering and evaluated it with datasets collected from UCI. Wang et al. [10] explored collaborative co-clustering and used datasets such as Reuters Multilingual dataset, WebKB and Cornell dataset.

6 Research Gaps

Clustering is an unsupervised problem of finding natural groups in the feature space of input data. There are many different clustering algorithms, and no single best method for all datasets. Essentially clustering is an unsupervised learning method that often saves time and effort in data mining operations. Co-clustering is data mining technique which allows simultaneous clustering of the rows and columns of a matrix. From the literature, it is understood that there are specific problems with recommender systems that are widely used in the contemporary era. Especially healthcare recommendations play vital role in different applications associated with the domain. The recommender systems in [35] and

[36] take care of co-clustering to enhance the performance of recommender systems. However, there are certain aspects to be enhanced. First, there is lack of consideration for short and long term preferences of users to generate more useful recommendations using co-clustering. Second, there is no adaptive user modelling that leverages performance of recommender systems with co-clustering. Third, there is problem of finding top-n recommendations so as to improve the recommender system performance using co-clustering. Moreover, there is abundant need for adapting the recommender systems to healthcare data so as to improve recommender systems to meet requirements of healthcare units in the real world.

7 Conclusion and Future Wor

In this paper, we review literature to ascertain useful facts pertaining to different approaches to make recommender systems. Since recommender systems lubricate the process of commercial or otherwise interactions with consumers, for business entities it is imperative to have applications with built-in recommender system. The literature review made in this paper provides different aspects of recommender systems such as datasets, methods and their utility in the current business scenarios. The review focused on different kinds of co-clustering to meet different requirements such as visualization, distributed data sources, multi-view scenarios and so on. From the review of literature, it is understood that co-clustering can be improved to build recommender systems. Finally, this paper throws light into the research gaps that help in further research and improvement based on novel data mining approaches. In future we intend to improve co-clustering for proposing an efficient healthcare recommender system.

References

1. Keuper, M., Tang, S., Andres, B., Brox, T., Schiele, B.: Motion segmentation & multiple object tracking by correlation co-clustering. IEEE Trans. Pattern Anal. Mach. Intell. **42**, 1–13 (2018)
2. Huang, S., Xu, Z., Tsang, I.W., Kang, Z.: Auto-weighted multi-view co-clustering with bipartite graphs. Inf. Sci. **512**, 1–21 (2019)
3. Huang, S., Wang, H., Li, D., Yang, Y., Li, T.: Spectral co-clustering ensemble. Knowl. Based Syst. **84**, 46–55 (2015)
4. Wang, H., Huang, Z., Zhang, D., Arief, J., Lyu, T., Tian, J.: Integrating co-clustering and interpretable machine learning for the prediction of intravenous immunoglobulin resistance in kawasaki disease. IEEE Access **8**, 97064–97071 (2020)
5. Salah, A., Nadif, M.: Directional co-clustering. Adv. Data Anal. Classif. **13**(3), 591–620 (2018). https://doi.org/10.1007/s11634-018-0323-4
6. Huang, S., Wang, H., Li, T., Yang, Y., Li, T.: Constraint co-projections for semi- supervised co-clustering. IEEE Trans. Cybern. **11**(4), 1–12 (2016)
7. Sun, J., Wang, Z., Sun, F., Li, H.: Sparse dual graph-regularized NMF for image co-clustering. Neurocomputing **316**, 156–165 (2018)
8. Lu, Y., Carin, L., Coifman, R., Shain, W., Roysam, B.: Quantitative arbor analytics: unsupervised harmonic co-clustering of populations of brain cell arbors based on L-measure. Neuroinformatics **13**, 1–17 (2014)

9. Cheng, X., Su, S., Gao, L., Yin, J.: Co-ClusterD: a distributed framework for data co-clustering with sequential updates. IEEE Trans. Knowl. Data Eng. **27**(12), 3231–3244 (2015)
10. Wang, F., Lin, S., Yu, P.S.: Collaborative co-clustering across multiple social media. In: 2016 17th IEEE International Conference on Mobile Data Management (MDM), pp. 142–151 (2016)
11. Tan, Q., Yang, P., He, J.: Feature co-shrinking for co-clustering, pp. 1–24 (2017)
12. Wang, F., Wang, G., Lin, S., Yu, P.S.: Concurrent goal-oriented co-clustering generation in social networks. In: Proceedings of the 2015 IEEE 9th International Conference on Semantic Computing (IEEE ICSC 2015), pp. 1–8 (2015)
13. Binh, L.T.C., Nha, P.V., Long, N.T., Long, P.T.: A new ensemble approach for hyper-spectral image segmentation. In: 2018 5th NAFOSTED Conference on Information and Computer Science (NICS), pp. 1–6 (2018)
14. Xu, P., Cao, N., Qu, H., Stasko, J.: Interactive visual co-cluster analysis of bipartite graphs. In: 2016 IEEE Pacific Visualization Symposium (PacificVis), pp. 1–8 (2016)
15. Skabar, A.: Clustering mixed-attribute data using random walk. Procedia Comput. Sci. **108**, 988–997 (2017)
16. Narmadha, N., Rathipriya, R.: Triclustering: an evolution of clustering, pp. 1–4. IEEE (2016)
17. Papp, D., Szucs, G., Knoll, Z.: Machine preparation for human labelling of hierarchical train sets by spectral clustering. In: 2019 10th IEEE International Conference on Cognitive Infocommunications (CogInfoCom), pp. 000157–000162 (2019)
18. Yamansavascilar, B., Guvensan, M.A., Yavuz, A.G., Karsligil, M.E.: Application identification via network traffic classification. In: 2017 International Conference on Computing, Networking and Communications (ICNC), pp. 1–6 (2017)
19. Tachaiya, J., Gharibshah, J., Papalexakis, E.E., Faloutsos, M.: RThread: a thread-centric analysis of security forums, pp. 1–5. IEEE (2020)
20. Qian, P., et al.: Multi-view maximum entropy clustering by jointly leveraging inter-view collaborations and intra- view-weighted attributes. IEEE Access **6**, 28594–28610 (2018)
21. Ahmed, M., Naser Mahmood, A., Hu, J.: A survey of network anomaly detection techniques. J. Netw. Comput. Appl. **60**, 19–31 (2016)
22. Yan, H.: Coclustering of multidimensional big data, pp. 23–30. IEEE (2017)
23. Patterson-Cross, R.B., Levine, A.J., Menon, V.: Selecting single cell clustering parameter values using subsampling-based robustness metrics. BMC Bioinform. **22**, 1–13 (2021)
24. Bu, F.: A high-order clustering algorithm based on dropout deep learning for heterogeneous data in cyber-physical-social systems. IEEE Access **6**, 11687–11693 (2018)

Machine Learning and Fuzzy Logic Based Intelligent Algorithm for Energy Efficient Routing in Wireless Sensor Networks

Sagar Mekala$^{(\boxtimes)}$ (iD), A. Mallareddy (iD), Rama Rao Tandu (iD), and Konduru Radhika

Department of CSE, CVR College of Engineering, Hyderabad, Telangana, India
arjunnannahi5@hotmail.com

Abstract. Energy efficiency is a crucial factor in wireless sensor networks and helps in driving the network for long time. The basic approach to increase energy efficiency is routing through clustering. With this approach, many clusters of sensor nodes in the network region are formed, and a cluster head (CH) is selected for every cluster. This CH receives data packets from the cluster's non-CH members and sends the data it has gathered to the base station (BS). But, after some transmissions, the CH can run out of energy. In this paper, we thus offer the Energy-efficient regression and Fuzzy based intelligent routing algorithm for Heterogeneous Wireless Sensor Network (HWSN). The Fine Cluster Head (FCH) has been chosen using the fuzzy inference system out of the selected CHs. Finally, the CH transfer the data gathered from the non-CH member to the chosen FCH. The hop-count from CHs to the FCH evaluated to build this effective route. Our simulation findings demonstrate that, in terms of Energy Efficiency, Packet Delivery Ratio, and Throughput, over without intelligence, and with regression models outperform the work currently being done.

Keywords: Regression · Fine Cluster Head (FCH) · Energy Efficiency · hop-count · Fuzzy Logic

1 Introduction

The recent advantages of Internet of Things (IoT) based apps have transformed people's lifestyle choices. Several of these IoT-based applications require excellent data communication and need to be able to precisely the node's position and location. The WSN, which allows numerous uses and permits the actively connecting of sensors to the network, is the essential element of IoT [1, 6]. There are hundreds of thousands of nodes in the WSN, and each node has the ability to connect with the base station (BS) or one another. It is crucial to have a routing plan for necessary communication between devices. Routing refers to the path that these sensors take to transfer the data to its BS. Every node comes with a battery with a restricted capacity at first. The nodes' energy is depleted as the data transmission continues. Hence, reducing energy consumption is the main obstacle to routing in WSN. Building communication channels between the WSN nodes and the BS is the goal of routing protocols. To overcome the WSN routing difficulty, a few energy-efficient routing techniques have been created [2].

© The Author(s), under exclusive license to Springer Nature Switzerland AG 2023
R. Morusupalli et al. (Eds.): MIWAI 2023, LNAI 14078, pp. 523–533, 2023.
https://doi.org/10.1007/978-3-031-36402-0_49

The rising need for integrating different IoT power-saving techniques has been crucial for tiny devices to implement energy efficient Internet of Things, which has increased the lifespan of gadgets. Compared to reception and idleness, more energy is lost during the distribution of wireless technologies. Energy conservation has become a crucial for communication in sensor networks. Algorithms based on artificial intelligence are appropriate. In this paper, we address energy-efficient communication tactics that draw on AI-based algorithms [4, 5] in tandem with the desire to lengthen device lifespans, and we thoroughly examine the condition of the most recent network energy-saving innovations. Future research should support the development of optimal AI algorithms as well as various methods for integrating these algorithms into WSNs [3]. The most of the results discussed here now use AI techniques to address distinct, constrained issues in select fields. Incompatibility between layers and heavy human contact are the main causes of difficulties. Self-adaptively is necessary for formulating and fine-tuning solutions. It is necessary to build hybrid strategies that maximize the exploitation of resources in WSN. A possible future avenue is the use of AI optimization techniques to tackle WSN difficulties. Several research issues, including as communication delay, balancing battery consumption, reliability, and Security of WSNs, are still largely unanswered. In the future, AI should be used with other optimization strategies. While optimizing WSNs, the cross-layer optimization model issues need to be handled more effectively. Future solutions to these issues may be further improved with the use of the findings from the study of biological traits connected to humans [4]. Future study might focus on the distributed and real-time use of lightweight algorithms to address the issues with dynamic MWSNs. In this paper we discuss energy-efficient communication strategies that use Artificial Intelligence based algorithms combined with the drive to increase the lifespan of devices and analyze the current state of the latest Internet energy-saving things in detail. Efficient routing is one of the crucial methods for extending the system lifetime in WSNs [5].

The ideal CH has the most neighbor nodes, the biggest amount of leftover energy, and is the closest to the BS. Yet, the selected cluster head can run out of energy after a few broadcasts. We introduce the Energy-efficient SoftMax Regression (SMR) and Fuzzy Logic based cluster heads with hop-count based routing for HWSN to address major problems. The contribution of this work is outlined in the next section.

- Cluster formation and head election performed using SoftMax Regression.
- According to the Fuzzy Logic, Fine Cluster Head (FCH) selected among CHs in the deployed nodes.
- Hop-count based shortest route to BS through CH and FCH is established.
- The proposed approach simulation results are compared with Without-Computational Intelligence routing, and With Regression routing.

The remainder of this article is structured as follows. Next section examines some earlier writings that examined fuzzy based routing in WSN. In Sect. 3, we present our suggested Energy-efficient Regression and Fuzzy-based Intelligence routing for WSN. The experiment findings of our suggested strategy are discussed in Sect. 4. Section 5 serves as the article conclusion.

2 Related Works

WSN research has become more active over time, and several initiatives have been carried out to enhance lifespan wireless sensor networks. Several surveys have been done based on various aspects to address the issues of WSN. Some recent research and demonstrated how recognizing the difficulties of WSN might improve energy efficiency. According to the survey, the majority of the currently utilized methodologies are based on simulations and generally targeted at static WSNs. Most literature cover the topic of bio-inspired computing's application to intelligent WSN optimization [3, 11]. They also discussed the use of hybrid Computing Intelligence (CI) techniques to some of the issues related to non-biological systems [4, 11]. Bello O et al. [5], present a thorough overview of Swam Intelligence (SI) based routing algorithms for WSN. They contrasted several Swam Intelligence based routing protocols to highlight the benefits and drawbacks of each method. The most well-known artificial intelligence schemes covered in this article include Ant Colony Optimization (ACO) [12], Bacterial Forging Optimization (BFO) [3], Particle Swarm Optimization (PSO) [14], Ant Bee Colony (ABC) [15], and many more. Authors in [8] claimed that ACO-based approaches perform better in network routing due to their lower overheads and real-time calculation capabilities. Researchers should thus come up with hybrid versions. In addition, they used Spider Monkey Optimization to offer a cluster-based strategy for routing in WSN. It enhances decision-making, uses less resource, and is appropriate for dealing with WSN problems including routing, data aggregation, security, localization, and deployment [6, 7].

Hamzah et al. [10] Fuzzy Logic (FL) may easily put up with inaccurate or unreliable readings. They promoted it as a simpler and more effective method. The drawback of this method is that storing takes a significant amount of additional memory, and when the number of variables rises, the number of rules also rises. They demonstrated how the FL technique may address the problems with the majority of algorithms. Since this strategy is dependent on rules and requires continual rule traversal, it might cause the technique for event discovery and recommendation to be slowed down. Constraints on energy, storage, communication, and computing capability present a significant obstacle to routing in WSNs [8, 17]. As a result, routing algorithms for WSNs should be simple, need little communication overhead, and be effective, scalable, and able to operate for an extended period of time. To carry out efficient WSN clustering, a multi-objective, distributed technique based on fuzzy theory is suggested. This multi-objective clustering approach attempts to address the issues of energy holes and hot spots in both stationary and developing WSNs. By appropriately adjusting the cluster radius based on three criteria, an energy dissipation balance is attained. For a WSN suggested adaptive fuzzy based clustering method, this protocol uses fuzzy to create clusters, to choose optimal CHs based on inputs such as number of nodes, distance to the BS, remaining energy, and distance from the cluster centroid. The fuzzy rules were appropriately tuned using the artificial bee colony algorithm (ABC), as opposed to manually updating the fuzzy rule basis table, designed to increase WSN lifetime in accordance with application requirements, the fitness function. It offers an adaptive, energy-efficient, and dependable routing strategy based on FL that takes into account transmission dependability, node-to-node communication delay, and energy efficiency. Hai et al. [9], proposed a fuzzy clustering strategy to acquire the clustering outcomes using a mathematical model, and it makes advantage of the FL's effectiveness to carry out CH selection in clusters. The suggested FL-based clustering system uses five basic criteria to choose the CH - the amount of energy still in the node, its compactness, its distance from the BS, its density, and its average local energy consumption [13, 16]. To quantify energy efficiency in terms of an algorithm's capacity and to achieve balanced energy usage the Gini index is used. As compared to existing methods, evaluation results show that the methodology has maximized energy efficiency and WSN lifespan.

3 Proposed Methodology

The Multiple Input - Multiple Output (MIMO) approach is a type of wireless technology that transmits multiple data streams simultaneously. The MIMO technique is crucial for 4G LTE, and 5G networks. Sensor Networks has encountered from challenges including often modifying the network architecture and congestion problems which influence bandwidth use. As a result, a new strategy is needed to improve data transmission and reduce latency. We present the Machine Learning and Fuzzy Logic based intelligent routing technique and its framework presented in Fig. 1. Initially, each deployed node energy is calculated based on the following method.

The proposed approach is provided as a system model, number of sensor nodes ($SN_i = SN_1, SN_3, SN_4, ...SN_n$) are deployed ($n * n$) area, and within the transmission range (TR). Devices are placed randomly and accumulate data from the deployed area, gathered data packets ($dpj = dp1, ..., dpm$) are forward to BS in energy-efficient manner. The regression analysis is a machine learning approaches to determine the relationship among dependent and independent variables. The proposed approach accomplishes the route categorization among devices (i.e., features). The sensor node characteristics are observed using the regression method (i.e., energy). The energy level is computed for each sensor node. Battery level is obtained as the product of node active time and power utilized, and all devices have a comparable battery level at the beginning of the sensing process.

$$E_{ni} = power(ni) * activeTime(ni)$$

Joules are used to measure "power(ni)" and seconds are used to measure "active Time" (sec). The power of the device is calculated in joules (J). Throughout the wireless network's detecting operation, the sensor's energy level decreases. As a result, the node's remaining energy is calculated as

$$E_{rem} = E_{ni} - ConsumedEnergy(ni)$$

The proposed method's regression analysis looks at the anticipated node battery level and identifies the battery efficient nodes. The logistic function is simplified to several dimensions using regression analysis. The sensor node output is categorized using it as the activation function according to the probability distribution of the expected output classes.

Average Distance - The mean distance between each device to clusters and BS, from the CH should be kept to a minimum to improve the nodes' energy efficiency. Hence,

$$E_{ni} = power(ni) * activeTime(ni)$$

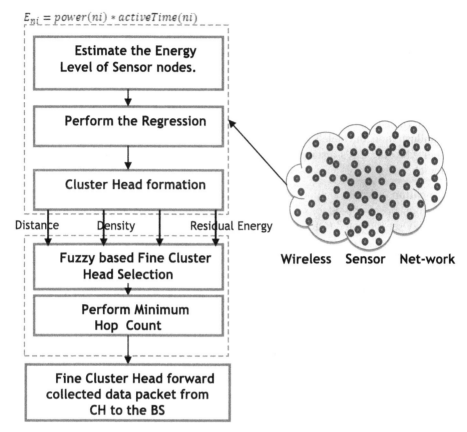

Fig. 1. Framework of Proposed MLFR based Routing Approach

the main goal of effective cluster head selection is to minimize the average device to cluster and BS distance of all the Clusters.

Residual Energy - The total remaining battery power of all CHs should be increased to choose the remarkable CH. Therefore, the last two functions are to decrease the reciprocal of the total remaining battery power of all to be chosen Clusters.

One Fine Cluster Head (FCH) is chosen from the selected cluster heads (CHs) once the CHs have been chosen. The data packet is forwarded to the base station by this FCH after being received from all CHs. The network's longevity and energy efficiency will be increased by using this FCH. Fuzzy Inference System is demonstrated for FCH selection. To choose the FCH, a fuzzy inference system is developed using the Mamdani model. The four steps of a fuzzy inference system are as follows.

Fuzzy variables - Fuzzy parameters Crisp input values are transformed into fuzzy variables, such as Near, Medium, and Far for distance to BS, and High, Medium, and Low for the fuzzy parameter of Clusters remaining battery power. Each fuzzy variable has a membership function established for it. The probability of choosing the FCH is one of this system's output parameters. The probability of being chosen as FCH is greater for the chance with a larger value. We use the trapezoidal and triangular membership function in our strategy, which produces good outcomes. After that, by sending the request and reply to messages, the route path between the source and BS is discovered. For effective routing, the shortest path is used.

Rules of If-Then - To achieve the fuzzy set out, the fuzzy variables are subjected to an if-then condition. These rules include the fuzzy operator and numerous inputs (AND). For each rule, a minimum of three membership values are chosen using this operator. As an illustration, the table's If-then rule is given as follows. If the CH's residual energy is high AND the CH's distance from the BS is short, the FCH choice output will be extremely large.

Aggregation - All the outputs obtained from all If-then rules are combined into this. Fuzzy logic operator used for selecting the highest rule probable outcomes, a new aggregate fuzzy set is created (OR). **Defuzzification -** The technique of defuzzification uses the accumulated fuzzy outcome set as an input to determine likelihood of selecting FCH. The Center of Gravity approach (COG) is employed for defuzzification. With this approach, we can take the input of fuzzy sets and produce a single crisp value.

Minimum Hop Count - An effective routing path among the devices and the BS will be built when the CHs and FCH have been successfully chosen. To choose the best path, a neighbors-based routing method is provided. In this method, each CH maintains its neighbor list with the data of other CHs and sends a HELLO message to its nearby CHs. The hop-count to the FCH is included in this HELLO beacon. The successive neighbor (hop) node or CH is chosen as the CH with the lowest intermediate node count (hop-count) value.

Where, min (hop-count) represents the least intermediate node count required for the neighbor CH to reach the BS. The minimum intermediate node count of neighbouring CHs in an equation is increased by one since CH hop count to its neighbor CH equals 1. Once a node receives a HELLO packet, new arrivals will be added to the Neighbour List (NL) of CHi and sorted in increasing order. Afterwards, the CH with the fewest intermediate node count is chosen to be the next CH, to transfer the data packet it has gathered device to the FCH. The following is a presentation of an intelligent routing algorithm based on machine learning and fuzzy logic.

Algorithm 1: *Regression and Fuzzy Logic based intelligence routing algorithm.*

Input: *Heterogeneous Wireless Sensor Network (HWSN) consist of N sensor nodes n_1, n_2, n_3, ..., ni and Base Station (BS) deployed into $n \times n$.*

Output: *Energy Efficient Routing among deployed nodes.*

1.   for each node in N
2.   Calculate node REN (n_i)   // to estimate node remaining energy
3.   Estimate SMR (REN (n_i)) //to obtain softmax regression value
4.   if SMR > 0.8 then:
5.   Node n_i can participate in CH selection.
6.   Append(n_i) to CH list.
7.   else
8.   Node n_i not energy efficient
9.   for each CH in CH List:
10.   Calculate REN(CH_i), Distance to BS.
11.   Estimate FL(CH_i) to find the Fine Cluster Head (FCH).
12.   Create the route path among CHs and FCH to BS.
13. CH_i can forward RREQ to BS through FCH.
14.   BS can transmit RREP to CH_i through FCH.
15.   Update the route paths.
16.   Attain the strong route path results.

---

4   Results and Discussions

The proposed Machine Learning and Fuzzy logic-based intelligent Routing (MLFR) algorithm implemented and evaluated using network simulator NS2. In this simulator 50, 150, 200, 250, 350, 400, 450, and 550 sensor nodes are conducted in the range 1000 m × 1000 m. Each device in the deployed area operates with a 0.66 W transmission power and a 0.395 W reception power. Each sensor node's transmission range is 50 m. In this study, the AODV routing protocol is employed. The proposed and parallel schemes performance is measured with different settings, the simulation and evaluation analysis of our model MLFR scheme and parallel schemes such as without computational Intelligence (WOI) model, and With Regression (WR) model values are discussed with three different metrics, they are throughput, packet delivery rate, and energy efficiency. The data from the source node is then gathered by a CH in a cluster. The source node transmits data to its associated CH, by deciding on the most effective path based on hop-count, the CH's acquired data are sent to the chosen FCH. The FCH then transmits the gathered data to the BS. The performance of FCHs are evaluated chosen utilizing our suggested fuzzy inference system from among the chosen CHs. The following measures are used to assess how well our suggested method performs. Performance indicators for our suggested strategy The MLFR is contrasted with the without AI (WOI) model, and With ML (WR) model values.

Packet Delivery Rate - It is the proportion between the number of packets successfully received and the overall number of packets delivered. The number of packets lost during data transmission is known as a packet drop. The number of packets lost during data transmission is known as a packet drop.

Package Delay - The network's latency indicates how long it takes for a bit to be sent to its destination. This parameter's unit is seconds (s).

Throughput - It refers to the volume of data that may be transmitted per second from sources to destinations. This parameter's unit is Mbps. Overhead - Amount of additional bytes that were added to the data packet as overhead to transmit the data.

Energy Consumption - The amount of battery power used during transmission by each node. Moreover, it is described as the difference between a node's original and current energy. This parameter's unit is the Joule (J).

Energy-Efficiency, Throughput, and Packet Delivery Ratio metrics of WSN, the proposed method MLFR is compared with WOI routing, and WR routing. Among these three approaches the proposed MLFR algorithm significantly increases the Packet Delivery Ratio, Throughput, and Energy-Efficiency even increasing the number of nodes in the area. Due to the efficient resource utilization, cluster formation, and route selection the energy efficiency of the MLFR scheme using 150 devices is 94.17%, while routing without Intelligence and only with regression is obtained as 80.4%, and 88.2% respectively. Similarly, the packet delivery ratio of the MLFR scheme for 150 devices is 91.9%, while routing without Intelligence and only with regression is obtained as 83.4%, and 88.2% respectively. Likewise, the throughput of the MLFR scheme using 150 devices is 96.2%, while routing without Intelligence and only with regression is obtained as 92.6%, and 91.2% respectively. Various Packet Delivery Ratio, Throughput, and Energy-Efficiency outcomes are observed by increasing number of nodes in the deployed area shown in Table 1, and Fig. 2.

Table 1. Proposed MLFR Model Simulations results compared with parallel research.

No of Nodes	Energy Efficiency (%)			Throughput (bps)			Packet Delivery Ratio (%)		
	WOI	*WR*	*MLFR*	*WOI*	*WR*	*MLFR*	*WOI*	*WR*	*MLFR*
50	72	76	85.2	67	82	133	79.21	86.16	89.03
150	80.41	88.2	98.17	140	170	195	80.4	88.2	91.9
200	80.92	88.76	98.12	205	222	267	81.90	90.43	93.05
250	81.38	89.1	98.7	255	286	311	83.04	90.78	94.26
300	83.2	89.9	98.02	324	340	376	84.8	92.5	94.90
350	86.16	92.4	98.4	384	405	442	87.09	95.97	98.18
400	87.2	92.6	98.65	440	482	510	91.9	96.08	98.68
450	87.92	94.32	98.1	510	560	572	92.1	97.4	98.9
550	89.61	92.45	98.47	573	633	664	94.23	97.9	99.12

Let assume 150 sensor nodes in deployed area, each node of a cluster is prevented from transmitting data to the destination independently by delivering effective cluster head and FCH selection utilizing the regression and fuzzy based algorithm. As a result, the packet delivery ratio of the MLFR is higher than the previous without intelligence and with regression by 12% and 4%, respectively. The network's throughput is enhanced by choosing the fine cluster heads among the cluster heads using a fuzzy logic algorithm, which increases the quantity of data that must be transferred from node to BS per second. The throughput of MLFR is enhanced to 28% and 12%, respectively, compared to the parallel research outcomes without intelligence (WOI) and with regression (WR). As per CHs, FCHs, and an efficient route utilize in our proposed MLFR, the network's energy consumption is decreased, hence increasing the network's energy efficiency. As a result, the energy efficiency of the MLFR is higher than that of the parallel research outcomes without intelligence (WOI) and with regression (WR) by 18% and 10%, respectively.

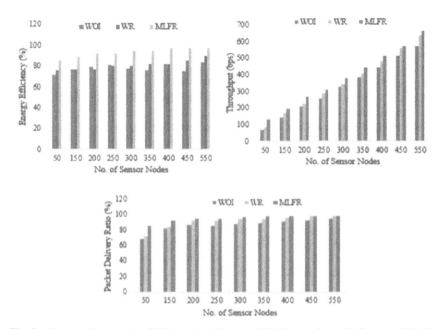

Fig. 2. Comparative results of Without Intelligence, With Regression with Proposed MLFR.

5 Conclusion

The Energy-efficient Machine Learning and Fuzzy logic based Fine Clustering and minimum hop-count Routing (MLFR) is presented for WSN in this work. CHs are chosen based on residual energy of sensor nodes using the SoftMax regression (ML) method. The remaining sensor nodes within its communication range are joined with chosen CHs to form a cluster. The Fine Cluster Head (FCH) has been chosen using the fuzzy inference system out of the selected CHs. Finally, the CH transfer the data gathered from the non-CH member to the chosen FCH. The hop-count from CHs to the FCH evaluated to build this effective route. Energy efficiency of the proposed MLFR algorithm has been assessed and compared to other parallel algorithms like Without Intelligence (WOI) and With Regression (WR) techniques. The proposed MLFR algorithm performed better in terms of Energy Efficiency, Packet Delivery Ratio, and Throughput. The findings of the simulation demonstrated that the proposed approach's energy efficiency and delivery ratio were better than those of the previous studies. When FCH are not accessible for specific CH, MLFR algorithm fundamental drawback is that it is useless for route finding and data forwarding. Additionally, it is not capable of creating Quality of Service (QoS) aware discovery schedules for a variety of duty cycles among CHs. It is a difficult challenge to solve; therefore we will take it into consideration for our future efforts.

References

1. Mekala, S., Chatrapati, K.S.: Present state-of-the-art of continuous neighbor discovery in asynchronous wireless sensor networks. EAI Endors. Trans. Energy Web **8**(33) (2021)
2. Mekala, S., Shahu Chatrapati, K.: A hybrid approach to neighbour discovery in wireless sensor networks. Intell. Autom. Soft Comput. **35**(1) (2023)
3. Mekala, S., Shahu Chatrapati, K.: Energy-efficient neighbor discovery using bacterial foraging optimization (BFO) algorithm for directional wireless sensor networks. In: Gopi, E.S. (ed.) Machine Learning, Deep Learning and Computational Intelligence for Wireless Communication. LNEE, vol. 749, pp. 93–107. Springer, Singapore (2021). https://doi.org/10.1007/978-981-16-0289-4_7
4. Goswami, P., et al.: Ai based energy efficient routing protocol for intelligent transportation system. IEEE Trans. Intell. Transp. Syst. **23**(2), 1670–1679 (2022). https://doi.org/10.1109/TITS.2021.3107527
5. Bello, O., Holzmann, J., Yaqoob, T., Teodoriu, C.: Application of artificial intelligence methods in drilling system design and operations: a review of the state of the art. J. Artif. Intell. Soft Comput. Res. **5**(2), 121–139 (2017). https://doi.org/10.1515/jaiscr-2015-0024
6. Chaudhry, R., Tapaswi, S., Kumar, N.: Fz enabled multi-objective pso for multicasting in IoT based wireless sensor networks. Inf. Sci. **498**(3), 1–20 (2019). https://doi.org/10.1016/j.ins.2019.05.002
7. Dorri, A., Kanhere, S.S., Jurdak, R.: Multi-agent systems: a survey. IEEE. Access **6**, 28573–28593 (2018). https://doi.org/10.1109/ACCESS.2018.2831228
8. Fanian, F., Rafsanjani, M.K.: A new fuzzy multi-hop clustering protocol with automatic rule tuning for wireless sensor networks. Appl. Soft Comput. **89**(11), 106115 (2020). https://doi.org/10.1016/j.asoc.2020.106115
9. Hai, D.T., Son, L.H., Vinh, T.L.: Novel fuzzy clustering scheme for 3D wireless sensor networks. Appl. Soft Comput. **54**(2), 141–149 (2017). https://doi.org/10.1016/j.asoc.2017.01.021
10. Hamzah, A., Shurman, M., Al-Jarrah, O., Taqieddin, E.: Energy-efficient fuzzy-logic-based clustering technique for hierarchical routing protocols in wireless sensor networks. Sensors **19**(3), 561 (2019). https://doi.org/10.3390/s19030561
11. Jabbar, W.A., Saad, W.K., Ismail, M.: Meqsaolsrv: a multicriteria-based hybrid multipath protocol for energy-efficient and QoS-aware data routing in manet-WSN convergence scenarios of IoT. IEEE Access **6**, 76546–76572 (2018). https://doi.org/10.1109/ACCESS.2018.2882853

12. Zhang, T., Chen, G., Zeng, Q., Song, G., Li, C., Duan, H.: Seamless clustering multi-hop routing protocol based on improved artificial bee colony algorithm. EURASIP J. Wirel. Commun. Netw. **2020**(1), 1–20 (2020). https://doi.org/10.1186/s13638-020-01691-8
13. Yu, X., Liu, Q., Liu, Y., Hu, M., Zhang, K., Xiao, R.: Uneven clustering routing algorithm based on glowworm swarm optimization. Ad Hoc Netw. **93**(3), 101923 (2019). https://doi.org/10.1016/j.adhoc.2019.101923
14. Yang, J., Liu, F., cao, J.: Greedy discrete particle swarm optimization based routing protocol for cluster-based wireless sensor networks. J. Ambient. Intell. Humaniz. Comput. **41**(7), 1–16 (2017). https://doi.org/10.1007/s12652-017-0515-3
15. Yang, X.-S.: Bat algorithm: literature review and applications. ArXiv preprint (2013). https://doi.org/10.48550/arXiv.1308.3900
16. Wang, C., Liu, X., Hu, H., Han, Y., Yao, M.: Energy-efficient and load-balanced clustering routing protocol for wireless sensor networks using a chaotic genetic algorithm. IEEE Access **8**, 158082–158096 (2020). https://doi.org/10.1109/ACCESS.2020.3020158
17. Verma, A., Kumar, S., Gautam, P.R., Rashid, T., Kumar, A.: Fuzzy logic based effective clustering of homogeneous wireless sensor networks for mobile sink. IEEE Sens. J. **20**(10), 5615–5623 (2020). https://doi.org/10.1109/JSEN.2020.2969697

Sentiment Analysis of Twitter Data on 'The Agnipath Yojana'

Vamsi Krishna Mulukutla$^{(\boxtimes)}$ (ID), Sai Supriya Pavarala (ID), Vinay Kumar Kareti (ID), Sujan Midatani (ID), and Sridevi Bonthu (ID)

Computer Science and Engineering Department, Vishnu Institute of Technology, Bhimavaram, Andhra Pradesh, India
{21pa1a05a3,21pa1a05do,21pa1a0574,21pa1a05a2,
sridevi.b}@vishnu.edu.in

Abstract. On June 14, 2022, India's government introduced "The Agnipath Recruitment Scheme" to allow Indian youth, called Agniveers, to serve in the armed forces for a four-year tenure. This scheme has been criticized for the lack of consultation and public debate. Democratic institutions must know the opinion of the public as it signals the public's preferences. This paper proposes a framework for determining the sentiment of the comments posted by the public. The comments related to our scheme are extracted from the Twitter platform with related tags. The sentiment identification for the cleaned comments is performed with the help of the Valence Aware Dictionary for Sentiment Reasoning technique. A base-line model is created by training Multinomial Naïve Bayes and RoBERTa models on the data. RoBERTa model has achieved a precision of 84% on the data. This work also performs topic modeling using the LDA algorithm to determine the most important vocabulary used in comments.

Keywords: Agnipath Scheme · Twitter · Sentiment Analysis · Naïve Bayes Classifier · Natural Language Toolkit · VADER · Topic Modeling

1 Introduction

The usage of social media is tremendously increasing, and analyzing social media content is gaining popularity [1]. People are expressing their views without any hesitation on the popular social media platforms such as Twitter, Facebook, and Instagram, etc. An analysis of these huge comments can give a clear picture of people's thoughts about a topic.

Every country's government takes several initiatives for the benefit of the nation. Some initiatives will be more beneficial than others, and a few of them may not reach the public. A system that collects and analyzes public opinion from social media is useful. This paper proposes a framework that leverages the content available on social media to extract the opinions of the public. To create and test a framework, we have taken an Indian government initiative titled "AGNIPATH".

© The Author(s), under exclusive license to Springer Nature Switzerland AG 2023
R. Morusupalli et al. (Eds.): MIWAI 2023, LNAI 14078, pp. 534–542, 2023.
https://doi.org/10.1007/978-3-031-36402-0_50

1.1 Agnipath Scheme

Now-a-days, every country is shedding light on defense-oriented training for young people with the aim of strengthening national security [2]. Of late, India saw a massive protest from the public on the sector of the Defense Force Recruitment System [3]. On June 14, 2022, India's Government launched a new regimental recruitment process called the "AGNIPATH YOJANA". This scheme paved a new way of joining the inspired youth of India, who want to serve the nation via the Defense Force. The Armed Forces of India include the Indian Navy, the Indian Air Force, and the Indian Army.

The after-benefits of this Yojana incorporate a financial package of about Rs. 12 lakh, which provides a head start in their lives [4]. Priority under bank loan schemes is provided for those who wish to be entrepreneurs. Class 12 equivalent certificates and bridge course certificates of requested subjects are provided to those that desire to continue their study. Additionally, for those who would like to work, priorities are provided in the Central Armed Police Forces (CAPF), Assam Rifles, and Police Allied Forces of several states.

However, the above benefits exclude any pension or health-insurance scheme, which were available in the previous recruitment process. This triggered an insecure feeling in the new recruits. Furthermore, the decision to replace the old recruitment process with the Agnipath Scheme was made by the Government of India without consulting the public. This caused protests and riots by the people, calling for the government to withdraw or modify the new recruitment process.

In this paper, we intend to analyze the *emotional level response* of the mob in view of this Yojana. The data we used for the analysis consists of comments under posts on the "Agnipath Scheme" across Twitter. Twitter is an online social media platform and social networking service, owned by an American company, Twitter Inc., on which various users post images and interact with others. Twitter used to have a count of 11.5 Million Indian users by 2013 and a drastic change is seen as the number raised to 34 million by 2019. Twitter is one of the most studied social media platforms by researchers in data science [5]. People can post text messages by extensively using hashtags, retweets, @mentions, etc. Twitter is considered a great source of data for the researchers studying the attitudes, beliefs, and behavior of consumers and opinion makers [6, 7]. Due to this massive usage, we have considered our collection of data that of Twitter.

Since this Yojana (scheme) has been criticized and has mass protest, we assume that the outcome of this analysis would be that the negative comments (Hating or Protest against the scheme) out-number the positive ones (Supporting and Accepting), while the neutral comments tend to be a majority.

The analysis done for extracting opinion from the comments would be classified as 'The Sentiment Analysis'. For this task, we followed MSD Boddapati et al., [8] and used lexicon-based Sentiment Analysis NLTK module that classifies the word data into emotions of negative, neutral, and positive.

We have also performed the process of 'Topic Modelling' via a generative statistical model that segregates a parameterized category count of most frequent words in the entire document. The crucial contributions of this work are

1. The assignment of Sentiment polarities to the English and English-translated Hindi tweets.

2. Summarizes the response of the public toward the Agnipath Scheme.
3. Helps the government to propose wise commitments in the future.

2 Methodology

The work mainly focuses on extracting the relevant tweets, assigning sentiment to them, and performing topic modeling. This work also trains a few baseline models on the labeled data. The entire architecture followed is shown in Fig. 1.

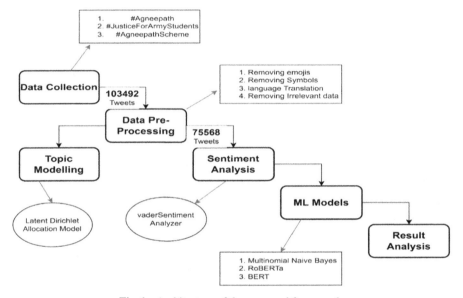

Fig. 1. Architecture of the proposed framework

2.1 Data Collection

The entire work is done on the collection of text data of tweets from the social media 'Twitter'. A twitter account is created to access the tweets of various people under a plethora of posts related to the 'Agnipath Yojana'. We were able to extract the tweets of various users with the help of Python's scraper modules such as *snsscrape*[1]. These modules handle the twitter API well and retrieve necessary information such as tweets, date & timestamp of tweet posts, etc. Tweets for the duration of six months from the initial launch of the scheme are extracted (June 2022 to December 2022). For the process of retrieval, hashtags are used as search parameters. The various hashtags utilized are *#agnipathscheme, #justiceforarmystudents, #agnipath* etc. The total number of extracted tweets are 103492 as shown in Table 1.

---

[1] https://pypi.org/project/snscrape/.

The results of extraction are available in the form of the tweet content along with date-timestamp of the user's posting. Since, we are primarily concerned with content of the tweet, we removed the column pertaining to the date-time. The extracted twitter data now contains only the text value of the tweet and it is stored in a CSV file format.

Table 1. Month-wise statistics of the extracted tweets

S.No.	Month	No.of Tweets
1	June	7382
2	July	32758
3	August	13007
4	September	7445
5	October	3367
6	November	6248
7	December	33162
	Total Tweets	**103492**

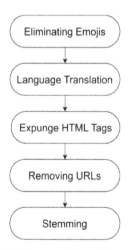

Fig. 2. Preprocessing of the tweets

The extracted data has many nonsensical values, noise and unrefined information. Example of one of the extracted tweet is *"@thinker 😅 😅 With What faced did #Arvin-dKejriwal, who fully supports #NarendraModi's anti-people armed foces recruitment scheme #agnipath #agniveer go bgging for votes in Rajasthan, where youths oppose it?"*. As the tweets come from different people, the language varies along many ways. Thus, raw extracted data can neither be used for analysis nor training a model or algorithm. The nonsensical values include different languages (Non-english), symbols, links and emojis. This noise data is rectified by applying the techniques listed in Fig. 2.

Table 2. Tweet before and after cleaning

	Tweet
Before Cleaning	@thinker 😜😜 With What faced did #ArvindKejriwal, who fully supports #NarendraModi's anti-people armed foces recruitment scheme #agnipath #agniveer go bgging for votes in Rajasthan, where youths oppose it?
After Cleaning	With What faced did who fully supports anti-people armed forces recruitment scheme #agnipath go begging for votes in Rajasthan where youths oppose it

Tweets with languages void of english are translated back to english via Google Translate function. With the help of various text pre-processing modules, we rectify the noise present in the data. With the support of powerful regular expression functions of python, we alter the data to retain information only with alpha-numeric values. As the next step, we deal with words in data. Stemming of data refers to the process of rounding words to the nearest English word, which may or may not make sense. Using powerful NLTK preprocessing text modules, we achieve our format. A raw before and after cleaning is presented in Table 2. The result is a cleaned CSV data file.

2.2 Sentiment Identification

Table 3. Statistics of month-wise tweets on *Agnipath* yojana after identifying the sentiment with Vader sentiment analyzer algorithm.

S.No.	Month	Sentiment			Total
		Positive	Negative	Neutral	
1	June	606	1618	4894	7118
2	July	1461	3688	22042	27191
3	August	720	2470	4937	8127
4	September	459	750	2538	3747
5	October	181	313	1253	1747
6	November	421	679	3069	4169
7	December	1277	2470	19902	23649
8	Total	**5125**	**11988**	**58635**	**75568**

For the Sentiment Analysis, we put the comment data through the SentimentIntensityAnalyser of the vaderSentiment Module[2]. VADER is an acronym that stands for Valance Aware Dictionary and sEntiment Reasoner. It is a lexicon and rule-based tool

---

[2] https://pypi.org/project/vaderSentiment/.

that is exclusively trained to perform the sentiment analysis of the social media comment data [9]. VaderSentiment class utilizes words of the dictionary which signify a particular emotion and this enables it to classify the comment (text) data into classes of Positive, Negative and Neutral Sentiments. Words such as support, stand with, appreciated, agree with, get along etc. enable the module to check whether the text has a positive-level response and words such as disagree, justice, protest, against, etc.... particularly signify a negative emotion for a sentence. Due to these features, we have utilized this algorithm.

With the help of this module, we create a dictionary with keys 'neg', 'neu', 'pos', 'compound' and their respective values. These values are the probabilities that represent a statement's sentiment. It fundamentally finds the ratio of negative, neutral and positive words present in a statement to a predefined set of words (lexicon-based).

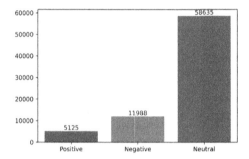

Fig. 3. Statistics of the identified sentiments

With the help of vaderSentiment, we have assigned a new column called "Target". This column consists of numbers belonging to set $\{-1, 0, 1\}$ where -1 represents that the corresponding tweet is a statement of negative sentiment, 0 indicating a neutral comment and 1 showing a positive tweet. This "Target" column has the labels for the corresponding "Tweet" column which makes the labelled data. This data acts as a classified reference for the Sentiment Analysis. Consider the temporal variation in sentiment analysis Month-wise results presented in Table 3. Specifically, the tweet count exhibited a noticeable fluctuation over the course of several months, with July having the highest count of 27191 tweets, and October having the lowest count of 1747 tweets. It is worth noting that this fluctuation is closely associated with external events in the physical world. Figure 3 presents the statistics of the assigned sentiment. Majority of the tweets are classified as neutral by the sentiment analyzer.

2.3 Topic Modeling

Topic modelling is a procedure of statistical text analysis that helps the user to find the necessary abstract information from a dataset. One of such topic modelling techniques is Latent Dirichlet Allocation (LDA) [10, 11]. It is used to classify text in a document to a particular topic. It builds a topic for document model and words for topic model, modelled as Dirichlet Distributions. We utilized this algorithm in comparison, as this can allocate probabilities to a word in the document which is more efficient, than the rest.

Only pre-processed data is suitable for Topic Modelling. The preprocessing involves performing Lemmatization which is the rectification of deprecated words in a document. The tweet data is read, and the recurring words are displayed for each tweet.

We made use of LDA Algorithm to perform topic modelling on the data and the result is presented in Fig. 4. This figure defines a set of topics, each of which is characterized by a distribution of words that most likely occurred in our extracted tweet data corpus. This modelling approach provide insights on emotions, attitude and opinions expressed in our data. We observe that term "supportagnipath" has the highest frequency, while terms like "student" and "right" has less repetitions.

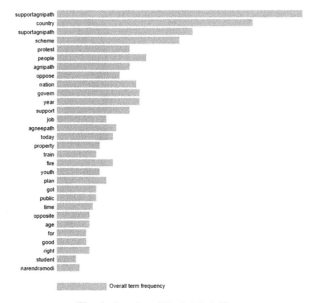

Fig. 4. Results of Topic Modelling

After the classification of the tweets, we come up with a baseline model that does prediction for the labelled Tweet data. This model should be used on Tweet text data on posts of Agnipath scheme. Since the main motto of this analysis lies in the classification of the tweet data into segments of sentiments i.e. negative, neutral and positive, we used a Multinomial Naïve Bayes Classifier (Multinomial NB Classifier) [12] from 'sklearn' library. Multinomial NB classifier is suitable for classification with discrete features. We split our data into training and testing batches and fit it to our model. We made sure to train our model with appropriate data by the removal of stopwords while fitting. Finally we calculated performance evaluation metrics for the model.

The model returns predicted labels with which we found the training data accuracy. After training the model and finding its accuracy, we have sent the split-test data to the model. The process of prediction repeats with the test data as well and the model returns the predicted label data. With this, we found the test data accuracy. We also took advantage of two pre-trained language models namely, BERT [13] and RoBERTa [14], for the purpose of twitter data classification. Unlike a general model, these can be used without a ML training process and hence are convenient to utilize. We tested our tweet data via these models and calculated their performance evaluation metrics such as F1_score, Precision and Recall as the data is unbalanced [15].

3   Results

In this paper, we study and examine Twitter's Tweet data on posts related to the Agnipath Scheme. We extracted and preprocessed the tweet data and performed sentiment identification with the help of vaderSentiment analysis. Table 3 and Fig. 3 presents the details of assigned sentiment. 36% of the tweets were made at the initial days of scheme launch (July, 2022) and 31% of the tweets were made in the month of December, 2022. We have observed that most people show neutral sentiment/emotion towards this scheme. Among the rest sentiment options, people displayed more negative emotion in comparison with positive. Out of all the tweets, 6% belong to positive category, 16% belong to negative, and 77% of the tweets carry neutral sentiment.

Table 4. Performance on the baseline models

S.No.	Model_Name	Precision	Recall	F1_Score
1	Naïve Bayes	0.64	0.5	0.64
2	BERT	0.79	0.64	0.79
3	RoBERTa	**0.84**	0.63	**0.84**

A general Multinomial Naive Bayes Model and pretrained models like RoBERTa and BERT models are employed to train a baseline model on the obtained data. Table 4 presents the performance of the three models. As the data is highly imbalanced, we have calculated Precision, Recall and F1-Score and the accuracy is not taken into account. The RoBERTa model generalized well with 84% of F1_score. The results can be improved my augmenting the data [16].

4   Conclusion and Future Work

This work proposes a framework that identifies the public sentiment and opinion toward the recently released scheme titled "Agnipath Yojana" by India's government. More than 1 lakh people posted their opinions on a popular social media platform such as Twitter. This work extracted and cleaned the tweets. Sentiment identification and topic modeling were performed on the extracted tweets. The majority of the public expressed neutral or negative feelings. Very few expressed their positive sentiments toward this scheme. We assume that due to the lack of appropriate public propaganda, the concept of this scheme was not well received, resulting in the rise of negative sentiment over positive. Three baseline models such as Naive Bayes, BERT, and RoBERTa are trained on the labeled data. The RoBERTa model generalized well, with 84% of the F1-score on the data. As future work, we want to build a dashboard to automate the process of extracting tweets and summarizing them.

References

1. Chakraborty, K., Bhattacharyya, S., Bag, R.: A survey of sentiment analysis from social media data. IEEE Trans. Comput. Soc. Syst. **7**(2), 450–464 (2020)
2. Urych, I., Matysiak, G.: Preparing youth for defence: socialisation, education, and training of young people in Europe for national security. Secur. Defence Q. **38** (2022)
3. Batra, J.: The youth must tread the Agni-path. The Times of India (2022)
4. Behera, L.K.: High on revenue, low on capital: India's defence budget 2023–24 (2023)
5. Antonakaki, D., Fragopoulou, P., Ioannidis, S.: A survey of Twitter research: data model, graph structure, sentiment analysis and attacks. Expert Syst. Appl. **164**, 114006 (2021)
6. Islam, M.R., et al.: Deep learning for misinformation detection on online social networks: a survey and new perspectives. Soc. Netw. Anal. Min. **10**(1), 1–20 (2020). https://doi.org/10.1007/s13278-020-00696-x
7. Kwak, E.J., Grable, J.E.: Conceptualizing the use of the term financial risk by non-academics and academics using twitter messages and ScienceDirect paper abstracts. Soc. Netw. Anal. Min. **11**(1), 1–14 (2021). https://doi.org/10.1007/s13278-020-00709-9
8. Boddapati, M.S.D., Chatradi, M.S., Bonthu, S., Dayal, A.: YouTube Comment Analysis Using Lexicon Based Techniques. In: Gupta, N., Pareek, P., Reis, M. (eds.) IC4S 2022. Lecture Notes of the Institute for Computer Sciences, Social Informatics and Telecommunications Engineering, vol. 472, pp. 76–85. Springer, Cham (2023). https://doi.org/10.1007/978-3-031-28975-0_7
9. Hutto, C., Gilbert, E.: VADER: a parsimonious rule-based model for sentiment analysis of social media text. In: Proceedings of the International AAAI Conference on Web and Social Media, vol. 8, no. 1 (2014)
10. Blei, D.M., Ng, A.Y., Jordan, M.I.: Latent dirichlet allocation. J. Mach. Learn. Res. **3**(Jan), 993–1022 (2003)
11. Chauhan, U., Shah, A.: Topic modeling using latent Dirichlet allocation: a survey. ACM Comput. Surv. (CSUR) **54**(7), 1–35 (2021)
12. Abbas, M., et al.: Multinomial Naive Bayes classification model for sentiment analysis. IJCSNS Int. J. Comput. Sci. Netw. Secur **19**(3), 62 (2019)
13. Devlin, J., et al.: BERT: pre-training of deep bidirectional transformers for language understanding. arXiv preprint arXiv:1810.04805 (2018)
14. Liu, Y., et al.: RoBERTa: a robustly optimized BERT pretraining approach. arXiv preprint arXiv:1907.11692 (2019)
15. Deshpande, A., Kamath, C., Joglekar, M.: A comparison study of classification methods and effects of sampling on unbalanced data. In: 2019 International Conference on Smart Systems and Inventive Technology (ICSSIT). IEEE (2019)
16. Bonthu, S., Rama Sree, S., Krishna Prasad, M.H.M.: Improving the performance of automatic short answer grading using transfer learning and augmentation. Eng. Appl. Artif. Intell. **123**, 106292 (2023)

Pixel Value Prediction Task: Performance Comparison of Multi-Layer Perceptron and Radial Basis Function Neural Network

Sabhapathy Myakal[1,2(✉)] [ID], Rajarshi Pal[2] [ID], and Nekuri Naveen[1] [ID]

[1] School of Computer and Information Sciences, University of Hyderabad, Hyderabad, India
[2] Institute for Development and Research in Banking Technology, Hyderabad, India
sabha.delight@gmail.com

Abstract. Pixel value prediction plays an important role in areas such as image compression and reversible data hiding. Many traditional pixel value predictors are available in literature. These predictors predict image pixel value using neighboring pixel values. These predictors establish a mathematical mapping from the neighboring pixel values to the predicted pixel value. Such heuristics may not handle the varied neighborhood that can occur in an image. Finding such kind of mapping is not a trivial task. On the contrary, a neural network can be trained for pixel value prediction. In this approach, a neural network takes neighborhood pixel values to produce the predicted value of the pixel as output. In this paper, the performances of two shallow neural networks - multilayer perceptron (MLP) and radial basis function (RBF) neural network - are investigated for pixel value prediction. Mean squared error (MSE) measure between original and predicted pixel values is used to compare the performances of pixel value predictors. Experiments reveal that the pixel predictors using these two shallow neural networks perform better than comparing state-of-the-art predictors. Moreover, MLP-based pixel predictor performs better than the RBF neural network based pixel predictor.

Keywords: pixel value prediction · multi-layer perceptron · radial basis function neural network · reversible data hiding

1 Introduction

Pixel value prediction is a task of predicting a pixel value using the values of its neighboring pixels. Pixel value prediction is an important part of image compression [1] and reversible data hiding (RDH) [2,3]. Most image compression methods [1,4] involve an initial pixel value prediction step which is followed by an encoding step. Difference between an original pixel value and corresponding predicted pixel value is termed as prediction error (PE). Low prediction error enables a good compression performance. In the context of reversible data hiding, the prediction error expansion based techniques [5–7] embed secret bits in the expanded prediction error. Similar to compression methods, a good reversible data hiding scheme requires low prediction error. Therefore, researchers focus on devising a suitable method for pixel value prediction in an image.

There are several pixel value predictors available in literature. Most of the existing traditional pixel value predictors use a mathematical relationship between neighboring pixel values and the pixel value being predicted. For example, a rhombus predictor [8] uses a simple average of the values at the 4-neighboring pixels. Depending on homogeneity of the neighboring pixel values, a predictor in [9] uses the average of either two vertical neighbors, two horizontal neighbors or all the four neighbors. Averages of pairs of neighboring pixels in specific orientations are considered to predict the center pixel value in [10]. A weighted average of 4-neighbors is considered to predict the center pixel value in [11]. Four predicted values are initially estimated in [12] as averages of pairwise neighboring pixel values in four directions (horizontal, vertical, diagonal and anti-diagonal) using a 3×3 window. Then, the directions with the least two diversities (between pairwise directional neighbors) are considered for obtaining the final predicted value. There also exist edge and gradient based approaches for pixel value prediction. For example, a median edge detection (MED) technique in [13] predicts a pixel value based on existence of an edge using 3-neighboring pixel values (right, bottom and bottom right). In a simplified gradient adjusted predictor (SGAP) [13], horizontal and vertical gradients are used to predict a pixel value. Instead of using only two directions for estimation of gradients, a gradient based selective weighting (GBSW) predictor [14] considers gradients in four directions, i.e. vertical, horizontal, diagonal and anti-diagonal. Among the four directions, two directions with the least gradients are used for predicting the pixel value. Then, a weighted average of the causal pixel values in the selected directions is utilized to compute the predicted pixel value. In an extended gradient-based selective weighting (EGBSW) scheme [15], the concept of gradient estimation is extended by considering a larger neighborhood than that of the GBSW predictor [14]. Other gradient-based approaches include an improvement to the gradient based approach in [16] and direction-based gradient methods in [17,18]. In few other approaches [19,20], a few reference pixel values are used to predict the other (non-reference) pixel values. In [19], the reference pixel values are used to interpolate the non-reference pixel values. In [20], weighted median of the neighboring reference pixel values predicts a center pixel value.

All of the above mathematical relationships between a pixel value being predicted and corresponding neighborhood pixel values may not handle the varied kind of neighborhood that can possibly occur in an image. Therefore, instead of using a mathematical based relationship, the pixel value can be predicted using a trained neural network. For example, pixel value is predicted in [21] and [22] using multi-layer perceptron (MLP). In [21], 8-neighbors in 3×3 window are used for pixel value prediction of the center pixel. In another similar MLP-based approach [22], 12 untraversed neighboring pixel values within a 5×5 window are considered for predicting the pixel value. A convolutional neural network based approach is also used for pixel prediction in [23]. In this method, an image is partitioned into two halves – a dot set and a cross set. The dot set pixel values are predicted using the cross set pixel values and vice-versa.

In line with the above neural network based approaches, this paper investigates pixel prediction performances of two shallow neural networks - MLP based predictor and RBF neural network based predictor. In this paper, investigating the performances of these two shallow neural networks is the primary contribution. Mean squared error between original pixel values and corresponding predicted pixel values is used as a measure to compare the pixel prediction performance. Moreover, pixel prediction performance of the neural network based predictors is compared with traditional predictors. Experimental results indicate that the two shallow neural network based predictors perform better than majority of the state-of-the art predictors. Experimental observation also reveals that the MLP-based pixel predictor performs better than the RBF neural network based pixel predictor.

Rest of this paper is structured as following: In Sect. 2, the considered pixel neighborhood and pixel selection criteria are described. Section 3 provides architecture details of the two shallow neural networks. Experimental setup and results are reported in Sect. 4. At last, the conclusion of the reported work is drawn in Sect. 5.

2   Pixel Prediction Task: Definition

Pixel prediction task T can be defined as a mapping from pixel neighborhood X to a predicted pixel value y. It can be represented as:

$$T : X \rightarrow y \tag{1}$$

The pixel neighborhood X is constituted of the set of neighboring pixel values, each of which is an integer in the range [0,255] for an 8-bit grayscale image. The predicted pixel value y is an integer in the range [0,255].

2.1   Considered Pixel Neighborhood

This subsection briefly describes the considered neighborhood for the pixel prediction task. The pixel neighborhood consisting of 12 untraversed neighbors in [22] is adopted in this work. It is illustrated in Fig. 1. In order to predict the pixel value at location (i, j), an input vector of size 12 is formed by concatenating the pixel values at the following locations in the order: $(i, j + 1)$, $(i + 1, j + 1)$, $(i+1, j)$, $(i+1, j-1)$, $(i, j+2)$, $(i+1, j+2)$, $(i+2, j+2)$, $(i+2, j+1)$, $(i+2, j)$, $(i+2, j-1)$, $(i+2, j-2)$ and $(i+1, j-2)$. In the current work, a neural network based approach is adopted to learn the mapping as in Eq. 1. The original pixel value at location (i, j) is the desired output for training the neural network. This trained neural network gives the predicted pixel value y as output.

		(i,j)	$(i, j+1)$	$(i, j+2)$
$(i+1, j-2)$	$(i+1, j-1)$	$(i+1, j)$	$(i+1, j+1)$	$(i+1, j+2)$
$(i+2, j-2)$	$(i+2, j-1)$	$(i+2, j)$	$(i+2, j+1)$	$(i+2, j+2)$

Fig. 1. 12 untraversed pixel neighborhood according to raster scan order traversal of an image

Justification of using such neighborhood in this work can be understood from the following discussion. In another shallow neural network based pixel value prediction task [21], a MLP-based predictor uses 8-neighbors to predict the center pixel value. A neural network based pixel value predictor needs same neighborhood pixel values during embedding and extraction phases of reversible data hiding (RDH). Therefore, in [21], alternate rows and columns of pixels are interleaved during embedding to retain the same pixel neighborhood for correct and successful extraction of data bits during extraction phase. This limits the embedding capacity of the RDH scheme. To overcome this limitation, an untraversed neighborhood of 12 neighboring pixel values is proposed in [22]. The considered untraversed neighborhood helps in maintaining the same neighborhood pixel values during embedding and extraction phases of RDH. This is possible because a raster scan order of pixel traversal is used at data embedding phase. A reverse raster scan order is used at data extraction phase which helps in restoring the same neighborhood pixels values as that of embedding phase.

2.2 Pixel Selection Criteria

As mentioned earlier, shallow neural network based predictor is trained with the pixel neighborhood tuples and the corresponding original pixel value (being predicted) as desired output. According to [24], existence of edge pixels in the neighborhood affects prediction performance of a neural network based predictor. Therefore, if there is an edge pixel in the considered neighborhood or if the pixel being predicted is an edge pixel, then such pixel neighborhoods are not included for training the neural network. Edge pixel detection is performed as follows:

- Initially, the input image is smoothed using a Gaussian low pass filter of size 7×7 for noise removal.
- A threshold is obtained using Otsu's method.
- Finally, a Canny edge detector is employed to get a binary image - indicating the edge pixels.

3   Neural Network Based Pixel Value Predictors

In this work, two shallow neural network based pixel value predictors - multilayer perceptron (MLP) based pixel value predictor and radial basis function (RBF) neural network based pixel value predictor - are investigated for the pixel value prediction task. The steps for edge pixel removal (Sect. 2.2) are performed for both the neural network based pixel value predictors. Both these predictors are trained using the considered pixel neighborhood tuples. Each tuple consists of the 12 untraversed neighboring pixel values (Fig. 1). The following two subsections describe the architecture details of the MLP-based predictor and the RBF network based predictor.

3.1 Multi-Layer Perceptron (MLP) Based Pixel Value Predictor

The architecture of the MLP based pixel value predictor (which has been adopted from the work in [22]) is described in this subsection. The architecture of the MLP is shown in Fig. 2. This architecture is adopted based on experimental observation in [21]. The MLP has an input layer of size 12, corresponding to the 12 untraversed neighboring pixel values. There are two hidden layers having 120 neurons each in the considered architecture. Output layer has a single neuron that produces the predicted pixel value as output. Activation function at the neurons in the hidden layers is rectified linear unit (ReLU).

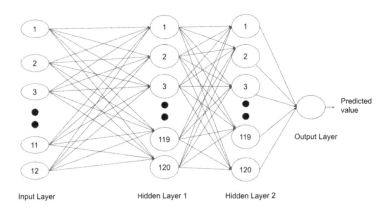

Fig. 2. Architecture of the MLP-based pixel value predictor

Back-propagation algorithm with Adam optimizer is used to train this MLP neural network. Learning rate of 0.0005 is used. The MLP is considered to be converged, if the validation loss (mean squared error) does not decrease for 50 consecutive epochs.

3.2 Radial Basis Function (RBF) Neural Network Based Pixel Value Predictor

This subsection describes the radial basis function neural network. The adopted RBF neural network has three layers: input, hidden and output layers. Similar to the stated MLP architecture (Sect. 3.1), the size of the input layer is 12 corresponding to the 12 untraversed neighboring pixel values. The hidden layer comprises of 64 RBF neurons. Output layer has a single neuron that produces predicted pixel value as output. Architecture of this RBF neural network is presented in Fig. 3.

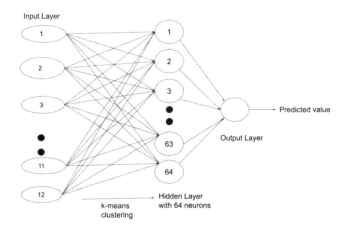

Fig. 3. Architecture of RBF neural network based pixel value predictor

The number of neurons in the hidden layer of the RBF network must be higher than the length of the input vector to follow the Cover's theorem in [25]. In the hidden layer, a Gaussian kernel is used as the radial basis function. Equation of Gaussian radial basis function in k^{th} neuron of the hidden layer is presented in Eq. 2.

$$f_k(X) = e^{-||X - \mu_k||^2 / 2\sigma^2} \tag{2}$$

As it is suggested in [26], the spread (σ) of the Gaussian function can be decided in two ways. One approach is to use a fixed spread for the Gaussian functions for all the neurons in the hidden layer. Another approach is to use different spreads for the Gaussian functions at different neurons. For the task of pixel value prediction, in this paper, a fixed spread Gaussian function is adopted. The suggested fixed spread of the Gaussian function in [26] is given by Eq. 3.

$$\sigma = \frac{d_{max}}{\sqrt{2k}} \tag{3}$$

Here, d_{max} is the maximum distance between any pair of centroids of the Gaussian kernels. The RBF network is trained in two phases. In phase one, k-means clustering on the input neighborhood tuples is performed and the cluster centers are fixed. The value of k is considered as 64 in this work. Once the clustering is performed, the cluster centers (i.e., the parameters of the radial basis function in each hidden neuron) are fixed. Then, in phase two, RBF neural network learns the synaptic weights between the hidden layer and the output layer through error correction learning. The value considered for the learning rate is 0.0005. Similar to the MLP, if there is no decrease in validation loss (mean squared error) for 50 epochs, the RBF network is then considered to be converged.

4   Experimental Setup and Results

The experimental setup and the performances of the two shallow neural network based pixel predictors are discussed in this section.

4.1   Experimental Setup

The training data consists of 400 randomly selected images from the episode-3 of the 2nd Break Our Watermarking System (BOWS-2) [27] data set. These 400 images are grayscale images having a dimension of 512×512. Nine such randomly selected images from the training data are shown in Fig. 4. Tuples in the training set are obtained from the pixels (and corresponding neighborhood) in 400 training images. The pixel selection strategy (Sect. 2.2) is followed for selecting the tuples in the training set. A total of 87,026,690 tuples are obtained as the training data set.

Fig. 4. Nine randomly selected sample images from the 400 training images.

For the training of the neural networks, 10-fold cross validation based approach is performed. The tuples in the training data are split into 10 non-overlapping partitions. At every fold, the neural network is trained using 9 partitions of the data consisting of 78, 324, 021 tuples and validation is done on one partition (validation set) consisting of 8,702,669 tuples.

Performances of the trained neural network based predictors are evaluated on a separate test set of 8 grayscale test images: namely Airplane, Boat, Elaine, Lake, Lena, Mandrill, Peppers and Tiffany. These images are shown in Fig. 5. The test set of 1, 680, 377 tuples (each of size 12) are formed in a similar manner as that of the training set tuples but from a separate set of 8 images (Fig. 5).

Fig. 5. Eight gray scale test images: (left to right in first row) Airplane, Boat and Elaine; (left to right in second row) Lake, Lena and Mandrill; (left to right in third row) Peppers and Tiffany

4.2   Comparison of Pixel Prediction Performance

In this subsection, the performances of the two neural network based pixel value predictors, i.e., MLP-based pixel value predictor and the RBF network based pixel value predictor, are compared. Adopted architecture for the MLP neural network is presented in Sect. 3.1. This architecture is adopted from the works in [22]. Similarly, the architecture of the RBF neural network is presented in Sect. 3.2. As mentioned earlier, mean squared error (MSE) measure is used to compare the pixel prediction performance of the predictors. MSE is defined as the mean of the squared differences between original pixel values and the corresponding predicted pixel values. Pixel prediction performance is compared on eight grayscale images in Fig 5. The pixel prediction performances of the two shallow neural networks are compared with four state-of-the-art prediction techniques: (i) simple computation based prediction in rhombus average predictor [8], (ii) Median Edge Detection (MED) predictor, (iii) Simplified Gradient Adjusted (SGAP) predictor in [13] and (iv) convolutional neural network (CNN) based prediction in [23]. The MSE values for each test image are presented in Table 1.

Table 1. Comparison of pixel prediction performances of various predictors

Test Image	MLP NN	RBF NN	CNN [23]	MED [13]	SGAP [13]	Rhombus [8]
Airplane	**13.11**	37.35	14.37	45.77	57.27	27.57
Boat	**42.78**	49.15	61.03	88.32	92.32	61.05
Elaine	78.23	**50.59**	114.83	100.70	76.95	54.42
Lake	60.30	**59.16**	93.45	122.60	120.29	67.62
Lena	**18.42**	26.78	22.80	50.91	41.89	24.90
Mandrill	**200.50**	306.32	295.06	432.66	434.65	273.98
Peppers	38.60	**30.36**	55.69	66.78	63.09	38.89
Tiffany	**28.77**	92.98	29.45	47.39	41.26	32.18
Average MSE	**60.09**	81.59	85.84	119.40	115.96	72.57

It can be observed from the MSE values in Table 1 that MLP based predictor performs better than the RBF neural network based predictor in following five test images: Airplane, Boat, Lena, Mandrill and Tiffany. On the contrary, the RBF neural network based predictor performs better than the MLP based predictor in the remaining three test images: Elaine, Lake and Peppers. Moreover, it can be observed that these two shallow neural network based pixel value predictors perform better than the comparing state-of-the-art approaches. It is interesting to observe that the proposed MLP based predictor outperforms a recent CNN-based approach [23]. The pixel value in an image is largely affected by its neighboring pixel values. The CNN-based approach [23] predicts a dot-set image using a cross-set image and vice versa. The entire dot-set (or cross-set) image is predicted considering the entire cross-set (or dot-set) image as input.

Therefore, the prediction error is higher for the CNN based approach [23] as compared to the local neighborhood based pixel prediction in the proposed shallow neural network based approach.

5   Conclusion

A neural network based pixel value predictor takes neighboring pixel values as input and produces the predicted pixel value as output. In this paper, the performances of two shallow neural networks, namely multi-layer perceptron (MLP) and radial basis function (RBF) neural network, are investigated for the pixel value prediction task.

Performance of the pixel prediction task is measured using mean squared error (MSE). MSE is defined as the mean of the squared differences between the original and the predicted pixel values. Eight standard gray scale test images are used to compare pixel prediction performances with several existing predictors. These predictors include both of the traditional mathematical relationship based predictors and neural network based predictors.

Experimental results show that the pixel predictors using these two shallow neural networks perform better than comparing state-of-the-art predictors. Moreover, the MLP-based pixel predictor performs better than the RBF neural network based pixel predictor. These results encourage to further explore neural network based pixel prediction. For example, effect of different neighborhoods as input to these shallow neural networks may be undertaken as a future work.

References

1. Leon, D., Balkir, S., Sayood, K., Hoffman, M.W.: A CMOS imager with pixel prediction for image compression. In: Proceedings of the International Symposium on Circuits and Systems, vol. 4, pp. IV-776-IV-779 (2003)
2. Thodi, D.M., Rodriguez, J.J.: Expansion embedding techniques for reversible watermarking. IEEE Trans. Image Process. **16**(3), 721–730 (2007)
3. Wu, H., Li, X., Luo, X., Zhang, X., Zhao, Y.: General expansion-shifting model for reversible data hiding: theoretical investigation and practical algorithm design. IEEE Trans. Circuits Syst. Video Technol. **32**(9), 5989–6001 (2022)
4. Ayoobkhan, M.U.A., Chikkannan, E., Ramakrishnan, K.: Lossy image compression based on prediction error and vector quantisation. EURASIP J. Image Video Process. **2017**(1), 1–13 (2017). https://doi.org/10.1186/s13640-017-0184-3
5. Kim, S., Qu, X., Sachnev, V., Kim, H.J.: Skewed histogram shifting for reversible data hiding using a pair of extreme predictions. IEEE Trans. Circuits Syst. Video Technol. **29**(11), 3236–3246 (2019)
6. Kumar, N., Kumar, R., Malik, A., Singh, S., Jung, K.-H.: Reversible data hiding with high visual quality using pairwise PVO and PEE. Multimed. Tools Appl. (2023)
7. Nguyen, N.-H., Pham, V.-A.: An efficient IPVO based reversible data hiding method using four pixel-pairs. Multimedia Tools and Applications (2023, In press)
8. Coltuc, D., Dragoi, I.C.: Context embedding for raster-scan rhombus based reversible watermarking. In: Proceedings of the ACM Workshop on Information Hiding and Multimedia Security, pp. 215–220 (2013)

9. Dragoi, C., Coltuc, D.: Improved rhombus interpolation for reversible watermarking by difference expansion. In: Proceedings of the 20th European Signal Processing Conference, pp. 1688–1692 (2012)

10. Kim, D.S., Yoon, E.J., Kim, C., Yoo, K.Y.: Reversible data hiding scheme with edge-direction predictor and modulo operation. J. Real-Time Image Proc. **14**, 137–145 (2018)

11. Jia, Y., Yin, Z., Zhang, X., Luo, Y.: Reversible data hiding based on reducing invalid shifting of pixels in histogram shifting. Signal Process. **163**, 238–246 (2019)

12. Uyyala, R., Pal, R.: Reversible data hiding with selected directional context based prediction using 8-neighborhood. In: Proceedings of IEEE International Conference on Electronics, Computing and Communication Technologies, pp. 1–6 (2020)

13. Coltuc, D.: Improved embedding for prediction-based reversible watermarking. IEEE Trans. Inf. Forensics Secur. **6**(3), 873–882 (2011)

14. Knezovic, J., Kovac, M.: Gradient based selective weighting of neighboring pixels for predictive lossless image coding. In: Proceedings of the 25th International Conference on Information Technology Interfaces, pp. 483–488 (2003)

15. Dragoi, I.C., Coltuc, D., Caciula, I.: Gradient based prediction for reversible watermarking by difference expansion. In: Proceedings of the 2nd ACM Workshop on Information Hiding and Multimedia Security, pp. 35–40 (2014)

16. Uyyala, R., Pal, R.: Reversible data hiding using improved gradient based prediction and adaptive histogram bin shifting. In: 7th International Conference on Signal Processing and Integrated Networks, pp. 720–726 (2020)

17. Chen, Y., Huang, D., Ma, G., Wang, J.: Gradient-based directional predictor for reversible data hiding. In: Proceedings of the 13th IEEE Conference on Industrial Electronics and Applications, pp. 1553–1556 (2018)

18. Shilpa, K., Aparna, P., Antony, A.: Gradient-oriented directional predictor for HEVC planar and angular intra prediction modes to enhance lossless compression. AEU - Int. J. Electron. Commun. (2018)

19. Uyyala, R., Pal, R., Prasad, M.V.N.K.: Reversible data hiding using B-tree triangular decomposition based prediction. IET Image Proc. **13**(11), 1986–1997 (2019)

20. Uyyala, R., Pal, R.: Reversible data hiding based on the random distribution of reference pixels. In: Proceedings of IEEE Region Ten Symposium, pp. 225–230 (2018)

21. Bhandari, A., Sharma, S., Uyyala, R., Pal, R., Verma, M.: Reversible data hiding using multi-layer perceptron based pixel prediction. In: Proceedings of the 11th International Conference on Advances in Information Technology, pp. 1–8 (2020)

22. Myakal, S., Pal, R., Naveen, N.: Reversible data hiding technique using multi-layer perceptron based prediction and adaptive histogram bin shifting. In: Proceedings of the 10th International Conference on Soft Computing for Problem Solving, pp. 231–243 (2020)

23. Hu, R., Xiang, S.: CNN prediction based reversible data hiding. IEEE Signal Process. Lett. **28**, 464–468 (2021)

24. Prabhakaran, A., Pal, R.: Image pixel prediction from neighborhood pixels using multilayer perceptron. In: Proceedings of the 7th International Conference on Soft Computing for Problem Solving, pp. 221–230 (2017)

25. Haykin, S.: Neural Networks and Learning Machines, 3/E. Pearson Education, India (2009)

26. Benoudjit, N., Verleysen, M.: On the kernel widths in radial-basis function networks. Neural Process. Lett. **18**, 139–154 (2003)

27. BOWS-2 data set: episode-3 of the 2nd Break Our Watermarking System contest data set. http://bows2.ec-lille.fr/BOWS2OrigEp3.tgz

A Yolo-Based Deep Learning Approach for Vehicle Class Classification

Lakshmi Kishore Kumar Nekkanti[1] and Varaprasad Rao[2(✉)]

[1] HARMAN Connected Services India Pvt. Ltd., Bangalore, India
[2] Department of Computer Science and Engineering, CVR College of Engineering, Hyderabad, India
varam78@gmail.com

Abstract. FASTag is an electronic toll system in India, operated by the NHAI. It uses RFID technology for making toll payments directly from the prepaid or savings accounts linked to it or directly from the toll owner. As per NHAI the toll collection on 25th February 2021 through FASTag has reached a record Rs.103.94 crore with 64.5 lakh daily transactions. Daily 5%–6% of breached data is handled manually. These violations are reported in a CSV file format along with the captured vehicle's images. We are looking forward to a solution that will identify whether the raised violation request is correct or not. Further, an action is taken on each case based on this result. In this paper, an attempt is made to build a POC (Proof of concept) model to detect using Yolo.v4, which harnesses the traffic rule enforcing system and also shows the classification in a web interface. The performance of the model has achieved 99.93% of accuracy.

Keywords: Deep Learning · RFID · Tollgate · Computer Vision · Cloud Deployment

1 Introduction

FASTag is an electronic toll system in India, operated by the NHAI. They utilize the RFID system for the payment of tolls directly from their prepayment or related savings accounts, or straight from the toll holder. The tag can be affixed to the vehicle's windscreen. The tag uses the RFID able to inevitably pay interchange costs without user involvement. In a day around on average 42 lakh toll transactions happen across the locations of the country. The vehicle Class is different to that of the class mentioned in the tag. In addition, because of this difference, the toll amount deducted is either less or more than the actual toll amount and the toll charge is also paid manually as the online payment deduction is not reflected immediately in a few cases.

Around 80 thousand violation data are received per day, which is now a manual process to sort out the claims. Several other organisations are having similar violation issues with FASTag. To address the same, a manual procedure is adapted to go through the violations and update the status. But this manual procedure resulted in the following.

a) The current turnaround time is 2 to 3 working days.
b) Human errors which may occur during manual verification.

The suggested strategy overcomes the aforementioned concerns as

i. Reduce the time in the process
ii. Automate the process of claims if occurs due to misclassification
iii. Utilize Computer Vision (AI/DL) and update the FASTag violations

2 Literature Review

For predictional analytics, most CNN object classifiers are used only. For example, city video cameras search for free parking spots is done with slow-care models, but vehicle crash warnings are associated with almost wrong models. Enhancing the precision of an object detector in real-time, not only allows them to generate recommendations but also to independently manage processes and reduce the input of humans. Effective operation of the object detector on standard GPUs allows their mass use at low prices. The most demanding contemporary neural networks are not available today and require significant training on GPUs. To solve these problems, need only a conventional CNN that runs on a regular GPU in real-time.

2.1 Previous Work

The major objective of this paper is to develop and optimize object identification with minimum time. A modern detector is usually composed of two parts, a backbone which is pre-trained on ImageNet and a head which is used to predict classes and bounding boxes of objects.

The core of detectors that run on GPU systems could be VGG [1], ResNet [2], ResNeXt [3], or DenseNet [4]. The backbone of detectors that run on a CPU platform could be SqueezeNet [5], MobileNet [6–9], or ShuffleNet [10, 11]. Most of the time, the head can be split into two types: one-stage and two-stage object detection. The most common type of two-stage object detector is the R-CNN [12] series, which includes fast R-CNN [13], faster R-CNN [14], R-FCN [15], and Libra R-CNN [16]. Like RepPoints [17], a two-stage object detector can also be changed into an anchor-free object detector. YOLO [18–20], SSD [21], and RetinaNet [22] are some of the most well-known models for one-stage object detection. In recent years, one-stage object detectors that don't need an anchor have been made. Some of these devices are CenterNet [23], CornerNet [24, 25], FCOS [26], and others. Object detectors made in the last few years often have layers between the backbone and the head. These layers are usually used to make feature maps at different stages. It is called the neck of an object tracker. A neck often has many routes that go from the bottom up and many that go from the top down. In networks like Feature Pyramid Networks (FPN) [27], Path Aggregation Networks (PAN) [28], BiFPN [29], and NAS-FPN [30].

3 Architecture for Vehicle Classification

This architecture of vehicle classification uses object detection algorithms in deep learning using YOLO. The same architecture is also used in many other methods like VGG, Inception, ResNet, EfficientNet, R-CNN, etc. In this proposed work, the authors have implemented ResNet, Inception, EfficientNet and MobilNet models to identify the objects.

We use the YOLOv4 model to detect objects in this project. Detection is a simple regression problem in YOLOv4, which takes an image as an input and learns the probability and bounding coordinates of the class. YOLOv4 was a model for real-time detection of objects published in April 2020 that delivered ultimate performance on the COCO data set. It works by breaking the detection task into two parts, regression, and the positioning of objects via bounding boxes and classification to determine the class of the object. YoloV4 uses the Darknet framework in this implementation.

CSPDarknet53 is an advanced network that uses a CSPNet strategy to divide the basic layer feature map into two parts and then fuse through a cross-stage hierarchy. The use of a split and merge strategy allows the network to flow more gradient. The architecture of YOLOv4 is shown in Fig. 1.

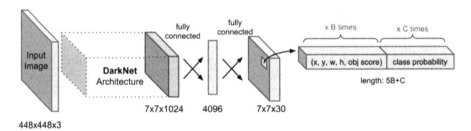

Fig. 1. Yolov4 Architecture

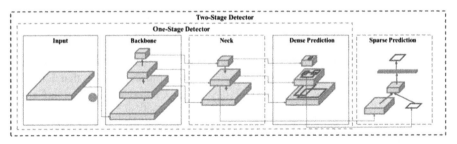

Fig. 2. Yolov4 Two-Stage Detector

From Fig. 1 (Source: https://www.analyticsvidhya.com), it is observed that the architecture contains layers that take inputs to additional layers. Depending on the application, the input can be any image. The DarkNet Architecture, an open-source neural network for which a framework is developed by C & CUDA, includes YOLO for object detection & object tracking. This framework is also available along with the input level. The architecture consists of the flattened layer that is densely connected to the coevolutionary layer, which is also densely connected to transfer data in the architecture from each node to other nodes. Different types of object detectors based on a shot can be observed in Fig. 2 (Source: https://www.analyticsvidhya.com).

3.1 Proposed Algorithm

1. Vehicle images dataset acquisition
2. Dataset preprocessing/Cleaning

   a. Deleting the duplicate images
   b. Deleting the unclear pics
   c. Image Annotation using LabelImg
   d. Image Augmentation

3. Train the model with Yolov4
4. Test the model
5. Tune the hyperparameters
6. Making Predictions/Object Classification with Yolov4

In the first step, we get images of 8 different types of vehicles to train and test the DL models. Second, we annotate and add to the whole dataset before we use it to increase the number of cases in the dataset. Image data enrichment is a way to add more data to a training set by slightly changing the images that are already there based on certain factors. Third, we use the YOLOv4 object recognition models to train on the dataset. Using the split dataset for validation, we checked how well the fine-tuned models could find things and analyze the results. Lastly, we test a model that works best for the classification.

4   Results and Discussion

The solution is implemented in two phases:

1. Local – Implemented and tested the images on the local PC
2. Heroku Cloud Platform– Implemented and deployed the solution in the cloud and results were shown in the web interface.

The images of the dataset were annotated with LabelImg (https://sourceforge.net/projects/labelimg.mirror/).

4.1 Phase I: Local Platform

Here, we are identifying the vehicle to which it belongs: Bus, Truck, MiniTruck, Van, Car, Jeep, and Lorry. As part of this, the first data is collected from Google images and Bing images in the.jpg format. The LabelImg is used further label the images for which the images were collected., and annotated as above listed classes. Metadata has been generated for these class labels such as object_id, center_x, center_y, width, and height.

Train the model for the collected over 10000 images by setting up the Google Colab GPU environment. The transfer learning using YOLOv4 is used to perform object detection. So, the number of classes is 8 (including Person), max_batches $= 2000 * 8 = 16000$, and the filters $= (8 + 5)*3 = 39$ are used.

Fig. 3. Yolov4 training snapshot with metrics like mAP, Precision, Recall and F1-Score

Here, we make yolov4_training_custom.cfg so that all the changes and configurations we will make for our custom model will be reflected in the copy, not the original file. We have applied Transfer Learning by adding our layers to a pre-trained model. So, we download the pre-trained weights called yolov4.conv.137. Thus, the model will be trained using these pre-trained weights instead of randomly initialized weights, which saves a lot of time and computations while training our model. The mean average precision, precision, recall and f1-score are displayed in Fig. 3 after training the data with the YOLOv4 algorithm.

The testing of the model is used the OpenCV DNN module to read weights and config files generated in the training step above, thus predicting the class of vehicle objects in the image. Here are the results and confidence values of the prediction locally from the command line shown below with Fig. 4 (a) to (i).

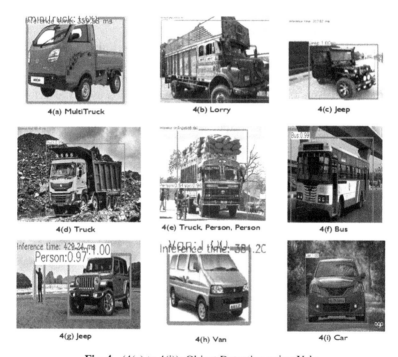

Fig. 4. (4(a) to 4(i)): Object Detection using Yolo

Figures 4(a) to (i) represent the following accuracy for object detection.

a) Inference (359.58 ms) and confidence value (1.00): Mini Truck
b) Inference (406.64 ms) and confidence value (1.00): Lorry
c) inference (337.82 ms) and confidence value (1.00): Jeep
d) Inference (401.45 ms) and confidence value (0.99): Truck
e) Inference (345.69 ms). Three Objects detected Confidence value:(0.99)-Truck, (0.84)- Person, (0.96) – Person
f) Inference (405.12 ms) and confidence value (0.99): Bus
g) Inference (429.24 ms). Two Objects detected Confidence value: (0.97) - Person, (1.00) – Jeep
h) Inference (381.2 ms) and confidence value (1.00): Van
i) Inference (403.49 ms) and confidence value (1.00): Car

4.2   Phase II: Cloud Platform

This section explains the deployment of the application on the cloud platform. The solution which is developed locally is deployed on the cloud. For this, using a Streamlit framework for developing a web interface and deploying it on Heroku Cloud Server is shown in Fig. 5. This web app shows vehicle classification using the Yolo model in two options: default – the input image is taken from the dataset and the latter is your choice – custom input image. The output of the object detection is shown in Figs. 6(a) to 6(d).

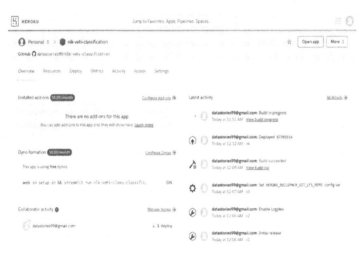

Fig. 5. Deployment of application on Heroku Cloud Server

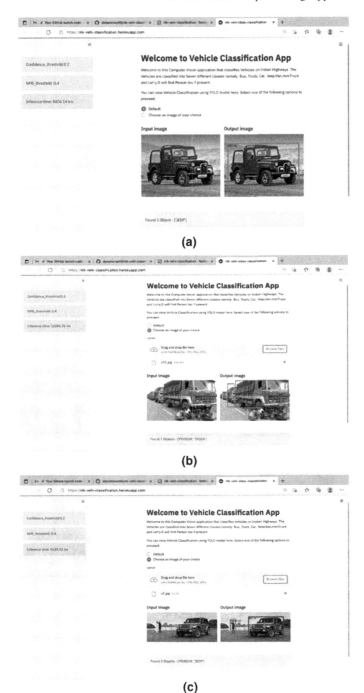

Fig. 6. (a). Default Image: 1 Jeep Object detected, (b). Custom Image: 3 Truck Objects and 4 Person Objects, (c). Custom Image: 1 Jeep Object and 1Person, (d) Custom Image: 1 Truck Object and 1 Person (6(a) to 6(d)): Object Detection using YOLOv4, on Cloud Platform

562   L. K. K. Nekkanti and M. Varaprasad Rao

(d)

Fig. 6. (*continued*)

4.3 Classification of Other Models

Apart from the Yolov4, for comparison study for image classification, used three other models ResNet50v2, InceptionV3 and EfficientNetB3 Figs. 7 and 8 show the various classes of the objects.

Fig. 7. Classes of Images-I

Fig. 8. Classes of Images-II

4.4 Comparison with Other Models

Apart from the Yolov4, for comparison study for image three other models were used for comparison study for image classification and EfficientNetB3. We considered around 10000+ images in various classes, here we considered Model-A as a functional layer with Adam optimizer and Model-B as a Keras layer with SGD optimizer for evaluating the image detection. The summary of the model training is shown in Table 1.

Table 1. Model Summary

Model Name	Layer Type	Output Shape	Trainable Params	Non-trainable Params
ResNet50v2	Model-A	(None, 7, 7, 2048)	263304	23564800
	Model-B	(None, 2048)	23535752	45440
Inception v3	Model-A	(None, 5, 5, 2048)	263304	21802784
	Model-B	(None, 2048)	21784744	34432
EfficientNetB3	Model-A	(None, 5, 5, 1536)	197768	10783535
	Model-B	(None, 1536)	10708528	87296

The testing accuracy with the ResNet50, Inception, EfficientNet and Mobilnetv2 models has been shown in Figs. 9, 10, 11 and 12, and model performance is shown in Table 2.

1. ResNet50V2

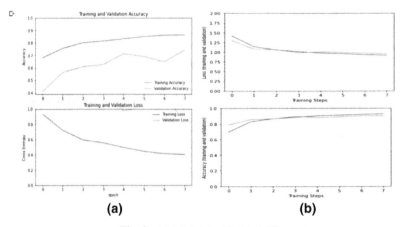

Fig. 9. (a) Model A, (b): Model B

2. InceptionV3

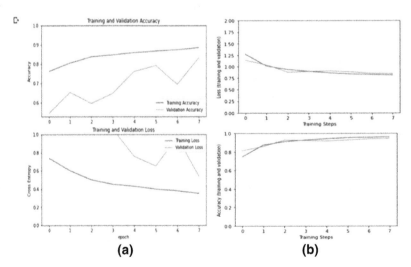

Fig. 10. (a) Model A, (b): Model B

3. EfficientNetB3

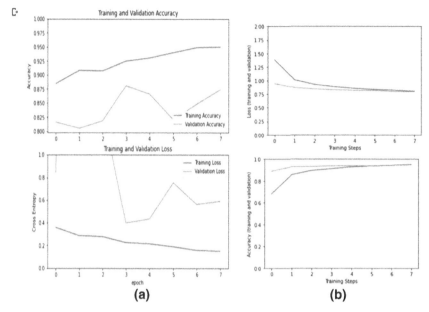

Fig. 11. (a) Model A, (b): Model B

4. Mobilenetv2

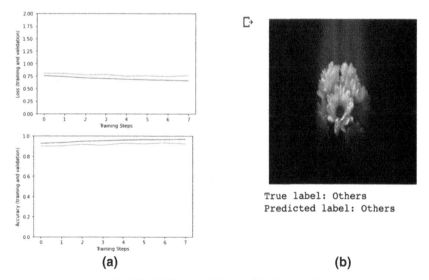

Fig. 12. (a) Training Metrics, (b). Test metrics

Table 2 shows that EfficientNetB3 is more accurate and the minimal loss among the three models using Model A and Adam Optimizer. EfficientNetB3 and InceptionV3 are both nearly accurate, and the loss of InceptionV3 is more than EfficientNetB3 using Model B and SGD Optimizer. Whereas the same is performed with the MobileNet model by SGD optimizer shown as more loss with good accuracy.

Table 2. Model Performance – Testing

Test Model	Model-A		Model-B	
	Accuracy	Loss	Accuracy	Loss
ResNet50v2	0.6805	1.0616	0.8962	0.9834
Inception v3	0.7085	0.8945	0.9311	0.8553
EfficientNetB3	**0.7888**	0.7190	**0.9437**	0.8007
MobileNetv2	-	-	0.9033	0.9577

5 Conclusion

After studying and using various image classification models, the following are the observations. The performance of Yolov4 is better (Accuracy is 99.93%) [18–20] than Restnetv50 (Accuracy is 89%), Inceptionv3 (Accuracy is 93%), EfficientnetB3 (Accuracy is 94%) and MobilenetV2(Accuracy is 90%) with [2, 6–9] compared. Models Restnetv50, Inceptionv2, and EfficientnetB3 performed better with Model-B than Model-A. The Yolov4 model is more robust and faster for real-time image classification. The Yolov4 performance is best even with less number of images (2500) too.

Yolov4 model size is greater than other models.

- Yolov4 - 256 MB
- RestnetV2_50 - 90.2 MB
- InceptionV3 – 83.6 MB
- EfficientnetB3 – 41.6 MB
- Mobilenetv2 – 8.9 MB

Mobilenetv2 is suitable for deployment in mobiles and devices with less processing power. The benefits from this work include a) it will automate the classification of the Vehicles, thus saving a lot of time, money and manpower in the process of settling the claims b) it will reduce the effort of their support team, so the number of support staff c) the same solution can be monetized as a service in the similar markets.

References

1. Simonyan, K., Zisserman, A.: Very deep convolutional networks for large-scale image recognition. arXiv preprint arXiv:1409.1556 (2014)
2. He, K., Zhang, X., Ren, S., Sun, J.: Deep Residual Learning for Image Recognition. In: 2016 IEEE Conference on Computer Vision and Pattern Recognition (CVPR), pp. 770–778. Las Vegas (2016). https://doi.org/10.1109/CVPR.2016.90
3. Xie, S., Girshick, R., Dollár, P., Tu, Z., He, K.: Aggregated residual transformations for deep neural networks. In: 2017 IEEE Conference on Computer Vision and Pattern Recognition (CVPR), pp. 5987–5995. Honolulu (2017). https://doi.org/10.1109/CVPR.2017.634
4. Huang, G., Liu, Z., Van Der Maaten, L., Weinberger, K.Q.: Densely connected convolutional networks. In: 2017 IEEE Conference on Computer Vision and Pattern Recognition (CVPR), pp. 2261–2269. Honolulu (2017). https://doi.org/10.1109/CVPR.2017.243
5. Iandola, F.N., Han, S., Moskewicz, M.W., Ashraf, K., Dally, W.J., Keutzer, K.: SqueezeNet: AlexNet-level accuracy with 50x fewer parameters and 0.5 MB model size. arXiv preprint arXiv:1602.07360 (2016)
6. Howard, A., et al.: Searching for MobileNetV3. In: 2019 IEEE/CVF International Conference on Computer Vision (ICCV), pp. 1314–1324. Seoul (2019). https://doi.org/10.1109/ICCV.2019.00140
7. Howard, A.G., et al.: MobileNets: Efficient convolutional neural networks for mobile vision applications. arXiv preprint arXiv:1704.04861 (2017)
8. Sandler, M., Howard, A., Zhu, M., Zhmoginov, A., Chen, L.C.:MobileNetV2: Inverted Residuals and Linear Bottlenecks. In: 2018 IEEE/CVF Conference on Computer Vision and Pattern Recognition, pp. 4510–4520. Salt Lake City (2018). https://doi.org/10.1109/CVPR.2018.00474
9. Tan, M., et al.: MNASnet: platform-aware neural architecture search for mobile. In: Proceedings of the IEEE Conference on Computer Vision and Pattern Recognition (CVPR), pp. 2820–2828 (2019)
10. Ma, N., Zhang, X., Zheng, H.T., Sun, J.: ShuffleNetV2: practical guidelines for efficient CNN architecture design. In: Proceedings of the European Conference on Computer Vision (ECCV), pp. 116–131 (2018)
11. Zhang, X., Zhou, X., Lin, M., Sun, J.: ShuffleNet: an extremely efficient convolutional neural network for mobile devices. In: Proceedings of the IEEE Conference on Computer Vision and Pattern Recognition (CVPR), pp. 6848–6856 (2018)
12. Girshick, R., Donahue, J., Darrell, T., Malik, J.:Rich feature hierarchies for accurate object detection and semantic segmentation. In: 2014 IEEE Conference on Computer Vision and Pattern Recognition, pp. 580–587. Columbus (2014). https://doi.org/10.1109/CVPR.2014.81
13. Girshick, R.: Fast R-CNN. In: Proceedings of the IEEE International Conference on Computer Vision (ICCV), pp. 1440–1448 (2015)
14. Ren, S., He, K., Girshick, R., Sun, J.: Faster R-CNN: towards real-time object detection with region proposal networks. In: Advances in Neural Information Processing Systems (NIPS), pp. 91–99 (2015)
15. Dai, J., Li, Y., He, K., Sun, J.: R-FCN: object detection via region-based fully convolutional networks. In: Advances in Neural Information Processing Systems (NIPS), pp. 379–387 (2016)
16. Pang, J., et al.: Libra R-CNN: towards balanced learning for object detection. In: 2019 IEEE/CVF Conference on Computer Vision and Pattern Recognition (CVPR), pp. 821–830 (2019)
17. Yang, Z., Liu, S., Hu, H., Wang, L., Lin, S.: RepPoints: point set representation for object detection. In: Proceedings of the IEEE International Conference on Computer Vision (ICCV), pp. 9657–9666 (2019)

18. Redmon, J., Divvala, S., Girshick, R., Farhadi, A.:You only look once: unified, real-time object detection. In: 2016 IEEE Conference on Computer Vision and Pattern Recognition (CVPR), pp. 779–788. Las Vegas (2016). https://doi.org/10.1109/CVPR.2016.91

19. Redmon, J., Farhadi, A.: YOLO9000: better, faster, stronger. In: Proceedings of the IEEE Conference on Computer Vision and Pattern Recognition (CVPR), pp. 7263–7271 (2017)

20. Redmon, J., Farhadi, A.: YOLOv3: an incremental improvement. arXiv preprint arXiv:1804.02767 (2018)

21. Liu, W., et al.: SSD: single shot multibox detector. In: Leibe, B., Matas, J., Sebe, N., Welling, M. (eds.) ECCV 2016. LNCS, vol. 9905, pp. 21–37. Springer, Cham (2016). https://doi.org/10.1007/978-3-319-46448-0_2

22. Lin, T.Y., Goyal, P., Girshick, R., He, K., Dollár, P.:Focal loss for dense object detection. In: 2017 IEEE International Conference on Computer Vision (ICCV), pp. 2999–3007. Venice (2017). https://doi.org/10.1109/ICCV.2017.324

23. Duan, K., Bai, S., Xie, L., Qi, H., Huang, Q., Tian, Q.: CenterNet: keypoint triplets for object detection. In: Proceedings of the IEEE International Conference on Computer Vision (ICCV), pp. 6569–6578 (2019)

24. Law, H., Deng, J.: CornerNet: detecting objects as paired key points. In: Proceedings of the European Conference on Computer Vision (ECCV), pp. 734–750 (2018)

25. Law, H., Teng, Y., Russakovsky, O., Deng, J.: CornerNet-Lite: efficient keypoint based object detection. arXiv preprint arXiv:1904.08900 (2019)

26. Tian, Z., Shen, C., Chen, H., He, T.: FCOS: fully convolutional one-stage object detection. In: Proceedings of the IEEE International Conference on Computer Vision (ICCV), pp. 9627–9636 (2019)

27. Lin, T. Y., Dollár, P., Girshick, R., He, K., Hariharan, B., Belongie, S.: Feature pyramid networks for object detection. In: Proceedings of the IEEE Conference on Computer Vision and Pattern Recognition (CVPR), pp. 2117–2125 (2017)

28. Liu, S., Qi, L., Qin, H., Shi, J., Jia, J.: Path aggregation network for instance segmentation. In: 2018 IEEE/CVF Conference on Computer Vision and Pattern Recognition, pp. 8759–8768. Salt Lake City (2018). https://doi.org/10.1109/CVPR.2018.00913

29. Tan, M., Pang, R., Le, Q. V.:EfficientDet: scalable and efficient object detection. In: 2020 IEEE/CVF Conference on Computer Vision and Pattern Recognition (CVPR) pp. 10778–10787. Seattle (2020).https://doi.org/10.1109/CVPR42600.2020.01079

30. Ghiasi, G., Lin, T. Y., Le, Q.V.: NAS-FPN: learning scalable feature pyramid architecture for object detection. In: Proceedings of the IEEE Conference on Computer Vision and Pattern Recognition (CVPR), pp. 7036–7045 (2019)

Rescheduling Exams Within the Announced Tenure Using Reinforcement Learning

Mohammed Ozair Omar[1] , D. Teja Santosh[1(✉)] , M. Raghava[1] ,
and Jyothirmai Joshi[2]

[1] Department of Computer Science and Engineering, CVR College of Engineering, Vastunagar,
Mangalpalli, Ibrahimpatnam, Telangana, India
mdozairomar@gmail.com, tejasantoshd@gmail.com,
raghava.m@cvr.ac.in
[2] Department of Electronics and Instrumentation Engineering, VNR Vignana Jyothi Institute of
Engineering and Technology, Pragathi Nagar, Nizampet(S.O), Hyderabad, Telangana, India
jyothirmai_j@vnrvjiet.in

Abstract. The academic examinations are scheduled as per the academic calendar. However, due to the occurrence of unprecedented events the exam schedule
will get disturbed which in turn impacts the academic calendar. In this paper, we
propose a temporally optimal and topic complexity balanced re-schedule model
in terms of a Markov Decision Process (MDP). This MDP is verified for the feasibility of a schedule using Bellman Equation with Temporal Difference Learning,
policy iteration and value iteration algorithms of Reinforcement Learning. The
objective of the proposed model is to find an optimal mapping from the state of
disturbed exam to the state of plausible date of the exam. The novelty of this
work is manifested in variable penalties assigned to various schedule slippage
scenarios. Rescheduling is optimally automated using Bellman Equation with
Temporal Difference Learning. These variable policy iteration and value iteration
algorithms have demonstrated that as the learning progresses the optimal schedule gets evolved. Also, it is shown that policy iteration has converged faster than
the value iteration while generating schedule. This instils confidence in utilizing the Reinforcement Learning algorithms on the grid environment-based exam
rescheduling problems.

Keywords: Academic exams · scheduling exams · events · rescheduling · MDP ·
Policy Iteration · Value Iteration · grid environment-based exam

1 Introduction

The provision of acceptable solution especially for Examination timetabling by following
the institution's academic calendar is a challenge based practical and research problem
[1]. The Examination timetable consists of examinations assigned in a way that all the
students attend and give their exam that they require as per the schedule. The examination
timings are usually split into a set of non-overlapping time slots. Also, the examination
schedule is prepared in such a way there will be enough time gap between the exams

which avoids the case of consecutive examinations (at least two tough subjects) in a day [2].

The schedule for these academic examinations is prepared by keeping in mind the aforementioned points and various soft and hard constraints and is circulated by the Examination wing. Nevertheless, this schedule might get disrupted due to the unanticipated occurrence of either endogenous or exogenous events. When this happens, the academic calendar will get impacted to a greater extent leading to adjusting the academic calendar. This is a loss [3] in terms of time and space allotments for smooth conduction of examinations and the academic calendar.

To alleviate this problem, the goal of examination rescheduling within the examination schedule is presented. A temporally optimal and topic complexity balanced re-schedule model is presented in terms of a Markov Decision Process (MDP). This MDP is verified for the feasibility of a schedule using Bellman Equation with Temporal Difference Learning, policy iteration and value iteration algorithms of Reinforcement Learning. Rescheduling is optimally automated using Bellman Equation with Temporal Difference Learning. The objective of the proposed model is to find an optimal mapping from the state of disturbed exam to the state of plausible date of the exam.

2 Motivation

The 2nd International Timetabling Competition (ITC2007) [4] is the inclination to this research work which is made up of three tracks namely examination timetabling, course timetabling and student sectioning. This work attempts to entail the underlining comprehension of the examinations timetabling track introduced as part of the competition. Both the model and the datasets are based on current real-world instances introduced by EventMAP Limited. In contrast, the researchers are incorporating the dataset from the examination department in the form of modelled MDP environment.

3 Related Works

Examination timetabling is a type of scheduling problem that has NP-hard complexity. Many approaches have been proposed to address this problem and find the optimal or near-optimal solutions. To start with, Glover proposed [5] Tabu search algorithm which is a representative local search algorithm. This algorithm starts with an initial solution to the problem and searches for the optimal solution based on the specific search direction. White and Xie designed [6] a four level Tabu search method for exam timetabling problem. Paquete and Stutzle proposed [7] a Tabu search for sorting priorities.

Evolutionary algorithms have research foundations in the field of examination timelines. Ergul implemented [8] a steady state genetic algorithm for solving the examination timetabling problem. Paquete and Fonseca designed [9] a multi-objective evolutionary algorithm to satisfy different types of conflicting constraints and find the solution to exam timetable schedule.

The hyper-heuristic method has emerged in the recent decade is a popular technology. Unlike traditional methods are discussed above, the hyper-heuristic methods are seen as utilizing the heuristic algorithm to find the right heuristic algorithm. Ross et al.

discussed [10] observations of exam timetabling problems of using Genetic Algorithm based approaches. Ahmadi et al. proposed [11] new ideas to find combinations of various heuristic methods to solve exam schedule problems. Ross et al. proposed [12] a steady-state genetic algorithm to solve the problems of curriculum scheduling and exam scheduling. In this algorithm, the search target of the genetic algorithm is to find a suitable heuristic algorithm.

The Reinforcement Learning (RL) techniques were used to influence heuristic selection for hyper-heuristics. McCollum et al. introduced [13] Extended Great Deluge algorithm for Examination Timetabling. This algorithm works similar to Simulated Annealing [14, 15] to escape local optima in finding the solution to the exam timetabling problem. Ozcan et al. explored [16] RL technique that rewards the successful actions that are chosen more often across the search space for providing automated exam timetabling solution. Ryan et al. proposed [2] the Directed Selection technique which improves solution of Examination timetabling problem by augmenting the stochastic method with weights.

It is observed from the above literature that examination timetabling is often addressed in two stages. At the first stage, one or more complete initial feasible solution(s) is constructed. At the second stage, the quality of the feasible solution(s) is improved [5, 8, 11]. These techniques are occasionally incapable of working effectively in generating the quality solution. Moreover, these works have been implemented on ITC 2007 benchmark datasets. RL techniques were modelled as heuristics. The exam rescheduling problem discussed in this research work is about rescheduling the disturbed exam within the examination schedule thereby the academic calendar runs smoothly without any deviation.

To the best of authors knowledge, no works have been concentrated on RL's Bellman principle of optimality with Temporal Difference Learning for solving exam timetabling problem which refers to the dynamic programming approach. The Policy iteration and Value iteration algorithms of dynamic programming also have not been leveraged to find the optimal exam scheduling policy. RL does not rely on static dataset as the data points are collected during training through trial-and-error interactions between the environment and a software agent. This is not the case with the existing literature.

The rest of the paper is structured as follows: Sect. 4 introduces the exam timetabling problem modelled as a Markov Decision Process (MDP) with corresponding terminology and its values. Section 5 presents the problem with the implementation of the Examination schedule and rescheduling with Bellman Equation, Policy Iteration and Value Iteration. The experimental setup for the examination timetabling problem and results are presented is shown in Sect. 6. Finally, the concluding remarks and the suggestions for future research are provided in Sect. 7.

4 Exam Timetabling Problem as a Markov Decision Process

The examination scheduling and rescheduling is treated as a RL problem having medium level of complexity with data collected continuously from the environment. The MDP of this problem is shown in Fig. 1 below.

Illustrating s1 through s12 as the states in the Exam timetabling environment and r1 through r11 as the rewards obtained after an action is performed in a state. The values

Initial State

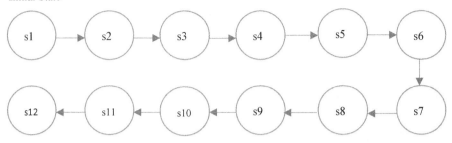

Final State

Fig. 1. Finite Scheduled Examination MDP

of these rewards are in the interval −1 to + 1 with + 1 being the reward for the exam slot among the list of states. The actions are not shown in this MDP. The actions in this environment are namely Up (U), Down (D), Left (L) and Right (R) respectively. These actions are presented in the problem instance which is shown in Table 1 below.

Table 1. Exam Schedule instance from MDP.

Day	Morning Session		Afternoon Session	
Monday	Exam Slot 1 (0,0)	D ↓	Empty Slot 1 (0,1)	
Tuesday	Exam Slot 2 (1,0)	R →	Exam Slot 3 (1,1)	D ↓
Wednesday	Empty Slot 2 (2,0)		Empty Slot 3 (2,1)	D ↓
Thursday	Empty Slot 4 (3,0)	D ↓	Exam Slot 4 (3,1)	L ←
Friday	Exam Slot 5 (4,0)		Empty Slot 5 (4,1)	
Saturday	Empty Slot 6 (5,1)		Empty Slot 7 (5,2)	

In the above table the character 'v' is considered as the arrow symbol to represent the sequence of actions from one exam slot state to the other exam slot state via connected empty exam slot state. Following is the below workflow that represents the MDP as shown in the Fig. 1 above.

(i) The agent (the implemented RL approach) is the one who navigates through the exam slots in the exams schedule.

(ii) The environment is the exam schedule.

(iii) The state is the position in the exam schedule (Forenoon or Afternoon exam slot or the empty slot) that the agent currently resides in. There will be no exam slots on Saturday in the considered exam schedule instance in order to reschedule the exam without any problem.

(iv) (An agent performs an action by moving from one state to another.

(v) An agent receives a positive reward (+1) when its action successfully completes the exam in the given exam slot and receives a negative reward when the exam in the given exam slot is disturbed (-0.25 when Monday or Tuesday exam slots are disturbed, -0.5 when Tuesday or Wednesday exam slots are disturbed, -0.75 when Wednesday or Thursday exam slots are disturbed and -1 when Thursday or Friday exam slots are disturbed) and a reward of zero when there is no action to be performed in a given slot.

The goal is to complete all the exams in the given exam schedule in the presence of raised event too. The algorithm for the assignment of variable penalties to various schedule slippage scenarios is presented below.

Algorithm Variable Penalty Assignment

Inputs:
   6-by-2 examination grid with 6 days (Monday through Saturday) and 2 exam
   slots
   Action (Up (U), Down (D), Left (L) and Right (R)) performed by the RL agent
   Exogenous Event (e)
Output:
   Positive Reward or Variable Penalty received by the RL agent
Algorithm:
   r ← 0, day ← {Monday through Saturday}
   foreach state si in the problem instance **Do**
      If Action in si leads to a new state s^1i Then r ←+1
      Else If e in si **and** [day ←Monday or day ←Tuesday] Then r ← -0.25
      Else If e in si **and** [day ←Tuesday or day ←Wednesday] Then r ← -0.5
      Else If e in si **and** [day ←Wednesday or day ←Thursday] Then r ← -0.75
      Else If e in si **and** [day ←Thursday or day ←Friday] Then r ← -1
   end

---

5 Implementation of the Examination Scheduling and Rescheduling Using Reinforcement Learning

The exam timetabling problem represented as a MDP in the previous section is solved initially with Bellman Equation. Bellman Equation connects value functions at consecutive timesteps.

5.1 Learning Exam Schedule Instance as a Policy Using Bellman Equation with Temporal Difference Learning (TDL)

Bellman Equation with TDL helps in estimating the optimal policy. The Bellman Equation is solved using two types of algorithms namely Policy Iteration and Value Iteration. These algorithms are used to find paths in grid world use cases. The Bellman Equation with TDL is given below.

$$V^{\Pi}(s) \rightarrow V^{\Pi}(s) + \alpha*(\text{sample} - V^{\Pi}(s)) \text{ with}$$
$$\text{sample} = R(s, \Pi(S), S^1) + \gamma*V_i^{\Pi}(S^1) \tag{1}$$

where $V^{\pi}(.)$ is the Value Function, R is the reward, γ is the discount factor, α is the learning rate, s and s^1 are states and $\pi(.)$ is the Policy.

Learning Optimal Exam Schedule using Policy Iteration
The Policy Iteration algorithm starts by:

1. Initializing the actions that the agent needs to take in the form of random policy.
2. Once the actions are decided then the values for these actions at the states are initialized.
3. Now until the convergence (till the policy is obtained) both the policy evaluation and policy improvement steps are iteratively computed.

The formulae for Policy Evaluation and Policy Improvement are given below.

(a) Policy Evaluation

$$V_{i+1\ k}^{\Pi}(s) = \sum_s^1 P(s^1|s, \Pi_k(s)) * [R(s, \Pi_k(s), s^1 + \gamma * V_1^{\Pi}{}_k(s^1)] \tag{2}$$

(b) Policy Improvement

$$\Pi_{k+1}(s) = \arg\max_a \sum_S^1 P\left(s^1|s, a\right) * \left[R\left(s, a, s^1\right) + \gamma * V_k^{\Pi}\left(s^1\right)\right] \tag{3}$$

The overall schema for Policy Iteration is illustrated in Fig. 2 below.

Fig. 2. Schema of Policy Iteration

Learning Optimal Exam Schedule using Value Iteration

The Value Iteration algorithm starts by:

(i) Initializing with the random value function. This means initially the values of the policy are randomly assigned.

Now until convergence (till the policy is obtained) the maximum value over all possible actions is determined. In this way the state values are updated in a single step instead of evaluating and improving them subsequently.

The formula for Value Iteration is given below.

$$V_{i+1}(s) = \max_{a \in A} \sum_{S}^{1} {}_{\varepsilon S} P\left(s^1 \mid s, a\right) * \left[R\left(s, a, s^1\right) + \gamma * V_k\left(s^1\right) \right] \qquad (4)$$

The final values and converged policy for the given exam schedule instance with Bellman Equation, Policy Iteration and Value Iteration are tabulated in Table 2 below.

Table 2. Exam schedule instance verification with Bellman Equation, Policy Iteration and Value Iteration.

Final Values and Converged Policy with Bellman Equation with TDL		Final Values and Converged Policy with Policy Iteration after 4 iterations		Final Values and Converged Policy with Value Iteration after 4 iterations	
Final Values:		Final Values:		Final Values:	
1.1	0	−0.11	0	−0.11	0
1.01	0.1	−0.11	−0.11	−0.11	−0.11
0	0.96	0	-0.1	0	−0.1
0.94	0.17	1	0	1	0
0	0	0	0	0	0
0	0	0	0	0	0
Final Policy:		Final Policy:		Final Policy:	
D		D		D	
R	D	R	D	R	D
	D		D		D
D	L	D	L	D	L

5.2 Learning the Rescheduled Examination Slot as an Optimal Policy Using Bellman Equation with Temporal Difference Learning

The exam rescheduling task considers the problem instance from the previous section. An event is raised at random on the available exam slots in the problem instance. Temporal Difference Learning aims to find an empty slot only after the raised event as the earlier empty slots before the event have already been elapsed in terms of time. This notion has helped to identify the optimal policy that suggests rescheduling the exam within the examination schedule. The final values and the optimal policy for the event raised at the slot (0, 0) i.e., on Monday morning session in the problem instance are shown in Table 3 below.

Table 3. Final Values and the Optimal Policy using Bellman Equation with TDL.

Final Values:	
0.93	0.00
0.00	0.00
0.00	0.00
0.00	0.00
0.00	0.00
0.00	0.00
Final Policy:	
R	---
---	---
---	---
---	---
---	---
---	---

6   Experimental Setup with Results and Discussions

The experimental setup for implementing the examination rescheduling using Reinforcement Learning is by considering the Python programming environment with colab as the development platform. As Reinforcement Learning is used to carry out this, the training data is generated by the agent's own behaviour. The Timetable scheduling environment contains 12 states, 4 actions and the corresponding rewards for the performed actions. The examination schedule is handled by defining a standard 6-by-2 grid holding the exam slots and empty slots during forenoon sessions and afternoon sessions for all the 6 days of the week. Whenever the agent navigates in this grid through actions the reward pertaining to that state is updated. The Exploration versus Exploitation dilemma is handled by carefully providing the small values for the parameter epsilon. This ensures that the agent visits all the states present in the grid. The epsilon values are modified in both policy iteration and value iteration to obtain the convergence plots. The convergence plots with cumulative values across the iterations with various epsilon values for both policy iteration and value iteration are shown in Figs. 3 and 4 respectively. These plots are for the above mentioned problem instance.

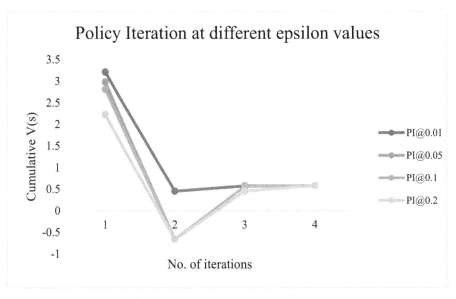

Fig. 3. Convergence Plot for Policy Iteration across different epsilon values

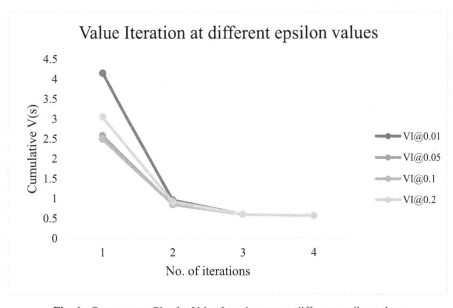

Fig. 4. Convergence Plot for Value Iteration across different epsilon values

It is observed from the above plots that both the PI and VI finds the optimal policy when the epsilon value is 0.05 or higher. The cumulative value when PI and VI reaches optimal policy are 0.57 and 0.57 respectively. As both the algorithms converge to optimal policy at same number of iterations and with same value, the time analysis is carried out on these two algorithms. The time taken by PI and VI across the iterations to find the optimal policy are tabulated in Table 4 below.

Table 4. Policy Iteration vs Value Iteration execution times across iterations.

Iterations	Policy Iteration (in seconds)	Value Iteration (in seconds)
1	0.699	0.1
2	0.721	0.17
3	0.723	0.2
4	0.725	2

It is clear from the above table that Policy Iteration has converged to optimal policy with smaller increments in time across the iterations whereas the Value Iteration has converged to optimal policy with larger increments in time across the iterations. In particular, the time taken by the Value Iteration algorithm towards finding the optimal policy from 3rd iteration to 4th iteration is considerably high in terms of CPU time. It is also observed that below 30% of the CPU time has been utilized when optimal policy is found with Policy Iteration and near 100% of CPU time has been utilized when optimal policy is found with Value Iteration. These time values make clear that Value Iteration algorithm is slower to converge than the Policy Iteration. It is also understood that the utilization of both of these algorithms for the task of exam rescheduling depends on the kind of states in the exam schedule instance. To the best of authors' knowledge there are no existing works in the literature that discussed about rescheduling the disturbed exam within the examination schedule by using Reinforcement Learning algorithms thereby the academic calendar runs smoothly without any deviation. Therefore, it is not possible to compare and claim the strength of this work.

7   Conclusion and Future Work

The task of rescheduling the exam within the examination timetable with variable penalties by using reinforcement learning has been carried out successfully. The objective is to find an optimal policy that provides the rescheduled exam without deviating from the examination schedule. This was achieved by starting with creating the grid environment as the instance of the examination schedule with exam slots and empty slots. This is represented as a MDP. This MDP is solved for the defined instance as a policy with the help of Bellman's equation with TDL by assuming that the transition probabilities and rewards are unknown. Further, this MDP is solved using Policy Iteration and Value Iteration by assuming that the transition probabilities and rewards are known. The cumulative values for both PI and VI algorithms are obtained as same. This is further analysed for the time taken by these algorithms in finding the optimal policy. It has been observed that PI algorithm is faster in converging towards optimal policy than VI algorithm. The experiments carried out and the obtained results from this research validate the objective that an optimal mapping from the state of disturbed exam to the state of plausible exam date has been succeeded. In future, the MDP is approached as a graph and Graph Representation Learning is implemented on the defined 6-by-2 examination schedule grid to find the optimal policy in the faster manner and achieving higher rewards much earlier.

References

1. Burke, E.K., Rudová, H. (eds.): PATAT 2006. LNCS, vol. 3867. Springer, Heidelberg (2007). https://doi.org/10.1007/978-3-540-77345-0
2. Hamilton-Bryce, R., McMullan, P., McCollum, B.: Directed selection using reinforcement learning for the examination timetabling problem. In: Proceedings of the PATAT 14 (2014)
3. Han, K.: Using reinforcement learning in solving exam timetabling problems. Diss. Queen's University Belfast. Faculty of Engineering and Physical Sciences (2018)
4. McCollum, B., et al.: Setting the research agenda in automated timetabling: The second international timetabling competition. Informs J. Comput. 22(1), 120–130 (2010)
5. Glover, F.: Tabu search—part I. ORSA J. Comput. 1(3), 190–206 (1989)
6. White, G.M., Xie, B.S.: Examination timetables and tabu search with longer-term memory. In: Burke, E., Erben, W. (eds.) PATAT 2000. LNCS, vol. 2079, pp. 85–103. Springer, Heidelberg (2001). https://doi.org/10.1007/3-540-44629-X_6
7. Paquete, L., Stützle, T.: An experimental investigation of iterated local search for coloring graphs. In: Cagnoni, S., Gottlieb, J., Hart, E., Middendorf, M., Raidl, G.R. (eds.) EvoWorkshops 2002. LNCS, vol. 2279, pp. 122–131. Springer, Heidelberg (2002). https://doi.org/10.1007/3-540-46004-7_13
8. Ergül, A.: GA-based examination scheduling experience at Middle East Technical University. In: Burke, E., Ross, P. (eds.) Practice and Theory of Automated Timetabling. PATAT 1995. Lecture Notes in Computer Science, vol. 1153, pp. 212–226. Springer, Heidelberg (1996). https://doi.org/10.1007/3-540-61794-9_61
9. Paquete, L.F., Fonseca, C.M.: A study of examination timetabling with multiobjective evolutionary algorithms. In: Proceedings of the 4th Metaheuristics International Conference (MIC 2001) (2001)
10. Ross, P., Hart, E., Corne, D.: Some observations about GA-based exam timetabling. In: Burke, E., Carter, M. (eds.) PATAT 1997. LNCS, vol. 1408, pp. 115–129. Springer, Heidelberg (1998). https://doi.org/10.1007/BFb0055884
11. Ahmadi, S., et al.: Perturbation based variable neighbourhood search in heuristic space for examination timetabling problem. In: Proceedings of Multidisciplinary International Scheduling: Theory and Applications (MISTA 2003), pp. 155–171 (2003)
12. Ross, P., Marín-Blázquez, J.G., Hart, E.: Hyper-heuristics applied to class and exam timetabling problems. In: Proceedings of the 2004 Congress on Evolutionary Computation (IEEE Cat. No. 04TH8753). IEEE, vol. 2. (2004)
13. McCollum, B., et al.: An extended great deluge approach to the examination timetabling problem. In: Proceedings of the 4th Multidisciplinary International Scheduling: Theory and Applications 2009 (MISTA 2009), pp. 424–434 (2009)
14. Bai, R., et al.: A simulated annealing hyper-heuristic methodology for flexible decision support. 4OR, 10, 43–66 (2012)
15. Burke, E., et al.: Using simulated annealing to study behaviour of various exam timetabling data sets (2003)
16. Özcan, E., et al.: A reinforcement learning: great-deluge hyper-heuristic for examination timetabling. In: Modeling, Analysis, and Applications in Metaheuristic Computing: Advancements and Trends. IGI Global, pp. 34–55 (2012)

AI Based Employee Attrition Prediction Tool

Swati Agarwal[1], Chetna Bhardwaj[1], Glory Gatkamani[1], Raghav Gururaj[1], Narayana Darapaneni[2], and Anwesh Reddy Paduri[1(✉)]

[1] Great Learning, Bangalore, India
anwesh@greatlearning.in
[2] Northwestern University/Great Learning, Evanston, USA

Abstract. Employee attrition is one of the key issues for every organization these days, because of its adverse effects on workplace productivity and achieving organizational goals. Employee attrition means not just the loss of an employee, but also leads to the loss of customers from the organization. This in turn results in more attrition among employees due to lesser workplace satisfaction. Hence it is important for every organization to understand how to attract potential employees, retain existing employees and predict attrition early to reduce significant loss of productivity among hiring managers, recruiters, and eventual loss of revenue. High employee attrition shows a failure of organizational effectiveness in terms of retaining qualified employees. To predict attrition among employees, we propose an AI-based solution as a SaaS, because of less investment of time, effort, and cost for the companies. We will be collecting the data from various sources like HRMS, Employee Pulse Surveys, Yammer, etc. as input to our model. We intend to utilize AI/ML models like Decision Tree, SVM, Random Forest, NLP. Our model will be trained to estimate attrition risk among employees in real-time with about 95% accuracy rate.

Keywords: Artificial Intelligence · Employee Attrition · NLP · Classification · Churn

1 Introduction

Attrition Status in India: India has been giving double-digit salary hikes since the pandemic, as demand for skilled workers increased. Despite the hikes, the attrition rate still stands at 20.3%, in 2022 which is marginally lower than last year's 21%, shows research by Aon, a leading global professional services firm. In its latest Salary Increase Survey in India, data across 1,300 companies from more than 40 industries in the country was analyzed. The attrition rate in India is steadily rising, going up more than 7% within the last two years. A majority of the attrition rate comes from voluntary resignation, i.e. when the employee leaves the job voluntarily, taking up 17.5% of the attrition percentage. The attrition rate is expected to remain in double-digits in 2023 as well [1] The Indian IT industry recorded 25.2% employee attrition in FY22 and that pain will continue as it loses talent to other industries, said a report by TeamLease. The attrition in the contract staffing industry is predicted to touch at least 50 per cent in FY23 compared to 49 per cent in FY22, said the report called 'Brain Drain: Tackling the great talent exodus in IT sector' [2].

Attrition Status in USA: Employee churn leads to a massive loss for an organization. The Society for Human Resource Management (SHRM) determines that USD 4129 is the average cost-per-hire for a new employee. According to recent stats, 57.3% is the attrition rate in the year 2021 [3] Since 2021, HR professionals in the US have been dealing with high employee turnover rates and resignations as people started to return to work following the start of the COVID-19 pandemic. Over a year on, the Great Resignation shows no sign of abatement. The number of new job openings vastly outweighs the number of potential new employees willing to fill those roles. According to the latest Job Openings and Labor Turnover Summary by the US Bureau of Labor Statistics (BLS), July 2022 saw 5.9 million total separations. Total separations refer to quits, layoffs, discharges, other involuntary turnover, and other separations. In December 2019, quits were registered at 3.5 million. In July 2022, the number of employees who quit their jobs was 4.2 million. That means that this is still 20% higher than the annual turnover rate at pre-pandemic levels [4].

The key is to accurately detect the flight risk as early as possible so that proactive action can be taken to retain the employee before it is too late.

I. Market Analysis

As per Employee Turnover Rates by Industry (2019, 2020, 2021) (award.co) below chart clearly indicates that almost every industry needs a tool to help predict employee attrition so that proactive efforts can be taken (Fig. 1).

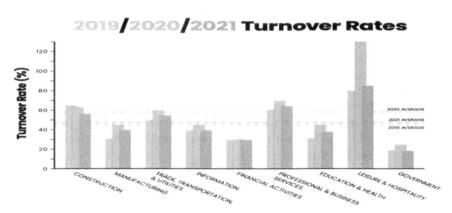

Fig. 1. 2021 Turnover Rates: Leisure and hospitality: 79%, Professional and business services: 63.5%, Information: 38.9%, Education and health: 33.4%, Government: 18.6%.

Target Customers: We would be targeting all companies having more than 1000 employees, which is a huge market in itself.

Current Market Competitors: There is no denying the fact that there are already many AI based solution providers for predicting employee churn, existing in the market.

Some of the competitors are as below:

- AI Based solution providers

  - Employee Retention Applications | No-Code AI - Akkio [5]
  - StarTree™ AI-Based Analytics - Powered by Apache Pinot [6]
  - Predicting Churn with AI: A Playbook - DataRobot AI Platform [7]

- Inhouse AI team who can develop the solution much faster as they will be having access to the database

  - IBM AI can predict with 95% accuracy [8]
  - Reducing Employee Churn with a Data Science Solution [9]

2 Detailed Solution

Churn prediction will be an automatic red flag generator as to which employees are likely to resign from the company. The solution consists of integrating all the data sources together, creating meaningful variables from raw data, applying AI/ML models and stating whether the employee will churn or not.

Benefits of predicting employee churn early:

- Help Managers & HR in planning employee retention strategies
- Save on recruitment cost
- Save on training cost of a new employee 6
- Prevent project delays
- Avoid loss of morale among other employees
- Avoid loss of information Employee churn could be broadly categorized into two segments: 1) voluntary churn due to reasons like salary, work environment, promotion etc. (2) when the company releases the employee. Here we are focusing on the voluntary churn part (Fig. 2).

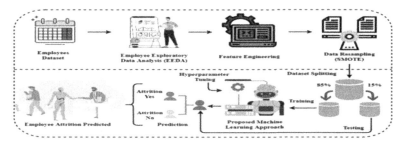

Fig. 2. The methodology analysis of our proposed research study for employee attrition prediction

Churn predictor will consist of the following 6 blocks:

1. **Data Integration:** In this step we will integrate all the data sources available to us for giving relevant information about the employee. We primarily have HR data about the employee, information from surveys opted by the employees & yammer publications. Here we will tag all the information at the employee id level which would be the unique identifier in our case.

2. **Feature engineering:** After obtaining these datasets together our main task here would be to create or extract meaningful information from data by creating relevant variables/features. These features could be either categorical or numerical depending on the information they would convey. Here we have broadly tried to cover the major aspects that would be relevant.

3. **Data Resampling:** Using all the features listed on the various source data (HRMS, RMS, PMS, HRIS, Employee Pulse surveys, Social Media platforms), could make the model over-fitting. Through the variable selection method, we would narrow down to the primary or key variables contributing to a major part of predictions. For feature selection, there are numerous techniques available, but we would primarily deal with those independent variables that are highly correlated with our target. The scores from different statistical tests help us in determining whether the response variables and predictors are related to one another or not. The primary reason for feature selection is to deal with multicollinearity. Some of the techniques used for variable selection are: (1) chi-square test for independence of variables (2) Spearman correlation (3) VIF method (Table 1).

Table 1. Key features leveraged within our AI model

S.No	Features	Data Type	Real-time Feed
1	Age	Numeric	No
2	Dept	Categorical	No
3	Highest Educational Qualifications	Categorical	No
4	Certifications	Categorical	No

(continued)

Table 1. (*continued*)

S.No	Features	Data Type	Real-time Feed
5	Distance from Home	Numeric	No
6	Gender	Categorical	No
7	Job Involvement	Categorical	Yes
8	Job level	Categorical	No
9	Job Role	Categorical	No
10	Monthly Income	Numeric	No
11	Marital status	Categorical	No
12	No. of companies worked	Numeric	No
13	No. of yrs in current company	Numeric	No
14	No. of yrs since last promotion	Numeric	No
15	Overtime	Categorical	Yes
16	Percent Salary Hike	Numeric	No
17	Rapport with manager	Categorical	yes
18	Business Travel	Categorical	No
19	Work Culture Satisfaction	Categorical	Yes
20	Performance Rating	Categorical	No
21	Stock Option level	Categorical	No
22	Sentiments on Yammer, LinkedIn, Twitter	Categorical	Yes
23	Employee Feedback (As per Employee Pulse survey)	Categorical (to be extracted thru NLP)	Yes
24	Location (Hybrid / On-site)	Categorical	No
25	Access to Flexible Work Options	Categorical	Yes
26	Flight Risk Status (As per Employee Pulse Surveys)	Categorical	Yes
27	Internal Mobility Options	Categorical	Yes
28	Access to required trainings	Categorical	Yes
29	Voluntary Stretch Assignments	Categorical	Yes
30	CSR Involvement	Categorical	Yes

* **Features that are not real time feed, will be updated every 6 months, from data sources.**

4. **AI/ML Model:** This is the most crucial and important part of the predictive analysis. Till date, research on predictive employee churn shows that Decision Tree delivers the highest accuracy of 98%, Random Forest second-highest accuracy of 97%,

while Support Vector Machine and Logistic Regression algorithms demonstrate 77% accuracy [10] As per other research paper citing binary classification techniques for employee churn prediction, the suggestion was to start with simple binary classification methods like Decision Tree, Naive Bayes, K-Nearest Neighbors methods and then, trying more complex methods as Support Vector Machines (SVM), Logistic Regression, and Random Forests.

The below chart demonstrates the comparison of classification methods in terms of accuracy metric on the test data: [11] (Fig. 3).

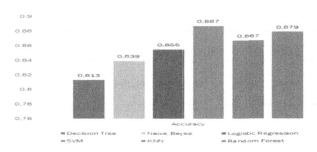

Fig. 3. Comparison as per accuracy

As per another paper, three ML models were applied & the results of the same are shown below: [12] (Table 2).

Table 2. Cross-validation results

Naïve Bayes		Decision Tree		Random Forest	
Parameter	Results	Parameter	Results	Parameter	Results
CA	0.969	CA	0.887	CA	0.975
F1	0.938	F1	0.749	F1	0.945
Precision	0.923	Precision	0.807	Precision	0.994
Recall	0.952	Recall	0.700	Recall	0.901

For our project, we split the data into a 70:30 ratio comprising of training and test data respectively. Then we intend to apply the binary classification techniques (Decision Tree, Naive Bayes, K-Nearest Neighbors, Support Vector Machines (SVM), Logistic Regression and Random Forests) to explore which one provides the highest accuracy.

5. **Evaluation of Results/Model Comparison:** As per paper [10], Decision Tree outperforms the other two models in terms of accuracy (98%). In paper [11], parameters like
   accuracy, precision and recall have been used to evaluate the model performance. The
   graphs w.r.t. [11] indicates that SVM outperforms the other models. In [12] Random
   Forest stands out when compared to others. With the addition of more parameters, we
   believe that our churn prediction [13] would end up performing slightly better. Since
   it's a binary classification model, we can stick to using accuracy, recall, precision as
   our evaluation metrics for model performance [14].
6. **Action-to-be-taken:** Once the red flag is generated against an employee the HR
   along with the manager can take necessary measures to retain the individual as per
   the company policy.

3   Conclusion and Future Directions

The key for our success is to prove to our customers how we are better than the solutions
that already exist.

3.1   USPs of Our Solution

1. While our competitors use specific & limited employee data for their analysis, we
   integrate real time employee data from **various HR tools** like HR Management Systems (HRMS), Resource Management Systems (RMS), Performance Management
   Systems (PMS), HR Information Systems (HRIS) for our analysis.
2. While the current competitors leverage historic data & limited employee demographics to predict attrition, our solution includes **employee sentiment analysis along with
   the historic data & employee demographics** to increase the prediction accuracy rate.
3. For effective sentiment analysis, our solution includes a) **Implementing periodic
   Employee Pulse Surveys** to gauge the employees' current sentiments about their
   company, job satisfaction, leadership and work culture. b) **Leveraging web-scraping
   tools/techniques** to capture employee tweets and comments about their job &
   company on Yammer, LinkedIn and Twitter.
4. Our AI model would leverage **the latest algorithms within Natural Language
   Processing (NLP), Machine Learning and sentiment analysis**, resulting in high
   accuracy prediction of flight risk among employees.
5. Leaders and Managers can **access Real time attrition analysis** which recalculates
   every time an employee submits feedback internally, on social media and every time
   any HR systems are updated.
6. Our solution includes **a Real time Dashboard & reports with insights** about reasons
   for flight risk among employees, which can be leveraged by the Leaders for planning
   long-term retention strategies. It also includes insights about company culture, effectiveness of retention strategies and recommendation of retention strategies as per the
   predicted attrition reasons.

Appendix: COST SUMMARY TO CLIENT

Dev & Run Costs	Y1	Y2	Y3	Y4	Y5	AOI assumptions
Platform cost	$20,206	$40,412	$81,074	$ 1,62,398	$ 3,25,046	Passthrough
Development Cost	$77,220	$25,740	$25,740	$25,740	$25,740	AOI baked in (service arbritage 30%)
Operate & maintenance Cost	$90,000	$90,000	$90,000	$90,000	$90,000	AOI baked in (service arbritage 30%)
SG&A	$ 1,50,000	$ 1,50,000	$ 1,50,000	$ 1,50,000	$ 1,50,000	AOI baked in (10%)
Sub Total Costs	$ 3,37,426	$ 3,06,152	$ 3,46,814	$ 4,28,138	$ 5,90,786	
Cumulative yearly cost	$ 3,37,426	$ 6,43,578	$ 9,90,392	$ 14,18,530	$ 20,09,316	

REVENUE MODEL

No. of Employees within the Company	Cost p.m in USD ($)	Y1		Y2		Y3		Y4		Y5	
		of custo mers	Yrly Reven ue	No. of custo mers	Yrly Revenue	No. of custo mers	Yrly Revenue	of custo mers	Yrly Revenue	of custo mers	Yrly Revenue
< 1,000	500	5	30,000	10	60,000	15	90,000	20	1,20,000	40	2,40,000
1,000 - 5,000	1,000			10	1,20,000	15	1,80,000	20	2,40,000	40	4,80,000
5,000 - 10,000	1,750			10	2,10,000	15	3,15,000	25	5,25,000	50	10,50,000
10,000 - 25,000	5,000			10	6,00,000	15	9,00,000	20	12,00,000	30	18,00,000
>25,000	10,000					5	6,00,000	10	12,00,000	20	24,00,000
Total			30,000		9,90,000		20,85,000		32,85,000		59,70,000
Cumulative yearly Revenue		-	30,000		10,20,000		31,05,000		63,90,000		1,23,60,000
AOI			-91%		58%		214%		350%		515%

Assumption:

- All the development & storage activities happen on the client network and systems
- Cloud platform will still be needed to support integration
- SaaS based on the employee population within a company
- Net Positive in year 2 of existence
- 5 year returns of 515%

References

1. Kapoor, E.: Great resignation impact being felt in India as attrition rate remains elevated at 20% in 2022. In: Business Insider India (2022). https://www.businessinsider.in/careers/news/great-resignation-impact-being-felt-in-india-as-attrition-rate-remains-elevated-at-20-in-2022/articleshow/94453768.cms. Accessed 02 May 2023

2. Shinde, S.: IT industry logged 25% attrition in FY22, trend to continue: Report. Business Standard (2022). https://www.business-standard.com/article/economy-policy/it-industry-log ged-25-attrition-in-fy22-trend-to-continue-report-122092900620_1.html. Accessed 02 May 2023

3. Raza, A., Munir, K., Almutairi, M., Younas, F., Fareed, M.M.S.: Predicting employee attrition using machine learning approaches. Appl. Sci. (Basel) **12**(13), 6424 (2022)

4. "7 statistics on employee turnover every HR manager should be aware of," Workforce.com. https://workforce.com/news/7-statistics-on-employee-turnover-in-2022-every-hr-manager-should-be-aware-of. Accessed 02 May 2023

5. "Employee retention," Akkio. https://www.akkio.com/applications/employee-retention. Accessed 02 May 2023

6. "Real-time analytics for a user-facing world," StarTree. https://startree.ai/. Accessed 02 May 2023

7. Plotnikov, A.: Predicting churn with AI: A playbook. DataRobot AI Platform (2020). https://www.datarobot.com/blog/predicting-churn-with-ai-a-playbook/. Accessed 02 May 2023

8. Rosenbaum, E.: IBM artificial intelligence can predict with 95% accuracy which workers are about to quit their jobs. CNBC (2019). https://www.cnbc.com/2019/04/03/ibm-ai-can-predict-with-95-percent-accuracy-which-employees-will-quit.html. Accessed 02 May 2023

9. Scanlon, N.: Reducing employee churn with a data science solution. Smartbridge (2023). https://smartbridge.com/reducing-employee-churn-data-science-solution/. Accessed 02 May 2023

10. Naz, K., Siddiqui, I.F., Koo, J., Khan, M.A., Qureshi, N.M.F.: Predictive modeling of employee churn analysis for IoT-enabled software industry. Appl. Sci. (Basel) **12**(20), 10495 (2022)

11. Researchgate.net. https://www.researchgate.net/profile/Ibrahim-Yigit-4/publication/320298 197_An_Approach_for_Predicting_Employee_Churn_by_Using_Data_Mining/links/59d c7932aca2728e201f79ba/An-Approach-for-Predicting-Employee-Churn-by-Using-Data-Mining.pdf. Accessed 02 May 2023

12. Academia.edu.   https://www.academia.edu/download/58244348/A_Comparative_S tudy_of_Empl%20oyee_Churn_Prediction_Model.pdf. Accessed 02 May 2023

13. Jain, A., et al.: Career support platform for older adults powered by AI. In: 2023 IEEE 13th Annual Computing and Communication Workshop and Conference (CCWC), pp. 47–53 (2023).

14. Darapaneni, N., et al.: A detailed analysis of AI models for predicting employee attrition risk. In: 2022 IEEE 10th Region 10 Humanitarian Technology Conference (R10-HTC), pp. pp. 243–246 (2022)

iSTIMULI: Prescriptive Stimulus Design for Eye Movement Analysis of Patients with Parkinson's Disease

S. Akshay[1]([✉]) [ID], J. Amudha[2] [ID], Nilima Kulkarni[3] [ID], and L. K. Prashanth[4,5] [ID]

[1] Department of Computer Science, School of Computing,
Amrita Vishwa Vidyapeetham, Mysuru, Karnataka, India
s_akshay@my.amrita.edu
[2] Department of Computer Science and Engineering, School of Computing,
Amrita Vishwa Vidyapeetham, Bengaluru, Karnataka, India
j_amudha@blr.amrita.edu
[3] Department of Computer Science and Engineering, MIT SOC, MIT Art,
Design and Technology University, Pune, India
[4] Parkinson's and Movement Disorders Clinic, Bengaluru, Karnataka, India
[5] Center for Parkinson's Disease and Movement Disorders, Manipal Hospital,
Miller's road, Bangalore, India

Abstract. With an increase in eye-tracking applications, there is a need for eye gaze data analytics to widen its scope to provide customized solutions. However, among several types of analytics such as predictive, descriptive, diagnostic, and prescriptive analytics providing insight into it is quite challenging. This work presents the need and role of prescriptive data analysis that can be carried out on eye gaze data pertaining to a specific study of research on the diagnosis of Parkinson's disease patients during visual search and visual attention tasks. We further look at the various aspects like the image stimulus used, a task performed by the viewer, and its relation to the viewer's eye movement behavior. iSTIMULI includes the design of the image stimuli used to classify the eye movements of Parkinson's disease patients from healthy controls. Visualizations of eye movements on the image stimulus designed are presented. A machine learning analysis is also provided that substantiates the significance of the stimuli with the highest f-measure of 73%. iSTIM-ULI establishes a relation between image stimulus and viewer behavior. As a prescriptive analysis model, iSTIMULI calculates the risk based on eye movements and recommends actions to be taken in the future to improve the ability of the participant.

Keywords: Parkinson's disease · Stimuli Design · Visual Search · Attention · Prescriptive analysis

1 Introduction

Eye-tracking applications are being incorporated both in industry and research which increases the need for the development of solid analytic methods to mea-

R. Morusupalli et al. (Eds.): MIWAI 2023, LNAI 14078, pp. 589–600, 2023.
https://doi.org/10.1007/978-3-031-36402-0_55

sure their efficiency. Eye movement research has several applications in health care. Since each application requires analyzing various aspects of a patient viewing behavior different image stimuli and different tasks are being used. The difference is the result of various gaze behaviors that are to be studied to infer about the participant. Even though the tasks performed are different it is possible to derive some commonality in terms of the task to be performed, the image stimulus to be used and the visualization to be considered. This article aims at supplying a prescriptive data analysis stage by explaining the existing analysis techniques. Prescriptive analysis in eye movement tracking refers to the use of eye-tracking technology to provide personalized recommendations or interventions for improving an individual's eye movements or visual behavior. Eye-tracking technology enables researchers to measure and analyze where a person looks, how long they look, and in what order they view visual stimuli. This information can be used to gain insights into how individuals process visual information and make decisions. In prescriptive analysis, this information is used to provide targeted interventions to improve visual behavior. Prescriptive analysis in eye movement tracking has the potential to provide personalized recommendations and interventions that can improve visual behavior and performance in a variety of contexts. It is seen that in the literature prescriptive analysis of the relationship between stages is not considered which leads to the development of application-specific technology. It is also clear in most of the applications where the visualization techniques supply insights for the statistical study of the metrics neglecting the visual stimulus. In literature, studies predict the task based on eye movement data but they do not emphasize the use of properties of stimuli. Various visualizations designed also lack a connection to the task performed and the stimulus given. This work aims at designing image stimuli that help in the identification of difficulties faced by PD patients in several aspects of visual cognition. A review of the literature that motivates the stimulus design and use of eye tracking in PD is provided in Sect. 2 The proposed method and stimuli designs are presented in Sects. 3 and 3.1. Section 3.2 explains the experimental setup. The results and discussion of the prescriptive analysis are depicted in Sect. 4 followed by the conclusion and future scope in Sect. 5.

2   Related Work

Eye movement analysis has become an increasingly important tool in the study of Parkinson's disease (PD). [5] Design a fuzzy expert system that generates a PD score to diagnose PD. It sets up the existence of a scale for assessing PD. Visual cognitive impairment is one of the first non-motor symptoms of PD. Multiple investigations have found that people with PD have impaired object perception and semantic classification. The evidence for Visual hallucinations in PD patients is provided by [7]. PD patients have problems with their memory for words, images, language, functions of vision and perception, fluency in speech, sustained concentration. PD patients show impairment in Brain Activation, Top-down and Bottom-up visual processing. Different stimulus, revealed that objects activate the brain in diverse ways thus establishing a connection between the stimulus and cognition approach. Patients with PD who were classed as "frontally impaired" had both efficient and inefficient search deficits. The pattern of eye movements for patients differed considerably from that of controls in various dimensions like the re-fixation, the average, the time between fixation, time spent on target, and on distractors. Bottom-up processing predominates allowing the target to "pop-out" from the backdrop of distractors. Disturbances in divided attention, selective attention, sustained attention, and visuospatial attention orientation are all examples of attention disorders in people with PD [14]. A study on orientation is presented with the help of Horizontal and Vertical neglect. Internal cueing error is detected during movement in PD [2]. [4] suggest that when the person is looking for a symbol rather than a letter, the impairment is severe. Identifying attentional deficiencies in non-demented PD patients can be utilized to detect early indicators of cognitive loss in these individuals. [16] study the exogenous and endogenous orientation of attention demonstrated a lack of inhibitory control of visual orienting in PD. The clinical value of contrast sensitivity in relation to attention, brain control, and spatial reasoning skills in PD was investigated by [1]. Patients with PD typically experience visual perception problems like reduced contrast sensitivity. In visual search tasks, patients with PD have trouble picking task-relevant stimuli in the presence of irrelevant stimuli. Deficiencies can vary depending as to whether choice would depend solely on the target's "bottom-up" salience in comparison to ambient stimulus, and whether "top-down" knowledge about the target's identification is available to influence selection [6]. Several applications by [8, 9, 15] and [13] explains the role of eye movements in understanding stress. [10] Investigated the relationship between eye movements and freezing of gait (FOG) in PD patients. [18] Provided an overview of the literature on eye movements in PD and their relationship to non-motor symptoms. Eye movements in PD and their potential use as a biomarker for disease progression and treatment efficacy [6]. It is clear from the above works that there is a relationship between the image stimulus used and the visual cognition abilities observed. Table 1 summarizes the significance of these stimuli with the respective visual cognition function. This motivates us to propose a set of stimuli that can reveal the visual cognition disability in PD patients. It explores the relationship between the viewing behavior to the stimulus used. Predicting future events using past data is prescriptive analytics. Prescriptive analytics can be applied to evaluate a patient's antecedent problems. It can predict the possibility of future complications and execute particular precautionary measures. Even though many healthcare systems use prescriptive analytics [11], there is still a lack of prescriptive studies based on eye movement in the literature. iSTIMULI provides the prescriptive analysis for PD patients by analyzing the eye movement features.

Table 1. An overview of image stimuli viewed by PD patients

Source	Image Stimulus	Target Question	Metrics	Inference (PD patients)
[2]	Visual cues	Will visual cues help to improve/correct gait?	Fixation	Visual cues are important to correct gait
[3]	Match-to-target test	Can engage dopamine-modulated brain regions?	Fixation	Visual search tasks were found to aid in engagement
[4]	Single-feature search, Dual-feature search	How is natural viewing behavior?	Omissions (target missed), Commissions (non-target item considered)	Slower to complete the task
[12]	Search for a "+" amongst rotated "L"s, or a search for a "T" amongst rotated "L"	Cognitive and visual deficits in PD	Fixation, Dwell time, Number of targets found	Miss more targets, more refixations, abnormally short dwell time
[14]	Cued target	horizontal and vertical orientation of attention	Reaction time, Vertical neglect, Horizontal neglect	Perform well in case when there are no distractors
[16]	Vertical Gabor patches	Specific loss of attentional mechanisms	Attention	Loss of inhibitory control of visual orientation
[17]	Unrelated scenes	To minimize predictability	Saccade amplitudes, Fixation durations	Demonstrated motor deficits

3   iSTIMULI

The iSTIMULI is depicted in Fig. 1. The first step is to design the image stimulus for the study. The next step is tracking the participant's eye gaze data with the help of an eye tracker. Once the participants look at the images the x and y coordinates of the participant's gaze are recorded along with the time stamp in a CSV file. These X and Y coordinates are processed to find the fixations and saccades. Once the eye movements are calculated they are visualized to understand the viewer's behavior. The data is then classified using machine learning models with respect to each stimulus. iSTIMULI then assigns a risk score based on the fixation duration, fixation count, and pupil dilation and prescriptively recommends actions. The machine learning results are then validated to show that iSTIMULI shows the expected viewing behavior of the participant.

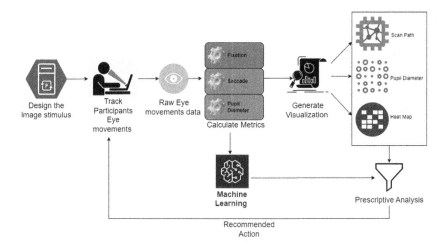

Fig. 1. iSTIMULI

3.1   Image Stimuli Design

In eye-tracking research the experiments are conducted by considering some random targets. Even if the stimulus is specific to the tasks performed by the participant, the relationship between the image stimulus and the viewing behavior of the participant is less explored. The stimuli used in iSTIMULI are designed in a specific way to capture various visual aspects of the participant. The stimulus can be categorized as Natural scenes (unbalanced), and artificial scenes (balanced). While conducting the experiment, screens should not cause center bias and it should not impact saccadic movements. Motion should not cause reflexive eye movements. Precision should not be affected by location, keeping brightness approximately constant. iSTIMULI majorly designs Visual Search Tasks and Scene perception that help in reflecting the difference between serial and parallel processing. Stimulus presented in this article holds variations in properties of targets/distractors, the distribution of targets/ distractors and the size of search array. The factors which vary the eye movements are word frequency, word length, and number of morphemes, measures, first fixation duration, first-pass duration, number of between-and within-word regressions, order of processing. Scene perception tasks define how one looks at visual scenes and bottom-up, top-down factors impact on gaze. The viewing behavior is influenced by the speed of forming a representation of a scene. When a viewer performs scene perception tasks low-level parameters based on luminance, color, and contrast can be tested. Some measures like the number of fixations, correlation between model-predicted and actual gaze.

1. **Horizontal and Vertical orientation:** The image stimulus 1 in Fig. 2a is made up of red-colored horizontal bars. All red-colored bars are horizontally placed with only one bar placed vertically as an exception. The horizontal

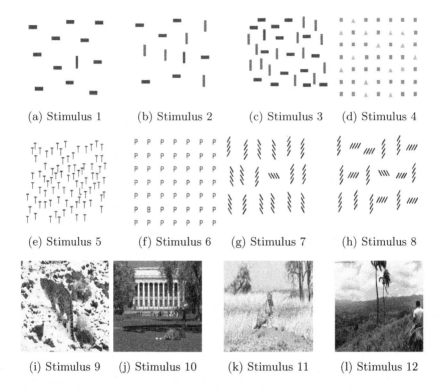

(a) Stimulus 1   (b) Stimulus 2   (c) Stimulus 3   (d) Stimulus 4

(e) Stimulus 5   (f) Stimulus 6   (g) Stimulus 7   (h) Stimulus 8

(i) Stimulus 9   (j) Stimulus 10   (k) Stimulus 11   (l) Stimulus 12

Fig. 2. Designed Image Stimulus (Color figure online)

bars act as distractors. Using this the vertical and horizontal attention of the participant can be captured. The image stimulus 2 in Fig. 2b consists again of horizontal and vertical bars. The participant is again asked to identify the vertical red bar. The image stimulus contains distractors that distract the horizontal and vertical orientation of the visual attention of the participant. The other distracts the participant with color. This can be used for capturing the visual orientation and the effect of color contrast on visual attention. The image stimulus 3 in Fig. 2b is also similar in nature. The images in Fig. 2g and Fig. 2h are made up of horizontal and vertical stripes. The orientation of the stripes differs. Figure 2g contains one horizontal stripe with vertical stripes. Similar stimuli aid the participants viewing behavior when they try to perform a task. The visual cue available in stimulus affects the way the participant performs a particular task.

2. **Color Contrast:** Image stimulus 4 in Fig. 2d is made of two different shapes a triangle and a square. The triangles are orange in color and the square are blue in color except for one orange-colored square. This helps us in understanding the response of the participant with respect to the impact of color contrast. The participant will be asked to identify the only orange-colored squares in the midst of orange-colored triangles and blue-colored squares.

The orange-colored triangles are perfect distractors as they help in revealing the color contrast abilities of the participant as the color of the square that the participant needs to search is also orange. The blue-colored squares deceive the participant as the user will get distracted by constantly looking at a larger number of blue squares while searching for an orange square.

3. **Top-down VS Bottom-up attention:** The image stimulus in Fig. 2e is made up of combination of English letters "L" and "T". The letters are placed randomly. There us is only one letter "L" in the midst of "T". The participant is a given a search task to search for the letter "L" among "T". The stimulus in Fig. 2f contains a set of English alphabet "P" which acts as a distractor as the participant will be asked to search for the letter "B" among the "P". It is seen in the studies that healthy controls use both top-down and bottom-up approaches for searching for the right letter among the distractors.

4. **Natural Scenes:** The images in Fig. 2i, 2j, 2k and 2l are natural scene images. Figure 2i includes a camouflage of a snow leopard with the background to deceive the participant. Other images are designed to understand the participant viewing behavior when the object of interest is at the center and at the edge of the stimulus.

3.2   Eye Tracking Experiment

For experimentation, eye tracking data from 20 participants (10 healthy controls and 10 PD patients) are considered, where the participants view 12 image stimuli. The eye tracking data is recorded using SMI (Senso Motoric Instruments) Red-m eye tracker with a sampling rate of 60 Hz, a Gaze position accuracy of $0.5°$, and a Spatial resolution RMS of $0.1°$. The data is collected in Binocular mode. The Operating distance of the device is between 50 cm to 75 cm with a Tracking range of 32 cm × 21 cm at a 60 cm distance. A 9-point calibration is used where the participant's view during the calibration is validated on these 9-points with a min accuracy of $0.4°$ to be acceptable. Both calibration and eye movement tracking are done using iView RED-m application. Once the calibration is done the participant will be viewing 1 of the 12 images. The eye movement data recorded contains details such as eye (left or right), start time, end time, duration, x and y coordinates of the participant's view, and pupil dilation. This raw data from the eye tracker is then preprocessed and given to the feature extraction model. IVT algorithm is used to extract the fixation and saccades from the raw eye-tracking data.

3.3   Classification of PD Patients Using Machine Learning

The fixations obtained in the previous step are then fed into the machine learning model where the data from all the participants is randomly divided into training and testing with a ratio of 80:20 respectively. The input data contains (x,y) coordinates, corresponding fixations, duration, and class labels. The class labels are 'Control' for healthy control and 'PD' for PD patients. Supervised machine learning algorithms such as KNN, SVM, Decision Tree, and Random

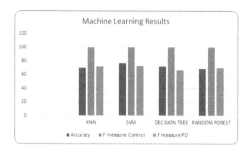

Fig. 3. Classification Accuracy

forest were applied to check if the stimulus designed is helpful in classifying PD patients with visual cognition disability. The results from different machine learning models clearly suggest that the study using the designed image stimulus is able to identify the difference in viewing behavior and accurately classify the PD patients and healthy controls. Figure 3 shows that the machine learning models accurately classify healthy controls. When it comes to the classification of PD patients SVM shows better performance with an F measure of 73%.

3.4   Visualization

In eye-tracking visualizations play a vital role in understanding the visual behavior of the participants. Generally, the eye trackers give data in CSV files that need to be visualized. Most commercial eye trackers come with their own visualization tool. But they are restricted by the parameters that are generally set by the software which is not changeable. The majority of eye-tracking research includes where the subject is looking, which can be represented using various visualization techniques.

1. Scan path visualization is obtained for PD patients for the stimulus used is depicted in the Fig. 4. It clearly shows the dispersed fixations are a result of the color contrast. It depicts the difficulty faced by PD patients while searching for an alphabet among the distractors.

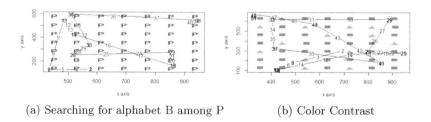

(a) Searching for alphabet B among P   (b) Color Contrast

Fig. 4. Scan path of patients with PD

2. Pupil dilation can provide valuable information about cognitive and physiological processes. PD patients show variation in pupil dilation in response
to increased cognitive load compared to healthy controls, indicating difficulties in cognitive processing. Pupil dilation is plotted against each fixation for
the designed image stimulus to understand the behaviour. Figure 5 shows the
pupil diameter for healthy control and for PD patient. Yellow color indicates
a smaller diameter and green color indicates a larger diameter. The variation
in pupil diameter is a clear indication of the difficulty faced by PD patients
in focusing their view on a particular object in the image.

   (a) Stimulus   (b) Control   (c) PD

Fig. 5. Pupil dilation plot that shows increased dilation in case of PD

3. Heatmaps are used to infer how people are visually processing information.
The heatmap shows areas of the visual stimulus that were fixated on more
frequently and for longer periods of time revealing which parts of the stimulus
are engaging to the viewer. The study shows that PD patients have longer
fixation durations and reduced saccadic velocity compared to healthy controls,
indicating slower and less efficient eye movements. PD patients also tend to
have more fixations in the central and lower parts of the visual field and
less in the upper parts, suggesting impaired visual exploration and attention
deficits. These heat maps provide valuable insights and can help in developing
interventions and treatments to improve cognitive function in PD patients.
The heat maps obtained from the fixations of raw data files are depicted in
Fig. 6. It is evident from the visualization that healthy controls are focusing
on the object of interest in the image. Heat map of the PD patients suggests
that the fixations are distributed around the object indicating inefficiency in
perceiving the image stimulus.

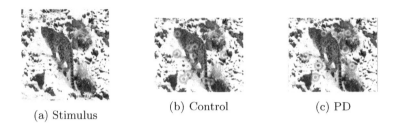

(a) Stimulus   (b) Control   (c) PD

Fig. 6. Heatmap Visualization that shows reduced attention

4   Results and Discussions

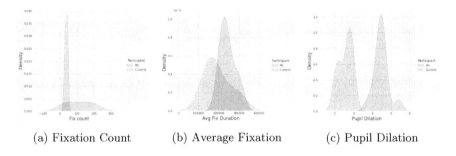

(a) Fixation Count   (b) Average Fixation   (c) Pupil Dilation

Fig. 7. Distributions of features as indicators of risk

In order to prescriptively identify the difficulty faced by PD patients in visual search, a risk score is obtained by considering the eye movement metrics of a patient for all the image stimuli. Figure 7 represents the distribution of features clearly indicating the difference between a PD patient and healthy control. The risk score obtained is a yield of eye movement. The risk score is calculated based on the distribution of average fixation, fixation count, and pupil dilation. A simple neural network model predicts the risk as low, medium, and high depending on the three inputs. The model is tested with a case study that included the data from a PD patient and control for all 12 image stimuli used. Out of 24 data points the neural network predicts 21 data points accurately with respective risk levels as depicted in the confusion matrix in Fig. 8. As a final step of the prescriptive analysis, recommendations is made to the participant based on the risk score with respect to each stimulus as shown in the Table 2.

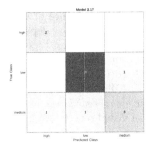

Fig. 8. Confusion matrix for risk prediction using Neural Network

Table 2. Recommendations by iSTIMULI

Stimulus	Predicted Risk score for PD	Recommendations
1	low	No problem with horizontal attention
2	high	Sensitive to color contrast
3	medium	Sensitive to color contrast
4	high	Sensitive to color contrast
5	medium	Difficulty in visual search
6	high	Difficulty in visual search
7	high	Difficulty in orientation of view
8	high	Difficulty in orientation of view
9	high	sensitive to camouflage image
10	high	Difficulty in visual search
11	medium	sensitive to camouflage image
12	low	no problem in viewing natural image

5   Conclusion and Future Scope

The method proposes to establish perseverance between the image stimulus and the eye movement behavior of a PD patient indicating any visual cognitive deficit. The visualizations obtained from an eye-tracking experiment also substantiate the fact that the designed stimuli are capable of identifying the visual cognition deficit. Machine learning results on the experiments with the image stimulus also prove that iSTIMULI serves the purpose of analyzing visual cognition abilities. It is evident that the approach to designing image stimuli based on prescriptive analysis is the future for eye movement experiments in various domains. In future, such systems can be used in medical applications.

References

1. Amick, M.M., Grace, J., Ott, B.: Visual and cognitive predictors of driving safety in Parkinson's disease patients. Arch. Clin. Neuropsychol. **22**(8), 957–967 (2007)

2. Azulay, J.P., Mesure, S., Blin, O.: Influence of visual cues on gait in Parkinson's disease: contribution to attention or sensory dependence? J. Neurol. Sci. **248**(1–2), 192–195 (2006)
3. Botha, H., Carr, J.: Attention and visual dysfunction in Parkinson's disease. Parkinsonism Relat. Disord. **18**(6), 742–747 (2012)
4. Filoteo, J.V., Williams, B.J., Rilling, L.M., Roberts, J.W.: Performance of Parkinson's disease patients on the visual search and attention test: impairment in single-feature but not dual-feature visual search. Arch. Clin. Neuropsychol. **12**(7), 621–634 (1997)
5. Geman, O.: A fuzzy expert systems design for diagnosis of Parkinson's disease. In: 2011 E-Health and Bioengineering Conference (EHB), pp. 1–4. IEEE (2011)
6. Horowitz, T.S., Choi, W.Y., Horvitz, J.C., Côté, L.J., Mangels, J.A.: Visual search deficits in Parkinson's disease are attenuated by bottom-up target salience and top-down information. Neuropsychologia **44**(10), 1962–1977 (2006)
7. Ibarretxe-Bilbao, N., Junque, C., Marti, M.J., Tolosa, E.: Cerebral basis of visual hallucinations in Parkinson's disease: structural and functional mri studies. J. Neurol. Sci. **310**(1–2), 79–81 (2011)
8. Jyotsna, C., Amudha, J., Ram, A., Nollo, G.: Inteleye an intelligent tool for the detection of stressful state based on eye gaze data while watching video. Procedia Comput. Sci. **218**, 1270–1279 (2023)
9. Jyotsna, C., Amudha, J.: Eye gaze as an indicator for stress level analysis in students. In: 2018 International Conference on Advances in Computing, Communications and Informatics (ICACCI), pp. 1588–1593. IEEE (2018)
10. Kim, J.S., Oh, Y.S., Lee, J.H., Lee, J.Y., Kim, J.S., Chung, S.J.: Eye movement abnormalities in Parkinson's disease with freezing of gait. Parkinsonism Relat. Disord. **72**, 46–51 (2020)
11. Lopes, J., Guimarães, T., Santos, M.F.: Predictive and prescriptive analytics in healthcare: a survey. Procedia Comput. Sci. **170**, 1029–1034 (2020)
12. Mannan, S.K., Hodgson, T.L., Husain, M., Kennard, C.: Eye movements in visual search indicate impaired saliency processing in Parkinson's disease. Prog. Brain Res. **171**, 559–562 (2008)
13. Navya, Y., SriDevi, S., Akhila, P., Amudha, J., Jyotsna, C.: Third eye: assistance for reading disability. In: Reddy, V.S., Prasad, V.K., Wang, J., Reddy, K.T.V. (eds.) ICSCSP 2019. AISC, vol. 1118, pp. 237–248. Springer, Singapore (2020). https://doi.org/10.1007/978-981-15-2475-2_22
14. Nys, G.M., Santens, P., Vingerhoets, G.: Horizontal and vertical attentional orienting in Parkinson's disease. Brain Cogn. **74**(3), 179–185 (2010)
15. Ramachandra, C.K., Joseph, A.: Ieyegase an intelligent eye gaze-based assessment system for deeper insights into learner performance. Sensors **21**(20), 6783 (2021)
16. Sampaio, J., et al.: Specific impairment of visual spatial covert attention mechanisms in Parkinson's disease. Neuropsychologia **49**(1), 34–42 (2011)
17. Tseng, P.H., Cameron, I.G., Pari, G., Reynolds, J.N., Munoz, D.P., Itti, L.: High-throughput classification of clinical populations from natural viewing eye movements. J. Neurol. **260**, 275–284 (2013)
18. Vandenbossche, J., Deroost, N., Soetens, E., Nieuwboer, A.: Eye movements as a non-motor biomarker in Parkinson's disease: a review. J. Neurol. **269**(1), 13–24 (2022)

EduKrishnaa: A Career Guidance Web Application Based on Multi-intelligence Using Multiclass Classification Algorithm

Shreyas Ajgaonkar, Pravin Tale, Yash Joshi, Pranav Jore, Mrunmayee Jakate[✉],
Snehal Lavangare, and Deepali Kadam

Information Technology, Datta Meghe College of Engineering Airoli, Navi Mumbai, India
mrunmayeej99@gmail.com

Abstract. Choosing the right career is one of the most crucial decisions in one's life. This decision should not be influenced by anyone's pressure and should be mainly your own choice. Selecting the right career ensures that you gain financial growth over time which eventually leads to a good well-being of an individual and hence a content society. Currently in India, we have over 250 career options available but according to a survey conducted by "India Today" in 2019, 93% of the student population of the country is familiar with hardly seven career options, as majority of the students and parents generally choose the most conventional careers like Engineering, Medical, Civil services, Management, Pharmacy. The reason for these appalling statistics is the lack of awareness and education about the varying professions available amongst the youth. Eventually pursuing a career that is not of your choice can lead to poor job satisfaction, a lack of skills, and an unsound mind. EduKrishnaa is a web-based career guidance system that analyzes user profiles with personality and technical tests and suggests diverse career options, provides informative materials on job opportunities and displays multiple skill-building courses, projects, internships, job opportunities, and startup options. The system uses multiclass classification algorithms, Random Forest provided the maximum accuracy of 95.45%. The system currently serves 8th–10th Std students, undergraduates (TE, BE) in Information Technology and Computer Science, and recruiters, but the aim is to extend it to all domains and become a one-stop solution for all career needs.

Keywords: career guidance system · multiclass classification · personality test · howard gardner test · unemployment

1 Introduction

Due to the recent advancements in technology, the job sector requirements have significantly changed then it was ten years ago. Many sectors have experienced consistent unemployment due to various factors such as overpopulation, automation, industrial conflict and the seasonal nature of agriculture. The unemployment rate in India has remained consistently high over time and is anticipated to increase in the coming years.

R. Morusupalli et al. (Eds.): MIWAI 2023, LNAI 14078, pp. 601–610, 2023.
https://doi.org/10.1007/978-3-031-36402-0_56

Some examples include low job availability in a certain sector due to oversaturation or a lack of skilled workers due to the majority of candidates not having the proper skills in a certain sector. This leads to a vicious cycle where the fresher candidates with job experience have difficulties in getting employed and due to this unemployment, they are unable to gather sufficient work experience [9].

The system aims to identify an individual's interests and natural instincts at an early stage and suggest a broad spectrum of career options to SSC and HSC students. This will make them aware of a wide variety of career options to choose from and also lead to the decentralization of the industry. The front end of our application is built using HTML, CSS, and Bootstrap framework and uses Flask API. The users will be evaluated based on standard test procedures: Howard Gardner's Multiple Intelligence (Personality/Psychometric) Test and Skill Test containing technical questions from their respective domains. Interconnectivity between frontend and backend has been established easily with the help of the SQLite database [1].

2 Literature Review

In May 2022, Ghimire et al. [3] used the Big Five Personality Trait index to predict college major preferences [1]. They surveyed 500 individuals aged 18–25 to capture traits and preferences, reducing dimensions with PCA and OCEAN indices. A decision tree model had over 90% accuracy.

Pandey and Maurya proposed an approach on 31 March 2022 to aid students in selecting the right courses based on interests and abilities [2]. Features like academic marks and communication skills were considered, and six machine learning algorithms were used. K-Nearest Neighbor had the highest accuracy at 63.4%, while Neural Network had the lowest at 45.45%.

Matheus and Takigawa [2] used multiclass classification algorithms in October 2021 to classify operator communication into 12 classes [3]. They compared the accuracy of Naive Bayes, Support Vector, K-nearest-neighbors, Multi-layer perceptron, and Random forest algorithms, with Multilayer Perceptron having the highest accuracy of 85%. The authors suggest that adding more samples to the dataset can prevent overfitting and improve results.

Vignesh et al. [4] developed a career counseling system in March 2021 with three modules, including a skill test assessment, prediction, and result analysis [4]. The system was designed for students to predict the most suitable department based on their skills, using KNN (94.10%), SVM, Naive Bayes, and K-mean models.

Alsafy et al. [3] compared multiple machine learning techniques, including KNN, SVM, decision tree, Naive Bayes, ANN, genetic algorithm, Fuzzy logic, k-mean, LDA, and QDA in December 2020 [5]. Their study identified the strengths and weaknesses of each algorithm in categorizing, recognizing, diagnosing, or clustering data, providing insights into their accuracy and limitations.

In December 2020, Hewage et al. [6] developed a smart HR management system using OCR to extract data from resumes and unsupervised learning algorithms for resume classification and skill assessment [6]. Supervised machine learning techniques were used to predict employee performance and attrition, maximizing productivity with minimal financial loss.

In September 2019, Akkaya and Çolakoğlu [2] proposed an approach for early diagnosis of heart diseases through analyzing various multi-class Classification Algorithms [7]. Logistic Regression, Gaussian Naïve Bayes, k-Nearest Neighbors, Support Vector Machines, Multilayer Perceptron, CART, Random Forest, Gradient Boosting Machine, and Extreme Gradient Boosting are among the suggested algorithms.

In August 2018, Anand et al. [3] created a system for assisting users in selecting a profession based on their human behavior and analysis [8]. The system used an MCQ module to classify traits with high accuracy and displayed career options mapped to broad domains obtained from aptitude analysis. Handwriting analysis was also performed with high accuracy.

In April 2017, Alimam et al. [4] proposed a system based on the Moroccan education system to classify high school students based on grades and skill set [9]. Two situations were considered: same subjects and different subjects. The system experimented with 50 final-year high school students to calculate their inclination to choose a field.

In February 2017, Min NIE1 et al. [7] analyzed university students' behavior and course selection data to study their career choices [10]. They used 4 classification algorithms to predict career choices, with Random Forest achieving the highest accuracy of 65% on 6 semesters of data, and suggested that the precision of the system can improve with more certainty in choices.

The papers [1, 2, 4, 8] provide an understanding of personality and interest tests for career assessment. Multiclass classification algorithms such as SVM, Naive Bayes, Random Forest, K-nearest-neighbor, and Decision trees can automate prediction, but their accuracy varies with data. The most accurate algorithm was implemented after testing the dataset.

3 Proposed Methodology

Current career guidance systems lack diverse career options and future employment information. Our solution, EduKrishnaa, offers all possible employment options (startups, government schemes, internships, higher education) to increase their employment probability. It's an interactive career guidance web application tool for students (14–22 years old) and recruiters. It aims at helping students find their strengths, weaknesses, skillsets and suggest them a flexible future career path. The users will be evaluated based on standard test procedures: Howard Gardner's Multiple Intelligence (Personality/Psychometric) Test and Skill Test containing technical questions from their respective domains. The recruiter portal connects recruiters with registered undergraduates (Fig. 1).

3.1 Test Modules

Personality Test: Personality tests are utilized to assess the traits of an individual. 1)their strengths/weaknesses, 2) areas of interest, 3) preferences, and style of interacting with people and situations, etc. These unique traits of a person are identified based on their responses to a set of questions. These questions are usually standard in format and do not have a definite right answer. It normally consists of a range of choices from which the candidate has to select the answer with which they agree the most. Some of

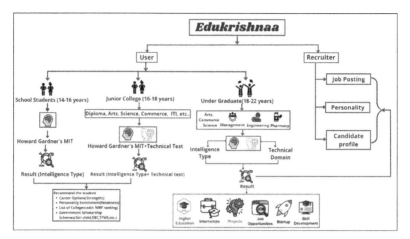

Fig. 1. System Overview

the common tests are Myers-Briggs Type Indicator (MBTI), Howard Gardner's Multiple Intelligence Test, 16 Personality Factor Questionnaire, DISC Test, Big 5 personality test, etc.

Howard Gardner's Multiple Intelligence Test:

Howard Gardner's theory of multiple intelligences proposes that humans are not born with a definite single type of intelligence but rather a person can be composed of multiple types of intelligence and each of them reflects a certain strength/liking the user has. Each intelligence type can be associated with an occupation/career choice.

Linguistic, Logical/Mathematical, Spatial, Bodily-Kinesthetic, Musical, Interpersonal, Intrapersonal, and Naturalist are the eight forms of intelligence that Gardner described.

Referring to this standard model we have presented 5 questions of each intelligence to the user on our interface. This use of this model for the different categories of users is stated below:

a) SSC Users: To give more generalized career options to 8-10th grade students, our system uses a personality test based on their natural abilities and suggests multiple career options according to their intelligence type. We make sure that the resultant career option is not limited to only one intelligence. We have listed 36 sets in our system. Each set corresponds to a list of job options. Each job role has a specific intelligence type that a student needs to have as best (must need), average and poor. If there are 5 job roles having the same group of intelligence types then they are clubbed into 1 set. In this manner, we have 36 sets and 72 career options created. Example: For example, a set has been created consisting of the following career options

   – {Geologist, Pilot. These 2 job roles have their best intelligence as {Bodily, Logical-Mathematical, Naturalist} hence they are grouped together.

b) other users: The result of the Personality test along with a technical test is used to assess and suggest flexible career options to this category of users (Table 1).

Table 1. Creation of Sets

Best Person-ality Trait (15-20)	Average Personality Trait (11-15)	Poor Personality Trait (5-10)	Output Set	Corresponding Job role
P3, P4, P7	P6, P1, P5,	P2, P8,	**SET1**	Librarian
P3, P4, P6	P1,P7, P8	P2, P5		Physician
P3, P4, P6	P5, P7, P8	P2, P1		Military
P3, P4, P6	P5, P7, P8	P2, P1	**SET 16**	Para Militry (https://en.wikipedia.org/wiki/Paramili-tary_forces_of_India)
P3, P4, P6	P5, P7,P8	P2, P1		Police Force (Spies, CBI officials, CID, Detectives)
P3, P4, P8,	P1, P5, P7	P2, P6	**SET17**	Geologist
P3, P4, P8,	P5, P6	P1, P2, P7		Pilot
P6, P7, P8,	P4, P3	P1, P2, P5	**SET23**	Fashion Designer
P6, P7, P8,	P1,P3, P4	P2, P5		Veterinarian

Technical Test: This test is for undergraduates to evaluate their knowledge in a specific field. Different tests will assess comprehension in different domains.

By incorporating personality tests and technical test results, the candidate will be recommended with a suitable career option. For instance, if a user excels in web development and has naturalist traits, our system recommends agricultural opportunities.

The technical test is at present designed only for Information Technology and Computer Science students. We have considered 6 major domains: Network and Infrastructure Management, Web Technology, AI ML, Data Science, IoT, Project Management, and Security for designing the test. There are approximately 5–6 questions framed for each domain and these are shuffled and presented to the user on the UI of the website. The result of the technical test (the highest scoring domain of the user) along with the personality test is combined and mapped to a job role. The table below will explain the mapping of technical expertise with the personality trait to provide the Set as an output which in turn corresponds to a list of job roles that are suggested to the user (Table 2).

3.2 Prediction Module

Machine learning algorithms, APIs, and datasets for training the machine learning model are only a few of the technologies used in the construction of this module.

Dataset:
The dataset used for the machine learning model is synthetic, as no appropriate data were available for the core concept of this application. Different datasets were used for each of the three categories of students, with separate machine-learning models built for each. The SSC student dataset consisted of over 3400 entries with eight features, including scores for personalities like linguistic, logical, spatial, bodily, musical, interpersonal, intrapersonal, and naturalist. The target label gave the recommended job set as an output. To verify the dataset's legitimacy, a career counselor was consulted to map the eight personalities to corresponding job roles.

Table 2. Mapping of Personality Trait with Technical domain

Dominant Personality Trait	Dominant Technical Domain	Output set	Corresponding Job role
Logical- Mathematical	Network and Infrastructure Management	set1	Network Engineer, Cryptographer (Junior), Network Analyst
Spatial- Visualization	Web Technology	set5	Frontend Developer, Frontend Engineer, Graphic Designer
Interpersonal	AI ML and Data Science	set9	Analytics Manager, Data Science Project Manager, LEAD / MANAGER - DATA SCIENCE AND BI, ML Engineer, Machine Learning-Consultant
Intrapersonal	Network and Infrastructure Management	set10	Network Consultant, Network Analyst

Likewise, for the UG category, the following datasets are used for building machine learning models for pre-final year and final-year engineering students of Information Technology and Computer Science.

TE Students (Engineering: IT Dept.): The dataset contains 1100+ entries which consist of scores of 4 personalities (Logical, Spatial, Interpersonal, Intrapersonal), 3 job domains scores (Network and Infrastructure Management, Web Technology, and AI/ML -Data Science) and the personality trait retrieved, these are the 8 features. There is one target label that gives the set as an output. A set is created by mapping a dominant personality with a strong technical domain and each set is mapped to a list of job roles. So basically, a set looks like {personality trait, best domain, list of job roles}, and there are 12 such sets for this category. For example, {Logical, AI/ML and Data Science, (Data Scientist, Computer Vision Engineer, ML Engineer, Computer Vision, and Machine Learning Researcher)} The dominant personality trait is Logical, strong technical domain is AI/ML and Data Science and job roles suggested are Data Scientist, Computer Vision Engineer, ML Engineer, Computer Vision, and Machine Learning Researcher.

BE Students (Engineering: IT Dept.): The dataset contains 1100+ entries which consist of scores of 4 personalities (Logical, Spatial, Interpersonal, Intrapersonal), and 6 job domains scores (IoT, Security, Network and Infrastructure Management, Web Technology, AI/ML-Data Science and Project Management) and personality trait retrieved, these are the 11 features. There is one target label that gives the set as an output (Table 3).

Table 3. SSC Dataset

Student	Linguistic	Musical	Bodily	Logical	Spatial	Interpersonal	Intrapersonal	Naturalist	Sets
S1	11	6	14	16	19	11	18	19	set18
S2	12	5	13	16	19	11	18	19	set18
S3	12	5	12	16	20	14	18	19	set18
S4	14	5	11	20	17	14	18	19	set18
S5	11	5	14	20	17	11	19	19	set18

Machine Learning Algorithms: Supervised machine learning was used to develop classifiers since the provided dataset was labelled with input and output. Multiclass classification was utilized as there were more than 2 output classes in the dataset. The SSC dataset had 36 class labels and the undergraduate dataset had 12, making multiclass classifiers more suitable for job role predictions, especially as the number of class labels may increase in the future.

The **K-Nearest Neighbor algorithm** estimates the distance between each neighbor to classify target values, using equations like Euclidean distance or cosine similarity measure.

The **Naive Bayes classifier** uses probabilistic learning based on Bayes theorem to perform classification problems, such as classifying whether a particular label is suitable for a student based on their personality and technical test scores.

Support Vector Machine creates the best decision boundary to segregate n-dimensional space into classes for classification problems in Machine Learning.

In our system, **One-vs-Rest classification** is used to solve multiclass problems, generating N-binary classifier models for N-class instances to predict a set based on student performance.

Random Forest classifier increases predictive accuracy by using many decision trees on different subsets of input data, with each tree giving a classification or "vote" for the forest to choose the majority vote classification.

The performance of multiple algorithms was evaluated on the SSC dataset, and K-Nearest Neighbor, Naive Bayes, Support Vector Machine, One-v-Rest, and Random Forest achieved accuracies of 96.21, 91.72, 94.34, 96.72, and 95.45, respectively. Random Forest outperformed the others in separate testing and was chosen for implementation in the system (Fig. 2).

Flask API: The Flask API facilitates communication between the front-end and back-end of the application. The machine learning model receives scores from the Test module

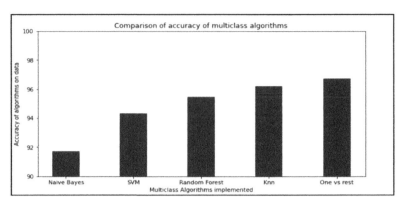

Fig. 2. Bar graph to represent the accuracy each multiclass algorithm

via the API to assign suitable personality traits and career options based on the candidate's performance. Python programming is utilized to implement this aspect of the API.

3.3 Result Module

Once the user completes the required tests on our platform they will be redirected to the results page. The distinctive factor of our system is the inclusion of multiple employment/skill-building options that we provide to our users. Users are given access to the following functionalities:

Personality Report and Career Prediction: Howard Gardner's Personality test results highlight dominant traits, strengths and weaknesses, and other characteristics of the user. Personality and technical test results predict career options for the users and provide a detailed career report.

Roadmaps along with Additional Courses: Along with the career option predicted for the user, information resources, and roadmaps of job roles are also provided. Employment requires appropriate skills which can be acquired through courses, projects, and internships. Trending courses hosted on nptel, swayam are linked on our platform using web scraping so that the user can navigate easily.

Startups and Government Schemes: Startups play a crucial role in self-employment and job creation. Times of India reports a surge from 471 to 72,993 recognized startups since 2016. However, youth awareness about the startup culture is low. Our system provides startup and mentor information to address this.

Internships, Job Opportunities and Resume Builder: Job openings posted on sites like Internshala, Naukri, Indeed, etc. are scraped and displayed to the user. Users can build resumes on our site, which display test results, personality strengths, and technical skills. Resumes can be downloaded in PDF format and uploaded to job postings (Fig. 3).

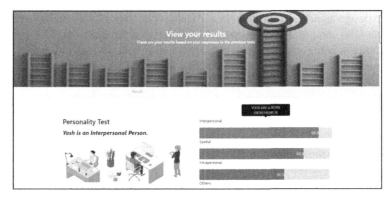

Fig. 3. Screenshot of website frontend

3.4 Recruiter Module

Our system connects the undergraduate students registered on our platform to the recruiters by allowing both the audience of users to see each other's data meaning the users of EduKrishnaa will be able to see the job openings posted by the recruiting companies and the talent acquisition teams will be able to access student data provided by EduKrishnaa. Using this method, we are trying to link talented candidates to the employing organizations.

4 Results

This system is currently working for the SSC category of students, undergraduates and recruiters. The students can give the personality and technical tests on the website and they can access their personalized results. Recruiters have the facility to post a job opening and see the candidate data. To obtain proper user feedback and test the system thoroughly the website is hosted live on the following URL: https://edukrishnaa-produc tion.up.railway.app/.

The easy accessibility of the website for the users is ensured by enabling its view to both desktop and mobile phones. The aim is to collect real time data of users, work on improving its accuracy and alter the features/functionalities based on the user's feedback.

5 Conclusion and Future Work

In the future the need for career guidance systems is going to increase with the exponential growth in career options and job opportunities. Access to proper information about available options is vital for educating the youth and should be accessible to all. This system is still under implementation. The following user categories: 14–16-year-olds, undergraduates (18–22-year-olds), and recruiters are currently supported by the system. For the undergraduate category, we have considered the Computer Science and Information Technology domain. Our aim is to include all the categories of career options available like Management, Science, Arts, etc. Expert guidance from career counselors is crucial to design technical questionnaires. We also want to work with multiple recruiting companies who can post their job openings regularly on our platform. This project has the capability of being converted into a business model with the integration of recruiters, startup mentors, and career counselors and that is exactly our ultimate goal.

References

1. Ghimire, A., Dorsch, T., Edwards, J.: Introspection with data: recommendation of academic majors based on personality traits. In: Intermountain Engineering, Technology and Computing (IETC), May 2022. ISBN:978-1-6654-8653-8
2. Pandey, A., Maurya, L.S.: Career prediction classifiers based on academic performance and skills using machine learning. SSRG Int. J. Comput. Sci. Eng. **9**(3), 5–20 (2022). ISSN: 2348 – 8387
3. Takigawa, de Lima, M.N.S., Takigawa, F.Y.K.: Evaluation of machine learning algorithms for multiclass classification of voice calls from power systems operations. In: 7th International Conference on Engineering and Emerging Technologies (ICEET), 27–28 October 2021, Istanbul, Turkey (2021)
4. Vignesh, S., Priyanka, C.S., Manju, H.S., Mythili, K.: An intelligent career guidance system using machine learning. In: International Conference on Advanced Computing & Communication Systems (ICACCS), March 2021. ISSN: 2575–7288
5. Alsafy, B.M., Aydam, Z.M., Mutlag, W.K.: Multiclass classification methods: a review. Int. J. Adv. Eng. Technol. Innov. Sci. (IJAETIS) **5**(3), 01–10 (2020). ISSN:24551651
6. Hewage, H.A.S.S, Hettiarachchi, K.U, Jayarathna, K.M.J.B, Hasintha, K.P.C., Senarathne, A.N., Wijekoon, J.: Smart human resource management system to maximize productivity. In: International Computer Symposium (ICS), December 2020. ISBN:978-1-7281-9255-0
7. Akkaya, B., Çolakoğlu, N.: Comparison of multi-class classification algorithms on early diagnosis of heart diseases. In: SBIS Young Business and Industrial Statisticians Workshop on Recent Advances in Data Science and Business Analytics, September 2019. ISBN:978-605-5005-95-5
8. Anand, A., Patil, D., Bhaawat, S., Karanje, S., Mangalvedhekar, V.: Automated career guidance using graphology, aptitude test and personality test. In: International Conference on Computing Communication Control and Automation (ICCUBEA), August 2018. ISBN:978-1-5386-5257-2
9. Alimam, M.A., Seghiouer, H., Alimam, M.A., Cherkaoui, M.: Automated system for matching scientific students to their appropriate career pathway based on science process skill model. In: IEEE Global Engineering Education Conference (EDUCON), April 2017. ISSN: 2165-9567
10. Nile, M., et al.: Advanced forecasting of career choices for college students based on campus big data. Higher Education Press and Springer-Verlag, Berlin, Heidelberg, February 2017

Multi-dimensional STAQR Indexing Algorithm for Drone Applications

Pappula Madhavi[1]($\boxtimes$) (ID) and K. P. Supreethi[2] (ID)

[1] CVR College of Engineering, Hyderabad, Telangana 501510, India
P.madhavi@cvr.ac.in
[2] Jawaharlal Nehru Technological University Hyderabad, Hyderabad, Telangana 500085, India
Supreethi.pujari@jntuh.ac.in

Abstract. No matter what you are employed in any field, spatial knowledge is usually enclosed with spacial data knowingly or unknowingly. Spatial data is encircled temporal knowledge with objects that change their location and position of access over the time. In present scenario, many applications which deals with spatial, temporal and altitude parameters required to index and get quick results in many applications. To represent spatial and temporal location, maps plays an important and vital role from large voluminous knowledge. Spatial data plays a main role to analyse and visualize current trends. STAQR algorithm provides indexing the data in multi level structure by using Quad and R tree in hybrid structure notation used to get query optimization quickly. Spatial temporal data with altitude contemplate for drone applications and multi stored building for data accessing. This manuscript provides drone tracking system for spatial queries by using STAQR algorithm with four parameters latitude, longitude, altitude, and time.

Keywords: Spatial Data · Temporal Data · Altitude · Indexing Tree structure · Spatial query · Drone trajectory

1 Introduction

1.1 Spatial Temporal Data

Spatial data provides information about object location exactly to identify the existence of the object in a given time. Query operations involved to extract the data about particular object. Different types of spatial queries used to gain information from spatial data are range queries, nearest neighbour queries, spatial joins and overlays, time slice queries and window queries. The extracted data used for the visualization, analysis, data sharing among peers to give report, mapping and comparison. Consequently data is used for Geographic Information Systems (GIS) and digital earth which manages large voluminous spatial data. To expedite region query for spatial data with indexing takes Minimum Bounding Rectangle (MBR) instead of original geometry of intersection [1]. Quad trees and R trees are used to index spatial data with timestamp and altitude

R. Morusupalli et al. (Eds.): MIWAI 2023, LNAI 14078, pp. 611–619, 2023.
https://doi.org/10.1007/978-3-031-36402-0_57

parameter which can be used in drone trajectory information system, flight trajectory, flight conflict detection system, and air cargo tracking system. Indexing consisting of Spatial databases, spatial concepts and data models, different query languages, storage and indexing, query processing and optimization. Spatial indexing includes grid files, R trees, cost model. Clustering goal is to reduce the seek time and latency time. Several mapping techniques are used to represent spatial data i.e. Z-order curves and Hilbert curves [2].

Measurements of temperature, pressure, air quality, traffic data etc., GPS data from mobile phones and data from radars that capture location information about people and other moving objects such as cars, trains produce a large amount of data. Spatial temporal data includes in the areas like Geological disaster monitoring, Geophysical exploration, predicting earthquakes and hurricanes, determining global warming trends, and public health (disease spread). Today's rapid advancements in computing hardware, tracking devices such as GPS receivers and sensors have become pervasive and generating a large amount of spatial temporal data. Environmental information systems, intelligent transport systems, geographic information system, traditional agriculture system, meteorological databases, Mobile tracking system, Global Positioning Systems, Internet-based map services, digital earth, epidemiology, and climatology are the other spatial temporal areas. Many indexing methods are proposed to index spatial, temporal and spatial-temporal data.

Many Indexing techniques are used for efficient data access. The indexing techniques reduce the frequent disk access. Many indexing structures exist for the spatial data to index set of objects, structures like Quad trees, R trees, R+ trees, R* trees and QR trees. A hybrid indexing structure STAQR tree implemented for spatial data with altitude parameter. Quad and R tree can be combined to index the spatial data which eliminates the problems of overlapping. Area is subdivided into quadrants if objects are present more than four still further divided into sub quadrants. STAQR Algorithm is used QR structure for 4 Dimensional data. Spatial data is converted from 4D to 1D and then encode it into string format. To insert nodes for STAQR tree 1D string data can be considered as node point in QR structure [3]. A hybrid indexing STAQR Tree structure method has implemented for spatial temporal objects with altitude parameter. A new algorithm improves query performance with less time. Tracking of location based vehicles with altitude can easily search the information like drones and flights. It finds anti-collision calculations for drone swarms. It identifies spatial temporal objects which behaves dissimilar with other objects in trajectory path. DBSCAN algorithm is used to find the object behaviour and identify the outlier from a set of objects. Sometimes outliers are good to identify thieves in cyber crime, suspicious transactions in credit card theft and speed of ambulance in traffic data.

COVID-19, COVID effected people information in different cities in a particular given time which gives large amount of data, history about recovered patients' information and updating data requires a proper storage structure. Contact Tracing Query (CTQ) method used for COVID-19 patients by using multilevel index QR-tree. Quad tree is used to identify user movements according to space and time. R-tree is used for space time mapping of traced users. CTQ identifies the people who is in close contact with COVID patient and monitor the further infected people for the last specified days (Preferably

14 days). It collected the mobility traces of patient by taking GPS-enabled cell phones through CDR-Call Data Record. Extended MBR used to identify infectious region [4]. GPS locations are not accurate in indoor locations. To eliminate these problems, use Wi-Fi localization in future works.

Managing spacial information can be a daunting task in today's world, especially with the vast and complex nature of such data. However, to optimize query performance and minimize memory access, compartmentalization can be implemented as a potential solution. Moreover, spatial-temporal classification can also be applied to various types of information systems, including multi-dimensional data systems, transmission systems, complex data systems, and even large-scale flight movement data. Transmitting data systems such as text, audio, images, and videos usually require significant storage. The collection of data in a spatial organization is done hierarchically and involves dividing the area into grid shapes.

The data is retrieved using area filling curves such as Z-order, Hilbert curves, and Piano curves. Geo-hash allows precision pricing as a prefix and gradually removes the top of the stream to reduce the size of the location. It shares a common prefix for Geo-hash codes that are spatially close to each other. To address the issue of organizing large data, researchers have proposed the integration of indexing structures in hybrid models. SFC (Space Filling Curves)s are used for ordering multi-dimensional data into one dimensional data to index spatial locations [5]. Using many applications for efficient accessing of range queries, KNN queries and join queries for spatial data. Z-order curves are considered for indexing spatial data for their mappings between spatial objects and efficient in building of quad trees. Space filling curves continuously record the numbering of object in sequence manner of a given region. Earth's surface is divided into different grid levels to encode each location. Geo hash divided the space into quadrants by giving geo codes in each level. Altitude is the additional parameter which can be used in multi stored building, drone trajectory and location based services. Ex. Unnamed Aerial Vehicles (UAV), Flight trajectory path.

A commonly used indexing structure is the QR tree which utilizes the quad area subdivision method along with the R tree region of objects falling within a Minimum Bounding Rectangle (MBR). The quad tree also facilitates multilevel indexing by dividing the entire index space into sub-index spaces. By combining Quad tree and R Tree, the hybrid data structure solves issues such as overlapping and node overflow that occur in individual structures. The QR tree divides the entire space into smaller sub space of 2k (where k is the number of dimensions of the space). Every node in the Quad tree is also a node in the R Tree and can be either an internal or leaf node. This combined structure partitions the space and creates a QR structure for the given objects in the space. Indexing in spatial dimension B-trees, B + trees, R trees, R + trees, R* trees, Quad trees and Oct trees, temporal dimension RT-tree, 3D R-tree, STR-tree, overlapping and multi-version structures like MR-tree, HR-tree, HR + -tree, MV3R-tree, PPR-tree, Trajectory oriented methods TB-tree [6], SETI, SEB-tree, CSE-tree indexing in multi-level 2 + 3 R-tree, 2–3 TR-tree, LUR-tree, Hashing, indexing in Quad trees PM-Quad tree, parametric spatial indexing PR-tree, TPR-tree techniques are used.

An efficient method spatial temporal index for trajectory data on No-SQL databases. No-SQL databases do not support trajectory data indexing, but it accelerates the time-consuming data with support of Geo-Hash algorithm. Geo hash divides Geo-space into hierarchical structure of latitude and longitude rectangles, and it will do continuous division into further rectangles until desired location is achieved. It codes each location into 1D string from 2D rectangle quad tree node. ST-Hash algorithm uses spatial temporal data and performs well for point query, range query and circle query. Altitude is the height of an object measured in meters or Centimeters. Applications of height parameter can be considered in multi stored building to deliver any item with a specific floor. Drones plays an important role nowadays, altitude is the main key parameter to check drone height and trajectory path. Flight conflict detection system and trajectory path is one of the main examples where altitude plays a main role. In this contribution altitude considered for multi stored building to deliver goods for packers and movers. Haversine distance [7] can be calculated to find the distance between two locations and height of a building.

Contribution of the paper, may be applicable to any types of queries in a drone trajectory path. STAQR indexing can be applied for drones and flight trajectory paths. This manuscript provides, Sect. 1: Introduction about spatial and temporal data, Sect. 2: Related work of the indexing algorithm, Sect. 3: Results and Analysis, and Sect. 4: Conclusion and Future work.

2 Related Work

Spatial data collected and re-processed by different processing techniques. To index the related information in a given area leads to prefix the common code in region wise which is similar to Geo code. Hybrid indexing structure STAQR algorithm defines that space is divided into quadrants and indexing can be done by sub quadrant Tree structure. Data is taken as multi dimensional model like four parameters latitude, longitude, altitude, and time considered to index in Tree model. Once the data is indexed processing and accessing is easy to find the locations of an object. 4D data is encoded into 1D string data to identify the object location. Many encoding techniques like Base 32, Base 64, Golomb Code, Elias Gamma, and Elias Delta are used to encode the spatial data into encrypted format. Spatial data is converted into binary string format by using ST Hash algorithm. This binary format is encoded into string format by encoding techniques [8]. Objects which are in same region will share the common prefix to index data at multiple levels. Quadrants are used to index the nodes at multiple levels like intermediate node level and leaf node level. Different objects are encoded with string format and need to be indexed with their indexing levels. Altitude parameter can be considered and added with latitude, longitude and time, data is encoded with string format. Altitude parameter [9] is used in flight trajectory and drone trajectory. Query performance is better when compared with less number of parameters index. By using trajectory path, drone exact location can be identified, we can track the drones which started at same time and many queries are applied on drones to access the data (Figs. 1 and 2).

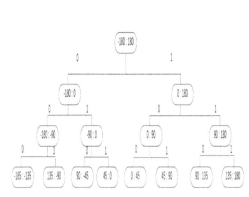

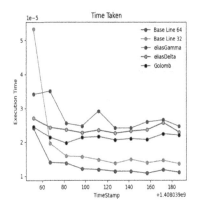

Fig. 1. Binary tree construction for data object dimensions

Fig. 2. Time complexity of different encoding techniques

Spatial data which contains latitude, longitude, altitude and time parameters can be converted into binary form by using of binary tree construction. A multidimensional data is able to access quickly and gives accurate results in less time. Time is converted by epoch time and altitude is suffixed with a binary stream Following is one example how multidimensional parameters are converted into binary form by using different encoding techniques.

Spatial and temporal point with altitude: **170^0, 780^0, 450m, 2022-March-10, 09:30:25 AM** is as follows:

Latitude	: 1000110000
Longitude	: 1011011110
Time	: 0100110001
1D stream	: 110001010010101111010010010001
Base 32 string conversion	: "YUV5ER4".
Base 64 string conversion	: "xSvSR4".
Elias Gamma code conversion: "9 12 1F 12 114".	
Elias Delta code conversion : " 23 25 1F 5 3 4".	
Golomb code conversion	: "10 11 E 11 10 4".

Encoding techniques are applied and analyzed for best encoding technique with less time. Base 64 is the suggestible to encode multidimensional data to convert it into unique code string format which is used for indexing.

Latitude	Longitude	Altitude	Geohash	Alt Geohash
17.4841877	78.3731065	482	teper7j93dz	teper7j93dz4
17.4629979	78.3476803	492	tepeqg5136b	tepeqg5136b4
17.4484363	78.3741361	563	teper2qk98r	teper2qk98r5
17.4359811	78.4193887	532	tepg0qp7bnq	tepg0qp7bnq5
17.439662	78.4248873	612	tepg0wg32kd	tepg0wg32kd6
17.439662	78.4248873	524	tepg0wg32kd	tepg0wg32kd5

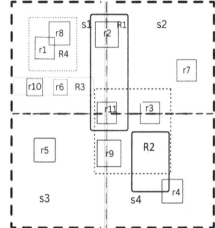

Fig. 3. Geo code for different locations data   **Fig. 4.** QR Structure for objects

Figure 3, shows different Geo hash codes for different parameters. All these codes are indexed by using of STAQR algorithm which follows hybrid notation of Quad and R tree in Fig. 4. Given region is divided into quadrants, R Tree is constructed by given objects at multiple levels. STAQR algorithm [10] performs all operations like insert, delete and search node to track the object location and its complexity is: O(Log N). Time and space complexities analyzed in results. Query performance is good for search operation.

The STAQR Tree with depth d contains the total number of nodes $n = \sum_{i=0}^{d-1} 4^i$.

3   Results and Analysis

STAQR algorithm is used for indexing multidimensional data objects in a sequence manner depending on the regions. A node can move from one quadrant to another which creates a trajectory pah. This can be applicable in drone trajectories and flight trajectories. Once the drone is moving from one point to another point we can track the drone location and access the data. Many queries will allowed to drone paths like speed, coverage area, any collision of drone, drone working nature and tracking of a drone.

STAQR Algorithm takes little bit more storage compared with 3 parameters in ST Hash algorithm. But time complexity is less and query performance is good compared with multidimensional data. STAQR Algorithm gives indexing structure of multi dimensional data which holds massive amount of data. Altitude parameter considered about the height of an object which is used to access spatial data accurately. Hybrid tree structure used to index the tree in multi level with multi dimensional data (Fig. 5).

Tracking of location based vehicles with altitude can easily search the information like drones and air vehicles. It finds anti-collision calculations for drone swarms. It identifies spatial-temporal objects which behaves dissimilar with other objects in trajectory path. ST Hash supports only three parameters to index and apply query operations.

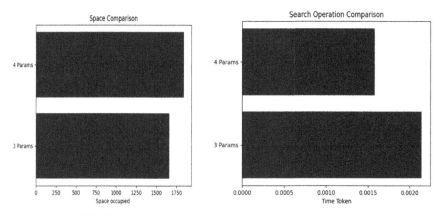

Fig. 5. Average space and Time taken for search operation

STAQR algorithm which takes Altitude parameter as multidimensional data and index the set of objects in a sequence by using Quad and R Trees.

Many query types are applied on drone trajectory path to run the STAQR algorithm. Query types are applied in path trajectory and finding an optimal path to access the details of given query. Manned Aerial Vehicles (MAVs) and Unmanned Aerial Vehicles (UAVs) are becoming popular in present scenario to get optimized results [11]. Query will give a optimized results compared with less dimension parameters. A multi dimensional data can easily access and gives quick query results.

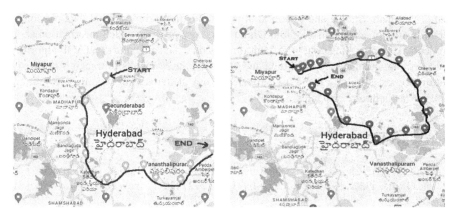

Fig. 6. A Trajectory paths for a drone in a given region

Figure 6, shows the trajectory paths of a given drone ids. A synthetic data set has taken for multiple drones and their trajectory path nodes in its journey. A graph can be taken for a drone movement path. Many queries like range query, window queries applied in their path and get optimized query results with in a given region by using STAQR Algorithm. The following graph indicates Three Drones moving paths in a given region.

Different queries can apply like drone travelling time, different locations drone has gone in a space of fixed region (Fig. 7).

Fig. 7. Multiple drones Trajectory Paths

4 Conclusion and Future Work

STAQR algorithm indexing multiple data objects which are having different location names in a path. Spatial and temporal objects holds multi dimensional data for correct identification of objects in a region. Drone trajectory provides much information about drones and their tracking system. A Multidimensional data indexing of STAQR algorithm used to store and access spatial data and got good query results in tracking of drones. Future drones are going to be used for delivering of items with specified weight and distance without any obstacles.

References

1. Yu, J., Wei, Y., Chu, Q., Wu, L.: QRB-tree indexing: optimized spatial index expanding upon the QR-tree index. ISPRS Int. J. Geo-Inf. **10**(11), 727 (2021). https://doi.org/10.3390/ijgi10110727
2. Jia, L., Liang, B., Li, M., Liu, Y., Chen, Y., Ding, J.: Efficient 3D Hilbert curve encoding and decoding algorithms. Chin. J. Electron. **31**, 277–284 (2022). https://doi.org/10.1049/cje.2020.00.171
3. Song, X.Y., et al.: The Study and Design of QR*-Tree Spatial Indexing Structure. Appl. Mech. Mater. 182–183 (2012). Trans Tech Publications, Ltd., pp. 2030–2034, Crossref https://doi.org/10.4028/www.scientific.net/amm.182-183.2030
4. Ali, M.E., Eusuf, S.S., Islam, K.A.: An Efficient Index for Contact Tracing Query in a Large Spatio-Temporal Database. https://arxiv.org/pdf/2006.12812.pdf/. arXiv:2006.12812 [cs.DB] (2020)

5. Narimani Rad, H., Karimipour, F.: Representation and generation of space-filling curves: a higher-order functional approach. J. Spat. Sci. **66**, 1–21 (2019). https://doi.org/10.1080/144 98596.2019.1668870
6. Tao, Y., Papadias, D.: MV3R-Tree: a spatio-temporal access method for timestamp and interval queries, pp. 431–440 (2001)
7. Alam, C.N., Manaf, K., Atmadja, A.R., Aurum, D.K.: Digital. Implementation of haversine formula for counting event visitor in the radius based on Android application, pp. 1–6 (2016). https://doi.org/10.1109/CITSM.2016.7577575
8. Zhang, Z., Sun, X., Chen, S., Liang, Y.: LPPS-AGC: location privacy protection strategy based on alt-geohash coding in location-based services. Wirel. Commun. Mob. Comput. 1–17 (2022). https://doi.org/10.1155/2022/3984099
9. Torres-Sospedra, J., et al.: UJIIndoorLoc: a new multi-building and multi-floor database for WLAN fingerprint-based indoor localization problems. In: Proceedings of the Fifth International Conference on Indoor Positioning and Indoor Navigation (2014)
10. Madhavi, P., Supreethi, K.P.: STAQR tree indexing for spatial temporal data with altitude. GIS Sci. J. **09**(11) (2022). GSJ/9190, ISSN NO: 1869-9391. https://doi.org/10.21203/rs.3.rs-2238587/v1
11. Eliker, K., Zhang, G., Grouni, S., Zhang, W.: An optimization problem for quad-copter reference flight trajectory generation. J. Adv. Transp. **2018**, 1–15 (2018). https://doi.org/10.1155/2018/657418

Low Light Image Illumination Adjustment Using Fusion of MIRNet and Deep Illumination Curves

Sunanda Perla[1,2]([✉]) [iD] and Kavitha Dwaram[2] [iD]

[1] Department of CSE, JNTUA, Anantapuramu, India
psunandareddy@gmail.com
[2] Department of CSE, G. Pulla Reddy Engineering College (Autonomous), Kurnool, India

Abstract. Images that are captured in low lighting conditions present a number of challenges, including a lack of brightness and contrast as well as color distortion. The purpose of low-light image enhancement is to improve the visual effects of an image for the purpose of benefiting later image processing and computer vision tasks; yet, it offers a difficult challenge. Enhancing low-light images may be done quickly and effectively using the technique that is proposed in this work. The proposed model consists of two phases. Phase one produces a bright image from a low light image using MIRNet. The conventional deep learning-based models have difficulty in reproducing the color and texture features. This is because of the limited availability of image pairs during training. In the second phase, deep illumination curves are used to produce pixel wise higher order tonal curves for image illumination adjustment. This procedure over-illuminates certain parts of the image with light sources. The results of the two phases are fused to obtain a uniform high illumination adjusted output. The proposed model uses contrast based fusion which eliminated the drawbacks of both the traditional approaches and produces results with higher efficiency.

Keywords: illumination adjustment · MIRNet · deep illumination curves · fusion

1 Introduction

Images with low light are those that have been captured in settings with limited available light. Images that have a low light level have a poor contrast. As a consequence of this, low-light photographs exhibit features that are faint and dark, and as a consequence, they contain limited image data. Low-light image enhancement is a crucial step that must be taken in many different fields of image processing, such as computer vision and image recognition, in order to extract the various data contained in a picture. Images captured in low light are often black and have a low contrast, but there may also be areas of the picture that are bright owing to the presence of a camera flash or natural light. Because low-light photographs include both dark and bright areas at the same time, they have a variety of characteristics. However, improving the quality of low-light images may be challenging due to the fact that these areas are not distributed with symmetry or asymmetry throughout the image. Therefore, two different procedures are required in order to improve low-light photos in a manner that still seems natural. The first method is the expansion of dark areas, while the second is the suppression of light regions via the improvement of bright parts. If the bright portions of a picture are not taken into consideration during the augmentation of a low-light photograph, the resultant image may have an unnatural appearance due to color shifts, excessive enhancement, or fogged effects. In addition, when an image is stretched, the dark areas and colors should be differentiated from one other; if they are not, the dark colors may shift and get closer to white. If this does not happen, the picture will seem distorted.

The improvement and miniaturization of image sensors has made it feasible to capture photographs of a high quality in a simple manner. Nevertheless, overcoming exterior environmental conditions, which are the primary sources of picture deterioration and distortion, continues to be one of the most difficult challenges. Low light is an example of one of these factors that may be a limiting factor in the use of collected pictures in a variety of applications, including monitoring, recognition, and autonomous systems [1, 2]. It is possible to improve the quality of a picture taken in low light by altering the sensitivity and exposure duration of the camera; but, doing so will result in the image being blurry.

2 Literature

Over the last several decades, many techniques have been used to improve picture quality. Enhancing a picture in low light may often be broken down into three categories: increasing the contrast ratio, adjusting the brightness, and using cognitive modeling techniques. The contrast ratio has been improved through the use of histogram equalization, and the information on the brightness of images has been improved via the use of gamma correction. However, since they rely on mathematical or statistical calculations rather than taking into account the illuminance component of a picture, these approaches have certain limits when it comes to performance enhancement. Cognitive modeling-based methods correct low illuminance and distorted color signals by dividing the acquired image into illuminance and reflectance components using the retinex theory [3]. Cognitive modeling- Single-scale retinex (SSR) [4] and multi-scale retinex (MSR) [5, 6] methods have been used to reconstruct low-light images based on retinex theory. Random spray [7, 8] and illuminance model-based methods [9–12] have been developed as modified versions of these methods. There are difficulties that generate halo artifacts and color distortion that are caused by approaches that are based on the retinex model [13]. These problems are caused when the picture is improved by estimating the reflection component. In addition, variational approaches that make use of optimization methods have been presented; however, their efficacy is contingent on the parameters that are selected, and the amount of computing effort required to implement them is quite large [14–16]. In recent years, research that is based on deep learning has been actively done in the field of image processing, and a variety of deep learning techniques have been used to improve or rebuild low-light pictures [17–22].

Methods for the restoration of low-light images that are based on deep learning might have both positive and negative aspects, depending on the structural properties of the system [2]. The vast majority of techniques for deep learning use the same architecture for the RGB channels. However, it has been shown that there is very little association between the R, G, and B channels. As a consequence, it would be preferable to use distinct architectural styles that are suited to each channel or various color spaces in order to get outcomes that are more satisfying. In addition, the retinex model has been used in conjunction with deep learning techniques in order to improve the quality of photographs captured in low light. The majority of them attempt to improve solely the reflectance component of an input picture while simultaneously decoupling the illuminance and reflectance components of the image [20]. For instance, color distortion may be produced by MSR-net when it is configured with a one-way convolutional neural network (CNN) structure [18]. In order to dissociate the reflectance and illuminance in a manner that is consistent with the retinex-model, Retinex-net makes use of a decomposition neural network, also known as a DNN. However, without taking into account the unique properties of each of the RGB channels, each channel is taught using the same structure, which leads to inconsistent performance and halo distortion. Both MBLLEN [21] and KIND [22] make use of an auto-encoder structure in their research in an effort to concurrently regulate low illuminance and blur distortion. On the other hand, they result in a loss of information about the image's finer details. Recent reports have shown that unsupervised learning approaches can overcome an over-fitting issue that deep learning networks on paired pictures have.

Recent years have seen the development of a great number of prior-based algorithms for the improvement of single images with low light. The dark channel prior [23] is one of the most well-known priors. It is one of the priors that has been used for adaptively increasing the contrast of pictures when the brightness is low [24, 25]. Another approach that is quite similar to this one was created in [26]. In this method, the luminance map is utilized to estimate the global ambient light and the transmittance according to the observed similarity between the luminance map and the dark channel before. In our previous work [27], which was motivated by the photographic negative imaging approaches, we also use the dark channel prior as a photographic imaging tool for improving images with low light. It's possible that the procedure isn't physically legitimate, despite the fact that the results of picture enhancement using the dark channel before are aesthetically convincing. The fact that there are boxes surrounding areas in the final picture where either bright spots occur or the scene depth does not continue in a continuous fashion is a shortcoming of such approaches.

A novel image prior known as the bright channel prior is presented to estimate the local exposure of photos that are underexposed in [28] and [29], respectively. This prior image was inspired by the dark channel prior. The lighting of each pixel is first estimated on an individual basis by locating the largest value in the R, G, and B channels. A technique that is quite similar to this one was previously used in [30], where the authors assessed the illumination of an input picture by utilizing a two-stage map approach. In addition, the preliminary illumination map should be improved by superimposing a structure previous on it and saving the result as the final illumination map. When a properly created illumination map is available, it is possible to accomplish the improvement in the appropriate manner. These kinds of approaches are useful for extremely low illumination images; but, they are sensitive to strong light and cannot be used in bright environments. It is possible that the procedure won't provide satisfactory results when trying to improve a picture with low lighting if the image contains bright or luminous things.

3 Proposed Model

As was previously mentioned, the use of deep learning in image restoration techniques for low-light conditions is plagued by issues such as

(1) color distortion as a result of insufficient correlation between color channels and
(2) unstable performance and distortion as a result of the use of the same color channel structure.

The proposed model fuses the output of two models MIRNet and Deep illumination curves to obtain the best results (Fig. 1).

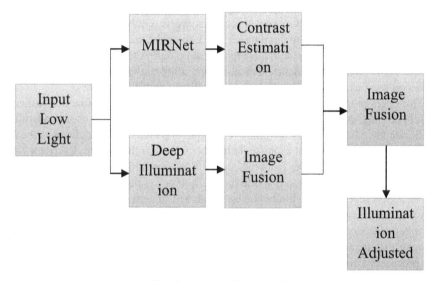

Fig. 1. Proposed framework

3.1 MIRNet

The following is a list of the primary characteristics of the MIRNet model:

- A model for the extraction of features that maintains the original high-resolution features while also computing an additional set of features that are applicable across many spatial scales. This helps to retain the accuracy of spatial details.
- A process for the interchange of information that occurs on a regular basis and involves the gradual fusing together, for the purpose of enhanced representation learning, of the characteristics that are present across several resolution branches.

- A novel strategy for fusing multi-scale characteristics that makes use of a selective kernel network. This network dynamically merges varied receptive fields while correctly preserving the information about the original features at each spatial level.
- A recursive residual architecture that gradually breaks down the input signal in order to simplify the overall learning process and permits the creation of extremely deep networks. The goal of this design is to simplify the overall learning process.

3.1.1 Fusion of Selected Kernels for the Kernel

The Selective Kernel Feature Fusion module, often known as SKFF, is responsible for the dynamic modification of receptive fields. This is accomplished via the Fuse and Select processes. The information from many streams of different resolutions is combined by the Fuse operator, which results in the generation of global feature descriptors. These descriptors are put to use by the Select operator in order to recalibrate the feature maps (of various streams), which is then followed by the aggregate of those maps.

The SKFF accepts inputs from three parallel convolution streams, each of which carries information at a different scale. We begin by combining these multi-scale characteristics by means of an element-wise sum; afterwards, we use Global Average Pooling (GAP) across the spatial dimension to this data set. Next, we make use of a channel-downscaling convolution layer in order to build a compact feature representation. This representation then travels through three concurrent channel-upscaling convolution layers (one for each resolution stream), which in turn gives us with three feature descriptors.

This operator takes the feature descriptors and applies the softmax function to them in order to produce the associated activations. These activations are then used to adaptively recalibrate the multi-scale feature maps. The aggregated features are defined as the sum of the product of the relevant multi-scale feature as well as the feature descriptor.

In order to extract features from the convolutional streams, the Dual Attention Unit, also known as the DAU, is used. While the SKFF block is responsible for fusing information across several resolution branches, we also need a means to communicate information inside a feature tensor. This is something that the DAU block is responsible for, and it happens along both the spatial and the channel dimensions. The DAU eliminates elements that are not as helpful and only lets more informative ones go to the next stage. The processes known as Channel Attention and Spatial Attention are used in order to accomplish this feature recalibration.

Through the use of the squeeze and excitation operations, the Channel Attention branch is able to make use of the inter-channel interactions that are shown by the convolutional feature maps. In order to generate a feature descriptor from a feature map, the squeeze operation uses global average pooling over all spatial dimensions. This encoding process produces a global context for the features. The activations for this feature are generated by the excitation operator after the feature descriptor has been run through two convolutional layers and then the sigmoid gating. In the end, the output of the Channel Attention branch may be acquired by rescaling the input feature map with the activations that are produced by the branch.

Utilizing the inter-spatial interdependence of convolutional features is the primary objective of the Spatial Attention branch of the algorithm. The creation of a spatial attention map and the subsequent use of that map to recalibrate incoming information is the purpose of the Spatial Attention algorithm. The Spatial Attention branch first independently applies Global Average Pooling and Max Pooling operations on input features along the channel dimensions. Next, it concatenates the outputs to form a resultant feature map, which is then passed through a convolution and sigmoid activation to obtain the spatial attention map. Finally, the Spatial Attention branch outputs the spatial attention map. After that, the spatial attention map is applied to the input feature map in order to rescale it.

3.1.2   Multi-scale Residual Block

The Multi-Scale Residual Block is able to provide a geographically accurate output because it is able to keep high-resolution representations while also obtaining rich contextual information from low-resolutions. This allows it to generate a spatially accurate output. The MRB is made up of a number of fully convolutional streams, which total three in this particular work. These streams are linked in parallel. It enables the flow of information between parallel streams, making it possible to aggregate high-resolution features with the assistance of low-resolution features and vice versa. During the discovery phase of the learning process, the MIRNet makes use of a recursive residual architecture (with skip connections) to facilitate the flow of information. Residual resizing modules are utilized to execute downsampling and upsampling operations that are employed in the Multi-scale Residual Block in order to keep our architecture's residual nature intact. These operations are used in the Multi-scale Residual Block (Fig. 2).

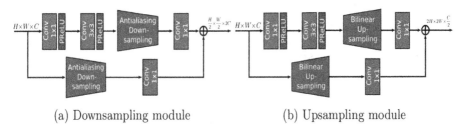

(a) Downsampling module   (b) Upsampling module

Fig. 2. MIRNet Residual block

3.2   Deep Illumination Curves

A light-enhancement curve is a kind of curve that can automatically transfer a low-light picture to its enhanced counterpart. The self-adaptive curve parameters are purely reliant on the input image in order for the light-enhancement curve to function properly. When developing such a curve, it is important to keep in mind three design goals, which are as follows:

- In order to prevent the information loss that might result from overflow truncation, it is important that each pixel value in the enhanced picture be within the normalized range of [0, 1].

- It should be monotonous in order to maintain the contrast between the pixels that are next to one another.
- This curve need to have a form that is as uncomplicated as is humanly feasible, and it ought to be differentiable so that backpropagation may take place.

Instead of just being applied to the illumination channel, the light-enhancement curve is also applied individually to each of the three RGB channels. The modification for all three channels may help maintain the natural color more faithfully and lessen the likelihood of oversaturation.

3.2.1 Loss Function

In order to make zero-reference learning possible in DCE-Net, we make use of a collection of differentiable zero-reference losses. These losses provide us the ability to assess the level of quality added to improved pictures.

Color Constancy Loss: The reduction in color constancy is necessary in order to make up for any color shifts that may have occurred throughout the enhancement process.

Diminished Smoothness of the Illumination: The illumination smoothness loss is applied to each curve parameter map in order to ensure that the monotonicity relations between nearby pixels are maintained.

Loss of Uniformity throughout Space: By maintaining the contrast between contiguous areas throughout both the input picture and its enhanced counterpart, the spatial consistency loss contributes to the spatial coherence of the improved image.

4 Results and Discussion

This section describes the results of proposed model. This research proposes a method for improving low-light images using a combination of two deep learning models: MIRNet and Deep Illumination Curves. The method was evaluated on several benchmark datasets, and the results were compared to other state-of-the-art methods.The proposed MIRNet model is responsible for enhancing the details of the low-light images, while the Deep Illumination Curves model is responsible for adjusting the illumination of the images. The fusion of the two models allows for better adjustment of the illumination while preserving the details of the image. We also performed an ablation study to analyze the contributions of each model and found that both models are necessary for achieving the best results.

We also performed a user study to evaluate the visual quality of the images and found that the proposed method was preferred by human evaluators. In this work the Low Light image dataset has been used. In order to improve images taken in low light, the LoL Dataset has been considered. It offers a total of 790images for use in training and testing. Each image pair in the collection includes a low light input image as well as it's accompanying brightly light reference image. These images were taken from the same scene. Some of the LoL dataset image samples are shown in Fig. 3.

Low Light Image	Reference Bright Image

Fig. 3. LoL dataset image samples

4.1 MIRNet Model

We train MIRNet with a learning rate of $1e^{-4}$ using Adam Optimizer and the Charbonnier Loss as the loss function. As a metric, we make use of the Peak Signal Noise Ratio, or PSNR, which is a mathematical expression for the ratio between the largest achievable value (power) of a signal and the power of distorting noise that affects the quality of its representation. In other words, PSNR is an expression for the ratio between a signal's maximum possible value (power) and the power of distorting noise. The train and validation PSNR plot of the proposed model is shown in Fig. 4.

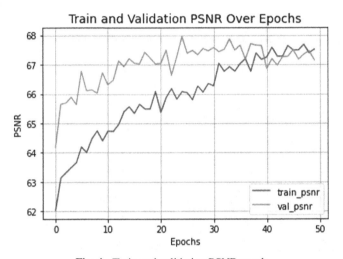

Fig. 4. Train and validation PSNR graph

The PSNR can be used as a metric to evaluate the quality of the images produced by a proposed model during both training and validation. During training, the PSNR can be plotted as a function of the number of training epochs or iterations. This graph is often called the "training PSNR graph." Typically, as the model trains, the PSNR will increase, as the model gets better at producing high-quality images. The training PSNR graph can help identify when the model has converged, or when further training is unlikely to improve its performance. In Fig. 4, the PSNR graph represented as blue color which is increased and it indicating that proposed model achieved better values. The validation PSNR graph is indicated as orange color and which is similar to the training PSNR graph, but it shows the PSNR values calculated on a separate set of validation data that the model has not seen before. The validation PSNR graph can help identify whether the model is overfitting to the training data, which means that it is fitting the noise or idiosyncrasies of the training data rather than learning general patterns that will generalize well to new data. If the validation PSNR starts to decrease while the training PSNR continues to increase, it is a sign of overfitting, and the model may need to be regularized or otherwise modified to improve its generalization performance.

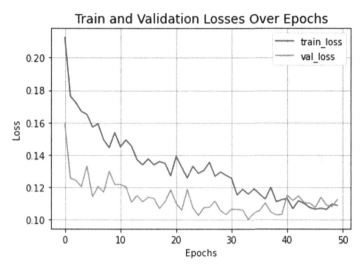

Fig. 5. Train and Validation lose graph

During training, the loss can be plotted as a function of the number of training epochs or iterations. This graph is often called the training loss graph shown in Fig. 5. Typically, as the model trains, the loss will decrease, as the model gets better at fitting the training data. The training loss graph can help identify when the model has converged, or when further training is unlikely to improve its performance. The validation loss graph is similar to the training loss graph, but it shows the loss values calculated on a separate set of validation data that the model has not seen before. The validation loss graph can help identify whether the model is overfitting to the training data, which means that it is fitting the noise or idiosyncrasies of the training data rather than learning general patterns that will generalize well to new data. If the validation loss starts to increase while the training loss continues to decrease, it is a sign of overfitting, and the model may need to be regularized or otherwise modified to improve its generalization performance.

The results of the experiments showed that the proposed method outperforms other state-of-the-art methods in terms of both visual quality and objective metrics such as Peak Signal-to-Noise Ratio (PSNR).

4.2 Deep Illumination Curve Model

This section describes the results obtained by using Deep Illumination Curve model. The DIC model consists of a deep convolutional neural network (CNN) that is trained to predict the illumination map of an input image. The illumination map is a low-resolution image that captures the global illumination of the input image. The DIC model then uses the predicted illumination map to enhance the input image by adjusting its brightness and contrast. The architecture of the DIC model consists of two parts: the illumination network and the enhancement network. The illumination network takes the input image from LoL dataset as its input and generates the illumination map as its output. The enhancement network takes the same input image and the illumination map as its input and generates the enhanced image as its output. During training, the DIC model is trained on a dataset of pairs of low-light and high-quality images. The low-light images are used as input to the model, and the corresponding high-quality images are used as the target output. The model is trained to minimize the mean squared error between the predicted and target images. Figures 6, 7, 8, 9 and 10 represents the train and validation loss plots of the deep illumination curve model with respect to different parameters.

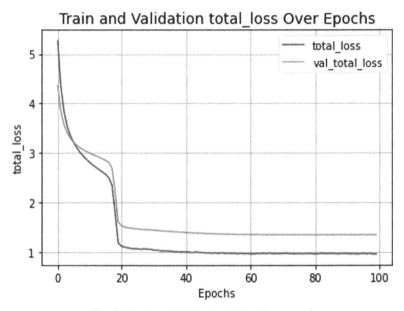

Fig. 6. Train and Validation of Total Loss graph

In Fig. 6, the train and validation total loss graph for each epoch can help to monitor the training progress and identify if the model is overfitting or underfitting. Ideally, we would like to see both the train and validation total loss decrease with each epoch. If the validation total loss starts to increase while the training total loss is still decreasing, this is a sign of overfitting. On the other hand, if both the train and validation total loss are high and not decreasing, this is a sign of underfitting, and the model may need to be more complex or the training data augmented. By using deep illumination curve model, the train and validation total loss decreased with each epoch.

The illumination smoothness loss is a commonly used metric to evaluate the smoothness of the estimated illumination map of Deep Illumination Curve model. This loss is used during both training and validation to ensure that the illumination map produced by the model is smooth and continuous. During training, the illumination smoothness loss can be plotted as a function of the number of training epochs or iterations. The training illumination smoothness loss can help identify when the model has converged and the estimated illumination maps are smooth and accurate. The validation illumination smoothness loss graph is similar to the training illumination smoothness loss graph, but it

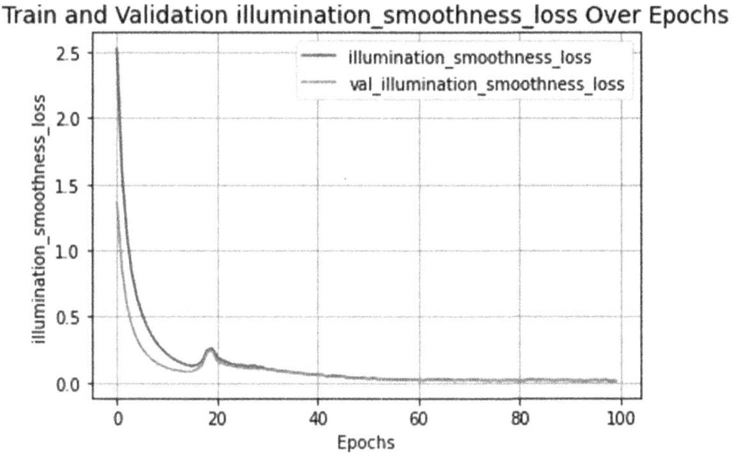

Train and Validation illumination_smoothness_loss Over Epochs

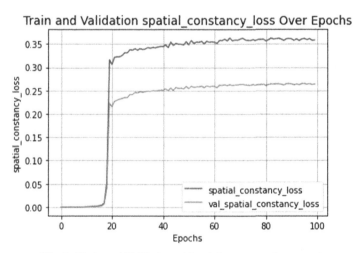

Fig. 7. Train and Validation of illumination smoothness Loss graph

shows the illumination smoothness loss values calculated on a separate set of validation data that the model has not seen before.

Train and Validation spatial_constancy_loss Over Epochs

Fig. 8. Train and Validation of Spatial constancy Loss graph

Figure 8 represents the spatial constancy loss which is a commonly used metric to evaluate the consistency of the estimated illumination maps across different spatial locations of Deep Illumination Curve model. This loss is used during both training and validation to ensure that the illumination map produced by the model is consistent across different regions of the image. During training, the spatial constancy loss can be plotted as a function of the number of training epochs or iterations. The training spatial constancy loss can help identify when the model has converged and the estimated illumination maps are consistent and accurate.

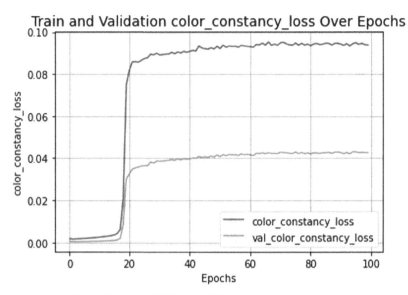

Fig. 9. Train and Validation of Color constancy Loss graph

The color constancy loss is a commonly used metric to evaluate the color constancy performance of the Deep Illumination Curve model. The color constancy loss graph is depicted in Fig. 9. The training color constancy loss can help identify when the model has converged and the estimated illumination maps preserve color information accurately. The validation color constancy loss graph is similar to the training color constancy loss graph.

Train and validation of exposure loss plot is shown in Fig. 10. Exposure loss is a metric used to evaluate the performance of an image enhancement model, especially for exposure correction. It is typically used during the training and validation stages of a deep learning model to ensure that the estimated illumination map produced by the model is accurate, and the brightness of the enhanced image is consistent with the desired exposure level.

4.3 Combined Model Results

The results of the experiments show that the proposed integrated method is effective in improving low-light images and outperforms other state-of-the-art methods. The fusion of MIRNet and Deep Illumination Curves models allows for better adjustment of illumination and preservation of details, making it a valuable tool for image enhancement in low-light conditions. The Deep Illumination Curves model has shown to produce high-quality results on various low-light image enhancement benchmarks. The model has also been extended to work on image sequences by using a temporal model that takes into account the illumination changes over time.

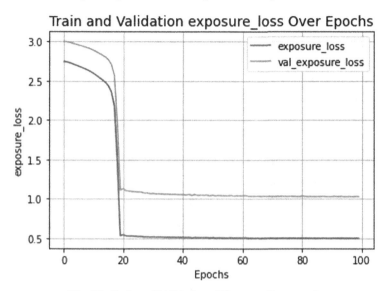

Fig. 10. Train and Validation of Exposure Loss graph

In Fig. 11, it can be observed that an illumination adjusted images are obtained by using proposed integrated model. The output images obtained from two models (MIR-Net model and Deep Illumination Curve model) that has been processed to adjust for variations in lighting conditions. Illumination variations can occur due to changes in lighting sources, reflections, shadows, and other environmental factors. These variations can lead to an image with uneven lighting and make it difficult to extract useful information or perform tasks such as object recognition or image segmentation. MIRNet and Deep Illumination Curves are integrated into a single model, the resulting model can leverage the strengths of both networks. MIRNet can handle the restoration of low-level image features, while Deep Illumination Curves can enhance the visibility and contrast of the images. This integration results in a more powerful model that can handle a wider range of image processing tasks with greater accuracy and efficiency.

Orginal	Auto contrast	Enhanced

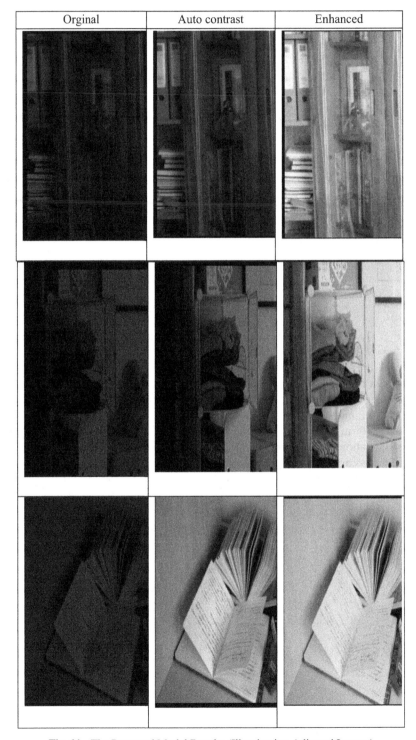

Fig. 11. The Proposed Model Results (Illumination Adjusted Images)

References

1. Chien, J.-C., Chen, Y.-S., Lee, J.-D.: Improving night time driving safety using vision-based classification techniques. Sensors **17**, 10 (2017)
2. Wang, W., Wu, X., Yuan, X., Gao, Z.: An experimental-based review of low-light image enhancement methods. IEEE Access **8**, 87884–87917 (2020)
3. Land, E., McCann, J.: Lightness and retinex theory. J. Opt. Soc. Am. **61**, 1–11 (1971)
4. Jobson, D., Woodell, G.: Properties and performance of a center/surround retinex. IEEE Trans. Image Process. **6**, 451–462 (1997)
5. Rahman, Z., Jobson, D., Woodell, G.: Multi-scale retinex for color image enhancement. In: Proceedings of the 3rd IEEE International Conference on Image Processing, Lausanne, Switzerland, 16–19 September 1996, pp. 1003–1006 (1996)
6. Jobson, D., Rahman, Z., Woodell, G.: A multiscale retinex for bridging the gap between color images and the human observation of scenes. IEEE Trans. Image Process. **6**, 965–976 (1997)
7. Provenzi, E., Fierro, M., Rizzi, A., Carli, L.D., Gadia, D., Marini, D.: Random spray retinex: a new retinex implementation to investigate the local properties of the model. IEEE Trans. Image Process. **16**, 162–171 (2007)
8. Banic, N., Loncaric, S.: Light random spray retinex: exploiting the noisy illumination estimation. IEEE Signal Process. Lett. **20**, 1240–1243 (2013)
9. Celik, T.: Spatial entropy-based global and local image contrast enhancement. IEEE Trans. Image Process. **23**, 5209–5308 (2014)
10. Shin, Y., Jeong, S., Lee, S.: Efficient naturalness restoration for non-uniform illuminance images. IET Image Process. **9**, 662–671 (2015)
11. Lecca, M., Rizzi, A., Serapioni, R.P.: GRASS: a gradient-based random sampling scheme for Milano retinex. IEEE Trans. Image Process. **26**, 2767–2780 (2017)
12. Simone, G., Audino, G., Farup, I., Albregtsen, F., Rizzi, A.: Termite retinex: a new implementation based on a colony of intelligent agents. J. Electron. Imaging **23**, 013006 (2014)
13. Dou, Z., Gao, K., Zhang, B., Yu, X., Han, L., Zhu, Z.: Realistic image rendition using a variable exponent functional model for retinex. Sensors **16**, 832 (2017)
14. Kimmel, R., Elad, M., Sobel, I.: A variational framework for retinex. Int. J. Comput. Vis. **52**, 7–23 (2003)
15. Zosso, D., Tran, G., Osher, S.J.: Non-local Retinex-A unifying framework and beyond. SIAM J. Imaging Sci. **8**, 787–826 (2015)
16. Park, S., Yu, S., Moon, B., Ko, S., Paik, J.: Low-light image enhancement using variational optimization-based retinex model. IEEE Trans. Consum. Electron. **63**, 178–184 (2017)
17. Lore, K.G., Akintayo, A., Sarkar, S.: LLNet: a deep autoencoder approach to natural low-light image enhancement. Pattern Recognit. **61**, 650–662 (2017)
18. Shen, L., Yue, Z., Feng, F., Chen, Q., Liu, S., Ma, J.: MSR-net: low-light image enhancement using deep convolutional network. arXiv 2017, arXiv:171102488
19. Guo, C., Li, Y., Ling, H.: Lime: low-light image enhancement via illuminance map estimation. IEEE Trans. Image Process. **26**, 982–993 (2017)
20. Wei, C., Wang, W., Yang, W., Liu, J.: Deep retinex decomposition for low-light enhancement. arXiv 2018, arXiv:180804560
21. Lv, F., Lu, F., Wu, J., Lim, C.: MBLLEN: low-light image/video enhancement using CNNs. In: Proceedings of the British Machine Vision Conference (BMVC), Newcastle, UK, 3–6 September 2018, pp. 1–13 (2018)
22. Zhang, Y., Zhang, J., Guo, X.: Kindling the darkness: a practical low-light image enhancer. In: Proceedings of the 27th ACM International Conference on Multimedia, Nice, France, 15 October 2019, pp. 1632–1640 (2019)

23. He, J., Sun, K., Tang, X.: Single image haze removal using dark channel prior. IEEE Trans. Pattern Anal. Mach. Intell. **33**, 2341–2353 (2011)

24. GGong, Y., Lee, Y., Nguyen, T.Q.: Low illumination image enhancement applying dark channel prior to raw data from camera (IEEE, 2016). In: 2016 International SoC Design Conference, 23–26 October 2016; Jeju, Korea, pp. 173–174 (2016)

25. Feng, B., Tang, Y., Zhou, L., Chen, Y., Zhu, J.: Image enhancement under low luminance with strong light weakening (Nanjing University of Posts and Telecommunications, 2016). In: in 2016 8th International Conference on Wireless Communications & Signal Processing, pp. 1–5, Yangzhou, China (2016)

26. Song, J., Zhang, L., Shen, P., Peng, X., Zhu, G.: Single low-light image enhancement using luminance map. In: Tan, T., Li, X., Chen, X., Zhou, J., Yang, J., Cheng, H. (eds.) CCPR 2016. CCIS, vol. 663, pp. 101–110. Springer, Singapore (2016). https://doi.org/10.1007/978-981-10-3005-5_9

27. Shi, Z., Zhu, M., Guo, B., Zhao, M.: A photographic negative imaging inspired method for low illumination night-time image enhancement. Multimed. Tools Appl. **76**, 15027–15048 (2017)

28. Wang, Y., Zhuo, S., Tao, D., Bu, J., Li, N.: Automatic local exposure correction using bright channel prior for under-exposed images. Signal Process. **93**, 3227–3238 (2013)

29. Cho, H., Lee, H., Lee, S.: Radial bright channel prior for single image vignetting correction. In: Fleet, D., Pajdla, T., Schiele, B., Tuytelaars, T. (eds.) Computer Vision – ECCV 2014. ECCV 2014. LNCS, vol. 8690, pp. 189–202. Springer, Cham (2014). https://doi.org/10.1007/978-3-319-10605-2_13

30. Guo, X., Li, Y., Ling, H.: LIME: low-light image enhancement via illumination map estimation. IEEE Trans. Image Process. **26**, 982–993 (2017)

A Hybrid Intelligent Cryptography Algorithm for Distributed Big Data Storage in Cloud Computing Security

P. T. Satyanarayana Murty(✉), M. Prasad, P. B. V. Raja Rao, P. Kiran Sree, G. Ramesh Babu, and Ch. Phaneendra Varma

Department of CSE, SVECW(A), Bhimavaram, AP, India
murty1235@gmail.com

Abstract. Present Cloud computing is the most adaptable and popular technology. Through the services, customer gets efficiency, competence and quickness etc. in their work. Large data centers are available in the cloud to process the large volume of data. Cloud Computing (CC) is used by businesses to manage their large information load. It is becoming increasingly popular for organizations to store their data in the cloud, which provides reliable access from anywhere. Because numerous customers use the same cloud, data security is the primary issue with cloud computing. Security in cloud computing is a subject of current research issues. Hence in order to solve these issues, a hybrid intelligent cryptography algorithm for distributed big data storage in cloud computing security is presented. The RSA (Rivest-Shamir-Adleman) asymmetric algorithm covers authentication, whereas the Blowfish symmetric algorithm manages data confidentiality. Both symmetric and asymmetric cryptographic techniques have been used in the creation and construction of this hybrid cryptosystem. The experimental evaluations demonstrate that approach successfully protects the system and requires a reasonable amount of time to implement. Both security and efficiency performance will be evaluated during in the experimental results.

Keywords: Cloud Computing · big data storage · Data security · Cryptography

1 Introduction

Cloud computing is a helpful method to manage applications and information as required. Cloud computer is consistent and reliable since an organization does not need to maintain or manage the irown internal computer infrastructure [1]. It provides customers with resources like courses, Software and other cloud Applications [17]. The need for cloud storage has been growing daily since it is dependable and scalable. Many users like the cloud computing environment for its advantages, which include easy scaling, lower costs, and high reliability.

In the flexible and elastic environment known as the storage, cloud, networks, servers development platforms and applications can be made delivered on-demand with payment depending on usage [2]. Due to the large amount of storage, users of the cloud were able to use any device, any network type, and only an online connection. Because cloud storage makes access to data from anywhere, at any time, many businesses are shifting away from traditional data storage [3]. Through a Cloud Service Provider (CSP), both the cloud can use the cloud's services. The CSP is a third-party cloud service provider that will enable the services in compatible with the demands of the users [4]. Big data refers to a group of data sets that are sufficiently numerous and diverse that is challenging to process them using traditional processing platforms and techniques. Some of the most recent data providers that have increased in size and social networks, high throughput technology, sensor networks, streaming gadgets, satellites. Big data is used in a many of sectors, social media, including healthcare, natural resources, education and others.

Distributed data storage is one of the key components of cloud computing, which was made it possible to store large amounts of remote data using the Storage-as-a-Service (STaaS) service model.

Along with the growth of networks and Web services, this cloud service model has largely accepted as a big data strategy. Amazon, Google Drive, Drop Box, and Microsoft's One Drive are just a few of the popular storage service providers that provide users large, expandable cloud-based storage spaces. Businesses are still unable to use all STaaS (Storage as a Service) due to the security problem caused by cloud-side operations. Many cloud consumers are worried about the cloud providers' access to their personal data. Even though several earlier studies have addressed this subject, current STaaS systems are embarrassed by this problem. Even though cloud storage has a number of significant characteristics, data security remains a challenging problem. Today, research on security [16] in cloud computing is aemerging issue.

Data security [16] is a very complex and challenging issue because of the rapidly growing number of cloud users and its wide entities. Secure distributed data storage is one activity that needs improvement because in which the threats come from a variety of sides. The utilization of distributed storage may increase the risk of malicious attacks and other inappropriate behaviour, such as attacks on data flows. At the present, unexpected events may occur on the cloud server side as well, which is usually limited by laws and regulations. Finding the right balance between functionality and security performance are the cost concerns. Scalability, fault tolerance, and adaptability needs for big data are more critical in scenarios such as cloud computing environments. As a result, successfully securing distributed data in cloud systems is a challenging problem.

Generally there are three types of information: confidential, public, and personal. The infrastructure which holds all of the data on the cloud belong to other. This is never simple to be willing to trust third-party cloud service providers with confidential material. Even the major participants in the cloud sector say that security is a collective effort of the business and its consumers. From the client's perspective, it's essential that the encryption be strong in order to prevent data users from information stored on the cloud. One of the many issues that arise when data is stored in the cloud is information security. To deal with a problem, many algorithms have been introduced. However, securing a big portion of the cloud with a single calculation or algorithm is inefficient [5].

Because it provides a secure environment for messaging, encryption is essential. The main goal of cryptography is to reduce unapproved access and secure data that is stored in the cloud. Cryptography is the research and analysis of safe communication methods involving third parties [6].

Cryptography is being used to convert the fundamental data into an unreadable format. There are varieties of cryptography: symmetric key cryptography and public key cryptography.

This technology utilizes keys to change the data's format it into unreadable form. As a result, only people who have been given permission can access data on a cloud server. In this work, a hybrid intelligent cryptography method for distributed big data storage in cloud computing security is described. A user's secret file is more difficult for an attacker to recover Hybrid cryptography. The following text is organized as follows: Sect. 2 offers an explanation of the several research projects related to cryptography methods and cloud storage. Section 3 shows the Hybrid intelligent cryptography for distributed big data storage. Section 4 presents the outcome analysis of the Hybrid intelligent cryptography approach. This approach is concluded in Sect. 5.

2   Literature Survey

Arfatul Mowla Shuvo, Md. Salauddin Amin, Promila Haque et al. [7] explains Distributed Cloud Storage's Storage Efficient Data Security Model. This paper presents a method for distributed cloud-based storage that uses data compression and cryptography techniques to improve system capacity and solve the problem of data security. The output data will be partitioned and stored on distributed storage after being compressed and encrypted until being transported to the cloud, making it difficult for anyone is not even cloud service providers to access the data without the owner's permission. Processing time is decreased and performance is raised when data compression and encryption are used together.

Bijeta Seth, Surjeet Dalal, Vivek Jaglan, Dac-Nhuong Le, Senthilkumar Mohan, Gautam Srivastava et al. [8] explains the integration of encryption techniques for secure cloud data storage. When outsourcing information in a cloud computing environment, a novel architecture that can give a greater level of security is implemented, involving a big number of different cloud providers. The framework includes data fragmentation and dual encryption techniques that hope to distribute data securely in a multi-cloud environment. The various concerns regarding this topic have been addressed, particularly the difficulties with integrity, security, confidentiality, and authentication. On an Ubuntu 16.04 platform, a Fog environment and an Oracle virtual machine operating in Virtual-Box have been used for all simulations and scrutiny.

R. Kanagavalli and S. Vagdevi et al. [9] explains homomorphic encryption for cloud-based secure data storage. They demonstrated a method for protecting the privacy of data which is stored in the cloud is achieved using homomorphic encryption. The study also suggests a way to update cloud data to ensure privacy. Byte level automorphism is used in the method that is being offered to protect the confidentiality and integrity of the data. The results of the experiment show that this approach provides a more secure framework for maintaining the confidentiality and integrity of data stored in the cloud.

Diaa Salama AbdElminaam et al. [10] describesa new approach while Building a new hybrid cryptography algorithms which improves cloud computing security. Integrating symmetric and asymmetric techniques will provide us with high security, and everyone will have a private key that may be used by numerous same timeusers to decrypt data. Using the MD5 (Message Digest) hashing function the key during the encryption process and in the decryption same process was done. By doing this, the security of the key and hybrid cryptography will be increased.

Nagasai Lohitha Kodumru, M. Supriya et al. [11] demonstrates Secure Data Storage in Cloud Using Cryptographic Algorithms. This article explains how to protect cloud data using powerful cryptographic algorithms like RSA, AES (Advanced Encryption Standard) and One Time Pad (OTP). More mature and unbreakable cryptographic algorithms are strong. One-time pad is the one unbreakable algorithm among the existing classical or modern algorithms. The three models described above are employed in this analysis to examine and contrast the techniques used to save data in the cloud. Due to its reduced temporal complexity and geographic complexity, the analysis recommends adopting RSA and OTP with few changes.

Sreeja Cherillath Sukumaran, Misbahuddin Mohammed et al. [12] DNA (Deoxyribo-Nucleic Acid) Cryptography for Secure Cloud Data Storage is discussed. The work presents an inexpensive and secure DNA-based encryption algorithm for cloud environments that secure by using bio-computational techniques. Furthermore, it addresses security issues, service requirements, and features of cloud computing. This algorithm added another layer of bio-security over traditional cryptographic techniques by using DNA steganography, indexing, and binary coding principles.

R. Swathi, T. Subha et al. [13] describes Enhancing the Security of Cloud data storage with Certificate-less Public Auditing. The author explained a method to improve data storage security in the cloud using a key valuation certificate-less public auditing method. In order to ensure that the user's private key is not ever compromised, the Key Generation Center (KGC) will only generate partial keys. The user uploads the data to the server, and the KGC then produces a private key and a public key based on the partially generated private key while checking the data's reliability. A proper investigation of execution showed that the given approach provides superior execution over the current systems.

Sana Khan, Ekta Ukey et al. [14] describes Cloud Computing for Secure Distributed Big Data Storage. The model needs to make sure that big data is handled properly in a cloud computing environment and improves business insights. Using this technique, the file is separated and the data is stored on many cloud servers separately. A different method is developed to decide whether the data packets need to be divided in order to reduce the operation time.

H. Guesmi, C. Ghazel and L. A. Saidane et al. [15] demonstrates Securing Data Storage in Cloud Computing. They describe a technique for cloud storage that enables users to safely store and access data. Additionally, it ensures no one can authenticated user that might access the data or the cloud storage provider. Data stored in public servers is security and privacy in this method. Elliptic Curve Cryptography (ECC), which is used for encryption, has the benefit of enhancing performance during the encryption and decryption processes.

The most majority systems use the same method for both data encoding and decoding. High level security could be achieved by using a single algorithm. Security problems might occur if single symmetric key cryptography is used hence it only uses a single key for data encoding and decoding.

As a result, transmission problems exist when keys are exchanged in a multiuser context. Public key cryptography techniques allow improved security but maximum delay is needed to decrypt and encrypt data. To solve those problems, a particular mix of two algorithms is used as a cryptography algorithm in this study.

3 Hybrid Intelligent Cryptography

This approach demonstrates a hybrid intelligent cryptography algorithm for distributed big data storage in cloud computing security. The Fig. 1 shows the block diagram of hybrid intelligent cryptography approach. Data management security which frequently focuses on encryption setup or data classification for security as it is the first part of protecting big cloud computing data. This technique is an effort for big data applications that necessitate higher levels of security. Ignoring the fact that the information is available to cloud operators, A formed distributed storage manner can enable the information to be secured in cloud servers. Big data means huge volumes of data that contains greater variety, arriving in increasing volumes and with more velocity.

Data can be split across multiple physical servers is often spread over various network infrastructure to use a distributed storage system. Typically, it assumes the form of a group of storage devices connected by synchronization and coordination for cluster nodes. An efficient large data storage system should be included in the latest data centres. File systems which form the basis of more complex applications for big data storage. The Google File System (GFS) is a robust, and dependable Distributed File System (DFS) for data-centric cloud applications [17]. GFS can be implemented on affordable servers to provide high performance and high reliability support for large-scale file applications. Another file system used by the MapReduce model, Hadoop Distributed File System (HDFS), enables data to be stored nearer to the center of execution.

The input data, which would be distributed among various distributed file systems, which is used to create functional units. There are two encrypted components, A and B, as seen in the image. There are several processes involved in completing this process. For an even better result, this hybrid cryptography technique combines both symmetric and asymmetric algorithms. The same encryption and decryption techniques are used in all forms of cryptography. The original data is changed during the encryption process into cipher data, which is unintelligible to humans or other living creatures. Data decryption is used to recover the old data from the encryption. In this analysis, symmetric and asymmetric methods are used to conduct two-time encryption and decryption procedures.

The block diagram of hybrid intelligent cryptography Fig. 1: takes input data and splits into two components component 'A' and component 'B'. Apply RSA encryption algorithm on secret key K, Apply Blowfish encryption algorithm on file f, using the secret key k. The Cloud Storage server 1 and Cloud Storage Server 2 are the output of Blowfish encryption algorithm, those outputs are merged into the single unit.

The encryption process changes the original data using the Blowfish technique. (i.e., components "A" and "B") into cipher data. The original data is encrypted by the Blowfish algorithm to use a secret key, which is transmitted together with the encrypted data to

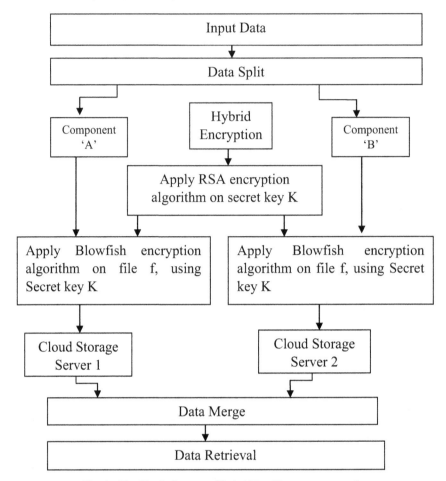

Fig. 1. The block diagram of hybrid intelligent cryptography

the receiver. The secret key being transmitted over a system is the risk associated with symmetric cryptography.

The RSA (Rivest-Shamir-Adleman) algorithm, that employs an asymmetric key encryption method, was established to solve the disadvantages of symmetric cryptography. Cloud computing provides a Hybrid intelligent cryptosystem, that includes symmetric and asymmetric data encryption to secure distributed big data.RSA is a popular public-key cryptosystem for safe data transmission. Ron Rivest, Adi Shamir, and Leonard Adleman are represented by the initials "RSA".

The data is encrypted using the Blowfish algorithm, which the user is selected. Blowfish is the symmetric block cipher algorithm and it encrypts the block information of 64-bits at a time. Blowfish was one of the first secure block ciphers not subject to any patents and therefore freely available for anyone to use. This benefit has contributed to its popularity in cryptographic software.

Blowfish has a 64-bit block size and keys which can be 32-bit or 448 bits wide. It has 16 iterations which resemble Feistel and Each one operates on a block containing 64 bits that is divided into two words of bits. There are two parts to the algorithm. One is the key expansion part and the second one for data encryption. Once it receives the request, the key expansion converts the 448 bits of a key into subkeys, leading the array to become 4168 bytes large. Blowfish is a fast block cipher, except when changing keys. Each new key requires the pre-processing equivalent of encrypting about 4 kilobytes of text, which is very slow compared to other block ciphers. This prevents its use in certain applications, but is not a problem in others. Encrypt and decrypt data using a single encryption key by Blowfish. The "secret key" is the term given to this key. The secret key should be encrypted because it is being transmitted over the internet with encrypted data. The RSA method, an asymmetric cryptographic technique, has been used to generate this secret encryption key. A unique key is used to encrypt and decryption with the RSA technique.

The hybrid intelligent cryptography encryption process is performed in following steps:

i) Choose a secret key K with such a length that really can range between 448 bits to 1024 bits.

ii) To use a secret key as well as the Blowfish algorithm, encrypt the selected file f.

The symmetric key cryptography algorithm is known as the blowfish that uses one key to transform the original data into cipher data and vice versa. Another name for this key is a secret or private key. The key size ranges from 32 bits to 448 bits, while the block size is 64 bits.

$$E_f = EBk(f) \tag{1}$$

Encrypt the secret key K that uses the RSA technique. RSA or other asymmetric key cryptography techniques use different key to encrypt and decrypt

$$E_k = ER(K) \tag{2}$$

Separate cloud servers collect the both encrypted data packets. The cloud server typically performs a dependable function in cloud service deployment models. Users need to get data packets from both cloud providers if they require data. After getting the data packets from the cloud sides, a series of actions need to be taken in order to acquire the original data. The new data string can be generated by first merging the matching data packets. To merge matching data packets from the cloud, and data retrieval based upon field matching query typically executed the following steps:

1. Retrieve the data packets: Access the cloud storage where the data packets are stored. This could be a cloud-based file storage service or a database.
2. Identify matching data packets: Determine the criteria for matching the data packets. It could be based on a specific field or attribute within the packets. For example, if each packet has a unique identifier, it can match packets with the same identifier.
3. Fetch and organize matching packets: Use a query or search mechanism to retrieve the matching packets based on the identified criteria. Retrieve the necessary data packets and store them in a suitable data structure or container for merging.
4. Merge the packets: Apply the desired merging logic to combine the matching packets. The merging process will depend on the structure and format of the packets.
5. Handle conflicts or duplicates: Address any conflicts or duplicates that may arise during the merging process. It may choose to prioritize certain fields or perform data reconciliation to ensure consistency if there are conflicts in matching packets.
6. Store or output the merged packets: Once the merging is complete, decide where to store or output the merged data packets. It could be in the same cloud storage location, a different storage system, or any other desired destination.
7. Validate and verify: After merging, it's crucial to validate and verify the merged data to ensure accuracy. Perform data integrity checks, cross-references, or any necessary validation steps based on the specific requirements of your application.
8. Clean up: If necessary, remove or archive the original data packets that were merged to maintain data cleanliness and prevent duplicate processing.
9. The data retrieval process transforms the cypher text into original data, so an user can read or access the data. The cypher text can be decoded by authorised users or those who have access to the data.

4   Result Analysis

In this section, a hybrid intelligent cryptography for distributed big data storage in cloud computing security is implemented. The result analysis of hybrid intelligent cryptography is demonstrated here.

In this hybrid approach of intelligent cryptography, the data from many distributed file systems is first split into two distinct components (i.e. component A and component B). Afterwards when, components are subjected to hybrid intelligent cryptography (a combination of RSA and Blowfish) to ensure big data before storing it in the cloud.

The information is stored on multiple cloud servers after encryption. Data from various cloud servers is merged for data retrieval, and using the secret key, the data is then decrypted. On this way, distributed bigdata is securely encrypted and decrypted in the cloud.

The expected performance dimensions of the hybrid intelligent cryptography model are evaluated by measuring its execution time as different input data sizes are being used.

Encryption Time: The encryption time is the amount of time required to encrypt the original data.

Decryption Time: The amount of time required to decrypt the cipher text and show the original message. Figure 2 shows the encryption rates for hybrid intelligent cryptography approach and the AES (Advanced Encryption Standard).

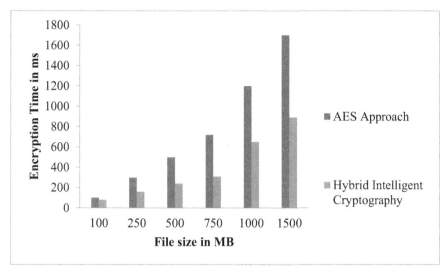

Fig. 2. Encryption Time Comparison

The encryption time consumptions for various data sizes are evaluated.

The x-axis in Fig. 2 shows different file sizes, and the y-axis demonstrates the encryption time in milliseconds. The hybrid intelligent cryptography approach requires less time to encrypt data as that AES approach requires. Figure 3 shows the decryption rates for the hybrid and AES cryptography algorithms.

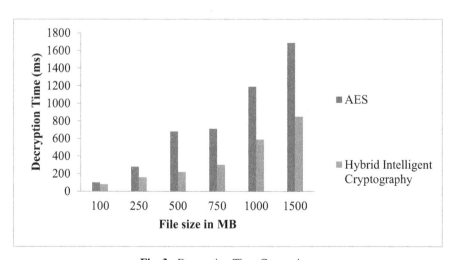

Fig. 3. Decryption Time Comparison

The x-axis in Fig. 3 shows different file sizes, and the y-axis demonstrates the decryption time in milliseconds. The hybrid intelligent cryptography approach requires less time to retrieve the data than AES approach. The RSA (Rivest-Shamir-Adleman) asymmetric algorithm manages an authentication whereas the Blowfish symmetric algorithm deals with data confidentiality, by improving security. The performance evaluation in terms of security is presented in Table 1.

Table 1. Performance Evaluation

Performance metrics	AES	Hybrid Intelligent cryptography
Security (%)	83%	95.6%

The Fig. 4 shows the security comparison between AES and Hybrid intelligent cryptography models.

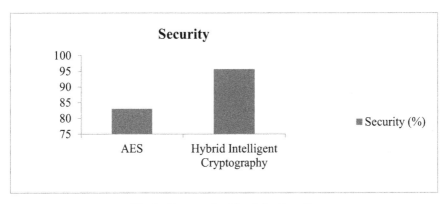

Fig. 4. Comparative Graph for Security

As a result, distributed big data storage has been better security that was provided by hybrid intelligent cryptography. Furthermore, compared to the earlier AES approach, this technique requires less time to encrypt and decrypt information.

5   Conclusion

This work presents a hybrid intelligent cryptography for distributed big data storage in cloud computing security. On this approach, a hybrid intelligent cryptography also known as a combination of symmetric (Blowfish) and asymmetric (Rivest-Shamir-Adleman) algorithms which are utilized to decrypt and encrypt distributed big data in the cloud. As the term indicates, there are huge volumes of data. The big data is first divided into two parts. These two components are encoded using hybrid intelligent cryptography, and the data is then stored on cloud servers. On cloud servers, a lot of data is stored. The data is again retrieved using the secret key. In order to increase the security of the cloud storage system, the RSA (Rivest-Shamir-Adleman) asymmetric algorithm handles authentication while the Blowfish symmetric method provides data confidentiality. The effectiveness of the hybrid cryptography approach is evaluated in terms of encryption time, decryption time, and security provided. In contrast to AES, hybrid cryptography offers better security and requires less time to encrypt and decrypt data.

References

1. Vidhya, A., Kumar, P.M.: Fusion-based advanced encryption algorithm for enhancing the security of Big Data in Cloud. Concurr. Eng. **30**(2), 171–180 (2022). https://doi.org/10.1177/1063293x221089086
2. El-Attar, N.E., El-Morshedy, D.S., Awad, W.A.: A new hybrid automated security framework to cloud storage system. Cryptography **5**(4), 37 (2021). https://doi.org/10.3390/cryptography5040037
3. Jayashri, N., Kalaiselvi, K.: Cloud cryptography for cloud data analytics in IoT. In: Machine Learning Approach for Cloud Data Analytics in IoT, pp. 119–142 (2021). https://doi.org/10.1002/9781119785873.ch6
4. Prathapkumar, K., Raja, D.A.T.: Double signature based cryptography using DS-SHA256 in cloud computing. NVEO - Nat. Volatiles Essent. Oils 9535–9541 (2021). https://www.nveo.org/index.php/journal/article/view/2639
5. Pronika, Tyagi, S.S.: Secure data storage in cloud using encryption algorithm. In: 2021 Third International Conference on Intelligent Communication Technologies and Virtual Mobile Networks (ICICV), pp. 136–141. IEEE (2021). https://doi.org/10.1109/ICICV50876.2021.9388388
6. Panyam, A.S., Jakkula, P.K., Neelakanta Rao, P.: Significant cloud computing service for secured heterogeneous data storing and its managing by cloud users. In: IEEE Xplore (2021). https://doi.org/10.1109/ICOEI51242.2021.9452970
7. Shuvo, A.M., Amin, M.S., Haque, P.: Storage efficient data security model for distributed cloud storage. In: 2020 IEEE 8th R10 Humanitarian Technology Conference (R10-HTC), pp. 1–6. IEEE (2020). https://doi.org/10.1109/r10-htc49770.2020.9356962
8. Seth, B., Dalal, S., Jaglan, V., Le, D.N., Mohan, S., Srivastava, G.: Integrating encryption techniques for secure data storage in the cloud. Trans. Emerg. Telecommun. Technol. **33**(4), e4108 (2022). https://doi.org/10.1002/ett.4108
9. Kanagavalli, R., Vagdevi, S.: Secured data storage in cloud using homomorphic encryption (2019). https://papers.ssrn.com/sol3/papers.cfm?abstract_id=3499579
10. AbdElminaam, D.S.: Improving the security of cloud computing by building new hybrid cryptography algorithms. Int. J. Electron. Inf. Eng. **8**(1), 40–48 (2018). https://doi.org/10.6636/IJEIE.201803.8(1).05
11. Kodumru, N.L., Supriya, M.: Secure data storage in cloud using cryptographic algorithms. In: 2018 Fourth International Conference on Computing Communication Control and Automation (ICCUBEA) (2018). https://doi.org/10.1109/iccubea.2018.8697550
12. Sukumaran, S.C., Misbahuddin, M.: DNA cryptography for secure data storage in cloud. Int. J. Netw. Secur. **20**(3), 447–454 (2018). https://doi.org/10.6633/IJNS.201805.20(3).06
13. Swathi, R., Subha, T.: Enhancing data storage security in Cloud using Certificate less public auditing. In: IEEE Xplore (2017). https://doi.org/10.1109/ICCCT2.2017.7972299
14. Khan, S., Ukey, E.: Secure distributed big data storage using cloud computing. IOSR J. Comput. Eng. **19**(4), 8–12 (2017). https://doi.org/10.9790/0661-1904050812
15. NagaRaju, P., Nagamalleswara Rao, N.: OB-MECC: an efficient confidentiality and security enhancement for cloud storage system. J. Cyber Secur. Mobil. (2021). https://doi.org/10.13052/jcsm2245-1439.944

16. Prasad, R., Rohokale, V.: Cyber security: the lifeline of information and communication technology. Springer, Cham (2020). https://doi.org/10.1007/978-3-030-31703-4
17. Prasad, M.: Advanced cloud computing techniques based on scientific computing applications. https://scholar.google.com/citations?user=Zlwl_SwAAAAJ&hl=en

An Ensemble Technique to Detect Stress in Young Professional

Rohit Ahuja(✉) and Rajendra Kumar Roul

Thapar Institute of Engineering and Technology, Patiala, India
{rohit.ahuja,raj.roul}@thapar.edu

Abstract. Mental health has become a major concern due to changing lifestyles and ever-increasing pressure at the workplace. Deadlines and goals are the prime reason for stress, which in turn leads to depression, anxiety as well as other mental illnesses. Hence, in the lure to improve the current situation, this paper proposed an ensemble stress detection mechanism that conveniently and accurately detects stress, depression as well anxiety. Few steps are conducted to detect the mental issue of any individual undertaking the test. The proposed ensemble mechanism comprises four basic detection modes: face detection, voice detection, Depression Anxiety Stress Scale (DASS), and a 22-parameter test. Face detection is a reliable source for detecting mental issues, whereas voice recognition confirms and aids the result provided by face detection. In addition, DASS test is a simple questionnaire conducted with a scaled answering system ranging from high to low, and finally, the 22-parameter test consists of 22 important physiological features of the patient. Experimental findings on different machine-learning datasets show that the proposed ensemble approach for stress detection is promising.

Keywords: Accuracy · Ensemble · F-measure · Machine Learning · Stress detection

1 Introduction

Stress is a natural reaction of the body to a demanding or challenging situation that causes emotional or physical tension. This response can be triggered by factors such as work pressure, personal issues, financial problems, or health concerns. However, if stress persists, it can harm an individual's mental and physical health, leading to anxiety, depression, mood swings, and difficulty concentrating. According to the World Health Organization (WHO)[1], around 7.5% of Indians have a mental illness, and by the end of 2025, 20% of Indians are expected to have a mental ailment. According to statistics, 56 million Indians will experience depression while the remaining 38% experience anxiety disorders. Thus, nearly 7% of the population in India is either suffering from mental illnesses or has encountered them by any means. Mental illnesses are taking their toll. Even if they are ill, they tend to ignore or, even worse, take it lightly, and as a result, they struggle with its devastating phase in later stages [12]. Everyone is extremely busy with

---

[1] https://apps.who.int/iris/bitstream/handle/10665/331901/9789240003910-eng.pdf.

R. Morusupalli et al. (Eds.): MIWAI 2023, LNAI 14078, pp. 649–658, 2023.
https://doi.org/10.1007/978-3-031-36402-0_60

doctor's appointments and considers mental health the least concern. Thus, it is crucial to manage stress through effective strategies such as exercise, relaxation techniques, mindfulness, time management, and seeking support from loved ones or a mental health professional when necessary[2]. Detecting stress in the early stage is imperative because it can have devastating and destructive effects on our bodies if left alone for a long time. Numerous studies [1, 2, 11] and everyday interactions suggest that an individual's facial expressions, tone of voice, and other physical indicators can convey their state of mind. Therefore, the objective is to create a system to detect an individual's stress state using these required parameters as input.

In the past many research works have already been done to detect stress [7, 9, 10]. Different machine learning techniques such as deep learning techniques such as Extreme Learning Machine (ELM) [17], Support Vector Machine (SVM), Decision Trees etc., and Multi-layer Extreme Learning Machine [13, 14], Convoluational Neural Network (CNN) [15, 16] etc. have been used for stress detection. The Mihai Garlasco-developed Facial Action Coding System (FACS) employs a special non-invasive design on three layers to measure depression, anxiety, and stress [3]. Fernando Bevilacqua et al. suggested a stress detection mechanism [5] in which seven facial features were identified to detect the activity of specific facial muscles. These features are mainly based on the Euclidean distance between facial landmarks. Many available technologies and works in this field use either one or a combination of a few facial features. Hijinx Zhang et al. [6], and Gavrilescu et al. [4] have merely employed facial expressions and action movements to detect stress. Few researchers have focused on the voice of an individual to detect the stress level of an individual [7]. However, researchers have not considered all the parameters to identify stress. Detection through voice or facial expression alone cannot serve the purpose. Often, voice testing or facial expression fails to provide whether a person is stressed. Furthermore, the detection of stress using traditional methods involving physiological conditions is contact based and requires high-quality costly sensors to be in contact with people to be tested for measurement.

Hence, this paper presents an ensemble approach to detect stress to address several concerns in the available work and hybridizes several parameters to identify stress in an individual and requires minimum contact with an individual undergoing a stress detection test. Moreover, the proposed system takes advantage of voice and facial expression along with DASS test and 22-parameters test, providing a better stress analysis result. The proposed approach consists of four stages for stress detection as discussed below:

- Facial Stress Recognition: A facial expression-based classification model to determine whether an individual is experiencing stress. Convolutional Neural Network (CNN) is used for this purpose.
- Voice Stress Detection: A basic model that utilizes an individual's voice which can be used to detect their stress level. Multi-layer perceptron (MLP) is used for this purpose.
- DASS test: By analyzing an individual's answers to a questionnaire, it is possible to determine their level of depression, anxiety, and stress on a scale. Google form is used for this purpose.

---

[2] https://www.who.int/news/item/28-09-2001-the-world-health-report-2001-mental-disorders-affect-one-in-four-people.

Table 1. Depression Anxiety Stress Scale (DASS) Test Scale

Sub-Scale	Depression	Anxiety	Stress
Normal	0–4	0–3	0–7
Mild	5–6	4–5	8–9
Moderate	6–7	10–12	–
Severe	11–13	8–9	13–16
Extremely Severe	14	10+	17+

- 22-Parameter test: Depending on individual's stress level, 22 parameters such as Blood pressure, calorie intake, body mass index (BMI) etc. are used using different Machine Learning (ML) classifiers.

Experimental results on various machine learning datasets show the effectiveness of the proposed approach.

2   Proposed Approach

2.1   Methodology

The steps employed for prediction of stress are discussed below:

- Face classification: The dataset for face recognition is filtered and analyzed using CNN, and the resulting data is saved in a file.
- Voice Classification: We use voice recognition to detect abnormal sounds in a person's voice and analyze the data using MLP to determine stress. If the analysis indicates stress, we proceed to the next step.
- Depression Anxiety Stress Scale(DASS) test: Those identified as stressed undergo a physical, psychological DASS test where they are given a questionnaire to answer. Their responses are evaluated, and their stress level is rated on a DASS scale, as shown in Table 1. If the subscale indicates a level of more than moderate, they are classified as stressed, and if in case of fake responses by the individual, we proceed further.
- 22-Parameter tests: This test is conducted to determine if a person is stressed. The patient submits the parameters as depicted in Fig. 1, and they are fed into a trained algorithm using a stress patient dataset collected from the hospital. This enables us to train the algorithm and obtain stress-level answers for new samples.

2.2   Proposed Solutions

1. Cameras scan the patient, and the data is uploaded to the cloud through a *Raspberry-Pi* connected to the camera.
2. The dataset with 35,888 images (including stressed and unstressed) was preprocessed and prepared using Keras, a high-level package installed on TensorFlow in Python. A Convolutional Neural Network (CNN) was trained on the pre-processed

Parameters			
Cardio	Frequent Cold	Minutes Lightly Active	Activity Calories
Calories	Upset Stomach	Minutes Very Active	Number of Awakenings
Stress Level	Calories Burned	Minutes Fairly Active	Aches
Fat Burn	Working Hours	Minutes Sedentary	Resting Heart Rate
Low Energy	Distance Travel	Minutes Awake	Body Mass Index (BMI)
Time in Bed	Pains		

Fig. 1. 22-Parameters for Psychological test

training and testing data-set (i.e., images) using Python. The dataset was divided into two parts in a ratio of 3:1, with the training data being 75% of the total data and the testing data being 25%. Furthermore, each ratio of stressed to unstressed data in the dataset was also 3:1.

3. For fitting images to CNN, Image Augmentation in Keras is used to reduce the problem of overfitting.
4. A machine learning model is prepared for voice recognition that plots a graph based on the voice tone and shivering to predict whether a person is stressed or not. The model uses a Multi-layer perceptron (MLP) classifier for this purpose.
5. To conduct a DASS Test: We asked the user to fill out a questionnaire. Based on the user's answers, our system will rate their stress level on the DASS scale using Google form and determine whether they are stressed or not. However, the accuracy of this method is not very high, so we will use it only for initial screening purposes. It is a fast method for mass detection.
6. If the initial screening indicates the person is stressed, we proceed to a 22-parameter test. The person reports on 22 different parameters, such as heart rate, skin color, blood pressure etc. An Machine Learning (ML) algorithm is trained on these parameters determines whether the person is stressed or not.
7. The algorithm is trained using different data samples. The model is then trained using this algorithm, and new samples are processed to test the model.
8. Compared to other available solutions, our approach has a significantly higher accuracy rate. We use cameras to filter out individuals, then utilize MLP to determine stress levels based on voice. We further improve precision and true positive ratio through the DASS and 22-parameters tests. This comprehensive approach results in a higher level of accuracy.

The overview of the proposed approach is depicted in Fig. 2.

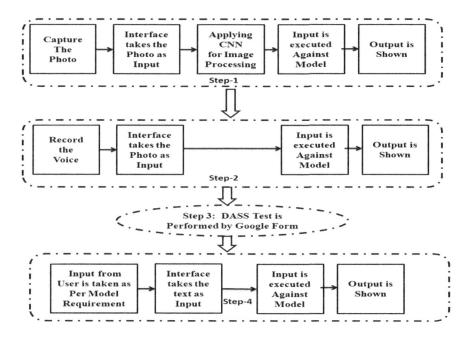

Fig. 2. Overview of the proposed approach

3   Implementation and Experimental Results

3.1   Datasets Used

After analyzing the data, similarities between facial expressions, physical and mental behavior, and stress have been figured out. We collected data from several sources, as mentioned below.

1. For face detection (Stage 1), Facial Expression Recognition 2013 (FER2013)[3] dataset is used. This dataset, whose size is limited to 48 × 48 facial RGB images of various emotions, comprises over 30,000 labels that can be categorised into seven categories: 0 means angry, 1, disgusted, 2, afraid, 3, happy, 4, sad, 5, surprised, and 6, neutral. 28,709 samples make up the training set, whereas 3,589 examples make up the public test set. The images were then converted to 40 × 40 pixel grayscale for ease of training.
2. For voice detection (Stage 2), Ravdess dataset[4] is used. There are 1440 files in this section of the RAVDESS. 60 trials per actor × 24 actors = 1440. 24 professional actors: 12 male and 12 female, perform two lexically similar phrases in The RAVDESS with a neutral North American accent. Speech expressions can be composed of expressions of calmness, joy, sadness, anger, fear, surprise, and disgust. There are two emotional intensity levels (normal and strong) and one neutral expression produced for each expression.

---

[3] https://www.kaggle.com/datasets/msambare/fer2013.
[4] https://www.kaggle.com/datasets/uwrfkaggler/ravdess-emotional-speech-audio.

3. No data was needed for Stage 3 since its outcome depends solely on user answers, which are evaluated using specific scores. We have used Google form for it.
4. In Stage 4, we partnered with a near Government Hospital (Rajendra Hospital, Patiala, Punjab-147001, India), to obtain confidential patient data for training our model. The data is available in the link[5] and is augmented using the NLPAUG[6], a python library. It does not contain any information that could reveal the patient's identity and is solely for research purposes.

3.2 Experimental Setup

This subsection discusses experiments conducted using the machine learning model and Python using the following stages:

Stage 1 We trained the CNN algorithm with over $28,000$ images and tested its accuracy using $3,500$ images for the FER2013 dataset used for face detection. Since the images were large and in RGB format, we converted them to greyscale and reduced their size to 40×40 pixels, making training faster. The greyscale values of the pixels were stored in a CSV file and used in the CNN algorithm.

Stage 2 User's voice and MLP[7] Classifier algorithm are employed for sound classification, with the help of Ravdess[8] dataset for training. The user's sound is recorded and saved in a .wav file format. If the sound is not already in .wav format, we convert it before feeding it into our system for prediction. For MLP, we set the parameter as follows: activation = relu, learning_rate_init = 0.1, random_state = 1, max_iter = 300.

Stage 3 DASS test is used to check depression, anxiety, and stress levels in an individual. We have used google forms to take user input, and then to use the formula, we calculate the score using a machine learning model and Python.

Stage 4 We have used different ML algorithms which are trained on the Hospital dataset. The dataset comprises 22 features and 1 output column. The dataset consists of data from the actual patient. User health-related data are required to make a prediction using this model.

3.3 Performance Parameters

Accuracy: It determines the number of stressed users correctly identified as stressed (true positive) and the number of unstressed users correctly identified as unstressed (true negative). The accuracy is influenced by the true positive and false negative values as shown in Eq. 1, where higher values lead to better results.

$$Accuracy = \frac{(TP + TN)}{(TP + TN + FP + FN)} \tag{1}$$

---

[5] https://www.mediafire.com/file/4m5j8h4rbl5rg69/fer2013.csv/file.

[6] https://www.analyticsvidhya.com/blog/2021/08/nlpaug-a-python-library-to-augment-your-text-data/.

[7] https://www.javatpoint.com/multi-layer-perceptron-in-tensorflow.

[8] https://www.kaggle.com/datasets/uwrfkaggler/ravdess-emotional-speech-audio.

where *TP=True Positives, TN = True Negatives, FP = False Positives* and *FN = False Negatives*

Precision: Precision is the ratio of true positives to the total number of predicted positives, expressed as

$$Precision = \frac{TP}{(TP + FP)},$$

where *Total number of predicted positives = TP + FP*

Recall/ Sensitivity: Recall is computed as the ratio of rightly predicted positives observation to all the observations that exists as shown below, i.e.,

$$Recall = \frac{TP}{(TP + FN)}$$

F-Score: The *F*-score is the weighted average of precision and Recall and is calculated using Eq. 2.

$$F = \frac{2 * (Precision * Recall)}{(Precision * Recall)} \tag{2}$$

3.4 Discussion

Procedural Workflow: This section presents the workflow of our proposed system through snapshot Fig. 3. The system consists of four stages. In stage 1, face classification is used to classify webcam-captured images as stressed or not stressed, followed by voice classification in stage 2 using MLP Classifier if the person is stressed. Stage 3 involves a psychological test. Specifically, the DASS test was administered via Google Forms and scored accordingly. Stage 4 is the most critical stage and involves sensitive patient data obtained from a hospital, with 22 parameters used to train the model for output prediction.

Performance Comparison of Different ML Algorithms: Table 2 shows the performance comparisons of various ML classifiers using different parameters for 22-parameters test. Figures 4 and 5 show the performance of CNN and MLP on face and voice detections, respectively. Figures 6 and 7 show different classifiers' precision and recall comparisons for 22-parameters test. The performance of Random forest dominates all other classifiers in terms of accuracy and F-measure. But the specificity of Decision trees is better compared to others. Similarly, linear SVM has a good precision value compared to other classifiers.

Fig. 3. Screenshot of face Detection

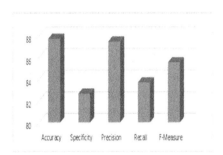

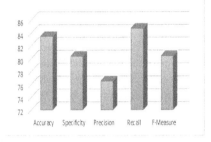

Fig. 4. Face detection using CNN   **Fig. 5.** Voice detection using MLP

Table 2. Performance Comparisons (bold indicates maximum)

Model	Accuracy (%)	Specificity (%)	F1-Score (%)
Linear SVM	82.33	74.77	81.76
SVM(RBF kernel)	74.32	63.44	75.67
k-NN	71.35	62.56	73.34
Gaussian NB	76.27	67.78	79.32
Multinomial NB	75.43	69.80	77.82
Decision Trees	81.23	**78.45**	81.39
Random Forest	**86.75**	77.54	**82.19**
Extra Trees	80.34	70.89	78.94
Ada Boost	82.53	72.10	79.31

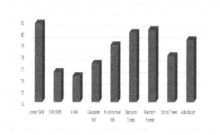

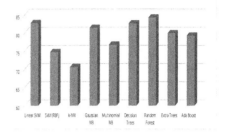

Fig. 6. Precision comparisons (22-parameters test)

Fig. 7. Recall comparisons (22-parameters test)

4 Conclusion

This paper presents a mechanism to detect stress in young professional in four stages. First, face detection is done, followed by voice recognition, then DASS test, and finally 22-parameters test are conducted in the final stage. CNN is used for face and voice recognition, and then different ML classifiers are trained using 22 parameters. Unlike existing techniques, the proposed approach used previously unused parameters and robust datasets, resulting in vastly improved accuracy. It's versatile, effective on all individuals regardless of age or gender, and has the potential for further development and application in industries, companies, surveys, and research. This work can also be extended by combining other ML classifiers, such as SVM, Random Forest, with CNN to reduce the training time and for better accuracy.

References

1. Investigation and evaluation of voice stress analysis technology. https://www.ojp.gov/pdffiles1/nij/193832.pdf. Accessed 18 Feb 2023
2. American Psychological Association Logo. https://www.apa.org/topics/stress/body. Accessed 18 Feb 2023
3. Zhang, H., Feng, L., Li, N., Jin, Z., Cao, L.: Video-based stress detection through deep learning. Sensors **20**(19), 5552 (2020)
4. Gavrilescu, M., Vizireanu, N.: Predicting depression, anxiety, and stress levels from videos using the facial action coding system. Sensors **19**(17), 3693 (2019)
5. Bevilacqua, F., Engström, H., Backlund, P.: Automated analysis of facial cues from videos as a potential method for differentiating stress and boredom of players in games. Int. J. Comput. Games Technol. (2018)
6. Zhang, J., Mei, X., Liu, H., Yuan, S., Qian, T.: Detecting negative emotional stress based on facial expression in real time. In: 2019 IEEE 4th International Conference on Signal and Image Processing (ICSIP), pp. 430–434. IEEE (2019)
7. Li, R., Liu, Z.: Stress detection using deep neural networks. BMC Med. Inform. Decis. Mak. **20**(Suppl 11), 285 (2020). https://doi.org/10.1186/s12911-020-01299-4
8. Depression anxiety stress scale calculator. https://www.thecalculator.co/health/DASS-21-Depression-Anxiety-Stress-Scale-Test-938.html. Accessed 18 Feb 2023

9. Qi, P., Chiaro, D., Giampaolo, F., Piccialli, F.: A blockchain-based secure Internet of medical things framework for stress detection. Inf. Sci. **628**, 377–390 (2023)

10. Kalra, P., Sharma, V.: Mental stress assessment using PPG signal a deep neural network approach. IETE J. Res. **69**, 879–885 (2023)

11. Dalmeida, K., Masala, G.: HRV features as viable physiological markers for stress detection using wearable devices. Sensors **21**, 2873 (2021)

12. Moya, I., et al.: Active in situ and passive airborne fluorescence measurements for water stress detection on a fescue field. Photosynth. Res. **155**, 159–175 (2023)

13. Roul, R.K., Asthana, S.R., Kumar, G.: Study on suitability and importance of multilayer extreme learning machine for classification of text data. Soft. Comput. **21**(15), 4239–4256 (2016). https://doi.org/10.1007/s00500-016-2189-8

14. Roul, R.K., Sahoo, J.K., Goel, R.: Deep learning in the domain of multi-document text summarization. In: Shankar, B.U., Ghosh, K., Mandal, D.P., Ray, S.S., Zhang, D., Pal, S.K. (eds.) PReMI 2017. LNCS, vol. 10597, pp. 575–581. Springer, Cham (2017). https://doi.org/10.1007/978-3-319-69900-4_73

15. Satyanath, G., Sahoo, J.K., Roul, R.K.: Smart parking space detection under hazy conditions using convolutional neural networks: a novel approach. Multimed. Tools Appl. **82**, 15415–15438 (2023). https://doi.org/10.1007/s11042-022-13958-x

16. Kaur, R., Roul, R.K., Batra, S.: A hybrid deep learning CNN-ELM approach for parking space detection in Smart Cities. Neural Comput. Appl. **35**, 13665–13683 (2023). https://doi.org/10.1007/s00521-023-08426-y

17. Roul, R.K., Gugnani, S., Kalpeshbhai, S.M.: Clustering based feature selection using extreme learning machines for text classification. In: 2015 Annual IEEE India Conference (INDICON), pp. 1–6. IEEE (2015)

iAOI: An Eye Movement Based Deep Learning Model to Identify Areas of Interest

S. Akshay[1]([✉]) [iD], J. Amudha[2] [iD], Nakka Narmada[2], Amitabh Bhattacharya[3],
Nitish Kamble[3], and Pramod Kumar Pal[3]

[1] Department of Computer Science, School of Computing, Amrita Vishwa
Vidyapeetham, Mysuru, Karnataka, India
s_akshay@my.amrita.edu
[2] Department of Computer Science and Engineering, School of Computing,
Amrita Vishwa Vidyapeetham, Bengaluru, Karnataka, India
j_amudha@blr.amrita.edu
[3] Department of Neurology, National Institute of Mental Health and Neuro Sciences,
Bangalore, Karnataka, India

Abstract. Eye Tracking is an important research technique used to analyze the movement of the eye and to recognize a pattern. Eye Tracking is a frequently used tool to understand the prognosis of a disease. iAOI is an Artificial Neural Network model that predicts the Area or Region of Interest viewed by a participant depending on the eye movement data. An eye-tracking experiment is conducted for participants with Parkinson's Disease and healthy controls for visual search tasks. From the eye movements recorded a higher-order dataset based on the Area of Interest is derived. This dataset is explored to understand the underlying AOI patterns for participants with Parkinson's Disease. This prediction from iAOI help in understanding the ability to search for a region of interest by patients suffering from Parkinson's Disease. iAOI predicts the viewed region of interest and how it deviates from the intended Area of Interest. iAOI provides offbeat visualizations that depict the higher-order Area of Interest. By applying the ANN model for this multi-class classification, an accuracy of 83% was observed.

Keywords: Eye Tracking · Parkinson's Disease · Artificial Neural Network · Area of Interest

1 Introduction

Parkinson's Disease (PD) is usually attributed to the degeneration of the nervous system. In PD, a person's movement is impacted. The first signs may be a barely perceptible tremor in one hand when they first appear. Although the disorder frequently results in tremors, it also frequently slows or stiffens movement. There is also a significant change in a visual pattern that can be observed in PD. In

R. Morusupalli et al. (Eds.): MIWAI 2023, LNAI 14078, pp. 659–670, 2023.
https://doi.org/10.1007/978-3-031-36402-0_61

PD, saccades are delayed and hence reading might be challenging if the eyes can't find the right spot on the following line. The blink rate, which is generally between 16 and 24 times per minute, lowers in PD patients, with rates of 12 and 14 blinks per minute being documented. Eye-tracking is a research technique to assess expert visual behavior and also aids in medical diagnosis by tracking illness progression over time. In this work, the participant's gaze statistics are used to determine the Area of Interest (AOI). This will help in analyzing the difference in visual patterns between healthy controls and PD participants. It will also aid in determining a pattern for PD participants based on the severity of the disease. iAOI does binary classification to determine if the participant is viewing within the AOI or outside the AOI. For multi-class classification, the Artificial Neural Network model - Multi-Layer Perceptron is utilized. The number of layers and the activation functions being used is varied to compare the performance metrics and to find the optimal model. Using Visualization tools, a plot is designed with different features of the participants to observe the AOI they are observing for a given instance of time. The related work is explained in Sect. 2. The proposed iAOI is explained in Sect. 3. The results of the iAOI model are represented in Sect. 4. The conclusion and future scope are provided in Sect. 5.

2   Related Work

[1] A study on the visual engagement and disengagement among participants of varied ages and ethnicity with mild cognitive impairments and Alzheimer's disease. They used the 'gap effect' and 'overlap effect'. It was observed that the mean reaction time decreased during the gap effect compared to the overlap condition. It concluded that age was an important aspect which affected visual engagement among the participants. [5] examines the gaze pattern of children to utilize it for intelligent attention enhancement therapies. The gaze pattern would vary between participants who performed the puzzle task better compared to those who performed poorly. [8] This study examined participants' gaze behaviour and performance while operating an aeroplane. Visual scanning of the cockpit, normal and abnormal flying situations, and distinctions between professional and beginner pilots were all regarded as important methodologies explaining aviation behaviour. These patterns served to improve piloting performance and distinguish between rookie and expert pilots. [2] To test visual attention while driving, the authors attempted to create a link between individuals with and without PD. The accuracy seen with a mirror in healthy participants was higher, but the accuracy observed with a mirror in PD patients was lower. They also discovered that when driving, people with PD had different visual attention than control participants. [12] The metric of measurement in this study was saccadic amplitude. Visual correction was also offered to the participants. Large vertical saccades were shown to be the least accurate, and visual corrective tools reduced accuracy and reliability. [4] Give an investigation on participants with PD and without PD to establish a relation between features like saccadic eye movements, gaze pattern and hand-reaction time. The participants were observed under two tasks - free viewing and time-optimal visual.

It was observed that PD patients did not have any statistical differences from control participants in saccade dynamics but there was a prominent difference observed in visual search tasks. [3] Use head-mounted eye-tracking for the control system involving visual attention in natural settings for toddlers. Methods to collect data that can be used to answer questions not only about visual attention, but also about a wide variety of other perceptual, cognitive, and social abilities and their development if this technique is applied successfully was presented. [11] The authors discuss how components such as the instrument, technique, environment, participant, and so on, impact the quality of the recorded eye-tracking data and the derived eye-movement and gaze metrics. A minimal and flexible reporting guideline was derived in the end. [15] This work uses r binocular vergence accuracy (i.e. fixation disparity) to explore pupillary artefact. The pupillary artefact can be corrected using a regression between records of pupil size and fixation disparity. The results offer a quantitative estimate of pupillary artefact on observed eye position as a function of viewing distance and brightness, for both monocular and binocular eye position measurements. Work by [7] examined the most commonly used eye-tracking metrics and demonstrated how they were employed in two studies. The first experiment used medical photos to examine perception in the diagnosing process. The second experiment looked at how participants' visual attention changed during psychomotor assessments. The authors provided a generic approach for visual attention analysis utilizing eye-tracking data and area of interest as a summary. [16] This research provides an overview of the current state of the art in terms of how video games and visual attention interact. A holistic glimpse into the future of visual attention and eye tracking in video games is provided. [10] The pupil signal from video-based eye trackers incorporates post-saccadic oscillations, according to a recent study. Using two high-quality video eye trackers, the authors evaluated PSOs in horizontal and vertical saccades of various sizes. Within observers, PSOs were fairly comparable, but not between observers. The incidence of PSOs is linked to deceleration at the conclusion of a saccade based on this data. Further [17] explain the steps in developing an eye movement-based application pertaining to real-world problems. Work by [6] explains how eye movements can be used for glaucoma. They establish an investigation using deep learning. Insights on PD can be obtained by [9] as it explains the affects of PD. The idea of using a simulation for the study of PD was given by [14]. The idea of giving a questionnaire task [13] motivated us to use a questionnaire-based task for the proposed iAOI.

3   iAOI

iAOI is a system that identifies the region of interest. The stages are explained in Fig. 1. The participant is asked to sit in front of an eye tracker and iAOI projects stimulus for visual search task to the participants. The AOI is manually marked before projecting the stimulus to the participant. Once the user starts the eye movement experiment the movements are recorded and the raw eye movements are obtained for all stimuli. This data is then processed to derive the higher-level features with respect to the AOI. The derived data set contains AOI-related statistics with 23 features. On this derived data set, EDA (Exploratory Data Analysis) is performed to understand the different features of the dataset. A hypothesis is then created based on the understanding from EDA. For this research, given the eye gaze statistics of a participant iAOI predicts the AOI name of the participant. This will help in understanding how far off or near is the actual fixation. A Multi-layer perceptron is used to determine the AOI name. After this step, PowerBI is used to draw a dashboard that explains the various insights from the dataset.

3.1 Recording Eye Movements

The dataset used in iAOI is obtained using a 1000 Hz eye-tracker. In this experiment, participants include both healthy control and patients suffering from PD. They are shown 12 different stimuli and their gazing pattern is observed. These readings are used to derive statistical features of importance which would further aid in analyzing the gaze pattern of the participants. For experimentation, participants were asked to look at a certain set of stimuli. The first stimulus (Fig. 2a) is to give instructions to the participant where the participant is asked to sit comfortably in front of the eye tracker. It also marks the beginning of the experiment for the participants. The next image stimulus (Fig. 2b) instructs the user about the calibration process and stimulus that is displayed for the purpose of calibration.

The calibration process prompts the user to look at the yellow dot on the left (Fig. 3a), right (Fig. 3b), center (Fig. 3c), top (Fig. 3c), and bottom (Fig. 3d) of the screen in order to calibrate the eye tracker with the participant's eye movements. Once the participant's eye movements are calibrated then another image consisting of the first set of instructions in Fig. 2a is shown. It says "Sit comfortably, When you are seated the experimenter will present before you the apparatus and clearly explain to you the method of the experiment". Once the participant reads it the second set of instructions as in Fig. 2b says "You will be seeing a fixation cross on your screen, you just have to look at it, Minimal movements will help the experimenter better analyze the data. We appreciate your time and effort to participate for the study, thanks" and makes the participant understand the importance of the experiment. Then the experimenter asks to find the number among the alphabet and the image stimulus in Fig. 2c is displayed. After the instruction, the next 3 stimuli with actual tasks are projected by the eye tracker. The image stimuli that include the visual search task are depicted in Fig. 4. All three image stimuli consist of a digit amongst alphabets that needs to be viewed by the participants. As the participant views the Stimulus, eye movements are tracked by the sensor, and the raw data is collected. From the features, all the categorical features are converted to a numerical form in order to pass them through an artificial neural network.

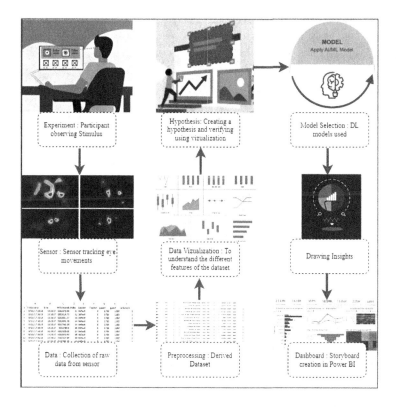

Fig. 1. iAOI

(a) Instructions set 1

(b) Instruction set 2

(c)

Fig. 2. Task Instructions

3.2 Deep Learning Analysis

In the Multi Layer Perceptron model, ReLu activation function, Leaky ReLU activation function and Softmax activation function are used. iAOI is a multiclass classification with 56 classes which are different AOI manually marked on the image stimulus. Activation functions defines which model information should be sent ahead and which should not at the end of the network. It introduces nonlinearity in the network. Some of the most often used activation functions include

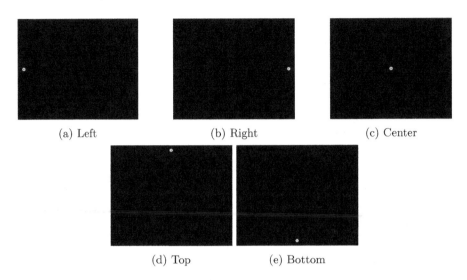

(a) Left   (b) Right   (c) Center

(d) Top   (e) Bottom

Fig. 3. Image Stimulus for Calibration

ReLU, Softmax, hyperbolic tan, and Sigmoid. For binary classification, sigmoid function is favoured, while softmax is widely used for multi-class classification. iAOI uses both ReLu and Softmax activation functions.

1. ReLu - ReLu is one of the activation functions which are non-linear, it stands for rectified linear unit. It ranges from (0,x). Not activating all the available neurons at the same time is the major benefit of using ReLu as an activation function in any model. It also avoids the vanishing gradient problem.
2. Leaky ReLU - The ReLU activation function has been upgraded to become the leaky ReLU function. It fixes the fading ReLU function issue. The ReLU activation function is specified as a very tiny linear component of x rather than as 0 for negative inputs(x).
3. Softmax - For the classification of multi-class problems, softmax is used as the activation function in the output layer. It is based on multinomial probability distribution.
4. Optimizers are functions that are used to modify a neural network's weights and learning rate. It contributes in improving the accuracy and reduce overall loss.
5. AdaGrad - The adaptive gradient descent algorithm, employs various learning rates for every iteration. The difference in the parameters during training determines the change in learning rate. The learning rate varies less noticeably the more the settings are altered. Real-world datasets include both dense and sparse features, therefore this change is quite advantageous.
6. RMSProp - Root Mean Squared Propagation, or RMSProp, is a variation on gradient descent that adapts the step size for each parameter using a

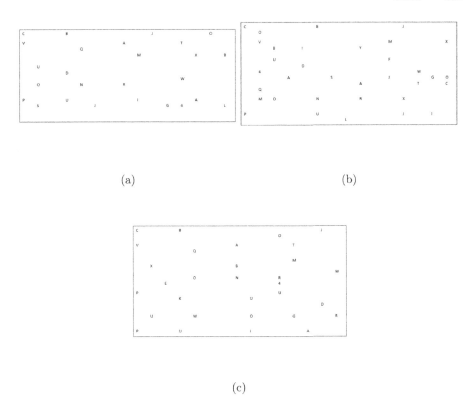

(a)   (b)

(c)

Fig. 4. Visual Search Task

declining average of partial gradients. The drawback of AdaGrad is overcome by using a decaying moving average, which enables the algorithm to ignore early gradients and focus on the recent recorded partial gradients detected as the search progresses.

7. Adam - Adaptive moment estimate is the source of the name Adam. Adam optimizer modifies the learning rate for each network weight independently as opposed to keeping a single learning rate during SGD training. Both Adagrad and RMS prop features are inherited by the Adam optimizer.

iAOI uses 4 models to predict the AOI at which the participant is looking based on the inputs given by the eye tracker. The models used train themselves on the eye movement metrics with respect to each AOI and trains for eye movement behavior in each of 56 manually marked AOIs. The data contains 23 features based on fixations, saccades, pupil diameter and AOI. Once the model is trained it predicts the AOI based on eye movement features as mentioned above.

3.3 Visualization

In eye movement research generally, the eye movements like fixation and saccades are visualized. The standard visualization techniques include fixation density maps, scan paths, and heat maps. Apart from the regular visualizations,
additional visualizations are proposed that reveal the eye movement behavior
with respect to the AOI. The histogram in Fig. 5 shows the number of observations inside AOI and the number of observations outside AOI. It can be observed
from the histogram that the number of fixations outside the AOI in each image
stimulus is always high compared to the number of fixations inside the AOI.
Another histogram in Fig. 6 shows the number of fixations in each AOI across
all the image stimuli. The visualization suggests that fixations in White space
and other unwanted parts of the image are high compared to the fixation in
other AOIs such as numbers and alphabets. Figure 7 shows the visualization for
the number of fixations inside and outside each AOI with respect to the estimated reaction time. As the reaction time increases the fixations inside the AOI
are less compared to the fixations outside the AOI. This implies that the PD
patients face difficulty in fixating within AOI. The Wordcloud visualization in
Fig. 8 depicts the name of the AOI which is viewed by the participant. It is clear

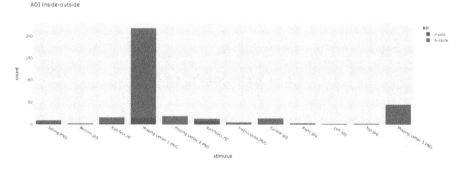

Fig. 5. Fixation Count: inside vs Outside AOI

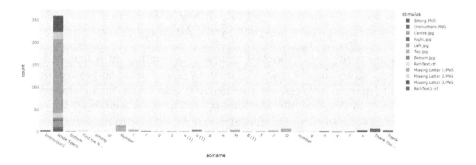

Fig. 6. Fixation Count in each AOI

that the whitespaces in the image take most of the fixations. Numbers that are the actual region of interest is observed to be less fixated. The size of the word that contains the name of the AOI represents the majority of fixation. The bigger the word in the word cloud more it is viewed by the participant. Even modern visualizations like word cloud also depict that the PD patients view whitespaces more as they find it difficult to fixate on the actual region of interest. General heatmaps are represented to understand the eye movements with respect to different AOI by plotting the superimposing heat signatures that relate directly to fixations. More fixations are depicted in high-intensity color patches on the superimposed image (Fig. 9).

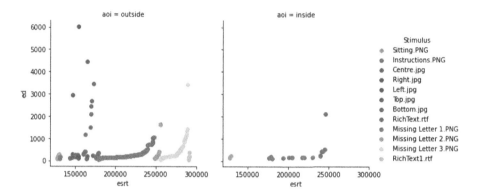

Fig. 7. Fixations inside and outise with respect to reaction time

Fig. 8. Wordcloud for AOI names based on fixation

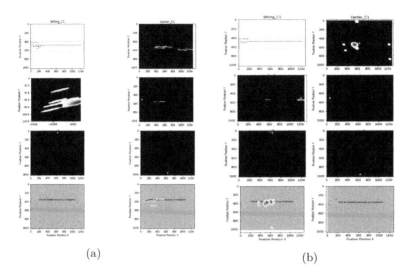

(a)   (b)

Fig. 9. Heatmaps

4   Results and Discussions

iAOI is an experimental setup for finding the AOI a participant is looking at given his gaze statistics. Through this, it is possible to help understand how different PD patients and normal people look at the designated Area of Interest. By analyzing how far off from the designated Area of Interest, the participant is viewing we could draw conclusions about the stage of PD a participant is suffering from. The ANN with 5 layers, with 3800 parameters using ReLu, LeakyReLu and Softmax achieves the maximum accuracy of 83.21% as depicted in Table 1. The PowerBI module helps in understanding the AOI-based eye movement behavior and the promising deep learning model helps in identifying the AOI. There are only three intended AOIs. That is to identify the number in the alphabet. It is observed by the visualizations provided that PD patients show a deficit and the same is learned by the deep learning model. The intended AOI in the three images that are used for visual search tasks is placed in different positions in three images. Once the participant's eye movements are recorded and the AOI is identified with the help of the model one can predict if the PD patient successfully identifies the AOI. If the identified AOI is different from the one which was supposed to be used then that clearly indicates the difficulty in the visual search task performed.

Table 1. Accuracy of different ANN Models

Model	Optimizer	Dropout	No. of parameters	No. of Layers	Activation Function	Accuracy
1	Adam	No	768	3	ReLu, Softmax	77.99%
2	Adam	No	3800	5	ReLu, LeakyReLu, Softmax	83.21%
3	AdaGrad	Yes	12416	5	ReLu, LeakyReLu, Softmax	77.61%
4	RMSprop	No	2192	3	ReLu, Softmax	82.84%

5 Conclusion and Future Scope

It is important to understand the visual search capabilities of patients with PD. The high-level AOI features derived from the iAOI provide important insights into the role of AOI analysis. The comparison of the intended AOI and the identified AOI reveals the difficulties faced by patients with PD. The Artificially intelligent model help in identifying the AOI based on the eye movements and it aids the comparison. In the future, the model can be further developed by considering various AOI visualization as the input, and using Convolution models, AOIs can be predicted.

Acknowledgement. We acknowledge the National Institute of Mental Health and Neuro-Sciences (NIMHANS), Bangalore, India for providing the eye movement tracker for experimentation and for allowing us to study the eye movements of PD patients at NIMHANS.

References

1. Doğan, M., Metin, Ö., Tek, E., Yumuşak, S., Öztoprak, K.: Speculator and influencer evaluation in stock market by using social media. In: 2020 IEEE International Conference on Big Data (Big Data), pp. 4559–4566. IEEE (2020)
2. Guan, C., Liu, W., Cheng, J.Y.C.: Using social media to predict the stock market crash and rebound amid the pandemic: the digital 'haves' and 'have-mores'. Ann. Data Sci. **9**(1), 5–31 (2022)
3. Hiransha, M., Gopalakrishnan, E.A., Menon, V.K., Soman, K.: NSE stock market prediction using deep-learning models. Procedia Comput. Sci. **132**, 1351–1362 (2018)
4. Jiao, P., Veiga, A., Walther, A.: Social media, news media and the stock market. J. Econ. Behav. Organ. **176**, 63–90 (2020)
5. Khan, W., Ghazanfar, M.A., Azam, M.A., Karami, A., Alyoubi, K.H., Alfakeeh, A.S.: Stock market prediction using machine learning classifiers and social media, news. J. Ambient. Intell. Humaniz. Comput. **13**, 3433–3456 (2022). https://doi.org/10.1007/s12652-020-01839-w
6. Krishnan, S., Amudha, J., Tejwani, S.: Gaze exploration index (GE i)-explainable detection model for glaucoma. IEEE Access **10**, 74334–74350 (2022)
7. Kuttichira, D.P., Gopalakrishnan, E., Menon, V.K., Soman, K.: Stock price prediction using dynamic mode decomposition. In: 2017 International Conference on

Advances in Computing, Communications and Informatics (ICACCI), pp. 55–60. IEEE (2017)

8. Li, D., et al.: Analyzing stock market trends using social media user moods and social influence. J. Am. Soc. Inf. Sci. **70**(9), 1000–1013 (2019)

9. Menon, B., et al.: Parkinson's disease, depression, and quality-of-life. Indian J. Psychol. Med. **37**(2), 144–148 (2015). pMID: 25969597

10. Nair, B.B., et al.: Forecasting short-term stock prices using sentiment analysis and artificial neural networks. J. Chem. Pharm. Sci. **9**(1), 533–536 (2016)

11. Nair, B.B., Minuvarthini, M., Sujithra, B., Mohandas, V.: Stock market prediction using a hybrid neuro-fuzzy system. In: 2010 International Conference on Advances in Recent Technologies in Communication and Computing, pp. 243–247. IEEE (2010)

12. Piñeiro-Chousa, J., Vizcaíno-González, M., Pérez-Pico, A.M.: Influence of social media over the stock market. Psychol. Mark. **34**(1), 101–108 (2017)

13. Radhakrishnan, S., Menon, U.K., Sundaram, K., et al.: Usefulness of a modified questionnaire as a screening tool for swallowing disorders in Parkinson disease: a pilot study. Neurol. India **67**(1), 118 (2019)

14. Sasidharakurup, H., Melethadathil, N., Nair, B., Diwakar, S.: A systems model of Parkinson's disease using biochemical systems theory. OMICS J. Integr. Biol. **21**(8), 454–464 (2017)

15. Selvin, S., Vinayakumar, R., Gopalakrishnan, E., Menon, V.K., Soman, K.: Stock price prediction using LSTM, RNN and CNN-sliding window model. In: 2017 International Conference on Advances in Computing, Communications and Informatics (ICACCI), pp. 1643–1647. IEEE (2017)

16. Unnithan, N.A., Gopalakrishnan, E.A., Menon, V.K., Soman, K.P.: A data-driven model approach for daywise stock prediction. In: Sridhar, V., Padma, M.C., Rao, K.A.R. (eds.) Emerging Research in Electronics, Computer Science and Technology. LNEE, vol. 545, pp. 149–158. Springer, Singapore (2019). https://doi.org/10.1007/978-981-13-5802-9_14

17. Venugopal, D., Amudha, J., Jyotsna, C.: Developing an application using eye tracker. In: 2016 IEEE International Conference on Recent Trends in Electronics, Information and Communication Technology (RTEICT), pp. 1518–1522 (2016)

Traffic Prediction in Indian Cities from Twitter Data Using Deep Learning and Word Embedding Models

Koyyalagunta Krishna Sampath$^{(\boxtimes)}$ ⓘ and M. Supriya ⓘ

Department of Computer Science and Engineering, Amrita School of Computing, Amrita Vishwa Vidyapeetham, Bengaluru 560035, Karnataka, India
`bl.en.p2cse21012@bl.students.amrita.edu,`
`m_supriya@blr.amrita.edu`

Abstract. Social media platforms, such as Twitter and Facebook, have become a significant part of modern society and have provided a significant amount of text data that can be utilized to enhance text classification research using machine learning approaches. These platforms often provide more in-depth views of real-world events by correlating tweet data along with the event and its geographical location. According to research, these correlations have potential applications in a variety of real-world scenarios, including the ability to predict critical events with high precision during emergency situations. The use of real-time geolocation data helps in mapping natural and social hazards in specific areas during national calamities. In addition, the data from tweets can be used to analyse weather patterns and the sentiment or mood of people in specific localities, such as Bengaluru and Delhi. This work aims to utilize the tweets from users to report on traffic conditions in a particular area and to identify the cause of traffic congestion, which is important for understanding the severity of the problem. The goal is to modernize the traffic information system and generate crowdsourced updates for traffic, and accidents using natural language processing and machine learning approaches in Indian cities like Bengaluru, Mumbai, Delhi etc. with the involvement of Twitter users.

Keywords: Twitter · Traffic prediction · BERT · Distil-BERT · Transformers · Deep Learning · Word Embedding · NLP

1 Introduction

Traffic congestion is a widespread issue that affects cities in India [1] as well as cities all over the world, causing delays, frustration, and economic losses. It can also have negative impacts on the environment, such as increased air pollution and greenhouse gas emissions. If you are in a traffic jam in Mumbai, Bengaluru, or Delhi, then you are in one of the Top 10 most crowded roads in the world and could lose an average of 100 h in the traffic, according to the most recent TomTom traffic index study [2]. According to another global study [3], Mumbai which is the financial capital of India, loses around 121 h annually due to traffic congestion, with congestion levels at 53%. Delhi and Bengaluru

R. Morusupalli et al. (Eds.): MIWAI 2023, LNAI 14078, pp. 671–682, 2023.
https://doi.org/10.1007/978-3-031-36402-0_62

also experience high levels of congestion. Istanbul, the capital of Turkey, is the most congested city in the world, losing 142 h annually to traffic. To address this issue, there are a number of strategies that have been planned or already implemented. These include, improving and expanding public transportation, implementing road pricing and intelligent transportation systems, encouraging telecommuting, investing in walking and biking infrastructure, considering land-use planning, and promoting carpooling. As cities continue to grow and urbanize, finding ways to alleviate traffic congestion as well as being able to predict traffic on several part of junctions becomes increasingly important. There are several organizations that offer information on various topics "Weather.com" and "Google Maps". However, accessing this information can be expensive and may come with limitations. In recent times there has been some research done to use data from social media like Twitter with or without addition of Maps data to analyze and predict traffic on a particular location.

According to research by Twitter [4], many people on Twitter engage with news and current events, with 94% expressing interest in these topics and 85% consuming news daily. They also frequently tweet about news, with 83% sharing news on the platform. Many people turn to Twitter for news, with 55% getting their news from the platform. In the first half of 2022, there were a total of 4.6 billion tweets about news in the US and 10.4 billion tweets about news globally. Twitter also connects people with news outlets and journalists, with 62% of news consumers saying it helps them discover new outlets to follow and over 80% of young journalists relying on Twitter for their job. It is also noted that people if given the opportunity and time to complaint/post about traffic or traffic related events or any other event, they are most likely to Tweet about on Twitter rather than using other social media platforms. Many people prefer Twitter because of its focus on real-time, short-form communication and the ability to follow a wide range of topics and people, because it allows them to stay up-to-date with current events and trends. Therefore, Twitter data should be used in conjunction with other sources of data, such as traffic cameras or sensors, to get a more comprehensive view of traffic conditions. In addition to identifying congestion hotspots and developing strategies to address them, Twitter data can also be used to evaluate the effectiveness of these strategies. By monitoring Twitter activity after implementing measures such as tolls or carpool lanes, researchers can determine whether they have had the desired effect on reducing congestion. This data can be used to refine and improve congestion management strategies over time. It is important to note, however, that Twitter data alone may not provide a complete picture of traffic conditions in a city. It is likely to be biased towards certain segments of the population, such as those who are more tech-savvy or have access to smartphones.

One more potential research would be to identify the times of day when traffic is heaviest and to develop strategies to alleviate congestion during those times. For example, by collecting tweets that mention traffic-related keywords, such as "traffic jam," "congestion," or "accident," researchers can gain insight into the areas of a city where traffic is heaviest and where problems are occurring. If analysis of Twitter data shows that traffic is particularly heavy during the morning and evening rush hours, cities might consider implementing measures such as variable tolls or carpool lanes to encourage people to drive at off-peak times. Another potential application is to identify the roads or intersections that are most prone to congestion, and to implement targeted measures to improve the flow of traffic. This might include improving road infrastructure, such as adding lanes of traffic signals, or implementing traffic management strategies such as smart traffic lights or intelligent transport systems.

Another recent advancement was Google announced that it is partnering with the Bengaluru traffic police to reduce traffic congestion in the city and to improve road safety [5]. The partnership will involve optimizing traffic light timings at key intersections using the data from Google Maps which is shared to the Bengaluru traffic police. The data from these tweets may also be used in addition to Maps data to better analyze traffic pattern and the sentiment or mood of the people in those localities depending upon the event and traffic in Indian cities like Bengaluru, Delhi etc. This work aims to use Twitter data analytics to provide information on traffic conditions and the causes of congestion in a specific area. Understanding the reason behind the traffic jam is important because it can indicate the severity of the issue. This work aims to modernize the Traffic information system and generate a crowdsourced update for traffic, accidents etc. using the involvement of Twitter users using Natural Language Processing and machine learning approaches for Indian cities.

2 Literature Review

There have been several studies that have used Twitter data to analyze traffic congestion in various cities around the world and some for Indian cities as well using several machine learning algorithms. In [6], the authors proposed a method for predicting traffic congestion the following morning by analyzing historical Twitter data and traffic data from sensors. Their approach involved using Twitter data to analyze the relationship between people's work and rest patterns and predict the next-day morning traffic conditions. The proposed work demonstrates the effectiveness of their approach through experiments on real-world data from Los Angeles, where a machine learning model was trained to predict traffic congestion the following morning and their method outperformed other state-of-the-art approaches, with an average absolute error of less than 10%. This work also explored the potential applications of their method in traffic management and transportation planning, where it could be used to take proactive measures to mitigate congestion, such as rerouting traffic or adjusting signal timings. Twitter data analytics can be used to track traffic in a specific area as a cost-effective method for monitoring congestion in real-time [7]. To create the system, the authors gathered Twitter feeds about traffic in a specific location and applied machine learning techniques such as Random Forest (RF) and K-Nearest Neighbors (KNN) to create a model. This work also had a real-time monitoring system that extracts tweets about transportation safety from Twitter, analyses public sentiment, and displays a map using OpenStreetMap. The research involved a dataset of 5000 tweets.

In [9], the authors developed a "real-time road traffic information system" that uses Tweets as their main source of information. To enhance the feature extraction process of the model, the authors used their own Bag of Words (BOW) and applied the Latent Dirichlet Allocation algorithm. They collected data on traffic flow in "Metropolitan Manila" and carried out data pre-processing, feature extraction, and data classification to produce traffic information patterns. The study included 250 filtered tweets. Twitter data was collected from the Twitter API using the "Twitter" package in R and was limited to Indonesian tweets. In [12], researchers developed a model for detecting traffic congestion in Indonesia, particularly in 'DKI Jakarta', by displaying the direction of street and classifying tweets based on the street name. The results showed that the highest accuracy rate was achieved using the SVM classification with the sigmoid kernel, at 96.24%. The average accuracy rate in similar studies using Twitter data for congestion detection was 96.24%. When tested against the Google Maps application, the system was able to identify similar traffic congestion conditions 17 times out of 25 tests. There were some works which focused on weather prediction using Tweets from users like Purwandari et al. [8] proposed on using Twitter data and Support Vector Machine (SVM) for weather classification in an information system which was able to display the weather conditions in Indonesia based on tweets posted by users. This study involved 88000 tweets. The work presented in [10] focuses on using machine learning models to classify the weather based on public Twitter data. The purpose of another work proposed in [11] was to determine how to identify the weather condition from the Twitter data. The research method used Term Frequency - Inverse Document Frequency (TF-IDF) on the pre-processed data and performed the classification task. Mastan Rao et al. in [13] conducted a study to evaluate the communication of Indian companies by utilizing sentiment analysis. They analyzed a sample of over 9,000 Tweets that were generated during a month using cloud-based technology. Machine learning (ML) algorithms namely Support Vector Machine, Decision Tree, Random Forest, Convolutional Neural Network (CNN), and Naive Bayes have been utilized to detect depression from the tweets of Twitter users' [14]. After evaluating these approaches, the Decision Tree Classifier emerged as the most effective, achieving 85.00% accuracy which aimed at detecting users' mental states. The objective of the work proposed in [15] was to conduct sentiment analysis on tweets from Twitter to gauge people's inclination towards adopting 5G technology. In [16], Hindi comments were gathered from social media platforms like YouTube and Twitter for sentiment analysis and various ML and deep learning models were trained using this corpus. The work in [17] mostly targeted to hinder the spread of hateful content in the form of blogs and tweets by training a Bidirectional Encoder Representations from Transformers (BERT) model for hate speech detection.

There were some studies which researched on the real time analysis on this topic. To perform the sentiment analysis using Twitter data, the authors discussed the usefulness of analyzing people's opinions on the social media platform [18]. They performed sentiment analysis on live tweets collected using the Twitter API and used bag of words for positive and negative analysis in the form of text files. The work in [19] presented a system for analyzing traffic jams that utilizes a real-time stream of Twitter data in multiple languages including English, Arabic, and dialect. The system extracts relevant features from the data to identify tweets related to traffic and classifies them based on the causes of traffic congestion. The system then visualizes the detected traffic events on a dynamic map that updates in real-time. The accuracy of the system's detection and prediction results are evaluated against data from relevant authorities in the UAE to validate its performance.

Eleonora et al. [20] developed a traffic detection system that used text analysis to identify traffic events in real-time by analyzing tweets. The system was designed to focus on small-scale traffic events and aimed to detect and analyses these possibilities by processing tweets from a specific area. To accomplish this, they used Latent Dirichlet Allocation (LDA) algorithm to extract real-time driving information from tweets based on keywords. They also utilized an SVM classifier to eliminate "noisy" tweets that were not related to traffic events. The study included 665 tweets with the traffic class, and the authors found that the SVM model had an accuracy of 95.75%. Another study aimed to provide an affordable solution for mapping natural and social hazards in real-time using geolocation data [21]. The data for this study was collected from Twitter using data mining techniques and filtered using sentiment analysis with machine learning algorithms. The results of the analysis were visualized through maps and a dashboard, which were tested for usability through human factor analysis techniques, eye tracking, and a survey. The work in [22] used text mining to extract traffic-related information from Twitter and displayed it in a spatial interface. The text mining approach involved classifying tweets to filter relevant data, extracting location information, and converting text-based locations into coordinates. They compared the performance of four supervised classification algorithms (Naive Bayes, Random Forest, Logistic Regression, and Support Vector Machine) using two different feature representations BOW and TF-IDF. Named Entity Recognition and Part-Of-Speech Tagging were used to extract the location data, and the ArcPy library was used for geocoding. With an F1-score of 93 percent, the Logistic Regression classifier with unigram and char n-gram features was found to be the best model for determining tweet relevance. The geocoding success rate for extracting location information was 68%, and the location extractor achieved an F1-score of 54% with a precision of 96%. The extracted traffic information was displayed in a web-based visualization tool.

There were other studies that used deep learning approaches as well. In [23], a deep learning model was proposed for predicting urban traffic parameters, such as traffic flow and congestion, using a combination of traffic data, weather information, and data from social media posts on Twitter. The model was based on a Bi-directional Long Short-Term Memory (LSTM) stacked autoencoder (SAE) architecture, and was trained on real-world data from an "urban road network" in "Greater Manchester, UK". The literature also suggests a way to categorize emotions expressed in text into six groups, including anger, fear, joy, love, sadness, and surprise [24]. It utilized cutting-edge pre-trained word embeddings and deep learning models. The Emotion Recognition dataset was used for this purpose and the findings of the experiments indicate that Distil Bert and CNN models achieved an impressive F-score of 98%. The model's explain ability modules offer insights into how the model is trained and how it makes predictions by examining the contextual significance of words in the classification process. The aim of [25] was to analyze the use unsupervised learning techniques to analyze traffic-related tweets from India and identify patterns and trends in the data. One of the key findings of this was that unsupervised learning techniques were able to effectively identify different types of traffic events from the tweets, including accidents, congestions, and road closures.

The work in [26] describes a study that used a deep learning model to detect traffic accidents from twitter data. They studied over 3 million tweets from "Northern Virginia" and "New York City" and found that paired tokens (combinations of words) were effective at capturing the rules in accident-related tweets and improving the performance of accident detection algorithm. The study also compared the performance of two deep learning methods Deep Belief Networks (DBN) and LSTM with two other methods SVM and supervised LDA in classifying the tweets. Finally, the study compared the tweets with traffic accident logs and traffic data to validate the results and found that the tweets were largely accurate and had useful information about location, time, and influential users and hashtags. Gary Goh and Jing Koh [27] have studied the use of Twitter data to predict future crowd flows in urban environments. They discovered that tweets can be beneficial in increasing the accuracy of crowd flow predictions by an average of 3.28%. They also found that processing tweets in multiple languages is particularly useful in cities like Singapore. They focused on predicting aggregated traffic flow across an entire city, rather than at specific road links.

There was a study done for Indian locations as well. Twitter data has been used to identify and locate traffic events in the Mumbai area [28]. The authors developed a model that first used a supervised method to classify tweets as relevant or not relevant to traffic. And then using a georeferencing module, they were able to identify the locations that were mentioned in the tweets to determine where traffic events were occurring. The study included 1330 tweets. To extract traffic locations from relevant tweets, the authors employed generalizable spatial rules and a lexicon-based approach instead of regular expressions. However, they observed that the OpenStreetMap API that was used, was not able to recognize the local Indian place names in about 30% of cases, highlighting the need of creating a detailed local place names dataset for this type of task. The authors suggested that building such a comprehensive dataset could improve performance in Mumbai and that future work should be to analyze this idea to better locate transport network events in other resource-constrained regions.

In conclusion, although there have been various studies on traffic prediction and developing real-time systems, there is a dearth of research focused on Indian cities. Furthermore, most of the previous work has relied heavily on machine learning and deep learning models that were trained using keywords such as "traffic jam" and "congestion." However, it is crucial to consider the context of the sentence to enable the model to understand and classify sentences even if they lack these keywords. We utilized word embedding models such as Word2Vec, GLoVe, and FastText for natural language processing and transformers models such as DistilBert and XLNet to identify the specific context in which a sentence was written and classify it accordingly. These transformers employ self-attention mechanisms, where each token in the input sequence is weighted based on its relevance to the other tokens, allowing the model to concentrate on the critical parts of the input vector and capture dependencies between tokens that are far apart in the sequence. In this study, we also analyzed the causes of traffic congestion as understanding the root cause of the problem can provide insight into its severity. We also tried to extract the location of the event from the tweet itself since geocoded tweets are not available from Twitter API due to privacy concerns.

3 System Implementation

3.1 Dataset

For the making of the proposed Twitter-based model, a dataset was created from scratch to analyze traffic conditions in the city of Bangalore using Twitter data. To obtain the data, the SNSCRAPE module was used to scrape more than 18000 tweets related to traffic in Bangalore for the period of March to September 2022. Data for other cities like Mumbai, Delhi were also scraped but were used separately. The dataset was then labelled into two classes: 0 for tweets related to traffic, 1 for tweets unrelated to traffic. The tweets were cleaned and pre-processed to extract relevant features, including the time the tweet was posted, the location of the tweet if given and the text of the post. Additional dataset was also created with three classes 0: for traffic and 1: for non-traffic, and 3: for tweets related to traffic containing some events like accident or weather which are causing the traffic for multiclass classification analysis.

3.2 Design

The process of building the proposed language model involves the following steps:

- Scraping and preparing a tweet dataset involves identifying the source of the tweets, setting up a Twitter developer account to obtain an API key, using a Twitter API client to access and download the tweets, and organizing them into a dataset format (such as CSV or JSON) for analysis.
- Pre-processing the dataset involves several steps to prepare the text data for analysis. Firstly, the text data is collected for analysis, which could be gathered from various sources like documents, websites, or social media platforms. Next, stop words, which are common words that do not contribute significantly to the meaning, are removed. Additionally, words can be stemmed or lemmatized to reduce dimensionality by reducing words to their root or base forms, respectively. Punctuation, special characters, and numbers are removed to eliminate noise. Finally, to ensure consistency, all the text is converted to lowercase. These pre-processing steps help clean and standardize the dataset, enabling more effective and accurate analysis in natural language processing tasks.
- Tokenization is the process of breaking down a sequence of text, such as a sentence or a document, into smaller units called tokens. There are two main approaches to train a tokenizer: rule-based tokenization, where splitting rules are defined, and machine learning-based tokenization using pre-trained tokenizers like BERT, DistilBERT, CountVectorizer, and others. The chosen tokenizer is then trained on the pre-processed tweet dataset, learning the patterns and structures within the text. This trained tokenizer will subsequently be used to tokenize new text data for further NLP analysis.
- Word embedding is the process of converting text into a numerical representation that captures the meaning of the words. To generate word vectors for the pre-processed tweet dataset, select a word embedding technique like Word2Vec, GLoVe, FastText, BERT, XLNet, or DistilBERT.

Word2Vec uses supervised embedding with CNN and skip-gram/CBOW approaches to learn word relationships.

GLoVe is an unsupervised method with predefined dense vectors for words. Fast-Text uses embedding with n-grams of characters, capturing the meaning of rare and shorter words.

BERT is a transformer-based model for contextual word representation.

XLNet is an auto-regressive model that combines permutation language modeling and T-XL for context understanding.

DistilBERT is a smaller variant of BERT that is faster yet retains accuracy.

After selecting the appropriate word embedding technique, initialize the language model using the chosen pre-trained model or train it from scratch and generate word vectors for the tweet dataset using the chosen word embedding technique.

- To train the language model, first, choose and experiment with different sets of hyperparameters. Identify the relevant hyperparameters for the chosen language model and explore various values for these hyperparameters to optimize the performance of the model. Once the hyperparameters are selected, initialize the language model with the chosen hyperparameters. Next, split the pre-processed dataset into training and validation sets. The training set will be used to train the language model using the generated word vectors. The model is trained by feeding the input data and adjusting its internal parameters to minimize the loss function.

- After training, the performance of the trained language model is evaluated using the validation set. This involves assessing metrics such as accuracy, precision, recall, or F1 score to measure the model's effectiveness. Fine-tuning or adjustments can be performed based on the validation results to further enhance the model's performance. Finally, the final trained model is tested on unseen or test data to evaluate its generalization ability. This step helps assess how well the model can handle new, unseen data and provides insights into its real-world applicability. The testing phase ensures that the model performs well beyond the data it was trained on and validates its effectiveness in practical scenarios (Fig. 1).

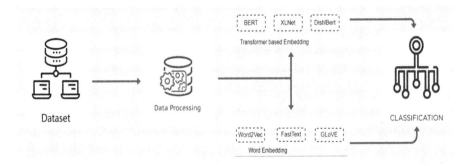

Fig. 1. Proposed Workflow

3.3 Results and Discussion

We trained and compared combinations of machine learning and deep learning models along with different word embedding models as mentioned below in the Table 1 and observed the different accuracies achieved. We observed that the ML algorithms like Random Forest Classifier, Logistic Regression, Multinomial NB with Tf-idf Vectorizer gave average results for classification with SVM giving best results of 94% for binary classification. SVM gave a very good accuracy on the classification problem but the model mostly depends on classifying based on keywords related to traffic like "traffic", "jam"," congestion" etc. But there can be tweets which does not contain these keywords and thus it is important to get the context behind the tweet and then classify if it belongs to traffic class or not. Deep learning models RNN, LSTM, GRU, Bi-LSTM with Glove word embedding maintained an accuracy of 91–93%. XL-Net also gave satisfying results with 90.9% accuracy. We utilized word embedding models such as Word2Vec, GLoVe, and FastText for natural language processing to identify the specific context in which a sentence was written and classify it accordingly. These employ self-attention mechanisms, where each token in the input sequence is weighted based on its relevance to the other tokens, allowing the model to concentrate on the critical parts of the input vector and capture dependencies between tokens that are far apart in the sequence. We also analyzed the causes of traffic congestion as understanding the root cause of the problem can provide insight into its severity. We also tried to extract the location of the event from the tweet itself since geocoded tweets are not available from Twitter API due to privacy concerns.

The transformer models BERT and FastText with Count Vectorizer also gave similar results of 91% accuracy but the DistilBert Tokenizer + DistilBert classifier gave the best results of 96% accuracy for both cases. Distil-BERT which is type of transformer takes into account about understanding the context behind the sentence and then classify and hence gave better accuracy. This is because transformers use self-attention mechanisms to process the input data. In self-attention, each token in the input sequence is weighted based on its relevance to the other tokens in the sequence. This allows the model to concentrate on only the important and specific parts of the input vector and capture dependencies between tokens that are far apart in the sequence. It was also observed that for getting the reason behind the traffic, it is much better to extract the reason from tweet traffic sentences rather than have multiple classes for traffic as this creates imbalance in the training dataset and the model will not learn accurately. The model was tested on different cases of tweets input to validate the classification into traffic and non-traffic classes and found to be accurate. When tested against the traffic events in Google Maps application, the model was able to identify similar traffic congestion status provided there were tweets available for that duration or event.

Table 1. Table of algorithms used, and their accuracies achieved

Algorithm/Technology Used	Accuracy
Random Forest Classifier with Tf-idf Vectorizer	~53%
Linear SVC with Tf-idf Vectorizer	83% multi class, 94% binary classes
Multinomial NB with Tf-idf Vectorizer	80%
Logistic Regression with Tf-idf Vectorizer	~91%
RNN with Glove	90%
LSTM with Glove	93%
GRU with Glove	91%
Bi-LSTM with Glove	92.58%
XL-Net	90.9%
Count Vectorizer + BERT	93%
Count Vectorizer + FastTEXT	91%
DistilBert Tokenizer + DistilBert	96%

4 Conclusion and Future Work

In conclusion by analysing Twitter data, it is possible to understand how online activity relates to real-world events and phenomena. This work aimed to predict the traffic using the involvement of Twitter users using Natural Language Processing and machine learning approaches for Indian cities to present information about traffic conditions in a specific location. The DistilBert Tokenizer + DistilBert classifier gave the best results of 96% accuracy. The work also included an analysis of the causes of traffic congestion, as the understanding of the source of the problem can provide insight into its severity. There were some limitations on which future research can be done, one is Twitter data may not be representative of the entire population, as not everyone uses Twitter or tweets about traffic. This can limit the generalizability of findings based on Twitter data to the broader population. Second is Twitter data may not be as accurate in providing the accurate location of where the traffic is or complete as other sources of traffic data, such as sensor data or traffic counts. This can limit the usefulness of Twitter data for certain applications, such as traffic forecasting or real-time traffic management. If we can come up with ways to give accurate or real time location using either geo-coded tweet dataset or using content from non-geo coded tweet dataset then this can help to develop systems that can use Twitter data in real-time to manage traffic. Third is that traffic-related tweets may be sparse in certain areas or at certain times of day and it may be a better approach to integrate Twitter data with other sources of traffic data, such as sensor data or traffic counts. Another possible feature that could be provided is giving personalized traffic recommendations to individuals based on their location, travel route and weather conditions.

References

1. Why is India's traffic still among the worst in the world? https://www.hindustantimes.com/. Accessed 29 Dec 2022
2. TomTom Traffic Index 2021. https://www.tomtom.com/traffic-index/india-country-traffic/. Accessed 29 Dec 2022
3. Mumbai 3rd Most Congested Traffic in World. www.india.com/news/india/. Accessed 29 Dec 2022
4. How many people come to Twitter for news? As it turns out, a LOT. Twitter News. https://blog.twitter.com/. Accessed 29 Dec 2022
5. Bengaluru traffic police, Google partner to reduce city's traffic congestion. Express News Service. https://indianexpress.com/article/. Accessed 29 Dec 2022
6. Yao, W., Qian, S.: From Twitter to traffic predictor: next-day morning traffic prediction using social media data. Transp. Res. C Emerg. Technol. **124**, 102938 (2021). https://doi.org/10.1016/j.trc.2020.102938
7. Leroke, G., Lall, M.: A (near) real-time traffic monitoring system using social media analytics. J. Eng. Appl. Sci. **14**, 8055–8060 (2020). https://doi.org/10.3923/jeasci.2019.8055.8060
8. Purwandari, K., Rahutomo, R., Sigalingging, J.W., Kusuma, M.A., Prasetyo, A., Pardamean, B.: Twitter-based text classification using SVM for weather information system. In: 2021 International Conference on Information Management and Technology (ICIMTech), vol. 1, pp. 27–32. IEEE (2021). https://doi.org/10.1109/ICIMTech53080.2021.9534945
9. Bondoc, E.R.P., Caparas, F.P.M., Macias, J.E.D., Naculangga, V.T., Estrada, J.E.: An intelligent road traffic information system using text analysis in the most congested roads in Metro Manila. In: 2018 IEEE 10th International Conference on Humanoid, Nanotechnology, Information Technology, Communication and Control, Environment and Management (HNICEM), pp. 1–6. IEEE (2018). https://doi.org/10.1109/HNICEM.2018.8666416
10. Dogariu, E., Garg, S., Khadan, B., Potts, A., Scornavacca, M.: Using machine learning to correlate Twitter data and weather patterns. In: 2019 IEEE MIT Undergraduate Research Technology Conference (URTC), pp. 1–4. IEEE (2019). https://doi.org/10.1109/URTC49097.2019.9660487
11. Purwandari, K., Sigalingging, J.W., Cenggoro, T.W., Pardamean, B.: Multi-class weather forecasting from Twitter using machine learning approaches. Procedia Comput. Sci. **179**, 47–54 (2021). https://doi.org/10.1016/j.procs.2020.12.006
12. Zulfikar, M., Suharjito, S.: Detection traffic congestion based on Twitter data using machine learning. Procedia Comput. Sci. **157**, 118–124 (2019). https://doi.org/10.1016/j.procs.2019.08.148
13. Rao, P.M., Babu, S.: Evaluating social responsible attitudes and opinions using sentiment analysis–an Indian sentiment. In: 2022 3rd International Conference on Computing, Analytics and Networks (ICAN), pp. 1–7. IEEE (2022). https://doi.org/10.1109/ICAN56228.2022.10007315
14. Kumar, S.K., Dinesh, N., Nitha, L.: Depression detection in Twitter tweets using machine learning classifiers. In: 2022 Second International Conference on Interdisciplinary Cyber Physical Systems (ICPS), pp. 81–86. IEEE (2022). https://doi.org/10.1109/ICPS55917.2022.00023
15. Mithillesh, K.P., Supriya, M.: Multi class sentiment analysis of 5G tweets. In: 2022 3rd International Conference for Emerging Technology (INCET), pp. 1–5. IEEE (2022). https://doi.org/10.1109/INCET54531.2022.9825160
16. Kumar, S.S., Kumar, S.S., Soman, K.P.: Deep learning-based emotion classification of Hindi text from social media. In: Gupta, D., Sambyo, K., Prasad, M., Agarwal, S. (eds.) Advanced Machine Intelligence and Signal Processing. LNEE, vol. 858, pp. 535–543. Springer, Singapore (2022). https://doi.org/10.1007/978-981-19-0840-8_40

17. Veerasamy, S., Khare, Y., Ramesh, A., Adarsh, S., Singh, P., Anjali, T.: Hate speech detection using mono BERT model in custom content-management-system. In: 2022 4th International Conference on Smart Systems and Inventive Technology (ICSSIT), pp. 1681–1686. IEEE (2022). https://doi.org/10.1109/ICSSIT53264.2022.9716428

18. Prakruthi, V., Sindhu, D., Kumar, S.A.: Real time sentiment analysis of Twitter posts. In: 2018 3rd International Conference on Computational Systems and Information Technology for Sustainable Solutions (CSITSS), pp. 29–34. IEEE (2018). https://doi.org/10.1109/CSITSS.2018.8768774

19. Alkouz, B., Al Aghbari, Z.: Traffic jam analysis using multi-language Twitter data. In: The 2021 3rd International Conference on Big Data Engineering, pp. 1–7. 29–31 May 2021, Shanghai, China. ACM, New York (2021). https://doi.org/10.1145/3468920.3468921

20. D'Andrea, E., Ducange, P., Lazzerini, B., Marcelloni, F.: Real-time detection of traffic from Twitter stream analysis. IEEE Trans. Intell. Transp. Syst. **16**(4), 2269–2283 (2015). https://doi.org/10.1109/TITS.2015.2404431

21. Albayrak, M.D., Gray-Roncal, W.: Data mining and sentiment analysis of real-time Twitter messages for monitoring and predicting events. In: 2019 IEEE Integrated STEM Education Conference (ISEC), pp. 42–43. IEEE (2019). https://doi.org/10.1109/ISECon.2019.8881956

22. Putra, P.K., Mahendra, R., Budi, I.: Traffic and road conditions monitoring system using extracted information from Twitter. J. Big Data **9**, 65 (2022). https://doi.org/10.1186/s40537-022-00621-3

23. Essien, A., Petrounias, I., Sampaio, P., Sampaio, S.: A deep-learning model for urban traffic flow prediction with traffic events mined from twitter. World Wide Web **24**(4), 1345–1368 (2020). https://doi.org/10.1007/s11280-020-00800-3

24. Abubakar, A.M., Gupta, D., Palaniswamy, S.: Explainable emotion recognition from tweets using deep learning and word embedding models. In: 2022 IEEE 19th India Council International Conference (INDICON), pp. 1–6. IEEE (2022). https://doi.org/10.1109/INDICON56171.2022.10039878

25. Kilaru, Y.S.C.G., Ghosh, I.: Traffic event description based on Twitter data using Unsupervised Learning Methods for Indian road conditions. arXiv preprint arXiv:2201.02738 (2021)

26. Zhang, Z., He, Q., Gao, J., Ni, M.: A deep learning approach for detecting traffic accidents from social media data. Transp. Res. C Emerg. Technol. **86**, 580–596 (2018). https://doi.org/10.1016/j.trc.2017.11.027

27. Goh, G., Koh, J.Y., Zhang, Y.: Twitter-informed crowd flow prediction. In: 2018 IEEE International Conference on Data Mining Workshops (ICDMW), pp. 624–631. IEEE (2018). https://doi.org/10.1109/ICDMW.2018.00097

28. Das, R.D., Purves, R.S.: Exploring the potential of Twitter to understand traffic events and their locations in Greater Mumbai, India. IEEE Trans. Intell. Transp. Syst. **21**(12), 5213–5222 (2019). https://doi.org/10.1109/TITS.2019.2950782

Interpretable Chronic Kidney Disease Risk Prediction from Clinical Data Using Machine Learning

Vijay Simha Reddy Chennareddy[1], Santosh Tirunagari[1],
Senthilkumar Mohan[2(✉)], David Windridge[1], and Yashaswini Balla[3]

[1] Department of Computer Science, Middlesex University, London, UK
vc381@live.mdx.ac.uk, {s.tirunagari,d.windridge}@mdx.ac.uk
[2] School of Information Technology and Engineering, Vellore Institute of Technology,
Vellore, India
senthilkumar.mohan@vit.ac.in
[3] Neurosciences Department, Alder Hey Children's NHS Foundation Trust,
Liverpool, UK
yashaswiniballa@doctors.org.uk

Abstract. Chronic Kidney Disease (CKD) is a major cause of illness and death worldwide, with over 2 million cases diagnosed in the U.K. and potentially up to 1.8 million undiagnosed. However, there is a lack of longitudinal studies on CKD in India, resulting in limited data on its prevalence. CKD is often asymptomatic until 70% of the kidneys are severely damaged, and once this occurs, there is no cure. Patients may require dialysis or a kidney transplant to survive. Detecting the risk of CKD early is therefore crucial. In developing countries like India, many people cannot afford regular laboratory blood tests. This study aims to develop machine learning models to predict the likelihood of CKD using limited blood test results collected in India, including blood pressure, albumin, red and white blood cell count, blood urea, serum creatinine, HbA1Cs, and other biomarkers. Decision Trees and Logistic Regression classification algorithms were used, with hyperparameter tuning, achieving an F-score of 1. These promising results suggest that state-of-the-art results may be achievable with just six laboratory tests.

Keywords: CKD · Classfication · Feature Selection

1 Introduction

Laboratory tests play a vital role in helping doctors and caregivers keep track of patients' health [1]. These tests can provide valuable insights into diseases like diabetes and chronic kidney disease. Typically, a laboratory appointment is taken to measure various parameters such as sugar levels, blood pressure, weight, and different cell counts. In India, millions of records from private labs are available, unlike in the UK, where records are not centralized [2]. It's essential for laboratory assistants to quickly identify any signs of disease progression from these records. However, reviewing each record manually is time-consuming and labour-intensive. Additionally, there are many other factors to consider when evaluating disease risk. For instance, serum creatinine levels less than 1.5 combined with abnormal protein albumin are a reliable indicator of acute kidney injury [3]. Evaluating these test results, along with various other factors, for millions of records is a significant challenge. Fortunately, machine learning can help overcome this bottleneck and make it possible to analyze these records more efficiently.

1.1   Motivation

CKD is a significant cause of morbidity and mortality in recent times. More than 2 million people in the UK are diagnosed with CKD, and a significant portion of the population, ranging from 1 to 1.8 million, is still undiagnosed, costing the NHS 1.4 billion [7]. Unfortunately, due to a lack of research, there is not enough data available to validate how many patients are affected by CKD in India. The major problem with CKD is that it is asymptomatic, and no deterioration of health is observed until 70% of the kidneys are already severely damaged. Currently, medical science cannot cure patients who experience CKD at any stage. The only possible solution is either dialysis or a kidney transplant, and without either of these, patients will eventually succumb to the disease. Therefore, AI may help us evaluate lab records and various other health information related to the patients. The techniques of machine learning can be quite vital for early CKD detection, and in the past, ML methods have proved to be quite effective for CKD analysis. These methods include OneR, ZeroR, clustering, Naïve Bayes, decision trees, K-Nearest Neighbors, and Support Vector Machines [4]. However, machine learning algorithms, such as SVMs, Logistic Regression, Decision Trees, and Adaboost algorithms, have not been widely utilized with this dataset, as mentioned in previous research articles [4]. Although previous studies have attempted to create a machine learning model for classifying laboratory test results as indicating CKD or not, they have not identified which laboratory tests are critical in diagnosing CKD [5,6].

1.2   Hypotheses and Limitations

The hypothesis of this study suggests that not all lab results are required for diagnosing CKD (chronic kidney disease), especially with the dataset used in this study. However, there are some limitations to this hypothesis, which are explained below.

   This paper uses a dataset of laboratory test results to predict the risk of Chronic Kidney Disease (CKD) rather than using Glomerular filtration rate (GFR) values, which are commonly used in hospitals to identify CKD stage. The dataset does include serum creatinine values, which could be used to calculate estimated GFR, but that is not the focus of this study.

It's important to note that the dataset used in this study only includes data from 400 patients, with 250 having CKD and 150 without. Also, all of the patients in the dataset are from India, so the classifiers used may be biased towards that population.

The study only uses machine learning classifiers like logistic regression and Decision Trees and not deep neural networks. This is because deep learning models require a large amount of data for training and are not feasible with this dataset. Additionally, deep learning models are not interpretable, and their predictions lack explainability.

1.3   Contributions

This section discusses the unique contributions of this study. Previous research on CKD mainly relied on estimated GFR and its progression, and the available datasets were also based on estimated GFR. However, this study uses a publicly available dataset with all laboratory tests labeled for CKD or not.

The hypothesis of this study is that not all 24 features (laboratory tests) in the dataset are necessary for diagnosing CKD. The contribution of this work is in investigating this hypothesis using machine learning models such as logistic regression and decision trees.

2   Data and Methods

This study utilized a dataset[1] that was collected at Apollo Hospitals in Tamil Nadu over the course of two months. This dataset, which contains information on 400 patients, has been made publicly available on the UCI machine learning repository for research purposes. Among the patients, 250 have been diagnosed with CKD, while the remaining 150 have not. The dataset includes a total of 24 variables, 11 of which contain numeric values and 13 of which are categorical.

Some of the numeric values recorded in the dataset include blood pressure, random blood glucose level, serum creatinine level, sodium, and potassium. For patients who suffer from hypertension or diabetes, their conditions are recorded as either 0 or 1, indicating no or yes respectively. On average, CKD patients in the dataset are around 60 years old.

In terms of other features recorded, there is a bi-modal distribution for some variables, meaning that there are only two unique values present. For instance, almost 250 patients have an albumin value of 0. The majority of the patients in the dataset have a good appetite, and around 90% do not have any coronary artery-related comorbidities. Since the dataset is focused on CKD, it was not surprising to find that serum creatinine values were less than 40 for 95% of the patients in the cohort. Additionally, it is interesting to note that 60% of the patients in the cohort were not diabetic.

---

[1] https://archive.ics.uci.edu/ml/datasets/Risk+Factor+prediction+of+Chronic+Kidney+Disease.

In this study, two classification techniques were utilized, namely Decision Trees (DT) and Logistic Regression (LR), to predict the risk factor of Chronic Kidney Disease (CKD) using patient data.

Decision Trees are a non-parametric supervised learning method that works by recursively splitting the data based on the features' values, resulting in a tree-like model. Each node in the tree represents a feature, and the branches represent the feature's possible values, leading to a final decision. DTs are robust to normalization and scaling of data, making them advantageous for this study. DTs can handle categorical and numerical data, and they are easy to interpret. However, they can be highly unstable and expensive to run, especially for complex datasets. DTs may overfit the training data, leading to low accuracy on new data.

On the other hand, Logistic Regression is a parametric supervised learning method that models the probability of a binary outcome. It works by finding a linear relationship between the input features and the log-odds of the output. Logistic Regression requires the data to be normalized and scaled, which can be time-consuming in the pre-processing stage. LR has a lower risk of overfitting and is more computationally efficient than DTs. However, LR is less robust to outliers and non-linear relationships in the data.

To tune the performance of the models, we need to adjust hyperparameters. For DT, hyperparameters like maximum depth, minimum samples split, and minimum samples leaf can be adjusted. For LR, hyperparameters like regularization strength, penalty type, and solver can be adjusted. Tuning hyperparameters can significantly affect the performance of the models. For example, increasing the maximum depth of the DT can lead to overfitting, while decreasing it can lead to underfitting. Similarly, increasing the regularization strength of LR can reduce overfitting, while decreasing it can lead to underfitting. Therefore, it is important to carefully choose and adjust hyperparameters to achieve the best performance for the models.

In summary, both DT and LR have their merits and demerits. DTs are advantageous for handling non-linear relationships and robust to normalization and scaling. However, they are unstable and can be expensive to run for complex datasets. On the other hand, LR is more computationally efficient and less prone to overfitting. However, it requires normalization and scaling and may not handle non-linear relationships well. DTs and LR are also known for their ability to handle imbalanced datasets, which is a common problem in medical datasets.

3   Experiments and Results

In this section, we will be discussing the experiments conducted and their results. Our hypothesis is that not all 24 laboratory tests are necessary when diagnosing CKD. We believe that fewer tests can potentially predict the risk of CKD. We also note that machine learning methods, such as logistic regression or decision trees, can automatically select features during the classifier learning process, making them interpretable.

We conducted three experiments in this section, which are as follows:

- **Baseline Performance:** Since the dataset is imbalanced, it is crucial to estimate the baseline performance of the machine learning classification algorithms. The baseline performance acts as a benchmark that the classification algorithms should perform better than.
- **Hyperparameter Tuning:** In this experiment, we tuned the classification algorithms to find the optimal parameter settings that maximize their performance. We considered various parameters such as criterion for splitting, maximum depth of the tree, minimum samples per leaf node, and minimum samples in split for the Decision Trees classifier.
- **Feature Selection and Classification:** In this experiment, we selected the features that contributed the most to the classification performance, while discarding others. We then performed classification using only the selected features.

We believe that these experiments can help us determine which laboratory tests are essential in diagnosing CKD and how machine learning algorithms can aid in this process.

3.1   Baseline Performance

In our dataset, out of the total 370 patient records (after removing missing values), 221 (59.73%) patients were diagnosed with CKD, while 149 (40.27%) patients did not have CKD. This indicates that there is an imbalance in the class distribution, with a higher number of CKD cases compared to non-CKD cases.

To estimate the baseline performance of our machine learning models, we need to consider this class imbalance. One simple approach is to use the "most frequent" representation, which means always predicting the most frequent class in the training set. In our case, this would be CKD. Thus, the baseline performance for our classification models would be 59.73%, which is the percentage of CKD cases in the dataset.

It is important to consider this imbalance when evaluating the performance of our models. A high accuracy rate alone does not necessarily indicate a good model, especially when dealing with imbalanced datasets. Therefore, we need to use appropriate evaluation metrics such as precision, recall, and F1-score, which take into account both true positive and false positive rates.

3.2   Hyperparameter Tuning

For the Logistic Regression classifier, we tested different values for the penalty parameter, C, and solver. The penalty parameter controls the regularization strength and the type of penalty used in the model. We tried L1 and L2 regularization penalties. The solver parameter specifies the algorithm to use in the optimization problem. We chose 'liblinear' solver as it is suitable for small datasets.

For the Decision Trees classifier, we tuned the criterion for splitting, maximum depth of the tree, minimum samples per leaf node, and minimum samples in split. The criterion parameter specifies the measure used to evaluate the quality of a split. We tried both 'gini' and 'entropy' criteria. The maximum depth parameter limits the depth of the tree. We considered depths of 4, 6, 8, and 12. The minimum samples per leaf node and minimum samples in split parameters determine the minimum number of samples required to be at a leaf node and in a split, respectively.

The best parameter values for Logistic Regression were a penalty of 'l1', C of 4.64, and solver of 'liblinear'. For Decision Trees, the best parameter values were a criterion of 'gini', maximum depth of 4, minimum samples per leaf of 1, and minimum samples in split of 2.

Overall, tuning the parameters of these classifiers helped us improve their performance in predicting the presence of Chronic Kidney Disease.

Table 1. Comparison of classification performance of Decision Trees and Logistic Regression.

Algorithm	Class	Precision	Recall	F1-Score	Support
Decision Trees	CKD	0.98	1	0.99	45
	non-CKD	1	0.99	0.99	66
Logistic Regression	CKD	0.93	0.96	0.95	45
	non-CKD	0.97	0.95	0.96	66
Weighted Avg F1-Score				0.97	111

Table 1 summarizes the performance of Decision Trees and Logistic Regression models in classifying patients as having Chronic Kidney Disease (CKD) or not. The results indicate that both models achieved good overall performance, with weighted average F1-score of 0.99 for Decision Trees and 0.96 for Logistic Regression.

Decision Trees achieved perfect recall for CKD patients, meaning that all patients with CKD were correctly identified by the model. The model also achieved a high precision score of 0.98, indicating that out of all patients classified as having CKD, 98% of them were correctly classified. Similarly, Logistic Regression achieved good recall and precision scores for CKD patients, with a recall score of 0.96 and a precision score of 0.93.

For Non-CKD patients, Decision Trees achieved a perfect recall score of 0.99 and a high precision score of 1, indicating that all Non-CKD patients were correctly classified by the model. On the other hand, Logistic Regression achieved a recall score of 0.95 and a precision score of 0.97 for Non-CKD patients, indicating that 95% of Non-CKD patients were correctly classified, out of all patients classified as Non-CKD.

Overall, both Decision Trees and Logistic Regression models performed well in classifying patients as having CKD or not. Decision Trees achieved slightly better overall performance, with perfect recall and high precision scores for both CKD and Non-CKD patients. However, Logistic Regression model achieved good performance as well and is faster to run, making it a good alternative for classification problems with categorical values.

3.3   Feature Selection and Classification

The Table 2 shown in this section displays the comparison of feature weights between two different classifiers, Decision Trees and Logistic Regression, for the classification of Chronic Kidney Disease (CKD) and non-CKD patients. The table contains 24 features with their respective weights assigned by each classifier, and the higher the weight, the more significant the feature is in the classification.

The Decision Tree classifier assigned higher weights to six features, namely, albumin, hemoglobin, packedCellVolume, redBloodCellCount, sodium, and specificGravity. These six features were considered for classification, while the other 18 features were discarded for this experiment. Logistic Regression is more suited for mixed data types, such as data containing continuous and categorical features, and provided weight coefficients for all 24 features. However, the interpretation of Logistic Regression weights is more complex than that of Decision Trees as it is multiplicative.

The results show that only a few laboratory tests are needed to accurately predict the risk of CKD, with an F-score of 1 obtained using only the six features identified by the Decision Trees. Therefore, it can be concluded that the remaining features are unnecessary for CKD risk prediction based on this dataset.

This section shows which features were important for the classification between CKD and non-CKD. The greater the weight, the more important the feature. Table 2 shows the features that are sorted in the highest of their weights on the Decision Tree classifier.

LR is better with mixed data types, i.e., data containing continuous features and categorical features. The beauty of the LR is its simplicity of providing the weight coefficients for the variables in model interpretation. Therefore, it is convenient to check what variables influence the prediction result. However, a drawback of LR model is that it is quite difficult to interpret as the weight representation is multiplicative. On the other hand, DTs are efficient in showing the weight representation.

According to Table 2, the Decision Tree classifier assigned weights to only 6 out of 24 features, namely: 1) hemoglobin, 2) specificGravity, 3) albumin, 4) sodium, 5) redBloodCellCount, and 6) packedCellVolume. Hence, these 6 features were considered for classification, while the other 18 features, including bacteria, serumCreatinine, potassium, whiteBloodCellCount, hypertension, diabetesMellitus, coronaryArteryDisease, appetite, pedalEdema, and anemia, were discarded for this experiment. Both the Decision Trees and Logistic regression classifiers were trained using these 6 features, and an **F-score of 1** was obtained,

Table 2. Comparison of feature weights in Decision Trees and Logistic Regression (sorted by Feature).

Feature	Decision Trees	Logistic Regression
albumin	0.032937429	78.99741
anemia	0	44.33313
appetite	0	10.61923
bacteria	0	−49.6613
bloodGlucoseRandom	0	45.03704
bloodPressure	0	−8.01845
bloodUrea	0	−2.34529
coronaryArteryDisease	0	3.083723
diabetesMellitus	0	28.2038
hemoglobin	0.708762166	−143.146
hypertension	0	73.90377
packedCellVolume	0.003614422	6.913668
pedalEdema	0	54.75435
potassium	0	−14.2495
pusCell	0	−5.05058
pusCellClumps	0	−31.1891
redBloodCellCount	0.015749964	−9.59441
redBloodCells	0	10.28026
serumCreatinine	0	102.3379
sodium	0.015974963	22.06235
specificGravity	0.222961056	12.74159
sugar	0	11.48266
whiteBloodCellCount	0	−68.9975
age	0	0.791261

validating our hypothesis that only a few laboratory tests were required to accurately predict the risk of CKD.

Thus, based on this dataset, only 6 laboratory tests are needed to detect the risk of CKD, and the remaining features are unnecessary.

4   Conclusion

This research highlights the potential of machine learning models in analyzing and detecting the risk of chronic kidney disease (CKD) from routinely collected laboratory tests. By automatically learning the interactions between different lab tests, it may be possible to accurately predict CKD risk with just a few tests, which could significantly reduce the cost and time associated with obtaining multiple tests. The study applied machine learning models on a dataset of 400 patients collected from Apollo hospitals in Tamil Nadu, India, and found that only six laboratory tests were required for an accurate prediction of CKD risk.

The findings of this study have important implications for healthcare professionals, as it could help them quickly identify patients at risk of CKD and provide them with appropriate interventions and treatments to prevent the progression of the disease. Moreover, the models developed in this study can be used to analyze large amounts of patient data and identify those at high risk of CKD in a hospital setting. However, more research is needed to validate the results of this study on a larger and more diverse population. Additionally, future studies should investigate the potential of other machine learning models and hyperparameters to improve the accuracy and generalization of the prediction models.

References

1. Faulkner, S.L., Trotter, S.P.: Data saturation. In: Matthes, J., Davis, C.S., Potter, R.F. (eds.) The International Encyclopedia of Communication Research Methods (2017). https://doi.org/10.1002/9781118901731.iecrm0060
2. Dalrymple, L.S., et al.: Chronic kidney disease and the risk of end-stage renal disease versus death. J. Gen. Intern. Med. **26**(4), 379–85 (2011)
3. Rule, A.D., Larson, T.S., Bergstralh, E.J., Slezak, J.M., Jacobsen, S.J., Cosio, F.G.: Using serum creatinine to estimate glomerular filtration rate: accuracy in good health and in chronic kidney disease. Ann. Int. Med. **141**(12), 929–937 (2004). https://doi.org/10.7326/0003-4819-141-12-200412210-00009. PMID: 15611490
4. Witten, I.H., Frank, E., Hall, M.A.: Data Mining: Practical Machine Learning Tools and Techniques, 3rd edn. Morgan Kaufmann Publishers Inc., San Francisco, CA (2011)
5. Reddy, M., Cho, J.: Detecting chronic kidney disease using machine learning. In: Qatar Foundation Annual Research Conference Proceedings 2016 (ICTSP1534) (2016). https://doi.org/10.5339/qfarc.2016.ICTSP1534
6. Bhattacharya, M., Jurkovitz, C., Shatkay, H.: Assessing chronic kidney disease from office visit records using hierarchical meta-classification of an imbalanced dataset. In: 2017 IEEE International Conference on Bioinformatics and Biomedicine (BIBM), pp. 663–670. IEEE (2017)
7. Tirunagari, S., Bull, S.C., Vehtari, A., Farmer, C., De Lusignan, S., Poh, N.: Automatic detection of acute kidney injury episodes from primary care data. In: 2016 IEEE Symposium Series on Computational Intelligence (SSCI), pp. 1–6. IEEE (2016)

Sign Language Interpretation Using Deep Learning

S. Suguna Mallika[1]([✉]) [iD], A. Sanjana[2] [iD], A. Vani Gayatri[3] [iD],
and S. Veena Naga Sai[4] [iD]

[1] CVR College of Engineering, Vastunagar, R.R. District, India
suguna.kishore@gmail.com
[2] Microsoft India, Gachibowli, Hyderabad, India
[3] GAP Inc., Hyderabad, India
[4] Oracle, Bangalore, India

Abstract. Sign language is used to communicate a particular message over some universally known and accepted gestures. The speech and hearing challenged people use a specific combination of hand gestures and movements to convey a message. Despite the extensive research progress in Sign Language Detection, cost effective and performance effective solutions are still need of the day. Deep learning, and computer vision can be used to provide an effective solution to the user. This can be very helpful for the hearing and speech impaired people in seamless communication with others around as knowing sign language is not something that is common to all. In this work, a sign detector is developed, which detects various signs of the Sign Language used by speech impaired people. Here, data taken as input in the form of images is extensively used for both training and testing using machine learning. A custom Convolutional Neural Network (CNN) model to identify the sign from an image frame using Open-CV is developed and sentence construction of the detected signs is accomplished. A lot of images have been used as input for the purposes of training and testing. Many of the symbols in sign language could be rightly identified. A series of gestures are translated as text to the recipient.

Keywords: CNN · sign language detection · machine learning for Sign detection

1 Introduction

Persons with hearing and speech disabilities are equally valuable human resources for a country. An environment must be created that provides identical prospects and protection of rights to these people [1]. They face many barriers like communicational, attitudinal, physical, and financial when trying to live an independent life [2]. Verbal communication is a fundamental necessity for a person to lead a normal life in society. Deaf and Dumb individuals use 'Sign Language', a form of non-verbal communication to communicate with one another, but people without knowledge of Sign Language find it tough to comprehend it [7, 17]. Similarly, hearing impaired people face difficulty with verbal communication [5, 19]. As a result, research was done for a vision-based interface system in which speech and hearing-impaired individuals can communicate without any hassles or dependencies on third person. Hence it is prudent to develop a system or device to mitigate the dependencies of the differently abled people on external people using the latest technologies. A simple Human Computer Interface (HCI) to identify sign language is proposed to serve the purpose of the afore mentioned. There are several sign languages used across the world, including Sign Languages like American, French, British, Japanese, Indian etc. among others [4, 20, 21].

In the current work, the main objective is to create a simple and user-friendly interface to detect and translate gestures into text with as high accuracy as possible. The activation function used is Rectified Linear Unit (ReLU) which is given by

$$F(x) = max(0, x)$$

where function always returns a 0 for a negative value of x and a positive value for a positive value of x. The performance measures taken into consideration are recall and accuracy.

In Sect. 2, a review of the existing solutions is presented. Section 3 presents a detailed proposal and implementation of a novel solution. Section 4 holds an elaborate discussion on the results. Section 5 presents some challenges faced during the implementation of this solution. Section 6 consolidates the findings and outcomes of the current work. Section 7 discusses the scope of future work.

2 Literature Review

The solution developed in [8] comprises of a system that can detect numbers between 1 to 10. This solution was developed using the OpenCV and Keras modules of Python. It was done by creating its own dataset. Two folders "test" and "train" were created in the directory named gesture. Each folder in turn contained ten sub-folders having images captured from live video feed using the create_gesture_date.py. CNN was used to train the created data set. Firstly, the data was loaded using ImageDataGenerator of Keras. The folder name represented the class name for the images that were loaded. Later, the accumulated_avg was calculated by finding the ROI and creating a bounding box around the identified foreground object in any data set. Then the max contour was searched for and if detected the threshold of the ROI was treated as test image. The previously saved model keras.models.load_model was used. The threshold image of the ROI consisting of the hand was used as input for the prediction model. This system can only recognize numbers from 1 to 10 only.

The solution implemented by rrupesh in [21] and Prof. Radha et al. in [22] used Indian Sign Language as the base. Rupesh segregated the dataset collected from UCI containing about 2,00,000 points. On the collected dataset, the approach was divided into 3 stages. In stage1, skin segment was extracted from the image while removing the remaining part. Stage 2 extracted appropriate features from skin segmented images. From stage 2 images were forwarded to stage 3 where key points were computed using Scale Inverse Feature Transform (SIFT). The skin segmentation image was observed using YUV-YIQ model. The third stage is for feeding the extracted features as input to various supervised models and later utilize the trained models to classify. For this, Support Vector Machine (SVM) was used by dividing the dataset into 2 parts, 70% for training and 30% for testing.

The solution implemented by Sreehari in [23] divided the problem into 2 parts, the first part is a multiclass classifier for static gesture recognition. The second part locates a hand in the raw image and feeds only this image to the first recognizer. For building this, a dataset was composed with coordinates indicating the boundary box for the detected hand in each image. To vectorize the images as part of feature extraction, Histogram of Oriented Gradients (HOG) approach was used [16, 18]. For building a localizer, building a dataset consisting of images of hands and values of bounding box for each image was constructed. Then, a binary classifier was used for training hand detection in the image. The region of interest was isolated by using the sliding window approach by the researchers. Lastly, a multi-class classifier was used for recognizing the gesture using those data sets.

There are several applications which were developed addressing gesture recognition [5]. However, some of the major limitations identified with them is that the existing solutions do not give meaningful well interpreted sentences for the user to easily comprehend [14].

Many models like [1, 2, 12, 13, 15, 22, 23] lack a user-friendly interface. Ease of use of technology encourage people with limited technology expertise also to adapt to the technology as well. Few models like [4] are adept with working on static data than on real time data.

As in [2] and [3], many models do not have proper functionalities that can provide output on the UI created. Though they have a UI to capture images, they just provide predicted solutions on IDE. The neural network model in sklearn is poor, due to lack of proper GPU support [9–11]. The Application developed by freecodecamp used scikit as the main building block of the model but there is no substantial assurance in outputs. The identified applications serving a similar purpose can be accessed at [18, 22, 23].

3 Proposed Gesture Recognition System

The current work attempts to make communication seamless between normal people and the speech impaired by taking American Sign Language as the base. The proposed system offers a self-reliant way of communicating with the outside world.

The idea is to create a platform for the recognition of sign language using Convolutional Neural Networks (CNN) to predict the hand gestures given by the user. The output will be displayed in the form of letters, words, and sentences by detecting blanks in the input. The system consists of two phases. In the first phase, the image is pre-processed and fed into a convolutional neural network (CNN) model for classification and recognition. The pre-processing steps include applying a Gaussian blur filter with a specific threshold to reduce noise and enhance the image quality. The CNN model then predicts the letter corresponding to each image segment and concatenates them to form a word. If a blank symbol is detected, the system inserts a space.

In the second phase, the system handles letters that have similar formation and may cause confusion. It uses additional classifiers to reclassify these letters and resolve any ambiguities. This improves the accuracy of gesture recognition.

3.1   Gesture Recognition System Architecture

Figure 1, shows the overall architecture of the current proposed gesture recognition system.

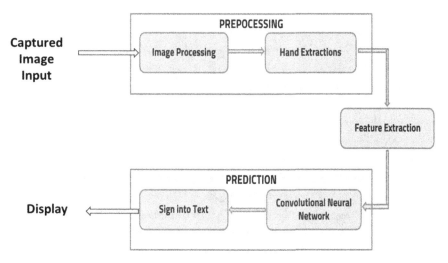

Fig. 1. Overview of System Architecture

Preprocessing Phase
The preprocessing phase comprises of the user giving a hand gesture as an input which in turn is fed as an image and processed internally to extract the hand gesture exclusively from the whole image. From this, the feature of hand image is extracted which is used to predict the intended letter.

Feature Extraction and Representation
After the pre-processing phase the image is fed to the feature extraction and representation phase. It is represented as a 3D matrix with dimensions equal to the image's height, breadth and depth equal to the value of each pixel (1 in Gray scale and 3 in RGB). The 3D matrix is now fed to the convolutional Neural Network.

Artificial Neural Networks
ANN transmits information from one layer to another until the final output layer through numerous hidden layers. ANN's and CNN's are used for further processing and identification of the gestures. The Gesture recognition happens with the help of various layers namely the pooling layer where window values are extracted using techniques like maxpooling or average pooling.

Convolutional Neural Networks
In contrast to normal Neural Networks, the neurons in CNN layers are arranged in three

dimensions: width, height, and depth. Instead of connecting all the neurons in a layer n by n, the neurons in a layer will only be connected to a tiny section of the next layer (Window size) preceding it [12]. Furthermore, as the complete image is condensed into a vector of class scores by the CNN, the final output layer has dimensions, i.e., number of classes. Detailed architecture of the proposed Gesture Recognition CNN is presented in Fig. 2.

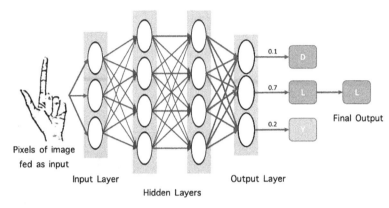

Fig. 2. Proposed CNN Architecture

Fully Connected Layer

In a convolution layer, neurons are only connected to a small region, however in a fully connected layer, all inputs to neurons are properly connected. Figure 3 shows a virtual representation of the Fully Connected Layer.

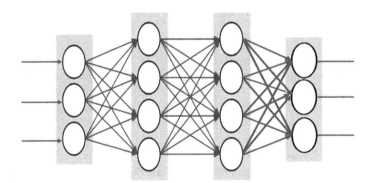

Fig. 3. Fully Connected Layer

Final Output Layer

After collecting values from the completely connected layer, connect them to the final layer of neurons [with a count equal to the total number of classes], which will forecast the likelihood of each image being classified into 27 different classes. In the current work, two layers of algorithm has been employed to identify the gesture applied by the user.

3.2 Implementation of LAYER 1 (CNN Model)

There are a few more layers as part of Layer 1 each of which are described as follows.

First Convolution Layer

The input image resolution is 128×128 pixels which is initially processed using 32 filter weights in the first layer of CNN creating a 128×128 pixel image one each for the filter weights.

First Pooling Layer

The 128×128 image has been reduced to 63×63 by down sampling using a 2×2 max pooling technique. As mentioned earlier max pooling technique employs highest value in the array's 2×2 square.

Second Convolution Layer

The 63×63 image received from first pooling layer is fed as input to second convolutional layer. The second convolutional layer uses 32 filter weights to process resulting in a 60×60 pixel image.

Second Pooling Layer

The 60×60 image is once again down sampled using the 2×2 max pooling to obtain a 30×30 image.

First Densely Connected Layer

The 30×30 images are now fed into a 128 neuron fully connected layer and the output of the second convolutional layer is transformed to $30 \times 30 \times 32$ which is a 28800-value array. The output of this layer is sent as input to the 2nd densely connected layer with 96 neurons. A threshold value of 0.5 is used to avoid overfitting.

Final Layer

The output from the 2nd Densely connected layer is then sent to the final layers. The final layers have as many neurons as the number of classes that have been identified. For instance, the input would be classified into alphabets, blank sign etc.

Activation Layer

Rectified Linear Unit Function (ReLU) was used in the activation function to compute $max(x,10)$. This function provided the formula with more nonlinearity making it easier to study intricate features. The vanishing gradient problem is addressed well. The training is accelerated due to lesser calculation time.

Dropout Layers

The dropout layers address the problems of overfitting by dropping out some set of activations randomly. Despite the drop in activations, the network should be able to predict correct categorization or output for a particular input.

Optimizer

The model was further updated using Adam Optimizer to the loss function's output. Adam Optimizer employs two stochastic gradient descent extensions, namely Adaptive Gradient Algorithm (ADA GRAD) and Root Mean Square Propagation (RMSProp). Adam optimizer was utilized to update the model in response to the loss function's output. Adam combines the benefits of two stochastic gradient descent extensions. The parameters of the neural network of the current proposed gesture recognition system are summarized in Table 1.

Table 1. Parameters of proposed Gestured Recognition CNN

Layer	Parametric Details
First CNN	128 × 128
First Pooling	63 × 63
Second CNN	60 × 60
Second Pooling	30 × 30
First Densely Connected Layer	28800-value Array
Second Densely Connected Layer	96 neurons
Activation Layer	ReLU
No. of Classes	27

3.3   Implementation of Layer 2

An additional two layers of algorithms to validate and predict symbols that are similar to each other have been used to validate and display symbols as accurately as possible. However, during testing phase it was discovered that symbols like D,U,I and S were not being rendered properly, For instance, R and U were being additionally displayed while D was supposed to be detected. Three more classifiers were designed to classify the misleading detections. Sets of symbols were created for this purpose namely {D R U}, {T K D I} and {S M N}.

3.4   User Interface

An easy-to-use simple user interface was created and OpenCV was used to capture signs to be recognized by the user and the design of the UI was made using Tkinter. The design involves a window for a camera live feed, a button that opens the chart of American sign language symbols, and sections to display the predicted letters, words, and sentences. The live camera capture is designed with a bounding box where certain image filters like Gaussian blur, and RGBA to Black and White are applied. The user must make sure to show the hand gestures in the bounding box.

3.5 Database

Data has been created by initially taking a few hand images with the signs of English alphabets. Later, they were processed by data augmentation using python. These processed images have been divided into folders, based on the alphabets (including space). The training and test data have been divided by 75% and 25% approximately. Around 500 images for each sign were used in training process. The test data consisted of 150–160 images for each sign letter.

3.6 Algorithm for Gesture Recognition

Layer 1:

Step 1: Post extraction of features, a gaussian blur filter is applied and threshold is computed for the frame using OpenCV to obtain the image.
Step 2: The image obtained in Step 1 is now forwarded to the CNN model for detection of any letter up to a count of 30. The letter identified is then added to the output word.
Step 3: Empty/Blank gesture symbolizes a space between words.

Layer 2:

Step 1: Sets of gestures which are uniformly detected are identified and segregated.
Step 2: Customized classifiers for those specific sets are then used to classify those sets of symbols.

4 Results and Discussion

The implementation involved printing and concatenating any letters detected over a certain number of times to the output string for display. It was ensured that no other letters were detected in the same vicinity, a threshold difference of 30 was used for this purpose. When dealing with a plain background, spaces are not identified if the number of blank spaces exceeds a specific threshold. Instead, a space indicates the end of a word, and the identified word was appended to the final output string. To overcome the noise present in the input images, the RGB images were transformed into grayscale and then subjected to Gaussian blur. The adaptive threshold technique was used to differentiate between the hand gesture and background, and the images were resized to 128×128 pixels before being fed into the model for training and testing.

The prediction layer calculates the likelihood of classifying an image into one of the categories. The softmax function is used to normalize the output, which ranges from 0 to 1 and sums up to 1 for all classes. However, the prediction layer's output may not precisely match the actual value. To improve accuracy, labelled data was used to train the networks. Cross-entropy, a classification metric, is positive when it differs from the labelled value and zero when it is the same. The goal was to minimize the cross-entropy and alter the weights of the neural network to achieve accuracy. TensorFlow's built-in function was used to calculate cross-entropy, and Gradient Descent was utilized to optimize the cross-entropy function. Adam Optimizer is best gradient descent optimizer.

Figure 4 is a screenshot taken during the testing phases of the work. Here the tester shows the gesture of the Letter L equivalent before the camera and the letter has been identified successfully. The identified letter is also appended to the output word. Similarly, the letters E and G are also appended to the word. Figures 5 and 6, show the identification of blank space and adding the word to the sentence as a final output. The Accuracy achieved by the proposed model is 86.35%.

Recall is how well the model can recognize the gestures from the trained data. Indicates how the positive samples are classified. Recall is calculated as in Eq. 1

$$\text{Recall} = \frac{TP}{TP + FN} \quad (1)$$

where TP – True Positives

FN – False Negatives from the confusion Matrix

Recall for the letters 'L' and 'V' are presented below by calculation from Eq. 1

$$\text{Recall(L)} = 0.5$$
$$\text{Recall(V)} = 0.5$$

Average recall computed for all alphabets in the sign language is arrived at 0.5.

Fig. 4. Output Screen Identifying Letter L   **Fig. 5.** Output Screen identifying Blank Space

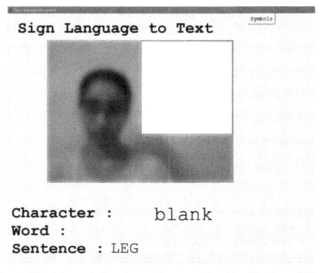

Fig. 6. Word Appended to Output Sentence after Identification of Blank

5 Challenges

The algorithm currently is failing to segregate noise in the captured image and rightly identify the gesture. It is mandatory to have a clear picture with the gesture rightly presented sans any shadows, lines or any background image etc. inorder for the output to be rendered accurately. The shadows, if any on the image added to the contour lines affecting accurate gesture recognition. Enough lighting needs to be ensured. Training phases were a challenge given the limited computing resources and it is highly recommended to have high computing power to achieve rapid and accurate results in a short time.

6 Conclusions

Few of the symbols were recognized successfully in the presence of proper light and minimal background disturbance. The user-interface is created in a simple and user-friendly manner, which displays the output in the form of characters, words and sentences, by detecting blanks in the input given by the user. A text message is delivered to the user after due recognition of the gestures.

7 Future Enhancements

Major extensions to this work shall include expanding the gesture recognition system to include all alphabets as well as non-alphabet gestures. Using different image preprocessing techniques, where dataset is taken and provided with different data augmentation techniques like changing orientation, size, etc. Including text-to-speech functionality, so that it would make the application more user-friendly and cater to more number of people. Including the gestures for common words, i.e., the words which are in daily usage like 'yes', 'no', 'thank you', etc. so that the user need not give the word letter by letter.

References

1. Bantupalli, K., Xie, Y.: American sign language recognition using deep learning and computer vision. In: 2018 IEEE International Conference on Big Data (Big Data), pp. 4896–4899. IEEE (2018). https://doi.org/10.1109/BigData.2018.8622141
2. Cabrera, M.E., Bogado, J.M., Fermin, L., Acuna, R., Ralev, D.: Glove-based gesture recognition system. In: Adaptive Mobile Robotics, pp. 747–753 (2012). https://doi.org/10.1142/978 9814415958_0095
3. He, S.: Research of a sign language translation system based on deep learning. In: 2019 International Conference on Artificial Intelligence and Advanced Manufacturing (AIAM), pp. 392–396. IEEE (2019). https://doi.org/10.1109/AIAM48774.2019.00083. International Conference on Trendz in Information Sciences and Computing (TISC 2012)
4. Herath, H.C.M., Kumari, W.A.L.V., Senevirathne, W.A.P.B., Dissanayake, M.B.: Image based sign language recognition system for Sinhala sign language. Sign 3(5), 2 (2013)
5. Geetha, M., Manjusha, U.C.: A vision based recognition of Indian sign language alphabets and numerals using b-spline approximation. Int. J. Comput. Sci. Eng. 4(3), 406–415 (2012)
6. Pigou, L., Dieleman, S., Kindermans, P.-J., Schrauwen, B.: Sign language recognition using convolutional neural networks. In: Agapito, L., Bronstein, M.M., Rother, C. (eds.) ECCV 2014. LNCS, vol. 8925, pp. 572–578. Springer, Cham (2015). https://doi.org/10.1007/978-3-319-16178-5_40
7. Escalera, S., et al.: ChaLearn looking at people challenge 2014: dataset and results. In: Agapito, L., Bronstein, M.M., Rother, C. (eds.) ECCV 2014. LNCS, vol. 8925, pp. 459–473. Springer, Cham (2015). https://doi.org/10.1007/978-3-319-16178-5_32
8. Huang, J., Zhou, W., Li, H.: Sign language recognition using 3D convolutional neural networks. In: IEEE International Conference on Multimedia and Expo (ICME), pp. 1–6. IEEE, Turin (2015)
9. Jaoa Carriera, A.Z.: Quo Vadis, action recognition? A new model and the kinetics dataset. In: 2017 IEEE Conference on Computer Vision and Pattern Recognition (CVPR), pp. 4724–4733. IEEE, Honolulu (2018)
10. Deng, J., Dong, W., Socher, R., Li, L.-J., Li, K., Fei-Fei, L.: ImageNet: a large-scale hierarchical image database. In: IEEE Conference on Computer Vision and Pattern Recognition (CVPR 2009), pp. 248–255. IEEE. Miami, FL, USA (2009)
11. Soomro, K., Zamir, A.R., Shah, M.: UCF101: a dataset of 101 human actions classes from videos in the wild. arXiv preprint arXiv:1212.0402 (2012)
12. Kuehne, H., Jhuang, H., Garrote, E., Poggio, T., Serre, T.: HMDB: a large video database for human motion recognition. In: 2011 IEEE International Conference on Computer Vision (ICCV), pp. 2556–2563. IEEE (2011)
13. Zhao, M., Bu, J., Chen, C.: Robust background subtraction in HSV color space. In: Proceedings of SPIE MSAV, vol. 1, p. 4861 (2002). https://doi.org/10.1117/12.456333
14. Chowdhury, A., Cho, S.J., Chong, U.P.: A background subtraction method using color information in the frame averaging process. In: Proceedings of 2011 6th International Forum on Strategic Technology, vol. 2, pp. 1275–1279. IEEE (2011). https://doi.org/10.1109/ifost.2011. 6021252
15. Mehreen, H., Mohammad, E.: Sign language recognition system using convolutional neural network and computer vision. Int. J. Eng. Res. Technol. 09(12) (2020). deeplearning-books.org: Convolutional Networks

16. https://learnopencv.com/. Accessed 03 Apr 2023
17. https://data-flair.training/blogs/sign-language-recognition-python-ml-opencv/. Accessed 03 Apr 2023
18. https://core.ac.uk/download/pdf/191337614.pdf. Accessed 03 Apr 2023
19. https://core.ac.uk/reader/191309220. Accessed 03 Apr 2023
20. https://www.acadpubl.eu/jsi/2017-117-20-22/articles/20/2.pdf. Accessed 03 Apr 2023
21. https://github.com/rrupeshh/Simple-Sign-Language-Detector. Accessed 03 Apr 2023
22. Shirbhate, R.S., Shinde, V.D., Metkari, S.A., Borkar, P.U., Khandge, M.A.: Sign language recognition using machine learning algorithm. Int. Res. J. Eng. Technol. **7**(03), 2122–2125 (2020)
23. https://www.freecodecamp.org/news/weekend-projects-sign-language-and-static-gesture-recognition-using-scikit-learn-60813d600e79/. Accessed 03 Apr 2023

Redefining the World of Medical Image Processing with AI – Automatic Clinical Report Generation to Support Doctors

Narayana Darapaneni[1], Anwesh Reddy Paduri[2(✉)], B. S. Sunil Kumar[3], S. Nivetha[3], Varadharajan Damotharan[3], Suman Sourabh[3], S. R. Abhishek[3], and V. Albert Princy[3]

[1] Northwestern University/Great Learning, Evanston, USA
[2] Great Learning, Bangalore, India
anwesh@greatlearning.in
[3] PES University, Bangalore, India

Abstract. In this study, we focus on generating readable automatic assisted clinical reports using medical scans/ images. This project is beneficial when it comes to quick analysis of the medical condition and providing on-time treatment. The challenge in this project is the achievement of clinical accuracy and reduce data bias. On the other hand, this endeavor is essential in meeting medical demands in nations with limited resources due to the shortage of radiologists and radiology training programs. Medical picture captioning or report production is the issue that we'll be solving in this case study. Fundamentally, we must use a Convolutional Neural Network (CNN) or a transfer learning algorithm to extract features (bottleneck features) from the photos (preferable as we have less amount of data). Use these traits that were extracted afterward to anticipate the captions. The result would be a string of words resembling a radiologist's report, where a typical report generated by radiologists includes a summary of the findings, a rationale for the examination, and a history of the patient. We were able to create the Python code with this goal in mind. The predictions were analyzed using greedy and beam search techniques. While beam search was shown to create proper phrases, a greedy search was discovered to be significantly faster. In conclusion, a custom final model that uses greedy search is determined to be the best model for this project based on the Bleu score.

Keywords: CNN · Image Processing · Radiology · X-ray · AI · ChexNet · convolutional neural network · transfer learning · bottleneck features · greedy search · beam search · radiologists

1 Introduction

Convolutional networks, in particular, have quickly emerged as the method of choice for analysing medical images, according to Litjens et al. [1]. The usage of rule-based image processing systems for medical image analysis has given way to supervised approaches, where a system is built using training data. As a result, wholly human-made systems are being replaced by ones that are taught by computers using test data that is used to construct feature vectors.

R. Morusupalli et al. (Eds.): MIWAI 2023, LNAI 14078, pp. 704–713, 2023.
https://doi.org/10.1007/978-3-031-36402-0_65

Many deep learning algorithms are based on the idea that computers can learn the characteristics of organs. These algorithms use models (networks) with many layers that convert input data (such as images) into outputs (such as the presence or absence of a disease) while learning ever-higher-level features. Convolutional neural networks have been the most effective sort of image analysis models to date (CNNs). The model does not need to learn distinct detectors for the same object occurring at different locations in an image because of CNNs share weights. Instead, the network executes convolution operations on the pictures. Consequently, the number of parameters is decreased and the number of weights is independent of the size of the input image as the network becomes equivariant with regard to translations of the input (refer Fig. 1).

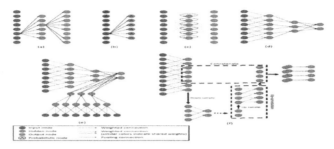

Fig. 1. Node graphs of 1D architectures for medical imaging.

2 Literature Review

A new feature map X_k is produced for each layer by convolving the input image with a set of K kernels $W = W_1, W_2, ...W_k$ and extra biases $B = b_1,....b_k$. Every convolutional layer l of these features goes through the identical element-by-element non-linear transform procedure:

$$X_k^l = \sigma(W_k^{l-1} * X^{l-1} + b_k^{l-1})$$

Moreover, CNNs incorporate pooling layers and aggregate pixel values using a permutation invariant function (max or mean operation). Via the induction of translation invariance, this lowers the number of parameters in the network. Fully connected layers (also known as normal neural network layers), where weights are no longer shared, they are frequently introduced after the network's convolutional stream.

In their study, Varoquaux & Cheplygina [2] determines the clinical implications of machine learning in medical imaging, and how to improve it. The size of medical databases is frequently in the hundreds or thousands, the author explains. Although the datasets are modest, the number of subjects is still important in medical imaging. A patient could have numerous images, for instance, taken at various times. Moreover, the datasets for a given medical condition only partially reflect the clinical environment, which leads in bias in the dataset, flaws in the results and diagnosis, and an inaccurate model. When compared to the test data, this model's distribution might be different.

Liu et al. [3] have conducted a study which generates chest x-ray reports using reinforcement learning (to aid better readability). In their investigation, Open-I and MIMIC-CXR datasets were employed. The largest matched image-report dataset currently accessible is MIMIC-CXR, whereas Open-I is a public radiography dataset gathered by Indiana University.

Deep neural networks were highlighted in a survey of automatic report generating techniques done by Messina Pablo et al. [4]. Datasets, architecture, explainability, and evaluation metrics are the categories into which the study is divided. The article also discusses explainable AI (XAI), which enables doctors to comprehend the reasoning behind black-box algorithms' automatic reports. Due to this, the model may provide results with clinical accuracy regardless of dataset bias (Guidotti et al. [5]). Additionally, they claim that the classification datasets just offer a list of clinical illnesses or anomalies that are present or absent rather than a report. Finally, this type of data is employed as a pre-training, an intermediate, or an auxiliary duty to produce the actual report.

Datasets for chest X-rays: Report Dataset (only English reports are considered): IU X-ray (7470 images); MIMIC-CXR (377110 images); Classification Dataset: CheXpert (224316 images); ChestX-ray14 (112120 images).

Figure 2 presents a summary of model design according to dimensions such as: Visual and linguistic components; input and output.

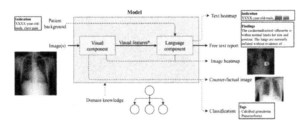

Fig. 2. General architecture representing inputs towards the left and outputs towards the right

Input and output: The features or anomalies from the image taken at different time steps or by using a sequence data is encoded using bidirectional long-short term memory (BiLSTM). Multi-task multi-attribute learning (MTMA) encodes the attributes from the image as indications/ findings. A software package such as Lucene is also used to generate the report in the defined template where the final report was generated by an encoder-decoder network (Fig. 3).

The output can take one of three forms: (1) generative multi-sentence (unstructured), in which the model is free to choose the words that go into each sentence; (2) generative multi-sentence structured, in which the output has a fixed number of sentences and each sentence always has a pre-defined topic; (3) generative single-sentence, in which the output is just one sentence. (4) The template-based report is created using a human-designed template, for instance, by conducting a classification operation [9] and then applying if-then rules; (5) The hybrid template will be free to create sentences word-by-word as well as employ templates.

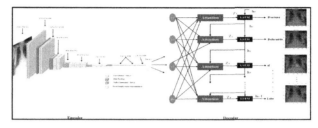

Fig. 3. Typical CNN architecture with encoder and decoder (Sirshar et al. [6])

Visual and linguistic components: Typically, a model architecture used to interpret an image has both a visual and linguistic component. Natural language processing (NLP) neural architecture serves as the language component, while CNN serves as the visual component. CNN analyses [10] the image and extracts its features. NLP analyses text and aids in the creation of reports. The results are a volume of feature maps with the dimensions W, H, and C, where W and H denote spatial (width and height) and C, respectively (depth or the number of feature maps).

The architecture used for visual and language components: CNN Architectures for chest X-ray: Dense Net; ResNet; VGG; InceptionV3; GoogLeNet;

Language component Architectures: Partial report encoding and FC layer (next word); Transformer; Hybrid template retrieval + generation/edition; GRU; LSTM; LSTM with attention; Hierarchical LSTM with attention; Dual Word LSTM (normal/abnormal) with Sentence LSTM; Recurrent BiLSTM-attention-LSTM.

The most popular methods are Dense Net, ResNet, and VGG, according to the literature review. The most prevalent is LSTM. An encoding vector is used to decode the entire report that LSTM obtains from the visual component at the beginning. Typically, the CNN outputs a vector of global characteristics like this encoding vector. Unfortunately, LSTM is only suitable for brief reports. The Hierarchical LSTM with attention can be used to unstructured reports containing several sentences.

Evaluation metrics of the reports are assessed into 3 categories: Text quality, medical precision/accuracy, and explainability.

Text quality: BLUE; ROUGE L; METEOR; CIDEr;

Medical Correctness/Accuracy: MIRQI; MeSH; Keyword accuracy; ROC-AUC;

The challenges that need attention: (1) Expert evaluation: The model and the report generation system be tested by medical experts who are board-certified experts. Their feedback carries immense value to better the model. (2) Explain ability.

A quantitative evaluation of the alignment between automated metrics and radiologists is studied by Yu et al. [6]. Radiology reports and automated metrics both receive scores. The automated metric uses the MIMIC CXR dataset. The metric oracle reports the test results, which are used to make applicant selections. The radiologist evaluation study design was carried out with the assistance of six board-certified radiologists, who scored the number of errors that various metric-oracle reports contained in contrast to the test report. Radiologists categorised errors as significant or insignificant. Radiologists subtyped each error into one of the following six categories: (1) False positive finding prediction (2) False negative inability to find (3) False positive location or discovery (4)

Wrong assessment of the severity (6) Omitting a comparison that demonstrates a shift from an earlier study; (5) mentioning a comparison that is not present in the reference impression. The MIMIC-CXR test set was randomly selected from 50 studies. The metrics RadGraph F1, BLEU, BERTScore, and CheXbert vector similarity were used to construct metric oracle reports (semb). BLEU calculates n-gram overlap within the family of text overlap-based natural language generation metrics, which also includes CIDEr, METEOR, and ROUGE. BERTScore has been suggested as a way to measure contextual similarity beyond simple text matches. Metrics like RadGraph F1 and CheXbert vector similarity are used to rate the precision of clinical data.

Metric scores and radiologists' reported errors are calculated by the use of the Kendall rank correlation coefficient (tau-b). The measures with the two best alignments with radiologists were BERTScore, and RadGraph F1. These results show that the metrics that are most closely aligned with radiologists are BERTScore, RadGraph, and BLEU. CheXbert is less concordant than the aforementioned metrics but has alignment with radiologists.

It was discovered that RadGraph and BLEU wrongly placed prior models above random retrieval, despite BERTScore having the strongest alignment with radiologists when it comes to evaluating metric-oracle reports. Several text overlap-based metrics than BLEU are extensively used in natural language generation, including CIDEr, METEOR, and ROUGE. These measurements might or might not produce reports with radiologist alignment and reliability that is better or worse than BLEU.

According to Sirshar et al. [7] study, by combining computer vision and natural language processing techniques, an auto medical report generator can be created. The automated report generator also employs long short-term memory and convolutional neural networks to identify symptoms, which are then followed by an attention mechanism to produce sequences based on these ailments. The accuracy of these models is evaluated using conventional Natural Language Processing (NLP) criteria as BLEU-1, BLEU-2, BLEU-3, and BLEU-4.

3   Foundation

The issue with the task of captioning images was addressed by Chempolil [8] in his article. A report in XML format and a few photos of various patients are provided for this dataset. The xml file contains data on the patients as well as the names of the images. Using regex, we extracted this data from the xml file and converted it into a data frame. Following that, we may utilise pre-trained models to extract information from images, and then LSTMs or GRUs can produce captions utilising this information.

Dual Language Evaluation score is referred to as understudy. The BLEU score will be the statistic in this situation. Each word in the predicted sentence is compared to each word in the reference sentence to determine how many words were predicted that were in the original sentence (also done in n-grams).

The data sets were acquired from the publicly available Indiana University Chest XRays dataset, which includes chest Xray images and reports (which are in XML format) that include information about the comparison, indication, results, and impressions radiologists made from those Xray images. The data set includes 7470 pictures (Figs. 4 and 5).

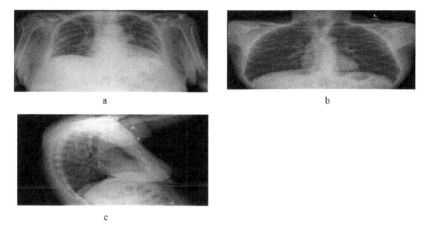

a

b

c

Fig. 4. a, b, c are typical X-ray images from dataset considered having different views (front and side).

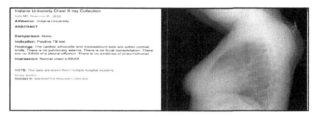

Fig. 5. Example report for respective X-ray image

This case study's objective is to create and train a model that creates impressions of the medical report accompanied by the X-ray images.

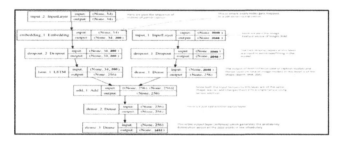

Fig. 6. Model architecture used for training

Using the above model architecture (refer to Fig. 6 Chempolil), the greedy search method was used.

Model Architecture and Training

The ChestX-ray 14 dataset was used to train the 121-layer Dense Convolutional Network (DenseNet) known as CheXNet. DenseNets enhance the network's row of information and gradients, making very deep network optimization manageable. After switching out the final fully linked layer for one with a single output, we add a sigmoid nonlinearity. The weights of the network are initialised using the weights from a model that has previously been trained on ImageNet. Adam is used to train the network using standard parameters from start to finish. We train the model with 16-piece micro batches. With an initial learning rate of 0:001 that decreases by a factor of 10 each time the validation loss reaches a plateau after an epoch, we select the model with the lowest validation loss.

Simple Encoder Decoder Model

The two images will be used by the encoder, which will turn them into the decoder's basic features. CheXNET model will be used for the encoder portion. We can input weights into that model and run photographs through it.

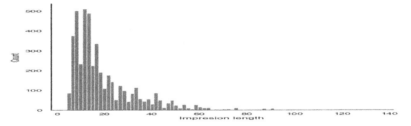

Fig. 7. Visualizing impression length

Figure 7 sets the max limit or value for the caption of respective medical condition.

Custom Model

Here, a unique encoder and decoder are being used. The backbone features for this model's encoder are taken from the output of the third last layer of the Chexnet model.

Global Flow and Context Flow

To extract image data, attention directed picture segmentation with chained context aggregation is used. The global flow will receive the outputs from the image encoder. The outputs from both the global flow and the chexNet will then be combined and forwarded to the context flow. As the dataset is short and using a more complex architecture could result in underfitting, only one context flow will be employed in this instance. In this case, the global flow extracts the image's global information while the local aspects of the images are obtained by the context flow. The following reshaping, applying batch norm, and dropout, the result of the context flow and global flow will be added before being given to the decoder.

4   Results

The predictions were examined using the beam search and greedy search approaches. In contrast to beam search, which multiplies the probabilities of each word at every time step to determine the sentence with the highest probability, greedy search only outputs the most likely word at each time step. While beam search is found to create valid phrases, greedy search is significantly faster (Table 1 and Fig. 8).

Table 1. BLEU score for Simple encoder and decoder model

	BLEU1	BLEU2	BLEU3	BLEU4
Greedy Search	0.317412	0.308454	0.333496	0.366244
Beam Search (top_K = 3)	0.317412	0.308454	0.333496	0.366244

```
test['prediction_gs'].value_counts()*100/test.shape[0] #greedy search

no acute cardiopulmonary abnormality .    100.0
Name: prediction_gs, dtype: float64

test['prediction_bm'].value_counts()*100/test.shape[0] #beam search

no acute cardiopulmonary abnormality .    100.0
Name: prediction_bm, dtype: float64
```

Fig. 8. Value counts of predicted captions

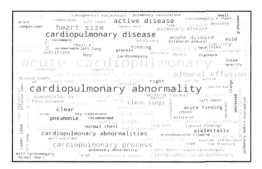

Fig. 9. Word Cloud of all clinical condition

It is observed from Fig. 9 that clinical condition with highest frequency or counts appears in large size as it is most recorded observation (Fig. 10).

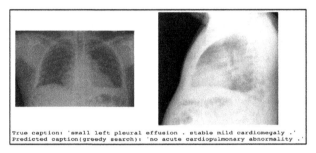

Fig. 10. Sample results from the test data.

5 Discussion and Conclusions

The research that has been evaluated focuses on deep learning models that use medical domain expertise for a variety of tasks.

Despite the fact that it is more common to incorporate medical domain information into deep learning models, there are still several challenges associated with the choice, representation, and incorporation of medical domain knowledge.

The data set to be selected is also an integral part of working of the model.

If the correct data set is not chosen, we need to spend more time in the data analysis (Table 2).

Table 2. BLEU score for Custom final lodel Simple encoder and decoder model

Sl.No	Model	BLEU1	BLEU2	BLEU3	BLEU4
1	**Custom Final Model (Greedy Search)**	0.214501	0.243265	0.303785	0.36675
2	**Simple Encoder Decoder (Greedy Search)**	0.317412	0.308454	0.333496	0.366244

Based on bleu score, the custom final model (greedy search) is found to be the best model.

This demonstration performed way better than other show (it was able to yield names of maladies and a few perceptions more accurately).

The fact that the straightforward encoder-decoder model could only produce one caption for the whole dataset suggests overfitting.

For the models to comprehend things better and to lessen bias to the "no disease category," additional data with greater variability, including X-rays of patients having disorders, can be very beneficial.

6   Future Scope

Based on this project we can see a possibility to extend methodologies for pathology images, 3D scans, etc. Improve clinical accuracy and less data bias.

Since the majority of the data in this dataset fell into the "no disease" category, more X-ray images with diseases are needed.

References

1. Litjens, G., et al.: A survey on deep learning in medical image analysis. Med. Image Anal. **42**, 60–88 (2017). https://doi.org/10.1016/J.MEDIA.2017.07.005
2. Varoquaux, G., Cheplygina, V.: Machine learning for medical imaging: methodological failures and recommendations for the future. NPJ Digit. Med. **5**(1), 1–8, (2022). https://doi.org/10.1038/s41746-022-00592-y
3. Liu, F., Yin, C., Wu, X., Ge, S., Zhang, P., Sun, X.: Contrastive attention for automatic chest X-ray report generation. Find. Assoc. Comput. Linguist. ACL-IJCNLP **2021**, 269–280 (2021). https://doi.org/10.18653/v1/2021.findings-acl.23
4. Messina, P., et al.: A survey on deep learning and explainability for automatic report generation from medical images. ACM Comput. Surv. **54**(10s), 1–40 (2022). https://doi.org/10.1145/3522747
5. Guidotti, R., Monreale, A., Ruggieri, S., Turini, F., Giannotti, F., Pedreschi, D.: A survey of methods for explaining black box models. ACM Comput. Surv. **51**(5), 1–42 (2018). https://doi.org/10.48550/arxiv.1802.01933
6. Yu, F., et al.: Evaluating progress in automatic chest X-ray radiology report generation. *medRxiv*, p. 2022.08.30.22279318 (2022). https://doi.org/10.1101/2022.08.30.22279318
7. Sirshar, M., Paracha, M.F.K., Akram, M.U., Alghamdi, N.S., Zaidi, S.Z.Y., Fatima, T.: Attention based automated radiology report generation using CNN and LSTM. PLoS ONE **17**(1), e0262209 (2022). https://doi.org/10.1371/JOURNAL.PONE.0262209
8. Chempolil, A.T.: Medical image captioning on chest X-Rays | by Ashish Thomas Chempolil | Towards Data Science.
9. Darapaneni, N., et al.: Inception C-net(IC-net): altered inception module for detection of covid-19 and pneumonia using chest X-rays. In: 2020 IEEE 15th International Conference on Industrial and Information Systems (ICIIS), pp. 393–398 (2020)
10. Darapaneni, N.: Explainable diagnosis, lesion segmentation and quantification of COVID-19 infection from CT images using convolutional neural networks. In: 2022 IEEE 13th Annual Information Technology Electronics and Mobile Communication Conference (IEMCON), pp. 0171–0178 (2022)

Statistical Analysis of the Monthly Costs of OPEC Crude Oil Using Machine Learning Models

V. Swapna[1(✉)], Srikanth Bethu[2], G. Vijaya Lakshmi[1], Kanthala Sampath Kumar[3], and V. V. Haragopal[4]

[1] H&S Department, CVR College of Engineering, Hyderabad, India
swapnacvr82@gmail.com
[2] Department of CSE, CVR College of Engineering, Hyderabad, India
[3] Department of Applied Statistics, Telanagna Univeristy, Nizamabad, India
[4] Department of Mathematics, Osmania University, Hyderabad, India

Abstract. In the present era of industrialization and technological advancement, all the countries economy including India depend on energy. The demand for energy has been increasing and, if more energy is consumed there will be more economic activity which leads to a larger economy. So, the energy industry plays an important role in the socio-economic growth, production and higher standards of living. The primary energy sources are plants, coal, petroleum, electricity, sun, geothermal steam and animals. The world is seriously concerned about the variations of crude oil because it is one of the most erratic commodities in the world. The aim of this study is to develop the best machine learning (ML) model and a potential unique-variant mathematical model that can estimate Organization of Petroleum Exporting Countries (OPEC) crude oil prices. In this work, machine learning and computational intelligence methodologies were empirically used to carry out features comparable to those of a decision support system for the human, and then they were applied to best mimic human anticipation. we have validated our results by evaluating the mean square error, root mean square error, mean absolute error, mean absolute percentage error and the R-square and the results obtained using the proposed model have significantly outperformed.

1 Introduction

The Organization of Petroleum Exporting Countries (OPEC) plays a great role in global oil market. The OPEC is an intergovernmental organization of oil producing nations accounted for nearly 44% of the world's oil production. This is the data which have been mined from the U.S Energy Information Administration (EIA) in the year 2016. Initially, Kuwait, Iran, Saudi Arabia, Iraq, and Venezuela joined together and formed OPEC in the year 1960. Later on, the number raised to a total of 13 countries.

As Oil is a vital income developing product for OPEC [1] member countries, national and international policies in these countries are inevitable and were affected by fluctuations in oil price. Hence, if the world oil market is in stable their foreign exchange is disturbed and is reflected in the investment, saving, expenditure and the projects which contribute to the growth of national income. Sometimes, it has been observed that even if there is an increase in the quality of oil exported or place there is no decrease in the inflation rate. Furthermore, the competitiveness of products of other sectors in world market has reduced. For instance, in Iran, when the value of petroleum export appreciated, the production index of the industrial sector increased oil revenues.

It has both advantages and disadvantages. From the positive side, they may result in a stronger economy and faster development plans. On the contrary, they may provoke ambitious and unrealistic investments, leading to economic imbalances, budget deficit and a large gap between investment and saving.

The consequences of the high and rising price of oil can be two-fold. Firstly, the standard of living decreases. Secondly, it affects the economy in ways that are difficult for policy makers to manage. Consequently, the hike in oil price hike not only stimulates general inflation but it also dwindles domestic demand and employment. Hence, OPEC controls the rise of oil prices.

In the presented context, the optimal monthly costs of OPEC crude oil are estimated using an autoregressive integrated moving average (ARIMA) [2] and a machine learning approach. Experiments on the proposed model are performed on datasets. Supervised machine learning is used for many efficient computations because it is used to obtain the best value for many alternatives. Crude oil prices are better predicted using this approach. Supervised machine learning [4] techniques like Linear regression, SVM, ANN, LSTM are compared in the results section.

The rest of the article is organized in the following manner like Sect. 2 discusses about related work, Sect. 3 discusses about Data and Methodology, Sect. 4 discusses about Results and Discussion.

2 Related Work

In this section we have highlighted the survey work done by the previous researchers and models used by them to generate the results.

Ying Xiang, Xiao Hong Zhuang [3]: Here the Brent crude oil prices were predicted with the help of time series modelling. They developed ARIMA (1,1,1) model for the study. It is identified that ARIMA (1,1,1) model was able to forecast the future international Brent crude oil price for the short-term data taken from November 2012 to April 2013. ARMA and GARCH were compared with ANN, and the results of the experiments reveal that ANN was a better method and provided a statistically significant forecast.

Azadeh et al. [7]: The authors proposed flexible artificial neural network (ANN) algorithm to forecast noisy oil price for long-term. Fuzzy regression (FR) algorithm is compared to the proposed algorithm. The study incorporates oil supply, crude oil distillation capacity, oil consumption of non-OECD, USA refinery capacity, and surplus capacity as the economic indicators. The authors applied Analysis of Variance (ANOVA) and Duncan's multiple range test (DMRT) for testing the accurateness of the projections with performance measure MAPE. Also, validation and verification of the outcomes is tested with Spearman correlation. ARIMA and BPNN approaches are compared to this ensemble model. They evaluated the predicting ability of SVM, and compared its performance with those of ARIMA and BPNN. They discovered that SVM is an effective technique for crude oil price prediction.

Bhattacharya et al. [9]: They investigated the co-movement between exchange rates (USD/INR and USD/EURO) and oil price volatility using the asymmetric univariate GARCH model and the DCC model. According to the analysis, the USD/EURO rate and the USD/INR rate both exhibited greater co-movement with oil prices before and throughout the financial crisis, but the USD/INR rate maintained its co-movement after oil prices began to decline in 2014. Performance metrics such as MAE, MAPE, RMSE, and R2 were used to evaluate the model's effectiveness.

The findings, according to the authors, have implications for risk management professionals who deal with the effects of negative oil stocks and exchange rate movements as well as policymakers who are tasked with limiting the real economy's negative effects from exchange rate fluctuations or the inflationary effects of oil prices.

Liu et al. [8]: They evaluated the predicting ability of SVM, and compared its performance with those of ARIMA and BPNN. Disadvantage is that Monthly crude oil prices data was only used for evaluation and prediction. Limitation is that the time span of data is very small.

Vo, A. H., Nguyen, T., & Le, T. [12]: The methods used in this study are Bidirectional Long Short-Term Memory (Bi-LSTM), Convolutional Neural Network (CNN) and combination of CNN and Bi-LSTM (CNN-Bi-LSTM). Disadvantage is Metrics including MSE, MAE, RMSE and MAPE were employed to assess the model's prediction ability. Limitation is Model's comparison is not available.

Nalini gupta, Shobhit Nigam [13]: The ANN has an approach which captures unstable patterns of the unstable pattern of the crude oil prices. Disadvantage is Metrics are not clearly mentioned. Limitation is that this work is carried out on the closing price of crude oil; however, there are various other factors which also affect the crude oil prices like change in the prices and quantities (demand and supply).

Fundamentally, in light of the fact that the econometric models expect the information to be fixed, normal and direct, they can't precisely demonstrate time series information that are irregular, perplexing and nonlinear.

2.1 Objectives and Contributions

This paper centers major contributions.

- Developing appropriate model and forecasting monthly cost of OPEC crude oil.
- Assessing the forecasting model accuracy using the error measures.
- Examining the linear and non-linear approaches for forecasting crude oil prices.

3 Data and Methodology

The proposed analysis incorporates the following developments: It employs a perceptibility chart computation to organize the informative collection and concentrate commotion from the informational index to determine the most compelling hubs. The model suggests estimating oil costs to gather information. As a result, LSTM is used to develop and test the model on the extracted dataset (Fig. 1).

Auxiliary information is considered for research purposes in this analysis. Here we address the existing ARIMA model and the proposed LSTM model.

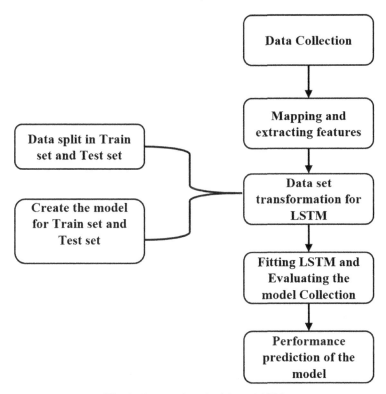

Fig. 1. Proposed methodology-LSTM

An ARIMA [11] model is usually used to represent a stationary time series Zt. The three components of this model are auto-regressive (p), number of differences (d), and moving averages (q). The ARIMA (p,d,q) model can be described as follows:

$$\varphi(B)\nabla^d Z_t = \theta(B)a_t \tag{1}$$

where $\varphi(B) = 1 - \varphi_1 B - \varphi_2 B^2 \dots \dots \dots \varphi_P B^p$ is referred to as the AR operator and is a polynomial in B of order "p", and $\theta(B) = 1 - \theta_1 B - \theta_2 B^2 - \theta_3 B^3 - \dots \dots \dots \dots \dots \theta_q B^q$ is referred to as the MA operator and is a polynomial in B of order 'q' and B is the Backward shift operator and is written as $B^k Z_t = Z_{t-k}$. Here the parameter 'd' is the number of differences required to obtain stationary.

Predictions can be generated when the LSTM matches the preparation data. When you match the model to all the preparation data at once, you may forecast each new time step independently of the test data. This is achieved by invoking the forecasting capacity of the model. The predictive accuracy of the model is evaluated using MSE, RMSE, MAE, MAPE, and R2.

$$RMSE = \sqrt{\frac{1}{N}\sum_{t=1}^{n}(S_t - O_t)^2} \tag{2}$$

where S_t and O_t are the real cost and estimate esteem at time t.

4   Results and Discussion

This study includes building a Linear Regression model and testing its accuracy by using the performance measures MSE, RMSE, MAE, MAPE and R^2.

Here the costs of OPEC crude oil have been taken from the source www.eia.gov. in for 47 years from 1973 to 2019. The data considered is assessed for fitting the best model using an ARIMA technique. The forecasts of crude oil prices are also explained with the best selected ARIMA model. Firstly, the time series plot of the actual OPEC crude oil prices was developed (Fig. 2).

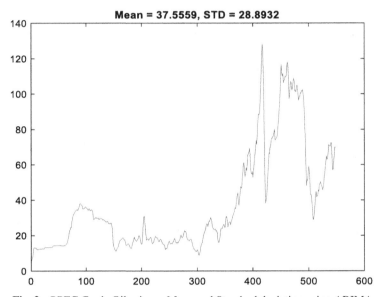

Fig. 2. OPEC Crude Oil prices - Mean and Standard deviation using ARIMA

Here, the stationarity of the considered time series data has been verified with the Dickey-Fuller test. Since, p value is 0.53668, which is greater than 0.05 indicates that the data with no unit root test is also not stationary. To make data stationary, we find the first difference (i.e., the difference at lag 1). The process of differencing will make the data stationary. After the data is made stationary, the period of sequence will be found and then we find the best forecasting model. We now discuss the ARIMA model fitting.

$$Z_t = 0.544\,Z_{t-1} + (1 - 0.195)\,a_t + 0.116$$

Based on MSE, RMSE, MAE, MAPE and R^2 the model is identified and best model fitted is selected. Among all these models selected, we found that ARIMA (1,1,1) is optimum when related to other models considered.

Table 1. OPEC crude oil prices- MSE, RMSE, MAE, MAPE and R^2 using ARIMA

S.NO	MODEL	MSE	RMSE	MAE	MAPE	R2
1	A	(5.345344)	(2.312)	(1.412)	(3.743)	(0.994)
2	B	(5.978025)	(2.445)	(1.474)	(3.877)	(0.993)
3	C	(5.230369)	(2.287)	(1.414)	(3.744)	(0.997)

Note: A stands for ARIMA (1 1 0), B stands for ARIMA (0 1 1), C stands for ARIMA (1 1 1).
From the above Table 1, only ARIMA (1,1,1) fits well according to MSE, RMSE, MAE, MAPE
and R2. Hence the most appropriate model observed as ARIMA (1,1,1). Therefore, the theoretical
model fitted for the data is ARIMA (1,1,1) thus, the fitted ARIMA model for the predicting the
costs of OPEC crude oil price is.

4.1 Predicting the OPEC Crude Oil Prices Using Long Short-Term Memory (LSTM)

This model is considering 80% for training data and 20% for testing data. The first
80% of the data were first developed in models and then the remaining 20% of the
data was utilized to evaluate the model and the model accuracy was then analyzed for
correctness, and MSE, RMSE, MAE, MAPE and R^2 have been used for measuring
model performance. The current, expected and residual data were taken to check the
mode performance.

Information about current, forecast values are incorporated into this Fig. 3, which
illustrate that the predicted and actual values are similar. The error values are close to
zero.

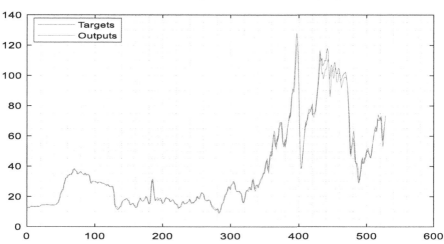

Fig. 3. OPEC Crude Oil price- Actual, predicted plot using LSTM

The time series values can be evaluated keeping in view the current and forecasted values that are correct even with dynamic predictions. Next, it has been described that the LSTM model will be applied to the prices of OPEC crude oil for future values (Fig. 4).

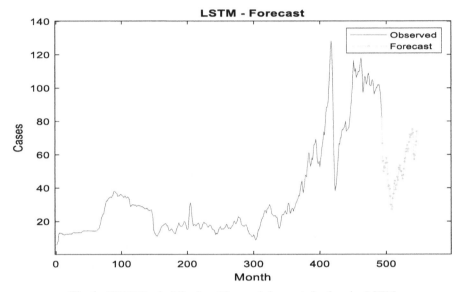

Fig. 4. OPEC Crude Oil price- Observed, forecasted values by LSTM

The above figure is being revealed that there is a slight decrease and increase of crude oil prices under the LSTM model in some months. Here we created a model on the training dataset and got the model trained and got the trend of the dataset. In evaluating current, predicted and error values, it has been demonstrated that the predicted and actual values of training dataset are similar. The error values are close to zero. Once model trained perfectly, we take test dataset and predict values for the same.

Table 2. OPEC crude oil prices- MSE, RMSE, MAE, MAPE and R^2 using LSTM

OPEC Crude Oil price (LSTM Results)	MSE	RMSE	MAE	MAPE	R2
	3.5894	1.8931455	0.5162	2.9841	0.9943

From the above Table 2, it is observed that the LSTM model has minimum MSE, RMSE, MAE, MAPE and higher R^2 value, therefore the LSTM model fits very well with the data of OPEC crude oil price.

4.2 Comparison of Linear Regression, ARIMA, ANN, SVM Linear, SVM Quadratic, Ensemble Boosted Trees, Ensemble Bagged Trees and LSTM for the Costs of OPEC Crude Oil

All twelve techniques should be measured for RMSE, MSE, MAE, MAPE and R Square in order to compare them.

Table 3. The monthly costs of OPEC Crude Oil – Comparison of Linear Regression, Exp. Smoothing, ARIMA, ANN, SVM Linear, SVM Quadratic, Ensemble Boosted Trees, Ensemble Bagged Trees and LSTM

S. No	Model	RMSE	MSE	MAE	MAPE	R Square
1	Linear- Regression	20.801559	432.7048428	17.07985	61.45141	0.481
2	Exp. Smoothing	3.0373313	9.225381204	1.673412	4.452876	0.988
3	ARIMA (0 1 0)	3.043	9.259849	1.669	4.464	0.989
4	ARIMA (1 1 0)	2.312	5.345344	1.412	3.743	0.994
5	ARIMA (0 1 1)	2.445	5.978025	1.474	3.877	0.993
6	ARIMA (1 1 1)	2.287	5.230369	1.414	3.744	0.997
7	ANN	7.3113807	53.45628724	3.961407	10.99859	0.952459
8	SVM Linear	116.01	13458	96.528	319.0275	0.46
9	SVM Quadratic	107.57	11572	85.876	295.8175	0.54
10	Ensemble Boosted Trees	89.425	7996.9	67.638	245.9188	0.68
11	Ensemble Bagged Trees	89.407	7993.6	64.834	245.8693	0.68
12	LSTM	1.8931455	3.5894	0.5162	2.9841	0.9943

From the above Comparative Table 3 of the methods, the RMSE, MSE, MAE, MAPE and R Square identify model identification and optimum model fit to data. Clearly, the LSTM model's RMSE, MSE, MAE, MAPE and R Square are superior to the Linear Regression, Exp. Smoothing, ARIMA, ANN, SVM Linear, SVM Quadratic, Ensemble Boosted Trees, Ensemble Bagged Trees models. The LSTM outperforms the others.

5 Conclusion

In this study, two prediction methods are presented for the costs of OPEC crude oil: Firstly, we applied traditional techniques, next we employed machine learning techniques. The traditional techniques include the Linear Regression, Exponential Smoothing and ARIMA, while the machine learning techniques include SVM, ANN, Ensemble models and LSTM. For evaluating the experimental results for every procedure considered here we employed the statistical measures such as MSE, RMSE, MAE, MAPE and

R-Squared. When we compare the predicting result, LSTM model has been found having lower errors and high accuracy. Hence, we concluded that, the LSTM model's forecasts are more reliable, and also the predictions will be more precise. The monthly costs of OPEC crude oil have been the subject of this investigation; However, as the media demonstrates, there are a number of additional factors that influence crude oil prices, including shifts in prices and quantities (demand and supply), changes in the economy, and current events. Capturing the shifting pattern of these prices is the primary benefit of this study. It is planned that fundamental indicators and market trends will be incorporated into a model in the not-too-distant future. This will make the proposed model work better.

References

1. Moshiri, S., Foroutan, F.: Forecasting nonlinear crude oil futures prices. Energy J. **27**(4) (2006)
2. Xie, W., Yu, L., Xu, S.: A new method for crude oil price forecasting based on support vector machine. In: Alexandrov, V.N., van Albada, G.D., Sloot, P.M.A., Dongarra, J. (eds.) Computational Science – ICCS 2006. ICCS 2006. Lecture Notes in Computer Science, vol. 3994, pp. 444–451. Springer, Berlin, Heidelberg (2006). https://doi.org/10.1007/11758549_63
3. Xiang, Y., Zhuang, X.H.: Application of ARIMA model in short-term prediction of international crude oil price. In: Advanced Materials Research (Vol. 798, pp. 979–982). Trans Tech Publications Ltd. (2013)
4. Kulkarni, S., Haidar, I.: Forecasting model for crude oil price using artificial neural networks and commodity futures prices. arXiv preprint arXiv:0906.4838. (2009)
5. Amin-Naseri, M.R., Gharacheh, E.A.: A hybrid artificial intelligence approach to monthly forecasting of crude oil price time series. In: The Proceedings of the 10th International Conference on Engineering Applications of Neural Networks, CEUR-WS284, (pp. 160–167) (2007)
6. Haidar, I., Kulkarni, S., Pan, H.: Forecasting model for crude oil prices based on artificial neural networks. In: 2008 International Conference on Intelligent Sensors, Sensor Networks and Information Processing, (pp. 103–108). IEEE (2008)
7. Azadeh, A., Moghaddam, M., Khakzad, M., Ebrahimipour, V.: A flexible neural network-fuzzy mathematical programming algorithm for improvement of oil price estimation and forecasting. Comput. Ind. Eng. **62**(2), 421–430 (2012)
8. Lizardo, R.A., Mollick, A.V.: Oil price fluctuations and US dollar exchange rates. Energy Econ. **32**(2), 399–408 (2010)
9. Bhattacharya, S.N., Jha, S.K., Bhattacharya, M.: Dependence between oil price and exchange rate volatility: an empirical analysis. J. Appl. Econ. Bus. Res. **9**(1), 15–26 (2019)
10. Swapna, V., Kumar, K.S., Hara Gopal, V.V.: Statistical analysis of the costs of OPEC crude oil. Int. J. Sc. Res. Math. Stat. Sci. **7**(4), 1–9 (2020)
11. Kumar, K.S., Swapna, V., JyothiRani, S.A., Hara Gopal, V.V.: Volatility of daily and weekly crude oil prices – a statistical perspective. Int. J. Sci. Res. Math. Stat. Sci. **5**(5), 108–113 (2018)
12. Vo, M.T., Vo, A.H., Nguyen, T., Sharma, R., Le, T.: Dealing with the class imbalance problem in the detection of fake job descriptions. Comput. Mater. Continua **68**(1), 521–535 2021
13. Gupta, N., Nigam, S.: Crude oil price prediction using artificial neural network. Procedia Comput. Sci. **170**, 642–647 (2020). ISSN 1877–0509. https://doi.org/10.1016/j.procs.2020.03.136

Conversational Artificial Intelligence in Digital Healthcare: A Bibliometric Analysis

P. R. Visakh[ID], P. N. Meena[ID], and V. S. Anoop[(✉)][ID]

School of Digital Sciences, Kerala University of Digital Sciences,
Innovation, and Technology, Thiruvananthapuram, India
{visakh.ds21,meena.ds21,anoop.vs}@duk.ac.in

Abstract. Conversational artificial intelligence is a subfield of the broader spectrum of AI that refers to tools and technologies, such as chatbots and virtual agents, that can converse with humans. Conversational AI uses natural language understanding, language processing, machine learning, and reasoning capabilities to mimic human cognition. These agents may find applications in sectors such as education, healthcare, and marketing, to name a few. Recent years witnessed exponential growth in conversational AI research and development, introducing more intelligent agents with near-human-like conversation capabilities. Healthcare is one area that witnessed the rapid adoption of healthcare agents, including patient-facing use cases. This bibliometric analysis summarizes and analyzes recent and prominent research in conversational AI in healthcare. This work poses many research questions and attempts to answer them using the derived insights. This may be highly useful for researchers and practitioners of various avenues of the digital healthcare sector to understand the research trends in conversational artificial intelligence.

Keywords: Conversational AI · Digital Healthcare · Virtual Agents · Chatbot · Bibliometric analysis

1 Introduction

Conversational AI is one of the most studied areas of artificial intelligence that tries to mimic human-like conversation abilities [25]. Right from Eliza [34], the very first chatbot, to the ChatGPT, that disrupts the current conversational artificial intelligence landscape, the conversational artificial intelligence has undergone tremendous developments [7,29]. These advancements are evident in areas such as healthcare [7,23], education [11,16], and finance [15,19], to name a few. The conversational virtual agents or chatbots may help automate the routine tasks humans perform, such as customer support and information seeking, thus significantly reducing human resource costs and time. Healthcare is considered one of the areas where a heavy amount of human effort is required, from patient

R. Morusupalli et al. (Eds.): MIWAI 2023, LNAI 14078, pp. 723–734, 2023.
https://doi.org/10.1007/978-3-031-36402-0_67

enquiry and appointment to post-discharge feedback systems. There are several attempts reported in the research and development arenas on using chatbots for automating this repetitive tasks [14,21]. While it is true that these artificial intelligence-enabled systems may not be able to replace humans, especially in areas such as healthcare, it is an undeniable fact that a lot of manual efforts and interventions may be eliminated.

The use of conversational artificial intelligence in healthcare is expected to grow exponentially in the coming years due to significant developments and advancements in the natural language understanding and natural language processing areas. The rise in the large language models and other pre-trained models contributes significantly to the advancements in conversational virtual agents that are gaining popularity due to their inherent ability to converse in a near-human manner. A careful analysis of the natural language processing literature and state-of-the-art systems suggested a need for consolidating recent and prominent approaches in using conversational virtual agents in the healthcare domain. This will be highly useful for healthcare workers and researchers to understand the landscape better. In this context, this work uses a bibliometric analysis of the existing literature on the role of conversational artificial intelligence in the healthcare domain to infer a thematic analysis. This work outlines three research questions, and then using the insights derived from the analysis, the answers to the questions are discussed. The research questions are outlined in Table 1. The major contributions of this paper are summarized as follows:

- Discusses some prominent and recent approaches in using conversational AI systems in healthcare.
- Conducts a bibliometric analysis of literature on healthcare conversational AI.
- Proposes research questions and finds the answers through thematic literature analysis.

Table 1. Research questions outlined in this bibliometric analysis

Research Question	Description
RQ1	What are the scholarly trends in scientific research about conversational AI in healthcare?
RQ2	What are the most important elements within the scientific research on conversational AI in healthcare?
RQ3	What are the hot research clusters and keywords in the conversational AI in healthcare?

The remainder of this manuscript is outlined as follows: Sect. 2 discusses some prominent and recent literature on conversational artificial intelligence in healthcare. Section 3 presents the methodology used in this paper for the bibliometric analysis. Section 4 presents the insights derived from the analysis and answers the research questions posed, followed by a detailed discussion. In Sect. 5, the authors conclude the paper.

2   Related Studies

Several studies have been conducted to understand the effectiveness of conversational agents, such as chatbots, avatars, and robots, in various healthcare applications. These agents are more practical, user-friendly, and efficient, saving time and resources. A review study was conducted on the chatbot characteristics available for anxiety and depression. It consisted of 42 studies, post-filtered from 1302 citations [1]. 25 of the 42 reviewed articles addressed anxiety and depression, with 16 addressing only depression. Chatbots' scalable and automated interactions can be used for mental health education and screening, referral, and treatment of addictions. These bots are made available using the internet and smartphones [5]. Smartphones are considered more affordable due to their easy availability, low cost, better service, and easy integration of data from multiple sensors. These agents use a taxonomy of technological attributes (such as agent design, setting, interaction, and data processing) to define different prototypes for effective patient care [9]. Many existing health chatbots depend on pre-written input and output from smartphones and function based on rules.

Chatbots such as SimSimi helped individuals to express their sentiments (negative or positive) and emotions (anger, anxiety, or sadness) during the COVID-19 outbreak [8]. The Latent Dirichlet Allocation algorithm modeled 18 topics, categorized under five common themes (outbreak, precautions, physical and psychological impact, life and people in the pandemic, and pandemic-related questions to chatbot) of COVID-19. Findings showed that the descriptions of masks, lockdowns, number of cases, and concerns about the pandemic reflected negative sentiments in users. The COVID-19 epidemic also brought about new factors related to mental health that elevated youth suicide tendencies. The impact of Artificial intelligence on mental health is assessed with the help of three social chatbots: Wysa, Woebot, and Happify [27]. The correlation between mental health distress, adoption of digital health, and COVID-19 case numbers was examined using Wysa between March 2020 and October 2021 by assessing user engagement patterns [32]. The Patient Health Questionnaire-9 and Generalized Anxiety Disorder-7 pre-post evaluations showed a statistically significant improvement with moderate effect size. Also, there was a substantial decrease in anxiety-depression symptoms in Wysa users.

The study examining 126,610 user reviews for the well-known and acclaimed conversational agent smartphone app Replika discovered several of its constraints [33]. This includes improved discussions and intelligent responses, avoiding doubtful and improper material, and an inclusive design. The effectiveness of coaching by a chatbot can be improved by personalizing the chatbot's conversations for each user. A blueprint topic model consisting of 30 topics and 115 actions a chatbot can perform for automatic topic selection is described to create a more intelligent virtual agent [4]. Integrating automatic topic selection with health coaching chatbots validated by experts can enhance user engagement by providing exciting and appropriate conversations. The feasibility and efficiency of a chatbot in analyzing the levels of depression were studied with the help of a conversation interface called Depression Analysis (DEPRA) using the Inventory of Depressive Symptomatology (IDS) and the Structured Interview Guide for the Hamilton Depression Rating Scale (SIGH-D) [13]. The study conducted on 50 participants to analyze their levels of depression was successful, with 79% of them impressed by the chatbot's performance. The effect of depression in university students was studied by comparing bibliotherapy (traditional self-help psychological intervention) with chatbot-based therapy [17]. Findings showed that the chatbot-based treatment was more effective than bibliotherapy in reducing depression and anxiety. It also achieved a better therapeutic alliance with the participants. Mental health distress in adolescents (aged 13 to 18) during the COVID-19 pandemic was studied using a virtual agent called Beth Bot [10]. Beth Bot, delivered through Facebook Messenger, gave psychoeducation on depression and coping mechanisms. The user experiences were assessed by Likert scale, open-ended, and net promoter score (NPS) questions. A considerable proportion accepted it; however, only 56% completed the study.

A chatbot named Vickybot was developed to test, monitor, and treat primary care patients and healthcare employees' work-related burnout and anxiety-depressive symptoms during the COVID-19 pandemic [2]. Vickybot was highly influential in screening anxiety and depression symptoms, reducing work-related burnout, and detecting suicidal risk, but it needed improvement in user engagement. Another chatbot, called ChatPal, was created to promote positive mental health among people living in rural areas [24]. ChatPal contains psychoeducational content and exercises on mindfulness and breathing, mood logging, gratitude, and thought diaries, available in English, Scottish Gaelic, Swedish, and Finnish. The study, on 348 participants aged 18–73, showed that mental well-being had a marginal improvement after using this app. Chatbot therapy can be an alternative to rehabilitation services for adults with brain-related neurological problems. Eleven publications on the design and application of rehabilitation conversational agents for adults (18 years or older) with neurological brain problems were examined [12]. The studies concluded that the conversational agents used for rehabilitation services have heterogeneous designs and are still in the early stages of development.

The mood of a chatbot participant can be improved by introducing expressive virtual agents. Virtual agents with and without expressive faces were used to test the efficacy of these agents [20]. Simulators boosted users' ability for empathy, and individuals who interacted with expressive virtual agents showed a discernible shift in perspective-taking. The virtual agents recognize users' automatic thoughts by creating a classifier framework of automatic thought-generating sentences using cognitive restructuring [31]. This framework used a support vector machine (linear kernel) classifier for training, bidirectional encoder representation from transformers, and term frequency-inverse document frequency for feature extraction. By including an example sentence from a self-help book, the classification performance of the learning data was enhanced. The effect of the human-AI relationships is studied by combining existing theoretical concepts and theories of human-computer interaction and interpersonal relationships [22]. Results demonstrate that chatbot attachment is higher among users who exhibit dominant social behavior.

The perceived ease of use, personalization, privacy loss, and anthropomorphism are essential determinants of public acceptance of an intelligent healthcare system [18]. Analyzing a clinical chatbot's service quality is relevant in identifying the best-performing chatbot. The quality of service is compared by cross-referencing ISO/IEC 25010 characteristics with the three dimensions: providing information, providing prescriptions, and process management [30]. The impact of several design factors on the efficacy of a healthcare chatbot is analyzed utilizing the chatbot's response complexity (e.g., technical or non-technical) and the provided qualifications of the persona (e.g., doctor, nurse, or nursing student). The analysis of 71 participants showed that those who received technical-language comments belonged to the high-effectiveness group and had higher test scores [6].

3 Method

This section details the research methods we employed to conduct bibliometric analysis and visualize the themes of "conversational AI for healthcare." The description of each of the subtasks, such as data collection, preprocessing, and bibliometric analysis, is outlined in this section.

3.1 Data Collection

This work primarily uses Web of Science (WoS) data, which provides reference and citation details from academic journals, conference proceedings, and other documents in various academic disciplines. We have used keywords such as "conversational artificial intelligence," "conversational AI," and "chatbot," along with the keyword "healthcare," and the results were restricted to the last three years. A total of 326 articles were returned, of which we have considered 179 articles for the thematic analysis. The WoS core collection website available at https://www.webofscience.com/wos/woscc/basic-search provides the keywords and collects the articles for analysis.

3.2 Text Preprocessing

We applied some preprocessing methods such as tokenization, stemming, and stop-word removal to improve the value of texts. The first step was tokenization, which inputs raw text and provides tokens or individual words as output. We have also removed special characters and stop-words from the results collected, and we have used Natural Language Toolkit (NLTK) available at https://www.

nltk.org/ for implementing the preprocessing techniques discussed. Stemming, the process of reducing a word to its root form (for example, "playing" to "play"), is also applied to the text collected for better analysis of the bibliography.

3.3 Bibliometric Analysis

Bibliometric analysis is a quantitative analysis of bibliometric data such as scientific literature to see trends and patterns. In recent years, bibliometric analysis has attained greater interest in analyzing the trends of scientific research, and many such studies have been reported [3,28,35]. As the number of literature is growing exponentially, manual analysis of such a vast body of text would be cumbersome and impractical. Thus, bibliometric analysis is crucial in automating the process, and innovative tools like CiteSpace available at http://cluster.ischool.drexel.edu/~cchen/citespace/download/ and VOS Viewer available at https://www.vosviewer.com/ may be employed for this purpose. The bibliometric analysis can be conducted using bibliographic coupling and co-citation analysis techniques. The visualization techniques may be distance-based, timeline-based, or graph-based. In this work, we used VOS Viewer, a bibliometric visualization tool that uses a distance-based mechanism for the visualization.

4   Results and Discussion

This section presents the findings from the bibliometric analysis conducted as outlined in Sect. 3. The answers to the research questions summarized in Table 1 are provided in this section using the insights derived from the analysis. Firstly, we answer the first research question (RQ1). The article publication year-wise on the theme "conversational AI in healthcare" is shown in Fig. 1(a). It shows a significant increase in research publications published in recent years, with the maximum number of publications in 2021. The number of citations received for these publications is also shown in the figure. The co-occurrence graph for the keywords from the research publications on "conversational AI in healthcare" shown in Fig. 3(a) and Fig. 3(b) shows the major trends in scientific research. These graphs show an increasing interest in using conversational AI techniques such as virtual agents and chatbots in the healthcare domain. Similarly, to answer RQ2 and RQ3, the insights derived from the analysis visualized in Fig. 1(b) and Fig. 1(c) are used. Figure 1(c) shows that healthcare sciences are the major category for publishing conversational AI-related research articles, followed by computer science, medical informatics, and engineering. Figurereffig:wholespsfigure(b) shows that Springer Nature publishes most research articles in conversational AI for the healthcare domain, followed by Elsevier, MDPI, and IEEE. Figure 2(a) depicts the author network showing the top authors publishing research articles on the conversational artificial intelligence and healthcare theme and the citations network for those articles. Figure 3(a) and Fig. 3(b) show the major keywords and their relations used by the authors and also extracted from the abstracts of the research articles. Major keywords are *chatbot, conversational agents, digital health, mental health, dialogue systems, depressions*, etc. This specifies that

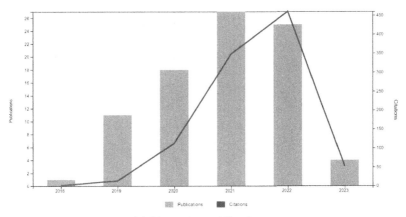

(a) Year-wise publications

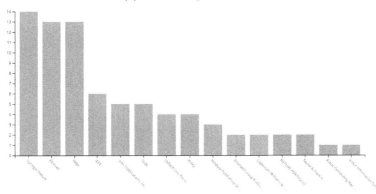

(b) Top publishers publishing research articles

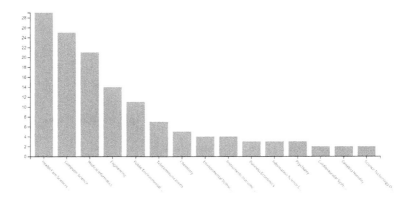

(c) Top publication categories

Fig. 1. Top publishers publishing research articles on the theme "Conversational AI in digital healthcare" and top publication categories

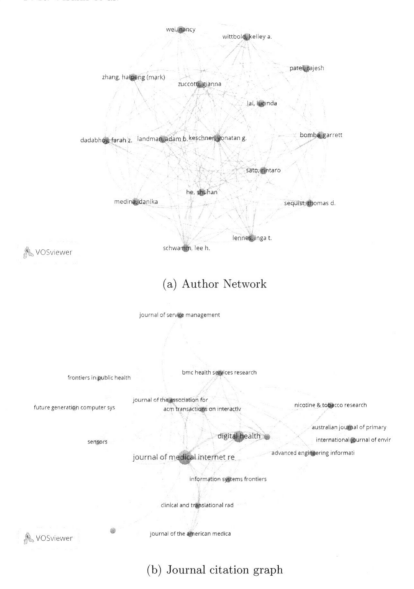

(a) Author Network

(b) Journal citation graph

Fig. 2. Author network graph and journal citation graph for the theme "cognitive artificial intelligence in digital healthcare"

conversational artificial intelligence agents are being heavily used for improving digital health access, and significant areas are mental health, depression, and other disorders. Figure 2(b) shows the journal citation graph for the top journals that publish research articles on conversational artificial intelligence in digital health. So, the analysis clearly shows a significant level of attention received recently on implementing medical chatbot systems to assist clinicians and other healthcare stakeholders.

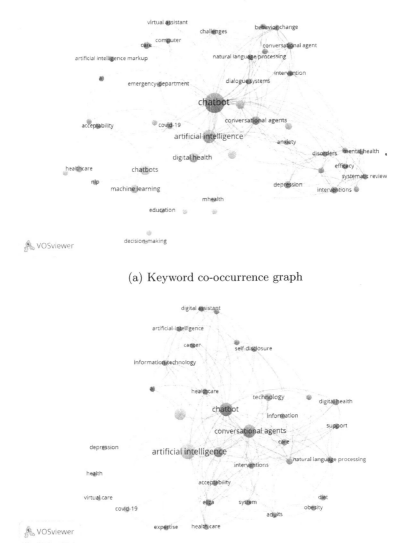

(a) Keyword co-occurrence graph

(b) Keyword co-occurrence graph

Fig. 3. Keyword co-occurrence graphs for the publications on the theme "cognitive artificial intelligence in digital healthcare"

4.1 The Future Trends in Conversational AI for Healthcare

The analysis shows that there will be considerable growth in conversational artificial intelligence systems in the healthcare domain, which is expected to grow exponentially. There are several use cases where conversational AI agents can bring in better services. Some of them are appointment scheduling, better patient care, health tracking and management, scaling of patient assistance, transforming access to healthcare, and multi-lingual patient support and information. With the recent developments in the pre-trained language models exclusively in the healthcare domain, such as Med-BERT [26], more innovative and context-aware virtual agents may be introduced. Digital conversational agents with near-human cognitive capabilities may be expected in the coming years to provide seamless patient services at scale.

5   Conclusions

This work reported the findings of a bibliometric analysis conducted using the research articles published in recent years on the theme "conversational AI for healthcare". The research, development, and adoption of virtual agents or chatbots in the healthcare domain have seen exponential growth due to the advances in natural language understanding and processing. This paper posed some research questions and answered them using the insights derived from the bibliometric analysis. The results showed that recent years witnessed a large number of research articles being published in the area of conversational artificial intelligence. This trend is expected to grow in the coming years due to the disruptions happening with the large language models and other deep learning techniques. These insights unearthed could be helpful for healthcare artificial intelligence researchers and practitioners.

References

1. Ahmed, A., et al.: Chatbot features for anxiety and depression: a scoping review. Health Inform. J. **29**(1), 14604582221146720 (2023)
2. Anmella, G., et al.: Vickybot, a chatbot for anxiety-depressive symptoms and work-related burnout in primary care and healthcare professionals: development, feasibility, and potential effectiveness studies. J. Med. Internet Res. **25**, e43293 (2023)
3. Bahuguna, P.C., Srivastava, R., Tiwari, S.: Two-decade journey of green human resource management research: a bibliometric analysis. Benchmarking Int. J. **30**(2), 585–602 (2023)
4. Beinema, T., Op den Akker, H., Hermens, H.J., van Velsen, L.: What to discuss?—A blueprint topic model for health coaching dialogues with conversational agents. Int. J. Hum.-Comput. Interact. **39**(1), 164–182 (2023)
5. Bickmore, T., O'Leary, T.: Conversational agents on smartphones and the web. In: Digital Therapeutics for Mental Health and Addiction, pp. 99–112. Elsevier (2023)
6. Biro, J., Linder, C., Neyens, D., et al.: The effects of a health care chatbot's complexity and persona on user trust, perceived usability, and effectiveness: mixed methods study. JMIR Hum. Factors **10**(1), e41017 (2023)
7. Budler, L.C., Gosak, L., Stiglic, G.: Review of artificial intelligence-based question-answering systems in healthcare. Wiley Interdiscip. Rev. Data Min. Knowl. Discov. e1487 (2023)
8. Chin, H., et al.: User-chatbot conversations during the COVID-19 pandemic: study based on topic modeling and sentiment analysis. J. Med. Internet Res. **25**, e40922 (2023)

9. Denecke, K., May, R.: Developing a technical-oriented taxonomy to define archetypes of conversational agents in health care: literature review and cluster analysis. J. Med. Internet Res. **25**, e41583 (2023)
10. Dosovitsky, G., Bunge, E.: Development of a chatbot for depression: adolescent perceptions and recommendations. Child Adolesc. Mental Health **28**(1), 124–127 (2023)
11. Essel, H.B., Vlachopoulos, D., Tachie-Menson, A., Johnson, E.E., Baah, P.K.: The impact of a virtual teaching assistant (chatbot) on students' learning in Ghanaian higher education. Int. J. Educ. Technol. High. Educ. **19**(1), 1–19 (2022)
12. Hocking, J., Oster, C., Maeder, A., Lange, B.: Design, development, and use of conversational agents in rehabilitation for adults with brain-related neurological conditions: a scoping review. JBI Evid. Synth. **21**(2), 326–372 (2023)
13. Kaywan, P., Ahmed, K., Ibaida, A., Miao, Y., Gu, B.: Early detection of depression using a conversational AI bot: a non-clinical trial. PLoS ONE **18**(2), e0279743 (2023)
14. Krishna, A.N., Anitha, A.C., Naveena, C.: Chatbot-an intelligent virtual medical assistant. In: Guru, D.S., Sharath Kumar, Y.H., Balakrishna, K., Agrawal, R.K., Ichino, M. (eds.) Cognition and Recognition (ICCR 2021). CCIS, vol. 1697, pp. 108–115. Springer, Cham (2022). https://doi.org/10.1007/978-3-031-22405-8_9
15. Krishnan, C., Gupta, A., Gupta, A., Singh, G.: Impact of artificial intelligence-based chatbots on customer engagement and business growth. In: Hong, T.P., Serrano-Estrada, L., Saxena, A., Biswas, A. (eds.) Deep Learning for Social Media Data Analytics. Studies in Big Data, vol. 113, pp. 195–210. Springer, Cham (2022). https://doi.org/10.1007/978-3-031-10869-3_11
16. Kuhail, M.A., Alturki, N., Alramlawi, S., Alhejori, K.: Interacting with educational chatbots: a systematic review. Educ. Inf. Technol. **28**(1), 973–1018 (2023)
17. Liu, H., Peng, H., Song, X., Xu, C., Zhang, M.: Using AI chatbots to provide self-help depression interventions for university students: a randomized trial of effectiveness. Internet Interv. **27**, 100495 (2022)
18. Liu, K., Tao, D.: The roles of trust, personalization, loss of privacy, and anthropomorphism in public acceptance of smart healthcare services. Comput. Hum. Behav. **127**, 107026 (2022)
19. Luo, B., Lau, R.Y., Li, C., Si, Y.W.: A critical review of state-of-the-art chatbot designs and applications. Wiley Interdiscip. Rev. Data Min. Knowl. Discov. **12**(1), e1434 (2022)
20. Milcent, A.S., Kadri, A., Richir, S.: Using facial expressiveness of a virtual agent to induce empathy in users. Int. J. Hum.-Comput. Interact. **38**(3), 240–252 (2022)
21. Moldt, J.A., Festl-Wietek, T., Madany Mamlouk, A., Nieselt, K., Fuhl, W., Herrmann-Werner, A.: Chatbots for future docs: exploring medical students' attitudes and knowledge towards artificial intelligence and medical chatbots. Med. Educ. Online **28**(1), 2182659 (2023)
22. Pentina, I., Hancock, T., Xie, T.: Exploring relationship development with social chatbots: a mixed-method study of replika. Comput. Hum. Behav. **140**, 107600 (2023)
23. Perez-Ramos, J.G., et al.: COVID-19 vaccine equity and access: case study for health care chatbots. JMIR Form. Res. **7**(1), e39045 (2023)
24. Potts, C., et al.: A multilingual digital mental health and wellbeing chatbot (ChatPal): pre-post multicenter intervention study. J. Med. Internet Res. (2023)
25. Ram, A., et al.: Conversational AI: the science behind the Alexa prize. arXiv preprint arXiv:1801.03604 (2018)

26. Rasmy, L., Xiang, Y., Xie, Z., Tao, C., Zhi, D.: Med-BERT: pretrained contextualized embeddings on large-scale structured electronic health records for disease prediction. NPJ Digit. Med. **4**(1), 86 (2021)
27. Rawat, B., Bist, A.S., Fakhrezzy, M., Octavyra, R.D., et al.: AI based assistance to reduce suicidal tendency among youngsters. APTISI Trans. Manag. **7**(2), 105–112 (2023)
28. Rojas-Sánchez, M.A., Palos-Sánchez, P.R., Folgado-Fernández, J.A.: Systematic literature review and bibliometric analysis on virtual reality and education. Educ. Inf. Technol. **28**(1), 155–192 (2023)
29. Saka, A.B., Oyedele, L.O., Akanbi, L.A., Ganiyu, S.A., Chan, D.W., Bello, S.A.: Conversational artificial intelligence in the AEC industry: a review of present status, challenges and opportunities. Adv. Eng. Inform. **55**, 101869 (2023)
30. Santa Barletta, V., Caivano, D., Colizzi, L., Dimauro, G., Piattini, M.: Clinical-chatbot AHP evaluation based on "quality in use" of ISO/IEC 25010. Int. J. Med. Inform. **170**, 104951 (2023)
31. Shidara, K., et al.: Automatic thoughts and facial expressions in cognitive restructuring with virtual agents. Front. Comput. Sci. **4**, 8 (2022)
32. Sinha, C., Meheli, S., Kadaba, M., et al.: Understanding digital mental health needs and usage with an artificial intelligence-led mental health app (Wysa) during the COVID-19 pandemic: retrospective analysis. JMIR Form. Res. **7**(1), e41913 (2023)
33. Wahbeh, A., Al-Ramahi, M.A., El-Gayar, O., El Noshokaty, A., Nasralah, T.: Conversational agents for mental health and well-being: discovering design recommendations using text mining (2023)
34. Weizenbaum, J.: ELIZA—a computer program for the study of natural language communication between man and machine. Commun. ACM **9**(1), 36–45 (1966)
35. Zhao, L., Yang, M.M., Wang, Z., Michelson, G.: Trends in the dynamic evolution of corporate social responsibility and leadership: a literature review and bibliometric analysis. J. Bus. Ethics **182**(1), 135–157 (2023)

Demand and Price Forecasting Using Deep Learning Algorithms

Narayana Darapaneni[1], Anwesh Reddy Paduri[2(✉)], Sourav Kundu[3], Lokesh Jayanna[3],
N. Balasubramaniam[3], M. P. Manohar[3], B. Rajesh[3], and Sudhakar Moses Munnangi[3]

[1] Northwestern University/Great Learning, Evanston, USA
[2] Great Learning, Bangalore, India
anwesh@greatlearning.in
[3] PES University, Bangalore, India

Abstract. Marketing agricultural products is always a challenge. The farmers are forced to sell their products at a very low price to the middlemen. Meanwhile, consumers are deprived of fresh farm products. Rythu Bazaar, the farmers' market, was established by the Andhra Pradesh government in the year 1999 to address this issue. Consumers can purchase fresh items directly from farmers, and farmers can sell their goods at the desired price. As a result, the present study examines various parameters where consumers and farmers have benefited from a varity of products such as vegetables, fruits, and so on. In this paper, we try to forecast the product price, which is going to help farmers as well as consumers. We are going to use some statistical approaches to prove that consumers are getting benefited from the Rythu Bazar. In our research, we want to forecast for a long time, i.e., 1 year. We are going to use normal machine learning algorithms along with a few Deep Learning algorithms like RNN (Recurrent neural networks), LSTM (Long short-term memory), and Bidirectional LSTM. We intend to investigate many techniques in this field, evaluate the existing algorithms, examine several Deep Learning models, and frame the best model enhancements that produce the greatest demand forecasting outcomes during our research.

Keywords: Rythu Bazaar · hypothesis testing · Forecasting · Recurrent neural networks · long short-term memory · Bidirectional LSTM

1 Introduction

There are several weak points in the production and disposal of agricultural goods. Market research is one of them. Customers who are denied access to fresh agricultural goods are another group of people that suffer greatly because of inadequate marketing infrastructure, in addition to farmers. Since it provides both more compensation for the farmers and improved customer happiness, direct marketing between farmers and consumers has long been thought to be necessary. This will reduce the need for commission-based salespeople and middlemen in marketing. Selling fresh produce and fruit needs a controlled market. The major goal of Rythu Bazaar is to assist farmers in getting their produce to consumers directly and in doing so without the use of middlemen. Farmers may come here and sell their goods at the correct price, and buyers can profit from the best deal and fresh items. The entire supply chain has been organized yet another time by the government for the Rythu Bazaar. Now that this market has been established for some time, it is necessary to determine whether the original motivation for its creation has been fulfilled. In the long run, this would increase customer happiness and farmer wealth.

2 Literature Survey

The research performed on the farmers to showcase if farmers are getting benefited [1, 2] out of the Rythu Bazaar. This research captures the satisfaction level of the farmers of Rythu Bazaar. A few hypothesis tests have been performed to know the satisfaction level. This research is completely exploratory. It has been done statistical way. However, no machine-learning algorithm has been used so far in this research.

The Warangal District [3] of Andhra Pradesh is where the study was conducted. The purpose of this study was to determine the key determinants of vegetable purchases, the demographics of Rythu Bazaar patrons, consumer purchasing habits, the impact of Rythu Bazaars on vegetable growers, and other related topics. This study is built around survey data. Through the sampling technique, 200 regular Rythu bazaar shoppers from the Warangal region were chosen as a sample. Once more, a structured survey was created for the consumers to gather the initial data. Newspapers, periodicals, journals, and other sources were used to gather the secondary data. This investigation is empirical. The effort to demonstrate the advantages of Rythu Bazaar's [4] supply chain management above that of conventional markets. They have examined how these two vary structurally. They have demonstrated how Rythu Bazaar's supply chain connects content farmers and buyers. Additionally, they have pointed out the flaws in the current models and offered solutions. In 1998, Govindasamy et al. examined the resurgence of farmers' markets in New Jersey. Farmers, consumers, and towns have all praised it. It gave the farmers a better understanding of how much money consumers spent on food. Consequently, their profits increased. According to the survey, the majority of farmer markets were situated in suburban areas, but too close to metropolitan areas. It was determined that essential considerations for market site selection include visibility, ease of access, parking availability, traffic flow, and room for farmers. This study aids in defining the characteristics necessary for a successful farmers' market as well as the obstacles these markets must overcome.

To identify correlations between meteorological data and wind power generation [5], the author developed a TCN-based model for day-ahead wind power prediction based on a casual convolution architecture with residual connections. The suggested method effectively tackles the long-distance dependency issue by incorporating a substantial amount of geographical and temporal series data [12], such as one year's worth of wind power data. The experimental results show that TCN models can extract features from long-term sequence data and have prediction accuracy comparable to or better than LSTM and GRU models. Overall, the suggested TCN-based technique performs better in terms of less convergence error and higher prediction accuracy than the models already in use that were employed in earlier studies on wind power forecasting.

TFT is a brand-new, intuitive attention-based deep learning model [6, 7] for highly successful multi-horizon forecasting. Across a range of multi-horizon forecasting datasets, TFT successfully manages static covariates, known inputs from the outset, and observed inputs by utilizing specialized components. Time-varying relationships are captured at multiple timescales by the sequence-to-sequence and attention-based temporal processing components [8]. The network is capable of configuring temporal forecasts based on static metadata [9] thanks to static covariate encoders.

There is a couple of more research on the same area, but none of those used any machine learning algorithms for their research [11]. In this research paper, we are going to use a Deep neural Network to understand the benefit that the farmers and consumers are getting through this [10]. We have also tried to forecast the price of the farm products through our research.

3   Challenges in Time Series Forecasting

Time series forecasting is not scalable and hence faces a variety of challenges. We learned about all these difficulties in-depth thanks to Inbal Tadeski, the Data Science Manager of Anodot, and her presentation on the subject at the Data-AI summit 2022.

These challenges are:

- Trends
- Seasonality
- Holiday or Special events
- Robustness for transient anomalies
- Adaptivity

These are the various difficulties we face when working on a time series forecast problem. There are several approaches to overcoming these obstacles by using machine learning methodologies. In many methods, Boosting Tree techniques, Linear Regression, Prophet, RNNs, etc., may be used to address problems like Trends, Seasonality more effectively (Table 1).

Table 1. Models Comparison

Model Properties Summary					
Challenges	Data Transformation	Features	Model built-in handling	External model	Sample weights
Trends	Boosting trees, RNNs	N/A	Linear regression, Linear Model, Prophet	N/A	N/A

(continued)

Table 1. (*continued*)

Model Properties Summary

Challenges	Data Transformation	Features	Model built-in handling	External model	Sample weights
Seasonality	Linear regression, Boosting trees, RNNs	Linear regression, Boosting trees	Linear Model, Prophet, RNNs	N/A	N/A
Holiday or Special events	N/A	Linear regression, Boosting trees, RNNs	Prophet, Linear Modelpartial	Linear regression, Boosting trees, RNNs, Prophet, Linear Model	N/A
Adaptivity	N/A	N/A	Linear Model	N/A	Linear regression, Boosting trees, RNNs
Robustness for transient anomalies	Linear regression, Boosting trees, RNNs, Prophet, Linear Model	N/A	N/A	N/A	N/A

As per the above table we can suggest using a hybrid model, which allows us to combine the strengths of several models in various segments, is our objective in the light of the explanation above. With all the algorithms' advantages and disadvantages considered, we would want to use LSTM as our price forecasting's base model.

4   Materials and Methods

4.1 Dataset

By cutting out middlemen, Rythu Bazaar (Farmers' Market) in Andhra Pradesh aims to establish a direct line of communication between farmers and consumers. One of the country's direct marketing programme that supports farmers is the Rythu Bazaar (Farmers' Market). The Rythu Bazaars will serve as the primary marketplace for all agricultural products. Vegetables, flowers, fruits, cereals, eggs, milk, meat, honey, seeds, saplings, etc. would all fall under this category.

Rythu Bazaars also offer all other goods that farmers require for their production in addition to the aforementioned (MG.1999). The dataset has been collected from http://183.82.5.184/rbzts/DailyPrices.aspx.

4.2 Source

Primary data has been collected from a website which is copyrighted @2010 by the Agricultural Marketing Department. The range lies between 2008 and 2021. This is Gold Data collected daily from the market. In total, Rythu bazaar has the latest count of 100 and counting in and around 13 Districts of the state.

The model operation method for the proposed Stacked LSTM model included the following three subphases: (i) data preprocessing; (ii) model training; and (iii) price forecasting.

4.3 Data Preparation

Data preprocessing for the Rythu Bazaar dataset is required by engineers before model training. Each record in the dataset includes information about the prices for vegetables at the Rythu Bazaar, the local market, and the daily datetime.

In terms of data preparation, we have identified that the data has a few missing values. We have used forward fill technique to handle the missing values. Also, we handled outliers and removed unnecessary columns. In addition to that we have done the feature engineering work and generated few additional columns which were required for our analysis.

4.4 Methods

We have used below methods or models on this dataset to compare the performance

1. Naive Forecasting
2. ARIMA
3. VAR
4. Decision Tree
5. Vanilla LSTM
6. Bi-Directional LSTM
7. Stacked LSTM

Out of above models, Stacked LSTM provides the best RMSE and MAPE values, so we have used Stacked LSTM for our forecasting.

(1) In the naïve forecasting, we just directly forecasted the price rate. Our intention is to compare the performance with the rest of the models.
(2) **ARIMA:** An Autoregressive Integrated Moving Average model is very good for predicting trend for time series data. It predicts future values based on historical values. Three terms—p, d, and q, define this model. p is the order of the AR term, d is the order of the MA term, and q is the quantity of differencing needed to make the time series stable. Let's understand Autoregressive (AR) and Moving average (MA) models first. In AR, we use linear combination of historical values of the variable to forecast. Autoregression means regression of the variables against themshelves. Here p can be written as

$$y_t = c + \phi_1 y_{t-1} + \phi_2 y_{t-2} + \cdots + \phi_p y_{t-p} + \varepsilon_t$$

where ε_t is noise.

In MA or Moving Average models, instead of using historical values in a regression, we use past forecast errors in a regression-like model.

$$y_t = c + \varepsilon_t + \Theta_1\varepsilon_{t-1} + \Theta_2\varepsilon_{t-2} + \cdots + \Theta_q\varepsilon_{t-q}$$

where ε_t is white noise.

Now if we combine differencing with AR and MA models, we obtain ARIMA model. The full model can be written as:

$$y't = c + \phi1y't - 1 + \cdots + \phi py't - p + \theta1\varepsilon t - 1 + \cdots + \theta q\varepsilon t - q + \varepsilon t$$

where $y't$ is the differenced series (it may have been differenced more than once). The "predictors" on the right hand side include both lagged values of y_t and lagged errors.

We call this an **ARIMA(p,d,q) model**

(3) **VAR:** For multivariate time series, the vector autoregressive model is utilized. Each variable in the structure is a linear function of its own and the other variables' past lags.

This is different from the univariate autoregressive models because they allow feedback between the variable in the model. This is a multi-step process which includes:

  i) Specifying and estimating a VAR model
  ii) Using inferences to check and revise the model
  iii) Forecasting
  iv) Structural analysis

(4) **Decision Tree:** This algorithm for supervised learning is non-parametric. This is for problems involving classification and regression. One root node, numerous internal nodes, and numerous leaf nodes make up the decision tree. Leaf nodes do not produce offspring. Each internal node in this diagram represents a test on an attribute, each branch a test result, and each leaf node (terminal node) a class label.

The goal is to create a model that predicts values by learning the simple or complex decision rules from the features. Also, it depends on the depth of the tree. The deeper the tree, the fitter the model will be (Fig. 1).

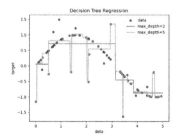

Fig. 1. Decision Tree Regression

In the above figure, the decision trees learn from features to approximate a sine curve with a set of decision rules.

There are two main type of DTs. Categorical variable DTs. This includes target variables that are divided into categories. And continuous variable DTs which have continuous target variables.

(5) A single hidden layer and a typical feedforward output layer make up the initial LSTM model. In contrast, Stacked LSTM uses a number of concealed LSTM layers. It can benefit from combining many LSTM layers, each of which has multiple memory cells. This deepens the model. It develops into a dependable method for sequence prediction models (Fig. 2).

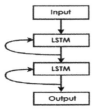

Fig. 2. Stacked Deep LSTM Network Architecture

Two hidden LSTM layers and one dense layer make up the stacked LSTM model that we utilized.

The architecture for our entire research work is given below (Fig. 3).

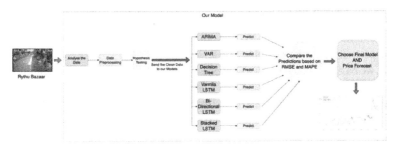

Fig. 3. Model architecture of price forecasting

The above picture shows the step-by-step approaches to forecast the Rythu Bazaar prices rates of all the vegetables. Here the data preparation part is very important as there were missing values and feature engineering had to be done to get more meaningful feature out of the dataset. We have also performed Hypothesis testing on the dataset to get more insights from the dataset. As we can see that all the different models' performance has been compared before forecast the price rates using Stacked LSTM model.

5   Results

The study has been conducted on the Rythu Bazar dataset using aforementioned models. As mentioned in the previous section, we have performed two business oriented Hypothesis testing on the dataset to get more insights of the data. This is explained below:

Hypothesis Testing:

Hypothesis 1: Rythu Bazaar rate is less than the local market rate.

H0: "RythuBazar Rate" mean standard deviation is less than or equal to Local Market Rate mean std.
H1: RythuBazar Rate" mean standard deviation is greater than Local Market Rate std.

We have used z-test and independent T-test for this test and found that p_value is greater than 0.05. So accept the null hypothesis and hence conclude that Rythu bazaar rate is cheaper than local market rate.

Hypothesis 2: Locally grown vegetables are at lesser price compared to imported.

H0: Mean price of imported vegetables is greater than or equal to local vegetables.
H1: Mean price of imported vegetables is less than local vegetables.

For this, we have used Wilcoxon test and found that p value is greater than 0.05. So accept the null hypothesis and hence conclude that locally grown vegetables are at lesser price compared to imported.

Model Comparison:

The model performance has been measured using RMSE and MAPE. It has been noticed that the RMSE and MAPE values of Stacked LSTM has given the best performance out of all the models.

First, we have predicted the price rates using models like ARIMA, VAR and Decision Tree, but none of them gave low RMSE and MAPE compared to LSTM models. We have noticed that LSTM models have performed 10%–17% better than the other models. Let's try to understand the difference between vanilla LSTM and Stacked LSTM model.

5.1   Figures and Tables

Here we want to show the predictions that we have done using different models (Fig. 4).

Table 2. Comparison of LSTM model performances

Models	RMSE	MAPE
Naive Forecasting	3.928	22.14
ARIMA	4.114	23.21
Decision Tree	4.343	23.89
Vanilla LSTM	4.819	24.82
Bidirectional LSTM	5.516	35.26
Stacked LSTM	4.491	24.53

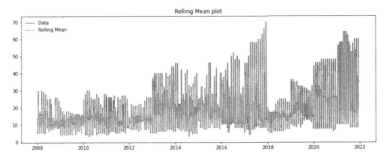

Fig. 4. ARIMA prediction with rolling mean as 3 days

The above figure shows that the tomato price increases as the years go on. In 2021 the price was the highest. So we can say that tomato is going to be increased in the next couple of years in Rythu Bazaar.

Now Let's start applying our different models and predict the prices of different vegetables. For simplicity, we have considered Anantapur district. However, the study can always be extended to other districts as well (Fig. 5).

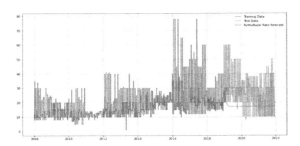

Fig. 5. Prediction with VAR with train-test data

The above figure shows that we fail to predict the price rates using VAR (Fig. 6).

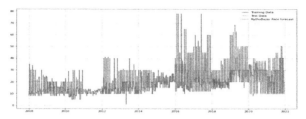

Fig. 6. Prediction with Decision Tree with train-test data

This figure shows that prediction with Decision Tree gives better result compare two VAR. However, the RMSE and MSE is bit higher with this (Fig. 7).

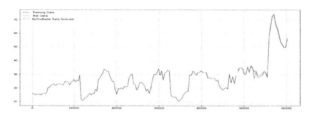

Fig. 7. Prediction with Vanilla LSTM with train-test data

The above figure also shows that vanilla LSTM performs even better than Decision Tree. Next, we would like to compare this chart with Bi-LSTM and Stacked LSTM (Fig. 8).

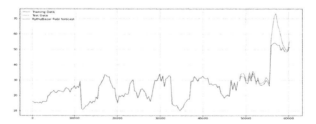

Fig. 8. Prediction with Bi-LSTM

This figure shows that Bi-LSTM does not perform well with the train-test data. The RMSE and MAPE values are even worse compare to the vanilla LSTM (Fig. 9).

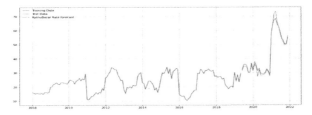

Fig. 9. Prediction with Stacked LSTM

The above figure shows that the prediction is almost similar with vanilla LSTM and better compare to Bi-LSTM.

If we see the Table 2 RMSE and MAPE comparison for the LSTM models, we would easily find out that Stacked LSTM stands out separate compare to other two and this also proved by the above plotting (Fig. 10).

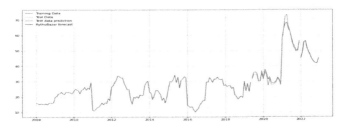

Fig. 10. Final Price forecasting for next one year

This is the final forecasting for Rythu Bazaar price rates using Stacked LSTM. We can see how the price rates vary compare to the previous years.

6 Discussions and Conclusions

Farmers are the backbone of the society. Every year a lot of farmers in India commit suicide due to poverty. We need to identify the root causes of this problem and try to eradicate those. One of the major concerns is farmers do not get correct price for the products that they produce. The middlemen take the advantage of the poor farmers and buy their products with lesser rate from them and sell to the customers at higher rates. A need has been raised to solve this problem. Also, due to the middlemen, customers are also getting rotten or damaged items. This in turn causes a lot of health-related problems. In order to solve this issue, the government of Andhra Pradesh had taken a major step in the year 1999 by introducing the concept of Rythu Bazaar. The government has redesigned the supply chain of the Rythu Bazaar for the farmers and consumers. They thought that both of these parties would get benefit out of it. Now it's almost 23 years since the inception of Rythu Bazaar. We need to analyze if both the parties got benefited.

The current or past studies on the Rythu Bzaar are all based on the sample collection. They did not use any Machine Learning technologies to analyze this. Machine learning is a state of the art technology and we need to use this in order to analyze the Rythu Bazar performance. In our study we have used Statistical and Deep learning techniques to analyze this. Out of all the techniques, we have preferred Stacked LSTM and forecasted the price of Rythu Bazaar rate for the next 1 year. Also, we have proved that customers and farmers are getting benefited using hypothesis testing.

1 year Data been predicted with the models build that both Farmers and Consumers can use to determine to farming and purchases preferences. Forecasting of 1-year Rythu Bazar data has given us a good understanding on when would be a particular item would have its Peake rates. Hence farmers can plan to cultivation accordingly.

From consumers point of view one can plan to buy vegetables that are at best and pocket friendly rates. With this algorithm run across markets will give a holistic view of prices and hence the demand to farmers that they can plan to transport to respective nearby markets for max benefit.

Adding demographic data like number of hectares available around a particular market farming vegetables/fruit, climatic change prediction we can predict a better result for framers and to the Government on crop rotations and optimal costs for consumers.

References

1. Dingli, A., Fournier, K.S.: Financial time series forecasting – a deep learning approach. Int. J. Mach. Learn. Comput. **7**, 118–122 (2017)
2. Clerk Maxwell, J.: A Treatise on Electricity and Magnetism, 3rd ed., vol. 2, pp.68–73. Clarendon, Oxford (1892)
3. Saibaba, R., Vadde, S., et al.: Consumer satisfaction and preferences towards rythu bazaar: a study in Warangal district Andhra Pradesh. Ind. J. Manag. Soc. Sci. **3**(1), 52–63 (2009)
4. Dey, S.: Rythu bazaar: a study of the supply chain of the farmers' markets of Andhra Pradesh. IUP J. Oper. Manag. **11**(3) (2012)
5. Lin, W.-H., et al.: Wind power forecasting with deep learning networks: time-series forecasting. Appl. Sci. **11**(21), 10335 (2021)
6. Lim, B., Arık, S.Ö., Loeff, N., Pfister, T.: Temporal fusion transformers for interpretable multi-horizon time series forecasting. Int. J. Forecast. **37**(4), 1748–1764 (2021)
7. Hochreiter, S., Schmidhuber, J.: Long short-term memory. Neural Comput. **9**(8), 1735–1780 (1997)
8. Young, M.: The Technical Writer's Handbook. University Science, Mill Valley, CA (1989)
9. Salinas, D., Flunkert, V., Gasthaus, J., Januschowski, T.: Deepar: probabilistic forecasting with autoregressive recurrent networks. Int. J. Forecast. **36**(3), 1181–1191 (2020)
10. Savitha, B.: Opinion of farmers about functioning of Rythu Bazaars. MANAGE Ext. Res. Rev. **4**, 53–57 (2003)
11. La Trobe, H.: Farmers' markets: consuming local rural produce. Int. J. Consum. Stud. **25**(3), 181–192 (2001)
12. Varner, T., Otto, D.: Factors affecting sales at farmers markets: an Iowa study. Rev. Agric. Econ. **30**(1), 176–189 (2004)

Hybrid Model Using Interacted-ARIMA and ANN Models for Efficient Forecasting

T. Baskaran$^{(\boxtimes)}$ ⓘ, Nimitha John ⓘ, and B. V Dhandra ⓘ

CHRIST (Deemed to be University), Hosur Road, Bengaluru 560029,
Karnataka, India
`t.baskaran@res.christuniversity.in`,
{`nimitha.john,basanna.veeranna`}`@christuniversity.in`

Abstract. When two models applied to the same dataset produce two different sets of forecasts, it is a good practice to combine the forecasts rather than using the better one and discarding the other. Alternatively, the models can also be combined to have a hybrid model to obtain better forecasts than the individual forecasts. In this paper, an efficient hybrid model with interacted ARIMA (INTARIMA) and ANN models is proposed for forecasting. Whenever interactions among the lagged variables exist, the INTARIMA model performs better than the traditional ARIMA model. This is validated through simulation studies. The proposed hybrid model combines forecasts obtained through the INTARIMA model from the dataset, and those through the ANN model from the residuals of INTARIMA, and produces better forecasts than the individual models. The quality of the forecasts is evaluated using three error metrics viz., Root Mean Square Error (RMSE), Mean Absolute Error (MAE) and Mean Absolute Percentage Error (MAPE). Empirical results from the application of the proposed model on the real dataset - lynx - suggest that the proposed hybrid model gives superior forecasts than either of the individual models when applied separately. The methodology is replicable to any dataset having interactions among the lagged variables. ...

Keywords: Interacted lagged variables · Time series · Interaction · INTARIMA

1 Introduction

Time series forecasting plays a significant role when it is required to predict the future value of a variable based only on the past values of the same variable. However, when prediction is required based on the influence of some other independent variables, regression is the choice. Several models exist for time series forecasting. Depending on the characteristics of the data series, appropriate model is applied to analyze and forecast. If the underlying process is propelled by a linear process or a non-linear process, then a linear or non-linear model respectively is suitable. When it is a combination of two processes, it

R. Morusupalli et al. (Eds.): MIWAI 2023, LNAI 14078, pp. 747–756, 2023.
https://doi.org/10.1007/978-3-031-36402-0_69

is prudent to use hybrid methods by combining the forecasts of more than one model so as to use the capabilities of each component-model in modeling the time series. From the literature survey, it is clear that hybrid models will enhance the forecasting performance significantly, as they combine the exclusive strengths of the models used. A review of the combination of forecasts during the last 50 years by [2] provides different methodologies in combining forecasts.

Autoregressive Integrated Moving Average (ARIMA) and Artificial Neural Network (ANN) are two popular techniques of time series forecasting. These models provide good forecasts, when the data generating process is either purely linear or purely non-linear respectively. However, in the real world problems, the nature of the data generating process is unknown, and may be only linear or only non-linear or a combination of both linear and non-linear processes. If the data generating process is unknown, generally linear process is assumed [1], though not appropriate.

In spite of the ARIMA model being popular for time series forecasting, it takes into account only the effects of the lagged variables, and not the potential interactions among them. While regression models use interactions among regressors, whenever required, it is not so in the case of time series models. Thus, the interactions among the lagged variables of a time series model will have the potentiality to increase the forecast accuracy, if the interactions among the lagged variables exist. In view of this, the present paper aims to extend the ARIMA model with interacted lagged variables (ILVs) and to construct a hybrid model by combining the forecasts derived from the interacted ARIMA (INTARIMA) and the ANN models.

2   Background and Review of Literature

When two different forecasts are available for the same data series from two different models, one tends to use the better forecast and discard the other. However, it is a good practice that the two forecasts should be combined so as to use the independent information available through each model for forecasting [3]. In this process, appropriate weights are required to be used for enhancing the robustness of the forecasts. Combining forecasts of different models has the potentiality for enhancing forecast accuracy [4]. On the other hand, it is also possible to combine two different models to have a hybrid model to forecast, and such a hybrid model has the efficiency to increase the forecast accuracy. The first attempt, in this direction, has been made by Zhang in 2003, wherein, he has combined the linear model ARIMA and the non-linear model ANN, under the assumption that the linear and the non-linear components are mixed up in an additive relationship in the data generating process [5]. Subsequently, several modifications have been suggested in Zhang's methodology. [6] improved upon Zhang's model by relaxing the additivity assumption. [7] upgraded Zhang's model by applying a Moving Average (MA) filter to separate the linear and non-linear components of the series and then building up the model. On the other hand, [8] used Discrete Wavelet Transform (DWT) decomposition to decompose the two processes of the series and bettered Zhang's model.

[9] constructed a hybrid ARIMA and Neural Networks model for pollution estimation in Chiang Mai city by utilizing the non-linear component in the ARIMA residuals and the linear part in the first differenced data. [10] extracted the two components using an MA filter and applied Zhang's methodology with Recurrent Neural Network (RNN) instead of ANN. [11] extracted the linear and non-linear components using DWT decomposition and applied Zhang's methodology with RNN instead of ANN. [12] improved upon Zhang's model by first decomposing the time series data into linear and non-linear components using an MA filter on the basis of Kurtosis and using ARIMA and ANN models to obtain the hybrid forecasts. They further enhanced the accuracy using Empirical Mode Decomposition (EMD). [13] constructed a hybrid model on the lines of [5], but examined both additive and multiplicative relationships between linear and non-linear components and proved that the multiplicative model was better. Thus, there has always been scope to increase the accuracy of forecasts by combining different models or the forecasts.

On the issue of including interactions for prediction, it is evident from the literature review that the inclusion of interactions among variables in regression models exist [14–17]. However, to the best of our knowledge, no evidence in the literature could be found to include interactions in a time series model, with particular reference to the ARIMA model. Recently, in an unpublished work of the authors, the ARIMA model has been extended to take into account the influence of interactions among the lagged variables. Empirical study shows that inclusion of interactions has been found to increase the accuracy of the forecasts.

Motivated by these, the present paper proposes a hybrid model by combining the INTARIMA and the ANN models using the methodology proposed by [5] and proves empirically the supremacy of the proposed hybrid model over other models.

3   Methodology

In this section, the Autoregressive Integrated Moving Average (ARIMA), Artificial Neural Network (ANN), Interacted ARIMA (INTARIMA) models and the Proposed Hybrid model are discussed.

3.1   Autoregressive Integrated Moving Average (ARIMA) Model

For the sake of simplicity, the ARIMA (p,0,0) model is considered for analysis. It can be written as:

$$y_t = \phi_0 + \phi_1 y_{t-1} + \phi_2 y_{t-2} + \cdots + \phi_p y_{t-p} + \epsilon_t \tag{1}$$

where $\phi_0, \phi_1, \ldots, \phi_p$ are the parameters, p is the number of lags in the model and ϵ_t is the white noise. The ARIMA is a linear model providing good forecasts, when the data generating process is linear. The model considers the influence of the past values or the lagged variables on the current value of the variable under study. However, it does not consider the interactions among the lagged variables, if exist. [18] provide an iterative approach, popularly known as the Box-Jenkins approach, to model building. It is a three stage iterative approach consisting of (i) identification of a plausible model, (ii) estimation of parameters conditional on the model identified and (iii) diagnostic checking of the adequacy of the fitted model. In case the model is not adequate, the approach is repeated till an adequate model is found. In the above approach, interactions among the lagged variables are not considered.

3.2   Artificial Neural Network (ANN) Model

ANN is another powerful technique for forecasting. This has become prominent due to its self-learning capability. The technique often becomes the first choice because of its ability to establish the relationship between the variables as well as its ease of implementation [19]. A Multi-layer feed forward or multi-layer perceptron (MLP) is the most frequently used network for forecasting, especially time series forecasting [20]. A single hidden layer feed forward Artificial Neural Network model ANN(p,q,1) with p input layer nodes, q hidden layer nodes and one output layer node is characterized by the Eq. (2):

$$y_t = \alpha_0 + \sum_{j=1}^{q} \alpha_j f\left(\beta_{0j} + \sum_{i=1}^{p} \beta_{ij} y_{t-i}\right) + \epsilon_t \qquad (2)$$

where α_j, $j = 1, 2, \cdots, q$ and β_{ij}, $i = 1, 2, \cdots, p$ & $j = 1, 2, \cdots, q$ are the connection weights, α_0, β_{0j} are the bias terms and f is the activation function - usually the logistic function - at the hidden layer.

3.3   Interacted ARIMA (INTARIMA) Model

The performance of any time series forecasting model depends on the inclusion of the right set of contributing-variables in the model [21]. The ARIMA model takes into account only the effects of the lagged variables and not the possible interactions among them. So, if interactions exist among the lagged variables and the ARIMA model is used, then the right set of variables - the interacted lagged variables - will be missing in the ARIMA model. This decreases the forecast accuracy. Hence, it is proposed to use the interacted ARIMA (INTARIMA) model to include the right set of interacted lagged variables and obtain the forecasts. In this paper, only the pairwise (second order) interactions among the autoregressive lagged variables are used, assuming that the effect of higher order interactions is negligible. Interactions are considered as the product of two lagged variables, since interactions go together simultaneously.

The INTARIMA (p,0,0)[a] model with only p lags in the AR component and $a = \binom{p}{2}$ pairwise interactions can be written as:

$$
\begin{aligned}
y_t = \phi_0 &+ \phi_1 y_{t-1} + \phi_2 y_{t-2} + \cdots + \phi_p y_{t-p} \\
&+ \phi_{12} y_{t-1} y_{t-2} + \phi_{23} y_{t-2} y_{t-3} + \cdots + \phi_{p-1,p} y_{t-(p-1)} y_{t-p} \\
&+ \phi_{13} y_{t-1} y_{t-3} + \phi_{24} y_{t-2} y_{t-4} + \cdots + \phi_{p-2,p} y_{t-(p-2)} y_{t-p} \\
&\ \vdots \\
&+ \phi_{1p} y_{t-1} y_{t-p} + \epsilon_t
\end{aligned} \tag{3}
$$

In this model, the interactions have been taken as the external regressors. For constructing the INTARIMA model the following algorithm has been adopted.

Step 1: Obtain the data , check for issues and pre-process the data for modeling.

Step 2: Identify the model parameters using Box-Jenkins approach and fit the appropriate ARIMA model.

Step 3: From Step 2, decide the number of lags used and the possible interactions.

Step 4: Select the pairwise interactions having significant correlation with the y variable for inclusion in the model.

Step 5: Fit the same ARIMA model of Step 2 with interactions as external regressors for different sets of interactions and identify the model with the lowest forecasting error.

Step 6: Check the significance of the parameters of the interactions and exclude any insignificant parameters, and repeat from Step 5, if need be, to reach a plausible model.

Step 7: Calculate the performance metrics and establish the model.

Step 8: Use the model for forecasting, taking the interacted lagged variables as external regressors.

3.4   Simulation Study for INTARIMA Model

In order to establish the veracity of the INTARIMA model, a simulation study has been conducted. For different values of ϕ_1, ϕ_2 and ϕ_{12}, data have been simulated for samples of sizes 50, 100, 200, 500 and 1000 using the INTARIMA model with two lags and one interaction, viz.

$$
y_t = \phi_1 y_{t-1} + \phi_2 y_{t-2} + \phi_{12} y_{t-1} y_{t-2} + \epsilon_t \tag{4}
$$

The parameters have been estimated using the model at Eq. (4) for the different samples. The procedure has been repeated 100 times and the mean of the estimates has been calculated along with its error (Mean Square Error). For the sake of brevity, the results of this simulation study only for the sample sizes 500 and 1000 are presented in the Table 1. It is seen from Table 1 that the estimates of the parameters for different sample sizes are consistent with true parameter values. Also, the error of estimation is reduced as the sample size increases. From this, one can infer that the INTARIMA model is suitable for time series forecasting, whenever there is an influence of interacted lagged variables.

Table 1. Parameter estimation by INTARIMA model

Sample Size	$\hat{\phi}_1(\text{MSE})$	$\hat{\phi}_2(\text{MSE})$	$\hat{\phi}_{12}(\text{MSE})$
Parameters: $\phi_1 = 0.7, \phi_2 = -0.2, \phi_{12} = 0.1$			
500	0.6884 (0.0021)	-0.2117 (0.0025)	0.0949 (0.0006)
1000	0.6961 (0.0010)	-0.2153 (0.0012)	0.0916 (0.0004)
Parameters: $\phi_1 = 0.2, \phi_2 = -0.7, \phi_{12} = 0.05$			
500	0.2025 (0.0009)	-0.6972 (0.0010)	0.0467 (0.0002)
1000	0.1997 (0.0006)	-0.6987 (0.0005)	0.0500 (0.0001)
Parameters: $\phi_1 = -0.5, \phi_2 = 0.2, \phi_{12} = 0.1$			
500	-0.4831 (0.0020)	0.2246 (0.0022)	0.1011 (0.0003)
1000	-0.4876 (0.0012)	0.2220 (0.0015)	0.1020 (0.0002)

3.5   Proposed Hybrid Model

The proposed hybrid model is a blend of the INTARIMA and ANN models. As the INTARIMA model has the potential for improving the accuracy of forecasts over the ARIMA model, the proposed model uses the INTARIMA in place of ARIMA model. The INTARIMA and ANN models extract the linear and non-linear components in the data. First, the INTARIMA is applied to the time series data and the linear forecasts are obtained. The INTARIMA residuals, therefore, are assumed to contain the non-linear component of the data. In order to extract the non-linear component, ANN is then applied to the INTARIMA residuals. The resultant non-linear forecasts from the ANN model are added with the linear forecasts obtained from the INTARIMA model to get the hybrid forecasts, in view of the assumed additive relationship between the components [5]. The methodology of the proposed hybrid model is given in the following algorithm.

(i) Pre-process and model the time series data y_t using the ARIMA model and obtain ARIMA-forecasts (F_{AR}) and ARIMA-residuals (R_{AR}).

(ii) Apply the ANN model on the time series data y_t and obtain the ANN-forecasts (F_{ANN}).

(iii) Apply the ANN on ARIMA-residuals (R_{AR}) and obtain the forecasts of ANN with ARIMA-Residuals $(F_{ANN,AR.res})$

(iv) Add the ARIMA-forecasts (F_{AR}) and the ANN-ARIMA-Residual-forecasts $(F_{ANN,AR.res})$ to obtain the Zhang's hybrid forecasts $(F_{ANN+AR.res})$ and compare the forecast accuracy of F_{AR}, F_{ANN} and $F_{ANN+AR.res}$ forecasts.

(v) Apply the INTARIMA model that has interactions with minimum error, on the time series y_t and obtain the INTARIMA-forecasts (F_{INTAR}) and INTARIMA-residuals (R_{INTAR})

(vi) Apply the ANN on the INTARIMA-residuals (R_{INTAR}) and obtain the forecasts $(F_{ANN,INTAR.res})$

(vii) Add the INTARIMA-forecasts F_{INTAR} and the ANN+ARIMA-Residual-forecasts $(F_{ANN,INTAR.res})$. This sum gives the proposed hybrid model forecasts $(F_{ANN+INTAR.res})$.

4 Experimental Analysis

The present paper uses the famous lynx data set to verify the efficiency of the proposed hybrid model. The dataset provides annual numbers of lynx trappings for 1821–1934 in Canada. The dataset is a stationary time series with 114 observations. Figure 1 presents the plot of the original lynx time series. In view of the cycle being very asymmetrical with a sharp and large peak and a relatively smooth and small trough [22], log10 transformation is applied. ARIMA(12,0,0) is fitted to the data, following earlier researchers [5, 23, 24]. Using the RMSE, MAE and MAPE the performance of the ARIMA model is noted along with its ARIMA forecasts and the ARIMA residuals. The ANN model is independently applied on the time series and the performance is noted along with ANN forecasts. Again, ANN is applied on the ARIMA residuals and forecasts are obtained. These ANN forecasts derived from the ARIMA residuals are added with the ARIMA forecasts to obtain Zhang's hybrid model forecasts. The performance evaluation of the ARIMA, ANN and the ARIMA+ANN models is presented in Table 3.

As the model has 12 lags, there are 66 possible pairwise interactions of which only 47 have significant correlations with the predictor variable. Different INTARIMA models with different number of interactions are applied to arrive

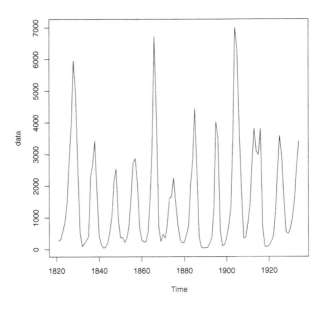

Fig. 1. Number of Lynx Captured during 1821–1934

at the adequate model. The performance of INTARIMA models with top one to eight interactions along with the model without interaction, is presented in Table (2). As the model INTARIMA (12,0,0)[6], which is the INTARIMA with 12 lags and the top six significant interactions has the lowest errors, it is concluded that the INTARIMA (12,0,0)[6] model is the appropriate INTARIMA model for the data. The forecasts and the residuals provided by this model are taken for further processing. ANN is applied on the INTARIMA residuals and the forecasts from this application and the INTARIMA forecasts are added together to obtain the proposed hybrid model forecasts.

Table 2. Errors on application of ARIMA and different INTARIMA models

Model	RMSE	MAE	MAPE
ARIMA(12,0,0)	0.3577276	0.2860144	9.472383
INTARIMA(12,0,0)[1]	0.4188392	0.3312271	10.970356
INTARIMA(12,0,0)[2]	0.3971861	0.3112433	10.334943
INTARIMA(12,0,0)[3]	0.3671634	0.2920865	9.710588
INTARIMA(12,0,0)[4]	0.2455551	0.2011070	6.917822
INTARIMA(12,0,0)[5]	0.2245469	0.1814330	6.189420
INTARIMA(12,0,0)[6]	**0.1999709**	**0.1582698**	**5.375780**
INTARIMA(12,0,0)[7]	0.2004741	0.1589809	5.402163
INTARIMA(12,0,0)[8]	0.2411917	0.2032628	6.841570

The forecast errors from the ARIMA, ANN, Zhang's ARIMA+ANN, INTARIMA models and the proposed hybrid model (INTARIMA+ANN) are presented in Table 3. The errors of ARIMA and the corresponding ANN models together with the ARIMA+ANN model evidence that the hybrid forecasts of ARIMA+ANN has less error than the individual models when applied individually. The INTARIMA forecasts has further less error when compared to the ARIMA+ANN model. The error gets further reduced in the case of the proposed hybrid model involving the INTARIMA and ANN models. Thus the proposed model is superior to the other models.

Table 3. Performance evaluation of different models

Model	RMSE	MAE	MAPE
ARIMA(12,0,0)	0.3577	0.2860	9.4724
ANN (11-6-1)	0.4197	0.3166	10.5485
Hybrid(ARIMA+ANN)	0.3396	0.2770	9.2396
INTARIMA(12,0,0)[6]	0.2000	0.1583	5.3758
Proposed Hybrid(INTARIMA+ANN)	0.1679	0.1229	4.2602

5 Conclusion

The objective of the paper is to develop a hybrid model combining INTARIMA and ANN models following Zhang's methodology, instead of the traditional ARIMA and ANN models. In the proposed methodology, the INTARIMA model is applied on the dataset, and the ANN model on the INTARIMA residuals. The resultant forecasts of the INTARIMA and the ANN models are summed up to get the hybrid forecasts. As evidenced from the lynx dataset, the proposed hybrid model gives the lowest forecast error. This proves that the proposed hybrid model with INTARIMA and ANN models can perform better than the traditional models, whenever the data have interactions among the lagged variables.

Acknowledgement. The authors thank the authorities of the CHRIST (Deemed to be University) for their constant support and encouragement for this research. The authors are also grateful to the reviewers for their suggestions and critical comments, which have helped in improving the paper to a large extent.

References

1. Medeiros, M.C., Veiga, Á.: A hybrid linear-neural model for time series forecasting. IEEE Trans. Neural Netw. **11**, 1402–1412 (2000)
2. Wang, X., Hyndman, R. J., Li, F., Kang, Y.: Forecast combinations: An over 50-year review(2022). https://doi.org/10.1016/j.ijforecast.2022.11.005
3. Bates, J.M., Granger, C.W.J.: The combination of forecasts. J. Oper. Res. Soc. **20**, 451–468 (1969)
4. Clemen, R.T.: Combining forecasts: a review and annotated bibliography. Int. J. Forecast. **5**, 559–583 (1989)
5. Zhang, G.P.: Time series forecasting using a hybrid ARIMA and neural network model. Neurocomputing **50**, 159–175 (2003)
6. Khashei, M., Bijari, M.: A novel hybridization of artificial neural networks and ARIMA models for time series forecasting. Appl. Soft Comput. J. **11**(2), 2664–2675 (2011). https://doi.org/10.1016/J.ASOC.2010.10.015
7. Babu, C.N., Reddy, B.E.: A moving-average filter based hybrid ARIMA-ANN model for forecasting time series data. Appl. Soft Comput. J. **23**, 27–38 (2014)
8. Khandelwal, I., Adhikari, R., Verma, G.: Time series forecasting using hybrid ARIMA and ANN models based on DWT Decomposition. Procedia Comput. Sci. **48**, 173–179 (2015)

9. Wongsathan, R., Seedadan, I.: A hybrid ARIMA and neural networks model for PM-10 pollution estimation: the case of Chiang Mai city moat area. Procedia Comput. Sci. **86**, 273–276 (2016)

10. Shui-Ling, Y.U., Li, Z.: Stock price prediction based on ARIMA-RNN combined model. In: 4th International Conference on Social Science (2017). ISBN: 978-1-60595-525-4

11. Madan, R., Mangipudi, P.S.: Predicting computer network traffic: A time series forecasting approach using DWT, ARIMA and RNN. In: Eleventh International Conference on Contemporary Computing (2018)

12. Büyükşahin, Ü.Ç., Ertekin, Ş: Improving forecasting accuracy of time series data using a new ARIMA-ANN hybrid method and empirical mode decomposition. Neurocomputing **361**, 151–163 (2019)

13. Wang, L., Zou, H., Su, J., Li, L., Chaudhry, S.: An ARIMA-ANN hybrid model for time series forecasting. Syst. Res. Behav. Sci. **30**, 244–259 (2013)

14. Vatcheva KP., Lee, M.: The effect of ignoring statistical interactions in regression analyses conducted in epidemiologic studies: An example with survival analysis using cox proportional hazards regression model. Epidemiol. **6** (2016). Open Access

15. Box, G.: Do interactions matter? J. Qual. Eng. **2**, 365–369 (1990)

16. Friedrich, R.J.: In defense of multiplicative terms in multiple regression equations. Am. J. Pol. Sci. **26**, 797–833 (1982)

17. Balli, H.O., Sørensen, B.E.: Interaction effects in econometrics. Empir. Econ. **45**, 583–603 (2013)

18. Box, G., Jenkins, G.: Time Series Analysis: Forecasting and Control (Holden-Day, 1976)

19. Tascikaraoglu, A., Uzunoglu, M.: A review of combined approaches for prediction of short-term wind speed and power. Renew. Sustain. Energy Rev. **34**, 243–254 (2014)

20. Zhang, G., Patuwo, B.E., Hu, M.Y.: Forecasting with artificial neural networks: the state of the art. Int. J. Forecast. **14**, 35–62 (1998)

21. Hyndman, R.J., Athanasopoulos, G.: Forecasting: Principles and Practice, 2nd edn. OTexts, Melbourne, Australia (2018)

22. Moran, P.A.P.: The statistical analysis of the Canadian Lynx cycle. Aust. J. Zool. **1**, 291–298 (1953)

23. Rao, T.S., Gabr, M.M.: An Introduction to Bispectral Analysis and Bilinear Time Series Models (1984)

24. Campbell, M.J., Walker, A.M.: A survey of statistical work on the Mackenzie river series of annual Canadian lynx trappings for the years 1821–1934 and a new analysis. Source J. R. Stat. Soc. Ser. A **140**, 411–431 (1977)

Addressing Challenges in Healthcare Big Data Analytics

Santosh Tirunagari[1], Senthilkumar Mohan[2(✉)], David Windridge[1],
and Yashaswini Balla[3]

[1] Department of Computer Science, Middlesex University, The Burroughs,
London, UK
{s.tirunagari,d.windridge}@mdx.ac.uk
[2] School of Information Technology and Engineering, Vellore Institute of Technology,
Vellore, India
senthilkumar.mohan@vit.ac.in
[3] Neurosciences Department, Alder Hey Children's NHS Foundation Trust,
Liverpool, UK
yashaswiniballa@doctors.org.uk

Abstract. The exponential growth of healthcare data poses significant
challenges for clinical researchers who strive to identify meaningful patterns and correlations. The complexity of this data arises from its high
dimensionality, sparsity, inaccuracy, incompleteness, longitudinality, and
heterogeneity. While conventional pattern recognition algorithms can
partially address issues related to high dimensionality, sparsity, inaccuracy, and longitudinality, the problems of incompleteness and heterogeneity remain a persistent challenge, particularly when analyzing electronic
health records (EHRs). EHRs often encompass diverse data types, such
as clinical notes (text), blood pressure readings (longitudinal numerical
data), MR scans (images), and DCE-MRIs (longitudinal video data), and
may only include a subset of data for each patient at any given time interval. To tackle these challenges, we propose a kernel-based framework as
the most suitable approach for handling heterogeneous data formats by
representing them as matrices of equal terms. Our research endeavours
to develop methodologies within this framework to construct a decision
support system (DSS). To achieve this, we advocate for the incorporation
of preprocessing mechanisms to address the challenges of incompleteness
and heterogeneity prior to integration into the kernel framework.

Keywords: Electronic health records · Kernel methods · Bigdata

1 Introduction

The implementation of electronic health records (EHRs) has accelerated greatly
in recent years, resulting in vast amounts of patient data being stored online and
easily accessible to healthcare professionals [11,12,31]. EHRs enable sharing of

© The Author(s), under exclusive license to Springer Nature Switzerland AG 2023
R. Morusupalli et al. (Eds.): MIWAI 2023, LNAI 14078, pp. 757–765, 2023.
https://doi.org/10.1007/978-3-031-36402-0_70

patient data across various healthcare settings, necessitating linking of individual patient records from different sources [13]. While the availability of EHRs presents new opportunities for big healthcare analytics, it also poses significant challenges [18,21].

Electronic health records (EHRs) present a unique set of challenges due to the diverse nature of data they contain, as well as their longitudinal and often incomplete nature [18]. This means that EHRs can include a range of data types, from handwritten notes, EEG signals [22] to medical images and videos [30], which may not be available for every patient or at every time interval. Additionally, EHRs contain longitudinal aspects of patient records, which means that they can include data taken over a period of several years or hours. However, missing values are common in EHRs due to irregular recording intervals and missed appointments [28,29]. All of these factors can create challenges when analyzing and interpreting EHR data.

Using traditional methods to analyze this data can result in oversimplified conclusions. To help doctors make informed decisions, an effective framework that can sort the aforementioned challenges. The current study advocates developing a kernel-based framework for analyzing EHRs, so doctors can have an efficient clinical decision support system (CDSS) to help them make the best possible decisions for their patients.

2   Background

In this section, we provide a brief summary of existing methods in three areas. In Fold 2.1, we discuss techniques for managing data that is collected over time (longitudinal). In Fold 2.2, we review techniques for handling different types of data (heterogeneity). Lastly, in Fold 3.4, we explore methods for dealing with missing data.

2.1   Handling Longitudinal Data

Clinicians use data collected over time to help diagnose and choose treatments for their patients. This data can include information like blood pressure readings, GFRs, HbA1C readings over several years, and videos taken over a period of time. Researchers have developed various methods for analyzing this type of data, some of which can also predict disease progression, even when some data is missing. [23,33].

2.2   Handling Heterogeneous Data

Considerable research has been devoted to addressing the challenges of handling heterogeneous data using multi-source learning. The literature can be broadly categorized into three types based on research methods [34].

Additive Classifier Models. This approach uses machine learning algorithms to learn patterns in different types of data, which are then combined using techniques like bagging or boosting. This method has been used in electronic health records to validate gene expression and protein-protein interaction data [7,15]. By combining multiple datasets, this approach can make more accurate predictions by finding the overlap between different sets of data.

Graph Models. Graph models are used to identify connections between different types of data and represent them as graphs. For example, gene expression data can be represented as graphs to identify protein-protein interactions and sequencing similarities. Graph algorithms can then be used to extract important information from these graphs. Nakaya *et al.*'s study used graph models to identify clusters of genes with shared similarities across different data sources [16]. Bayesian networks and Markov models are examples of specific graph models used in this type of analysis.

Fusion Techniques. Two methods of combining data sources are Bayesian fusion and kernel fusion. In Bayesian fusion, each data source is turned into a conditional probabilistic model and then combined through Bayesian networks [20]. For example, Deng*et al* [6] used this method to predict protein-protein interactions and functions using three types of data. However, one downside of Bayesian fusion is that it discards training data during the prediction phase.

On the other hand, in kernel fusion, each data source is represented using matrices called kernels and then combined through linear combinations. This method has the advantage of considering the training data during the prediction phase.

3   Addressing Challenges Through Kernel Framework

In this study, we propose utilizing the kernel fusion techniques depicted in Fig. 1 due to two primary reasons:

- All data formats can be represented using Mercer Kernels.
- A Mercer Kernel can be expressed as a linear combination of a group of Mercer Kernels.

3.1   Mercer Kernels for Different Data Types

Kernel methods are a type of machine learning technique used to classify and analyze data. They use a mathematical tool called a kernel, which is a matrix that allows for comparisons between pairs of objects in a dataset. By transforming data into a higher-dimensional space through non-linear maps, kernel methods make it easier to classify and analyze data that may be difficult to work with in lower dimensions [4,25]. This is because the mapping helps to transform

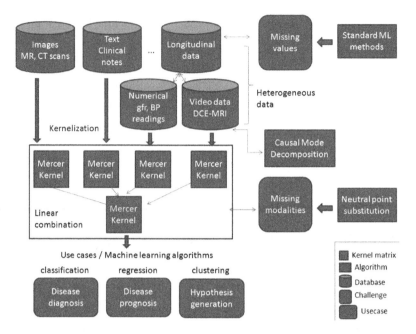

Fig. 1. The suggested framework for big data analysis in healthcare.

data into a format that is easier to work with, making classification and regression operations possible. The most widely used classifier in kernel methods is Support Vector Machines (SVM). One of the primary benefits of kernel methods is that they do not require the coordinates of the higher-dimensional space to be explicitly computed, only the kernel matrix of intra-object comparisons is needed.

Mercer kernels are a type of mathematical function which satisfy Mercer's properties [14, 35] that can be used to analyze different types of healthcare data. They have properties that make them suitable for a variety of formats, such as text, graphs, sequences, shapes, and real numbers. For example, clinical notes and patient information can be handled using NLP parse-tree kernels/LSA kernels [1, 3], while string kernels and random walk kernels are useful for analyzing gene expression data [2, 10]. Edit distance kernels [5] are useful for analyzing shapes, while dot product kernels and polynomial kernels [27] can be used for real number data like blood pressure and glucose levels. With the use of efficient match kernels and pyramid match kernels [9], even sets of pixels/voxels can be processed, such as renal perfusion quantification in DCE-MRI. Fisher kernels [17] are another useful tool for dealing with stochastic data. By using kernel methods, most of the medical data archives can potentially be represented in a kernelized form.

3.2   Linear Combination of Mercer Kernels

When combining multiple Mercer kernels, it is possible to create a new Mercer kernel through linear combination while taking care of the kernel weighting problem [8]. This allows for combining different kernels that handle various medical data formats, leading to more linear separability in the data. Additionally, 'meta' kernels can be constructed from these kernels, which further extends the range of possible representations.

To combine multiple kernels, two categories of linear combination methods exist: non-weighted sum and weighted sum methods. The former involves adding or averaging the kernels, while the latter involves linearly parameterizing the combination function using kernel weights. Specifically, given p Mercer kernels $k_1, \ldots, k_p$, the combined kernel function can be defined as:

$$k_\eta(\mathbf{x}_i, \mathbf{x}_j) = f_\eta(\{\mathbf{x}_i^m, \mathbf{x}_j^m\}_{m=1}^p | \eta) = \sum_{m=1}^p \eta_m k_m(\mathbf{x_i^m}, \mathbf{x_j^m}) \tag{1}$$

where $\eta = (\eta_1, \ldots, \eta_p)$ are the kernel weights, and $\mathbf{x}^m$ denotes the data in the mth format. We can also define the corresponding feature space mapping $\phi_\eta(\mathbf{x})$ as:

$$\phi_\eta(\mathbf{x}) = \begin{pmatrix} \sqrt{\eta_1}\phi_1(\mathbf{x}^1) \\ \sqrt{\eta_2}\phi_2(\mathbf{x}^2) \\ \vdots \\ \sqrt{\eta_p}\phi_p(\mathbf{x}^p) \end{pmatrix}. \tag{2}$$

where ϕ_m is the feature space mapping corresponding to kernel k_m. The combined kernel function can then be computed in terms of the dot product in the combined feature space:

$$< \phi_\eta(\mathbf{x}_i), \phi_\eta(\mathbf{x}_j) >= \begin{pmatrix} \sqrt{\eta_1}\phi_1(\mathbf{x}_i^1) \\ \sqrt{\eta_2}\phi_2(\mathbf{x}_i^2) \\ \vdots \\ \sqrt{\eta_p}\phi_p(\mathbf{x}_i^p) \end{pmatrix}^T \begin{pmatrix} \sqrt{\eta_1}\phi_1(\mathbf{x}_j^1) \\ \sqrt{\eta_2}\phi_2(\mathbf{x}_j^2) \\ \vdots \\ \sqrt{\eta_p}\phi_p(\mathbf{x}_j^p) \end{pmatrix} = \sum_{m=1}^p \eta_m k_m(\mathbf{x}_i^m), \mathbf{x}_j^m)$$

$$\tag{3}$$

Non-linear combinations using exponentiation or multiplication can also be considered as alternatives to linear combinations.

3.3   Advantages of the Kernel Framework

Using the kernel framework offers several benefits:

Keeps the Heterogeneity (Diversity) of Data Intact: The kernel trick transforms different types of data into kernel matrices of equal sizes, which allows for easy integration using linear combination methods. This ensures that the original data's diversity is preserved.

Openness, Flexibility, and Extendability: The linear combination of kernel matrices allows for the effortless addition or removal of various data types. Additionally, the compatibility of Support Vector Machines (SVMs) in statistical modelling makes it possible to use these algorithms in the kernel framework.

Ability to Solve Large Convex Optimization Problems: Many algorithms have been developed over the past two decades to solve convex optimization problems efficiently. These include interior point methods [24], which make it possible to solve kernel convex optimization problems on a large scale.

3.4   Dealing with Missing Values

When working with a kernel-based framework, there are two main things to consider when dealing with missing data: (1) dealing with missing values over time (longitudinal)in the data and (2) handling missing types of data when integrating different kernels.

Missing Values in Longitudinal Data. Electronic health records (EHRs) may have missing information due to irregular recording intervals, such as when blood pressure is measured only during appointments. This can result in missing data due to appointment cancellations or rescheduling. One solution to handle missing numerical data in EHRs is through kernel methods, specifically Gaussian processes (GP). Gaussian processes can predict patient outcomes [26] and interpolate or extrapolate missing data in longitudinal data. By using Gaussian process regression, the best linear unbiased prediction of extrapolation points can be produced, making it useful for modelling time-series data. In a medical context, Gaussian processes can help predict disease progression indicators, such as tumour size, which is a primary outcome variable.

Missing Values in Heterogeneous Data. Kernel methods are useful for combining different types of data, but they can encounter a problem when some of the data is missing. This is known as the missing inter-modal data problem, which means that some data in one modality may be missing for certain individuals. This problem is not easily solvable with traditional statistical or machine learning algorithms, but a method called "neutral point substitution" has been developed by Windridge *et al* [32] to address this challenge. This method replaces missing values with a neutral placeholder object in a multi-modal Support Vector Machine (SVM) combination. It is more tractable than other state-of-the-art methods that use imputation or naive Bayes fusion [19]. The neutral point substitution method can help overcome the challenges posed by big medical data by providing the necessary expertise and tools.

4   Conclusion

This study has highlighted the challenges faced by big healthcare analytics due to the increasing volumes of electronic health records (EHRs) in the healthcare industry. However, overcoming these challenges could present new opportunities for efficient DSS. To address these challenges, we propose a kernel-based framework that accommodates a variety of heterogeneous data present in EHRs represented as Mercer Kernels at equal terms.

To deal with heterogeneous data, we suggest using existing kernel methods independently for each of the data types and then combining them linearly to form a single kernel matrix effectively. The missing modality problem can be solved using methods such as neutral point substitution (NPS). For longitudinal numerical data with missing values, GP-based regression methods can be employed.

In conclusion, this kernel-based framework could prove to be useful in tackling the challenges faced by big healthcare analytics. It can enable more efficient DSS by effectively accommodating heterogeneous data present in EHRs. Additionally, by using existing kernel methods independently for each data type and combining them linearly, we can obtain a single Mercer kernel matrix that can be used for various machine-learning tasks. Overall, this framework can provide a promising path towards improved healthcare analytics.

References

1. Aseervatham, S.: A local latent semantic analysis-based kernel for document similarities. In: 2008 IEEE International Joint Conference on Neural Networks. IJCNN 2008. (IEEE World Congress on Computational Intelligence), pp. 214–219. IEEE (2008)
2. Borgwardt, K.M., Kriegel, H.P.: Shortest-path kernels on graphs. In: Fifth IEEE International Conference on Data Mining, pp. 8-pp. IEEE (2005)
3. Collins, M., Duffy, N.: Convolution kernels for natural language. In: Advances in Neural Information Processing Systems, pp. 625–632 (2001)
4. Cristianini, N., Shawe-Taylor, J.: An Introduction to Support Vector Machines and other Kernel-Based Learning Methods. Cambridge University Press, Cambridge (2000)
5. Daliri, M.R., Torre, V.: Shape recognition based on kernel-edit distance. Comput. Vis. Image Underst. **114**(10), 1097–1103 (2010)
6. Deng, M., Sun, F., Chen, T.: Assessment of the reliability of protein-protein interactions and protein function prediction. In: Pacific Symposium Biocomputing (PSB 2003), pp. 140–151 (2002)
7. Ge, H., Liu, Z., Church, G.M., Vidal, M.: Correlation between transcriptome and interactome mapping data from saccharomyces cerevisiae. Nat. Genet. **29**(4), 482–486 (2001)
8. Gönen, M., Alpaydın, E.: Multiple kernel learning algorithms. J. Mach. Learn. Res. **12**, 2211–2268 (2011)
9. Grauman, K., Darrell, T.: The pyramid match kernel: efficient learning with sets of features. J. Mach. Learn. Res. **8**, 725–760 (2007)
10. Hofmann, T., Schölkopf, B., Smola, A.J.: A review of kernel methods in machine learning. Mac-Planck-Institut für biologische, Kybernetik, Technical report 156 (2006)

11. Holzinger, A., Schantl, J., Schroettner, M., Seifert, C., Verspoor, K.: Biomedical text mining: state-of-the-art, open problems and future challenges. In: Holzinger, A., Jurisica, I. (eds.) Interactive Knowledge Discovery and Data Mining in Biomedical Informatics. LNCS, vol. 8401, pp. 271–300. Springer, Heidelberg (2014). https://doi.org/10.1007/978-3-662-43968-5_16

12. Krebs, K., Milani, L.: Harnessing the power of electronic health records and genomics for drug discovery. Annu. Rev. Pharmacol. Toxicol. **63**, 65–76 (2023)

13. de Lusignan, S., Navarro, R., Chan, T., Parry, G., Dent-Brown, K., Kendrick, T.: Detecting referral and selection bias by the anonymous linkage of practice, hospital and clinic data using secure and private record linkage (SAPREL): case study from the evaluation of the improved access to psychological therapy (IAPT) service. BMC Med. Inform. Decis. Mak. **11**(1), 61 (2011)

14. Lyu, S.: Mercer kernels for object recognition with local features. In: 2005 IEEE Computer Society Conference on Computer Vision and Pattern Recognition. CVPR 2005, vol. 2, pp. 223–229. IEEE (2005)

15. Mrowka, R., Liebermeister, W., Holste, D.: Does mapping reveal correlation between gene expression and protein-protein interaction? Nat. Genet. **33**(1), 15–16 (2003)

16. Nakaya, A., Goto, S., Kanehisa, M.: Extraction of correlated gene clusters by multiple graph comparison. Genome Inform. Ser. **12**, 44–53 (2001)

17. Nicotra, L., Micheli, A., Starita, A.: Fisher kernel for tree structured data. In: Proceedings of the IEEE International Joint Conference on Neural Networks, pp. 1917–1922. Citeseer (2004)

18. Nwegbu, N., Tirunagari, S., Windridge, D.: A novel kernel based approach to arbitrary length symbolic data with application to type 2 diabetes risk. Sci. Rep. **12**(1), 4985 (2022)

19. Panov, M., Tatarchuk, A., Mottl, V., Windridge, D.: A modified neutral point method for kernel-based fusion of pattern-recognition modalities with incomplete data sets. In: Sansone, C., Kittler, J., Roli, F. (eds.) MCS 2011. LNCS, vol. 6713, pp. 126–136. Springer, Heidelberg (2011). https://doi.org/10.1007/978-3-642-21557-5_15

20. Poh, N., Merati, A., Kittler, J.: Heterogeneous information fusion: a novel fusion paradigm for biometric systems. In: 2011 International Joint Conference on Biometrics (IJCB), pp. 1–8. IEEE (2011)

21. Poh, N., Tirunagari, S., Windridge, D.: Challenges in designing an online healthcare platform for personalised patient analytics. In: 2014 IEEE Symposium on Computational Intelligence in Big Data (CIBD), pp. 1–6. IEEE (2014)

22. Ramanna, S., Tirunagari, S., Windridge, D.: Epileptic seizure detection using constrained singular spectrum analysis and 1D-local binary patterns. Health Technol. **10**(3), 699–709 (2020). https://doi.org/10.1007/s12553-019-00395-4

23. Ripoll, V.J.R., et al.: On the intelligent management of sepsis in the intensive care unit (2012)

24. Roos, C., Terlaky, T., Vial, J.P.: Interior Point Methods for Linear Optimization. Springer, Berlin (2006)

25. Scholkopf, B., Smola, A.J.: Learning with Kernels: Support Vector Machines, Regularization, Optimization, and Beyond. MIT press, Cambridge (2001)

26. Shen, Y., et al.: Socialized gaussian process model for human behavior prediction in a health social network. In: ICDM, vol. 12, pp. 1110–1115. Citeseer (2012)

27. Smola, A.J., Ovari, Z.L., Williamson, R.C.: Regularization with dot-product kernels. In: Advances in Neural Information Processing Systems, pp. 308–314 (2001)

28. Tirunagari, S., Bull, S., Poh, N.: Automatic classification of irregularly sampled time series with unequal lengths: a case study on estimated glomerular filtration rate. In: 2016 IEEE 26th International Workshop on Machine Learning for Signal Processing (MLSP), pp. 1–6. IEEE (2016)

29. Tirunagari, S., Bull, S.C., Vehtari, A., Farmer, C., De Lusignan, S., Poh, N.: Automatic detection of acute kidney injury episodes from primary care data. In: 2016 IEEE Symposium Series on Computational Intelligence (SSCI), pp. 1–6. IEEE (2016)

30. Tirunagari, S., Poh, N., Wells, K., Bober, M., Gorden, I., Windridge, D.: Movement correction in DCE-MRI through windowed and reconstruction dynamic mode decomposition. Mach. Vis. Appl. **28**, 393–407 (2017)

31. Windridge, D., Bober, M.: A kernel-based framework for medical big-data analytics. In: Holzinger, A., Jurisica, I. (eds.) Interactive Knowledge Discovery and Data Mining in Biomedical Informatics. LNCS, vol. 8401, pp. 197–208. Springer, Heidelberg (2014). https://doi.org/10.1007/978-3-662-43968-5_11

32. Windridge, D., Mottl, V., Tatarchuk, A., Eliseyev, A.: The neutral point method for kernel-based combination of disjoint training data in multi-modal pattern recognition. In: Haindl, M., Kittler, J., Roli, F. (eds.) MCS 2007. LNCS, vol. 4472, pp. 13–21. Springer, Heidelberg (2007). https://doi.org/10.1007/978-3-540-72523-7_2

33. Yarkiner, Z., Hunter, G., O'Neil, R., de Lusignan, S.: Applications of mixed models for investigating progression of chronic disease in a longitudinal dataset of patient records from general practice. J. Biomet. Biostat. S **9**, 2 (2013)

34. Yu, S., Tranchevent, L.C., Moor, B., Moreau, Y.: Kernel-Based Data Fusion for Machine Learning: Methods and Applications in Bioinformatics and Text Mining, vol. 345. Springer, Heidelberg (2011). https://doi.org/10.1007/978-3-642-19406-1

35. Zhou, D.X.: The covering number in learning theory. J. Complex. **18**(3), 739–767 (2002)

Assessing Reading Patterns of Learners Through Eye Tracking

Agashini V. Kumar$^{(\boxtimes)}$, Atharwa Wagh,
Abdulqahar Mukhtar Abubakar, J. Amudha$^{(\boxtimes)}$, and K. R. Chandrika

Amrita School of Computing, Amrita Vishwa Vidyapeetham,
Kasavanahalli, Bangalore, India
{bl.en.p2dsc21002,bl.en.p2dsc21005,
bl.en.p2dsc21028}@bl.students.amrita.edu,
{j_amudha,kr_chandrika}@blr.amrita.edu

Abstract. Advancement in technology brings about the advent of E-learning which replaces the traditional way of conducting examination using paper and pen. Determining student academic growth merely based on assessment scores is inadequate to help them learn and grow from their mistakes. Non-verbal inkling such as eye gaze can provide insights on the motive and contemplation of the participants that may have affected their performance. The addition of this knowledge can help in obtaining a more realistic system for determining participant performance. This research focuses on 3 different reading patterns of participants and to label them into various categories. It was observed that most of the participants belonged to the novice category, while there was an equal distribution among the participants exhibiting organized and unorganized reading pattern classes, and participants that employed the scanning method tend to answer questions correctly.

Keywords: Eye gaze · Reading patterns · Machine Learning · MCQ

1 Introduction

With the advent of E-learning, most institutions are moving from the traditional way of assessing students which involves the use of paper and pen, to the use of computer-based platforms [1]. This traditional method is characterized as time consuming and does not efficiently monitor the internal cognitive and decision making factors of students when answering such questions. However, the use of computer-based platforms to conduct such examinations has made it possible to easily track such facets. Multiple choice questions (MCQ) have become the most popular way to conduct exams online. During such examination, many students exhibit different reading strategies [10]. Tracking the eye movement during the examination can be used to provide feedback on such reading strategies based on certain hypotheses. This research focuses on labeling the participant reading behaviour as experts, novice, and partial knowledge using the dwell time on

R. Morusupalli et al. (Eds.): MIWAI 2023, LNAI 14078, pp. 766–777, 2023.
https://doi.org/10.1007/978-3-031-36402-0_71

options, organized and unorganized reading behaviour based on raw data such as y coordinate, and skimming, scanning and careful readers using the number of fixation counts aided with heatmap. Following sections contain details on the experimental set up, results, conclusions and future scope.

1.1   Literature Survey

The use of eye gaze tracking data has been applied in many areas in the education field [8] and intelligent tutoring [9] such as stress detection [3] , fatigue detection [4,5], cross talk elimination [6], misbehaviour/ cheating detection [2]. [11] analyses the reading strategies applied by university students who are English language speakers at C1 level. Based on their results it was observed that university students differ in the strategies they use in reading comprehension and that not all competent and successful students use the topic structure method. Also highlighting the need for training of students in order to improve their topic processing skills in text reading [11]. Various visualization graphs were encountered in the literature. Heat map were used to represent the fixation duration and fixation location to show a better representation of visual processing. It is a visual form that displays visual behavior features by super imposing eye movement data of multiple participants [12]. Line chart contains circles to indicate the fixation trajectory and the number of fixations; the size of the circle indicates the fixation duration; and the lines between the circles indicate the saccade amplitude. By examining the fixation trajectory map, the complete reading process can be observed [13]. Gaze plots visualizes areas of interest (AOIs) as well as fixation duration [14]. Contour maps visualizes AOIs on the background stimulus, clustered on the represented map. Bar charts visualizes fixations and their duration with a different graphic compared to the line chart, so that new or other insights can be found [12]. The current work is carried forward and inspired from a work called IEyeGASE that focused on other factors affecting the participant performance such as level of knowledge acquired, intentional blindness and confusion [7], to address the research gap of identifying some more hypotheses addressing observable reading patterns in learners impacting their performance.

2   Methodology

2.1   Experimental Setup

Materials Used: The final year students from Amrita College of Engineering, Bangalore, were informed to take up an MCQ test based on fundamental programming languages like C. The Bloom's taxonomic levels of recall and understanding were considered for setting up the questions for the test. The MCQs were framed with 7 questions, 4 options, keyword, covering the already mentioned concept for the level of Bloom's Taxonomy.

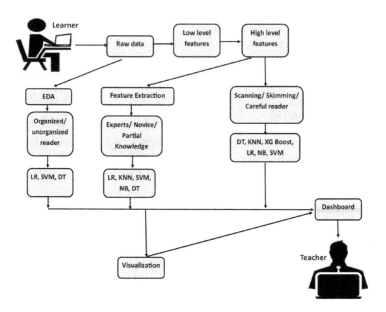

Fig. 1. System architecture

Apparatus: The open source GazeRecorder platform was chosen to reach out to a large number of participants. The mentioned technology uses a simple webcam and turns it into an accurate eye-tracker, which helped to take the research outside the lab, especially during the pandemic. For this experiment GazeRecorder 30 Hz 60 Hz, and eye calibration of 16 points were used. The participants were provided with details on what the experiment was and were presented the stimulus which had video of the MCQs, 30 s given for reading question, 6 s for answering, wherein 1 s was for transition and 5 s were for answering. The participants were provided with three parts: [a] An animated short film which was provided in order to reduce the stress levels in the participants, the analysis of which is not in our scope. [b] Two MCQs were provided for the participants to get comfortable with the platform. [c] The Assessment consisted of 7 questions. One screen (first screen) had the question, while another one (second screen) was used to record the answer. Over all, the tests were for 10 min that comprised of both the video and assessment. There were some challenges such as lost connection, lost calibration, head movements, blockage due to objects/hand and each question participant data was recorded. The identity of the participant was kept anonymous to assure privacy.

Data Collection: A pre-study survey was done where the participants were provided with the link for the same. A video of short film and practice session MCQ were provided to the participants before they could move on to the actual MCQs. The data was collected for the actual MCQs. Following which, a post-study survey was done in similar procedure to the pre-study survey. The data was recorded and stored in the GazeRecorder Cloud. The entire procedure was done adhering to the EMA Ethical committee (Fig. 1).

Dataset: The raw data consisted of various fields such as participant details, calibration details, calibration area, system details, timestamp, trial number, gaze position, pupil position, pupil diameter, and quality values. For eye gaze data analysis, the data points of interest were timestamp and gaze position represented using Raw X and Raw Y coordinates. The raw low-level features from the sensory data were extracted in terms of low-level features like fixations and saccades. Fixations were the fixed gazes over AOI, and saccades were rapid eye movements between fixations. To understand the reading behavior of the participants, these low-level features were converted into high level features. The Fixation count indicates how many times the learner has viewed the information of interest. Fixation duration indicates how long they have viewed the information of interest. The scanpath of the learner represents the sequence of gaze on the area of interest. There were a total of 75 observations.

2.2   Expert, Novice, and Partial Knowledge Behaviour from Reading Patterns

Table 1. Existing feature set

	Description	Features
AOI_First_View where AOI: question, option a, option b, option c, and option d.	The first time in seconds at the which the AOI was gazed	Q_First_View, option_A_First_view, option_B_First_view, option_C_First_view, option_D_First_view
AOI_Dwell% where AOI: question, option a, option b, option c, and option d.	Ratio of Dwell time of AOI in seconds to the sum of Dwell time of all the AOIs in seconds	Q_Dwell_%, option_A_Dwell_%, option_B_Dwell_%, option_C_Dwell_%, option_D_Dwell_%
AOI_Dwell_time where AOI: question, option a, option b, option c, and option d.	Total time dwelt in an AOI in seconds	Q_Dwell_time, option_A_Dwell_time, option_B_Dwell_time, option_C_Dwell_time, option_D_Dwell_time

The maximum and second maximum time each participant gazed at an option while reading and answering the questions were taken from the high level data and their difference was obtained. The mean of the differences for each case were taken as the threshold. Using this threshold, the participants were classified as

Table 2. Derived feature set

	Description	Features
Max_n_Q/A where Q= question, A = Answer, n:1-7	Maximum time given to an option while reading question/ answering the question by the participant.	Max_1_Q, Max_1_A, Max_2_Q, Max_2_A, Max_3_Q, Max_3_A, Max_4_Q, Max_4_A, Max_5_Q, Max_5_A, Max_6_Q,Max_6_A, Max_7_Q, Max_7_A
Sec_max_n_Q/A where Q= question, A = Answer, n:1-7	Second maximum time given to an option while reading question/ answering the question by the participant.	Sec_max_1_Q, Sec_max_1_A, Sec_max_2_Q, Sec_max_2_A, Sec_max_3_Q, Sec_max_3_A, Sec_max_4_Q, sec_max_4_A, Sec_max_5_Q, Sec_max_5_A, Sec_max_6_Q, Sec_max_6_A, Sec_max_7_Q, Sec_max_7_A
Difference_n_Q/A where Q= question, A = Answer, n:1-7	Difference between maximum and second maximum obtained while reading the question/ answering the question by the participant.	Difference_1_Q, Difference_1_A, Difference_2_Q, Difference_2_A, Difference_3_Q, Difference_3_A, Difference_4_Q, Difference_4_A, Difference_5_Q, Difference_5_A, Difference_6_Q, Difference_6_A, Difference_7_Q, Difference_7_A
Class_n_Q/A where Q= question, A = Answer, n:1-7	Behavior exhibited as expert or not for question while reading the question/ answering the question by the participant. Label "1" = Expert, Label "0" = Not Expert	Class_1_Q, Class_1_A, Class_2_Q, Class_2_A, Class_3_Q, Class_3_A, Class_4_Q, Class_4_A, Class_5_Q, Class_5_A, Class_6_Q, Class_6_A, Class_7_Q, Class_7_A
Level_n where n:1-7	Behavior exhibited as expert, partial knowledge, or novice for the question by the participant	Level_1, Level_2, Level_3, Level_4, Level_5, Level_6, Level_7
Category	Overall Behavior of the participant as expert, partial knowledge, or novice.	Category

Well prepared: "1" or not so well prepared: "0", which gave the momentary description of each student's preparation status. The options that each participant gazed at for the maximum time while reading the questions and answering them were recorded. If both those options were the correct choice, then their

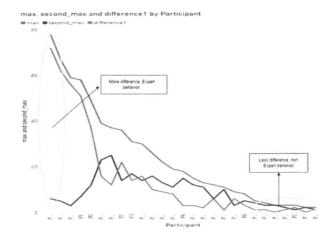

Fig. 2. Experts and non-expert behavior while reading question 1

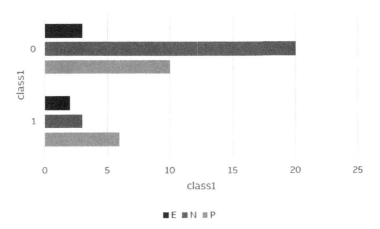

Fig. 3. Level Distribution based on class for question 1 while reading the question.

level for that question was taken as "Expert". If both the options were wrong, the level was "Novice". If one of them was correct and the other wrong, their level was "Partial Knowledge". Based on the aggregation of the levels for the participants at each question, they were categorized as Experts, Novice or students with Partial Knowledge, which described the overall stand of each participant at the end of the assessment.

Feature Extraction and Visual Analysis: From the available features in Table 1, 64 new features were extracted for the study. The new feature set and their descriptions are tabulated in Table 2. Figure 2 shows the trend of the maximum and second maximum gaze percentage of the participants while reading question 1. When the difference between maximum and second maxi-

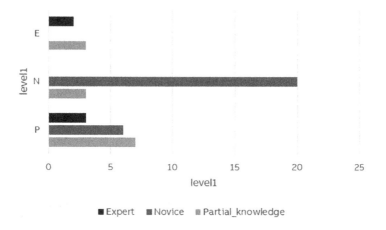

Fig. 4. Participant Level Distribution based on category for question 1 while reading the question.

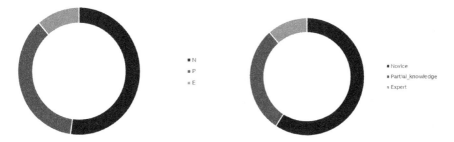

Fig. 5. Participant level distribution for question 1

Fig. 6. Participant distribution based on the category.

mum is more, the participants were classified as showing Expert behavior for the scenario of reading the question. Similarly, they were classified as showing non-Expert behavior when the difference is less. The participants were classified into the following levels:"Experts" when they exhibit an Expert behavior for both scenarios of reading and answering the question, "Partial knowledge" when the behavior of one of the scenarios is Expert and the other is non-Expert, and "Novice" when both the scenarios have non-Expert behavior exhibited. This leads to the extraction of "levels" feature for each of the questions. Figure 3 show how the participants are distributed into the different levels based on the behaviors exhibited while reading question 1 as explained above. Similarly, the level of each participant for each question is obtained. And based on the combination of the levels of all the participants for each question, the overall category of the participants is identified as Experts, Novice, and Partial knowledge. Figure 4 shows how the participants were distributed into the various categories based on their level for question 1. It can be observed that the participants belonging to the novice category were either in the novice or partial knowledge level at question 1. Similarly, the participants belonging to the expert category were either in the expert or partial knowledge level, and the participants belonging to the partial knowledge category belonged to either of all the levels for the same question. Figure 5 shows the distribution of the participants based on their levels for question 1 (combination of behaviors exhibited while reading and answering the questions). Figure 6 shows the overall distribution of the participants into the category they belonged to. 59.09% of the participants belong to the novice, 36.36% belong to the partial knowledge, and 11.36% of the participants belong to the expert category. The data was trained using LR, KNN, SVM, DT, and NB. A dashboard was created to reflect the participant analysis to the teacher.

2.3   Organized and Unorganized Reading Patterns

The raw data was subjected to exploratory data analysis (EDA) using various types of plots, such as line plots, scatter plots, and stacked bar charts, to visualize the data distribution and feature relationships. EDA helped to uncover hidden insights about the data that would have been difficult to see in the raw excel data sheets. The y-coordinate of the left eye was used for this study, as the tracking pattern of both eyes were almost similar. Line plots were used to determine the gazing pattern of each student, and they were labeled as either organized or unorganized readers based on their gaze path. Heatmap plots were then created to analyze whether students spent time reading the keywords or not. The heatmap showed the areas where the participant gazed for a longer period, which were mapped onto the MCQ image to determine if the keywords were present in those areas. It was further trained using LR, SVM, and DT. An interactive dashboard was created that summarized the entire process from raw data exploration to the machine learning models' end results.

Dashboard in Fig. 8 comprises a range of visual representations of data such as line graphs, heatmap plots, bar charts, and pie charts. These graphics illustrated the overall performance of the participants and provided insight into their understanding of the subject. The pallet on the dashboard referred to the total time spent by the participant on the question, yielding the percentage of thinking or off-screen time spent, y-coordinate span which is nothing but the difference between the maximum and minimum value of the y - coordinate, class being an organized or unorganized reader, and the participant being Confident, Confused, Skipped, Methodical. Participant belonging to organized reader category with less time consumption and negligible off-screen time were labelled as Confident. Unorganized readers that took a lot of time and had high percentage of off-screen time from the total time of the question were labelled as Confused. Skipped label was given to those participants who did not answer the question and were unorganized. Methodical were the ones who were organized readers, yet took a lot of time, also had good amount of off-screen, but carefully read the question, thought it through by taking their own time and answered correctly.

2.4   Scanning, Careful Reading, and Skimming Reading Patterns

The hypothesis used for this use case is the Reading Strategy Hypothesis which aims to find significant relationship between student reading habits and their overall performance. The three kinds of reading habits observed are careful reading, scanning reading, and skimming reading as defined by Feng Liu (Reading Abilities and Strategies: A Short Introduction, Feng Liu ,2010). The number of fixation counts on the AOI and heatmap serve as the suitable visualization tool for this hypothesis. Figure 9 shows the different reading style exhibit by students during the exams. The results of the participants were recorded which was then analyzed based on the hypothesis mentioned above. The derived high level features such as the fixation count were passed onto the machine learning model for classification. It was observed that most of the students were performing the Scanning method for the visualization as compare to the Skimming and Careful reading habit. This led to an imbalanced dataset, thus a smote technique was applied to handle such data imbalance. The class distribution is shown in Fig. 7. A dashboard to visualize and analysis the hypothesis was created. The dashboard contained several visualization plots such as the the gaze plot with respect to time, how the student visualize a particular question. The dashboard is shown in Fig. 10.

3   Results and Analysis

Table 3. Performance metric of classifiers for experts, novice, and partial knowledge

Classifier	Expert			Partial Knowledge			Novice			Micro F1	Macro F1
	P	R	F1	P	R	F1	P	R	F1		
LR	0.64	0.55	0.59	0.71	0.66	0.68	0.84	0.91	0.87	0.78	0.71
KNN	0.39	0.39	0.39	0.51	0.38	0.43	0.71	0.83	0.76	0.62	0.53
SVM	0.66	0.55	0.60	0.70	0.62	0.66	0.81	0.90	0.85	0.76	0.70
NB	0.42	0.71	0.53	0.53	0.37	0.43	0.76	0.80	0.78	0.64	0.58
DT	0.42	0.45	0.44	0.55	0.57	0.56	0.81	0.78	0.80	0.67	0.59

Performance metrics for experts, novice, and partial knowledge are tabulated in Table 3. Among all the classification models, Logistic Regression was able to yield the best result followed by Support Vector Machines with the best f1 scores of 0.78 and 0.765 respectively. Expert had 0.59 F1score, 0.64 Precision, and 0.55 Recall. Novice had 0.87 F1score, 0.84 Precision, and 0.91 Recall. Partial Knowledge had 0.68 F1score, 0.71 Precision, and 0.66 Recall. Performance metrics for organized and unorganized readers are tabulated in Table 4. A false positive would be when the reader was actually organized, but the model mistakenly identified them as unorganized. Hence, precision becomes crucial as it helps in handling false positives. The algorithm with the highest precision was SVM

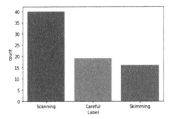

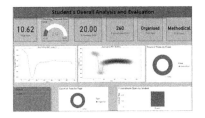

Fig. 7. Distribution of Classes

Fig. 8. Organized and unorganized reading pattern dashboard for participant 1

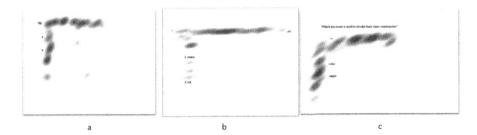

a   b   c

Fig. 9. (a.) Careful (b) Scanning (c) Skimming

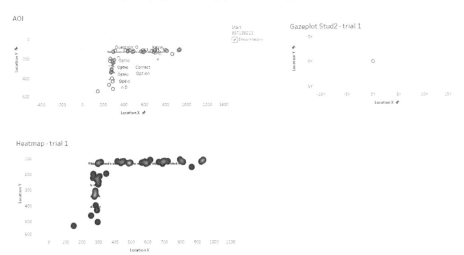

Fig. 10. Interactive dashboard to monitor skimming, scanning, and careful readers

with 64.51%. In contrast, a false negative would be when the reader was unorganized, but the model incorrectly labeled them as organized. For this case, recall becomes crucial and Decision Tree algorithm had the best recall, with 95.65%. Table 5 contains the performance metrics for the scanning, skimming, and care-

776 A. V. Kumar et al.

Table 4. Performance metric of classifiers for organized and unorganized readers

Classifier	Accuracy	F1 score	Precision	Recall
SVM	68.18	74.07	64.51	78.95
DT	63.63	73.33	59.45	95.65
NB	63.63	72.41	60.00	91.30

Table 5. Performance metric classifiers for skimming, scanning, and careful readers

Classifier	Accuracy
DT	74.5
KNN	63.8
XGBoost	81
LR	68.1
NB	66
SVM	74.5

ful reader use case. From the experimental results, KNN algorithm obtained the lowest accuracy with about 63.8%, while XGBoost achieved the highest accuracy of 81.0%. Thus, XGboost model was selected for deployment into the dashboard.

4 Conclusion

The dashboard allows teachers and participants to optimize the learning process by visualizing the study's results. From this study, it can be observed that after applying the proposed labelling techniques based on the three use cases, the distribution of the participants was as follows- most of the participants belonged to the novice category and opted for the scanning method for reading the questions, while equal number of participants exhibited organized and unorganized reading patterns. Participants that employed the scanning method tend to answer questions correctly. Training the models with more samples and development of real time dashboard to track the performance of the learners however, is the future scope of the study.

References

1. Elzainy, A., El Sadik, A., Al Abdulmonem, W.: Experience of e-learning and online assessment during the COVID-19 pandemic at the college of medicine, Qassim university. J. Taibah Univ. Med. Sci. **15**(6), 456–462 (2020)
2. Dilini, N., Senaratne, A., Yasarathna, T., Warnajith, N., Seneviratne, L.: Cheating detection in browser-based online exams through eye gaze tracking. In: 2021 6th International Conference on Information Technology Research (ICITR), pp. 1–8 (2021). https://doi.org/10.1109/ICITR54349.2021.9657277
3. Li, X., Liu, W., Wang, W., Zhong, J., Yu, M.: Assessing students' behavior in error finding programming tests: an eye-tracking based approach. In: 2019 IEEE International Conference on Engineering, Technology and Education (TALE), pp. 1–6 (2019). https://doi.org/10.1109/TALE48000.2019.9225906
4. Akshay, S., Abhishek, M. B., Sudhanshu, D., Anuvaishnav, C.: Drowsy driver detection using eye-tracking through machine learning. In: 2021 Second

International Conference on Electronics and Sustainable Communication Systems (ICESC), pp. 1916–1923 (2021). https://doi.org/10.1109/ICESC51422.2021.9532928

5. Jyotsna, C., Amudha, J.: Eye gaze as an indicator for stress level analysis in students. In: 2018 International Conference on Advances in Computing, Communications and Informatics (ICACCI) (2018). https://doi.org/10.1109/ICACCI.2018.8554715

6. Ye, B., Fujimoto, Y., Uchimine, Y., Sawabe, T., Kanbara, M., Kato, H.: Crosstalk elimination for lenslet array near eye display based on eye-gaze tracking. Opt. Express **30**, 16196–16216 (2022)

7. Ramachandra, C. K., Joseph, A.: IEyeGASE: an intelligent eye gaze-based assessment system for deeper insights into learner performance. Sensors **21**(20), 6783 (2021). https://doi.org/10.3390/s21206783

8. Haridas, M., Vasudevan, N., Gayathry, S., Gutjahr, G., Raman, R., Nedungadi, P.: Feature-aware knowledge tracing for generation of concept-knowledge reports in an intelligent tutoring system. In: Proceedings of the 2019 IEEE Tenth International Conference on Technology for Education (T4E), Goa, India, 9–11 December 2019, pp. 142–145

9. Haridas, M., Gutjahr, G., Raman, R., Ramaraju, R., Nedungadi, P.: Predicting school performance and early risk of failure from an intelligent tutoring system. Educ. Inf. Technol. **25**(5), 3995–4013 (2020). https://doi.org/10.1007/s10639-020-10144-0

10. Liu, F.: Reading abilities and strategies: a short introduction. Int. Educ. Stud. **3**(3), 153–157 (2010)

11. Vanitha, V., Sabariraja, V., Rajalakshmi, K.: The power of pleasure reading in digital era-an exhilarating journey to promote success in learning environment among youth. Turk. Online J. Qual. Inq. **12**(7), 7136–7151 (2021)

12. SAkshay, S., Rames, A.A.: Visual search capability using heatmaps (2019). Corpus ID: 212522840

13. Bayrak, M., Demirel, T., Kurşun, E.: Examination of different reading strategies with eye tracking measures in paragraph questions. Hacettepe Üniv. Eğitim Fakültesi Dergisi, **35**(1), 92–106

14. Chandrika, K.R., Amudha, J., Sudarsan, S.D.: Recognizing eye tracking traits for source code review. In: 2017 22nd IEEE International Conference on Emerging Technologies and Factory Automation (ETFA), pp. 1–8 (2017). https://doi.org/10.1109/ETFA.2017.8247637

Comparison of Deep Learning Algorithms for Early Detection of Melanoma Skin Cancer on Dermoscopic and Non-dermoscopic Images

Niharika Wamane🅳, Aishwarya Yadav$^{(\boxtimes)}$ 🅳, Jidnyasa Bhoir$^{(\boxtimes)}$ 🅳,
Deep Shelke$^{(\boxtimes)}$ 🅳, and Deepali Kadam$^{(\boxtimes)}$ 🅳

Information Technology, Datta Meghe College of Engineering, Mumbai University, Navi
Mumbai, India
wamaneniharika@gmail.com, aishwaryayadav235@gmail.com,
jidnyasab11@gmail.com, shelkedeep0404@gmail.com,
deepalikadam15387@gmail.com

Abstract. Our research suggests a deep-learning method for automated recognition of melanoma utilizing dermoscopic and non-dermoscopic pictures. The methodology entails creating CNN and ResNet-50 models as well as using a number of pre-processing methods. With the use of hair removal and augmentation procedures, the CNN and ResNet-50 models accurately identified melanoma with dermoscopic photographs with 98.07% and 99.83% accuracy, respectively. The CNN and ResNet-50 models used the hair removal method to obtain accuracy for non-dermoscopic images of 97.06% and 100%, respectively. An accuracy of 96.40% was achieved using CNN through the adoption of age and sex as additional criteria in the identification of melanoma in dermoscopic images. The generated models can be a useful tool in the early identification of melanoma, which is essential for its effective treatment as well as the prevention of fatalities. This can be accomplished by combining the models with multiple methods of pre-processing and the inclusion of age and sex.

Keywords: Malignant · Benign · Dermoscopic · Non-dermo- scopic · Convolutional Neural Network · ResNet50 · Melanoma Skin Cancer

1 Introduction

Sun-exposed skin is the most prevalent site for skin cancer or an atypical growth of skin cells [1]. However, this typical type of cancer can even arise gradually in parts of the human body that infrequently are exposed to the rays of the sun [1].

Melanoma is a potentially fatal type of skin cancer [2, 3]. When melanoma is discovered at an initial stage, it may be possible to treat it surgically using a simpler technique [4]. Dermoscopy is one of the imaging techniques that dermatologists employ the most frequently [2]. It magnifies the skin lesion's surface, enhancing its structure so that the dermatologist can study it.

Only medical experts who have received adequate training may properly use this procedure because it only depends on the practitioner's eye acuity and knowledge [2].

R. Morusupalli et al. (Eds.): MIWAI 2023, LNAI 14078, pp. 778–785, 2023.
https://doi.org/10.1007/978-3-031-36402-0_72

These restrictions are what drive the scientific community to develop new melanoma visualization and detection techniques. A computer-aided diagnostic (CAD) system may improve the accuracy of melanoma cancer diagnosis [11]. For dermatologists with minimal or no prior knowledge, the CAD program provides a welcoming and simple user interface. Evidence suggests that a CAD diagnostic device might be used as a second opinion for identifying melanoma malignancy.

The two fundamental types of skin cancer tumors are benign and malignant. A common finding in benign lesions (common nevi) is the presence of melanin deposits in the epidermal layer. Melanin has reproduced very abnormally in malignant tumors.

2 Literature Survey

In 2009, José Fernández Alcón and colleagues [3] employed computer vision approaches to automate the classification of melanoma skin cancer. They achieved an 86% accuracy rate by categorizing melanoma into benign and malignant types based on the ABCD features. Their study revealed that individuals with light skin tones and the elderly are at higher risk for developing melanoma, and the occurrence of melanoma varies by age and gender.

Enakshi Jana and her team [4] proposed various skin classification algorithms and image pre-processing techniques in 2017. The median filter approach for hair removal and picture noise reduction, along with sharpening filters to increase image edge definition, were used in their pre-processing procedures.

Shetu Rani Guha et al. [5] suggested a CNN-based machine learning approach in 2019. They improved the confidence of the ISIC dataset using transfer learning and CNN. The study used 1137 images for training and 197 images for testing. Transfer learning surmounts the CNN model in terms of accuracy, improving it by 11.65%.

B. Sreedhar et al.'s [2] 2020 paper discusses the progress in detecting melanoma skin cancer using skin lesion analysis. The paper compares the accuracy of traditional image processing methods with deep learning algorithms like CNNs. The limitations of traditional methods and the effectiveness of current image processing techniques for detecting melanoma skin cancer are highlighted.

In 2020, Tasneem Alkarakatly and colleagues [6] created a CNN model for diagnosing skin cancer using the PH2 dataset, which featured two hundred dermoscopic pictures of 3 categories - melanoma, common and atypical nevus. They utilized a 5-layer CNN architecture and tested various image sizes before selecting the best size to feed to the neural network. The model achieved 95% accuracy through cross-validation.

Hari Kishan Kondaveeti and Prabhat Edupuganti's [7] work also presented research in 2020 on the application of transfer learning for skin cancer categorization. The authors of this work employed transfer learning for building a deep neural networks approach to skin cancer categorization. The results showed that the transfer learning approach outperformed traditional deep learning methods in terms of accuracy and efficiency, highlighting the potential of transfer learning for skin cancer classification.

Aman Kamboj and Shalu [8] developed an approach to use digital pictures to diagnose skin cancer with melanoma. The MED-NODE dataset was preprocessed and the segmented part was used to distinguish the region of interest. Classifiers were used to assess the system's performance, with a accuracy of 82.35%.

3   Proposed Solution

3.1   Dataset

A dermoscopic picture dataset was utilized in this study [9]. The dataset utilized in skin cancer diagnostic research and development comprises 1497 melanoma and 1800 benign photos from the Kaggle International Skin Imaging Collaboration (ISIC).

The dataset used in the investigation and spread of skin cancer detection from macroscopic pictures includes seventy melanoma and hundred nevus samples [10] from the University Medical Center Groningen's (UMCG) digital image repository.

3.2   Preprocessing

The goal of image pre-processing is to eliminate unwanted artifacts like noise, air bubbles, and fine hair.

Sharpening. It is used to produce precise images. This may be achieved using a variety of techniques, including unsharp masking, highpass filtering, etc. A typical method for sharpening a picture is convolution using a sharpening kernel.

Normalization. It is an approach for adjusting the intensity range of pixels in a picture to build a more homogeneous and visually appealing result. It is necessary to convert the intensity values to a certain range. It is essential for producing high-quality pictures and increasing the interpretation of image-based models. Its purpose is to reduce irregularities in size, illumination, and contrast to allow for exact picture comparison and analysis.

Hair Removal. The hair removal procedure entails scaling the image to 224 by 224 pixels and transforming it into gray scale. The blackhat morphological method is used on a 17×17 matrix to reduce noise, and the image is thresholded at a value of 10. Finally, by filling in the thresholded parts, the inpainting procedure is used to restore the image's integrity.

Augmentation. It is the process of producing new training data sets from current ones through random modifications such as rotations, translations, scaling, and flipping. The purpose of picture augmentation is to enhance the quantity and variety of the training dataset, resulting in better model generalization and less overfitting. There are a variety of image-enhancing techniques available. The dataset allows for rotation, vertical flipping, or a combination of the two (Fig. 1).

(1)   (2)   (3)   (4)   (5)

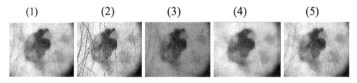

Fig. 1. Image sample (1) Original Image, (2) image after sharpening, (3) image after normalization, (4) image after hair removal, (5) image after augmentation

3.3   Algorithms

Convolutional Neural Networks
CNN is a form of neural network commonly used in computer vision. This is an algorithm that takes a picture as input and allocates significance to various aspects of the image in order to distinguish them.

Architecture for Dermoscopic Pictures using Normalization and Sharpening Preprocessing Methods

The model uses both convolutional and dense layers for image classification. The Conv2D layer is the foremost with thirty-two filters using ReLU activation function. The inserted picture size is (225,225,3). The following layers are MaxPooling layers that lessen the feature maps' size by a factor of 2 using a pool size of (2, 2). The next three Conv2D layers have 64 and 128 filters with a kernel dimension of (3, 3) and use ReLU actuation. The Flatten layer converts the 3D feature maps into 1D vectors, which are fed into the dense layers.

Architecture for Dermoscopic and Non-Dermoscopic Images with Hair Removal and Augmentation Preprocessing Methods

The model begins with a Conv2D layer that has thirty-two filters and the ReLU function. It expects color images with a size of 150×150 pixels. A BatchNormalization layer follows the input layer to normalize the activations and prevent overfitting. A MaxPooling layer is used to decrease the spatial proportions of the feature maps. The Flatten layer is employed to flatten the previous layer's output into a 1D array. Following that are 2 Dense layers with ReLU functions, the first of which is a 512-unit layer with BatchNormalization. For binary classification, the final Dense layer contains one unit and uses the sigmoid activating function. A binary cross-entropy loss function is used to train the model.

ResNet50
ResNet50 is a type of CNN that makes use of residual connections to make training easier and more efficient. ResNet50 is composed of Fifty layers, comprising convolution and fully connected layers, it was trained on massive datasets such as ImageNet, which contains millions of images.

Architecture for Dermoscopic Images with Sharpening and Normalization Pre-processing Methods

The model, which performs well in image classification, is utilized. The weights are initialized using pre-trained ImageNet weights, and the maximum value of each feature map is calculated with a dense layer that contains one output node and uses sigmoid activation. The Adam boost approach updates the model parameters using the loss function's gradients to enhance the model's predictions. The binary cross-entropy loss function computes the discrepancy between the anticipated and actual probability, while the accuracy metric determines how well the model performs in binary classification tasks.

The Architecture of Dermoscopic and Non-Dermoscopic with Hair Removal and Augmentation Preprocessing Methods

The model is divided into two sections: a ResNet50 convolutional basis and an associated layer with an activation function that is sigmoid. Most of the stages in the ResNet50 base are frozen, and only the last eight may be trained to fine-tune the algorithm. The model utilizes a flattened layer to transform the trait maps into a one-dimensional vector, provided by a fully connected layer using a ReLU activation function. A Dropout layer with a rate of 0.5 is included preceding the final output layer (Fig. 2).

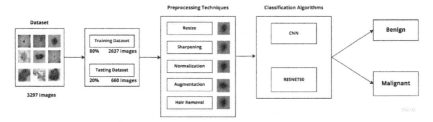

Fig. 2. Methodology For Dermoscopic Images

Dermoscopic images are used to detect melanoma skin disease, with pre-processing techniques to improve image quality and CNN and ResNet50 models are used to classify them (Fig. 3).

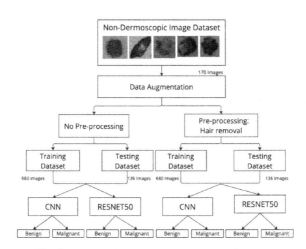

Fig. 3. Methodology For Non-Dermoscopic Image

Non-dermoscopic pictures are utilized to forecast melanoma skin disease, data augmentation techniques are employed to boost data, and hairs are removed using a preprocessing method. The CNN and ResNet50 models categorize the pictures as benign or malignant (Table 1).

4 Results and Discussion

Table 1. Dermoscopic image dataset performance comparison

Models	Pre-processing	Train Accuracy	Test Accuracy
CNN	No Pre-processing	82.71	82.73
CNN	Sharpening	83.45	80.00
CNN	Normalization	89.09	89.08
CNN	Augmentation	91.48	97.98
CNN	Hair Removal	90.61	98.07
CNN (age, gender)	No Pre-processing	98.50	96.40
ResNet50	No Pre-processing	74.02	77.73
ResNet50	Sharpening	88.84	88.72
ResNet50	Normalization	75.18	58.89
ResNet50	Augmentation	94.31	99.83
ResNet50	Hair Removal	94.04	99.74
ResNet50(age, gender)	No Pre-processing	68.20	68.20

The table displays the findings of an analysis of various models developed using the Dermoscopic Images Dataset. Train Accuracy and Test Accuracy are the evaluation measures employed. CNN and ResNet50 models were evaluated in the study utilizing different preprocessing approaches such as sharpening, normalization, augmentation, and hair removal. The models' performance is also assessed both with and without taking into account their age and gender.

The findings shown in the table indicate that the CNN model, which was trained using the Hair Removal preprocessing strategy, has the highest Test accuracy. of 98.07%. The ResNet50 model, which was trained using a preprocessing approach Augmentation, obtained the highest Test Accuracy of 99.83%. Utilizing age and gender data, the CNN model yielded an impressive Train Accuracy of 98.50%, but the Testing Accuracy was substantially lower at 96.40%.

The dataset of non-dermoscopic image training and testing outcomes are shown in the table. In order to increase the variety of the training set for the CNN model, the dataset was extended. As a consequence, the training accuracy for the CNN model was 87.65%, and the test accuracy was 93.43% (Table 2).

The same model from CNN was then preprocessed for hair removal, which resulted in a substantial boost in performance with an accuracy in training of 96.77% and testing accuracy of 97.06%. On the same dataset, the pre-trained ResNet50 model was also

Table 2. Non-Dermoscopic image dataset performance comparison

Models	Pre-processing	Train Accuracy	Test Accuracy
CNN	Augmentation	87.65	93.43
CNN	Hair Removal	96.77	97.06
ResNet50	Augmentation	96.95	100
ResNet50	Hair Removal	99.85	100

assessed using both hair removal and augmentation methods. A training accuracy of 96.95% and a perfect test accuracy of 100% were obtained using the supplemented dataset. The preprocessing method for hair removal, however, produced even better performance, with training accuracy of 99.85% and faultless test accuracy of 100%. The high degree of classification accuracy attained by both models implies that the preprocessing step of hair removal was successful in enhancing the models' classification abilities.

5 Conclusion

According to the findings of this study, when suitable preprocessing approaches are utilized, deep learning models, notably CNN and ResNet50, can recognize pictures with high accuracy. Hair removal and Augmentation preprocessing were shown to be quite beneficial in improving model performance. The ResNet50 model constantly outperformed the CNN model in terms of accuracy, achieving near-perfect accuracy. These findings imply that architecture and preprocessing approaches should be cautiously selected.

6 Future Scope

This technology might be developed to help in the early diagnosis of numerous skin illnesses. CNN and ResNet50, two well-known deep-learning models, were evaluated in the study. Future studies may examine the effectiveness of several deep-learning models, such as VGG or Inception, to determine which architecture is best suited for image classification tasks. To assess performance, a huge dataset might be employed.

References

1. Skin cancer - Symptoms and causes. Mayo Clinic (2022). https://www.mayoclinic.org/dis eases-conditions/skin-cancer/symptoms-causes/syc20377605
2. Sreedhar, B., BE, M.S., Kumar, M.S.:A comparative study of melanoma skin cancer detection in traditional and current image processing techniques. In: 2020 Fourth International Conference on I-SMAC (IoT in Social, Mobile, Analytics and Cloud) (I- SMAC), pp. 654–658. Palladam (2020). https://doi.org/10.1109/I-SMAC49090.2020.9243501

3. Fernandez Alcon, J., et al.: Automatic imaging system with decision support for inspection of pigmented skin lesions and melanoma diagnosis. IEEE J. Sel. Top. Sign. Process. **3**(1), 14–25 (2009). https://doi.org/10.1109/JSTSP.2008.2011156
4. Jana, E., Subban, R., Saraswathi, S.: Research on skin cancer cell detection using image processing. In: 2017 IEEE International Conference on Computational Intelligence and Computing Research (ICCIC), pp. 1–8. Coimbatore (2017). https://doi.org/10.1109/ICCIC.2017.8524554
5. Guha, S.R., Haque, S.R.: Convolutional neural network based skin lesion analysis for classifying melanoma. In: 2019 International Conference on Sustainable Technologies for Industry 4.0 (STI), pp. 1–5. Dhaka (2019). https://doi.org/10.1109/STI47673.2019.9067979
6. Alkarakatly, T., Eidhah, S., Al-Sarawani, M., Al-Sobhi, A., Bilal, M.: Skin lesions identification using deep convolutional neural network. In: 2019 International Conference on Advances in the Emerging Computing Technologies (AECT), pp. 1–5. Al Madinah Al Munawwarah (2020). https://doi.org/10.1109/AECT47998.2020.9194205
7. Kondaveeti, H.K., Edupuganti, P.: Skin cancer classification using transfer learning. In: 2020 IEEE International Conference on Advent Trends in MultidisciplinaryResearch and Innovation (ICATMRI), pp. 1–4. Buldhana (2020). https://doi.org/10.1109/ICATMRI51801.2020.9398388
8. Kamboj, A.: A color-based approach for melanoma skin cancer detection. In: 2018 First International Conference on Secure Cyber Computing and Communication (ICSCCC), pp. 508–513. Jalandhar, (2018). https://doi.org/10.1109/ICSCCC.2018.8703309
9. Claudio Kaggle, F.: Skin Cancer: Malignant vs. Benign (2018). https://www.kaggle.com/datasets/fanconic/skin-cancer-malignant-vsbenign
10. MED-NODE dataset (2015). https://www.cs.rug.nl/~imaging/databases/melanoma_naevi/
11. Naeem, A., Farooq, M.S., Khelifi, A., Abid, A.: Malignant melanoma classification using deep learning: datasets, performance measurements, challenges and opportunities. IEEE Access **8**, 110575–110597 (2020). https://doi.org/10.1109/ACCESS.2020.300150

Author Index

A

Abhishek, S. R.   704
Abubakar, Abdulqahar Mukhtar   766
Acharya, Aniruddh   159
Afroz, Suhail   421
Agarwal, Swati   580
Ahuja, Rohit   265, 649
Aithu, Sanath   368
Ajgaonkar, Shreyas   601
Akhil., M. R.   159
Akshay, S.   589, 659
Alam, Mahpara Yasmin Mohd Minhaz   192
Amudha, J.   589, 659, 766
Anand Krishna, R.   68
Anirudh, Ch. Ram   60
Anoop, V. S.   147, 723
Aran, Anmol   297
Aravind, M.   245
Arefin, Nazmul   297
Asifa Tazeem, P.   421

B

Babu, P. Ashok   169
Badola, Akshay   101
Balasubramaniam, N.   735
Balla, Yashaswini   683, 757
Basavaraj, G. M.   475
Baskaran, T.   747
Bethu, Srikanth   714
Bhardwaj, Chetna   580
Bhattacharya, Amitabh   659
Bhoir, Jidnyasa   778
Bhukya, Wilson Naik   112
Bhusnurmath, Rohini A.   407
Bolla, Bharath Kumar   48
Bonthu, Sridevi   534

C

Chakkaravarthy, Midhun   496
Chandrika, K. R.   766

Chennareddy, Vijay Simha Reddy   683
Chereddy, Nagarjuna Venkata   48
Chitra, N. Thulasi   336
Choudhury, Anirban   356

D

Damotharan, Varadharajan   704
Danni, Vijai   429
Darapaneni, Narayana   255, 368, 503, 580, 704, 735
Devrani, Sneha   265
Dhandra, B. V   747
Doddamani, Shaila   407
Durga Bhavani, S.   91
Durgesh, D. V. S.   442
Dwaram, Kavitha   620

E

Ezhilarasan, M.   179

G

Ganesh, G. V.   169
Gatadi, Ashwitha   203
Gatkamani, Glory   580
Gautam, Rahul Kumar   91
Ghimire, Sandesh   297
Goel, Anirudh   265
Gosala, Bethany   449
Gosala, Emmanuel Raj   449
Govindarajan, Usharani Hareesh   147
Gudapati, Maneesha   236
Gulani, Jayesh   368
Guntupalli, Neelima   309
Gupta, Manjari   449
Gururaj, Raghav   580

H

Hanimi Reddy, M.   421
Haragopal, V. V.   714

R. Morusupalli et al. (Eds.): MIWAI 2023, LNAI 14078, pp. 787–789, 2023.
https://doi.org/10.1007/978-3-031-36402-0

J

Jadda, Vijetha   421
Jain, Pravar   316
Jain, Samyak   316
Jakate, Mrunmayee   601
Jayanna, Lokesh   735
John, Nimitha   747
Jore, Pranav   601
Joshi, Jyothirmai   135, 569
Joshi, Yash   601

K

Kadam, Deepali   601, 778
Kalva, Sudhakar   484
Kamble, Nitish   659
KanthaSamy, Balassubramamian   503
Kare, Anjeneya Swami   91
Kareti, Vinay Kumar   534
Katiyar, Sheetal   255
Kavi, Narayana Murthy   60
Khanna, Manju   214
Kharbanda, Sahajdeep Singh   265
Kiran Sree, P.   637
Kolhe, Sujata   380
Kota, Nageswar Rao   112
Krishna Dutt, R. V. S.   68
Krishna, R.   255
Krishnamurthy, K. T.   475
Krisnakumar, R.   503
Kulkarni, Nilima   589
Kumar, Agashini V.   766
Kumar, B. S. Sunil   704
Kumar, Bharath Raj Anand   255
Kumar, Dudla Anil   179
Kumar, Kanthala Sampath   714
Kumar, Naresh   513
Kundu, Sourav   735
Kuruva, Harinath   285

L

Lakshmi, G. Vijaya   714
Lakumarapu, Srikanth   348
Lal, Rajendra Prasad   101
Lavangare, Snehal   601
Lingada, Prasanth   255

M

Madhav, K. Venu   336
Madhavi, Pappula   611

Majumder, Sebanti   25
Malhotra, D. K.   277
Malhotra, Rashmi   277
Mallareddy, A.   523
Manohar, M. P.   735
Mattaparthi, Karunakar   255
Meena, P. N.   723
Meenakshi, B. Akhila   390
Mekala, Sagar   523
Midatani, Sujan   534
Mittal, Shruti   316
Mohan, Senthilkumar   683, 757
Mohanty, Hrushikesha   1
Moiz, Salman Abdul   285
Mridha, Krishan   297
Mudlapur, Chetan   316
Mulukutla, Vamsi Krishna   534
Munnangi, Sudhakar Moses   735
Myakal, Sabhapathy   324, 543

N

Nagarjuna, N.   399
Naik, Wilson   192
Nair, Namrata   245
Narmada, Nakka   659
Nath, Keshab   429
Naveen, Nekuri   324, 543
Neerugatti, Vikram   316
Nekkanti, Lakshmi Kishore Kumar   554
Nerkar, Neeraj   380
Nivetha, S.   704

O

Omar, Mohammed Ozair   569

P

Padmanabhan, Vineet   101, 112
Paduri, Anwesh Reddy   255, 368, 503, 580, 704, 735
Pal, Pramod Kumar   659
Pal, Rajarshi   324, 543
Pandey, Aashish Prashad   297
Pandit, Rugved   380
Pavarala, Sai Supriya   534
Perla, Sunanda   620
Phaneendra Varma, Ch.   637
Poornachandran, Prabaharan   245
Prakash, Gnana   255
Prasad, M.   637

Prashanth, L. K.   589
Premchand, P.   68
Princy, V. Albert   704

R
Radhika, C.   169
Radhika, Konduru   523
Raghava, M.   225, 569
Raj, N. Prabhas   225
Raja Rao, P. B. V.   637
Rajesh, B.   735
Rajeswarappa, G.   348
Ramana Reddy, B.   442
Ramana, P. V.   390
Ramesh Babu, G.   637
Rani, A. Sandhya   124
Rani, K. Swarupa   124
Ranjan, Ashish   503
Rao, B. Naga Malleswara   390
Rao, Varaprasad   554
Reddy, B. Krishna   79
Reddy, D. Sudheer   79
Reddy, E. Uma   399
Reddy, Y. Subba   336
Riyazuddin, Y. Md.   421
Rohith, S.   475
Roul, Rajendra Kumar   649
Roy, Sudipta   356
Rudramalla, Vasantha   309

S
Saket, M. V. S.   442
Sampath, Koyyalagunta Krishna   671
Sanjana, A.   692
Santhosh, M. M.   368
Santosh, D. Teja   225, 569
Sarkar, Shakil   297
Sathyanarayana, Anirudh B.   159
Satuluri, Naganjaneyulu   484
Satyamurty, Ch. V. S.   421
Satyanarayana Murty, P. T.   637
Senthil Kumar, G.   496
Shashank, H. S.   159
Sheeba, Merlin   513
Shelke, Deep   778
Shravani, M.   79
Singh, Alok   25

Sirisala, Srinivasulu   348
Sombattheera, Chattrakul   459
Sourabh, Suman   704
Sreenivasulu, G.   336
Subalie, Adhella   36
Sudkhot, Panich   459
Suguna Mallika, S.   692
Suhartono, Derwin   36
Sujadevi, V. G.   245
Supreeth, S.   475
Supreethi, K. P.   611
Supriya, M.   671
Swapna, V.   714
Swarupa Rani, K.   203, 236, 285
Swathi, S.   475

T
Tale, Pravin   601
Tandu, Rama Rao   523
Tank, Rishi   380
Tank, Umesh   503
Tarun, G.   225
Thanuja, V.   336
Thekkiniath, Jose   147
Tirunagari, Santosh   683, 757
Tola, Fitsum Getachew   297

U
Upadhyaya, Sujatha R.   159
Uyyala, Ravi   135

V
Vani Gayatri, A.   692
Varghese, Shaji   368
Veena Naga Sai, S.   692
Visakh, P. R.   723
Vuppaladhadiam, Dileep   255

W
Wagh, Atharwa   214, 766
Walunj, Parmesh   380
Wamane, Niharika   778
Windridge, David   683, 757

Y
Yadav, Aishwarya   778

Printed in the United States
by Baker & Taylor Publisher Services